THE
CONCISE OXFORD
DICTIONARY
OF
QUOTATIONS

DOMI MINA
NUS TIO
ILLU MEA

OXFORD UNIVERSITY PRESS
LONDON   OXFORD   NEW YORK

Oxford University Press

OXFORD LONDON NEW YORK
GLASGOW TORONTO MELBOURNE WELLINGTON
CAPE TOWN IBADAN NAIROBI DAR ES SALAAM LUSAKA ADDIS ABABA
DELHI BOMBAY CALCUTTA MADRAS KARACHI LAHORE DACCA
KUALA LUMPUR SINGAPORE HONG KONG TOKYO

ISBN 0 19 281022 7

Selection and arrangement
© *Oxford University Press, 1964*

First issued as an Oxford University Press paperback 1964
Reprinted 1965, 1967 (twice), 1969 (twice), 1970, 1971, and
1972 (twice)

Printed in Great Britain
at the University Press, Oxford
by Vivian Ridler
Printer to the University

CONTENTS

PUBLISHER'S FOREWORD

The Oxford Dictionary of Quotations, published in 1941, quickly established itself as a standard work of reference and was seven times reprinted with occasional revisions. In 1953 a second edition appeared, which has also been reprinted. The compilers of *The Concise Oxford Dictionary of Quotations* have had the latest revised impression before them in preparing this abridgement.

The *Concise O.D.Q.* is not to be considered as displacing, superseding, or providing even a tolerable substitute for its parent volume. A comparison between the thousand large pages of the *Dictionary* and the many fewer small pages of the present volume will make this clear enough. The *Concise O.D.Q.* has been undertaken to meet the demand for a shorter dictionary containing such quotations as might be used daily by the 'man in the street' rather than by the literary specialist. The intention has been to reduce, not to add; but some additions have nevertheless been made, with the idea of keeping the work up to date, from sources as far apart as Lord Hewart, Dorothy Parker, Adlai Stevenson, and Beatrix Potter.

The Oxford Dictionary of Quotations is graced by an introduction from the late Bernard Darwin. 'Quotation brings to many people one of the intensest joys of living', he begins, and even the members of the Amen House committee who have spent many hours weighing one quotation against another—to test their merits for possible inclusion in this book—rose from their labours with the love of quotation unimpaired. Few can emulate Bernard Darwin's dexterity with a quotation; but others beside leader-writers and crossword zealots will turn to these pages with enthusiasm, for dictionaries of quotations are fields of paradise for the browser. It is the hope of the compilers that the joy of this book will remain intense in its concise form.

One further warning may be added: proverbs and phrases are not included either in this dictionary or in its parent volume, but they are fully dealt with in the *Oxford Dictionary of English Proverbs*.

SIR J. E. E. DALBERG ACTON, FIRST BARON ACTON 1834–1902

1 Power tends to corrupt and absolute power corrupts absolutely.
> *Letter in* Life of Mandell Creighton (1904), i. 372

SAMUEL ADAMS 1722–1803

2 A Nation of shop-keepers are very seldom so disinterested.
> *Oration said to have been delivered at Philadelphia,* 1776, p. 10 (*see also 151:15, 217:12*)

JOSEPH ADDISON 1672–1719

3 And, pleas'd th' Almighty's orders to perform,
Rides in the whirl-wind, and directs the storm. *The Campaign,* l. 291

4 'Tis not in mortals to command success,
But we'll do more, Sempronius; we'll deserve it. *Cato,* ii. 43

5 When vice prevails, and impious men bear sway,
The post of honour is a private station.
> *Ib.* 140

6 From hence, let fierce contending nations know
What dire effects from civil discord flow. *Ib.* iv. 111

7 Thus I live in the world rather as a spectator of mankind than as one of the species. *The Spectator,* No. 1

8 When I am in a serious humour, I very often walk by myself in Westminster Abbey. *Ib.* No. 26

9 I have often thought, says Sir Roger, it happens very well that Christmas should fall out in the Middle of Winter. *Ib.* No. 269

10 The Knight in the triumph of his heart made several reflections on the greatness of the *British* Nation; as, that one *Englishman* could beat three *Frenchmen;* that we cou'd never be in danger of Popery so long as we took care of our fleet; that the *Thames* was the noblest river in *Europe;* that *London Bridge* was a greater piece of work than any of the Seven Wonders of the World; with many other honest prejudices which naturally cleave to the heart of a true *Englishman.*
> *Ib.* No. 383

11 The spacious firmament on high,
With all the blue ethereal sky.
> *The Spectator,* No. 465. Ode

12 Soon as the evening shades prevail,
The moon takes up the wondrous tale,
And nightly to the listening Earth
Repeats the story of her birth. *Ib.*

13 Whilst all the stars that round her burn,
And all the planets, in their turn,
Confirm the tidings as they roll,
And spread the truth from pole to pole. *Ib.*

14 In Reason's ear they all rejoice,
And utter forth a glorious Voice,
For ever singing as they shine,
'The Hand that made us is Divine.'
> *Ib.*

15 If we may believe our logicians, man is distinguished from all other creatures by the faculty of laughter.
> *Ib.* No. 494

16 'We are always doing', says he, 'something for Posterity, but I would fain see Posterity do something for us.'
> *Ib.* No. 583

THOMAS ADY c. 1655

17 Matthew, Mark, Luke, and John,
The Bed be blest that I lie on.
Four angels to my bed,
Four angels round my head,
One to watch, and one to pray,
And two to bear my soul away.
> Quoted in part by Ady in A Candle in the Dark (1656)

AESOP c. 550 B.C.

18 Beware that you do not lose the substance by grasping at the shadow.
> *Fables. The Dog and the Shadow*

19 The gods help them that help themselves. *Ib. Hercules and the Waggoner*

20 It is not only fine feathers that make fine birds.
> *Ib. The Jay and the Peacock*

21 Don't count your chickens before they are hatched.
> *Ib. The Milkmaid and her Pail*

AGATHON 447?–401 B.C.

22 Even God cannot change the past.
> *Attr. by Aristotle in* The Nicomachean Ethics, vi.

CHARLES HAMILTON AÏDÉ
1830–1906

1 I sit beside my lonely fire,
  And pray for wisdom yet—
  For calmness to remember
  Or courage to forget.
  Remember or Forget

ALFRED AINGER 1837–1904

2 No flowers, by request.
  At a dinner given to the contri-
  butors to the Dict. of Nat. Biog.,
  8 July 1897: his summary of their
  editor's instructions.

ARTHUR CAMPBELL AINGER
1841–1919

3 God is working His purpose out as
    year succeeds to year,
  God is working His purpose out and
    the time is drawing near;
  Nearer and nearer draws the time, the
    time that shall surely be,
  When the earth shall be fill'd with the
    glory of God as the waters cover the
    sea.
    God is Working His Purpose Out
    (1894)

ALCUIN 735–804

4 Vox populi, vox dei.
    The voice of the people is the voice
    of God.
    Letter to Charlemagne, A.D. 800.
    Works, Epis. 127

HENRY ALDRICH 1648–1710

5 If all be true that I do think,
  There are five reasons we should drink;
  Good wine—a friend—or being dry—
  Or lest we should be by and by—
  Or any other reason why.
    Reasons for Drinking

ALEXANDER 356–323 B.C.

6 εἰ μὴ Ἀλέξανδρος ἤμην, Διογένης ἂν ἤμην.
    If I were not Alexander, I would be
    Diogenes.
    Plutarch, *Life of Alexander,* xiv. 3

CECIL FRANCES ALEXANDER
1818–1895

7 All things bright and beautiful,
  All creatures great and small,
  All things wise and wonderful,
  The Lord God made them all.
    All Things Bright and Beautiful
    (1848)

8 The rich man in his castle,
  The poor man at his gate,
  God made them, high or lowly,
  And order'd their estate. *Ib.*

9 Do no sinful action,
  Speak no angry word;
  Ye belong to Jesus,
  Children of the Lord.
    Do No Sinful Action (1848)

10 Once in royal David's city
  Stood a lowly cattle shed,
  Where a Mother laid her Baby
  In a manger for His bed:
  Mary was that Mother mild,
  Jesus Christ her little Child.
    Once in Royal David's City (1848)

11 We are but little children weak
  Not born in any high estate.
    We are but Little Children Weak
    (1850)

SIR WILLIAM ALEXANDER,
EARL OF STIRLING 1567?–1640

12 The weaker sex, to piety more prone.
    Doomsday, Hour v, lv

HENRY ALFORD 1810–1871

13 Come, ye thankful people, come,
  Raise the song of Harvest-home:
  All is safely gathered in,
  Ere the winter storms begin.
    Come, Ye Thankful People, Come
    (1844)

14 Ten thousand times ten thousand,
  In sparkling raiment bright.
    Ten Thousand Times Ten Thou-
    sand (1867)

ABBÉ D'ALLAINVAL 1700–1753

15 L'embarras des richesses.
    The more alternatives, the more
    difficult the choice.
    Title of Comedy (1726)

GRANT ALLEN 1848–1899

16 The Woman who Did.
    Title of Novel (1895)

WILLIAM ALLINGHAM
1824–1889

17 Up the airy mountain,
  Down the rushy glen,
  We daren't go a-hunting,
  For fear of little men. *The Fairies*

18 Four ducks on a pond,
  A grass-bank beyond,
  A blue sky of spring,
  White clouds on the wing:
  What a little thing
  To remember for years—
  To remember with tears! *A Memory*

ST. AMBROSE c. 340–397

1 Si fueris Romae, Romano vivito more;
Si fueris alibi, vivito sicut ibi.

If you are at Rome live in the
Roman style; if you are else-
where live as they live elsewhere.
Quoted by Jeremy Taylor, Ductor
Dubitantium, *I. i. 5*

MAXWELL ANDERSON 1888–1959

2 What Price Glory, *Title of Play* (1924)

SIR NORMAN ANGELL 1874–1967

3 The Great Illusion
Title of book on the futility of war

ARCHIBALD DOUGLAS, FIFTH EARL OF ANGUS 1449?–1514

4 I shall bell the cat.
Attr. by J. Man in Buchanan's
Rerum Scoticarum Historia
(1762), *bk. xii, § 41, note*

ANONYMOUS

English

5 A beast, but a just beast.
*Of Dr. Temple, Headmaster of
Rugby, 1857–69*

6 Absence makes the heart grow fonder.
Davison, *Poetical Rhapsody* (1602)
(see 19:3)

7 Adam
Had 'em.
*On the Antiquity of Microbes.
(Said to be the shortest poem.)*

8 All present and correct.
*King's Regulations (Army). Re-
port of the Orderly Sergeant to the
Officer of the Day*

9 An abomination unto the Lord, but
a very present help in time of trouble.
[A lie.]
*(Cf. Proverbs xii. 22; the second
half is from Psalms xlvi. I)*

10 An Austrian army, awfully arrayed,
Boldly by battery besieged Belgrade;
Cossack commanders cannonading
come,
Dealing destruction's devastating
doom.
Siege of Belgrade. The Trifler, 1817

11 A place within the meaning of the Act.
The Betting Act

12 Appeal from Philip drunk to Philip
sober.
See Valerius Maximus, Facta et
Dicta Memorabilia *(c. A.D. 15),
bk. vi, ch. ii*

13 Are we downhearted? No!
*Expression much used by British
soldiers in War of 1914–18, probably based on remark of Joseph
Chamberlain, q.v.*

14 As I sat on a sunny bank,
On Christmas Day in the morning,
I spied three ships come sailing by.
*Carol: As I sat on a Sunny Bank.
Oxford Book of Carols*

15 A swarm of bees in May
Is worth a load of hay;
A swarm of bees in June
Is worth a silver spoon;
A swarm of bees in July
Is not worth a fly. *Old Rhyme*

16 Begone, dull care! I prithee begone
from me!
Begone, dull care, you and I shall
never agree. *Begone Dull Care*

17 Be happy while y'er leevin,
For y'er a lang time deid.
Scottish Motto for a house. Notes
and Queries, 7 Dec. 1901, p. 469

18 Born 1820, still going strong.
*Advertisement for Johnnie Walker
Whisky*

19 Bovril prevents that sinking feeling.
Advertisement

20 Christmas is coming, the geese are
getting fat,
Please to put a penny in the old man's
hat;
If you haven't got a penny, a ha'penny
will do,
If you haven't got a ha'penny, God
bless you! *Beggar's Rhyme*

21 Come, landlord, fill the flowing bowl
Until it doth run over. . . .
For to-night we'll merry be,
To-morrow we'll be sober.
*Come, Landlord, Fill the Flowing
Bowl.* Oxford Song Book

22 Come lasses and lads, get leave of
your dads,
And away to the Maypole hie,
For every he has got him a she,
And the fiddler's standing by.
For Willie shall dance with Jane,
And Johnny has got his Joan,
To trip it, trip it, trip it, trip it, trip
it up and down.
*Come Lasses and Lads (c. 1670).
Oxford Song Book*

23 Conduct . . . to the prejudice of good
order and military discipline.
Army Act, § 40

1 Dear Sir, Your astonishment's odd:
I am always about in the Quad.
   And that's why the tree
   Will continue to be,
Since observed by Yours faithfully,
  God.
     Reply to limerick on Idealism,
     'There was once a man who said
     "God . . ." ' (see 129:2)

2 Dollar Diplomacy.
     Term applied to Secretary Knox's
     activities in securing opportunities
     for the investment of American
     capital abroad, particularly in
     Latin America and China. See
     Harper's Weekly, 23 Apr. 1910,
     p. 8.

3 Dr. Williams' pink pills for pale people.
     Advertisement

4 Early one morning, just as the sun was
   rising,
I heard a maid sing in the valley below:
'Oh, don't deceive me; Oh, never leave
  me!
How could you use a poor maiden so?'
     Early One Morning. Oxford Song
     Book

5 Earned a precarious living by taking
in one another's washing.
     In The Commonweal, 6 Aug.
     1887, William Morris suggested
     that this was an invention of Mark
     Twain's

6 Esau selleth his birthright for a mess
of potage.
     Genevan Bible: chapter-heading to
     Genesis, ch. 25

7 An intelligent Russian once remarked
to us, 'Every country has its own constitution; ours is absolutism moderated by assassination.'
     Georg Herbert, Count Münster,
     Political Sketches of the State of
     Europe, 1814–1867, ed. 1868, p.
     19

8 Frankie and Johnny were lovers, my
   gawd, how they could love,
Swore to be true to each other, true
   as the stars above;
He was her man, but he done her
   wrong.   *Frankie and Johnny,* st. 1

9 From ghoulies and ghosties and long-
   leggety beasties
And things that go bump in the night,
   Good Lord, deliver us!   *Cornish*

10 God be in my head,
   And in my understanding;

God be in my eyes,
   And in my looking;

God be in my mouth,
   And in my speaking;

God be in my heart,
   And in my thinking;

God be at my end,
   And at my departing.   *Sarum Missal*

11 God rest you merry, Gentlemen,
Let nothing you dismay.
     Carol: God Rest You Merry.
     Oxford Book of Carols

12 O tidings of comfort and joy.   *Ib.*

13 God's own country.
     Sir St. V. Troubridge (Notes and
     Queries, 26 Sept. 1942) quotes
     from Sir W. Craigie's Dictionary
     of American English:
       'A special part of the U.S. or
       the country as a whole, viewed
       nostalgically as almost a para-
       dise.'
     The earliest example without 'own'
     given is 1865, the earliest with
     'own' is 1921

14 Great Chatham with his sabre drawn
Stood waiting for Sir Richard
   Strachan;
Sir Richard, longing to be at 'em,
Stood waiting for the Earl of Chatham.
     At Walcheren, 1809

15 Greensleeves was all my joy,
   Greensleeves was my delight,
Greensleeves was my heart of gold,
   And who but Lady Greensleeves?
     A new Courtly Sonnet of the Lady
     Greensleeves, to the new tune of
     'Greensleeves'. From A Handful
     of Pleasant Delites (1584)

16 Ha-ha-ha, you and me,
Little brown jug, don't I love thee.
     The Little Brown Jug. Oxford
     Song Book

17 Here lies Fred,
Who was alive and is dead:
Had it been his father,
I had much rather;
Had it been his brother,
Still better than another;
Had it been his sister,
No one would have missed her;
Had it been the whole generation,
Still better for the nation:
But since 'tis only Fred,
Who was alive and is dead,—
There's no more to be said.
     Horace Walpole, *Memoirs of*
     George II (1847), vol. i, p. 436

18 Here we come a-wassailing. *Old Song*

19 Here we come gathering nuts in May
   Nuts in May,
On a cold and frosty morning.
     Children's Song

1 He that fights and runs away
   May live to fight another day.
   Musarum Deliciae, collected by
   Sir John Mennes and Dr. James
   Smith, 1656

2 He won't be happy till he gets it.
   Advertisement for Pears' Soap

3 Hierusalem, my happy home,
   When shall I come to thee?
   When shall my sorrows have an end,
   Thy joys when shall I see?
   Hierusalem. See Songs of Praise
   Discussed

4 'How different, how very different
   from the home life of our own dear
   Queen!'
   Irvin S. Cobb, *A Laugh a Day*

   As Cleopatra, Sarah Bernhardt
   stabbed the slave who bore to her
   the tidings of Mark Antony's
   defeat at Actium; she stormed,
   raved, wrecked some of the scenery
   in her frenzy and finally, as the
   curtain fell, dropped in a shud-
   dering, convulsive heap.
   As the applause died, a middle-
   aged British matron was heard to
   say to her neighbour: 'How
   different, how very different from
   the home life of our own dear
   Queen!' (Victoria).

5 I feel no pain dear mother now
   But oh, I am so dry!
   O take me to a brewery
   And leave me there to die.
   C. Fox-Smith's *Book of Shanties*
   (1927)

6 If you your lips would keep from slips
   Of five things have a care:
   To whom you speak, of whom you
     speak,
   And how, and when, and where.
   Quoted in Augustus Hare, Story
   of My Life

7 I know two things about the horse,
   And one of them is rather coarse.
   The Week-End Book

8 In Dublin's fair city, where girls are so
     pretty,
   I first set my eyes on sweet Molly
     Malone,
   As she wheeled her wheelbarrow
     through streets broad and narrow,
   Crying, Cockles and mussels! alive,
     alive, oh!
   Cockles and Mussels. Oxford
   Song Book

9 In good King Charles's golden days,
   When loyalty no harm meant;
   A furious High-Churchman I was,
   And so I gain'd preferment.
   Unto my flock I daily preach'd,
   Kings are by God appointed,

And damned are those who dare resist,
Or touch the Lord's Anointed.
And this is law, I will maintain,
Unto my dying day, Sir,
That whatsoever King shall reign,
I will be the Vicar of Bray, Sir!
   The Vicar of Bray. Brit. Musical
   Miscellany (1734), i

10 I saw three ships a-sailing there,
   —A-sailing there, a-sailing there,
   Jesu, Mary and Joseph they bare
     On Christ's Sunday at morn.
   I saw three ships. Oxford Book of
   Carols

11 I sing of a maiden
     That is makeless;
   King of all kings
     To her son she ches.
   Carol: I Sing of a Maiden (15th
   cent.). Oxford Book of Carols

12 The children of Lord Lytton organized
   a charade. The scene displayed a
   Crusader knight returning from the
   wars. At his gate he was welcomed by
   his wife to whom he recounted his
   triumphs and the number of heathen
   he had slain. His wife, pointing to a
   row of dolls of various sizes, replied
   with pride, 'And I too, my lord, have
   not been idle'.
   G. W. E. Russell's *Collections*
   and Recollections, ch. 31

13 It's a long time between drinks.
   The Governor of South Carolina re-
   quired the return of a fugitive slave.
   The Governor of North Carolina
   hesitated because of powerful
   friends of the fugitive. He gave a
   banquet to his official brother. The
   Governor of South Carolina in a
   speech demanded the return of the
   slave and ended with 'What do
   you say?' The Governor of North
   Carolina replied as above

14 It is good to be merry and wise,
   It is good to be honest and true,
   It is best to be off with the old love,
   Before you are on with the new.
   Songs of England and Scotland.
   London (1835), vol. ii, p. 73

15 It's love, it's love that makes the
   world go round.
   Chansons Nationales et Popu-
   laires de France, vol. ii, p. 180

16 I wish I were single again.
   I Married a Wife (19th cent.)

17 Jesus Christ is risen to-day,
   Our triumphant holy day;
   Who did once upon the cross
   Suffer to redeem our loss.
     Hallelujah!
   Jesus Christ is Risen To-day.
   From a Latin Hymn of the 15th
   cent. Translator unknown

1 King Charles the First walked and
talked
Half an hour after his head was cut off.
*See Peter Puzzlewell, A Choice
Collection of Riddles, Charades
and Rebusses (1792)*

2 Like a fine old English gentleman,
All of the olden time.
*The Fine Old English Gentleman.
Oxford Song Book*

3 Lizzie Borden took an axe
And gave her mother forty whacks;
When she saw what she had done
She gave her father forty-one!
*After an American murder trial of
the 1890's in which Miss Borden
was acquitted of murdering her
father and stepmother*

4 Love me little, love me long,
Is the burden of my song.
*Love me Little, Love me Long
(1569–70)*

5 March winds and April showers
Bringeth vo'th May flowers.
*West Somerset Word-Book, ed.
Frederick Thomas Elworthy
(1886), March*

6 Miss Buss and Miss Beale
Cupid's darts do not feel.
How different from us,
Miss Beale and Miss Buss.
*Of the Headmistress of the North
London Collegiate School and the
Principal of the Ladies' College,
Cheltenham. 19th cent.*

7 Most Gracious Queen, we thee implore
To go away and sin no more,
But if that effort be too great,
To go away at any rate.
*Epigram on Queen Caroline,
1820. Quoted in Lord Colchester's
Diary, 15 Nov. 1820; sent to him
by Francis Burton*

8 Multiplication is vexation,
Division is as bad;
The Rule of three doth puzzle me,
And Practice drives me mad.
Elizabethan MS. dated 1570

9 My name is George Nathaniel Curzon,
I am a most superior person.
*The Masque of Balliol, composed
by and current among members of
Balliol College in the late 1870's
(see also 20:5, 219:19 and 20)*

10 My face is pink, my hair is sleek,
I dine at Blenheim once a week.
Ib. (a later addition)

11 Now I lay me down to sleep;
I pray the Lord my soul to keep.
If I should die before I wake,
I pray the Lord my soul to take.
*First printed in a late edition of the
New England Primer, 1781*

12 O Death, where is thy sting-a-ling-a-
ling,
O Grave, thy victoree?
The bells of Hell go ting-a-ling-a-ling
For you but not for me.
*Song popular in the British Army,
1914–18*

13 O God, if there be a God, save my soul,
if I have a soul!
*Prayer of a common soldier
before the battle of Blenheim (see
Notes and Queries, clxxiii. 264).
Quoted in Newman's Apologia*

14 Oh, Shenandoah, I long to hear you.
Away, you rolling river,
Oh, Shenandoah, I long to hear you.
Away, I'm bound to go
'Cross the wide Missouri.
Shenandoah. Oxford Song Book

15 Oh! the oak, and the ash, and the
bonny ivy-tree,
They flourish at home in my own
country.
*O The Oak and The Ash (c.
1650). Oxford Song Book*

16 Oh, 'tis my delight on a shining night,
in the season of the year.
*The Lincolnshire Poacher. Oxford
Song Book*

17 Oh, 'twas in the broad Atlantic,
'Mid the equinoctial gales,
That a young fellow fell overboard
Among the sharks and whales.
And down he went like a streak of
light,
So quickly down went he,
Until he came to a mer-ma-id
At the bottom of the deep blue sea.
Singing, Rule Britannia, Britannia,
rule the waves!
Britons never, never, never shall be
mar-ri-ed to a mer-ma-id
At the bottom of the deep blue sea.
*Oh! 'Twas in the Broad Atlantic.
Oxford Song Book.*

18 Oh! where is my wandering boy to-
night?
The boy who was bravest of all.
Oh! Where is My Boy To-night?

19 Old soldiers never die;
They only fade away!
*War song of the British Soldiers,
1914–18*

20 One Friday morn when we set sail,
And our ship not far from land,
We there did espy a fair pretty maid,
With a comb and a glass in her hand.
While the raging seas did roar,
And the stormy winds did blow,
And we jolly sailor-boys were all up
aloft
And the land-lubbers lying down
below.
The Mermaid. Oxford Song Book

1 O No John! No John! No John! No!
O No, John. Oxford Song Book

2 O Paddy dear, an' did ye hear the news
that's goin' round?
The shamrock is by law forbid to grow
on Irish ground!
No more St. Patrick's Day we'll keep,
his colour can't be seen,
For there's a cruel law agin the
wearin' o' the Green!
*The Wearin' o' the Green.
(Famous street ballad, later added
to by Boucicault.)*

3 Please to remember the Fifth of
November,
Gunpowder Treason and Plot.
*Traditional since seventeenth cent.
(see also 157 : 12)*

4 O ye'll tak' the high road, and I'll
tak' the low road,
And I'll be in Scotland afore ye,
But me and my true love will never
meet again,
On the bonnie, bonnie banks o' Loch
Lomon'.
*The Bonnie Banks o' Loch
Lomon'. Oxford Song Book*

5 She was poor but she was honest,
And her parents was the same,
Till she met a city feller,
And she lost her honest name.
*1914–18 War song. There are
many versions*

6 Its the same the whole world over,
Its the poor wot gets the blame,
Its the rich wot gets the pleasure,
Ain't it all a blooming shame.　　*Ib.*

7 Some talk of Alexander, and some of
Hercules;
Of Hector and Lysander, and such
great names as these;
But of all the world's brave heroes,
there's none that can compare
With a tow, row, row, row, row, row,
for the British Grenadier.
The British Grenadiers

8 Spheres of influence.
*'Spheres of action', found in Earl
Granville's letter to Count Mün-
ster, 29 Apr. 1885. Hertslet's
Map of Africa by Treaty, 3rd
edn., p. 868 (see 132:2)*

9 Sumer is icumen in
Lhude sing cuccu!
Groweth sed, and bloweth med,
And springth the wude nu.
Cuckoo Song (c. 1250)

10 Swing low, sweet chariot—
Comin' for to carry me home;
I looked over Jordan and what did I
see?
A band of angels comin' after me—
Comin' for to carry me home.
American Negro Spiritual (c. 1850)

11 That schoolgirl complexion.
Advertisement for Palmolive Soap

12 The almighty dollar is the only object
of worship.
*Philadelphia Public Ledger,
2 Dec. 1836*

13 The animals went in one by one,
There's one more river to cross.
*One More River. Oxford Song
Book*

14 The Campbells are comin', oho, oho.
*The Campbells are Comin' (c.
1715). Oxford Song Book*

15 The eternal triangle.
Book review in The Daily Chronicle, *5 Dec. 1907*

16 The girl I left behind me.
*Title of song (c. 1759). Oxford Song
Book*

17 The holly and the ivy,
When they are both full grown,
Of all the trees that are in the wood,
The holly bears the crown:
The rising of the sun
And the running of the deer,
The playing of the merry organ,
Sweet singing in the choir.
*The Holly and the Ivy. Oxford
Book of Carols*

18 The King over the Water.
Jacobite Toast, eighteenth cent.

19 The ministry of all the talents.
*A name given ironically to Gren-
ville's coalition of 1806; also
applied to later coalitions*

20 And Vilikins and his Dinah
Lie a-buried in one grave.
In Henry Mayhew's The Wander-
ing Minstrels *(1834)*

21 The noble Duke of York,
He had ten thousand men,
He marched them up to the top of the
hill,
And he marched them down again.
And when they were up, they were up,
And when they were down, they were
down,
And when they were only half way up,
They were neither up nor down.
*The Noble Duke of York, first
printed in A. Rackham,* Mother
Goose *(1913)*

22 There is a lady sweet and kind,
Was never face so pleased my mind;
I did but see her passing by,
And yet I love her till I die.
*Found on back of leaf 53 of
'Popish Kingdome or reigne of
Antichrist', in Latin verse by
Thomas Naogeorgus, and Eng-
lished by Barnabe Googe. Printed
1570. See* Notes and Queries, *9th
series, x. 427*

1 There is a tavern in the town,
   And there my dear love sits him down,
   And drinks his wine 'mid laughter free,
   And never, never thinks of me.
      Fare thee well, for I must leave thee,
      Do not let this parting grieve thee,
      And remember that the best of
      friends must part.

      Adieu, adieu, kind friends, adieu,
      adieu, adieu,
      I can no longer stay with you.
      I'll hang my harp on a weeping
      willow-tree,
      And may the world go well with
      thee.
        There is a Tavern in the Town.
        Oxford Song Book

2 There's nae luck about the house,
   There's nae luck at a',
   There's nae luck about the house
   When our gudeman's awa'.
        The Mariner's Wife

3 There was an old man of Boulogne,
   Who sang a most topical song.
      It wasn't the words
      Which frightened the birds,
   But the horrible double entendre.
        Langford Reed, *The Limerick
        Book*, p. 51

4 There was a young lady of Riga,
   Who rode with a smile on a tiger;
      They returned from the ride
      With the lady inside,
   And the smile on the face of the tiger.
        Ib. p. 103

5 They came as a boon and a blessing to
   men,
   The Pickwick, the Owl, and the
      Waverley pen.   *Advertisement*

6 To change the name, and not the
   letter,
   Is a change for the worse, and not for
   the better.
        Book of Days (ed. Robert
        Chambers, 1802–71), vol. i, June,
        p. 723

7 Wash me in the water
   That you washed the colonel's daugh-
   ter
   And I shall be whiter
   Than the whitewash on the wall.
        *Song popular among the British
        troops in France, 1914–18*

8 We don't want to fight; but, by Jingo,
   if we do,
   We won't go to the front ourselves,
   but we'll send the mild Hindoo.
        *1878 parody, on hearing that
        Indian troops were being sent to
        Malta to help the English.*
        G. W. E. Russell's *Collections
        and Recollections*, ch. 28

9 We hold these truths to be self-evident, that all men are created equal,
   that they are endowed by their Creator
   with certain unalienable rights, that
   among these are life, liberty, and the
   pursuit of happiness.
        *The American Declaration of In-
        dependence, 4 July 1776 (see
        113:2)*

10 Western wind, when wilt thou blow,
   The small rain down can rain?
   Christ, if my love were in my arms
   And I in my bed again!
        Oxford Book of 16th Cent. Verse

11 What did you do in the Great War,
   daddy?
        Recruiting placard, 1914–18 War

12 What shall we do with the drunken
   sailor?
   Early in the morning?
   Hoo-ray and up she rises
   Early in the morning.
        *What shall we do with the Drunken
        Sailor? Oxford Song Book*

13 When Adam delved, and Eve span,
   Who was then a gentleman?
        *Text of Ball's revolutionary ser-
        mon at Blackheath in Wat Tyler's
        Rebellion, 1381.* See J. R. Green,
        Short Hist. (1893), ii. 484 (*see
        99:11*)

14 When Johnny Comes Marching Home
   Again.
        Title of Song. Oxford Song Book

15 When the wind is in the east,
   'Tis neither good for man nor beast;
   When the wind is in the north,
   The skilful fisher goes not forth;
   When the wind is in the south,
   It blows the bait in the fishes' mouth;
   When the wind is in the west,
   Then 'tis at the very best.
        See J. O. Halliwell, *Popular
        Rhymes* (1849)

16 Workers of the world, unite!
        Common form of 'Working men
        of all countries, unite!' *This is the
        English Translation* (1888) *by
        Samuel Moore, revised by Engels,
        of* 'Proletarier aller Länder,
        vereinigt euch!' *which concludes
        The* Communist Manifesto
        (1848), *by Marx and Engels, and
        is quoted as the final words of the
        programme of the Communist
        International* (1928). *Another
        common form is* 'Proletarians of
        the world, unite!'

17 Worth a guinea a box.
        Advertisement for Beecham's Pills

French

1 An army marches on its stomach.
> *Attr. to Napoleon in, e.g.,*
> *Windsor Magazine (1904) p. 268*
>
> *Probably condensed from a long*
> *passage in Las Cases, Mémo-*
> *rial de Ste-Hélène (Nov. 1816)*

2 Ça ira.
> Untranslatable phrase, meaning
> 'That will certainly happen'. *Re-*
> *frain of French Revolutionary Song*

3 Cet animal est très méchant,
Quand on l'attaque il se défend.
> This animal is very mischievous;
> when it is attacked it defends it-
> self.
> *La Ménagerie, by Théodore*
> *P. K. (1868)*

4 Chevalier sans peur et sans reproche.
> Knight without fear and without
> blemish.
> *Description in contemporary*
> *chronicles of Pierre Bayard,*
> *1476–1524*

5 Il ne faut pas être plus royaliste que le
roi.
> One must not be more royalist than
> the king.
> *Phrase originated under Louis*
> *XVI. Chateaubriand, La Monar-*
> *chie selon la Charte (ed. 1876),*
> *p. 94*

6 Le monde est plein de fous, et qui n'en
veut pas voir
Doit se tenir tout seul, et casser son
miroir.
> The world is full of fools, and he who
> would not see it
> Should live alone and smash his
> mirror.
> *An adaptation from an original*
> *form attributed to Claude Le*
> *Petit (1640–1665) in Discours*
> *Satiriques (1686)*

7 Liberté! Égalité! Fraternité!
> Liberty! Equality! Fraternity!
> *Phrase of unknown origin dating*
> *from before the French Revolu-*
> *tion. Aulard in Études et Leçons*
> *sur la Révolution Française (6ᵉ*
> *série) gives the first official use of*
> *the phrase in the motion passed*
> *by the Club des Cordeliers (30*
> *June 1793): 'que les proprié-*
> *taires seront invités, . . . de faire*
> *peindre sur la façade de leurs*
> *maisons, en gros caractères, ces*
> *mots: Unité, indivisibilité de la*
> *République, Liberté, Égalité,*
> *Fraternité ou la mort.'*
> **(Journal de Paris, No. 182)**

8 Retournons à nos moutons.
> Let us return to our sheep. (Let us
> get back to the subject.)
> *Maistre Pierre Pathelin, l. 1191*

9 Taisez-vous! Méfiez-vous! Les oreilles
ennemies vous écoutent.
> Be quiet! Be on your guard!
> Enemy ears are listening to you.
> *Official Notice in France in 1915*

10 Tout passe, tout casse, tout lasse.
> Everything passes, everything
> perishes, everything palls.
> *Cahier, Quelques six mille pro-*
> *verbes*

Greek

11 μηδὲν ἄγαν.
> Nothing in excess.
> *Written up in the temple at Delphi*
> *by Cleobulus, according to some*
> *accounts. Quoted by Plato in*
> *Protagoras, 343 b*

12 γνῶθι σεαυτόν.
> From the gods comes the saying
> 'Know thyself'.
> *Juvenal, Satires, xi. 27. The*
> *saying was written up in the*
> *temple of Delphi*

Italian

13 Se non è vero, è molto ben trovato.
> If it is not true, it is a happy in-
> vention.
> *Apparently a common saying in*
> *the sixteenth century. Found in*
> *Giordano Bruno (1585) in the*
> *above form, and in Antonio Doni*
> *(1552) as 'Se non è vero, egli*
> *è stato un bel trovato'*

Latin

14 Adeste, fideles,
Laeti triumphantes;
Venite, venite in Bethlehem.
> O come, all ye faithful,
> Joyful and triumphant,
> O come, ye, O come ye to Bethle-
> hem.
> *French or German hymn of eigh-*
> *teenth cent. Trans. by Oakeley in*
> *Murray's Hymnal (1852). See*
> *Songs of Praise Discussed*

15 Ad majorem Dei gloriam.
> To the greater glory of God.
> *Motto of the Society of Jesus*

16 Ave Caesar, morituri te salutant.
> Hail Caesar; those who are about to
> die salute you.
> *Salutation of Roman gladiators on*
> *entering the arena*

1 Et in Arcadia ego.

> *Inscription on a tomb, frequently reproduced in paintings, e.g. by Guercino, Poussin, and Reynolds*

> Usually translated: 'And I too [the occupant of the tomb] was in Arcadia.' But perhaps rather, 'I too [the tomb itself] am in Arcadia': even in Arcadia there am I (Death). (See E. Panofsky in *Philosophy and History*: essays presented to E. Cassirer (1936).)

2 Gaudeamus igitur,
Juvenes dum sumus
Post jucundam juventutem,
Post molestam senectutem,
Nos habebit humus.

> Let us live then and be glad
> While young life's before us
> After youthful pastime had,
> After old age hard and sad,
> Earth will slumber o'er us.
> *Medieval students' song, traced to 1267, but revised in the eighteenth cent.*

3 Nemo me impune lacessit.

> No one provokes me with impunity.
> *Motto of the Crown of Scotland and of all Scottish regiments*

4 Orare est laborare, laborare est orare.

> To pray is to work, to work is to pray.
> *See* Notes and Queries, 6th series, vol. xi, p. 477

5 Quidquid agas, prudenter agas, et respice finem.

> Whatever you do, do cautiously, and look to the end.
> *Gesta Romanorum*, cap. 103. init.

6 Te Deum laudamus.

> We praise thee, O God.
> *First words and title of Canticle attr. to St. Ambrose*

7 Tempora mutantur, et nos mutamur in illis.

> Times change, and we change with them.
> Harrison, *Description of Britain* (1577), part III, ch. iii, p. 99.

CHRISTOPHER ANSTEY
1724–1805

8 How he welcomes at once all the world and his wife,
And how civil to folk he ne'er saw in his life.

> *Ib.* (1766), *letter 13, A Public Breakfast*

THOMAS APPLETON 1812–1884

9 Good Americans, when they die, go to Paris.

> O. W. Holmes, *Autocrat of the Breakfast Table*, ch. 6

ARABIAN NIGHTS

10 Who will change old lamps for new ones? . . . new lamps for old ones?

> *The History of Aladdin*

11 Open Sesame!

> *The History of Ali Baba*

ARCHIMEDES 287–212 B.C.

12 εὕρηκα.

> Eureka! (I have found!)
> Vitruvius Pollio, *De Architectura*, ix. 215

13 δός μοι ποῦ στῶ καὶ κινῶ τὴν γῆν.

> Give me but one firm spot on which to stand, and I will move the earth.
> Pappus Alexandr., *Collectio*, lib. viii, prop. 10, § xi (ed. Hultsch, Berlin, 1878)

COMTE D'ARGENSON 1652–1721

14 L'ABBÉ GUYOT DESFONTAINES: Il faut que je vive.
D'ARGENSON: Je n'en vois pas la nécessité.

> DESFONTAINES: I must live.
> D'ARGENSON: I do not see the necessity.
> Voltaire, *Alzire, Discours Préliminaire (see 178:1)*

ARISTOTLE 384–322 B.C.

15 ἄνθρωπος φύσει πολιτικὸν ζῷον.

> Man is by nature a political animal.
> *Politics*, i. 2. 9. 1253 a (ed. W. L. Newman)

16 ἔστιν οὖν τραγῳδία μίμησις πράξεως
σπουδαίας καὶ τελείας μέγεθος ἐχούσης . . .
δι᾽ ἐλέου καὶ φόβου περαίνουσα τὴν τῶν
τοιούτων παθημάτων κάθαρσιν.

> A tragedy is the imitation of an action that is serious and also, as having magnitude, complete in itself . . . with incidents arousing pity and fear, wherewith to accomplish its purgation of such emotions.
> *Poetics*, 6. 1449 b. Trans. by Bywater

17 Amicus Plato, sed magis amica veritas

> Plato is dear to me, but dearer still is truth.
> *Original ascribed to Aristotle*

SIR JOHN ARKWRIGHT
1872–1954

1 O valiant hearts who to your glory
  came.   *Hymn*

ROBERT ARMIN *fl.* 1610

2 A flea in his ear.
       Foole upon Foole (1605), c. 3

JOHN ARMSTRONG 1709–1779

3 Of right and wrong he taught
  Truths as refin'd as ever Athens heard;
  And (strange to tell!) he practis'd
      what he preach'd.
         Art of Preserving Health (1744),
                      bk. iv, l. 303

4 'Tis not too late to-morrow to be
  brave.   *Ib.* l. 460

SIR EDWIN ARNOLD 1832–1904

5   Nor ever once ashamed
       So we be named
  Press-men; Slaves of the Lamp;
       Servants of Light.
            The Tenth Muse, st. 18

GEORGE ARNOLD 1834–1865

6 The living need charity more than the
  dead.   *The Jolly Old Pedagogue*

MATTHEW ARNOLD 1822–1888

7 And we forget because we must
  And not because we will.   *Absence*

8 The Sea of Faith
  Was once, too, at the full, and round
      earth's shore
  Lay like the folds of a bright girdle
      furl'd.
  But now I only hear
  Its melancholy, long, withdrawing
      roar,
  Retreating, to the breath
  Of the night-wind, down the vast edges
      drear
  And naked shingles of the world.
            Dover Beach, l. 21

9 And we are here as on a darkling plain
  Swept with confused alarms of struggle
      and flight,
  Where ignorant armies clash by night.
                    Ib. l. 35

10 Come, dear children, let us away;
   Down and away below.
           The Forsaken Merman, l. 1

11 Where great whales come sailing by,
   Sail and sail, with unshut eye,
   Round the world for ever and aye.
                    Ib. l. 41

12 Children dear, was it yesterday
   (Call yet once) that she went away?
                    Ib. l. 48

13 Singing, 'Here came a mortal,
   But faithless was she!
   And alone dwell for ever
   The kings of the sea.'
           The Forsaken Merman, l. 120

14 Who saw life steadily, and saw it
       whole:
   The mellow glory of the Attic stage;
   Singer of sweet Colonus, and its child.
         Sonnet to a Friend: 'Who prop,
                      thou ask'st.'

15 Wandering between two worlds, one
       dead,
   The other powerless to be born.
         The Grande Chartreuse, l. 85

16 He bears the seed of ruin in himself.
                 Merope, l. 856

17 We cannot kindle when we will
   The fire which in the heart resides,
   The spirit bloweth and is still,
   In mystery our soul abides:
   But tasks in hours of insight will'd
   Can be through hours of gloom fulfill'd.
                 Morality, st. 1

18 Listen, Eugenia—
   How thick the bursts come crowding
       through the leaves!
   Again—thou hearest!
   Eternal Passion!
   Eternal Pain!   *Philomela*, l. 28

19 Strew on her roses, roses,
   And never a spray of yew.
   In quiet she reposes:
   Ah! would that I did too.
                      Requiescat

20 Others abide our question. Thou art
       free.
   We ask and ask: Thou smilest and art
       still,
   Out-topping knowledge.   *Shakespeare*

21 Truth sits upon the lips of dying men.
         Sohrab and Rustum, l. 656

22 Go, for they call you, Shepherd, from
   the hill.   *The Scholar-Gipsy*, l. 1

23 All the live murmur of a summer's day.
                    Ib. l. 20

24 Crossing the stripling Thames at
       Bab-lock-hithe,
   Trailing in the cool stream thy
       fingers wet,
   As the slow punt swings round.
                    Ib. l. 74

25 Thou waitest for the spark from
       heaven! and we,
   Light half-believers in our casual
       creeds   *Ib.* l. 171

26 This strange disease of modern life.
                    Ib. l. 203

27 Still nursing the unconquerable hope,
   Still clutching the inviolable shade.
                    Ib. l. 211

1 And that sweet City with her dreaming
   spires,
      She needs not June for beauty's
      heightening.   *Thyrsis, l. 19*

2 So have I heard the cuckoo's parting
   cry,
      From the wet field, through the
      vext garden-trees,
      Come with the volleying rain and
      tossing breeze:
   'The bloom is gone, and with the
      bloom go I.'   *Ib. l. 57*

3 [Oxford] [Beautiful city! so venerable,
   so lovely, so unravaged by the fierce
   intellectual life of our century, so
   serene! . . . whispering from her
   towers the last enchantments of the
   Middle Age.] . . . Home of lost causes,
   and forsaken beliefs, and unpopular
   names, and impossible loyalties!
      Essays in Criticism, First Series,
      Preface

4 Philistinism!—We have not the expression in English. Perhaps we have
   not the word because we have so
   much of the thing.   *Ib. Heinrich Heine*

5 In poetry, no less than in life, he is 'a
   beautiful and ineffectual angel, beating in the void his luminous wings in
   vain'.   *Ib. Second Series, Shelley*
      [Quoting his own sentence in his
      essay on Byron, *Essays in Criti-
      cism, Second Series*]

6 The pursuit of perfection, then, is the
   pursuit of sweetness and light . . .
   He who works for sweetness and light
   united, works to make reason and the
   will of God prevail.
      Culture and Anarchy, p. 47

7 Miracles do not happen.
      Literature and Dogma, preface to
      1883 edition, last words

8 The true meaning of religion is thus
   not simply morality, but morality
   touched by emotion.   *Ib. ch. 1, § 2*

9 Conduct is three-fourths of our life
   and its largest concern.   *Ib. § 3*

10 Let us put into their 'Eternal' and
   'God' no more science than they [the
   Hebrew writers] did:—the enduring
   power, not ourselves, which makes for
   righteousness.   *Ib. § 5*

11 But there remains the question: what
   righteousness really is. The method
   and secret and sweet reasonableness
   of Jesus.   *Ib. ch. xii, § 2*

SAMUEL JAMES ARNOLD
1774–1852

12 Our ships were British oak,
   And hearts of oak our men.
      Death of Nelson

THOMAS ARNOLD 1795–1842

13 My object will be, if possible, to form
   Christian men, for Christian boys I
   can scarcely hope to make.
      *Letter, in 1828, on appointment
      to Headmastership of Rugby*

GEORGE ASAF [GEORGE H. POWELL] 1880–1951

14 What's the use of worrying?
      It never was worth while,
   So, pack up your troubles in your old
      kit-bag,
      And smile, smile, smile.
      *Pack Up Your Troubles in Your
      Old Kit-Bag*

JOHN DUNNING, BARON ASHBURTON 1731–1783

15 The influence of the Crown has increased, is increasing, and ought to be
   diminished.
      *Motion passed in the House of
      Commons, 1780*

HERBERT HENRY ASQUITH, EARL OF OXFORD 1852–1928

16 Wait and see.
      *Phrase used repeatedly in speeches
      in 1910.* Spender and Cyril
      Asquith's *Life of Lord Oxford
      and Asquith*, vol. i, p. 275

SIR JACOB ASTLEY 1579–1652

17 O Lord! thou knowest how busy I
   must be this day: if I forget thee, do
   not thou forget me.
      *Prayer before the Battle of Edge-
      hill* (Sir Philip Warwick,
      Memoires, 1701, p. 229)

EDWARD L. ATKINSON
and
APSLEY CHERRY-GARRARD

18 A very gallant gentleman.
      Inscription on the burial place of
      Capt. L. E. G. Oates *in the
      Antarctic*, Nov. 1912. *Being al-
      most crippled, he walked to his
      death in a blizzard to enable his
      companions to proceed on their
      journey more quickly.*

JOHN AUBREY 1626–1697

19 When he killed a calf he would do it in
   a high style, and make a speech.
      Brief Lives. William Shakespeare

20 Anno 1670 not far from Cirencester
   was an apparition. Being demanded
   whether a good spirit or a bad? returned no answer but disappeared with
   a curious Perfume and most melodious
   Twang. Mr. W. Lilley believes it was
   a Farie.   *Ib. Nicholas Towes*

ÉMILE AUGIER 1820–1889

1 La nostalgie de la boue.

Homesickness for the gutter.
Le Mariage d'Olympe, I. i

ST. AUGUSTINE 354–430

2 Fecisti nos ad te et inquietum est cor nostrum, donec requiescat in te.

Thou hast created us for thyself, and our heart cannot be quieted till it may find repose in thee.
Confessions, bk. i, ch. I. Trans. by Watts

3 Da mihi castitatem et continentiam, sed noli modo.

Give me chastity and continency, but do not give it yet.
Ib. bk. viii, ch. 7

4 Tolle lege, tolle lege.

Take up and read, take up and read.
Ib. ch. 12

5 Da quod iubes et iube quod vis. Imperas nobis continentiam.

Give what thou commandest, and command what thou wilt.
Thou imposest continency upon us.
Ib. ch. 29

6 Securus iudicat orbis terrarum.

The verdict of the world is conclusive.
Contra Epist. Parmen. iii. 24

7 Salus extra ecclesiam non est.

No salvation exists outside the church.
De Bapt. IV, c. xvii. 24, referring back to St. Cyprian's 'Habere non potest Deum patrem qui ecclesiam non habet matrem' (He cannot have God for his Father who has not the church for his mother), *De Cath. Eccl. Unitate.* vi

8 Audi partem alteram.

Hear the other side.
De Duabus Animabus, XIV. ii

9 Ama et fac quod vis.

Love and do what you will.
Popular version of St. Augustine's 'Dilige et quod vis fac' (Love and do what you will), *In Epist. Johann. Hom.* vii. 8

10 Multi quidem facilius se abstinent ut non utantur, quam temperent ut bene utantur.

To many, total abstinence is easier than perfect moderation.
On the Good of Marriage, xxi

11 Roma locuta est; causa finita est.

Rome has spoken; the case is concluded. *Sermons*, bk. i

JANE AUSTEN 1775–1817

12 An egg boiled very soft is not unwholesome. [*Mr. Woodhouse.*]
Emma, ch. 3

13 One half of the world cannot understand the pleasures of the other. [*Emma.*] *Ib.* ch. 9

14 A basin of nice smooth gruel, thin, but not too thin. *Ib.* ch. 12

15 Let other pens dwell on guilt and misery. *Mansfield Park*, ch. 48

16 'And what are you reading, Miss —?' 'Oh! it is only a novel!' replies the young lady: while she lays down her book with affected indifference, or momentary shame.—'It is only Cecilia, or Camilla, or Belinda:' or, in short, only some work in which the most thorough knowledge of human nature, the happiest delineation of its varieties, the liveliest effusions of wit and humour are conveyed to the world in the best chosen language.
Northanger Abbey, ch. 5

17 Sir Walter Elliot, of Kellynch-hall, in Somersetshire, was a man who, for his own amusement, never took up any book but the Baronetage; there he found occupation for an idle hour, and consolation in a distressed one; . . . this was the page at which the favourite volume always opened: ELLIOT OF KELLYNCH-HALL. *Persuasion*, ch. 1

18 It is a truth universally acknowledged, that a single man in possession of a good fortune, must be in want of a wife. *Pride and Prejudice*, ch. 1

19 You have delighted us long enough. [*Mr. Bennet.*] *Ib.* ch. 18

20 Nobody is on my side, nobody takes part with me: I am cruelly used, nobody feels for my poor nerves. [*Mrs. Bennet.*] *Ib.* ch. 20

21 Lady Middleton . . . exerted herself to ask Mr. Palmer if there was any news in the paper.
'No, none at all,' he replied, and read on. *Sense and Sensibility*, ch. 19

ALFRED AUSTIN 1835–1913

22 Across the wires the electric message came:
'He is no better, he is much the same.'
On the Illness of the Prince of Wales, afterwards Edward VII. Attr. to Austin, but probably not his. *See* J. Lewis May in the *Dublin Review*, July 1937

WILLIAM EDMONDSTOUNE AYTOUN 1813–1865

1 They bore within their breasts the grief
   That fame can never heal—
The deep, unutterable woe
   Which none save exiles feel.
                     The Island of the Scots, xii

2 Fhairshon swore a feud
   Against the clan M'Tavish;
Marched into their land
   To murder and to rafish;
For he did resolve
   To extirpate the vipers,
With four-and-twenty men
   And five-and-thirty pipers.
                  The Massacre of the Macpherson, i

3 Fhairshon had a son,
   Who married Noah's daughter,
And nearly spoiled ta Flood,
   By trinking up ta water: *Ib.* vii

4 Come hither, Evan Cameron!
   Come, stand beside my knee.
                  The Execution of Montrose, i

FRANCIS BACON 1561–1626

5 All good moral philosophy is but an handmaid to religion.
       Advancement of Learning, II, xxii, 14

6 Pyrrhus, when his friends congratulated to him his victory over the Romans, under the conduct of Fabricius, but with great slaughter of his own side, said to them again: 'Yes, but if we have such another victory, we are undone.'   *Apothegms* 193

7 Silence is the virtue of fools.
       De Dignitate et Augmentis Scientiarium, pt. 1, bk. vii, ch. 31 (ed. 1640, trans. Gilbert Watts)

8 There is no excellent beauty that hath not some strangeness in the proportion.   *Essays*, 43. *Of Beauty*

9 Mahomet made the people believe that he would call a hill to him, and from the top of it offer up his prayers for the observers of his law. The people assembled: Mahomet called the hill to come to him again and again; and when the hill stood still, he was never a whit abashed, but said, 'If the hill will not come to Mahomet, Mahomet will go to the hill.'   *Ib.* 12. *Of Boldness*

10 A wise man will make more opportunities than he finds.
       Ib. 52. *Of Ceremonies and Respects*

11 In things that are tender and unpleasing, it is good to break the ice by some whose words are of less weight, and to reserve the more weighty voice to come in as by chance.
                     Essays, 22. *Of Cunning*

12 Men fear death as children fear to go in the dark; and as that natural fear in children is increased with tales, so is the other.   *Ib.* 2. *Of Death*

13 Lookers-on many times see more than gamesters.
       Ib. 48. *Of Followers and Friends*

14 A crowd is not company, and faces are but a gallery of pictures, and talk but a tinkling cymbal, where there is no love.   *Ib.* 27. *Of Friendship*

15 Cure the disease and kill the patient.
                                          Ib.

16 God Almighty first planted a garden; and, indeed, it is the purest of human pleasures.   *Ib.* 46. *Of Gardens*

17 He that hath wife and children hath given hostages to fortune; for they are impediments to great enterprises, either of virtue or mischief.
       Ib. 8. *Of Marriage and Single Life*

18 Wives are young men's mistresses, companions for middle age, and old men's nurses.   *Ib.*

19 He was reputed one of the wise men that made answer to the question when a man should marry? 'A young man not yet, an elder man not at all.' *Ib.*

20 Children sweeten labours, but they make misfortunes more bitter.
       Ib. 7. *Of Parents and Children*

21 Revenge is a kind of wild justice, which the more man's nature runs to, the more ought law to weed it out.
       Ib. 4. *Of Revenge*

22 Money is like muck, not good except it be spread.
       Ib. 15. *Of Seditions and Troubles*

23 The remedy is worse than the disease.
                                          Ib.

24 Studies serve for delight, for ornament, and for ability.
                     Ib. 50. *Of Studies*

25 Some books are to be tasted, others to be swallowed, and some few to be chewed and digested; that is, some books are to be read only in parts; others to be read but not curiously; and some few to be read wholly, and with diligence and attention. Some books also may be read by deputy, and extracts made of them by others. *Ib.*

26 Reading maketh a full man; conference a ready man and writing an exact man.   *Ib.*

27 Histories make men wise; poets, witty; the mathematics, subtile; natural philosophy, deep; moral,

grave; logic and rhetoric, able to contend.
Essays, 50. Of Studies

1 There is a superstition in avoiding superstition. *Ib. 17. Of Superstition*

2 Neither is money the sinews of war (as it is trivially said).
Ib. 29. Of The True Greatness of Kingdoms

3 Thus much is certain; that he that commands the sea is at great liberty, and may take as much and as little of the war as he will. *Ib.*

4 Travel, in the younger sort, is a part of education; in the elder, a part of experience. He that travelleth into a country before he hath some entrance into the language, goeth to school, and not to travel.
Ib. 18. Of Travel

5 What is truth? said jesting Pilate; and would not stay for an answer.
Ib. 1. Of Truth

6 It is the wisdom of the crocodiles, that shed tears when they would devour.
Ib. 23. Of Wisdom for a Man's Self

7 He is the fountain of honour.
Essay of a King

8 Lucid intervals and happy pauses.
History of King Henry VII, par. 3

9 I have taken all knowledge to be my province.
Letter to Lord Burleigh, 1592

10 Opportunity makes a thief.
Letter to the Earl of Essex, 1598

11 There are four classes of Idols which beset men's minds. To these for distinction's sake I have assigned names —calling the first class, Idols of the Tribe; the second, Idols of the Cave; the third, Idols of the Market-place; the fourth, Idols of the Theatre.
Novum Organon, Aphor. xxxix. Trans. Spedding

12 Nam et ipsa scientia potestas est.

Knowledge itself is power.
Religious Meditations. Of Heresies

13 De Sapientia Veterum.

The wisdom of the ancients.
Title of Work. Trans. Sir Arthur Gorges, 1619

14 Who then to frail mortality shall trust, But limns the water, or but writes in dust. *The World*

15 What then remains, but that we still should cry,
Not to be born, or being born, to die?
Ib.

KARL BAEDEKER 1801–1859

16 Oxford is on the whole more attractive than Cambridge to the ordinary visitor; and the traveller is therefore recommended to visit Cambridge first, or to omit it altogether if he cannot visit both.
Baedeker's Great Britain (1887), 30. From London to Oxford

WALTER BAGEHOT 1826–1877

17 It has been said that England invented the phrase, 'Her Majesty's Opposition'.
The English Constitution, ch. i. The Cabinet

18 The *Times* has made many ministries.
Ib.

CHARLES BRUCE BAIRNSFATHER 1888–1959

19 Well, if you knows of a better 'ole, go to it.
Fragments from France, No. 1 (1915)

HENRY WILLIAMS BAKER 1821–1877

20 The King of Love my Shepherd is, Whose goodness faileth never.
Hymns Ancient and Modern. The King of Love my Shepherd is (1868)

MICHAEL BAKUNIN 1814–1876

21 We wish, in a word, equality—equality in fact as corollary, or, rather, as primordial condition of liberty. From each according to his faculties, to each according to his needs; that is what we wish sincerely and energetically.
Declaration signed by forty-seven anarchists on trial after the failure of their uprising at Lyons in 1870. See J. Morrison Davidson, The Old Order and the New (1890) (see 140:15)

STANLEY BALDWIN, EARL BALDWIN 1867–1947

22 When you think about the defence of England you no longer think of the chalk cliffs of Dover. You think of the Rhine. That is where our frontier lies to-day.
Speech, House of Commons, 30 July 1934

ARTHUR JAMES BALFOUR FIRST EARL OF BALFOUR, 1848–1930

23 Defence of philosophic doubt.
Article in Mind (1878)

1 Frank Harris ... said ...: 'The fact is, Mr. Balfour, all the faults of the age come from Christianity and journalism.' 'Christianity, of course, but why journalism?'
Autobiography of Margot Asquith,
vol. i, ch. 10

BALLADS

2 In Scarlet town, where I was born, There was a fair maid dwellin', Made every youth cry *Well-a-way!* Her name was Barbara Allen.
*The Oxford Book of Ballads.
Barbara Allen's Cruelty*

3 'But I hae dream'd a dreary dream, Beyond the Isle of Sky; I saw a dead man win a fight, And I think that man was I.'
Ib. Chevy Chase (xix in the Scottish version, but not included in the Oxford Book version)

4 Clerk Saunders and may Margaret Walk'd owre yon garden green; And deep and heavy was the love That fell thir twa between.

'A bed, a bed,' Clerk Saunders said, 'A bed for you and me!' 'Fye na, fye na,' said may Margaret, 'Till anes we married be!'
Ib. Clerk Saunders

5 She hadna sail'd a league, a league, A league but barely three, Till grim, grim grew his countenance And gurly grew the sea.
Ib. The Daemon Lover

6 Goodman, you've spoken the foremost word! Get up and bar the door.
Ib. Get Up and Bar the Door

7 I wish I were where Helen lies, Night and day on me she cries; O that I were where Helen lies, On fair Kirkconnell lea!

Curst be the heart that thought the thought, And curst the hand that fired the shot, When in my arms burd Helen dropt, And died to succour me!
Ib. Helen of Kirkconnell

8 'What gat ye to your dinner, Lord Randal, my Son? What gat ye to your dinner, my handsome young man?' 'I gat eels boil'd in broo'; mother, make my bed soon, For I'm weary wi' hunting, and fain wald lie down.' *Ib. Lord Randal*

9 When captains couragious whom death could not daunte, Did march to the siege of the city of Gaunt They mustered their soldiers by two and by three, And the foremost in battle was Mary Ambree.
*The Oxford Book of Ballads.
Mary Ambree*

10 Yestreen the Queen had four Maries, The night she'll hae but three; There was Marie Seaton, and Marie Beaton, And Marie Carmichael, and me.
Ib. The Queen's Maries

11 There are twelve months in all the year, As I hear many men say, But the merriest month in all the year Is the merry month of May.
Ib. Robin Hood and the Widow's Three Sons

12 The king sits in Dunfermline town Drinking the blude-red wine.
Ib. Sir Patrick Spens

13 'To Noroway, to Noroway, To Noroway o'er the faem; The king's daughter o' Noroway, 'Tis thou must bring her hame.' *Ib.*

14 I saw the new moon late yestreen Wi' the auld moon in her arm; And if we gang to sea, master, I fear we'll come to harm.' *Ib.*

15 And lang, lang may the maidens sit Wi' their gowd kames in their hair, A-waiting for their ain dear loves! For them they'll see nae mair. *Ib.*

16 And till seven years were gane and past, True Thomas on earth was never seen. *Ib. Thomas the Rhymer, xx*

17 There were three ravens sat on a tree, They were as black as they might be. The one of them said to his make, 'Where shall we our breakfast take?'
Ib. The Three Ravens

18 All the trees they are so high, The leaves they are so green, The day is past and gone, sweetheart, That you and I have seen. It is cold winter's night, You and I must bide alone: Whilst my pretty lad is young And is growing.
Ib. The Trees so High

19 As I was walking all alane, I heard twa corbies[1] making a mane: The tane unto the tither did say, 'Where sall we gang and dine the day?'
Ib. The Twa Corbies

[1] corbies = ravens

1 'The wind doth blow to-day, my love,
   And a few small drops of rain;
I never had but one true love;
   In cold grave she was lain.
         The Oxford Book of Ballads.
         The Unquiet Grave

2 O waly, waly, up the bank,
   And waly, waly, doun the brae,
And waly, waly, yon burn-side,
   Where I and my Love wont to gae!
         Ib. Waly, Waly

3 But had I wist, before I kist,
   That love had been sae ill to win,
I had lock'd my heart in a case o'
   gowd,
And pinn'd it wi' a siller pin.   *Ib.*

4 'Tom Pearse, Tom Pearse, lend me
   your grey mare,
All along, down along, out along, lee.
For I want for to go to Widdicombe
   Fair,
Wi' Bill Brewer, Jan Stewer, Peter
   Gurney, Peter Davey, Dan'l Whid-
   don, Harry Hawk,
      Old Uncle Tom Cobbleigh and
         all.
      Old Uncle Tom Cobbleigh and
         all.'   *Ib. Widdicombe Fair*

EDWARD BANGS *fl.* 1775

5 Yankee Doodle, keep it up,
   Yankee Doodle dandy;
Mind the music and the step,
   And with the girls be handy.
         Yankee Doodle; or Father's Re-
         turn to Camp. See Nicholas
         Smith, Stories of Great National
         Songs

6 Yankee Doodle came to town
   Riding on a pony;
Stuck a feather in his cap
   And called it Macaroni.   *Ib.*

THÉODORE DE BANVILLE
                              1823–1891

7 Nous n'irons plus aux bois, les lauriers
   sont coupés.
   We will go no more to the woods,
   the laurel-trees are cut.
         Les Cariatides, Les Stalactites
         (Nursery rhyme, earlier than Ban-
         ville)

ANNA LETITIA BARBAULD
                              1743–1825

8 Life! we've been long together,
   Through pleasant and through cloudy
      weather;
   'Tis hard to part when friends are
      dear,
Perhaps 'twill cost a sigh, a tear;

Then steal away, give little warning;
   Choose thine own time;
Say not 'Good-night'; but in some
   brighter clime
Bid me 'Good-morning'.
         Ode to Life

REV. RICHARD HARRIS
BARHAM 1788–1845

9 What Horace says is,
   Eheu fugaces
   Anni labuntur, Postume, Postume!
Years glide away, and are lost to me,
   lost to me!
         The Ingoldsby Legends. Epigram:
         Eheu fugaces

10 What *was* to be done?—'twas per-
      fectly plain
That they could not well hang the
      man over again;
What *was* to be done?—The man was
      dead!
Nought *could* be done—nought could
      be said;
So—my Lord Tomnoddy went home
      to bed!
         Ib. Hon. Mr. Sucklethumbkin's
         Story

11 The Jackdaw sat on the Cardinal's
      chair!
Bishop, and abbot, and prior were
      there;
   Many a monk, and many a friar,
   Many a knight, and many a squire,
With a great many more of lesser
      degree,—
In sooth a goodly company;
And they served the Lord Primate on
      bended knee.
         Never, I ween,
         Was a prouder seen,
   Read of in books, or dreamt of in
      dreams,
Than the Cardinal Lord Archbishop
      of Rheims!
         Ib. The Jackdaw of Rheims

12 And six little Singing-boys,—dear
      little souls!
In nice clean faces, and nice white
      stoles.   *Ib.*

13 Never was heard such a terrible curse!
   But what gave rise to no little sur-
      prise,
Nobody seem'd one penny the worse!
         Ib.

14 Heedless of grammar, they all cried,
   'That's him!'   *Ib.*

15   A German,
Who smoked like a chimney.
         Ib. Lay of St. Odille

16 So put that in your pipe, my Lord
   Otto, and smoke it!   *Ib.*

1 'Twas in Margate last July, I walk'd
    upon the pier,
  I saw a little vulgar Boy—I said,
  'What make you here?'
        The Ingoldsby Legends. Mis-
        adventures at Margate

2 He had no little handkerchief to wipe
  his little nose!   *Ib.*

3 But when the Crier cried, 'O Yes!' the
  people cried, 'O No!'   *Ib.*

4 He smiled and said, 'Sir, does your
  mother know that you are out?'   *Ib.*

5 They were a little less than 'kin', and
  rather more than 'kind'.
                Ib. Nell Cook

SABINE BARING-GOULD
1834-1924

6 Now the day is over,
    Night is drawing nigh,
  Shadows of the evening
    Steal across the sky.
      Hymns Ancient and Modern.
      Now the Day is Over

7 Onward, Christian soldiers,
    Marching as to war,
  With the Cross of Jesus
    Going on before.
      Ib. Onward, Christian Soldiers

8 Through the night of doubt and sorrow
  Onward goes the pilgrim band,
  Singing songs of expectation,
  Marching to the Promised Land.
      Ib. Tr. from the Danish of B. S.
      Ingemann, 1789–1862. *Through*
      the Night of Doubt and Sorrow

9 Brother clasps the hand of brother,
  Stepping fearless through the night.
                    Ib.

WILLIAM BARNES 1801–1886

10 An' there vor me the apple tree
  Do lean down low in Linden Lea.
      My Orcha'd in Linden Lea

11 Since I noo mwore do zee your feäce.
          The Wife A-Lost

RICHARD BARNFIELD 1574–1627

12 As it fell upon a day,
  In the merry month of May,
  Sitting in a pleasant shade,
  Which a grove of myrtles made.
  Beasts did leap and birds did sing,
  Trees did grow and plants did spring,
  Everything did banish moan,
  Save the nightingale alone.
  She, poor bird, as all forlorn,
  Lean'd her breast up-till a thorn,
  And there sung the dolefull'st ditty
  That to hear it was great pity.
  Fie, fie, fie, now would she cry;
  Tereu, Tereu, by and by.
      Poems: in Divers Humors, An Ode

13 King Pandion, he is dead,
  All thy friends are lapp'd in lead.
      Poems: in Divers Humors, An Ode

PHINEAS T. BARNUM 1810–1891

14 There's a sucker born every minute.
                    Attr.

SIR JAMES MATTHEW BARRIE
1860–1937

15 His lordship may compel us to be
  equal upstairs, but there will never be
  equality in the servants' hall.
      The Admirable Crichton, Act I

16 I don't want to be a might-have-been!
            Dear Brutus, Act II

17 Never ascribe to an opponent motives
  meaner than your own.
      'Courage', Rectorial Address, St.
      Andrews, 3 May 1922

18 Courage is the thing. All goes if
  courage goes.   *Ib.*

19 When the first baby laughed for the
  first time, the laugh broke into a
  thousand pieces and they all went
  skipping about, and that was the
  beginning of fairies.   *Peter Pan, Act I*

20 Every time a child says 'I don't believe
  in fairies' there is a little fairy somewhere that falls down dead.   *Ib.*

21 To die will be an awfully big adventure.   *Ib. Act III*

22 Do you believe in fairies? . . . If you
  believe, clap your hands!   *Ib. Act IV*

23 The Twelve-pound Look.
                Title of Play

24 It's a sort of bloom on a woman. If
  you have it [charm], you don't need
  to have anything else; and if you
  don't have it, it doesn't much matter
  what else you have.
      What Every Woman Knows, Act I

25 There are few more impressive sights
  in the world than a Scotsman on the
  make.   *Ib. Act II*

GEORGE BARRINGTON b. 1755

26 True patriots we; for be it understood,
  We left our country for our country's
  good.
      Prologue for the opening of the
      Playhouse, Sydney, New South
      Wales, 16 Jan. 1796. The com-
      pany was composed of convicts.

EDGAR BATEMAN
nineteenth century

27 Wiv a ladder and some glasses,
  You could see to 'Ackney Marshes,
  If it wasn't for the 'ouses in between.
      If it wasn't for the 'ouses in
      between

RICHARD BAXTER 1615–1691

1 I preach'd as never sure to preach
again,
And as a dying man to dying men!
*Love Breathing Thanks and
Praise*, pt. ii

2 In necessary things, unity; in doubtful things, liberty; in all things,
charity. *Motto*

THOMAS HAYNES BAYLY
1797–1839

3 Absence makes the heart grow fonder,
Isle of Beauty, Fare thee well!
Isle of Beauty (see 3:6)

4 The mistletoe hung in the castle hall,
The holly branch shone on the old oak
wall. *The Mistletoe Bough*

5 She wore a wreath of roses,
The night that first we met.
She Wore a Wreath of Roses

6 Gaily the Troubadour
Touch'd his guitar.
Welcome Me Home

PIERRE-AUGUSTIN DE
BEAUMARCHAIS 1732–1799

7 Je me presse de rire de tout, de peur
d'être obligé d'en pleurer.

I make myself laugh at everything,
for fear of having to weep.
Le Barbier de Séville, I. ii

8 Parce que vous êtes un grand seigneur,
vous vous croyez un grand génie! . . .
Vous vous êtes donné la peine de
naître, et rien de plus.

Because you are a great lord, you
believe yourself to be a great
genius! . . . You took the trouble
to be born, but no more.
Mariage de Figaro, v. iii

FRANCIS BEAUMONT 1584–1616

9   What things have we seen,
Done at the Mermaid! heard words
that have been
So nimble, and so full of subtil flame,
As if that every one from whence they
came,
Had meant to put his whole wit in
a jest,
And had resolv'd to live a fool, the rest
Of his dull life. *Letter to Ben Jonson*

FRANCIS BEAUMONT 1584–1616
and
JOHN FLETCHER 1579–1625

10 You are no better than you should be.
The Coxcomb, IV. iii

11 I care not two-pence. *Ib.* v. i

12 It is always good
When a man has two irons in the fire.
The Faithful Friends, I. ii

13 Let's meet, and either do, or die.
The Island Princess, II. ii

14 Deeds, not words shall speak me.
The Lovers' Progress, III. vi

15 I find the medicine worse than the
malady. *Ib.* ii

16 Faith, Sir, he went away with a flea
in 's ear. *Ib.* IV. iii

17 I'll put on my considering cap.
The Loyal Subject, II. i

18 I'll put a spoke among your wheels.
The Mad Lover, III. vi

19 Those have most power to hurt us that
we love. *The Maid's Tragedy*, v. iv

20   All your better deeds
Shall be in water writ, but this in
marble. *The Nice Valour*, v. iii

21 'Tis virtue, and not birth that makes
us noble.
Great actions speak great minds, and
such should govern.
The Prophetess, II. iii

22 I'll have a fling.
Rule a Wife and have a Wife,
III. v

23 Kiss till the cow comes home.
Scornful Lady, II. ii

24 Daisies smell-less, yet most quaint.
Two Noble Kinsmen, I. i

25 Though I say't, that should not say't.
Wit at Several Weapons, II. ii

26 Whistle and she'll come to you.
Wit Without Money, IV. iv

27 Let the world slide. *Ib.* v. ii

LORD BEAVERBROOK 1879–1964

28 Responsible for this work of development were 'the boys in the back
rooms' who 'do not sit in the limelight, but are the men who do the
work'.
Glasgow Herald 24 March 1941,
p. 6, col. 4 (report of broadcast
by Lord Beaverbrook)

CARL BECKER 1873–1945

29 Twice tricked by the British into a
European war in order to pull their
chestnuts out of the fire.
Progress and Power (1935)

THOMAS BECON 1512–1567

30 For when the wine is in, the wit is out.
Catechism, 375

THOMAS LOVELL BEDDOES
1798–1851

1 If there were dreams to sell,
　What would you buy?
　Some cost a passing bell;
　Some a light sigh,
　That shakes from Life's fresh crown
　Only a roseleaf down.
　If there were dreams to sell,
　Merry and sad to tell,
　And the crier rung the bell,
　What would you buy?
　　　　　Dream-Pedlary

BEDE 673–735

2 'Such,' he said, 'O King, seems to me
the present life of men on earth, in
comparison with that time which to us
is uncertain, as if when on a winter's
night you sit feasting with your ealdor-
men and thegns,—a single sparrow
should fly swiftly into the hall, and
coming in at one door, instantly fly
out through another. In that time in
which it is indoors it is indeed not
touched by the fury of the winter, but
yet, this smallest space of calmness
being passed almost in a flash, from
winter going into winter again, it is
lost to your eyes. Somewhat like this
appears the life of man; but of what
follows or what went before, we are
utterly ignorant.'
　　Ecclesiastical History, bk. ii, ch. 13

BERNARD ELLIOTT BEE
1823–1861

3 Let us determine to die here, and we
will conquer. There is Jackson standing like a stone wall. Rally behind the
Virginians.
　　First Battle of Bull Run, 1861.
　　Poore, *Reminiscences of Metropolis*, ii. 85.

HENRY CHARLES BEECHING
1859–1919

4 With lifted feet, hands still,
I am poised, and down the hill
Dart, with heedful mind;
The air goes by in a wind.
　　Going Down Hill on a Bicycle

5 First come I; my name is Jowett.
There's no knowledge but I know it.
I am Master of this college:
What I don't know isn't knowledge.
　　*The Masque of Balliol, composed
by and current among members of
Balliol College in the late 1870's*
　　(see also 6:9, 219:19 and 20)

SIR MAX BEERBOHM 1872–1956

6 Most women are not so young as they
are painted.　*A Defence of Cosmetics*

7 To give an accurate and exhaustive
account of that period would need a
far less brilliant pen than mine.　*1880*

8 Not that I had any special reason for
hating school. Strange as it may seem
to my reader, I was not unpopular
there. I was a modest, good-humoured
boy. It was Oxford that has made me
insufferable.　*Going back to School*

9 The Nonconformist Conscience makes
cowards of us all.
　　King George the Fourth

10 'Ah, say that again,' she murmured.
'Your voice is music.'
　He repeated his question.
　'Music!' she said dreamily; and such
is the force of habit that 'I don't', she
added, 'know anything about music,
really. But I know what I like.'
　　Zuleika Dobson, ch. 16

APHRA BEHN 1640–1689

11 Faith, Sir, we are here to-day, and
gone to-morrow.
　　The Lucky Chance, IV

12 Beauty unadorn'd.
　　The Rover, Part II, IV. ii

W. H. BELLAMY *nineteenth century*

13 Old Simon the Cellarer keeps a rare
store
Of Malmsey and Malvoisie.
　　Song: Simon the Cellarer

JOACHIM DU BELLAY 1515–1560

14 France, mère des arts, des armes et
des loix.
　　France, mother of arts, of warriors,
　　and of laws.　　　*Sonnets*

15 Heureux qui comme Ulysse a fait un
beau voyage.
　　Happy the wanderer, like Ulysses,
　　who has come happily home at
　　last.　　　　　　*Ib.*

HILAIRE BELLOC 1870–1953

16 Your little hands were made to take
The better things and leave the worse
ones:
They also may be used to shake
The massive paws of elder persons.
　　Bad Child's Book of Beasts, dedi-
cation

17 When people call this beast to mind,
They marvel more and more
At such a little tail behind,
So large a trunk before.
　　Ib. The Elephant

18 I shoot the Hippopotamus
With bullets made of platinum,
Because if I use leaden ones
His hide is sure to flatten 'em.
　　Ib. The Hippopotamus

1 The nicest child I ever knew
Was Charles Augustus Fortescue.
Cautionary Tales. Charles Augustus Fortescue

2 Godolphin Horne was nobly born;
He held the human race in scorn.
Ib. Godolphin Horne

3 The chief defect of Henry King
Was chewing little bits of string.
Ib. Henry King

4 'Oh, my friends, be warned by me,
That breakfast, dinner, lunch, and tea
Are all the human frame requires . . .'
With that, the wretched child expires.
Ib.

5 Lord Lundy from his earliest years
Was far too freely moved to tears.
Ib. Lord Lundy

6 Towards the age of twenty-six,
They shoved him into politics. *Ib.*

7 We had intended you to be
The next Prime Minister but three:
The stocks were sold; the Press was squared;
The Middle Class was quite prepared.
But as it is! . . . My language fails!
Go out and govern New South Wales!
Ib.

8 Matilda told such Dreadful Lies,
It made one Gasp and Stretch one's Eyes;
Her Aunt, who, from her Earliest Youth,
Had kept a Strict Regard for Truth,
Attempted to Believe Matilda:
The effort very nearly killed her.
Ib. Matilda

9 For every time she shouted 'Fire!'
They only answered 'Little liar!' *Ib.*

10 It happened that a few Weeks later
Her Aunt was off to the Theatre
To see that Interesting Play
The Second Mrs. Tanqueray. *Ib.*

11 She was not really bad at heart,
But only rather rude and wild;
She was an aggravating child.
Ib. Rebecca

12 From quiet homes and first beginning,
Out to the undiscovered ends,
There's nothing worth the wear of winning,
But laughter and the love of friends.
Dedicatory Ode

13 The moon on the one hand, the dawn on the other:
The moon is my sister, the dawn is my brother.
The moon on my left and the dawn on my right.
My brother, good morning: my sister, good night. *The Early Morning*

14 They died to save their country and they only saved the world.
The English Graves

15 When I am dead, I hope it may be said:
'His sins were scarlet, but his books were read.' *Epigrams. On his Books*

16 Of this bad world the loveliest and the best
Has smiled and said 'Good Night,' and gone to rest.
Ib. On a Dead Hostess

17 I said to Heart, 'How goes it?' Heart replied:
'Right as a Ribstone Pippin!' But it lied. *Ib. The False Heart*

18 The accursed power which stands on Privilege
(And goes with Women, and Champagne, and Bridge)
Broke—and Democracy resumed her reign:
(Which goes with Bridge, and Women and Champagne).
Ib. On a Great Election

19 The Devil, having nothing else to do,
Went off to tempt my Lady Poltagrue.
My Lady, tempted by a private whim,
To his extreme annoyance, tempted him.
Ib. On Lady Poltagrue, a Public Peril

20 Remote and ineffectual Don
That dared attack my Chesterton.
Lines to a Don

21 Don different from those regal Dons!
With hearts of gold and lungs of bronze,
Who shout and bang and roar and bawl
The Absolute across the hall,
Or sail in amply billowing gown.
Enormous through the Sacred Town.
Ib.

22 The Llama is a woolly sort of fleecy hairy goat,
With an indolent expression and an undulating throat
Like an unsuccessful literary man.
More Beasts for Worse Children. The Llama

23 I had an aunt in Yucatan
Who bought a Python from a man
And kept it for a pet.
She died, because she never knew
These simple little rules and few;—
The Snake is living yet.
Ib. The Python

24 When I am living in the Midlands
That are sodden and unkind

. . . . .

the great hills of the South Country
Come back into my mind.
The South Country

1 If I ever become a rich man,
  Or if ever I grow to be old,
  I will build a house with deep thatch
  To shelter me from the cold,
  And there shall the Sussex songs be
    sung
  And the story of Sussex told.
  I will hold my house in the high wood
  Within a walk of the sea,
  And the men that were boys when I
    was a boy
  Shall sit and drink with me.
    The South Country

2 Do you remember an Inn,
  Miranda? *Tarantella*

3 The fleas that tease in the high Pyrenees. *Ib.*

JULIEN BENDA 1868–1956

4 La trahison des clercs.
    The treason of the educated classes.
      Attr.

ENOCH ARNOLD BENNETT
1867–1931

5 Journalists say a thing that they know
  isn't true, in the hope that if they keep
  on saying it long enough it *will* be
  true. *The Title*, Act II

S. R. BENNETT 1836–1898

6 In the sweet by-and-by,
  We shall meet on that beautiful shore.
    *Sacred Songs and Solos. Sweet
    By-and-By*

ARTHUR CHRISTOPHER
BENSON 1862–1925

7 Land of Hope and Glory, Mother of
    the Free,
  How shall we extol thee, who are born
    of thee?
  Wider still and wider shall thy bounds
    be set;
  God who made thee mighty, make
    thee mightier yet.
    Song from Pomp and Circum-
    stance *by* Elgar, op. 39, No. 1

JEREMY BENTHAM 1748–1832

8 The greatest happiness of the greatest
  number is the foundation of morals
  and legislation. (see *112:10*)
    The Commonplace Book (Works,
    vol. x, p. 142)

EDMUND CLERIHEW BENTLEY
1875–1956

9 The art of Biography
  Is different from Geography.
  Geography is about maps,
  But Biography is about chaps.
    Biography for Beginners

10 What I like about Clive
  Is that he is no longer alive.
  There is a great deal to be said
  For being dead.
    Biography for Beginners. Clive

11 John Stuart Mill
  By a mighty effort of will
  Overcame his natural bonhomie
  And wrote 'Principles of Political
    Economy.' *Ib. John Stuart Mill*

12 Sir Christopher Wren
  Said, 'I am going to dine with some
    men.
  If anybody calls
  Say I am designing St. Paul's.'
    Ib. Sir Christopher Wren

13 George the Third
  Ought never to have occurred.
  One can only wonder
  At so grotesque a blunder.
    More Biographies. George the Third

THOMAS BENTLEY 1693?–1742

14 No man is demolished but by himself.
    A Letter to Mr. Pope, 1735

PIERRE-JEAN DE BÉRANGER
1780–1857

15 Nos amis, les ennemis.
    Our friends, the enemy.
      L'Opinion de ces demoiselles

BISHOP GEORGE BERKELEY
1685–1753

16 Westward the course of empire takes
    its way;
  The four first acts already past,
  A fifth shall close the drama with the
    day:
  Time's noblest offspring is the last.
    *On the Prospect of Planting Arts
    and Learning in America*

IRVING BERLIN 1888–

17 Come on and hear, come on and hear,
  Alexander's Ragtime Band.
    Alexander's Ragtime Band

WILLIAM BAYLE BERNARD
1807–1875

18 A Storm in a Teacup.
    Title of farce (1854)

RICHARD BETHELL, BARON
WESTBURY 1800–1873

19 His Lordship says he will turn it over
  in what he is pleased to call his mind.
    Nash, *Life of Westbury*, i. 158

THEOBALD VON BETHMANN HOLLWEG 1856–1921

1 Just for a word—'neutrality', a word which in wartime has so often been disregarded, just for a scrap of paper—Great Britain is going to make war.
To Sir Edward Goschen, 4 Aug. 1914. Dispatch by Sir Edward Goschen to the British Foreign Office

JACOB BEULER *nineteenth century*

2 If I had a donkey wot wouldn't go,
D'ye think I'd wollop him? no, no, no.
Music Hall Song (c. 1822)

WILLIAM, LORD BEVERIDGE 1879–1963

3 The object of government in peace and in war is not the glory of rulers or of races, but the happiness of the common man. *Social Insurance*

HOLY BIBLE

Old Testament

4 In the beginning God created the heaven and the earth. *Genesis i. 1*

5 And God said, Let there be light: and there was light. *Ib. 3*

6 Fiat lux.
Let there be light. *Ib. 3 (Vulgate)*

7 And God saw that it was good. *Ib. 10*

8 Male and female created he them. *Ib. 27*

9 Be fruitful, and multiply, and replenish the earth. *Ib. 28*

10 But of the tree of the knowledge of good and evil, thou shalt not eat of it: for in the day that thou eatest thereof thou shalt surely die. *Ib. ii. 17*

11 It is not good that the man should be alone; I will make him an help meet for him. *Ib. 18*

12 And the Lord God caused a deep sleep to fall upon Adam, and he slept: and he took one of his ribs, and closed up the flesh instead thereof;
And the rib, which the Lord God had taken from man, made he a woman. *Ib. 21*

13 Bone of my bones, and flesh of my flesh. *Ib. 23*

14 Therefore shall a man leave his father and his mother, and shall cleave unto his wife: and they shall be one flesh. *Ib. 24*

15 And they sewed fig leaves together, and made themselves aprons [breeches in *Genevan Bible*, 1560].
And they heard the voice of the Lord God walking in the garden in the cool of the day. *Genesis iii. 7*

16 In the sweat of thy face shalt thou eat bread. *Ib. 19*

17 For dust thou art, and unto dust shalt thou return. *Ib.*

18 Am I my brother's keeper? *Ib. iv. 9*

19 Dwelt in the land of Nod. *Ib. 16*

20 And Noah begat Shem, Ham, and Japheth. *Ib. v. 32*

21 There were giants in the earth in those days. *Ib. vi. 4*

22 Whoso sheddeth man's blood, by man shall his blood be shed. *Ib. ix. 6*

23 I do set my bow in the cloud. *Ib. 13*

24 Even as Nimrod the mighty hunter before the Lord. *Ib. x. 9*

25 His hand will be against every man, and every man's hand against him. *Ib. xvi. 12*

26 But his wife looked back from behind him, and she became a pillar of salt. *Ib. xix. 26*

27 And he sold his birthright unto Jacob. *Ib. xxv. 33*

28 Behold, Esau my brother is a hairy man, and I am a smooth man. *Ib. xxvii. 11*

29 And he [Jacob] dreamed, and behold a ladder set up on the earth, and the top of it reached to heaven: and behold the angels of God ascending and descending on it. *Ib. xxviii. 12*

30 And Jacob served seven years for Rachel; and they seemed unto him but a few days, for the love he had to her. *Ib. xxix. 20*

31 Mizpah; for he said, The Lord watch between me and thee, when we are absent one from another. *Ib. xxxi*

32 Now Israel loved Joseph more than all his children, because he was the son of his old age; and he made him a coat of many colours. *Ib. xxxvii. 3*

33 Behold, this dreamer cometh. *Ib. 19*

34 Jacob saw that there was corn in Egypt. *Ib. xlii. 1*

35 Bring down my gray hairs with sorrow to the grave. *Ib. 38*

36 Ye shall eat the fat of the land. *Ib. xlv. 18*

37 I have been a stranger in a strange land. *Exodus ii. 22*

38 Behold, the bush burned with fire, and the bush was not consumed. *Ib. iii. 2*

1 Put off thy shoes from off thy feet, for the place whereon thou standest is holy ground. *Exodus* iii. 5

2 A land flowing with milk and honey; unto the place of the Canaanites, and the Hittites, and the Amorites, and the Perizzites, and the Hivites, and the Jebusites. *Ib.* 8

3 I AM THAT I AM. *Ib.* 14

4 Darkness which may be felt. *Ib.* x. 21

5 With your loins girded, your shoes on your feet, and your staff in your hand; and ye shall eat it in haste; it is the Lord's passover. *Ib.* xii. 11

6 Would to God we had died by the hand of the Lord in the land of Egypt, when we sat by the flesh pots, and when we did eat bread to the full. *Ib.* xvi. 3

7 Life for life,
Eye for eye, tooth for tooth, hand for hand, foot for foot,
Burning for burning, wound for wound, stripe for stripe. *Ib.* xxi. 23

8 A stiffnecked people. *Ib.* xxxiii. 3

9 Joshua the son of Nun. *Ib.* 11

10 There shall no man see me, and live. *Ib.* 20

11 Let him go for a scapegoat into the wilderness. *Leviticus* xvi. 10

12 Thou shalt love thy neighbour as thyself. *Ib.* xix. 18; *St. Matthew* xix. 19

13 The Lord bless thee, and keep thee:
The Lord make his face shine upon thee, and be gracious unto thee:
The Lord lift up his countenance upon thee, and give thee peace. *Numbers* vi. 24

14 Sent to spy out the land. *Ib.* xiii. 16

15 Smote him with the edge of the sword. *Ib.* xxi. 24

16 Be sure your sin will find you out. *Ib.* xxxii. 23

17 Man doth not live by bread only, but by every word that proceedeth out of the mouth of the Lord doth man live. *Deuteronomy* viii. 3

18 A dreamer of dreams. *Ib.* xiii. 1

19 The wife of thy bosom. *Ib.* 6

20 Thou shalt not muzzle the ox when he treadeth out the corn. *Ib.* xxv. 4

21 Cursed be he that removeth his neighbour's landmark. *Ib.* xxvii. 17

22 In the waste howling wilderness. *Ib.* xxxii. 10

23 Jeshurun waxed fat, and kicked. *Ib.* 15

24 As thy days, so shall thy strength be. *Deuteronomy* xxxiii. 25

25 The eternal God is thy refuge, and underneath are the everlasting arms. *Ib.* 27

26 Be strong and of a good courage; be not afraid, neither be thou dismayed: for the Lord thy God is with thee, whithersoever thou goest. *Joshua* i. 9

27 Hewers of wood and drawers of water. *Ib.* ix. 21

28 The stars in their courses fought against Sisera. *Judges* v. 20

29 She brought forth butter in a lordly dish. *Ib.* 25

30 Faint, yet pursuing. *Ib.* viii. 4

31 Out of the eater came forth meat, and out of the strong came forth sweetness. *Ib.* xiv. 14

32 He smote them hip and thigh. *Ib.* xv. 8

33 From Dan even to Beer-sheba. *Ib.* xx. 1

34 The people arose as one man. *Ib.* 8

35 Intreat me not to leave thee, or to return from following after thee: for whither thou goest, I will go; and where thou lodgest, I will lodge: thy people shall be my people, and thy God my God: *Ruth* i. 16

36 The flower of their age. *1 Samuel* ii. 33

37 Speak, Lord; for thy servant heareth. *Ib.* iii. 9

38 Quit yourselves like men. *Ib.* iv. 9

39 I-chabod, saying, The glory is departed from Israel. *Ib.* 21

40 God save the king. *Ib.* x. 24

41 A man after his own heart. *Ib.* xiii. 14

42 Agag came unto him delicately. And Agag said, Surely the bitterness of death is past. *Ib.* xv. 32

43 Now he was ruddy, and withal of a beautiful countenance, and goodly to look to. *Ib.* xvi. 12

44 Go, and the Lord be with thee. *Ib.* xvii. 37

45 Saul hath slain his thousands, and David his ten thousands. *Ib.* xviii. 7

46 I have played the fool. *Ib.* xxvi. 21

47 The beauty of Israel is slain upon thy high places: how are the mighty fallen! Tell it not in Gath, publish it not in the streets of Askelon. *2 Samuel* i. 19

48 Saul and Jonathan were lovely and pleasant in their lives, and in their death they were not divided: they

were swifter than eagles, they were stronger than lions. *2 Samuel* i. 23

1 How are the mighty fallen in the midst of the battle! O Jonathan, thou wast slain in thine high places.
I am distressed for thee, my brother Jonathan: very pleasant hast thou been unto me: thy love to me was wonderful, passing the love of women. How are the mighty fallen, and the weapons of war perished! *Ib.* 25

2 Smote him under the fifth rib.
Ib. ii. 23

3 The poor man had nothing, save one little ewe lamb. *Ib.* xii. 3

4 Would God I had died for thee, O Absalom, my son, my son!
Ib. xviii. 33

5 The sweet psalmist of Israel.
Ib. xxiii. 1

6 Went in jeopardy of their lives. *Ib.* 17

7 A proverb and a byword among all people. *1 Kings* ix. 7

8 Behold, the half was not told me.
Ib. x. 7

9 Ivory, and apes, and peacocks. *Ib.* 22

10 My father hath chastised you with whips, but I will chastise you with scorpions. *Ib.* xii. 11

11 He slept with his fathers. *Ib.* xiv. 20

12 There ariseth a little cloud out of the sea, like a man's hand. *Ib.* xviii. 44

13 Sat down under a juniper tree.
Ib. xix. 4

14 But the Lord was not in the wind: and after the wind an earthquake; but the Lord was not in the earthquake:
And after the earthquake a fire: but the Lord was not in the fire: and after the fire a still small voice. *Ib.* 11

15 Elijah passed by him, and cast his mantle upon him. *Ib.* 19

16 Feed him with bread of affliction and with water of affliction, until I come in peace. *Ib.* xxii. 27

17 And a certain man drew a bow at a venture, and smote the king of Israel between the joints of the harness.
Ib. 34

18 I bow myself in the house of Rimmon.
2 Kings v. 18

19 Is thy servant a dog, that he should do this great thing? *Ib.* viii. 13

20 The driving is like the driving of Jehu, the son of Nimshi; for he driveth furiously. *Ib.* ix. 20

21 She painted her face, and tired her head, and looked out at a window.
Ib. 30

22 Thou trustest upon the staff of this bruised reed, even upon Egypt, on which if a man lean, it will go into his hand, and pierce it. *2 Kings* xviii. 21

23 He died in a good old age, full of days, riches, and honour.
1 Chronicles xxix. 28

24 And the Lord said unto Satan, Whence comest thou? Then Satan answered the Lord, and said, From going to and fro in the earth, and from walking up and down in it. *Job* i. 7

25 Doth Job fear God for naught? *Ib.* 9

26 The Lord gave, and the Lord hath taken away; blessed be the name of the Lord. *Ib.* 21

27 Curse God, and die. *Ib.* ii. 9

28 There the wicked cease from troubling, and there the weary be at rest.
Ib. iii. 17

29 Man is born unto trouble, as the sparks fly upward. *Ib.* v. 7

30 Canst thou by searching find out God?
Ib. xi. 7

31 Man that is born of a woman is of few days, and full of trouble. *Ib.* xiv. 1

32 Miserable comforters are ye all.
Ib. xvi. 2

33 I am escaped with the skin of my teeth. *Ib.* xix. 20

34 Oh that my words were now written! oh that they were printed in a book!
Ib. 23

35 I know that my redeemer liveth, and that he shall stand at the latter day upon the earth. *Ib.* 25

36 Seeing the root of the matter is found in me. *Ib.* 28

37 The price of wisdom is above rubies.
Ib. xxviii. 18

38 My desire is . . . that mine adversary had written a book. *Ib.* xxxi. 35

39 Who is this that darkeneth counsel by words without knowledge?
Ib. xxxviii. 2

40 Gird up now thy loins like a man. *Ib.* 3

41 Where wast thou when I laid the foundations of the earth? *Ib.* 4

42 When the morning stars sang together, and all the sons of God shouted for joy. *Ib.* 7

43 Canst thou bind the sweet influences of Pleiades, or loose the bands of Orion? *Ib.* 31

44 He saith among the trumpets, Ha, ha; and he smelleth the battle afar off, the thunder of the captains, and the shouting. *Ib.* xxxix. 25

1 Behold now behemoth, which I made with thee; he eateth grass as an ox.
Job xl. 15

2 Canst thou draw out leviathan with an hook? *Ib.* xli. 1

3 Dominus illuminatio mea.
The Lord is my light.
Psalms xxvii. 1 (Vulgate)

4 Nisi dominus frustra.
Except the Lord keep the city the watchman waketh but in vain.
Ib. cxxvii. 1 (Vulgate) abridged
(*Motto of the City of Edinburgh*)

For psalms in the Book of Common Prayer see Prayer Book

5 Surely in vain the net is spread in the sight of any bird. *Proverbs* i. 17

6 Length of days is in her right hand; and in her left hand riches and honour.
Ib. iii. 16

7 Her ways are ways of pleasantness, and all her paths are peace. *Ib.* 17

8 Go to the ant, thou sluggard; consider her ways, and be wise. *Ib.* vi. 6

9 Yet a little sleep, a little slumber, a little folding of the hands to sleep.
Ib. 10

10 As an ox goeth to the slaughter.
Ib. vii. 22

11 Stolen waters are sweet, and bread eaten in secret is pleasant. *Ib.* ix. 17

12 In the multitude of counsellors there is safety. *Ib.* xi. 14

13 Hope deferred maketh the heart sick.
Ib. xiii. 12

14 The way of transgressors is hard.
Ib. 15

15 He that spareth his rod hateth his son.
Ib. 24

16 A soft answer turneth away wrath.
Ib. xv. 1

17 A merry heart maketh a cheerful countenance. *Ib.* 13

18 Better is a dinner of herbs where love is, than a stalled ox and hatred therewith. *Ib.* 17

19 A word spoken in due season, how good is it! *Ib.* 23

20 Pride goeth before destruction, and an haughty spirit before a fall.
Ib. xvi. 18

21 There is a friend that sticketh closer than a brother. *Ib.* xviii. 24

22 Train up a child in the way he should go: and when he is old, he will not depart from it. *Ib.* xxii. 6

23 Look not thou upon the wine when it is red, when it giveth his colour in the cup. *Proverbs* xxiii. 31

24 Heap coals of fire upon his head.
Ib. xxv. 22

25 As cold waters to a thirsty soul, so is good news from a far country. *Ib.* 25

26 Answer a fool according to his folly.
Ib. xxvi. 5

27 As a dog returneth to his vomit, so a fool returneth to his folly. *Ib.* 11

28 Boast not thyself of to morrow; for thou knowest not what a day may bring forth. *Ib.* xxvii. 1

29 The wicked flee when no man pursueth: but the righteous are bold as a lion. *Ib.* xxviii. 1

30 Where there is no vision, the people perish. *Ib.* xxix. 18

31 The way of an eagle in the air; the way of a serpent upon a rock; the way of a ship in the midst of the sea; and the way of a man with a maid. *Ib.* xxx. 19

32 Who can find a virtuous woman? for her price is far above rubies.
Ib. xxxi. 10

33 Her children arise up, and call her blessed. *Ib.* 28

34 Vanity of vanities, saith the Preacher, vanity of vanities; all is vanity.
What profit hath a man of all his labour which he taketh under the sun? One generation passeth away, and another generation cometh.
Ecclesiastes i. 2

35 The thing that hath been, it is that which shall be; and that which is done is that which shall be done: and there is no new thing under the sun. *Ib.* 8

36 All is vanity and vexation of spirit.
Ib. 14

37 He that increaseth knowledge increaseth sorrow. *Ib.* 18

38 To every thing there is a season, and a time to every purpose under the heaven:
A time to be born, and a time to die.
Ib. iii. 1

39 As the crackling of thorns under a pot, so is the laughter of a fool. *Ib.* vii. 6

40 Be not righteous over much. *Ib.* 16

41 God hath made man upright; but they have sought out many inventions.
Ib. 29

42 There is no discharge in that war.
Ib. viii. 8

43 A man hath no better thing under the sun, than to eat, and to drink, and to be merry. *Ib.* 15

1 A living dog is better than a dead lion.
Ecclesiastes ix. 4

2 Whatsoever thy hand findeth to do,
do it with thy might; for there is no
work, nor device, nor knowledge, nor
wisdom, in the grave, whither thou
goest. *Ib.* 10

3 The race is not to the swift, nor the
battle to the strong. *Ib.* 11

4 He that diggeth a pit shall fall into it.
Ib. x. 8

5 Cast thy bread upon the waters: for
thou shalt find it after many days.
Ib. xi. 1

6 In the place where the tree falleth,
there it shall be. *Ib.* 3

7 Remember now thy Creator in the
days of thy youth, while the evil
days come not, nor the years draw
nigh, when thou shalt say, I have no
pleasure in them; *Ib. xii.* 1

8 Or ever the silver cord be loosed, or
the golden bowl be broken, or the
pitcher be broken at the fountain, or
the wheel broken at the cistern.
Then shall the dust return to the earth
as it was: and the spirit shall return
unto God who gave it. *Ib. xii.* 6

9 Of making many books there is no
end; and much study is a weariness of
the flesh. *Ib.* 12

10 Fear God, and keep his commandments: for this is the whole duty of
man. *Ib.* 13

11 The song of songs, which is Solomon's.
The Song of Solomon i. 1

12 I am black, but comely, O ye daugh-
ters of Jerusalem, as the tents of
Kedar, as the curtains of Solomon.
Ib. 5

13 I am the rose of Sharon, and the lily
of the valleys. *Ib. ii.* 1

14 His banner over me was love. *Ib.* 4

15 Stay me with flagons, comfort me with
apples: for I am sick of love.
His left hand is under my head, and
his right hand doth embrace me. *Ib.* 5

16 Rise up, my love, my fair one, and
come away.
For, lo, the winter is past, the rain is
over and gone;
The flowers appear on the earth; the
time of the singing of birds is come,
and the voice of the turtle is heard in
our land. *Ib.* 10

17 Take us the foxes, the little foxes, that
spoil the vines. *Ib.* 15

18 My beloved is mine, and I am his:
he feedeth among the lilies.
Until the day break, and the shadows
flee away. *Ib.* 16

19 Who is she that looketh forth as the
morning, fair as the moon, clear as the
sun, and terrible as an army with
banners. *The Song of Solomon vi.* 10

20 Many waters cannot quench love,
neither can the floods drown it: if
a man would give all the substance of
his house for love, it would utterly be
contemned. *Ib. viii.* 7

21 Though your sins be as scarlet, they
shall be as white as snow. *Isaiah i.* 18

22 They shall beat their swords into
plowshares, and their spears into
pruninghooks: nation shall not lift up
sword against nation, neither shall
they learn war any more. *Ib. ii.* 4

23 Grind the faces of the poor. *Ib. iii.* 15

24 My wellbeloved hath a vineyard in a
very fruitful hill. *Ib. v.* i

25 Woe unto them that join house to
house, that lay field to field, till there
be no place. *Ib.* 8

26 Woe unto them that call evil good,
and good evil. *Ib.* 20

27 In the year that king Uzziah died I
saw also the Lord sitting upon a
throne, high and lifted up, and his
train filled the temple.
Above it stood the seraphims: each
one had six wings; with twain he
covered his face, and with twain he covered his feet, and with twain he did
fly.
And one cried unto another, and said,
Holy, holy, holy, is the Lord of hosts:
the whole earth is full of his glory.
And the posts of the door moved at
the voice of him that cried, and the
house was filled with smoke.
Then said I, Woe is me! for I am undone; because I am a man of unclean
lips, and I dwell in the midst of a
people of unclean lips. *Ib. vi.* 1

28 Whom shall I send, and who will go
for us? Then said I, Here am I; send
me. *Ib.* 8

29 Then said I, Lord, how long? *Ib.* 11

30 Behold, a virgin shall conceive, and
bear a son, and shall call his name
Immanuel. *Ib. vii.* 14

31 The people that walked in darkness
have seen a great light; they that
dwell in the land of the shadow of
death, upon them hath the light
shined. *Ib. ix.* 2

32 For unto us a child is born, unto us a
son is given: and the government shall
be upon his shoulder: and his name
shall be called Wonderful, Counsellor,
The mighty God, The everlasting
Father, The Prince of Peace.
Of the increase of his government and
peace there shall be no end. *Ib.* 6

1 And there shall come forth a rod out
of the stem of Jesse, and a Branch
shall grow out of his roots:
And the spirit of the Lord shall rest
upon him, the spirit of wisdom and
understanding, the spirit of counsel
and might, the spirit of knowledge and
of the fear of the Lord.　　*Isaiah* xi. 1

2 The wolf also shall dwell with the
lamb, and the leopard shall lie down
with the kid; and the calf and the
young lion and the fatling together;
and a little child shall lead them.
　　　　　　　　　　　　Ib. 6

3 for the earth shall be full of the knowledge of the Lord, as the waters cover
the sea.　　　　　　　　*Ib.* 9

4 How art thou fallen from heaven, O
Lucifer, son of the morning!
　　　　　　　　　　Ib. xiv. 12

5 Watchman, what of the night?
Watchman, what of the night?
The watchman said, The morning
cometh, and also the night.
　　　　　　　　　　Ib. xxi. 11

6 Let us eat and drink; for to morrow
we shall die.　　　　*Ib.* xxii. 13

7 For precept must be upon precept,
precept upon precept; line upon line,
line upon line; here a little, and there
a little.　　　　　　*Ib.* xxviii. 10

8 The bread of adversity.　*Ib.* xxx. 20

9 This is the way, walk ye in it.　*Ib.* 21
The wilderness and the solitary place
shall be glad for them; and the desert
shall rejoice, and blossom as the rose.
　　　　　　　　　　Ib. xxxv. 1

10 Set thine house in order.
　　　　　　　　　Ib. xxxviii. 1

11 Comfort ye, comfort ye my people,
saith your God. Speak ye comfortably
to Jerusalem, and cry unto her, that
her warfare is accomplished.　*Ib.* xl. 1

12 The voice of him that crieth in the
wilderness, Prepare ye the way of the
Lord, make straight in the desert a
highway for our God.
Every valley shall be exalted, and
every mountain and hill shall be made
low: and the crooked shall be made
straight, and the rough places plain:
And the glory of the Lord shall be revealed, and all flesh shall see it together: for the mouth of the Lord
hath spoken it.　　　　　　*Ib.* 3

13 The voice said, Cry. And he said,
What shall I cry? All flesh is grass,
and all the goodliness thereof is as the
flower of the field:
The grass withereth, the flower fadeth:
because the spirit of the Lord bloweth
upon it: surely the people is grass.
　　　　　　　　　　　　Ib. 6

14 He shall feed his flock like a shepherd:
he shall gather the lambs with his arm,
and carry them in his bosom, and shall
gently lead those that are with young.
　　　　　　　　　　Isaiah xl. 11

15 But they that wait upon the Lord shall
renew their strength: they shall
mount up with wings as eagles; they
shall run, and not be weary; and they
shall walk, and not faint.
　　　　　　　　　　　　Ib. 31

16 A bruised reed shall he not break, and
the smoking flax shall he not quench.
　　　　　　　　　　Ib. xlii. 3

17 There is no peace, saith the Lord, unto
the wicked.　　　　　　*Ib.* 22

18 How beautiful upon the mountains
are the feet of him that bringeth good
tidings, that publisheth peace; that
bringeth good tidings of good, that
publisheth salvation; that saith unto
Zion, Thy God reigneth!　*Ib.* lii. 7

19 For they shall see eye to eye, when the
Lord shall bring again Zion.
Break forth into joy, sing together, ye
waste places of Jerusalem: for the
Lord hath comforted his people, he
hath redeemed Jerusalem.　*Ib.* 8

20 He is despised and rejected of men;
a man of sorrows, and acquainted with
grief: and we hid as it were our faces
from him; he was despised, and we
esteemed him not.
Surely he hath borne our griefs, and
carried our sorrows.　　*Ib.* liii. 3

21 But he was wounded for our transgressions, he was bruised for our iniquities: the chastisement of our peace
was upon him; and with his stripes we
are healed.
All we like sheep have gone astray; we
have turned every one to his own way;
and the Lord hath laid on him the
iniquity of us all.
He was oppressed, and he was afflicted,
yet he opened not his mouth: he is
brought as a lamb to the slaughter,
and as a sheep before her shearers is
dumb, so he openeth not his mouth.
　　　　　　　　　　　　Ib. 5

22 He was cut off out of the land of the
living.　　　　　　　　*Ib.* 8

23 He was numbered with the transgressors.　　　　　　　*Ib.* 12

24 Seek ye the Lord while he may be
found, call ye upon him while he is
near.　　　　　　　　*Ib.* lv. 6

25 For my thoughts are not your
thoughts, neither are your ways my
ways, saith the Lord.　　*Ib.* 8

26 Peace to him that is far off, and to
him that is near.　　*Ib.* lvii. 19

1 Arise, shine; for thy light is come, and the glory of the Lord is risen upon thee.
Isaiah lx. 1

2 To bind up the brokenhearted, to proclaim liberty to the captives, and the opening of the prison to them that are bound;
Ib. lxi. 1

3 For, behold, I create new heavens and a new earth.
Ib. lxv. 17

4 Saying, Peace, peace; when there is no peace.
Jeremiah vi. 14

5 Is there no balm in Gilead?
Ib. viii. 22

6 Can the Ethiopian change his skin, or the leopard his spots?
Ib. xiii. 23

7 The heart is deceitful above all things, and desperately wicked.
Ib. xvii. 9

8 Is it nothing to you, all ye that pass by? behold, and see if there be any sorrow like unto my sorrow.
Lamentations i. 12

9 The wormwood and the gall.
Ib. iii. 19

10 It is good for a man that he bear the yoke in his youth.
Ib. 27

11 As is the mother, so is her daughter.
Ezekiel xvi. 44

12 The fathers have eaten sour grapes, and the children's teeth are set on edge.
Ib. xviii. 2

13 When the wicked man turneth away from his wickedness that he hath committed, and doeth that which is lawful and right, he shall save his soul alive.
Ib. 27

14 The valley which was full of bones.
Ib. xxxvii. 1

15 Can these bones live?
Ib. 3

16 The sound of the cornet, flute, harp, sackbut, psaltery, dulcimer, and all kinds of musick.
Daniel iii. 5

17 Cast into the midst of a burning fiery furnace.
Ib. 6

18 MENE, MENE, TEKEL, UPHARSIN.
This is the interpretation of the thing: MENE; God hath numbered thy kingdom, and finished it.
TEKEL; Thou art weighed in the balances, and art found wanting.
PERES; Thy kingdom is divided, and given to the Medes and Persians.
Ib. v. 25

19 The Ancient of days.
Ib. vii. 9

20 They have sown the wind, and they shall reap the whirlwind.
Hosea viii. 7

21 I will restore to you the years that the locust hath eaten.
Joel ii. 25

22 And it shall come to pass afterward, that I will pour out my spirit upon all flesh; and your sons and your daughters shall prophesy, your old men shall dream dreams, your young men shall see visions.
Joel ii. 28

23 Multitudes in the valley of decision.
Ib. iii. 14

24 A firebrand plucked out of the burning.
Amos iv. 11

25 Come, and let us cast lots, that we may know for whose cause this evil is upon us. So they cast lots, and the lot fell upon Jonah.
Jonah i. 7

26 Jonah was in the belly of the fish three days and three nights.
Ib. 17

27 They shall sit every man under his vine and under his fig tree.
Micah iv. 4

28 But thou, Beth-lehem Ephratah, though thou be little among the thousands of Judah, yet out of thee shall he come forth unto me that is to be ruler in Israel.
Ib. v. 2

29 What doth the Lord require of thee, but to do justly, and to love mercy, and to walk humbly with thy God?
Ib. vi. 8

Apocrypha

30 I shall light a candle of understanding in thine heart, which shall not be put out.
2 Esdras xiv. 25

31 Magna est veritas et praevalet.
Great is Truth, and mighty above all things.
3 Esdras iv. 41 (Vulgate)

32 But the souls of the righteous are in the hand of God, and there shall no torment touch them.
The Wisdom of Solomon iii. 1

33 For though they be punished in the sight of men, yet is their hope full of immortality.
And having been a little chastised, they shall be greatly rewarded: for God proved them, and found them worthy for himself.
Ib. 4

34 And in the time of their visitation they shall shine, and run to and fro like sparks among the stubble.
Ib. 7

35 He that toucheth pitch shall be defiled therewith.
Ecclesiasticus xiii. 1

36 Leave off first for manners' sake.
Ib. xxxi. 17

37 Let us now praise famous men, and our fathers that begat us.
Ib. xliv. 1

38 And some there be, which have no memorial.
Ib. 9

39 When he was at the last gasp.
2 Maccabees vii. 9

New Testament

1 There came wise men from the east
to Jerusalem,
Saying, Where is he that is born King
of the Jews? for we have seen his star
in the east, and are come to worship
him. *St. Matthew ii. 1*

2 They presented unto him gifts; gold,
and frankincense, and myrrh. *Ib. 11*

3 Repent ye: for the kingdom of heaven
is at hand. *Ib. iii. 2*

4 The voice of one crying in the wilderness, Prepare ye the way of the Lord,
make his paths straight. *Ib. 3*

5 O generation of vipers, who hath
warned you to flee from the wrath to
come? *Ib. 7*

6 And now also the axe is laid unto the
root of the trees. *Ib. 10*

7 This is my beloved Son, in whom I
am well pleased. *Ib. 17*

8 Man shall not live by bread alone,
but by every word that proceedeth
out of the mouth of God. *Ib. iv. 4*

9 Thou shalt not tempt the Lord thy
God. *Ib. 7*

10 Fishers of men. *Ib. 19*

11 Blessed are the poor in spirit: for
theirs is the kingdom of heaven.
Blessed are they that mourn: for they
shall be comforted.
Blessed are the meek: for they shall
inherit the earth.
Blessed are they which do hunger and
thirst after righteousness: for they
shall be filled.
Blessed are the merciful: for they shall
obtain mercy.
Blessed are the pure in heart: for they
shall see God.
Blessed are the peacemakers: for they
shall be called the children of God.
Ib. v. 3

12 Ye are the salt of the earth: but if the
salt have lost his savour, wherewith
shall it be salted? *Ib. 13*

13 Ye are the light of the world. A city
that is set on an hill cannot be hid.
Ib. 14

14 Let your light so shine before men,
that they may see your good works.
Ib. 16

15 Think not that I am come to destroy
the law, or the prophets: I am come
not to destroy, but to fulfil. *Ib. 17*

16 Till thou hast paid the uttermost
farthing. *Ib. 26*

17 Let your communication be, Yea, yea;
Nay, nay. *Ib. 37*

18 Resist not evil: but whosoever shall
smite thee on thy right cheek, turn to
him the other also.
St. Matthew v. 39

19 He maketh his sun to rise on the evil
and on the good, and sendeth rain on
the just and on the unjust. *Ib. 45*

20 When thou doest alms, let not thy left
hand know what thy right hand doeth.
Ib. vi. 3

21 Use not vain repetitions, as the
heathen do: for they think that they
shall be heard for their much speaking.
Ib. 7

22 After this manner therefore pray ye:
Our Father which art in heaven,
Hallowed be thy name.
Thy kingdom come. Thy will be done
in earth, as it is in heaven.
Give us this day our daily bread.
And forgive us our debts, as we forgive
our debtors.
And lead us not into temptation, but
deliver us from evil: For thine is the
kingdom, and the power, and the
glory, for ever. Amen. *Ib. 9*

23 Lay not up for yourselves treasures
upon earth, where moth and rust doth
corrupt, and where thieves break
through and steal. *Ib. 19*

24 Lay up for yourselves treasures in
heaven. *Ib. 20*

25 Where your treasure is, there will your
heart be also. *Ib. 21*

26 No man can serve two masters. *Ib. 24*

27 Ye cannot serve God and mammon.
Ib.

28 Consider the lilies of the field, how
they grow; they toil not, neither do
they spin:
And yet I say unto you, That even
Solomon in all his glory was not
arrayed like one of these. *Ib. 28*

29 Take therefore no thought for the
morrow: for the morrow shall take
thought for the things of itself.
Sufficient unto the day is the evil
thereof. *Ib. 34*

30 Judge not, that ye be not judged.
Ib. vii. 1

31 Why beholdest thou the mote that is
in thy brother's eye, but considerest
not the beam that is in thine own eye?
Ib. 3

32 Neither cast ye your pearls before
swine. *Ib. 6*

33 Ask, and it shall be given you; seek,
and ye shall find; knock, and it shall
be opened unto you. *Ib. 7*

34 Or what man is there of you, whom if
his son ask bread, will he give him
a stone? *Ib. 9*

1 Wide is the gate, and broad is the way, that leadeth to destruction, and many there be that go in thereat.
St. Matthew vii. 13

2 Strait is the gate, and narrow is the way, which leadeth unto life, and few there be that find it. *Ib.* 14

3 Beware of false prophets, which come to you in sheep's clothing, but inwardly they are ravening wolves.
Ib. 15

4 By their fruits ye shall know them.
Ib. 20

5 I am a man under authority, having soldiers under me: and I say to this man, Go, and he goeth; and to another, Come, and he cometh; and to my servant, Do this, and he doeth it. *Ib.* viii. 9

6 But the children of the kingdom shall be cast out into outer darkness: there shall be weeping and gnashing of teeth.
Ib. 12

7 The foxes have holes, and the birds of the air have nests; but the Son of man hath not where to lay his head.
Ib. 20

8 Let the dead bury their dead. *Ib.* 22

9 Sitting at the receipt of custom.
Ib. ix. 9

10 Why eateth your Master with publicans and sinners? *Ib.* 11

11 Neither do men put new wine into old bottles. *Ib.* 17

12 When ye depart out of that house or city, shake off the dust of your feet.
Ib. x. 14

13 Be ye therefore wise as serpents, and harmless as doves. *Ib.* 16

14 The very hairs of your head are all numbered. *Ib.* 30

15 I came not to send peace, but a sword.
Ib. 34

16 He that findeth his life shall lose it: and he that loseth his life for my sake shall find it. *Ib.* 39

17 Whosoever shall give to drink unto one of these little ones a cup of cold water only in the name of a disciple, verily I say unto you, he shall in no wise lose his reward. *Ib.* 42

18 What went ye out into the wilderness to see? A reed shaken with the wind?
Ib. xi. 3

19 We have piped unto you, and ye have not danced; we have mourned unto you, and ye have not lamented. *Ib.* 17

20 Come unto me, all ye that labour and are heavy laden, and I will give you rest. *Ib.* 28

21 For my yoke is easy, and my burden is light. *St. Matthew* xi. 30

22 He that is not with me is against me.
Ib. xii. 30

23 Empty, swept, and garnished. *Ib.* 44

24 Then goeth he, and taketh with himself seven other spirits more wicked than himself, and they enter in and dwell there: and the last state of that man is worse than the first. *Ib.* 45

25 Some seeds fell by the wayside.
Ib. xiii. 4

26 An enemy hath done this. *Ib.* 28

27 The kingdom of heaven is like to a grain of mustard seed. *Ib.* 31

28 One pearl of great price. *Ib.* 46

29 A prophet is not without honour, save in his own country, and in his own house. *Ib.* 57

30 They be blind leaders of the blind. And if the blind lead the blind, both shall fall into the ditch. *Ib.* xv. 14

31 The dogs eat of the crumbs which fall from their masters' table. *Ib.* 27

32 The signs of the times. *Ib.* xvi. 3

33 Thou art Peter, and upon this rock I will build my church; and the gates of hell shall not prevail against it.
Ib. 18

34 Get thee behind me, Satan. *Ib.* 23

35 What is a man profited, if he shall gain the whole world, and lose his own soul? *Ib.* 26

36 If ye have faith as a grain of mustard seed, ye shall say unto this mountain, Remove hence to yonder place; and it shall remove. *Ib.* xvii. 20

37 Except ye be converted, and become as little children, ye shall not enter into the kingdom of heaven.
Ib. xviii. 3

38 But whoso shall offend one of these little ones which believe in me, it were better for him that a millstone were hanged about his neck, and that he were drowned in the depth of the sea.
Ib. 6

39 If thine eye offend thee, pluck it out, and cast it from thee. *Ib.* 9

40 For where two or three are gathered together in my name, there am I in the midst of them. *Ib.* 20

41 What therefore God hath joined together, let not man put asunder.
Ib. xix. 6

42 Thou shalt love thy neighbour as thyself. *Ib.* 19

1 It is easier for a camel to go through the eye of a needle, than for a rich man to enter into the kingdom of God.
St. Matthew xix. 24

2 With men this is impossible; but with God all things are possible. *Ib.* 26

3 But many that are first shall be last; and the last shall be first. *Ib.* 30

4 Borne the burden and heat of the day.
Ib. xx. 12

5 I will give unto this last, even as unto thee.
Is it not lawful for me to do what I will with mine own? *Ib.* 14

6 For many are called, but few are chosen. *Ib.* xxii. 14

7 Render therefore unto Cæsar the things which are Cæsar's. *Ib.* 21

8 Blind guides, which strain at a gnat, and swallow a camel. *Ib.* xxiii. 24

9 Whited sepulchres, which indeed appear beautiful outward, but are within full of dead men's bones.
Ib. 27

10 Wars and rumours of wars.
Ib. xxiv. 6

11 For nation shall rise against nation, and kingdom against kingdom. *Ib.* 7

12 Abomination of desolation. *Ib.* 15

13 Wheresoever the carcase is, there will the eagles be gathered together.
Ib. 28

14 Well done, thou good and faithful servant. *Ib.* xxv. 21

15 Unto every one that hath shall be given, and he shall have abundance: but from him that hath not shall be taken away even that which he hath.
Ib. 29

16 I was a stranger, and ye took me in: Naked, and ye clothed me: I was sick, and ye visited me: I was in prison, and ye came unto me. *Ib.* 35

17 Inasmuch as ye have done it unto one of the least of these my brethren, ye have done it unto me. *Ib.* 40

18 What will ye give me, and I will deliver him unto you? And they covenanted with him for thirty pieces of silver. *Ib.* xxvi. 15

19 This night, before the cock crow, thou shalt deny me thrice. *Ib.* 34

20 If it be possible, let this cup pass from me. *Ib.* 39

21 The spirit indeed is willing, but the flesh is weak. *Ib.* 41

22 Hail, master; and kissed him. *Ib.* 49

23 All they that take the sword shall perish with the sword. *Ib.* 52

24 He saved others; himself he cannot save. *St. Matthew* xxvii. 42

25 Eli, Eli, lama sabachthani? . . . My God, my God, why hast thou forsaken me? *Ib.* 46

26 The sabbath was made for man, and not man for the sabbath.
St. Mark ii. 27

27 If a house be divided against itself, that house cannot stand. *Ib.* iii. 25

28 He that hath ears to hear, let him hear. *Ib.* iv. 9

29 My name is Legion: for we are many.
Ib. v. 9

30 Clothed, and in his right mind. *Ib.* 15

31 I see men as trees, walking. *Ib.* viii. 24

32 For what shall it profit a man, if he shall gain the whole world, and lose his own soul? *Ib.* 36

33 Lord, I believe; help thou mine unbelief. *Ib.* ix. 24

34 Suffer the little children to come unto me, and forbid them not: for of such is the kingdom of God. *Ib.* x. 14

35 And there came a certain poor widow, and she threw in two mites. *Ib.* xii. 42

36 Hail, thou that art highly favoured, the Lord is with thee: blessed art thou among women. *St. Luke* i. 28

37 My soul doth magnify the Lord,
And my spirit hath rejoiced in God my Saviour.
For he hath regarded the low estate of his handmaiden: for, behold, from henceforth all generations shall call me blessed. *Ib.* 46

38 He hath shewed strength with his arm; he hath scattered the proud in the imagination of their hearts.
He hath put down the mighty from their seats, and exalted them of low degree.
He hath filled the hungry with good things; and the rich he hath sent empty away. *Ib.* 51

39 To give light to them that sit in darkness and in the shadow of death, to guide our feet into the way of peace.
Ib. 79

40 Because there was no room for them in the inn. *Ib.* ii. 7

41 And, lo, the angel of the Lord came upon them, and the glory of the Lord shone round about them: and they were sore afraid. *Ib.* 9

42 Be not afraid; for behold, I bring you good tidings of great joy. *Ib.* 10

43 Glory to God in the highest, and on earth peace, good will toward men.
Ib. 14

1 Lord, now lettest thou thy servant depart in peace, according to thy word. *St. Luke* ii. 29

2 Physician, heal thyself. *Ib.* iv. 23

3 Judge not, and ye shall not be judged. *Ib.* vi. 37

4 Peace be to this house. *Ib.* x. 5

5 For the labourer is worthy of his hire. *Ib.* 7

6 Fell among thieves. *Ib.* 30

7 He passed by on the other side. *Ib.* 31

8 Go, and do thou likewise. *Ib.* 37

9 But Martha was cumbered about much serving. *Ib.* 40

10 When a strong man armed keepeth his palace, his goods are in peace. *Ib.* xi. 21

11 All his armour wherein he trusted. *Ib.* 22

12 Woe unto you, lawyers! for ye have taken away the key of knowledge. *Ib.* 52

13 Are not five sparrows sold for two farthings, and not one of them is forgotten before God? *Ib.* xii. 6

14 Friend, go up higher. *Ib.* xiv. 10

15 For whosoever exalteth himself shall be abased; and he that humbleth himself shall be exalted. *Ib.* 11

16 I have married a wife, and therefore I cannot come. *Ib.* 20

17 The poor, and the maimed, and the halt, and the blind. *Ib.* 21

18 Go out into the highways and hedges, and compel them to come in. *Ib.* 23

19 Rejoice with me; for I have found my sheep which was lost. *Ib.* xv. 6

20 Joy shall be in heaven over one sinner that repenteth, more than over ninety and nine just persons, which need no repentance. *Ib.* 7

21 Wasted his substance with riotous living. *Ib.* 13

22 I will arise and go to my father, and will say unto him, Father, I have sinned against heaven, and before thee,
And am no more worthy to be called thy son: make me as one of thy hired servants. *Ib.* 18

23 Bring hither the fatted calf, and kill it. *Ib.* 23

24 This my son was dead, and is alive again; he was lost, and is found. *Ib.* 24

25 I cannot dig; to beg I am ashamed. *Ib.* xvi. 3

26 Make to yourselves friends of the mammon of unrighteousness. *St. Luke* xvi. 9

27 The crumbs which fell from the rich man's table. *Ib.* 21

28 Carried by the angels into Abraham's bosom. *Ib.* 22

29 Between us and you there is a great gulf fixed. *Ib.* 26

30 It were better for him that a millstone were hanged about his neck, and he cast into the sea. *Ib.* xvii. 2

31 The kingdom of God is within you. *Ib.* 21

32 Remember Lot's wife. *Ib.* 32

33 God, I thank thee, that I am not as other men are. *Ib.* xviii. 11

34 God be merciful to me a sinner. *Ib.* 13

35 If these should hold their peace, the stones would immediately cry out. *Ib.* xix. 40

36 In your patience possess ye your souls. *Ib.* xxi. 19

37 Nevertheless, not my will, but thine, be done. *Ib.* xxii. 42

38 For if they do these things in a green tree, what shall be done in the dry? *Ib.* xxiii. 31

39 Father, forgive them; for they know not what they do. *Ib.* 34

40 Lord, remember me when thou comest into thy kingdom. *Ib.* 42

41 To day shalt thou be with me in paradise. *Ib.* 43

42 Father, into thy hands I commend my spirit. *Ib.* 46

43 In the beginning was the Word, and the Word was with God, and the Word was God. *St. John* i. 1

44 And the light shineth in darkness; and the darkness comprehended it not. *Ib.* 5

45 He came unto his own, and his own received him not. *Ib.* 11

46 And the Word was made flesh, and dwelt among us. *Ib.* 14

47 Who coming after me is preferred before me, whose shoe's latchet I am not worthy to unloose. *Ib.* 27

48 Can there any good thing come out of Nazareth? *Ib.* 46

49 Woman, what have I to do with thee? mine hour is not yet come. *Ib.* ii. 4

50 The wind bloweth where it listeth, and thou hearest the sound thereof, but canst not tell whence it cometh, and whither it goeth. *Ib.* iii. 8

1 God so loved the world, that he gave his only begotten Son, that whosoever believeth in him should not perish, but have everlasting life. *St. John* iii. 16

2 God is a Spirit: and they that worship him must worship him in spirit and in truth. *Ib.* iv. 24

3 Rise, take up thy bed, and walk. *Ib.* v. 8

4 What are they among so many? *Ib.* vi. 9

5 Him that cometh to me I will in no wise cast out. *Ib.* 37

6 He that is without sin among you, let him first cast a stone at her. *Ib.* viii. 7

7 Neither do I condemn thee: go, and sin no more. *Ib.* 11

8 The truth shall make you free. *Ib.* 32

9 There is no truth in him. *Ib.* 44

10 He is a liar, and the father of it. *Ib.*

11 The night cometh, when no man can work. *Ib.* ix. 4

12 The good shepherd giveth his life for the sheep. *Ib.* x. 11

13 I am the resurrection, and the life. *Ib.* xi. 25

14 It is expedient for us, that one man should die for the people. *Ib.* 50

15 The poor always ye have with you. *Ib.* xii. 8

16 Let not your heart be troubled: ye believe in God, believe also in me. *Ib.* xiv. 1

17 In my Father's house are many mansions. *Ib.* 2

18 I go to prepare a place for you. *Ib.*

19 I am the way, the truth, and the life: no man cometh unto the Father, but by me. *Ib.* 6

20 Greater love hath no man than this, that a man lay down his life for his friends. *Ib.* xv. 13

21 Quo vadis? Whither goest thou? *Ib.* xvi. 5 (Vulgate) and the Apocryphal *Acts of Peter*

22 In the world ye shall have tribulation: but be of good cheer; I have overcome the world. *Ib.* 33

23 Pilate saith unto him, What is truth? *Ib.* xviii. 38

24 Now Barabbas was a robber. *Ib.* 40

25 Ecce homo.
Behold the man.
Ib. xix. 5 (Vulgate)

26 What I have written I have written. *Ib.* 22

27 Woman, behold thy son! . . .
Behold thy mother! *St. John* xix. 26

28 Consummatum est.
It is finished. *Ib.* 30 (Vulgate)

29 Noli me tangere.
Touch me not. *Ib.* xx. 17 (Vulgate)

30 The disciple whom Jesus loved. *Ib.* xxi. 20

31 A rushing mighty wind. *The Acts of the Apostles* ii. 2

32 Silver and gold have I none; but such as I have give I thee. *Ib.* iii. 6

33 We ought to obey God rather than men. *Ib.* v. 29

34 Breathing out threatenings and slaughter. *Ib.* ix. 1

35 Saul, Saul, why persecutest thou me? *Ib.* 4

36 It is hard for thee to kick against the pricks. *Ib.* 5

37 Full of good works. *Ib.* 36

38 God is no respecter of persons. *Ib.* x. 34

39 Come over into Macedonia, and help us. *Ib.* xvi. 9

40 Certain lewd fellows of the baser sort. *Ib.* xvii. 5

41 These that have turned the world upside down. *Ib.* 6

42 Ye men of Athens, I perceive that in all things ye are too superstitious.
For as I passed by, and beheld your devotions, I found an altar with this inscription, TO THE UNKNOWN GOD. Whom therefore ye ignorantly worship, him declare I unto you. *Ib.* 22

43 For in him we live, and move, and have our being. *Ib.* 28

44 Gallio cared for none of those things. *Ib.* xviii. 17

45 All with one voice about the space of two hours cried out, Great is Diana of the Ephesians. *Ib.* xix. 34

46 It is more blessed to give than to receive. *Ib.* xx. 35

47 A citizen of no mean city. *Ib.* xxi. 39

48 I appeal unto Cæsar. *Ib.* xxv. 11

49 Hast thou appealed unto Cæsar? unto Cæsar shalt thou go. *Ib.* 12

50 Paul, thou art beside thyself; much learning doth make thee mad. *Ib.* xxvi. 24

51 Almost thou persuadest me to be a Christian. *Ib.* 28

52 The just shall live by faith. *The Epistle of Paul to the Romans* i. 17

1 Let us do evil, that good may come.
Romans iii. 8

2 Who against hope believed in hope.
Ib. iv. 18

3 Shall we continue in sin, that grace
may abound? *Ib. vi.* 1

4 Christ being raised from the dead
dieth no more; death hath no more
dominion over him. *Ib.* 9

5 The wages of sin is death. *Ib.* 23

6 For the good that I would I do not:
but the evil which I would not, that
I do. *Ib. vii.* 19

7 For ye have not received the spirit of
bondage again to fear; but ye have
received the Spirit of adoption,
whereby we cry, Abba, Father.
Ib. viii. 15

8 All things work together for good to
them that love God. *Ib.* 28

9 If God be for us, who can be against
us? *Ib.* 31

10 For I am persuaded, that neither
death, nor life, nor angels, nor principalities, nor powers, nor things present, nor things to come,
Nor height, nor depth, nor any other
creature, shall be able to separate us
from the love of God, which is in
Christ Jesus our Lord. *Ib.* 38

11 Vengeance is mine; I will repay, saith
the Lord. *Ib. xii.* 19

12 Be not overcome of evil, but overcome
evil with good. *Ib.* 21

13 The powers that be are ordained of
God. *Ib. xiii.* 1

14 Now it is high time to awake out of
sleep: for now is our salvation nearer
than when we believed.
The night is far spent, the day is at
hand: let us therefore cast off the
works of darkness, and let us put on
the armour of light. *Ib.* 11

15 Absent in body, but present in spirit.
*The First Epistle of Paul to the
Corinthians* v. 3

16 It is better to marry than to burn.
Ib. vii. 9

17 I am made all things to all men.
Ib. ix. 22

18 All things are lawful for me, but all
things are not expedient. *Ib. x.* 23

19 For the earth is the Lord's, and the
fulness thereof. *Ib.* 26

20 Though I speak with the tongues of
men and of angels, and have not
charity, I am become as sounding
brass, or a tinkling cymbal. *Ib. xiii.* 1

21 Though I have all faith, so that I could
remove mountains, and have not
charity, I am nothing.
And though I bestow all my goods to
feed the poor, and though I give my
body to be burned, and have not
charity, it profiteth me nothing.
Charity suffereth long, and is kind;
charity envieth not; charity vaunteth
not itself, is not puffed up,
Doth not behave itself unseemly,
seeketh not her own, is not easily
provoked, thinketh no evil;
Rejoiceth not in iniquity, but rejoiceth in the truth;
Beareth all things, believeth all
things, hopeth all things, endureth all
things.
Charity never faileth: but whether
there be prophecies, they shall fail;
whether there be tongues, they shall
cease; whether there be knowledge, it
shall vanish away.
For we know in part, and we prophesy
in part. *1 Corinthians* xiii. 2

22 When I was a child, I spake as a
child, I understood as a child, I
thought as a child: but when I became
a man, I put away childish things.
For now we see through a glass,
darkly; but then face to face; now
I know in part; but then shall I know
even as also I am known.
And now abideth faith, hope, charity,
these three; but the greatest of these
is charity. *Ib. xiii.* 11

23 Let all things be done decently and in
order. *Ib. xiv.* 40

24 Last of all he was seen of me also, as
of one born out of due time. *Ib. xv.* 8

25 The last enemy that shall be destroyed
is death. *Ib.* 26

26 Let us eat and drink; for to morrow
we die. *Ib.* 32

27 Evil communications corrupt good
manners. *Ib.* 33

28 The first man is of the earth, earthy.
Ib. 47

29 Behold, I shew you a mystery; We
shall not all sleep, but we shall all be
changed,
In a moment, in the twinkling of an
eye, at the last trump. *Ib.* 51

30 For this corruptible must put on incorruption, and this mortal must put
on immortality. *Ib.* 53

31 O death, where is thy sting? O grave,
where is thy victory? *Ib.* 55

32 Quit you like men, be strong.
Ib. xvi. 13

1 Not of the letter, but of the spirit: for the letter killeth, but the spirit giveth life.
The Second Epistle of Paul to the Corinthians iii. 6

2 God loveth a cheerful giver. *Ib.* ix. 7

3 For ye suffer fools gladly, seeing ye yourselves are wise. *Ib.* xi. 19

4 There was given to me a thorn in the flesh, the messenger of Satan to buffet me. *Ib.* xii. 7

5 The right hands of fellowship.
The Epistle of Paul to the Galatians ii. 9

6 Ye are fallen from grace. *Ib.* v. 4

7 But the fruit of the Spirit is love, joy, peace, longsuffering, gentleness, goodness, faith,
Meekness, temperance. *Ib.* 22

8 Be not deceived; God is not mocked: for whatsoever a man soweth, that shall he also reap. *Ib.* vi. 7

9 To be strengthened with might by his Spirit in the inner man.
The Epistle of Paul to the Ephesians iii. 16

10 Carried about with every wind of doctrine. *Ib.* iv. 14

11 We are members one of another.
Ib. 25

12 Be ye angry, and sin not: let not the sun go down upon your wrath. *Ib.* 26

13 Put on the whole armour of God.
Ib. vi. 11

14 For we wrestle not against flesh and blood, but against principalities, against powers, against the rulers of the darkness of this world, against spiritual wickedness in high places.
Wherefore take unto you the whole armour of God, that ye may be able to withstand in the evil day, and having done all, to stand. *Ib.* 12

15 Given him a name which is above every name:
That at the name of Jesus every knee should bow.
The Epistle of Paul to the Philippians ii. 9

16 Work out your own salvation with fear and trembling. *Ib.* 12

17 Whose God is their belly, and whose glory is in their shame. *Ib.* iii. 19

18 Rejoice in the Lord alway: and again I say, Rejoice. *Ib.* iv. 4

19 The peace of God, which passeth all understanding. *Ib.* 7

20 Whatsoever things are true, whatsoever things are honest, whatsoever things are just, whatsoever things are pure, whatsoever things are lovely, whatsoever things are of good report; if there be any virtue, and if there be any praise, think on these things.
Philippians iv. 8

21 I can do all things through Christ which strengtheneth me. *Ib.* 13

22 Set your affection on things above, not on things on the earth.
The Epistle of Paul to the Colossians iii. 2

23 Labour of love.
The First Epistle of Paul to the Thessalonians i. 3

24 Prove all things; hold fast that which is good. *Ib.* v. 21

25 Be not weary in well doing.
The Second Epistle of Paul to the Thessalonians iii. 13

26 Not greedy of filthy lucre.
The First Epistle of Paul to Timothy iii. 3

27 Old wives' fables. *Ib.* iv. 7

28 Drink no longer water, but use a little wine for thy stomach's sake and thine often infirmities. *Ib.* v. 23

29 For we brought nothing into this world, and it is certain we can carry nothing out. *Ib.* vi. 7

30 The love of money is the root of all evil. *Ib.* 10

31 Fight the good fight of faith, lay hold on eternal life. *Ib.* 12

32 Rich in good works. *Ib.* 18

33 I have fought a good fight, I have finished my course, I have kept the faith.
The Second Epistle of Paul to Timothy iv. 7

34 Unto the pure all things are pure.
The Epistle of Paul to Titus i. 15

35 Wherefore seeing we also are compassed about with so great a cloud of witnesses, let us lay aside every weight, and the sin which doth so easily beset us, and let us run with patience the race that is set before us,
Looking unto Jesus the author and finisher of our faith.
The Epistle of Paul to the Hebrews xii. 1

36 Whom the Lord loveth he chasteneth.
Ib. 6

37 Be not forgetful to entertain strangers; for thereby some have entertained angels unawares. *Ib.* xiii. 1

38 Jesus Christ the same yesterday, and to day, and for ever. *Ib.* 8

39 Faith without works is dead.
The General Epistle of James ii. 20

1 Ye have heard of the patience of Job.
James v. 11

2 Let your yea be yea; and your nay, nay. *Ib.* 12

3 All flesh is as grass, and all the glory of man as the flower of grass. The grass withereth, and the flower thereof falleth away.
The First Epistle General of Peter i. 24

4 Honour all men. Love the brotherhood. Fear God. Honour the king.
Ib. ii. 17

5 Giving honour unto the wife, as unto the weaker vessel. *Ib.* iii. 7

6 Charity shall cover the multitude of sins. *Ib.* iv. 8

7 Be sober, be vigilant; because your adversary the devil, as a roaring lion, walketh about, seeking whom he may devour. *Ib.* v. 8

8 If we say that we have no sin, we deceive ourselves, and the truth is not in us.
The First Epistle General of John i. 8

9 He that loveth not knoweth not God; for God is love. *Ib.* iv. 8

10 No man hath seen God at any time.
Ib. 12

11 There is no fear in love; but perfect love casteth out fear. *Ib.* 18

12 If a man say, I love God, and hateth his brother, he is a liar: for he that loveth not his brother whom he hath seen, how can he love God whom he hath not seen? *Ib.* 20

13 I am Alpha and Omega, the beginning and the ending, saith the Lord.
The Revelation of John the Divine i. 8

14 Be thou faithful unto death, and I will give thee a crown of life.
Ib. ii. 10

15 Behold, I stand at the door, and knock. *Ib.* iii. 20

16 They were full of eyes within: and they rest not day and night, saying, Holy, holy, holy, Lord God Almighty, which was, and is, and is to come.
Ib. iv. 8

17 And I looked, and behold a pale horse: and his name that sat on him was Death. *Ib.* vi. 8

18 God shall wipe away all tears from their eyes. *Ib.* vii. 17

19 And there were stings in their tails.
Ib. ix. 10

20 And that no man might buy or sell, save he that had the mark, or the name of the beast, or the number of his name. *Revelation* xiii. 17

21 Babylon is fallen, is fallen, that great city. *Ib.* xiv. 8

22 MYSTERY, BABYLON THE GREAT, THE MOTHER OF HARLOTS AND ABOMINATIONS OF THE EARTH.
And I saw the woman drunken with the blood of the saints. *Ib.* xvii. 5

23 The key of the bottomless pit. *Ib.* xx. 1

24 And the sea gave up the dead which were in it. *Ib.* 13

25 And I saw a new heaven and a new earth: for the first heaven and the first earth were passed away; and there was no more sea.
And I John saw the holy city, new Jerusalem, coming down from God out of heaven, prepared as a bride adorned for her husband. *Ib.* xxi. 1

26 And God shall wipe away all tears from their eyes; and there shall be no more death, neither sorrow, nor crying, neither shall there be any more pain: for the former things are passed away.
And he that sat upon the throne said, Behold, I make all things new. And he said unto me, Write: for these words are true and faithful. *Ib.* 4

27 I will give unto him that is athirst of the fountain of the water of life freely. *Ib.* 6

28 The twelve gates were twelve pearls.
Ib. 21

ISAAC BICKERSTAFFE
1735?–1812?

29 There was a jolly miller once,
Lived on the river Dee;
He worked and sang from morn till night;
No lark more blithe than he.
Love in a Village, I. v

30 And this the burthen of his song,
For ever us'd to be,
I care for nobody, not I,
If no one cares for me. *Ib.*

31 We all love a pretty girl—under the rose. *Ib.* II. ii

32 In every port he finds a wife.
Thomas and Sally (1761), ii

EDWARD HENRY BICKERSTETH 1825–1906

33 Peace, perfect peace, in this dark world of sin?
The Blood of Jesus whispers peace within.
Songs in the House of Pilgrimage (1875)

JOSH BILLINGS
see HENRY WHEELER SHAW

LAURENCE BINYON 1869–1943

1 With proud thanksgiving, a mother
  for her children,
  England mourns for her dead across
  the sea.   *Poems for the Fallen*

2 They shall grow not old, as we that
  are left grow old:
  Age shall not weary them, nor the
  years condemn.
  At the going down of the sun and in
  the morning
  We will remember them.   *Ib.*

OTTO VON BISMARCK 1815–1898

3 Nach Canossa gehen wir nicht.
  We will not go to Canossa.
          Speech, Reichstag, 14 May 1872

4 Blut und Eisen.
  Blood and iron.
          Speech, Prussian House of Deputies, 28 Jan. 1886
  (Legt eine möglichst starke militärische Kraft . . . in die Hand des
  Königs von Preussen, dann wird er
  die Politik machen können, die Ihr
  wünscht; mit Reden und Schützenfesten und Leidern macht sie sich
  nicht, sie macht sich nur durch
  Blut und Eisen.
  Place in the hands of the King of
  Prussia the strongest possible
  military power, then he will be
  able to carry out the policy you
  wish; this policy cannot succeed
  through speeches, and shooting-
  matches, and songs; it can only
  be carried out through blood and
  iron.)

VALENTINE BLACKER 1778–1823

5 'Put your trust in God, my boys, and
  keep your powder dry.'
          Oliver's Advice

SIR WILLIAM BLACKSTONE
1723–1780

6 The king never dies.
          *Commentaries on the Laws of
          England,* bk. i. 7

7 That the king can do no wrong, is a
  necessary and fundamental principle
  of the English constitution. *Ib.* iii. 17

8 It is better that ten guilty persons
  escape than one innocent suffer.
          Ib. iv. 27

CHARLES DUPEE BLAKE
1846–1903

9 Rock-a-bye-baby on the tree top,
  When the wind blows the cradle will
  rock,

When the bough bends the cradle will
  fall,
Down comes the baby, cradle and all.
          Attr. But see Oxford Dictionary
          of Nursery Rhymes

WILLIAM BLAKE 1757–1827

10 To see a World in a Grain of Sand,
  And a Heaven in a Wild Flower,
  Hold Infinity in the palm of your hand,
  And Eternity in an hour.
          Auguries of Innocence

11 A Robin Redbreast in a Cage
  Puts all Heaven in a Rage.   *Ib.*

12 The harlot's cry from street to street
  Shall weave old England's winding
  sheet.   *Ib.*

13 'What,' it will be questioned, 'when
  the sun rises, do you not see a round
  disc of fire somewhat like a guinea?'
  'O no, no, I see an innumerable company of the heavenly host crying,
  "Holy, Holy, Holy is the Lord God
  Almighty!"'
          Descriptive Catalogue, 1810. *The
          Vision of Judgment*

14 [On Cromek]
  A petty sneaking knave I knew—
  O! Mr. Cr—, how do ye do?
          On Friends and Foes, xxi

15 Great things are done when men and
  mountains meet,
  This is not done by jostling in the
  street.   *Gnomic Verses,* i

16 And did those feet in ancient time
  Walk upon England's mountains
  green?
  And was the holy Lamb of God
  On England's pleasant pastures seen?

  And did the Countenance Divine
  Shine forth upon our clouded hills?
  And was Jerusalem builded here
  Among these dark Satanic mills?

  Bring me my bow of burning gold!
  Bring me my arrows of desire!
  Bring me my spear! O clouds, unfold!
  Bring me my chariot of fire!

  I will not cease from Mental Fight,
  Nor shall my Sword sleep in my hand,
  Till we have built Jerusalem,
  In England's green & pleasant Land.
          Milton, preface

17 Mock on, mock on, Voltaire, Rousseau;
  Mock on, mock on, 'tis all in vain!
  You throw the sand against the wind,
  And the wind blows it back again.
          Mock on, mock on, Voltaire

18 Hear the voice of the Bard!
  Who present, past, and future sees.
          Songs of Experience, introduction

1 Tyger! Tyger! burning bright
  In the forests of the night,
  What immortal hand or eye
  Could frame thy fearful symmetry?
  Songs of Experience. The Tyger

2 And what shoulder, and what art,
  Could twist the sinews of thy heart?
  And when thy heart began to beat,
  What dread hand? and what dread
  feet?

  What the hammer? What the chain?
  In what furnace was thy brain?
  What the anvil? what dread grasp
  Dare its deadly terrors clasp?   *Ib.*

3 Did he who made the Lamb make
  thee?   *Ib.*

4 Tyger! Tyger! burning bright
  In the forests of the night,
  What immortal hand or eye,
  Dare frame thy fearful symmetry? *Ib.*

5 Love seeketh not itself to please,
  Nor for itself hath any care,
  But for another gives its ease,
  And builds a Heaven in Hell's despair.
       Ib. The Clod and the Pebble

6 Love seeketh only Self to please,
  To bind another to its delight,
  Joys in another's loss of ease,
  And builds a Hell in Heaven's despite.
                                    Ib.

7 Ah, Sun-flower! weary of time,
  Who countest the steps of the Sun;
  Seeking after that sweet golden clime,
  Where the traveller's journey is done;
       Ib. Ah, Sun-Flower!

8 Piping down the valleys wild,
  Piping songs of pleasant glee,
  On a cloud I saw a child,
  And he laughing said to me:

  'Pipe a song about a Lamb!'
  So I piped with merry cheer.
  'Piper, pipe that song again;'
  So I piped: he wept to hear.

  'Drop thy pipe, thy happy pipe;
  Sing thy songs of happy cheer:'
  So I sang the same again,
  While he wept with joy to hear.

  'Piper, sit thee down and write
  In a book, that all may read.'
  So he vanish'd from my sight,
  And I pluck'd a hollow reed.

  And I made a rural pen,
  And I stain'd the water clear,
  And I wrote my happy songs
  Every child may joy to hear.
       Songs of Innocence, introduction

9 Little Lamb, who made thee?
       Ib. The Lamb

10 My mother bore me in the southern
   wild,
   And I am black, but O! my soul is
   white;

White as an angel is the English child,
But I am black, as if bereav'd of light.
       *Songs of Innocence. The Little
       Black Boy*

11 When the voices of children are heard
   on the green,
   And laughing is heard on the hill.
              Ib. Nurse's Song

12 To Mercy, Pity, Peace, and Love
   All pray in their distress.
              Ib. The Divine Image

13 For Mercy has a human heart,
   Pity a human face,
   And Love, the human form divine,
   And Peace, the human dress.
                            Ib.

14 Can I see another's woe,
   And not be in sorrow too?
   Can I see another's grief,
   And not seek for kind relief?
              Ib. On Another's Sorrow

15 Energy is Eternal Delight.
       *The Marriage of Heaven and Hell:
       The Voice of the Devil*

16 The reason Milton wrote in fetters
   when he wrote of Angels and God, and
   at liberty when of Devils and Hell, is
   because he was a true Poet, and of the
   Devil's party without knowing it.
                            Ib. note

17 A fool sees not the same tree that a
   wise man sees.   *Ib. Proverbs of Hell*

18 Eternity is in love with the productions of time.   *Ib.*

19 If the fool would persist in his folly
   he would become wise.   *Ib.*

20 Damn braces. Bless relaxes.   *Ib.*

21 If the doors of perception were
   cleansed everything would appear to
   man as it is, infinite.
       The Marriage of Heaven and Hell

PHILIPP BLISS 1838–1876

22 Hold the fort, for I am coming.
       *The Charm. Ho, My Comrades,
       See the Signal!*

23 Pull for the shore, sailor, pull for the
   shore!
   Heed not the rolling waves, but bend to
   the oar.
       *Sacred Songs and Solos. The Life-
       boat*

GEBHARD LEBERECHT BLÜCHER 1742–1819

24 Was für plündern!
   What a place to plunder!
       On his visit to London in 1814.
   Attr.

EDMUND BLUNDEN 1896–

25 Undertones of War   *Title of Book*

BOETHIUS 480?–524

1 For truly in adverse fortune the worst sting of misery is to *have been* happy.
　　Consolation of Philosophy, bk. ii, prose 4 (H. R. James's translation) (*see 72:7*)

NICOLAS BOILEAU 1636–1711

2 Enfin Malherbe vint, et, le premier en France,
Fit sentir dans les vers une juste cadence.

At last comes Malherbe, and, the first to do so in France, makes verse run smoothly.
　　L'Art Poétique, i. 131–2

HENRY ST. JOHN, VISCOUNT BOLINGBROKE 1678–1751

3 The Idea of a Patriot King.
　　Title of Book

4 Truth lies within a little and certain compass, but error is immense.
　　Reflections upon Exile

5 They make truth serve as a stalking-horse to error.
　　On the Study of History, letter 1

CARRIE JACOBS BOND 1862–1946

6 And we find at the end of a perfect day
The soul of a friend we've made.
　　A Perfect Day, st. 2

'GENERAL' WILLIAM BOOTH 1829–1912

7 This Submerged Tenth—is it, then, beyond the reach of the nine-tenths in the midst of whom they live.
　　In Darkest England (1890), I. ii. 23

GEORGE BORROW 1803–1881

8 There's night and day, brother, both sweet things; sun, moon, and stars, brother, all sweet things; there's likewise a wind on the heath. Life is very sweet, brother; who would wish to die?
　　Lavengro, ch. 25

9 Youth will be served, every dog has his day, and mine has been a fine one.
　　Ib. ch. 92

MARÉCHAL BOSQUET 1810–1861

10 C'est magnifique, mais ce n'est pas la guerre.
It is magnificent, but it is not war.
　　Remark on the Charge of the Light Brigade, 1854

JOHN COLLINS BOSSIDY
1860–1928

11 And this is good old Boston,
The home of the bean and the cod,
Where the Lowells talk to the Cabots,
And the Cabots talk only to God.
　　On the Aristocracy of Harvard

BOULAY DE LA MEURTHE
1761–1840

12 C'est pire qu'un crime, c'est une faute.
It is worse than a crime, it is a blunder.
　　On hearing of the execution of the Duc d'Enghien, 1804

FRANCIS WILLIAM BOURDILLON 1852–1921

13 The night has a thousand eyes,
And the day but one;
Yet the light of the bright world dies,
With the dying sun.

The mind has a thousand eyes,
And the heart but one;
Yet the light of a whole life dies,
When love is done. *Light*

CHARLES, BARON BOWEN
1835–1894

14 The rain it raineth on the just
And also on the unjust fella:
But chiefly on the just, because
The unjust steals the just's umbrella.
　　Walter Sichel, *Sands of Time*

EDWARD ERNEST BOWEN
1836–1901

15 Forty years on, when afar and asunder
Parted are those who are singing to-day.
　　Forty Years On. Harrow School Song

16 Follow up! Follow up! Follow up!
Follow up! Follow up!
Till the field ring again and again,
With the tramp of the twenty-two men,
Follow up! *Ib.*

JOHN BRADFORD 1510?–1555

17 But for the grace of God there goes John Bradford.
　　Exclamation on seeing some criminals taken to execution. Dict. of Nat. Biog.

JOHN BRAHAM 1774?–1856

18 England, home and beauty.
　　The Americans (1811). Song, *The Death of Nelson*

HARRY BRAISTED
nineteenth century

1 If you want to win her hand,
Let the maiden understand
That she's not the only pebble on the
beach.
*You're Not the Only Pebble on
the Beach*

REV. JAMES BRAMSTON
1694?–1744

2 What's not destroy'd by Time's
devouring hand?
Where's Troy, and where's the Maypole in the Strand?
Art of Politics, l. 71

RICHARD BRATHWAITE
1588?–1673

3 To Banbury came I, O profane one!
Where I saw a Puritane-one
Hanging of his cat on Monday,
For killing of a mouse on Sunday.
Barnabee's Journal, pt. i

NICHOLAS BRETON 1545?–1626?

4 We rise with the lark and go to bed
with the lamb.
The Court and the Country, par. 8

5 A Mad World, My Masters.
Title of Dialogue (1635)

ROBERT BRIDGES 1844–1930

6 I love all beauteous things,
I seek and adore them;
God hath no better praise,
And man in his hasty days
Is honoured for them.
I Love All Beauteous Things

7 When men were all asleep the snow
came flying,
In large white flakes falling on the
city brown,
Stealthily and perpetually settling
and loosely lying.
London Snow

8 Whither, O splendid ship, thy white
sails crowding,
Leaning across the bosom of the urgent West,
That fearest nor sea rising, nor sky
clouding,
Whither away, fair rover, and what
thy quest?   *A Passer-By*

JOHN BRIGHT 1811–1889

9 My opinion is that the Northern
States will manage somehow to muddle
through.
During the American Civil War.
Quoted in Justin McCarthy,
Reminiscences (1899)

10 The angel of death has been abroad
throughout the land; you may almost
hear the beating of his wings.
*Speech, House of Commons,
23 Feb. 1855*

11 I am for 'Peace, retrenchment, and
reform', the watchword of the great
Liberal party 30 years ago.
Ib. Birmingham, 28 Apr. 1859

12 England is the mother of Parliaments.
Ib. 18 Jan. 1865

EMILY BRONTË 1818–1848

13 No coward soul is mine,
No trembler in the world's storm-
troubled sphere:
I see Heaven's glories shine,
And faith shines equal, arming me
from fear.   *Last Lines*

14 Vain are the thousand creeds
That move men's hearts: unutterably
vain;
Worthless as withered weeds,
Or idlest froth amid the boundless
main.   *Ib.*

15 Cold in the earth—and fifteen wild
Decembers,
From those brown hills, have melted
into spring.   *Remembrance*

RUPERT BROOKE 1887–1915

16 Blow out, you bugles, over the rich
Dead!
There's none of these so lonely and
poor of old,
But, dying, has made us rarer gifts
than gold.
These laid the world away; poured out
the red
Sweet wine of youth; gave up the
years to be
Of work and joy, and that unhoped
serene,
That men call age; and those who
would have been,
Their sons, they gave, their immor-
tality.   *The Dead*

17 The cool kindliness of sheets, that soon
Smooth away trouble; and the rough
male kiss of blankets.
The Great Lover

18 The benison of hot water.   *Ib.*

19 Fish say, they have their stream and
pond;
But is there anything beyond?
Heaven

20 One may not doubt that, somehow,
good
Shall come of water and of mud;
And, sure, the reverent eye must see
A purpose in liquidity.   *Ib.*

C

1 But somewhere, beyond space and
time,
Is wetter water, slimier slime; *Heaven*

2 Immense, of fishy form and mind,
Squamous, omnipotent, and kind;
And under that Almighty Fin,
The littlest fish may enter in.   *Ib.*

3 Unfading moths, immortal flies,
And the worm that never dies.
And in that Heaven of all their wish,
There shall be no more land, say fish.
Ib.

4 Breathless, we flung us on the windy
hill,
Laughed in the sun, and kissed the
lovely grass.   *The Hill*

5 Here tulips bloom as they are told;
Unkempt about those hedges blows
An English unofficial rose.
The Old Vicarage, Grantchester

6 Curates, long dust, will come and go
On lissom, clerical, printless toe;
And oft between the boughs is seen
The sly shade of a Rural Dean.   *Ib.*

7 God! I will pack, and take a train,
And get me to England once again;
For England's the one land, I know,
Where men with splendid hearts may
go;
And Cambridgeshire, of all England,
The shire for men who understand;
And of *that* district I prefer
The lovely hamlet Grantchester.   *Ib.*

8 For Cambridge people rarely smile,
Being urban, squat, and packed with
guile.   *Ib.*

9 Stands the Church clock at ten to
three?
And is there honey still for tea?   *Ib.*

10 Now, God be thanked Who has
matched us with His hour,
And caught our youth, and wakened
us from sleeping.   *Peace*

11 If I should die, think only this of me:
That there's some corner of a foreign
field
That is for ever England. There shall
be
In that rich earth a richer dust con-
cealed;
A dust whom England bore, shaped,
made aware,
Gave, once, her flowers to love, her
ways to roam,
A body of England's, breathing Eng-
lish air,
Washed by the rivers, blest by suns of
home.
And think, this heart, all evil shed
away,
A pulse in the eternal mind, no less
Gives somewhere back the thoughts by
England given,
Her sights and sounds; dreams happy
as her day;

And laughter, learnt of friends; and
gentleness,
In hearts at peace, under an English
heaven.   *The Soldier*

THOMAS BROOKS 1608–1680

12 For (magna est veritas et prævalebit)
great is truth, and shall prevail.
*The Crown and Glory of Chris-
tianity* (1662), p. 407

JOHN BROWN 1715–1766

13 Altogether upon the high horse.
*Letter to Garrick, 27 Oct. 1765.
Correspondence of Garrick* (1831),
vol. i, p. 205

JOHN BROWN 1800–1859

14 I, John Brown, am now quite certain
that the crimes of this guilty land
will never be purged away but with
blood.
Last Statement, 2 Dec. 1859.
R. J. Hinton, *John Brown and
His Men*

THOMAS BROWN 1663–1704

15 A little before you made a leap into the
dark.   *Letters from the Dead*

16 I do not love you, Dr. Fell,
But why I cannot tell;
But this I know full well,
I do not love you, Dr. Fell.
(Trans. of Martial, *Epigrams*,
i. 32.) *Works* (1719), vol. iv,
p. 113

THOMAS EDWARD BROWN
1830–1897

17 A garden is a lovesome thing, God wot!
My Garden

18 Not God! in gardens! when the eve is
cool?
Nay, but I have a sign;
'Tis very sure God walks in mine.   *Ib.*

CHARLES FARRAR BROWNE
see ARTEMUS WARD

SIR THOMAS BROWNE 1605–1682

19 I love to lose myself in a mystery; to
pursue my reason to an *O altitudo!*
Religio Medici, pt. i, § 10

20 Charity begins at home, is the voice
of the world.   *Ib. pt. ii, § 4*

21 For the world, I count it not an inn,
but an hospital, and a place, not to
live, but to die in.   *Ib.* § 12

22 There is surely a piece of divinity in
us, something that was before the
elements, and owes no homage unto
the sun.   *Ib.*

1 What song the Syrens sang, or what
name Achilles assumed when he hid
himself among women, though puzzling questions, are not beyond all
conjecture.   *Urn Burial*, ch. 5

WILLIAM BROWNE 1591–1643

2 Underneath this sable hearse
Lies the subject of all verse,
Sidney's sister, Pembroke's mother;
Death, ere thou hast slain another,
Fair and learn'd, and good as she,
Time shall throw a dart at thee.
    *Epitaph. On the Countess of
    Pembroke*

SIR WILLIAM BROWNE
                              1692–1774

3 The King to Oxford sent a troop of
horse,
For Tories own no argument but force:
With equal skill to Cambridge books
he sent,
For Whigs admit no force but argument.
    Reply to Trapp's epigram 'The
    King, observing with judicious
    eyes' *(see 234:3)
    Nichols' Literary Anecdotes*, vol.
    iii, p. 330

ELIZABETH BARRETT
BROWNING 1806–1861

4   Earth's crammed with heaven,
And every common bush afire with
God;   *Aurora Leigh*, bk. vii

5 What was he doing, the great god
Pan,
Down in the reeds by the river?
    A Musical Instrument

ROBERT BROWNING 1812–1889

6 On the earth the broken arcs; in the
heaven, a perfect round.
    Abt Vogler, ix

7 The high that proved too high, the
heroic for earth too hard,
The passion that left the ground to
lose itself in the sky,
Are music sent up to God by the lover
and the bard;
Enough that he heard it once: we
shall hear it by and by.   *Ib.* x

8 Ah, but a man's reach should exceed
his grasp,
Or what's a heaven for?
    Andrea del Sarto

9 Just when we're safest, there's a sun-
set-touch,
A fancy from a flower-bell, some one's
death,

A chorus-ending from Euripides,
And that's enough for fifty hopes and
fears,—
The grand Perhaps.
    Bishop Blougram's Apology

10 Gigadibs the literary man.   *Ib.*

11 Oh, the little more, and how much it
is!
And the little less, and what worlds
away!   *By the Fireside*, xxxix

12 Kentish Sir Byng stood for his King,
Bidding the crop-headed Parliament
swing:
And, pressing a troop unable to stoop
And see the rogues flourish and honest
folk droop,
Marched them along, fifty-score
strong,
Great-hearted gentlemen, singing this
song.
    Cavalier Tunes, 1. *Marching Along*

13 Boot, saddle, to horse, and away!
    Ib. 3. *Boot and Saddle*

14 Dauntless the slug-horn to my lips
I set,
And blew.
    *Childe Roland to the Dark Tower
    came. Childe Roland*, xxxiv

15 How sad and bad and mad it was—
But then, how it was sweet!
    Confessions

16 Stung by the splendour of a sudden
thought. *A Death in the Desert*, l. 59

17 He said, 'What's time? leave now for
dogs and apes!
Man has Forever
    A Grammarian's Funeral, l. 83

18 That low man seeks a little thing to
do,
Sees it and does it:
This high man, with a great thing to
pursue,
Dies ere he knows it.
That low man goes on adding one to
one,
His hundred's soon hit:
This high man, aiming at a million,
Misses an unit.
That, has the world here—should he
need the next,
Let the world mind him!
This, throws himself on God, and
unperplext
Seeking shall find Him.   *Ib.* l. 113

19 He settled *Hoti's* business—let it be!—
Properly based *Oun*—
Gave us the doctrine of the enclitic
De,
Dead from the waist down.
                              Ib. l. 129

20 This is Ancona, yonder is the sea.
    The Guardian Angel

1 Oh, to be in England
  Now that April's there,
And whoever wakes in England
  Sees, some morning, unaware,
That the lowest boughs and the
    brushwood sheaf
  Round the elm-tree bole are in tiny
    leaf,
While the chaffinch sings on the or-
    chard bough
  In England—now!
    Home-thoughts, from Abroad

2 Nobly, nobly Cape St. Vincent to the
    North-west died away;
Sunset ran, one glorious blood-red,
  reeking into Cadiz Bay.
    Home-thoughts, from the Sea

3 'Here and here did England help me:
  how can I help England?'—say,
Whoso turns as I, this evening, turn
  to God to praise and pray,
While Jove's planet rises yonder,
  silent over Africa.   *Ib.*

4   'With this same key
Shakespeare unlocked his heart' once
    more!
Did Shakespeare? If so, the less Shake-
  speare he!   *House*, x

5 I sprang to the stirrup, and Joris, and
    he;
I galloped, Dirck galloped, we galloped
    all three.
    *How they brought the Good News
    from Ghent to Aix*

6 You know, we French stormed Ratisbon.   *Incident of the French Camp*

7 'You're wounded!' 'Nay,' the soldier's
    pride
Touched to the quick, he said:
'I'm killed, Sire!' And his chief beside
Smiling the boy fell dead.   *Ib.*

8 Escape me?
  Never—
  Beloved!   *Life in a Love*

9 Just for a handful of silver he left us,
  Just for a riband to stick in his coat.
    The Lost Leader

10 We that had loved him so, followed
    him, honoured him,
  Lived in his mild and magnificent
    eye,
  Learned his great language, caught his
    clear accents,
  Made him our pattern to live and to
    die!   *Ib.*

11 Shakespeare was of us, Milton was
    for us,
  Burns, Shelley, were with us—they
    watch from their graves!   *Ib.*

12 Never glad confident morning again!
      Ib.

13 Ah, did you once see Shelley plain,
  And did he stop and speak to you
And did you speak to him again?
  How strange it seems, and new!
    Memorabilia

14 That's my last Duchess painted on
the wall.   *My Last Duchess*, I. i

15 Never the time and the place
  And the loved one all together!
    Never the Time and the Place

16 Round the Cape of a sudden came the
    sea,
And the sun looked over the moun-
    tain's rim;
And straight was a path of gold for
    him,
And the need of a world of men for me.
    Parting at Morning

17 It was roses, roses, all the way.
    The Patriot

18 Hamelin Town's in Brunswick,
  By famous Hanover city;
The river Weser, deep and wide,
  Washes its walls on the southern
    side.
    The Pied Piper of Hamelin, st. i

19 Shrieking and squeaking
In fifty different sharps and flats.
    Ib. ii

20 Anything like the sound of a rat
Makes my heart go pit-a-pat!   *Ib.* iv

21 In did come the strangest figure!
    Ib. v

22 So munch on, crunch on, take your
    nuncheon,
Breakfast, supper, dinner, luncheon.
    Ib. vii

23 So, Willy, let me and you be wipers
Of scores out with all men, especially
  pipers!   *Ib.* xv

24 The year's at the spring,
And day's at the morn;
Morning's at seven;
The hill-side's dew-pearled;
The lark's on the wing;
The snail's on the thorn:
  God's in his heaven—
All's right with the world!
    Pippa Passes, pt. I

25 In the morning of the world,
When earth was nigher heaven than
  now.   *Ib.* pt. III

26   Who fished the murex up?
What porridge had John Keats?
    Popularity

27   All her hair
In one long yellow string I wound
Three times her little throat around,
And strangled her. No pain felt she;
I am quite sure she felt no pain.
    Porphyria's Lover

1 And all night long we have not stirred,
And yet God has not said a word! *Ib.*

2 Fear death?—to feel the fog in my throat,
The mist in my face. *Prospice*

3 Where he stands, the Arch Fear in a visible form. *Ib.*

4 Grow old along with me!
The best is yet to be,
The last of life, for which the first was made:
Our times are in His hand
Who saith, 'A whole I planned,
Youth shows but half; trust God: see all, nor be afraid!'
Rabbi ben Ezra, i

5 Time's wheel runs back or stops:
potter and clay endure. *Ib.* xxvii

6 O lyric Love, half angel and half bird
And all a wonder and a wild desire.
The Ring and the Book, bk. 1, l. 1391

7 Gr-r-r- there go, my heart's abhorrence!
Water your damned flower-pots, do!
Soliloquy of the Spanish Cloister

8 The sin I impute to each frustrate ghost
Is—the unlit lamp and the ungirt loin,
Though the end in sight was a vice,
I say. *The Statue and the Bust*

9 Greet the unseen with a cheer.
Summum Bonum (Asolando), epilogue

10 One who never turned his back but marched breast forward,
Never doubted clouds would break,
Never dreamed, though right were worsted, wrong would triumph,
Held we fall to rise, are baffled to fight better,
Sleep to wake. *Ib.*

11 What of soul was left, I wonder, when the kissing had to stop?
A Toccata of Galuppi's, xiv

12 Dear dead women, with such hair, too—what's become of all the gold
Used to hang and brush their bosoms?
I feel chilly and grown old. *Ib.* xv

13 What's become of Waring
Since he gave us all the slip?
Waring, i. i

GEORGE BRYAN BRUMMELL
1778–1840

14 Who's your fat friend? [Of the Prince of Wales.]
Gronow, *Reminiscences* (1862), p. 63

WILLIAM JENNINGS BRYAN
1860–1925

15 You shall not press down upon the brow of labor this crown of thorns, you shall not crucify mankind upon a cross of gold.
Speech at the National Democratic Convention, Chicago, 1896

WILLIAM CULLEN BRYANT
1794–1878

16 They seemed
Like old companions in adversity.
A Winter Piece, l. 26

ROBERT WILLIAMS BUCHANAN 1841–1901

17 The Fleshly School of Poetry.
Title of article in The Contemporary Review, *Oct. 1871. (Applied to Swinburne, William Morris, D. G. Rossetti, and others.)*

GEORGE VILLIERS, SECOND DUKE OF BUCKINGHAM
1628–1687

18 The world is made up for the most part of fools and knaves.
To Mr. Clifford, on his Humane Reason

19 Ay, now the plot thickens very much upon us. *The Rehearsal* iii. i

HENRY J. BUCKOLL 1803–1871

20 Lord, behold us with Thy blessing
Once again assembled here.
Psalms and Hymns for the Use of Rugby School Chapel. Lord, Behold us with Thy Blessing

21 Lord, dismiss us with Thy blessing,
Thanks for mercies past receive.
Ib. Lord, Dismiss us with Thy Blessing

GEORGES-LOUIS LECLERC DE BUFFON 1707–1788

22 Le style est l'homme même.
Style is the man himself.
Discours sur le Style

23 Le génie n'est qu'une grande aptitude à la patience.
Genius is only a great aptitude for patience.
Attr. to Buffon by Hérault de Séchelles in Voyage à Montbard

ARTHUR BULLER 1874–1944

24 There was a young lady named Bright,
Whose speed was far faster than light;

She set out one day
In a relative way,
And returned home the previous night.
Limerick in Punch, *19 Dec. 1923*

ALFRED BUNN 1796?–1860

1 Alice, where art thou?   *Title of Song*

2 I dreamt that I dwelt in marble halls,
With vassals and serfs at my side.
Bohemian Girl, Act II

JOHN BUNYAN 1628–1688

3 As I walk'd through the wilderness of
this world.   *Pilgrim's Progress, pt.* i

4 The name of the slough was Despond.
Ib.

5 The gentleman's name was Mr.
Wordly-Wise-Man.   *Ib.*

6 And behold there was a very stately
palace before him, the name of which
was Beautiful.   *Ib.*

7 The valley of Humiliation.   *Ib.*

8 A foul Fiend coming over the field to
meet him; his name is Apollyon.   *Ib.*

9 It beareth the name of Vanity-Fair,
because the town where 'tis kept, is
lighter than vanity.   *Ib.*

10 Hanging is too good for him, said Mr.
Cruelty.   *Ib.*

11 A castle, called Doubting-Castle, the
owner whereof was Giant Despair.
Ib.

12 They came to the Delectable Mountains.   *Ib.*

13 Sleep is sweet to the labouring man.
Ib.

14 So I awoke, and behold it was a dream.
Ib.

15 A man that could look no way but
downwards, with a muckrake in his
hand.   *Ib.* pt. ii

16 One Great-heart.   *Ib.*

17 He that is down needs fear no fall,
He that is low no pride.
He that is humble ever shall
Have God to be his guide.
*Ib. Shepherd Boy's Song in the
Valley of Humiliation*

18 An ornament to her profession.   *Ib.*

19 Whose name is Valiant-for-Truth. *Ib.*

20 Who would true valour see,
Let him come hither;
One here will constant be,
Come wind, come weather.
There's no discouragement
Shall make him once relent
His first avow'd intent
To be a pilgrim.
Then fancies flee away!

I'll fear not what men say,
I'll labour night and day
To be a pilgrim.
Pilgrim's Progress, pt. ii.
*Shepherd Boy's Song in the Valley
of Humiliation*

21 Mr. Standfast.   *Ib.*

22 My sword, I give to him that shall
succeed me in my pilgrimage, and my
courage and skill to him that can get
it. [*Mr. Valiant-for-Truth.*]   *Ib.*

23 So he passed over, and all the trumpets
sounded for him on the other side.   *Ib.*

GELETT BURGESS 1866–1951

24 I never saw a Purple Cow,
I never hope to see one;
But I can tell you, anyhow,
I'd rather see than be one!
*Burgess Nonsense Book. The
Purple Cow*

25 Ah, yes! I wrote the 'Purple Cow'—
I'm sorry, now, I wrote it!
But I can tell you anyhow,
I'll kill you if you quote it!   *Ib.*

REV. JOHN WILLIAM BURGON
1813–1888

26 A rose-red city—'half as old as Time'!
Petra, l. 132

EDMUND BURKE 1729–1797

27 Parliament is not a *congress* of ambassadors from different and hostile interests; which interests each must
maintain, as an agent and advocate,
against other agents and advocates;
but parliament is a *deliberative* assembly of *one* nation, with *one* interest, that of the whole; where, not
local purposes, not local prejudices
ought to guide, but the general good,
resulting from the general reason of
the whole. You choose a member indeed; but when you have chosen him,
he is not member of Bristol, but he is
a member of *parliament.*
*Speech to the Electors of Bristol,
3 Nov. 1774*

28 Young man, there is America—which
at this day serves for little more than
to amuse you with stories of savage
men, and uncouth manners; yet shall,
before you taste of death, show itself
equal to the whole of that commerce
which now attracts the envy of the
world.
*Speech on Conciliation with
America, 22 Mar. 1775*

29 The use of force alone is but *temporary.*
It may subdue for a moment; but it
does not remove the necessity of sub-
duing again: and a nation is not
governed, which is perpetually to be
conquered.   *Ib.*

1 All protestantism, even the most cold and passive, is a sort of dissent. But the religion most prevalent in our northern colonies is a refinement on the principle of resistance: it is the dissidence of dissent, and the protestantism of the Protestant religion.
Speech on Conciliation with America, 22 Mar. 1775

2 I do not know the method of drawing up an indictment against an whole people. *Ib.*

3 It is the love of the people; it is their attachment to their government, from the sense of the deep stake they have in such a glorious institution, which gives you your army and your navy, and infuses into both that liberal obedience, without which your army would be a base rabble, and your navy nothing but rotten timber. *Ib.*

4 Magnanimity in politics is not seldom the truest wisdom; and a great empire and little minds go ill together. *Ib.*

5 By adverting to the dignity of this high calling, our ancestors have turned a savage wilderness into a glorious empire: and have made the most extensive, and the only honourable conquests, not by destroying, but by promoting the wealth, the number, the happiness of the human race. *Ib.*

6 My hold of the colonies is in the close affection which grows from common names, from kindred blood, from similar privileges, and equal protection. These are ties which, though light as air, are as strong as links of iron. *Ib.*

7 Corrupt influence, which is itself the perennial spring of all prodigality, and of all disorder; which loads us, more than millions of debt; which takes away vigour from our arms, wisdom from our councils, and every shadow of authority and credit from the most venerable parts of our constitution.
Speech on the Economical Reform, 1780

8 The people are the masters. *Ib.*

9 A rapacious and licentious soldiery.
Speech on Fox's East India Bill, 1783

10 An event has happened, upon which it is difficult to speak, and impossible to be silent.
Impeachment of Warren Hastings, 5 May 1789

11 I impeach him in the name of the people of India, whose rights he has trodden under foot, and whose country he has turned into a desert. Lastly, in the name of human nature itself, in the name of both sexes, in the name of every age, in the name of every rank, I impeach the common enemy and oppressor of all!
Impeachment of Warren Hastings, as recorded by Macaulay in his essay on Warren Hastings

12 Well stored with pious frauds, and, like most discourses of the sort, much better calculated for the private advantage of the preacher than the edification of the hearers.
Observations on a Publication, 'The present state of the nation'

13 People will not look forward to posterity, who never look backward to their ancestors.
Reflections on the Revolution in France

14 It is now sixteen or seventeen years since I saw the Queen of France, then the Dauphiness, at Versailles; and surely never lighted on this orb, which she hardly seemed to touch, a more delightful vision. I saw her just above the horizon, decorating and cheering the elevated sphere she just began to move in,—glittering like the morning star, full of life, and splendour, and joy. . . . Little did I dream that I should have lived to see disasters fallen upon her in a nation of gallant men, in a nation of men of honour, and of cavaliers. I thought ten thousand swords must have leaped from their scabbards to avenge even a look that threatened her with insult. But the age of chivalry is gone. That of sophisters, economists, and calculators, has succeeded; and the glory of Europe is extinguished for ever. *Ib.*

15 Vice itself lost half its evil, by losing all its grossness. *Ib.*

16 Superstition is the religion of feeble minds. *Ib.*

17 And having looked to government for bread, on the very first scarcity they will turn and bite the hand that fed them.
Thoughts and Details on Scarcity

18 Somebody has said, that a king may make a nobleman, but he cannot make a gentleman.
Letter to Wm. Smith, 29 Jan. 1795

19 Not merely a chip of the old 'block', but the old block itself.
On Pitt's First Speech, 1781

BISHOP GILBERT BURNET
1643–1715

20 There was a sure way never to see it lost, and that was to die in the last ditch.
History of his own Times (1715), i. 457 (1766)

1 He [Halifax] had said he had known many kicked down stairs, but he never knew any kicked up stairs before.
Original Memoirs, c. 1697

JOHN BURNS 1858–1943

2 Every drop of the Thames is liquid 'istory.
Attr. by Sir Frederick Whyte, K.C.S.I.

ROBERT BURNS 1759–1796

3 Ae fond kiss, and then we sever.
Ae Fond Kiss

4 But to see her was to love her, Love but her, and love for ever. *Ib.*

5 Had we never lov'd sae kindly, Had we never lov'd sae blindly, Never met—or never parted, We had ne'er been broken-hearted. *Ib.*

6 Should auld acquaintance be forgot, And never brought to mind?
Auld Lang Syne

7 We'll tak a cup o' kindness yet, For auld lang syne. *Ib.*

8 And there's a hand, my trusty fiere, And gie 's a hand o' thine. *Ib.*

9 To make a happy fire-side clime To weans and wife, That's the true pathos and sublime Of human life. *To Dr. Blacklock*

10 Bonnie wee thing, cannie wee thing, Lovely wee thing, wert thou mine, I wad wear thee in my bosom, Lest my jewel it should tine.
The Bonnie Wee Thing

11 Gin a body meet a body Coming through the rye; Gin a body kiss a body, Need a body cry?
Coming through the Rye (taken from an old song The Bob-tailed Lass)

12 They never sought in vain that sought the Lord aright!
The Cottar's Saturday Night, vi

13 I wasna fou, but just had plenty.
Death and Dr. Hornbook, iii

14 On ev'ry hand it will allow'd be, He's just—nae better than he should be.
A Dedication to Gavin Hamilton, l. 25

15 The De'il's Awa' Wi' the Exciseman.
Title of Song

16 The rank is but the guinea's stamp; The man's the gowd for a' that!
For a' that and a' that

17 A man's a man for a' that. *Ib.*

18 Go fetch to me a pint o' wine, An' fill it in a silver tassie.
Go Fetch to Me a Pint

19 Green grow the rashes O, Green grow the rashes O; The sweetest hours that e'er I spend, Are spent amang the lasses O!
Green Grow the Rashes

20 John Anderson my jo, John, When we were first acquent, Your locks were like the raven, Your bonny brow was brent.
John Anderson My Jo

21 Now we maun totter down, John, And hand in hand we'll go, And sleep thegither at the foot, John Anderson, my jo. *Ib.*

22 There were three kings into the east, Three kings both great and high; And they hae sworn a solemn oath John Barleycorn should die.
John Barleycorn

23 O wad some Pow'r the giftie gie us To see oursels as others see us! It wad frae mony a blunder free us, And foolish notion. *To a Louse*

24 Man's inhumanity to man Makes countless thousands mourn!
Man was made to Mourn

25 Wee, sleekit, cow'rin', tim'rous beastie, O what a panic's in thy breastie! Thou need na start awa sae hasty, Wi' bickering brattle! I wad be laith to rin an' chase thee, Wi' murd'ring pattle!
To a Mouse

26 The best laid schemes o' mice an' men Gang aft a-gley. *Ib.*

27 My heart's in the Highlands, my heart is not here; My heart's in the Highlands a-chasing the deer; Chasing the wild deer, and following the roe, My heart's in the Highlands, wherever I go.
My Heart's in the Highlands

28 O, my Luve's like a red red rose That's newly sprung in June: O my Luve's like the melodie That's sweetly play'd in tune.
My Love is like a Red Red Rose

29 If there's a hole in a' your coats, I rede you tent it: A chield's amang you taking notes, And, faith, he'll prent it.
On Captain Grose's Peregrinations

30 Scots, wha hae wi' Wallace bled, Scots, wham Bruce has aften led, Welcome to your gory bed, Or to victorie.

Now's the day, and now's the hour; See the front o' battle lour! See approach proud Edward's power— Chains and slaverie!
Scots, Wha Hae

1 Liberty's in every blow!
    Let us do or die!
        Scots, Wha Hae

2 The mirth and fun grew fast and
furious. *Tam O'Shanter, l. 143*

3 O whistle, and I'll come to you, my
    lad:
    O whistle, and I'll come to you, my
    lad:
    Tho' father and mither and a' should
    gae mad,
    O whistle, and I'll come to you, my
    lad.
        Whistle, and I'll come to you, my
        Lad

4 Ye banks and braes o' bonny Doon,
    How can ye bloom sae fresh and
    fair?
    How can ye chant, ye little birds,
    And I sae weary fu' o' care?
        Ye Banks and Braes o' Bonny
        Doon

5 Thou minds me o' departed joys,
    Departed never to return. *Ib.*

6 Don't let the awkward squad fire over
me.
    A. Cunningham's *Works of*
    Burns; with his Life (1834), vol. i,
    p. 344

BENJAMIN HAPGOOD BURT
nineteenth century

7 When you're all dressed up and no
place to go. *Title of Song*

ROBERT BURTON 1577–1640

8 I had no time to lick it into form, as
she [a bear] doth her young ones.
    Anatomy of Melancholy, Demo-
    critus to the Reader

9 What is a ship but a prison?
    Ib. pt. ii, § 3, memb. 4

10 To these crocodile's tears, they will
add sobs, fiery sighs, and sorrowful
countenance.
    Ib. pt. iii, § 2, memb. 2, subsect. 4

11 England is a paradise for women, and
hell for horses: Italy a paradise for
horses, hell for women, as the diverb
goes. *Ib. § 3, memb. 1, subsect. 2*

12 One religion is as true as another.
    Ib. § 4, memb. 2, subsect. 1

13 Be not solitary, be not idle.
    Ib. Last words

COMTE DE BUSSY-RABUTIN
1681–1693

14 L'absence est à l'amour ce qu'est au
feu le vent; il éteint le petit, il
allume le grand.
    Absence is to love what wind is to
fire; it extinguishes the small, it enkindles the great.
        Histoire amoureuse des Gaules,
        Maximes d'Amours

BISHOP JOSEPH BUTLER
1692–1752

15 Things and actions are what they are,
and the consequences of them will be
what they will be: why then should we
desire to be deceived?
    Fifteen Sermons. No. 7, § 16

SAMUEL BUTLER 1612–1680

16 What ever sceptic could inquire for;
For every why he had a wherefore.
    Hudibras, pt. i, c. 1, l. 131

17 He knew what's what, and that's as
high
As metaphysic wit can fly. *Ib. l. 149*

18 'T was Presbyterian true blue.
    Ib. l. 189

19 Compound for sins, they are inclin'd to
By damning those they have no mind
to. *Ib. l. 213*

20 He ne'er consider'd it, as loth
To look a gift-horse in the mouth.
    Ib. l. 483

21 Quoth Hudibras, I smell a rat;
Ralpho, thou dost prevaricate.
    Ib. l. 815

22 Through perils both of wind and limb,
Through thick and thin she follow'd
him. *Ib. c. 2, l. 369*

23   I'll make the fur
Fly 'bout the ears of the old cur.
    Ib. l. 277

24 These reasons made his mouth to
water. *Ib. l. 379*

25 Then while the honour thou hast got
Is spick and span-new, piping hot.
    Ib. l. 398

26 Love is a boy, by poets styl'd,
Then spare the rod, and spoil the
child. *Ib. pt. ii, c. 1, l. 844*

27 Have always been at daggers-drawing,
And one another clapper-clawing.
    Ib. c. 2, l. 79

28   As the ancients
Say wisely, Have a care o' th' main
chance,
And look before you ere you leap;
For, as you sow, you are like to reap.
    Ib. l. 501

29 Doubtless the pleasure is as great
Of being cheated, as to cheat.
As lookers-on feel most delight,
That least perceive a juggler's sleight,
And still the less they understand,
The more th' admire his sleight of
hand. *Ib. c. 3, l. 1*

1 To swallow gudgeons ere th'are
    catch'd,
  And count their chickens ere th'are
    hatch'd.
          Hudibras, pt. ii, c. 3, l. 923

2 For in what stupid age or nation
  Was marriage ever out of fashion?
          Ib. pt. iii, c. 1, l. 817

3 He that complies against his will,
  Is of his own opinion still.
          Ib. c. 3, l. 547

4 All love at first, like generous wine,
  Ferments and frets until 'tis fine;
  But when 'tis settled on the lee,
  And from th' impurer matter free,
  Becomes the richer still the older,
  And proves the pleasanter the colder.
          Miscellaneous Thoughts

SAMUEL BUTLER 1835–1902

5 Genius . . . has been defined as a
  supreme capacity for taking trouble.
  . . . It might be more fitly described
  as a supreme capacity for getting its
  possessors into trouble of all kinds
  and keeping them therein so long as
  the genius remains.
          Notebooks, Genius, i

6 The phrase 'unconscious humour' is
  the one contribution I have made to
  the current literature of the day.
        Ib. The Position of a Homo Unius
        Libri. Myself and 'Unconscious
        Humour'

7 An honest God's the noblest work of
  man.
        Further Extracts from the Note-
        books (1934), p. 26. *See also*
        Festing Jones, *Memoir* (1919),
        vol. i, p. 212.

8 The advantage of doing one's praising
  for oneself is that one can lay it on so
  thick and exactly in the right places.
        The Way of All Flesh, ch. 34

9 There's many a good tune played on
  an old fiddle.   *Ib.* ch. 61

10 O God! Oh Montreal!
        Psalm of Montreal

WILLIAM BUTLER 1535–1618

11 Doubtless God could have made a
  better berry [strawberry], but doubtless God never did.
        Walton, *Compleat Angler*, pt. i,
        ch. 5

JOHN BYROM 1692–1763

12 Some say, that Signor Bononcini,
  Compar'd to Handel's a mere ninny;

Others aver, to him, that Handel
Is scarcely fit to hold a candle.
Strange! that such high dispute shou'd
  be
'Twixt Tweedledum and Tweedledee.
        Epigram on the Feuds between
        Handel and Bononcini

13 I shall prove it—as clear as a whistle.
        Epistle to Lloyd, I. xii

14 Christians awake, salute the happy
  morn,
  Whereon the Saviour of the world was
  born.   *Hymn for Christmas Day*

15 God bless the King, I mean the Faith's
  Defender;
  God bless—no harm in blessing—the
  Pretender;
  But who Pretender is, or who is King,
  God bless us all—that's quite another
  thing.   *To an Officer in the Army*

GEORGE GORDON BYRON, LORD BYRON 1788–1824

16 In short, he was a perfect cavaliero,
  And to his very valet seem'd a hero.
        Beppo, xxxiii

17 His heart was one of those which most
  enamour us,
  Wax to receive, and marble to retain.
        Ib. xxxiv

18 Mark! where his carnage and his conquests cease!
  He makes a solitude, and calls it—
  peace!   *Bride of Abydos*, c. II. xx

19 Hark! to the hurried question of
  Despair:
  'Where is my child?'—an echo answers
  —'Where?'   *Ib.* xxvii

20 War, war is still the cry, 'War even
  to the knife!'
        Childe Harold, c. I. lxxxvi

21 A schoolboy's tale, the wonder of an
  hour!   *Ib.* c. II. ii

22 Where'er we tread 'tis haunted, holy
  ground.   *Ib.* lxxxviii

23 There was a sound of revelry by night,
  And Belgium's capital had gather'd
  then
  Her beauty and her chivalry, and
  bright
  The lamps shone o'er fair women and
  brave men;
  A thousand hearts beat happily; and
  when
  Music arose with its voluptuous
  swell,
  Soft eyes look'd love to eyes which
  spake again,
  And all went merry as a marriage
  bell;
  But hush! hark! a deep sound strikes
  like a rising knell!   *Ib.* c. III. xxi

1 Did ye not hear it?—No; 'twas but the
    wind,
  Or the car rattling o'er the stony
    street;
  On with the dance! let joy be uncon-
    fined;
  No sleep till morn, when Youth and
    Pleasure meet
  To chase the glowing Hours with
    flying feet.
            Childe Harolde, c. III. xxii

2 Arm! Arm! it is—it is—the cannon's
    opening roar!   *Ib.*

3 He rush'd into the field, and, foremost
    fighting, fell.   *Ib.*

4 Yet, Freedom! yet thy banner, torn,
    but flying,
  Streams like the thunder-storm *against*
    the wind.   *Ib.* c. IV. xcviii

5 He reck'd not of the life he lost nor
    prize,
  But where his rude hut by the Danube
    lay,
  There were his young barbarians all
    at play,
  There was their Dacian mother—he,
    their sire,
  Butcher'd to make a Roman holiday.
                              Ib. cxli

6 While stands the Coliseum, Rome
    shall stand;
  When falls the Coliseum, Rome shall
    fall;
  And when Rome falls—the World.
                              Ib. cxlv

7 There is a pleasure in the pathless
    woods,
  There is a rapture on the lonely shore,
  There is society, where none intrudes,
  By the deep sea, and music in its roar:
  I love not man the less, but Nature
    more,
  From these our interviews, in which
    I steal
  From all I may be, or have been before,
  To mingle with the Universe, and feel
  What I can ne'er express, yet cannot
    all conceal.   *Ib.* clxxviii

8 Roll on, thou deep and dark blue
    Ocean—roll!
  Ten thousand fleets sweep over thee
    in vain;   *Ib.* clxxix

9 Eternal spirit of the chainless mind!
  Brightest in dungeons, Liberty! thou
    art.   *Sonnet on Chillon*

10 Her stature tall—I hate a dumpy
    woman.   *Don Juan*, c. I. lxi

11 What men call gallantry, and gods
    adultery,
  Is much more common where the
    climate's sultry.   *Ib.* lxiii

12 A little still she strove, and much
    repented,
  And whispering 'I will ne'er consent'—
    consented.   *Ib.* cxvii

13 'Tis sweet to hear the watch-dog's
    honest bark
  Bay deep-mouth'd welcome as we
    draw near home;
  'Tis sweet to know there is an eye
    will mark
  Our coming, and look brighter when
    we come.   *Don Juan*, c. I. cxxiii

14 Man's love is of man's life a thing
    apart,
  'Tis woman's whole existence.
                              Ib. cxciv

15 Let us have wine and women, mirth
    and laughter,
  Sermons and soda-water the day after.
                     Ib. c. II. clxxviii

16 He was the mildest manner'd man
  That ever scuttled ship or cut a
    throat,
  With such true breeding of a gentle-
    man,
  You never could divine his real
    thought.   *Ib.* c. III. xli

17 The isles of Greece, the isles of Greece!
  Where burning Sappho loved and
    sung,
  Where grew the arts of war and peace,
  Where Delos rose, and Phœbus
    sprung!
  Eternal summer gilds them yet,
  But all, except their sun, is set.
                         Ib. lxxxvi. 1

18 The mountains look on Marathon—
  And Marathon looks on the sea;
  And musing there an hour alone,
    I dream'd that Greece might still be
      free.   *Ib.* 3

19 A king sate on the rocky brow
  Which looks o'er sea-born Salamis;
  And ships, by thousands, lay below,
    And men in nations;—all were his!
  He counted them at break of day—
  And when the sun set where were they?
                              Ib. 4

20 Earth! render back from out thy breast
  A remnant of our Spartan dead!
  Of the three hundred grant but three,
  To make a new Thermopylæ!   *Ib.* 7

21 Fill high the cup with Samian wine!
                         Ib. lxxxvi. 9

22 And if I laugh at any mortal thing,
  'Tis that I may not weep.   *Ib.* c. IV. iv

23 A lady in the case.   *Ib.* c. V. xix

24 That all-softening, overpowering knell,
  The tocsin of the soul—the dinner-bell.
                              Ib. xlix

25 John Keats, who was kill'd off by one
    critique,
  Just as he really promised something
    great,
  If not intelligible, without Greek
  Contrived to talk about the Gods of
    late,

Much as they might have been supposed to speak.
Poor fellow! His was an untoward
fate;
'Tis strange the mind, that very fiery
particle,
Should let itself be snuff'd out by an
article. *Don Juan*, c. XI. lx

1 A finish'd gentleman from top to toe.
Ib. c. XII. lxxxiv

2 'Tis strange—but true; for truth is
always strange;
Stranger than fiction. *Ib*. c. XIV. ci

3 With just enough of learning to misquote.
*English Bards and Scotch Re-
viewers* l. 66

4 Or lend fresh interest to a twice-told
tale. *Hints from Horace*, l. 184

5 Though women are angels, yet wedlock's the devil.
Hours of Idleness. To Eliza

6 Who killed John Keats?
'I,' says the Quarterly,
So savage and Tartarly;
"Twas one of my feats.' *John Keats*

7 Oh, talk not to me of a name great in
story;
The days of our youth are the days of
our glory;
And the myrtle and ivy of sweet
two-and-twenty
Are worth all your laurels, though
ever so plenty.
*Stanzas Written on the Road be-
tween Florence and Pisa.*

8 I am the very slave of circumstance
And impulse—borne away with every
breath! *Sardanapalus*, iv. i

9 The Assyrian came down like the wolf
on the fold,
And his cohorts were gleaming in
purple and gold;
And the sheen of their spears was like
stars on the sea,
When the blue wave rolls nightly on
deep Galilee.
Destruction of Sennacherib

10 For the Angel of Death spread his
wings on the blast. *Ib.*

11 And the might of the Gentile, unsmote
by the sword,
Hath melted like snow in the glance of
the Lord! *Ib.*

12 She walks in beauty, like the night
Of cloudless climes and starry
skies;
*Hebrew Melodies. She Walks in
Beauty*

13 So, we'll go no more a roving
So late into the night,
Though the heart be still as loving,
And the moon be still as bright.
So, We'll Go No More a Roving

14 For the sword outwears its sheath,
And the soul wears out the breast.
And the heart must pause to breathe,
And love itself have rest. *Ib.*

15 Though the night was made for loving,
And the day returns too soon,
Yet we'll go no more a-roving
By the light of the moon. *Ib.*

16 When we two parted
In silence and tears,
Half broken-hearted
To sever for years,
Pale grew thy cheek and cold,
Colder thy kiss.
When We Two Parted

17 If I should meet thee
After long years,
How should I greet thee?—
With silence and tears. *Ib.*

18 As he [Lord Byron] himself briefly
described it in his Memoranda, 'I
awoke one morning and found myself famous.'—Moore's *Life of Byron*
(1830), vol. i, p. 347 (referring to the
instantaneous success of *Childe
Harold*)

JAMES BRANCH CABELL 1879–

19 The optimist proclaims that we live
in the best of all possible worlds; and
the pessimist fears this is true.
The Silver Stallion, bk. iv, ch. 26

AUGUSTUS CAESAR
63 B.C.–A.D. 14

20 Quintili Vare, legiones redde.
Quintilius Varus, give me back my
legions.
Suetonius, *Divus Augustus*, 23

21 Urbem . . . excoluit adeo, ut iure sit
gloriatus marmoream se relinquere,
quam latericiam accepisset.
He so improved the city that he
justly boasted that he found it
brick and left it marble. *Ib.* 28

22 Ad Graecas Kalendas soluturos.
They will pay at the Greek Kalends.
Ib. 87

JULIUS CAESAR 102?–44 B.C.

23 Gallia est omnis divisa in partes tres.
Gaul as a whole is divided into three
parts. *De Bello Gallico*, I. i

1 Et tu, Brute?
   You also, Brutus?
      Of unknown origin. Quoted by
      Shakespeare, 'Julius Caesar',
      III. i, perhaps from the (lost) Latin
      play 'Caesar Interfectus', prob-
      ably from 'The True Tragedie
      of Richard Duke of York.'
      'Some have written that as M.
      Brutus came running upon him,
      he said "καὶ σύ, τέκνον", "and
      you, my son." '
      (Holland's *Suetonius*, p. 33)

2 Veni, vidi, vici.
   I came, I saw, I conquered.
      Suetonius, *Divus Julius*, xxxvii.
      2.
      (Inscription displayed in Caesar's
      Pontic triumph, or, according to
      Plutarch, l. 2, written in a letter
      by Caesar, announcing the victory
      of Zela which concluded the Pontic
      campaign)

3 Iacta alea est.
      The die is cast.   *Ib.* xxxii
         At the crossing of the Rubicon

CALIGULA A.D. 12–41

4 Utinam populus Romanus unam
   cervicem haberet!
      Would that the Roman people had
      but one neck!
         Suetonius, *Life of Caligula*, 30

CALLIMACHUS fl. 250 B.C.

5 μέγα βιβλίον μέγα κακόν.
      Great book, great evil.
         Proverb derived from Calli-
         machus, *Fragments*, 359

CHARLES STUART CALVERLEY
1831–1884

6 The farmer's daughter hath soft
   brown hair;
      (*Butter and eggs and a pound of*
      cheese)
   And I met with a ballad, I can't say
   where,
      Which wholly consisted of lines like
      these.   *Ballad*

7 A bare-legg'd beggarly son of a gun.
      The Cock and the Bull

8 Life is with such all beer and skittles;
   They are not difficult to please
   About their victuals.   *Contentment*

9 Sweet, when the morn is grey;
   Sweet, when they've cleared away
   Lunch; and at close of day
   Possibly sweetest.   *Ode to Tobacco*

PIERRE-JACQUES, BARON DE CAMBRONNE 1770–1842

10 La Garde meurt, mais ne se rend pas.
      The Guards die but do not sur-
      render.
         Attr. to Cambronne when called
         upon to surrender by Col. Halkett.
         Cambronne denied the saying at
         a banquet at Nantes, 1835

WILLIAM CAMDEN 1551–1623

11 My friend, judge not me,
   Thou seest I judge not thee.
   Betwixt the stirrup and the ground
   Mercy I asked, mercy I found.
         Remains. Epitaph for a Man
         Killed by Falling from His Horse

JANE MONTGOMERY CAMPBELL 1817–1878

12 We plough the fields, and scatter
   The good seed on the land,
   But it is fed and watered
   By God's Almighty Hand;
   He sends the snow in winter,
   The warmth to swell the grain,
   The breezes and the sunshine,
   And soft refreshing rain.
   All good gifts around us
   Are sent from Heaven above,
   Then thank the Lord, O thank the
   Lord,
   For all His love.
         We Plough the Fields. Trans. from
         the German. C. S. Bere's Gar-
         land of Songs

THOMAS CAMPBELL 1777–1844

13 O leave this barren spot to me!
   Spare, woodman, spare the beechen
   tree.   *The Beech-Tree's Petition*

14 To live in hearts we leave behind
   Is not to die.   *Hallowed Ground*

15 On Linden, when the sun was low,
   All bloodless lay the untrodden snow,
   And dark as winter was the flow
   Of Iser, rolling rapidly.   *Hohenlinden*

16 'Tis the sunset of life gives me mystical lore,
   And coming events cast their shadows
   before.   *Lochiel's Warning*

17 A chieftain to the Highlands bound
   Cries, 'Boatman, do not tarry!
   And I'll give thee a silver pound
   To row us o'er the ferry.'
         Lord Ullin's Daughter

18 'O, I'm the chief of Ulva's isle,
   And this Lord Ullin's daughter.'
                              Ib.

1 'Come back! come back!' he cried in
   grief
     Across the stormy water:
   'And I'll forgive your Highland chief,
     My daughter! oh my daughter!'
                 Lord Ullin's Daughter

2 With Freedom's lion-banner
   Britannia rules the waves.
                 Ode to the Germans

3 'Tis distance lends enchantment to the
     view,
   And robes the mountain in its azure
     hue.   *Pleasures of Hope*, pt. i, l. 7

4 The proud, the cold untroubled heart
     of stone,
   That never mused on sorrow but its
     own.   *Ib.* l. 185

5 Hope, for a season, bade the world
     farewell,
   And Freedom shrieked—as Kosciusko
     fell!   *Ib.* l. 381

6 Ye Mariners of England
   That guard our native seas,
   Whose flag has braved, a thousand
     years,
   The battle and the breeze—
   Your glorious standard launch again
   To match another foe!
   And sweep through the deep,
   While the stormy winds do blow,—
   While the battle rages loud and long,
   And the stormy winds do blow.
                 Ye Mariners of England

7 Britannia needs no bulwarks,
   No towers along the steep;
   Her march is o'er the mountain waves,
   Her home is on the deep.   *Ib.*

8 The meteor flag of England
   Shall yet terrific burn,
   Till danger's troubled night depart
   And the star of peace return.   *Ib.*

9 Now Barabbas was a publisher.
                 Often attr. to Byron

THOMAS CAMPION *d.* 1620

10 Good thoughts his only friends,
     His wealth a well-spent age,
   The earth his sober inn
     And quiet pilgrimage.
                 A Book of Airs, xviii

11 There is a garden in her face,
   Where roses and white lilies grow;
   A heav'nly paradise is that place,
   Wherein all pleasant fruits do flow.
   There cherries grow, which none may
     buy
   Till 'Cherry ripe' themselves do cry.
                 Fourth Book of Airs, vii

GEORGE CANNING 1770–1827

12 In matters of commerce the fault of
     the Dutch
   Is offering too little and asking too
     much.

The French are with equal advantage
   content,
So we clap on Dutch bottoms just
   twenty per cent.
       *Dispatch, in Cipher, To Sir
       Charles Bagot, English Ambas-
       sador at The Hague, 31 Jan. 1826*

13 A steady patriot of the world alone,
   The friend of every country but his
   own. [The Jacobin.]
                 New Morality, l. 113

14 Give me the avowed, erect and manly
     foe;
   Firm I can meet, perhaps return the
     blow;
   But of all plagues, good Heaven, thy
     wrath can send,
   Save me, oh, save me, from the candid
     friend.   *Ib.* l. 207

15 Pitt is to Addington
   As London is to Paddington.
                 The Oracle, c. 1803–4

16 A sudden thought strikes me, let us
   swear an eternal friendship.
                 The Rovers, I. i

17 (*Pitt:*)
   When our perils are past, shall our
     gratitude sleep?
   No,—here's to the pilot that
   weathered the storm.
       *Song for the inauguration of the
       Pitt Club, 25 May 1802*

18 I called the New World into existence,
   to redress the balance of the Old.
                 Speech, 12 Dec. 1826

FRANCESCO CARACCIOLI
                       1752–1799

19 Il y a en Angleterre soixante sectes
   religieuses différentes, et une seule
   sauce.

     In England there are sixty different
     religions, and only one sauce.
                               Attr.

THOMAS CAREW 1595?–1639?

20 Here lies a King that rul'd, as he
     thought fit
   The universal monarchy of wit;
   Here lies two Flamens, and both those
     the best:
   Apollo's first, at last the true God's
     priest.   *Elegy on the Death of Donne*

21 An untimely grave.
       *Inscription on Tomb of the Duke
       of Buckingham*

HENRY CAREY 1693?–1743

22 God save our gracious king!
   Long live our noble king!
     God save the king!
                 God Save the King

1 Confound their politics,
Frustrate their knavish tricks.   *Ib.*

2 Of all the girls that are so smart
There's none like pretty Sally,
She is the darling of my heart,
And she lives in our alley.
                Sally in our Alley

3 When she is by I leave my work,
(I love her so sincerely)
My master comes like any Turk,
And bangs me most severely.   *Ib.*

4 Of all the days that's in the week
I dearly love but one day—
And that's the day that comes betwixt
A Saturday and Monday.   *Ib.*

THOMAS CARLYLE 1795–1881

5 The three great elements of modern
civilization, Gunpowder, Printing, and
the Protestant Religion.
*Critical and Miscellaneous
Essays, vol. i. State of German
Literature*

6 To the very last, he [Napoleon] had
a kind of idea; that, namely, of
La carrière ouverte aux talents, The
tools to him that can handle them.
Ib. vol. iv. Sir Walter Scott

7 A witty statesman said, you might
prove anything by figures.
Ib. Chartism, ch. 2

8 In epochs when cash payment has become the sole nexus of man to man.
Ib. ch. 6

9 'Genius' (which means transcendent
capacity of taking trouble, first of all).
Frederick the Great, bk. iv, ch. 3

10 Happy the people whose annals are
blank in history-books!
Ib. bk. xvi, ch. 1

11 A whiff of grapeshot.
History of the French Revolution,
pt. 1, bk. v, ch. 3

12 The seagreen Incorruptible. [Robespierre.]   *Ib.* pt. ii, ch. 4

13 No great man lives in vain. The history of the world is but the biography of great men.
Heroes and Hero Worship, i. *The
Hero as Divinity*

14 The true University of these days is a
collection of books.
Ib. v. *The Hero as Man of
Letters*

15 Burke said there were Three Estates
in Parliament; but, in the Reporters'
Gallery yonder, there sat a *Fourth
Estate* more important far than they
all.   *Ib.*

16 A Parliament speaking through reporters to Buncombe and the twenty-
seven millions mostly fools.
Latter-Day Pamphlets No. 6.
Parliaments

17 The unspeakable Turk should be immediately struck out of the question.
Letter to G. Howard, 24 Nov. 1876

18 Transcendental moonshine.
Life of John Sterling, pt. i, ch. 15

19 Captains of industry.
Past and Present, bk. iv, title of
ch. 4

20 Man is a tool-using animal. . . .
Without tools he is nothing, with
tools he is all.
Sartor Resartus, bk. i, ch. 5

21 I don't pretend to understand the
Universe—it's a great deal bigger
than I am. . . . People ought to be
modester.
Remark to Wm. Allingham. D. A.
Wilson's and D. Wilson Mac-
Arthur *Carlyle in Old Age*

22 Macaulay is well for a while, but one
wouldn't *live* under Niagara.
Remark. R. M. Milnes's *Notebook* (1838)

23 Who never ate his bread in sorrow,
Who never spent the darksome hours
Weeping and watching for the morrow
He knows ye not, ye heavenly Powers.
*Translation of Goethe's Wilhelm
Meister's Apprenticeship,* bk. ii,
ch. 13

24 MARGARET FULLER:
I accept the universe.
CARLYLE:
Gad! she'd better!   *Attr.*

DALE CARNEGIE 1888–1955

25 How to win Friends and influence
People.   *Title of Book*

JULIA CARNEY 1823–1908

26 Little drops of water, little grains of
sand,
Make the mighty ocean, and the
pleasant land.
So the little minutes, humble though
they be,
Make the mighty ages of eternity.
Little Things. (Attr. also to E. C.
Brewer, D. C. Colesworthy, and
F. S. Osgood)

JOSEPH EDWARDS CARPENTER 1813–1885

27 What are the wild waves saying
Sister, the whole day long,
That ever amid our playing,
I hear but their low lone song?
What are the Wild Waves Saying?

LEWIS CARROLL [CHARLES LUTWIDGE DODGSON] 1832–1898

1 What I tell you three times is true.
Hunting of the Snark, Fit 1.
The Landing

2 He would answer to 'Hi!' or to any
loud cry,
Such as 'Fry me!' or 'Fritter-my-
wig!'   *Ib.*

3 His intimate friends called him
'Candle-ends',
And his enemies, 'Toasted-cheese'
Ib.

4 But oh, beamish nephew, beware of
the day,
If your Snark be a Boojum! For
then
You will softly and suddenly vanish
away,
And never be met with again!
Ib. Fit 3. *The Baker's Tale*

5 They sought it with thimbles, they
sought it with care;
They pursued it with forks and
hope;
They threatened its life with a rail-
way-share;
They charmed it with smiles and
soap.
Ib. Fit 5. *The Beaver's Lesson*

6 For the Snark *was* a Boojum, you see.
Ib. Fit 8. *The Vanishing*

7 He thought he saw an Elephant,
That practised on a fife:
He looked again, and found it was
A letter from his wife.
'At length I realize,' he said,
'The bitterness of life!'
Sylvie and Bruno, ch. 5

8 He thought he saw a Rattlesnake
That questioned him in Greek,
He looked again and found it was
The Middle of Next Week.
'The one thing I regret,' he said,
'Is that it cannot speak!' *Ib.* ch. 6

9 He thought he saw a Banker's Clerk
Descending from the bus:
He looked again, and found it was
A Hippopotamus:
'If this should stay to dine,' he said,
'There won't be much for us.'
Ib. ch. 7

10 'What is the use of a book,' thought
Alice, 'without pictures or conversations?'   *Alice in Wonderland*, ch. 1

11 Do cats eat bats? . . . Do bats eat
cats?   *Ib.*

12 'Curiouser and curiouser!' cried Alice.
Ib. ch. 2

13 How doth the little crocodile
Improve his shining tail,
And pour the waters of the Nile
On every golden scale!   *Ib.*

14 'I'll be judge, I'll be jury,' said cunning old Fury;
'I'll try the whole cause, and condemn you to death.'
Alice in Wonderland, ch. 3

15 The Duchess! The Duchess!
O my dear paws! Oh my fur and whiskers!   *Ib.* ch. 4

16 'You are old, Father William,' the
young man said,
'And your hair has become very
white;
And yet you incessantly stand on your
head—
Do you think, at your age, it is
right?'

'In my youth,' Father William replied
to his son.
'I feared it might injure the brain;
But now that I'm perfectly sure I have
none,
Why, I do it again and again.'
Ib. ch. 5

17 'I have answered three questions, and
that is enough,'
Said his father; 'don't give yourself
airs!
Do you think I can listen all day to
such stuff?
Be off, or I'll kick you downstairs!'
Ib.

18 'If everybody minded their own
business,' said the Duchess in a hoarse
growl, 'the world would go round a
deal faster than it does.' *Ib.* ch. 6

19 Speak roughly to your little boy,
And beat him when he sneezes;
He only does it to annoy,
Because he knows it teases.   *Ib.*

20 For he can thoroughly enjoy
The pepper when he pleases!   *Ib.*

21 This time it vanished quite slowly,
beginning with the end of the tail, and
ending with the grin, which remained
some time after the rest of it had gone.
[The Cheshire Cat.]   *Ib.*

22 'Then you should say what you mean,'
the March Hare went on. 'I do,'
Alice hastily replied; 'at least—at
least I mean what I say—that's the
same thing, you know.'
'Not the same thing a bit!' said the
Hatter. 'Why, you might just as well
say that "I see what I eat" is the same
thing as "I eat what I see!"' '
Ib. ch. 7

23 'It was the *best* butter,' the March
Hare meekly replied.   *Ib.*

24 Twinkle, twinkle, little bat!
How I wonder what you're at!
Up above the world you fly!
Like a teatray in the sky.   *Ib.*

1 The Queen was in a furious passion,
and went stamping about, and shouting, 'Off with his head!' or 'Off with
her head!' about once in a minute.
Alice in Wonderland, ch. 8

2 'A cat may look at a king,' said Alice.
Ib.

3 And the moral of that is—'Oh, 'tis
love, 'tis love, that makes the world
go round!' *Ib.* ch. 9

4 Take care of the sense, and the sounds
will take care of themselves. *Ib.*

5 I only took the regular course . . .
the different branches of Arithmetic—
Ambition, Distraction, Uglification,
and Derision. *Ib.*

6 'That's the reason they're called
lessons,' the Gryphon remarked: 'because they lessen from day to day.' *Ib.*

7 'Will you walk a little faster?' said
a whiting to a snail,
'There's a porpoise close behind us,
and he's treading on my tail.'
Ib. ch. 10

8 Will you, won't you, will you, won't
you, will you join the dance? *Ib.*

9 The further off from England the
nearer is to France—
Then turn not pale, beloved snail,
but come and join the dance. *Ib.*

10 'Tis the voice of the lobster; I heard
him declare,
'You have baked me too brown, I
must sugar my hair.' *Ib.*

11 Soup of the evening, beautiful Soup!
Ib.

12 The Queen of Hearts, she made some
tarts,
All on a summer day:
The Knave of Hearts, he stole those
tarts,
And took them quite away!
Ib. ch. 11

13 'Where shall I begin, please your
Majesty?' he asked.
'Begin at the beginning,' the King
said, gravely, 'and go on till you
come to the end: then stop.' *Ib.*

14 'Twas brillig, and the slithy toves
Did gyre and gimble in the wabe;
All mimsy were the borogoves,
And the mome raths outgrabe.

'Beware the Jabberwock, my son!
The jaws that bite, the claws that
catch!
Beware the Jubjub bird, and shun
The frumious Bandersnatch!'

He took his vorpal sword in hand:
Long time the manxome foe he
sought—
So rested he by the Tumtum tree,
And stood awhile in thought.

And as in uffish thought he stood,
The Jabberwock, with eyes of flame,
Came whiffling through the tulgey
wood,
And burbled as it came!

One, two! One, two! And through and
through
The vorpal blade went snicker-
snack!
He left it dead, and with its head
He went galumphing back.

'And hast thou slain the Jabberwock?
Come to my arms, my beamish boy!
O frabjous day! Callooh! Callay!'
He chortled in his joy.
Through the Looking-Glass, ch. 1

15 Curtsey while you're thinking what
to say. It saves time. *Ib.* ch. 2

16 Speak in French when you can't think
of the English for a thing. *Ib.*

17 Now, *here* you see, it takes all the
running *you* can do, to keep in the
same place. If you want to get somewhere else, you must run at least
twice as fast as that! *Ib.*

18 Tweedledum and Tweedledee
Agreed to have a battle;
For Tweedledum said Tweedledee
Had spoiled his nice new rattle.

Just then flew down a monstrous crow,
As black as a tar-barrel;
Which frightened both the heroes so,
They quite forgot their quarrel.
Ib. ch. 4

19 'Contrariwise,' continued Tweedledee,
'if it was so, it might be; and if it
were so, it would be: but as it isn't,
it ain't. That's logic.' *Ib.*

20 The sun was shining on the sea,
Shining with all his might:
He did his very best to make
The billows smooth and bright—
And this was odd, because it was
The middle of the night.
Ib. The Walrus and the Carpenter

21 The Walrus and the Carpenter
Were walking close at hand;
They wept like anything to see
Such quantities of sand:
'If this were only cleared away,'
They said, 'it would be grand!'

'If seven maids with seven mops
Swept it for half a year,
Do you suppose,' the Walrus said,
'That they could get it clear?'
'I doubt it,' said the Carpenter,
And shed a bitter tear. *Ib.*

22 'The time has come,' the Walrus said,
'To talk of many things:
Of shoes—and ships—and sealing
wax—
Of cabbages—and kings—
And why the sea is boiling hot—
And whether pigs have wings.' *Ib.*

1   But answer came there none—
    And this was scarcely odd because
    They'd eaten every one.
            Through the Looking-Glass.
        The Walrus and the Carpenter

2   'Let's fight till six, and then have
    dinner,' said Tweedledum.   *Ib.*

3   The rule is, jam to-morrow and jam
    yesterday—but never jam to-day.
                        Ib. ch. 5

4   They gave it me,—for an un-birthday
    present.   *Ib. ch. 6*

5   'There's glory for you!' 'I don't know
    what you mean by "glory",' Alice
    said. 'I meant, "there's a nice knock-
    down argument for you!"' 'But
    "glory" doesn't mean "a nice knock-
    down argument",' Alice objected.
    'When I use a word,' Humpty Dumpty
    said in a rather scornful tone, 'it means
    just what I choose it to mean,—
    neither more nor less.'   *Ib.*

6   I said it very loud and clear;
    I went and shouted in his ear.

    But he was very stiff and proud;
    He said 'You needn't shout so loud!'

    And he was very proud and stiff;
    He said 'I'd go and wake them, if——'
                                Ib.

7   You see it's like a portmanteau—there
    are two meanings packed up into one
    word.   *Ib.*

8   He's an Anglo-Saxon Messenger—
    and those are Anglo-Saxon attitudes.
                            Ib. ch. 7

9   It's as large as life, and twice as
    natural!   *Ib.*

10 The [White] Knight said . . . 'It's my
    own invention.'   *Ib.*

11 I'll tell thee everything I can:
        There's little to relate.
    I saw an aged, aged man,
        A-sitting on a gate.   *Ib.*

12 He said, 'I hunt for haddocks' eyes
        Among the heather bright,
    And work them into waistcoat-buttons
        In the silent night.   *Ib.*

13 I sometimes dig for buttered rolls,
        Or set limed twigs for crabs;
    I sometimes search the grassy knolls
        For wheels of hansom-cabs.'   *Ib.*

14 Or madly squeeze a right-hand foot
        Into a left-hand shoe.   *Ib.*

15 'Speak when you're spoken to!' the
    Red Queen sharply interrupted her.
                            Ib. ch. 9

16 It isn't etiquette to cut any one you've
    been introduced to. Remove the joint.
                                Ib.

WILLIAM HERBERT CARRUTH
1859–1924

17 Some call it evolution,
    And others call it God.
        *Each In His Own Tongue, and
        Other Poems* (1908)

PHOEBE CARY 1824–1871

18 And though hard be the task,
    'Keep a stiff upper lip'.
            Keep a Stiff Upper Lip

HARRY CASTLING

19 What-Ho! She bumps!   *Title of Song*

20 Let's all go down the Strand.
                    Title of Song

REV. EDWARD CASWALL
1814–1878
(As adapted in 'Hymns Ancient and
Modern'):

21 Days and moments quickly flying,
        Blend the living with the dead;
    Soon will you and I be lying
        Each within our narrow bed.
            *Hymns and Poems. Days and
            Moments Quickly Flying*

22 Earth has many a noble city;
    Bethlehem, thou dost all excel.
        Ib. Earth Has Many a Noble City

23 Jesu, the very thought of Thee
    With sweetness fills the breast.
        *Ib. Jesu, The Very Thought of
        Thee (trans. from Latin)*

CATO THE ELDER 234–149 B.C.

24 Delenda est Carthago.
    Carthage must be destroyed.
            Plutarch, Life of Cato

CATULLUS 84?–54? B.C.

25 Lugete, O Veneres Cupidinesque,
    Et quantum est hominum venusti-
        orum.
    Passer mortuus est meae puellae,
    Passer, deliciae meae puellae.

    Come, all ye Loves and Cupids,
        haste
    To mourn, and all ye men of taste;
    My lady's sparrow, O, he's sped,
    The bird my lady loved is dead!
        *Carmina, iii, trans. by Sir W.
        Marris*

26 Vivamus, mea Lesbia, atque amemus,
    Rumoresque senum severiorum
    Omnes unius aestimemus assis.
    Soles occidere et redire possunt:
    Nobis cum semel occidit brevis lux
    Nox est perpetua una dormienda.

    Lesbia mine, let's live and love!
    Give no doit for tattle of
    Crabbed old censorious men;

Suns may set and rise again,
But when our short day takes flight
Sleep we must one endless night.
Carmina, v

1 Da mi basia mille.
Kiss me times a thousand o'er. *Ib.*

2 Odi et amo: quare id faciam, fortasse
requiris.
Nescio, sed fieri sentio et excrucior.
I hate, I love—the cause thereof
Belike you ask of me:
I do not know, but feel 'tis so,
And I'm in agony. *Ib.* lxxxv

3 Accipe fraterno multum manantia
fletu,
Atque in perpetuum, frater, ave atque vale.

A brother's tears have wet them
o'er and o'er;
And so, my brother, hail, and farewell evermore! *Ib.* ci

EDITH CAVELL 1865–1915

4 I realize that patriotism is not enough.
I must have no hatred or bitterness
towards anyone.
*Last Words, 12 Oct. 1915. The
Times, 23 Oct. 1915*

ROBERT CECIL
see SALISBURY

THOMAS OF CELANO *c.* 1250

5 Dies irae, dies illa
Solvet saeclum in favilla,
Teste David cum Sibylla.

Day of wrath and doom impending,
David's word with Sibyl's blending
Heaven and earth in ashes ending!
Analecta Hymnica, liv, p. 269.
(Trans. by Dr. W. J. Irons in
The English Hymnal)

SUSANNAH CENTLIVRE
1667?–1723

6 The real Simon Pure.
Bold Stroke for a Wife, v. i.

7 And lash the vice and follies of the age.
The Man's Bewitched, prologue

MIGUEL DE CERVANTES
1547–1616

8 El Caballero de la Triste Figura.
The Knight of the Sorrowful Countenance.
Don Quixote, pt. i, ch. 19. *Trans.
by* Smollett

9 La mejor salsa del mundo es el hambre.
The best sauce in the world is
hunger. *Ib.* pt. ii, ch. 5

10 Muchos pocos hacen un mucho.
Many a pickle makes a mickle.
Don Quixote, pt. ii, ch. 7

11 Dos linages sólos hay en el mundo,
como decía una abuela mia, que son el
tenir y el no tenir.
There are but two families in the
world, as my grandmother used to
say, the Haves and the Have-
nots. *Ib.* ch. 20

PATRICK REGINALD CHALMERS
1872–1942

12 What's lost upon the roundabouts we
pulls up on the swings!
*Green Days and Blue Days:
Roundabouts and Swings*

JOSEPH CHAMBERLAIN
1836–1914

13 Provided that the City of London remains as it is at present, the clearing-
house of the world.
*Speech, Guildhall, London, 19
Jan. 1904*

14 We are not downhearted. The only
trouble is, we cannot understand what
is happening to our neighbours.
Ib. Smethwick, 18 Jan. 1906

NEVILLE CHAMBERLAIN
1869–1940

15 In war, whichever side may call itself
the victor, there are no winners, but all
are losers.
Speech at Kettering, 3 July 1938

16 I believe it is peace for our time . . .
peace with honour.
*Radio Speech after Munich Agree-
ment. 1 Oct. 1938*

CHARLES HADDON
CHAMBERS 1860–1921

17 The long arm of coincidence.
Captain Swift, Act ii

JOHN CHANDLER 1806–1876

18 Conquering kings their titles take
From the foes they captive make:
Jesu, by a nobler deed,
From the thousands He hath freed.
As in Hymns Ancient and
Modern. *Conquering Kings Their
Titles Take,* trans. from Latin

GEORGE CHAPMAN 1559?–1634?

19 Speed his plough.
Bussy D'Ambois, i. i

20 And let a scholar all Earth's volumes
carry,
He will be but a walking dictionary.
Tears of Peace, l. 266

CHARLES II OF GREAT BRITAIN
1630–1685

1 It is upon the navy under the Providence of God that the safety, honour, and welfare of this realm do chiefly attend.   *Articles of War*. Preamble

2 Better than a play.
(*On the Debates in the House of Lords on Lord Ross's Divorce Bill, 1670.*) A. Bryant, *King Charles II*

3 Let not poor Nelly starve.
Burnet, *History of My Own Time*, vol. II, bk. iii, ch. 17

4 Brother, I am too old to go again to my travels.
Hume's *History of Great Britain*, vol. ii (1757), ch. 7

5 He had been, he said, an unconscionable time dying; but he hoped that they would excuse it.
Macaulay's *Hist. England* (1849), vol. i, ch. 4, p. 437.

CHARLES V 1500–1558

6 Je parle espagnol à Dieu, italien aux femmes, français aux hommes et allemand à mon cheval.

To God I speak Spanish, to women Italian, to men French, and to my horse—German.   *Attr.*

EARL OF CHATHAM
see WILLIAM PITT

THOMAS CHATTERTON
1752–1770

7 O' synge untoe mie roundelaie,
O! droppe the brynie teare wythe mee,
Daunce ne moe atte hallie daie,
Lycke a reynynge ryver bee;
Mie love ys dedde,
Gon to hys death-bedde,
Al under the wyllowe-tree.
Mynstrelles Songe

GEOFFREY CHAUCER 1340?–1400

8 Whanne that Aprille with his shoures sote
The droghte of Marche hath perced to the rote.
Canterbury Tales. Prologue, l. 1

9 And smale fowles maken melodye,
That slepen al the night with open yë,
(So priketh hem nature in hir corages):
Than longen folk to goon on pilgrimages.   *Ib.* l. 9

10 He was a verray parfit gentil knight.
Ib. l. 72

11 He was as fresh as is the month of May.   *Ib.* l. 92

12 Ful wel she song the service divyne,
Entuned in hir nose ful semely;
And Frensh she spak ful faire and fetisly,
After the scole of Stratford atte Bowe,
For Frensh of Paris was to hir unknowe.
Canterbury Tales. Prologue, l. 122

13 A Clerk ther was of Oxenford also.
Ib. l. 285

14 And gladly wolde he lerne, and gladly teche.   *Ib.* l. 308

15 No-wher so bisy a man as he ther nas,
And yet he semed bisier than he was.
Ib. l. 321

16 She was a worthy womman al hir lyve,
Housbondes at chirche-dore she hadde fyve,   *Ib.* l. 459

17 The smyler with the knyf under the cloke.   *Ib.* l. 1141

18 What is this world? what asketh men to have?
Now with his love, now in his colde grave
Allone, with-outen any companye.
Ib. Knightes Tale, l. 1919

19 So was hir joly whistle wel y-wet.
Ib. The Reves Tale, l. 235

20 The bacoun was nat fet for hem, I trowe,
That som men han in Essex at Dunmowe.
Ib. The Prologue of the Wyves' Tale of Bathe, l. 217

21 Farwel my book and my devocion.
Legend of Good Women. Prologue, l. 29

22 And she was fair as is the rose in May.
Ib. Legend of Cleopatra, l. 34

23 Thou shalt make castels than in Spayne,
And dreme of joye, al but in vayne.
Romaunt of the Rose, B. l. 2573

24 Til crowes feet be growe under your yë.   *Troilus and Criseyde*, ii, l. 403

25 And we shal speke of thee som-what, I trowe,
Whan thou art goon, to do thyne eres glowe!   *Ib.* l. 1021

26 It is nought good a sleping hound to wake.   *Ib.* iii, l. 764

27 Right as an aspes leef she gan to quake.   *Ib.* l. 1200

28 Oon ere it herde, at the other out it wente.   *Ib.* iv, l. 434

29 But manly set the world on sixe and sevene;
And, if thou deye a martir, go to hevene.   *Ib.* l. 622

30 For tyme y-lost may not recovered be.
Ib. l. 1283

1 Go, litel book, go litel myn tragedie.
Troilus and Criseyde, iv, l. 1786

2 O yonge fresshe folkes, he or she.
Ib. l. 1835

PHILIP DORMER STANHOPE, EARL OF CHESTERFIELD
1694–1773

3 Unlike my subject will I frame my song,
It shall be witty and it sha'n't be long.
Epigram on 'Long' Sir Thomas Robinson. D.N.B.

4 The picture plac'd the busts between,
Adds to the thought much strength;
Wisdom and Wit are little seen,
But Folly's at full length.
Wit and Wisdom of Lord Chesterfield. Epigrams. On the Picture of Richard Nash . . . between the Busts of . . . Newton and . . . Pope . . . at Bath. (*Attr. also to Mrs. Jane Brereton*)

5 There is a Spanish proverb, which says very justly, Tell me whom you live with, and I will tell you who you are.
Letter to his Son, 9 Oct. 1747

6 Take the tone of the company that you are in.
Ib.

7 Do as you would be done by is the surest method that I know of pleasing.
Ib. 16 Oct. 1747

8 I recommend you to take care of the minutes: for hours will take care of themselves.
Ib. 6 Nov. 1747

9 It must be owned, that the Graces do not seem to be natives of Great Britain; and I doubt, the best of us here have more of rough than polished diamond.
Ib. 18 Nov. 1748

10 Idleness is only the refuge of weak minds.
Ib. 20 July 1749

11 A chapter of accidents.
Ib. 16 Feb. 1753

12 Religion is by no means a proper subject of conversation in a mixed company.
Undated Letter to his Godson, No. 112

GILBERT KEITH CHESTERTON 1874–1936

13 Talk about the pews and steeples
And the cash that goes therewith!
But the souls of Christian peoples . . .
Chuck it, Smith!
Antichrist, or the Reunion of Christendom

14 I tell you naught for your comfort,
Yea, naught for your desire,
Save that the sky grows darker yet
And the sea rises higher.
Ballad of the White Horse, bk. i

15 For the great Gaels of Ireland
Are the men that God made mad,
For all their wars are merry,
And all their songs are sad. *Ib.* bk. ii

16 When fishes flew and forests walked
And figs grew upon thorn,
Some moment when the moon was blood
Then surely I was born.

With monstrous head and sickening cry
And ears like errant wings,
The devil's walking parody
On all four-footed things.
The Donkey

17 Fools! For I also had my hour;
One far fierce hour and sweet:
There was a shout about my ears,
And palms before my feet. *Ib.*

18 White founts falling in the courts of the sun,
And the Soldan of Byzantium is smiling as they run. *Lepanto*

19 Don John of Austria is going to the war. *Ib.*

20 From all the easy speeches
That comfort cruel men.
O God of Earth and Altar

21 Before the Roman came to Rye or out to Severn strode,
The rolling English drunkard made the rolling English road.
The Rolling English Road

22 That night we went to Birmingham by way of Beachy Head. *Ib.*

23 For there is good news yet to hear and fine things to be seen,
Before we go to Paradise by way of Kensal Green. *Ib.*

24 Smile at us, pay us, pass us; but do not quite forget.
For we are the people of England, that never have spoken yet.
The Secret People

25 God made the wicked Grocer
For a mystery and a sign,
That men might shun the awful shop
And go to inns to dine.
Song Against Grocers

26 They haven't got no noses,
The fallen sons of Eve.
The Song of Quoodle

27 And goodness only knowses
The Noselessness of Man. *Ib.*

28 And Noah he often said to his wife when he sat down to dine,
'I don't care where the water goes if it doesn't get into the wine.'
Wine and Water

1 The human race, to which so many of
my readers belong . . .
The Napoleon of Notting Hill,
ch. 1

2 Hardy went down to botanize in the
swamp, while Meredith climbed towards the sun. Meredith became, at his
best, a sort of daintily dressed Walt
Whitman: Hardy became a sort of
village atheist brooding and blaspheming over the village idiot.
The Victorian Age in Literature,
ch. 2

ALBERT CHEVALIER 1861–1923

3 'Wot's the good of Hanyfink? Why—
Nuffink!'   *Cockney Complaint*

4 We've been together now for forty
years,
An' it don't seem a day too much;
There ain't a lady livin' in the land
As I'd 'swop' for my dear old Dutch!
My Old Dutch

5 Knocked 'em in the Old Kent Road.
Title of Song

DAVID CHRISTY 1802–?

6 Cotton is King.   *Title of Book* (1855)

CHARLES CHURCHILL 1731–1764

7   Be England what she will,
With all her faults, she is my country
still.   *The Farewell*, l. 27

8 Just to the windward of the law.
The Ghost, bk. iii, l. 56

9 By different methods different men
excel;
But where is he who can do all things
well?
Epistle to William Hogarth, l. 573

10 Keep up appearances; there lies the
test;
The world will give thee credit for
the rest.   *Night*, l. 311

11 Who often, but without success, have
pray'd
For apt Alliteration's artful aid.
The Prophecy of Famine, l. 85

LORD RANDOLPH SPENCER CHURCHILL 1849–1894

12 Ulster will fight; Ulster will be right.
Letter, 7 May 1886

13 The old gang. [Members of the Conservative Government.]
*Speech, House of Commons,
7 Mar. 1878*

14 An old man in a hurry. [Gladstone.]
*Ib. To the Electors of South Pad-
dington, June 1886*

15 All great men make mistakes. Napo-
leon forgot Blücher, I forgot Goschen.
*Leaves from the Notebooks of
Lady Dorothy Nevill, p. 21*

16 The duty of an Opposition is to
oppose.
*1830. Quoted by Lord Randolph
Churchill. W. S. Churchill, Lord
Randolph Churchill* (1906), vol.
i, ch. 5

17 (Decimal points:) I never could make
out what those damned dots meant.
Ib. vol. ii, p. 184

SIR WINSTON CHURCHILL 1874–1965

18 It cannot in the opinion of His
Majesty's Government be classified as
slavery in the extreme acceptance of
the word without some risk of terminological inexactitude.
*Speech, House of Commons,
22 Feb. 1906*

19 The maxim of the British people is
'Business as usual'.
Speech at Guildhall, 9 Nov. 1914

20 I would say to the House, as I said
to those who have joined this Government, 'I have nothing to offer but
blood, toil, tears and sweat'.
*Speech, House of Commons,
13 May 1940*

21 We shall not flag or fail. We shall fight
in France, we shall fight on the seas
and oceans, we shall fight with growing
confidence and growing strength in the
air, we shall defend our island, whatever the cost may be, we shall fight
on the beaches, we shall fight on the
landing grounds, we shall fight in the
fields and in the streets, we shall
fight in the hills; we shall never
surrender.   *Ib. 4 June 1940*

22 Let us therefore brace ourselves to our
duty and so bear ourselves that if
the British Commonwealth and Empire
lasts for a thousand years men will
still say, 'This was their finest hour.'
Ib. 18 June 1940

23 Never in the field of human conflict
was so much owed by so many to so
few.
Ib. 20 Aug. 1940

24 Give us the tools, and we will finish
the job.
*Radio Broadcast. (Addressing
President Roosevelt.) 9 Feb. 1941*

25 What kind of people do they [the
Japanese] think we are?
*Speech to U.S. Congress, 24 Dec.
1941*

1 When I warned them [the French Government] that Britain would fight on alone whatever they did, their Generals told their Prime Minister and his divided Cabinet: 'In three weeks England will have her neck wrung like a chicken.'
Some chicken! Some neck!
Speech to the Canadian Parliament, 30 Dec. 1941

2 This is not the end. It is not even the beginning of the end. But it is, perhaps, the end of the beginning.
Speech at the Mansion House, 10 Nov. 1942. (Of the Battle of Egypt)

3 I have not become the King's First Minister in order to preside over the liquidation of the British Empire. *Ib.*

4 The soft under-belly of the Axis.
Report on the War Situation, House of Commons, 11 Nov. 1942

5 An iron curtain is drawn down upon their front. We do not know what is going on behind.
Telegram to President Truman, 12 May 1945. (Printed in W. S. Churchill, Triumph and Tragedy (1954), p. 498.) But see also 94:11 and 234:5.

COLLEY CIBBER 1671–1757

6 Off with his head—so much for Buckingham.
Richard III, altered, IV. iii

7 Conscience avaunt, Richard's himself again: *Ib.*

8 Perish the thought! *Ib.* v

9 Stolen sweets are best.
The Rival Fools, Act 1

10 This business will never hold water.
She Would and She Would Not, Act IV

MARCUS TULLIUS CICERO 106–43 B.C.

11 Salus populi suprema est lex.
The good of the people is the chief law. *De Legibus, III. iii. 8*

12 'Ipse dixit.' 'Ipse' autem erat Pythagoras.
'He himself said it', and this 'he himself', it seems, was Pythagoras.
De Natura Deorum, I. v. 10

13 Summum bonum.
The highest good.
De Officiis, I. ii. 5

14 Cedant arma togae, concedat laurea laudi.
Let wars yield to peace, laurels to paeans. *De Officiis, I. xxii. 82*

15 Numquam se minus otiosum esse quam cum otiosus, nec minus solum quam cum solus esset.
Never less idle than when wholly idle, nor less alone than when wholly alone. *Ib. III. i. 1*

16 Quousque tandem abutere, Catilina, patientia nostra?
How long will you abuse our patience, Catiline?
In Catilinam, I. i. 1

17 O tempora, O mores!
O what times, O what habits! *Ib.*

18 Civis Romanus sum.
I am a Roman citizen.
In Verrem, v. lvii. 147

19 Oderint, dum metuant.
Let them hate so long as they fear.
Philippic, I. 14 (quoted from the tragedian Accius)

20 Quod di omen avertant.
May the gods avert this omen.
Ib. III. xiv. 35

21 Silent enim leges inter arma.
Laws are inoperative in war.
Pro Milone, IV. xi

22 Cui bono.
To whose profit. *Ib. XII. xxxii*

23 Ne quid res publica detrimenti caperet.
That no harm come to the state.
Ib. XXVI. lxx, quoting the senatorial 'ultimate decree', beginning 'caveant consules' (let the consuls see to it).

24 O fortunatam natam me consule Romam!
O happy Rome, born when I was consul! *Quoted in Juvenal, x. 122*

EDWARD HYDE, EARL OF CLARENDON 1609–1674

25 Without question, when he [Hampden] first drew the sword, he threw away the scabbard.
History of the Rebellion, ed. W. Dunn Macray (1888), III. vii. 84

26 So enamoured on peace that he would have been glad the King should have bought it at any price. *Ib. 233*

JOHN CLARKE *fl.* 1639

27 Home is home, though it be never so homely.
Parœmiologia Anglo-Latina (1639)

SAMUEL LANGHORNE CLEMENS
see MARK TWAIN

**STEPHEN GROVER
CLEVELAND** 1837–1908

1 I have considered the pension list of
the republic a roll of honour.
*Veto of Dependent Pension Bill,
5 July 1888*

ROBERT CLIVE, LORD CLIVE
1725–1774

2 By God, Mr. Chairman, at this
moment I stand astonished at my own
moderation!
*Reply during Parliamentary
cross-examination, 1773*

ARTHUR HUGH CLOUGH
1819–1861

3 How pleasant it is to have money,
heigh-ho!
How pleasant it is to have money.
Dipsychus, pt. I. iv

4 'There is no God,' the wicked saith,
'And truly it's a blessing,
For what he might have done with us
It's better only guessing.'   *Ib. v.*

5 Thou shalt have one God only; who
Would be at the expense of two?
The Latest Decalogue

6 Thou shalt not kill; but need'st not
strive
Officiously to keep alive.   *Ib.*

7 Do not adultery commit;
Advantage rarely comes of it.   *Ib.*

8 Thou shalt not steal; an empty feat,
When it's so lucrative to cheat.   *Ib.*

9 Thou shalt not covet; but tradition
Approves all forms of competition.
Ib.

10 Say not the struggle naught availeth,
The labour and the wounds are vain,
The enemy faints not, nor faileth,
And as things have been, things
remain.

If hopes were dupes, fears may be
liars;
It may be, in yon smoke concealed,
Your comrades chase e'en now the
fliers,
And, but for you, possess the field.

For while the tired waves, vainly
breaking,
Seem here no painful inch to gain,
Far back through creeks and inlets
making
Comes silent, flooding in, the main.

And not by eastern windows only,
When daylight comes, comes in the
light,
In front the sun climbs slow, how
slowly,
But westward, look, the land is
bright.
*Say Not the Struggle Naught
Availeth*

11 That out of sight is out of mind
Is true of most we leave behind.
*Songs in Absence, That Out of
Sight*

12 Where lies the land to which the ship
would go!
Far, far ahead, is all her seamen know.
And where the land she travels from?
Away,
Far, far behind, is all that they can
say.   *Ib. Where Lies the Land*

SIR WILLIAM LAIRD CLOWES
1856–1905

13 The Glorious First of June.
Page-heading in The Royal
Navy: a History (1899), vol. iv,
p. 225. Taken from explanatory
pamphlet accompanying Cleve-
ley's prints of the action: *Two
prints . . . representing the
Glorious and Memorable Action
of the First of June 1794*

WILLIAM COBBETT 1762–1835

14 But what is to be the fate of the great
wen [London] of all? The monster,
called . . . 'the metropolis of the
empire'?   *Rural Rides, 1821*

**CHARLES COBORN
[C. W. McCALLUM]** 1852–1945

15 Two lovely black eyes,
Oh! what a surprise!
Only for telling a man he was wrong,
Two lovely black eyes!
Two Lovely Black Eyes

ALISON COCKBURN 1713–1794

16 For the flowers of the forest are
withered away.
The Flowers of the Forest

DESMOND F. T. COKE 1879–1931

17 His blade struck the water a full
second before any other . . . until . . .
as the boats began to near the
winning-post, his own was dipping
into the water *twice* as often as any
other.
*Sandford of Merton (1903), ch.
xii. Often quoted as* 'All rowed fast
but none so fast as stroke', *and
attr. to* Ouida.

SIR EDWARD COKE 1552–1634

1 For a man's house is his castle, *et domus sua cuique est tutissimum refugium.*
  Institutes: Commentary upon Littleton. Third Institute, cap. 73

HARTLEY COLERIDGE 1796–1849

2 She is not fair to outward view
  As many maidens be;
  Her loveliness I never knew
  Until she smiled on me.
  Oh! then I saw her eye was bright,
  A well of love, a spring of light.
  Song. She is not Fair

MARY ELIZABETH COLERIDGE
1861–1907

3 We were young, we were merry, we
  were very, very wise,
  And the door stood open at our feast,
  When there passed us a woman with
  the West in her eyes,
  And a man with his back to the East.
  Unwelcome

SAMUEL TAYLOR COLERIDGE
1772–1834

4 It is an ancient Mariner,
  And he stoppeth one of three.
  'By thy long grey beard and glittering
  eye,
  Now wherefore stopp'st thou me?'
  The Ancient Mariner, pt. i

5 He holds him with his skinny hand,
  'There was a ship,' quoth he.
  'Hold off! unhand me, grey-beard
  loon!'
  Eftsoons his hand dropt he.

  He holds him with his glittering eye—
  The Wedding-Guest stood still,
  And listens like a three years' child:
  The Mariner hath his will.   *Ib.*

6 The Sun came up upon the left,
  Out of the sea came he!
  And he shone bright, and on the right
  Went down into the sea.   *Ib.*

7 The Wedding-Guest here beat his
  breast,
  For he heard the loud bassoon.   *Ib.*

8 The ice was here, the ice was there,
  The ice was all around:
  It cracked and growled, and roared
  and howled,
  Like noises in a swound!   *Ib.*

9 And a good south wind sprung up
  behind;
  The Albatross did follow,
  And every day, for food or play,
  Came to the mariner's hollo!   *Ib.*

10 'God save thee, ancient Mariner!
  From the fiends that plague thee
  thus!—
  Why look'st thou so?—With my cross-
  bow
  I shot the Albatross.
  The Ancient Mariner, pt. i

11 We were the first that ever burst
  Into that silent sea.   *Ib.* pt. ii

12 All in a hot and copper sky,
  The bloody Sun, at noon,
  Right up above the mast did stand,
  No bigger than the Moon.   *Ib.*

13 As idle as a painted ship
  Upon a painted ocean.   *Ib.*

14 Water, water, every where,
  And all the boards did shrink;
  Water, water, every where,
  Nor any drop to drink.

  The very deep did rot: O Christ!
  That ever this should be!
  Yea, slimy things did crawl with legs
  Upon the slimy sea.

  I bit my arm, I sucked the blood,
  And cried, A sail! a sail!   *Ib.* pt. iii

15 The Sun's rim dips; the stars rush out:
  At one stride comes the dark;
  With far-heard whisper, o'er the sea,
  Off shot the spectre-bark.   *Ib.*

16 The hornèd Moon, with one bright
  star
  Within the nether tip.   *Ib.*

17 Each turned his face with a ghastly
  pang,
  And cursed me with his eye.   *Ib.*

18 'I fear thee, ancient Mariner!
  I fear thy skinny hand!
  And thou art long, and lank, and
  brown,
  As is the ribbed sea-sand.'   *Ib.* pt. iv

19 Alone, alone, all, all alone,
  Alone on a wide wide sea!
  And never a saint took pity on
  My soul in agony.   *Ib.*

20 And a thousand thousand slimy
  things
  Lived on; and so did I.   *Ib.*

21 An orphan's curse would drag to hell
  A spirit from on high;
  But oh! more horrible than that
  Is the curse in a dead man's eye.   *Ib.*

22 The moving Moon went up the sky,
  And no where did abide:
  Softly she was going up,
  And a star or two beside.   *Ib.*

23 Oh Sleep! it is a gentle thing,
  Beloved from pole to pole,
  To Mary Queen the praise be given!
  She sent the gentle sleep from Heaven,
  That slid into my soul.   *Ib.* pt. v

1 The silly buckets on the deck,
That had so long remained,
I dreamt that they were filled with
dew;
And when I awoke, it rained.
The Ancient Mariner, pt. v.

2 We were a ghastly crew.   *Ib.*

3 It ceased; yet still the sails made on
A pleasant noise till noon,
A noise like of a hidden brook
If the leafy month of June,
That to the sleeping woods all night
Singeth a quiet tune.   *Ib.*

4 Quoth he, 'The man hath penance
done,
And penance more will do.'   *Ib.*

5 Like one, that on a lonesome road
Doth walk in fear and dread,
And having once turned round walks on,
And turns no more his head;
Because he knows, a frightful fiend
Doth close behind him tread.
Ib. pt. vi

6 O sweeter than the marriage-feast,
'Tis sweeter far to me,
To walk together to the kirk
With a goodly company.
To walk together to the kirk,
And all together pray,
While each to his great Father bends,
Old men, and babes, and loving friends
And youths and maidens gay!
Ib. pt. vii

7 He prayeth well, who loveth well
Both man and bird and beast.

He prayeth best, who loveth best
All things both great and small;
For the dear God who loveth us,
He made and loveth all.   *Ib.*

8 A sight to dream of, not to tell!
Christabel, pt. i

9 In Köhln, a town of monks and bones,
And pavements fang'd with murderous
stones
And rags, and hags, and hideous
wenches;
I counted two and seventy stenches,
All well defined, and several stinks!
Ye Nymphs that reign o'er sewers and
sinks,
The river Rhine, it is well known,
Doth wash your city of Cologne;
But tell me, Nymphs, what power
divine
Shall henceforth wash the river
Rhine?   *Cologne*

10 His jacket was red and his breeches
were blue,
And there was a hole where the tail
came through. *The Devil's Thoughts*

11 With Donne, whose muse on dromedary trots,
Wreathe iron pokers into true-love
knots.   *On Donne's Poetry*

12 What is an Epigram? a dwarfish whole,
Its body brevity, and wit its soul.
Epigram

13 Swans sing before they die—'twere
no bad thing
Did certain persons die before they
sing.
Epigram on a Volunteer Singer

14 In Xanadu did Kubla Khan
A stately pleasure-dome decree:
Where Alph, the sacred river, ran
Through caverns measureless to man
Down to a sunless sea.
So twice five miles of fertile ground
With walls and towers were girdled
round:
And there were gardens bright with
sinuous rills,
Where blossomed many an incense-
bearing tree;
And here were forests ancient as the
hills,
Enfolding sunny spots of greenery.
But oh! that deep romantic chasm
which slanted
Down the green hill athwart a cedarn
cover!
A savage place! as holy and enchanted
As e'er beneath a waning moon was
haunted
By woman wailing for her demon-
lover!
And from this chasm, with ceaseless
turmoil seething,
As if this earth in fast thick pants
were breathing,
A mighty fountain momently was
forced.   *Kubla Khan*

15 And 'mid these dancing rocks at once
and ever
It flung up momently the sacred river.
Five miles meandering with a mazy
motion
Through wood and dale the sacred
river ran,
Then reached the caverns measureless
to man,
And sank in tumult to a lifeless ocean:
And 'mid this tumult Kubla heard
from far
Ancestral voices prophesying war!

The shadow of the dome of pleasure
Floated midway on the waves;
Where was heard the mingled
measure
From the fountain and the caves.
It was a miracle of rare device,
A sunny pleasure-dome with caves of
ice!

A damsel with a dulcimer
In a vision once I saw:
It was an Abyssinian maid,
And on her dulcimer she played,
Singing of Mount Abora.

Could I revive within me
Her symphony and song,
To such a deep delight 'twould win
me,
That with music loud and long,
I would build that dome in air,
That sunny dome! those caves of ice!
And all who heard should see them
there,
And all should cry, Beware! Beware!
His flashing eyes, his floating hair!
Weave a circle round him thrice,
And close your eyes with holy dread,
For he on honey-dew hath fed,
And drunk the milk of Paradise.
Kubla Khan

1 Trochee trips from long to short.
Metrical Feet

2 Iambics march from short to long;—
With a leap and a bound the swift
Anapaests throng.   *Ib.*

3 Like some poor nigh-related guest,
That may not rudely be dismist;
Yet hath outstay'd his welcome while,
And tells the jest without the smile.
Youth and Age

4 He who begins by loving Christianity
better than Truth will proceed by
loving his own sect or church better
than Christianity, and end by loving
himself better than all.
*Aids to Reflection: Moral and
Religious Aphorisms*, xxv

5 That willing suspension of disbelief
for the moment, which constitutes
poetic faith.
Biographia Literaria, ch. 14

6 Summer has set in with its usual
severity.
*Remark quoted in Lamb's Letter
to V. Novello, 9 May 1826*

7 To see him [Kean] act, is like reading
Shakespeare by flashes of lightning.
Table Talk, 27 Apr. 1823

8 I wish our clever young poets would
remember my homely definitions of
prose and poetry; that is, prose =
words in their best order;—poetry =
the *best* words in the best order.
Ib. 12 July 1827

JESSE COLLINGS 1831–1920

9 Three acres and a cow.
*Phrase used in his land-reform
propaganda of 1885.*

MORTIMER COLLINS 1827–1876

10 A man is as old as he's feeling,
A woman as old as she looks.
The Unknown Quantity

WILLIAM COLLINS 1721–1759

11 If aught of oaten stop, or pastoral
song,
May hope, O pensive Eve, to soothe
thine ear.   *Ode to Evening*

12 Now air is hush'd, save where the
weak-ey'd bat,
With short shrill shriek flits by on
leathern wing,
Or where the beetle winds
His small but sullen horn   *Ib.*

13 Hamlets brown, and dim-discover'd
spires.   *Ib.*

14 How sleep the brave, who sink to rest,
By all their country's wishes blest!
Ode Written in the Year 1746

15 By fairy hands their knell is rung,
By forms unseen their dirge is sung;
There Honour comes, a pilgrim grey,
To bless the turf that wraps their clay
And Freedom shall awhile repair,
To dwell a weeping hermit there! *Ib*

GEORGE COLMAN 1732–1794

16 Love and a cottage! Eh, Fanny! Ah,
give me indifference and a coach and
six!   *The Clandestine Marriage*, I. ii

GEORGE COLMAN 1762–1836

17 Mum's the word.
Battle of Hexham, II. i

18 Lord help you! Tell 'em Queen Anne's
dead.   *Heir-at-Law*, I. i

19 Oh, London is a fine town,
A very famous city,
Where all the streets are paved with
gold,
And all the maidens pretty. *Ib.* ii

20 Not to be sneezed at.   *Ib.* II. i

21 Says he, 'I am a handsome man, but
I'm a gay deceiver.'
Love Laughs at Locksmiths, Act II,
Song

22 Johnson's style was grand and
Gibbon's elegant; the stateliness of
the former was sometimes pedantic,
and the polish of the latter was oc-
casionally finical. Johnson marched to
kettle-drums and trumpets; Gibbon
moved to flutes and hautboys: Johnson hewed passages through the Alps,
while Gibbon levelled walks through
parks and gardens.
Random Records (1830), i. 121

23 His heart runs away with his head.
Who Wants a Guinea?, I. i

24 When taken, To be well shaken.
*My Nightgown and Slippers.
Newcastle Apothecary*

CHARLES CALEB COLTON
1780?–1832

1 When you have nothing to say, say
nothing.   *Lacon*, vol. i, No. 183

2 Man is an embodied paradox, a bundle
of contradictions.
                    Ib. No. 408

WILLIAM CONGREVE 1670–1729

3 She lays it on with a trowel.
          The Double Dealer, III. x

4 See how love and murder will out.
                    Ib. IV. vi

5 If I can give that Cerberus a sop, I
shall be at rest for one day.
          Love for Love, I. iv

6 I warrant you, if he danced till doomsday, he thought I was to pay the piper.
                    Ib. II. v

7 Has he not a rogue's face? . . . a
hanging-look to me . . . has a damn'd
Tyburn-face, without the benefit o'
the Clergy. . . .   *Ib.* vii

8 Oh fie, Miss, you must not kiss and
tell.   *Ib.* x

9 Music has charms to sooth a savage
breast.   *The Mourning Bride*, I. i

10 Heav'n has no rage, like love to hatred
turn'd,
Nor Hell a fury, like a woman
scorn'd.   *Ib.* III. viii

11 Now am I slap-dash down in the
mouth.   *The Old Bachelor*, IV. ix

12 Well, Sir Joseph, you have such a
winning way with you.   *Ib.* v. vii

13 SHARPER.
    Thus grief still treads upon the
    heels of pleasure:
    Marry'd in haste, we may repent at
    leisure.
SETTER.
    Some by experience find those
    words mis-plac'd:
    At leisure marry'd, they repent in
    haste.   *Ib.* viii *and* ix

14 O Sleep, why dost thou leave me?
Why thy visionary joys remove?
O Sleep, again deceive me,
To my arms restore my wand'ring
Love.   *Semele*, II. ii

15 Alack he's gone the way of all flesh.
    Squire Bickerstaff Detected. (Attr.
    to Congreve)

16 Say what you will, 'tis better to be
left than never to have been loved.
          The Way of the World, II. i

17 Here she comes i' faith full sail, with
her fan spread and streamers out, and
a shoal of fools for tenders.   *Ib.* iv

18 I nauseate walking; 'tis a country
diversion, I loath the country.   *Ib.*

19 These articles subscrib'd, if I continue
to endure you a little longer, I may
by degrees dwindle into a wife.
          The Way of the World, IV. v

20 O horrid provisos!   *Ib.*

T. W. CONNOR *nineteenth century*

21 She was one of the early birds,
And I was one of the worms.
    She Was A Dear Little Dickie-bird

CONSTANTINE c. 274–337

22 In hoc signo vinces.
    In this sign shalt thou conquer.
        Words of Constantine's vision.
    Eusebius, *Life of Constantine*, i. 28

ELIZA COOK 1818–1889

23 I love it, I love it; and who shall dare
To chide me for loving that old arm-
chair?   *The Old Arm-chair*

CALVIN COOLIDGE 1872–1933

24 He said he was against it.
    *On being asked what had been said
    by a clergyman who preached on
    sin*

25 The business of America is business.
    *Speech before Society of American
    Newspaper Editors*, 17 Jan. 1925

JAMES FENIMORE COOPER
1789–1851

26 The Last of the Mohicans.
                    Title of Novel

BISHOP RICHARD CORBET
1582–1635

27 Farewell rewards and fairies.
          The Fairy's Farewell

FRANCES CROFTS CORNFORD
1886–1960

28 O fat white woman whom nobody
loves,
Why do you walk through the fields in
gloves,
    .   .   .
Missing so much and so much?
    To a Fat Lady Seen from a Train

MME CORNUEL 1605–1694

29 Il n'y a point de héros pour son valet
de chambre.
    No man is a hero to his valet.
        Lettres de Mlle Aissé, xii, 13
        August 1728

CORONATION SERVICE

1 We present you with this Book, the
most valuable thing that this world
affords. Here is wisdom; this is the
royal Law; these are the lively Oracles
of God.
The Presenting of the Holy Bible

WILLIAM JOHNSON CORY
1823–1892

2 They told me, Heraclitus, they told
me you were dead,
They brought me bitter news to hear
and bitter tears to shed. *Heraclitus*

3   How often you and I
Had tired the sun with talking and
sent him down the sky.   *Ib.*

4 A handful of grey ashes, long long
ago at rest.   *Ib.*

ÉMILE COUÉ 1857–1926

5 Tous les jours, à tous points de vue,
je vais de mieux en mieux.

Every day, in every way, I am getting better and better.
Formula in his clinic at Nancy

VICTOR COUSIN 1792–1867

6 L'art pour l'art.

Art for art's sake.
Lecture at the Sorbonne

THOMAS COVENTRY, BARON
COVENTRY 1578–1640

7 The wooden walls are the best walls
of this kingdom.
*Speech to the Judges, 17 June
1635, given in Rushworth's Hist.
Coll. (1680), vol. ii, p. 297.*

NOEL COWARD 1899–

8 Mad dogs and Englishmen go out in
the mid-day sun;
The Japanese don't care to, the
Chinese wouldn't dare to;
Hindus and Argentines sleep firmly
from twelve to one,
But Englishmen detest a siesta.
Mad Dogs and Englishmen

9 Don't put your daughter on the stage,
Mrs. Worthington.   *Title of Song*

10 Dance, Little Lady.   *Ib.*

11 Twentieth-Century Blues.   *Ib.*

12 Poor Little Rich Girl.   *Ib.*

13 Don't let 's be beastly to the Germans.
Ib.

14 In Which We Serve.   *Title of Film*
Taken from the Book of Common Prayer

15 Strange how potent cheap music is.
Private Lives, Act I

16 Very flat, Norfolk.   *Ib.*

17 Certain women should be struck
regularly, like gongs.   *Ib.* Act II

ABRAHAM COWLEY 1618–1667

18 God the first garden made, and the
first city Cain   *The Garden*

19 Life is an incurable disease.
To Dr. Scarborough, vi

WILLIAM COWPER 1731–1800

20 Regions Caesar never knew
Thy posterity shall sway,
Where his eagles never flew,
None invincible as they.   *Boadicea*

21 John Gilpin was a citizen
Of credit and renown,
A train-band captain eke was he
Of famous London town.
John Gilpin

22 To-morrow is our wedding-day,
And we will then repair
Unto the Bell at Edmonton
All in a chaise and pair.   *Ib.*

23 I am a linen-draper bold,
As all the world doth know,
And my good friend the calender
Will lend his horse to go.   *Ib.*

24 O'erjoy'd was he to find
That, though on pleasure she was bent,
She had a frugal mind.   *Ib.*

25   And all agog
To dash through thick and thin!   *Ib.*

26 John Gilpin at his horse's side
Seiz'd fast the flowing mane,
And up he got, in haste to ride,
But soon came down again.   *Ib.*

27 Away went Gilpin, neck or nought,
Away went hat and wig!   *Ib*

28 The dogs did bark, the children
scream'd.
Up flew the windows all;
And ev'ry soul cried out—Well done!
As loud as he could bawl.

Away went Gilpin—who but he?
His fame soon spread around—
He carries weight! he rides a race!
'Tis for a thousand pound!   *Ib.*

29 My hat and wig will soon be here—
They are upon the road.   *Ib.*

30 Said John—It is my wedding-day,
And all the world would stare,
If wife should dine at Edmonton
And I should dine at Ware.   *Ib.*

31 Now let us sing—Long live the king,
And Gilpin long live he;
And, when he next doth ride abroad,
May I be there to see!   *Ib.*

1 Beware of desp'rate steps. The darkest
    day
    (Live till to-morrow) will have pass'd
    away.   *The Needless Alarm*, l. 132

2 What peaceful hours I once enjoy'd!
    How sweet their mem'ry still!
    But they have left an aching void,
    The world can never fill.
                    Olney Hymns, I

3 Hark, my soul! it is the Lord;
    'Tis thy Saviour, hear his word;
    Jesus speaks, and speaks to thee;
    'Say, poor sinner, lov'st thou me?'
                    Ib. 18

4 'Can a woman's tender care
    Cease, towards the child she bare?
    Yes, she may forgetful be,
    Yet will I remember thee.'   *Ib.*

5 God moves in a mysterious way
    His wonders to perform;
    He plants his footsteps in the sea,
    And rides upon the storm.   *Ib.* 35

6 Ye fearful saints fresh courage take,
    The clouds ye so much dread
    Are big with mercy, and shall break
    In blessings on your head.   *Ib.*

7 The poplars are fell'd, farewell to the
    shade
    And the whispering sound of the cool
    colonnade.   *The Poplar-Field*

8 Talks of darkness at noon-day.
                    Progress of Error, l. 451

9 Toll for the brave—
    The brave! that are no more:
    All sunk beneath the wave,
    Fast by their native shore.
                    Loss of the Royal George

10 Toll for the brave—
    Brave Kempenfelt is gone.   *Ib.*

11 His sword was in the sheath,
    His fingers held the pen,
    When Kempenfelt went down
    With twice four hundred men.   *Ib.*

12 As if the world and they were hand
    and glove.   *Table Talk*, l. 173

13 I sing the Sofa.
                    The Task, bk. i, *The Sofa*, l. 1

14 God made the country, and man made
    the town.   *Ib.* l. 749

15 England, with all thy faults, I love
    thee still—
    My country!
            Ib. bk. ii, *The Timepiece*, l. 206

16 Variety's the very spice of life,
    That gives it all its flavour.
                    Ib. l. 606

17 I was a stricken deer, that left the
    herd
    Long since.
            Ib. bk. iii, *The Garden*, l. 108

18 Now stir the fire, and close the shutters
    fast,
    Let fall the curtains, wheel the sofa
    round,
    And, while the bubbling and loud-
    hissing urn
    Throws up a steamy column, and the
    cups,
    That cheer but not inebriate, wait
    on each,
    So let us welcome peaceful ev'ning in.
            The Task, bk. iv, *The Winter
            Evening*, l. 34

19 I am monarch of all I survey,
    My right there is none to dispute;
            *Verses Supposed to be Written by
            Alexander Selkirk*

GEORGE CRABBE 1754–1832

20 And mighty folios first, a lordly band,
    Then quartos, their well-order'd ranks
    maintain,
    And light octavos fill a spacious plain;
    See yonder, ranged in more frequented
    rows,
    A humbler band of duodecimos.
                    The Library, l. 128

21 When from the cradle to the grave
    I look,
    Mine I conceive a melancholy book.
            The Parish Register, pt. iii,
            Burials, l. 21

22 When the coarse cloth she saw, with
    many a stain,
    Soil'd by rude hinds who cut and came
    again.
            Tales, vii, *The Widow's Tale*,
            l. 25

23 I sought the simple life that Nature
    yields.   *The Village*, bk. i, l. 110

STEPHEN CRANE 1871–1900

24 The Red Badge of Courage.   *Title*

ARCHBISHOP THOMAS
CRANMER 1489–1556

25 This hand hath offended.
            Strype's *Memorials of Cranmer*
            (1694), vol. iii

RICHARD CRASHAW 1612?–1649

26 By all the eagle in thee, all the dove.
            *The Flaming Heart upon the
            Book of Saint Teresa*, l. 95

27 Whoe'er she be,
    That not impossible she
    That shall command my heart and
    me;
            Wishes to His Supposed Mistress

MRS. EDMUND CRASTER d. 1874

1 The Centipede was happy quite,
Until the Toad in fun
Said 'Pray which leg goes after which?'
And worked her mind to such a pitch,
She lay distracted in the ditch
Considering how to run. *Attr.*

JULIA CRAWFORD *fl.* 1835

2 Kathleen Mavourneen! the grey dawn
is breaking,
The horn of the hunter is heard on
the hill;
The lark from her light wing the bright
dew is shaking;
Kathleen Mavourneen! what, slumbering still?
Oh! hast thou forgotten how soon we
must sever?
Oh! hast thou forgotten this day we
must part?
It may be for years, and it may be
for ever,
Oh! why art thou silent, thou voice
of my heart?
*Kathleen Mavourneen. Metro-
politan Magazine*, London, 1835

BISHOP MANDELL CREIGHTON
1843–1901

3 No people do so much harm as those
who go about doing good.
Life (1904), vol. ii, p. 503

JOHN WILSON CROKER
1780–1857

4 A game which a sharper once played
with a dupe, entitled, 'Heads I win,
tails you lose.' *Croker Papers*, iii. 59

OLIVER CROMWELL 1599–1658

5 Such men as had the fear of God before
them and as made some conscience of
what they did . . . the plain russet-
coated captain that knows what he
fights for and loves what he knows.
*Letter of Sept. 1643. In Carlyle,
Letters and Speeches of Oliver
Cromwell*

6 I beseech you, in the bowels of Christ,
think it possible you may be mistaken.
*Letter to the General Assembly of
the Church of Scotland, 3 Aug.
1650*

7 The dimensions of this mercy are
above my thoughts. It is, for aught I
know, a crowning mercy.
*Letter for the Honourable William
Lenthall, 4 Sept. 1651*

8 Not what they want but what is good
for them. *Attr. remark*

9 Mr. Lely, I desire you would use all
your skill to paint my picture truly
like me, and not flatter me at all;
but remark all these roughnesses,
pimples, warts, and everything as you
see me, otherwise I will never pay
a farthing for it.
*Remark, Walpole's Anecdotes of
Painting*, ch. 12

10 Take away these baubles.
Remark, Sydney Papers (1825),
p. 141

11 It is not fit that you should sit here
any longer! . . . you shall now give
place to better men.
*Speech to the Rump Parliament,
22 Jan. 1654*

12 Necessity hath no law. Feigned necessities, imaginary necessities, . . . are
the greatest cozenage that men can put
upon the Providence of God, and make
pretences to break known rules by.
*Speech to Parliament, 12 Sept.
1654*

13 My design is to make what haste I can
to be gone.
Last Words. Morley, Life, v,
ch. 10

JOHANN CRÜGER 1598–1662

14 Nun danket alle Gott.
Now thank we all our God. *Hymn*

BISHOP RICHARD CUMBER-
LAND 1631–1718

15 It is better to wear out than to rust
out.
G. Horne, *The Duty of Contending for the Faith*

ALLAN CUNNINGHAM 1784–1842

16 A wet sheet and a flowing sea,
A wind that follows fast
And fills the white and rustling sail
And bends the gallant mast.
A Wet Sheet and a Flowing Sea

JOHN PHILPOT CURRAN
1750–1817

17 The condition upon which God hath
given liberty to man is eternal vigilance; which condition if he break,
servitude is at once the consequence of
his crime, and the punishment of his
guilt.
*Speech on the Right of Election
of Lord Mayor of Dublin,
10 July 1790*

HARRY DACRE *fl.* 1892

1 Daisy, Daisy, give me your answer, do!
I'm half crazy, all for the love of you!
It won't be a stylish marriage,
I can't afford a carriage,
But you'll look sweet upon the seat
Of a bicycle made for two! *Daisy Bell*

CHARLES ANDERSON DANA
1819–1897

2 When a dog bites a man that is not
news, but when a man bites a dog
that is news.
*What is News? The New York
Sun, 1882*

SAMUEL DANIEL 1562–1619

3 Unless above himself he can
Erect himself, how poor a thing is
man!
*To the Lady Margaret, Countess
of Cumberland,* xii

DANTE ALIGHIERI 1265–1321

4 Nel mezzo del cammin di nostra vita.
In the middle of the road of our life.
Divine Comedy. Inferno, i.

5 Lasciate ogni speranza voi ch'entrate!
All hope abandon, ye who enter
here. *Ib.* iii. 9

6 Il gran rifiuto.
The great refusal. *Ib.* 60

7 Nessun maggior dolore,
Che ricordarsi del tempo felice
Nella miseria.
There is no greater sorrow than to
recall a time of happiness in misery.
Ib. v. 121

GEORGES JACQUES DANTON
1759–1794

8 De l'audace, et encore de l'audace,
et toujours de l'audace!
Boldness, and again boldness, and
always boldness!
*Speech to the Legislative Com-
mittee of General Defence, 2 Sept.
1792. Le Moniteur, 4 Sept. 1792*

CHARLES ROBERT DARWIN
1809–1882

9 I have called this principle, by which
each slight variation, if useful, is
preserved, by the term of Natural
Selection.
The Origin of Species, ch. 3

CHARLES DAVENANT 1656–1714

10 Custom, that unwritten law,
By which the people keep even kings
in awe. *Circe,* II. iii

SIR WILLIAM DAVENANT
1606–1668

11 I shall sleep like a top.
The Rivals, Act III

JOHN DAVIDSON 1857–1909

12 A runnable stag, a kingly crop.
A Runnable Stag

WILLIAM HENRY DAVIES
1870–1940

13 What is this life if, full of care,
We have no time to stand and stare?
Leisure

STEPHEN DECATUR 1779–1820

14 Our country! In her intercourse with
foreign nations, may she always be
in the right; but our country, right
or wrong.
*A. S. Mackenzie, Life of Decatur,
ch.* xiv.

MARQUISE DU DEFFAND
1697–1780

15 La distance n'y fait rien; il n'y a que
le premier pas qui coûte.
The distance is nothing; it is only
the first step that is difficult.
*Remark on the legend that St.
Denis, carrying his head in his
hands, walked two leagues. Letter
to d'Alembert, 7 July 1763*

DANIEL DEFOE 1661?–1731

16 The good die early, and the bad die
late.
*Character of the late Dr. S.
Annesley*

17 I takes my man Friday with me.
*The Life and Adventures of
Robinson Crusoe,* pt. i

THOMAS DEKKER 1570?–1641?

18 Art thou poor, yet hast thou golden
slumbers?
Oh sweet content!
Art thou rich, yet is thy mind per-
plexed?
Oh, punishment!
Dost thou laugh to see how fools are
vexed
To add to golden numbers, golden
numbers?
O, sweet content, O, sweet, O, sweet
content!
Work apace, apace, apace, apace;
Honest labour bears a lovely face;
Then hey nonny, nonny; hey nonny,
nonny. *Patient Grissil,* Act I

1 Golden slumbers kiss your eyes,
Smiles awake you when you rise:
Sleep, pretty wantons, do not cry,
And I will sing a lullaby:
Rock them, rock them, lullaby.
Patient Grissil, Act IV. ii

WALTER DE LA MARE 1873–1956

2 Oh, no man knows
Through what wild centuries
Roves back the rose. *All That's Past*

3 Look thy last on all things lovely,
Fare Well, iii

4 'Is there anybody there?' said the
traveller,
Knocking on the moonlit door.
The Listeners

5 'Tell them I came, and no one answered,
That I kept my word,' he said. *Ib.*

6 Ay, they heard his foot upon the
stirrup,
And the sound of iron on stone,
And how the silence surged softly
backward,
When the plunging hoofs were gone.
Ib.

7 It's a very odd thing—
As odd as can be—
That whatever Miss T. eats
Turns into Miss T. *Miss T.*

8 Three jolly Farmers
Once bet a pound
Each dance the others would
Off the ground. *Off the Ground*

9 Slowly, silently, now the moon
Walks the night in her silver shoon.
Silver

10 Some one came knocking
At my wee, small door;
Some one came knocking,
I'm sure—sure—sure. *Some One*

THOMAS, LORD DENMAN 1779–1854

11 Trial by jury itself, instead of being
a security to persons who are accused,
will be a delusion, a mockery, and a
snare.
*Judgement in O'Connell v. the
Queen, 4 Sept. 1844*

CLARENCE JAMES DENNIS 1876–1938

12 Me name is Mud.
*The Sentimental Bloke: A Spring
Song, st. 2 (1916)*

JOHN DENNIS 1657–1734

13 Damn them! They will not let my play
run, but they steal my thunder!
*W. S. Walsh, Handy-Book of
Literary Curiosities*

THOMAS DE QUINCEY 1785–1859

14 Murder Considered as One of the
Fine Arts. *Title of Essay*

RENÉ DESCARTES 1596–1650

15 Cogito, ergo sum.
I think, therefore I am.
Le Discours de la Méthode

PHILIPPE NÉRICAULT dit DESTOUCHES 1680–1754

16 Les absents ont toujours tort.
The absent are always in the wrong.
L'Obstacle imprévu, I. vi

CHARLES DIBDIN 1745–1814

17 In every mess I finds a friend,
In every port a wife.
Jack in his Element

18 But the standing toast that pleased
the most
Was—The wind that blows, the ship
that goes,
And the lass that loves a sailor!
The Round Robin

19 Here, a sheer hulk, lies poor Tom
Bowling,
The darling of our crew.
Tom Bowling

THOMAS JOHN DIBDIN 1771–1841

20 Oh! what a snug little Island,
A right little, tight little Island!
The Snug Little Island

CHARLES DICKENS 1812–1870

21 Jarndyce and Jarndyce still drags its
dreary length before the Court, perennially hopeless. *Bleak House, ch. 1*

22 This is a London particular. . . . A fog,
miss. *Ib. ch. 3*

23 Educating the natives of Borrioboola-Gha, on the left bank of the
Niger. [Mrs. Jellyby.] *Ib. ch. 4*

24 'Not to put too fine a point upon it'—
a favourite apology for plain-speaking
with Mr. Snagsby. *Ib. ch. 11*

25 He wos wery good to me, he wos! [Jo.]
Ib.

26 'It is', says Chadband, 'the ray of
rays, the sun of suns, the moon of
moons, the star of stars. It is the
light of Terewth.' *Ib. ch. 25*

27 England has been in a dreadful state
for some weeks. Lord Coodle would go
out, and Sir Thomas Doodle wouldn't
come in, and there being nobody in

Great Britain (to speak of) except
Coodle and Doodle, there has been no
Government. *Bleak House*, ch. 40

1 A smattering of everything, and a
knowledge of nothing. [*Minerva
House.*]
Sketches by Boz. Tales, ch. 3.
Sentiment

2 O let us love our occupations,
Bless the squire and his relations,
Live upon our daily rations,
And always know our proper stations.
The Chimes, 2nd Quarter

3 'Glod bless us every one!' said Tiny
Tim, the last of all.
A Christmas Carol, stave 3

4 It *was* a turkey! He could never have
stood upon his legs, that bird. He
would have snapped 'em off short in
a minute, like sticks of sealing-wax.
Ib., stave 5

5 'I am a lone lorn creetur',' were Mrs.
Gummidge's words, . . . 'and every-
think goes contrary with me.'
David Copperfield, ch. 3

6 Barkis is willin'. *Ib.* ch. 5

7 I have known him [Micawber] come
home to supper with a flood of tears,
and a declaration that nothing was
now left but a jail; and go to bed making a calculation of the expense of
putting bow-windows to the house,
'in case anything turned up,' which
was his favourite expression. *Ib.* ch. 11

8 Annual income twenty pounds, annual
expenditure nineteen nineteen six,
result happiness. Annual income
twenty pounds, annual expenditure
twenty pounds ought and six, result
misery. [*Mr. Micawber.*] *Ib.* ch. 12

9 I am well aware that I am the
'umblest person going. . . . My mother
is likewise a very 'umble person. We
live in a numble abode. [*Uriah Heep.*]
Ib. ch. 16

10 The mistake was made of putting
some of the trouble out of King
Charles's head into my head. *Ib.* ch. 17

11 I only ask for information. [*Miss Rosa
Dartle.*] *Ib.* ch. 20

12 Accidents will occur in the best-regulated families; and in families not
regulated by that pervading influence
which sanctifies while it enhances the
—a—I would say, in short, by the
influence of Woman, in the lofty
character of Wife, they may be expected with confidence, and must be
borne with philosophy. [*Mr.
Micawber.*] *Ib.* ch. 28

13 Mrs. Crupp had indignantly assured
him that there wasn't room to swing
a cat there; but, as Mr. Dick justly
observed to me, sitting down on the
foot of the bed, nursing his leg, 'You
know, Trotwood, I don't want to
swing a cat. I never do swing a cat.
Therefore, what does that signify to
me!' *David Copperfield*, ch. 35

14 It's only my child-wife. [*Dora.*]
Ib. ch. 44

15 'Wal'r, my boy,' replied the Captain,
'in the Proverbs of Solomon you will
find the following words, "May we
never want a friend in need, nor
a bottle to give him!" When found,
make a note of.' [*Captain Cuttle.*]
Dombey and Son, ch. 15

16 On the Rampage, Pip, and off the
Rampage, Pip; such is Life! [*Joe
Gargery.*] *Great Expectations*, ch. 15

17 You don't object to an aged parent,
I hope? [*Wemmick.*] *Ib.* ch. 25

18 Whatever was required to be done,
the Circumlocution Office was before-
hand with all the public departments
in the art of perceiving—HOW NOT
TO DO IT. *Little Dorrit*, bk. i, ch. 10

19 Father is rather vulgar, my dear.
The word Papa, besides, gives a pretty
form to the lips. Papa, potatoes,
poultry, prunes and prism, are all
very good words for the lips; especially
prunes and prism. [*Mrs. General.*]
Ib. bk. ii, ch. 5

20 With affection beaming in one eye,
and calculation shining out of the
other. [*Mrs. Todgers.*]
Martin Chuzzlewit, ch. 8

21 'Mrs. Harris,' I says, 'leave the bottle
on the chimley-piece, and don't ask
me to take none, but let me put my
lips to it when I am so disposed.'
[*Mrs. Gamp.*] *Ib.* ch. 19

22 Some people . . . may be Rooshans,
and others may be Prooshans; they
are born so, and will please themselves.
Them which is of other naturs thinks
different. [*Mrs. Gamp.*] *Ib.*

23 He'd make a lovely corpse. [*Mrs.
Gamp.*] *Ib.* ch. 25

24 'Bother Mrs. Harris!' said Betsey
Prig. . . . 'I don't believe there's no
sich a person!' *Ib.* ch. 49

25 EDUCATION.—At Mr. Wackford
Squeers's Academy, Dotheboys Hall,
at the delightful village of Dotheboys,
near Greta Bridge in Yorkshire, Youth
are boarded, clothed, booked, furnished with pocket-money, provided
with all necessaries, instructed in all
languages living and dead, mathematics, orthography, geometry, astro-
nomy, trigonometry, the use of the
globes, algebra, single stick (if re-

quired), writing, arithmetic, fortification, and every other branch of classical literature. Terms, twenty guineas per annum. No extras, no vacations, and diet unparalleled.
Nicholas Nickleby, ch. 3

1 Here's richness! [*Mr. Squeers.*]
Ib. ch. 5

2 C-l-e-a-n, clean, verb active, to make bright, to scour. W-i-n, win, d-e-r, der, winder, a casement. When the boy knows this out of the book, he goes and does it. [*Mr. Squeers.*] *Ib.* ch. 8

3 As she frequently remarked when she made any such mistake, it would be all the same a hundred years hence. [*Mrs. Squeers.*] *Ib.* ch. 9

4 Language was not powerful enough to describe the infant phenomenon.
Ib. ch. 23

5 All is gas and gaiters. [*The Gentleman in the Small-clothes.*] *Ib.* ch. 49

6 He has gone to the demnition bow-wows. [*Mr. Mantalini.*] *Ib.* ch. 64

7 Oliver Twist has asked for more! [*Bumble.*] *Oliver Twist*, ch. 2

8 Known by the *sobriquet* of 'The Artful Dodger.' *Ib.* ch. 8

9 'Hard,' replied the Dodger. 'As nails,' added Charley Bates. *Ib.* ch. 9

10 'If the law supposes that,' said Mr. Bumble . . . 'the law is a ass—a idiot.'
Ib. ch. 51

11 The question [with Mr. Podsnap] about everything was, would it bring a blush into the cheek of the young person?
Our Mutual Friend, bk. i, ch. 11

12 I think . . . that it is the best club in London. [*Mr. Tremlow, on the House of Commons.*] *Ib.* bk. ii, ch. 3

13 Queer Street is full of lodgers just at present. [*Fledgeby.*] *Ib.* bk. iii, ch. 1

14 He'd be sharper than a serpent's tooth, if he wasn't as dull as ditch water. [*Fanny Cleaver.*] *Ib.* ch. 10

15 He had used the word in its Pickwickian sense. . . . He had merely considered him a humbug in a Pickwickian point of view. [*Mr. Blotton.*]
Pickwick Papers, ch. 1

16 Kent, sir—everybody knows Kent—apples, cherries, hops, and women. [*Jingle.*] *Ib.* ch. 2

17 I wants to make your flesh creep. [*The Fat Boy.*] *Ib.* ch. 8

18 'It's always best on these occasions to do what the mob do.' 'But suppose there are two mobs?' suggested Mr. Snodgrass. 'Shout with the largest,' replied Mr. Pickwick. *Ib.* ch. 13

19 'Can I unmoved see thee dying
   On a log,
   Expiring frog!' [*Mrs. Leo Hunter.*]
Pickwick Papers, ch. 15

20 Mr. Weller's knowledge of London was extensive and peculiar. *Ib.* ch. 20

21 Be wery careful o' vidders all your life. [*Mr. Weller.*] *Ib.*

22 Keep yourself *to* yourself. [*Mr. Raddle.*] *Ib.* ch. 32

23 She's a swellin' wisibly before my wery eyes. [*Mr. Weller.*] *Ib.* ch. 33

24 Chops and Tomata sauce. Yours, Pickwick. *Ib.* ch. 34

25 Put it down a we, my Lord, put it down a we. [*Mr. Weller.*] *Ib.*

26 'Little to do, and plenty to get, I suppose?' said Sergeant Buzfuz, with jocularity.
'Oh, quite enough to get, sir, as the soldier said ven they ordered him three hundred and fifty lashes,' replied Sam.
'You must not tell us what the soldier, or any other man, said, sir,' interposed the judge; 'it's not evidence.' *Ib.*

27 'Yes, I have a pair o' eyes,' replied Sam, 'and that's just it. If they wos a pair o' patent double million magnifyin' gas microscopes of hextra power, p'raps I might be able to see through a flight o' stairs and a deal door; but bein' only eyes, you see my wision's limited.' *Ib.*

28 Oh Sammy, Sammy, vy worn't there a alleybi! [*Mr. Weller.*] *Ib.*

29 Miss Bolo rose from the table considerably agitated, and went straight home, in a flood of tears and a Sedan chair. *Ib.* ch. 35

30 A friendly swarry, consisting of a boiled leg of mutton with the usual trimmings. *Ib.* ch. 37

31 'That 'ere young lady,' replied Sam. 'She knows wot's wot, she does.' *Ib.*

32 The have-his-carcase, next to the perpetual motion, is vun of the blessedest things as wos ever made. [*Sam Weller.*]
Ib. ch. 43

33 Anythin' for a quiet life, as the man said wen he took the sitivation at the lighthouse. [*Sam Weller.*] *Ib.*

34 It is a far, far better thing that I do, than I have ever done; it is a far, far better rest that I go to, than I have ever known. [*Sydney Carton.*]
A Tale of Two Cities, bk. iii, ch. 15

JOHN DICKINSON 1732–1808

1 Then join in hand brave Americans all,
By uniting we stand, by dividing we fall.
> *The Liberty Song. Memoirs of the Historical Soc. of Pennsylvania, vol. xiv*

DENIS DIDEROT 1713–1784

2 L'esprit de l'escalier.
Staircase wit.
> *An untranslatable phrase, the meaning of which is that one only thinks on one's way downstairs of the smart retort one might have made in the drawing-room.*
> *Paradoxe sur le Comédien*

WENTWORTH DILLON, EARL OF ROSCOMMON 1633?–1685

3 The multitude is always in the wrong.
> *Essay on Translated Verse, l. 183*

DIOGENES fl. c. 380 B.C.

4 Alexander . . . asked him if he lacked anything. 'Yea,' said he, 'that I do: that you stand out of my sun a little.'
> *Plutarch, Life of Alexander, 14 (North's translation)*

BENJAMIN DISRAELI, EARL OF BEACONSFIELD 1804–1881

5 Though I sit down now, the time will come when you will hear me.
> *Maiden Speech, 7 Dec. 1837. Meynell, Disraeli, i. 43*

6 The Continent will not suffer England to be the workshop of the world.
> *Speech, House of Commons, 15 Mar. 1838*

7 The right hon. Gentleman [Sir Robert Peel] caught the Whigs bathing, and walked away with their clothes.
> *Ib. 28 Feb. 1845*

8 Is man an ape or an angel? Now I am on the side of the angels.
> *Ib. at Meeting of Society for Increasing Endowments of Small Livings in the Diocese of Oxford, 25 Nov. 1864*

9 As I sat opposite the Treasury Bench the ministers reminded me of one of those marine landscapes not very unusual on the coasts of South America. You behold a range of exhausted volcanoes. *Ib. Manchester, 3 Apr. 1872*

10 Lord Salisbury and myself have brought you back peace—but a peace I hope with honour.
> *Ib. House of Commons, 16 July 1878*

11 A sophistical rhetorician, inebriated with the exuberance of his own verbosity. [Gladstone.]
> *Speech at Banquet in Riding School, Knightsbridge, 27 July 1878*

12 Damn your principles! Stick to your party.
> *Attr. Remark to Bulwer Lytton (Latham, Famous Sayings)*

13 There is no reason to doubt the story which represents him as using more than once, in conversation with Her Majesty on literary subjects, the words: 'We authors, Ma'am.'
> *Monypenny and Buckle, Life of Disraeli, v. 49*

14 She is an excellent creature, but she never can remember which came first, the Greeks or the Romans. [Of his wife.] *G. W. E. Russell, Collections and Recollections, ch. 1*

15 Everyone likes flattery; and when you come to Royalty you should lay it on with a trowel.
> *Remark to Matthew Arnold. Ib. ch. 23*

16 His Christianity was muscular.
> *Endymion, bk. i, ch. 14*

17 Time is the great physician.
> *Ib. bk. vi, ch. 9*

18 The blue ribbon of the turf. [The Derby.]
> *Life of Lord George Bentinck, ch. 26*

19 Every woman should marry—and no man. *Lothair, ch. 30*

20 Little things affect little minds.
> *Sybil, bk. iii, ch. 2*

21 I was told that the Privileged and the People formed Two Nations.
> *Ib. bk. iv, ch. 8*

22 The microcosm of a public school.
> *Vivian Grey, bk. i, ch. 2*

23 A *dark* horse, which had never been thought of, and which the careless St. James had never even observed in the list, rushed past the grand stand in sweeping triumph.
> *The Young Duke, bk. ii, ch. 5*

HENRY AUSTIN DOBSON 1840–1921

24 I intended an Ode,
And it turned to a Sonnet.
It began à la mode,
I intended an Ode;
But Rose crossed the road
In her latest new bonnet;
I intended an Ode;
And it turned to a Sonnet.
> *Rose-Leaves*

CHARLES LUTWIDGE DODGSON
see LEWIS CARROLL

JOHN DONNE 1571?–1631

1 All other things, to their destruction
   draw,
   Only our love hath no decay;
   This, no to-morrow hath, nor yester-
   day,
   Running it never runs from us away,
   But truly keeps his first, last, ever-
   lasting day. *The Anniversary*

2 For God's sake hold your tongue, and
   let me love. *The Canonization*

3 She, and comparisons are odious.
   Elegies, No. 8. *The Comparison*

4 No Spring, nor Summer beauty hath
   such grace,
   As I have seen in one Autumnal face.
   Ib. No. 9. *The Autumnal*

5 O my America! my new-found-land.
   Ib. No. 19. *On Going to Bed*

6 Where, like a pillow on a bed,
   A pregnant bank swelled up, to rest
   The violet's reclining head,
   Sat we two, one another's best.
   The Extasy

7 I wonder by my troth, what thou, and
   I
   Did, till we lov'd? were we not wean'd
   till then?
   But suck'd on country pleasures,
   childishly? *The Good-Morrow*

8 At the round earth's imagined corners,
   blow
   Your trumpets, Angels, and arise,
   arise. *Holy Sonnets*, vii

9 Death be not proud, though some have
   called thee
   Mighty and dreadful, for, thou art not
   so,
   For, those, whom thou think'st, thou
   dost overthrow,
   Die not, poor death. *Ib.* x

10 One short sleep past, we wake eternally,
   And death shall be no more; death,
   thou shalt die. *Ib.*

11 What if this present were the world's
   last night? *Ib.* xiii

12 Batter my heart, three person'd God;
   for, you
   As yet but knock, breathe, shine, and
   seek to mend. *Ib.* xiv

13 I long to talk with some old lover's
   ghost,
   Who died before the god of love was
   born. *Love's Deity*

14 A bracelet of bright hair about the
   bone. *The Relic*

15 Sweetest love, I do not go,
   For weariness of thee,
   Nor in hope the world can show
   A fitter Love for me;
   But since that I
   Must die at last, 'tis best,
   To use my self in jest
   Thus by feigned deaths to die. *Song*

16 Go, and catch a falling star,
   Get with child a mandrake root,
   Tell me, where all past years are,
   Or who cleft the Devil's foot.
   Song, Go and Catch a Falling Star

17 And swear
   No where
   Lives a woman true and fair. *Ib.*

18 Busy old fool, unruly Sun,
   Why dost thou thus,
   Through windows, and through cur-
   tains call on us?
   Must to thy motions lovers' seasons
   run? *The Sun Rising*

19 I am two fools, I know,
   For loving, and for saying so
   In whining Poetry. *The Triple Fool*

20 Dull sublunary lovers' love
   (Whose soul is sense) cannot admit
   Absence, because it doth remove
   Those things which elemented it.
   *A Valediction Forbidding Mourn-
   ing*

21 But I do nothing upon my self, and
   yet I am mine own *Executioner*.
   Devotions

22 No man is an *Island*, entire of it self.
   Ib.

23 Any man's *death* diminishes *me*, because I am involved in *Mankind*;
   And therefore never send to know for
   whom the *bell* tolls; It tolls for *thee*.
   Ib.

24 John Donne, Anne Donne, Un-done.
   Letter to his Wife

WILLIAM DOUGLAS 1672–1748

25 And for bonnie Annie Laurie
   I'd lay me doun and dee.
   Annie Laurie

ERNEST DOWSON 1867–1900

26 I have been faithful to thee, Cynara!
   in my fashion. *Non Sum Qualis Eram*

27 I have forgot much, Cynara! gone with
   the wind,
   Flung roses, roses, riotously, with the
   throng,
   Dancing, to put thy pale, lost lilies out
   of mind. *Ib.*

SIR ARTHUR CONAN DOYLE
1859–1930

1 What of the bow?
The bow was made in England:
Of true wood, of yew-wood,
The wood of English bows.
Song of the Bow

2 It is quite a three-pipe problem.
The Adventures of Sherlock Holmes. The Red-Headed League

3 To Sherlock Holmes she [Irene Adler] is always *the* woman.
Ib. Scandal in Bohemia

4 It is a capital mistake to theorize before one has data. *Ib.*

5 You know my methods, Watson.
The Memoirs of Sherlock Holmes. The Crooked Man

6 'Excellent!' I [Dr. Watson] cried. 'Elementary,' said he [Holmes]. *Ib.*

7 'It is my duty to warn you that it will be used against you,' cried the Inspector, with the magnificent fair play of the British criminal law.
Ib. Dancing Men

8 He [Professor Moriarty] is the Napoleon of crime. *Ib. The Final Problem*

9 These are much deeper waters than I had thought. *Ib. Reigate Squires*

10 A long shot, Watson; a very long shot!
Ib. Silver Blaze

11 'Is there any point to which you would wish to draw my attention?'
'To the curious incident of the dog in the night-time.'
'The dog did nothing in the night-time.'
'That was the curious incident,' remarked Sherlock Holmes. *Ib.*

12 Good old Watson! You are the one fixed point in a changing age.
His Last Bow. His Last Bow.

13 But here, unless I am mistaken, is our client. *Ib. Wisteria Lodge*

14 There is but one step from the grotesque to the horrible. *Ib.*

15 An experience of women which extends over many nations and three separate continents. *The Sign of Four*

16 How often have I said to you that when you have eliminated the impossible, whatever remains, *however improbable*, must be the truth? *Ib.*

17 The vocabulary of 'Bradshaw' is nervous and terse but limited.
The Valley of Fear

18 Mediocrity knows nothing higher than itself, but talent instantly recognizes genius. *Ib.*

19 The Baker Street irregulars. *Ib.*

20 London, that great cesspool into which all the loungers of the Empire are irresistibly drained.
A Study in Scarlet

21 'Wonderful!' I [Dr. Watson] ejaculated. 'Commonplace,' said Holmes. *Ib.*

SIR FRANCIS HASTINGS CHARLES DOYLE 1810–1888

22 Last night, among his fellow roughs, He jested, quaff'd, and swore.
The Private of the Buffs

23 To-day, beneath the foeman's frown, He stands in Elgin's place,
Ambassador from Britain's crown And type of all her race. *Ib.*

24 His creed no parson ever knew, For this was still his 'simple plan,' To have with clergymen to do As little as a Christian can.
The Unobtrusive Christian

SIR FRANCIS DRAKE 1540?–1596

25 There is plenty of time to win this game, and to thrash the Spaniards too. *Attr. in the Dict. of Nat. Biog.*

'The tradition goes, that Drake would needs see the game up; but was soon prevail'd on to go and play out the rubber with the Spaniards.' W. Oldys' *Life of Ralegh* in Ralegh's *Hist. of the World* (1736)

26 I remember Drake, in the vaunting style of a soldier, would call the Enterprise [of Cadiz, 1587] the singeing of the King of Spain's Beard.
Bacon, *Considerations touching a War with Spain (Harleian Misc.* (1745), vol. v, p. 85, col. 1)

27 I must have the gentleman to haul and draw with the mariner, and the mariner with the gentleman. . . . I would know him, that would refuse to set his hand to a rope, but I know there is not any such here.
Corbett, *Drake and the Tudor Navy*, i. 249

MICHAEL DRAYTON 1563–1631

28 Fair stood the wind for France When now we our sails advance,
Nor now to prove our chance Longer will tarry.
To the Cambro-Britons. Agincourt

29 Since there's no help, come let us kiss and part. *Sonnets*, lxi

WILLIAM DRENNAN 1754–1820

30 The men of the Emerald Isle. *Erin*

THOMAS DRUMMOND 1797–1840

1 Property has its duties as well as its rights.
*Letter to the Earl of Donoughmore,
22 May 1838*

JOHN DRYDEN 1631–1700

2 In pious times, ere priestcraft did begin,
Before polygamy was made a sin.
Absalom and Achitophel, pt. i, l. 1

3 And, wide as his command,
Scatter'd his Maker's image through the land. *Ib. l. 9*

4 The Jews, a headstrong, moody, murmuring race
As ever tried the extent and stretch of grace,
God's pampered people, whom, debauched with ease,
No king could govern nor no God could please. *Ib. l. 45*

5 A fiery soul, which working out its way,
Fretted the pigmy body to decay:
And o'er informed the tenement of clay. *Ib. l. 156*

6 Great wits are sure to madness near alli'd,
And thin partitions do their bounds divide. *Ib. l. 163*

7 But far more numerous was the herd of such
Who think too little and who talk too much. *Ib. l. 533*

8 A man so various that he seem'd to be
Not one, but all mankind's epitome.
Stiff in opinions, always in the wrong;
Was everything by starts, and nothing long:
But, in the course of one revolving moon,
Was chemist, fiddler, statesman, and buffoon. *Ib. l. 545*

9 During his office treason was no crime,
The sons of Belial had a glorious time. *Ib. l. 597*

10 Doeg, though without knowing how or why,
Made still a blund'ring kind of melody;
Spurr'd boldly on, and dash'd through thick and thin,
Through sense and nonsense, never out nor in. *Ib. pt. ii, l. 412*

11 None but the brave deserves the fair.
Alexander's Feast, l. 15

12 Drinking is the soldier's pleasure.
Ib. l. 57

13 All For Love, or the World Well Lost.
Title of Play

14 A knock-down argument; 'tis but a word and a blow. *Amphitryon, I. i*

15 Whistling to keep myself from being afraid. *Amphitryon, III. i*

16 From harmony, from heavenly harmony
This universal frame began:
From harmony to harmony
Through all the compass of the notes it ran,
The diapason closing full in Man.
St. Cecilia's Day, i

17 The soft complaining flute. *Ib. iv*

18 The trumpet shall be heard on high,
The dead shall live, the living die,
And Music shall untune the sky.
Ib. Grand Chorus

19 I am as free as nature first made man,
Ere the base laws of servitude began,
When wild in woods the noble savage ran.
The Conquest of Granada, pt. i, I. i

20 Here lies my wife: here let her lie!
Now she's at rest, and so am I.
Epitaph Intended for Dryden's Wife

21 He had brought me to my last dregs;
I was fighting as low as ever was Squire Widdrington.
An Evening's Love, II. i

22 Either to be wholly slaves or wholly free.
The Hind and the Panther, pt. ii, l. 285

23 Fairest Isle, all isles excelling,
Seat of pleasures, and of loves;
Venus here will choose her dwelling,
And forsake her Cyprian groves.
King Arthur, v. Song of Venus

24 The rest to some faint meaning make pretence,
But Shadwell never deviates into sense.
Some beams of wit on other souls may fall,
Strike through and make a lucid interval;
But Shadwell's genuine night admits no ray,
His rising fogs prevail upon the day.
Mac Flecknoe, l. 19

25 I am to be married within these three days; married past redemption.
Marriage à la Mode, I. i

26 But treason is not own'd when 'tis descried;
Successful crimes alone are justified.
The Medal, l. 207

27 And Antony, who lost the world for love.
Palamon and Arcite, bk. ii, l. 607

28 Like pilgrims to th' appointed place we tend;
The world's an inn, and death the journey's end. *Ib. bk. iii, l. 887*

1 There is a pleasure sure,
In being mad, which none but mad-
men know!
The Spanish Friar, I. i

2 We must beat the iron while it is hot,
but we may polish it at leisure.
Dedication of the Aeneis

3 He was the man who of all modern,
and perhaps ancient poets, had the
largest and most comprehensive soul.
. . . He was naturally learn'd; he
needed not the spectacles of books to
read Nature; he looked inwards, and
found her there. . . . He is many times
flat, insipid; his comic wit degenerating into clenches, his serious swelling
into bombast. But he is always great,
when some occasion is presented to
him. [Shakespeare.]
Essay of Dramatic Poesy

4 The consideration of this made Mr.
Hales of Eaton say, that there was
no subject of which any poet ever
writ, but he would produce it much
better done in Shakespeare. *Ib.*

5 What judgment I had increases rather
than diminishes; and thoughts, such
as they are, come crowding in so fast
upon me, that my only difficulty is
to choose or reject; to run them into
verse or to give them the other
harmony of prose. *Preface to Fables*

6 'Tis sufficient to say [of Chaucer],
according to the proverb, that here is
God's plenty. *Ib.*

7 He [Chaucer] is a perpetual fountain
of good sense. *Ib.*

GEORGE DUFFIELD 1818–1888

8 Stand up!—stand up for Jesus!
*The Psalmist. Stand Up, Stand
Up for Jesus*

ALEXANDRE DUMAS 1802–1870

9 Cherchons la femme.
Let us look for the woman.
Les Mohicans de Paris, vol. ii,
ch. 2
(Cherchez la femme. Attr. to Joseph
Fouché.)

10 Tous pour un, un pour tous.
All for one, one for all.
Les Trois Mousquetaires, passim

MARÉCHAL DUMOURIEZ
1739–1823

11 Les courtisans qui l'entourent n'ont
rien oublié et n'ont rien appris.
The courtiers who surround him

have forgotten nothing and learnt
nothing.
*Of Louis XVIII, at the time of the
Declaration of Verona, Sept. 1795.
Examen. See also Talleyrand*

WILLIAM DUNBAR 1465?–1530?

12 Timor mortis conturbat me.
Lament for the Makaris

13 London, thou art of townes A per se.
London, l. 1

14 London, thou art the flower of cities
all!
Gemme of all joy, jasper of jocunditie.
Ib. l. 16

JAMES DUPORT 1606–1679

15 Quem Juppiter vult perdere dementat
prius.
Whom God would destroy He first
sends mad.

THOMAS D'URFEY 1653–1723

16 Neighbours o'er the Herring Pond.
*Pills to Purge Melancholy (1719),
vol. ii, p. 333. Fable of the Lady,
the Lurcher, and the Marrow-
Puddings, xiv*

SIR EDWARD DYER c. 1540–1607

17 My mind to me a kingdom is,
Such present joys therein I find,
That it excels all other bliss
That earth affords or grows by kind.
Though much I want which most
would have,
Yet still my mind forbids to crave.
My Mind to Me a Kingdom Is

JOHN DYER 1700?–1758

18 A little rule, a little sway,
A sunbeam in a winter's day,
Is all the proud and mighty have
Between the cradle and the grave.
Grongar Hill, l. 89

JOHN DYER fl. 1714

19 And he that will this health deny,
Down among the dead men let him lie.
Toast: Here's a Health to the King

MARIA EDGEWORTH 1767–1849

20 Well! some people talk of morality,
and some of religion, but give me a
little snug property.
The Absentee, ch. 2

21 Come when you're called;
And do as you're bid;
Shut the door after you;
And you'll never be chid.
The Contrast, ch. 1

THOMAS ALVA EDISON
1847–1931

1 Genius is one per cent. inspiration and ninety-nine per cent. perspiration.
Newspaper Interview. Life (1932), ch. 24

JAMES EDMESTON 1791–1867

2 Lead us, Heavenly Father, lead us
O'er the world's tempestuous sea;
Guard us, guide us, keep us, feed us,
For we have no help but Thee.
Sacred Lyrics, Set 2. Lead Us, Heavenly Father

EDWARD III OF ENGLAND
1312–1377

3 Let the boy win his spurs.
Of the Black Prince at Crécy, 1345

4 Also say to them, that they suffre hym this day to wynne his spurres, for if god be pleased, I woll this iourney be his, and the honoure therof.
Lord Berners, *Froissart's Chron.* (1812), I. cxxx. 158.

EDWARD VIII OF GREAT BRITAIN 1894–

5 I have found it impossible to carry the heavy burden of responsibility and to discharge my duties as King as I would wish to do without the help and support of the woman I love.
Broadcast, 11 Dec. 1936

JONATHAN EDWARDS 1629–1712

6 The bodies of those that made such a noise and tumult when alive, when dead, lie as quietly among the graves of their neighbours as any others.
Procrastination

OLIVER EDWARDS 1711–1791

7 I have tried too in my time to be a philosopher; but, I don't know how, cheerfulness was always breaking in.
Boswell's *Johnson*, 17 Apr. 1778

'GEORGE ELIOT' [MARY ANN CROSS] 1819–1880

8 I'm not denyin' the women are foolish: God Almighty made 'em to match the men. *Adam Bede*, ch. 53

9 The happiest women, like the happiest nations, have no history.
The Mill on the Floss, bk. vi, ch. 3

THOMAS STEARNS ELIOT 1888–1965

10 Time present and time past
Are both perhaps present in time future,
And time future contained in time past. *Burnt Norton*

11 In the seventeenth century a dissociation of sensibility set in from which we have never recovered.
Essay on Dryden

12 We are the hollow men
We are the stuffed men
Leaning together. *The Hollow Men*

13 This is the way the world ends
Not with a bang but a whimper. *Ib.*

14 When the evening is spread out against the sky
Like a patient etherized upon a table.
Love Song of J. Alfred Prufrock

15 In the room the women come and go
Talking of Michelangelo. *Ib.*

16 The yellow fog that rubs its back upon the window-panes. *Ib.*

17 I have measured out my life with coffee spoons. *Ib.*

18 I should have been a pair of ragged claws
Scuttling across the floors of silent seas. *Ib.*

19 I grow old . . . I grow old . . .
I shall wear the bottoms of my trousers rolled. *Ib.*

20 I am aware of the damp souls of housemaids
Sprouting despondently at area gates.
Morning at the Window

21 The last temptation is the greatest treason:
To do the right deed for the wrong reason.
Murder in the Cathedral, pt. 1

22 The nightingales are singing near
The Convent of the Sacred Heart
And sang within the bloody wood
When Agamemnon cried aloud.
Sweeney Among the Nightingales

23 April is the cruellest month, breeding
Lilacs out of the dead land, mixing
Memory and desire, stirring
Dull roots with spring rain.
The Waste Land, i. *The Burial of the Dead*

24 And I will show you something different from either
Your shadow at morning striding behind you,
Or your shadow at evening rising to meet you
I will show you fear in a handful of dust. *Ib.*

1 O the moon shone bright on Mrs.
  Porter
  And on her daughter
  They wash their feet in soda water.
  The Waste Land, iii. *The Fire Sermon*

2 When lovely woman stoops to folly
  and
  Paces about her room again, alone,
  She smoothes her hair with automatic
  hand,
  And puts a record on the gramophone.
  Ib.

3 Webster was much possessed by death.
  Whispers of Immortality

QUEEN ELIZABETH I 1533–1603

4 'Twas God the word that spake it,
  He took the Bread and brake it;
  And what the word did make it;
  That I believe, and take it.
  *Answer on being asked her opinion
  of Christ's presence in the Sacra-
  ment.* S. Clarke's *Marrow of
  Ecclesiastical History*, pt. ii, *Life
  of Queen Elizabeth* (ed. 1675)

5 The queen of Scots is this day leichter
  of a fair son, and I am but a barren
  stock.
  Memoirs of Sir James Melville
  (1549–93)

6 God may forgive you, but I never can.
  [To the Countess of Nottingham.]
  The Queen . . . crying to her that
  God might pardon her, but she
  never could.
  Hume, *History of England under
  the House of Tudor*, vol. ii, ch. 7

7 If thy heart fails thee, climb not at
  all.
  *Lines written on a window after
  Sir Walter Ralegh's line* 'Fain
  would I climb, yet fear I to fall.'
  Fuller, *Worthies of England*,
  vol. i, p. 419

8 Semper eadem.   *Motto*

9 I know I have the body of a weak and
  feeble woman, but I have the heart
  and stomach of a king, and of a king
  of England too; and think foul scorn
  that Parma or Spain, or any prince of
  Europe, should dare to invade the
  borders of my realm.
  *Speech to the Troops at Tilbury
  on the Approach of the Armada,
  1588*

10 Must! Is *must* a word to be addressed
  to princes? Little man, little man!
  thy father, if he had been alive, durst
  not have used that word.
  To Robert Cecil. On her death-bed.
  J. R. Green, *A Short History of
  the English People*, ch. vii

JOHN ELLERTON 1826–1893

11 The day Thou gavest, Lord, is ended,
  The darkness falls at Thy behest.
  *A Liturgy for Missionary Meet-
  ings. The Day Thou Gavest*

JANE ELLIOT 1727–1805

12 I've heard them lilting, at the ewe
  milking,
  Lasses a' lilting, before dawn of day;
  But now they are moaning, on ilka
  green loaning;
  The flowers of the forest are a' wede
  away.   *The Flowers of the Forest*

GEORGE ELLIS

see SIR GREGORY GANDER

RALPH WALDO EMERSON
1803–1882

13 If the red slayer think he slays,
  Or if the slain think he is slain,
  They know not well the subtle ways
  I keep, and pass, and turn again.
  Brahma

14 By the rude bridge that arched the
  flood,
  Their flag to April's breeze unfurled,
  Here once the embattled farmers
  stood,
  And fired the shot heard round the
  world.
  *Hymn Sung at the Completion
  of the Concord Monument*

15 The hand that rounded Peter's dome,
  And groined the aisles of Christian
  Rome,
  Wrought in a sad sincerity;
  Himself from God he could not free;
  He builded better than he knew;—
  The conscious stone to beauty grew.
  The Problem

16 Art is a jealous mistress.
  Conduct of Life. Wealth

17 The louder he talked of his honour,
  the faster we counted our spoons.
  Ib. Worship

18 There is properly no history; only
  biography.   *Essays, i. History*

19 All mankind love a lover. *Ib. v. Love*

20 In skating over thin ice, our safety is
  in our speed.   *Ib. vii. Prudence*

21 Is it so bad, then, to be misunderstood? Pythagoras was misunderstood, and Socrates, and Jesus, and
  Luther, and Copernicus, and Galileo,
  and Newton, and every pure and wise
  spirit that ever took flesh. To be great
  is to be misunderstood.
  Ib. ii. Self-Reliance

1 I have heard with admiring submission the experience of the lady who declared that the sense of being well-dressed gives a feeling of inward tranquillity which religion is powerless to bestow. [Miss C. F. Forbes, 1817–1911.]
Letters and Social Aims. Social Aims

2 Hitch your wagon to a star.
Society and Solitude. Civilization

3 We boil at different degrees.
Ib. Eloquence

4 If a man write a better book, preach a better sermon, or make a better mouse-trap than his neighbour, tho' he build his house in the woods, the world will make a beaten path to his door.
Mrs. Sarah S. B. Yule (1856–1916) credits the quotation to Emerson in her Borrowings *(1889), stating in* The Docket, *Feb. 1912, that she copied this in her handbook from a lecture delivered by Emerson. The 'mouse-trap' quotation was the occasion of a long controversy, owing to Elbert Hubbard's claim to its authorship.*

ENNIUS 239–169 B.C.

5 Unus homo nobis cunctando restituit rem.
One man by delaying saved the state for us.
Cicero, De Senectute, iv. 10

HENRY ERSKINE 1746–1817

6 In the garb of old Gaul, wi' the fire of old Rome. *In the Garb of Old Gaul*

THOMAS ERSKINE, BARON ERSKINE 1750–1823

7 The uncontrouled licentiousness of a brutal and insolent soldiery.
Report (1796) of Erskine's defence of William Stone

HENRI ESTIENNE 1531–1598

8 Si jeunesse savoit; si vieillesse pouvoit.
If youth knew; if age could.
Les Prémices, Épigramme cxci

EUCLID *fl. c.* 300 B.C.

9 Quod erat demonstrandum (trans. from the Greek).
Which was to be proved.

10 A line is length without breadth.

EURIPIDES 485?–406? B.C.

11 ἡ γλῶσσ' ὀμώμοχ', ἡ δὲ φρὴν ἀνώμοτος.
'Twas but my tongue, 'twas not my soul that swore.
Hippolytus, 612. Trans. by Gilbert Murray

ABEL EVANS 1679–1737

12 Under this stone, Reader, survey
Dead Sir John Vanbrugh's house of clay.
Lie heavy on him, Earth! for he
Laid many heavy loads on thee!
Epitaph on Sir John Vanbrugh, Architect of Blenheim Palace

WILLIAM NORMAN EWER 1885–

13 How odd
Of God
To choose
The Jews. *How Odd*

FREDERICK WILLIAM FABER
1814–1863

14 My God, how wonderful Thou art!
Thy majesty how bright,
How beautiful Thy mercy-seat
In depths of burning light!
Jesus and Mary. My God, How Wonderful Thou Art!

ROBERT FABYAN *d.* 1513

15 Finally he paid the debt of nature.
Chronicles, pt. ii, xli

LUCIUS CARY, VISCOUNT FALKLAND 1610?–1643

16 When it is not necessary to change, it is necessary not to change.
A Speech concerning Episcopacy [delivered 1641]. *A Discourse of Infallibility* (1660)

AUGUST HEINRICH HOFFMANN VON FALLERSLEBEN
1798–1874

17 Deutschland, Deutschland über alles.
Germany, Germany over all.
Title of Song

GEORGE FARQUHAR 1678–1707

18 My Lady Bountiful.
The Beaux' Stratagem, I. i

19 He answered the description the page gave to a T, Sir.
Love and a Bottle, IV. iii

REV. FREDERICK WILLIAM FARRAR 1831–1903

20 Russell, let me always call you Edwin, and call me Eric.
Eric, or Little by Little, pt. i, ch. 4

GUY FAWKES 1570–1606

1 Desperate diseases require desperate
remedies.
(Gunpowder plot) *Dict. of Nat.
Biog.*

EUGENE FIELD 1850–1895

2 Listen to my tale of woe.
The Little Peach

3 Wynken, Blynken, and Nod one night
Sailed off in a wooden shoe—
Sailed on a river of crystal light,
Into a sea of dew.
Wynken, Blynken, and Nod

HENRY FIELDING 1707–1754

4 One of my illustrious predecessors.
*Covent-Garden Journal, No. 3,
11 Jan. 1752*

5 I am as sober as a Judge.
Don Quixote in England, III. xiv

6 Oh! The roast beef of England,
And old England's roast beef.
The Grub Street Opera, III. iii

7 Public schools are the nurseries of all
vice and immorality.
Joseph Andrews, bk. iii, ch. 5

8 Some folks rail against other folks,
because other folks have what some
folks would be glad of.
Ib. bk. iv, ch. 6

9 An amiable weakness.
Tom Jones, bk. x, ch. 8

10 To sun my self in Huncamunca's eyes.
Tom Thumb the Great, I. iii

11 The dusky night rides down the sky,
And ushers in the morn;
The hounds all join in glorious cry,
The huntsman winds his horn:
And a-hunting we will go.
A-Hunting We Will Go

L'ABBÉ EDGEWORTH DE FIRMONT 1745–1807

12 Fils de Saint Louis, montez au ciel.
Son of Saint Louis, ascend to heaven.
*Attr. words to Louis XVI as he
mounted the steps of the guillotine
at his execution, 1793. No docu-
mentary proof at all.*

JOHN ARBUTHNOT FISHER, LORD FISHER 1841–1920

13 Sack the lot!
The Times, 2 Sept. 1919

ALBERT H. FITZ

14 You are my honey, honey-suckle,
I am the bee.
The Honey-Suckle and the Bee

EDWARD FITZGERALD 1809–1883

15 Awake! for Morning in the Bowl of
Night
Has flung the Stone that puts the
Stars to Flight:
And Lo! the Hunter of the East has
caught
The Sultan's Turret in a Noose of
Light.   *Omar Khayyám*, ed. 1, i

16 Iram indeed is gone with all its Rose,
And   Jamshyd's   Sev'n-ring'd   Cup
where no one knows;
But still the Vine her ancient Ruby
yields,
And still a Garden by the Water
blows.   *Ib.* ed. 1, v

17 Come, fill the Cup, and in the Fire
of Spring
The Winter Garment of Repentance
fling:
The Bird of Time has but a little
way
To fly—and Lo! the Bird is on the
Wing.   *Ib.* ed. 1, vii

18 Here with a Loaf of Bread beneath the
bough,
A Flask of Wine, a Book of Verse—
and Thou
Beside me singing in the Wilder-
ness—
And Wilderness is Paradise enow.
Ib. ed. 1, xi

19 A Book of Verses underneath the
Bough,
A Jug of Wine, a Loaf of Bread—and
Thou
Beside me singing in the Wilder-
ness—
Oh, Wilderness were Paradise enow!
Ib. ed. 4, xii

20 Ah, take the Cash in hand and
waive the Rest;
Oh, the brave Music of a *distant*
Drum!   *Ib.* ed. 1, xii

21 Ah, take the Cash, and let the
Credit go,
Nor heed the rumble of a distant
Drum!   *Ib.* ed. 4, xiii

22 Think, in this batter'd Caravanserai
Whose Doorways are alternate Night
and Day,
How Sultan after Sultan with his
Pomp
Abode his Hour or two, and went his
way.   *Ib.* ed. 1, xv

23 Think, in this batter'd Caravanserai
Whose Portals are alternate Night and
Day,
How Sultan after Sultan with his
Pomp
Abode his destin'd Hour, and went his
way.   *Ib.* ed. 4, xvii

1 They say the Lion and the Lizard keep
The Courts where Jamshyd gloried
and drank deep:
And Bahram, that great Hunter—
the Wild Ass
Stamps o'er his Head, and he lies fast
asleep.
Omar Khayyám, ed. 1, xvii

2 I sometimes think that never blows so
red
The Rose as where some buried Caesar
bled;
That every Hyacinth the Garden
wears
Dropt in her Lap from some once
lovely Head.
Ib. ed. 1, xviii; ed. 4, xix

3 Ah, my Belovéd, fill the Cup that
clears
To-DAY of past Regrets and Future
Fears:
To-morrow!—Why, To-morrow I
may be
Myself with Yesterday's Sev'n
thousand Years.
Ib. ed. 1, xx; ed. 4, xxi

4 Lo! some we loved, the loveliest and
best
That Time and Fate of all their
Vintage prest,
Have drunk their Cup a Round or
two before,
And one by one crept silently to Rest.
Ib. ed. 1, xxi

5 Ah, make the most of what we yet
may spend,
Before we too into the Dust descend;
Dust into Dust, and under Dust, to
lie,
Sans Wine, sans Song, sans Singer,
and—sans End!
Ib. ed. 1, xxiii; ed. 4, xxiv

6 Oh, come with old Khayyám, and
leave the Wise
To talk; one thing is certain, that Life
flies;
One thing is certain, and the Rest
is Lies;
The Flower that once hath blown
for ever dies. *Ib.* ed. 1, xxvi

7 Myself when young did eagerly fre-
quent
Doctor and Saint, and heard great
argument
About it and about: but evermore
Came out by the same Door as in
I went. *Ib.* xxvii

8 Ah, fill the Cup:—what boots it to
repeat
How Time is slipping underneath our
Feet:
Unborn To-MORROW, and dead
YESTERDAY,
Why fret about them if To-DAY be
sweet!
Ib. ed. 1, xxxvii. Not in ed. 4

9 One Moment in Annihilation's Waste,
One Moment, of the Well of Life to
taste—
The Stars are setting and the Cara-
van
Starts for the Dawn of Nothing—Oh,
make haste!
Omar Khayyám, ed. 1, xxxviii

10 'Tis all a Chequer-board of Nights and
Days
Where Destiny with Men for Pieces
plays:
Hither and thither moves, and
mates, and slays,
And one by one back in the Closet
lays. *Ib.* ed. 1, xlix

11 The Ball no question makes of Ayes
and Noes,
But Here or There as strikes the
Player goes;
And He that toss'd you down into
the Field,
He knows about it all—HE knows—
HE knows! *Ib.* ed. 4, lxx

12 The Moving Finger writes; and, hav-
ing writ,
Moves on: nor all thy Piety nor Wit
Shall lure it back to cancel half a
Line,
Nor all thy Tears wash out a Word of
it. *Ib.* ed. 1, li
[Ed. 4, lxxi, reads 'your' instead of
'thy'.]

13 And that inverted Bowl we call The
Sky,
Whereunder crawling coop't we live
and die,
Lift not thy hands to It for help—
for It
Rolls impotently on as Thou or I.
Ib. lii

14 Said one—'Folks of a surly Tapster
tell,
And daub his Visage with the Smoke
of Hell;
They talk of some strict Testing of
us—Pish!
He's a Good Fellow, and 'twill all be
well.' *Ib.* lxiv; ed. 4, lxxxviii

15 Indeed the Idols I have loved so long
Have done my credit in this World
much wrong:
Have drown'd my Glory in a
Shallow Cup
And sold my Reputation for a Song.
Ib. ed. 4, xciii

16 And much as Wine has play'd the
Infidel,
And robb'd me of my Robe of Honour
—Well,
I often wonder what the Vintners
buy
One half so precious as the Goods they
sell. *Ib.* ed. 1, lxxi

1 Ah Love! could thou and I with Fate
  conspire
To grasp this sorry Scheme of Things
  entire,
Would not we shatter it to bits—
  and then
Re-mould it nearer to the Heart's
  Desire!
        Omar Khayyám, ed. 1, xxiii

2 Ah, Moon of my Delight who know'st
  no wane,
The Moon of Heav'n is rising once
  again:
How oft hereafter rising shall she
  look
Through this same Garden after me—
  in vain!   *Ib. ed. 1, lxxiv*

3 And when Thyself with shining Foot
  shall pass
Among the Guests Star-scattered on
  the Grass,
And in thy joyous Errand reach the
  Spot
Where I made one—turn down an
  empty Glass!   *Ib. ed. 1, lxxv*

4 And when like her, O Saki, you shall
  pass.   *Ib. ed. 4, ci*

JAMES ELROY FLECKER
1884–1915

5 The dragon-green, the luminous, the
  dark, the serpent-haunted sea.
    *The Gates of Damascus. West
    Gate*

6 How splendid in the morning glows
  the lily; with what grace he throws
  His supplication to the rose.
        Hassan, I. i

7 For one night or the other night
Will come the Gardener in white, and
  gathered flowers are dead, Yasmin.
        Ib. ii

8 For lust of knowing what should not
  be known,
We take the Golden Road to Samarkand.   *Ib. v. ii*

9 It was so old a ship—who knows, who
  knows?
And yet so beautiful, I watched in
  vain
To see the mast burst open with a
  rose,
And the whole deck put on its leaves
  again.   *The Old Ships*

10 A ship, an isle, a sickle moon—
  With few but with how splendid
  stars
The mirrors of the sea are strewn
  Between their silver bars.
    A Ship, an Isle, and a Sickle Moon

MARJORIE FLEMING 1803–1811

11 O lovely O most charming pug
Thy graceful air and heavenly mug....
His noses cast is of the roman
He is a very pretty weoman
I could not get a rhyme for roman
And was oblidged to call it weoman.
        Poems

ANDREW FLETCHER OF
SALTOUN 1655–1716

12 I knew a very wise man so much of
Sir Chr—'s sentiment, that he believed if a man were permitted to
make all the ballads, he need not care
who should make the laws of a nation.
    *Letter to the Marquis of Montrose,
    and Others. Political Works*

JOHN FLORIO 1553?–1625

13 England is the paradise of women, the
purgatory of men, and the hell of
horses.   *Second Frutes*

MARÉCHAL FOCH 1851–1929

14 Mon centre cède, ma droite recule,
situation excellente. J'attaque!
  My centre is giving way, my right
  is in retreat; situation excellent.
  I shall attack.
    Sir G. Aston, *Biography of Foch*
    (1929), ch. 13, p. 122

JEAN DE LA FONTAINE
1621–1695

15 Aide-toi, le ciel t'aidera.
  Help yourself, and heaven will help
  you.
    *Fables, vi. 18. Le Chartier Em-
    bourbé*

16 Je plie et ne romps pas.
  I bend and I break not.
    Ib. i. 22. Le Chêne et le Roseau

17 Il connaît l'univers et ne se connaît
pas.
  He knows the world and does not
  know himself.
    *Ib. viii. 26. Démocrite et les
    Abdéritains*

18 La raison du plus fort est toujours la
meilleure.
  The reason of the strongest is always the best.
    Ib. i. 10. Le Loup et l'Agneau

SAMUEL FOOTE 1720–1777

19 So she went into the garden to cut a
cabbage-leaf, to make an apple-pie;
and at the same time a great she-bear,
coming up the street, pops its head
into the shop. 'What! no soap?' So

he died, and she very imprudently married the barber; and there were present the Picninnies, and the Joblillies, and the Garyalies, and the grand Panjandrum himself, with the little round button at top, and they all fell to playing the game of catch as catch can, till the gun powder ran out at the heels of their boots.

> *In Maria Edgeworth, Harry and Lucy Concluded*

1 He is not only dull in himself, but the cause of dullness in others.

> *Remark. Boswell's Life of Johnson, ed. Powell, iv, p. 178. Parody of Shakespeare, Henry IV, Part II, I. ii. 7*

HENRY FORD 1863–1947

2 History is bunk.

> *In the witness-box during his libel suit v. the Chicago Tribune, July 1919*

JOHN FORD 1586–1639?

3 'Tis Pity She's a Whore.   *Title of Play*

LENA GUILBERT FORD d. 1916?

4 Keep the home fires burning, while your hearts are yearning,
Though your lads are far away they dream of home;
There's a silver lining through the dark cloud shining:
Turn the dark cloud inside out, till the boys come home.

> *Keep the Home Fires Burning*

HOWELL FORGY 1908–

5 Praise the Lord, and pass the ammunition.

> *Attr. when a Naval Lt., at Pearl Harbour, 7 Dec. 1941*

E. M. FORSTER 1879–

6 Only connect.   *Howard's End, ch. xxii*

VENANTIUS FORTUNATUS
c. 535–c. 600

7 Vexilla regis prodeunt
Fulget crucis mysterium.

The royal banners forward go
The cross shines forth in mystic glow.

> *Durham Rituale. Trans. by J. M. Neale*

STEPHEN COLLINS FOSTER
1826–1864

8 I come down dah wid my hat caved in,
Doodah! doodah!
I go back home wid a pocket full of tin,
Oh! doodah day!

Gwine to run all night!
Gwine to run all day!
I'll bet my money on de bob-tail nag,
Somebody bet on de bay.

> *Camptown Races*

9 De blind hoss stick'n in a big mud hole,
Doodah! doodah!
Can't touch de bottom wid a ten-foot pole,
Oh! doodah day!   *Ib.*

10 Weep no more, my lady,
Oh! weep no more to-day!
We will sing one song for the old Kentucky Home,
For the old Kentucky Home far away.   *My Old Kentucky Home*

11 'Way down upon de Swanee Ribber,
Far, far away,
Dere's where my heart is turning ebber:
Dere's where de old folks stay.
All up and down de whole creation
Sadly I roam,
Still longing for de old plantation,
And for de old folks at home.

> *Old Folks at Home (Swanee Ribber)*

12 I'm coming, I'm coming,
For my head is bending low,
I hear their gentle voices calling
'Poor old Joe.'   *Poor Old Joe*

13 He had no wool on de top of his head,
In de place where de wool ought to grow.   *Uncle Ned*

14 Dere's no more hard work for poor old Ned,
He's gone whar de good niggers go.
                                          Ib.

15 I dream of Jeanie with the light brown hair.

> *Jeanie With the Light Brown Hair*

16 Beautiful Dreamer   *Song Title*

CHARLES JAMES FOX 1749–1806

17 How much the greatest event it is that ever happened in the world! and how much the best!

> *On the Fall of the Bastille. Letter to Fitzpatrick, 30 July 1789. Russell's Life and Times of C. J. Fox, vol. ii, p. 361*

FRANÇOIS IER 1494–1547

18 Tout est perdu fors l'honneur.

All is lost save honour.

> *Traditional words in a letter to his mother after his defeat at Pavia, 1525. The actual words were: 'De toutes choses ne m'est demeuré que l'honneur et la vie qui est saulve.' Collection des Documents Inédits sur l'Histoire de France, vol. i (1847), p. 129*

BENJAMIN FRANKLIN 1706–1790

1 Remember, that time is money.
*Advice to Young Tradesman,
1748. Writings,* vol. ii.

2 No nation was ever ruined by trade.
*Essays. Thoughts on Commercial
Subjects*

3 There never was a good war, or a bad
peace. *Letter to Quincy, 11 Sept. 1783*

4 But in this world nothing can be said
to be certain, except death and taxes.
*Letter to Jean Baptiste Le Roy,
13 Nov. 1789. Writings,* vol. x

5 A little neglect may breed mischief,
. . . for want of a nail, the shoe was
lost; for want of a shoe the horse was
lost; and for want of a horse the rider
was lost.
Maxims . . . Prefixed to Poor
Richard's Almanac *(1758)*

6 We must indeed all hang together, or,
most assuredly, we shall all hang
separately.
*Remark to John Hancock, at
Signing of the Declaration of Independence, 4 July 1776*

FREDERICK THE GREAT
1712–1786

7 Ihr Racker, wollt ihr ewig leben?
Rascals, would you live for ever?
*When the Guards hesitated, at
Kolin, 18 June 1757*

JOHN HOOKHAM FRERE
1769–1846

8 The feather'd race with pinions skim
the air—
Not so the mackerel, and still less the
bear!
Progress of Man, l. 34. *Poetry
of the Anti-Jacobin (1799)*

ROBERT FROST 1875–1963

9 My apple trees will never get across
And eat the cones under his pines,
I tell him.
He only says, 'Good fences make
good neighbours.'
North of Boston. Mending Wall

JAMES ANTHONY FROUDE
1818–1894

10 Wild animals never kill for sport.
Man is the only one to whom the
torture and death of his fellow-
creatures is amusing in itself.
Oceana, ch. 5

THOMAS FULLER 1608–1661

11 Worldly wealth he cared not for, desiring only to make both ends meet.
[Of Edmund Grindall.]
*Worthies of England. Worthies
of Cumberland*

ROSE FYLEMAN 1877–1957

12 There are fairies at the bottom of our
garden. *Fairies and Chimneys. Fairies*

THOMAS GAINSBOROUGH
1727–1788

13 We are all going to heaven, and Vandyke is of the company.
Attr. Last Words. Boulton, *Thomas Gainsborough,* ch. 9

GAIUS *fl. c.* 110–*c.* 180

14 Damnosa hereditas.
Ruinous inheritance.   *Inst.* ii. 163

GALILEO GALILEI 1564–1642

15 E pur si muove.
But it does move.
*Attr. to Galileo after his recan-
tation in 1632. The Earliest
appearance of the phrase is 1761
(see E. R. Hull,* Galileo), *and it
is generally conceded to be apocryphal.*

SIR GREGORY GANDER
[GEORGE ELLIS] 1745–1815

16 Snowy, Flowy, Blowy,
Showery, Flowery, Bowery,
Hoppy, Croppy, Droppy,
Breezy, Sneezy, Freezy.
The Twelve Months

AUGUSTUS P. GARDNER
1865–1918

17 Wake up, America.
Speech, 16 Oct. 1916

DAVID GARRICK 1717–1779

18 Come, cheer up, my lads! 'tis to glory
we steer,
To add something more to this
wonderful year;
To honour we call you, not press you
like slaves,
For who are so free as the sons of the
waves?
Heart of oak are our ships,
Heart of oak are our men:
We always are ready;
Steady, boys, steady;
We'll fight and we'll conquer again
and again.   *Heart of Oak*

1 Here lies Nolly Goldsmith, for shortness call'd Noll,
Who wrote like an angel, but talk'd
like poor Poll.
Impromptu Epitaph

2 A fellow-feeling makes one wond'rous
kind.
*An Occasional Prologue on Quit-
ting the Theatre, 10 June 1776*

WILLIAM LLOYD GARRISON
1805–1879

3 I am in earnest—I will not equivocate
—I will not excuse—I will not retreat
a single inch—and I will be heard!
*Salutatory Address of The Libera-
tor, 1 Jan. 1831*

SIR SAMUEL GARTH 1661–1719

4 A barren superfluity of words.
The Dispensary, c. 2, l. 95

ELIZABETH CLEGHORN
GASKELL 1810–1865

5 Get her a flannel waistcoat and flannel
drawers, ma'am, if you wish to keep
her alive. But my advice is, kill the
poor creature at once. [*Capt. Brown on
Miss Betsey Barker's cow.*]
Cranford, ch. 1

GAVARNI 1801–1866

6 Les enfants terribles.
The embarrassing young.
Title of a series of prints

JOHN GAY 1685–1732

7   I rage, I melt, I burn,
The feeble God has stabb'd me to the
heart.   *Acis and Galatea, ii*

8 O ruddier than the cherry,
O sweeter than the berry.   *Ib.*

9 Do you think your mother and I
should have liv'd comfortably so long
together, if ever we had been married?
*The Beggar's Opera, Act I, sc.
viii, air vii*

10 O Polly, you might have toy'd and
kist,
By keeping men off, you keep them
on.   *Ib. air ix*

11 Well, Polly; as far as one woman can
forgive another, I forgive thee.
Ib.

12 The comfortable estate of widowhood,
is the only hope that keeps up a wife's
spirits.   *Ib. x*

13 Away, hussy. Hang your husband and
be dutiful.   *Ib. xii*

14 I sipt each flower,
I chang'd ev'ry hour,
But here ev'ry flower is united
*The Beggar's Opera, Act I, sc.
xiii, air xv*

15 If with me you'd fondly stray
Over the hills and far away. *Ib. air xvi*

16 O what pain it is to part!   *Ib. air xvii*

17 Fill ev'ry glass, for wine inspires us,
And fires us
With courage, love and joy.
Women and wine should life employ.
Is there aught else on earth desirous?
Ib. II, ii, air xix

18 If the heart of a man is deprest with
cares,
The mist is dispell'd when a woman
appears.   *Ib. iii, air xxi*

19 Youth's the season made for joys,
Love is then our duty.
Ib. iv, air xxii

20 So he that tastes woman, woman,
woman,
He that tastes woman, ruin meets.
Ib. viii, air xxvi

21 How happy could I be with either,
Were t'other dear charmer away!
But while ye thus tease me together,
To neither a word will I say.
Ib. xiii, air xxxv

22 She who has never lov'd, has never
liv'd.   *The Captives, II. i*

23 If e'er your heart has felt the tender
passion
You will forgive this just, this pious
fraud.   *Ib. IV. x*

24 Behold the bright original appear.
Epistle to a Lady, l. 85

25 One always zealous for his country's
good.   *Ib. l. 118*

26 Life is a jest; and all things show it.
I thought so once; but now I know it.
My Own Epitaph

27 Whence is thy learning? Hath thy toil
O'er books consum'd the midnight
oil?
Fables. Series 1, introduction, l. 15

28 Where there is life, there's hope, he
cried,
Then why such haste? so groan'd and
died.
*Ib. xxvii. The Sick Man and the
Angel, l. 49*

29 And when a lady's in the case,
You know, all other things give place.
*Ib. l. The Hare and Many Friends,
l. 41*

30 All in the Downs the fleet was moor'd,
The streamers waving in the wind,
When black-ey'd Susan came aboard.
*Sweet William's Farewell to Black-
Ey'd Susan*

1 They'll tell thee, sailors, when away,
In ev'ry port a mistress find.
Sweet William's Farewell to Black-Eyed Susan

SIR ERIC GEDDES 1875–1937

2 We will get everything out of her [Germany] that you can squeeze out of a lemon and a bit more. . . . I will squeeze her until you can hear the pips squeak.
Speech at the Drill Hall, Cambridge, 9 Dec. 1918

DAVID LLOYD GEORGE, EARL OF DWYFOR 1863–1945

3 What is our task? To make Britain a fit country for heroes to live in.
Speech, Wolverhampton, 24 Nov. 1918

GEORGE I OF GREAT BRITAIN 1660–1727

4 I hate all Boets and Bainters.
Campbell, *Lives of the Chief Justices*, ch. 30, Lord Mansfield

GEORGE II OF GREAT BRITAIN 1683–1760

5 Non, j'aurai des maîtresses.

No, I shall have mistresses.
Reply to Queen Caroline when, as she lay dying, she urged him to marry again. Her reply to this was 'Ah! mon Dieu! cela n'empêche pas'. Hervey, Memoirs of George the Second (1848), vol. ii.

6 Oh! he is mad, is he? Then I wish he would *bite* some other of my generals.
Reply to one who complained that General Wolfe was a madman. F. Thackeray, History of William Pitt, vol. i, ch. 15, note

GEORGE III OF GREAT BRITAIN 1738–1820

7 Born and educated in this country I glory in the name of Briton.
Speech from the Throne, 1760

8 'Was there ever', cried he, 'such stuff as great part of Shakespeare? Only one must not say so! But what think you?—what?—Is there not sad stuff? what?—what?
To Fanny Burney (in her Diary, 19 Dec. 1785)

GEORGE V OF GREAT BRITAIN 1865–1936

9 Wake up, England.
Title of a reprint in 1911 of a speech made by the King when Prince of Wales in the Guildhall on 5 Dec. 1901 on his return from a tour of the Empire

EDWARD GIBBON 1737–1794

10 I sighed as a lover, I obeyed as a son.
Autobiography (World's Classics ed.), p. 83

11 Crowds without company, and dissipation without pleasure.   *Ib.* p. 90

12 It was at Rome, on the 15th of October, 1764, as I sat musing amidst the ruins of the Capitol, while the barefoot friars were singing vespers in the Temple of Jupiter, that the idea of writing the decline and fall of the city first started to my mind.
Ib. p. 160

13 My English text is chaste, and all licentious passages are left in the decent obscurity of a learned language.
Ib. p. 212

14 Titus Antoninus Pius. . . . His reign is marked by the rare advantage of furnishing very few materials for history; which is, indeed, little more than the register of the crimes, follies, and misfortunes of mankind.
Decline and Fall of the Roman Empire, ch. 3

STELLA GIBBONS 1902–

15 Something nasty in the woodshed.
Cold Comfort Farm, passim

FRED GILBERT 1850–1903

16 At Trinity Church I met my doom.
Title of Song

17 As I walk along the Bois Bou-long,
With an independent air,
You can hear the girls declare,
'He must be a millionaire';
You can hear them sigh and wish to die,
You can see them wink the other eye
At the man who broke the Bank at Monte Carlo.
The Man Who Broke the Bank at Monte Carlo

SIR HUMPHREY GILBERT 1539?–1583

18 We are as near to heaven by sea as by land!
Hakluyt's Voyages, iii (1600), p. 159

SIR WILLIAM SCHWENCK GILBERT 1836–1911

19 He had often eaten oysters, but had never had enough.
The Bab Ballads. Etiquette

20 The padre said, 'Whatever have you been and gone and done?'
Ib. Gentle Alice Brown

1 Which is pretty, but I don't know
what it means. *The Bab Ballads.*
The Story of Prince Agib

2 Then they began to sing
That extremely lovely thing,
'*Scherzando! ma non troppo ppp.*' *Ib.*

3 Oh, I am a cook and a captain bold,
And the mate of the *Nancy* brig,
And a bo'sun tight, and a midshipmite,
And the crew of the captain's gig.
Ib. The Yarn of the 'Nancy Bell'

4 In all the woes that curse our race
There is a lady in the case.
Fallen Fairies, II

5 He led his regiment from behind—
He found it less exciting.
The Gondoliers, I

6 That celebrated,
Cultivated,
Underrated
Nobleman,
The Duke of Plaza Toro! *Ib.*

7 Of that there is no manner of doubt—
No probable, possible shadow of
doubt—
No possible doubt whatever. *Ib.*

8 Oh, 'tis a glorious thing, I ween,
To be a regular Royal Queen!
No half-and-half affair, I mean,
But a right-down regular Royal
Queen! *Ib.*

9 All shall equal be.
The Earl, the Marquis, and the Dook,
The Groom, the Butler, and the Cook,
The Aristocrat who banks with Coutts,
The Aristocrat who cleans the boots.
Ib.

10 But the privilege and pleasure
That we treasure beyond measure
Is to run on little errands for the
Ministers of State. *Ib.* II

11 With the gratifying feeling that our
duty has been done! *Ib.*

12 Take a pair of sparkling eyes. *Ib.*

13 Dukes were three a penny. *Ib.*

14 When every one is somebodee,
Then no one's anybody. *Ib.*

15 For I'm to be married to-day—
to-day—
Yes, I'm to be married to-day!
Iolanthe, I

16 Bow, bow, ye lower middle classes!
Bow, bow, ye tradesmen, bow, ye
masses. *Ib.*

17 The Law is the true embodiment
Of everything that's excellent.
It has no kind of fault or flaw,
And I, my Lords, embody the Law.
Ib.

18 A pleasant occupation for
A rather susceptible Chancellor! *Ib.*

19 Hearts just as pure and fair
May beat in Belgrave Square
As in the lowly air
Of Seven Dials. *Iolanthe*

20 When I went to the Bar as a very
young man,
(Said I to myself, said I). *Ib.*

21 I often think it's comical
How Nature always does contrive
That every boy and every gal,
That's born into the world alive,
Is either a little Liberal,
Or else a little Conservative! *Ib.*

22 The House of Peers, throughout the
war,
Did nothing in particular,
And did it very well:
Yet Britain set the world ablaze
In good King George's glorious days!
Ib.

23 When you're lying awake with a dismal headache, and repose is taboo'd
by anxiety,
I conceive you may use any language
you choose to indulge in, without
impropriety. *Ib.*

24 For you dream you are crossing the
Channel, and tossing about in a
steamer from Harwich—
Which is something between a large
bathing machine and a very small
second class carriage. *Ib.*

25 And you're giving a treat (penny ice
and cold meat) to a party of friends
and relations—
They're a ravenous horde—and they
all came on board at Sloane Square
and South Kensington Stations.
And bound on that journey you find
your attorney (who started that
morning from Devon);
He's a bit undersized, and you don't
feel surprised when he tells you he's
only eleven. *Ib.*

26 Faint heart never won fair lady!
Nothing venture, nothing win—
Blood is thick, but water's thin—
In for a penny, in for a pound—
It's Love that makes the world go
round! *Ib.*

27 A wandering minstrel I—
A thing of shreds and patches,
Of ballads, songs and snatches,
And dreamy lullaby! *The Mikado,* I

28 I can trace my ancestry back to a
protoplasmal primordial atomic globule. Consequently, my family pride
is something in-conceivable. I can't
help it. I was born sneering. *Ib.*

29 It revolts me, but I do it! *Ib.*

30 As some day it may happen that a
victim must be found,
I've got a little list—I've got a little
list

Of society offenders who might well
be under ground
And who never would be missed—
who never would be missed!
The Mikado, I

1 The idiot who praises, with enthusiastic tone,
All centuries but this, and every
country but his own. *Ib.*

2 Three little maids from school are we,
Pert as a schoolgirl well can be,
Filled to the brim with girlish glee.
Ib.

3 Three little maids who, all unwary,
Come from a ladies' seminary. *Ib.*

4 Modified rapture! *Ib.*

5 Awaiting the sensation of a short,
sharp shock,
From a cheap and chippy chopper on
a big black block. *Ib.*

6 For he's going to marry Yum-Yum—
Yum-Yum. *Ib.*

7 Here's a how-de-doo! *Ib.*

8 My object all sublime
I shall achieve in time—
To let the punishment fit the crime—
The punishment fit the crime. *Ib.* II

9 The billiard sharp whom any one
catches,
His doom's extremely hard—
He's made to dwell—
In a dungeon cell
On a spot that's always barred.
And there he plays extravagant
matches
In fitless finger-stalls
On a cloth untrue
With a twisted cue
And elliptical billiard balls. *Ib.*

10 I drew my snickersnee! *Ib.*

11 I have a left shoulder-blade that is
a miracle of loveliness. People come
miles to see it. My right elbow has a
fascination that few can resist. *Ib.*

12 Something lingering, with boiling oil
in it, I fancy. *Ib.*

13 Merely corroborative detail, intended
to give artistic verisimilitude to an
otherwise bald and unconvincing
narrative. *Ib.*

14 The flowers that bloom in the spring,
Tra la,
Have nothing to do with the case.
Ib.

15 I've got to take under my wing,
Tra la,
A most unattractive old thing,
Tra la,
With a caricature of a face.
And that's what I mean when I say,
or I sing,
'Oh bother the flowers that bloom in
the spring.' *Ib.*

16 On a tree by a river a little tom-tit
Sang 'Willow, titwillow, titwillow!'
And I said to him, 'Dicky-bird, why
do you sit
Singing 'Willow, titwillow, titwillow?'
The Mikado, II

17 'Is it weakness of intellect, birdie?'
I cried,
'Or a rather tough worm in your little
inside?'
With a shake of his poor little head
he replied,
'Oh, willow, titwillow, titwillow!'
Ib.

18 Twenty love-sick maidens we,
Love-sick all against our will.
Patience, I

19 When I first put this uniform on. *Ib.*

20 If you're anxious for to shine in the
high aesthetic line as a man of
culture rare. *Ib.*

21 You must lie upon the daisies and
discourse in novel phrases of your
complicated state of mind,
The meaning doesn't matter if it's
only idle chatter of a transcendental
kind.
And everyone will say,
As you walk your mystic way,
'If this young man expresses himself
in terms too deep for *me*,
Why, what a very singularly deep
young man this deep young man
must be!' *Ib.*

22 Then a sentimental passion of a vegetable fashion must excite your
languid spleen,
An attachment à la Plato for a bashful young potato, or a not too
French French bean!
Though the Philistines may jostle, you
will rank as an apostle in the high
aesthetic band,
If you walk down Piccadilly with a
poppy or a lily in your medieval
hand.
And everyone will say,
As you walk your flowery way,
'If he's content with a vegetable love
which would certainly not suit *me*,
Why, what a most particularly pure
young man this pure young man
must be!' *Ib.*

23 Prithee, pretty maiden—prithee, tell
me true. *Ib.*

24 Prithee, pretty maiden, will you
marry me?
(Hey, but I'm hopeful, willow, willow,
waly!)
I may say, at once, I'm a man of
propertee—
Hey willow waly O!
Money, I despise it;
Many people prize it,
Hey willow waly O! *Ib.*

1 There will be too much of me
In the coming by and by! *Patience*, II

2 Sing 'Hey to you—good day to you'—
Sing 'Bah to you—ha! ha! to you'—
Sing 'Booh to you—pooh, pooh to
you.'   *Ib.*

3 Francesca di Rimini, miminy, piminy,
Je-ne-sais-quoi young man!   *Ib.*

4 A greenery-yallery, Grosvenor Gallery,
Foot-in-the-grave young man!   *Ib.*

5 I'm called Little Buttercup—dear
Little Buttercup,
Though I could never tell why.
H.M.S. Pinafore, I

6 I am the Captain of the *Pinafore*;
And a right good captain too!   *Ib.*

7 And I'm never, never sick at sea!
What, never?
No, never!
What, *never?*
Hardly ever!
He's hardly ever sick at sea!
Then's give three cheers, and one cheer
more,
For the hardy Captain of the *Pinafore!*
Ib.

8 I never use a big, big D.   *Ib.*

9 And so do his sisters, and his cousins
and his aunts!
His sisters and his cousins,
Whom he reckons up by dozens,
And his aunts!   *Ib.*

10 When I was a lad I served a term
As office boy to an Attorney's firm.
I cleaned the windows and I swept the
floor,
And I polished up the handle of the
big front door.
I polished up that handle so care-
fullee
That now I am the Ruler of the
Queen's Navee!   *Ib.*

11 Stick close to your desks and never
go to sea,
And you all may be Rulers of the
Queen's Navee!   *Ib.*

12 It was the cat!   *Ib.* II

13 He is an Englishman!
For he himself has said it,
And it's greatly to his credit,
That he is an Englishman!   *Ib.*

14 For he might have been a Roosian,
A French, or Turk, or Proosian,
Or perhaps Ital-ian!
But in spite of all temptations
To belong to other nations,
He remains an Englishman!   *Ib.*

15 The other, upper crust,
A regular patrician.   *Ib.*

16 It is, it is a glorious thing
To be a Pirate King.
Pirates of Penzance, I

17 Poor wandering one!
Though thou hast surely strayed,
Take heart of grace,
Thy steps retrace,
Poor wandering one!
Pirates of Penzance, I

18 I am the very model of a modern
Major-General.   *Ib.*

19 I'm very good at integral and differential calculus;
I know the scientific names of beings
animalculous.   *Ib.*

20 When the foeman bares his steel,
Tarantara, tarantara!
We uncomfortable feel,
Tarantara.   *Ib.* II

21 When constabulary duty's to be done,
The policeman's lot is not a happy one.
Ib.

22 When the enterprising burglar's not
a-burgling.   *Ib.*

23 When the coster's finished jumping on
his mother—
He loves to lie a-basking in the sun.
Ib.

24 You must stir it and stump it,
And blow your own trumpet,
Or trust me, you haven't a chance.
Ruddigore, I

25 He combines the manners of a Marquis
with the morals of a Methodist.   *Ib.*

26 When he's excited he uses language
that would make your hair curl.   *Ib.*

27 Desperate deeds of derring do. *Ib.* II

28 Some word that teems with hidden
meaning—like Basingstoke.   *Ib.*

29 This particularly rapid, unintelligible
patter
Isn't generally heard, and if it is it
doesn't matter.   *Ib.*

30 I was a pale young curate then.
The Sorcerer, I

31 Oh! My name is John Wellington
Wells,
I'm a dealer in magic and spells.   *Ib.*

32 If anyone anything lacks,
He'll find it all ready in stacks,
If he'll only look in
On the resident Djinn,
Number seventy, Simmery Axe!   *Ib.*

33 So I fell in love with a rich attorney's
Elderly ugly daughter.
Trial by Jury

34 She may very well pass for forty-three
In the dusk with a light behind her!
Ib.

35 For now I am a Judge
And a good Judge too.   *Ib.*

36 'Tis ever thus with simple folk—an
accepted wit has but to say 'Pass the
mustard', and they roar their ribs
out!   *The Yeomen of the Guard*

JAMES GILLRAY 1757–1815

1 Political Ravishment, or, The Old
Lady of Threadneedle Street in
Danger.   *Title of Caricature, 1797*

WILLIAM EWART GLADSTONE
1809–1898

2 You cannot fight against the future.
Time is on our side.
Speech on the Reform Bill, 1866

3 [The Turks] one and all, bag and
baggage, shall, I hope, clear out from
the province they have desolated and
profaned.
Speech,   House   of   Commons,
7 May 1877

4 Out of the range of practical politics.
Ib. at Dalkeith, 26 Nov. 1879

5 All the world over, I will back the
masses against the classes.
Ib. Liverpool, 28 June 1886

HANNAH GLASSE *fl.* 1747

6 Take your hare when it is cased. . . .
Art of Cookery
Usually misquoted as 'First catch
your hare'.

WILLIAM HENRY, DUKE OF
GLOUCESTER 1743–1805

7 Another damned, thick, square book!
Always scribble, scribble, scribble!
Eh! Mr. Gibbon?
Best's Literary Memorials. (Bos-
well's *Johnson,* vol. ii, p. 2, n.)

JOHN A. GLOVER-KINDE d. 1918

8 I Do Like To Be Beside the Seaside.
Title of Song (1909)

ALFRED DENIS GODLEY
1856–1925

9 What is this that roareth thus?
Can it be a Motor Bus?
Yes, the smell and hideous hum
Indicat Motorem Bum

How shall wretches live like us
Cincti Bis Motoribus?
Domine, defende nos
Contra hos Motores Bos!
The   Motor   Bus.   Letter   to
C.R.L.F., 10 Jan. 1914

WILLIAM GODWIN 1756–1836

10 The log was burning brightly,
'Twas a night that should banish all
sin,
For the bells were ringing the Old
Year out,
And the New Year in.
The Miner's Dream of Home

JOSEF GOEBBELS 1897–1945

11 Wenn das deutsche Volk die Waffen
niederlegte, würden die Sowjets, auch
nach den Abmachungen zwischen
Roosevelt, Churchill und Stalin, ganz
Ost- und Südosteuropa zuzüglich des
grössten Teiles des Reiches besetzen.
Vor diesem einschliesslich der Sowjet-
union riesigen Territorium würde sich
sofort ein eiserner Vorhang herunter-
senken.

Should the German people lay down
its arms, the agreement between
Roosevelt, Churchill and Stalin
would allow the Soviets to occupy
all Eastern and South-eastern
Europe together with the major
part of the Reich. An iron curtain would at once descend on
this territory which, including
the Soviet Union, would be of
enormous dimensions.
Das Reich, 25 February 1945.
Cf. Mrs. Philip Snowden, *Through*
Bolshevik Russia (1920), ii, p. 32.
We were behind the 'iron curtain'
at last!
See also 63:5 and 234:5

HERMANN GOERING 1893–1946

12 Guns will make us powerful; butter
will only make us fat.
Radio Broadcast, summer of 1936
See also Hanns Johst

JOHANN WOLFGANG VON
GOETHE 1749–1832

13 Meine Ruh' ist hin,
Mein Herz ist schwer.
My peace is gone,
My heart is heavy.
Faust, pt. i. Gretchen am Spinnrad

14 Die Tat ist alles, nicht der Ruhm.
The deed is everything, its repute
nothing.   *Ib. pt. ii. Großer Vorhof*

15 Über allen Gipfeln
Ist Ruh'.
Over all the mountain tops is peace.
Wanderers Nachtlied

16 Kennst du das Land, wo die Zitronen
blühn?
Im dunkeln Laub die Gold-Orangen
glühn,
Ein sanfter Wind vom blauen Himmel
weht,
Die Myrte still und hoch der Lorbeer
steht —
Kennst du es wohl?
Dahin! Dahin!
Möcht ich mit dir, o mein Geliebter,
ziehn!
Know you the land where the
lemon-trees bloom? In the dark

foliage the gold oranges glow; a soft wind hovers from the sky, the myrtle is still and the laurel stands tall—do you know it well? There, there, I would go, O my beloved, with thee!
Wilhelm Meisters Lehrjahre, III. i

1 Mehr Licht!

More light!
Attr. dying words. (Actually: 'Macht doch den zweiten Fensterladen auch auf, damit mehr Licht hereinkomme': 'Open the second shutter, so that more light can come in.')

OLIVER GOLDSMITH 1728–1774

2 For he who fights and runs away
    May live to fight another day;
But he who is in battle slain
    Can never rise and fight again.
        Art of Poetry on a New Plan.
        Written by Newbery, revised
        by Goldsmith

3 Sweet Auburn! loveliest village of the plain.   *The Deserted Village*, l. 1

4 Ill fares the land, to hast'ning ills a prey,
Where wealth accumulates, and men decay;
Princes and lords may flourish, or may fade;
A breath can make them, as a breath has made;
But a bold peasantry, their country's pride,
When once destroy'd, can never be supplied.   *Ib.* l. 51

5 The watchdog's voice that bay'd the whisp'ring wind,
And the loud laugh that spoke the vacant mind.   *Ib.* l. 121

6 A man he was to all the country dear,
And passing rich with forty pounds a year;   *Ib.* l. 141

7 Truth from his lips prevail'd with double sway,
And fools, who came to scoff, remain'd to pray.   *Ib.* l. 179

8 In arguing too, the parson own'd his skill,
For e'en though vanquish'd, he could argue still;

And still they gaz'd, and still the wonder grew,
That one small head could carry all he knew.   *Ib.* l. 211

9 Man wants but little here below,
    Nor wants that little long.
        Edwin and Angelina, or The Hermit

10 Good people all, of every sort,
    Give ear unto my song;
And if you find it wond'rous short,
    It cannot hold you long.
        Elegy on the Death of a Mad Dog

11 That still a godly race he ran,
    Whene'er he went to pray.   *Ib.*

12 The naked every day he clad,
    When he put on his clothes.   *Ib.*

13 And in that town a dog was found,
    As many dogs there be,
Both mongrel, puppy, whelp, and hound,
    And curs of low degree.   *Ib.*

14 The dog, to gain some private ends,
    Went mad and bit the man.   *Ib.*

15 And swore the dog had lost his wits,
    To bite so good a man.   *Ib.*

16 The man recover'd of the bite,
    The dog it was that died.   *Ib.*

17 Who, born for the Universe, narrow'd his mind,
And to party gave up what was meant for mankind.
        [Edmund Burke] *Retaliation*, l. 31

18 Who, too deep for his hearers, still went on refining,
And thought of convincing, while they thought of dining.
        [Edmund Burke] *Ib.* l. 35

19 When they talk'd of their Raphaels, Correggios, and stuff,
He shifted his trumpet, and only took snuff.   [Reynolds] *Ib.* l. 145

20 Let schoolmasters puzzle their brain,
    With grammar, and nonsense, and learning,
Good liquor, I stoutly maintain,
    Gives genius a better discerning.
        She Stoops to Conquer, I. i, song

21 When lovely woman stoops to folly
    And finds too late that men betray,
What charm can soothe her melancholy,
    What art can wash her guilt away?
The only art her guilt to cover,
    To hide her shame from every eye,
To give repentance to her lover.
    And wring his bosom—is to die.
        Song. From *The Vicar of Wakefield*, ch. 29

22 I'm now no more than a mere lodger in my own house.
        The Good-Natured Man, I

23 She stoops to conquer.   *Title of play*

24 I love everything that's old; old friends, old times, old manners, old books, old wines.
        She Stoops to Conquer, I

25 The very pink of perfection.   *Ib.*

26 This is Liberty-Hall, gentlemen.   *Ib.* II

1 As for murmurs, mother, we grumble
a little now and then, to be sure. But
there's no love lost between us.
She Stoops to Conquer, IV

2 By the living jingo, she was all of a
muck of sweat.
The Vicar of Wakefield, ch. 9

3 There is no arguing with Johnson; for
when his pistol misses fire, he knocks
you down with the butt end of it.
Remark. Boswell's *Life of Johnson, 26 Oct. 1769*

4 [To Johnson who was laughing when
he said that the little fishes in a
proposed fable should talk like little
fishes.]
Why, Dr. Johnson, this is not so
easy as you seem to think; for if
you were to make little fishes
talk, they would talk like whales.
Ib. 27 Apr. 1773

SAMUEL GOLDWYN 1882–

5 In two words: im-possible.
Quoted in Alva Johnson, *The
Great Goldwyn*

ADAM LINDSAY GORDON
1833–1870

6 Life is mostly froth and bubble,
Two things stand like stone,
Kindness in another's trouble,
Courage in your own.
Ye Wearie Wayfarer, Fytte 8

GEORGE JOACHIM, FIRST
VISCOUNT GOSCHEN 1831–1907

7 We have stood alone in that which is
called isolation—our splendid isolation, as one of our colonial friends
was good enough to call it. [See G. E.
Foster.]
Speech at Lewes, 26 Feb. 1896

RICHARD GRAFTON ?–1572?

8 Thirty days hath November,
April, June, and September,
February hath twenty-eight alone,
And all the rest have thirty-one.
*Abridgement of the Chronicles of
England* (1570), introductory
matter, sig. 1 ¶ j. b

HARRY GRAHAM 1874–1936

9 Auntie, did you feel no pain
Falling from that willow-tree?
Would you do it, please, again?
Cos my friend here didn't see.
*Ruthless Rhymes for Heartless
Homes. Appreciation*

10 O'er the rugged mountain's brow
Clara threw the twins she nursed,
And remarked, 'I wonder now
Which will reach the bottom first?'
*Ruthless Rhymes for Heartless Homes.
Calculating Clara*

11 Aunt Jane observed, the second time
She tumbled off a bus,
The step is short from the Sublime
To the Ridiculous. *Ib. Equanimity*

12 'There's been an accident!' they said,
'Your servant's cut in half; he's dead!'
'Indeed!' said Mr. Jones, 'and please
Send me the half that's got my keys.'
Ib. Mr. Jones

13 Billy, in one of his nice new sashes,
Fell in the fire and was burnt to ashes;
Now, although the room grows chilly,
I haven't the heart to poke poor Billy.
Ib. Tender-Heartedness

14 When Baby's cries grew hard to bear
I popped him in the Frigidaire.
I never would have done so if
I'd known that he'd be frozen stiff.
My wife said: 'George, I'm so unhappé!
Our darling's now completely frappé!
*More Ruthless Rhymes. L'Enfant
Glacé*

15 When Mrs. Gorm (Aunt Eloise)
Was stung to death by savage bees,
Her husband (Prebendary Gorm)
Put on his veil and took the swarm.
He's publishing a book, next May,
On 'How to Make Bee-keeping Pay'.
Ib. Opportunity

KENNETH GRAHAME 1859–1932

16 Believe me, my young friend, there is
nothing—absolutely nothing—half so
much worth doing as simply messing
about in boats.
The Wind in the Willows, ch. 1

17 The clever men at Oxford
Know all that there is to be
knowed.
But they none of them know one half
as much
As intelligent Mr. Toad. *Ib. ch. x*

SIR ROBERT GRANT 1779–1838

18 The Ancient of Days,
Pavilioned in splendour,
And girded with praise.
Bickersteth's *Church Psalmody.
O Worship the King*

19 His chariots of wrath The deep
thunder clouds form,
And dark is his path On the wings of
the storm. *Ib.*

20 Frail children of dust,
And feeble as frail. *Ib.*

ULYSSES SIMPSON GRANT
1822–1885

1 No terms except unconditional and immediate surrender can be accepted. I propose to move immediately upon your works.
To Simon Bolivar Buckner, whom he was besieging in Fort Donelson, 16 Feb. 1862

JOHN WOODCOCK GRAVES
1795–1886

2 D'ye ken John Peel with his coat so gray?
D'ye ken John Peel at the break of day?
D'ye ken John Peel when he's far far away
With his hounds and his horn in the morning?
'Twas the sound of his horn called me from my bed,
And the cry of his hounds has me oft-times led;
For Peel's view-hollo would waken the dead,
Or a fox from his lair in the morning.
John Peel

ROBERT GRAVES 1895–

3 Goodbye to all that. *Title of book*

THOMAS GRAY 1716–1771

4 Ruin seize thee, ruthless King!
Confusion on thy banners wait,
Tho' fann'd by Conquest's crimson wing
They mock the air with idle state.
The Bard, I. i

5 Weave the warp, and weave the woof,
The winding-sheet of Edward's race.
Give ample room, and verge enough
The characters of hell to trace.
Ib. II. i

6 Youth on the prow, and Pleasure at the helm; *Ib. ii*

7 Ye towers of Julius, London's lasting shame,
With many a foul and midnight murther fed. *Ib. iii*

8 The curfew tolls the knell of parting day,
The lowing herd wind slowly o'er the lea,
The ploughman homeward plods his weary way,
And leaves the world to darkness and to me.
Now fades the glimmering landscape on the sight,
And all the air a solemn stillness holds,

Save where the beetle wheels his droning flight,
And drowsy tinklings lull the distant folds.
Elegy Written in a Country Churchyard, i–ii

9 Save that from yonder ivy-mantled tow'r,
The moping owl does to the moon complain. *Ib. iii*

10 Each in his narrow cell for ever laid,
The rude forefathers of the hamlet sleep. *Ib. iv*

11 The breezy call of incense-breathing Morn,
The swallow twitt'ring from the straw-built shed,
The cock's shrill clarion, or the echoing horn,
No more shall rouse them from their lowly bed. *Ib. v*

12 Let not ambition mock their useful toil,
Their homely joys, and destiny obscure;
Nor grandeur hear with a disdainful smile,
The short and simple annals of the poor.
The boast of heraldry, the pomp of pow'r,
And all that beauty, all that wealth e'er gave,
Awaits alike th' inevitable hour,
The paths of glory lead but to the grave. *Ib. viii–ix*

13 Can storied urn or animated bust
Back to its mansion call the fleeting breath?
Can honour's voice provoke the silent dust,
Or flatt'ry soothe the dull cold ear of death? *Ib. xi*

14 Hands, that the rod of empire might have sway'd,
Or wak'd to ecstasy the living lyre. *Ib. xii*

15 Full many a gem of purest ray serene,
The dark unfathom'd caves of ocean bear:
Full many a flower is born to blush unseen,
And waste its sweetness on the desert air.
Some village-Hampden, that with dauntless breast
The little tyrant of his fields withstood;
Some mute inglorious Milton here may rest,
Some Cromwell guiltless of his country's blood. *Ib. xiv–xv*

1 Far from the madding crowd's ig-
noble strife,
Their sober wishes never learn'd to
stray;
Along the cool sequester'd vale of life
They kept the noiseless tenor of
their way.
*Elegy Written in a Country
Churchyard, xix;*

2 What female heart can gold despise?
What cat's averse to fish?
*Ode on the Death of a Favourite
Cat*

3 A fav'rite has no friend! *Ib.*

4 Not all that tempts your wand'ring
eyes
And heedless hearts, is lawful prize;
Nor all, that glisters, gold. *Ib.*

5 Ye distant spires, ye antique towers,
That crown the wat'ry glade.
*Ode on a Distant Prospect of
Eton College, l. 1*

6 Urge the flying ball. *Ib. l. 30*

7 Still as they run they look behind,
They hear a voice in every wind,
And snatch a fearful joy. *Ib. l. 38*

8 Alas regardless of their doom,
The little victims play!
No sense have they of ills to come,
Nor care beyond to-day. *Ib. l. 51*

9 To each his suff'rings: all are men,
Condemn'd alike to groan;
The tender for another's pain,
Th' unfeeling for his own. *Ib. l. 91*

10 . . . Where ignorance is bliss
'Tis folly to be wise. *Ib. l. 99*

11 He saw; but blasted with excess of
light,
Closed his eyes in endless night.
[Milton.]
The Progress of Poesy, iii. 2

ROBERT GREENE 1560?–1592

12 Friar Bacon and Friar Bungay.
Title of Play

13 For there is an upstart crow, beautified with our feathers, that with his
tiger's heart wrapped in a player's
hide, supposes he is as well able to
bumbast out a blank verse as the best
of you; and being an absolute *Iohannes
fac totum*, is in his own conceit the
only Shake-scene in a country.
*The Groatsworth of Wit Bought
with a Million of Repentance*

GREGORY I 540–604

14 Responsum est, quod Angli vocarentur. At ille: 'Bene,' inquit; 'nam et
angelicam habent faciem, et tales

angelorum in caelis decet esse co-
heredes.'
They answered that they were
called Angles. 'It is well,' he said,
'for they have the faces of angels,
and such should be the co-heirs
of the angels in heaven.'
Traditionally quoted: 'Non Angli
sed Angeli.'
Bede, Historia Ecclesiastica, ii. i

STEPHEN GRELLET 1773–1855

15 I expect to pass through this world but
once; any good thing therefore that
I can do, or any kindness that I can
show to any fellow-creature, let me
do it now; let me not defer or neglect
it, for I shall not pass this way again.
*Attr. 'Treasure Trove', collected
by John o' London, 1925.* Many
other claimants to authorship

FULKE GREVILLE, FIRST
BARON BROOKE 1554–1628

16 Fulke Greville, Servant to Queen
Elizabeth, Councillor to King James,
and Friend to Sir Philip Sidney.
*Epitaph Written for Himself, on
his Monument in Warwick*

EDWARD, VISCOUNT GREY OF
FALLODON 1862–1933

17 The lamps are going out all over
Europe; we shall not see them lit
again in our lifetime.
*3 Aug. 1914. Twenty-Five Years,
vol. ii, ch. 18*

GEORGE GROSSMITH 1847–1912
and
WALTER WEEDON GROSSMITH
1854–1919

18 I left the room with silent dignity, but
caught my foot in the mat.
The Diary of a Nobody, ch. 12

19 What's the matter with Gladstone?
He's all right. *Ib. ch. 17*

PHILIP GUEDALLA 1889–1944

20 The work of Henry James has always
seemed divisible by a simple dynastic
arrangement into three reigns:
James I, James II, and the Old Pretender.
*Collected Essays, vol. iv. Men of
Letters: Mr. Henry James*

YVETTE GUILBERT 1867–1944

21 Linger longer Lucy,
Linger longer Lou. *Song*

TEXAS GUINAN 1884–1933

1 Fifty million Frenchmen can't be wrong.
> Attr. *New York World-Telegram,*
> *21 Mar. 1931*

DOROTHY FRANCES GURNEY
1858–1932

2 The kiss of the sun for pardon,
The song of the birds for mirth,
One is nearer God's Heart in a garden
Than anywhere else on earth.
> *God's Garden*

HADRIAN A.D. 76–138

3 Animula vagula blandula,
Hospes comesque corporis,
Quae nunc abibis in loca
Pallidula rigida nudula,
Nec ut soles dabis iocos!

> Little soul, wandering, pleasant,
> guest and companion of the body,
> into what places wilt thou now
> go, pale, stiff, naked, nor wilt thou
> play any longer as thou art wont.
> Duff, *Minor Latin Poems* (Loeb,
> 1934), 445

DOUGLAS HAIG, EARL HAIG
1861–1928

4 Every position must be held to the last man: there must be no retirement. With our backs to the wall, and believing in the justice of our cause, each one of us must fight on to the end.
> *Order to the British Troops,*
> *12 Apr. 1918. The Times, 13 Apr.*

SARAH JOSEPHA HALE
1788–1879

5 Mary had a little lamb,
Its fleece was white as snow,
And everywhere that Mary went
The lamb was sure to go.

> 'What makes the lamb love Mary so?'
> The eager children cry.
> 'Oh, Mary loves the lamb, you know,'
> The teacher did reply.
> *Poems for Our Children. Mary's*
> *Little Lamb*

CHARLES SPRAGUE HALL
fl. 1860

6 John Brown's body lies a mould'ring in the grave,
His soul is marching on!
> *John Brown's Body.* Nicholas
> Smith's *Stories of Great National*
> *Songs*

BISHOP JOSEPH HALL 1574–1656

7 All his dealings are square, and above the board.
> *Virtues and Vices* (1608), bk. 1,
> p. 15

OWEN HALL [JAMES DAVIS]
d. 1907

8 Tell me, pretty maiden, are there any more at home like you?
> *Florodora,* Act II

FRIEDRICH HALM [FRANZ VON MÜNCH-BELLINGHAUSEN]
1806–1871

9 Mein Herz ich will dich fragen:
Was ist denn Liebe? Sag'!—
'Zwei Seelen und ein Gedanke,
Zwei Herzen und ein Schlag!'

> What love is, if thou wouldst be taught,
> Thy heart must teach alone,—
> Two souls with but a single thought,
> Two hearts that beat as one.
> *Der Sohn der Wildnis,* Act II
> *ad fin.* Trans. by Maria Lovell
> in *Ingomar the Barbarian*

OSCAR HAMMERSTEIN II
1895–1960

10 The last time I saw Paris, her heart was warm and gay,
I heard the laughter of her heart in every street café.
> *Song. The Last Time I Saw Paris*

RICHARD ROLLE DE HAMPOLE
1290?–1349

11 When Adam dalfe and Eve spane
So spire if thou may spede,
Whare was than the pride of man,
That nowe merres his mede?
> *Religious Pieces in Prose and*
> *Verse,* vii. *Early English Text*
> *Society, Original Series, No. 26.*
> *An altered form was used by John*
> *Ball (d. 1381) as the text of his*
> *revolutionary sermon on the out-*
> *break of the Peasants' Revolt,*
> *1381:*

> > When Adam delved, and Eve span,
> > Who was then a gentleman?

MINNY MAUD HANFF fl. 1900

12 Since then they called him Sunny Jim.
> *Sunny Jim. Advertisement for*
> *Force, a breakfast food.*

KATHERINE HANKEY 1834–1911

13 Tell me the old, old story,
Of unseen things above.
> *The Story Wanted. Tell Me the*
> *Old, Old Story*

SIR WILLIAM HARCOURT
1827–1904

1 We are all Socialists now.
   See Fabian Essays (*1889*) *ed.*
   Shaw (p. 194 in 1948 edition)

E. J. HARDY 1849–1920

2 How To Be Happy Though Married.
   Title of Book (1910)

THOMAS HARDY 1840–1928

3 William Dewy, Tranter Reuben,
   Farmer Ledlow late at plough,
   Robert's kin, and John's, and Ned's,
   And the Squire, and Lady Susan, lie
   in Mellstock churchyard now!
   Friends Beyond

4 Only a man harrowing clods
   In a slow silent walk
   With an old horse that stumbles and
   nods
   Half asleep as they stalk.

   Only thin smoke without flame
   From the heaps of couch grass;
   Yet this will go onward the same
   Though Dynasties pass.

   Yonder a maid and her wight
   Come whispering by:
   War's annals will cloud into night
   Ere their story die.
   *In Time of 'The Breaking of
   Nations'*

5 This is the weather the cuckoo likes,
   And so do I.   *Weathers*

6 When I set out for Lyonnesse,
   A hundred miles away.
   When I Set Out for Lyonnesse

7 When I came back from Lyonnesse
   With magic in my eyes.   *Ib.*

8 Life's Little Ironies.   *Title*

9 Michael Henchard's Will.
   That Elizabeth-Jane Farfrae be not
      told of my death, or made to
      grieve on account of me.
      & that I be not buried in consecrated
      ground.
      & that no sexton be asked to toll
      the bell.
      & that nobody is wished to see my
      dead body.
      & that no murners walk behind me
      at my funeral.
      & that no flours be planted on my
      grave.
      & that no man remember me.
   To this I put my name.
   The Mayor of Casterbridge, ch. 45

10 The President of the Immortals (in
   Æschylean phrase) had ended his
   sport with Tess.
   Tess of the D'Urbervilles, ch. 59

JULIUS CHARLES HARE 1795–1855
and
AUGUSTUS WILLIAM HARE
1792–1834

11 Man without religion is the creature
   of circumstances.
   Guesses at Truth, Series 1

MAURICE EVAN HARE 1889–1967

12 There once was a man who said,
      'Damn!
   It is borne in upon me I am
   An engine that moves
   In predestinate grooves,
   I'm not even a bus I'm a tram.'
   *Written, as above, at St. John's
   College, Oxford, in 1905*

WILLIAM HARGREAVES d. 1941

13 I'm Burlington Bertie:
   I rise at ten-thirty.
   Burlington Bertie. First Sung by
   Ella Shields in October 1914 at
   the Argyle Theatre, Birkenhead.

SIR JOHN HARINGTON
1561–1612

14 Treason doth never prosper: what's
   the reason?
   For if it prosper, none dare call it
   treason.
   Epigrams, bk. iv, No. 5. *Of
   Treason*

CHARLES K. HARRIS 1865–1930

15 After the ball is over.   *After the Ball*

16 Somewhere the sun is shining.
   Somewhere

CLIFFORD HARRIS d. 1949

17 You called me Baby Doll a year ago.
   A Broken Doll.

JOEL CHANDLER HARRIS
1848–1908

18 A contrapshun what he call a Tar-
   Baby.
   *Uncle Remus. Legends of the
   Old Plantation,* ch. 2. *Tar-Baby
   Story*

19 Tar-baby ain't sayin' nuthin', en
   Brer Fox, he lay low.   *Ib.*

20 Bred en bawn in a brier-patch!
   Ib. ch. 4

1 Oh, whar shill we go w'en de great day
    comes,
 Wid de blowin' er de trumpits en de
    bangin' er de drums?
 How many po' sinners'll be kotched
    out late
 En find no latch ter de golden gate?
        Uncle Remus. His Songs, i

FRANCIS BRETT HART *or* BRET HARTE 1839–1902

2 If, of all words of tongue and pen,
 The saddest are, 'It might have been,'
 More sad are these we daily see:
 'It is, but hadn't ought to be!'
        Mrs. Judge Jenkins

3 Which I wish to remark,
 And my language is plain,
 That for ways that are dark
 And for tricks that are vain,
 The heathen Chinee is peculiar,
 Which the same I would rise to explain.
        *Plain Language from Truthful
        James*

4 And he smiled a kind of sickly smile,
    and curled up on the floor,
 And the subsequent proceedings in-
    terested him no more.
        The Society upon the Stanislaus

MINNIE LOUISE HASKINS 1875–1957

5 And I said to the man who stood at
 the gate of the year: 'Give me a light
 that I may tread safely into the unknown.' And he replied: 'Go out into
 the darkness and put your hand into
 the hand of God. That shall be to you
 better than light and safer than a
 known way.'
        *God Knows. Quoted by King
        George VI in a Christmas Broad-
        cast, 25 Dec. 1939*

ROBERT STEPHEN HAWKER 1803–1875

6 And have they fixed the where and
    when?
 And shall Trelawny die?
 Here's twenty thousand Cornish men
 Will know the reason why!
        *Song of the Western Men. The
        last three lines have existed since
        the imprisonment by James II,
        1688, of the seven Bishops, includ-
        ing Trelawny, Bishop of Bristol.*

SIR ANTHONY HOPE HAWKINS *see* ANTHONY HOPE

LORD CHARLES HAY ?–1760

7 Gentlemen of the French Guard, fire
 first! (Messieurs les gardes françaises,
 tirez.)
        Battle of Fontenoy, 1745. E.
        Fournier, *L'Esprit dans l'His-
        toire* (1883), ch. 52, p. 349

IAN HAY [JOHN HAY BEITH] 1876–1952

8 Funny peculiar, or funny ha-ha?
        The Housemaster, Act III

WILLIAM HAZLITT 1778–1830

9 His worst is better than any other
 person's best.
        English Literature, ch. xiv. *Sir
        Walter Scott*

10 He [Coleridge] talked on for ever;
 and you wished him to talk on for
 ever.
        Lectures on the English Poets.
        Lecture viii, *On the Living Poets*

11 Give me the clear blue sky over my
 head, and the green turf beneath my
 feet, a winding road before me, and
 a three hours' march to dinner—and
 then to thinking! It is hard if I cannot
 start some game on these 'lone heaths.
        Table Talk, xix. *On Going a
        Journey*

12 The English (it must be owned) are
 rather a foul-mouthed nation.
        Ib. xxii. *On Criticism*

13 We can scarcely hate anyone that we
 know.   *Ib.*

BISHOP REGINALD HEBER 1783–1826

14 Brightest and best of the sons of the
 morning!
 Dawn on our darkness and lend us
 Thine aid!
        Hymns, &c. Brightest and Best

15 From Greenland's icy mountains,
 From India's coral strand,
 Where Afric's sunny fountains
 Roll down their golden sand.
        *Ib. From Greenland's Icy Moun-
        tains*

16 What though the spicy breezes
 Blow soft o'er Ceylon's isle;
 Though every prospect pleases,
 And only man is vile:

 In vain with lavish kindness
 The gifts of God are strown;
 The heathen in his blindness
 Bows down to wood and stone.
        *This is the most familiar version.
        Bishop Heber originally wrote
        'The savage in his blindness'.
        He altered this, and also altered
        'Ceylon's' to 'Java's'. Ib.*

1 Holy, Holy, Holy; Lord God Al-
mighty!
Early in the morning our song shall
rise to Thee:
Holy, Holy, Holy! Merciful and
Mighty;
God in Three Persons, Blessed Trinity!

Holy, Holy, Holy; all the Saints adore
Thee,
Casting down their golden crowns
around the glassy sea.
Hymns, &c. Holy, Holy, Holy!

GEORG WILHELM HEGEL
1770–1831

2 What experience and history teach is
this—that people and governments
never have learned anything from
history, or acted on principles deduced
from it.
Philosophy of History. Introduction. Used by Shaw in his
Revolutionist's Handbook and in
the Preface to *Heartbreak House*

HEINRICH HEINE 1797–1856

3 Ich grolle nicht, und wenn das Herz
auch bricht.

I do not murmur, even if my heart
break.
Buch der Lieder. Title of Song

4 Ich weiss nicht, was soll es bedeuten,
Dass ich so traurig bin;
Ein Märchen aus alten Zeiten,
Das kommt mir nicht aus dem Sinn.

I know not why I am so sad; I
cannot get out of my head a
fairy-tale of olden times.
Die Lorelei

5 Auf Flügeln des Gesanges.

On the wings of song. *Title of Song*

6 Dieu me pardonnera. C'est son métier.

God will pardon me. It is His trade.
On his Deathbed

FELICIA DOROTHEA HEMANS
1793–1835

7 The boy stood on the burning deck
Whence all but he had fled;
The flame that lit the battle's wreck
Shone round him o'er the dead.
Casabianca

8 There came a burst of thunder sound—
The boy—oh! where was he? *Ib.*

9 They grew in beauty, side by side,
They fill'd one home with glee;—
Their graves are sever'd, far and wide,
By mount, and stream, and sea.
The Graves of a Household

10 He Never Smiled Again! *Title of poem*

11 The stately homes of England,
How beautiful they stand!
Amidst their tall ancestral trees,
O'er all the pleasant land.
The Homes of England

12 In the busy haunts of men.
Tale of the Secret Tribunal, pt. i,
l. 203

WILLIAM ERNEST HENLEY
1849–1903

13 Out of the night that covers me,
Black as the Pit from pole to pole,
I thank whatever gods may be
For my unconquerable soul.

In the fell clutch of circumstance,
I have not winced nor cried aloud:
Under the bludgeonings of chance
My head is bloody, but unbowed.
*Echoes, iv. Invictus. In Mem.
R. T. H. B.*

14 It matters not how strait the gate,
How charged with punishments the
scroll,
I am the master of my fate:
I am the captain of my soul. *Ib.*

15 Or ever the Knightly years were gone
With the old world to the grave,
I was a King in Babylon
And you were a Christian Slave.
Ib. xxxvii. To W. A.

16 What have I done for you,
England, my England?
What is there I would not do,
England, my own?
*For England's Sake, iii. Pro Rege
Nostro*

17 Ever the faith endures,
England, my England:—
'Take and break us: we are yours,
England, my own!
Life is good, and joy runs high
Between English earth and sky;
Death is death; but we shall die
To the Song on your bugles blown,
England.' *Ib.*

HENRI IV 1553–1610

18 Je veux qu'il n'y ait si pauvre paysan
en mon royaume qu'il n'ait tous les
dimanches sa poule au pot.

I want there to be no peasant in
my kingdom so poor that he is
unable to have a chicken in his
pot ever Sunday.
Hardouin de Péréfixe, *Hist. de
Henry le Grand* (1681)

1 Pends-toi, brave Crillon; nous avons
combattu à Arques et tu n'y étais pas.
Hang yourself, brave Crillon; we
fought at Arques and you were
not there.
*Traditional form given by Voltaire
to a letter of Henri to Crillon.
Lettres missives de Henri IV,
Collection des documents inédits
de l'histoire de France, vol. iv
(1847), p. 848*

2 Paris vaut bien une messe.
Paris is well worth a mass.
*Attr. either to Henry IV or to his
minister Sully, in conversation
with Henry. Caquets de l'Accou-
chée, 1622*

3 The wisest fool in Christendom.
*Of James I of England. Remark
attr. to Henry IV and Sully.
The French is not known*

MATTHEW HENRY 1662–1714

4 Many a dangerous temptation comes
to us in gay, fine colours, that are but
skin-deep.
Commentaries, Genesis iii. 1

5 To their own second and sober
thoughts. *Ib. Job vi. 29*

6 They that die by famine die by inches.
Ib. Ps. lix. 15

7 Men of polite learning and a liberal
education. *Ib. Acts x. 1*

8 All this and heaven too.
Life of Philip Henry, p. 70

PATRICK HENRY 1736–1799

9 Caesar had his Brutus—Charles the
First, his Cromwell—and George the
Third—('Treason,' cried the Speaker)
. . . may profit by their example. If this
be treason, make the most of it.
*Speech in the Virginia Convention,
1765. W. Wirt's Patrick Henry
(1818), p. 65*

10 I know not what course others may
take; but as for me, give me liberty,
or give me death!
*Ib. 23 Mar. 1775. W. Wirt's
Patrick Henry (1818), p. 123.*

PHILIP HENRY 1631–1696

11 They are not amissi, but praemissi.
[Not lost, but gone before.]
*Matthew Henry, Life of Philip
Henry, ch. 5 (ed. 1825), p. 111*

HENRY II OF ENGLAND
1133–1189

12 Who will free me from this turbulent
priest? [Becket.] *History books*

13 What a parcel of fools and dastards
have I nourished in my house, that
not one of them will avenge me of
this one upstart clerk!
K. Norgate, in Dict. of Nat. Biog.

HENRY VIII OF ENGLAND
1491–1547

14 [*Anne of Cleves.*] The King found her
so different from her picture . . . that
. . . he swore they had brought him
a Flanders mare.
*Smollett, Hist. of England (ed. 3,
1759), vi. 68*

HERACLEITUS *fl.* 513 B.C.

15 πάντα ῥεῖ, οὐδὲν μένει.
All is flux, nothing is stationary.
*Alluded to by Aristotle in De Caelo,
3. 1. 18 (ed. Weise) and elsewhere*

SIR ALAN PATRICK HERBERT
1890–1971

16 Let's stop somebody from doing something! *Let's Stop Somebody*

17 Holy Deadlock.
*Title of a novel satirizing the
Divorce Law*

GEORGE HERBERT 1593–1633

18 Let all the world in ev'ry corner sing
My God and King.
The heav'ns are not too high,
His praise may thither fly;
The earth is not too low,
His praises there may grow.
Let all the world in ev'ry corner sing
My God and King.
The Church with psalms must shout,
No door can keep them out:
But above all, the heart
Must bear the longest part.
The Temple. Antiphon

19 I struck the board, and cried, 'No
more;
I will abroad.' *Ib. The Collar*

20 Methought I heard one calling, 'Child';
And I replied, 'My Lord.'
Ib.

21 Teach me, my God and King,
In all things Thee to see,
And what I do in any thing
To do it as for Thee.
A man that looks on glass,
On it may stay his eye;
Or if he pleaseth, through it pass,
And then the heaven espy.
Ib. The Elixir

22 A servant with this clause
Makes drudgery divine;
Who sweeps a room as for Thy laws
Makes that and th' action fine. *Ib.*

1 Love bade me welcome; yet my soul
    drew back,
        Guilty of dust and sin.
But quick-ey'd Love, observing me
    grow slack
        From my first entrance in,
Drew nearer to me, sweetly questioning
    If I lack'd any thing.
              The Temple. Love

2 King of glory, King of peace,
    I will love Thee;
And, that love may never cease,
    I will move Thee.
              Ib. Praise

3 Sev'n whole days, not one in seven,
    I will praise Thee;
In my heart, though not in heaven,
    I can raise Thee.   *Ib.*

4 The God of love my Shepherd is,
And He that doth me feed,
While He is mine, and I am His,
What can I want or need?
            Ib. 23rd Psalm

5 Lord, make me coy and tender to
    offend.   *Ib. Unkindness*

6 Sweet day, so cool, so calm, so bright,
The bridal of the earth and sky,
The dew shall weep thy fall to-night;
        For thou must die.
               Ib. Virtue

7 Sweet spring, full of sweet days and
    roses,
A box where sweets compacted lie. *Ib.*

ROBERT HERRICK 1591–1674

8 Cherry ripe, ripe, ripe, I cry,
Full and fair ones; come and buy:
If so be, you ask me where
They do grow? I answer, there,
Where my Julia's lips do smile;
There's the land, or cherry-isle.
        Hesperides. Cherry Ripe

9 Get-up, sweet Slug-a-bed, and see
The dew bespangling herb and tree.
      Ib. Corinna's Going a-Maying

10 Fair daffodils, we weep to see
You haste away so soon:
As yet the early-rising sun
Has not attain'd his noon.
    Stay, stay,
Until the hasting day
    Has run
But to the even-song;
And, having pray'd together, we
Will go with you along.
             Ib. Daffodils

11 A sweet disorder in the dress
Kindles in clothes a wantonness:
A lawn about the shoulders thrown
Into a fine distraction:
An erring lace, which here and there
Enthrals the crimson stomacher:
A cuff neglectful, and thereby
Ribbands to flow confusedly:

A winning wave (deserving note)
In the tempestuous petticoat:
A careless shoe-string, in whose tie
I see a wild civility:
Do more bewitch me, than when Art
Is too precise in every part.
    Hesperides. Delight in Disorder

12 You say, to me-wards your affection's
    strong;
Pray love me little, so you love me long.
    Ib. Love me Little, Love me Long

13 Her eyes the glow-worm lend thee,
The shooting-stars attend thee;
    And the elves also,
    Whose little eyes glow,
Like the sparks of fire, befriend thee.

No Will-o'-th'-Wisp mislight thee;
Nor snake, or slow-worm bite thee:
    But on, on thy way
    Not making a stay,
Since ghost there's none to affright
thee.   *Ib. The Night-Piece, to Julia*

14 Gather ye rosebuds while ye may,
Old Time is still a-flying:
And this same flower that smiles to-day,
To-morrow will be dying.
    *Ib. To Virgins, to Make Much of
    Time*

15 Whenas in silks my Julia goes,
Then, then (methinks) how sweetly
    flows
That liquefaction of her clothes.

Next, when I cast mine eyes and see
That brave vibration each way free;
O how that glittering taketh me!
    Ib. Upon Julia's Clothes

16 Here a little child I stand,
Heaving up my either hand;
Cold as paddocks though they be,
Here I lift them up to Thee,
For a benison to fall
On our meat, and on us all. Amen.
    *Noble Numbers. Another Grace for
    a Child*

JAMES HERVEY 1714–1758

17 E'en crosses from his sov'reign hand
Are blessings in disguise.
    *Works. Reflections on a Flower-
    Garden*

HESIOD c. 735 B.C.

18 πλέον ἥμισυ παντός.
    The half is greater than the whole.
          Works and Days, 40

GORDON HEWART, LORD HEWART 1870–1943

19 Justice should not only be done, but
manifestly and undoubtedly be seen
to be done.
    *Rex v. Sussex Justices, 9 Nov.
    1923 (King's Bench Reports,
    1924, vol. i, p. 259)*

THOMAS HEYWOOD d. 1650?

1 Seven cities warr'd for Homer, being
  dead,
  Who, living, had no roof to shroud his
  head.
        Hierarchie of the Blessed Angels

2 Pack, clouds, away, and welcome day,
  With night we banish sorrow;
  Sweet air blow soft, mount larks aloft
  To give my Love good-morrow!
        Pack, Clouds, Away, st. 1

3 A Woman Killed with Kindness.
        Title of Play

WILLIAM EDWARD HICKSON
1803–1870

4 'Tis a lesson you should heed,
  Try, try again.
  If at first you don't succeed,
  Try, try again.   *Try and Try Again*

'DR. BREWSTER HIGLEY'
nineteenth century

5 Oh give me a home where the buffalo
  roam,
  Where the deer and the antelope play,
  Where seldom is heard a discouraging
  word
  And the skies are not cloudy all day.
        Home on the Range (1873)

HIPPOCRATES c. 460–357 B.C.

6 ὁ βίος βραχύς, ἡ δὲ τέχνη μακρή.
    The life so short, the craft so long
    to learn.
        Aphorisms, I. i. Trans. by
        Chaucer

ADOLF HITLER 1889–1945

7 My patience is now at an end.
        Speech, 26 Sept. 1938

8 It is the last territorial claim which I
  have to make in Europe.   *Ib.*

THOMAS HOBBES 1588–1679

9 No arts; no letters; no society; and
  which is worst of all, continual fear
  and danger of violent death; and the
  life of man, solitary, poor, nasty,
  brutish, and short.
        Leviathan, pt. i, ch. 13

10 I am about to take my last voyage,
   a great leap in the dark.
        Last Words. Watkins, *Anecdotes
        of Men of Learning*

JOHN CAM HOBHOUSE, BARON BROUGHTON 1786–1869

11 When I invented the phrase 'His
   Majesty's Opposition' [Canning] paid
   me a compliment on the fortunate hit.
        Recollections of a Long Life, ii,
        ch. 12

EDWARD WALLIS HOCH
1849–1925

12 There is so much good in the worst of
   us,
   And so much bad in the best of us,
   That it hardly becomes any of us
   To talk about the rest of us.
        Good and Bad. Attr. to many
        other authors

RALPH HODGSON 1871–1962

13 'Twould ring the bells of Heaven
   The wildest peal for years,
   If Parson lost his senses
   And people came to theirs,
   And he and they together
   Knelt down with angry prayers
   For tamed and shabby tigers
   And dancing dogs and bears,
   And wretched, blind, pit ponies,
   And little hunted hares.
        Poems. The Bells of Heaven

14 Time, you old gypsy man,
   Will you not stay,
   Put up your caravan
   Just for one day?
        Ib. Time, You Old Gypsy Man

HEINRICH HOFFMAN 1809–1874

15 Augustus was a chubby lad;
   Fat ruddy cheeks Augustus had:
   And everybody saw with joy
   The plump and hearty, healthy boy.
   He ate and drank as he was told,
   And never let his soup get cold.
   But one day, one cold winter's day,
   He screamed out, 'Take the soup
   away!
   O take the nasty soup away!
   I won't have any soup to-day.'
        Struwwelpeter. Augustus

16 Here is cruel Frederick, see!
   A horrid wicked boy was he.
        Ib. Cruel Frederick

17 Let me see if Philip can
   Be a little gentleman;
   Let me see, if he is able
   To sit still for once at table.
        Ib. Fidgety Philip

18 But fidgety Phil,
   He won't sit still;
   He wriggles
   And giggles,
   And then, I declare,
   Swings backwards and forwards,
   And tilts up his chair.   *Ib.*

E

1 It almost makes me cry to tell
   What foolish Harriet befell.
   Struuwelpeter. Harriet and the Matches

2 Look at Little Johnny there,
   Little Johnny Head-In-Air!
                  Ib. Johnny Head-in-Air

3 The door flew open, in he ran,
   The great, long, red-legged scissor-
   man.   *Ib. The Little Suck-a-Thumb*

4 'Ah!' said Mamma, 'I knew he'd come
   To naughty little Suck-a-Thumb.' *Ib.*

5 Anything to me is sweeter
   Than to see Shock-headed Peter.
                  Ib. Shock-Headed Peter

JAMES HOGG 1770–1835

6 We'll o'er the water, we'll o'er the sea,
   We'll o'er the water to Charlie;
   Come weel, come wo, we'll gather and
   go,
   And live or die wi' Charlie.
       Jacobite Relics of Scotland, ii. 76.
       O'er the Water to Charlie

7 'Twas on a Monday morning,
   Right early in the year,
   That Charlie came to our town,
   The young Chevalier.
   And Charlie he's my darling,
   My darling, my darling.
   And Charlie he's my darling,
   The young Chevalier.
       Ib. 93. *The Young Chevalier*

8 Will you no come back again?
   Better lo'ed you'll never be,
   And will you no come back again?
       Ib. 195. *Will You No Come Back
       Again?*

9 My love she's but a lassie yet.
                       Title of Song

JOHN HAYNES HOLMES 1879–

10 The universe is not hostile, nor yet
   is it friendly. It is simply indifferent.
       Sensible Man's View of Religion

OLIVER WENDELL HOLMES
                       1809–1894

11 We love the precepts for the teacher's
   sake.
       Poems. A Rhymed Lesson
       (Urania)

12 Man wants but little drink below,
   But wants that little strong.
       Ib. A Song of other Days. Parody
       on Goldsmith

13 Man has his will,—but woman has her
   way.
       *The Autocrat of the Breakfast-
       Table*, ch. 1

JOHN HOME 1722–1808

14 My name is Norval; on the Grampian
   hills
   My father feeds his flocks; a frugal
   swain,
   Whose constant cares were to increase
   his store.   *Douglas*, II. i

HOMER c. 900 B.C.

15 μῆνιν ἄειδε, θεά, Πηληϊάδεω Ἀχιλῆος
   οὐλομένην, ἣ μυρί' Ἀχαιοῖς ἄλγε' ἔθηκε.

   The wrath of Peleus' son, the direful
   spring
   Of all the Grecian woes, O Goddess,
   sing!   *Iliad*, i. 1. Trans. by Pope

16 ἄνδρα μοι ἔννεπε, Μοῦσα, πολύτροπον.

   Tell me, Muse, of the man of many
   wiles. [Odysseus.]   *Odyssey*, i. 1

17 πολλῶν δ' ἀνθρώπων ἴδεν ἄστεα καὶ νόον
   ἔγνω.

   He saw the cities of many men, and
   knew their mind.   *Ib.* 3

WILLIAM HONE 1780–1842

18 John Jones may be described as 'one
   of the *has beens*'.
       Every-Day Book, vol. ii, p. 820

THOMAS HOOD 1799–1845

19 It was not in the winter
   Our loving lot was cast!
   It was the time of roses,
   We plucked them as we passed!
       Ballad: It Was Not in the Winter

20 One more Unfortunate,
   Weary of breath,
   Rashly importunate,
   Gone to her death!

   Take her up tenderly,
   Lift her with care;
   Fashion'd so slenderly,
   Young, and so fair!
              The Bridge of Sighs

21 Two stern-faced men set out from
   Lynn,
   Through the cold and heavy mist;
   And Eugene Aram walked between,
   With gyves upon his wrist.
              The Dream of Eugene Aram

22 Ben Battle was a soldier bold,
   And used to war's alarms:
   But a cannon-ball took off his legs,
   So he laid down his arms!
              Faithless Nelly Gray

23 His death, which happen'd in his
   berth,
   At forty-odd befell:
   They went and told the sexton, and
   The sexton toll'd the bell.
              Faithless Sally Brown

1 I remember, I remember,
The house where I was born,
The little window where the sun
Came peeping in at morn.
I Remember

2 He never spoils the child and spares
the rod,
But spoils the rod and never spares
the child.
The Irish Schoolmaster, xii

3 With fingers weary and worn,
With eyelids heavy and red,
A woman sat, in unwomanly rags,
Plying her needle and thread—
Stitch! stitch! stitch!
In poverty, hunger, and dirt.
The Song of the Shirt

4 Oh! God! that bread should be so
dear,
And flesh and blood so cheap! *Ib.*

5 There are three things which the public will always clamour for sooner or
later: namely, Novelty, novelty,
novelty.
*Announcement for Comic Annual
for 1836*

ELLEN STURGIS HOOPER
1816–1841

6 I slept, and dreamed that life was
Beauty;
I woke, and found that life was Duty.
Life a Duty

HERBERT CLARK HOOVER
1874–1964

7 The American system of rugged individualism.
*Campaign speech, New York,
22 Oct. 1928*

ANTHONY HOPE [SIR
ANTHONY HOPE HAWKINS]
1863–1933

8 His foe was folly and his weapon wit.
*Inscription on the tablet to W. S.
Gilbert, Victoria Embankment,
London (1915)*

LAURENCE HOPE [ADELA
FLORENCE NICOLSON] 1865–1904

9 Pale hands I loved beside the Shali-
mar,
Where are you now? Who lies beneath
your spell?
*Indian Love Lyrics. Pale Hands
I Loved*

10 Less than the dust beneath thy chariot
wheel,
Less than the weed that grows beside
thy door,
Less than the rust that never stained
thy sword,

Less than the need thou hast in life of
me,
Even less am I.
*Indian Love Lyrics. Less than the
Dust*

GERARD MANLEY HOPKINS
1844–1889

11 Towery city and branchy between
towers. *Duns Scotus' Oxford*

12 The world is charged with the grandeur of God. *God's Grandeur*

13 Elected Silence, sing to me
And beat upon my whorlèd ear,
Pipe me to pastures still and be
The music that I care to hear.
The Habit of Perfection

14 Glory be to God for dappled things.
Pied Beauty

15 All things counter, original, spare,
strange;
Whatever is fickle, freckled (who
knows how?)
With swift, slow; sweet, sour; adazzle,
dim;
He fathers-forth whose beauty is past
change:
Praise him. *Ib.*

16 Look at the stars! look, look up at the
skies!
O look at all the fire-folk sitting in the
air!
The bright boroughs, the circle-citadels there! *The Starlight Night*

17 I caught this morning morning's
minion, kingdom of daylight's dauphin, dapple-dawn-drawn Falcon.
The Windhover

HORACE 65–8 B.C.

18 Inceptis gravibus plerumque et magna
professis
Purpureus, late qui splendeat, unus
et alter
Adsuitur pannus.
Often on a work of grave purpose
and high promises is tacked a
purple patch or two to give an
effect of colour. *Ars Poetica, 14*

19 Proicit ampullas et sesquipedalia
verba.
Throws aside his paint-pots and his
words a foot and a half long.
Ib. 97

20 Si vis me flere, dolendum est
Primum ipsi tibi.
If you wish to draw tears from me,
you must first feel pain yourself.
Ib. 102

21 Parturient montes, nascetur ridiculus
mus.
Mountains will be in labour, the
birth will be a single laughable
little mouse. *Ib. 139*

1 Semper ad eventum festinat et in
medias res
Non secus ac notas auditorem rapit.

He ever hastens to the issue, and
hurries his hearers into the
midst of the story as if they knew
it before.   Ars Poetica, 148.

2 Laudator temporis acti   Ib. 173
Inclined to praise the way the world
went.

3 Indignor quandoque bonus dormitat
Homerus.

But if Homer, usually good, nods
for a moment, I think it shame.
Ib. 359

4 Ut pictura poesis.

As with the painter's work, so with
the poet's.   Ib. 361

5 Nonumque prematur in annum.

Let it be kept quiet till the ninth
year.   Ib. 388

6 Si possis recte, si non, quocumque
modo rem.

Money by right means if you can,
if not, by any means, money.
Epistles, I. i. 66

7 Dimidium facti qui coepit habet:
sapere aude.

He who has begun his task has half
done it. Have the courage to be
wise.   Ib. ii. 40

8 Naturam expellas furca, tamen usque
recurret.

If you drive nature out with a pitchfork, she will soon find a way back.
Ib. x. 24

9 Caelum non animum mutant qui
trans mare currunt.
Strenua nos exercet inertia: navibus
atque
Quadrigis petimus bene vivere. Quod
petis hic est,
Est Ulubris, animus si te non deficit
aequus.

They change their sky, not their
soul, who run across the sea.
We work hard at doing nothing:
we seek happiness in yachts and
four-horse coaches. What you
seek is here—is at Ulubrae—if
an even soul does not fail you.
Ib. xi. 27

10 Concordia discors.
Harmony in discord.   Ib. xii. 19

11 Principibus placuisse viris non ultima
laus est.
Non cuivis homini contingit adire
Corinthum.

To have found favour with leaders
of mankind is not the meanest of
glories. It is not every one that
can get to Corinth.   Ib. xvii. 35

12 Si foret in terris, rideret Democritus.

If he were on earth, Democritus
would laugh at the sight.
Epistles, II. i. 194

13 Quid te exempta iuvat spinis de
pluribus una?
Vivere si recte nescis, decede peritis.
Lusisti satis, edisti satis atque bibisti:
Tempus abire tibi est.

How does it relieve you to pluck one
thorn out of many? If you do not
know how to live aright, make
way for those who do. You have
played enough, have eaten and
drunk enough. It is time for you
to leave the scene.   Ib. ii. 212

14 Beatus ille, qui procul negotiis,
Ut prisca gens mortalium,
Paterna rura bubus exercet suis,
Solutus omni faenore.

Happy the man who far from
schemes of business, like the early
generations of mankind, ploughs
and ploughs again his ancestral
land with oxen of his own breeding, with no yoke of usury on
his neck!
Epodes, ii. I. Trans. by Wickham

15 Nil mortalibus ardui est.

No height is too arduous for mortal
men.   Odes, I. iii. 37

16 Pallida Mors aequo pulsat pede pauperum tabernas
Regumque turris.

Pale Death with impartial foot
knocks at the doors of poor men's
hovels and of kings' palaces.
Ib. iv. 13

17 Vitae summa brevis spem nos vetat
incohare longam.

Life's short span forbids us to enter
on far-reaching hopes.   Ib. 15

18 Quis multa gracilis te puer in rosa
Perfusus liquidis urget odoribus
Grato, Pyrrha, sub antro?
Cui flavam religas comam,
Simplex munditiis?

What delicate stripling is it, Pyrrha,
that now, steeped in liquid perfumes, is wooing thee on the
heaped rose-leaves in some
pleasant grot? For whose eyes
dost thou braid those flaxen
locks, so trim, so simple? Ib. v. 1

19 Nil desperandum Teucro duce et
auspice Teucro.

No lot is desperate under Teucer's
conduct and Teucer's star.
Ib. vii. 27

1 Quid sit futurum cras fuge quaerere et
Quem Fors dierum cumque dabit
lucro
Appone.

What shall be to-morrow, think not
of asking. Each day that Fortune
gives you, be it what it may, set
down for gain. *Odes*, I. ix. 13

2 Tu ne quaesieris, scire nefas.

Pray, ask not,—such knowledge is
not for us. *Ib*. xi. 1

3 Dum loquimur, fugerit invida
Aetas: carpe diem, quam minimum
credula postero.

Even while we speak, Time, the
churl, will have been running.
Snatch the sleeve of to-day and
trust as little as you may to
to-morrow. *Ib*. 7

4 O matre pulchra filia pulchrior.

O fairer daughter of a fair mother.
Ib. xvi. 1

5 Integer vitae scelerisque purus.

He that is unstained in life and
pure from guilt. *Ib*. xxii. 1

6 Dulce ridentem Lalagen amabo,
Dulce loquentem.

Still shall I love Lalage and her
sweet laughter, Lalage and her
sweet prattle. *Ib*. 23

7 Quis desiderio sit pudor aut modus
Tam cari capitis?

What shame or measure should
there be in grief for one so dear?
Ib. xxiv. 1

8 Nunc est bibendum, nunc pede libero
Pulsanda tellus.

Now we must drink, now beat the
earth with free step.
Ib. xxxvii. 1

9 Persicos odi, puer, apparatus.

Persian luxury, boy, I hate.
Ib. xxxviii. 1

10 Aequam memento rebus in arduis
Servare mentem.

Remember when life's path is steep
to keep your mind even.
Ib. II. iii. 1

11 Omnes eodem cogimur.

We all are driven one road. *Ib*. 25

12 Ille terrarum mihi praeter omnis
Angulus ridet.

That nook of earth's surface has a
smile for me before all other
places. *Ib*. vi. 13

13 Auream quisquis mediocritatem
Diligit.

Whoso loves well the golden mean.
Ib. x. 5

14 Eheu fugaces, Postume, Postume,
Labuntur anni.

Ah me, Postumus, Postumus, the
fleeting years are slipping by.
Odes, II. xiv. 1

15 Credite posteri.

Believe it, after-years! *Ib*. xix. 2

16 Odi profanum vulgus et arceo;
Favete linguis; carmina non prius
Audita Musarum sacerdos
Virginibus puerisque canto.

I hate the uninitiate crowd and
bid them avaunt. Listen all in
silence! Strains unheard before
I, the Muses' hierophant, now
chant to maidens and to boys.
Ib. III. i. 1

17 Post equitem sedet atra Cura.

Black Care mounts on the horseman's pillion. *Ib*. 40

18 Dulce et decorum est pro patria mori.

To die for fatherland is a sweet
thing and becoming. *Ib*. ii. 13

19 Iustum et tenacem propositi virum
Non civium ardor prava iubentium,
Non vultus instantis tyranni
Mente quatit solida.

The just man and firm of purpose,
not the heat of fellow citizens
clamouring for what is wrong, nor
presence of threatening tyrant
can shake in his rocklike soul.
Ib. iii. 1

20 Fratresque tendentes opaco
Pelion imposuisse Olympo.

The brothers who strove to leave
Pelion set on the top of leafy
Olympus. *Ib*. iv. 51

21 Vis consili expers mole ruit sua.

Force without mind falls by its
own weight. *Ib*. 65

22 Delicta maiorum immeritus lues.

For the sins of your sires albeit you
had no hand in them, you must
suffer. *Ib*. vi. 1

23 Aetas parentum peior avis tulit
Nos nequiores, mox daturos
Progeniem vitiosiorem.

Our sires' age was worse than our
grandsires'. We their sons are
more worthless than they: so in
our turn we shall give the world a
progeny yet more corrupt. *Ib*. 46

24 O fons Bandusiae splendidior vitro.

O spring of Bandusia, more brilliant
than glass. *Ib*. xiii. 1

25 Non ego hoc ferrem calidus iuventa
Consule Planco.

I should not have borne it in my
youth's hot blood when Plancus
was consul. *Ib*. xiv. 27

1 Magnas inter opes inops.
> A pauper in the midst of wealth.
> *Odes*, III. xvi. 28

2 Vixi puellis nuper idoneus
Et militavi non sine gloria;
> Nunc arma defunctumque bello
> Barbiton hic paries habebit.

> Though that life is past, I was but
> now still meet for ladies' love,
> and fought my battles not with-
> out glory. Now my armour and
> the lute, whose campaigns are
> over, will hang here on yonder
> wall.   *Ib.* xxvi. 1

3 Non omnis moriar.
> I shall not all die.   *Ib.* xxx, 6

4 Non sum qualis eram bonae
Sub regno Cinarae. Desine, dulcium
Mater saeva Cupidinum.
> I am other than I was when poor
> Cinara was queen. Try no more,
> 'imperious mother of sweet loves'.
> *Ib.* IV. i. 3

5 Diffugere nives, redeunt iam gramina
campis
> Arboribusque comae.

> The snows have scattered and fled;
> already the grass comes again in
> the fields and the leaves on the
> trees.   *Ib.* vii. 1

6 Damna tamen celeres reparant caelestia lunae:
> Nos ubi decidimus
> Quo pater Aeneas, quo Tullus dives
> et Ancus,
> Pulvis et umbra sumus.

> Yet change and loss in the heavens
> the swift moons make up again.
> For us, when we have descended
> where is father Aeneas, where
> are rich old Tullus and Ancus,
> we are but some dust and a
> shadow.   *Ib.* 13

7 Misce stultitiam consiliis brevem:
> Dulce est desipere in loco.

> Mix with your sage counsels some
> brief folly. In due place to forget
> one's wisdom is sweet. *Ib.* xii. 27

8   Mutato nomine de te
Fabula narratur.
> Change but the name, and it is of
> yourself that tale is told.
> *Satires*, I. i. 69. Trans. by Wickham

9 Hoc genus omne.
> All their kith and kin.   *Ib.* ii. 2

10 Stans pede in uno.
> Without effort.   *Ib.* iv. 10

11 Etiam disiecti membra poetae.
> Even in his dismembered state, the
> limbs of a poet.   *Ib.* 62

12   Credat Iudaeus Apella,
Non ego.
> Apella the Jew must believe it,
> not I.   *Satires*, v. 100

13 O noctes cenaeque deum!
> O nights and suppers of gods!
> *Ib.* II. vi. 65

RICHARD MONCKTON MILNES, BARON HOUGHTON 1809–1885

14 A fair little girl sat under a tree,
Sewing as long as her eyes could see;
Then smoothed her work, and folded
it right,
And said, 'Dear work! Good Night!
Good Night!'
> *Good Night and Good Morning*

ALFRED EDWARD HOUSMAN
1859–1936

15 Loveliest of trees, the cherry now
Is hung with bloom along the bough,
And stands about the woodland ride
Wearing white for Eastertide.

Now, of my threescore years and ten,
Twenty will not come again,
And take from seventy springs a
score,
It only leaves me fifty more.

And since to look at things in bloom
Fifty springs are little room,
About the woodlands I will go
To see the cherry hung with snow.
> *A Shropshire Lad*, ii

16 When I was one-and-twenty
I heard a wise man say,
'Give crowns and pounds and guineas
But not your heart away.'   *Ib.* xiii

17 When I was one-and-twenty
I heard him say again,
'The heart out of the bosom
Was never given in vain;
'Tis paid with sighs a plenty
And sold for endless rue.'
And I am two-and-twenty,
And oh, 'tis true, 'tis true.   *Ib.*

18 Oh, when I was in love with you,
Then I was clean and brave,
And miles around the wonder grew
How well did I behave.   *Ib.* xiv

19 In summertime on Bredon
The bells they sound so clear;
Round both the shires they ring them
In steeples far and near,
A happy noise to hear.

Here of a Sunday morning
My love and I would lie,
And see the coloured counties,
And hear the larks so high
About us in the sky.   *Ib.* xxi

1 The bells they sound on Bredon,
And still the steeples hum.
'Come all to church, good people,'—
Oh, noisy bells, be dumb;
I hear you, I will come.
A Shropshire Lad, xxi

2 The lads that will die in their glory
and never be old. *Ib.* xxiii

3 Is my team ploughing,
That I was used to drive? *Ib.* xxvii

4 The goal stands up, the keeper
Stands up to keep the goal. *Ib.*

5 Into my heart an air that kills
From yon far country blows.
What are those blue remembered hills,
What spires, what farms are those?

That is the land of lost content,
I see it shining plain,
The happy highways where I went
And cannot come again. *Ib.* xl

6 Many a rose-lipt maiden
And many a lightfoot lad. *Ib.* liv

7 Malt does more than Milton can,
To justify God's ways to man.
Ib. lxii

8 We'll to the woods no more,
The laurels all are cut.
Last Poems, introductory.

9 I, a stranger and afraid
In a world I never made. *Ib.* xii

10 The candles burn their sockets,
The blinds let through the day,
The young man feels his pockets
And wonders what's to pay.
Ib. xxi

11 These, in the day when heaven was
falling,
The hour when earth's foundations
fled,
Followed their mercenary calling
And took their wages and are dead.

Their shoulders held the sky suspended;
They stood, and earth's foundations
stay;
What God abandoned, these defended,
And saved the sum of things for
pay.
Ib. xxxvii. *Epitaph on an Army
of Mercenaries*

**BISHOP WILLIAM WALSHAM
HOW** 1823–1897

12 For all the Saints who from their
labours rest,
Who Thee by faith before the world
confess'd,
Thy name, O Jesu, be for ever blest,
Alleluia!
Earl Nelson's *Hymns For Saints'
Days: For All the Saints*

13 O Lord, stretch forth thy mighty
hand
And guard and bless our fatherland.
Church Hymns (1871). *To Thee,
Our God, We Fly*

14 O Jesu, thou art standing
Outside the fast-closed door.
Psalms and Hymns, 1867

JULIA WARD HOWE 1819–1910

15 Mine eyes have seen the glory of the
coming of the Lord:
He is trampling out the vintage where
the grapes of wrath are stored.
*Battle Hymn of the American
Republic*

16 As He died to make men holy, let us
die to make men free. *Ib.*

MARY HOWITT 1799–1888

17 Buttercups and daisies,
Oh, the pretty flowers.
Buttercups and Daisies

18 'Will you walk into my parlour?' said
a spider to a fly:
''Tis the prettiest little parlour that
ever you did spy.'
The Spider and the Fly

EDMOND HOYLE 1672–1769

19 When in doubt, win the trick.
*Hoyle's Games. Whist. Twenty-
four Short Rules for Learners*

ELBERT HUBBARD 1859–1915

20 Life is just one damned thing after
another.
A Thousand and One Epigrams,
p. 137

THOMAS HUGHES 1822–1896

21 It's more than a game. It's an institution. [Cricket.]
Tom Brown's Schooldays, pt. ii,
ch. 7

DAVID HUME 1711–1776

22 Never literary attempt was more un-
fortunate than my Treatise of Human
Nature. It fell *dead-born from the press.*
My Own Life, ch. 1

**MARGARET WOLFE HUNGER-
FORD** 1855?–1897

23 Beauty is in the eye of the beholder.
Quoted in Molly Bawn (1878)
(*see 238:2*)

G. W. HUNT *fl.* 1878

1 We don't want to fight, but, by jingo
  if we do,
  We've got the ships, we've got the
    men, we've got the money too.
       We Don't Want to Fight. Music
       Hall Song, 1878

JAMES HENRY LEIGH HUNT
                    1784–1859

2 Abou Ben Adhem (may his tribe
  increase!)
  Awoke one night from a deep dream of
    peace
      Abou Ben Adhem and the Angel

3   'I pray thee then,
  Write me as one that loves his fellow-
    men.'   *Ib.*

4 Jenny kissed me when we met,
  Jumping from the chair she sat in;
  Time, you thief, who love to get
  Sweets into your list, put that in:
  Say I'm weary, say I'm sad,
  Say that health and wealth have
    missed me,
  Say I'm growing old, but add,
  Jenny kissed me.   *Rondeau*

5 Stolen sweets are always sweeter,
  Stolen kisses much completer,
  Stolen looks are nice in chapels,
  Stolen, stolen, be your apples.
    Song of Fairies Robbing an Or-
    chard

6 The two divinest things this world
  has got,
  A lovely woman in a rural spot!
      The Story of Rimini

7 This Adonis in loveliness was a corpulent man of fifty. [The Prince
  Regent.]
      The Examiner, 22 Mar. 1812

ANNE HUNTER 1742–1821

8 My mother bids me bind my hair
  With bands of rosy hue,
  Tie up my sleeves with ribbons rare,
  And lace my bodice blue.
    My Mother Bids Me Bind My
    Hair

JOHN HUSS 1373–1415

9 O sancta simplicitas!
  O holy simplicity!
    At the stake, seeing an old peasant
    bringing a faggot to throw on the
    pile. Zincgreff-Weidner, *Apo-*
    phthegmata (Amsterdam, 1653),
    pt. iii, p. 383. Geo. Büchmann,
    Geflügelte Worte (1898), p. 509

FRANCIS HUTCHESON 1694–1746

10 That action is best, which procures
  the greatest happiness for the greatest
  numbers.
    Inquiry into the Original of our
    Ideas of Beauty and Virtue,
    Treatise II. *Concerning Moral*
    Good and Evil, sec. 3, § 8 (*see*
    22:8)

THOMAS HENRY HUXLEY
                    1825–1895

11 It is the customary fate of new truths
  to begin as heresies and to end as
  superstitions.
    Science and Culture, xii. *The*
    Coming of Age of the Origin of
    Species

12 I took thought, and invented what I
  conceived to be the appropriate title
  of 'agnostic'.
    Science and Christian Tradition,
    ch. 7

EDWARD HYDE
see EARL OF CLARENDON

HENRIK IBSEN 1828–1906

13 The minority is always right.
    An Enemy of the People, Act IV

14 One should never put on one's best
  trousers to go out to battle for freedom
  and truth.   *Ib.* Act V

15 Vine-leaves in his hair.
    Hedda Gabler, Act II

WASHINGTON IRVING
                    1783–1859

16 The almighty dollar, that great object
  of universal devotion throughout our
  land, seems to have no genuine devotees in these peculiar villages.
    Wolfert's Roost. The Creole Vil-
    lage

RICHARD JAGO 1715–1781

17 With leaden foot time creeps along
  While Delia is away.
    Absence: With Leaden Foot

**JAMES I OF ENGLAND AND VI
OF SCOTLAND** 1566–1625

18 Dr. Donne's verses are like the peace
  of God; they pass all understanding.
    Saying recorded by Archdeacon
    Plume (1630–1704)

WILLIAM JAMES 1842–1910

1 [Letter to H. G. Wells.] A symptom of the moral flabbiness born of the exclusive worship of the bitch-goddess SUCCESS.
   1906 in *Letters*, ed. Henry James (1920), ii, 260

THOMAS JEFFERSON 1743–1826

2 We hold these truths to be sacred and undeniable; that all men are created equal and independent, that from that equal creation they derive rights inherent and inalienable, among which are the preservation of life, and liberty, and the pursuit of happiness.
   Original draft for the *Declaration of Independence* (see 8:9)

3 The tree of liberty must be refreshed from time to time with the blood of patriots and tyrants. It is its natural manure.
   Letter to W. S. Smith, 13 Nov. 1787

4 No duty the Executive had to perform was so trying as to put the right man in the right place.
   J. B. MacMaster, *History of the People of the U.S.* vol. ii, ch. 13, p. 586

FRANCIS, LORD JEFFREY 1773–1850

5 This will never do.
   On Wordsworth's 'Excursion'. *Edinburgh Review, Nov. 1814*, p. 1

JEROME KLAPKA JEROME 1859–1927

6 Love is like the measles; we all have to go through it.
   Idle Thoughts of an Idle Fellow. On Being in Love

7 George goes to sleep at a bank from ten to four each day, except Saturdays, when they wake him up and put him outside at two.
   Three Men in a Boat, ch. 2

8 I like work: it fascinates me. I can sit and look at it for hours. I love to keep it by me: the idea of getting rid of it nearly breaks my heart.
   Ib. ch. 15

9 The Passing of the Third Floor Back.
   Title of Play

DOUGLAS WILLIAM JERROLD 1803–1857

10 Mrs. Caudle's Curtain Lectures.
   Title of Book

11 Love's like the measles—all the worse when it comes late in life.
   Wit and Opinions of Douglas Jerrold (1859), p. 6. A *Philanthropist*

12 We love peace, as we abhor pusillanimity; but not peace at any price. There is a peace more destructive of the manhood of living man than war is destructive of his material body. Chains are worse than bayonets.
   A Charitable Man, p. 155. *Peace*

PHILANDER CHASE JOHNSON 1866–1939

13 Cheer up, the worst is yet to come.
   Shooting Stars. See *Everybody's Magazine, May 1920*

SAMUEL JOHNSON 1709–1784

14 *Johnson*: I had no notion that I was wrong or irreverent to my tutor.
   Boswell: That, Sir, was great fortitude of mind.
   Johnson: No, Sir: stark insensibility.
   Boswell's *Life of Johnson*, vol. i, p. 60. *5 Nov. 1728*

15 Sir, we are a nest of singing birds.
   Ib. p. 75. *1730*

16 If you call a dog *Hervey*, I shall love him.
   Ib. p. 106. *1737*

17 A man may write at any time, if he will set himself doggedly to it.
   Ib. p. 203. *Mar. 1750*

18 [Of F. Lewis]
   Sir, he lived in London, and hung loose upon society.
   Ib. p. 226. *1750*

19 [On being knocked up at 3 a.m. by Beauclerk and Langton]
   What, is it you, you dogs! I'll have a frisk with you.
   Ib. p. 250. *1752*

20 I had done all I could; and no man is well pleased to have his all neglected, be it ever so little.
   Ib. p. 261. *Letter to Lord Chesterfield, 7 Feb. 1755*

21 The shepherd in Virgil grew at last acquainted with Love, and found him a native of the rocks.
   Ib.

22 Is not a Patron, my Lord, one who looks with unconcern on a man struggling for life in the water, and, when he has reached ground, encumbers him with help? The notice which you have been pleased to take of my labours, had it been early, had been kind; but it has been delayed till I am indifferent, and cannot enjoy it; till I am solitary, and cannot impart it; till I am known, and do not want it.
   Ib.

1 [Of Lord Chesterfield]
This man I thought had been a Lord
among wits; but, I find, he is only
a wit among Lords. Boswell's *Life of
Johnson*, vol. i, p. 266. *1754*

2 [Of Lord Chesterfield's *Letters*]
They teach the morals of a whore, and
the manners of a dancing master. *Ib.*

3 [When asked by a lady why he defined 'pastern' as the 'knee' of a
horse, in his Dictionary]
Ignorance, madam, pure ignorance.
Ib. p. 293. *1755*

4 Lexicographer: a writer of dictionaries, a harmless drudge.
Ib. p. 296. *1755*

5 A man, Sir, should keep his friendship
in constant repair. *Ib.* p. 300. *1755*

6 No man will be a sailor who has con-
trivance enough to get himself into
a jail; for being in a ship is being in
a jail, with the chance of being
drowned. . . . A man in a jail has
more room, better food, and commonly
better company.
Ib. p. 348. *16 Mar. 1759*

7 *Boswell*: I do indeed come from Scotland, but I cannot help it.
Johnson: That, Sir, I find, is what a
very great many of your countrymen
cannot help. *Ib.* p. 392. *16 May 1763*

8 [On Dr. Blair's asking whether any
man of a modern age could have
written *Ossian*]
Yes, Sir, many men, many women,
and many children.
Ib. p. 396. *24 May 1763*

9 He insisted on people praying with
him; and I'd as lief pray with Kit
Smart as any one else.
Ib. p. 397. *24 May 1763*

10 [Of Kit Smart]
He did not love clean linen; and I have
no passion for it. *Ib.*

11 [Of literary criticism]
You may scold a carpenter who has
made you a bad table, though you
cannot make a table. It is not your
trade to make tables.
Ib. p. 409. *25 June 1763*

12 [Of Dr. John Campbell]
I am afraid he has not been in the
inside of a church for many years; but
he never passes a church without
pulling off his hat. This shews that he
has good principles.
Ib. p. 418. *1 July 1763*

13 Norway, too, has noble wild prospects;
and Lapland is remarkable for prodi-
gious noble wild prospects. But, Sir,
let me tell you, the noblest prospect
which a Scotchman ever sees, is the
high road that leads him to England!
Ib. p. 425. *6 July 1763*

14 A man ought to read just as inclination leads him; for what he reads as
a task will do him little good.
Boswell's *Life of Johnson*, vol. i,
p. 428. *14 July 1763*

15 Your levellers wish to level *down* as far
as themselves; but they cannot bear
levelling *up* to themselves.
Ib. p. 448. *21 July 1763*

16 Sir, it is no matter what you teach
them [children] first, any more than
what leg you shall put into your
breeches first.
Ib. p. 452. *26 July 1763*

17 Why, Sir, Sherry [Thomas Sheridan]
is dull, naturally dull; but it must
have taken him a great deal of pains
to become what we now see him. Such
an excess of stupidity, Sir, is not in
Nature. *Ib.* p. 453. *28 July 1763*

18 [Of Thomas Sheridan's influence on
the English language]
Sir, it is burning a farthing candle at
Dover, to shew light at Calais.
Ib. p. 454. *28 July 1763*

19 Sir, a woman's preaching is like a
dog's walking on his hinder legs. It is
not done well; but you are surprised
to find it done at all.
Ib. p. 463. *31 July 1763*

20 I look upon it, that he who does not
mind his belly will hardly mind
anything else.
Ib. p. 467. *5 Aug. 1763*

21 [Talking of Bishop Berkeley's theory
of the non-existence of matter, Boswell observed that though they were
satisfied it was not true, they were unable to refute it. Johnson struck his
foot against a large stone, till he re-
bounded from it, saying]
I refute it *thus*.
Ib. p. 471. *6 Aug. 1763*

22 [Of Sir John Hawkins]
A very unclubable man.
Ib. p. 480 n. *1764*

23 It was not for me to bandy civilities
with my Sovereign.
Ib. vol. ii, p. 35. *Feb. 1767*

24 Sir, We *know* our will is free, and
there's an end on't.
Ib. p. 82. *16 Oct. 1769*

25 Inspissated gloom. *Ib.*

26 I would not *coddle* the child.
Ib. p. 101. *26 Oct.* 1769

27 A gentleman who had been very unhappy in marriage, married immediately after his wife died: Johnson
said, it was the triumph of hope over
experience. *Ib.* p. 128. *1770*

28 [To Sir Adam Fergusson]
Sir, I perceive you are a vile Whig.
Ib. p. 170. *31 Mar. 1772*

1 [Quoting a college tutor]
Read over your compositions, and
where ever you meet with a passage
which you think is particularly fine,
strike it out.
Boswell's *Life of Johnson*, vol. ii,
p. 237. *30 Apr. 1773*

2 I think the full tide of human existence is at Charing-Cross.
Ib. p. 337. *2 Apr. 1775*

3 Most vices may be committed very
genteelly: a man may debauch his
friend's wife genteelly: he may cheat
at cards genteelly.
Ib. p. 340. *6 Apr. 1775*

4 Patriotism is the last refuge of a
scoundrel. *Ib.* p. 348. *7 Apr. 1775*

5 In lapidary inscriptions a man is not
upon oath. *Ib.* p. 407. *1775*

6 Sir, it is a great thing to dine with the
Canons of Christ-Church.
Ib. p. 445. *20 Mar. 1776*

7 There is nothing which has yet been
contrived by man, by which so much
happiness is produced as by a good
tavern or inn.
Ib. p. 452. *21 Mar. 1776*

8 No man but a blockhead ever wrote,
except for money.
Ib. vol. iii, p. 19. *5 Apr. 1776*

9 'Sir, what is poetry?'
'Why, Sir, it is much easier to say
what it is not. We all *know* what light
is; but it is not easy to *tell* what it is.'
Ib. p. 38. *12 Apr. 1776*

10 Dine with Jack Wilkes, Sir! I'd as
soon dine with Jack Ketch.
Ib. p. 66. (This has been circu-
lated as if actually said by Johnson; when the truth is, it was
only supposed by me. *Boswell's
note, Ib.* p. 66. *May 1776*)

11 Olivarii Goldsmith, Poetae, Physici,
Historici, Qui nullum fere scribendi
genus non tetigit, Nullum quod tetigit
non ornavit.
To Oliver Goldsmith, A Poet,
Naturalist, and Historian, who
left scarcely any style of writing
untouched, and touched none
that he did not adorn.
Ib. p. 82. *22 June 1776*. Epitaph
on Goldsmith

12 If I had no duties, and no reference to
futurity, I would spend my life in
driving briskly in a post-chaise with a
pretty woman.
Ib. p. 162. *19 Sept. 1777*

13 Depend upon it, Sir, when a man
knows he is to be hanged in a fortnight, it concentrates his mind wonderfully.
Ib. p. 167. *19 Sept. 1777*

14 No, Sir, when a man is tired of London,
he is tired of life; for there is in London
all that life can afford.
Boswell's *Life of Johnson*, vol. iii,
p. 178. *20 Sept. 1777*

15 John Wesley's conversation is good,
but he is never at leisure. He is always obliged to go at a certain hour.
This is very disagreeable to a man who
loves to fold his legs and have out his
talk as I do.
Ib. p. 230. *31 Mar. 1778*

16 Every man thinks meanly of himself
for not having been a soldier, or not
having been at sea.
Ib. p. 265. *10 Apr. 1778*

17 Johnson had said that he could repeat
a complete chapter of 'The Natural
History of Iceland', from the Danish
of Horrebow, the whole of which was
exactly thus:—'CHAP. LXXII. *Concerning snakes.* 'There are no snakes to
be met with throughout the whole
island.' *Ib.* p. 279. *13 Apr. 1778*

18 As the Spanish proverb says, 'He,
who would bring home the wealth of
the Indies, must carry the wealth of
the Indies with him.' So it is in
travelling; a man must carry know-
lege with him, if he would bring home
knowledge. *Ib.* p. 302. *17 Apr. 1778*

19 I have always said, the first Whig was
the Devil. *Ib.* p. 326. *28 Apr. 1778*

20 Claret is the liquor for boys; port for
men; but he who aspires to be a
hero must drink brandy.
Ib. p. 381. *7 Apr. 1779*

21 *Boswell*: Is not the Giant's-Causeway
worth seeing?
Johnson: Worth seeing? yes; but not
worth going to see.
Ib. p. 410. *12 Oct. 1779*

22 If you are idle, be not solitary; if you
are solitary, be not idle.
Ib. p. 415. *Letter to Boswell,
27 Oct. 1779*

23 This merriment of parsons is mighty
offensive.
Ib. vol. iv, p. 76. *Mar. 1781*

24 [At the sale of Thrale's brewery]
We are not here to sell a parcel of
boilers and vats, but the potentiality
of growing rich, beyond the dreams of
avarice. *Ib.* p. 87. *6 Apr. 1781*

25 'The woman had a bottom of good
sense.'
The word *'bottom'* thus introduced,
was so ludicrous, . . . that most of us
could not forbear tittering . . .
Where's the merriment? . . . I say
the *woman* was *fundamentally* sensible.' *Ib.* p. 99. *20 Apr. 1781*

1 [To Maurice Morgann who asked him whether he reckoned Derrick or Smart the better poet]
Sir, there is no settling the point of precedency between a louse and a flea.
Boswell's Life of Johnson, vol. iv, p. 192. *1783*

2 When I observed he was a fine cat, saying, 'why yes, Sir, but I have had cats whom I liked better than this'; and then as if perceiving Hodge to be out of countenance, adding, 'but he is a very fine cat, a very fine cat indeed.' *Ib.* p. 197. *1783*

3 Clear your *mind* of cant.
Ib. p. 221. *15 May 1783*

4 Boswell is a very clubable man.
Ib. p. 254 n. *1783*

5 [To Miss Hannah More, who had expressed a wonder that the poet who had written *Paradise Lost* should write such poor Sonnets]
Milton, Madam, was a genius that could cut a Colossus from a rock; but could not carve heads upon cherry-stones. *Ib.* p. 305. *13 June 1784*

6 [On Sir Joshua Reynolds's observing that the real character of a man was found out by his amusements]
Yes, Sir; no man is a hypocrite in his pleasures. *Ib.* p. 316. *June 1784*

7 Blown about by every wind of criticism. *Ib.* p. 319. *June 1784*

8 Sir, I look upon every day to be lost, in which I do not make a new acquaintance. *Ib.* p. 374. *Nov. 1784*

9 If the man who turnips cries,
Cry not when his father dies,
'Tis a proof that he had rather
Have a turnip than his father.
Johnsonian Miscellanies, vol. i, p. 193. *Burlesque of Lopez de Vega's lines, 'Se acquien los leones vence,' &c.*

10 What is written without effort is in general read without pleasure.
Ib. vol. ii, p. 309

11 As with my hat upon my head
I walk'd along the Strand,
I there did meet another man
With his hat in his hand.
Ib. Anecdotes by George Steevens, p. 315

12 Fly fishing may be a very pleasant amusement; but angling or float fishing I can only compare to a stick and a string, with a worm at one end and a fool at the other.
Attr. to Johnson by Hawker in Instructions to Young Sportsmen (1859), p. 197. *Not found in his works. See Notes and Queries, 11 Dec. 1915*

13 To make dictionaries is dull work.
Dictionary of the English Language. Dull. 8

14 *Excise.* A hateful tax levied upon commodities. *Ib.*

15 *Net.* Anything reticulated or decussated at equal distances, with interstices between the intersections. *Ib.*

16 *Oats.* A grain, which in England is generally given to horses, but in Scotland supports the people. *Ib.*

17 *Patron.* Commonly a wretch who supports with insolence, and is paid with flattery. *Ib.*

18 *Pension.* An allowance made to anyone without an equivalent. In England it is generally understood to mean pay given to a state hireling for treason to his country. *Ib.*

19 *Whig.* The name of a faction. *Ib.*

20 When two Englishmen meet, their first talk is of the weather.
The Idler, No. 11

21 The father of English criticism. [Dryden]
Lives of the English Poets (1905), ed. G. B. Hill, vol. i, *Dryden*, § 193, p. 410

22 But what are the hopes of man! I am disappointed by that stroke of death, which has eclipsed the gaiety of nations and impoverished the public stock of harmless pleasure. [Garrick's death.]
Ib. vol. ii, *Edmund Smith*, § 76, p. 21

23 Human life is everywhere a state in which much is to be endured, and little to be enjoyed. *Rasselas*, ch. 11

24 Marriage has many pains, but celibacy has no pleasures. *Ib.* ch. 26

25 Example is always more efficacious than precept. *Ib.* ch. 29

26 Notes are often necessary, but they are necessary evils.
Shakespeare (1765), preface.

27 This mournful truth is ev'rywhere confess'd,
Slow rises worth by poverty depress'd.
London, l. 176

28 The stage but echoes back the public voice.
The drama's laws the drama's patrons give,
For we that live to please, must please to live.
Prologue at the Opening of Drury Lane

1 Let observation with extensive view,
Survey mankind, from China to Peru;
Remark each anxious toil, each eager
strife,
And watch the busy scenes of crowded
life. *Vanity of Human Wishes*, l. 1

2 Deign on the passing world to turn
thine eyes,
And pause awhile from letters to be
wise;
There mark what ills the scholar's
life assail,
Toil, envy, want, the patron, and the
jail.
See nations slowly wise, and meanly
just,
To buried merit raise the tardy bust.
Ib. l. 157

3 His fall was destined to a barren
strand,
A petty fortress, and a dubious hand;
He left the name, at which the world
grew pale,
To point a moral, or adorn a tale.
Ib. l. 219

JOHN BENN JOHNSTONE
1803–1891

4 I want you to assist me in forcing her
on board the lugger; once there, I'll
frighten her into marriage.
(*Since quoted as*: Once aboard the
lugger and the maid is mine.)
The Gipsy Farmer

HANNS JOHST 1890–

5 Wenn ich Kultur höre . . . entsichere
ich meinen Browning.
Whenever I hear the word culture,
I release the safety catch on my
revolver.
Schlageter (1934), Act I, sc. i.
Attr. to Goering in the form, When
I hear anyone talk of culture I
reach for my revolver.

AL JOLSON 1886–1950

6 You ain't heard nothin' yet, folks.
*Remark in the first talking film,
'The Jazz Singer', July 1927*

JOHN PAUL JONES 1747–1792

7 I have not yet begun to fight.
*Remark on being hailed to know
whether he had struck his flag as
his ship was sinking, 23 Sept.
1779.* De Koven's *Life and Letters
of J. P. Jones*, vol. i

BEN JONSON 1573–1637

8 Fortune, that favours fools.
The Alchemist, prologue

9 Thou look'st like Anti-Christ in that
lewd hat! *The Alchemist*, Act IV

10 Slow, slow, fresh fount, keep time
with my salt tears:
Yet, slower, yet; O faintly, gentle
springs:
List to the heavy part the music bears,
Woe weeps out her division, when
she sings. *Cynthia's Revels*, I. i

11 Queen and huntress, chaste and fair,
Now the sun is laid to sleep,
Seated in thy silver chair,
State in wonted manner keep:
Hesperus entreats thy light,
Goddess, excellently bright.
Ib. v. iii

12 I remember the players have often
mentioned it as an honour to Shakespeare that in his writing (whatsoever
he penned) he never blotted out a
line. My answer hath been 'Would he
had blotted a thousand'. Which they
thought a malevolent speech. I had
not told posterity this, but for their
ignorance, who chose that circumstance to commend their friend by
wherein he most faulted; and to
justify mine own candour: for I
loved the man, and do honour his
memory, on this side idolatry, as
much as any.
*Discoveries. De Shakespeare Nos-
trati. Augustus in Haterium*

13 Alas, all the castles I have, are built
with air, thou know'st.
Eastward Ho!, II. ii. 226

14 Helter skelter, hang sorrow, care'll
kill a cat, up-tails all, and a louse for
the hangman.
Every Man in his Humour, I. iii

15 I have it here in black and white.
Ib. IV. ii

16 It must be done like lightning. *Ib.* v

17 There shall be no love lost.
Every Man out of his Humour,
II. i

18 Follow a shadow, it still flies you,
Seem to fly it, it will pursue:
So court a mistress, she denies you;
Let her alone, she will court you.
Say, are not women truly, then,
Styl'd but the shadows of us men?
The Forest, vii. *Song: That Women
are but Men's Shadows*

19 Drink to me only with thine eyes,
And I will pledge with mine;
Or leave a kiss but in the cup,
And I'll not look for wine.
The thirst that from the soul doth rise
Doth ask a drink divine:
But might I of Jove's nectar sup,
I would not change for thine.

I sent thee late a rosy wreath,
Not so much honouring thee,
As giving it a hope that there
It could not wither'd be.
But thou thereon didst only breathe,
And sent'st it back to me;
Since when it grows and smells, I
swear,
Not of itself, but thee.
The Forest, ix. *To Celia*

1 Ramp up my genius, be not retro-
grade;
But boldly nominate a spade a spade.
The Poetaster, v. i

2 This is Mab, the Mistress-Fairy
That doth nightly rob the dairy.
The Satyr

3 This figure that thou here seest put,
It was for gentle Shakespeare cut,
Wherein the graver had a strife
With Nature, to out-do the life:
O could he but have drawn his wit
As well in brass, as he has hit
His face; the print would then surpass
All that was ever writ in brass:
But since he cannot, reader, look
Not on his picture, but his book.
*On the Portrait of Shakespeare,
To the Reader*

4   Soul of the Age!
The applause! delight! the wonder of
our stage!
My Shakespeare, rise; I will not lodge
thee by
Chaucer, or Spenser, or bid Beaumont
lie
A little further, to make thee a room:
Thou art a monument, without a
tomb,
And art alive still, while thy book
doth live,
And we have wits to read, and praise
to give.
*To the Memory of My Beloved,
the Author, Mr. William Shakespeare*

5 Marlowe's mighty line.   *Ib.*

6 And though thou hadst small Latin,
and less Greek.   *Ib.*

7 He was not of an age, but for all time!
Ib.

8 For a good poet's made, as well as
born.   *Ib.*

9 Sweet Swan of Avon! what a sight it
were
To see thee in our waters yet appear,
And make those flights upon the banks
of Thames,
That so did take Eliza, and our James!
Ib.

10   Hark you, John Clay, if you have
Done any such thing, tell troth and
shame the devil.
Tale of a Tub, II. i

11 Have you seen but a bright lily grow,
Before rude hands have touch'd it?
Have you mark'd but the fall o' the
snow
Before the soil hath smutch'd it?
.   .   .   .   .
O so white! O so soft! O so sweet is she!
*Underwoods Celebration of Cha-
ris*, IV. *Her Triumph*

12 Come, my Celia, let us prove,
While we can, the sports of love.
Volpone, III. v

13 Suns, that set, may rise again;
But if once we lose this light,
'Tis with us perpetual night.   *Ib.*

14 O rare Ben Jonson.
*Epitaph written on his tombstone
in Westminster Abbey, by Jack
Young. See Aubrey's Brief Lives,
Ben Jonson*

DOROTHEA JORDAN 1762–1816

15 'Oh where, and Oh! where is your
Highland laddie gone?'
'He's gone to fight the French, for
King George upon the throne,
And it's Oh! in my heart, how I wish
him safe at home!'
The Blue Bells of Scotland. Prop-
erly *The Blue Bell of Scotland*
but popularly known as *Blue
Bells*

BENJAMIN JOWETT 1817–1893

16 The lie in the Soul is a true lie.
*From the Introduction to his
translation of* Plato's *Republic,
bk.* ii

JAMES JOYCE 1882–1941

17 A portrait of the artist as a young
man.   *Title of Book*

JULIAN THE APOSTATE
c. 331–363

18 Vicisti, Galilæe.
Thou hast conquered, O Galilean.
Dying words. Latin translation
of Theodoret, *Hist. Eccles.* iii. 20

JUVENAL A.D. 60–c. 130

19 Si natura negat, facit indignatio
versum.
If nature denies the power, indig-
nation would give birth to verses.
Satires, i. 79. Trans. by Lewis
Evans.

1 Quidquid agunt homines, votum timor
 ira voluptas
Gaudia discursus nostri farrago libelli
est.

> All that men are engaged in, their
> wishes, fears, anger, pleasures,
> joys, and varied pursuits, form
> the hotch-potch of my book.
> *Satires*, i. 85

2 Nemo repente fuit turpissimus.

> No one ever reached the climax of
> vice at one step. *Ib.* ii. 83

3 Haud facile emergunt quorum virtuti-
 bus obstat
Res angusta domi.

> Difficult indeed is it for those to
> emerge from obscurity whose
> noble qualities are cramped by
> narrow means at home.
> *Ib.* iii. 164

4 Rara avis in terris nigroque simillima
 cycno.

> A rare bird on the earth and very
> like a black swan. *Ib.* vi. 165

5 'Pone seram, prohibe.' Sed quis custo-
 diet ipsos
Custodes? Cauta est et ab illis incipit
uxor.

> 'Put on a lock! keep her in confine-
> ment!' But who is to guard the
> guards themselves? Your wife is
> as cunning as you, and begins
> with them. *Ib.* 347

6   Tenet insanabile multos
Scribendi cacoethes et aegro in corde
senescit.

> An inveterate itch of writing, now
> incurable, clings to many, and
> grows old in their distempered
> body. *Ib.* vii. 51

7   Verbosa et grandis epistula venit
A Capreis.

> A wordy and lengthy epistle came
> from Capreae. *Ib.* x. 71

8 Duas tantum res anxius optat,
Panem et circenses.

> Limits its [i.e. the Roman people's]
> anxious longings to two things
> only—bread, and the games of the
> circus. *Ib.* 80

9 Orandum est ut sit mens sana in
corpore sano.

> Your prayer must be that you may
> have a sound mind in a sound
> body. *Ib.* 356

IMMANUEL KANT 1724–1804

10 Zwei Dinge erfüllen das Gemüth mit
immer neuer und zunehmender Be-
wunderung und Ehrfurcht, je öfter
und anhaltender sich das Nach-
denken damit beschäftigt: der bestirnte Himmel über mir, und das
moralische Gesetz in mir.

> Two things fill the mind with ever-
> increasing wonder and awe, the
> more often and the more in-
> tensely the mind of thought is
> drawn to them: the starry
> heavens above me and the moral
> law within me.
> *Critique of Practical Reason*, con-
> clusion

11 There is . . . but one categorical imperative: 'Act only on that maxim
 whereby thou canst at the same time
 will that it should become a universal
 law.'
> *Trans. by A. D. Lindsay, from*
> *Fundamental Principles of . . .*
> *Morals*, p. 421

12 I ought, therefore I can. *Attr.*

ALPHONSE KARR 1808–1890

13 Plus ça change, plus c'est la même
chose.

> The more things change, the more
> they are the same.
> *Les Guêpes, Jan. 1849*, vi

14 Si l'on veut abolir la peine de mort en
ce cas, que MM. les assassins commencent.

> If we are to abolish the death
> penalty, I should like to see the
> first step taken by our friends the
> murderers. *Ib.*

TED KAVANAGH 1892–1958

15 It's that man again.
> *B.B.C., Itma* programmes

DENIS KEARNEY 1847–1907

16 Horny-handed sons of toil.
> *Speech. San Francisco, c. 1878*

JOHN KEATS 1795–1821

17 Season of mists and mellow fruitfulness,
Close bosom-friend of the maturing
sun;
Conspiring with him how to load and
bless
With fruit the vines that round the
thatch-eaves run. *To Autumn*

18 Who hath not seen thee oft amid thy
store?
Sometimes whoever seeks abroad may
find
Thee sitting careless on a granary floor,
Thy hair soft-lifted by the winnowing
wind;

Or on a half-reap'd furrow sound
asleep,
Drows'd with the fume of poppies,
while thy hook
Spares the next swath and all its
twined flowers.   *To Autumn*

1 A thing of beauty is a joy for ever:
Its loveliness increases; it will never
Pass into nothingness; but still will
keep
A bower quiet for us, and a sleep
Full of sweet dreams, and health,
and quiet breathing.
               Endymion, bk. i, l. 1

2 St. Agnes' Eve—Ah, bitter chill it was!
The owl, for all his feathers, was
a-cold;
The hare limp'd trembling through the
frozen grass,
And silent was the flock in woolly
fold.   *The Eve of Saint Agnes*, i

3 The silver, snarling trumpets 'gan to
chide.   *Ib.* iv

4 A casement high and triple-arch'd
there was,
All garlanded with carven imag'ries
Of fruits, and flowers, and bunches of
knot-grass,
And diamonded with panes of quaint
device,
Innumerable of stains and splendid
dyes,
As are the tiger-moth's deep-damask'd
wings;
And in the midst, 'mong thousand
heraldries,
And twilight saints, and dim emblazonings,
A shielded scutcheon blush'd with
blood of queens and kings.
                         Ib. xxiv

5 And they are gone: aye, ages long ago
These lovers fled away into the storm.
                         Ib. xlii

6 Ever let the fancy roam,
Pleasure never is at home. *Fancy,* l. 1

7   No stir of air was there,
Not so much life as on a summer's day
Robs not one light seed from the
feather'd grass,
But where the dead leaf fell, there did
it rest.   *Hyperion*, bk. i, l. 7

8 So the two brothers and their murder'd
man
Rode past fair Florence.
                  Isabella, xxvii

9 I stood tip-toe upon a little hill.
                             Title

10 Oh what can ail thee, Knight at arms
Alone and palely loitering;
The sedge is wither'd from the lake,
And no birds sing.
          La Belle Dame Sans Merci

11 I see a lily on thy brow,
With anguish moist and fever dew;
And on thy cheek a fading rose
Fast withereth too.
          La Belle Dame Sans Merci

12 She look'd at me as she did love,
And made sweet moan.   *Ib.*

13 And there I shut her wild, wild eyes
With kisses four.
          Ib. (Ld. Houghton's version)

14   La belle Dame sans Merci
Hath thee in thrall!   *Ib.*

15 Love in a hut, with water and a crust,
Is—Love, forgive us!—cinders, ashes,
dust;
Love in a palace is perhaps at last
More grievous torment than a hermit's
fast.   *Lamia*, pt. ii, l. 1

16 Philosophy will clip an Angel's wings.
                         Ib. l. 234

17 Souls of poets dead and gone,
What Elysium have ye known,
Happy field or mossy cavern,
Choicer than the Mermaid Tavern?
Have ye tippled drink more fine
Than mine host's Canary wine?
          Lines on the Mermaid Tavern

18 Thou still unravish'd bride of quietness,
Thou foster-child of silence and slow
time.   *Ode on a Grecian Urn*

19 Heard melodies are sweet, but those
unheard
Are sweeter; therefore, ye soft pipes,
play on;
Not to the sensual ear, but, more
endear'd,
Pipe to the spirit ditties of no tone. *Ib.*

20 For ever wilt thou love, and she be
fair!   *Ib.*

21 Who are these coming to the sacrifice?
To what green altar, O mysterious
priest,
Lead'st thou that heifer lowing at the
skies,
And all her silken flanks with garlands
drest?
What little town by river or sea shore,
Or mountain-built with peaceful cita-
del,
Is emptied of this folk, this pious
morn?   *Ib.*

22 O Attic shape! Fair attitude!   *Ib.*

23 'Beauty is truth, truth beauty,'—
that is all
Ye know on earth, and all ye need to
know.   *Ib.*

24 She dwells with Beauty—Beauty that
must die;
And Joy, whose hand is ever at his lips
Bidding adieu; and aching Pleasure
nigh,
Turning to Poison while the bee-
mouth sips:

Ay, in the very temple of delight
Veil'd Melancholy has her sovran
  shrine.
Though seen of none save him whose
  strenuous tongue
Can burst Joy's grape against his
  palate fine;
His soul shall taste the sadness of her
  might,
And be among her cloudy trophies
  hung.   *Ode on Melancholy*

1 My heart aches, and a drowsy numbness pains
My sense.   *Ode to a Nightingale*

2 'Tis not through envy of thy happy lot,
But being too happy in thine happiness,—
That thou, light-winged Dryad of the
  trees,
    In some melodious plot
Of beechen green, and shadows numberless,
Singest of summer in full-throated
  ease.   *Ib.*

3 O, for a draught of vintage! that hath
  been
Cool'd a long age in the deep-delved
  earth,
Tasting of Flora and the country
  green,
Dance, and Provençal song, and sun-
  burnt mirth!
O for a beaker full of the warm South,
Full of the true, the blushful Hippo-
  crene,
With beaded bubbles winking at the
  brim,
And purple-stained mouth;
That I might drink, and leave the
  world unseen,
And with thee fade away into the
  forest dim.   *Ib.*

4 Fade far away, dissolve, and quite
  forget
What thou among the leaves hast
  never known,
The weariness, the fever, and the fret,
Here, where men sit and hear each
  other groan.   *Ib.*

5 Fast fading violets cover'd up in
  leaves;
And mid-May's eldest child,
The coming musk-rose, full of dewy
  wine,
The murmurous haunt of flies on
  summer eves.   *Ib.*

6 Darkling I listen; and, for many a
  time
I have been half in love with easeful
  Death,
Call'd him soft names in many a
  mused rhyme,
To take into the air my quiet breath;

Now more than ever seems it rich to
  die,
To cease upon the midnight with no
  pain,
While thou art pouring forth thy soul
  abroad
    In such an ecstasy!
Still wouldst thou sing, and I have
  ears in vain—
To thy high requiem become a sod.

Thou wast not born for death, im-
  mortal Bird!
No hungry generations tread thee
  down;
The voice I hear this passing night
  was heard
In ancient days by emperor and
  clown:
Perhaps the self-same song that found
  a path
Through the sad heart of Ruth, when
  sick for home,
She stood in tears amid the alien corn;
    The same that oft-times hath
Charm'd magic casements, opening on
  the foam
Of perilous seas, in faery lands forlorn.
          Ode to a Nightingale

7 Forlorn! the very word is like a bell
To toll me back from thee to my sole
  self!
Adieu! the fancy cannot cheat so well
As she is fam'd to do, deceiving elf.
Adieu! adieu! thy plaintive anthem
  fades
Past the near meadows, over the still
  stream,
Up the hill-side; and now 'tis buried
  deep
    In the next valley-glades:
Was it a vision, or a waking dream?
Fled is that music:—Do I wake or
  sleep?   *Ib.*

8 Bright star, would I were steadfast
  as thou art—
Not in lone splendour hung aloft the
  night
And watching, with eternal lids apart,
Like nature's patient, sleepless Eremite,
The moving waters at their priestlike
  task
Of pure ablution round earth's human
  shores.   *Sonnet. Bright Star*

9 Much have I travell'd in the realms of
  gold,
And many goodly states and kingdoms
  seen;
Round many western islands have I
  been
Which bards in fealty to Apollo hold.
Oft of one wide expanse had I been
  told
That deep-brow'd Homer ruled as his
  demesne;
Yet did I never breathe its pure serene

Till I heard Chapman speak out loud
   and bold:
Then felt I like some watcher of the
   skies
When a new planet swims into his ken;
Or like stout Cortez when with eagle
   eyes
He star'd at the Pacific—and all his
   men
Look'd at each other with a wild
   surmise—
Silent, upon a peak in Darien.
   *Sonnets. On First Looking into
   Chapman's Homer*

1 Glory and loveliness have pass'd away.
   Ib. To Leigh Hunt

2 To one who has been long in city pent;
'Tis very sweet to look into the fair
And open face of heaven.
   Ib. To One Who Has Been Long

3 When I have fears that I may cease to
   be
Before my pen has glean'd my teeming
   brain.   *Ib. When I Have Fears*

4 When I behold upon the night's
   starr'd face,
Huge cloudy symbols of a high
   romance.   *Ib.*

5   Then on the shore
Of the wide world I stand alone, and
   think
Till love and fame to nothingness do
   sink.   *Ib.*

6 In a drear-nighted December,
Too happy, happy tree,
Thy branches ne'er remember
Their green felicity.
   *Stanzas. In a Drear-nighted
   December*

7 I am certain of nothing but the holiness of the heart's affections and the
   truth of imagination—what the imagination seizes as beauty must be truth
   —whether it existed before or not.
   Letters (ed. M. B. Forman), 31.
   *To Benjamin Bailey, 22 Nov.
   1817*

8 O for a life of sensations rather than
   of thoughts!   *Ib.*

9 There is an awful warmth about my
   heart like a load of immortality.
   *Ib. 87. To J. H. Reynolds, 22
   Sept. 1818*

10 I think I shall be among the English
   Poets after my death.
   *Ib. 94. To George and Georgiana
   Keats, 14 Oct. 1818*

11 You, I am sure, will forgive me for
   sincerely remarking that you might
   curb your magnanimity, and be more
   of an artist, and load every rift of
   your subject with ore.
   Ib. 227. To Shelley, Aug. 1820

12 Here lies one whose name was writ in
   water.
   Epitaph. Lord Houghton, *Life
   of Keats*, ii. 91

JOHN KEBLE 1792–1866

13 New every morning is the love
Our wakening and uprising prove.
   The Christian Year. Morning

14 The trivial round, the common task,
Would furnish all we ought to ask;
Room to deny ourselves; a road
To bring us, daily, nearer God.   *Ib.*

15 And help us, this and every day,
To live more nearly as we pray.   *Ib.*

16 Sun of my soul! Thou Saviour dear,
It is not night if Thou be near.
   Ib. Evening

17 Like infant slumbers, pure and light.
   Ib.

18 There is a book, who runs may read,
Which heavenly truth imparts,
And all the lore its scholars need,
Pure eyes and Christian hearts.
   Ib. Septuagesima

19 Bless'd are the pure in heart,
For they shall see our God.
   Ib. The Purification

20 The voice that breathed o'er Eden.
   Poems. Holy Matrimony

THOMAS KELLY 1769–1854

21 The Head that once was crowned with
   thorns
Is crowned with glory now.
   *Hymns on Various Passages of
   Scripture* (1820). *The Head that
   Once Was Crowned*

THOMAS À KEMPIS 1380–1471

22 Nam homo proponit, sed Deus disponit.
   Man proposes but God disposes.
   Imitatio Christi, Bk. 1, ch. xix.
   § 2

23 Sic transit gloria mundi.
   O, how quickly doth the glory of
   the world pass away!
   Ib. ch. iii. § 6

JOHN KEMPTHORNE 1775–1838

24 Praise the Lord! ye heavens adore
   Him,
Praise Him, Angels in the height;
Sun and moon, rejoice before Him,
Praise Him, all ye stars and light.
   *Hymns of Praise. For Foundling
   Apprentices* (1796). *Praise the
   Lord! Ye Heavens Adore Him*

BISHOP THOMAS KEN 1637-1711

1 Awake my soul, and with the sun
Thy daily stage of duty run;
Shake off dull sloth, and joyful rise
To pay thy morning sacrifice.
Morning Hymn (1709). *Awake
My Soul*

2 Teach me to live, that I may dread
The grave as little as my bed.
*Evening Hymn. Glory to Thee
My God This Night*

3 Praise God, from whom all blessings
flow,
Praise Him, all creatures here below,
Praise Him above, ye heavenly host,
Praise Father, Son, and Holy Ghost.
Morning and Evening Hymn

JOSEPH KESSELRING 1902–

4 Arsenic and Old Lace.
Title of Play (1941)

WILLIAM KETHE d. 1608?

5 All people that on earth do dwell,
Sing to the Lord with cheerful voice;
Him serve with fear, His praise forth
tell,
Come ye before Him, and rejoice.

The Lord, ye know, is God indeed;
Without our aid He did us make.
Daye's Psalter (1560). *All People
That on Earth*

6 For it is seemly so to do.   *Ib.*

FRANCIS SCOTT KEY 1779-1843

7 'Tis the star-spangled banner; O long
may it wave
O'er the land of the free, and the
home of the brave!
The Star-Spangled Banner

JOYCE KILMER 1888-1918

8 I think that I shall never see
A poem lovely as a tree.
Poems, Essays, and Letters (1917),
i. *Trees*

9 Poems are made by fools like me,
But only God can make a tree.   *Ib.*

BENJAMIN FRANKLIN KING
1857-1894

10 Nothing to do but work,
Nothing to eat but food,
Nothing to wear but clothes
To keep one from going nude.
The Pessimist

BISHOP HENRY KING 1592-1669

11 But hark! My pulse like a soft drum
Beats my approach, tells thee I come;
And slow howe'er my marches be,
I shall at last sit down by thee.
The Exequy

STODDARD KING 1889-1933

12 There's a long, long trail a-winding
Into the land of my dreams,
Where the nightingales are singing
And a white moon beams:
There's a long, long night of waiting
Until my dreams all come true;
Till the day when I'll be going down
That long long trail with you.
The Long, Long Trail

ALEXANDER WILLIAM KING-LAKE 1809-1891

13 Soon the men of the column began to
see that though the scarlet line was
slender, it was very rigid and exact.
Invasion of the Crimea, vol. ii,
p. 455

CHARLES KINGSLEY 1819-1875

14 Be good, sweet maid, and let who can
be clever;
Do lovely things, not dream them, all
day long;
And so make Life, and Death, and
that For Ever,
One grand sweet song.
A Farewell. To C. E. G.

15 What we can we will be,
Honest Englishmen.
Do the work that's nearest,
Though it's dull at whiles,
Helping, when we meet them,
Lame dogs over stiles.
Letter to Thomas Hughes

16 Welcome, wild North-easter!
Shame it is to see
Odes to every zephyr;
Ne'er a verse to thee.
Ode to the North-East Wind

17 I once had a sweet little doll, dears,
The prettiest doll in the world;
Her cheeks were so red and so white,
dears,
And her hair was so charmingly
curled.
*Songs from The Water Babies.
My Little Doll*

18 When all the world is young, lad,
And all the trees are green;
And every goose a swan, lad,
And every lass a queen;
Then hey for boot and horse, lad,
And round the world away:
Young blood must have its course, lad,
And every dog his day.

When all the world is old, lad,
And all the trees are brown;
And all the sport is stale, lad,
And all the wheels run down;
Creep home, and take your place
there,
The spent and maimed among:
God grant you find one face there,
You loved when all was young.
*Songs from The Water Babies.
Young and Old*

1 'O Mary, go and call the cattle home,
and call the cattle home,
And call the cattle home,
Across the sands of Dee:'
The western wind was wild and dank
with foam,
And all alone went she.
The Sands of Dee

2 Three fishers went sailing away to the
west,
Away to the west as the sun went
down;
Each thought on the woman who
loved him the best,
And the children stood watching
them out of the town.
The Three Fishers

3 For men must work, and women must
weep.   *Ib.*

4 To be discontented with the divine
discontent, and to be ashamed with
the noble shame, is the very germ
and first upgrowth of all virtue.
Health and Education (1874),
p. 20

5 Mrs. Bedonebyasyoudid is coming.
The Water Babies, ch. 5

6 The loveliest fairy in the world; and
her name is Mrs. Doasyouwouldbedoneby.   *Ib.*

7 More ways of killing a cat than
choking her with cream.
Westward Ho!, ch. 20

8 Some say that the age of chivalry is
past, that the spirit of romance is
dead. The age of chivalry is never past,
so long as there is a wrong left unredressed on earth.
Life (1879), vol. ii, ch. 28

RUDYARD KIPLING 1865–1936

9 When you've shouted 'Rule Britannia', when you've sung 'God save
the Queen',
When you've finished killing Kruger
with your mouth.
The Absent-Minded Beggar

10 He's an absent-minded beggar, and
his weaknesses are great.   *Ib.*

11 Duke's son—cook's son—son of a
hundred Kings—
(Fifty thousand horse and foot going
to Table Bay!)   *Ib.*

12 Rolling down the Ratcliffe Road
drunk and raising Cain.
The Ballad of the 'Bolivar'

13 Oh, East is East, and West is West,
and never the twain shall meet,
Till Earth and Sky stand presently at
God's great Judgment Seat;
But there is neither East nor West,
Border, nor Breed, nor Birth,
When two strong men stand face to
face, though they come from the
ends of the earth!
The Ballad of East and West

14 And a man is only a woman, but
a good cigar is a Smoke.
The Betrothed

15 'Oh, where are you going to, all you
Big Steamers,
With England's own coal, up and
down the salt seas?'
'We are going to fetch you your bread
and your butter,
Your beef, pork, and mutton, eggs,
apples, and cheese.'   *Big Steamers*

16 We're   foot—slog—slog—slog—slog-
gin' over Africa—
Foot—foot—foot—foot—sloggin' over
Africa—
(Boots — boots — boots — boots —
movin' up an' down again!)
There's no discharge in the war!
Boots

17 Land of our birth, we pledge to thee
Our love and toil in the years to be;
When we are grown and take our
place,
As men and women with our race.

Father in Heaven who lovest all,
Oh, help Thy children when they call;
That they may build from age to age
An undefilèd heritage.

Teach us to bear the yoke in youth,
With steadfastness and careful truth;
That, in our time, Thy Grace may give
The truth whereby the nations live.
The Children's Song

18 Teach us delight in simple things,
And mirth that has no bitter springs;
Forgiveness free of evil done,
And love to all men 'neath the sun!

Land of our birth, our faith, our pride,
For whose dear sake our fathers died;
O Motherland, we pledge to thee
Head, heart, and hand through the
years to be!   *Ib.*

19 Gold is for the mistress—silver for the
maid—
Copper for the craftsman cunning at
his trade.
'Good!' said the Baron, sitting in his
hall,
'But Iron—Cold Iron—is master of
them all.'   *Cold Iron*

1 Our father Adam sat under the Tree
and scratched with a stick in the
mould;
And the first rude sketch that the
world had seen was joy to his
mighty heart.
Till the Devil whispered behind the
leaves, 'It's pretty, but is it Art?'
*The Conundrum of the Work-
shops*

2 'For they're hangin' Danny Deever,
you can hear the Dead March play,
The Regiment's in 'ollow square—
they're hangin' 'im to-day;
They've taken of 'is buttons off an'
cut 'is stripes away,
An' they're hangin' Danny Deever in
the mornin'.' *Danny Deever*

3 The 'eathen in 'is blindness bows down
to wood an' stone;
'E don't obey no orders unless they is
'is own;
'E keeps 'is side-arms awful: 'e leaves
'em all about,
An' then comes up the Regiment an'
pokes the 'eathen out. *The 'Eathen*

4 Winds of the World, give answer!
They are whimpering to and fro—
And what should they know of Eng-
land who only England know?
The English Flag

5 When the Himalayan peasant meets
the he-bear in his pride,
He shouts to scare the monster, who
will often turn aside.
But the she-bear thus accosted rends
the peasant tooth and nail
For the female of the species is more
deadly than the male.
The Female of the Species

6 To the legion of the lost ones, to the
cohort of the damned.
Gentlemen Rankers

7 Gentlemen-rankers out on the spree,
Damned from here to Eternity. *Ib.*

8 Our England is a garden that is full of
stately views,
Of borders, beds and shrubberies and
lawns and avenues,
With statues on the terraces and peacocks strutting by;
But the Glory of the Garden lies in
more than meets the eye.
The Glory of the Garden

9 Our England is a garden, and such
gardens are not made
By singing:—'Oh, how beautiful!' and
sitting in the shade,
While better men than we go out and
start their working lives
At grubbing weeds from gravel paths
with broken dinner-knives. *Ib.*

10 Oh, Adam was a gardener, and God
who made him sees
That half a proper gardener's work is
done upon his knees,
So when your work is finished, you
can wash your hands and pray
For the Glory of the Garden, that it
may not pass away!
And the Glory of the Garden it shall
never pass away!
The Glory of the Garden

11 You may talk o' gin an' beer
When you're quartered safe out 'ere,
An' you're sent to penny-fights an'
Aldershot it;
But when it comes to slaughter
You will do your work on water,
An' you'll lick the bloomin' boots of
'im that's got it. *Gunga Din*

12 Though I've belted you an' flayed you,
By the livin' Gawd that made you,
You're a better man than I am,
Gunga Din! *Ib.*

13 There are nine and sixty ways of
constructing tribal lays,
And—every—single—one—of—them
—is—right! *In the Neolithic Age*

14 If you can keep your head when all
about you
Are losing theirs and blaming it on
you,
If you can trust yourself when all men
doubt you,
But make allowance for their doubt-
ing too;
If you can wait and not be tired by
waiting,
Or being lied about, don't deal in lies,
Or being hated, don't give way to
hating,
And yet don't look too good, nor
talk too wise:
If you can dream—and not make
dreams your master;
If you can think—and not make
thoughts your aim;
If you can meet with Triumph and
Disaster
And treat those two impostors just
the same. *If*

15 If you can make one heap of all your
winnings
And risk it on one turn of pitch-
and-toss,
And lose, and start again at your
beginnings
And never breathe a word about
your loss. *Ib.*

16 If you can talk with crowds and keep
your virtue,
Or walk with Kings—nor lose the
common touch,
If neither foes nor loving friends can
hurt you,
If all men count with you, but none
too much;

If you can fill the unforgiving minute
With sixty seconds' worth of distance run,
Yours is the Earth and everything that's in it,
And—which is more—you'll be a Man, my son! *If*

1 Then ye returned to your trinkets;
then ye contented your souls
With the flannelled fools at the wicket or the muddied oafs at the goals. *The Islanders*

2 The Camel's hump is an ugly lump
Which well you may see at the Zoo;
But uglier yet is the Hump we get
From having too little to do.
Just-So Stories. How the Camel Got his Hump

3 We get the Hump—
Cameelious Hump—
The Hump that is black and blue! *Ib.*

4 The cure for this ill is not to sit still,
Or frowst with a book by the fire;
But to take a large hoe and a shovel also,
And dig till you gently perspire. *Ib.*

5 Old Man Kangaroo first, Yellow-Dog Dingo behind.
Ib. Sing-Song of Old Man Kangaroo

6 'Confound Romance!' . . . And all unseen
Romance brought up the nine-fifteen.
The King

7 I've taken my fun where I've found it,
An' now I must pay for my fun,
For the more you 'ave known o' the others
The less will you settle to one;
An' the end of it 's sittin' an' thinkin',
An' dreamin' Hell-fires to see.
So be warned by my lot (which I know you will not),
An' learn about women from me!
The Ladies

8 For the Colonel's Lady an' Judy O'Grady
Are sisters under their skins! *Ib.*

9 Now this is the Law of the Jungle—
as old and as true as the sky.
The Law of the Jungle

10 Ye thought? Ye are not paid to think.
McAndrew's Hymn

11 By the old Moulmein Pagoda, lookin' eastward to the sea,
There's a Burma girl a-settin', and I know she thinks o' me;
For the wind is in the palm-trees, an' the temple-bells they say:
'Come you back, you British soldier; come you back to Mandalay!'
Come you back to Mandalay,
Where the old Flotilla lay:

Can't you 'ear their paddles chunkin' from Rangoon to Mandalay?
On the road to Mandalay,
Where the flyin'-fishes play,
An' the dawn comes up like thunder outer China 'crost the Bay!
Mandalay

12 An' I seed her first a-smokin' of a whackin' white cheroot,
An' a-wastin' Christian kisses on an 'eathen idol's foot. *Ib.*

13 But that 's all shove be'ind me—long ago an' fur away,
An' there ain' no 'buses runnin' from the Bank to Mandalay;
An' I'm learnin' 'ere in London wot the ten-year soldier tells:
'If you've 'eard the East a-callin', you won't never 'eed naught else.'
Ib.

14 I am sick o' wastin' leather on these gritty pavin'-stones,
An' the blasted English drizzle wakes the fever in my bones;
Tho' I walks with fifty 'ousemaids outer Chelsea to the Strand,
An' they talks a lot o' lovin', but wot do they understand?
Beefy face an' grubby 'and—
Law! Wot do they understand?
I've a neater, sweeter maiden in a cleaner, greener land! *Ib.*

15 Ship me somewheres east of Suez, where the best is like the worst,
Where there aren't no Ten Commandments, an' a man can raise a thirst:
For the temple-bells are callin', an' it 's there that I would be—
By the old Moulmein Pagoda, looking lazy at the sea. *Ib.*

16 If I were hanged on the highest hill,
Mother o' mine, O mother o' mine!
I know whose love would follow me still,
Mother o' mine, O mother o' mine!
Mother O' Mine

17 And the epitaph drear: 'A Fool lies here who tried to hustle the East.'
Naulahka, heading of ch. 5

18 The Saxon is not like us Normans.
His manners are not so polite.
Norman and Saxon

19 A Nation spoke to a Nation,
A Throne sent word to a Throne:
'Daughter am I in my mother's house,
But mistress in my own.
Our Lady of the Snows

20 The toad beneath the harrow knows
Exactly where each tooth-point goes;
The butterfly upon the road
Preaches contentment to that toad.
Pagett M.P.

21 Pagett, M.P., was a liar, and a fluent liar therewith. *Ib.*

1 Can't! Don't! Sha'n't! Won't!
Pass it along the line!
Somebody's pack has slid from his
back,
'Wish it were only mine!
Somebody's load has tipped off in the
road—
Cheer for a halt and a row!
Urrh! Yarrh! Grr! Arrh!
Somebody's catching it now!
*Parade-Song of the Camp-Ani-
mals. Commissariat Camels*

2 Brothers and Sisters, I bid you beware
Of giving your heart to a dog to tear.
The Power of the Dog

3 God of our fathers, known of old,
Lord of our far-flung battle-line,
Beneath whose awful Hand we hold
Dominion over palm and pine—
Lord God of Hosts, be with us yet,
Lest we forget—lest we forget!

4 The tumult and the shouting dies;
The Captains and the Kings depart:
Still stands Thine ancient sacrifice,
An humble and a contrite heart.
Lord God of Hosts, be with us yet,
Lest we forget—lest we forget!
Recessional

5 Lo, all our pomp of yesterday
Is one with Nineveh and Tyre!   *Ib.*

6 If, drunk with sight of power, we loose
Wild tongues that have not Thee in
awe,
Such boastings as the Gentiles use,
Or lesser breeds without the Law. *Ib.*

7 For heathen heart that puts her trust
In reeking tube and iron shard,
All valiant dust that builds on dust,
And, guarding, calls not Thee to guard,
For frantic boast and foolish word—
Thy mercy on Thy People, Lord! *Ib.*

8 And I've lost Britain, and I've lost
Gaul,
And I've lost Rome and, worst of all,
I've lost Lalage!   *Rimini*

9 Shillin' a day,
Bloomin' good pay—
Lucky to touch it, a shillin' a day!
Shillin' a Day

10 Them that asks no questions isn't told
a lie.
Watch the wall, my darling, while the
Gentlemen go by!
Five and twenty ponies
Trotting through the dark—
Brandy for the Parson,
'Baccy for the Clerk;
Laces for a lady, letters for a spy,
Watch the wall, my darling, while the
Gentlemen go by!
A Smuggler's Song

11 I am all that ever went with evening
dress!   *The Song of the Banjo*

12 If blood be the price of admiralty,
Lord God, we ha' paid in full!
The Song of the Dead, ii

13 Through the Jungle very softly flits
a shadow and a sigh—
He is Fear, O Little Hunter, he is
Fear!
The Song of the Little Hunter

14 Mithras, God of the Morning, our
trumpets waken the Wall!
'Rome is above the Nations, but
Thou art over all!' *A Song to Mithras*

15 'Let us now praise famous men—
Men of little showing—
For their work continueth,
And their work continueth,
Broad and deep continueth,
Greater than their knowing!
Stalky & Co. A School Song

16 A Jelly-bellied Flag-flapper.   *Ib.*

17 You may carve it on his tombstone,
you may cut it on his card,
That a young man married is a young
man marred.
The Story of the Gadsbys

18 God gives all men all earth to love,
But, since man's heart is small,
Ordains for each one spot shall prove
Belovèd over all.
Each to his choice, and I rejoice
The lot has fallen to me
In a fair ground—in a fair ground—
Yea, Sussex by the sea!   *Sussex*

19 One man in a thousand, Solomon says,
Will stick more close than a brother.
The Thousandth Man

20 Oh, it's Tommy this, an' Tommy that,
an' 'Tommy, go away';
But it's 'Thank you, Mister Atkins,'
when the band begins to play.
Tommy

21 It's Tommy this, an' Tommy that,
an' 'Chuck him out, the brute!'
But it's 'Saviour of 'is country' when
the guns begin to shoot.   *Ib.*

22 Then it's Tommy this, an' Tommy
that, an' 'Tommy 'ow 's yer soul?'
But it's 'Thin red line of 'eroes' when
the drums begin to roll.   *Ib.*

23 We aren't no thin red 'eroes, nor we
aren't no blackguards too.
But single men in barricks, most remarkable like you;
An' if sometimes our conduck isn't
all your fancy paints,
Why, single men in barricks don't
grow into plaster saints.   *Ib.*

24 Of all the trees that grow so fair,
Old England to adorn,
Greater are none beneath the Sun,
Than Oak, and Ash, and Thorn.
A Tree Song

1 A fool there was and he made his
prayer
    (Even as you and I!)
To a rag and a bone and a hank of hair
(We called her the woman who did not
    care)
But the fool he called her his lady
    fair—
    (Even as you and I!) *The Vampire*

2 They shut the road through the woods
Seventy years ago.
    The Way Through the Woods

3 Steadily cantering through
The misty solitudes,
As though they perfectly knew
The old lost road through the woods—
But there is no road through the
    woods! *Ib.*

4 When 'Omer smote 'is bloomin' lyre,
'E'd 'eard men sing by land an' sea;
An' what 'e thought 'e might require,
'E went an' took—the same as me!
    *When 'Omer Smote. (Barrack-
    Room Ballads: Introduction)*

5 Take up the White Man's burden—
    Send forth the best ye breed—
Go, bind your sons to exile
    To serve your captives' need;
To wait in heavy harness
    On fluttered folk and wild—
Your new-caught, sullen peoples,
    Half-devil and half-child.
    The White Man's Burden

6 'Ave you 'eard o' the Widow at
    Windsor
With a hairy gold crown on 'er 'ead?
She 'as ships on the foam—she 'as
    millions at 'ome,
An' she pays us poor beggars in red.
    The Widow at Windsor

7 Down to Gehenna or up to the Throne,
He travels the fastest who travels
    alone. *The Winners*

8 When the 'arf-made recruity goes out
    to the East
'E acts like a babe an' 'e drinks like
    a beast,
An' 'e wonders because 'e is frequent
    deceased
Ere 'e's fit for to serve as a soldier.
    The Young British Soldier

9 Good hunting!
    The Jungle Book. Kaa's Hunting

10 We be of one blood, thou and I. *Ib.*

11 Most 'scruciating idle.
    *Just-So Stories. How the Camel
    Got His Hump*

12 'Humph yourself!'
And the Camel humphed himself.
    Ib.

13 An Elephant's Child—who was full of
'satiable curiosity.
    Ib. The Elephant's Child

14 The great grey-green, greasy Limpopo River, all set about with fever-
trees.
    *Just-So Stories. The Elephant's
    Child*

15 Led go! You are hurtig be! *Ib.*

16 The Cat. He walked by himself, and
all places were alike to him.
    *Ib. The Cat That Walked By
    Himself*

17 He went back through the Wet Wild
Woods, waving his wild tail, and
walking by his wild lone. But he never
told anybody. *Ib.*

18 What's the good of argifying?
    *Life's Handicap. On Greenhow
    Hill*

19 The Light that Failed. *Title of Novel*

20 But that is another story.
    *Plain Tales from the Hills. Three
    and an Extra*

21 Lalun is a member of the most ancient
profession in the world.
    Soldiers Three. On the City Wall

22 Steady the Buffs.
    *Ib. The Gadsbys. Poor Dear
    Mamma*

23 I gloat! Hear me gloat!
    Stalky & Co., ch. i

24 Your Uncle Stalky. *Ib.*

25 Once upon a time there was a Man and
his Wife and a Tertium Quid.
    *Wee Willie Winkie. At the Pit's
    Mouth*

26 Gawd knows, an' 'E won't split on a
pal. *Ib. Drums of the Fore and Aft*

FRIEDRICH VON KLINGER
1752–1831

27 Sturm und Drang.
    Storm and stress.
    Title of Play (1775)

CHARLES KNIGHT

28 Here we are! here we are!! here we
    are again!!!
There's Pat and Mac and Tommy and
    Jack and Joe.
When there's trouble brewing,
When there's something doing,
Are we downhearted?
No! let 'em all come!
    *Here We Are! Here We Are
    Again!!*

MARY KNOWLES 1733–1807

29 He [Dr. Johnson] gets at the substance of a book directly; he tears
out the heart of it.
    *Boswell's Johnson (ed. 1934),
    vol. iii, p. 284. 15 Apr. 1778*

JOHN KNOX 1505–1572

1 The First Blast of the Trumpet Against the Monstrous Regiment of Women.
Title of Pamphlet (1558)

RONALD ARBUTHNOT KNOX 1888–1957

2 There was once a man who said 'God
    Must think it exceedingly odd
    If he finds that this tree
    Continues to be
When there's no one about in the
    Quad.'
Attr. Langford Reed, *The Limerick Book*

ARTHUR J. LAMB 1870–1928

3 She's a bird in a gilded cage.
Song (1900)

LADY CAROLINE LAMB 1785–1828

4 Mad, bad, and dangerous to know.
Of Byron, in her Journal

CHARLES LAMB 1775–1834

5 I am, in plainer words, a bundle of prejudices—made up of likings and dislikings.
Essays of Elia. Imperfect Sympathies

6 'A clear fire, a clean hearth, and the rigour of the game.' This was the celebrated wish of old Sarah Battle (now with God), who, next to her devotions, loved a good game at whist.
Ib. Mrs. Battle's Opinions on Whist

7 I mean your *borrowers of books*—those mutilators of collections, spoilers of the symmetry of shelves, and creators of odd volumes.
Ib. The Two Races of Men

8 I could forgive a man for not enjoying Milton; but I would not call that man my friend who should be offended with 'the divine chit-chat of Cowper'.
Quoting Coleridge's own phrase in Letter to Coleridge, 5 Dec. 1796

9 The scene for the most part laid in a Brothel. O tempora, O mores! but as friend Coleridge said when he was talking bawdy to Miss — 'to the pure all things are pure'.
Letter to Southey, July 1798

10 I came home . . . hungry as a hunter.
Letter to Coleridge, probably 16 or 17 Apr. 1800

11 A little thin, flowery border round, neat, not gaudy.
Letter to Wordsworth, June 1806

12 His face when he repeats his verses hath its ancient glory, an Archangel a little damaged. [Coleridge.]
Letter to W. Wordsworth, 26 Apr. 1816

13 You are knee deep in clover.
Letter to C. C. Clarke, Dec. 1828

14 When my sonnet was rejected, I exclaimed, 'Damn the age; I will write for Antiquity!'
Letter to B. W. Procter, 22 Jan. 1829

15 The greatest pleasure I know, is to do a good action by stealth, and to have it found out by accident.
Table Talk by the late Elia. The Athenaeum, 4 Jan. 1834

16 I have had playmates, I have had companions,
In my days of childhood, in my joyful school-days,—
All, all are gone, the old familiar faces.
The Old Familiar Faces

17 I do not [know the lady]; but damn her at a venture.
E. V. Lucas, *Charles Lamb* (1905), vol. i, p. 320, note

JOHN GEORGE LAMBTON, FIRST EARL OF DURHAM 1792–1840

18 . . . one of his sublimities . . . too good to be lost . . . he said he considered £40,000 a year a moderate income—such a one as a man *might jog on with.*
The Creevey Papers (13 Sept. 1821), ii. 32

WALTER SAVAGE LANDOR 1775–1864

19 Ah, what avails the sceptred race!
Ah, what the form divine!
What every virtue, every grace!
Rose Aylmer, all were thine.
Rose Aylmer

20 I strove with none; for none was worth my strife;
Nature I loved, and, next to Nature, Art;
I warmed both hands before the fire of life;
It sinks, and I am ready to depart.
Finis

21 Mother, I cannot mind my wheel. *Title*

22 There are no fields of amaranth on this side of the grave: there are no voices, O Rhodopè! that are not soon mute, however tuneful: there is no name, with whatever emphasis of passionate love repeated, of which the echo is not faint at last.
Imaginary Conversations, Æsop and Rhodope, ii

ANDREW LANG 1844–1912

1 The surge and thunder of the Odyssey.
*As One that for a Weary Space
has Lain*

2 If the wild bowler thinks he bowls,
Or if the batsman thinks he's
bowled,
They know not, poor misguided souls,
They too shall perish unconsoled.
I am the batsman and the bat,
I am the bowler and the ball,
The umpire, the pavilion cat,
The roller, pitch, and stumps, and
all.
Brahma (in imitation of Emerson)

FREDERICK LANGBRIDGE
1849–1923

3 Two men look out through the same
bars:
One sees the mud, and one the stars.
*A Cluster of Quiet Thoughts
(1896) (Religious Tract Society
Publication)*

WILLIAM LANGLAND
1330?–1400?

4 In a somer seson whan soft was the
sonne.
*The Vision of William concerning
Piers the Plowman* (ed. Skeat),
B Text, Prologue, l. 1.

ARCHBISHOP STEPHEN
LANGTON d. 1228

5 Veni, Sancte Spiritus,
Et emitte coelitus
Lucis tuae radium.

Come, thou holy Paraclete,
And from thy celestial seat
Send thy light and brilliancy.
Trans. by J. M. Neale

BISHOP HUGH LATIMER
1485?–1555

6 Be of good comfort Master Ridley,
and play the man. We shall this day
light such a candle by God's grace in
England, as (I trust) shall never be
put out.
Foxe, *Actes and Monuments*
(1570), p. 1937

SIR HARRY LAUDER 1870–1950

7 I love a lassie. *Title of Song*

8 Just a wee deoch-an-doris
Before we gang awa' . . .
If you can say, 'It's a braw, bricht,
moonlicht nicht',
Ye're a' richt, ye ken. *Song*

9 Keep right on to the end of the road.
Song

10 O! it's nice to get up in the mornin'
But it's nicer to lie in bed. *Song*

11 Roamin' in the Gloamin'.
Title of Song

STEPHEN BUTLER LEACOCK
1869–1944

12 Lord Ronald . . . flung himself upon
his horse and rode madly off in all
directions.
*Nonsense Novels. Gertrude the
Governess*

13 A pie may be produced any number of
times.
*Literary Lapses. Boarding House
Geometry*

14 The landlady can be reduced to her
lowest terms by a series of propositions. *Ib.*

EDWARD LEAR 1812–1888

15 There was an Old Man with a beard,
Who said, 'It is just as I feared!—
Two Owls and a Hen,
Four Larks and a Wren,
Have all built their nests in my beard!'
Book of Nonsense

16 There was an old man who said,
'Hush!
I perceive a young bird in this bush!'
When they said, 'Is it small?'
He replied, 'Not at all!'
It is four times as big as the bush!'
Ib.

17 'How pleasant to know Mr. Lear!'
Who has written such volumes of
stuff!
Some think him ill-tempered and
queer,
But a few think him pleasant
enough. *Nonsense Songs*, preface

18 His body is perfectly spherical,
He weareth a runcible hat. *Ib.*

19 On the coast of Coromandel
Where the early pumpkins blow,
In the middle of the woods
Lived the Yonghy-Bonghy-Bò.
Two old chairs, and half a candle,—
One old jug without a handle,—
These were all his worldly goods.
*Ib. The Courtship of the Yonghy-
Bonghy-Bò*

20 When awful darkness and silence reign
Over the great Gromboolian plain,
Through the long, long wintry
nights.
When the angry breakers roar
As they beat on the rocky shore;—
When Storm-clouds brood on the
towering heights
Of the Hills of the Chankly Bore.
*Ib. The Dong with the Luminous
Nose*

1 'The Dong!—the Dong!
The wandering Dong through the forest goes!
The Dong!—the Dong!
The Dong with the Luminous Nose!'
Nonsense Songs. The Dong with the Luminous Nose

2 And who so happy,—O who,
As the Duck and the Kangaroo?
Ib. The Duck and the Kangaroo

3 O My agèd Uncle Arly!
Sitting on a heap of Barley
Thro' the silent hours of night,—
Close beside a leafy thicket:—
On his nose there was a Cricket,—
In his hat a Railway-Ticket;—
(But his shoes were far too tight.)
Ib. Incidents in the Life of my Aged Uncle Arly

4 Far and few, far and few,
Are the lands where the Jumblies live;
Their heads are green, and their hands are blue,
And they went to sea in a Sieve.
Ib. The Jumblies

5 In spite of all their friends could say,
On a winter's morn, on a stormy day,
In a Sieve they went to sea! *Ib.*

6 The Owl and the Pussy-Cat went to sea
In a beautiful pea-green boat.
They took some honey, and plenty of money,
Wrapped up in a five-pound note.
The Owl looked up to the Stars above
And sang to a small guitar,
'O lovely Pussy! O Pussy, my love,
What a beautiful Pussy you are.'
Ib. The Owl and the Pussy-Cat

7 Pussy said to the Owl, 'You elegant fowl!
How charmingly sweet you sing!
O let us be married! too long we have tarried:
But what shall we do for a ring?'
They sailed away for a year and a day,
To the land where the Bong-tree grows,
And there in a wood a Piggy-wig stood
With a ring at the end of his nose.
Ib.

8 'Dear Pig, are you willing to sell for one shilling
Your ring?' Said the Piggy, 'I will'.
Ib.

9 They dined on mince, and slices of quince,
Which they ate with a runcible spoon;
And hand in hand, on the edge of the sand,
They danced by the light of the moon. *Ib.*

10 The Pobble who has no toes
Had once as many as we;
When they said, 'Some day you may lose them all';—
He replied,—'Fish fiddle de-dee!'
Nonsense Songs. The Pobble Who Has No Toes

11 His Aunt Jobiska made him drink
Lavender water tinged with pink,
For she said, 'The world in general knows
There's nothing so good for a Pobble's toes!' *Ib.*

12 He has gone to fish, for his Aunt Jobiska's
Runcible Cat with crimson whiskers!
Ib.

13 It's a fact the whole world knows,
That Pobbles are happier without their toes. *Ib.*

14 Who, or why, or which, or what,
Is the Akond of Swat?
Ib. 1888 edn. *The Akond of Swat*

15 There was an old man of Thermopylae,
Who never did anything properly;
But they said, 'If you choose
To boil eggs in your shoes,
You shall never remain in Thermopylae.'
One Hundred Nonsense Pictures and Rhymes

MARY ELIZABETH LEASE
1853–1933

16 Kansas had better stop raising corn and begin raising hell. *Attr.*

HENRY LEE 1756–1818

17 First in war, first in peace, first in the hearts of his fellow citizens.
Resolution in the House of Representatives on the death of Washington, 26 Dec. 1799

NATHANIEL LEE 1653?–1692

18 When Greeks joined Greeks, then was the tug of war!
The Rival Queens, IV. ii

CHARLES GODFREY LELAND
1824–1903

19 Hans Breitmann gife a barty—
Vhere ish dat barty now?
Hans Breitmann's Party

WILLIAM LENTHALL 1591–1662

20 I have neither eye to see, nor tongue to speak here, but as the House is pleased to direct me.
Rushworth's *Historical Collections*, iv. 238

SIR ROGER L'ESTRANGE
1616–1704

1 It is with our passions as it is with fire and water, they are good servants, but bad masters.
Æsop's Fables, no. 38, *Reflection*

GEORGE LEVESON-GOWER, EARL GRANVILLE 1815–1891

2 Spheres of action.
Letter to Count Münster, 29 Apr. 1885 (Sir Edward Hertslet, *Map of Africa by Treaty* (1894), vol. ii, p. 596) (*see* 7:8)

DUC DE LÉVIS 1764–1830

3 Noblesse oblige.
Nobility carries its obligations.
Maximes et réflexions

GEORGE LEYBOURNE d. 1884

4 O, he flies through the air with the greatest of ease,
This daring young man on the flying trapeze.
The Man on the Flying Trapeze

CHARLES-JOSEPH, PRINCE DE LIGNE 1735–1814

5 Le congrès ne marche pas, il danse.
The Congress makes no progress; but it dances.
Comment on the Congress of Vienna to Comte Auguste de La Garde-Chambonas. La Garde-Chambonas, *Souvenirs du Congrès de Vienne, 1814–1815*, ch. 1

ABRAHAM LINCOLN 1809–1865

6 The ballot is stronger than the bullet.
Speeches and Letters (1907). *Speech, 19 May 1856*

7 'A house divided against itself cannot stand.' I believe this government cannot endure permanently, half slave and half free.
Ib. Speech, 16 June 1858

8 Fourscore and seven years ago our fathers brought forth upon this continent a new nation, conceived in liberty, and dedicated to the proposition that all men are created equal. Now we are engaged in a great civil war, testing whether that nation, or any nation so conceived and so dedicated, can long endure. We are met on a great battlefield of that war. We have come to dedicate a portion of that field as a final resting-place of those who here gave their lives that that nation might live. It is altogether fitting and proper that we should do this. But in a larger sense we cannot dedicate, we cannot consecrate, we cannot hallow this ground. The brave men, living and dead, who struggled here, have consecrated it far above our power to add or detract. The world will little note, nor long remember, what we say here, but it can never forget what they did here. It is for us, the living, rather to be dedicated here to the unfinished work they have thus far so nobly advanced. It is rather for us to be here dedicated to the great task remaining before us, that from these honoured dead we take increased devotion to that cause for which they here gave the last full measure of devotion; that we here highly resolve that the dead shall not have died in vain, that this nation, under God, shall have a new birth of freedom; and that government of the people, by the people, and for the people, shall not perish from the earth.
Address at Dedication of National Cemetery at Gettysburg, 19 Nov. 1863

9 With malice toward none; with charity for all; with firmness in the right, as God gives us to see the right.
Ib. Second Inaugural Address, 4 Mar. 1865

10 You can fool all the people some of the time, and some of the people all the time, but you can not fool all the people all of the time.
Attr. words in a speech at Clinton, 8 Sept. 1858. N. W. Stephenson, *Autobiography of A. Lincoln* (1927). *Attr. also to Phineas Barnum, 1810–91*

11 It is not best to swap horses while crossing the river.
Reply to National Union League, 9 June 1864. J. E. Nicolay and J. Hay, *Abraham Lincoln*, bk. ix

12 People who like this sort of thing will find this the sort of thing they like.
Judgement on a book. G. W. E. Russell, *Collections and Recollections*, ch. 30

GEORGE LINLEY 1798–1865

13 Among our ancient mountains,
And from our lovely vales,
Oh, let the prayer re-echo:
'God bless the Prince of Wales!'
Poems. God Bless the Prince of Wales

SIR THOMAS LITTLETON
1422–1481

14 [From] time whereof the memory of man runneth not to the contrary.
Tenures (?1481), § 170

LIVY 59 B.C.–A.D. 17

1 Vae victis.
   Woe to the vanquished.
   History, v. xlviii. 9

MARIE LLOYD 1870–1922

2 A little of what you fancy does you
   good.   *Title of Song*

3 I'm one of the ruins that Cromwell
   knocked about a bit.   *Ib.*

4 Oh, mister porter, what shall I do?
   Ib. (*words actually by* Thomas Le
   Brunn)

ROBERT LLOYD 1733–1764

5 Slow and steady wins the race.
   Poems. The Hare and the Tortoise

JOHN LOCKE 1632–1704

6 New opinions are always suspected,
   and usually opposed, without any
   other reason but because they are not
   already common.
   *Essay on the Human Under-
   standing*, dedicatory epistle.

7 It is one thing to show a man that he
   is in an error, and another to put him
   in possession of truth.
   Ib. bk. iv, ch. 7, sec. 11

8 All men are liable to error; and most
   men are, in many points, by passion or
   interest, under temptation to it.
   Ib. ch. 20, sec. 17

FREDERICK LOCKER-LAMPSON 1821–1895

9 If you lift a guinea-pig up by the tail
   His eyes drop out!   *A Garden Lyric*

THOMAS LODGE 1558?–1625

10 Devils are not so black as they are
   painted.   *A Margarite of America*

JACK LONDON [JOHN GRIFFITH LONDON] 1876–1916

11 The Call of the Wild.   *Title*

HENRY WADSWORTH LONGFELLOW 1807–1882

12 I shot an arrow into the air,
   It fell to earth, I knew not where.
   The Arrow and the Song

13 Thou, too, sail on, O Ship of State!
   Sail on, O Union, strong and great!
   Humanity with all its fears,
   With all the hopes of future years,
   Is hanging breathless on thy fate!
   The Building of the Ship

14 The bards sublime,
   Whose distant footsteps echo
   Through the corridors of Time.
   The Day is Done

15 The cares that infest the day
   Shall fold their tents, like the Arabs,
   And as silently steal away.   *Ib.*

16 This is the forest primeval.
   Evangeline, introduction, l. 1

17 The shades of night were falling fast,
   As through an Alpine village passed
   A youth, who bore, 'mid snow and ice,
   A banner with the strange device,
   Excelsior!   *Excelsior*

18 'O stay,' the maiden said, 'and rest
   Thy weary head upon this breast!' *Ib.*

19 'Beware the pine-tree's withered
   branch!
   Beware the awful avalanche!'   *Ib.*

20 A traveller, by the faithful hound,
   Half-buried in the snow was found.
   Ib.

21 I like that ancient Saxon phrase, which
   calls
   The burial-ground God's-Acre!
   God's-Acre

22 The heights by great men reached and
   kept
   Were not attained by sudden flight,
   But they, while their companions
   slept,
   Were toiling upward in the night.
   The Ladder of Saint Augustine

23 Standing, with reluctant feet,
   Where the brook and river meet,
   Womanhood and childhood fleet!
   Maidenhood

24 A boy's will is the wind's will,
   And the thoughts of youth are long,
   long thoughts.   *My Lost Youth*

25 Listen, my children, and you shall hear
   Of the midnight ride of Paul Revere,
   On the eighteenth of April in Seventy-
   five.   *Paul Revere's Ride*

26 Tell me not, in mournful numbers,
   Life is but an empty dream!
   For the soul is dead that slumbers,
   And things are not what they seem.

   Life is real! Life is earnest!
   And the grave is not its goal;
   Dust thou art, to dust returnest,
   Was not spoken of the soul.
   A Psalm of Life

27 Lives of great men all remind us
   We can make our lives sublime,
   And, departing, leave behind us
   Footprints on the sands of time. *Ib.*

28 Let us, then, be up and doing,
   With a heart for any fate;
   Still achieving, still pursuing,
   Learn to labour and to wait.   *Ib.*

1 There is no flock, however watched
       and tended,
   But one dead lamb is there!
   There is no fireside, howsoe'er de-
       fended,
   But has one vacant chair!
                           Resignation

2 Though the mills of God grind slowly,
       yet they grind exceeding small;
   Though with patience he stands wait-
       ing, with exactness grinds he all.
       Retribution. From the Sinnge-
       dichte of Friedrich von Logau

3 Beside the ungather'd rice he lay,
   His sickle in his hand.
                           The Slave's Dream

4 By the shores of Gitche Gumee,
   By the shining Big-Sea-Water,
   Stood the wigwam of Nokomis,
   Daughter of the Moon, Nokomis.
   Dark behind it rose the forest,
   Rose the black and gloomy pine-trees,
   Rose the firs with cones upon them;
   Bright before it beat the water,
   Beat the clear and sunny water,
   Beat the shining Big-Sea-Water.
       The Song of Hiawatha, iii. *Hia-*
       watha's Childhood

5 Ewa-yea! my little owlet!
   Who is this, that lights the wigwam?
   With his great eyes lights the wigwam?
                           Ib.

6 From the waterfall he named her,
   Minnehaha, Laughing Water.
       Ib. iv. *Hiawatha and Mudje-*
       keewis

7 As unto the bow the cord is,
   So unto the man is woman;
   Though she bends him, she obeys him,
   Though she draws him, yet she
       follows;
   Useless each without the other!
       Ib. x. *Hiawatha's Wooing*

8 Onaway! Awake, beloved!
       Ib. xi. *Hiawatha's Wedding*

   Ships that pass in the night, and
       speak each other in passing;
   Only a signal shown and a distant
       voice in the darkness;
   So on the ocean of life we pass and
       speak one another,
   Only a look and a voice; then darkness
       again and a silence.
       Tales of a Wayside Inn, pt. III.
       The Theologian's Tale. Elizabeth,
       iv

0 Under the spreading chestnut tree
   The village smithy stands;
   The smith, a mighty man is he,
   With large and sinewy hands;
   And the muscles of his brawny arms
   Are strong as iron bands.
                       The Village Blacksmith

11 Something   attempted,   something
       done,
   Has earned a night's repose.
                       The Village Blacksmith

12 It was the schooner Hesperus,
   That sailed the wintry sea;
   And the skipper had taken his little
       daughter,
   To bear him company.
                   The Wreck of the Hesperus

13 But the father answered never a word,
   A frozen corpse was he.   *Ib.*

14 There was a little girl
   Who had a little curl
   Right in the middle of her forehead,
   When she was good
   She was very, very good,
   But when she was bad she was horrid.
       B. R. T. Machetta, *Home Life of*
       Longfellow

ANITA LOOS 1893–

15 Gentlemen Prefer Blondes.
                           Title of Novel

LOUIS XIV 1638–1715

16 Il n'y a plus de Pyrénées.
       The Pyrenees have ceased to exist.
       At the accession of his grandson
       to the throne of Spain, 1700. Attr.
       by Voltaire in Siècle de Louis
       XIV, ch. 28

17 L'État c'est moi.
       I am the State.
       Attr. remark before the Parlement
       de Paris, 13 Apr. 1655. Dulaure,
       Histoire de Paris

LOUIS XVIII 1755–1824

18 L'exactitude est la politesse des rois.
       Punctuality is the politeness of
       kings.   *Attr.*

RICHARD LOVELACE 1618–1658

19 Stone walls do not a prison make
       Nor iron bars a cage;
   Minds innocent and quiet take
       That for an hermitage;
   If I have freedom in my love,
       And in my soul am free;
   Angels alone, that soar above,
       Enjoy such liberty.
                   To Althea, From Prison

20 Tell me not (Sweet) I am unkind,
       That from the nunnery
   Of thy chaste breast, and quiet mind,
       To war and arms I fly.

   True; a new mistress now I chase,
       The first foe in the field;
   And with a stronger faith embrace
       A sword, a horse, a shield.

Yet this inconstancy is such,
As you too shall adore;
I could not love thee (Dear) so much,
Lov'd I not honour more.
To Lucasta, Going to the Wars

JAMES RUSSELL LOWELL
1819–1891

1 You've a darned long row to hoe.
The Biglow Papers, First Series,
No. 1

2 I *don't* believe in princerple,
But O, I *du* in interest.
Ib. No. 6. *The Pious Editor's
Creed*

3 Once to every man and nation comes
the moment to decide,
In the strife of Truth with Falsehood,
for the good or evil side.
The Present Crisis

4 New occasions teach new duties: Time
makes ancient good uncouth;
They must upward still, and onward,
who would keep abreast of Truth.
Ib.

LUCAN A.D. 39–65

5 Stat magni nominis umbra.
There stands the shadow of a
glorious name.   *Works,* i. 135

6 Nil actum credens, dum quid superesset agendum.
Thinking nothing done while anything remained to be done.
Ib. ii. 657

LUCRETIUS 99–55 B.C.

7 Tantum religio potuit suadere malorum.
Such evil deeds could religion
prompt.
De Rerum Natura, i. 101. Trans.
by Bailey

8   Nil posse creari
De nilo
Nothing can be created out of
nothing.   *Ib.* 155

9 Inque brevi spatio mutantur saecla
animantum
Et quasi cursores vitai lampada
tradunt.
And in a short space the tribes of
living things are changed, and like
runners hand on the torch of life.
Ib. ii. 78

MARTIN LUTHER 1483–1546

10 Ich kann nicht anders.
I can do no other.
*Speech at the Diet of Worms,
18 Apr. 1521. On his monument
at Worms*

11 Wer nicht liebt Wein, Weib und
Gesang,
Der bleibt ein Narr sein Leben lang.
Who loves not woman, wine, and song
Remains a fool his whole life long.
*Attr. to Luther. Written in the
Luther room in the Wartburg, but
no proof exists of its authorship*

12 Ein feste Burg ist unser Gott,
Ein gute Wehr und Waffen.
A safe stronghold our God is still,
A trusty shield and weapon.
Klug'sches Gesangbuch (1529),
Ein feste Burg. Trans. by Car-
lyle

JOHN LYLY 1554?–1606

13 CAMPASPE:
Were women never so fair, men would
be false.
APELLES:
Were women never so false, men
would be fond.   *Campaspe,* III. iii

14 Cupid and my Campaspe play'd
At cards for kisses, Cupid paid; *Ib.* v

15 Night hath a thousand eyes.
Maides Metamorphose, III. i

HENRY FRANCIS LYTE 1793–1847

16 Abide with me; fast falls the eventide;
The darkness deepens; Lord, with me
abide;
When other helpers fail, and comforts
flee,
Help of the helpless, O, abide with me.

Swift to its close ebbs out life's little
day;
Earth's joys grow dim, its glories pass
away;
Change and decay in all around I see;
O Thou, who changest not, abide with
me.   *Remains. Abide with Me*

17 I fear no foe with Thee at hand to
bless;
Ills have no weight, and tears no
bitterness;
Where is death's sting? Where, grave,
thy victory?
I triumph still, if Thou abide with me.

Hold Thou Thy Cross before my closing eyes;
Shine through the gloom, and point
me to the skies;
Heaven's morning breaks, and earth's
vain shadows flee;
In life, in death, O Lord, abide with
me.   *Ib.*

EDWARD GEORGE BULWER-LYTTON, BARON LYTTON 1803-1873

1 Here Stanley meets,—how Stanley
scorns, the glance!
The brilliant chief, irregularly great,
Frank, haughty, rash,—the Rupert
of Debate.
The New Timon, pt. I. vi

2 Beneath the rule of men entirely great
The pen is mightier than the sword.
Richelieu, II. ii

3 Poverty has strange bedfellows.
The Caxtons, pt. iv, ch. 4

4 There is no man so friendless but what
he can find a friend sincere enough to
tell him disagreeable truths.
What Will He Do With It?, bk.
iii, ch. 15 (heading)

THOMAS BABINGTON MACAULAY, BARON MACAULAY 1800-1859

5 Attend, all ye who list to hear our
noble England's praise;
I tell of the thrice famous deeds she
wrought in ancient days.
The Armada

6 And the red glare on Skiddaw roused
the burghers of Carlisle. *Ib.*

7 For God! for the Cause! for the
Church! for the laws!
For Charles King of England, and
Rupert of the Rhine!
The Battle of Naseby

8 Lars Porsena of Clusium
By the nine gods he swore
That the great house of Tarquin
Should suffer wrong no more.
By the Nine Gods he swore it,
And named a trysting day,
And bade his messengers ride forth,
East and west and south and north,
To summon his array.
Lays of Ancient Rome. Horatius, i

9 Then out spake brave Horatius,
The Captain of the Gate:
'To every man upon this earth
Death cometh soon or late.
And how can man die better
Than facing fearful odds,
For the ashes of his fathers,
And the temples of his Gods?'
Ib. xxvii

10 To save them from false Sextus
That wrought the deed of shame.
Ib. xxviii

11 'Now who will stand on either hand,
And keep the bridge with me?'
Ib. xxix

12 Then none was for a party;
Then all were for the state;
Then the great man helped the poor,
And the poor man loved the great;
Then lands were fairly portioned;
Then spoils were fairly sold:
The Romans were like brothers
In the brave days of old.
Lays of Ancient Rome. Horatius,
xxxi

13 Was none who would be foremost
To lead such dire attack;
But those behind cried 'Forward!'
And those before cried 'Back!'
Ib. l

14 'Oh, Tiber! father Tiber!
To whom the Romans pray,
A Roman's life, a Roman's arms,
Take thou in charge this day!'
Ib. lix

15 And even the ranks of Tuscany
Could scarce forbear to cheer.
Ib. lx

16 With weeping and with laughter
Still is the story told,
How well Horatius kept the bridge
In the brave days of old. *Ib.* lxx

17 Those trees in whose dim shadow
The ghastly priest doth reign,
The priest who slew the slayer,
And shall himself be slain.
Ib. The Battle of Lake Regillus, x

18 The business of everybody is the business of nobody.
*Historical Essays Contributed to
the 'Edinburgh Review'. Hallam's
Constitutional History* (Sept.
1828)

19 The gallery in which the reporters sit
has become a fourth estate of the
realm. *Ib.*

20 Every schoolboy knows who imprisoned Montezuma, and who
strangled Atahualpa.
Ib. Lord Clive (Jan. 1840)

21 When some traveller from New
Zealand shall, in the midst of a vast
solitude, take his stand on a broken
arch of London Bridge to sketch the
ruins of St. Paul's.
Ib. Von Ranke (Oct. 1840)

22 The great Proconsul.
Ib. Warren Hastings (Oct. 1841)

23 We know no spectacle so ridiculous as
the British public in one of its periodical fits of morality.
*Literary Essays contributed to the
'Edinburgh Review'. Moore's Life
of Lord Byron* (June 1830)

24 He was a rake among scholars, and a
scholar among rakes. [Richard Steele.]
Ib. Aikin's Life of Addison (July
1843)

1 The Puritan hated bear-baiting, not because it gave pain to the bear, but because it gave pleasure to the spectators.
History of England, vol. i, ch. 2

2 There were gentlemen and there were seamen in the navy of Charles the Second. But the seamen were not gentlemen; and the gentlemen were not seamen. *Ib.* ch. 3

3 The English Bible, a book which, if everything else in our language should perish, would alone suffice to show the whole extent of its beauty and power.
Edinburgh Review, Jan. 1828. *On John Dryden*

4 Thank you, madam, the agony is abated. [Reply, aged four.]
Trevelyan's *Life and Letters of Macaulay*, ch. 1

5 I shall not be satisfied unless I produce something which shall for a few days supersede the last fashionable novel on the tables of young ladies.
Ib. ch. 9

JOSEPH McCARTHY d. 1944

6 You made me love you,
I didn't want to do it.
You Made Me Love You

GEORGE McCLELLAN 1826–1885

7 All quiet along the Potomac.
Attr. in the American Civil War

JOHN McCRAE d. 1918

8 We shall not sleep, though poppies grow
In Flanders fields.
In Flanders Fields. (*Punch*, vol. cxlix, 8 Dec. 1915)

GEORGE MACDONALD 1824–1905

9 Where did you come from, baby dear?
Out of the everywhere into here.
At the Back of the North Wind, xxxiii, *Song*

CHARLES MACKAY 1814–1889

10 Cheer! Boys, cheer! *Title of Song*

11 There's a good time coming, boys,
A good time coming.
The Good Time Coming

SIR JAMES MACKINTOSH 1765–1832

12 The Commons, faithful to their system, remained in a wise and masterly inactivity. *Vindiciæ Gallicæ*, § 1

IRENE RUTHERFORD McLEOD 1891–

13 I'm a lean dog, a keen dog, a wild dog, and alone. *Lone Dog*, st. 1

MAURICE DE MACMAHON 1808–1893

14 J'y suis, j'y reste.
Here I am, and here I stay.
Attr. remark at the taking of the Malakoff, 8 Sept. 1855

LEONARD McNALLY 1752–1820

15 This lass so neat, with smiles so sweet,
Has won my right good-will,
I'd crowns resign to call thee mine,
Sweet lass of Richmond Hill.
The Lass of Richmond Hill. E. Duncan, *Minstrelsy of England* (1905), i. 254. Attr. also to W. Upton in *Oxford Song Book*, and to W. Hudson in Baring-Gould, *English Minstrelsie* (1895), iii. 54

MAURICE DE MAETERLINCK 1862–1949

16 Il n'y a pas de morts.
There are no dead.
L'Oiseau bleu, IV. ii

MAGNA CARTA 1215

17 Nisi per legale iudicium parium suorum vel per legem terrae.
Except by the legal judgement of his peers or the law of the land.
Clause 39

ALFRED THAYER MAHAN 1840–1914

18 Those far distant, storm-beaten ships, upon which the Grand Army never looked, stood between it and the dominion of the world.
The Influence of Sea Power upon the French Revolution and Empire, 1793–1812 (1892), ii. 118

FRANCIS SYLVESTER MAHONY
see FATHER PROUT

JOSEPH DE MAISTRE 1753–1821

19 Toute nation a le gouvernement qu'elle mérite.
Every country has the government it deserves.
Lettres et Opuscules Inédits, i, p. 215, 15 August 1811

SIR THOMAS MALORY *fl.* 1470

20 The questing beast.
Le Morte D'Arthur, bk. ix, ch. 12

THOMAS ROBERT MALTHUS
1766–1834

1 Population, when unchecked, increases in a geometrical ratio. Subsistence only increases in an arithmetical ratio.
The Principle of Population, 1

W. R. MANDALE *nineteenth century*

2 Up and down the City Road,
In and out the Eagle,
That's the way the money goes—
Pop goes the weasel!
Pop Goes the Weasel

MRS. MARY DE LA RIVIERE MANLEY 1663–1724

3 No time like the present.
The Lost Lover, IV. i

LORD JOHN MANNERS, DUKE OF RUTLAND 1818–1906

4 Let wealth and commerce, laws and learning die,
But leave us still our old nobility!
England's Trust, pt. III, l. 227

WILLIAM MURRAY, EARL OF MANSFIELD 1705–1793

5 Consider what you think justice requires, and decide accordingly. But never give your reasons; for your judgement will probably be right, but your reasons will certainly be wrong.
Advice. Campbell's *Lives of the Chief Justices* (1874), vol. iv, p. 26

RICHARD MANT 1776–1848

6 Bright the vision that delighted
Once the sight of Judah's seer.
Ancient Hymns. Bright the Vision

WILLIAM LEARNED MARCY
1786–1857

7 To the victor belong the spoils of the enemy.
Parton's *Life of Jackson* (1860), vol. iii, p. 378

MARIE-ANTOINETTE 1755–1793

8 Qu'ils mangent de la brioche.
Let them eat cake.
On being told that her people had no bread. Attr. to Marie-Antoinette, but much older. Rousseau refers in his Confessions, *1740, to a similar remark, as a well-known saying*

CHRISTOPHER MARLOWE
1564–1593

9 My men, like satyrs grazing on the lawns,
Shall with their goat feet dance an antic hay.   *Edward II*, I. i. 59

10 MEPHISTOPHELES:
O by aspiring pride and insolence,
For which God threw him from the face of heaven.   *Faustus*, l. 303

11 Why this is hell, nor am I out of it:
Thinkst thou that I who saw the face of God,
And tasted the eternal joys of heaven,
Am not tormented with ten thousand hells
In being deprived of everlasting bliss!
Ib. l. 312

12 Was this the face that launch'd a thousand ships,
And burnt the topless towers of Ilium?
Sweet Helen, make me immortal with a kiss!
Her lips suck forth my soul: see, where it flies!
Come Helen, come give me my soul again.
Here will I dwell, for heaven be in these lips,
And all is dross that is not Helena.
Ib. l. 1328

13 O thou art fairer than the evening air,
Clad in the beauty of a thousand stars,
Brighter art thou than flaming Jupiter,
When he appeared to hapless Semele,
More lovely than the monarch of the sky
In wanton Arethusa's azured arms,
And none but thou shalt be my paramour.   *Ib.* l. 1341

14 Now hast thou but one bare hour to live,
And then thou must be damned perpetually;
Stand still you ever-moving spheres of heaven,
That time may cease, and midnight never come.
Fair nature's eye, rise, rise again and make
Perpetual day, or let this hour be but
A year, a month, a week, a natural day,
That Faustus may repent and save his soul.
O *lente, lente currite noctis equi:*
The stars move still, time runs, the clock will strike,
The devil will come, and Faustus must be damn'd.
O I'll leap up to my God: who pulls me down?
See see where Christ's blood streams in the firmament.
One drop would save my soul, half a drop, ah my Christ.   *Ib.* l. 1420

1 O soul, be changed into little water
   drops,
And fall into the ocean, ne'er be found:
My God, my God, look not so fierce on
   me. *Faustus*, l. 1472

2 Cut is the branch that might have
   grown full straight,
And burnèd is Apollo's laurel bough,
That sometimes grew within this
   learned man. *Ib*. l. 1478

3 Who ever loved that loved not at first
   sight?
   Hero and Leander. First Sestiad,
   l. 176

4 I count religion but a childish toy,
And hold there is no sin but ignorance.
   The Jew of Malta, l. 14

5 And as their wealth increases, so en-
   close
Infinite riches in a little room. *Ib*. l. 71

6 Come live with me, and be my love,
And we will all the pleasures prove,
That valleys, groves, hills and fields,
Woods or steepy mountain yields.
   *The Passionate Shepherd to his
   Love*

7 By shallow rivers, to whose falls
Melodious birds sing madrigals. *Ib*.

8 Jigging veins of rhyming mother wits.
   Conquests of Tamburlaine, Prologue

9 Is it not passing brave to be a King,
And ride in triumph through Persepolis? *Ib*. pt. I, l. 758

10 Nature that fram'd us of four ele-
   ments,
Warring within our breasts for regi-
   ment,
Doth teach us all to have aspiring
   minds:
Our souls, whose faculties can com-
   prehend
The wondrous Architecture of the
   world:
And measure every wand'ring planet's
   course,
Still climbing after knowledge infinite,
And always moving as the restless
   Spheres,
Will us to wear ourselves and never
   rest,
Until we reach the ripest fruit of all,
That perfect bliss and sole felicity,
The sweet fruition of an earthly
   crown. *Ib*. l. 869

11 What is beauty saith my sufferings
   then?
If all the pens that ever poets held,
Had fed the feeling of their masters'
   thoughts,
And every sweetness that inspir'd
   their hearts,
Their minds, and muses on admired
   themes: *Ib*. l. 1941

12 Now walk the angels on the walls of
   heaven,
As sentinels to warn th' immortal
   souls,
To entertain divine Zenocrate.
   Conquests of Tamburlaine,
   pt. II, l. 2983

13 Holla, ye pampered Jades of Asia:
What, can ye draw but twenty miles
   a day? *Ib*. l. 3980

14 Tamburlaine, the Scourge of God,
   must die. *Ib*. l. 4641

15 I'm arm'd with more than complete
   steel—
The justice of my quarrel.
   Lust's Dominion, IV. iii.
   (*Authorship doubtful*)

DONALD ROBERT PERRY MARQUIS 1878–1937

16 toujours gai, archy, toujours gai.
   archy's life of mehitabel, i. *the
   life of mehitabel the cat*

FREDERICK MARRYAT 1792–1848

17 If you please, ma'am, it was a very
   little one. [The nurse excusing her ille-
   gitimate baby.]
   Midshipman Easy, ch. 3

18 As savage as a bear with a sore head.
   The King's Own, ch. 26

19 I never knows the children. It's just
   six of one and half-a-dozen of the
   other. *The Pirate*, ch. 4

20 I think it much better that . . . every
   man paddle his own canoe.
   Settlers in Canada, ch. 8

21 I haven't the gift of the gab, my sons
   —because I'm bred to the sea.
   The Old Navy, st. 1

MARTIAL b. A.D. 43

22 Non amo te, Sabidi, nec possum dicere
   quare:
   Hoc tantum possum dicere, non
   amo te.
   I do not love you, Sabidius, and I
   can't say why. This only I can
   say, I do not love you.
   Epigrammata, I. xxxii. Trans.
   by Ker

23 Laudant illa sed ista legunt.
   Those they praise, but they read
   the others. *Ib*. IV. xlix

24 Rus in urbe.
   The country in town. *Ib*. XII. lvii

ANDREW MARVELL 1621–1678

25 Where the remote Bermudas ride
In th' ocean's bosom unespied.
   Bermudas

1 Echo beyond the Mexique Bay.
Bermudas

2 My love is of a birth as rare
As 'tis for object strange and high:
It was begotten by despair
Upon impossibility. *Definition of Love*

3 All this fair, and soft, and sweet,
Which scatteringly doth shine,
Shall within one Beauty meet,
And she be only thine.
*Dialogue between the Resolved
Soul and Created Pleasure*

4 How vainly men themselves amaze
To win the palm, the oak, or bays;
The Garden

5 Fair quiet, have I found thee here,
And Innocence thy Sister dear! *Ib.*

6 What wond'rous life is this I lead!
Ripe apples drop about my head;
The luscious clusters of the vine
Upon my mouth do crush their wine;
The nectarine and curious peach,
Into my hands themselves do reach;
Stumbling on melons, as I pass,
Insnar'd with flow'rs, I fall on grass.
Ib.

7 Annihilating all that's made
To a green thought in a green shade.
Ib.

8 [*Charles I*]
He nothing common did or mean
Upon that memorable scene:
But with his keener eye
The axe's edge did try.
*Horatian Ode upon Cromwell's
Return from Ireland*, l. 57

9 But bowed his comely head,
Down as upon a bed. *Ib.*

10 Who can foretell for what high cause
This darling of the Gods was born?
The Picture of Little T.C.

11 Had we but world enough, and time,
This coyness, Lady, were no crime.
We would sit down, and think which
way
To walk, and pass our long love's day.
Thou by the Indian Ganges' side
Shouldst rubies find: I by the tide
Of Humber would complain. I would
Love you ten years before the Flood:
And you should if you please refuse
Till the conversion of the Jews.
My vegetable love should grow
Vaster than empires, and more slow.
To His Coy Mistress

12 But at my back I always hear
Time's wingèd chariot hurrying near.
And yonder all before us lie
Deserts of vast eternity.
Thy beauty shall no more be found;
Nor, in thy marble vault, shall sound
My echoing song: then worms shall
try

That long preserved virginity:
And your quaint honour turn to dust;
And into ashes all my lust.
The grave's a fine and private place,
But none I think do there embrace.
To His Coy Mistress

13 Thrice happy he who, not mistook,
Hath read in Nature's mystic book.
*Upon Appleton House. To My
Lord Fairfax*, lxxiii

KARL MARX 1818–1883

14 Die Proletarier haben nichts in ihr
zu verlieren als ihre Ketten. Sie
haben eine Welt zu gewinnen.
Proletarier aller Länder, vereinigt
euch!

The workers have nothing to lose in
this [revolution] but their chains.
They have a world to gain.
Workers of the world, unite!
The Communist Manifesto
(1848), last words

15 Jeder nach seinen Fähigkeiten, jedem
nach seinen Bedürfnissen.

From each according to his abilities,
to each according to his needs.
Criticism of the Gotha programme
(1875) (*see 15:21*)

16 Die Religion . . . ist das Opium des
Volkes.

Religion . . . is the opium of the
people.
*Kritik der Hegelschen Rechts-
philosophie*, Introduction

17 The dictatorship of the proletariat.
'*Used more than once*', *according
to Mr. and Mrs. Sidney Webb*

MARY TUDOR 1516–1558

18 When I am dead and opened, you
shall find 'Calais' lying in my heart.
Holinshed, Chron. iii. 1160

JOHN MASEFIELD 1878–1967

19 Coming in solemn beauty like slow old
tunes of Spain. *Beauty*

20 Quinquereme of Nineveh from distant
Ophir
Rowing home to haven in sunny Pales-
tine,
With a cargo of ivory,
And apes and peacocks,
Sandalwood, cedarwood, and sweet
white wine. *Cargoes*

21 Dirty British coaster with a salt-
caked smoke stack,
Butting through the Channel in the
mad March days,
With a cargo of Tyne coal,
Road-rail, pig-lead,
Firewood, iron-ware, and cheap tin
trays. *Ib.*

1 Oh some are fond of Spanish wine, and
   some are fond of French,
   And some'll swallow tay and stuff fit
   only for a wench.
   Captain Stratton's Fancy

2 I must down to the seas again, to the
   lonely sea and the sky,
   And all I ask is a tall ship and a star
   to steer her by,
   And the wheel's kick and the wind's
   song and the white sail's shaking,
   And a grey mist on the sea's face and
   a grey dawn breaking.   *Sea Fever*

3 I must down to the seas again, for the
   call of the running tide
   Is a wild call and a clear call that may
   not be denied.   *Ib.*

4 I must down to the seas again, to the
   vagrant gypsy life,
   To the gull's way and the whale's way
   where the wind's like a whetted
   knife;
   And all I ask is a merry yarn from a
   laughing fellow-rover,
   And quiet sleep and a sweet dream
   when the long trick's over.   *Ib.*

5 Friends and loves we have none, nor
   wealth nor blessed abode,
   But the hope of the City of God at the
   other end of the road.   *The Seekers*

6 It's a warm wind, the west wind, full
   of birds' cries;
   I never hear the west wind but tears
   are in my eyes.
   For it comes from the west lands, the
   old brown hills,
   And April's in the west wind, and
   daffodils.   *The West Wind*

WALT MASON 1862–1939

7 He's the Man Who Delivers the Goods.
   The Man Who Delivers the Goods

PHILIP MASSINGER 1583–1640

8 He that would govern others, first
   should be
   The master of himself.
                       The Bondman, I. iii

9   I am driven
   Into a desperate strait and cannot
   steer
   A middle course.
             Great Duke of Florence, III. i

10 A New Way to Pay Old Debts.
                            Title of Play

11 What pity 'tis, one that can speak so
   well,
   Should in his actions be so ill!
                   Parliament of Love, III. iii

12 There are a thousand doors to let out
   life.   *Ib.* IV. ii

13   Serves and fears
   The fury of the many-headed monster,
   The giddy multitude.
             The Unnatural Combat, III. ii

CHARLES ROBERT MATURIN
1782–1824

14 'Tis well to be merry and wise,
   'Tis well to be honest and true;
   'Tis well to be off with the old love,
   Before you are on with the new.
                        Bertram. Motto

GEORGE LOUIS PALMELLA
BUSSON DU MAURIER 1834–1896

15 Life ain't all beer and skittles, and
   more's the pity; but what's the odds,
   so long as you're happy?
                            Trilby, pt. 1

TERENTIANUS MAURUS
fl. c. A.D. 200

16 Pro captu lectoris habent sua fata
   libelli.

   The fate of books depends on the
   capacity of the reader.
        De Literis, Syllabis, &c., l. 1286

HUGHES MEARNS 1875–

17 As I was going up the stair
   I met a man who wasn't there.
   He wasn't there again to-day.
   I wish, I wish he'd stay away.
             The Psychoed (Antigonish)

WILLIAM LAMB, VISCOUNT
MELBOURNE 1779–1848

18 I wish I was as cocksure of anything
   as Tom Macaulay is of everything.
       Earl Cowper's *Preface to Lord
       Melbourne's Papers* (1889), p. xii

19 I like the Garter; there is no damned
   merit in it.
          On the Order of the Garter

20 Things have come to a pretty pass
   when religion is allowed to invade the
   sphere of private life.
       *Remark on hearing an Evangelical
       Sermon.* G. W. E. Russell's
       Collections and Recollections, ch. 6

THOMAS MELLOR 1880–1926

21 I wouldn't leave my little wooden hut
   for you!
   I've got one lover and I don't want
   two.
       *I Wouldn't Leave My Little
       Wooden Hut for You*

GEORGE MEREDITH 1828–1909

1 On a starred night Prince Lucifer up-
rose.
Tired of his dark dominion swung the
fiend . . .
He reached a middle height, and at
the stars,
Which are the brain of heaven, he
looked, and sank.
Around the ancient track marched,
rank on rank,
The army of unalterable law.
Lucifer in Starlight

2 Not till the fire is dying in the grate,
Look we for any kinship with the
stars.   *Modern Love, iv*

3 And if I drink oblivion of a day,
So shorten I the stature of my soul.
Ib. xii

4   In tragic life, God wot,
No villain need be! Passions spin the
plot:
We are betrayed by what is false
within.   *Ib. xliii*

5 We saw the swallows gathering in the
sky.   *Ib. xlvii*

6 The pilgrims of the year waxed very
loud
In multitudinous chatterings.   *Ib.*

7 Ah, what a dusty answer gets the soul
When hot for certainties in this our
life!   *Ib.*

8 Enter these enchanted woods,
You who dare.
The Woods of Westermain

9 Men may have rounded Seraglio Point:
they have not yet doubled Cape Turk.
Diana of the Crossways, ch. 1

10 You see he has a leg.
The Egoist, ch. 2

11 A dainty rogue in porcelain. *Ib. ch. 5*

12 I expect that Woman will be the last
thing civilized by Man.
*The Ordeal of Richard Feverel,
ch. 1*

OWEN MEREDITH [EDWARD ROBERT BULWER, EARL OF LYTTON] 1831–1891

13 Genius does what it must, and Talent
does what it can.
*Poems. Last words of a Sensitive
Second-rate Poet*

DIXON LANIER MERRITT 1879–

14 A wonderful bird is the pelican,
His bill will hold more than his belican.
He can take in his beak
Food enough for a week,
But I'm damned if I see how the
helican.   *The Pelican*

JEAN MESSELIER
eighteenth century

15 Je voudrais, et ce sera le dernier et le
plus ardent de mes souhaits, je
voudrais que le dernier des rois fût
étranglé avec les boyaux du dernier
prêtre.

I should like to see, and this will be
the last and the most ardent of
my desires, I should like to see
the last king strangled with the
guts of the last priest.
*In his Will, 1733, published by
Voltaire*

PRINCE METTERNICH 1773–1859

16 Italien ist ein geographischer Begriff.

Italy is a geographical expression.
Letter, 19 Nov. 1849

HUGO MEYNELL 1727–1808

17 The chief advantage of London is,
that a man is always so near his
burrow.
*Boswell's Johnson (ed. 1934),
vol. iii, p. 379, 1 Apr. 1779*

THOMAS MIDDLETON
1570?–1627

18 By many a happy accident.
*No Wit, No Help, Like a
Woman's, iv. i. 66*

19 Though I be poor, I'm honest.
The Witch, iii. ii

ALBERT MIDLANE 1825–1909

20 There's a Friend for little children
Above the bright blue sky
Good News for the Little Ones

JOHN STUART MILL 1806–1873

21 Unearned increment.
*Dissertations and Discussions, vol.
iv, p. 299*

22 The liberty of the individual must be
thus far limited; he must not make
himself a nuisance to other people.
Liberty, ch. 3

23 The worth of a State, in the long run,
is the worth of the individuals com-
posing it.   *Ib.*

24 When the land is cultivated entirely
by the spade and no horses are kept,
a cow is kept for every three acres of
land.
*Political Economy. A Treatise on
Flemish Husbandry*

EDNA ST. VINCENT MILLAY
1892–1950

1 My candle burns at both ends;
  It will not last the night;
  But oh, my foes, and oh, my friends—
  It gives a lovely light. *Poems* (1923)

ALICE DUER MILLER 1874–1942

2 I am American bred,
  I have seen much to hate here—much
      to forgive,
  But in a world where England is
      finished and dead,
  I do not wish to live.
            The White Cliffs (1940)

MRS. EMILY MILLER 1833–1913

3 I love to hear the story
  Which angel voices tell.
        The Little Corporal. I Love to Hear

WILLIAM MILLER 1810–1872

4 Wee Willie Winkie
  Rins through the town,
  Upstairs and doon stairs
  In his nicht-gown,
  Tirling at the window,
  Crying at the lock,
  'Are the weans in their bed,
  For it's now ten o'clock?'
            Willie Winkie

A. J. MILLS

5 Just like the ivy I'll cling to you.
            Title of Song

REV. HENRY HART MILMAN
1791–1868

6 Ride on! ride on in majesty!
  In lowly pomp ride on to die.
            Hymns. Ride On!

ALAN ALEXANDER MILNE
1882–1956

7 They're changing guard at Bucking-
      ham Palace—
  Christopher Robin went down with
      Alice.
        When We Were Very Young.
        Buckingham Palace

8 John had
  Great Big
  Waterproof
  Boots on;
  John had a
  Great Big
  Waterproof
  Hat;
  John had a
  Great Big
  Waterproof
  Mackintosh.
  And that
  (Said John)
  Is That.   *Ib. Happiness*

9 James James
  Morrison Morrison
  Weatherby George Dupree
  Took great
  Care of his Mother
  Though he was only three.
        When We Were Very Young.
        Disobedience

10 You must never go down to the end of
   the town if you don't go down with
   me.   *Ib.*

11 *What* is the matter with Mary Jane?
   She's crying with all her might and
       main,
   And she won't eat her dinner—rice
       pudding again—
   What *is* the matter with Mary Jane?
            Ib. Rice Pudding

12 *What* is the matter with Mary Jane?
   She's perfectly well and she hasn't a
       pain
   *And it's lovely rice pudding for dinner
       again!*
   What *is* the matter with Mary Jane?
                              Ib.

13 The King asked
   The Queen, and
   The Queen asked
   The Dairymaid:
   'Could we have some butter for
   The Royal slice of bread?'
            Ib. The King's Breakfast

14 I do like a little bit of butter to my
   bread!   *Ib.*

15 Little Boy kneels at the foot of the
       bed,
   Droops on the little hands, little gold
       head;
   Hush! Hush! Whisper who dares!
   Christopher Robin is saying his
   prayers.   *Ib. Vespers*

16 Isn't it funny
   How a bear likes honey?
   Buzz! Buzz! Buzz!
   I wonder why he does?
            Winnie-the-Pooh, ch. 1

17 I am a Bear of Very Little Brain, and
   long words Bother me.   *Ib. ch. 4*

18 Time for a little something. *Ib. ch. 6*

ALFRED, LORD MILNER
1854–1925

19 [*The Peers and the Budget*] If we believe
   a thing to be bad, and if we have a
   right to prevent it, it is our duty to
   try to prevent it and to damn the
   consequences.
        Speech at Glasgow, 26 Nov. 1909

JOHN MILTON 1608–1674

20 What hath night to do with sleep?
            Comus, l. 122

1 Come, knit hands, and beat the ground,
In a light fantastic round. *Comus*, l. 143

2 How charming is divine philosophy!
Not harsh, and crabbed as dull fools suppose,
But musical as is Apollo's lute,
And a perpetual feast of nectared sweets,
Where no crude surfeit reigns.
Ib. l. 476

3 Sabrina fair,
Listen where thou art sitting
Under the glassy, cool, translucent wave,
In twisted braids of lilies knitting
The loose train of thy amber-dropping hair. *Ib.* l. 859

4 Hence, vain deluding joys,
The brood of Folly without father bred. *Il Penseroso*, l. 1

5 Hail divinest Melancholy. *Ib.* l. 12

6 Sweet bird, that shunn'st the noise of folly,
Most musical, most melancholy!
Ib. l. 61

7 Where glowing embers through the room
Teach light to counterfeit a gloom,
Far from all resort of mirth,
Save the cricket on the hearth.
Ib. l. 79

8 Sometime let gorgeous Tragedy
In sceptred pall come sweeping by,
Presenting Thebes, or Pelops' line,
Or the tale of Troy divine. *Ib.* l. 97

9 With antique pillars massy proof,
And storied windows richly dight,
Casting a dim religious light.
There let the pealing organ blow,
To the full-voiced quire below,
In service high, and anthems clear
As may, with sweetness, through mine ear,
Dissolve me into ecstasies,
And bring all Heaven before mine eyes. *Ib.* l. 158

10 Hence, loathed Melancholy,
Of Cerberus, and blackest Midnight born,
In Stygian cave forlorn,
'Mongst horrid shapes, and shrieks, and sights unholy.
L'Allegro, l. 1

11 So buxom, blithe, and debonair.
Ib. l. 24

12 Haste thee Nymph, and bring with thee
Jest and youthful jollity,
Quips and cranks, and wanton wiles,
Nods, and becks, and wreathed smiles.
Ib. l. 25

13 Sport that wrinkled Care derides,
And Laughter holding both his sides.
Come, and trip it as ye go
On the light fantastic toe.
L'Allegro, l. 31

14 Meadows trim with daisies pied,
Shallow brooks and rivers wide.
Towers, and battlements it sees
Bosom'd high in tufted trees,
Where perhaps some beauty lies,
The cynosure of neighbouring eyes.
Ib. l. 75

15 Of herbs, and other country messes,
Which the neat-handed Phyllis dresses. *Ib.* l. 85

16 To many a youth, and many a maid,
Dancing in the chequered shade.
And young and old come forth to play
On a sunshine holiday. *Ib.* l. 95

17 Then to the spicy nut-brown ale.
Ib. l. 100

18 Towered cities please us then,
And the busy hum of men. *Ib.* l. 117

19 And pomp, and feast, and revelry,
With mask, and antique pageantry,
Such sights as youthful poets dream,
On summer eves by haunted stream.
Then to the well-trod stage anon,
If Jonson's learnèd sock be on,
Or sweetest Shakespeare, Fancy's child,
Warble his native wood-notes wild,
And ever against eating cares,
Lap me in soft Lydian airs,
Married to immortal verse
Such as the meeting soul may pierce
In notes, with many a winding bout
Of linked sweetness long drawn out.
Ib. l. 127

20 Yet once more, O ye laurels, and once more
Ye myrtles brown, with ivy never sere,
I come to pluck your berries harsh and crude,
And with forc'd fingers rude,
Shatter your leaves before the mellowing year.
Bitter constraint and sad occasion dear
Compels me to disturb your season due,
For Lycidas is dead, dead ere his prime,
Young Lycidas and hath not left his peer.
Who would not sing for Lycidas? he knew
Himself to sing and build the lofty rhyme.
He must not float upon his watery bier
Unwept, and welter to the parching wind
Without the meed of some melodious tear. *Lycidas*, l. 1

21 Whom universal Nature did lament.
Ib. l. 60

1 Alas! what boots it with uncessant care
To tend the homely, slighted, shep-
  herd's trade,
And strictly meditate the thankless
  Muse?
Were it not better done, as others use,
To sport with Amaryllis in the shade,
Or with the tangles of Neæra's hair.
Fame is the spur that the clear spirit
  doth raise
(That last infirmity of noble mind)
To scorn delights, and live laborious
  days;
But the fair guerdon when we hope
  to find,
And think to burst out into sudden
  blaze,
Comes the blind Fury with th' ab-
  horred shears
And slits the thin-spun life.
                          Lycidas, l. 64

2 Last came, and last did go,
The Pilot of the Galilean lake,
Two massy keys he bore of metals
  twain,
The golden opes, the iron shuts amain.
                          Ib. l. 108

3   Their lean and flashy songs
Grate on their scrannel pipes of
  wretched straw,
The hungry sheep look up, and are not
  fed,
But, swoln with wind and the rank
  mist they draw,
Rot inwardly and foul contagion
  spread;
Besides what the grim wolf with privy
  paw
Daily devours apace, and nothing
  said.
But that two-handed engine at the
  door
Stands ready to smite once, and smite
  no more.   *Ib. l. 123*

4 For Lycidas your sorrow is not dead,
Sunk though he be beneath the watery
  floor;
So sinks the day-star in the ocean bed,
And yet anon repairs his drooping
  head,
And tricks his beams, and with new
  spangled ore,
Flames in the forehead of the morning
  sky:
So Lycidas sunk low, but mounted
  high,
Through the dear might of Him that
  walked the waves.   *Ib. l. 166*

5 At last he rose, and twitch'd his
  mantle blue;
To-morrow to fresh woods, and
  pastures new.   *Ib. l. 192*

6 This is the month, and this the happy
  morn,
Wherein the Son of Heaven's eternal
  King,

Of wedded maid, and virgin mother
  born,
Our great redemption from above did
  bring;
For so the holy sages once did sing,
That He our deadly forfeit should
  release,
And with His Father work us a perpetual peace.
    *Hymn. On the Morning of
    Christ's Nativity, l. 1*

7   It was the winter wild
While the Heav'n-born child
All meanly wrapt in the rude manger
  lies,
Nature in awe to him
Had doff't her gawdy trim
With her great Master so to sympa-
  thize.   *Ib. l. 29*

8 Time will run back, and fetch the age
  of gold.   *Ib. l. 135*

9 Of Man's first disobedience, and the
  fruit
Of that forbidden tree, whose mortal
  taste
Brought death into the world, and all
  our woe,
With loss of Eden.
          Paradise Lost, bk. i, l. 1

10 Things unattempted yet in prose or
  rhyme.   *Ib. l. 16*

11   What in me is dark
Illumine, what is low raise and support;
That to the height of this great argu-
  ment
I may assert eternal Providence,
And justify the ways of God to Men.
                        Ib. l. 22

12   Him the Almighty Power
Hurled headlong flaming from th'
  ethereal sky
With hideous ruin and combustion
  down
To bottomless perdition, there to
  dwell
In adamantine chains and penal fire
Who durst defy th' Omnipotent to
  arms.   *Ib. l. 44*

13 No light, but rather darkness visible.
                        Ib. l. 62

14   But O how fall'n! how changed
From him who, in the happy realms of
  light,
Clothed with transcendent brightness
  didst outshine
Myriads though bright.   *Ib. l. 84*

15   What though the field be lost?
All is not lost; th' unconquerable will,
And study of revenge, immortal hate,
And courage never to submit or yield:
And what is else not to be overcome?
                        Ib. l. 105

1 Fall'n Cherub, to be weak is miserable
Doing or suffering; but of this be sure,
To do aught good never will be our
  task,
But ever to do ill our sole delight.
  Paradise Lost, bk. i, l. 157

2 The mind is its own place, and in it self
Can make a Heav'n of Hell, a Hell
of Heav'n. *Ib.* l. 254

3 Here we may reign secure, and in my
  choice
To reign is worth ambition though in
  hell:
Better to reign in hell, than serve in
heav'n. *Ib.* l. 261

4 Thick as autumnal leaves that strow
the brooks
In Vallombrosa, where th' Etrurian
  shades
High over-arch'd imbower. *Ib.* l. 302

5 And when night
Darkens the streets, then wander
forth the sons
Of Belial, flown with insolence and
wine. *Ib.* l. 500

6 A shout that tore hell's concave, and
beyond
Frighted the reign of Chaos and old
Night. *Ib.* l. 542

7 Who overcomes
By force, hath overcome but half his
foe. *Ib.* l. 648

8 Let none admire
That riches grow in hell; that soil may
best
Deserve the precious bane. *Ib.* l. 690

9 From morn
To noon he fell, from noon to dewy
eve,
A summer's day; and with the setting
sun
Dropt from the zenith like a falling
star. *Ib.* l. 742

10 Satan exalted sat, by merit raised
To that bad eminence; *Ib.* bk. ii, l. 5

11 But all was false and hollow; though
his tongue
Dropt manna, and could make the
worse appear
The better reason. *Ib.* l. 112

12 Who shall tempt with wand'ring feet
The dark unbottom'd infinite abyss
And through the palpable obscure
find out
His uncouth way. *Ib.* l. 404

13 With ruin upon ruin, rout on rout
Confusion worse confounded.
  Ib. l. 995

14 So farewell hope, and with hope farewell fear,
Farewell remorse: all good to me is
lost;
Evil be thou my Good. *Ib.* bk. iv, l. 108

15 A heaven on earth.
  Paradise Lost, bk. iv, l. 208

16 For contemplation he and valour
formed;
For softness she and sweet attractive
grace,
He for God only, she for God in him:
His fair large front and eye sublime
declared
Absolute rule. *Ib.* l. 297

17 Adam, the goodliest man of men since
born
His sons; the fairest of her daughters
Eve. *Ib.* l. 323

18 But wherefore thou alone? Wherefore
with thee
Came not all hell broke loose?
  Ib. l. 917

19 Hear all ye Angels, progeny of light,
Thrones, Dominations, Princedoms,
Virtues, Powers. *Ib.* bk. v, l. 600

20 Standing on earth, not rapt above the
Pole,
More safe I sing with mortal voice,
unchang'd
To hoarse or mute, though fall'n on
evil days,
On evil days though fall'n, and evil
tongues.
In darkness, and with dangers com-
pass'd round,
And solitude; yet not alone, while
thou
Visit'st my slumbers nightly, or when
morn
Purples the east: still govern thou
my song,
Urania, and fit audience find, though
few:
But drive far off the barb'rous dis-
sonance
Of Bacchus and his revellers.
  Ib. bk. vii, l. 23

21 The sum of earthly bliss.
  Ib. bk. viii, l. 522

22 As one who long in populous city pent,
Where houses thick and sewers annoy
the air,
Forth issuing on a summer's morn to
breathe
Among the pleasant villages and
farms
Adjoin'd, from each thing met conceives delight. *Ib.* bk. ix, l. 445

23 She fair, divinely fair, fit love for
Gods. *Ib.* l. 489

24 Demoniac frenzy, moping melan-
choly,
And moon-struck madness.
  Ib. bk. xi, l. 485

25 The world was all before them, where
to choose
Their place of rest, and Providence
their guide:

They hand in hand with wandering
steps and slow
Through Eden took their solitary way.
Paradise Lost, bk. xii, 1. 646

1 Of whom to be dispraised were no
small praise.
Paradise Regained, bk. iii, 1. 56

2 Eyeless in Gaza, at the mill with
slaves. *Samson Agonistes*, 1. 41

3 O dark, dark, dark, amid the blaze
of noon,
Irrecoverably dark, total eclipse
Without all hope of day! *Ib.* 1. 80

4 To live a life half dead, a living death.
Ib. 1. 100

5 But who is this, what thing of sea or
land?
Female of sex it seems,
That so bedeck'd, ornate, and gay,
Comes this way sailing
Like a stately ship
Of Tarsus, bound for th' isles
Of Javan or Gadier,
With all her bravery on, and tackle
trim,
Sails fill'd, and streamers waving,
Courted by all the winds that hold
them play,
An amber scent of odorous perfume
Her harbinger. *Ib.* 1. 710

6 O how comely it is, and how reviving
To the spirits of just men long opprest,
When God into the hands of their
deliverer
Puts invincible might,
To quell the mighty of the earth, th'
oppressor. *Ib.* 1. 1268

7 He's gone, and who knows how he may
report
Thy words by adding fuel to the
flame? *Ib.* 1. 1350

8 For evil news rides post, while good
news baits. *Ib.* 1. 1538

9 Samson hath quit himself
Like Samson, and heroically hath
finish'd
A life heroic. *Ib.* 1. 1709

10 Nothing is here for tears, nothing to
wail
Or knock the breast; no weakness, no
contempt,
Dispraise or blame; nothing but well
and fair,
And what may quiet us in a death so
noble. *Ib.* 1. 1721

11 His servants he with new acquist
Of true experience from this great
event
With peace and consolation hath dis-
miss'd,
And calm of mind all passion spent.
Ib. 1. 1755

12 What needs my Shakespeare for his
honour'd bones,
The labour of an age in piled stones,
Or that his hallow'd relics should be
hid
Under a star-y-pointing pyramid?
Dear son of memory, great heir of
fame,
What need'st thou such weak witness
of thy name?
[Epitaph] on Shakespeare

13 Blest pair of Sirens, pledges of
Heaven's joy,
Sphere-born harmonious sisters, Voice
and Verse. *At a Solemn Music*

14 Where the bright Seraphim in burning
row
Their loud up-lifted Angel trumpets
blow. *Ib.*

15 All is, if I have grace to use it so,
As ever in my great Task-Master's eye.
*Sonnet ii. On his having arrived
at the age of twenty-three*

16 Avenge, O Lord, thy slaughtered
saints, whose bones
Lie scattered on the Alpine mountains
cold;
Ev'n them who kept thy truth so pure
of old,
When all our fathers worshipped
stocks and stones,
Forget not. In thy book record their
groans
Who were thy sheep, and in their
ancient fold
Slain by the bloody Piedmontese, that
rolled
Mother with infant down the rocks.
Ib. xv. *On the late Massacre in
Piedmont*

17 When I consider how my light is spent,
E're half my days, in this dark world
and wide,
And that one Talent which is death
to hide,
Lodg'd with me useless, though my
Soul more bent
To serve therewith my Maker, and
present
My true account, lest He returning
chide;
'Doth God exact day-labour, light
deny'd?'
I fondly ask; But Patience, to prevent
That murmur, soon replies, 'God doth
not need
Either man's work or his own gifts. Who
best
Bear his mild yoke, they serve him
best, his State
Is Kingly. Thousands at his bidding
speed
And post o'er Land and Ocean without
rest:
They also serve who only stand and
wait.' *Ib.* xvi. *On His Blindness*

1 Methought I saw my late espousèd
Saint
Brought to me like Alcestis from the
grave.
Sonnet xix. *On His Deceased Wife*

2 But O as to embrace me she inclined,
I waked, she fled, and day brought
back my night. *Ib.*

3 New Presbyter is but old Priest writ
large.
*Ib. On the New Forcers of Con-
science under the Long Parliament*

4 For what can war but endless war still
breed?
Ib. On the Lord General Fairfax

5 Peace hath her victories
No less renowned than war.
Ib. [*To the Lord General Crom-
well, May 1652*]

6 Fly, envious Time, till thou run out
thy race:
Call on the lazy leaden-stepping
hours. *On Time,* l. 1

7 As good almost kill a man as kill a
good book: who kills a man kills a
reasonable creature, God's image;
but he who destroys a good book, kills
reason itself, kills the image of God,
as it were in the eye. *Areopagitica*

8 A good book is the precious life-blood
of a master spirit, embalmed and
treasured up on purpose to a life
beyond life. *Ib.*

9 I cannot praise a fugitive and cloistered virtue, unexercised and unbreathed, that never sallies out and
sees her adversary, but slinks out of
the race, where that immortal garland
is to be run for, not without dust and
heat. Assuredly we bring not innocence into the world, we bring impurity much rather: that which purifies us is trial, and trial is by what is
contrary. *Ib.*

10 Methinks I see in my mind a noble
and puissant nation rousing herself
like a strong man after sleep, and
shaking her invincible locks. Methinks
I see her as an eagle mewing her
mighty youth, and kindling her undazzled eyes at the full midday beam.
Ib.

11 Let not England forget her prece-
dence of teaching nations how to live.
*The Doctrine and Discipline of
Divorce*

MISSAL

12 O felix culpa, quae talem ac tantum
meruit habere Redemptorem.
O happy fault, which has deserved
to have such and so mighty a
Redeemer.
'*Exsultet*' *on Holy Saturday*

EMILIO MOLA d. 1936

13 La quinta columna.
The fifth column.
*Radio Address given when a
General in the Spanish Civil
War, 1936–1939*

JEAN BAPTISTE POQUELIN,
called MOLIÈRE 1622–1673

14 Il faut manger pour vivre et non pas
vivre pour manger.
One should eat to live, not live to
eat. *L'Avare,* III. v

15 M. JOURDAIN: Quoi? quand je dis:
'Nicole, apportez-moi mes pantoufles,
et me donnez mon bonnet de nuit',
c'est de la prose?
MAÎTRE DE PHILOSOPHIE: Oui, monsieur.
M. JOURDAIN: Par ma foi! il y a plus
de quarante ans que je dis de la prose
sans que j'en susse rien.

M. JOURDAIN: What? when I say:
'Nicole, bring me my slippers, and
give me my night-cap,' is that
prose?
PROFESSOR OF PHILOSOPHY: Yes, Sir.
M. JOURDAIN: Good Heavens! For
more than forty years I have been
speaking prose without knowing
it.
Le Bourgeois Gentilhomme, II. iv

16 Tout ce qui n'est point prose est vers;
et tout ce qui n'est point vers est prose.
All that is not prose is verse; and
all that is not verse is prose. *Ib.*

17 Que diable allait-il faire dans cette
galère?
What the devil was he doing in that
galley?
Les Fourberies de Scapin, II. vii

18 Vous l'avez voulu, Georges Dandin,
vous l'avez voulu.
You asked for it, George Dandin,
you asked for it.
Georges Dandin, I. ix

19 Oui, cela était autrefois ainsi, mais
nous avons changé tout cela.
Yes, it used to be so, but we have
changed all that.
Le Médecin malgré lui, II. vi. *Said
by the pretended doctor to justify
his mistake as to the relative
positions of heart and liver.*

20 Ils commencent ici [Paris] par faire
pendre un homme et puis ils lui font
procès.
Here, in Paris, they hang a man first,
and try him afterwards.
Monsieur de Pourceaugnac, III. ii

**JOHN SAMUEL BEWLEY MON-
SELL** 1811–1875

1 Fight the good fight with all thy might,
  Christ is thy strength, and Christ thy
    right;
  Lay hold on life, and it shall be
  Thy joy and crown eternally.

  Run the straight race through God's
    good grace,
  Lift up thine eyes, and seek His Face;
  Life with its way before us lies,
  Christ is the path, and Christ the
    prize.
       *Hymns of Love and Praise. Fight
       of Faith*

MICHEL EYQUEM MONTAIGNE
                1533–1592

2 [*Of his friend, Étienne de la Boétie*]
  Si l'on me presse de dire pourquoi je
  l'aimais, je sens que cela ne se peut
  exprimer qu'en répondant, Parce que
  c'était lui; parce que c'était moi.

  If you press me to say why I loved
    him, I can say no more than it
    was because he was he and I was
    I.   *Essais*, I. xxviii

3 La plus grande chose du monde c'est
  de savoir être à soi.

  The greatest thing in the world is
    to know how to be sufficient unto
    oneself.   *Ib.* xxxix

4 Que sais-je?

  What do I know?   *Ib.* II. xii

ROBERT MONTGOMERY
                1807–1855

5 The soul aspiring pants its source to
    mount,
  As streams meander level with their
    fount.
       The Omnipresence of the Deity
       (ed. 1830), pt. i, l. 339

**JAMES GRAHAM, MARQUIS OF
MONTROSE** 1612–1650

6 He either fears his fate too much,
  Or his deserts are small,
  That puts it not unto the touch,
  To win or lose it all.
       My Dear and Only Love

PERCY MONTROSE
        nineteenth century

7 In a cavern, in a canyon,
    Excavating for a mine,
  Dwelt a miner, Forty-niner,
  And his daughter, Clementine.
  Oh, my darling, oh my darling, oh
    my darling Clementine!
  Thou art lost and gone for ever, dread-
    ful sorry, Clementine. *Clementine*

8 Light she was and like a fairy,
    And her shoes were number nine;
  Herring boxes without topses,
  Sandals were for Clementine.
                Clementine

9 But I kissed her little sister,
  And forgot my Clementine. *Ib.*

EDWARD MOORE 1712–1757

10 This is adding insult to injuries.
       The Foundling, v. ii

11 I am rich beyond the dreams of
  avarice.   *The Gamester*, II. ii

THOMAS MOORE 1779–1852

12 Believe me, if all those endearing
    young charms,
  Which I gaze on so fondly to-day.
     Irish Melodies. Believe Me, if All

13 The harp that once through Tara's
    halls
    The soul of music shed,
  Now hangs as mute on Tara's walls
    As if that soul were fled.—
  So sleeps the pride of former days,
    So glory's thrill is o'er;
  And hearts, that once beat high for
    praise,
  Now feel that pulse no more.
       Ib. The Harp that Once

14 No, there's nothing half so sweet in
    life
    As love's young dream.
       Ib. Love's Young Dream

15 The Minstrel Boy to the war is gone,
    In the ranks of death you'll find
      him;
  His father's sword he has girded on,
    And his wild harp slung behind him.
       Ib. The Minstrel Boy

16 Oh! blame not the bard.
       Ib. Oh! Blame Not

17 She is far from the land where her
    young hero sleeps,
  And lovers are round her, sighing:
  But coldly she turns from their gaze,
    and weeps,
  For her heart in his grave is lying.
       Ib. She is Far

18 'Tis the last rose of summer
    Left blooming alone;
  All her lovely companions
    Are faded and gone.
       Ib. 'Tis the Last Rose

19 I never nurs'd a dear gazelle,
    To glad me with its soft black eye,
  But when it came to know me well,
    And love me, it was sure to die!
    *Lalla Rookh. The Fire-Wor-
    shippers*, i, l. 279

1 Oft, in the stilly night,
  Ere Slumber's chain has bound me,
Fond Memory brings the light
  Of other days around me;
    The smiles, the tears,
    Of boyhood's years,
The words of love then spoken;
    The eyes that shone,
    Now dimm'd and gone,
The cheerful hearts now broken!
    National Airs. Oft in the Stilly Night

2 Faintly as tolls the evening chime
  Our voices keep tune and our oars
    keep time.
Soon as the woods on shore look dim,
We'll sing at St. Ann's our parting
  hymn.
Row, brothers, row, the stream runs
  fast,
The Rapids are near and the daylight's
  past.
    *Poems Relating to America.
    Canadian Boat Song*

THOMAS OSBERT MORDAUNT
1730–1809

3 Sound, sound the clarion, fill the fife,
  Throughout the sensual world pro-
    claim,
One crowded hour of glorious life
Is worth an age without a name.
    *The Bee, 12 Oct. 1791. Verses
    Written During the War, 1756–
    1763*

SIR THOMAS MORE 1478–1535

4 I pray you, master Lieutenant, see me
safe up, and my coming down let me
shift for myself. [On mounting the
scaffold.]
    Roper, *Life of Sir Thomas More*
    (1935), p. 103

5 Pluck up thy spirits, man, and be not
afraid to do thine office; my neck is
very short; take heed therefore thou
strike not awry, for saving of thine
honesty. [To the Executioner.]
    Ib. p. 103

6 This hath not offended the king. [As
he drew his beard aside on placing his
head on the block.]
    Bacon, *Apophthegms*, 22

7 Yea, marry, now it is somewhat, for
now it is rhyme; before, it was neither
rhyme nor reason. [Advising an
author to put his ill-written work into
verse.]
    A. Cayley's *Memoirs of Sir Thos.
    More* (1808), vol. i, p. 247

8 They roll and rumble,
They turn and tumble,
As pigges do in a poke.
    Works (1557), ¶ ii. 6. *How a
    Sergeant would learn to Play the
    Frere*

9 This is a fair tale of a tub told us of
his elects.
    Works (1557), p. 576. *Confutation
    of Tyndale's Answers*

THOMAS MORELL 1703–1784

10 See, the conquering hero comes!
Sound the trumpets, beat the drums!
    Joshua, pt. iii

AUGUSTUS DE MORGAN
1806–1871

11 Great fleas have little fleas upon their
  backs to bite 'em,
And little fleas have lesser fleas, and
  so *ad infinitum.*
    A Budget of Paradoxes (1872),
    p. 377

GEORGE POPE MORRIS
1802–1867

12 Woodman, spare that tree!
  Touch not a single bough!
In youth it sheltered me,
  And I'll protect it now.
    Woodman, Spare that Tree

WILLIAM MORRIS 1834–1896

13 The idle singer of an empty day.
    The Earthly Paradise. An Apology

14 Forget six counties overhung with
  smoke,
Forget the snorting steam and piston
  stroke,
Forget the spreading of the hideous
  town;
Think rather of the pack-horse on the
  down,
And dream of London, small and white
  and clean,
The clear Thames bordered by its
  gardens green.
    Ib. Prologue. *The Wanderers*, l. 1

THOMAS MORTON 1764?–1838

15 Approbation from Sir Hubert Stanley
is praise indeed.
    A Cure for the Heartache, v. ii

16 Always ding, dinging Dame Grundy
into my ears—what will Mrs. Grundy
zay? What will Mrs. Grundy think?
    Speed the Plough, I. i

JOHN LOTHROP MOTLEY
1814–1877

17 As long as he lived, he was the guiding-
star of a whole brave nation, and when
he died the little children cried in the
streets. [William of Orange.]
    Rise of the Dutch Republic, pt. vi,
    ch. vii

1 Give us the luxuries of life, and we
will dispense with its necessities.
> *Remark.* O. W. Holmes, *Auto-
> crat of the Breakfast-Table*, ch. 6

PETER ANTHONY MOTTEUX
1660–1718

2 The devil was sick, the devil a monk
wou'd be;
The devil was well, and the devil a
monk he'd be.
> Translation of Rabelais. *Gar-
> gantua and Pantagruel*, bk. iv,
> ch. 24

HENRY PHIPPS, EARL OF MULGRAVE 1755–1831

3 And toast before each martial tune—
'Howe, and the Glorious First of
June!'   *Our Line was Formed*

HECTOR HUGH MUNRO
see SAKI

C. W. MURPHY

4 Has anybody here seen Kelly?
Kelly from the Isle of Man?
> *Has Anybody Here seen Kelly?*

FRED MURRAY

5 Carve a little bit off the top for me!
> *A Little Bit Off The Top*

6 Our lodger's such a nice young man.
> *Title of Song*

ALFRED DE MUSSET 1810–1857

7 Mon verre n'est pas grand mais je
bois dans mon verre.
> The glass I drink from is not large,
> but at least it is my own.
> *La Coupe et les lèvres*

8 Le seul bien qui me reste au monde
Est d'avoir quelquefois pleuré.
> The only good thing left to me
> Is knowledge that I, too, have
> wept.   *Poèmes*

9 Malgré moi l'infini me tourmente.
> I can't help it, the idea of the in-
> finite is a torment to me.
> *Premières Poésies, L'Espoir en
> Dieu*

IAN NAIRN 1930–

10 By the end of the century Great
Britain will consist of isolated oases
of preserved monuments in a desert
of wire, concrete roads, cosy plots and
bungalows. . . . Upon this new Britain

the REVIEW bestows a name in the
hope that it will stick—SUBTOPIA.
> *Architectural Review* (June 1955),
> p. 365

CAROLINA, BARONESS NAIRNE
1766–1845

11 Will ye no come back again?
Better lo'ed ye canna be,
Will ye no come back again?
> *Life and Songs* (1869), *Bonnie
> Charlie's now awa'*

12 Charlie is my darling, my darling, my
darling,
Charlie is my darling, the young
Chevalier.
> *Ib. Charlie is My Darling*

13 Wi' a hundred pipers an' a', an' a',
Wi' a hundred pipers an' a', an' a',
We'll up an' gie them a blaw, a blaw,
Wi' a hundred pipers an' a', an' a'.
> *Ib. The Hundred Pipers*

SIR WILLIAM NAPIER 1785–1860

14 Then was seen with what a strength
and majesty the British soldier fights.
> *History of the War in the Penin-
> sula*, bk. xii, ch. 6, *Albuera*

NAPOLEON I 1769–1821

15 L'Angleterre est une nation de boutiquiers.
> England is a nation of shopkeepers.
> *Attr. by* B. B. E. O'Meara,
> *Napoleon at St. Helena*, vol. ii.
> *The original is probably 'sono
> mercanti', a phrase of Paoli,
> quoted by Napoleon; see* Gour-
> gaud, *Journal Inédit de Sainte-
> Hélène*, i. 69 (*see 1:2, 217:12*)

16 Tout soldat français porte dans sa
giberne le bâton de maréchal de
France.
> Every French soldier carries in his
> cartridge-pouch the baton of a
> marshal of France.
> E. Blaze, *La Vie Militaire sous
> l'Empire*, I. v

17 Quant au courage moral, il avait
trouvé fort rare, disait-il, celui de
deux heures après minuit; c'est-à-dire
le courage de l'improviste.
> As to moral courage, I have very
> rarely met with *the two o'clock in
> the morning courage*: I mean un-
> prepared courage.
> Las Cases, *Mémorial de Sainte-
> Hélène, Dec. 4–5, 1815*

18 La carrière ouverte aux talents.
> The career open to talents.
> O'Meara, *Napoleon in Exile*
> (1822), vol. i, p. 103

1 Soldats, songez que, du haut de ces
pyramides, quarante siècles vous con-
templent.
Think of it, soldiers; from the
summit of these pyramids, forty
centuries look down upon you.
*Speech to the Army of Egypt on
21 July 1798, before the Battle
of the Pyramids.* Gourgaud,
Mémoires, Guerre d'Orient, i,
p. 160

2 Du sublime au ridicule il n'y a qu'un
pas.
There is only one step from the
sublime to the ridiculous.
*To De Pradt, Polish ambassador,
after the retreat from Moscow in
1812.* De Pradt, *Histoire de
l'Ambassade dans le grand-duché
de Varsovie en 1812* (ed. 1815),
p. 215.

3 Voilà le soleil d'Austerlitz
There rises the sun of Austerlitz.
*To his officers, before Moscow,
7 Sept. 1812*

4 Tête d'Armée.   *Last words*

THOMAS NASHE 1567–1601

5 Brightness falls from the air;
Queens have died young and fair;
Dust hath closed Helen's eye.
I am sick, I must die.
Lord have mercy on us.
In Time of Pestilence

6 Spring, the sweet spring, is the year's
pleasant king;
Then blooms each thing, then maids
dance in a ring,
Cold doth not sting, the pretty birds
do sing:
Cuckoo, jug-jug, pu-we, to-witta-
woo!   *Spring*

JOHN MASON NEALE 1818–1866

7 All glory, laud, and honour
To Thee, Redeemer, King,
To whom the lips of children
Made sweet Hosannas ring.
All Glory, Laud, and Honour,
trans. from Latin *Gloria, Laus et
Honor tibi sit.*

8 Around the throne of God a band
Of glorious Angels always stand.
*Around the Throne of God.
Hymns for Children, First Series*
(1842)

9 Art thou weary, art thou languid,
Art thou sore distressed?
Art Thou Weary, trans. from
Greek

10 Brief life is here our portion;
Brief sorrow, short-lived care.
Brief Life is here, trans. from
Latin, *Hic breve Vivitur*

11 Christian, dost thou see them
On the holy ground,
How the troops of Midian
Prowl and prowl around?
Christian, Dost Thou See Them,
trans. from Greek

12 Good Christian men, rejoice
With heart, and soul, and voice.
Good Christian Men, Helmore
and Neale, *Carols for Christmas-
tide*

13 Good King Wenceslas look'd out,
On the Feast of Stephen;
When the snow lay round about,
Deep and crisp and even.
Good King Wenceslas. Helmore
and Neale, *Carols for Christmas-
tide*

14 Jerusalem the golden,
With milk and honey blest,
Beneath thy contemplation
Sink heart and voice opprest.
Jerusalem the Golden, trans.
from Latin, *Urbs Syon Aurea*

15 O come, O come, Emmanuel,
And ransom captive Israel.
O Come, O Come, Emmanuel,
trans. from Latin, *Veni, Veni,
Emmanuel*

16 O happy band of pilgrims,
Look upward to the skies,
Where such a light affliction
Shall win you such a prize!
*O Happy Band of Pilgrims.
Hymns of the Eastern Church*

HORATIO, VISCOUNT NELSON
1758–1805

17 Palmam qui meruit, ferat.
Let him who merits bear the palm.
Motto

18 Before this time to-morrow I shall
have gained a peerage, or Westminster
Abbey.
Battle of the Nile. Southey's *Life
of Nelson,* ch. 5

19 I have only one eye,—I have a right
to be blind sometimes: . . . I really do
not see the signal!
At the battle of Copenhagen. Ib.

20 England expects that every man will
do his duty.
At the battle of Trafalgar. Ib.

21 This is too warm work, Hardy, to last
long.   *Ib.*

22 Thank God, I have done my duty. *Ib.*

1 Kiss me, Hardy.
> *At the battle of Trafalgar.*
> Southey's *Life of Nelson*, ch. 5

2 Such a band of brothers [of his officers].
> *Letter to Earl Howe, 8 Jan. 1799, about the battle of the Nile. See Henry V, iv. 3.*

NERO A.D. 37–68

3 Qualis artifex pereo!
What an artist dies with me!
> Suetonius, *Life of Nero*, xlix. 1

SIR HENRY JOHN NEWBOLT
1862–1938

4 'Take my drum to England, hang et by the shore,
> Strike et when your powder's runnin' low;
> If the Dons sight Devon, I'll quit the port o' Heaven,
> An' drum them up the Channel as we drummed them long ago.'
> *The Island Race. Drake's Drum*

5 Drake he's in his hammock till the great Armadas come.
> (Capten, art tha sleepin' there below?)
> Slung atween the round shot, listenin' for the drum,
> An' dreamin' arl the time o' Plymouth Hoe.
> Call him on the deep sea, call him up the Sound,
> Call him when ye sail to meet the foe;
> Where the old trade's plyin' an' the old flag flyin'
> They shall find him ware an' wakin', as they found him long ago! *Ib.*

6 There's a breathless hush in the Close to-night—
> Ten to make and the match to win—
> A bumping pitch and a blinding light,
> An hour to play and the last man in.
> And it's not for the sake of a ribboned coat,
> Or the selfish hope of a season's fame,
> But his Captain's hand on his shoulder smote—
> 'Play up! play up! and play the game!' *Ib. Vitaï Lampada*

7 But cared greatly to serve God and the King,
> And keep the Nelson touch.
> *Minora Sidera*

JOHN HENRY, CARDINAL NEWMAN 1801–1890

8 It is very difficult to get up resentment towards persons whom one has never seen.
> *Apologia pro Vita Sua* (1864). *Mr. Kingsley's Method of Disputation*

9 There is such a thing as legitimate warfare: war has its laws; there are things which may fairly be done, and things which may not be done. . . . He has attempted (as I may call it) to *poison the wells.*
> *Apologia pro Vita Sua* (1864). *Mr. Kingsley's Method of Disputation*

10 I will vanquish, not my Accuser, but my judges.
> *Ib. True Mode of meeting Mr. Kingsley*

11 Trinity had never been unkind to me. There used to be much snap-dragon growing on the walls opposite my freshman's rooms there, and I had for years taken it as the emblem of my own perpetual residence even unto death in my University.
> On the morning of the 23rd I left the Observatory. I have never seen Oxford since, excepting its spires, as they are seen from the railway.
> *Ib. History of My Religious Opinions from 1841 to 1845*

12 May He support us all the day long, till the shades lengthen, and the evening comes, and the busy world is hushed, and the fever of life is over, and our work is done! Then in His mercy may He give us a safe lodging, and a holy rest, and peace at the last.
> *Sermon, 1834. Wisdom and Innocence*

13 Firmly I believe and truly
> God is Three, and God is One;
> And I next acknowledge duly
> Manhood taken by the Son.
> *The Dream of Gerontius*

14 Praise to the Holiest in the height,
> And in the depth be praise;
> In all his words most wonderful,
> Most sure in all His ways. *Ib.*

15 Lead, kindly Light, amid the encircling gloom,
> Lead thou me on;
> The night is dark, and I am far from home,
> Lead thou me on.
> Keep Thou my feet; I do not ask to see
> The distant scene; one step enough for me.
> *The Pillar of Cloud. Lead Kindly Light*

16 And with the morn those Angel faces smile,
> Which I have loved long since, and lost awhile. *Ib.*

SIR ISAAC NEWTON 1642–1727

17 I do not know what I may appear to the world, but to myself I seem to have been only a boy playing on the seashore, and diverting myself in now and

then finding a smoother pebble or a
prettier shell than ordinary, whilst
the great ocean of truth lay all undiscovered before me.
> Brewster's *Memoirs of Newton*,
> vol. ii, ch. 27

JOHN NEWTON 1725–1807

1 How sweet the name of Jesus sounds
In a believer's ear!
It soothes his sorrows, heals his
wounds,
And drives away his fear.
> *Olney Hymns* (1779), *How Sweet
> the Name*

2 Glorious things of thee are spoken,
Zion, city of our God.
> *Ib. Glorious Things of Thee*

NICHOLAS I OF RUSSIA
1796–1855

3 Nous avons sur les bras un homme
malade — un homme gravement
malade.
> We have on our hands a sick man—
> a very sick man.
> [The sick man of Europe, the
> Turk.]
> *Parliamentary Papers. Accounts
> and Papers*, vol. lxxi, pt. 5.
> *Eastern Papers*, p. 2. *Sir G. H.
> Seymour to Lord John Russell,
> 11 Jan. 1853*

4 Russia has two generals in whom she
can confide—Generals Janvier and
Février.
> *Punch, 10 Mar. 1853. Speech of
> the late Emperor of Russia*

ADELA FLORENCE NICOLSON
see LAURENCE HOPE

FRIEDRICH WILHELM
NIETZSCHE 1844–1900

5 Herren-Moral und Sklaven-Moral.
> The morality of masters and the
> morality of slaves.
> *Jenseits von Gut und Böse*

6 Ich lehre euch den Übermenschen. Der
Mensch ist Etwas, das überwunden
werden soll.
> I teach you the superman. Man is
> something to be surpassed.
> *Thus Spake Zarathustra*. Pro-
> logue

7 Blonde Bestie.
> Blonde beast.
> *Zur Genealogie der Moral*

THOMAS NOEL 1799–1861

8 Rattle his bones over the stones;
He's only a pauper, whom nobody
owns!
> *Rhymes and Roundelays, The
> Pauper's Drive*

CHRISTOPHER NORTH [JOHN
WILSON] 1785–1854

9 His Majesty's dominions, on which the
sun never sets.
> *Noctes Ambrosianae*, No. 20
> (Apr. 1829)

10 Laws were made to be broken.
> *Ib.* No. 24 (May 1830)

SIR STAFFORD HENRY NORTH-
COTE, EARL OF IDDESLEIGH
1818–1887

11 Argue as you please, you are nowhere, that grand old man, the Prime
Minister, insists on the other thing.
> *Speech at Liverpool, 12 Apr. 1882*

CAROLINE ELIZABETH SARAH
NORTON 1808–1877

12 My beautiful, my beautiful! that
standest meekly by,
With thy proudly-arched and glossy
neck, and dark and fiery eye!
Fret not to roam the desert now, with
all thy winged speed:
I may not mount on thee again!—
thou'rt sold, my Arab steed!
> *The Arab's Farewell to His Steed*

13 For death and life, in ceaseless strife,
Beat wild on this world's shore,
And all our calm is in that balm—
Not lost but gone before.
> *Not Lost but Gone Before*

NOVALIS [FRIEDRICH VON
HARDENBERG] 1772–1801

14 Ein Gott-betrunkener Mensch.
> A God-intoxicated man.
> *Remark about Spinoza*

IVOR NOVELLO 1893–1951

15 Keep the home fires burning.
> *Title and first line of Song*

ALFRED NOYES 1880–1958

16 Go down to Kew in lilac-time, in
lilac-time, in lilac-time;
Go down to Kew in lilac-time (it
isn't far from London!)
And you shall wander hand in hand
with love in summer's wonderland;
Go down to Kew in lilac-time (it isn't
far from London!) *Barrel Organ*

1 The wind was a torrent of darkness
   among the gusty trees,
The moon was a ghostly galleon tossed
   upon cloudy seas,
The road was a ribbon of moonlight
   over the purple moor,
And the highwayman came riding—
   Riding—riding—
The highwayman came riding, up to
   the old inn-door. *The Highwayman*

NURSERY RHYMES

(Earliest known sources are given)

2 A was an apple-pie;
   B bit it;
   C cut it.
      Quoted by John Eachard, *Some
      Observations* (1671)

3 As I was going to St. Ives,
   I met a man with seven wives,
   Each wife had seven sacks,
   Each sack had seven cats,
   Each cat had seven kits:
   Kits, cats, sacks, and wives,
   How many were there going to St.
   Ives? *Harley MS., 1316* (c. 1730)

4 Baa, baa, black sheep,
   Have you any wool?
   Yes, sir, yes, sir,
   Three bags full:
   One for the master,
   And one for the dame,
   And one for the little boy
   Who lives down the lane.
      *Tommy Thumb's Pretty Song
      Book* (c. 1744)

5 Boys and girls come out to play,
   The moon doth shine as bright as day.
      In William King, *Useful Trans-
      actions in Philosophy* (1708–9)

6 Bye, baby bunting,
   Daddy's gone a-hunting,
   Gone to get a rabbit skin
   To wrap the baby bunting in.
      Gammer Gurton's Garland (1784)

7 Cock a doodle doo!
   My dame has lost her shoe;
   My master's lost his fiddling-stick,
   And knows not what to do.
      *Quoted in The Most Cruel And
      Bloody Murder Committed by an
      Innkeepers Wife* (1606)

8 Come, let's to bed, says Sleepy-head;
   Tarry a while, says Slow;
   Put on the pot, says Greedy-gut,
   We'll sup before we go.
      Gammer Gurton's Garland (1784)

9 Cross-patch,
   Draw the latch,
   Sit by the fire and spin:
   Take a cup,
   And drink it up,
   Then call your neighbours in.
      Mother Goose's Melody (c. 1765)

10 Cry, baby, cry,
   Put your finger in your eye,
   And tell your mother it wasn't I.
      Nursery Rhymes, ed. J. O. Halli-
      well (1853)

11 Curly locks, Curly locks,
   Wilt thou be mine?
   Thou shalt not wash dishes
   Nor yet feed the swine.
   But sit on a cushion
   And sew a fine seam,
   And feed upon strawberries,
   Sugar and cream.
      Infant Institutes (1797)

12 Daffy-down-dilly is new come to
      town,
   With a yellow petticoat, and a green
      gown. *Songs for the Nursery* (1805)

13 Ding, dong, bell,
   Pussy's in the well.
   Who put her in?
   Little Johnny Green.
      Mother Goose's Melody (c. 1765)

14 A frog he would a-wooing go.
   'Heigh ho!' says Rowley.
      In Thomas Ravenscroft, *Melis-
      mata* (1611)

15 Georgie Porgie, pudding and pie,
   Kissed the girls and made them cry;
   When the boys came out to play
   Georgie Porgie ran away.
      Nursery Rhymes, ed. J. O. Halli-
      well (1842)

16 Goosey goosey gander,
   Whither shall I wander?
   Upstairs and downstairs,
   And in my lady's chamber;
   There I met an old man
   That would not say his prayers;
   I took him by the left leg,
   And threw him down the stairs.
      Gammer Gurton's Garland (1784)

17 Hey diddle diddle,
   The cat and the fiddle,
   The cow jumped over the moon;
   The little dog laughed
   To see such sport,
   And the dish ran away with the spoon.
      Mother Goose's Melody (c. 1765)

18 Hickory, dickory, dock,
   The mouse ran up the clock,
   The clock struck one,
   The mouse ran down;
   Hickory, dickory, dock.
      *Tommy Thumb's Pretty Song
      Book* (c. 1744)

19 How many miles to Babylon?
   Threescore miles and ten.
   Can I get there by candle-light?
   Yes, and back again.
   If your heels are nimble and light,
   You may get there by candle-light.
      Songs for the Nursery (1805)

1 Humpty Dumpty sat on a wall,
Humpty Dumpty had a great fall;
All the king's horses,
And all the king's men,
Couldn't put Humpty together again.
    From MS. addition to a copy of
    Mother Goose's Melody (c. 1803)

2 I had a little nut tree, nothing would
it bear
But a silver nutmeg and a golden pear;
The king of Spain's daughter came to
visit me,
And all for the sake of my little nut
tree.
    Newest Christmas Box (c. 1797)

3 I like little pussy, her coat is so warm,
And if I don't hurt her, she'll do me
no harm.
So I'll not pull her tail, nor drive her
away,
But pussy and I very gently will play.
    Only True Mother Goose Melodies
    (Boston, c. 1843)

4 Jack and Jill went up the hill
To fetch a pail of water;
Jack fell down and broke his crown,
And Jill came tumbling after.
    Mother Goose's Melody (c. 1765)

5 Jack Sprat could eat no fat,
His wife could eat no lean;
And so between them both, you see,
They licked the platter clean.
    In John Clarke, *Paroemiologia*
    Anglo-Latina (1639)

6 The King of France went up the hill,
With forty thousand men;
The King of France came down the
hill,
And ne'er went up again.
    Quoted by James Howell in a
    letter to Sir James Crofts, 12 May
    1620

7 Ladybird, ladybird, fly away home,
Your house is on fire, and your children all gone.
    Tommy Thumb's Pretty Song
    Book (c. 1744)

8 The lion and the unicorn
Were fighting for the crown;
The lion beat the unicorn
All round about the town.
Some gave them white bread,
And some gave them brown;
Some gave them plum cake,
And sent them out of town.
    In William King, *Useful Trans-*
    actions in Philosophy (1708–9)

9 Little Bo-Peep has lost her sheep,
And can't tell where to find them;
Leave them alone, and they'll come
home,
And bring their tails behind them.
    Douce MS. (c. 1805)

10 Little boy blue, come blow up your
horn,
The sheep's in the meadow, the cow's
in the corn;
But where is the boy that looks after
the sheep?
He's under the haycock fast asleep.
Will you wake him? No, not I,
For if I do, he'll be sure to cry.
    The Famous Tommy Thumb's
    Little Story Book (c. 1760)

11 Little Jack Horner sat in the corner,
Eating a Christmas pie:
He put in his thumb, and pulled out a
plum,
And said, 'What a good boy am I!'
    Quoted by Henry Carey, *Namby*
    Pamby (c. 1720)

12 Little Polly Flinders
Sat among the cinders,
Warming her pretty little toes;
Her mother came and caught her,
And whipped her little daughter
For spoiling her nice new clothes.
    Original Ditties for the Nursery
    (c. 1805)

13 Little Tommy Tucker
Sings for his supper;
What shall we give him?
White bread and butter.
    Tommy Thumb's Pretty Song
    Book (c. 1744)

14 London bridge is broken down,
My fair lady.
    Quoted by Henry Carey, *Namby*
    Pamby (c. 1720)

15 The man in the wilderness asked me,
How many strawberries grow in the
sea?
I answered him, as I thought good,
As many as red herrings grow in the
wood.
    MS. addition, dated 1744, to the
    Bath Municipal Library's copy
    of *The Whole Duty of Man* (1733)

16 Mary, Mary, quite contrary,
How does your garden grow?
With silver bells, and cockle shells,
And pretty maids all in a row.
    Tommy Thumb's Pretty Song
    Book (c. 1744)

17 Monday's child is fair of face,
Tuesday's child is full of grace,
Wednesday's child is full of woe,
Thursday's child has far to go,
Friday's child is loving and giving,
Saturday's child works hard for its
living,
And a child that's born on the
Sabbath day
Is fair and wise and good and gay.
    Quoted by A. E. Bray, *Traditions*
    of Devonshire (1838), ii. 288

1 The north wind doth blow,
And we shall have snow,
And what will poor robin do then?
          Poor thing!
He'll sit in a barn,
To keep himself warm,
And hide his head under his wing.
          Poor thing!
    Songs for the Nursery (1805)

2 Old King Cole
Was a merry old soul,
And a merry old soul was he,
He called for his pipe,
And he called for his bowl,
And he called for his fiddlers three.
    Quoted by William King, *Useful Transactions in Philosophy* (1708–9)

3 Old Mother Hubbard
Went to the cupboard,
To get her poor dog a bone;
But when she came there
The cupboard was bare,
And so the poor dog had none.
    Sarah Catherine Martin, *The Comic Adventures of Old Mother Hubbard* (1805)

4 One a penny, two a penny, hot cross-buns;
If your daughters do not like them, give them to your sons.
    Christmas Box (1797)

5 One, two,
Buckle my shoe;
Three, four,
Knock at the door;
Five, six,
Pick up sticks.
Seven, eight,
Lay them straight;
Nine, ten,
A big fat hen.
    Songs for the Nursery (1805)

6 Oranges and lemons
Say the bells of St. Clement's.
    Tommy Thumb's Pretty Song Book (c. 1744)

7 When will you pay me?
Say the bells of Old Bailey.
When I grow rich,
Say the bells of Shoreditch.   *Ib.*

8 Here comes a candle to light you to bed,
Here comes a chopper to chop off your head.   *Ib.*

9 Pat-a-cake, pat-a-cake, baker's man,
Bake me a cake as fast as you can;
Pat it and prick it, and mark it with B,
Put it in the oven for baby and me.
    Quoted in Tom D'Urfey, *The Campaigners* (1698)

10 Pease-porridge hot, pease-porridge cold,
Pease-porridge in the pot, nine days old. *Newest Christmas Box* (c. 1797)

11 Peter Piper picked a peck of pickled pepper;
A peck of pickled pepper Peter Piper picked;
If Peter Piper picked a peck of pickled pepper,
Where's the peck of pickled pepper Peter Piper picked?
    Peter Piper's Practical Principles of Plain and Perfect Pronunciation (1819)

12 Please to remember
The Fifth of November,
Gunpowder treason and plot;
We know no reason
Why gunpowder treason
  Should ever be forgot.
    Anonymous broadsheet (1826). *See* Wm. Hone, *The Every-Day Book* (1841) (*see also* 7:3)

13 Polly put the kettle on, we'll all have tea. [*Grip.*]   *Barnaby Rudge*, ch. 17

14 Pussy cat, pussy cat, where have you been?
I've been up to London to look at the queen.
Pussy cat, pussy cat, what did you there?
I frightened a little mouse under the chair. *Songs for the Nursery* (1805)

15 The Queen of Hearts
She made some tarts,
All on a summer's day;
The Knave of Hearts
He stole the tarts,
  And took them clean away.
    The European Magazine (Apr. 1782)

16 Rain, rain, go away,
Come again another day.
    In James Howell, *Proverbs* (1659)

17 Ride a cock-horse to Banbury Cross,
To see a fine lady upon a white horse,
Rings on her fingers and bells on her toes,
And she shall have music wherever she goes.
    Gammer Gurton's Garland (1784)

18 See-saw, Margery Daw,
Jacky shall have a new master;
Jacky must have but a penny a day,
Because he can't work any faster.
    Mother Goose's Melody (c. 1765)

19 Simple Simon met a pieman
  Going to the fair:
Says Simple Simon to the pieman,
'Let me taste your ware.'
    Simple Simon (a chapbook advertisement, 1764)

1 Sing a song of sixpence,
   A pocket full of rye,
Four and twenty blackbirds,
   Baked in a pie;
When the pie was opened,
   The birds began to sing;
Was not that a dainty dish
   To set before the king?

The king was in his counting-house
   Counting out his money;
The queen was in the parlour
   Eating bread and honey;
The maid was in the garden
   Hanging out the clothes,
There came a little blackbird,
   And snapped off her nose.
     Tommy Thumb's Pretty Song
     Book (c. 1744)

2 Solomon Grundy,
Born on a Monday,
Christened on Tuesday,
Married on Wednesday,
Took ill on Thursday,
Worse on Friday,
Died on Saturday,
Buried on Sunday:
This is the end
Of Solomon Grundy.
     Nursery Rhymes, ed. J. O.
     Halliwell (1842)

3 Taffy was a Welshman, Taffy was a
   thief;
Taffy came to my house and stole a
   piece of beef:
I went to Taffy's house, Taffy was not
   at home;
Taffy came to my house and stole a
   marrow-bone.
     Nancy Cock's Pretty Song Book
     (c. 1780)

4 Tell tale, tit!
Your tongue shall be split,
And all the dogs in the town
Shall have a little bit.
     Nursery Rhymes, ed. J. O.
     Halliwell (1842)

5 There was a crooked man, and he
   walked a crooked mile,
He found a crooked sixpence against a
   crooked stile:
He bought a crooked cat, which caught
   a crooked mouse,
And they all lived together in a little
   crooked house.   *Ib.*

6 There was an old woman who lived in
   a shoe,
She had so many children she didn't
   know what to do;
She gave them some broth without
   any bread,
She whipped them all soundly and put
   them to bed.
     Gammer Gurton's Garland (1784)

7 Thirty days hath September,
April, June, and November;
All the rest have thirty-one,
Excepting February alone,
And that has twenty-eight days clear
And twenty-nine in each leap year.
     Stevins MS. (c. 1555) (*see 96:8*)

8 This is the farmer sowing his corn,
That kept the cock that crowed in the
   morn,
That waked the priest all shaven and
   shorn,
That married the man all tattered
   and torn,
That kissed the maiden all forlorn,
That milked the cow with the
   crumpled horn,
That tossed the dog,
That worried the cat,
That killed the rat,
That ate the malt
That lay in the house that Jack built.
     Nurse Truelove's New-Year's-
     Gift (1755)

9 This little pig went to market;
This little pig stayed at home;
This little pig had roast beef;
And this little pig had none;
And this little pig cried, Wee, wee,
   wee!
I can't find my way home.
     The Famous Tommy Thumb's
     Little Story Book (c. 1760)

10 Three blind mice, see how they run!
They all ran after the farmer's wife,
Who cut off their tails with a carving-
   knife,
Did you ever see such a thing in your
   life
     As three blind mice?
     In Thomas Ravenscroft, *Deute-*
     romelia (1609)

11 Three wise men of Gotham
Went to sea in a bowl:
And if the bowl had been stronger,
My song would have been longer.
     Mother Goose's Melody (c. 1765)

12 Tom he was a piper's son,
He learned to play when he was
   young,
But all the tune that he could play,
Was 'Over the hills and far away.'
     Tom, the Piper's Son (c. 1795)

13 Tom, Tom, the piper's son,
Stole a pig, and away he run;
The pig was eat, and Tom was beat,
And Tom went howling down the
   street.   *Ib.*

14 What are little boys made of?
What are little boys made of?
Frogs and snails, and puppy-dogs'
   tails;
That's what little boys are made of.

What are little girls made of?
What are little girls made of?
Sugar and spice, and all that's nice;
That's what little girls are made of.
Nursery Rhymes, ed. J. O.
Halliwell (1844)

1 Where are you going to, my pretty
maid?
Quoted by William Pryce,
Archaeologia Cornu-Britannica
(1790)

2 'My face is my fortune, sir,' she said.
Ib.

3 'Nobody asked you, sir,' she said. *Ib.*

4 'Who killed Cock Robin?'
'I,' said the Sparrow,
'With my bow and arrow,
I killed Cock Robin.'
All the birds of the air fell a-sighing
and a-sobbing
When they heard of the death of poor
Cock Robin.
*Tommy Thumb's Pretty Song
Book (c. 1744)*

5 'Who saw him die?'
'I,' said the Fly,
'With my little eye,
I saw him die.' *Ib.*

FREDERICK OAKELEY 1802–1880

6 O come, all ye faithful,
Joyful and triumphant,
O come ye, O come ye to Bethlehem.
O Come, All Ye Faithful, trans.
from Latin, *Adeste Fideles*

SEAN O'CASEY 1884–1964

7 The whole world is in a state of chassis.
Juno and the Paycock, I. i

ADOLPH S. OCHS 1858–1935

8 All the news that's fit to print.
Motto of the New York Times

JOHN O'KEEFFE 1747–1833

9 Amo, amas, I love a lass
Agreeable Surprise, II. ii. *Song:
Amo, Amas*

10 Fat, fair and forty were all the toasts
of the young men. *Irish Minnie*, ii

11 You should always except the present
company. *London Hermit*, I. ii

DENNIS O'KELLY 1720?–1787

12 Eclipse first, the rest nowhere.
*Epsom, 3 May 1769. Annals of
Sporting*, vol. ii, p. 271

BARONESS ORCZY [MRS. MON-TAGUE BARSTOW] 1865–1947

13 We seek him here, we seek him there,
Those Frenchies seek him everywhere.
Is he in heaven?—Is he in hell?
That demmed, elusive Pimpernel?
The Scarlet Pimpernel, ch. 12

META ORRED

14 In the gloaming, O, my darling!
When the lights are dim and low,
And the quiet shadows falling
Softly come and softly go.
In the Gloaming

GEORGE ORWELL [ERIC BLAIR] 1903–1950

15 All animals are equal, but some animals are more equal than others.
Animal Farm, ch. 10

16 Big brother is watching you.
1984, pt. I, i

17 Double think means the power of
holding two contradictory beliefs in
one's mind simultaneously, and accepting both of them. *Ib.* pt. II, ix

ARTHUR WILLIAM EDGAR O'SHAUGHNESSY 1844–1881

18 We are the music makers,
We are the dreamers of dreams,
Ode: 'We are the Music Makers'

19 For each age is a dream that is dying,
Or one that is coming to birth. *Ib.*

JOHN O'SULLIVAN 1813–1895

20 Our manifest destiny to overspread
the continent allotted by Providence
for the free development of our yearly
multiplying millions.
*U.S. Magazine and Democratic
Review*, vol. xvii, p. 5

JAMES OTIS 1725–1783

21 Taxation without representation is
tyranny.
*Watchword of the American
Revolution. Attr.*

THOMAS OTWAY 1652–1685

22 Oh woman! lovely woman! Nature
made thee
To temper man: we had been brutes
without you;
Venice Preserved, Act I, l. 337

SIR THOMAS OVERBURY
1581–1613

1 He disdains all things above his reach, and preferreth all countries before his own.
Miscellaneous Works. An Affectate Traveller

OVID 43 B.C.–A.D. 18?

2 Cetera quis nescit?
The rest who does not know?
Amores, I. v. 25. Trans. by Showerman

3 Procul omen abesto!
Far from us be the omen!
Ib. xiv. 41

4 Iam seges est ubi Troia fuit.
Now are fields of corn where Troy once was. *Heroides*, I. i. 53

5 Rudis indigestaque moles.
An unformed and confused mass.
Metamorphoses, i. 7

6 Medio tutissimus ibis.
You will go most safely in the middle. *Ib.* ii. 137

7 Video meliora, proboque;
Deteriora sequor.
I see and approve better things, but follow worse. *Ib.* vii. 20

8 Tempus edax rerum.
Time the devourer of all things.
Ib. xv. 234

9 Tu quoque.
Thou also. *Tristia*, ii. 39

JOHN OWEN 1560?–1622

10 Tempora mutantur nos et mutamur in illis:
Quomodo? fit semper tempore pejor homo.
Times change, and we change with them too. How so?
With time men only the more vicious grow. *Epigrams*

THOMAS PAINE 1737–1809

11 The sublime and the ridiculous are often so nearly related, that it is difficult to class them separately. One step above the sublime, makes the ridiculous; and one step above the ridiculous, makes the sublime again.
Age of Reason (1795), pt. II, p. 20

12 These are the times that try men's souls.
The American Crisis, No. 1. *Writings* (1894), vol. i, p. 170

13 Government, even in its best state, is but a necessary evil; in its worst state, an intolerable one.
Common Sense, ch. 1

14 The religion of humanity.
Attr. by Edmund Gosse

REV. WILLIAM PALEY 1743–1805

15 Who can refute a sneer?
Moral Philosophy, bk. v, ch. 9

HENRY JOHN TEMPLE, VISCOUNT PALMERSTON 1784–1865

16 Accidental and fortuitous concurrence of atoms.
Speech, House of Commons, 5 Mar. 1857

17 Die, my dear Doctor, that's the last thing I shall do! *Attr. last words*

DOROTHY PARKER 1893–

18 Men seldom make passes
At girls who wear glasses.
The Best of Dorothy Parker, News Item

MARTIN PARKER d. 1656?

19 You gentlemen of England
Who live at home at ease,
How little do you think
On the dangers of the seas.
The Valiant Sailors (Early Naval Ballads [Percy Society, 1841], p. 34)

20 But all's to no end, for the times will not mend
Till the king enjoys his own again.
Upon Defacing of Whitehall (The Loyal Garland, 1671). Later title: *When the King Enjoys His Own Again.* Ritson's *Ancient Songs* (1792), p. 231

ROSS PARKER 1914–
and
HUGHIE CHARLES 1907–

21 There'll always be an England
While there's a country lane,
Wherever there's a cottage small
Beside a field of grain.
Song of Second World War (1939)

THEODORE PARKER 1810–1860

22 A democracy, that is, a government of all the people, by all the people, for all the people; of course, a government after the principles of eternal justice, the unchanging law of God; for shortness' sake, I will call it the idea of freedom.
The American Idea. Speech at N.E. Anti-Slavery Convention, Boston, 29 May 1850. Discourses of Slavery (1863), i

CHARLES STEWART PARNELL
1846–1891

1 No man has a right to fix the boundary of the march of a nation; no man has a right to say to his country—thus far shalt thou go and no further.
Speech at Cork, 21 Jan. 1885

THOMAS PARNELL 1679–1718

2 We call it only pretty Fanny's way.
Poems (1894). An Elegy, to an Old Beauty, l. 34

BLAISE PASCAL 1623–1662

3 Quand on voit le style naturel, on est tout étonné et ravi, car on s'attendait de voir un auteur, et on trouve un homme.

When we encounter a natural style we are always astonished and delighted, for we expected to see an author, and find a man.
Pensées, § i. 29

4 Le nez de Cléopâtre: s'il eût été plus court, toute la face de la terre aurait changé.

Had Cleopatra's nose been shorter, the whole history of the world would have been different.
Ib. § ii. 162

5 Le silence éternel de ces espaces infinis m'effraie.

The eternal silence of these infinite spaces [the heavens] terrifies me.
Ib. § iii. 206

6 On mourra seul.

We shall die alone.   *Ib. 211*

7 Le cœur a ses raisons que la raison ne connaît point.

The heart has its reasons which reason knows nothing of.
Ib. § iv. 277

8 L'homme n'est qu'un roseau, le plus faible de la nature; mais c'est un roseau pensant.

Man is only a reed, the weakest thing in nature; but he is a thinking reed.
Ib. § vi. 347

WALTER HORATIO PATER
1839–1894

9 She is older than the rocks among which she sits; like the vampire, she has been dead many times, and learned the secrets of the grave; and has been a diver in deep seas, and keeps their fallen day about her; and trafficked for strange webs with Eastern merchants; and, as Leda, was the mother of Helen of Troy, and, as Saint Anne, the mother of Mary; and all this has been to her but as the sound of lyres and flutes, and lives only in the delicacy with which it has moulded the changing lineaments, and tinged the eyelids and the hands.
The Renaissance. Leonardo da Vinci

10 All art constantly aspires towards the condition of music.
Ib. The School of Giorgione

11 To burn always with this hard, gem-like flame, to maintain this ecstasy, is success in life.   *Ib. Conclusion*

ANDREW PATERSON 1864–1941

12 Once a jolly swagman camped by a billabong,
Under the shade of a coolibah tree,
And he sang as he sat and waited till his billy boiled
'You'll come a-waltzing, Matilda, with me.'   *Waltzing Matilda*

COVENTRY PATMORE 1823–1896

13 For dear to maidens are their rivals dead.   *Amelia, l. 135*

14 I, singularly moved
To love the lovely that are not beloved,
Of all the Seasons, most
Love Winter.
The Unknown Eros, bk. I. iii. Winter, l. 1

15 My little Son, who look'd from thoughtful eyes
And moved and spoke in quiet grown-up wise,
Having my law the seventh time disobey'd,
I struck him, and dismiss'd
With hard words and unkiss'd,
His Mother, who was patient, being dead.   *Ib. x. The Toys, l. 1*

JAMES PAYN 1830–1898

16 I had never had a piece of toast
Particularly long and wide,
But fell upon the sanded floor,
And always on the buttered side.
Chambers's Journal, 2 Feb. 1884

JOHN HOWARD PAYNE
1791–1852

17 Mid pleasures and palaces though we may roam,
Be it ever so humble, there's no place like home;
A charm from the sky seems to hallow us there,
Which, seek through the world, is ne'er met with elsewhere.
Home, home, sweet, sweet home!
There's no place like home! there's no place like home!
Clari, the Maid of Milan. Home, Sweet Home

THOMAS LOVE PEACOCK
1785–1866

1 The mountain sheep are sweeter,
    But the valley sheep are fatter;
  We therefore deemed it meeter
    To carry off the latter.
        *The Misfortunes of Elphin, ch.
        11. The War-Song of Dinas
        Vawr*

2 In a bowl to sea went wise men three,
    On a brilliant night in June:
  They carried a net, and their hearts
      were set
    On fishing up the moon.
        *The Wise Men of Gotham. Paper
        Money Lyrics*

WILLIAM PENN 1644–1718

3 No Cross, No Crown.
        Title of Pamphlet, 1669

SAMUEL PEPYS 1633–1703

4 And so to bed.   *Diary, 20 Apr. 1660*

5 I went out to Charing Cross, to see
  Major-general Harrison hanged,
  drawn, and quartered, which was done
  there, he looking as cheerful as any
  man could do in that condition.
        Ib. 13 Oct. 1660

6 My wife, who, poor wretch, is troubled
  with her lonely life.   *Ib. 19 Dec. 1662*

7 Pretty witty Nell. [Nell Gwynne.]
        Ib. 3 Apr. 1665

CHARLES PERRAULT 1628–1703

8 'Anne, ma sœur Anne, ne vois-tu
  rien venir?' Et la sœur Anne lui
  répondit, 'Je ne vois rien que le
  soleil qui poudroye, et l'herbe qui
  verdoye.'

    'Anne, sister Anne, do you see any-
    thing coming?' And her sister
    Anne replied, 'I see nothing but
    the sun which makes a dust, and
    the grass looking green.'
        Perrault, *Histoires et contes du
        temps passé* (1697). Trans. by
        R. Samber, 1764

PERSIUS A.D. 34–62

9 Venienti occurrite morbo.
    Meet the disease at its first stage.
        Satires, iii. 64

10 De nihilo nihilum, in nihilum nil posse
   reverti.
    Nothing can come out of nothing,
    nothing can go back to nothing.
        Ib. 84. Trans. by Conington

MARÉCHAL PÉTAIN 1856–1951

11 Ils ne passeront pas.
    They shall not pass.
        Verdun, Feb. 1916

PETRONIUS d. c. A.D. 66

12 Cave canem.
    Beware of the dog.
        *Petronii Arbitri Satyricon, 29, 1.
        Found with picture of a dog on
        a mosaic floor in Pompeii.*

13 Abiit ad plures.
    He has joined the great majority.
        Cena Trimalchionis, xlii. 5

EDWARD JOHN PHELPS
1822–1900

14 The man who makes no mistakes does
   not usually make anything.
        *Speech at Mansion House, 24 Jan.
        1899*

WENDELL PHILLIPS 1811–1884

15 Every man meets his Waterloo at last.
        *Speeches (1880), Lecture at Brook-
        lyn, N.Y., 1 Nov. 1859*

EDEN PHILLPOTTS 1862–1960

16 His father's sister had bats in the
   belfry and was put away.
        Peacock House. My First Murder

WILLIAM PITT, EARL OF
CHATHAM 1708–1778

17 The atrocious crime of being a young
   man . . . I shall neither attempt to
   palliate or deny.
        *Speech, House of Commons,
        27 Jan. 1741*

18 Unlimited power is apt to corrupt the
   minds of those who possess it.
        Ib. House of Lords, 9 Jan. 1770

19 You cannot conquer America.
        Ib. 18 Nov. 1777

20 I invoke the genius of the Constitution!   *Ib.*

21 It was a saying of Lord Chatham, that
   the parks were the lungs of London.
        *William Windham, in a Speech
        in House of Commons, 30 June
        1808*

WILLIAM PITT 1759–1806

22 England has saved herself by her
   exertions, and will, as I trust, save
   Europe by her example.
        Speech, at the Guildhall, 1805

1 Roll up that map; it will not be
wanted these ten years.
On a map of Europe, after hearing the news of the Battle of
Austerlitz. Stanhope's Life of
the Rt. Hon. William Pitt (1862),
vol. iv, p. 369

2 Oh, my country! how I love my
country.   Attr. last words. Ib. p. 382

3 Oh, my country! how I leave my
country!
Attr. last words. Ib. (1879),
vol. iii, p. 391

4 My country! oh, my country!
Attr. last words. G. Rose, Diary,
23 Jan. 1806

5 I think I could eat one of Bellamy's
veal pies.
Alternative attr. last words

JAMES ROBINSON PLANCHÉ
1796–1880

6 It would have made a cat laugh.
Extravaganzas (1879), The Queen
of the Frogs, I. iv

PLATO c. 429–347 B.C.

7 Σωκράτη φησὶν ἀδικεῖν τούς τε νέους
διαφθείροντα καὶ θεοὺς οὓς ἡ πόλις νομίζει
οὐ νομίζοντα, ἕτερα δὲ δαιμόνια καινά.

Socrates is charged with corrupting
the youth of the city, and with
rejecting the gods of Athens and
introducing new divinities.
Apologia, 24ᵇ 9

PLAUTUS B.C. 254–184

8 Quem di diligunt
Adulescens moritur.

He whom the gods favour dies
young.   Bacchides iv. 816

PLINY A.D. 23–79

9 Ex Africa semper aliquid novi.

There is always something new from
Africa. Proverbial from Pliny:
Unde etiam vulgare Graeciae
dictum 'semper aliquid novi
Africam adferre'.
Whence it is commonly said
among the Greeks that 'Africa
always offers something new'.
Naturalis Historia, II. viii. 42

10 In vino veritas.

Truth comes out in wine. Proverbial
from Pliny: Vulgoque veritas iam
attributa vino est.
Now truth is commonly said to
be in wine.   Ib. xiv. 141

11 Sal Atticum.

Attic wit.   Ib. xxxi. 87

12 Nulla dies sine linea.

Not a day without a line. Proverbial from Pliny: Apelli fuit alioqui
perpetua consuetudo numquam
tam occupatam diem agendi, ut
non lineam ducendo exerceret
artem, quod ab eo in proverbium
venit.

It was moreover a regular habit
of Apelles never to be so
occupied in the business of the
day that he could not practise
his art by drawing a line, and
this gave rise to the proverb.
Naturalis Historia, xxxv. 36. 12

13 Ne supra crepidam sutor iudicaret.

The cobbler should not judge above
his last.   Ib. 85

EDGAR ALLAN POE 1809–1849

14 I was a child and she was a child,
In this kingdom by the sea;
But we loved with a love that was
more than love—
I and my Annabel Lee.   Annabel Lee

15 The fever call'd 'Living'
Is conquer'd at last.   For Annie

16 Helen, thy beauty is to me
Like those Nicean barks of yore,
That gently, o'er a perfumed sea,
The weary, wayworn wanderer bore
To his own native shore.

On desperate seas long wont to roam,
Thy hyacinth hair, thy classic face,
Thy Naiad airs have brought me
home
To the glory that was Greece
And the grandeur that was Rome.
To Helen, l. 1

17 Take thy beak from out my heart, and
take thy form from off my door!
Quoth the Raven, 'Nevermore'.
The Raven, xvii

JOHN POMFRET 1667–1703

18 We live and learn, but not the wiser
grow.   Reason, l. 112

MME DE POMPADOUR 1721–1764

19 Après nous le déluge.

After us the deluge.
Madame de Hausset, Mémoires,
p. 19

JOHN POOLE 1786?–1872

20 I hope I don't intrude?
Paul Pry, I. ii

ALEXANDER POPE 1688–1744

1 Poetic Justice, with her lifted scale,
Where, in nice balance, truth with
gold she weighs,
And solid pudding against empty
praise.   *The Dunciad*, bk. i, l. 52

2 May you, my Cam and Isis, preach it
long!
The Right Divine of Kings to govern
wrong.   *Ib.* bk. iv, l. 187

3 Lo! thy dread empire, Chaos! is
restor'd;
Light dies before thy uncreating word;
Thy hand, great Anarch! lets the
curtain fall,
And universal darkness buries all.
Ib. l. 653

4 Is it, in heav'n, a crime to love too
well?
*Elegy to the Memory of an Un-
fortunate Lady*, l. 6

5 Is there no bright reversion in the sky,
For those who greatly think, or
bravely die?   *Ib.* l. 9

6 How happy is the blameless vestal's
lot!
The world forgetting, by the world
forgot.   *Eloisa to Abelard*, l. 207

7 I am his Highness' dog at Kew;
Pray tell me, sir, whose dog are you?
*Epigrams. On the Collar of a
Dog which I gave to his Royal
Highness*

8 Nature and Nature's laws lay hid in
night:
God said, *Let Newton be!* and all was
light.
*Epitaphs. Intended for Sir Isaac
Newton*

9 A little learning is a dang'rous thing;
Drink deep, or taste not the Pierian
spring.
An Essay on Criticism, l. 215

10 True wit is nature to advantage
dressed,
What oft was thought, but n'er so well
expressed.   *Ib.* l. 297

11 A needless Alexandrine ends the song,
That, like a wounded snake, drags its
slow length along.   *Ib.* l. 356

12 To err is human, to forgive, divine.
Ib. l. 525

13 For fools rush in where angels fear to
tread.   *Ib.* l. 625

14 Hope springs eternal in the human
breast;
Man never is, but always to be
blessed.
The soul, uneasy, and confined from
home,
Rests and expatiates in a life to come.

Lo, the poor Indian! whose untutored
mind
Sees God in clouds, or hears him in the
wind;
His soul proud science never taught
to stray
Far as the solar walk or milky way;
Yet simple nature to his hope has giv'n,
Behind the cloud-topped hill, an
humbler heav'n.
An Essay on Man. Epistle i, l. 95

15 Die of a rose in aromatic pain?
Ib. l. 200

16 The spider's touch how exquisitely
fine!
Feels at each thread, and lives along
the line.   *Ib.* l. 217

17 And, spite of pride, in erring reason's
spite,
One truth is clear, Whatever is, is
right.   *Ib.* l. 288

18 Know then thyself, presume not
God to scan,
The proper study of mankind is man.
Placed on this isthmus of a middle
state,
A being darkly wise, and rudely
great:
With too much knowledge for the
sceptic side.   *Ib.* Ep. ii, l. 1

19 Created half to rise, and half to fall;
Great lord of all things, yet a prey to
all;
Sole judge of truth, in endless error
hurled;
The glory, jest, and riddle of the
world!   *Ib.* l. 15

20 An honest man's the noblest work of
God.   *Ib.* Ep. iv, l. 247

21 Thou wert my guide, philosopher, and
friend.   *Ib.* l. 390

22 And you, brave Cobham! to the latest
breath,
Shall feel your ruling passion strong in
death.
Moral Essays, Ep. i, *To Lord
Cobham*, l. 262

23 The ruling passion, be it what it will,
The ruling passion conquers reason
still.
Ib. Ep. iii. *To Lord Bathurst*,
l. 153

24 Rise, honest Muse! and sing the Man
of Ross!   *Ib.* l. 250

25 Statesman, yet friend to truth! of soul
sincere,
In action faithful, and in honour
clear;
Who broke no promise, served no
private end,
Who gained no title, and who lost no
friend.
Ib. Ep. vii. *To Mr. Addison*, l. 67

1 Where'er you walk cool gales shall
fan the glade;
Trees, where you sit, shall crowd into
a shade;
Where'er you tread, the blushing
flow'rs shall rise,
And all things flourish where you turn
your eyes. *Pastorals, Summer*, l. 73

2 Fair tresses man's imperial race insnare,
And beauty draws us with a single
hair.
The Rape of the Lock, c. ii, l. 27

3 Here thou, great Anna! whom three
realms obey,
Dost sometimes counsel take—and
sometimes tea. *Ib. c. iii, l. 7*

4 As yet a child, nor yet a fool to fame,
I lisped in numbers, for the numbers
came.
*Epistles and Satires of Horace
Imitated. Prologue, Epistle to
Dr. Arbuthnot, l. 127*

5 This long disease, my life. *Ib. l. 132*

6 Damn with faint praise, assent with
civil leer,
And, without sneering, teach the rest
to sneer;
Willing to wound, and yet afraid to
strike,
Just hint a fault, and hesitate dislike.
Alike reserved to blame, or to commend. *Ib. l. 201*

7 Let Sporus tremble.—A. What? that
thing of silk,
Sporus, that mere white curd of ass's
milk!
Satire or sense, alas! can Sporus feel?
Who breaks a butterfly upon a wheel?
Ib. l. 305

8 Yet let me flap this bug with gilded
wings—
This painted child of dirt, that stinks
and stings. *Ib. l. 309*

9 Wit that can creep, and pride that
licks the dust. *Ib. l. 333*

10 There St. John mingles with my
friendly bowl
The feast of reason and the flow of
soul.
*Ib. I. Hor. II, Sat. 1. To Mr.
Fortescue, l. 127*

11 For I, who hold sage Homer's rule the
best,
Welcome the coming, speed the going
guest.
*Ib. II. Hor. II, Sat. 2. To Mr.
Bethel, l. 159. (In Odyssey, xv.
83, with 'parting' for 'going'.)*

12 There still remains to mortify a wit,
The many-headed monster of the pit.
On Paradise Lost, l. 304

13 Let humble Allen, with an awkward
shame,
Do good by stealth, and blush to find
it fame.
On Paradise Lost, Epilogue, Dial. i, l. 136

14 Happy the man whose wish and care
A few paternal acres bound,
Content to breathe his native air,
In his own ground. *Ode on Solitude*

15 This is the Jew
That Shakspeare drew.
*Of Macklin's performance of
Shylock, 14 Feb. 1741. Baker,
Reed, & Jones, Biographia
Dramatica (1812), vol. 1, pt. ii,
p. 469*

16 'Blessed is the man who expects
nothing, for he shall never be disappointed', was the ninth beatitude
which a man of wit (who, like a man
of wit, was a long time in gaol) added
to the eighth.
Letters. To Fortescue, 23 Sept. 1725

RICHARD PORSON 1759–1808

17 The Germans in Greek
Are sadly to seek:
Not five in five score,
But ninety-five more:
All, save only Herman,
And Herman's a German.
*M. L. Clarke, Life of Porson,
ch. vii*

18 I went to Frankfort, and got drunk
With that most learn'd professor,
Brunck;
I went to Worts, and got more drunken
With that more learn'd professor,
Ruhnken.
Facetiæ Cantabrigienses (1825)

BEILBY PORTEUS 1731–1808

19 War its thousands slays, Peace its
ten thousands. *Death, l. 179*

20 Teach him how to live,
And, oh! still harder lesson! how to
die. *Ib. l. 319*

FRANCIS POTT 1832–1909

21 The strife is o'er, the battle done;
Now is the Victor's triumph won;
O let the song of praise be sung.
Alleluia!
*The Strife is O'er. Hymns fitted
to the Order of Common Prayer
(1861), trans. of Latin Finita
Iam Sunt Praelia*

BEATRIX POTTER 1866–1943

22 Once upon a time there were four
little Rabbits, and their names were
Flopsy, Mopsy, Cotton-tail, and Peter.
The Tale of Peter Rabbit

1 No more twist!
The Tailor of Gloucester

2 It is said that the effect of eating too
much lettuce is 'soporific'.
The Tale of the Flopsy Bunnies

STEPHEN POTTER 1900–

3 Gamesmanship. *Book Title*

JOHN O'CONNOR POWER

4 The mules of politics: without pride
of ancestry, or hope of posterity.
*Quoted in H. H. Asquith's
Memories and Reflections, i. 123*

WINTHROP MACKWORTH
PRAED 1802–1839

5 His talk was like a stream, which runs
With rapid change from rocks to
roses:
It slipped from politics to puns,
It passed from Mahomet to Moses;
Beginning with the laws which keep
The planets in their radiant courses,
And ending with some precept deep
For dressing eels, or shoeing horses.
The Vicar

THE BOOK OF COMMON
PRAYER

6 A Table of the Moveable Feasts.
*Section Heading in Introductory
Pages, p. xxxi*

7 Dearly beloved brethren, the Scripture moveth us in sundry places to
acknowledge and confess our manifold
sins and wickedness.
*Morning Prayer. Priest's Opening
Exhortation*

8 We have erred, and strayed from thy
ways like lost sheep.
Ib. General Confession

9 We have left undone those things
which we ought to have done; And
we have done those things which we
ought not to have done; And there
is no health in us. *Ib.*

10 A godly, righteous, and sober life. *Ib.*

11 And forgive us our trespasses, As we
forgive them that trespass against us.
Ib. The Lord's Prayer

12 The noble army of martyrs.
Ib. Te Deum Laudamus

13 Give peace in our time, O Lord.
Because there is none other that
fighteth for us, but only thou, O God.
Ib. Versicles

14 The author of peace and lover of concord, in knowledge of whom standeth
our eternal life, whose service is perfect freedom.
Ib. Second Collect, for Peace

15 Neither run into any kind of danger.
*Morning Prayer. Third Collect,
for Grace*

16 In Quires and Places where they sing.
Ib. Rubric after Third Collect

17 When two or three are gathered together in thy Name thou wilt grant
their requests.
Ib. Prayer of St. Chrysostom

18 From whom all holy desires, all good
counsels, and all just works do proceed. *Evening Prayer. Second Collect*

19 That peace which the world cannot
give. *Ib.*

20 Lighten our darkness, we beseech
thee, O Lord; and by thy great mercy
defend us from all perils and dangers
of this night. *Ib. Third Collect*

21 Have mercy upon us miserable sinners.
The Litany

22 Envy, hatred, and malice, and all
uncharitableness. *Ib.*

23 Deceits of the world, the flesh, and the
devil. *Ib.*

24 Agony and bloody Sweat. *Ib.*

25 The kindly fruits of the earth, so as in
due time we may enjoy them. *Ib.*

26 Our Mediator and Advocate.
*Prayers and Thanksgivings, upon
Several Occasions. 'O God, whose
nature and property'*

27 All sorts and conditions of men.
*Ib. Prayer for All Conditions of
Men*

28 All who profess and call themselves
Christians. *Ib.*

29 Any ways afflicted, or distressed, in
mind, body, or estate. *Ib.*

30 A happy issue out of all their afflictions. *Ib.*

31 Our creation, preservation, and all the
blessings of this life.
*Ib. Thanksgiving. A General
Thanksgiving*

32 For the means of grace, and for the
hope of glory. *Ib.*

33 Cast away the works of darkness, and
put upon us the armour of light, now
in the time of this mortal life.
Collects. 1st Sunday in Advent

34 Hear them, read, mark, learn, and inwardly digest them.
Ib. 2nd Sunday in Advent

35 The unruly wills and affections of
sinful men.
Ib. 4th Sunday after Easter

36 We may so pass through things temporal, that we finally lose not the
things eternal.
Ib. 4th Sunday after Trinity

1 Such good things as pass man's understanding.
   Collects. 6th Sunday after Trinity

2 The author and giver of all good things.   *Ib. 7th Sunday after Trinity*

3 An open and notorious evil liver.
   Holy Communion: Introductory Rubric

4 Unto whom all hearts be open, all desires known, and from whom no secrets are hid.   *Ib. Collect for Purity*

5 Thou shalt have none other gods but me.   *Ib. 1st Commandment*

6 Incline our hearts to keep this law.
   Ib. Response to Commandments

7 Thou shalt not make to thyself any graven image, nor the likeness of any thing that is in heaven above, or in the earth beneath, or in the water under the earth. Thou shalt not bow down to them, nor worship them: for I the Lord thy God am a jealous God, and visit the sins of the fathers upon the children unto the third and fourth generation.   *Ib. 2nd Commandment*

8 Thou shalt not take the Name of the Lord thy God in vain.
   Ib. 3rd Commandment

9 Remember that thou keep holy the Sabbath-day. Six days shalt thou labour, and do all that thou hast to do; but the seventh day is the Sabbath of the Lord thy God.
   Ib. 4th Commandment

10 The stranger that is within thy gates.
   Ib.

11 In six days the Lord made heaven and earth, the sea, and all that in them is, and rested the seventh day.   *Ib.*

12 Honour thy father and thy mother; that thy days may be long in the land which the Lord thy God giveth thee.
   Ib. 5th Commandment

13 Thou shalt do no murder.
   Ib. 6th Commandment

14 Thou shalt not commit adultery.
   Ib. 7th Commandment

15 Thou shalt not steal.
   Ib. 8th Commandment

16 Thou shalt not bear false witness against thy neighbour.
   Ib. 9th Commandment

17 Thou shalt not covet thy neighbour's wife, nor his servant, nor his maid, nor his ox, nor his ass, nor any thing that is his.   *Ib. 10th Commandment*

18 All things visible and invisible.
   Ib. Nicene Creed

19 One Catholick and Apostolick Church.
   Ib.

20 The whole state of Christ's Church militant here in earth.
   Holy Communion: Prayer for the Church Militant

21 All them, who in this transitory life are in trouble, sorrow, need, sickness, or any other adversity.   *Ib.*

22 Ye that do truly and earnestly repent you of your sins, and are in love and charity with your neighbours, and intend to lead a new life.
   Ib. The Invitation

23 It is meet and right so to do.
   Ib. Versicles

24 This our bounden duty and service.
   Ib. Prayer of Oblation, 1

25 The peace of God, which passeth all understanding.   *Ib. The Blessing*

26 Be amongst you and remain with you always.   *Ib.*

27 All the changes and chances of this mortal life.
   Ib. Collects after the Offertory, 1

28 Prevent us, O Lord, in all our doings.
   Ib. 4

29 All our works begun, continued, and ended in thee.   *Ib.*

30 Grant that the old Adam in this Child may be so buried, that the new man may be raised up in him.
   Publick Baptism of Infants. Invocation of Blessing on the Child

31 Ministration of Baptism to Such as are of Riper Years.   *Title*

32 What is your name?
   N. or *M.*
   Who gave you this name?
   My Godfathers and Godmothers in my Baptism; wherein I was made a member of Christ, the child of God, and an inheritor of the kingdom of heaven.
   What did your Godfathers and Godmothers then for you?
   They did promise and vow three things in my name. First, that I should renounce the devil and all his works, the pomps and vanity of this wicked world, and all the sinful lusts of the flesh. Secondly, that I should believe all the Articles of the Christian Faith. And thirdly, that I should keep God's holy will and commandments, and walk in the same all the days of my life.   *The Catechism*

33 My duty towards God, and my duty towards my Neighbour.   *Ib.*

34 To keep my hands from picking and stealing, and my tongue from evil-speaking, lying, and slandering.   *Ib.*

1 To learn and labour truly to get mine own living, and to do my duty in that state of life, unto which it shall please God to call me.   *The Catechism*

2 An outward and visible sign of an inward and spiritual grace.   *Ib.*

3 Being now come to the years of discretion.   *Confirmation*

4 Defend, O Lord, this thy child [*or* this thy servant] with thy heavenly grace that *he* may continue thine for ever; and daily increase in thy holy Spirit more and more, until *he* come unto thy everlasting kingdom.   *Ib.*

5 If any of you know cause, or just impediment, why these two persons should not be joined together in holy Matrimony, ye are to declare it. This is the first time of asking.   *Solemnization of Matrimony. The Banns*

6 First, it was ordained for the procreation of children.   *Ib.*

7 A remedy against sin.   *Ib.*

8 Such persons as have not the gift of continency.   *Ib.*

9 Let him now speak, or else hereafter for ever hold his peace.   *Ib.*

10 Wilt thou have this woman to thy wedded wife, to live together after God's ordinance in the holy estate of Matrimony?   *Ib. Betrothal*

11 Forsaking all other, keep thee only unto her, so long as ye both shall live.   *Ib.*

12 To have and to hold from this day forward, for better for worse, for richer for poorer, in sickness and in health, to love and to cherish, till death us do part, according to God's holy ordinance; and thereto I plight thee my troth.   *Ib.*

13 To love, cherish, and to obey.   *Ib.*

14 With this Ring I thee wed, with my body I thee worship, and with all my worldly goods I thee endow.   *Ib. The Wedding*

15 Those whom God hath joined together let no man put asunder.   *Ib. The Prayer*

16 Unto God's gracious mercy and protection we commit thee.   *Visitation of the Sick*

17 The inner man.   *Ib.*

18 Laid violent hands upon themselves.   *Burial of the Dead. Introductory Rubric*

19 In the midst of life we are in death.   *Ib. First Anthem*

20 We therefore commit *his* body to the ground; earth to earth, ashes to ashes, dust to dust; in sure and certain hope of the Resurrection to Eternal life.   *Burial of the Dead. First Anthem*

21 Why do the heathen so furiously rage together: and why do the people imagine a vain thing?   *Psalms ii. 1*

22 Out of the mouth of very babes and sucklings hast thou ordained strength, because of thine enemies: that thou mightest still the enemy, and the avenger.   *Ib. viii. 2*

23 What is man, that thou art mindful of him: and the son of man, that thou visitest him?   *Ib. 4*

24 The fowls of the air, and the fishes of the sea.   *Ib. 8*

25 Up, Lord, and let not man have the upper hand.   *Ib. ix. 19*

26 The fool hath said in his heart: There is no God.   *Ib. xiv. 1*

27 Lord, who shall dwell in thy tabernacle: or who shall rest upon thy holy hill?
Even he, that leadeth an uncorrupt life: and doeth the thing which is right, and speaketh the truth from his heart.   *Ib. xv. 1*

28 Keep me as the apple of an eye: hide me under the shadow of thy wings.   *Ib. xvii. 8*

29 The heavens declare the glory of God: and the firmament sheweth his handywork.
One day telleth another: and one night certifieth another.   *Ib. xix. 1*

30 In them hath he set a tabernacle for the sun: which cometh forth as a bridegroom out of his chamber, and rejoiceth as a giant to run his course. It goeth forth from the uttermost part of the heaven, and runneth about unto the end of it again: and there is nothing hid from the heat thereof.   *Ib.*

31 Let the words of my mouth, and the meditation of my heart: be alway acceptable in thy sight,
O Lord, my strength, and my redeemer.   *Ib. 14*

32 Some put their trust in chariots, and some in horses: but we will remember the name of the Lord our God.   *Ib. xx. 7*

33 Thou hast given him his heart's desire: and hast not denied him the request of his lips.   *Ib. xxi. 2*

34 Many oxen are come about me: fat bulls of Basan close me in on every side.   *Ib. xxii. 12*

1 Deliver my soul from the sword: my darling from the power of the dog. Save me from the lion's mouth: thou hast heard me also from the horns of the unicorns. *Psalms* xxii. 20

2 The Lord is my shepherd: therefore can I lack nothing.
He shall feed me in a green pasture: and lead me forth beside the waters of comfort.
He shall convert my soul: and bring me forth in the paths of righteousness, for his Name's sake.
Yea, though I walk through the valley of the shadow of death, I will fear no evil: for thou art with me; thy rod and thy staff comfort me.
Thou shalt prepare a table before me against them that trouble me: thou hast anointed my head with oil, and my cup shall be full.
But thy loving-kindness and mercy shall follow me all the days of my life: and I will dwell in the house of the Lord for ever. *Ib.* xxiii

3 The earth is the Lord's, and all that therein is: the compass of the world, and they that dwell therein.
Ib. xxiv. 1

4 Lift up your heads, O ye gates, and be ye lift up, ye everlasting doors: and the King of glory shall come in.
Ib. 7

5 Who is the King of glory: even the Lord of hosts, he is the King of glory.
Ib. 10

6 O remember not the sins and offences of my youth. *Ib.* xxv. 6

7 I should utterly have fainted: but that I believe verily to see the goodness of the Lord in the land of the living. *Ib.* xxvii. 15

8 Give thanks unto him for a remembrance of his holiness.
For his wrath endureth but the twinkling of an eye, and in his pleasure is life: heaviness may endure for a night, but joy cometh in the morning. *Ib.* xxx. 4

9 Into thy hands I commend my spirit.
Ib. xxxi. 6

10 I am clean forgotten, as a dead man out of mind. *Ib.* 14

11 Sing unto the Lord a new song: sing praises lustily unto him with a good courage. *Ib.* xxxiii. 3

12 Eschew evil, and do good: seek peace, and ensue it. *Ib.* xxxiv. 14

13 I have been young, and now am old: and yet saw I never the righteous forsaken, nor his seed begging their bread. *Ib.* xxxvii. 25

14 I myself have seen the ungodly in great power: and flourishing like a green bay-tree. *Psalms* xxxvii. 36

15 Like as the hart desireth the water-brooks: so longeth my soul after thee, O God. *Ib.* xlii. 1

16 One deep calleth another, because of the noise of the water-pipes: all thy waves and storms are gone over me.
Ib. 9

17 While mine enemies that trouble me cast me in the teeth. *Ib.* 12

18 My heart is inditing of a good matter: I speak of the things which I have made unto the King.
My tongue is the pen of a ready writer. *Ib.* xlv. 1

19 The King's daughter is all glorious within: her clothing is of wrought gold.
Ib. 14

20 God is our hope and strength: a very present help in trouble.
Therefore will we not fear, though the earth be moved: and though the hills be carried into the midst of the sea. *Ib.* xlvi. 1

21 He maketh wars to cease in all the world: he breaketh the bow, and knappeth the spear in sunder, and burneth the chariots in the fire.
Be still then, and know that I am God.
Ib. 9

22 God is gone up with a merry noise: and the Lord with the sound of the trump. *Ib.* xlvii. 5

23 Walk about Sion, and go round about her: and tell the towers thereof.
Ib. xlviii. 11

24 Man being in honour hath no understanding: but is compared unto the beasts that perish. *Ib.* xlix. 20

25 Behold, I was shapen in wickedness: and in sin hath my mother conceived me. *Ib.* li. 5

26 Thou shalt purge me with hyssop, and I shall be clean: thou shalt wash me, and I shall be whiter than snow.
Ib. 7

27 Make me a clean heart, O God: and renew a right spirit within me. *Ib.* 10

28 For thou desirest no sacrifice, else would I give it thee: but thou delightest not in burnt-offerings.
The sacrifice of God is a troubled spirit: a broken and contrite heart, O God, shalt thou not despise. *Ib.* 16

29 Even like the deaf adder that stoppeth her ears;
Which refuseth to hear the voice of the charmer: charm he never so wisely. *Ib.* lviii. 4

G

1 They grin like a dog, and run about through the city. *Psalms* lix. 6

2 Moab is my wash-pot; over Edom will I cast out my shoe. *Ib.* lx. 8

3 The folds shall be full of sheep: the valleys also shall stand so thick with corn, that they shall laugh and sing. *Ib.* lxv. 14

4 God be merciful unto us, and bless us: and shew us the light of his countenance, and be merciful unto us.
That thy way may be known upon earth: thy saving health among all nations. *Ib.* lxvii. 1

5 Then shall the earth bring forth her increase: and God, even our own God, shall give us his blessing. *Ib.* 6

6 Let God arise, and let his enemies be scattered: let them also that hate him flee before him. *Ib.* lxviii. 1

7 Thou art gone up on high, thou hast led captivity captive, and received gifts for men. *Ib.* 18

8 The zeal of thine house hath even eaten me. *Ib.* lxix. 9

9 His enemies shall lick the dust. *Ib.* lxxii. 9

10 For promotion cometh neither from the east, nor from the west: nor yet from the south. *Ib.* lxxv. 7

11 A faithless and stubborn generation. *Ib.* lxxviii. 9

12 So the Lord awaked as one out of sleep: and like a giant refreshed with wine.
He smote his enemies in the hinder parts: and put them to a perpetual shame. *Ib.* 66

13 O how amiable are thy dwellings: thou Lord of hosts!
My soul hath a desire and longing to enter into the courts of the Lord: my heart and my flesh rejoice in the living God.
Yea, the sparrow hath found her an house, and the swallow a nest where she may lay her young: even thy altars, O Lord of hosts, my King and my God. *Ib.* lxxxiv. 1

14 Who going through the vale of misery use it for a well: and the pools are filled with water.
They will go from strength to strength. *Ib.* 6

15 For one day in thy courts: is better than a thousand. I had rather be a door-keeper in the house of my God: than to dwell in the tents of ungodliness. *Ib.* 10

16 Lord, thou hast been our refuge from one generation to another. *Ib.* xc. 1

17 For a thousand years in thy sight are but as yesterday: seeing that is past as a watch in the night.
As soon as thou scatterest them they are even as a sleep: and fade away suddenly like the grass.
In the morning it is green, and groweth up: but in the evening it is cut down, dried up, and withered.
Psalms xc. 4

18 For when thou art angry all our days are gone: we bring our years to an end, as it were a tale that is told.
The days of our age are threescore years and ten; and though men be so strong that they come to fourscore years: yet is their strength then but labour and sorrow; so soon passeth it away, and we are gone. *Ib.* 9

19 For he shall deliver thee from the snare of the hunter: and from the noisome pestilence.
He shall defend thee under his wings, and thou shalt be safe under his feathers: his faithfulness and truth shall be thy shield and buckler.
Thou shalt not be afraid for any terror by night: nor for the arrow that flieth by day.
For the pestilence that walketh in darkness: nor for the sickness that destroyeth in the noon-day.
A thousand shall fall beside thee, and ten thousand at thy right hand: but it shall not come nigh thee. *Ib.* xci. 3

20 There shall no evil happen unto thee: neither shall any plague come nigh thy dwelling.
For he shall give his angels charge over thee: to keep thee in all thy ways.
They shall bear thee in their hands: that thou hurt not thy foot against a stone. *Ib.* 10

21 Shew ourselves glad in him with psalms. *Ib.* xcv. 2

22 In his hand are all the corners of the earth: and the strength of the hills is his also.
The sea is his, and he made it: and his hands prepared the dry land. *Ib.* 4

23 O come, let us worship and fall down: and kneel before the Lord our Maker. *Ib.* 6

24 For he is the Lord our God: and we are the people of his pasture, and the sheep of his hand. *Ib.* 7

25 To-day if ye will hear his voice, harden not your hearts: as in the provocation, and as in the day of temptation in the wilderness. *Ib.* 8

26 When your fathers tempted me: proved me, and saw my works. *Ib.* 9

1 The days of man are but as grass: for he flourisheth as a flower of the field. For as soon as the wind goeth over it, it is gone: and the place thereof shall know it no more. *Psalms* ciii. 15

2 Wine that maketh glad the heart of man: and oil to make him a cheerful countenance. *Ib.* civ. 15

3 Man goeth forth to his work, and to his labour: until the evening. *Ib.* 23

4 So is the great and wide sea also: wherein are things creeping innumerable, both small and great beasts. There go the ships, and there is that Leviathan: whom thou hast made to take his pastime therein. These wait all upon thee: that thou mayest give them meat in due season. *Ib.* 25

5 Whose feet they hurt in the stocks: the iron entered into his soul. *Ib.* cv. 18

6 Their soul abhorred all manner of meat: and they were even hard at death's door. *Ib.* cvii. 18

7 They that go down to the sea in ships: and occupy their business in great waters; These men see the works of the Lord: and his wonders in the deep. *Ib.* 23

8 They reel to and fro, and stagger like a drunken man: and are at their wit's end. So when they cry unto the Lord in their trouble: he delivereth them out of their distress. *Ib.* 27

9 Then are they glad, because they are at rest: and so he bringeth them unto the haven where they would be. *Ib.* 30

10 The Lord said unto my Lord: Sit thou on my right hand, until I make thine enemies thy footstool. *Ib.* cx. 1

11 The fear of the Lord is the beginning of wisdom: a good understanding have all they that do thereafter; the praise of it endureth for ever. *Ib.* cxi. 10

12 The mountains skipped like rams: and the little hills like young sheep. *Ib.* cxiv. 4

13 They have mouths, and speak not: eyes have they, and see not. They have ears, and hear not: noses have they, and smell not. They have hands, and handle not; feet have they, and walk not: neither speak they through their throat. *Ib.* cxv. 5

14 I said in my haste, All men are liars. *Ib.* cxvi. 10

15 The same stone which the builders refused: is become the head-stone in the corner. *Ib.* cxviii. 22

16 I will lift up mine eyes unto the hills: from whence cometh my help. *Psalms* cxxi. 1

17 The Lord himself is thy keeper: the Lord is thy defence upon thy right hand; So that the sun shall not burn thee by day: neither the moon by night. *Ib.* 5

18 The Lord shall preserve thy going out, and thy coming in: from this time forth for evermore. *Ib.* 8

19 I was glad when they said unto me: We will go into the house of the Lord. *Ib.* cxxii. 1

20 O pray for the peace of Jerusalem: they shall prosper that love thee. Peace be within thy walls: and plenteousness within thy palaces. *Ib.* 6

21 Turn our captivity, O Lord: as the rivers in the south. They that sow in tears: shall reap in joy. He that now goeth on his way weeping, and beareth forth good seed: shall doubtless come again with joy, and bring his sheaves with him. *Ib.* cxxvi. 5

22 Except the Lord build the house: their labour is but lost that build it. Except the Lord keep the city: the watchman waketh but in vain. *Ib.* cxxvii. 1

23 Like as the arrows in the hand of the giant: even so are the young children. Happy is the man that hath his quiver full of them: they shall not be ashamed when they speak with their enemies in the gate. *Ib.* 5

24 Thy wife shall be as the fruitful vine upon the walls of thine house. Thy children like the olive-branches round about thy table. *Ib.* cxxviii. 3

25 Out of the deep have I called unto thee, O Lord: Lord, hear my voice. *Ib.* cxxx. 1

26 Behold, how good and joyful a thing it is, brethren, to dwell together in unity! *Ib.* cxxxiii. 1

27 His mercy endureth for ever. *Ib.* cxxxvi. 1

28 By the waters of Babylon we sat down and wept: when we remembered thee, O Sion. As for our harps, we hanged them up: upon the trees that are therein. For they that led us away captive required of us then a song, and melody, in our heaviness: Sing us one of the songs of Sion. How shall we sing the Lord's song in a strange land?

If I forget thee, O Jerusalem: let my right hand forget her cunning.
If I do not remember thee, let my tongue cleave to the roof of my mouth: yea, if I prefer not Jerusalem in my mirth. *Psalms* cxxxvii. 1

1 If I take the wings of the morning and remain in the uttermost parts of the sea;
Even there also shall thy hand lead me: and thy right hand shall hold me.
If I say, Peradventure the darkness shall cover me: then shall my night be turned to day.
Yea, the darkness is no darkness with thee, but the night is as clear as the day: the darkness and light to thee are both alike. *Ib.* cxxxix. 8

2 I will give thanks unto thee, for I am fearfully and wonderfully made. *Ib.* 13

3 The Lord is gracious, and merciful: long-suffering, and of great goodness.
Ib. cxlv. 8

4 O put not your trust in princes, nor in any child of man: for there is no help in them. *Ib.* cxlvi. 2

5 The Lord careth for the strangers; he defendeth the fatherless and widow: as for the way of the ungodly, he turneth it upside down. *Ib.* 9

6 Young men and maidens, old men and children, praise the Name of the Lord: for his Name only is excellent, and his praise above heaven and earth.
Ib. cxlviii. 12

7 To bind their kings in chains: and their nobles with links of iron.
Ib. cxlix. 8

8 Praise him upon the well-tuned cymbals: praise him upon the loud cymbals.
Let every thing that hath breath: praise the Lord. *Ib.* cl. 5

9 Such as pass on the seas upon their lawful occasions.
Forms of Prayer to be Used at Sea. 'O Eternal Lord God'

10 We therefore commit his body to the deep, to be turned into corruption, looking for the resurrection of the body (when the Sea shall give up her dead).
Ib. At the Burial of their Dead at Sea

11 Come, Holy Ghost, our souls inspire, And lighten with celestial fire.
Thou the anointing Spirit art, Who dost thy seven-fold gifts impart.
Ordering of Priests. Veni, Creator Spiritus

12 All things necessary to salvation.
Articles of Religion, vi. *Of the Sufficiency of the Holy Scriptures*

13 Of Works of Supererogation.
Articles of Religion. Title of Article xiv

14 Understanded of the people.
Ib. xxiv. *Of Speaking in the Congregation*

15 It is lawful for Christian men, at the commandment of the Magistrate, to wear weapons, and serve in the wars.
Ib. Of the Civil Magistrates

16 Table of Kindred and Affinity. *Title*

17 A Man may not marry his Grandmother. *Table of Kindred*

ARCHIBALD PHILIP PRIMROSE, EARL OF ROSEBERY
see ROSEBERY

MATTHEW PRIOR 1664–1721

18 All jargon of the schools.
*On Exod. iii. 14. I am that I am.
An Ode,* l. 65

19 No longer shall the bodice, aptly lac'd
From thy full bosom to thy slender waist,
That air and harmony of shape express,
Fine by degrees and beautifully less.
Henry and Emma, l. 427

20 I never strove to rule the roast, She ne'er refus'd to pledge my toast.
Turtle and Sparrow, l. 334

21 A Rechabite poor Will must live, And drink of Adam's ale.
The Wandering Pilgrim, iii

ADELAIDE ANN PROCTER 1825–1864

22 Seated one day at the organ, I was weary and ill at ease, And my fingers wandered idly Over the noisy keys.
Legends and Lyrics. A Lost Chord

23 But I struck one chord of music, Like the sound of a great Amen.
Ib.

PROTAGORAS c. 481–411 B.C.

24 πάντων χρημάτων ἄνθρωπον μέτρον εἶναι.
Man is the measure of all things.
Quoted by Plato in Theaetetus, 160d

PIERRE-JOSEPH PROUDHON
1809–1865

25 La propriété c'est le vol.
Property is theft.
Qu'est-ce que la propriété? ch. 1

FATHER PROUT [FRANCIS SYLVESTER MAHONY] 1804–1866

1 'Tis the bells of Shandon,
That sound so grand on
The pleasant waters
Of the River Lee.
The Bells of Shandon

JOHN PUDNEY 1909–

2 Do not despair
For Johnny head-in-air;
He sleeps as sound
As Johnny underground.
For Johnny, st. 1

PUNCH

3 Advice to persons about to marry.—
'Don't.' *Punch*, vol. viii, p. 1. 1845

4 You pays your money and you takes
your choice.
Ib. vol. x, p. 17. 1846. *A quotation from what appears to be a peepshow rhyme. See* V. S. Lean, Collectanea (1902–4).

5 Never do to-day what you can put off
till to-morrow.
Ib. vol. xvii, p. 241. 1849

6 Who's 'im, Bill?
A stranger!
'Eave 'arf a brick at 'im.
Ib. vol. xxvi, p. 82. 1854

7 What is Matter?—Never mind.
What is Mind?—No matter.
Ib. vol. xxix, p. 19. 1855

8 'Peccavi—I've Scinde' wrote Lord
Ellen so proud.
More briefly Dalhousie wrote—'Vovi
—I've Oude'.
Ib. vol. xxx, p. 141. 1856

9 It ain't the 'unting as 'urts 'un, it's
the 'ammer, 'ammer, 'ammer along
the 'ard 'igh road.
Ib. vol. xxx, p. 218. 1856

10 Mun, a had na' been the-erre abune
two hours when—*bang*—went saxpence!!! *Ib.* vol. liv, p. 235. 1868

11 Go directly—see what she's doing, and
tell her she mustn't.
Ib. vol. lxiii, p. 202. 1872

12 There was one poor tiger that hadn't
got a Christian.
Ib. vol. lxviii, p. 143. 1875

13 Here was an old owl liv'd in an oak
The more he heard, the less he spoke;
The less he spoke, the more he heard
O, if men were all like that wise bird!
Ib. p. 155. 1875

14 It's worse than wicked, my dear, it's
vulgar. *Ib. Almanac.* 1876

15 'Is Life worth living?' . . . he suspects
it is, in a great measure, a question of
the Liver. *Ib.* vol. lxxiii, p. 207. 1877

16 What sort of a doctor is he?
Oh, well, I don't know very much
about his ability; but he's got a very
good bedside manner!
Punch, vol. lxxxvi, p. 121. 1884

17 I used your soap two years ago; since
then I have used no other.
Ib. p. 197. 1884

18 Don't look at me, Sir, with—ah—in
that tone of voice.
Ib. vol. lxxxvii, p. 38. 1884

19 Oh yes! I'm sure he's not so fond of
me as at first. He's away so much, neglects me dreadfully, and he's so cross
when he comes home. What *shall* I do?
Feed the brute!
Ib. vol. lxxxix, p. 206. 1886

20 Nearly all our best men are dead!
Carlyle, Tennyson, Browning, George
Eliot!—I'm not feeling very well
myself. *Ib.* vol. civ, p. 210. 1893

21 I'm afraid you've got a bad egg, Mr.
Jones.
Oh no, my Lord, I assure you!
Parts of it are excellent!
Ib. vol. cix, p. 222, 1895

ISRAEL PUTNAM 1718–1790

22 Men, you are all marksmen—don't
one of you fire until you see the whites
of their eyes.
Bunker Hill, 1775. Frothingham, *History of the Siege of Boston* (1873), ch. 5, note. *Also attr. to* William Prescott (1726–95)

ERNIE PYLE 1900–1945

23 The worm's eye point of view.
Here Is Your War

FRANCIS QUARLES 1592–1644

24 We spend our midday sweat, our midnight oil;
We tire the night in thought, the day
in toil. *Emblems*, bk. ii, No. 2, l. 33

25 Be wisely worldly, be not worldly wise.
Ib. l. 46

26 Our God and soldiers we alike adore
Ev'n at the brink of danger; not
before:
After deliverance, both alike requited,
Our God's forgotten, and our soldiers
slighted. *Epigram*

27 My soul, sit thou a patient looker-on;
Judge not the play before the play is
done:
Her plot hath many changes; every
day
Speaks a new scene; the last act
crowns the play.
Epigram. Respice Finem

1 He that had no cross deserves no
crown.   *Esther*, Sect. 9, Medit. 9

FRANÇOIS QUESNAY 1694–1774

2 Laissez faire, laissez passer.
No interference, and complete free-
dom of movement.
*Of Government interference. Also
attr.* to Marquis d'Argenson,
Mémoires (1736)

SIR ARTHUR QUILLER-COUCH
1863–1944

3 Know you her secret none can utter?
Hers of the Book the tripled Crown?
Poems. Alma Mater

FRANÇOIS RABELAIS 1494?–1553

4 L'appétit vient en mangeant.
The appetite grows by eating.
Gargantua, I. v

5 Fay ce que vouldras.
Do what thou wilt.   *Ib.* I. lvii

6 Tirez le rideau, la farce est jouée.
Ring down the curtain, the farce
is over.
Attr. to Rabelais on his death-bed

7 Je m'en vais chercher un grand peut-
être.
I go to seek a great perhaps.   *Ib.*

8 Vogue la galère!
Let her rip!
[Literally, the words mean 'loose
the galley' or 'hoist sail'.]
Works, bk. i, ch. 40

JEAN RACINE 1639–1699

9 Elle flotte, elle hésite; en un mot, elle
est femme.
She is all wavering and hesitation:
in short, she is a woman.
Athalie, iii. 3

10 Ce n'est plus une ardeur dans mes
veines cachée:
C'est Vénus tout entière à sa proie
attachée.
It is no longer a passion hidden in
my veins: it is the goddess Venus
herself fastened on her prey.
Phèdre, I. iii

11 Point d'argent, point de Suisse.
No money, no Swiss [soldiers].
Les Plaideurs, I. i

THOMAS RAINBOROWE d. 1648

12 The poorest he that is in England hath
a life to live as the greatest he.
*In the Army debates at Putney,
29 Oct. 1647.* Peacock, *Life of
Rainborowe*

SIR WALTER RALEGH 1552?–1618

13 Give me my scallop-shell of quiet,
My staff of faith to walk upon,
My scrip of joy, immortal diet,
My bottle of salvation,
My gown of glory, hope's true gage,
And thus I'll take my pilgrimage.
The Passionate Man's Pilgrimage

14 Fain would I climb, yet fear I to fall.
Line Written on a Window-Pane.
Queen Elizabeth wrote under it,
'If thy heart fails thee, climb
not at all.' Fuller, *Worthies*
(1840), i. 419

15 Even such is time, which takes in
trust
Our youth, our joys, and all we have,
And pays us but with age and dust,
Who in the dark and silent grave,
When we have wandered all our ways,
Shuts up the story of our days.
And from which earth, and grave, and
dust,
The Lord shall raise me up, I trust.
*Written the night before his death.
Found in his Bible in the Gate-
house at Westminster*

16 O eloquent, just, and mighty Death!
whom none could advise, thou has
persuaded; what none hath dared,
thou hast done; and whom all the
world hath flattered, thou only hast
cast out of the world and despised:
thou hast drawn together all the far-
stretched greatness, all the pride,
cruelty, and ambition of man, and
covered it all over with these two
narrow words, *Hic jacet*.
A History of the World, bk. v,
ch. vi, § 12

17 [Feeling the edge of the axe before his
execution:]
'Tis a sharp remedy, but a sure one for
all ills.
Hume, *History of Great Britain*
(1754), vol. i, ch. iv, p. 72

18 [When asked which way he preferred
to lay his head on the block:]
So the heart be right, it is no matter
which way the head lies.
W. Stebbing, *Sir Walter Raleigh*,
ch. xxx

SIR WALTER A. RALEIGH
1861–1922

19 I wish I loved the Human Race;
I wish I loved its silly face;
I wish I liked the way it walks;
I wish I liked the way it talks;
And when I'm introduced to one
I wish I thought *What Jolly Fun!*
Laughter from a Cloud (1923),
p. 228. *Wishes of an Elderly Man*

JULIAN RALPH 1853–1903

1 News value.
> Lecture to Brander Matthews's English Class, Columbia, 1892.
> Thomas Beer's Mauve Decade

JEREMIAH EAMES RANKIN
1828–1904

2 God be with you, till we meet again,
By His counsels guide, uphold you,
With His sheep securely fold you:
God be with you, till we meet again.
> Hymn

CHARLES READE 1814–1884

3 Courage, mon ami, le diable est mort!
> The Cloister and the Hearth, ch. 24, and passim

4 Sow an act, and you reap a habit.
Sow a habit, and you reap a character.
Sow a character, and you reap a destiny.
> Attr. See Notes and Queries, 9th series, vol. 12, p. 377

ERICH MARIA REMARQUE
1898–

5 Im Westen nichts Neues.
> All Quiet on the Western Front.
> Title of Novel. Trans. by A. W. Wheen

EBEN REXFORD 1848–1916

6 Darling, I am growing old,
Silver threads among the gold
Shine upon my brow to-day;
Life is fading fast away.
> Silver Threads among the Gold

FREDERIC REYNOLDS 1764–1841

7 How goes the enemy? [Said by Mr. Ennui, 'the time-killer'.]
> The Dramatist, I. i

ARCHBISHOP WALTER REYNOLDS [De REYNEL or REGINALD] d. 1327

8 Vox Populi, vox Dei.
> The voice of the people, the voice of God.
> Text of Sermon when Edward III ascended the throne, 1 Feb. 1327.
> Walsingham, Historia Anglicana (ed. 1863), i. 186

CECIL JOHN RHODES 1853–1902

9 So little done, so much to do.
> Last words. L. Michell, Life, vol. ii, ch. 39

GRANTLAND RICE 1880–1954

10 For when the One Great Scorer comes
To write against your name,
He marks—not that you won or lost—
But how you played the game.
> Alumnus Football

SIR STEPHEN RICE 1637–1715

11 Sir Stephen Rice . . . having been often heard to say, before he was a judge, that he will drive a coach and six horses through the Act of Settlement.
> W. King, State of the Protestants of Ireland (1672), ch. 3, § 3, par. 6

ROBERT LEROY RIPLEY
1893–1949

12 Believe it or not.
> Title of newspaper feature

ANTOINE DE RIVAROL 1753–1801

13 Ce qui n'est pas clair n'est pas français.
> What is not clear is not French.
> De l'universalité de la langue française (1784)

SIR BOYLE ROCHE 1743–1807

14 He regretted that he was not a bird, and could not be in two places at once.
> Attr.

15 Mr. Speaker, I smell a rat; I see him forming in the air and darkening the sky; but I'll nip him in the bud.
> Attr.

DUC DE LA ROCHEFOUCAULD
1613–1680

16 Dans l'adversité de nos meilleurs amis, nous trouvons quelque chose qui ne nous déplaît pas.
> In the misfortune of our best friends, we find something which is not displeasing to us.
> Maximes supprimées, 583

DUC DE LA ROCHEFOUCAULD-LIANCOURT 1747–1827

17 LOUIS XVI: C'est une révolte?
LA ROCHEFOUCAULD-LIANCOURT: Non, Sire, c'est une révolution.
> LOUIS XVI: Is it a revolt?
> LA R.-LIANCOURT: No, Sire, it is a revolution.
> When the news arrived at Versailles of the Fall of the Bastille, 1789

JOHN WILMOT, EARL OF ROCHESTER 1647–1680

1 A merry monarch, scandalous and poor.
   Works (1926). *A Satire on King
   Charles II for which he was
   banished from the Court*, l. 19

2 Here lies a great and mighty king
   Whose promise none relies on;
   He never said a foolish thing,
   Nor ever did a wise one.
   *The King's Epitaph. An alterna-
   tive version of the first line is:*
   'Here lies our sovereign lord
   the King.'

E. W. ROGERS

3 Ev'ry member of the force
   Has a watch and chain, of course;
   If you want to know the time,
   Ask a P'liceman!   *Ask A P'liceman*

JAMES EDWIN THOROLD ROGERS 1823–1890

4 While ladling butter from alternate
   tubs
   Stubbs butters Freeman, Freeman
   butters Stubbs.
   Attr. in Hutton's *Letters of Bishop
   Stubbs*

SAMUEL ROGERS 1763–1855

5 Think nothing done while aught remains to do.   *Human Life*, l. 49

6 But there are moments which he calls
   his own,
   Then, never less alone than when
   alone,
   Those whom he loved so long and sees
   no more,
   Loved and still loves—not dead—
   but gone before,
   He gathers round him.   *Ib.* l. 755

7 Sheridan was listened to with such
   attention that you might have heard
   a pin drop.   *Table Talk*

MME ROLAND 1754–1793

8 O liberté! O liberté! que de crimes on
   commet en ton nom!

   O liberty! O liberty! what crimes are
   committed in thy name!
   Lamartine, *Histoire des Giron-
   dins*, bk. li, ch. 8

9 The more I see of men, the better I
   like dogs.   *Attr.*

JAMES ROLMAZ

10 'Where did you get that hat?
   Where did you get that tile?
   Isn't it a nobby one, and just the
   proper style?
   I should like to have one just the
   same as that!'

Where'er I go they shout, 'Hello!
Where did you get that hat?'
   Where Did You Get That Hat?

PIERRE RONSARD 1529–1585

11 Quand vous serez bien vieille, au soir,
   à la chandelle,
   Assise auprès du feu, dévidant et
   filant,
   Direz, chantant mes vers, en vous
   émerveillant,
   Ronsard me célébrait du temps que
   j'étais belle.

   When you are very old, and sit in
   the candle-light at evening spinning by the fire, you will say, as
   you murmur my verses, a wonder
   in your eyes, 'Ronsard sang of
   me in the days when I was fair.'
   Sonnets pour Hélène, ii. 43

FRANKLIN DELANO ROOSEVELT 1882–1945

12 I pledge you—I pledge myself—to a
   new deal for the American people.
   *Speech at Convention, Chicago,
   2 July 1932*. (*New York Times,
   3 July, sect. 1, p. 8, col. 7.)*
   E. K. Lindley, *The Roosevelt
   Revolution*, ch. 1

13 Let me assert my firm belief that the
   only thing we have to fear is fear itself.
   *First Inaugural Address, 4 March
   1933*

14 In the field of world policy; I would
   dedicate this nation to the policy of
   the good neighbour.   *Ib.*

15 I see one-third of a nation ill-housed,
   ill-clad, ill-nourished.
   *Second Inaugural Address, 20 Jan.
   1937*

16 We must be the great arsenal of
   democracy.   *Fireside Chat, 29 Dec. 1940*

17 In the future days, which we seek to
   make secure, we look forward to a
   world founded upon four essential
   freedoms.
   The first is freedom of speech and
   expression—everywhere in the world.
   The second is freedom of every person
   to worship God in his own way—
   everywhere in the world.
   The third is freedom from want. . . .
   The fourth is freedom from fear.
   Speech, 6 Jan. 1941

THEODORE ROOSEVELT 1858–1919

18 Speak softly and carry a big stick.
   *Speech, Minnesota State Fair,
   2 Sept. 1901*

1 The first requisite of a good citizen in this Republic of ours is that he shall be able and willing to pull his weight.
Speech, New York, 11 Nov. 1902

2 The men with the muck-rakes are often indispensable to the well-being of society; but only if they know when to stop raking the muck.
Ib. At the laying of the Cornerstone of the Office Building of House of Representatives, 14 Apr. 1906

3 There can be no fifty-fifty Americanism in this country. There is room here for only 100 per cent. Americanism, only for those who are Americans and nothing else.
Ib. Republican Convention, Saratoga

4 We demand that big business give the people a square deal; in return we must insist that when any one engaged in big business honestly endeavors to do right he shall himself be given a square deal.
Autobiography (1913), p. 615

ARCHIBALD PHILIP PRIMROSE, EARL OF ROSEBERY
1847–1929

5 There is no need for any nation, however great, leaving the Empire, because the Empire is a Commonwealth of Nations.
Speech at Adelaide, 18 January 1884

6 I must plough my furrow alone.
Speech, City of London Liberal Club, 19 July 1901

ALAN STRODE CAMPBELL ROSS 1907–

7 U and non-U.
'Upper Class English Usage', Bulletin de la Société neo-philologique de Helsinki (1954). See also Nancy Mitford, 'The English Aristocracy', Encounter (September 1955)

CHRISTINA GEORGINA ROSSETTI 1830–1894

8 My heart is like a singing bird
Whose nest is in a watered shoot;
My heart is like an apple-tree
Whose boughs are bent with thickset fruit;
My heart is like a rainbow shell
That paddles in a halcyon sea;
My heart is gladder than all these
Because my love is come to me.
A Birthday

9 In the bleak mid-winter
Frosty wind made moan,
Earth stood hard as iron,
Water like a stone;
Snow had fallen, snow on snow,
Snow on snow,
In the bleak mid-winter,
Long ago.   *Mid-Winter*

10 In the bleak mid-winter
A stable-place sufficed
The Lord God almighty,
Jesus Christ.   *Ib.*

11 Better by far you should forget and smile
Than that you should remember and be sad.   *Remember*

12 When I am dead, my dearest,
Sing no sad songs for me;
Plant thou no roses at my head,
Nor shady cypress tree:
Be the green grass above me
With showers and dewdrops wet;
And if thou wilt, remember,
And if thou wilt, forget.
Song: When I am Dead

13 Does the road wind up-hill all the way?
Yes, to the very end.
Will the day's journey take the whole long day?
From morn to night, my friend.
Up-Hill

DANTE GABRIEL ROSSETTI
1828–1882

14 Mother of the Fair Delight,
Thou handmaid perfect in God's sight.
Ave, l. 1

15 The blessed damozel leaned out
From the gold bar of Heaven;
Her eyes were deeper than the depth
Of waters stilled at even;
She had three lilies in her hand,
And the stars in her hair were seven.
The Blessed Damozel, i

16 Her hair that lay along her back
Was yellow like ripe corn.   *Ib. ii*

ROUGET DE LISLE 1760–1836

17 Allons, enfants de la patrie,
Le jour de gloire est arrivé.
Come, children of our country, the day of glory has arrived.
La Marseillaise

JEAN-JACQUES ROUSSEAU
1712–1778

18 L'homme est né libre, et partout il est dans les fers.
Man was born free, and everywhere he is in chains.
Du Contrat Social, ch. 1

1 'Monseigneur, il faut que je vive,'
disait un malheureux auteur satirique
au ministre qui lui reprochait l'in-
famie de ce métier. 'Je n'en vois pas la
nécessité,' lui repartit froidement
l'homme en place.

'My Lord—I must live'—once said
a wretched author of satire to a
minister who had reproached
him for following so degrading a
profession. 'I fail to see why,'
replied the Great Man coldly.
Émile, iii (see *10:14*)

MARTIN JOSEPH ROUTH
1755–1854

2 You will find it a very good practice
always to verify your references, sir!
Burgon, *Memoir of Dr. Routh*.
Quarterly Review (July 1878),
vol. cxlvi

NICHOLAS ROWE 1674–1718

3 The evening of my age.
The Fair Penitent, IV. i

4 I feel the pangs of disappointed love.
Ib.

5 Is this that haughty, gallant, gay
Lothario? *Ib.* v. 1

'RED ROWLEY'

6 Mademoiselle from Armenteers,
Hasn't been kissed in forty years,
Hinky, dinky, parley-voo.
Song of the First World War

DAMON RUNYON 1884–1946

7 More than somewhat. *Title of Book*

JOHN RUSKIN 1819–1900

8 [On Whistler's 'Nocturne in Black and
Gold']
I have seen, and heard, much of
Cockney impudence before now; but
never expected to hear a coxcomb ask
two hundred guineas for flinging a
pot of paint in the public's face.
Fors Clavigera, letter lxxix,
18 June 1877

9 All violent feelings . . . produce in us
a falseness in all our impressions of
external things, which I would
generally characterize as the 'Pathetic
Fallacy'.
Modern Painters (1888), vol. iii

10 There is really no such thing as bad
weather, only different kinds of good
weather. *Quoted by Lord Avebury*

LORD JOHN RUSSELL 1792–1878

11 Among the defects of the Bill, which
were numerous, one provision was
conspicuous by its presence and
another by its absence.
*Speech to the electors of the City of
London, Apr. 1859*

SIR WILLIAM HOWARD
RUSSELL 1820–1907

12 [The Russians] dash on towards that
thin red line tipped with steel.
*The British Expedition to the
Crimea* (1877), p. 156

W. ST. LEGER 1850–c. 1915

13 There is a fine stuffed chavender,
A chavender, or chub,
That decks the rural pavender,
The pavender, or pub,
Wherein I eat my gravender,
My gravender, or grub.
The Chavender, or Chub, st. 1

CHARLES-AUGUSTIN
SAINTE-BEUVE 1804–1869

14   Et Vigny plus secret,
Comme en sa tour d'ivoire, avant
midi rentrait.
    And Vigny more reserved,
Returned ere noon, within his ivory
tower.
Quoted in Paléologue's *Vigny*,
p. 71

'SAKI' [HECTOR HUGH MUNRO]
1870–1916

15 The cook was a good cook, as cooks go;
and as cooks go she went.
*Reginald. Reginald on Besetting
Sins*

16 Women and elephants never forget
an injury. *Ib.*

ROBERT CECIL, LORD
SALISBURY 1830–1903

17 By office boys for office boys.
Remark about The Daily Mail.
*See H. Hamilton Fyfe, North-
cliffe, an Intimate Biography,
ch. 4*

SALLUST 86–34 B.C.

18 Pro patria, pro liberis, pro aris atque
focis suis.
On behalf of their country, their
children, their altars, and their
hearths. *Catiline, 59*

1 Urbem venalem et mature perituram,
si emptorem invenerit.

The venal city soon to perish, if
a buyer can be found.
Jugurtha, 35

2 Punica fide.

With Carthaginian faith [i.e. treach-
ery.] *Ib.* 108, 3

EPES SARGENT 1813–1880

3 A life on the ocean wave,
A home on the rolling deep.
A Life on the Ocean Wave

SIEGFRIED SASSOON 1886–1967

4 If I were fierce and bald and short of
breath,
I'd live with scarlet Majors at the
Base,
And speed glum heroes up the line
to death. *Base Details*

5 And when the war is done and youth
stone dead
I'd toddle safely home and die—in
bed. *Ib.*

6 Everyone suddenly burst out singing.
Everyone Sang

7 The song was wordless;
The singing will never be done. *Ib.*

RICHARD SAVAGE d. 1743

8 No tenth transmitter of a foolish
face. *The Bastard*, l. 8

HENRY J. SAYERS d. 1932

9 Ta-ra-ra-boom-de-ay!
Title of Song (1891)

FRIEDRICH VON SCHELLING
1775–1854

10 Architecture in general is frozen
music. *Philosophie der Kunst*

FRIEDRICH VON SCHILLER
1759–1805

11 Freude, schöner Götterfunken,
Tochter aus Elysium,
Wir betreten Feuertrunken,
Himmlische, dein Heiligtum.
Deine Zauber binden wieder,
Was die Mode streng geteilt,
Alle Menschen werden Brüder
Wo dein sanfter Flügel weilt.

Thou radiance sprung from God
Himself,
Thou daughter of Elysium, Joy,
Thy shrine we tread, Thou Maid
Divine,
Though light's excess our sense
destroy.

What harsh world-use has rent
apart,
Thy healing spells restore again;
Where'er Thy gentle wings may
rest,
Brothers we find our fellow-men.
An die Freude

12 Die Sonne geht in meinem Staat nicht
unter.

The sun does not set in my
dominions.
[Philip II.] *Don Carlos*, Act 1, sc. 6

13 Mit der Dummheit kämpfen Götter
selbst vergebens.

With stupidity the gods themselves
struggle in vain.
Jungfrau von Orleans, III. vi

14 Die Weltgeschichte ist das Welt-
gericht.

The world's history is the world's
judgement.
*First lecture as Professor of His-
tory, Jena, 26 May 1789*

MAX SCHNECKENBURGER
1819–1849

15 Die Wacht am Rhein.
The watch on the Rhine.
Title of Song

LOUIS SCHNEIDER

16 O Tannenbaum, O Tannenbaum,
Wie grün sind deine Blätter!

O pine-tree, O pine-tree,
How green are thy leaves!
Der Kurmärker und die Picarde

CHARLES PRESTWICH SCOTT
1846–1932

17 Comment is free but facts are sacred.
In the Manchester Guardian, *6 May
1926*

ROBERT FALCON SCOTT
1868–1912

18 For God's sake look after our people.
Journal, 25 March 1912

19 Had we lived, I should have had a tale
to tell of the hardihood, endurance,
and courage of my companions which
would have stirred the heart of every
Englishman. These rough notes and
our dead bodies must tell the tale.
Message to the Public

SIR WALTER SCOTT 1771–1832

20 Come fill up my cup, come fill up my
can,
Come saddle your horses, and call
up your men;

Come open the West Port, and let me
gang free,
And it's room for the bonnets of
Bonny Dundee!'
  Bonny Dundee. (*The Doom of
  Devorgoil,* Act II, sc. ii)

1 But answer came there none.
  Bridal of Triermain, can. III. x

2 He is gone on the mountain,
  He is lost to the forest,
  Like a summer-dried fountain,
  When our need was the sorest.
  The Lady of the Lake, can. III. xvi

3 Like the dew on the mountain,
  Like the foam on the river,
  Like the bubble on the fountain,
  Thou art gone, and for ever! *Ib.*

4 The way was long, the wind was cold,
  The Minstrel was infirm and old;
  His wither'd cheek and tresses grey,
  Seem'd to have known a better day.
  The harp, his sole remaining joy,
  Was carried by an orphan boy.
  The last of all the Bards was he,
  Who sung of Border chivalry.
  The Lay of the Last Minstrel,
  introduction, l. 1

5 If thou would'st view fair Melrose
  aright,
  Go visit it by the pale moonlight;
  For the gay beams of lightsome day
  Gild, but to flout, the ruins grey.
  Ib. c. II. i

6 Breathes there the man, with soul so
  dead,
  Who never to himself hath said,
  This is my own, my native land!
  Whose heart hath ne'er within him
  burn'd,
  As home his footsteps he hath turn'd
  From wandering on a foreign strand!
  If such there breathe, go, mark him
  well;
  For him no Minstrel raptures swell;
  High though his titles, proud his
  name,
  Boundless his wealth as wish can
  claim;
  Despite those titles, power, and pelf,
  The wretch, concentred all in self,
  Living, shall forfeit fair renown,
  And, doubly dying, shall go down
  To the vile dust, from whence he
  sprung,
  Unwept, unhonour'd, and unsung.

  O Caledonia! stern and wild,
  Meet nurse for a poetic child!
  Land of brown heath and shaggy
  wood,
  Land of the mountain and the flood,
  Land of my sires! what mortal hand
  Can e'er untie the filial band
  That knits me to thy rugged strand!
  Ib. can. VI. i–ii

7 That day of wrath, that dreadful day,
  When heaven and earth shall pass
  away.
  The Lay of the Last Minstrel, can. VI. xxxi

8 O, young Lochinvar is come out of the
  west,
  Through all the wide Border his steed
  was the best. *Marmion,* can. V. xii

9 So faithful in love, and so dauntless in
  war,
  There never was knight like the young
  Lochinvar. *Ib.*

10 For a laggard in love, and a dastard
  in war,
  Was to wed the fair Ellen of brave
  Lochinvar. *Ib.*

11 'O come ye in peace here, or come ye
  in war,
  Or to dance at our bridal, young Lord
  Lochinvar?' *Ib.*

12 O what a tangled web we weave,
  When first we practise to deceive!
  Ib. can. VI. xvii

13 O Woman! in our hours of ease,
  Uncertain, coy, and hard to please,
  And variable as the shade
  By the light quivering aspen made;
  When pain and anguish wring the
  brow,
  A ministering angel thou! *Ib.* xxx

14 You . . . whirl'd them to the back o'
  beyont. *The Antiquary,* ch. 2

15 Look not thou on beauty's charm-
  ing,—
  Sit thou still when kings are arming,—
  Taste not when the wine-cup
  glistens,—
  Speak not when the people listens,—
  Stop thine ear against the singer,—
  From the red gold keep thy finger;—
  Vacant heart and hand, and eye,—
  Easy live and quiet die.
  The Bride of Lammermoor, ch. 3

16 [He] was ever after designated as a
  'stickit minister.'
  Guy Mannering, ch. 2

17 The ancient and now forgotten pastime of high jinks. *Ib.* ch. 36

18 Proud Maisie is in the wood,
  Walking so early,
  Sweet Robin sits in the bush,
  Singing so rarely.
  The Heart of Midlothian, ch. 40

19 Come, trowl the brown bowl to me,
  Bully boy, bully boy,
  Come, trowl the brown bowl to me:
  Ho! jolly Jenkin, I spy a knave in
  drinking,
  Come, trowl the brown bowl to me.
  Ivanhoe, ch. 20

20 But, my lord, there is a Southern proverb,—fine words butter no parsnips.
  The Legend of Montrose, ch. 3

1 But with the morning cool repentance
came.   *Rob Roy*, ch. 12

2 There's a gude time coming.
                    Ib. ch. 29, note

3 Fair, fat, and forty.
                    St. Ronan's Well, ch. 7

4 The play-bill, which is said to have
announced the tragedy of Hamlet,
the character of the Prince of Denmark
being left out.
        The Talisman, introduction. *For
        an earlier report of this anecdote
        see* Times Literary Supplement,
        3 June 1939

5 The Big Bow-Wow strain I can do
myself like any now going; but the
exquisite touch, which renders ordinary commonplace things and characters interesting, from the truth of the
description and the sentiment, is
denied to me. [On Jane Austen.]
                    Journal, 14 Mar. 1826

6 I would like to be there, were it but to
see how the cat jumps.
                    Ib. 7 Oct. 1826

7 From the lone shieling of the misty
        island
    Mountains divide us, and the waste
        of seas—
Yet still the blood is strong, the heart
    is Highland,
And we in dreams behold the
    Hebrides!
Fair these broad meads, these hoary
    woods are grand;
But we are exiles from our fathers'
    land.
        *Canadian Boat Song. Of disputed
        authorship. See* Times Literary
        Supplement, *23 Dec. 1904*, G. M.
        Fraser's article.

SCOTTISH METRICAL PSALMS
1650

8 The Lord's my shepherd, I'll not
        want.
    He makes me down to lie
In pastures green: he leadeth me
    the quiet waters by.
My soul he doth restore again;
    and me to walk doth make
Within the paths of righteousness,
    ev'n for his own name's sake.

Yea, though I walk in death's dark vale,
    yet will I fear none ill:
For thou art with me; and thy rod
    and staff me comfort still.
My table thou hast furnished
    in presence of my foes;
My head thou dost with oil anoint,
    and my cup overflows.
                    Psalm xxiii. 1

9 The race that long in darkness pin'd
have seen a glorious light.
                    Paraphrase 19. Isaiah ix. 2–8

EDMUND HAMILTON SEARS
1810–1876

10 It came upon the midnight clear,
    That glorious song of old,
From Angels bending near the earth
    To touch their harps of gold;
'Peace on the earth, good will to man
    From Heaven's all gracious King.'
The world in solemn stillness lay
    To hear the angels sing.
        The Christian Register (1850).
        That Glorious Song of Old

ALAN SEEGER 1888–1916

11 I have a rendezvous with Death
At some disputed barricade.
        I Have a Rendezvous with Death

SIR JOHN ROBERT SEELEY
1834–1895

12 We [the English] seem, as it were, to
have conquered and peopled half the
world in a fit of absence of mind.
        The Expansion of England, Lec-
        ture I

JOHN SELDEN 1584–1654

13 Ignorance of the law excuses no man;
not that all men know the law, but
because 'tis an excuse every man will
plead, and no man can tell how to confute him.   *Table Talk*, p. 99. *Law*

14 Take a straw and throw it up into the
air, you shall see by that which way
the wind is.   *Ib.* 105. *Libels*

15 Pleasure is nothing else but the intermission of pain.   *Ib.* 132. *Pleasure*

WALTER CARRUTHERS
SELLAR 1898–1951
and
ROBERT JULIAN YEATMAN
contemporary

16 1066, And All That.   *Title of Book*

17 The Roman Conquest was, however,
a *Good Thing*.
                    1066, And All That, ch. 1

18 Napoleon's armies always used to
march on their stomachs, shouting:
'Vive l'Intérieur!'   *Ib.* ch. 48

19 A Bad Thing: America was thus
clearly top nation, and History came
to a .   *Ib.* ch. 62

SENECA d. A.D. 65

20 Contra bonum morem.
    Against good custom.
                    Dialogues, VI. i. 2

ROBERT WILLIAM SERVICE
1874–

1 The lady that's known as Lou.
Songs of a Sourdough. The Shooting of Dan McGrew

EDWARD SEXBY d. 1658

2 Killing no Murder Briefly Discourst in Three Questions.
Title of Pamphlet (1657)

RICHARD SHACKLOCK c. 1575

3 Proud as peacocks.
Hatchet of Heresies (1565), p. 26b

THOMAS SHADWELL 1642?–1692

4 'Tis the way of all flesh.
The Sullen Lovers, v. ii

5 And wit's the noblest frailty of the mind. *A True Widow, II. i*

6 I am, out of the ladies' company, like a fish out of the water. *Ib.*

WILLIAM SHAKESPEARE
1564–1616

In the references the line number is given without brackets where the scene is all verse up to the quotation and the line number is certain. It is given in square brackets where prose makes it variable, and the references are to the Oxford Standard Authors Shakespeare in one volume.

7   It were all one
That I should love a bright particular star
And think to wed it, he is so above me.
All's Well That Ends Well, I. i. [97]

8 My friends were poor but honest.
Ib. iii. [203]

9 They say miracles are past.
Ib. II. iii. [1]

10 A young man married is a man that's marred. *Ib. [315]*

11 I know a man that had this trick of melancholy sold a goodly manor for a song. *Ib. III. ii. [8]*

12 Where's my serpent of old Nile?
Antony and Cleopatra, I. v. 25

13 My salad days,
When I was green in judgment. *Ib. 73*

14 I do not much dislike the matter, but The manner of his speech.
Ib. II. ii. 117

15 The barge she sat in, like a burnish'd throne,
Burn'd on the water; the poop was beaten gold,
Purple the sails, and so perfumed, that The winds were love-sick with them, the oars were silver,

Which to the tune of flutes kept stroke, and made
The water which they beat to follow faster,
As amorous of their strokes. For her own person,
It beggar'd all description; she did lie In her pavilion,—cloth-of-gold of tissue,—
O'er-picturing that Venus where we see
The fancy outwork nature; on each side her
Stood pretty-dimpled boys, like smiling Cupids,
With divers-colour'd fans, whose wind did seem
To glow the delicate cheeks which they did cool,
And what they undid did.
Antony and Cleopatra, II. ii. [199]

16 Age cannot wither her, nor custom stale
Her infinite variety; other women cloy
The appetites they feed, but she makes hungry
Where most she satisfies. *Ib. [243]*

17 Let's have one other gaudy night.
Ib. III. xi. 182

18 Unarm, Eros; the long day's task is done,
And we must sleep. *Ib. IV. xii. 35*

19 I am dying, Egypt, dying; only I here importune death awhile, until Of many thousand kisses the poor last
I lay upon thy lips. *Ib. xiii. 18*

20   A Roman by a Roman
Valiantly vanquished. *Ib. 57*

21   O! see my women,
The crown o' the earth doth melt. My lord!
O! wither'd is the garland of the war, The soldier's pole is fall'n; young boys and girls
Are level now with men; the odds is gone,
And there is nothing left remarkable Beneath the visiting moon. *Ib. 62*

22   What's brave, what's noble,
Let's do it after the high Roman fashion,
And make death proud to take us.
Ib. 86

23 Finish, good lady; the bright day is done,
And we are for the dark.
Ib. v. ii. 192

24   Antony
Shall be brought drunken forth, and I shall see
Some squeaking Cleopatra boy my greatness
I' the posture of a whore. *Ib. 217*

1 I know that a woman is a dish for the
gods, if the devil dress her not.
Antony and Cleopatra, v. ii. [274]

2   I have
Immortal longings in me.   *Ib.* [282]

3   Husband, I come:
Now to that name my courage prove
my title!
I am fire and air; my other elements
I give to baser life.   *Ib.* [289]

4 CLEOPATRA:
Come, thou mortal wretch
With thy sharp teeth this knot intrin-
sicate
Of life at once untie; poor venomous
fool,
Be angry, and dispatch. O! couldst
thou speak,
That I might hear thee call great
Cæsar ass
Unpolicied.
CHARMIAN:
O eastern star!
CLEOPATRA: Peace! peace!
Dost thou not see my baby at my
breast,
That sucks the nurse asleep?   *Ib.* [305]

5 Now boast thee, death, in thy possession lies
A lass unparallel'd.   *Ib.* [317]

6 It is well done, and fitting for a
princess
Descended of so many royal kings.
Ib. [328]

7 Well said: that was laid on with a
trowel.   *As You Like It*, I. ii. [113]

8 Hereafter, in a better world than this,
I shall desire more love and knowledge
of you.   *Ib.* [301]

9 Sweet are the uses of adversity,
Which like the toad, ugly and venomous,
Wears yet a precious jewel in his
head;
And this our life, exempt from public
haunt,
Finds tongues in trees, books in the
running brooks,
Sermons in stones, and good in
everything.   *Ib.* II. i. 12

10 Ay, now am I in Arden; the more fool
I. When I was at home I was in a
better place; but travellers must be
content.   *Ib.* iv. [16]

11   As true a lover
As ever sigh'd upon a midnight pillow.
Ib. [26]

12 Thou speakest wiser than thou art
ware of.   *Ib.* [57]

13 Under the greenwood tree
Who loves to lie with me,
And turn his merry note
Unto the sweet bird's throat,

Come hither, come hither, come
hither:
Here shall he see
No enemy
But winter and rough weather.
As You Like It, II. v. 1

14 I can suck melancholy out of a song
as a weasel sucks eggs.   *Ib.* [12]

15 Who doth ambition shun
And loves to live i' the sun,
Seeking the food he eats,
And pleas'd with what he gets.
Ib. [38]

16 'Call me not fool till heaven hath
sent me fortune.'
And then he drew a dial from his
poke,
And, looking on it with lack-lustre eye,
Says very wisely, 'It is ten o'clock;
Thus may we see,' quoth he, 'how the
world wags.'   *Ib.* vii. 19

17 And so, from hour to hour, we ripe
and ripe,
And then from hour to hour, we rot
and rot:
And thereby hangs a tale.   *Ib.* 26

18 A worthy fool! Motley's the only wear.
Ib. 34

19 If ever you have look'd on better days,
If ever been where bells have knoll'd
to church,
If ever sat at any good man's feast,
If ever from your eyelids wip'd a tear,
And know what 'tis to pity, and be
pitied,
Let gentleness my strong enforcement
be.   *Ib.* 109

20   All the world's a stage,
And all the men and women merely
players:
They have their exits and their en-
trances;
And one man in his time plays many
parts,
His acts being seven ages. At first the
infant,
Mewling and puking in the nurse's
arms.
And then the whining schoolboy,
with his satchel,
And shining morning face, creeping
like snail
Unwillingly to school. And then the
lover,
Sighing like furnace, with a woful
ballad
Made to his mistress' eyebrow. Then
a soldier,
Full of strange oaths, and bearded
like the pard,
Jealous in honour, sudden and quick
in quarrel,
Seeking the bubble reputation
Even in the cannon's mouth. And
then the justice,

In fair round belly with good capon
 lin'd,
With eyes severe, and beard of formal
 cut,
Full of wise saws and modern in-
 stances;
And so he plays his part. The sixth
 age shifts
Into the lean and slipper'd pantaloon,
With spectacles on nose and pouch on
 side,
His youthful hose well sav'd a world
 too wide
For his shrunk shank; and his big
 manly voice,
Turning again towards childish treble,
 pipes
And whistles in his sound. Last scene
 of all,
That ends this strange eventful history,
Is second childishness, and mere
 oblivion,
Sans teeth, sans eyes, sans taste, sans
 everything.
              As You Like It, II. vii. 139

1 Blow, blow, thou winter wind,
  Thou art not so unkind
       As man's ingratitude:
  Thy tooth is not so keen,
  Because thou art not seen,
       Although thy breath be rude.
  Heigh-ho! sing, heigh-ho! unto the
   green holly:
  Most friendship is feigning, most
   loving mere folly.
       Then heigh-ho! the holly!
       This life is most jolly.

2 Freeze, freeze, thou bitter sky,
  That dost not bite so nigh
       As benefits forgot:
  Though thou the waters warp,
  Thy sting is not so sharp
       As friend remember'd not.   *Ib.* 174

3 Run, run, Orlando: carve on every tree
  The fair, the chaste, and unexpressive
   she.   *Ib.* III. ii. 9

4 Thou art in a parlous state.   *Ib.* [46]

5 Let us make an honourable retreat;
  though not with bag and baggage, yet
  with scrip and scrippage.   *Ib.* [170]

6   Down on your knees,
  And thank heaven, fasting, for a good
  man's love.   *Ib.* v. 57

7 Dead shepherd, now I find thy saw of
   might:
  'Who ever lov'd that lov'd not at first
   sight?'   *Ib.* 81

8 For now I am in a holiday humour.
              Ib. IV. i [70]

9 When you were gravelled for lack of
  matter.   *Ib.* [76]

10 Men have died from time to time, and
   worms have eaten them, but not for
   love.   *Ib.* [110]

11 Men are April when they woo,
   December when they wed: maids are
   May when they are maids, but the
   sky changes when they are wives.
              As You Like It, IV. i. [153]

12 It was a lover and his lass,
       With a hey, and a ho, and a hey
        nonino,
   That o'er the green cornfield did pass,
       In the spring time, the only pretty
        ring time,
   When birds do sing, hey ding a ding,
        ding;
   Sweet lovers love the spring.

   Between the acres of the rye,
       With a hey, and a ho, and a hey
        nonino,
   These pretty country folks would lie,
   In the spring time, &c.   *Ib.* v. iii. [18]

13 An ill-favoured thing, sir, but mine
   own.   *Ib.* iv. [60]

14 The retort courteous . . . the quip
   modest . . . the reply churlish . . . the
   reproof valiant . . . the countercheck
   quarrelsome . . . the lie circumstantial
   . . . the lie direct.   *Ib.* [96]

15 He uses his folly like a stalking-horse,
   and under the presentation of that he
   shoots his wit.   *Ib.* [112]

16 If it be true that 'good wine needs no
   bush', 'tis true that a good play
   needs no epilogue.   *Ib. Epilogue* [3]

17   They threw their caps
   As they would hang them on the
    horns o' the moon,
   Shouting their emulation.
              Coriolanus, I. i. [218]

18 Hear you this Triton of the minnows?
    mark you
   His absolute 'shall'?   *Ib.* III. i. 88

19 If you have writ your annals true, 'tis
    there,
   That, like an eagle in a dove-cot, I
   Flutter'd your Volscians in Corioli:
   Alone I did it.   *Ib.* v. v. 114

20 Hark! hark! the lark at heaven's gate
    sings,
   And Phœbus 'gins arise,
   His steeds to water at those springs
       On chalic'd flowers that lies;
   And winking Mary-buds begin
       To ope their golden eyes:
   With everything that pretty is,
       My lady sweet, arise!
              Cymbeline, II. iii. [22]

21 I have not slept one wink.   *Ib.* iv. [103]

22 Fear no more the heat o' the sun,
   Nor the furious winter's rages;
   Thou thy worldly task hast done,
   Home art gone and ta'en thy wages:
   Golden lads and girls all must,
   As chimney-sweepers, come to dust.
              Ib. IV. ii. 258

1 You come most carefully upon your
hour. *Hamlet*, I. i. 6

2 For this relief much thanks; 'tis bitter
cold,
And I am sick at heart. *Ib.* 8

3 In the most high and palmy state of
Rome,
A little ere the mightiest Julius fell,
The graves stood tenantless and the
sheeted dead
Did squeak and gibber in the Roman
streets. *Ib.* 113

4 It faded on the crowing of the cock.
Some say that ever 'gainst that season
comes
Wherein our Saviour's birth is celebrated,
The bird of dawning singeth all night
long;
And then, they say, no spirit can walk
abroad;
The nights are wholesome; then no
planets strike,
No fairy takes, nor witch hath power
to charm,
So hallow'd and so gracious is the
time. *Ib.* 157

5 But, look, the morn, in russet mantle
clad,
Walks o'er the dew of yon high eastern
hill. *Ib.* 166

6 The memory be green. *Ib.* ii. 2

7 A little more than kin, and less than
kind. *Ib.* 65

8 Not so, my lord; I am too much i'
the sun. *Ib.* 67

9 Seems, madam! Nay, it is; I know not
'seems'. *Ib.* 76

10 But I have that within which passeth
show;
These but the trappings and the suits
of woe. *Ib.* 85

11 O! that this too too solid flesh would
melt,
Thaw, and resolve itself into a dew;
Or that the Everlasting had not fix'd
His canon 'gainst self-slaughter! O
God! O God!
How weary, stale, flat, and unprofit-
able
Seem to me all the uses of this world.
Fie on't! O fie! 'tis an unweeded
garden,
That grows to seed; things rank and
gross in nature
Possess it merely. That it should
come to this!
But two months dead: nay, not so
much, not two:
So excellent a king; that was, to this,
Hyperion to a satyr: so loving to my
mother,
That he might not beteem the winds
of heaven

Visit her face too roughly. Heaven and
earth!
Must I remember? Why, she would
hang on him,
As if increase of appetite had grown
But what it fed on; and yet, within
a month,
Let me not think on't: Frailty, thy
name is woman!
A little month; or ere those shoes were
old
With which she follow'd my poor
father's body,
Like Niobe, all tears; why she, even
she,—
O God! a beast, that wants discourse
of reason,
Would have mourn'd longer,—married
with mine uncle,
My father's brother, but no more like
my father
Than I to Hercules. *Hamlet*, I. ii.

12 We'll teach you to drink deep ere you
depart. *Ib.* 175

13 Thrift, thrift, Horatio! the funeral
bak'd meats
Did coldly furnish forth the marriage
tables.
Would I had met my dearest foe in
heaven
Ere I had ever seen that day, Horatio!
Ib. 180

14 In my mind's eye, Horatio. *Ib.* 185

15 He was a man, take him for all in all,
I shall not look upon his like again.
Ib. 187

16 In the dead vast and middle of the
night. *Ib.* 198

17 But answer made it none. *Ib.* 215

18 A countenance more in sorrow than
in anger. *Ib.* 231

19 All is not well;
I doubt some foul play. *Ib.* 254

20 Do not, as some ungracious pastors do,
Show me the steep and thorny way to
heaven,
Whiles, like a puff'd and reckless
libertine,
Himself the primrose path of dalliance
treads,
And recks not his own rede. *Ib.* iii. 47

21 And these few precepts in thy memory
Look thou character. Give thy
thoughts no tongue,
Nor any unproportion'd thought his
act.
Be thou familiar, but by no means
vulgar;
The friends thou hast, and their adoption tried,
Grapple them to thy soul with hoops
of steel;
But do not dull thy palm with entertainment

Of each new-hatch'd, unfledg'd comrade. Beware
Of entrance to a quarrel; but, being in,
Bear't that th' opposed may beware of thee.
Give every man thine ear, but few thy voice;
Take each man's censure, but reserve thy judgment.
Costly thy habit as thy purse can buy,
But not express'd in fancy; rich, not gaudy;
For the apparel oft proclaims the man,
And they in France of the best rank and station
Are most select and generous, chief in that.
Neither a borrower, nor a lender be;
For loan oft loses both itself and friend,
And borrowing dulls the edge of husbandry,
This above all: to thine own self be true,
And it must follow, as the night the day,
Thou canst not then be false to any man.
Farewell; my blessing season this in thee! *Hamlet*, I. iii. 58

1   You speak like a green girl,
Unsifted in such perilous circumstance.   *Ib.* 101

2 HAMLET:
The air bites shrewdly; it is very cold.
HORATIO:
It is a nipping and an eager air.
             Ib. iv. 1

3 But to my mind,—though I am native here,
And to the manner born,—it is a custom
More honour'd in the breach than the observance.   *Ib.* 14

4 Angels and ministers of grace defend us!   *Ib.* 39

5   Unhand me, gentlemen,
By heaven! I'll make a ghost of him that lets me.   *Ib.* 84

6 Something is rotten in the state of Denmark.   *Ib.* 90

7   But that I am forbid
To tell the secrets of my prison-house,
I could a tale unfold whose lightest word
Would harrow up thy soul, freeze thy young blood,
Make thy two eyes, like stars, start from their spheres,
Thy knotted and combined locks to part,
And each particular hair to stand an end,
Like quills upon the fretful porpentine.   *Ib.* v. 13

8 Murder most foul, as in the best it is;
But this most foul, strange, and unnatural.   *Hamlet*, I. v. 27

9 And duller shouldst thou be than the fat weed
That rots itself in ease on Lethe wharf.   *Ib.* 32

10   O my prophetic soul!
My uncle!   *Ib.* 40

11 But, soft! methinks I scent the morning air.   *Ib.* 58

12 Cut off even in the blossoms of my sin,
Unhousel'd, disappointed, unanel'd,
No reckoning made, but sent to my account
With all my imperfections on my head:
O, horrible! O, horrible! most horrible!
If thou hast nature in thee, bear it not.
           Ib. 76

13   Leave her to heaven,
And to those thorns that in her bosom lodge,
To prick and sting her.   *Ib.* 86

14 O most pernicious woman!
O villain, villain, smiling, damned villain!
My tables,—meet it is I set it down,
That one may smile, and smile, and be a villain;
At least I'm sure it may be so in Denmark.   *Ib.* 105

15 Well said, old mole! canst work i' the earth so fast?   *Ib.* 162

16 There are more things in heaven and earth, Horatio,
Than are dreamt of in your philosophy.   *Ib.* 166

17 To put an antic disposition on.
          Ib. 172

18 Rest, rest, perturbed spirit!   *Ib.* 182

19 The time is out of joint; O cursed spite,
That ever I was born to set it right!
          Ib. 188

20 By indirections find directions out.
       Ib. II. i. 66

21 Brevity is the soul of wit.   *Ib.* ii. 90

22 More matter with less art.   *Ib.* 95

23 That he is mad, 'tis true; 'tis true 'tis pity;
And pity 'tis 'tis true: a foolish figure;
But farewell it, for I will use no art.
          Ib. 97

24 Still harping on my daughter.
         Ib. [190]

25 POLONIUS:
What do you read, my lord?
HAMLET:
Words, words, words.   *Ib.* [195]

26 Though this be madness, yet there is method in it.   *Ib.* [211]

1 HAMLET:
Then you live about her waist, or in
the middle of her favours?
GUILDENSTERN:
Faith, her privates we.
Hamlet, II. ii. 240

2 There is nothing either good or bad,
but thinking makes it so. *Ib.* [259]

3 O God! I could be bounded in a nut-
shell, and count myself a king of infinite space, were it not that I have
bad dreams. *Ib.* [263]

4 It goes so heavily with my disposition
that this goodly frame, the earth,
seems to me a sterile promontory; this
most excellent canopy, the air, look
you, this brave o'erhanging firmament, this majestical roof fretted with
golden fire, why, it appears no other
thing to me but a foul and pestilent
congregation of vapours. What a
piece of work is a man! How noble in
reason! how infinite in faculty! in
form, in moving, how express and
admirable! in action how like an
angel! in apprehension how like a
god! the beauty of the world! the
paragon of animals! And yet, to me,
what is this quintessence of dust? man
delights not me; no, nor woman
neither, though, by your smiling,
you seem to say so. *Ib.* [316]

5 I am but mad north-north-west;
when the wind is southerly, I know
a hawk from a handsaw.[1] *Ib.* [405]

[1] = heron-shaw, or heron.

6 One fair daughter and no more,
The which he loved passing well.
Ib. [435]

7 The play, I remember, pleased not
the million; 'twas caviare to the
general. *Ib.* [465]

8 The mobled queen. *Ib.* [533]

9 Good my lord, will you see the players
well bestowed? Do you hear, let them
be well used; for they are the abstracts
and brief chronicles of the time: after
your death you were better have a
bad epitaph than their ill report while
you live. *Ib.* [553]

10 Use every man after his desert, and
who should 'scape whipping?
Ib. [561]

11 O, what a rogue and peasant slave am I:
Is it not monstrous that this player
here,
But in a fiction, in a dream of passion,
Could force his soul so to his own con-
ceit
That from her working all his visage
wann'd,
Tears in his eyes, distraction in 's
aspect,

A broken voice, and his whole function
suiting
With forms to his conceit? and all for
nothing!
For Hecuba!
What's Hecuba to him or he to
Hecuba
That he should weep for her?
Hamlet, II. ii. [584]

12 The play's the thing
Wherein I'll catch the conscience of
the king. *Ib.* [641]

13 To be, or not to be: that is the ques-
tion:
Whether 'tis nobler in the mind to
suffer
The slings and arrows of outrageous
fortune,
Or to take arms against a sea of
troubles,
And by opposing end them? To die:
to sleep;
No more; and, by a sleep to say we end
The heart-ache and the thousand
natural shocks
That flesh is heir to, 'tis a consum-
mation
Devoutly to be wish'd. To die, to
sleep;
To sleep: perchance to dream: ay,
there's the rub;
For in that sleep of death what dreams
may come
When we have shuffled off this mortal
coil,
Must give us pause. There's the re-
spect
That makes calamity of so long life;
For who would bear the whips and
scorns of time,
The oppressor's wrong, the proud
man's contumely,
The pangs of dispriz'd love, the law's
delay,
The insolence of office, and the spurns
That patient merit of the unworthy
takes,
When he himself might his quietus
make
With a bare bodkin? Who would
fardels bear,
To grunt and sweat under a weary
life,
But that the dread of something after
death,
The undiscover'd country from whose
bourn
No traveller returns, puzzles the will,
And makes us rather bear those ills
we have,
Than fly to others that we know not
of?
Thus conscience doth make cowards
of us all;
And thus the native hue of resolution
Is sicklied o'er with the pale cast of
thought,

And enterprises of great pith and
moment
With this regard their currents turn
awry,
And lose the name of action.
                    Hamlet, III. i. 56

1   Nymph, in thy orisons
Be all my sins remember'd.   *Ib.* 89

2   For, to the noble mind,
Rich gifts wax poor when givers prove
unkind.   *Ib.* 100

3 Get thee to a nunnery.   *Ib.* [124]

4 I am myself indifferent honest.
                    Ib. [125]

5 Be thou as chaste as ice, as pure as
snow, thou shalt not escape calumny.
                    Ib. [142]

6 O! what a noble mind is here o'er-
thrown:
The courtier's, soldier's, scholar's, eye,
tongue, sword;
The expectancy and rose of the fair
state,
The glass of fashion, and the mould of
form,
The observed of all observers, quite,
quite down!
And I, of ladies most deject and
wretched,
That suck'd the honey of his music
vows,
Now see that noble and most sovereign
reason,
Like sweet bells jangled, out of tune
and harsh;
That unmatch'd form and figure of
blown youth,
Blasted with ecstasy: O! woe is me,
To have seen what I have seen, see
what I see!   *Ib.* [159]

7 Speak the speech, I pray you, as I
pronounced it to you, trippingly on the
tongue; but if you mouth it, as many
of your players do, I had as lief the
town-crier spoke my lines. Nor do not
saw the air too much with your hand,
thus; but use all gently: for in the
very torrent, tempest, and—as I may
say—whirlwind of passion, you must
acquire and beget a temperance, that
may give it smoothness. O! it offends
me to the soul to hear a robustious
periwig-pated fellow tear a passion to
tatters, to very rags, to split the ears
of the groundlings, who for the most
part are capable of nothing but inexplicable dumb-shows and noise: I
would have such a fellow whipped for
o'erdoing Termagant; it out-herods
Herod: pray you, avoid it.   *Ib.* ii. 1

8 Be not too tame neither, but let your
own discretion be your tutor: suit the
action to the word, the word to the
action; with this special observance,

that you o'erstep not the modesty of
nature.   *Hamlet*, III. ii. [19]

9 The purpose of playing, whose end,
both at the first and now, was and is,
to hold, as 'twere, the mirror up to
nature.   *Ib.* [24]

10 To show . . . the very age and body
of the time his form and pressure.
                    Ib. [26]

11   Give me that man
That is not passion's slave, and I will
wear him
In my heart's core, ay, in my heart of
heart,
As I do thee. Something too much of
this.   *Ib.* [76]

12 Here's metal more attractive.
                    Ib. [117]

13 The lady doth protest too much, methinks.   *Ib.* [242]

14 We that have free souls, it touches us
not: let the galled jade wince, our
withers are unwrung.   *Ib.* [255]

15 What! frighted with false fire?
                    Ib. [282]

16 So runs the world away.   *Ib.* [289]

17 You would play upon me; you would
seem to know my stops; you would
pluck out the heart of my mystery;
you would sound me from my lowest
note to the top of my compass.
                    Ib. [387]

18 HAMLET:
Do you see yonder cloud that's al-
most in shape of a camel?
POLONIUS:
By the mass, and 'tis like a camel,
indeed.
HAMLET:
Methinks it is like a weasel.
POLONIUS:
It is backed like a weasel.
HAMLET:
Or like a whale?
POLONIUS:
Very like a whale.   *Ib.* [400]

19 They fool me to the top of my bent.
                    Ib. [408]

20 'Tis now the very witching time of
night.   *Ib.* [413]

21 Let me be cruel, not unnatural;
I will speak daggers to her, but use
none.   *Ib.* [420]

22 O! my offence is rank, it smells to
heaven.   *Ib.* iii. 36

23 Now might I do it pat, now he is
praying.   *Ib.* 73

24 How now! a rat? Dead, for a ducat,
dead!   *Ib.* iv. 23

25 Look here, upon this picture, and on
this.   *Ib.* 53

1   Speak no more;
Thou turn'st mine eyes into my very
     soul.   *Hamlet*, III. iv. 88

2 A king of shreds and patches.   *Ib.* 102

3   Mother, for love of grace,
Lay not that flattering unction to your
     soul.   *Ib.* 144

4 I must be cruel, only to be kind.
                   Ib. 178

5 For 'tis the sport to have the engi-
ner
Hoist with his own petar.   *Ib.* 206

6 How all occasions do inform against
me,
And spur my dull revenge!
             Ib. IV. iv. 32

7   Rightly to be great
Is not to stir without great argument,
But greatly to find quarrel in a straw
When honour's at the stake.   *Ib.* 53

8 How should I your true love know?
From another one?
By his cockle hat and staff,
And his sandal shoon.   *Ib.* v. [23]

9 He is dead and gone, lady,
He is dead and gone,
At his head a grass-green turf;
At his heels a stone.   *Ib.* [29]

10 Come, my coach! Good-night, ladies;
good-night, sweet ladies; good night,
good-night.   *Ib.* [72]

11 When sorrows come, they come not
single spies,
But in battalions.   *Ib.* [78]

12   We have done but greenly
In hugger-mugger to inter him.
             Ib. [83]

13 There's such divinity doth hedge a
king,
That treason can but peep to what it
would.   *Ib.* [123]

14 There's rosemary; that's for remembrance; pray, love, remember: and
there is pansies, that's for thoughts.
             Ib. [174]

15 You must wear your rue with a difference. There's a daisy; I would give
you some violets, but they withered
all when my father died.   *Ib.* [181]

16 They say he made a good end.
             Ib. [184]

17 And where the offence is let the great
axe fall.   *Ib.* [218]

18 There is a willow grows aslant a brook,
That shows his hoar leaves in the
glassy stream;
There with fantastic garlands did she
come,
Of crow-flowers, nettles, daisies, and
long purples,

That liberal shepherds give a grosser
name,
But our cold maids do dead men's
fingers call them:
There, on the pendent boughs her
coronet weeds
Clambering to hang, an envious sliver
broke,
When down her weedy trophies and
herself
Fell in the weeping brook. Her clothes
spread wide,
And, mermaid-like, awhile they bore
her up;
Which time she chanted snatches of
old tunes,
As one incapable of her own distress.
          Hamlet, IV. vii. 167

19 Cudgel thy brains no more about it,
for your dull ass will not mend his
pace with beating.   *Ib.* v. i. [61]

20 Alas! poor Yorick. I knew him,
Horatio; a fellow of infinite jest, of
most excellent fancy; he hath borne
me on his back a thousand times; and
now, how abhorred in my imagination
it is! my gorge rises at it. Here hung
those lips that I have kissed I know
not how oft. Where be your gibes now?
your gambols? your songs? your
flashes of merriment, that were wont to
set the table on a roar? Not one now,
to mock your own grinning? quite
chap-fallen? Now get you to my lady's
chamber, and tell her, let her paint
an inch thick, to this favour she must
come.   *Ib.* [201]

21 Imperious Cæsar, dead, and turn'd to
clay,
Might stop a hole to keep the wind
away.   *Ib.* [235]

22   Lay her i' the earth;
And from her fair and unpolluted
flesh
May violets spring! I tell thee, chur-
lish priest,
A ministering angel shall my sister be,
When thou liest howling.   *Ib.* [260]

23 Sweets to the sweet: farewell!
             Ib. [265]

24 There's a divinity that shapes our
ends,
Rough-hew them how we will.
             Ib. ii. 10

25 It did me yeoman's service.   *Ib.* 36

26 Not a whit, we defy augury; there's
a special providence in the fall of a
sparrow. If it be now, 'tis not to come;
if it be not to come, it will be now;
if it be not now, yet it will come: the
readiness is all.   *Ib.* [232]

27 A hit, a very palpable hit.   *Ib.* [295]

28   This fell sergeant, death,
Is strict in his arrest.   *Ib.* [350]

1 Report me and my cause aright.
Hamlet, v. ii. [353]

2 I am more an antique Roman than a Dane. *Ib.* [355]

3 Horatio, what a wounded name,
Things standing thus unknown, shall
live behind me.
If thou didst ever hold me in thy heart,
Absent thee from felicity awhile,
And in this harsh world draw thy
breath in pain,
To tell my story. *Ib.* [358]

4 The rest is silence. *Ib.* [372]

5 Now cracks a noble heart. Good-
night, sweet prince,
And flights of angels sing thee to thy
rest! *Ib.* [373]

6 Let us be Diana's foresters, gentlemen
of the shade, minions of the moon.
King Henry IV, Part I, i. ii. [28]

7 Old father antick, the law. *Ib.* 69

8 O! the blood more stirs
To rouse a lion than to start a hare.
Ib. iii. 192

9 By heaven methinks it were an easy
leap
To pluck bright honour from the
pale-fac'd moon,
Or dive into the bottom of the deep,
Where fathom-line could never touch
the ground,
And pluck up drowned honour by the
locks;
So he that doth redeem her thence
might wear
Without corrival all her dignities:
But out upon this half-fac'd fellow-
ship! *Ib.* 201

10 I know a trick worth two of that.
Ib. ii. i. [40]

11 Falstaff sweats to death
And lards the lean earth as he walks
along. *Ib.* ii. [119]

12 Out of this nettle, danger, we pluck
this flower, safety. *Ib.* iii. [11]

13 Show it a fair pair of heels.
Ib. iv. [52]

14 Nay that's past praying for. *Ib.* [214]

15 No, my good lord; banish Peto, banish
Bardolph, banish Poins; but for
sweet Jack Falstaff, kind Jack Falstaff, true Jack Falstaff, valiant Jack
Falstaff, and therefore more valiant,
being, as he is, old Jack Falstaff,
banish not him thy Harry's company:
banish not him thy Harry's company:
banish plump Jack and banish all the
world. *Ib.* [528]

16 O monstrous! but one half-penny-
worth of bread to this intolerable deal
of sack! *Ib.* [598]

17 GLENDOWER:
I can call spirits from the vasty deep.
HOTSPUR:
Why, so can I, or so can any man;
But will they come when you do call
for them?
King Henry IV, Part I, iii. i. [53]

18 O! while you live, tell truth, and
shame the devil! *Ib.* [62]

19 Now I perceive the devil understands
Welsh. *Ib.* [233]

20 My near'st and dearest enemy.
Ib. ii. 123

21 Shall I not take mine ease in mine inn?
Ib. iii. [91]

22 But thought's the slave of life, and
life time's fool;
And time, that takes survey of all the
world,
Must have a stop. *Ib.* iv. iv. [81]

23 Fare thee well, great heart!
Ill-weav'd ambition, how much art
thou shrunk!
When that this body did contain a
spirit,
A kingdom for it was too small a
bound;
But now two paces of the vilest earth
Is room enough: this earth, that bears
thee dead,
Bears not alive so stout a gentleman.
Ib. [87]

24 Poor Jack, farewell!
I could have better spar'd a better
man. *Ib.* v. iv. [103]

25 The better part of valour is discretion.
Ib. [120]

26 Lord, Lord, how this world is given to
lying! I grant you I was down and out
of breath; and so was he; but we rose
both at an instant, and fought a long
hour by Shrewsbury clock. *Ib.* [148]

27 I am not only witty in myself, but the
cause that wit is in other men.
King Henry IV, Part II, i. ii. [10]

28 I am as poor as Job, my lord, but not
so patient. *Ib.* [145]

29 He hath eaten me out of house and
home. *Ib.* ii. i. [82]

30 Then, happy low, lie down!
Uneasy lies the head that wears a
crown. *Ib.* iii. i. 30

31 We have heard the chimes at midnight. *Ib.* ii. [231]

32 I care not; a man can die but once;
we owe God a death. *Ib.* [253]

33 Thy wish was father, Harry, to that
thought. *Ib.* iv. v. 91

34 Under which king, Bezonian? speak,
or die! *Ib.* v. iii. [115]

1 I know thee not, old man: fall to thy
prayers;
How ill white hairs become a fool and
jester!
   King Henry IV, Part II, IV. v. [52]

2 O! for a Muse of fire, that would
ascend
The brightest heaven of invention.
   King Henry V, Chorus, 1

3   Can this cockpit hold
The vasty fields of France? or may we
cram
Within this wooden O the very casques
That did affright the air at Agincourt?
   Ib. 11

4 His present and your pains we thank
you for:
When we have match'd our rackets to
these balls,
We will in France, by God's grace,
play a set
Shall strike his father's crown into the
hazard.   *Ib.* I. ii. 260

5 Now all the youth of England are on
fire,
And silken dalliance in the wardrobe
lies;
Now thrive the armourers, and
honour's thought
Reigns solely in the breast of every
man:
They sell the pasture now to buy the
horse,
Following the mirror of all Christian
kings,
With winged heels, as English Mer-
curies.
For now sits Expectation in the air
And hides a sword from hilts unto the
point
With crowns imperial, crowns and
coronets,
Promis'd to Harry and his followers.
   Ib. II. Chorus, 1

6 He's in Arthur's bosom, if ever man
went to Arthur's bosom. A' made a
finer end, and went away an it
had been any christom child; a'
parted even just between twelve and
one, even at the turning o' the tide:
for after I saw him fumble with the
sheets and play with flowers and
smile upon his fingers' ends, I knew
there was but one way; for his nose
was as sharp as a pen, and a' babbled
of green fields. [Theobald's emen-
dation of the Folio's reading: 'A
table of green fields'.]   *Ib.* iii. [9]

7 Yes, that a' did; and said they were
devils incarnate.   *Ib.* [33]

8 Once more unto the breach, dear
friends, once more;
Or close the wall up with our English
dead!
In peace there's nothing so becomes a
man

As modest stillness and humility:
But when the blast of war blows in our
ears,
Then imitate the action of the tiger;
Stiffen the sinews, summon up the
blood,
Disguise fair nature with hard-
favour'd rage;
Then lend the eye a terrible aspect.
   King Henry V, III. i. 1

9 I see you stand like greyhounds in
the slips,
Straining upon the start. The game's
afoot:
Follow your spirit; and, upon this
charge
Cry 'God for Harry! England and
Saint George!'   *Ib.* 31

10 Men of few words are the best men.
   Ib. ii. [40]

11 A little touch of Harry in the night.
   Ib. IV. Chorus, 47

12 I think the king is but a man, as I am:
the violet smells to him as it doth to
me.   *Ib.* i. [106]

13 Every subject's duty is the king's; but
every subject's soul is his own.
   Ib. [189]

14   What infinite heart's ease
Must kings neglect, that private men
enjoy!   *Ib.* [256]

15 'Tis not the balm, the sceptre and the
ball,
The sword, the mace, the crown im-
perial,
The intertissued robe of gold and pearl,
The farced title running 'fore the king,
The throne he sits on, nor the tide of
pomp
That beats upon the high shore of this
world,
No, not all these, thrice-gorgeous
ceremony,
Not all these, laid in bed majestical,
Can sleep so soundly as the wretched
slave,
Who with a body fill'd and vacant
mind
Gets him to rest, cramm'd with dis-
tressful bread;
Never sees horrid night, the child of
hell,
But, like a lackey, from the rise to set
Sweats in the eye of Phœbus, and all
night
Sleeps in Elysium; next day after
dawn,
Doth rise and help Hyperion to his
horse,
And follows so the ever-running year
With profitable labour to his grave:
And, but for ceremony, such a wretch,
Winding up days with toil and nights
with sleep,
Hath the forehand and vantage of a
king.   *Ib.* [280]

1 O God of battles! steel my soldiers'
hearts;
Possess them not with fear.
King Henry V, IV. i. [309]

2 O! that we now had here
But one ten thousand of those men in
England
That do no work to-day. *Ib.* iii. 16

3 If we are mark'd to die, we are enow
To do our country loss; and if to live,
The fewer men, the greater share of
honour. *Ib.* 20

4 He which hath no stomach to this fight,
Let him depart; his passport shall be
made,
And crowns for convoy put into his
purse:
We would not die in that man's com-
pany
That fears his fellowship to die with us.
This day is called the feast of Crispian:
He that outlives this day and comes
safe home,
Will stand a tip-toe when this day is
nam'd,
And rouse him at the name of
Crispian.
He that shall live this day, and see old
age,
Will yearly on the vigil feast his neigh-
bours,
And say, 'To-morrow is Saint Cris-
pian:'
Then will he strip his sleeve and
show his scars,
And say, 'These wounds I had on
Crispin's day.'
Old men forget: yet all shall be forgot,
But he'll remember with advantages
What feats he did that day. Then
shall our names,
Familiar in his mouth as household
words,
Harry the King, Bedford and Exeter,
Warwick and Talbot, Salisbury and
Gloucester,
Be in their flowing cups freshly re-
member'd.
This story shall the good man teach
his son;
And Crispin Crispian shall ne'er go by,
From this day to the ending of the
world,
But we in it shall be remembered;
We few, we happy few, we band of
brothers;
For he to-day that sheds his blood
with me
Shall be my brother; be he ne'er so vile
This day shall gentle his condition:
And gentlemen in England, now a-bed
Shall think themselves accurs'd they
were not here,
And hold their manhoods cheap whiles
any speaks
That fought with us upon Saint
Crispin's day. *Ib.* 35

5 Expect Saint Martin's summer, halcyon days.
King Henry VI, Part I, I. ii. 131

6 Unbidden guests
Are often welcomest when they are
gone. *Ib.* II. ii. 55

7 What stronger breastplate than a
heart untainted!
Thrice is he arm'd that hath his
quarrel just,
And he but naked, though lock'd up
in steel,
Whose conscience with injustice is
corrupted.
King Henry VI, Part II, III. ii.
232

8 Forbear to judge, for we are sinners
all.
Close up his eyes, and draw the curtain
close;
And let us all to meditation.
Ib. iii. 31

9 The first thing we do, let's kill all the
lawyers. *Ib.* IV. ii. [86]

10 And Adam was a gardener. *Ib.* [146]

11 O tiger's heart wrapp'd in a woman's
hide!
King Henry VI, Part III, I. iv.
137

12 The mirror of all courtesy.
King Henry VIII, II. i. 53

13 Orpheus with his lute made trees,
And the mountain-tops that freeze,
Bow themselves when he did sing.
Ib. III. i. 3

14 Farewell! a long farewell, to all my
greatness!
This is the state of man: to-day he
puts forth
The tender leaves of hope; to-morrow
blossoms,
And bears his blushing honours thick
upon him;
The third day comes a frost, a killing
frost;
And, when he thinks, good easy man,
full surely
His greatness is a-ripening, nips his
root,
And then he falls, as I do. I have
ventur'd,
Like little wanton boys that swim on
bladders,
This many summers in a sea of glory,
But far beyond my depth: my high-
blown pride
At length broke under me, and now
has left me
Weary and old with service, to the
mercy
Of a rude stream that must for ever
hide me.
Vain pomp and glory of this world,
I hate ye:

I feel my heart new open'd. O how wretched
Is that poor man that hangs on princes' favours!
There is, betwixt that smile we would aspire to,
That sweet aspect of princes, and their ruin,
More pangs and fears than wars or women have;
And when he falls, he falls like Lucifer,
Never to hope again.
King Henry VIII, ii. 352

1 Had I but serv'd my God with half the zeal
I serv'd my king, he would not in mine age
Have left me naked to mine enemies.
Ib. 456

2 To dance attendance on their lordships' pleasures. *Ib.* v. ii. 30

3 Mad world! Mad kings! Mad composition! *King John*, II. i. 561

4 Bell, book, and candle shall not drive me back,
When gold and silver becks me to come on. *Ib.* III. iii. 12

5 Life is as tedious as a twice-told tale,
Vexing the dull ear of a drowsy man.
Ib. iv. 108

6 To gild refined gold, to paint the lily,
To throw a perfume on the violet,
To smooth the ice, or add another hue
Unto the rainbow, or with taper light
To seek the beauteous eye of heaven to garnish,
Is wasteful and ridiculous excess.
Ib. IV. ii. 11

7 I beg cold comfort. *Ib.* v. vii. 42

8 This England never did, nor never shall,
Lie at the proud foot of a conqueror,
But when it first did help to wound itself.
Now these her princes are come home again,
Come the three corners of the world in arms,
And we shall shock them: nought shall make us rue,
If England to itself do rest but true.
Ib. 112

9 You blocks, you stones, you worse than senseless things!
O you hard hearts, you cruel men of Rome,
Knew you not Pompey?
Julius Cæsar, I. i [39]

10 Beware the ides of March. *Ib.* ii. 18

11 Why, man, he doth bestride the narrow world
Like a Colossus; and we petty men
Walk under his huge legs, and peep about

To find ourselves dishonourable graves.
Men at some time are masters of their fates:
The fault, dear Brutus, is not in our stars,
But in ourselves, that we are underlings. *Julius Cæsar*, I. i. 134

12 For mine own part, it was Greek to me.
Ib. [288]

13 Let's carve him as a dish fit for the gods,
Not hew him as a carcass fit for hounds. *Ib.* II. i. 173

14 CALPHURNIA:
When beggars die, there are no comets seen;
The heavens themselves blaze forth the death of princes.
CÆSAR:
Cowards die many times before their deaths;
The valiant never taste of death but once.
Of all the wonders that I yet have heard,
It seems to me most strange that men should fear;
Seeing that death, a necessary end,
Will come when it will come.
Ib. ii. 30

15 CÆSAR:
The ides of March are come.
SOOTHSAYER:
Ay, Cæsar; but not gone. *Ib.* III. i. 1

16 If I could pray to move, prayers would move me;
But I am constant as the northern star,
Of whose true-fix'd and resting quality
There is no fellow in the firmament.
Ib. 59

17 Et tu, Brute? *Ib.* 77

18 O mighty Cæsar! dost thou lie so low?
Are all thy conquests, glories, triumphs, spoils,
Shrunk to this little measure? *Ib.* 148

19 Though last, not least in love. *Ib.* 189

20 O! pardon me, thou bleeding piece of earth,
That I am meek and gentle with these butchers;
Thou art the ruins of the noblest man
That ever lived in the tide of times.
Ib. 254

21 And Cæsar's spirit ranging for revenge,
With Ate by his side, come hot from hell,
Shall in these confines, with a monarch's voice
Cry, 'Havoc!' and let slip the dogs of war. *Ib.* 270

1 Not that I loved Cæsar less, but that
I loved Rome more.
Julius Cæsar, III. ii. [22]

2 As he was valiant, I honour him: but,
as he was ambitious, I slew him.
Ib. [27]

3 Friends, Romans, countrymen, lend
me your ears;
I come to bury Cæsar, not to praise
him.
The evil that men do lives after them,
The good is oft interred with their
bones;
So let it be with Cæsar. The noble
Brutus
Hath told you Cæsar was ambitious;
If it were so, it was a grievous fault;
And grievously hath Cæsar answer'd
it. *Ib.* [79]

4 For Brutus is an honourable man;
So are they all, all honourable men.
Ib. [88]

5 He was my friend, faithful and just to
me:
But Brutus says he was ambitious;
And Brutus is an honourable man.
Ib. [91]

6 But yesterday the word of Cæsar
might
Have stood against the world; now
lies he there,
And none so poor to do him reverence.
Ib. [124]

7 If you have tears, prepare to shed them
now.
You all do know this mantle: I re-
member
The first time ever Cæsar put it on;
'Twas on a summer's evening, in his
tent,
That day he overcame the Nervii.
Ib. [174]

8 See what a rent the envious Casca
made. *Ib.* [180]

9 This was the most unkindest cut of all.
Ib. [188]

10 O! what a fall was there, my countrymen;
Then I, and you, and all of us fell
down,
Whilst bloody treason flourish'd over
us,
O! now you weep, and I perceive you
feel
The dint of pity; these are gracious
drops. *Ib.* [195]

11 I come not, friends, to steal away
your hearts:
I am no orator, as Brutus is;
But, as you know me all, a plain,
blunt man,
That love my friend. *Ib.* [220]

12 For I have neither wit, nor words, nor
worth,

Action, nor utterance, nor power of
speech,
To stir men's blood; I only speak
right on;
I tell you that which you yourselves
do know. *Julius Cæsar*, III. ii. [225]

13   But were I Brutus,
And Brutus Antony, there were an
Antony
Would ruffle up your spirits, and put
a tongue
In every wound of Cæsar, that should
move
The stones of Rome to rise and
mutiny. *Ib.* [230]

14 Here was a Cæsar! when comes such
another? *Ib.* [257]

15 Let me tell you, Cassius, you yourself
Are much condemn'd to have an
itching palm. *Ib.* IV. iii. 9

16 Remember March, the ides of March
remember. *Ib.* 18

17 I had rather be a dog, and bay the
moon,
Than such a Roman. *Ib.* 27

18   All his faults observ'd,
Set in a note-book, learn'd, and conn'd
by rote,
To cast into my teeth. *Ib.* 96

19 There is a tide in the affairs of men,
Which, taken at the flood, leads on to
fortune;
Omitted, all the voyage of their life
Is bound in shallows and in miseries.
On such a full sea are we now afloat,
And we must take the current when it
serves,
Or lose our ventures. *Ib.* 217

20 BRUTUS:
Then I shall see thee again?
GHOST:
Ay, at Philippi.
BRUTUS:
Why, I will see thee at Philippi, then.
Ib. 283

21 For ever, and for ever, farewell,
Cassius!
If we do meet again, why, we shall
smile!
If not, why then, this parting was well
made. *Ib.* V. i. 117

22   O! that a man might know
The end of this day's business, ere it
come;
But it sufficeth that the day will end,
And then the end is known. *Ib.* 123

23 This was the noblest Roman of them
all. *Ib.* V. 68

24 His life was gentle, and the elements
So mix'd in him that Nature might
stand up
And say to all the world, 'This was a
man!' *Ib.* 73

1 LEAR:
So young, and so untender?
CORDELIA:
So young, my lord, and true.
King Lear, I. i. [108]

2 This is the excellent foppery of the
world. *Ib.* ii. [132]

3 How sharper than a serpent's tooth
it is
To have a thankless child!
Ib. iv. [312]

4 Blow, winds, and crack your cheeks!
rage! blow!
You cataracts and hurricanoes, spout
Till you have drench'd our steeples,
drown'd the cocks!
You sulphurous and thought-execut-
ing fires,
Vaunt-couriers   to   oak-cleaving
thunderbolts,
Singe my white head! And thou, all-
shaking thunder,
Strike flat the thick rotundity o' the
world!
Crack nature's moulds, all germens
spill at once
That make ingrateful man!
Ib. III. ii. 1

5 I tax not you, you elements, with un-
kindness;
I never gave you kingdom, call'd you
children,
You owe me no subscription: then,
let fall
Your horrible pleasure; here I stand,
your slave,
A poor, infirm, weak, and despis'd old
man.
But yet I call you servile ministers,
That have with two pernicious daugh-
ters join'd
Your high-engender'd battles 'gainst
a head
So old and white as this. *Ib.* [16]

6   I am a man
More sinned against than sinning.
Ib. [59]

7 O! that way madness lies; let me shun
that. *Ib.* iv. 21

8 Poor naked wretches, wheresoe'er you
are,
That bide the pelting of this pitiless
storm,
How shall your houseless heads and
unfed sides,
Your looped and window'd raggedness, defend you
From seasons such as these? *Ib.* 28

9   Take physic, pomp;
Expose thyself to feel what wretches
feel. *Ib.* 33

10 Tom's a-cold. *Ib.* [57]

11 Keep thy foot out of brothels, thy
hand out of plackets, thy pen from
lenders' books, and defy the foul
fiend. *King Lear*, III. iv. [96]

12 Thou art the thing itself; unaccommodated man is no more but such
a poor, bare, forked animal as thou
art. *Ib.* [109]

13 The prince of darkness is a gentleman.
Ib. [148]

14 Child Roland to the dark tower came,
His word was still, Fie, foh, and fum,
I smell the blood of a British man.
Ib. [185]

15   The little dogs and all,
Tray, Blanch, and Sweet-heart, see,
they bark at me. *Ib.* vi. 65

16 I am tied to the stake, and I must
stand the course. *Ib.* vii. [54]

17 Out, vile jelly! *Ib.* [83]

18 As flies to wanton boys, are we to the
gods;
They kill us for their sport.
Ib. IV. i. 36

19 How fearful
And dizzy 'tis to cast one's eyes so
low!
The crows and choughs that wing the
midway air
Show scarce so gross as beetles; half-
way down
Hangs one that gathers samphire,
dreadful trade!
Methinks he seems no bigger than his
head.
The fishermen that walk upon the
beach
Appear like mice, and yond tall an-
choring bark
Diminish'd to her cock, her cock a
buoy
Almost too small for sight. The mur-
muring surge,
That on the unnumber'd idle pebbles
chafes,
Cannot be heard so high. *Ib.* vi. 12

20 GLOUCESTER:
Is't not the king?
LEAR:
    Ay, every inch a king.
Ib. [110]

21 Give me an ounce of civet, good
apothecary, to sweeten my imagination. *Ib.* [133]

22   Get thee glass eyes;
And, like a scurvy politician, seem
To see the things thou dost not.
Ib. [175]

23   Mine enemy's dog,
Though he had bit me, should have
stood that night
Against my fire. *Ib.* vii. 36

1 Thou art a soul in bliss; but I am
    bound
Upon a wheel of fire, that mine own
    tears
Do scald like molten lead.
                    King Lear, IV. vii. 46

2 I am a very foolish, fond old man,
Fourscore and upward, not an hour
    more or less;
And, to deal plainly,
I fear I am not in my perfect mind.
                                    Ib. 60

3 For, as I am a man, I think this lady
To be my child Cordelia.   *Ib.* 69

4 Pray you now, forget and forgive.
                                Ib. [85]

5   Men must endure
Their going hence, even as their com-
    ing hither:
Ripeness is all.   *Ib.* v. ii. 9

6   Come, let's away to prison;
We two alone will sing like birds i' the
    cage:
When thou dost ask me blessing, I'll
    kneel down,
And ask of thee forgiveness: and we'll
    live,
And pray, and sing, and tell old tales,
    and laugh
At gilded butterflies, and hear poor
    rogues
Talk of court news; and we'll talk
    with them too,
Who loses, and who wins; who's in,
    who's out;
And take upon's the mystery of
    things,
As if we were God's spies; and we'll
    wear out,
In a wall'd prison, packs and sets of
    great ones
That ebb and flow by the moon.
                              Ib. iii. 8

7 The gods are just, and of our pleasant
    vices
Make instruments to plague us.
                              Ib. [172]

8 The wheel is come full circle.
                              Ib. [176]

9   Her voice was ever soft,
Gentle and low, an excellent thing in
    woman.   *Ib.* [274]

10 I have seen the day, with my good
    biting falchion
I would have made them skip.
                              Ib. [278]

11 And my poor fool is hang'd! No, no,
    no life!
Why should a dog, a horse, a rat,
    have life,
And thou no breath at all? Thou'lt
    come no more,
Never, never, never, never, never!
Pray you, undo this button. *Ib.* [307]

12 Vex not his ghost: O! let him pass;
    he hates him
That would upon the rack of this
    tough world
Stretch him out longer.
                    King Lear, v. iii. [314]

13 Spite of cormorant devouring Time.
                    Love's Labour's Lost, I. i. 4

14 He hath not fed of the dainties that
    are bred in a book; he hath not eat
    paper, as it were; he hath not drunk
    ink.   *Ib.* IV. ii. [25]

15 Never durst poet touch a pen to
    write
Until his ink were temper'd with
    Love's sighs.   *Ib.* iii. [346]

16 From women's eyes this doctrine I
    derive:
They sparkle still the right Prome-
    thean fire;
They are the books, the arts, the
    academes,
That show, contain, and nourish all
    the world.   *Ib.* [350]

17 MOTH:
They have been at a great feast of
    languages, and stolen the scraps.
COSTARD:
O! they have lived long on the alms-
    basket of words. I marvel thy master
    hath not eaten thee for a word; for
    thou art not so long by the head as
    honorificabilitudinitatibus: thou art
    easier swallowed than a flap-dragon.
                          Ib. v. i. [39]

18 A jest's prosperity lies in the ear
Of him that hears it, never in the
    tongue
Of him that makes it.   *Ib.* ii. [869]

19 When daisies pied and violets blue
    And lady-smocks all silver-white
And cuckoo-buds of yellow hue
    Do paint the meadows with delight,
The cuckoo then, on every tree,
Mocks married men; for thus sings he,
                              Cuckoo;
Cuckoo, cuckoo; O, word of fear,
Unpleasing to a married ear!
                              Ib. [902]

20 When icicles hang by the wall,
    And Dick, the shepherd, blows his
        nail,
And Tom bears logs into the hall,
    And milk comes frozen home in
        pail,
When blood is nipp'd and ways be
    foul,
Then nightly sings the staring owl,
                              Tu-who;
Tu-whit, tu-who—a merry note,
While greasy Joan doth keel the pot.
When all aloud the wind doth blow,
And coughing drowns the parson's
    saw;
And birds sit brooding in the snow,

And Marion's nose looks red and raw,
When roasted crabs hiss in the bowl.
Love's Labour's Lost, v. ii. [920]

1 The words of Mercury are harsh after
the songs of Apollo.   *Ib.* [938]

2 FIRST WITCH:
When shall we three meet again
In thunder, lightning, or in rain?
SECOND WITCH:
When the hurly-burly's done,
When the battle's lost and won.
THIRD WITCH:
That will be ere the set of sun.
FIRST WITCH:
Where the place?
SECOND WITCH:
                Upon the heath.
THIRD WITCH:
There to meet with Macbeth.
FIRST WITCH:
I come, Graymalkin!
SECOND WITCH:
                Paddock calls.
THIRD WITCH:
Anon!
ALL:
Fair is foul, and foul is fair:
Hover through the fog and filthy air.
                Macbeth, I. i. 1

3 DUNCAN:
What bloody man is that? . . .
MALCOLM:
        This is the sergeant. *Ib.* ii. 1

4 Disdaining fortune, with his brandish'd steel,
Which smok'd with bloody execution,
Like valour's minion carv'd out his
passage.   *Ib.* 17

5 A sailor's wife had chestnuts in her
lap,
And munch'd, and munch'd, and
munch'd: 'Give me,' quoth I:
'Aroint thee, witch!' the rump-fed
ronyon cries.
Her husband's to Aleppo gone, master
o' the Tiger:
But in a sieve I'll thither sail,
And, like a rat without a tail,
I'll do, I'll do, and I'll do. *Ib.* iii. 4

6 Sleep shall neither night nor day
Hang upon his pent-house lid.
He shall live a man forbid.
Weary se'nnights nine times nine
Shall he dwindle, peak, and pine:
Though his bark cannot be lost,
Yet it shall be tempest-tost. *Ib.* 19

7 So foul and fair a day I have not seen.
                Ib. 38

8   What are these,
So withered, and so wild in their
attire,
That look not like th' inhabitants o'
the earth,
And yet are on 't?   *Ib.* 39

9   Two truths are told,
As happy prologues to the swelling act
Of the imperial theme.
                Macbeth, I. iii. 127

10 This supernatural soliciting
Cannot be ill, cannot be good. *Ib.* 130

11   Present fears
Are less than horrible imaginings.
                Ib. 137

12   Come what come may,
Time and the hour runs through the
roughest day.   *Ib.* 146

13 MALCOLM:
                Nothing in his life
Became him like the leaving it; he died
As one that had been studied in his
death
To throw away the dearest thing he
owed
As 'twere a careless trifle.
DUNCAN:
                There's no art
To find the mind's construction in the
face;
He was a gentleman on whom I built
An absolute trust.   *Ib.* iv. 7

14 Glamis thou art, and Cawdor; and
shalt be
What thou art promis'd. Yet do I fear
thy nature;
It is too full o' the milk of human
kindness
To catch the nearest way; thou
wouldst be great.   *Ib.* v. [16]

15   The raven himself is hoarse
That croaks the fatal entrance of
Duncan
Under my battlements. Come, you
spirits
That tend on mortal thoughts! unsex
me here,
And fill me from the crown to the toe
top full
Of direst cruelty; make thick my
blood,
Stop up the access and passage to
remorse,
That no compunctious visitings of
nature
Shake my fell purpose, nor keep
peace between
The effect and it! Come to my
woman's breasts,
And take my milk for gall, you mur-
dering ministers,
Wherever in your sightless sub-
stances
You wait on nature's mischief! Come,
thick night,
And pall thee in the dunnest smoke of
hell,
That my keen knife see not the
wound it makes,
Nor heaven peep through the blanket
of the dark,
To cry 'Hold, hold!'   *Ib.* [38]

1 Your face, my thane, is as a book
where men
May read strange matters. To beguile
the time,
Look like the time; bear welcome in
your eye,
Your hand, your tongue: look like the
innocent flower,
But be the serpent under't.
Macbeth, I. v. [63]

2 DUNCAN:
This castle hath a pleasant seat; the air
Nimbly and sweetly recommends itself
Unto our gentle senses.

BANQUO:
This guest of summer,
The temple-haunting martlet, does
approve
By his lov'd mansionry that the
heaven's breath
Smells wooingly here: no jutty,
frieze,
Buttress, nor coign of vantage, but
this bird
Hath made his pendent bed and pro-
creant cradle:
Where they most breed and haunt,
I have observ'd,
The air is delicate. *Ib.* vi. 1

3 If it were done when 'tis done, then
'twere well
It were done quickly: if the assassination
Could trammel up the consequence,
and catch
With his surcease success; that but
this blow
Might be the be-all and the end-all
here,
But here, upon this bank and shoal
of time,
We'd jump the life to come. *Ib.* vii. 1

4 Besides, this Duncan
Hath borne his faculties so meek,
hath been
So clear in his great office, that his
virtues
Will plead like angels trumpet-
tongu'd, against
The deep damnation of his taking-off;
And pity, like a naked new-born babe,
Striding the blast, or heaven's cheru-
bim, hors'd
Upon the sightless couriers of the air,
Shall blow the horrid deed in every
eye,
That tears shall drown the wind.
I have no spur
To prick the sides of my intent, but
only
Vaulting ambition, which o'erleaps
itself,
And falls on the other. *Ib.* 16

5 He hath honour'd me of late; and I
have bought
Golden opinions from all sorts of
people. *Ib.* 32

6 Letting 'I dare not' wait upon 'I
would,'
Like the poor cat i' the adage.
Macbeth, I. vii. 44

7 MACBETH:
If we should fail,—
LADY MACBETH:
We fail!
But screw your courage to the stick-
ing-place,
And we'll not fail. *Ib.* 60

8 There's husbandry in heaven;
Their candles are all out. *Ib.* II. i. 4

9 Is this a dagger which I see before me,
The handle toward my hand? Come,
let me clutch thee:
I have thee not, and yet I see thee still.
Art thou not, fatal vision, sensible
To feeling as to sight! or art thou but
A dagger of the mind, a false creation,
Proceeding from the heat-oppressèd
brain? *Ib.* 33

10 Hear it not, Duncan; for it is a knell
That summons thee to heaven or to
hell. *Ib.* 64

11 Consider it not so deeply. *Ib.* ii. 31

12 I had most need of blessing, and
'Amen'
Stuck in my throat. *Ib.* 33

13 Methought I heard a voice cry, 'Sleep
no more!
Macbeth does murder sleep,' the innocent sleep,
Sleep that knits up the ravell'd sleave
of care,
The death of each day's life, sore
labour's bath,
Balm of hurt minds, great nature's
second course,
Chief nourisher in life's feast. *Ib.* 36

14 Glamis hath murder'd sleep, and
therefore Cawdor
Shall sleep no more, Macbeth shall
sleep no more! *Ib.* 43

15 Will all great Neptune's ocean wash
this blood
Clean from my hand? No, this my
hand will rather
The multitudinous seas incarnadine,
Making the green one red. *Ib.* 61

16 A little water clears us of this deed.
Ib. 68

17 The primrose way to the everlasting
bonfire. *Ib.* iii. [22]

18 The labour we delight in physics
pain. *Ib.* [56]

19 All is but toys; renown and grace is
dead,
The wine of life is drawn, and the mere
lees
Is left this vault to brag of. *Ib.* [101]

20 There's daggers in men's smiles.
Ib. [147]

1 A falcon, towering in her pride of place,
Was by a mousing owl hawk'd at and kill'd. *Macbeth*, II. iv. 12

2   Thy soul's flight,
If it find heaven, must find it out to-night. *Ib.* III. i. 141

3 LADY MACBETH:
        Things without all remedy
Should be without regard: what's done is done.
MACBETH:
We have scotch'd the snake, not killed it. *Ib.* ii. 11

4   Duncan is in his grave;
After life's fitful fever he sleeps well;
Treason has done his worst: nor steel, nor poison,
Malice domestic, foreign levy, nothing,
Can touch him further. *Ib.* 22

5 A deed of dreadful note. *Ib.* 44

6 Be innocent of the knowledge, dearest chuck,
Till thou applaud the deed. Come, seeling night,
Scarf up the tender eye of pitiful day,
And with thy bloody and invisible hand,
Cancel and tear to pieces that great bond
Which keeps me pale! Light thickens, and the crow
Makes wing to the rooky wood;
Good things of day begin to droop and drowse,
Whiles night's black agents to their preys do rouse. *Ib.* 45

7 Now spurs the lated traveller apace
To gain the timely inn. *Ib.* iii. 6

8 But now I am cabin'd, cribb'd, confin'd, bound in
To saucy doubts and fears. *Ib.* iv. 24

9 Now good digestion wait on appetite,
And health on both! *Ib.* 38

10 Stand not upon the order of your going,
But go at once. *Ib.* 119

11 It will have blood, they say; blood will have blood. *Ib.* 122

12   I am in blood
Stepp'd in so far that, should I wade no more,
Returning were as tedious as go o'er. *Ib.* 136

13 Double, double toil and trouble;
Fire burn, and cauldron bubble. *Ib.* IV. i. 10

14 Eye of newt and toe of frog,
Wool of bat and tongue of dog. *Ib.* 14

15   Slips of yew
Sliver'd in the moon's eclipse. *Ib.* 27

16 Finger of birth-strangled babe,
Ditch-deliver'd by a drab,
Make the gruel thick and slab.
Macbeth, IV. i. 30

17 By the pricking of my thumbs,
Something wicked this way comes.
        Open, locks,
        Whoever knocks. *Ib.* 44

18 How now, you secret, black, and midnight hags! *Ib.* 48

19 A deed without a name. *Ib.* 49

20 Be bloody, bold, and resolute; laugh to scorn
The power of man, for none of woman born
Shall harm Macbeth. *Ib.* 79

21 But yet I'll make assurance double sure,
And take a bond of fate. *Ib.* 83

22 Macbeth shall never vanquish'd be until
Great Birnam wood to high Dunsinane hill
Shall come against him. *Ib.* 90

23 What! will the line stretch out to the crack of doom? *Ib.* 117

24 The weird sisters. *Ib.* 136

25 His flight was madness: when our actions do not,
Our fears do make us traitors.
Ib. ii. 3

26 Stands Scotland where it did?
Ib. iii. 164

27   All my pretty ones?
Did you say all? O hell-kite! All?
What! all my pretty chickens and their dam,
At one fell swoop? *Ib.* 216

28 Out, damned spot! out, I say! One; two: why then, 'tis time to do't. Hell is murky! Fie, my lord, fie! a soldier, and afeard? What need we fear who knows it, when none can call our power to account? Yet who would have thought the old man to have had so much blood in him? *Ib.* v. i. [38]

29 The Thane of Fife had a wife: where is she now? What! will these hands ne'er be clean? *Ib.* [46]

30 All the perfumes of Arabia will not sweeten this little hand. *Ib.* [56]

31 The devil damn thee black, thou cream-faced loon!
Where gott'st thou that goose look?
Ib. iii. 11

32 I have lived long enough: my way of life
Is fall'n into the sear, the yellow leaf;
And that which should accompany old age,
As honour, love, obedience, troops of friends,

I must not look to have; but, in their
    stead,
Curses, not loud but deep, mouth-
    honour, breath,
Which the poor heart would fain deny,
    and dare not.   *Macbeth*, v. iii. 22

1 MACBETH:
Canst thou not minister to a mind
    diseas'd,
Pluck from the memory a rooted
    sorrow,
Raze out the written troubles of the
    brain,
And with some sweet oblivious anti-
    dote
Cleanse the stuff'd bosom of that
    perilous stuff
Which weighs upon the heart?
DOCTOR:
                Therein the patient
Must minister to himself.
MACBETH:
Throw physic to the dogs; I'll none
    of it.   *Ib.* 40

2 Hang out our banners on the outward
    walls;
The cry is still, 'They come;' our
    castle's strength
Will laugh a siege to scorn.   *Ib.* v. 1

3 I have supp'd full with horrors.
                               Ib. 13

4 SEYTON:
The queen, my lord, is dead.
MACBETH:
She should have died hereafter;
There would have been a time for
    such a word.
To-morrow, and to-morrow, and
    to-morrow,
Creeps in this petty pace from day to
    day,
To the last syllable of recorded time;
And all our yesterdays have lighted
    fools
The way to dusty death. Out, out,
    brief candle!
Life's but a walking shadow, a poor
    player,
That struts and frets his hour upon
    the stage,
And then is heard no more; it is a tale
Told by an idiot, full of sound and
    fury,
Signifying nothing.   *Ib.* 16

5 I pull in resolution, and begin
To doubt the equivocation of the
    fiend
That lies like truth: 'Fear not, till
    Birnam wood
Do come to Dunsinane.'   *Ib.* 42

6 I 'gin to be aweary of the sun,
And wish the estate o' the world
    were now undone.   *Ib.* 49

7   Blow, wind! come, wrack!
At least we'll die with harness on our
    back.   *Ib.* 51

8 They have tied me to a stake; I cannot
    fly.
But bear-like I must fight the course.
                       Macbeth, v. vii. 1

9 Why should I play the Roman fool,
    and die
On mine own sword?   *Ib.* 30

10 I bear a charmed life.   *Ib.* 41

11 And let the angel whom thou still
    hast served
Tell thee, Macduff was from his
    mother's womb
Untimely ripp'd.   *Ib.* 43

12   Lay on, Macduff;
And damn'd be him that first cries,
    'Hold, enough!'   *Ib.* 62

13   Spirits are not finely touch'd
But to fine issues.
           Measure for Measure, I. i. 35

14 And liberty plucks justice by the nose.
                            Ib. iii. 29

15 'Tis one thing to be tempted, Escalus,
Another thing to fall.   *Ib.* II. i. 17

16 Some rise by sin, and some by virtue
    fall.   *Ib.* 38

17 This will last out a night in Russia,
When nights are longest there.
                            Ib. [144]

18   O! it is excellent
To have a giant's strength, but it is
    tyrannous
To use it like a giant.   *Ib.* ii. 107

19   But man, proud man,
Drest in a little brief authority,
Most ignorant of what he's most
    assur'd,
His glassy essence, like an angry ape,
Plays such fantastic tricks before
    high heaven,
As make the angels weep.   *Ib.* 117

20   Thou hast nor youth nor age;
But, as it were, an after-dinner's sleep,
Dreaming on both.   *Ib.* III. i. 32

21   Dar'st thou die?
The sense of death is most in appre-
    hension,
And the poor beetle, that we tread
    upon,
In corporal sufferance finds a pang
    as great
As when a giant dies.   *Ib.* 75

22   If I must die,
I will encounter darkness as a bride,
And hug it in mine arms.   *Ib.* 81

23 CLAUDIO:
           Death is a fearful thing.
ISABELLA:
And shamed life a hateful.
CLAUDIO:
Ay, but to die, and go we know not
    where;

To lie in cold obstruction and to rot;
This sensible warm motion to become
A kneaded clod; and the delighted
spirit
To bathe in fiery floods, or to reside
In thrilling region of thick-ribbèd
ice;
To be imprisoned in the viewless
winds,
And blown with restless violence
round about
The pendant world!
    Measure for Measure, III. i. 114

1 The weariest and most loathèd worldly
life
That age, ache, penury, and im-
prisonment
Can lay on nature, is a paradise
To what we fear of death.   *Ib.* 127

2 There, at the moated grange, resides
this dejected Mariana.   *Ib.* [279]

3 Take, O take those lips away,
That so sweetly were forsworn;
And those eyes, the break of day,
Lights that do mislead the morn:
But my kisses bring again, bring again
Seals of love, but seal'd in vain, seal'd
in vain.   *Ib.* IV. i. 1

4 I am a kind of burr; I shall stick.
  Ib. iii. [193]

5 They say best men are moulded out of
faults,
And, for the most, become much more
the better
For being a little bad. *Ib.* v. i. [440]

6 In sooth I know not why I am so sad:
It wearies me; you say it wearies you;
But how I caught it, found it, or came
by it,
What stuff 'tis made of, whereof it is
born,
I am to learn.
    The Merchant of Venice, I. i. 1

7 There are a sort of men whose visages
Do cream and mantle like a standing
pond.   *Ib.* 88

8 As who should say, 'I am Sir Oracle,
And when I ope my lips let no dog
bark!'
O, my Antonio, I do know of these,
That therefore only are reputed wise,
For saying nothing.   *Ib.* 93

9 If to do were as easy as to know what
were good to do, chapels had been
churches, and poor men's cottages
princes' palaces.   *Ib.* ii. [13]

10 It is a good divine that follows his
own instructions; I can easier teach
twenty what were good to be done,
than be one of the twenty to follow
mine own teaching.   *Ib.* [15]

11 He doth nothing but talk of his horse.
  Ib. [43]

12 God made him, and therefore let him
pass for a man.
    The Merchant of Venice, I. ii. [59]

13 I will buy with you, sell with you,
talk with you, walk with you, and so
following; but I will not eat with you,
drink with you, nor pray with you.
What news on the Rialto? *Ib.* iii. [36]

14 How like a fawning publican he looks!
I hate him for he is a Christian.
    Ib. [42]

15 If I can catch him once upon the hip,
I will feed fat the ancient grudge I
bear him.   *Ib.* [47]

16 The devil can cite Scripture for his
purpose.   *Ib.* [99]

17 Signior Antonio, many a time and oft
In the Rialto you have rated me.
    Ib. [107]

18 For sufferance is the badge of all our
tribe.   *Ib.* [111]

19 Mislike me not for my complexion,
The shadow'd livery of the burnished
sun.   *Ib.* II. i. 1

20 The very staff of my age, my very
prop.   *Ib.* ii. [71]

21 It is a wise father that knows his own
child.   *Ib.* [83]

22 Truth will come to light; murder
cannot be hid long.   *Ib.* [86]

23 But love is blind, and lovers cannot
see
The pretty follies that themselves
commit.   *Ib.* vi. 36

24 My daughter! O my ducats! O my
daughter!
Fled with a Christian! O my Christian
ducats!   *Ib.* viii. 15

25 The portrait of a blinking idiot.
    Ib. ix. 54

26 Let him look to his bond.
    Ib. III. i. [51, 52, 54]

27 Hath not a Jew eyes? hath not a Jew
hands, organs, dimensions, senses,
affections, passions! fed with the same
food, hurt with the same weapons, subject to the same diseases, healed by
the same means, warmed and cooled
by the same winter and summer, as
a Christian is? If you prick us, do we
not bleed? if you tickle us, do we not
laugh? if you poison us, do we not
die? and if you wrong us, shall we not
revenge?   *Ib.* [63]

28 TUBAL:
One of them showed me a ring that he
had of your daughter for a monkey.
SHYLOCK:
I would not have given it for a wilder-
ness of monkeys.   *Ib.* [126]

H

1 Tell me where is fancy bred,
   Or in the heart or in the head?
How begot, how nourished?
   Reply, reply.

It is engender'd in the eyes,
With gazing fed; and fancy dies
In the cradle where it lies.
   Let us all ring fancy's knell:
   I'll begin it,—Ding, dong, bell.
   The Merchant of Venice, III. ii. 63

2   Rash-embrac'd despair,
And shuddering fear, and green-ey'd
   jealousy.   *Ib.* 109

3 I will have my bond.   *Ib.* iii. 17

4 A harmless necessary cat. *Ib.* IV. i. 55

5 The quality of mercy is not strain'd,
It droppeth as the gentle rain from
   heaven
Upon the place beneath: it is twice
   bless'd;
It blesseth him that gives and him
   that takes:
'Tis mightiest in the mightiest: it
   becomes
The throned monarch better than his
   crown;
His sceptre shows the force of tem-
   poral power,
The attribute to awe and majesty,
Wherein doth sit the dread and fear of
   kings;
But mercy is above this sceptred
   sway,
It is enthroned in the hearts of kings,
It is an attribute to God himself,
And earthly power doth then show
   likest God's
When mercy seasons justice. There-
   fore, Jew,
Though justice be thy plea, consider
   this,
That in the course of justice none of us
Should see salvation: we do pray for
   mercy,
And that same prayer doth teach us
   all to render
The deeds of mercy.   *Ib.* [184]

6 A Daniel come to judgment! yea, a
   Daniel!
O wise young judge, how I do honour
   thee!   *Ib.* [223]

7 'Tis not in the bond.   *Ib.* [263]

8 A second Daniel, a Daniel, Jew!
Now, infidel, I have thee on the hip.
              Ib. [334]

9   In such a night
Troilus methinks mounted the Troyan
   walls,
And sigh'd his soul towards the
   Grecian tents,
Where Cressid lay that night.
            Ib. v. i. 3

10   In such a night
Stood Dido with a willow in her hand
Upon the wild sea-banks, and waft
   her love
To come again to Carthage.
    The Merchant of Venice, v. i. 9

11 How sweet the moonlight sleeps upon
   this bank!
Here will we sit, and let the sounds of
   music
Creep in our ears: soft stillness and
   the night
Become the touches of sweet harmony.
Sit, Jessica: look, how the floor of
   heaven
Is thick inlaid with patines of bright
   gold:
There's not the smallest orb which
   thou behold'st
But in his motion like an angel sings,
Still quiring to the young-eyed cheru-
   bins;
Such harmony is in immortal souls;
But, whilst this muddy vesture of
   decay
Doth grossly close it in, we cannot
   hear it.   *Ib.* 54

12 I am never merry when I hear sweet
   music.   *Ib.* 69

13 The man that hath no music in him-
   self,
Nor is not mov'd with concord of
   sweet sounds,
Is fit for treasons, stratagems, and
   spoils;
The motions of his spirit are dull as
   night,
And his affections dark as Erebus:
Let no such man be trusted. *Ib.* 83

14 PORTIA:
How far that little candle throws his
   beams!
So shines a good deed in a naughty
   world.
NERISSA:
When the moon shone, we did not see
   the candle.
PORTIA:
So doth the greater glory dim the less.
            Ib. 90

15 Here will be an old abusing of God's
patience, and the king's English.
    The Merry Wives of Windsor,
   I. iv. [5]

16 There's the humour of it. *Ib.* II. i. [139]

17 Why, then the world's mine oyster,
Which I with sword will open.
            Ib. ii. 2

18 Marry, this is the short and the long
of it.   *Ib.* [62]

19 I cannot tell what the dickens his
name is.   *Ib.* III. ii. [20]

20 As good luck would have it. *Ib.* v. [86]

21 A man of my kidney.   *Ib.* [119]

1 But earthlier happy is the rose dis-
till'd,
Than that which withering on the
virgin thorn
Grows, lives, and dies, in single
blessedness.
A Midsummer Night's Dream,
I. i. 76

2 Ay me! for aught that ever I could
read,
Could ever hear by tale or history,
The course of true love never did run
smooth. *Ib.* 132

3 A part to tear a cat in, to make all
split. *Ib.* ii. [32]

4 I will aggravate my voice so that I
will roar you as gently as any sucking dove; I will roar you as 'twere any
nightingale. *Ib.* [84]

5 A proper man, as one shall see in a
summer's day. *Ib.* [89]

6 Over hill, over dale,
Thorough bush, thorough brier,
Over park, over pale,
Thorough flood, thorough fire.
Ib. II. i. 2

7 But I might see young Cupid's fiery
shaft
Quench'd in the chaste beams of
the wat'ry moon,
And the imperial votaress passed on,
In maiden meditation, fancy-free.
Yet mark'd I where the bolt of Cupid
fell:
It fell upon a little western flower,
Before milk-white, now purple with
love's wound,
And maidens call it, Love-in-idleness.
Ib. 161

8 I'll put a girdle round about the
earth
In forty minutes. *Ib.* 175

9 I know a bank whereon the wild
thyme blows,
Where oxlips and the nodding violet
grows
Quite over-canopied with luscious
woodbine,
With sweet musk-roses, and with
eglantine:
There sleeps Titania some time of the
night,
Lull'd in these flowers with dances and
delight;
And there the snake throws her
enamell'd skin,
Weed wide enough to wrap a fairy in.
Ib. 249

10 You spotted snakes with double
tongue,
Thorny hedge-hogs, be not seen;
Newts, and blind-worms, do no wrong;
Come not near our fairy queen.
Ib. ii. 9

11 Weaving spiders come not here;
Hence, you long-legg'd spinners,
hence!
Beetles black, approach not near;
Worm nor snail, do no offence.
A Midsummer Night's Dream, II. ii. 20

12 What hempen home-spuns have we
swaggering here,
So near the cradle of the fairy queen?
Ib. III. i. [82]

13 Bless thee, Bottom! bless thee! thou
art translated. *Ib.* [124]

14 Lord what fools these mortals be!
Ib. ii. 115

15 So we grew together,
Like to a double cherry, seeming
parted,
But yet an union in partition,
Two lovely berries moulded on one
stem. *Ib.* 208

16 Jack shall have Jill;
Nought shall go ill;
The man shall have his mare again,
And all shall be well. *Ib.* 461

17 I have had a dream, past the wit of
man to say what dream it was.
Ib. IV. i. [211]

18 The eye of man hath not heard, the
ear of man hath not seen, man's hand
is not able to taste, his tongue to conceive, nor his heart to report, what
my dream was. *Ib.* [218]

19 The lunatic, the lover, and the poet,
Are of imagination all compact:
One sees more devils than vast hell
can hold,
That is, the madman; the lover, all
as frantic,
Sees Helen's beauty in a brow of
Egypt:
The poet's eye, in a fine frenzy rolling,
Doth glance from heaven to earth,
from earth to heaven;
And, as imagination bodies forth
The forms of things unknown, the
poet's pen
Turns them to shapes, and gives to
airy nothing
A local habitation and a name.
Such tricks hath strong imagination,
That, if it would but apprehend some
joy,
It comprehends some bringer of that
joy;
Or in the night, imagining some fear,
How easy is a bush suppos'd a bear!
Ib. v. i. 7

20 That is the true beginning of our end.
Consider then we come but in despite.
We do not come as minding to content
you,
Our true intent is. All for your
delight,
We are not here. *Ib.* [111]

1 Whereat, with blade, with bloody
   blameful blade,
   He bravely broach'd his boiling
   bloody breast.
      A Midsummer Night's Dream, v. i. [148]

2 The best in this kind are but shadows,
   and the worst are no worse, if imagination amend them.   *Ib.* [215]

3 Well roared, Lion.   *Ib.* [272]
   Now the hungry lion roars,
   And the wolf behowls the moon;
   Whilst the heavy ploughman snores,
   All with weary task fordone.
                                  Ib. ii. 1

4   Not a mouse
   Shall disturb this hallow'd house:
   I am sent with broom before,
   To sweep the dust behind the door.
                                  Ib. 17

5 He is a very valiant trencher-man.
      Much Ado About Nothing,
      i. i. [52]

6 BEATRICE:
   I wonder that you will still be talking,
   Signior Benedick: nobody marks you.
   BENEDICK:
   What! my dear Lady Disdain, are
   you yet living?   *Ib.* [121]

7 I will live a bachelor.   *Ib.* [256]

8 There was a star danced, and under
   that was I born.   *Ib.* ii. i. [351]

9 Sigh no more, ladies, sigh no more,
      Men were deceivers ever;
   One foot in sea, and one on shore,
   To one thing constant never.
         Then sigh not so,
         But let them go,
   And be you blithe and bonny,
   Converting all your sounds of woe
      Into Hey nonny, nonny.

   Sing no more ditties, sing no mo
      Of dumps so dull and heavy;
   The fraud of men was ever so,
      Since summer first was leavy.
                                  Ib. iii. [65]

10 Sits the wind in that corner? *Ib.* [108]

11 He hath a heart as sound as a bell,
   and his tongue is the clapper; for
   what his heart thinks his tongue
   speaks.   *Ib.* iii. ii. [12]

12 Are you good men and true? *Ib.* iii. 1

13 Comparisons are odorous. *Ib.* v. [18]

14 A good old man, sir; he will be
   talking: as they say, 'when the age is
   in, the wit is out.'   *Ib.* [36]

15 For there was never yet philosopher
   That could endure the toothache
   patiently.   *Ib.* v. i. 35

16 But I will wear my heart upon my
   sleeve
   For daws to peck at: I am not what
   I am.   *Othello,* I. i. 64

17 Your daughter and the Moor are now
   making the beast with two backs.
                         Othello, I. i. [117]

18 The gross clasps of a lascivious Moor.
                                  Ib. [127]

19 Keep up your bright swords, for the
   dew will rust them.   *Ib.* ii. 59

20   Rude am I in my speech,
   And little bless'd with the soft phrase
   of peace.   *Ib.* iii. 81

21   Yet, by your gracious patience,
   I will a round unvarnish'd tale deliver.
                                  Ib. 90

22 It was my hint to speak, such was the
   process;
   And of the Cannibals that each other
   eat,
   The Anthropophagi, and men whose
   heads
   Do grow beneath their shoulders. This
   to hear
   Would Desdemona seriously incline.
                                  Ib. 142

23   My story being done,
   She gave me for my pains a world of
   sighs:
   She swore, in faith, 'twas strange,
   'twas passing strange;
   'Twas pitiful, 'twas wondrous pitiful.
                                  Ib. 158

24 Virtue! a fig! 'tis in ourselves that we
   are thus, or thus.   *Ib.* [323]

25 Put money in thy purse.   *Ib.* [345]

26   Do not put me to 't,
   For I am nothing if not critical.
                         Ib. II. i. 118

27 To suckle fools and chronicle small
   beer.   *Ib.* 160

28   If it were now to die,
   'Twere now to be most happy, for
   I fear
   My soul hath her content so absolute
   That not another comfort like to this
   Succeeds in unknown fate.   *Ib.* [192]

29 And let me the canakin clink:
      A soldier's a man;
      A life's but a span;
   Why then let a soldier drink.
                                  Ib. iii. [73]

30 'Tis pride that pulls the country down.
                                  Ib. [99]

31 Silence that dreadful bell! it frights
   the isle
   From her propriety.   *Ib.* [177]

32 Thy honesty and love doth mince this
   matter.   *Ib.* [249]

33 Reputation, reputation, reputation!
   O! I have lost my reputation. I have
   lost the immortal part of myself, and
   what remains is bestial. My reputation,
   Iago, my reputation!   *Ib.* [264]

1 O! thereby hangs a tail.
Othello, III. i. [8]

2 Talk him out of patience. *Ib.* iii. 23

3 Excellent wretch! Perdition catch my
soul
But I do love thee! and when I love
thee not,
Chaos is come again. *Ib.* 90

4 Good name in man and woman, dear
my lord,
Is the immediate jewel of their souls;
Who steals my purse steals trash; 'tis
something, nothing;
'Twas mine, 'tis his, and has been
slave to thousands;
But he that filches from me my good
name
Robs me of that which not enriches
him,
And makes me poor indeed. *Ib.* 155

5 O! beware, my lord, of jealousy;
It is the green-ey'd monster which
doth mock
The meat it feeds on. *Ib.* 165

6 For I am declin'd
Into the vale of years. *Ib.* 265

7 O curse of marriage!
That we can call these delicate crea-
tures ours,
And not their appetites. I had rather
be a toad,
And live upon the vapour of a dun-
geon,
Than keep a corner in the thing I love
For others' uses. *Ib.* 268

8 Trifles light as air
Are to the jealous confirmations strong
As proofs of holy writ. *Ib.* 323

9 Not poppy, nor mandragora,
Nor all the drowsy syrups of the
world,
Shall ever medicine thee to that sweet
sleep
Which thou ow'dst yesterday. *Ib.* 331

10 O! now, for ever
Farewell the tranquil mind; farewell
content!
Farewell the plumed troop and the
big wars
That make ambition virtue! O, fare-
well!
Farewell the neighing steed and the
shrill trump,
The spirit-stirring drum, the ear-
piercing fife,
The royal banner, and all quality,
Pride, pomp, and circumstance of
glorious war!
And, O you mortal engines, whose
rude throats
The immortal Jove's dread clamours
counterfeit,
Farewell! Othello's occupation's gone!
Ib. 348

11 But this denoted a foregone conclusion. *Othello*, III, iii. 429

12 But yet the pity of it, Iago! O! Iago,
the pity of it, Iago! *Ib.* IV. i. [205]

13 But, alas! to make me
The fixed figure for the time of scorn
To point his slow and moving finger
at;
Yet could I bear that too. *Ib.* ii. 52

14 DESDEMONA:
Mine eyes do itch;
Doth that bode weeping?
EMILIA:
'Tis neither here nor there. *Ib.* iii. [59]

15 It is the cause, it is the cause, my
soul;
Let me not name it to you, you chaste
stars!
It is the cause. *Ib.* v. ii. 1

16 Put out the light, and then put out
the light. *Ib.* 7

17 Here is my journey's end, here is my
butt,
And very sea-mark of my utmost sail.
Ib. 266

18 Blow me about in winds! roast me in
sulphur!
Wash me in steep-down gulfs of liquid
fire!
O Desdemona! Desdemona! dead!
Ib. 278

19 An honourable murderer, if you will;
For nought did I in hate, but all in
honour. *Ib.* 293

20 I have done the state some service,
and they know't;
No more of that. I pray you, in your
letters,
When you shall these unlucky deeds
relate,
Speak of me as I am; nothing ex-
tenuate,
Nor set down aught in malice: then,
must you speak
Of one that lov'd not wisely but too
well;
Of one not easily jealous, but, being
wrought,
Perplex'd in the extreme; of one whose
hand,
Like the base Indian, threw a pearl
away
Richer than all his tribe; of one whose
subdu'd eyes
Albeit unused to the melting mood,
Drop tears as fast as the Arabian trees
Their med'cinable gum. Set you down
this;
And say besides, that in Aleppo once,
Where a malignant and a turban'd
Turk
Beat a Venetian and traduc'd the
state,

I took by the throat the circumcised dog,
And smote him thus. *Othello*, v. ii. 338

1 Old John of Gaunt, time-honour'd Lancaster. *King Richard II*, I. i. 1

2 The purest treasure mortal times afford
Is spotless reputation; that away,
Men are but gilded loam or painted clay.
A jewel in a ten-times-barr'd-up chest
Is a bold spirit in a loyal breast.
Mine honour is my life; both grow in one;
Take honour from me, and my life is done. *Ib.* 177

3 We were not born to sue, but to command. *Ib.* 196

4 Teach thy necessity to reason thus;
There is no virtue like necessity.
Ib. iii. 275

5 O, no! the apprehension of the good
Gives but the greater feeling to the worse. *Ib.* 300

6 Methinks I am a prophet new inspir'd,
And thus expiring do foretell of him:
His rash fierce blaze of riot cannot last,
For violent fires soon burn out themselves;
Small showers last long, but sudden storms are short;
He tires betimes that spurs too fast betimes. *Ib.* II. i. 31

7 This royal throne of kings, this scepter'd isle,
This earth of majesty, this seat of Mars,
This other Eden, demi-paradise,
This fortress built by Nature for herself
Against infection and the hand of war,
This happy breed of men, this little world,
This precious stone set in the silver sea,
Which serves it in the office of a wall,
Or as a moat defensive to a house,
Against the envy of less happier lands,
This blessed plot, this earth, this realm, this England,
This nurse, this teeming womb of royal kings,
Fear'd by their breed and famous by their birth,
Renowned for their deeds as far from home,—
For Christian service and true chivalry,—
As is the sepulchre in stubborn Jewry
Of the world's ransom, blessed Mary's Son:
This land of such dear souls, this dear, dear land. *Ib.* 40

8 England, bound in with the triumphant sea. *King Richard II*, II. i. 61

9 That England, that was wont to conquer others,
Hath made a shameful conquest of itself. *Ib.* 65

10 I count myself in nothing else so happy
As in a soul remembering my good friends. *Ib.* iii. 46

11 Grace me no grace, nor uncle me no uncle. *Ib.* 87

12 Not all the water in the rough rude sea
Can wash the balm from an anointed king. *Ib.* III. ii. 54

13 O! call back yesterday, bid time return. *Ib.* 69

14   Of comfort no man speak:
Let's talk of graves, of worms, and epitaphs;
Make dust our paper, and with rainy eyes
Write sorrow on the bosom of the earth.
Let's choose executors, and talk of wills. *Ib.* 144

15 For God's sake, let us sit upon the ground
And tell sad stories of the death of kings:
How some have been depos'd, some slain in war,
Some haunted by the ghosts they have depos'd,
Some poison'd by their wives, some sleeping kill'd;
All murder'd: for within the hollow crown
That rounds the mortal temples of a king
Keeps Death his court, and there the antick sits,
Scoffing his state and grinning at his pomp;
Allowing him a breath, a little scene,
To monarchize, be fear'd, and kill with looks,
Infusing him with self and vain conceit
As if this flesh which walls about our life
Were brass impregnable; and humour'd thus
Comes at the last, and with a little pin
Bores through his castle wall, and farewell king! *Ib.* 155

16 What must the king do now? Must he submit?
The king shall do it: must he be depos'd?
The king shall be contented: must he lose

The name of king? o' God's name, let
  it go.
I'll give my jewels for a set of beads,
My gorgeous palace for a hermitage,
My gay apparel for an almsman's
  gown,
My figur'd goblets for a dish of wood,
My sceptre for a palmer's walking
  staff,
My subjects for a pair of carved saints,
And my large kingdom for a little
  grave,
A little little grave, an obscure grave;
Or I'll be buried in the king's highway,
Some way of common trade, where
  subjects' feet
May hourly trample on their sove-
  reign's head;
For on my heart they tread now
  whilst I live;
And buried once, why not upon my
  head?   *King Richard II*, III. iii. 143

1 You make a leg.   *Ib.* 175

2   And there at Venice gave
His body to that pleasant country's
  earth,
And his pure soul unto his captain
  Christ,
Under whose colours he had fought so
  long.   *Ib.* IV. i. 97

3 As in a theatre, the eyes of men,
After a well-grac'd actor leaves the
  stage,
Are idly bent on him that enters next,
Thinking his prattle to be tedious.
                  Ib. v. ii. 23

4 Now is the winter of our discontent
Made glorious summer by this sun of
  York.   *King Richard III*, I. i. 1

5 This weak piping time of peace.
                  Ib. 24

6 And therefore, since I cannot prove a
  lover, . . .
I am determined to prove a villain.
                  Ib. 28

7 Was ever woman in this humour
  woo'd?
Was ever woman in this humour won?
                  Ib. ii. 229

8 Clarence is come,—false, fleeting, perjur'd Clarence.   *Ib.* iv. 55

9 I am not in the giving vein to-day.
                  Ib. IV. ii. 115

10 Harp not on that string.   *Ib.* iv. 365

11 The king's name is a tower of strength.
                  Ib. v. iii. 12

12 A horse! a horse! my kingdom for a
  horse!   *Ib.* iv. 7

13 A pair of star-cross'd lovers.
              Romeo and Juliet, Prologue, 6

14 The two hours' traffic of our stage.
                  Ib. 12

15 Come, we burn daylight, ho!
              Romeo and Juliet, I. iv. 43

16 For you and I are past our dancing
  days.   *Ib.* v. [35]

17 O! she doth teach the torches to
  burn bright.
It seems she hangs upon the cheek of
  night
Like a rich jewel in an Ethiop's ear;
Beauty too rich for use, for earth too
  dear.   *Ib.* [48]

18 My only love sprung from my only
  hate!   *Ib.* [142]

19 Young Adam Cupid, he that shot so
  trim
When King Cophetua lov'd the
  beggar-maid.   *Ib.* II. i. 13

20 He jests at scars, that never felt a
  wound.
But, soft, what light through yonder
  window breaks?
It is the east, and Juliet is the sun.
                  Ib. ii. 1

21 See! how she leans her cheek upon her
  hand:
O! that I were a glove upon that hand,
That I might touch that cheek.
                  Ib. 23

22 O Romeo, Romeo! wherefore art thou
  Romeo?   *Ib.* 33

23 What's in a name? that which we call
  a rose
By any other name would smell as
  sweet.   *Ib.* 43

24 ROMEO:
Lady, by yonder blessed moon I swear
That tips with silver all these fruit-
  tree tops,—
JULIET:
O! swear not by the moon, the in-
  constant moon,
That monthly changes in her circled
  orb,
Lest that thy love prove likewise
  variable.   *Ib.* 107

25 Good-night, good-night! parting is
  such sweet sorrow
That I shall say good-night till it be
  morrow.   *Ib.* 184

26 O flesh, flesh, how art thou fishified!
                  Ib. iv. [41]

27 I am the very pink of courtesy.
                  Ib. [63]

28 Thy head is as full of quarrels as an
  egg is full of meat.   *Ib.* III. i. [23]

29 A word and a blow.   *Ib.* [43]

30 A plague o' both your houses!
                  Ib. [112]

31 O! I am Fortune's fool.   *Ib.* [142]

32 Gallop apace, you fiery-footed steeds,
Towards Phœbus' lodging.   *Ib.* ii. 1

1 Give me my Romeo: and, when he
    shall die,
  Take him and cut him out in little
    stars,
  And he will make the face of heaven
    so fine
  That all the world will be in love with
    night,
  And pay no worship to the garish sun.
              Romeo and Juliet, III. ii. 21

2 Night's candles are burnt out, and
    jocund day
  Stands tiptoe on the misty mountain
    tops.   *Ib.* v. 9

3 Tempt not a desperate man.
                         Ib. v. iii. 59

4   Beauty's ensign yet
  Is crimson in thy lips and in thy
    cheeks,
  And death's pale flag is not ad-
    vanced there.   *Ib.* 94

5   Eyes, look your last!
  Arms, take your last embrace! and,
    lips, O you
  The doors of breath, seal with a
    righteous kiss
  A dateless bargain to engrossing
    death!   *Ib.* 112

6 And thereby hangs a tale.
           The Taming of the Shrew, IV. i.
    [60]

7   She shall watch all night:
  And if she chance to nod I'll rail and
    brawl,
  And with the clamour keep her still
    awake.
  This is the way to kill a wife with
    kindness.   *Ib.* [208]

8   What seest thou else
  In the dark backward and abysm of
    time?   *The Tempest*, I. ii. 49

9 Come unto these yellow sands,
    And then take hands:
  Curtsied when you have, and kiss'd,—
    The wild waves whist,—
  Foot it featly here and there;
  And, sweet sprites, the burden bear.
    Hark, hark!
              Bow, wow,
  The watch-dogs bark:
              Bow, wow,
  Hark, hark! I hear
  The strain of strutting Chanticleer
              Cock-a-diddle-dow.
                          Ib. 375

10 This music crept by me upon the
    waters,
  Allaying both their fury, and my
    passion,
  With its sweet air.   *Ib.* 389

11 Full fathom five thy father lies;
  Of his bones are coral made:
  Those are pearls that were his eyes:
  Nothing of him that doth fade,

12 But doth suffer a sea-change
  Into something rich and strange.
  Sea-nymphs hourly ring his knell:
              Ding-dong,
  Hark! now I hear them,—ding-dong,
    bell.   *The Tempest*, I. ii. 394

13 A very ancient and fish-like smell.
                      Ib. II. ii. [27]

14 Misery acquaints a man with strange
  bedfellows.   *Ib.* [42]

15 Thou deboshed fish thou.
                      Ib. III. ii. [30]

16 Flout 'em, and scout 'em; and scout
    'em, and flout 'em;
  Thought is free.   *Ib.* [133]

17 He that dies pays all debts. *Ib.* [143]

18   The isle is full of noises,
  Sounds and sweet airs, that give
    delight, and hurt not.   *Ib.* [147]

19 Deeper than did ever plummet sound,
  I'll drown my book.   *Ib.* v. i. 56

20 Where the bee sucks, there suck I
  In a cowslip's bell I lie;
  There I couch when owls do cry.
  On the bat's back I do fly
  After summer merrily:
  Merrily, merrily shall I live now
  Under the blossom that hangs on the
    bough.   *Ib.* 88

21   O brave new world,
  That has such people in 't. *Ib.* 183

22   Retire me to my Milan, where
  Every third thought shall be my grave.
                         Ib. [310]

23 Uncover, dogs, and lap.
           Timon of Athens, III. vi. [96]

24 We have seen better days.
                      Ib. IV. ii. 27

25 She is a woman, therefore may be
    woo'd;
  She is a woman, therefore may be
    won;
  She is Lavinia, therefore must be lov'd.
           Titus Andronicus, II. i. 82

26 Men prize the thing ungain'd more
    than it is.
           Troilus and Cressida, I. ii. [313]

27 Time hath, my lord, a wallet at his
    back,
  Wherein he puts alms for oblivion,
  A great-size'd monster of ingratitudes:
  Those scraps are good deeds past;
    which are devour'd
  As fast as they are made, forgot as
    soon
  As done.   *Ib.* III. iii. 145

28 One touch of nature makes the whole
    world kin,
  That all with one consent praise new-
    born gawds.   *Ib.* 175

1   The end crowns all,
And that old common arbitrator, Time,
Will one day end it.
    Troilus and Cressida, III. iv. 223

2 If music be the food of love, play on;
Give me excess of it, that, surfeiting,
The appetite may sicken, and so die.
That strain again! it had a dying fall:
O! it came o'er my ear like the sweet
    sound
That breathes upon a bank of violets,
Stealing and giving odour! Enough!
    no more:
'Tis not so sweet now as it was before.
    Twelfth Night, I. i. 1

3 A plague o' these pickle herring!
    Ib. v. [127]

4 Make me a willow cabin at your gate,
And call upon my soul within the
    house.   *Ib.* [289]

5 O mistress mine! where are you roam-
    ing?
O! stay and hear; your true love's
    coming,
That can sing both high and low.
Trip no further, pretty sweeting;
Journeys end in lovers meeting,
Every wise man's son doth know.

What is love? 'tis not hereafter;
Present mirth hath present laughter;
What 's to come is still unsure.
In delay there lies no plenty;
Then come kiss me, sweet and twenty,
Youth's a stuff will not endure.
    Ib. II. iii. [42]

6 Is there no respect of place, persons,
nor time, in you?   *Ib.* [100]

7 SIR TOBY:
Dost thou think, because thou art
    virtuous, there shall be no more cakes
    and ale?
CLOWN:
Yes, by Saint Anne, and ginger shall be
hot i' the mouth too.   *Ib.* [124]

8 My purpose is, indeed, a horse of that
colour.   *Ib.* [184]

9 Come away, come away, death,
    And in sad cypress let me be laid;
Fly away, fly away, breath:
    I am slain by a fair cruel maid.
My shroud of white, stuck all with yew,
    O! prepare it.
My part of death no one so true
    Did share it.

Not a flower, not a flower sweet,
    On my black coffin let there be
    strown;
Not a friend, not a friend greet
    My poor corse, where my bones shall
    be thrown.
A thousand thousand sighs to save,
    Lay me, O! where
Sad true lover never find my grave,
    To weep there.   *Ib.* iv. 51

10 DUKE:
And what 's her history?
VIOLA:
A blank, my lord. She never told her
    love,
But let concealment, like a worm i' the
    bud,
Feed on her damask cheek: she pin'd
    in thought;
And with a green and yellow melan-
    choly,
She sat like patience on a monument,
Smiling at grief.
    Twelfth Night, II. iv. [111]

11 I am all the daughters of my father's
house,
And all the brothers too.   *Ib.* [122]

12 But be not afraid of greatness: some
men are born great, some achieve
greatness, and some have greatness
thrust upon them.   *Ib.* v. [158]

13 Remember who commended thy
yellow stockings, and wished to see
thee ever cross-gartered.   *Ib.* [168]

14 He will come to her in yellow stockings, and 'tis a colour she abhors;
and cross-gartered, a fashion she
detests.   *Ib.* [220]

15 In the south suburbs, at the Elephant.
    Ib. III. iii. 39

16 Why, this is very midsummer madness.   *Ib.* iv. [62]

17 Still you keep o' the windy side of the
law.   *Ib.* [183]

18 He is a knight dubbed with unhatched rapier, and on carpet consideration.   *Ib.* [260]

19 And thus the whirligig of time brings
in his revenges.   *Ib.* v. i. [388]

20 When that I was and a little tiny boy,
    With hey, ho, the wind and the rain;
A foolish thing was but a toy,
    For the rain it raineth every day.

But when I came to man's estate,
    With hey, ho, the wind and the rain;
'Gainst knaves and thieves men shut
    their gates,
    For the rain it raineth every day.

But when I came, alas! to wive,
    With hey, ho, the wind and the rain;
By swaggering could I never thrive,
    For the rain it raineth every day.

But when I came unto my beds,
    With hey, ho, the wind and the rain;
With toss-pots still had drunken
    heads,
    For the rain it raineth every day.

A great while ago the world begun,
    With hey, ho, the wind and the
    rain;
But that 's all one, our play is done,
    And we'll strive to please you every
    day.   *Ib.* [401]

1 O! how this spring of love resembleth
The uncertain glory of an April day.
   The Two Gentlemen of Verona,
   III. iii. 84

2 Who is Sylvia? what is she,
   That all our swains commend her?
Holy, fair, and wise is she;
   The heaven such grace did lend her,
That she might admired be.

Is she kind as she is fair?
   For beauty lives with kindness:
Love doth to her eyes repair,
   To help him of his blindness;
And, being help'd, inhabits there.

Then to Silvia let us sing,
   That Silvia is excelling;
She excels each mortal thing
   Upon the dull earth dwelling;
To her let us garlands bring.
                        Ib. IV. ii. 40

3   A sad tale's best for winter.
I have one of sprites and goblins.
   The Winter's Tale, II. i. 24

4 *Exit, pursued by a bear.*
   Ib. III. iii. *Stage Direction*

5 When daffodils begin to peer,
   With heigh! the doxy, over the dale,
Why, then comes in the sweet o' the
      year;
   For the red blood reigns in the
      winter's pale.

The white sheet bleaching on the
      hedge,
   With heigh! the sweet birds, O,
      how they sing!
Doth set my pugging tooth on edge;
   For a quart of ale is a dish for a
      king.

The lark, that tirra-lirra chants,
   With, heigh! with, heigh! the
      thrush and the jay,
Are summer songs for me and my
      aunts,
   While we lie tumbling in the
      hay.   *Ib.* IV. ii. 1

6 A snapper-up of unconsidered trifles.
                              Ib. [26]

7 Jog on, jog on the foot-path way,
   And merrily hent the stile-a:
A merry heart goes all the day,
   Your sad tires in a mile-a.
                              Ib. [133]

8   Daffodils,
That come before the swallow dares,
      and take
The winds of March with beauty;
      violets dim,
But sweeter than the lids of Juno's
      eyes
Or Cytherea's breath; pale prime-
      roses,
That die unmarried, ere they can
      behold

Bright Phœbus in his strength,—a
      malady
Most incident to maids; bold oxlips
      and
The crown imperial; lilies of all
      kinds,
The flower-de-luce being one.
      The Winter's Tale, IV. iii. 118

9 Lawn as white as driven snow.
                              Ib. [220]

10 Crabbed age and youth cannot live
      together:
   Youth is full of pleasance, age is full of
      care.   *The Passionate Pilgrim,* xii

11 Age, I do abhor thee, youth, I do
      adore thee.   *Ib.*

12 Shall I compare thee to a summer's
      day?
Thou art more lovely and more temper-
      ate:
Rough winds do shake the darling buds
      of May,
And summer's lease hath all too short
      a date:
Sometimes too hot the eye of heaven
      shines,
And often is his gold complexion
      dimm'd;
And every fair from fair sometime
      declines,
By chance, or nature's changing course
      untrimm'd;
But thy eternal summer shall not fade,
Nor lose possession of that fair thou
      ow'st,
Nor shall death brag thou wander'st
      in his shade,
When in eternal lines to time thou
      grow'st;
So long as men can breathe, or eyes
      can see,
So long lives this, and this gives life
      to thee.   *Sonnets,* 18

13 When in disgrace with fortune and
      men's eyes
I all alone beweep my outcast state,
And trouble deaf heaven with my
      bootless cries,
And look upon myself, and curse my
      fate,
Wishing me like to one more rich in
      hope
Featur'd like him, like him with
      friends possess'd,
Desiring this man's art, and that man's
      scope,
With what I most enjoy contented
      least;
Yet in these thoughts myself almost
      despising,
Haply I think on thee,—and then
      my state,
Like to the lark at break of day
      arising
From sullen earth, sings hymns at
      heaven's gate;

For thy sweet love remember'd such
  wealth brings
That then I scorn to change my state
  with kings.   *Sonnets*, 29

1 When to the sessions of sweet silent
  thought
I summon up remembrance of things
  past,
I sigh the lack of many a thing I
  sought,
And with old woes new wail my dear
  times' waste.   *Ib.* 30

2 Full many a glorious morning have
  I seen
Flatter the mountain-tops with sove-
  reign eye,
Kissing with golden face the meadows
  green,
Gilding pale streams with heavenly
  alchymy.   *Ib.* 33

3 Why didst thou promise such a
  beauteous day,
And make me travel forth without my
  cloak?   *Ib.* 34

4 Not marble, nor the gilded monuments
Of princes, shall outlive this powerful
  rhyme.   *Ib.* 55

5 Like as the waves make towards the
  pebbled shore,
So do our minutes hasten to their end.
                         Ib. 60

6 When I have seen by Time's fell hand
  defac'd
The rich-proud cost of outworn buried
  age.   *Ib.* 64

7 No longer mourn for me when I am
  dead
Than you shall hear the surly sullen
  bell
Give warning to the world that I am
  fled
From this vile world, with vilest
  worms to dwell.   *Ib.* 71

8 That time of year thou mayst in me
  behold
When yellow leaves, or none, or few,
  do hang
Upon those boughs which shake
  against the cold,
Bare ruin'd choirs, where late the
  sweet birds sang.   *Ib.* 73

9 Farewell! thou art too dear for my
  possessing,
And like enough thou know'st thy
  estimate:
The charter of thy worth gives thee
  releasing;
My bonds in thee are all determinate.
                         Ib. 87

10 Thus have I had thee, as a dream doth
  flatter,
In sleep a king, but, waking, no such
  matter.   *Ib.*

11 Lilies that fester smell far worse than
  weeds.   *Sonnets*, 94

12 How like a winter hath my absence been
From thee, the pleasure of the fleeting
  year!
What freezings have I felt, what dark
  days seen!
What old December's bareness every
  where!   *Ib.* 97

13 To me, fair friend, you never can be old,
For as you were when first your eye
  I ey'd,
Such seems your beauty still. Three
  winters cold
Have from the forests shook three
  summers' pride,
Three beauteous springs to yellow
  autumn turn'd
In process of the seasons have I seen,
Three April perfumes in three hot
  Junes burn'd,
Since first I saw you fresh, which yet
  are green.
Ah! yet doth beauty, like a dial-hand,
Steal from his figure, and no pace
  perceiv'd;
So your sweet hue, which methinks
  still doth stand,
Hath motion, and mine eye may be
  deceiv'd:
For fear of which, hear this, thou
  age unbred:
Ere you were born was beauty's sum-
  mer dead   *Ib.* 104

14 Not mine own fears, nor the prophetic soul
Of the wide world dreaming on things
  to come,
Can yet the lease of my true love
  control.   *Ib.* 107

15 Alas! 'tis true I have gone here and
  there,
And made myself a motley to the
  view.   *Ib.* 110

16 Let me not to the marriage of true
  minds
Admit impediments. Love is not love
Which alters when it alteration finds,
Or bends with the remover to remove:
O, no! it is an ever-fixed mark,
That looks on tempests and is never
  shaken;
It is the star to every wandering bark,
Whose worth's unknown, although his
  height be taken.
Love's not Time's fool, though rosy
  lips and cheeks
Within his bending sickle's compass
  come;
Love alters not with his brief hours
  and weeks,
But bears it out even to the edge of
  doom.
If this be error, and upon me prov'd,
I never writ, nor no man ever lov'd.
                         Ib. 116

1 The expense of spirit in a waste of
shame
Is lust in action; and till action, lust
Is perjur'd, murderous, bloody, full
of blame,
Savage, extreme, rude, cruel, not to
trust.   *Sonnets*, 129

2 Mad in pursuit, and in possession so;
Had, having, and in quest to have,
extreme;
A bliss in proof,—and prov'd, a very
woe;
Before, a joy propos'd; behind, a
dream.
All this the world well knows; yet
none knows well:
To shun the heaven that leads men
to this hell.   *Ib.*

3 My mistress' eyes are nothing like the
sun;
Coral is far more red than her lips'
red:
If snow be white, why then her
breasts are dun;
If hairs be wires, black wires grow on
her head.   *Ib.* 130

4 Two loves I have of comfort and despair,
Which like two spirits do suggest me
still:
The better angel is a man right fair,
The worser spirit a woman colour'd
ill.   *Ib.* 144

5 Good friend, for Jesu's sake forbear
To dig the dust enclosed here.
Blest be the man that spares these
stones,
And curst be he that moves my bones.
*Shakespeare's Epitaph (chosen by
himself for his tomb at Stratford-
on-Avon)*

6 Item, I give unto my wife my second
best bed, with the furniture.
Will, 1616

DAVID TAYLOR SHAW 1813–1890

7 O Britannia, the pride of the ocean,
The home of the brave and the free,
The shrine of the sailor's devotion,
No land can compare unto thee!
*The Red, White, and Blue. First
line changed to* 'Columbia, the
gem of the ocean', *when sung by
Shaw in America. Attr. also to
Thomas à Becket, 1850*

GEORGE BERNARD SHAW
1856–1950

8 You can always tell an old soldier by
the inside of his holsters and cartridge-
boxes. The young ones carry pistols
and cartridges: the old ones, grub.
Arms and the Man, Act I

9 I never apologize.
Arms and the Man, Act III

10 You're not a man, you're a machine.
Ib.

11 I'm only a beer teetotaller, not a
champagne teetotaller.
Candida, Act III

12 The British soldier can stand up to
anything except the British War
Office.   *The Devil's Disciple*, Act III

13 Stimulate the phagocytes.
The Doctor's Dilemma (1906),
Act I

14 With the single exception of Homer,
there is no eminent writer, not even
Sir Walter Scott, whom I can despise
so entirely as I despise Shakespeare
when I measure my mind against
his. . . . It would positively be a
relief to me to dig him up and throw
stones at him.
Dramatic Opinions and Essays
(1907), vol. ii, p. 52

15 Go anywhere in England, where there
are natural, wholesome, contented,
and really nice English people; and
what do you always find? That the
stables are the real centre of the
household.
Heartbreak House (1919), Act III

16 The greatest of evils and the worst of
crimes is poverty.
Major Barbara (1907), Preface

17 Wot prawce Selvytion nah?   *Ib.* Act II

18 Nothing is ever done in this world
until men are prepared to kill one
another if it is not done.   *Ib.* Act III

19 A lifetime of happiness: no man alive
could bear it: it would be hell on
earth.
Man and Superman (1903), Act I

20 The true artist will let his wife starve,
his children go barefoot, his mother
drudge for his living at seventy,
sooner than work at anything but his
art.   *Ib.*

21 An Englishman thinks he is moral
when he is only uncomfortable.
Ib. Act III

22 There are two tragedies in life. One is
not to get your heart's desire. The
other is to get it.   *Ib.* Act IV

23 The golden rule is that there are no
golden rules.
Ib. Maxims for Revolutionists,
p. 227

24 He who can, does. He who cannot,
teaches.   *Ib.* p. 230

25 Marriage is popular because it combines the maximum of temptation
with the maximum of opportunity.
Ib. p. 231

1 Home is the girl's prison and the
woman's workhouse.
Man and Superman (1903),
Maxims for Revolutionists, p. 240

2 Every man over forty is a scoundrel.
Ib. p. 242

3 Not bloody likely.
Pygmalion (1912), Act II

HENRY WHEELER SHAW ['JOSH BILLINGS'] 1818–1885

4 Thrice is he armed that hath his
quarrel just,
But four times he who gets his blow
in fust.
Josh Billings, his Sayings (1865)

RICHARD SHEALE *sixteenth century*

5 For Witherington needs must I wail,
As one in doleful dumps;
For when his legs were smitten off,
He fought upon his stumps.
Ballad of Chevy Chase, pt. II, x

PERCY BYSSHE SHELLEY
1792–1822

6 I weep for Adonais—he is dead!
O, weep for Adonais! though our tears
Thaw not the frost which binds so
dear a head!   *Adonais,* 1

7 A pard-like Spirit, beautiful and
swift—   *Ib.* XXXII

8 He has out-soared the shadow of our
night;
Envy and calumny and hate and pain,
And that unrest which men miscall
delight,
Can touch him not and torture not
again;
From the contagion of the world's
slow stain
He is secure, and now can never mourn
A heart grown cold, a head grown grey
in vain.   *Ib.* XL

9 He is a portion of the loveliness
Which once he made more lovely.
Ib. XLIII

10 The One remains, the many change
and pass;
Heaven's light forever shines, Earth's
shadows fly;
Life, like a dome of many-coloured
glass,
Stains the white radiance of Eternity.
Ib. LII

11 A widow bird sate mourning for her
love
Upon a wintry bough;
The frozen wind crept on above,
The freezing stream below.

There was no leaf upon the forest bare,
No flower upon the ground,
And little motion in the air
Except the mill-wheel's sound.
Charles the First, sc. v, 1. 10

12 The world's great age begins anew,
The golden years return,
The earth doth like a snake renew
Her winter weeds outworn;
Heaven smiles, and faiths and empires
gleam,
Like wrecks of a dissolving dream.

A brighter Hellas rears its mountains
From waves serener far;
A new Peneus rolls his fountains
Against the morning star.
Where fairer Tempes bloom, there
sleep
Young Cyclads on a sunnier deep.

A loftier Argo cleaves the main,
Fraught with a later prize;
Another Orpheus sings again,
And loves, and weeps, and dies.
A new Ulysses leaves once more
Calypso for his native shore.
Hellas, 1. 1060

13 I arise from dreams of thee
In the first sweet sleep of night,
When the winds are breathing low,
And the stars are shining bright:
I arise from dreams of thee,
And a spirit in my feet
Hath led me—who knows how?
To thy chamber window, Sweet!
The Indian Serenade

14 Best and brightest, come away!
Fairer far than this fair day.
To Jane: The Invitation

15 O world! O life! O time!
On whose last steps I climb,
Trembling at that where I had stood
before;
When will return the glory of your
prime?
No more—Oh, never more! *A Lament*

16 When the lamp is shattered
The light in the dust lies dead—
When the cloud is scattered
The rainbow's glory is shed.
When the lute is broken,
Sweet tones are remembered not;
When the lips have spoken,
Loved accents are soon forgot.
Lines: When the Lamp

17 Underneath Day's azure eyes
Ocean's nursling, Venice lies,
A peopled labyrinth of walls,
Amphitrite's destined halls.
*Lines written amongst the
Euganean Hills,* 1. 94

18 I met Murder in the way—
He had a mask like Castlereagh.
The Mask of Anarchy, II

19 Ye are many—they are few.
Ib. XXXVIII

20 Swiftly walk over the western wave,
Spirit of Night!
Out of the misty eastern cave,

Where, all the long and lone daylight,
Thou wovest dreams of joy and fear,
Which make thee terrible and dear,—
　　Swift be thy flight!　　*To Night*

1 O wild West Wind, thou breath of
　　Autumn's being,
Thou, from whose unseen presence the
　　leaves dead
Are driven, like ghosts from an en-
　　chanter fleeing,

Yellow, and black, and pale, and
　　hectic red,
Pestilence-stricken multitudes: O thou,
Who chariotest to their dark wintry
　　bed

The winged seeds, where they lie cold
　　and low,
Each like a corpse within its grave,
　　until
Thine azure sister of the spring shall
　　blow

Her clarion o'er the dreaming earth,
　　and fill
(Driving sweet buds like flocks to feed
　　in air)
With living hues and odours plain and
　　hill:

Wild Spirit, which art moving every-
　　where;
Destroyer and preserver; hear, oh,
　　hear!　　*Ode to the West Wind*, l. 1

2 Thou who didst waken from his
　　summer dreams
　　The blue Mediterranean, where he
　　　　lay,
Lulled by the coil of his crystalline
　　streams

　　Beside a pumice isle in Baiae's bay,
And saw in sleep old palaces and
　　towers
　　Quivering within the wave's in-
　　　　tenser day,

All overgrown with azure moss and
　　flowers
So sweet, the sense faints picturing
　　them.　　*Ib.* l. 29

3 If I were a dead leaf thou mightest
　　bear;
If I were a swift cloud to fly with
　　thee;
A wave to pant beneath thy power,
　　and share

The impulse of thy strength, only less
　　free
Than thou, O uncontrollable! If even
I were as in my boyhood, and could be

The comrade of thy wanderings over
　　Heaven,
As then, when to outstrip thy skiey
　　speed
Scarce seemed a vision; I would
　　ne'er have striven

As thus with thee in prayer in my
　　sore need,
Oh, lift me as a wave, a leaf, a cloud!
I fall upon the thorns of life! I bleed!
　　　　Ode to the West Wind, l. 43

4 Make me thy lyre, even as the forest is:
What if my leaves are falling like its
　　own?
The tumult of thy mighty harmonies
Will take from both a deep, autumnal
　　tone,
Sweet though in sadness. Be thou,
　　Spirit fierce,
My spirit! Be thou me, impetuous one!

Drive my dead thoughts over the
　　universe
Like withered leaves to quicken a
　　new birth!
And, by the incantation of this verse,

Scatter, as from an unextinguished
　　hearth
Ashes and sparks, my words among
　　mankind!
Be through my lips to unawakened
　　earth

The trumpet of a prophecy! O, Wind,
If Winter comes, can Spring be far
　　behind?　　　　*Ib.* l. 57

5 I met a traveller from an antique land
Who said: Two vast and trunkless
　　legs of stone
Stand in the desert.　　*Ozymandias*

6 My name is Ozymandias, king of
　　kings:
Look on my works, ye Mighty, and
　　despair!　　　　　　　　*Ib.*

7 Nothing beside remains. Round the
　　decay
Of that colossal wreck, boundless and
　　bare
The lone and level sands stretch far
　　away.　　　　　　　　*Ib.*

8 The dust of creeds outworn.
　　　　Prometheus Unbound, I. 697

9 On a poet's lips I slept
Dreaming like a love-adept
In the sound his breathing kept;
Nor seeks nor finds he mortal blisses,
But feeds on the aërial kisses
Of shapes that haunt thought's wilder-
　　nesses.
He will watch from dawn to gloom
The lake-reflected sun illume
The yellow bees in the ivy-bloom,
Nor heed, nor see, what things they
　　be;
But from these create he can
Forms more real than living man,
Nurslings of immortality!　　*Ib.* 737

10 A traveller from the cradle to the
　　grave
Through the dim night of this im-
　　mortal day.　　　*Ib.* IV. 551

1 To suffer woes which Hope thinks
   infinite;
To forgive wrongs darker than death
   or night;
To defy Power, which seems omni-
   potent;
To love, and bear; to hope till Hope
   creates
From its own wreck the thing it con-
   templates;
   Neither to change, nor falter, nor
     repent;
This, like thy glory, Titan, is to be
Good, great and joyous, beautiful and
   free;
This is alone Life, Joy, Empire and
   Victory.
     Prometheus Unbound, IV. 570

2 A Sensitive Plant in a garden grew.
     The Sensitive Plant, pt. I, l. 1

3 Hail to thee, blithe Spirit!
   Bird thou never wert,
That from Heaven, or near it,
   Pourest thy full heart
In profuse strains of unpremeditated
   art.   *To a Skylark*

4 Like a Poet hidden
   In the light of thought,
   Singing hymns unbidden,
     Till the world is wrought
To sympathy with hopes and fears it
   heeded not.   *Ib.*

5 We look before and after;
   We pine for what is not;
   Our sincerest laughter
     With some pain is fraught;
Our sweetest songs are those that tell
   of saddest thought.   *Ib.*

6 Teach me half the gladness
   That thy brain must know,
   Such harmonious madness
   From my lips would flow
The world should listen then—as I am
   listening now.   *Ib.*

7 Rarely, rarely, comest thou,
   Spirit of Delight!
     Song: Rarely, Rarely, Comest
     Thou

8 An old, mad, blind, despised, and
   dying king.   *Sonnet: England in 1819*

9 Lift not the painted veil which those
   who live
Call Life.
   Sonnet: Lift not the Painted Veil

10 Music, when soft voices die,
   Vibrates in the memory—
Odours, when sweet violets sicken,
   Live within the sense they quicken.

   Rose leaves, when the rose is dead,
   Are heaped for the beloved's bed;
And so thy thoughts, when thou art
   gone,
Love itself shall slumber on.
     To——. Music, When Soft Voices

11 I fear thy kisses, gentle maiden,
   Thou needest not fear mine;
My spirit is too deeply laden
   Ever to burthen thine.

I fear thy mien, thy tones, thy motion,
   Thou needest not fear mine;
Innocent is the heart's devotion
   With which I worship thine.
     To——. I Fear Thy Kisses

12 One word is too often profaned
   For me to profane it,
One feeling too falsely disdained
   For thee to disdain it.
     To——. One Word is too often
     Profaned

13 The desire of the moth for the star,
   Of the night for the morrow,
The devotion to something afar
   From the sphere of our sorrow. *Ib.*

14 And like a dying lady, lean and pale,
   Who totters forth, wrapped in a
   gauzy veil.   *The Waning Moon*

15 Poets are the unacknowledged legislators of the world.
     A Defence of Poetry

16 The rich have become richer, and the
   poor have become poorer; and the
   vessel of the state is driven between
   the Scylla and Charybdis of anarchy
   and despotism.   *Ib.*

17 Poetry is the record of the best and
   happiest moments of the happiest and
   best minds.   *Ib.*

WILLIAM SHENSTONE 1714–1763

18 Whoe'er has travell'd life's dull round,
   Where'er his stages may have been,
May sigh to think he still has found
   The warmest welcome, at an inn.
     At an Inn at Henley

ROBERT LOWE, VISCOUNT SHERBROOKE 1811–1892

19 I believe it will be absolutely necessary
   that you should prevail on our future
   masters to learn their letters.
     Speech in House of Commons
     (on the passing of the Reform Bill),
     15 July 1867. Popularized as
     'We must educate our masters'

PHILIP HENRY SHERIDAN
                      1831–1888

20 The only good Indian is a dead Indian.
     Attr., at Fort Cobb, Jan. 1869

RICHARD BRINSLEY SHERIDAN 1751–1816

21 Not a translation—only *taken from
the French*.   *The Critic*, I. i

1 Yes, sir, puffing is of various sorts; the principal are, the puff direct, the puff preliminary, the puff collateral, the puff collusive, and the puff oblique, or puff by implication.   *The Critic*, I. ii

2 No scandal about Queen Elizabeth, I hope?   *Ib.* II. i

3 Where they do agree on the stage, their unanimity is wonderful!   *Ib.* ii

4 O Lord, sir, when a heroine goes mad she always goes into white satin.
                   Ib. III. i

5 An oyster may be crossed in love. *Ib.*

6 I loved him for himself alone.
             The Duenna, I. iii.

7 I was struck all of a heap.   *Ib.* II. ii

8 Madam, a circulating library in a town is as an evergreen tree of diabolical knowledge! It blossoms through the year! And depend on it, Mrs. Malaprop, that they who are so fond of handling the leaves, will long for the fruit at last.   *The Rivals*, I. ii

9 You gentlemen's gentlemen are so hasty.   *Ib.* II. ii

10 An aspersion upon my parts of speech!
                Ib. III. iii

11 If I reprehend any thing in this world, it is the use of my oracular tongue, and a nice derangement of epitaphs!
                      Ib.

12 She's as headstrong as an allegory on the banks of the Nile.   *Ib.*

13 Too civil by half.   *Ib.* iv

14 I own the soft impeachment. *Ib.* v. iv

15 You shall see them on a beautiful quarto page, where a neat rivulet of text shall meander through a meadow of margin.   *The School for Scandal*, I. i

16 MRS. CANDOUR:
I'll swear her colour is natural: I have seen it come and go.
LADY TEAZLE:
I dare swear you have ma'am: it goes off at night, and comes again in the morning.   *Ib.* II. ii

17 I'm called away by particular business. But I leave my character behind me.   *Ib.*

18 Oh! plague of his sentiments!   *Ib.* iii

19 Here's to the maiden of bashful fifteen;
Here's to the widow of fifty;
Here's to the flaunting, extravagant quean;
And here's to the housewife that's thrifty.
        Let the toast pass,—
        Drink to the lass,
I'll warrant she'll prove an excuse for the glass.   *Ib.* III. iii. Song

20 Damned disinheriting countenance.
        The School for Scandal, IV. i

21 CHARLES SURFACE:
Lady Teazle, by all that's wonderful!
SIR PETER TEAZLE:
Lady Teazle, by all that's damnable!
                   Ib. iii

22 It was an amiable weakness. *Ib.* v. i

23 The Right Honourable gentleman is indebted to his memory for his jests, and to his imagination for his facts.
     Speech in Reply to Mr. Dundas.
     T. Moore, *Life of Sheridan* (1825),
     ii. 471

JAMES SHIRLEY 1596–1666

24 The glories of our blood and state
Are shadows, not substantial things;
There is no armour against fate:
Death lays his icy hand on kings:
       Sceptre and crown
       Must tumble down,
And in the dust be equal made
With the poor crooked scythe and spade.
     The Contention of Ajax and Ulysses, I. iii

25 Only the actions of the just
Smell sweet, and blossom in their dust.
                    Ib.

THE SHORTER CATECHISM

26 'What is the chief end of man?'
'To glorify God and to enjoy him for ever.'

ALGERNON SIDNEY 1622–1683

27 Liars ought to have good memories.
     Discourses on Government, ch. 2,
     § xv

28 'Tis not necessary to light a candle to the sun.   *Ib.* § xxiii

SIR PHILIP SIDNEY 1554–1586

29 My true love hath my heart and I have his,
By just exchange one for the other giv'n;
I hold his dear, and mine he cannot miss,
There never was a better bargain driv'n.   *The Arcadia*, bk. iii *ad fin.*

30 With how sad steps, O Moon, thou climb'st the skies!
How silently, and with how wan a face!
What! may it be that even in heavenly place
That busy archer his sharp arrows tries?
     Astrophel and Stella, *Certain Sonnets*. *Sonnet XXXI*

1 Come, Sleep! O Sleep, the certain
  knot of peace,
  The baiting-place of wit, the balm of
  woe,
  The poor man's wealth, the prisoner's
  release,
  Th' indifferent judge between the
  high and low.
    *Astrophel and Stella, Certain Son-
    nets, Sonnet XXXIX*

2 With a tale forsooth he cometh unto
  you, with a tale which holdeth
  children from play, and old men from
  the chimney corner.
    The Defence of Poesy (1595)

3 Thy necessity is yet greater than mine.
    *On giving his water-bottle to a
    dying soldier on the battlefield of
    Zutphen, 1586.* Sir Fulke Gre-
    ville's *Life* (1907), ch. 12. *The
    word 'necessity' is more often
    quoted as 'need'*

SIMONIDES 556–468 B.C.

4 ὦ ξεῖν', ἀγγειλον Λακεδαιμονίοις ὅτι τῇδε
  κείμεθα, τοῖς κείνων ῥήμασι πειθόμενοι.

  Go, tell the Spartans, thou who
    passest by,
      That here obedient to their
      laws we lie.
    Select Epigrams (ed. Mackail), iii. 4

GEORGE R. SIMS 1847–1922

5 It is Christmas Day in the workhouse.   *The Dagonet Ballads*

SIR OSBERT SITWELL 1892–1969

6 The British Bourgeoisie
  Is not born,
  And does not die,
  But, if it is ill,
  It has a frightened look in its eyes.
    At the House of Mrs. Kinfoot

JOHN SKELTON 1460?–1529

7 For the soul of Philip Sparrow,
  That was late slain at Carrow
  Among the Nunnes Black,
  For that sweet soul's sake
  And for all sparrows' souls
  Set in our bead-rolls,
  Pater noster qui
  With an *Ave Mari.*
    The Sparrow's Dirge

8 The Tunning of Elynour Rumming.
    Title of Poem

CHRISTOPHER SMART 1722–1771

9 And now the matchless deed's
  achiev'd,
  Determined, dared, and done.
    Song to David, st. 86

FRANCIS EDWARD SMEDLEY
1818–1864

10 You are looking as fresh as paint.
    Frank Fairlegh, ch. 41

SAMUEL SMILES 1812–1904

11 A place for everything, and everything
   in its place.   *Thrift,* ch. 5

ADAM SMITH 1723–1790

12 To found a great empire for the sole
   purpose of raising up a people of
   customers, may at first sight appear a
   project fit only for a nation of shop-
   keepers. It is, however, a project
   altogether unfit for a nation of shop-
   keepers; but extremely fit for a
   nation that is governed by shop-
   keepers.
     Wealth of Nations, vol. II, bk. iv,
     ch. 7, pt. iii (see *1:2, 151:15*)

LOGAN PEARSALL SMITH
1865–1946

13 Thank heavens, the sun has gone in,
   and I don't have to go out and enjoy
   it.   *All Trivia.* Last Words

SAMUEL FRANCIS SMITH
1808–1895

14 My country, 'tis of thee,
   Sweet land of liberty,
   Of thee I sing:
   Land where my fathers died,
   Land of the pilgrims' pride,
   From every mountain-side
   Let freedom ring.   *America*

REV. SYDNEY SMITH 1771–1845

15 Looked as if she had walked straight
   out of the Ark.
     Lady Holland, *Memoir* (1st ed.
     1855), vol. i, ch. 7, p. 157

16 Madam, I have been looking for a
   person who disliked gravy all my life;
   let us swear eternal friendship.
     Ib. ch. 9, p. 257

17 As the French say, there are three
   sexes—men, women, and clergymen.
     Ib. p. 262

18 Serenely full, the epicure would say,
   Fate cannot harm me, I have dined
   to-day.
     Ib. ch. 11, p. 373, *Recipe for
     Salad*

19 You remember Thurlow's answer . . .
   you never expected justice from a
   company, did you? They have neither
   a soul to lose, nor a body to kick.
     Ib. p. 376

20 Deserves to be preached to death by
   wild curates.   *Ib.* p. 384

1 I never read a book before reviewing
it; it prejudices a man so.
 H. Pearson, *The Smith of Smiths*
 (1934), ch. 3, p. 5

2 ——'s idea of heaven is, eating *pâtés
de foie gras* to the sound of trumpets.
 Ib. ch. 10, p. 236

3 I am just going to pray for you at
St. Paul's, but with no very lively
hope of success.   *Ib.* ch. 13, p. 308

4 Dame Partington . . . was seen . . .
with mop and pattens . . . vigorously
pushing away the Atlantic Ocean.
The Atlantic Ocean beat Mrs. Partington.
 Peter Plymley's Letters (1929),
 p. 228

TOBIAS GEORGE SMOLLETT
1721–1771

5 That great Cham of literature, Samuel
Johnson.
 *Letter to John Wilkes, 16 Mar.
 1759.* Boswell's *Johnson* (1934),
 vol. i, p. 348

GEORGE HUNT SMYTTAN
1822–1870
and
FRANCIS POTT 1832–1909

6 Forty days and forty nights
Thou wast fasting in the wild,
Forty days and forty nights
Tempted, and yet undefiled.
 *Hymn: Forty Days and Forty
 Nights. The Penny Post* (1856)

SOCRATES 469–399 B.C.

7 ὦ Κρίτων, τῷ Ἀσκληπιῷ ὀφείλομεν ἀλεκτρυόνα. ἀλλὰ ἀπόδοτε καὶ μὴ ἀμελήσητε.
 Crito, we owe a cock to Aesculapius;
 pay it, therefore, and do not
 neglect it.
 Last words, 399 B.C. Plato,
 Phaedo, 118a

SOLON c. 640–c. 558 B.C.

8 πρὶν δ᾽ ἂν τελευτήσῃ, ἐπισχεῖν μηδὲ καλέειν
κω ὄλβιον, ἀλλ᾽ εὐτυχέα.
 Call no man happy till he dies, he
 is at best but fortunate.
 Herodotus, *Histories,* i. 32

SOPHOCLES 495–406 B.C.

9 πολλὰ τὰ δεινὰ κοὐδὲν ἀνθρώπου δεινότερον πέλει.
 Wonders are many, and none is
 more wonderful than man.
 Antigone, 332. Trans. by Jebb

10 μὴ φῦναι τὸν ἅπαντα νικᾷ λόγον.
 Not to be born is best.
 Oedipus Coloneus, 1225

JOHN BABSONE LANE SOULE
1815–1891

11 Go west, young man.
 Article in the Terre Haute, In-
 diana, Express (1851)

ROBERT SOUTHEY 1774–1843

12 It was a summer evening,
 Old Kaspar's work was done,
And he before his cottage door
 Was sitting in the sun,
And by him sported on the green
 His little grandchild Wilhelmine.
 The Battle of Blenheim

13 But what they fought each other for,
 I could not well make out.   *Ib.*

14 'And everybody praised the Duke,
 Who this great fight did win.'
 'But what good came of it at last?'
 Quoth little Peterkin.
 'Why that I cannot tell,' said he,
 'But 'twas a famous victory.'   *Ib.*

15 Curses are like young chickens, they
always come home to roost.
 The Curse of Kehama. Motto

16 His coat was red and his breeches were
 blue,
And there was a hole where his tail
 came through.
 The Devil's Walk, iii

17 He passed a cottage with a double
 coach-house,
 A cottage of gentility!
And he owned with a grin
That his favourite sin
 Is pride that apes humility.   *Ib.* viii

18 No stir in the air, no stir in the sea,
The ship was still as she could be.
 The Inchcape Rock

19 And then they knew the perilous rock,
And blest the Abbot of Aberbrothok.
 Ib.

20 O Christ! It is the Inchcape Rock!
 Ib.

21 Sir Ralph the Rover tore his hair;
He curst himself in his despair.   *Ib.*

22 You are old, Father William, the
 young man cried,
The few locks which are left you are
 grey;
You are hale, Father William, a
 hearty old man,
Now tell me the reason, I pray.
 *The Old Man's Comforts, and
 how he Gained them*

1 You are old, Father William, the
young man cried
And pleasures with youth pass
away,
And yet you lament not the days that
are gone,
Now tell me the reason, I pray.
*The Old Man's Comforts, and how
he Gained them*

2 The death of Nelson was felt in England as something more than a public
calamity; men started at the intelligence, and turned pale, as if they had
heard of the loss of a dear friend.
The Life of Nelson, ch. 9

HERBERT SPENCER 1820–1903

3 This survival of the fittest.
*Principles of Biology, pt. iii, ch.
12, Indirect Equilibration, § 165*

4 Progress, therefore, is not an accident,
but a necessity. . . . It is a part of
nature. *Social Statics, pt. i, ch. 2, § 4*

5 It was remarked to me by the late
Mr. Charles Roupell . . . that to play
billiards well was a sign of an ill-spent
youth.
*Remark. Duncan, Life and
Letters of Spencer (1908), ch. 20,
p. 298*

STEPHEN SPENDER 1909–

6 I think continually of those who were
truly great—
The names of those who in their lives
fought for life,
Who wore at their hearts the fire's
centre.
I Think Continually of Those

7 Born of the sun they travelled a short
while towards the sun,
And left the vivid air signed with their
honour. *Ib.*

EDMUND SPENSER 1552?–1599

8 Triton blowing loud his wreathed
horn.
*Colin Clout's Come Home Again,
l. 245*

9 A gentle knight was pricking on the
plain.
The Faerie Queene, bk. I, c. I. i

10 Sleep after toil, port after stormy seas,
Ease after war, death after life does
greatly please. *Ib. c. IX. xl*

11 And all for love, and nothing for
reward. *Ib. bk. II, c. VIII. ii*

12 For all that nature by her mother wit
Could frame in earth.
Ib. bk. IV, c. X. xxi

13 Sweet Thames, run softly, till I end
my Song. *Prothalamion, l. 18*

14 At length they all to merry London
came,
To merry London, my most kindly
nurse,
That to me gave this life's first native
source. *Prothalamion, l. 127*

15 So now they have made our English
tongue a gallimaufry or hodgepodge
of all other speeches.
*The Shepherd's Calendar. Letter
to Gabriel Harvey*

REV. WILLIAM ARCHIBALD SPOONER 1844–1930

16 Kinquering Congs their titles take.
*Announcing the hymn in New
College Chapel, 1879 (see 59:18)*

17 You have deliberately tasted two
worms and you can leave Oxford by
the town drain.
Dismissing a student. Attr.

SIR CECIL ARTHUR SPRING-RICE 1858–1918

18 I vow to thee, my country—all
earthly things above—
Entire and whole and perfect, the
service of my love. *Last Poem*

19 I am the Dean of Christ Church, Sir:
There's my wife; look well at her.
She's the Broad and I'm the High;
We are the University.
*The Masque of Balliol, composed
by and current among members of
Balliol College, Oxford, in the
late 1870's. This first couplet
(identified as by C. A. Spring-
Rice) was unofficially altered to:*

20 I am the Dean, and this is Mrs. Liddell;
She is the first and I the second fiddle.
(See also 6:9, 20:5)

SIR JOHN COLLINGS SQUIRE 1884–

21 It did not last: the Devil howling 'Ho!
Let Einstein be!' restored the status
quo.
*Answer to Pope's epitaph for Sir
Isaac Newton*

MME DE STAËL 1766–1817

22 Tout comprendre rend très indulgent.
To know all makes one tolerant.
Corinne (1807), lib. iv, ch. 3

EDWARD STANLEY, EARL OF DERBY 1799–1869

23 When I first came into Parliament,
Mr. Tierney, a great Whig authority,
used always to say that the duty of
an Opposition was very simple—it

was, to oppose everything, and propose nothing.
House of Commons, 4 June 1841.
Hansard, 3rd ser., lviii. 1188

1 Don't you see that we have dished the Whigs?
With reference to the Reform Bill of 1867. Monypenny and Buckle, *Life of Disraeli,* ii. 285

SIR HENRY MORTON STANLEY
1841–1904

2 Dr. Livingstone, I presume?
How I found Livingstone, ch. 11

FRANK LEBBY STANTON
1857–1927

3 Sweetest li'l feller, everybody knows;
Dunno what to call him, but he's mighty lak' a rose;
Lookin' at his mammy wid eyes so shiny blue
Mek' you think that Heav'n is comin' clost ter you.   *Mighty Lak' a Rose*

SIR RICHARD STEELE 1672–1729

4 There are so few who can grow old with a good grace.
The Spectator, No. 263

5 Though her mien carries much more invitation than command, to behold her is an immediate check to loose behaviour; to love her is a liberal education.   *The Tatler,* No. 49

6 Reading is to the mind what exercise is to the body.   *Ib.* No. 147

JAMES KENNETH STEPHEN
1859–1892

7 Two voices are there: one is of the deep;

And one is of an old half-witted sheep
Which bleats articulate monotony,

And Wordsworth, both are thine.
Lapsus Calami. Sonnet

8 When the Rudyards cease from kipling
And the Haggards ride no more.
Ib. To R.K.

JAMES STEPHENS 1882–1950

9 I heard a sudden cry of pain!
There is a rabbit in a snare.
The Snare

10 Little One! Oh, Little One!
I am searching everywhere!   *Ib.*

LAURENCE STERNE 1713–1768

11 They order, said I, this matter better in France.
A Sentimental Journey, l. 1

12 God tempers the wind, said Maria, to the shorn lamb.
Ib. Maria. From a French proverb, but familiar in Sterne's form of words

13 'Pray, my dear,' quoth my mother, 'have you not forgot to wind up the clock?'—'Good G——!' cried my father, making an exclamation, but taking care to moderate his voice at the same time,—'Did ever woman, since the creation of the world, interrupt a man with such a silly question?'
Tristram Shandy, bk. i, ch.1

14 My uncle Toby would never offer to answer this by any other kind of argument, than that of whistling half a dozen bars of Lillabullero.
Ib. ch. 21

15 I should have no objection to this method, but that I think it must smell too strong of the lamp.
Ib. ch. 23

16 That's another story. *Ib.* bk. ii, ch. 18

17 The nonsense of the old women (of both sexes).   *Ib.* bk. iv, ch. 16

18 Said my mother, 'what is all this story about?'—
'A Cock and a Bull,' said Yorick.
Ib. bk. ix, ch. 33

ADLAI EWING STEVENSON
1900–1965

19 [Mr. Stevenson] derided the Secretary [of State] for 'boasting of his brinkmanship—the art of bringing us to the edge of the nuclear abyss'.
New York Times, 26 Feb. 1956, p. 1, col. 5 (reporting a speech by Mr. Adlai Stevenson).

ROBERT LOUIS STEVENSON
1850–1894

20 Every one lives by selling something.
Across the Plains, ix. *Beggars,* iii

21 Am I no a bonny fighter? [*Alan Breck.*]
Kidnapped, ch. 10

22 I have thus played the sedulous ape to Hazlitt, to Lamb, to Wordsworth, to Sir Thomas Browne, to Defoe, to Hawthorne, to Montaigne, to Baudelaire and to Obermann.
Memories and Portraits, ch. 4

23 I own I like definite form in what my eyes are to rest upon; and if landscapes were sold, like the sheets of characters of my boyhood, one penny plain and twopence coloured, I should

go the length of twopence every day of my life.
Travels with a Donkey. Father Apollinaris

1 Fifteen men on the dead man's chest
Yo-ho-ho, and a bottle of rum!
Drink and the devil had done for the rest—
Yo-ho-ho, and a bottle of rum!
Treasure Island, ch. 1

2 Tip me the black spot. *Ib. ch. 3*

3 Pieces of eight! *Ib. ch. 10*

4 Many 's the long night I've dreamed of cheese—toasted, mostly. [*Ben Gunn.*]
Ib. ch. 15

5 Marriage is like life in this—that it is a field of battle, and not a bed of roses. *Virginibus Puerisque, 1. i*

6 To travel hopefully is a better thing than to arrive, and the true success is to labour. *Ib. VI. El Dorado*

7 Though we are mighty fine fellows nowadays, we cannot write like Hazlitt. *Ib. X. Walking Tours*

8 You must not fancy I am sick, only over-driven and under the weather.
The Wrecker, ch. 4

9 Nothing like a little judicious levity.
[*Michael Finsbury.*] *The Wrong Box, ch. 7*

10 'The "Athæneum", that was the name! Golly, what a paper!' ' "Athenæum", you mean,' said Morris.
Ib. ch. 15

11 A child should always say what's true,
And speak when he is spoken to,
And behave mannerly at table:
At least as far as he is able.
A Child's Garden of Verses. V. Whole Duty of Children

12 The pleasant land of counterpane.
Ib. XVI. The Land of Counterpane

13 The friendly cow, all red and white,
I love with all my heart:
She gives me cream with all her might,
To eat with apple-tart.
Ib. XXIII. The Cow

14 The world is so full of a number of things,
I'm sure we should all be as happy as kings. *Ib. XXIV. Happy Thought*

15 Give to me the life I love,
Let the lave go by me,
Give the jolly heaven above
And the byway nigh me.
Bed in the bush with stars to see,
Bread I dip in the river—
There 's the life for a man like me,
There 's the life for ever.
Songs of Travel. I. The Vagabond

16 The untented Kosmos my abode,
I pass, a wilful stranger;
My mistress still the open road
And the bright eyes of danger.
Songs of Travel, II. Youth and Love

17 I will make you brooches and toys for your delight
Of bird-song at morning and star-shine at night.
I will make a palace fit for you and me
Of green days in forests and blue days at sea. *Ib. XI*

18 Bright is the ring of words
When the right man rings them,
Fair the fall of songs
When the singer sings them. *Ib. XIV*

19 Trusty, dusky, vivid, true,
With eyes of gold and bramble-dew,
Steel-true and blade-straight,
The great artificer
Made my mate. *Ib. XXV. My Wife*

20 Sing me a song of a lad that is gone,
Say, could that lad be I?
Merry of soul he sailed on a day
Over the sea to Skye. *Ib. XLII*

21 Mull was a-stern, Rum on the port,
Eigg on the starboard bow;
Glory of youth glowed in his soul,
Where is that glory now? *Ib.*

22 Go, little book, and wish to all
Flowers in the garden, meat in the hall,
A bin of wine, a spice of wit,
A house with lawns enclosing it,
A living river by the door,
A nightingale in the sycamore!
Underwoods, bk. I. i. Envoy

23 Under the wide and starry sky
Dig the grave and let me lie.
Glad did I live and gladly die,
And I laid me down with a will.
This be the verse you grave for me:
'Here he lies where he longed to be;
Home is the sailor, home from sea,
And the hunter home from the hill.'
Ib. xxi. Requiem

24 If I have faltered more or less
In my great task of happiness;
If I have moved among my race
And shown no glorious morning face;
If beams from happy human eyes
Have moved me not; if morning skies,
Books, and my food, and summer rain
Knocked on my sullen heart in vain:—
Lord, thy most pointed pleasure take
And stab my spirit broad awake;
Or, Lord, if too obdurate I,
Choose thou, before that spirit die,
A piercing pain, a killing sin,
And to my dead heart run them in!
Ib. xxii. The Celestial Surgeon

WILLIAM STEVENSON
1530?–1575

25 I stuff my skin, so full within,
Of jolly good ale and old,

Back and side go bare, go bare,
Both foot and hand go cold:
But belly God send thee good ale
    enough,
Whether it be new or old.
    Gammer Gurton's Needle, Act II,
    Song

SAMUEL JOHN STONE 1839–1900

1 The Church's one foundation
Is Jesus Christ her Lord;
She is His new creation
By water and the Word.
    Lyra Fidelium (1866). *The
    Church's One Foundation*

2 Yet Saints their watch are keeping,
Their cry goes up, 'How long?'
And soon the night of weeping
Shall be the morn of song.   *Ib.*

HARRIET BEECHER STOWE
1811–1896

3 'Who was your mother?' 'Never had
none!' said the child, with another
grin. 'Never had any mother? What
do you mean? Where were you born?'
'Never was born!' persisted Topsy.
    Uncle Tom's Cabin, ch. 20

4 'Do you know who made you?' 'Nobody, as I knows on,' said the child,
with a short laugh. . . . 'I 'spect I
grow'd.'   *Ib.*

SIR JOHN SUCKLING 1609–1642

5 Why so pale and wan, fond lover?
    Prithee, why so pale?
Will, when looking well can't move her,
    Looking ill prevail?
    Prithee, why so pale?
    Aglaura, IV. i. *Song*

6 Her feet beneath her petticoat,
Like little mice, stole in and out,
As if they fear'd the light.
    Ballad. Upon a Wedding, viii

7 The Prince of Darkness is a gentleman.
    The Goblins, Act III, *A Catch*

8 Out upon it, I have loved
    Three whole days together;
And am like to love three more,
    If it prove fair weather.

Time shall moult away his wings,
    Ere he shall discover
In the whole wide world again
    Such a constant lover.
    A Poem with the Answer

SUETONIUS *fl. c.* A.D. 120

9 Festina lente. [σπεῦδε βραδέως.]
    Hasten slowly. *Divus Augustus,* 25

10 Ave, Imperator, morituri te salutant.
    Hail, Emperor, those about to die
    salute thee. *Life of Claudius,* 21

MAXIMILIAN DE BETHUNE,
DUC DE SULLY 1559–1641

11 Les anglais s'amusent tristement
selon l'usage de leur pays.
    The English take their pleasures
    sadly after the fashion of their
    country.   *Memoirs, c.* 1630

ROBERT SMITH SURTEES
1803–1864

12 The only infallible rule we know is,
that the man who is always talking
about being a gentleman never is one.
    Ask Mamma (1858), ch. 1

13 'Unting is all that's worth living for—
all time is lost wot is not spent in
'unting—it is like the hair we breathe
—if we have it not we die—it's the
sport of kings, the image of war
without its guilt, and only five-and-
twenty per cent. of its danger.
    Handley Cross (1843), ch. 7

14 'Unting fills my thoughts by day, and
many a good run I have in my sleep.
Many a dig in the ribs I gives Mrs. J.
when I think they're running into the
warmint (renewed cheers). No man
is fit to be called a sportsman wot
doesn't kick his wife out of bed on
a haverage once in three weeks!
    Ib. ch. 11

15 Come Hup! I say, you hugly beast!
    Ib. ch. 13

16 He will bring his nightcap with him,
for where the M.F.H. dines he sleeps,
and where the M.F.H. sleeps he breakfasts.   *Ib.* ch. 15

17 It ar'n't that I loves the fox less, but
that I loves the 'ound more. *Ib.* ch. 16

18 Full o' beans and benevolence!
    Ib. ch. 27

19 Hellish dark, and smells of cheese!
    Ib. ch. 50

20 And a nod or a wink for every pretty
maid that showed at the windows;
for . . . , as he says, 'there is no harm
in looking'.
    Jorrocks's Jaunts and Jollities
    (1838), *No. 4. Surrey Stag-
    Hounds*

21 No one knows how ungentlemanly he
can look, until he has seen himself
in a shocking bad hat.
    Mr. Facey Romford's Hounds
    (1865), ch. 9

22 He was a gentleman who was generally
spoken of as having nothing a-year,
paid quarterly.
    Mr. Sponge's Sporting Tour
    (1853), ch. 24

JONATHAN SWIFT 1667–1745

1 Instead of dirt and poison we have rather chosen to fill our hives with honey and wax; thus furnishing mankind with the two noblest of things, which are sweetness and light.
The Battle of the Books, preface

2 And he gave it for his opinion, that whoever could make two ears of corn or two blades of grass to grow upon a spot of ground where only one grew before, would deserve better of mankind, and do more essential service to his country than the whole race of politicians put together.
Gulliver's Travels. Voyage to Brobdingnag, ch. 7

3 With my own fair hands.
Journal to Stella, 4 Jan. 1711

4 Will she pass in a crowd? Will she make a figure in a country church?
Ib. 9 Feb. 1711

5 Not die here in a rage, like a poisoned rat in a hole.
Letter to Bolingbroke, 21 Mar. 1729

6 I have ever hated all nations, professions and communities, and all my love is towards individuals. . . . But principally I hate and detest that animal called man; although I heartily love John, Peter, Thomas, and so forth.
Letter to Pope, 29 Sept. 1725

7 What they call 'running a man down'.
Letter to a Young Lady on her Marriage (1723)

8 Promises and pie-crust are made to be broken.
Polite Conversation. Dialogue 1

9 The sight of you is good for sore eyes.
Ib.

10 You were half seas over.   *Ib.*

11 I won't quarrel with my bread and butter.   *Ib.*

12 I swear, she's no chicken; she's on the wrong side of thirty, if she be a day.   *Ib.*

13 She wears her clothes, as if they were thrown on her with a pitchfork.   *Ib.*

14 You must take the will for the deed.
Ib. Dialogue 2

15 She has more goodness in her little finger, than he has in his whole body.
Ib.

16 I know Sir John will go, though he was sure it would rain cats and dogs.
Ib.

17 There's none so blind as they that won't see.   *Ib. Dialogue 3*

18 She watches him, as a cat would watch a mouse.
Polite Conversation. Dialogue 3

19 She pays him in his own coin.   *Ib.*

20 All the world and his wife.   *Ib.*

21 Party is the madness of many, for the gain of a few.
Thoughts on Various Subjects

22 They never would hear,
But turn the deaf ear,
As a matter they had no concern in.
Dingley and Brent, ii

23 Hail, fellow, well met,
All dirty and wet:
Find out, if you can,
Who's master, who's man.
My Lady's Lamentation, l. 171

24 Philosophy, the lumber of the schools.
Ode to Sir W. Temple, ii

25 Walls have tongues, and hedges ears.
Pastoral Dialogue, l. 8

26 So, naturalists observe, a flea
Hath smaller fleas that on him prey;
And these have smaller fleas to bite 'em,
And so proceed *ad infinitum*.
Thus every poet, in his kind,
Is bit by him that comes behind.
On Poetry, l. 337

27 Ubi saeva indignatio ulterius cor lacerare nequit.

Where fierce indignation can no longer tear his heart.
Swift's Epitaph

ALGERNON CHARLES SWINBURNE 1837–1909

28 When the hounds of spring are on winter's traces,
The mother of months in meadow or plain
Fills the shadows and windy places
With lisp of leaves and ripple of rain;
And the brown bright nightingale amorous
Is half assuaged for Itylus,
For the Thracian ships and the foreign faces,
The tongueless vigil and all the pain.
Atalanta in Calydon. Collected Poetical Works (1924), vol. ii. Chorus, p. 249

29 And time remembered is grief forgotten,
And frosts are slain and flowers begotten,
And in green underwood and cover
Blossom by blossom the spring begins.   *Ib. p. 250*

1 Before the beginning of years
   There came to the making of man
Time with a gift of tears,
   Grief with a glass that ran.
Pleasure with pain for leaven,
   Summer with flowers that fell,
Remembrance fallen from heaven,
   And Madness risen from hell,
Strength without hands to smite,
   Love that endures for a breath;
Night, the shadow of light,
   And Life, the shadow of death.
        Atalanta in Calydon. Collected
        Poetical Works (1924), vol. ii,
        Chorus, p. 258

2 Eyesight and speech they wrought
   For the veil of the soul therein,
A time for labour and thought,
   A time to serve and to sin;
They gave him light in his ways,
   And love, and a space for delight,
And beauty and length of days,
   And night, and sleep in the night.
His speech is a burning fire;
   With his lips he travaileth;
In his heart is a blind desire,
   In his eyes foreknowledge of death;
He weaves, and is clothed with deri-
   sion;
   Sows, and he shall not reap;
His life is a watch or a vision
   Between a sleep and a sleep.
                Ib. p. 259

3 We shift and bedeck and bedrape us,
   Thou art noble and nude and
   antique.   *Dolores,* vii

4   Change in a trice
The lilies and languors of virtue
   For the raptures and roses of vice.
                  Ib. ix

5 O splendid and sterile Dolores,
   Our Lady of Pain.   *Ib.*

6 From too much love of living,
   From hope and fear set free,
We thank with brief thanksgiving
   Whatever gods may be
That no man lives forever,
That dead men rise up never;
That even the weariest river
   Winds somewhere safe to sea.
      The Garden of Persephone

7 Swallow, my sister, O sister swallow,
   How can thine heart be full of the
   spring?
A thousand summers are over and
   dead.
   What hast thou found in the spring
   to follow?
What hast thou found in thine heart
   to sing?
What wilt thou do when the summer
   is shed?   *Itylus*

8 Glory to Man in the highest! for Man
is the master of things. *Hymn of Man*

9 Wilt thou yet take all, Galilean? but
   these thou shalt not take,
The laurel, the palms and the paean,
   the breasts of the nymphs in the
   brake;
Breasts more soft than a dove's, that
   tremble with tenderer breath;
And all the wings of the Loves, and all
   the joy before death.
          Hymn to Proserpine

10 Thou hast conquered, O pale Galilean;
   the world has grown grey from Thy
   breath;
We have drunken of things Lethean,
   and fed on the fullness of death.
Laurel is green for a season, and love
   is sweet for a day;
But love grows bitter with treason,
   and laurel outlives not May.   *Ib.*

11 There lived a singer in France of old
By the tideless dolorous midland sea.
In a land of sand and ruin and gold
There shone one woman, and none but
she.   *The Triumph of Time*

PUBLILIUS SYRUS
                     fl. first century B.C.

12 Bis dat qui cito dat.
   He gives twice who gives soon.
          Proverbial, attr. to Syrus

13 Necessitas non habet legem.
   Necessity has no law.
          Proverbial, attr. to Syrus

TACITUS c. A.D. 55–c. 117

14 Atque omne ignotum pro magnifico
   est; sed nunc terminus Britanniae
   patet.
    For wonder grows where knowledge
      fails. But now the very bounds of
      Britain are laid bare.
      Agricola, 30. Trans. by Fyfe

15 Ubi solitudinem faciunt, pacem appellant.
    When they make a wilderness they
      call it peace.   *Ib.*

16 Felix . . . opportunitate mortis.
    Fortune favoured him . . . in the
      opportune moment of his death.
                    Ib. 45

17 Editis annalibus laudatoque M. Bruto
   C. Cassium Romanorum ultimum
   dixisset.
    In his history he had praised Brutus
      and had called Cassius the last
      of the Romans.   *Annals,* iv. 34

18 Elegantiae arbiter. [Petronius.]
   Judge of taste.   *Ib.* xvi. 18

1 Maior privato visus dum privatus fuit,
et omnium consensu capax imperii
nisi imperasset.

When he was a commoner he seemed
too big for his station, and had he
never been emperor, no one would
have doubted his ability to reign.
[Servius Galba.]
Histories, I. xlix. Trans. by Fyfe

CHARLES-MAURICE DE
TALLEYRAND 1754–1838

2 Ils n'ont rien appris, ni rien oublié.

They have learnt nothing, and forgotten nothing.
*Attributed to Talleyrand by the
Chevalier de Panat in a letter to
Mallet du Pan, Jan. 1796, 'Personne n'est corrigé, personne n'a
su ni rien oublier ni rien ap-
prendre.' (Mémoires et corre-
spondance de Mallet du Pan
(1851), ii. 196.) See also 80:11*

3 N'ayez pas de zèle.

Not too much zeal.
Sainte-Beuve, *Portraits de
femmes, Madame de Staël*, p. 131

4 Voilà le commencement de la fin.

This is the beginning of the end.
*On the announcement of
Napoleon's defeat at Borodino,
1812*

5 War is much too serious a thing to be
left to military men.
*Quoted by Briand to Lloyd George
during the First World War*

NAHUM TATE 1652–1715
and
NICHOLAS BRADY 1659–1726

6 As pants the hart for cooling streams
When heated in the chase.
*New Version of the Psalms (1696).
As Pants the Hart*

7 Through all the changing scenes of
life. *Ib. Through all the Changing*

8 Fear Him, ye saints, and you will then
Have nothing else to fear. *Ib.*

9 While shepherds watch'd their flocks
by night,
All seated on the ground,
The Angel of the Lord came down,
And glory shone around.

'Fear not,' said he, for mighty dread
Had seized their troubled mind;
'Glad tidings of great joy I bring
To you and all mankind.'
*Supplement to the New Version of
the Psalms (1700). While Shep-
herds Watched*

ANN TAYLOR 1782–1866
and
JANE TAYLOR 1783–1824

10 Twinkle, twinkle, little star,
How I wonder what you are!
Up above the world so high,
Like a diamond in the sky!
*Rhymes for the Nursery. The
Star. (By Jane Taylor)*

BISHOP JEREMY TAYLOR
1613–1667

11 Every school-boy knows it.
On the Real Presence, § v, par. 1

JOHN TAYLOR 1580–1653

12 'Tis a mad world, my masters.
Western Voyage, l. 1

ARCHBISHOP WILLIAM
TEMPLE 1881–1944

13 We have . . . seen that in place of the
conception of the Power-State we are
led to that of the Welfare-State.
*Citizen and Churchmen (1941),
p. 35*

ALFRED, LORD TENNYSON
1809–1892

14 Break, break, break,
On thy cold gray stones, O Sea!
And I would that my tongue could
utter
The thoughts that arise in me.
Break, Break, Break

15 And the stately ships go on
To their haven under the hill;
But O for the touch of a vanish'd hand,
And the sound of a voice that is still!

Break, break, break,
At the foot of thy crags, O Sea!
But the tender grace of a day that is
dead
Will never come back to me. *Ib.*

16 A happy bridesmaid makes a happy
bride. *The Bridesmaid, l. 4*

17 I come from haunts of coot and hern,
I make a sudden sally
And sparkle out among the fern,
To bicker down a valley.
The Brook, l. 23

18 For men may come and men may go,
But I go on for ever. *Ib. l. 33*

19 That petitionary grace
Of Sweet Seventeen. *Ib. l. 112*

20 Half a league, half a league,
Half a league onward.
The Charge of the Light Brigade

21 'Forward, the Light Brigade!'
Was there a man dismay'd? *Ib.*

1 Some one had blunder'd.
The Charge of the Light Brigade

2 Their's not to make reply,
Their's not to reason why,
Their's but to do and die:
Into the valley of Death
Rode the six hundred.   *Ib.*

3 Cannon to right of them
Cannon to left of them,
Cannon in front of them
Volley'd and thunder'd.   *Ib.*

4 Into the jaws of Death,
Into the mouth of Hell.   *Ib.*

5 When can their glory fade?
O the wild charge they made!
All the world wonder'd.   *Ib.*

6 Sunset and evening star,
And one clear call for me!
And may there be no moaning of the
bar,
When I put out to sea,

But such a tide as moving seems
asleep,
Too full for sound and foam,
When that which drew from out the
boundless deep
Turns again home.

Twilight and evening bell,
And after that the dark!
And may there be no sadness of fare-
well,
When I embark;

For tho' from out our bourne of Time
and Place
The flood may bear me far,
I hope to see my Pilot face to face
When I have crost the bar.
Crossing the Bar

7 Gray metropolis of the North. [Edin-
burgh.]   *The Daisey,* xxvi

8 A daughter of the gods, divinely tall
And most divinely fair.
A Dream of Fair Women, l. 87

9 He clasps the crag with crooked
hands;
Close to the sun in lonely lands,
Ring'd with the azure world, he
stands.
The wrinkled sea beneath him crawls;
He watches from his mountain walls,
And like a thunderbolt he falls.
The Eagle

10 And when they buried him the little
port
Had seldom seen a costlier funeral.
Enoch Arden

11 The mellow lin-lan-lone of evening
bells.   *Far-Far-Away*

12 Flower in the crannied wall,
I pluck you out of the crannies,
I hold you here, root and all, in my
hand,

Little flower—but *if* I could under-
stand
What you are, root and all, and all in
all,
I should know what God and man is.
Flower in the Crannied Wall

13 More black than ashbuds in the front
of March.
The Gardener's Daughter, l. 28

14 Pray God our greatness may not fail
Thro' craven fears of being great.
Hands All Round, iii

15 Wearing the white flower of a blame-
less life,
Before a thousand peering littlenesses,
In that fierce light which beats upon
a throne,
And blackens every blot.
The Idylls of the King, Dedica-
tion, l. 24

16 Clothed in white samite, mystic,
wonderful.
Ib. l. 284, and *The Passing of
Arthur,* l. 199

17 Live pure, speak true, right wrong,
follow the King—
Else, wherefore born?
Ib. Gareth and Lynette, l. 117

18 The children born of thee are sword
and fire,
Red ruin, and the breaking up of
laws.   *Ib. Guinevere,* l. 422

19 It was my duty to have loved the
highest:
It surely was my profit had I known:
It would have been my pleasure had
I seen.
We needs must love the highest when
we see it,
Not Lancelot, nor another. *Ib.* l. 652

20 God make thee good as thou art
beautiful.   *Ib. The Holy Grail,* l. 136

21 Elaine the fair, Elaine the loveable,
Elaine, the lily maid of Astolat.
Ib. Lancelot and Elaine, l. 1

22 The shackles of an old love straiten'd
him,
His honour rooted in dishonour stood,
And faith unfaithful kept him falsely
true.   *Ib.* l. 870

23 It is the little rift within the lute,
That by and by will make the music
mute,
And ever widening slowly silence all.
Ib. Merlin and Vivien, l. 388

24 Man dreams of fame while woman
wakes to love.   *Ib.* l. 458

25 So all day long the noise of battle
roll'd
Among the mountains by the winter
sea.

Ib. The Passing of Arthur, l. 170

1 And slowly answer'd Arthur from the barge:
'The old order changeth, yielding place to new,
And God fulfils himself in many ways,
Lest one good custom should corrupt the world.' *The Idylls of the King.*
The Passing of Arthur, l. 407

2 If thou shouldst never see my face again,
Pray for my soul. More things are wrought by prayer
Than this world dreams of. Wherefore, let thy voice
Rise like a fountain for me night and day.
For what are men better than sheep or goats
That nourish a blind life within the brain,
If, knowing God, they lift not hands of prayer
Both for themselves and those who call them friend?
For so the whole round earth is every way
Bound by gold chains about the feet of God. *Ib. l.* 414

3 I am going a long way
With these thou seest—if indeed I go
(For all my mind is clouded with a doubt)—
To the island-valley of Avilion;
Where falls not hail, or rain, or any snow,
Nor ever wind blows loudly; but it lies
Deep-meadow'd, happy, fair with orchard lawns
And bowery hollows crown'd with summer sea,
Where I will heal me of my grievous wound. *Ib. l.* 424

4 Thou madest man, he knows not why,
He thinks he was not made to die;
And thou hast made him: thou art just.
In Memoriam, prologue. (*The numbering of the Cantos follows that of the latest edition, and includes the additional Canto No. xxxix, first published in 1869.*)

5 Our little systems have their day;
They have their day and cease to be:
They are but broken lights of thee,
And thou, O Lord, art more than they. *Ib.*

6 I held it truth, with him who sings
To one clear harp in divers tones,
That men may rise on stepping-stones
Of their dead selves to higher things.
In Memoriam, i

7 Never morning wore
To evening, but some heart did break. *Ib.* vi

8 The last red leaf is whirl'd away,
The rooks are blown about the skies.
In Memoriam, xv

9 'Tis better to have loved and lost
Than never to have loved at all. *Ib.* xxvii

10 Oh yet we trust that somehow good
Will be the final goal of ill. *Ib.* liv

11 But what am I?
An infant crying in the night:
An infant crying for the light:
And with no language but a cry. *Ib.* liv

12 So careful of the type she seems,
So careless of the single life. *Ib.* lv

13 Nature, red in tooth and claw. *Ib.* lvi

14 So many worlds, so much to do,
So little done, such things to be. *Ib.* lxxiii

15 Dusty purlieus of the law. *Ib.* lxxxix

16 There lives more faith in honest doubt,
Believe me, than in half the creeds. *Ib.* xcvi

17 He seems so near and yet so far. *Ib.* xcvii

18 Ring out, wild bells, to the wild sky. *Ib.* cvi

19 Ring out the old, ring in the new,
Ring, happy bells, across the snow:
The year is going, let him go;
Ring out the false, ring in the true. *Ib.*

20 Ring out old shapes of foul disease;
Ring out the narrowing lust of gold;
Ring out the thousand wars of old,
Ring in the thousand years of peace.
Ring in the valiant man and free,
The larger heart, the kindlier hand;
Ring out the darkness of the land;
Ring in the Christ that is to be. *Ib.*

21 Wearing all that weight
Of learning lightly like a flower.
Ib. Conclusion, st. x

22 Kind hearts are more than coronets,
And simple faith than Norman blood.
Lady Clara Vere de Vere, vi

23 On either side the river lie
Long fields of barley and of rye.
The Lady of Shalott, pt. i

24 'Tirra lirra,' by the river
Sang Sir Lancelot. *Ib.*

25 She left the web, she left the loom,
She made three paces thro' the room,
She saw the water-lily bloom,
She saw the helmet and the plume,
She look'd down to Camelot.
Out flew the web and floated wide;
The mirror crack'd from side to side;
'The curse is come upon me,' cried
The Lady of Shalott. *Ib.*

1 Heard a carol, mournful, holy,
Chanted loudly, chanted lowly,
Till her blood was frozen slowly,
And her eyes were darken'd wholly,
Turn'd to tower'd Camelot.
The Lady of Shalott, pt. i

2 But Lancelot mused a little space;
He said, 'She has a lovely face;
God in his mercy lend her grace,
The Lady of Shalott.'   *Ib.*

3 Airy, fairy Lilian.   *Lilian*

4 Comrades, leave me here a little,
while as yet 'tis early morn:
Leave me here, and when you want
me, sound upon the bugle-horn.
Locksley Hall, l. i

5 In the Spring a livelier iris changes on
the burnish'd dove;
In the Spring a young man's fancy
lightly turns to thoughts of love.
Ib. l. 19

6 He will hold thee, when his passion
shall have spent its novel force.
Something better than his dog, a
little dearer than his horse. *Ib.* l. 49

7 This is truth the poet sings,
That a sorrow's crown of sorrow is
remembering happier things.
Ib. l. 75

8 For I dipt into the future, far as
human eye could see,
Saw the Vision of the world, and all
the wonder that would be.
Ib. l. 119

9 Heard the heavens fill with shouting,
and there rain'd a ghastly dew
From the nations' airy navies grappling
in the central blue. *Ib.* l. 123

10 In the Parliament of man, the Federation of the world. *Ib.* l. 128

11 Yet I doubt not thro' the ages one increasing purpose runs,
And the thoughts of men are widen'd
with the process of the suns.
Ib. l. 137

12 Knowledge comes, but wisdom lingers.
Ib. l. 143

13 I the heir of all the ages, in the foremost files of time. *Ib.* l. 178

14 Forward, forward let us range,
Let the great world spin for ever down
the ringing grooves of change.
Ib. l. 181

15 Better fifty years of Europe than a
cycle of Cathay. *Ib.* l. 184

16 A land
In which it seemed always afternoon.
The Lotus-Eaters

17 Music that gentlier on the spirit lies,
Than tir'd eyelids upon tir'd eyes.
Ib. Choric Song, i

18 She only said, 'My life is dreary,
He cometh not,' she said;
She said, 'I am aweary, aweary.
I would that I were dead!' *Mariana*

19 Faultily faultless, icily regular, splendidly null. *Maud,* Pt. I. ii

20 Come into the garden, Maud,
For the black bat, night, has flown;
Come into the garden, Maud,
I am here at the gate alone;
And the woodbine spices are wafted
abroad,
And the musk of the rose is blown.
Ib. XXII. i.

There has fallen a splendid tear
From the passion-flower at the gate.
She is coming, my dove, my dear;
She is coming, my life, my fate;
The red rose cries, 'She is near, she is
near;'
And the white rose weeps, 'She is
late;'
The larkspur listens, 'I hear, I hear;
And the lily whispers, 'I wait.'

She is coming, my own, my sweet;
Were it ever so airy a tread,
My heart would hear her and beat,
Were it earth in an earthy bed;
My dust would hear her and beat,
Had I lain for a century dead;
Would start and tremble under her
feet,
And blossom in purple and red.
Ib. x–xi

21 You must wake and call me early,
call me early, mother dear;
To-morrow 'ill be the happiest time
of all the glad New-year;
Of all the glad New-year, mother, the
maddest merriest day;
For I'm to be Queen o' the May,
mother, I'm to be Queen o' the May.
The May Queen

22 In after-dinner talk,
Across the walnuts and the wine.
The Miller's Daughter

23 But I knaw'd a Quaäker feller as often
'as towd me this:
'Doänt thou marry for munny, but
goä wheer munny is!'
Northern Farmer. New Style

24 Bury the Great Duke
With an empire's lamentation,
Let us bury the Great Duke
To the noise of the mourning of a
mighty nation.
*Ode on the Death of the Duke of
Wellington,* i

25 Foremost captain of his time,
Rich in saving common-sense,
And, as the greatest only are,
In his simplicity sublime.
O good grey head which all men knew!
Ib. iv

1 O fall'n at length that tower of strength
Which stood four-square to all the winds that blew!
Ode on the Death of the Duke of Wellington, iv.

2 Not once or twice in our rough island-story,
The path of duty was the way to glory. *Ib. viii*

3 O mother Ida, many-fountain'd Ida.
Œnone, l. 22

4 Dear mother Ida, harken ere I die.
It was the deep midnoon: one silvery cloud
Had lost his way between the piney sides
Of this long glen. Then to the bower they came,
Naked they came to that smooth-swarded bower,
And at their feet the crocus brake like fire,
Violet, amaracus, and asphodel,
Lotos and lilies. *Ib. l. 89*

5 I built my soul a lordly pleasure-house,
Wherein at ease for aye to dwell.
The Palace of Art, i

6 With prudes for proctors, dowagers for deans,
And sweet girl-graduates in their golden hair.
The Princess, prologue, l. 141

7 As thro' the land at eve we went,
And pluck'd the ripen'd ears,
We fell out, my wife and I,
O we fell out I know not why,
And kiss'd again with tears.
And blessings on the falling out
That all the more endears,
When we fall out with those we love
And kiss again with tears!
Ib. ii. Introd. Song

8 O hard, when love and duty clash!
Ib. ii. l. 273

9 Sweet and low, sweet and low,
Wind of the western sea,
Low, low, breathe and blow,
Wind of the western sea!
Over the rolling waters go,
Come from the dying moon, and blow,
Blow him again to me;
While my little one, while my pretty one, sleeps. *Ib. iii. Introd. Song*

10 The splendour falls on castle walls
And snowy summits old in story:
The long light shakes across the lakes,
And the wild cataract leaps in glory.
Blow, bugle, blow, set the wild echoes flying,
Blow, bugle; answer, echoes, dying, dying, dying. *Ib. iv. Introd. Song*

11 O hark, O hear! how thin and clear,
And thinner, clearer, farther going!
O sweet and far from cliff and scar
The horns of Elfland faintly blowing!
The Princess, iv. Introd. Song

12 O love, they die in yon rich sky,
They faint on hill or field or river:
Our echoes roll from soul to soul,
And grow for ever and for ever.
Ib.

13 Tears, idle tears, I know not what they mean,
Tears from the depth of some divine despair
Rise in the heart, and gather to the eyes,
In looking on the happy Autumn-fields,
And thinking of the days that are no more. *Ib. l. 21*

14 O tell her, Swallow, thou that knowest each,
That bright and fierce and fickle is the South,
And dark and true and tender is the North. *Ib. l. 78*

15 Home they brought her warrior dead.
She nor swoon'd, nor utter'd cry:
All her maidens, watching, said,
'She must weep or she will die.'
Ib. vi. Introd. Song

16 Now sleeps the crimson petal, now the white;
Nor waves the cypress in the palace walk;
Nor winks the gold fin in the porphyry font:
The fire-fly wakens: waken thou with me.
Now droops the milk-white peacock like a ghost,
And like a ghost she glimmers on to me. *Ib. l. 61*

17 Now folds the lily all her sweetness up,
And slips into the bosom of the lake:
So fold thyself, my dearest, thou, and slip
Into my bosom and be lost in me.
Ib. l. 171

18 Come down, O maid, from yonder mountain height:
What pleasure lives in height?
Ib. l. 177

19 Sweet is every sound,
Sweeter thy voice, but every sound is sweet;
Myriads of rivulets hurrying thro' the lawn,
The moan of doves in immemorial elms,
And murmuring of innumerable bees.
Ib. l. 203

1　Her court was pure; her life serene;
　　God gave her peace; her land
　　　reposed;
　　A thousand claims to reverence
　　　closed
　In her as Mother, Wife, and Queen;
　　　To the Queen (1851), 'Revered,
　　　beloved'

2　At Flores in the Azores Sir Richard
　　Grenville lay,
　And a pinnace, like a fluttered bird,
　　came flying from far away:
　'Spanish ships of war at sea! we have
　　sighted fifty-three!' *The Revenge*, i

3　And they blest him in their pain, that
　　they were not left to Spain,
　To the thumbscrew and the stake, for
　　the glory of the Lord.　　*Ib.* iii

4　'Shall we fight or shall we fly?
　Good Sir Richard, tell us now,
　For to fight is but to die!
　There'll be little of us left by the time
　　this sun be set.'
　And Sir Richard said again: 'We be all
　　good English men.
　Let us bang these dogs of Seville, the
　　children of the devil,
　For I never turn'd my back upon Don
　　or devil yet.'　　　　　*Ib.* iv

5　And they praised him to his face with
　　their courtly foreign grace;
　But he rose upon their decks, and he
　　cried:
　'I have fought for Queen and Faith
　　like a valiant man and true;
　I have only done my duty as a man is
　　bound to do:
　With a joyful spirit I Sir Richard
　　Grenville die!'
　And he fell upon their decks, and he
　　died.　　　　　　　*Ib.* xiii

6　What does little birdie say
　In her nest at peep of day?
　　　　　　Sea Dreams, 1. 281

7　Birdie, rest a little longer,
　Till the little wings are stronger.
　So she rests a little longer,
　Then she flies away.　　*Ib.* 1. 285

8　My strength is as the strength of ten,
　Because my heart is pure.
　　　　　　　　Sir Galahad

9　Alone and warming his five wits,
　The white owl in the belfry sits.
　　　　　　　Song. The Owl

10　The woods decay, the woods decay and
　　fall,
　The vapours weep their burthen to the
　　ground,
　Man comes and tills the field and lies
　　beneath,
　And after many a summer dies the
　　swan.　　　　　*Tithonus*, 1. 1

11　Here at the quiet limit of the world.
　　　　　　　　　Ib. 1. 7

12　It little profits that an idle king,
　By this still hearth, among these
　　barren crags,
　Match'd with an aged wife, I mete and
　　dole
　Unequal laws unto a savage race.
　　　　　　　　Ulysses, 1. 1

13　　　　　　I will drink
　Life to the lees: all times I have en-
　　joy'd
　Greatly, have suffer'd greatly, both
　　with those
　That loved me, and alone; on shore,
　　and when
　Thro' scudding drifts the rainy Hyades
　Vext the dim sea: I am become a
　　name;
　For always roaming with a hungry
　　heart
　Much have I seen and known; cities
　　of men
　And manners, climates, councils,
　　governments,
　Myself not least, but honour'd of them
　　all;
　And drunk delight of battle with my
　　peers,
　Far on the ringing plains of windy
　　Troy.
　I am a part of all that I have met;
　Yet all experience is an arch where-
　　thro'
　Gleams that untravell'd world, whose
　　margin fades
　For ever and for ever when I move.
　How dull it is to pause, to make an end,
　To rust unburnish'd, not to shine in
　　use!
　As tho' to breathe were life. Life
　　piled on life
　Were all too little, and of one to me
　Little remains: but every hour is
　　saved
　From that eternal silence, something
　　more,
　A bringer of new things.　　*Ib.* 1. 6

14　This gray spirit yearning in desire
　To follow knowledge like a sinking
　　star,
　Beyond the utmost bound of human
　　thought.　　　　　*Ib.* 1. 30

15　　　　　My mariners,
　Souls that have toil'd, and wrought,
　　and thought with me—
　That ever with a frolic welcome took
　The thunder and the sunshine, and
　　opposed
　Free hearts, free foreheads—you and
　　I are old;
　Old age hath yet his honour and his
　　toil;
　Death closes all: but something ere
　　the end,
　Some work of noble note, may yet
　　be done,
　Not unbecoming men that strove with
　　gods.

The lights begin to twinkle from the
rocks:
The long day wanes: the slow moon
climbs: the deep
Moans round with many voices. Come,
my friends,
'Tis not too late to seek a newer world.
Push off, and sitting well in order
smite
The sounding furrows; for my pur-
pose holds
To sail beyond the sunset, and the
baths
Of all the western stars, until I die.
It may be that the gulfs will wash us
down:
It may be we shall touch the Happy
Isles,
And see the great Achilles, whom we
knew.
Tho' much is taken, much abides;
and tho'
We are not now that strength which
in old days
Moved earth and heaven; that which
we are, we are;
One equal temper of heroic hearts,
Made weak by time and fate, but
strong in will
To strive, to seek, to find, and not to
yield. *Ulysses, l. 45*

1 I salute thee, Mantovano,
I that loved thee since my day began,
Wielder of the stateliest measure ever
moulded by the lips of man.
To Virgil, x

2 Every moment dies a man,
Every moment one is born.
The Vision of Sin, ix

3 Sea-King's daughter from over the
sea, Alexandra!
Saxon and Norman and Dane are we,
But all of us Danes in our welcome of
thee, Alexandra!
A Welcome to Alexandra

4 O plump head-waiter at the Cock
To which I most resort.
*Will Waterproof's Lyrical Mono-
logue, i*

5 A louse in the locks of literature.
*Said of Churton Collins to Ed-
mund Gosse. Evan Charteris's
Life and Letters of Sir Edmund
Gosse, ch. xiv*

TERENCE c. 195–159 B.C.

6 Homo sum; humani nil a me alienum
puto.

I am a man, I count nothing human
alien from me.
Heauton Timorumenos, 77

7 Fortis fortuna adiuvat.

Fortune aids the brave.
Phormio, 203

8 Quot homines tot sententiae: suo'
quoique mos.

So many men, so many opinions; his
own a law to each. *Phormio, 454*

TERTULLIAN A.D. c. 160–c. 225

9 O testimonium animae naturaliter
Christianae.

O witness of the soul naturally
Christian. *Apol. xvii*

10 Plures efficimus quoties metimur a
vobis, semen est sanguis Christianorum.

The more ye mow us down, the
more we grow, the blood of Christians is seed. (*Traditionally ren-
dered as* 'The blood of the martyrs is the seed of the Church'.)
Ib. 1 ad fin.

11 Certum est quia impossibile est.

It is certain because it is impossible.
De Carne Christi, 5

EDWARD TESCHEMACHER
nineteenth century

12 Where my caravan has rested,
Flowers I leave you on the grass.
Where My Caravan Has Rested

WILLIAM MAKEPEACE
THACKERAY 1811–1863

13 Kind, cheerful, merry Dr. Brighton.
The Newcomes, bk. i

14 Rake's progress.
*Pendennis, title of ch. 19. Used
earlier by Hogarth*

15 Business first; pleasure afterwards.
[Queen of Paflagonia.]
The Rose and the Ring, ch. 1

16 Them's my sentiments! [Fred Bullock.]
Vanity Fair, ch. 21

17 Darkness came down on the field and
city: and Amelia was praying for
George, who was lying on his face,
dead, with a bullet through his heart.
Ib. ch. 32

18 How to live well on nothing a year.
Ib. Title of ch. 36

19 There were three sailors of Bristol
City
Who took a boat and went to sea.
But first with beef and captain's
biscuits
And pickled pork they loaded she.
There was gorging Jack and guzzling
Jimmy,
And the youngest he was little Billee.
Now when they got as far as the
Equator
They'd nothing left but one split pea.
Little Billee

1 Says gorging Jim to guzzling Jacky,
 We have no wittles, so we must eat
   we.   *Little Billee*

2 There's little Bill as is young and
   tender,
 We're old and tough—so let's eat *he*.
                                    Ib.

3 He scarce had said his Catechism,
 When up he jumps: 'There's land
   I see!
 There's Jerusalem and Madagascar,
 And North and South Ameri*key*.
 There's the British Fleet a-riding at
   anchor,
 With Admiral Napier, K.C.B.' *Ib.*

4 Werther had a love for Charlotte
 Such as words could never utter;
 Would you know how first he met her?
 She was cutting bread and butter.

 Charlotte was a married lady,
 And a moral man was Werther,
 And for all the wealth of Indies,
 Would do nothing for to hurt her.

 So he sighed and pined and ogled,
 And his passion boiled and bubbled,
 Till he blew his silly brains out
 And no more was by it troubled.

 Charlotte, having seen his body
 Borne before her on a shutter,
 Like a well-conducted person,
 Went on cutting bread and butter.
                     Sorrows of Werther

WILLIAM MAKEPEACE THAYER

5 Log-cabin to White House.
   *Title of a biography (1910) of
   James Garfield (1831–1881)*

BRANDON THOMAS 1848–1914

6 Brazil, where the nuts come from.
                        Charley's Aunt

FRANCIS THOMPSON 1859–1907

7 I fled Him, down the nights and down
     the days;
 I fled Him, down the arches of the
     years;
 I fled Him, down the labyrinthine
     ways
 Of my own mind; and in the mist of
     tears
 I hid from Him, and under running
   laughter.   *The Hound of Heaven*

8 But with unhurrying chase,
 And unperturbèd pace,
 Deliberate speed, majestic instancy,
 They beat—and a Voice beat
 More instant than the Feet—
 'All things betray thee, who betrayest
   Me.'   *Ib.*

9 O world invisible, we view thee,
 O world intangible, we touch thee,
 O world unknowable, we know thee,
 Inapprehensible, we clutch thee!
                     The Kingdom of God

10 The angels keep their ancient
     places;—
 Turn but a stone, and start a wing!
 'Tis ye, 'tis your estrangèd faces,
 That miss the many-splendoured
   thing.

 But (when so sad thou canst not
   sadder)
 Cry;—and upon thy so sore loss
 Shall shine the traffic of Jacob's ladder
 Pitched betwixt Heaven and Charing
   Cross.

 Yea, in the night, my Soul, my
     daughter,
 Cry,—clinging Heaven by the hems;
 And lo, Christ walking on the water
 Not of Gennesareth, but Thames! *Ib.*

11 It is little I repair to the matches of
     the Southron folk,
 Though my own red roses there may
     blow;
 It is little I repair to the matches of
     the Southron folk,
 Though the red roses crest the caps
     I know.
 For the field is full of shades as I near
     the shadowy coast,
 And a ghostly batsman plays to the
     bowling of a ghost,
 And I look through my tears on a
     soundless-clapping host
 As the run-stealers flicker to and fro,
     To and fro:—
   O my Hornby and my Barlow long
     ago!   *At Lord's*

WILLIAM HEPWORTH
THOMPSON 1810–1886

12 We are none of us infallible—not
   even the youngest of us.
     *Remark referring to G. W. Bal-
     four, then Junior Fellow of
     Trinity. G. W. E. Russell's
     Collections and Recollections, ch.
     18*

JAMES THOMSON 1700–1748

13 When Britain first, at heaven's
     command,
 Arose from out the azure main,
 This was the charter of the land,
 And guardian angels sung this strain:
   'Rule, Britannia, rule the waves;
   Britons never will be slaves.'
     *Alfred: a Masque (1740), Act II,
     Scene the last*

14 Delightful task! to rear the tender
     thought,
 To teach the young idea how to shoot.
     The Seasons, Spring, l. 1152

1 Or sighed and looked unutterable things.
The Seasons, Summer, l. 1188

2 Oh! Sophonisba! Sophonisba! Oh!
Sophonisba, III. iii

JAMES THOMSON 1834–1882

3 The City of Dreadful Night.
Title of Poem

4 As we rush, as we rush in the train,
The trees and the houses go wheeling back,
But the starry heavens above that plain
Come flying on our track.
Sunday at Hampstead, x

5 Give a man a horse he can ride,
Give a man a boat he can sail.
Sunday up the River, xv

HENRY DAVID THOREAU
1817–1862

6 As for Doing-good, that is one of the professions which are full. Moreover, I have tried it fairly, and, strange as it may seem, am satisfied that it does not agree with my constitution.
Walden. Economy

7 The three-o'-clock in the morning courage, which Bonaparte thought was the rarest.
Ib. Sounds

8 It takes two to speak the truth,— one to speak, and another to hear.
A Week on the Concord and Merrimack Rivers, Wednesday

9 Some circumstantial evidence is very strong, as when you find a trout in the milk.
Unpublished MSS. in Miscellanies, Biographical Sketch (1918), vol. x, p. 30

ROSE HARTWICK THORPE
1850–1939

10 Curfew must not ring to-night.
Title of Poem

THUCYDIDES c. 460–c. 400 B.C.

11 κτῆμα ἐς ἀεί.
A possession for ever. *History*, i, § 4

12 ἀνδρῶν γὰρ ἐπιφανῶν πᾶσα γῆ τάφος.
The whole earth is the sepulchre of famous men. *Ib.* ii. 43, § 3

JAMES THURBER 1894–1961

13 The War Between Men and Women.
Title of Series of Cartoons

14 Is Sex Necessary? *Title of Book*

EDWARD, FIRST BARON THURLOW 1731–1806

15 Did you ever expect a corporation to have a conscience, when it has no soul to be damned, and no body to be kicked?
Attr. See Sydney Smith, Recipe for Salad, p. 376, and John Poynder, Literary Extracts from English and Other Works (1884)

TIBULLUS 54?–18? B.C.

16 Iuppiter pluvius.
Jupiter the rain-bringer.
Ib. I. vii. 26

THOMAS TICKELL 1686–1740

17 There taught us how to live; and (oh! too high
The price for knowledge) taught us how to die.
Epitaph. On the Death of Mr. Addison, l. 81. Addison's *Works* (1721), preface, p. xx

HARRY TILZER

18 Come, Come, Come and have a drink with me
Down at the old 'Bull and Bush'.
Song sung by Florrie Ford

19 Come, Come, Come and make eyes at me. *Ib.*

TITUS VESPASIANUS
A.D. 39–81

20 Amici, diem perdidi.
Friends, I have lost a day.
Suetonius, *Titus*, ch. 8, 1

JACOPONE DA TODI d. 1306

21 Stabat mater dolorosa
Iuxta crucem lacrimosa.
At the cross her station keeping
Stood the mournful mother weeping.
Pacheu, *Jacopone de Todi. Trans. in English Hymnal. Also ascribed to Innocent III*

LEO TOLSTOY 1828–1910

22 All happy families resemble each other, each unhappy family is unhappy in its own way.
Anna Karenina, pt. i, ch. 1.
Trans. by Maude

AUGUSTUS MONTAGUE TOPLADY 1740–1778

23 Rock of ages, cleft for me,
Let me hide myself in thee.
The Gospel Magazine, Oct. 1775.
Rock of Ages

I

1 Nothing in my hand I bring,
  Simply to thy Cross I cling;
  Naked, come to thee for dress;
  Helpless, look to thee for grace;
  Foul, I to the Fountain fly;
  Wash me, Saviour, or I die.
  The Gospel Magazine, Oct. 1775.
  Rock of Ages

THOMAS TRAHERNE 1637?–1674

2 The corn was orient and immortal
  wheat, which never should be reaped,
  nor was ever sown. I thought it had
  stood from everlasting to everlasting.
  Centuries of Meditations. Cent.
  iii, § 3

JOSEPH TRAPP 1679–1747

3 The King, observing with judicious
  eyes
  The state of both his universities,
  To Oxford sent a troop of horse, and
  why?
  That learned body wanted loyalty;
  To Cambridge books, as very well
  discerning
  How much that loyal body wanted
  learning.
  *On George I's Donation of the
  Bishop of Ely's Library to Cam-
  bridge University.* Nichols's *Liter-
  ary Anecdotes*, vol. iii, p. 330.
  For the reply see 43:3

ANTHONY TROLLOPE 1815–1882

4 It's dogged as does it. It ain't thinking about it.
  Last Chronicle of Barset, ch. 61

ST. VINCENT TROUBRIDGE 1895–1963

5 There is an iron curtain across Europe.
  Sunday Empire News, 21 Oct.
  1945 (*see also 63:5 and 94:11*)

WALTER JAMES REDFERN TURNER 1889–1946

6 Chimborazo, Cotopaxi,
  They had stolen my soul away!
  Romance, vii

THOMAS TUSSER 1524?–1580

7 At Christmas play and make good
  cheer,
  For Christmas comes but once a
  year.
  *Five Hundred Points of Good
  Husbandry*, ch. 12. *The Farmer's
  daily Diet*

8 It is an ill wind turns none to good.
  Ib. ch. 13. *Description of the
  Properties of Winds*

9 Who goeth a borrowing
  Goeth a sorrowing.
  Few lend (but fools)
  Their working tools.
  *Five Hundred points of Good
  Husbandry*, ch. 15. *September's
  Abstract*

10 In doing of either, let wit bear a stroke,
   For buying or selling of pig in a poke.
   Ib. September's Husbandry

11 Naught venture, naught have.
   Ib. ch. 16. *October's Abstract*

12 To dog in the manger some liken I
   could.
   Ib. ch. 28. *Against Fantastical
   Scrupleness*

13 Feb, fill the dyke
   With what thou dost like.
   Ib. ch. 34. *February's Husbandry*

14 Sweet April showers
   Do spring May flowers.
   Ib. ch. 38. *April's Husbandry*

15 Look ere thou leap, see ere thou go.
   Ib. ch. 56. *Dialogue of Wiving and
   Thriving*

16 The stone that is rolling can gather no
   moss.   *Ib. Housewifely Admonitions*

MARK TWAIN [SAMUEL LANG-HORNE CLEMENS] 1835–1910

17 There was things which he stretched,
   but mainly he told the truth.
   *The Adventures of Huckleberry
   Finn*, ch. 1

18 The statements was interesting, but
   tough.   *Ib.* ch. 17

19 There's plenty of boys that will come
   hankering and gruvveling around
   when you've got an apple, and beg
   the core off you; but when *they've* got
   one, and you beg for the core and
   remind them how you give them a
   core one time, they make a mouth at
   you and say thank you 'most to death,
   but there ain't-a-going to *be* no core.
   Tom Sawyer Abroad, ch. 1

20 This poor little one-horse town.
   The Undertaker's Chat

21 The report of my death was an
   exaggeration.
   *Cable from Europe to the Asso-
   ciated Press*

HENRY TWELLS 1823–1900

22 At even ere the sun was set,
   The sick, O Lord, around thee lay.
   Hymns Ancient and Modern
   (1868), Appendix. *At Even Ere
   the Sun Was Set*

EDWARD SMITH UFFORD
1851–1929

1 Throw out the life-line across the dark
wave,
There is a brother whom someone
should save,
Throw out the life-line, throw out the
life-line,
Someone is sinking to-day.
Revivalist Hymn (1884)

MRS. C. UNWIN

2 The Hungry Forties.
Title of Book (1905)

RALPH R. UPTON

3 Stop; look; listen.
*Slogan devised in 1912 to replace
the old U.S. railway-crossing
signs of* 'Look out for the loco-
motive'

W. UPTON

4 This lass so neat, with smile so sweet,
Has won my right good will,
I'd crowns resign to call thee mine,
Sweet lass of Richmond Hill.
The Lass of Richmond Hill.
Oxford Song Book (see 137 : 15)

SIR JOHN VANBRUGH 1664–1726

5 Much of a muchness.
The Provok'd Husband, I. i

6 The want of a thing is perplexing
enough, but the possession of it is
intolerable.   *The Confederacy,* I. ii

HENRY VAUGHAN 1622–1695

7 My soul, there is a country
Far beyond the stars,
Where stands a wingèd sentry
All skilful in the wars:
There, above noise and danger,
Sweet Peace is crown'd with smiles,
And One born in a manger
Commands the beauteous files.
Silex Scintillans. Peace

8 If thou canst get but thither,
There grows the flower of Peace,
The Rose that cannot wither,
Thy fortress, and thy ease.
Leave then thy foolish ranges;
For none can thee secure,
But One, who never changes,
Thy God, thy life, thy cure.   *Ib.*

9 They are all gone into the world of
light,
And I alone sit lingering here;
Their very memory is fair and bright,
And my sad thoughts doth clear.
Ib. They Are All Gone

10 I see them walking in an air of glory,
Whose light doth trample on my
days:
My days, which are at best but dull
and hoary,
Mere glimmering and decays.
Silex Scintillans. They Are All Gone

11 I saw Eternity the other night,
Like a great ring of pure and endless
light,
All calm, as it was bright;
And round beneath it, Time in hours,
days, years,
Driv'n by the spheres
Like a vast shadow mov'd; in which
the world
And all her train were hurl'd.
Ib. The World

VEGETIUS *fourth century* A.D.

12 Qui desiderat pacem, praeparet bellum.
Let him who desires peace, prepare
for war.   *De Re Mil.* 3, prologue

PIERRE VERGNIAUD 1753–1793

13 Il a été permis de craindre que la
Révolution, comme Saturne, dévorât
successivement tous ses enfants.
There was reason to fear that the
Revolution, like Saturn, might
devour in turn each one of her
children.
Lamartine, *Histoire des Giron-
dins,* bk. xxxviii, ch. 20

PAUL VERLAINE 1844–1896

14 Et tout le reste est littérature.
All the rest is mere fine writing.
Jadis et Naguère

QUEEN VICTORIA 1819–1901

15 I will be good.
*Letter from the Baroness Lehzen
to Her Majesty, 2 Dec. 1867.
Martin's The Prince Consort*
(1875), vol. i, p. 13

16 We are not amused.
*Notebooks of a Spinster Lady,
2 Jan. 1900*

17 We are not interested in the possi-
bilities of defeat.
*To A. J. Balfour, in 'Black Week',
Dec. 1899*

18 He [Mr. Gladstone] speaks to Me as if
I was a public meeting.
G. W. E. Russell's *Collections and
Recollections,* ch. 14

ALFRED DE VIGNY 1797–1863

1 Seul le silence est grand; tout le reste
est faiblesse . . .
Fais énergiquement ta longue et
lourde tâche . . .
Puis, après, comme moi, souffre et
meurs sans parler.

Silence alone is great; all else is
feebleness . . .
Perform with all your heart your
long and heavy task. . . .
Then as do I, say naught, but suffer
and die.   *La Mort du Loup*

FRANÇOIS VILLON b. 1431

2 Mais où sont les neiges d'antan?
But where are the snows of yester-
year?
*Le Grand Testament, Ballade des
Dames du Temps Jadis.* Trans.
by D. G. Rossetti

VIRGIL 70–19 B.C.

3 Arma virumque cano, Troiae qui
primus ab oris
Italiam fato profugus Lavinaque venit
Litora—multum ille et terris iactatus
et alto
Vi superum, saevae memorem Iunonis
ob iram.

Arms I sing, and the man, who first
from the shores of Troy came,
Fate-exiled, to Italy and her
Lavinian strand—much buffeted
he on flood and field by constraint
of Heaven and fell Juno's unslumbering ire.
Aeneid, i. 1. Trans. by Jackson

4 Fidus quae tela gerebat Achates.
The weapons which loyal Achates bore.
Ib. 188

5 Forsan et haec olim meminisse iuvabit.
The day may dawn when this plight
shall be sweet to remember.
Ib. 203

6 Vera incessu patuit dea.
The goddess indubitable was revealed in her step.   *Ib.* 405

7 Sunt hic etiam sua praemia laudi;
Sunt lacrimae rerum et mentem mor-
talia tangunt.
Even here, virtue hath her rewards, and mortality her tears:
even here, the woes of man touch
the heart of man!   *Ib.* 461

8 Mens sibi conscia recti.
A mind conscious of the right.
Ib. 604

9 Timeo Danaos et dona ferentis.
I fear the Danaans, though their
hands proffer gifts.   *Ib.* ii. 49

10 Horresco referens.
I shudder to recall it.
Aeneid, ii. 204

11 Dis aliter visum.
Heaven's thought was otherwise.
Ib. 428

12 Non tali auxilio nec defensoribus istis
Tempus eget.
The hour calls not for such succour,
nor such defenders.   *Ib.* 521

13 Monstrum horrendum, informe, ingens, cui lumen ademptum.
A monster fearful and hideous, vast
and eyeless.   *Ib.* iii. 658

14 Varium et mutabile semper
Femina.
A fickle thing and changeful is
woman always!   *Ib.* iv. 569

15 Facilis descensus Averni:
Light is the descent to Avernus!
Ib. vi. 126

16 Procul, o procul este, profani.
Hence, O hence, . . . ye that are
uninitiated.   *Ib.* 258

17 Tendebantque manus ripae ulterioris
amore.
Their hands outstretched in yearning for the farther shore. *Ib.* 314

18 Tu regere imperio populos, Romane,
memento
(Hae tibi erunt artes), pacisque imponere morem,
Parcere subiectis et debellare superbos.
Roman, be this thy care—these
thine arts—to bear dominion over
the nations and to impose the
law of peace, to spare the humbled
and to war down the proud!
Ib. 851

19 Geniumque loci . . .
precatur.
Implored the Genius of the place.
Ib. vii. 136

20 Flectere si nequeo superos, Acheronta
movebo.
And if Heaven be inflexible, Hell
shall be unleashed!   *Ib.* 312

21 Macte nova virtute, puer, sic itur ad
astra.
Good speed to thy youthful valour,
child! So shalt thou scale the
stars!   *Ib.* ix. 641

22 Audentis Fortuna iuvat.
Fortune is ally to the brave.
Ib. x. 284

23 Experto credite.
Believe the man with experience.
Ib. xi. 283

24 Latet anguis in herba.
A snake lurks in the grass!
Eclogues, iii. 93

1 Ultima Cumaei venit iam carminis
    aetas;
Magnus ab integro saeclorum nascitur
    ordo.
Iam redit et virgo, redeunt Saturnia
    regna,
Iam nova progenies caelo demittitur
    alto.

> The last age, heralded in Cumean
> song, is come, and the great
> march of the centuries, begins
> anew. Now the Virgin returns:
> now Saturn is king again, and a
> new and better race descends
> from on high.   *Eclogues*, iv. 5

2 Non omnia possumus omnes.
> All power is not to all.   *Ib.* viii. 63

3 Omnia vincit Amor: et nos cedamus
    Amori.
> Love is lord of all: yield we, too, to
> Love!   *Ib.* x. 69

4 Ultima Thule.
> Farthest Thule.
>   *Georgics*, i. 30. *Trans. by Jackson*

5   Labor omnia vicit
Improbus et duris urgens in rebus
    egestas.
> Never-flinching labour proved lord
> of all, and the stress of need in
> a life of struggles.   *Ib.* 145

6   Imponere Pelio Ossam
Scilicet, atque Ossae frondosum invol-
    vere Olympum.
> In sooth . . . to pile Ossa on Pelion
> and roll leaf-crowned Olympus on
> Ossa.   *Ib.* 281

7 Felix qui potuit rerum cognoscere
    causas.
> Happy he, who has availed to read
> the causes of things.   *Ib.* ii. 490

8 Sed fugit interea, fugit inreparabile
    tempus.
> Meanwhile, Time is flying—flying,
> never to return.   *Ib.* iii. 284

9 At genus immortale manet, multos-
    que per annos
Stat fortuna domus, et avi numerantur
    avorum.
> Yet the race abides immortal, the
> star of their house sets not
> through many years, and grand-
> sire's grandsire is numbered in
> the roll.   *Ib.* iv. 208

10 Sic vos non vobis mellificatis apes.
Sic vos non vobis nidificatis aves.
Sic vos non vobis vellera fertis oves.
> So you bees make your honey, not
> for yourselves.
> So you birds make nests, not for
> yourselves.
> So you sheep bear fleeces, not for
> yourselves.
>   *Attr. On Bathyllus' claiming the
> authorship of certain lines by Virgil*

VOLTAIRE 1694–1778

11 Dans ce pays-ci il est bon de tuer de
temps en temps un amiral pour
encourager les autres.
> In this country [England] it is
> thought well to kill an admiral
> from time to time to encourage
> the others.   *Candide*, ch. 23

12 Tout est pour le mieux dans le meilleur
des mondes possibles.
> All is for the best in the best of
> possible worlds.   *Ib.* 30

13 Cela est bien dit, répondit Candide,
mais il faut cultiver notre jardin.
> 'That is well said,' replied Candide,
> 'but we must cultivate our gar-
> den.' (We must attend to our own
> affairs.)   *Ib.*

14 Le mieux est l'ennemi du bien.
> The best is the enemy of the good.
>   *Dict. Philosophqiue*, art. *Art Dra-*
>   *matique*

15 Si Dieu n'existait pas, il faudrait
l'inventer.
> If God did not exist, it would be
> necessary to invent him.
>   *Épîtres*, xcvi. *A l'Auteur du
> Livre des Trois Imposteurs*

16 Ce corps qui s'appelait et qui s'appelle
encore le saint empire romain n'était
en aucune manière ni saint, ni romain,
ni empire.
> This agglomeration which was called
> and which still calls itself the Holy
> Roman Empire was neither holy,
> nor Roman, nor an empire.
>   *Essai sur les Mœurs et l'Esprit
> des Nations*, lxx

17 Quoi que vous fassiez, écrasez l'infâme, et aimez qui vous aime.
> Whatever you do, trample down
> abuses, and love those who love
> you.
>   *Lettres. A M. d'Alembert, 28 Nov.
> 1762*

18 On dit que Dieu est toujours pour les
gros bataillons.
> It is said that God is always for the
> big battalions.
>   *Ib. A M. Le Riche, 6 Feb. 1770*

19 Le secret d'ennuyer est . . . de tout dire.
> The way to be a bore [for an author]
> is to say everything.
>   *Sept Discours en vers sur
> l'Homme*, vi. *Sur la Nature de
> l'Homme*. v. 174–5

20 I disapprove of what you say, but
I will defend to the death your right
to say it.
>   *Attr. in* S. G. Tallentyre, *The
> Friends of Voltaire* (1907), p. 199

HENRY WALLACE 1888–

1 The century on which we are entering
—the century which will come out of
this war—can be and must be the
century of the common man.
*Address: The Price of Free World
Victory, 8 May 1942*

LEW WALLACE 1827–1905

2 Beauty is altogether in the eye of the
beholder.
The Prince of India (1893), III.
vi. 78 (see *111:23*)

WILLIAM ROSS WALLACE
d. 1881

3 The hand that rocks the cradle
Is the hand that rules the world.
John o' London's Treasure Trove

EDMUND WALLER 1606–1687

4   Go, lovely Rose!
Tell her, that wastes her time and me,
  That now she knows,
When I resemble her to thee,
  How sweet and fair she seems to be.
Song: Go, Lovely Rose!

**HORACE WALPOLE, FOURTH
EARL OF ORFORD** 1717–1797

5 [Strawberry Hill] is a little plaything-
house that I got out of Mrs. Chene-
vix's shop, and is the prettiest bauble
you ever saw. It is set in enamelled
meadows, with filigree hedges.
Letters. To Conway, 8 June 1747

6 One of the greatest geniuses that ever
existed, Shakespeare, undoubtedly
wanted taste.
Ib. To Wren, 9 Aug. 1764

7 This world is a comedy to those that
think, a tragedy to those that feel.
*Ib. To the Countess of Upper
Ossory, 16 Aug. 1776*

8 All his [Sir Joshua Reynolds's] own
geese are swans, as the swans of others
are geese.
*Ib. To the Countess of Upper
Ossory, 1 Dec. 1786*

**SIR ROBERT WALPOLE, FIRST
EARL OF ORFORD** 1676–1745

9 They now *ring* the bells, but they will
soon *wring* their hands.
*Remark on the declaration of war
with Spain, 1739.* W. Coxe,
Memoirs of Sir Robert Walpole
(1798), vol. i, p. 618

10 All those men have their price.
Ib. p. 757

11 Madam, there are fifty thousand men
slain this year in Europe, and not one
Englishman.
Remark to Queen Caroline, 1734.
Hervey, *Memoirs* (1848), vol. i,
p. 398

12 The balance of power.
*Speech in the House of Commons,
13 Feb. 1741*

WILLIAM WALSH 1663–1708

13 I can endure my own despair,
But not another's hope.
Song. 'Of All the Torments'

IZAAK WALTON 1593–1683

14 I remember that a wise friend of mine
did usually say, 'that which is everybody's business is nobody's business.'
Compleat Angler, pt. i, ch. 2

15 Look to your health; and if you have
it, praise God, and value it next to
a good conscience; for health is the
second blessing that we mortals are
capable of; a blessing that money
cannot buy. *Ib.* ch. 21

BISHOP WILLIAM WARBURTON
1698–1779

16 Orthodoxy is my doxy; heterodoxy is
another man's doxy.
Remark to Lord Sandwich. Priest-
ley, *Memoirs* (1807), vol. i,
p. 372

**ARTEMUS WARD [CHARLES
FARRAR BROWNE]** 1834–1867

17 Shall we sell our birthrite for a mess of
potash?
*Artemus Ward His Book. The
Crisis*

18 Do me eyes deceive me earsight? Is
it some dreams? *Ib. Moses, the Sassy*

19 It is a pity that Chawcer, who had
geneyus, was so unedicated. He's the
wuss speller I know of.
Artemus Ward in London, ch. 4.
At the Tomb of Shakespeare

20 He [Brigham Young] is dreadfully
married. He's the most married man
I ever saw in my life.
Artemus Ward's Lecture

21 Why is this thus? What is the reason
of this thusness? *Ib.*

MRS. HUMPHRY WARD 1851–1920

22 'Propinquity does it'—as Mrs. Thorn-
burgh is always reminding us.
Robert Elsmere, bk. i, ch. 2

SUSAN WARNER 1819–1885

1 Jesus loves me—this I know,
  For the Bible tells me so.
                    The Love of Jesus

GEORGE WASHINGTON
                        1732–1799

2 Father, I cannot tell a lie, I did it
  with my little hatchet.
        Attr. remark. Mark Twain's
        Mark Twain as George Washing-
        ton. Another version is: I can't
        tell a lie, Pa; you know I can't
        tell a lie. I did cut it with my
        hatchet.
        Weems, *Washington* (1800) (5th
        ed., 1806)

3 We must consult Brother Jonathan.
        Said to have been a frequent re-
        mark of his during the American
        Revolution, referring to Jonathan
        Trumbull, 1710–85, Governor of
        Connecticut. Norwich Evening
        Courier, 12 Nov. 1846, No. 797,
        p. 2. (*Publications of the Colonial*
        Society of Massachusetts (1905),
        vol. vii, p. 94)

WILLIAM WATSON 1559?–1603

4 Fiat justitia et ruant coeli.
      Let justice be done though the
      heavens fall.
        Quodlibets of Religion and State
        (1602)

SIR WILLIAM WATSON 1858–1936

5 April, April,
  Laugh thy girlish laughter;
  Then, the moment after,
  Weep thy girlish tears!   *April*

ISAAC WATTS 1674–1748

6 Let dogs delight to bark and bite,
  For God hath made them so;
  Let bears and lions growl and fight,
  For 'tis their nature too.
        Divine Songs for Children, xvi.
        Against Quarrelling

7 But, children, you should never let
    Such angry passions rise;
  Your little hands were never made
    To tear each other's eyes.   *Ib.*

8 Birds in their little nests agree
  And 'tis a shameful sight,
  When children of one family
  Fall out, and chide, and fight.   *Ib.*

9 How doth the little busy bee
    Improve each shining hour,
  And gather honey all the day
    From every opening flower!
        Ib. xx. *Against Idleness and Mis-*
        chief

10 In works of labour, or of skill,
     I would be busy too;
   For Satan finds some mischief still
     For idle hands to do.
        Divine Songs for Children, xx.
        Against Idleness and Mischief

11 Hush! my dear, lie still and slumber,
     Holy angels guard thy bed!
   Heavenly blessings without number
     Gently falling on thy head.
            Ib. xxxv. *Cradle Hymn*

12 'Tis the voice of the sluggard; I heard
     him complain,
   'You have wak'd me too soon, I must
     slumber again.'
   As the door on its hinges, so he on his
     bed,
   Turns his sides and his shoulders and
     his heavy head.
            Moral Songs, i. *The Sluggard*

13 Jesus shall reign where e'er the sun
     Does his successive journeys run;
   His kingdom stretch from shore to
     shore
       Till moons shall wax and wane no
         more.   *Psalms,* lxxii

14 Our God, our help in ages past
   Our hope for years to come,
   Our shelter from the stormy blast,
   And our eternal home.

   Beneath the shadow of Thy Throne
   Thy saints have dwelt secure;
   Sufficient is Thine Arm alone,
   And our defence is sure.

   Before the hills in order stood,
   Or earth received her frame,
   From everlasting Thou art God,
   To endless years the same.

   A thousand ages in Thy sight
   Are like an evening gone;
   Short as the watch that ends the night
   Before the rising sun.

   Time, like an ever-rolling stream,
   Bears all its sons away;
   They fly forgotten, as a dream
   Dies at the opening day.
            Ib. xc. *First line altered by John*
            Wesley to 'O God . . .'

15 There is a land of pure delight,
     Where saints immortal reign;
   Infinite day excludes the night,
     And pleasures banish pain.
        Hymns and Spiritual Songs, bk. ii,
        No. 66. *There is a Land of Pure*
        Delight

16 When I survey the wondrous Cross,
     On which the Prince of glory died,
   My richest gain I count but loss
   And pour contempt on all my pride.
        Hymns and Spiritual Songs,
        bk. iii, No. 7. *When I Survey the*
        Wondrous Cross

17 Were the whole realm of nature mine,
   That were a present far too small;
   Love so amazing, so Divine,
   Demands my soul, my life, my all. *Ib.*

FREDERIC EDWARD WEATHERLY 1848–1929

1 Where are the boys of the Old Brigade?
The Old Brigade

SIDNEY WEBB, LORD PASSFIELD 1859–1947

2 The inevitability of gradualness.
Presidential address to the annual conference of the Labour Party, 1920

WILLIAM WEBB *fl.* 1839

3 His throat they cut from ear to ear,
His brains they pun*ch*ed in,
His name was Mr. William Weare,
Wot lived in Lyon's Inn.
Ballad. See Lord William Lennox in *The Sporting Review*, July 1839, vol. ii, p. 42. Also attr. to Theodore Hook (1788–1841). See C. Hindley's *Life and Times of James Catnach* (1878), p. 145

DANIEL WEBSTER 1782–1852

4 There is always room at the top.
When advised not to become a lawyer as the profession was overcrowded

5 Fearful concatenation of circumstances.
Argument on the Murder of Captain Joseph White

JOHN WEBSTER 1580?–1625?

6 I am Duchess of Malfi still.
The Duchess of Malfi, IV. ii, l. 146

7 I know death hath ten thousand several doors
For men to take their exits. *Ib.* l. 222

8 Cover her face; mine eyes dazzle: she died young. *Ib.* l. 267

9 I saw him even now going the way of all flesh. *Westward Hoe*, II. ii

10 A mere tale of a tub, my words are idle. *The White Devil*, II. i. 92

11 Call for the robin redbreast and the wren,
Since o'er shady groves they hover,
And with leaves and flowers do cover
The friendless bodies of unburied men. *Ib.* v. iv. 100

12 I am i' th' way to study a long silence.
Ib. vi. l. 204

13 I have caught
An everlasting cold; I have lost my voice
Most irrecoverably. *Ib.* l. 270

ARTHUR WELLESLEY, DUKE OF WELLINGTON 1769–1852

14 It has been a damned serious business
—Blücher and I have lost 30,000 men.
It has been a damned nice thing—the nearest run thing you ever saw in your life. . . . By God! I don't think it would have done if I had not been there.
Creevey Papers, ch. x, p. 236

15 All the business of war, and indeed all the business of life, is to endeavour to find out what you don't know by what you do; that's what I called 'guessing what was at the other side of the hill'.
Croker Papers (1885), vol. iii, p. 276

16 I never saw so many shocking bad hats in my life.
On seeing the first Reformed Parliament. Sir William Fraser, *Words on Wellington* (1889), p. 12

17 The battle of Waterloo was won in the playing fields of Eton.
Montalembert, *De l'Avenir Politique de l'Angleterre* (1855). *The attribution has been refuted by the 7th Duke.*

18 In refusing the dedication of a song [the Duke of Wellington] informed Mrs. Norton that he had been obliged to make a rule of refusing dedications, 'because, in his situation as Chancellor of the University of Oxford, he had been much exposed to authors'.
G. W. E. Russell's *Collections and Recollections*, ch. 2

19 Hard pounding this, gentlemen; let's see who will pound longest.
At Waterloo. Sir W. Scott, *Paul's Letters* (1815)

20 I used to say of him [Napoleon] that his presence on the field made the difference of forty thousand men.
Stanhope, *Notes of Conversations with the Duke of Wellington*, 2 Nov. 1831

21 What is the best to be done for the country? How can the Government be carried on? *Ib.* 18 May 1839
('The Queen's Government must be carried on'—*and variants—was used by him on several occasions.*)

22 I don't know what effect these men will have upon the enemy, but, by God, they terrify me.
On a draft of troops sent to him in Spain, 1809. (Also attr. to George III)

23 [*To a gentleman who accosted him in the street saying,* 'Mr. Jones, I believe?']
If you believe that you will believe anything. *Attr.*

1 Up Guards and at them again!
> *Attr. to Wellington during the Battle of Waterloo. Capt. Batty's letter, 22 June 1815, in Booth's Battle of Waterloo. J. W. Croker, in a letter to A. Greville, 14 Mar. 1852, wrote 'Perhaps I might also venture to ask his Grace whether he did say, "Up Guards and at them".' Wellington replied in an undated letter to Croker which is in* Croker Correspondence and Diaries *(1884), vol. iii, p. 280: 'What I must have said and possibly did say was, Stand up, Guards! and then gave the commanding officers the order to attack'*

2 Publish and be damned.   *Attr.*

HERBERT GEORGE WELLS
1866–1946

3 'I expect,' he said, 'I was thinking jest what a Rum Go everything is. I expect it was something like that.'
> *Kipps, bk. iii, ch. 3, § 8*

4 The Shape of Things to Come.
> *Title of Book (1933)*

5 The Time-Machine.
> *Title of Novel (1895)*

6 The War that will end War.
> *Title of Book (1914)*

CHARLES WESLEY 1707–1788

7 'Christ, the Lord, is risen to-day,'
Sons of men and angels say,
Raise your joys and triumphs high,
Sing, ye heavens, and earth reply.
> *Hymns and Sacred Poems (1739). Christ, the Lord, is Risen To-day*

8 Jesu, Lover of my soul,
Let me to Thy Bosom fly,
While the nearer waters roll,
While the tempest still is high;
Hide me, O my Saviour, hide,
Till the storm of life is past;
Safe into the haven guide,
O receive my soul at last.
> *Ib. (1740), Jesu, Lover of My Soul*

9 Other refuge have I none;
Hangs my helpless soul on Thee.   *Ib.*

10 Cover my defenceless head
With the shadow of Thy wing.   *Ib.*

11 Thou of Life the Fountain art;
Freely let me take of Thee;
Spring Thou up within my heart,
Rise to all eternity.   *Ib.*

12 Gentle Jesus, meek and mild,
Look upon a little child;
Pity my simplicity,
Suffer me to come to thee.
> *Ib. (1742), Gentle Jesus, Meek and Mild*

13 Soldiers of Christ, arise,
And put your armour on.
> *Hymns and Sacred Poems (1749). Soldiers of Christ, Arise*

14 Lift up your heart, lift up your voice;
Rejoice, again I say, rejoice.
> *Hymns for Our Lord's Resurrection (1746): Rejoice, the Lord is King*

15 Hark! the herald-angels sing
Glory to the new-born King:
Peace on earth, and mercy mild,
God and sinners reconciled.
> *Ib. Christmas Hymn: Hark! the Herald Angels Sing. First two lines altered by George Whitefield in 1753 from Wesley's original*
> Hark, how all the welkin rings,
> 'Glory to the King of kings'.

16 Lo! he comes with clouds descending.
> *Hymns of Intercession for all Mankind (1758): Lo! He Comes with Clouds. New Version of John Cennick's 'Lo! He cometh, countless trumpets', in Collection of Sacred Hymns (1752)*

17 Let saints on earth in concert sing.
> *Funeral Hymns (1759): Let saints on earth. Altered by F. H. Murray in his Hymnal for Use in the English Church (1852), from 'Let all the saints terrestrial sing'*

JOHN WESLEY 1703–1791

18 I look upon all the world as my parish.
> *Journal, 11 June 1739*

19 Let it be observed, that slovenliness is no part of religion; that neither this, nor any text of Scripture, condemns neatness of apparel. Certainly this is a duty, not a sin. 'Cleanliness is, indeed, next to godliness.'
> *Sermons, No. xciii. On Dress*

REV. SAMUEL WESLEY 1662–1735

20 Style is the dress of thought; a modest dress,
Neat, but not gaudy, will true critics please.
> *An Epistle to a Friend concerning Poetry (1700)*

MAE WEST 1893–

21 Come up and see me sometime.
> *Diamond Lil (1932)*

EDITH WHARTON 1862–1937

22 Mrs. Ballinger is one of the ladies who pursue Culture in bands, as though it were dangerous to meet it alone.
> *Xingu, ch. 1*

JAMES ABBOTT McNEILL WHISTLER 1834–1903

1 I am not arguing with you—I am telling you.
> *Gentle Art of Making Enemies*

2 'I only know of two painters in the world,' said a newly introduced feminine enthusiast to Whistler, 'yourself and Velasquez.' 'Why,' answered Whistler in dulcet tones, 'why drag in Velasquez?'
> O. C. Seitz, *Whistler Stories* (1913), p. 27

3 [*In answer to the question* 'For two days' labour, you ask two hundred guineas?']
No, I ask it for the knowledge of a lifetime.   *Ib.* p. 40

4 [*Answering Oscar Wilde's* 'I wish I had said that']
You will, Oscar, you will.
> L. C. Ingleby, *Oscar Wilde*, p. 67

HENRY KIRKE WHITE 1785–1806

5 Oft in danger, oft in woe,
Onward, Christians, onward go.
> W. J. Hall's *Mitre Hymn Book* (1836). *Adapted by Dr. W. B. Collyer from White's original* 'Much in sorrow, oft in woe'

WILLIAM ALLEN WHITE 1868–1944

6 All dressed up, with nowhere to go.
> *On the Progressive Party in the U.S.A. in 1916, after Theodore Roosevelt had retired from the Presidential campaign*

WILLIAM LINDSAY WHITE 1900–

7 They Were Expendable.
> *Title of Book* (1942)

GEORGE WHITEFIELD 1714–1770

8 I had rather wear out than rust out.
> *Attr. by Robert Southey*

WILLIAM WHITING 1825–1878

9 O hear us when we cry to Thee
For those in peril on the sea.
> *Hymn: Eternal Father Strong to Save*

WALT WHITMAN 1819?–1892

10 O Captain! my Captain! our fearful trip is done,
The ship has weather'd every rack, the prize we sought is won,
The port is near, the bells I hear, the people all exulting.
> *O Captain! My Captain! i*

11 Exult O shores, and ring O bells!
But I with mournful tread
Walk the deck my Captain lies, Fallen cold and dead.
> *O Captain! My Captain! iii*

12 Out of the cradle endlessly rocking,
Out of the mocking-bird's throat, the musical shuttle,
.   .   .   .   .
A reminiscence sing.
> *Out of the Cradle endlessly Rocking*

13 Pioneers! O Pioneers.   *Title of Poem*

14 I think I could turn and live with animals, they are so placid and self-contain'd,
I stand and look at them long and long.
They do not sweat and whine about their condition,
They do not lie awake in the dark and weep for their sins,
They do not make me sick discussing their duty to God,
Not one is dissatisfied, not one is demented with the mania of owning things,
Not one kneels to another, nor to his kind that lived thousands of years ago,
Not one is respectable or unhappy over the whole earth.
> *Song of Myself, 32*

15 Do I contradict myself?
Very well then I contradict myself,
(I am large, I contain multitudes.)
> *Ib. 50*

JOHN GREENLEAF WHITTIER 1807–1892

16 'Shoot, if you must, this old gray head,
But spare your country's flag,' she said.
> *Barbara Frietchie, l. 35*

17 For all sad words of tongue or pen,
The saddest are these: 'It might have been!'
> *Maud Muller, l. 105*

18 Dinna ye hear it?—Dinna ye hear it?
The pipes o' Havelock sound!
> *Pipes at Lucknow, iv*

CORNELIUS WHURR c. 1845

19 What lasting joys the man attend
Who has a polished female friend.
> *The Accomplished Female Friend*

GEORGE JOHN WHYTE-MELVILLE 1821–1878

20 Then drink, puppy, drink, and let ev'ry puppy drink,
That is old enough to lap and to swallow;
For he'll grow into a hound, so we'll pass the bottle round,
And merrily we'll whoop and we'll holloa. *Drink, Puppy, Drink, chorus*

1 Wrap me up in my tarpaulin jacket,
And say a poor buffer lies low,
And six stalwart lancers shall carry
me,
With steps solemn, mournful, and
slow.　*The Tarpaulin Jacket*

BISHOP SAMUEL WILBERFORCE 1805–1873

2 If I were a cassowary
On the plains of Timbuctoo,
I would eat a missionary,
Cassock, band, and hymn-book too.
Impromptu verse, Ascribed

ELLA WHEELER WILCOX 1855–1919

3 Laugh and the world laughs with you;
Weep, and you weep alone;
For the sad old earth must borrow its
mirth,
But has trouble enough of its own.
Solitude

OSCAR WILDE 1854–1900

4 I never saw a man who looked
With such a wistful eye
Upon that little tent of blue
Which prisoners call the sky.
*The Ballad of Reading Gaol
(1898), pt. I. iii*

5 Yet each man kills the thing he loves,
By each let this be heard,
Some do it with a bitter look,
Some with a flattering word.
The coward does it with a kiss,
The brave man with a sword!
Ib. vii

6 And the wild regrets, and the bloody
sweats,
None knew so well as I:
For he who lives more lives than one
More deaths than one must die.
Ib. III. xxxvii

7 The truth is rarely pure, and never
simple.　*The Importance of Being
Earnest* (1895), Act I

8 In married life three is company and
two none.　*Ib.*

9 I have invented an invaluable permanent invalid called Bunbury, in
order that I may be able to go down
into the country whenever I choose.
Ib.

10 To lose one parent, Mr. Worthing,
may be regarded as a misfortune; to
lose both looks like carelessness. *Ib.*

11 All women become like their mothers.
That is their tragedy. No man does.
That's his.　*Ib.*

12 The chapter on the Fall of the Rupee
you may omit. It is somewhat too
sensational.　*Ib.* Act II

13 On an occasion of this kind it becomes
more than a moral duty to speak one's
mind. It becomes a pleasure.
*The Importance of Being Earnest,
Act II*

14 Please do not shoot the pianist. He
is doing his best.
*Impressions of America. Lead-
ville*

15 I couldn't help it. I can resist every-
thing except temptation.
Lady Windermere's Fan (1891),
Act I

16 We are all in the gutter, but some of us
are looking at the stars.　*Ib.* Act III

17 There is nothing in the whole world
so unbecoming to a woman as a Nonconformist conscience.　*Ib.*

18 CECIL GRAHAM:
What is a cynic?
LORD DARLINGTON:
A man who knows the price of every-
thing and the value of nothing.　*Ib.*

19 There is no such thing as a moral or an
immoral book. Books are well written,
or badly written.
Picture of Dorian Gray (1891),
preface

20 There is only one thing in the world
worse than being talked about, and
that is not being talked about.
Ib. ch. 1

21 The only way to get rid of a temptation is to yield to it.　*Ib.* ch. 2

22 Anybody can be good in the country.
Ib. ch. 19

23 MRS. ALLONBY:
They say, Lady Hunstanton, that
when good Americans die they go to
Paris.
LADY HUNSTANTON:
Indeed? And when bad Americans die,
where do they go to?
LORD ILLINGWORTH:
Oh, they go to America.
A Woman of No Importance
(1893), Act I (*see* 10:9)

24 The English country gentleman gallop-
ing after a fox—the unspeakable in
full pursuit of the uneatable.　*Ib.*

25 One should never trust a woman who
tells one her real age. A woman who
would tell one that, would tell one
anything.　*Ib.*

26 LORD ILLINGWORTH:
The Book of Life begins with a man
and a woman in a garden.
MRS. ALLONBY:
It ends with Revelations.　*Ib.*

27 Children begin by loving their parents;
after a time they judge them; rarely,
if ever, do they forgive them.　*Ib.*

1 [*At the New York Custom House*]
I have nothing to declare except my
genius.
F. Harris, *Oscar Wilde* (1918),
p. 75

2 [*A huge fee for an operation was mentioned*]
'Ah, well, then,' said Oscar, 'I suppose that I shall have to die beyond
my means.'
R. H. Sherard, *Life of Oscar
Wilde* (1906), p. 421

JOHN WILKES 1727–1797

3 The chapter of accidents is the longest
chapter in the book.
*Attr. to John Wilkes by Southey
in* The Doctor (1837), *vol. iv,
p. 166*

EMMA HART WILLARD
1787–1876

4 Rocked in the cradle of the deep. *Song*

WILLIAM III OF GREAT
BRITAIN 1650–1702

5 I will die in the last ditch.
Hume, *History of Great Britain*,
vol. ii (1757), p. 226. *Charles II,
ch. 3*

6 Every bullet has its billet.
John Wesley, *Journal, 6 June
1765*

HARRY WILLIAMS
and
JACK JUDGE

7 It's a long way to Tipperary, it's a
long way to go;
It's a long way to Tipperary, to the
sweetest girl I know!
Good-bye Piccadilly, Farewell Leices-
ter Square;
It's a long, long way to Tipperary, but
my heart's right there!
*It's a Long Way to Tipperary.
Chorus claimed by Alice Smythe
B. Jay. Written in 1908. See
New York Times, 20 Sept. 1907*

8 In the shade of the old apple tree.
Title of Song

NATHANIEL PARKER WILLIS
1806–1867

9 At present there is no distinction
among the upper ten thousand of the
city.   *Necessity for a Promenade Drive*

W. G. WILLS *nineteenth century*

10 I'll sing thee songs of Araby,
And tales of wild Cashmere,
Wild tales to cheat thee of a sigh,
Or charm thee to a tear.   *Lalla Rookh*

D. EARDLEY WILMOT
contemporary

11 It's a corner of heaven itself,
Though it's only a tumble-down
nest,
But with love brooding there, why,
no place can compare,
With my little grey home in the
west.   *My Little Grey Home*

JOHN WILSON 1785–1854
see CHRISTOPHER NORTH

THOMAS WOODROW WILSON
1856–1924

12 Armed neutrality.
*Message to Congress, 26 Feb.
1917*

13 The world must be made safe for
democracy.
Address to Congress, 2 Apr. 1917

ARTHUR WIMPERIS 1874–1953

14 Gilbert, the Filbert,
The Colonel of the Knuts.
Gilbert the Filbert

ANNE FINCH, LADY
WINCHILSEA d. 1720

15 Now the Jonquille o'ercomes the
feeble brain;
We faint beneath the aromatic pain.
The Spleen

WILLIAM WINDHAM 1750–1810

16 Those entrusted with arms . . .
should be persons of some substance
and stake in the country.
*Speech in the House of Commons,
22 July 1807*

CATHERINE WINKWORTH
1829–1878

17 Now thank we all our God,
With heart and hands and voices
Who wondrous things hath done
In whom His world rejoices.
Trans. of Martin Rinkart: Nun
danket alle Gott

GEORGE WITHER 1588–1667

18 Shall I, wasting in despair,
Die because a woman's fair?
Or make pale my cheeks with care,
'Cause another's rosy are?
Be she fairer than the day,
Or the flow'ry meads in May;
If she think not well of me,
What care I how fair she be?
Sonnet

PELHAM GRENVILLE WODEHOUSE 1881–

1 He spoke with a certain what-is-it in his voice, and I could see that, if not actually disgruntled, he was far from being gruntled.
The Code of the Woosters

2 Donning the soup-and-fish in preparation for the evening meal.
Jeeves and the Impending Doom

CHARLES WOLFE 1791–1823

3 Not a drum was heard, not a funeral note,
As his corse to the rampart we hurried.
The Burial of Sir John Moore at Corunna, i

4 We buried him darkly at dead of night,
The sods with our bayonets turning.
Ib. ii

5 But he lay like a warrior taking his rest,
With his martial cloak around him.
Ib. iii

6 Few and short were the prayers we said,
And we spoke not a word of sorrow;
But we steadfastly gazed on the face that was dead,
And we bitterly thought of the morrow. *Ib.* iv

7 We carved not a line, and we raised not a stone—
But we left him alone with his glory. *Ib.* viii

JAMES WOLFE 1727–1759

8 The General . . . repeated nearly the whole of Gray's Elegy . . . adding, as he concluded, that he would prefer being the author of that poem to the glory of beating the French to-morrow.
J. Playfair, *Biogr. Acc. of J. Robinson* in *Transactions R. Soc. Edinb. 1814*, vii. p. 499

9 Now God be praised, I will die in peace.
Dying words. J. Knox, *Historical Journal of Campaigns, 1757–60.* Published 1769. Ed. 1914, vol. ii, p. 114

THOMAS, CARDINAL WOLSEY 1475?–1530

10 Father Abbot, I am come to lay my bones amongst you.
Cavendish, *Negotiations of Thomas Wolsey* (1641), p. 108

11 Had I but served God as diligently as I have served the king, he would not have given me over in my gray hairs.
Ib. p. 113

MRS. HENRY WOOD 1814–1887

12 Dead! and . . . never called me mother.
East Lynne (dramatized version by T. A. Palmer, 1874). These words do not occur in the novel

ELIZABETH WORDSWORTH 1840–1932

13 If all the good people were clever,
And all clever people were good,
The world would be nicer than ever
We thought that it possibly could.

But somehow, 'tis seldom or never
The two hit it off as they should;
The good are so harsh to the clever,
The clever so rude to the good!
St. Christopher and Other Poems: Good and Clever

WILLIAM WORDSWORTH 1770–1850

14 A slumber did my spirit seal;
I had no human fears:
She seemed a thing that could not feel
The touch of earthly years.

No motion has she now, no force;
She neither hears nor sees;
Rolled round in earth's diurnal course,
With rocks, and stones, and trees.
A Slumber did My Spirit Seal

15 O blithe new-comer! I have heard,
I hear thee and rejoice.
O Cuckoo! Shall I call thee bird,
Or but a wandering voice?
To the Cuckoo: O Blithe New-comer!

16 Thrice welcome, darling of the Spring!
Ib.

17 Still glides the Stream, and shall for ever glide;
The Form remains, the Function never dies.
The River Duddon, xxxiv. *After-Thought*

18 And if, as toward the silent tomb we go,
Through love, through hope, and faith's transcendent dower,
We feel that we are greater than we know. *Ib.*

19 Stern daughter of the voice of God!
O Duty! if that name thou love
Who art a light to guide, a rod
To check the erring and reprove.
Ode to Duty

20 Not in the lucid intervals of life
That come but as a curse to party strife.
Evening Voluntaries, iv. *Not in the Lucid Intervals*

1 Bliss was it in that dawn to be alive,
But to be young was very heaven!
*French Revolution, as it Appeared
to Enthusiasts*, and *The Prelude*,
bk. xi, l. 108

2 Who is the happy Warrior? Who is he
That every man in arms should wish
to be?
Character of the Happy Warrior

3 The rapt one, of the godlike forehead,
The heaven-eyed creature sleeps in
earth:
And Lamb, the frolic and the gentle,
Has vanished from his lonely hearth.
*Extempore Effusion upon the
Death of James Hogg*

4 Him whom you love, your Idiot Boy.
The Idiot Boy

5   All shod with steel
We hissed along the polished ice, in
games
Confederate.
Influence of Natural Objects and
The Prelude, bk. i, l. 414

6   'Yet still the solitary cliffs
Wheeled by me—even as if the earth
had rolled
With visible motion her diurnal round!'
Ib. and *The Prelude*, bk. i, l. 458

7 There was a time when meadow,
grove, and stream,
The earth, and every common sight,
To me did seem
Apparelled in celestial light,
The glory and the freshness of a dream.
It is not now as it hath been of yore;—
Turn wheresoe'er I may,
By night or day,
The things which I have seen I now
can see no more.
Ode. Intimations of Immortality, i

8   The rainbow comes and goes,
And lovely is the rose,
The moon doth with delight
Look round her when the heavens are
bare,
Waters on a starry night
Are beautiful and fair;
The sunshine is a glorious birth:
But yet I know, where'er I go,
That there hath passed away a glory
from the earth.   *Ib.* ii

9 And the babe leaps up on his mother's
arm.   *Ib.* iv

10 —But there's a tree, of many, one
A single field which I have looked
upon,
Both of them speak of something that
is gone:
The pansy at my feet
Doth the same tale repeat:
Whither is fled the visionary gleam?
Where is it now, the glory and the
dream?   *Ib.*

11 Our birth is but a sleep and a for-
getting:
The Soul that rises with us, our
life's Star,
Hath had elsewhere its setting,
And cometh from afar:
Not in entire forgetfulness,
And not in utter nakedness,
But trailing clouds of glory do we
come
From God, who is our home:
Heaven lies about us in our infancy!
Shades of the prison-house begin to
close
Upon the growing boy,
But he beholds the light, and whence
it flows,
He sees it in his joy;
The youth, who daily farther from the
east
Must travel, still is Nature's priest,
And by the vision splendid
Is on his way attended;
At length the man perceives it die
away,
And fade into the light of common
day.
Ode. Intimations of Immortality, v

12 Hence in a season of calm weather
Though inland far we be,
Our souls have sight of that immortal
sea
Which brought us hither,
Can in a moment travel thither,
And see the children sport upon the
shore,
And hear the mighty waters rolling
evermore.   *Ib.* ix

13 Though nothing can bring back the
hour
Of splendour in the grass, of glory in
the flower;
We will grieve not, rather find
Strength in what remains behind;
In the primal sympathy
Which having been must ever be;
In the soothing thoughts that spring
Out of human suffering;
In the faith that looks through death,
In years that bring the philosophic
mind.   *Ib.*

14 Another race hath been, and other
palms are won.
Thanks to the human heart by which
we live,
Thanks to its tenderness, its joys, and
fears,
To me the meanest flower that blows
can give
Thoughts that do often lie too deep
for tears.   *Ib.* xi

15 It is a beauteous evening, calm and
free,
The holy time is quiet as a nun,
Breathless with adoration.
Miscellaneous Sonnets, pt. I, xxx.
It is a Beauteous Evening

1 We must be free or die, who speak the
  tongue
  That Shakespeare spake; the faith
  and morals hold
  Which Milton held.
    *National Independence and Lib-
    erty,* pt. I, xvi. *It is not to be thought
    of*

2 I travelled among unknown men
  In lands beyond the sea;
  Nor, England! did I know till then
  What love I bore to thee.
    I Travelled among Unknown Men

3 I wandered lonely as a cloud
  That floats on high o'er vales and hills,
  When all at once I saw a crowd,
  A host, of golden daffodils;
  Beside the lake, beneath the trees,
  Fluttering and dancing in the breeze.
    I Wandered Lonely as a Cloud

4 Continuous as the stars that shine
  And twinkle on the milky way.   *Ib.*

5 For oft, when on my couch I lie
  In vacant or in pensive mood,
  They flash upon that inward eye
  Which is the bliss of solitude;
  And then my heart with pleasure fills,
  And dances with the daffodils.   *Ib.*

6 Give all thou canst; high Heaven
  rejects the lore
  Of nicely-calculated less or more.
    Ecclesiastical Sonnets, pt. III,
    xliii. *King's College Chapel. Tax
    not the Royal Saint*

7 Milton! thou shouldst be living at
  this hour:
  England hath need of thee; she is a fen
  Of stagnant waters.
    *National Independence and
    Liberty,* pt. I, xiv. *London.
    Milton! thou shouldst*

8 Plain living and high thinking are
  no more:
    Ib. xiii. *Written in London.* O
    Friend! I Know Not

9   The cattle are grazing,
    Their heads never raising;
  There are forty feeding like one!
    Written in March

10 My heart leaps up when I behold
   A rainbow in the sky:
  So was it when my life began;
  So is it now I am a man;
  So be it when I shall grow old,
   Or let me die!
  The Child is father of the Man;
  And I could wish my days to be
  Bound each to each by natural piety.
    My Heart Leaps Up

11 Another year!—another deadly blow!
  Another mighty Empire overthrown!
  And we are left, or shall be left, alone.
    *National Independence and
    Liberty,* pt. I, xxvii. *November.
    Another Year!*

12 Nuns fret not at their convent's
   narrow room;
  And hermits are contented with their
  cells.
    Miscellaneous Sonnets, pt. I, i.
    Nuns Fret Not

13 The light that never was, on sea or
   land,
  The consecration, and the poet's
  dream.
    *Elegiac Stanzas Suggested by a
    Picture of Peele Castle in a Storm*

14 A primrose by a river's brim
  A yellow primrose was to him,
  And it was nothing more.
    Peter Bell, pt. i, l. 249

15 Is it a party in a parlour?
  Cramm'd just as they on earth were
   cramm'd—
  Some sipping punch, some sipping
   tea,
  But, as you by their faces see,
  All silent and all damned!
    Ib. pt. i, l. 516 (later omitted)

16 The dew was falling fast, the stars
   began to blink;
  I heard a voice; it said, 'Drink, pretty
   creature, drink!'   *The Pet Lamb*

17   Where the statue stood
  Of Newton, with his prism and silent
   face,
  The marble index of a mind for ever
  Voyaging through strange seas of
   thought alone.
    The Prelude, bk. iii, l. 61

18 Sweet Spenser, moving through his
   clouded heaven
  With the moon's beauty and the
   moon's soft pace,
  I called him Brother, Englishman, and
   Friend!   *Ib.* l. 280

19 I thought of Chatterton, the mar-
   vellous boy,
  The sleepless soul, that perished in his
   pride;
  Of him who walked in glory and in joy,
  Following his plough, along the moun-
   tain side:
  By our own spirits are we deified:
  We poets in our youth begin in glad-
   ness;
  But thereof comes in the end des-
   pondency and madness.
    Resolution and Independence, vii

20   The good old rule
  Sufficeth them, the simple plan,
  That they should take, who have the
   power,
  And they should keep who can.
    *Memorials of a Tour in Scotland,
    1803.* xi. *Rob Roy's Grave*

1 Scorn not the Sonnet; Critic, you have
frowned,
Mindless of its just honours; with
this key
Shakespeare unlocked his heart.
*Miscellaneous Sonnets, pt. II, i.
Scorn Not the Sonnet*

2   And when a damp
Fell round the path of Milton, in his
hand
The Thing became a trumpet; whence
he blew
Soul-animating strains,—alas! too few.
Ib.

3 She dwelt among the untrodden ways
Beside the springs of Dove,
A maid whom there were none to
praise
And very few to love:

A violet by a mossy stone
Half hidden from the eye!
Fair as a star, when only one
Is shining in the sky.

She lived unknown, and few could
know
When Lucy ceased to be;
But she is in her grave, and, oh,
The difference to me!
*She Dwelt Among the Untrodden
Ways*

4 She was a phantom of delight
When first she gleamed upon my sight;
A lovely apparition, sent
To be a moment's ornament.
She was a Phantom of Delight

5 A perfect woman, nobly planned,
To warn, to comfort, and command;
And yet a spirit still, and bright
With something of angelic light.   *Ib.*

6 Type of the wise who soar, but never
roam;
True to the kindred points of heaven
and home!   *To a Skylark*

7 Behold her, single in the field,
Yon solitary Highland lass!
*Memorials of a Tour in Scotland,
1803, ix. The Solitary Reaper*

8 A voice so thrilling ne'er was heard
In spring-time from the Cuckoo-bird,
Breaking the silence of the seas
Among the farthest Hebrides.   *Ib.*

9 Will no one tell me what she sings?—
Perhaps the plaintive numbers flow
For old, unhappy, far-off things,
And battles long ago.   *Ib.*

10 Spade! with which Wilkinson hath
tilled his lands.
To the Spade of a Friend

11 And much it grieved my heart to
think
What man has made of man.
Lines Written in Early Spring

12 And 'tis my faith that every flower
Enjoys the air it breathes.   *Ib.*

13 Two Voices are there; one is of the sea,
One of the mountains; each a mighty
Voice,
In both from age to age thou didst
rejoice,
They were thy chosen music, Liberty!
*National Independence and
Liberty, xii. Thought of a Briton
on the Subjugation of Switzerland:
Two Voices are There*

14 And hark! how blithe the throstle sings!
He, too, is no mean preacher
Come forth into the light of things,
Let Nature be your teacher.
The Tables Turned

15 One impulse from a vernal wood
May teach you more of man,
Of moral evil and of good,
Than all the sages can.   *Ib.*

16 I've measured it from side to side:
'Tis three feet long, and two feet wide.
The Thorn, iii [early reading]

17   Sensations sweet,
Felt in the blood, and felt along the
heart.
*Lines composed a few miles above
Tintern Abbey, l. 27*

18   That best portion of a good man's
life,
His little, nameless, unremembered
acts
Of kindness and of love.   *Ib. l. 33*

19   I have learned
To look on nature, not as in the hour
Of thoughtless youth; but hearing
often-times
The still, sad music of humanity,
Nor harsh nor grating, though of
ample power
To chasten and subdue. And I have felt
A presence that disturbs me with the joy
Of elevated thoughts; a sense sublime
Of something far more deeply inter-
fused,
Whose dwelling is the light of setting
suns,
And the round ocean and the living air,
And the blue sky, and in the mind of
man.   *Ib. l. 88*

20   Thou hast left behind
Powers that will work for thee; air,
earth, and skies;
There's not a breathing of the common
wind
That will forget thee; thou hast great
allies;
Thy friends are exultations, agonies,
And love, and man's unconquerable
mind.
*National Independence and
Liberty, pt. I, viii. To Toussaint
L'Ouverture: Toussaint, the Most
Unhappy*

1 Once did she hold the gorgeous East
   in fee,
   And was the safeguard of the West.
      Ib. vi. *On the Extinction of the
      Venetian Republic: Once Did
      She Hold*

2 And when she took unto herself a
   Mate,
   She must espouse the everlasting Sea.
      Ib.

3 I take my little porringer
   And eat my supper there.
      We are Seven

4 Earth has not anything to show more
   fair:
   Dull would he be of soul who could
   pass by
   A sight so touching in its majesty:
   This City now doth, like a garment,
   wear
   The beauty of the morning; silent,
   bare,
   Ships, towers, domes, theatres, and
   temples lie
   Open unto the fields, and to the sky;
   All bright and glittering in the smoke-
   less air.
   Never did sun more beautifully steep
   In his first splendour, valley, rock, or
   hill!
   Ne'er saw I, never felt, a calm so
   deep!
   The river glideth at his own sweet will:
   Dear God! the very houses seem
   asleep;
   And all that mighty heart is lying still!
      Miscellaneous Sonnets, pt. II,
      xxxvi. *Composed upon West-
      minster Bridge*

5 The world is too much with us; late
   and soon,
   Getting and spending, we lay waste
   our powers:
   Little we see in Nature that is ours;
   We have given our hearts away, a
   sordid boon!
   This Sea that bares her bosom to the
   moon;
   The winds that will be howling at all
   hours,
   And are up-gathered now like sleeping
   flowers;
   For this, for everything, we are out of
   tune;
   It moves us not; Great God! I'd
   rather be
   A Pagan suckled in a creed outworn,
   So might I, standing on this pleasant
   lea,
   Have glimpses that would make me
   less forlorn;
   Have sight of Proteus rising from the
   sea,
   Or hear old Triton blow his wreathed
   horn.
      Ib. xxxiii. *The World is Too
      Much with Us*

6 Every great and original writer, in
   proportion as he is great and original,
   must himself create the taste by which
   he is to be relished.
      Letter to Lady Beaumont

HENRY CLAY WORK 1832–1884

7 Bring the good old bugle, boys, we'll
   sing another song;
   Sing it with a spirit that will start the
   world along,
   Sing it as we used to sing it—fifty
   thousand strong,
   As we were marching through
   Georgia.
      Marching Through Georgia

8 'Hurrah! hurrah! we bring the Jubilee!
   Hurrah! hurrah! the flag that makes
   you free!'
   So we sang the chorus from Atlanta
   to the sea,
   As we were marching through
   Georgia.   *Ib. Chorus*

9 Father, dear father, come home with
   me now,
   The clock in the belfry strikes one.
      Temperance song (1864)

SIR HENRY WOTTON 1568–1639

10 How happy is he born and taught
   That serveth not another's will;
   Whose armour is his honest thought,
   And simple truth his utmost skill!
      Character of a Happy Life, i

11 This man is freed from servile bands,
   Of hope to rise, or fear to fall:—
   Lord of himself, though not of lands,
   And having nothing, yet hath all.
      Ib. vi

12 He first deceas'd; she for a little tri'd
   To live without him: lik'd it not, and
   di'd.
      *Death of Sir Albertus Moreton's
      Wife*

13 You meaner beauties of the night,
   That poorly satisfy our eyes,
   More by your number, than your
   light;
   You common people of the skies,
   What are you when the moon shall
   rise?
      *On His Mistress, the Queen of
      Bohemia*

14 An ambassador is an honest man sent
   to lie abroad for the good of his
   country.
      *Written in the Album of Christo-
      pher Fleckmore* (1604)

SIR CHRISTOPHER WREN
1632–1723

1 Si monumentum requiris, circumspice.
If you would see his monument
look around.
*Inscription over the interior of the
North Door in St. Paul's Cathe-
dral, London. Attr. to Wren's son*

SIR THOMAS WYATT 1503?–1542

2 They flee from me, that sometime did
me seek. *Remembrance*

WILLIAM WYCHERLEY
1640?–1716

3 QUAINT:
With sharp invectives—
WIDOW:
Alias, Billingsgate.
Plain Dealer, Act III

XENOPHON b. *c*. 430 B.C.

4 θάλαττα θάλαττα.
The sea! the sea!
Anabasis, IV. vii. 24

WILLIAM BUTLER YEATS
1865–1939

5 Down by the salley gardens my love
and I did meet;
She passed the salley gardens with
little snow-white feet.
She bid me take love easy, as the
leaves grow on the tree;
But I, being young and foolish, with
her would not agree.
Down by the Salley Gardens

6 I have spread my dreams under your
feet;
Tread softly, because you tread on my
dreams.
*He Wishes for the Cloths of
Heaven*

7 Nor law, nor duty bade me fight,
Nor public men, nor cheering crowds,
A lonely impulse of delight
Drove to this tumult in the clouds;
I balanced all, brought all to mind,
The years to come seemed waste of
breath,
A waste of breath the years behind
In balance with this life, this death.
*An Irish Airman Foresees His
Death*

8 When I play on my fiddle in Dooney
Folk dance like a wave of the sea.
The Fiddler of Dooney

9 I will arise and go now, and go to
Innisfree,
And a small cabin build there, of clay
and wattles made:
Nine bean-rows will I have there, a
hive for the honey-bee,
And live alone in the bee-loud glade.
The Lake Isle of Innisfree

10 And pluck till time and times are done
The silver apples of the moon
The golden apples of the sun.
The Song of Wandering Ængus

11 When you are old and gray and full of
sleep,
And nodding by the fire, take down
this book,
And slowly read, and dream of the
soft look
Your eyes had once, and of their
shadows deep;
How many loved your moments of
glad grace,
And loved your beauty with love
false or true,
But one man loved the pilgrim soul in
you,
And loved the sorrows of your changing face.
And bending down beside the glowing
bars,
Murmur, a little sadly, how Love fled
And paced upon the mountains over-
head
And hid his face amid a crowd of
stars. *When you are Old*

ANDREW YOUNG 1807–1889

12 There is a happy land,
Far, far away,
Where Saints in glory stand,
Bright, bright as day.
Hymn: There is a Happy Land.
C. H. Bateman's *Sacred Song
Book* (1843)

EDWARD YOUNG 1683–1765

13 Be wise with speed;
A fool at forty is a fool indeed.
Love of Fame, Sat. ii, l. 281

14 How commentators each dark passage
shun,
And hold their farthing candle to the
sun. *Ib.* Sat. vii, l. 97

15 Tir'd Nature's sweet restorer, balmy
sleep!
*The Complaint: Night Thoughts,
Night i, l. 1*

16 Procrastination is the thief of time.
Ib. l. 393

17 Man wants but little; nor that little,
long. *Ib.* Night iv, l. 118

18 By night an atheist half believes a
God. *Ib.* Night v, l. 176

1 Life is the desert, life the solitude;
Death joins us to the great majority.
The Revenge, Act IV

2 You are so witty, profligate, and thin,
At once we think thee Milton, Death,
and Sin. *Epigram on Voltaire*

ISRAEL ZANGWILL 1864–1926

3 America is God's Crucible, the great
Melting-Pot where all the races of
Europe are melting and reforming! ...
God is making the American.
The Melting Pot, Act I

ÉMILE ZOLA 1840–1902

4 J'accuse.
I accuse.
Title of an open letter to the President of the Republic, in connexion with the Dreyfus case, published in L'Aurore, 13 Jan. 1898

INDEX

A

A was an apple-pie   155:2
Abandoned: What God a.   111:11
Abased: shall be a.   33:15
Abba, Father   35:7
Abbot of Aberbrothok: blest the A.   218:19
Abhor: Age, I do a. thee   210:11
Abhorred: a. all manner of meat   171:6
  how a. in my imagination 189:20
  with th'a. shears   145:1
Abhorrence: my heart's a.!   45:7
Abhors: a colour she a.   209:14
Abide: a. with me   135:16, 17
  no where did a.   65:22
Abides: much a.   230:15
  race a. immortal   237:9
Abiit ad plures   162:13
Abilities: according to his a.   140:15
Ability: about his a.   173:16
  doubted his a. to reign   225:1
  Studies serve. .for a.   14:24
Able: as far as he is a.   221:11
  if he is a.   105:17
Ablution: Of pure a.   121:8
Aboard: black-ey'd Susan came a.   89:30
Abode: A. his Hour or two   84:22
  a numble a.   74:9
  nor blessed a.   141:5
Abolish the death penalty   119:14
Abomination of desolation   32:12
Abominations of the earth   37:22
Abou Ben Adhem (may his tribe in-
  crease!)   112:2
Abound: that grace may a.?   35:3
About: A. it and a.   85:7
  go round a. her   169:23
  oxen are come a. me   168:34
Above: a. every name   36:15
  Praise Him a.   123:3
  so a. me   182:7
  Unless a. himself   72:3
Abraham: into A.'s bosom   33:28
Abreast: keep a. of Truth   135:4
Abroad:
  angel of death has been a. 41:10
  I will a.   103:19
  no spirit can walk a.   185:4
  pouring forth thy soul a. 121:6
  seeks a. may find   119:18
  spices are wafted a.   228:20
  to lie a.   249:14
Absence:
  A. makes the heart grow fonder
                   3:6, 19:3
  cannot admit A.   77:20
  conspicuous. .by its a.   178:11
  hath my a. been   211:12
Absence: L'a. est à l'amour ce qu'est
  au feu le vent   49:14
Absent: a. are always in the wrong   73:16
  A. in body   35:15
  a. one from another   23:31
  A. thee from felicity awhile 190:3
Absent-minded beggar   124:10
Absents: Les a. ont toujours tort   73:16
Absolom: O A., my son   25:4
Absolute:
  A. across the hall   21:21
  a. power corrupts absolutely 1:1
  declared a. rule   146:16
  her content so a.   204:28

Absolutism moderated by assas-
  sination   4:7
Abstinent: facilius se a. ut non
  utantur   13:10
Abstracts and brief chronicles   187:9
Abundance: he shall have a.   32:15
Abuse our patience   63:16
Abuses: trample down a.   237:17
Abusing of God's patience   202:15
Abutere: quousque. .a. . .patientia
  nostra?   63:16
Abysm of time?   208:8
Abyss: dark unbottom'd infinite
  a.   146:12
  edge of the nuclear a.   220:19
Abyssinian: It was an A. maid   66:15
Academes: arts, the a.   196:16
Accents: caught his clear a.   44:10
  Loved a. are soon forgot   213:16
Acceptable in thy sight   168:31
Access: Stop up the a. . .to re-
  morse   197:15
Accident: found out by a.   129:15
  happy a.   142:18
  Progress . .is not an a.   219:4
  There's been an a.!   96:12
Accidental and fortuitous   160:16
Accidents: A. will occur   74:12
  chapter of a.   61:11, 244:3
Accipe fraterno multum manantia
  fletu   59:3
Accomplished: her warfare is a.   28:11
According to the proverb   80:6
Accordingly: decide a.   138:5
Accosted: she-bear thus a.   125:5
Account: an accurate and exhaus-
  tive a.   20:7
  call our power to a.?   199:28
  present My true a.   147:17
  sent to my a.   186:12
Accumulates: Where wealth a.   95:4
Accursed: a. power   21:18
  think themselves a.   192:4
Accuse: j'accuse   251:4
Accused: who are a.   73:11
Accuser: vanquish, not my A.   153:10
Achates: Loyal A.   236:4
Ache: age, a., penury   201:1
Acheronta movebo   236:20
Aches: My heart a.   121:1
Achieve: I shall a. in time   92:8
Achieving: Still a.   133:28
Achilles: And see the great A.   230:15
  what name A. assumed   43:1
Aching void   70:2
Acknowledge: I next a. duly   153:13
A-cold: Tom's a.   195:10
Acquaintance: make a new a.   116:8
  Should auld a.   48:6
Acquainted: a. with love   113:21
Acquaints: Misery a. a man   208:14
Acquent: we were first a.   48:20
Acquire: a. and beget a temperance 188:7
Acquist: a. Of true experience   147:11
Acres: a. of the rye   184:12
  Cow for every three a.   142:24
  few paternal a.   165:14
  Three a. and a cow   67:9
Across: never get a.   88:9
Act: A. of Settlement   175:11
  last a. crowns the play   173:27

Act (cont.)
Sow an a. 175:4
To see him [Kean] a. 67:7
to the swelling a. 197:9
within the meaning of the A. 3:11
Acted on principles 102:2
Action: A., nor utterance 194:12
a. of the tiger 191:8
do a good a. by stealth 129:15
Do no sinful a. 2:9
In a. faithful 164:25
in a. how like an angel! 187:4
lose the name of a. 187:13
lust in a. 212:1
Makes that th' a. fine 103:22
Spheres of a. 132:2
suit the a. to the word 188:8
That a. is best 112:10
Actions: a. are what they are 49:15
a. do not. .make us traitors 199:25
a. of the just 216:25
Great a. speak great minds 19:21
in his a. be so ill! 141:11
Actor: well-grac'd a. 207:3
Acts: His a. being seven ages 183:20
unremembered a. 248:18
Actum: nil a. credens 135:6
ad infinitum 223:26
Adage: i' the a. 198:6
Adam: A.'s ale 172:21
A. Had 'em 3:7
A., the goodliest man 146:17
A. was a gardener 125:10, 192:10
old A. in this Child 167:30
Our father A. 125:1
When A. dalfe 99:11
When A. delved 8:13
Adamantine: In a. chains 145:12
Adazzle: a., dim 107:15
Add: to a. or detract 132:8
To a. something more 88:18
Adder: deaf a. 169:29
Adding: a. fuel to the flame? 147:7
a. insult to injuries 149:10
goes on a. one to one 43:18
Addington: Pitt is to A. 54:15
Addressed: a. to princes? 82:10
Adeste, fideles 9:14
Adieu: a., a., kind friends, a., a., a.
Bidding a. 8:1
Admirable: how express and a.! 120:24
Admiral: to kill an a. 187:4
Admiralty: price of a. 237:11
Admire: Let none a. 127:12
Admired: she might a. be 146:8
Admiring: with a. submission 210:2
Admit: cannot a. Absence 83:1
Admits: a. no ray 77:20
Adonais: I weep for A. 79:24
Adonis: This A. in loveliness 213:6
Adoption: and their a. tried 112:7
Spirit of a. 185:21
Adoration: Breathless with a. 35:7
Adore: all the Saints a. 246:15
I seek and a. them 102:1
we alike a. 41:6
ye heavens a. Him 173:26
you too shall a. 122:24
Youth, I do a. thee 134:20
Adorn: Old England to a. 210:11
or a. a tale 127:24
that he did not a. 117:3
Adorned: bride a. for her husband 115:11
Adultery: and gods (call) a. 37:25
Do not a. commit 51:11
Thou shalt not commit a. 64:7
Advance: we our sails a. 167:14
Advanced: is not a. there 78:28
so nobly a. 208:4
132:8

Advantage: a. rarely comes of it 64:7
by the rare a. 90:14
chief a. of London 142:17
Advantages: remember with a. 192:4
Adventure: To die. .an awfully big a. 18:21
Adversary: never. .sees her a. 148:9
your a. the devil 37:7
Adverse: in a. fortune 40:1
Adversité de nos meilleurs amis 175:16
Adversity: any other a. 167:21
bread of a. 28:8
old companions in a. 45:16
Sweet are the uses of a. 183:9
Advice to persons about to marry 173:3
Advise: none could a. 174:16
Advocate: Mediator and A. 166:26
Aeneas: where is father A. 110:6
Aequam memento. . Servare mentem 109:10
Aërial: feeds on the a. kisses 214:9
Aesthetic: high a. band 92:22
high a. line 92:20
Aetas parentum peior avis tulit 109:23
Afar: cometh from a. 246:11
devotion to something a. 215:13
when a. and asunder 40:15
Afeard: a soldier, and a.? 199:28
Affairs: in the a. of men 194:19
Affection: a. beaming in one eye 74:20
close a. which grows from com-
mon names 47:6
Set your a. on things above 36:22
your a.'s strong 104:12
Affections: his a. dark as Erebus 202:13
of the heart's a. 122:7
wills and a. 166:35
Affinity: Kindred and A. 172:16
Afflicted: Any ways a. 166:29
he was a. 28:21
Affliction: bread of a. 25:16
such a light a. 152:16
Afflictions: out of all their a. 166:30
Afford: can't a. a carriage 72:1
mortal times a. 206:2
that life can a. 115:14
Affords: That earth a. 80:17
Affright: a. the air 191:3
none to a. thee 104:13
Afire: common bush a. with God 43:4
Afloat: are we now a. 194:19
A-flying: Old Time is still a. 105:14
Afoot: game's a. 191:9
Afraid: a. for any terror 170:19
a. to strike 165:6
Be not a. 24:26, 32:42
be not a. of greatness 209:12
be not a. to do thine office 150:5
I, a stranger and a. 111:9
nor be a.! 45:4
they were sore a. 32:41
to keep myself from being a. 79:15
Afric: A.'s sunny fountains 101:15
Africa: silent over A. 44:3
sloggin' over A. 124:16
Africa: ex A. semper aliquid novi 163:9
After-dinner talk 228:22
Afternoon: seemed always a. 228:16
After-years: Believe it, a.! 109:15
Agag came unto him 24:42
Again: conquer a. and a. 88:18
do it a. and a. 56:16
do it, please, a.? 96:9
I shall not pass this way a. 98:15
It's that man a. 119:15
Against: A. good custom 181:20
every man's hand a. him 23:25
He said he was a. it 68:24
not with me is a. me 31:22
used a. you 78:7
who can be a. us? 35:9

Agamemnon: When A. cried aloud 81:22
Agas: Quidquid a., prudenter a. 10:5
Age: a., ache, penury 201:1
a. and body of the time 188:10
A. cannot wither her 182:16
A., I do abhor thee 210:11
a. is full of care 210:10
a. of chivalry is past 124:8
A. shall not weary them 38:2
a. without a name 150:3
at your a. 56:16
build from a. to a. 124:17
cool'd a long a. 121:3
Crabbed a. and youth 210:10
Damn the a. 129:14
days of our a. 170:18
died in a good old a. 25:23
each a. is a dream 159:19
evening of my a. 178:3
faults of the a. come from
  Christianity 16:1
fetch the a. of gold 145:8
flower of their a. 24:36
if a. could 83:8
in a changing a. 78:12
in mine a. 193:1
in the name of every a. 47:11
labour of an a. 147:12
last a. 237:1
nor youth nor a. 200:20
not of an a. 118:7
Old a. hard and sad 10:2
Old a. hath yet his honour 230:15
Our sires' a. was worse 109:23
outworn buried a. 211:6
pays us but with a. 174:15
see old a. 192:4
son of his old a. 23:32
Soul of the A.! 118:4
staff of my a. 201:20
That men call a. 41:16
thou a. unbred 211:13
Towards the a. of twenty-six 21:6
vice and follies of the a. 59:7
well-spent a. 54:10
when the a. is in 204:14
which should accompany old a. 199:32
woman who tells one her real a. 243:25
world's great a. 213:12
Aged: an a., a. man 58:11
an a. parent 74:17
Agendum: dum quid superesset a. 135:6
Agents: night's black a. 199:6
Ages: aye, a. long ago 120:5
being seven a. 183:20
heir of all the a. 228:13
in a. past 239:14
Make the mighty a. 55:26
Rock of a. 233:23
thousand a. in Thy sight 239:14
thro' the a. 228:11
Agglomeration: This a. 237:16
Aggravate my voice 203:4
Aggravating: She was an a. child 21:11
Agincourt: affright the air at A.? 191:3
Agitated: considerably a. 75:29
A-gley: Gang aft a. 48:26
Agnes: St. A.' Eve 120:2
Agnostic: title of 'a.' 112:12
Ago: long, long a. 69:4
Agog: And all a. 69:25
Agonies: exultations, a. 248:20
Agony: A. and bloody Sweat 166:24
a. is abated 137:4
And I'm in a. 59:2
My soul in a. 65:19
Agree: Birds. .a. 239:8
Where they do a. 216:3
with her would not a. 250:5

Agunt: Quidquid a. homines 119:1
Aid: and lend us Thine a.! 101:14
apt Alliteration's artful a. 62:11
Without our a. 123:5
Aide-toi, le ciel t'aidera 86:15
Ail: what can a. thee 120:10
Aim: not make thoughts your a. 125:14
Aiming: a. at a million 43:18
Air: affright the a. at Agincourt? 191:3
a. and harmony 172:19
a., earth, and skies 248:20
a. goes by in a wind 20:4
A. is delicate 198:2
a. is hush'd 67:12
a. it breathes 248:12
a. that kills 111:5
all the a. a solemn stillness holds 97:8
arrow into the a. 133:12
As in the lowly a. 91:19
birds of the a. fell a-sighing 159:4
birds of the a. have nests 31:7
breathe his native a. 165:14
breathing English a. 42:11
Brightness falls from the a. 152:5
build that dome in a. 66:15
built with a. 117:13
canopy, the a. 187:4
couriers of the a. 198:4
eagle in the a. 26:31
fairer than the evening a. 138:13
filthy a. 197:2
flies through the a. 132:4
forming in the a. 175:15
fowls of the a. 168:24
graceful a. 86:11
growing strength in the a. 62:21
I am fire and a. 183:3
in an a. of glory 235:10
in the smokeless a. 249:4
left the vivid a. 219:7
like the a. we breathe 222:13
little motion in the a. 213:11
living a. 248:19
nipping and an eager a. 186:2
No stir in the a. 218:18
No stir of a. 120:7
on the desert a. 97:15
saw the a…with your hand 188:7
scent the morning a. 186:11
sewers annoy the a. 146:22
sits Expectation in the a. 191:5
sitting in the a.! 107:16
skim the a. 88:8
Sweet a. blow soft 105:2
take into the a. 121:6
They mock the a. 97:4
though light as a. 47:6
throw it up into the a. 181:14
to feed in a. 214:1
Trifles light as a. 205:8
wing the midway a. 195:19
With an independent a. 90:17
With its sweet a. 208:10
Airs: don't give yourself a. 56:17
Naiad a. 163:16
soft Lydian a. 144:19
Sounds and sweet a. 208:18
Airy: a., fairy Lilian 228:3
gives to a. nothing 203:19
so a. a tread 228:20
Aisles: And groined the a. 82:15
Alarms: used to war's a. 106:22
Albatross: A. did follow 65:9
I shot the A. 65:10
Alcestis: like A. from the grave 148:1
Alchemy: with heavenly a. 211:2
Aldershot: an' A. it 125:11
Ale: Adam's a. 172:21
For a quart of a. 201:5

Ale (*cont.*)
  jolly good a. 221:25
  no more cakes and a.? 209:7
  spicy nut-brown a. 144:17
Alea: Iacta a. est 53:3
Aleppo: in A. once 205:20
  to A. gone 197:5
Alexander: If I were not A. 2:6
  Some talk of A. 7:7
Alexander's Ragtime Band 22:17
Alexandra: Sea-King's daughter..A.! 231:3
Alexandrine: needless A. 164:11
Alibi: vy worn't there a a.! 75:28
Alice, where art thou? 46:1
Alien: amid the a. corn 121:6
  nothing human a. from me 231:6
Alike: all places were a. to him 128:16
  to thee are both a. 172:1
Alive: And art a. still 118:4
  Bears not a. 190:23
  Bliss..to be a. 246:1
  he had been a. 82:10
  he is no longer a. 22:10
  is a. again 33:24
  made such a noise .. when a. 81:6
  no man a. could bear it 212:19
  Officiously to keep a. 64:6
  wish to keep her a. 89:5
All: a. along, down along 17:4
  a. but he had fled 102:7
  A. For Love 79:13
  A. for one, one for all 80:10
  A. is not lost 145:15
  A. power is not to a. 237:2
  Demands..my a. 239:17
  last of a. 74:3
  Loving himself better than a. 67:4
  prey to a. 164:19
  take him for a. in a. 185:15
  This above a. 185:21
  Thou art over a.! 127:14
  with charity for a. 132:9
  yet hath a. 249:11
Allaying both their fury and my passion 208:10
Allegory: headstrong as an a. 216:12
Allen: humble A. 165:13
Alley: she lives in our a. 55:2
Allied: wits are sure to madness near a. 79:6
Allies: thou hast great a. 248:20
Alliteration: apt A.'s artful aid 62:11
Allowance: a. made to anyone 116:18
  But make a. 125:14
All-shaking thunder 195:4
All-softening: a., overpowering knell 51:24
Ally: a. to the brave 236:22
Almighty: a. dollar 112:16
  A. Power 145:12
  And, pleas'd th' A.'s orders to perform 1:3
  And under that A. Fin 42:2
  Lord God A. 37:16, 38:13, 102:1
Alms: a. for oblivion 208:27
  When thou doest a. 30:20
Alms-basket of words 196:17
Almsman: for an a.'s gown 206:16
Aloft: mount larks a. 105:2
Alone: all a. went she 124:1
  A., a., all, all a. 65:19
  A. and warming his five wits 230:9
  A. I did it 184:19
  A., with-outen any companye 60:18
  I a. sit lingering 235:9
  Left blooming a. 149:18
  left him a. with his glory 245:7
  less a. than when a. 63:15, 176:6
  live a. 250:9
  loved him for himself a. 216:6

man should be a. 23:11
  plough my furrow a. 177:6
  seas of thought a. 247:17
  stand a., and think 122:5
  We are left,..a. 247:11
  We have stood a. 96:7
  weep a. 243:3
  wherefore thou a.? 146:18
  who travels a. 128:7
  wild dog, and a. 137:13
  yet not a. 146:20
  You and I must bide a. 16:18
Along: a. the mountain side 247:19
  Will go with you a. 104:10
Aloud: all a. the wind 196:20
Alph the sacred river 66:14
Alpha: I am A. and Omega 37:13
Alpine: A. mountains cold 147:16
  through an A. village 133:17
Alps: hewed passages through the A. 67:22
Altar: an a. with this inscription 34:42
  To what green a. 120:21
Altars: even thy a. 170:13
  on behalf of..their a. 178:18
Alteration: when it a. finds 211:16
Alternatives: more a., the more difficult the choice 2:15
Alters: Which a. when it alteration finds 211:16
Always in the wrong 79:8
Am: Here I a. 137:14
  I a. that I a. 24:3
  I think, therefore I a. 73:15
Ama et fac quod vis 13:9
Amaracus, and asphodel 229:4
Amaranth: no fields of a. 129:22
Amaryllis: To sport with A. 145:1
Amaze: men themselves a. 140:4
Ambassador: A. from Britain's crown 78:23
  a. is an honest man 249:14
Ambassadors: not a *congress* of a. 46:27
Amber-dropping hair 144:3
Amber scent 147:5
Ambition: A., Distraction 57:5
  a. of man 174:16
  ill-weav'd a. 190:23
  Let not a. mock 97:12
  make a. virtue! 205:10
  To reign is worth a. 146:3
  Vaulting a. 198:4
  Who doth a. shun 183:15
Ambitious: as he was a. 194:2
  Caesar was a. 194:3
Amelia was praying 231:17
Amen: 'A.' stuck in my throat 198:12
  sound of a great A. 172:23
America: is A. God's Crucible 251:3
  A. was thus clearly top nation 181:19
  business of A. 68:25
  cannot conquer A. 162:19
  O my A.! 77:5
  there is A. 46:28
  Wake up, A. 88:17
American: A. system 107:7
  I am A. bred 143:2
  making the A. 251:3
Americanism: fifty-fifty A. 177:3
Americans: A. and nothing else 177:3
  bad A. 243:23
  brave A. all 76:1
  good A.,..go to Paris 10:9, 243:23
Amerikey: North and South A. 232:3
Amiable: a. are thy dwellings 170:13
  An a. weakness 84:9, 216:22
Amicus Plato 10:17
Amidst their tall ancestral trees 102:11
Amis: nos a., les ennemis 22:15

Amissi: They are not a. 103:11
Ammunition: and pass the a. 87:5
Amo: A. amas, I love a lass 159:9
Non a. te, Sabidi 139:22
Amongst: Be a. you 167:26
Amor: Omnia vincit A. 237:3
Amorous: a. of their strokes 182:15
Amphitrite's destined halls 213:17
Ample: of a. power 248:19
Ampullas: Proicit a. 107:19
Amused: We are not a. 235:16
Amusement: very pleasant a. 116:12
Amusing: is a. in itself 88:10
Anapaests: swift A. throng 67:2
Anarch: Thy hand, great A.! 164:3
Anarchy: of a. and despotism 215:16
Ancestors: look backward to their a. 47:13
Ancestral: A. voices prophesying 66:15
ploughs again his a. land 108:14
tall a. trees 102:11
Ancestry: I can trace my a. 91:18
pride of a. 166:4
Anchor: British Fleet a-riding at a. 232:3
Anchoring: tall a. bark 195:19
Ancient: an a. Mariner 65:4
a. and fish-like smell 208:13
a. and now forgotten 180:17
a. as the hills 66:14
A. of Days 29:19, 96:18
Around the a. track 142:1
hath its a. glory 129:12
heard In a. days 121:6
in a. time 38:16
in their a. fold 147:16
keep their a. places 232:10
Ancients: wisdom of the a. 15:13
Ancona: This is A. 43:20
Ancus: rich old Tullus and A. 110:6
Anders: Ich kann nicht a. 135:11
Anderson: John A. my jo 48:20
Anew: begins a. 213:12
Angel: And let the a. 200:11
A. of Death 41:10, 52:10
A. of the Lord 32:41, 225:9
beautiful and ineffectual a. 12:5
better a. 212:4
clip and A.'s wings 120:16
half a. 45:6
how like an a.! 187:4
like an a. sings 202:11
man an ape or an a.? 76:8
ministering a. 180:13, 189:22
those A. faces smile 153:16
up-lifted A. trumpets 147:14
Which a. voices tell 143:3
White as an a. 39:10
Who wrote like an A. 89:1
Angelic: something of a. light 248:5
Angels: A. alone 134:19
A. and ministers of grace 186:4
A. bending near the earth 181:10
a. keep their ancient places 232:10
a. of God ascending 23:29
a. sung this strain 232:13
band of a. comin' after me 7:10
band of glorious A. 152:8
blow Your trumpets, A. 77:8
Carried by the a. 33:28
entertained a. unawares 36:37
faces of a. 98:14
Flights of a., sing thee 190:5
Four a. to my bed 1:17
give his a. charge 170:20
Hear all ye A. 146:19
hear the a. sing 181:10
Holy a. guard thy bed! 239:11
like a. trumpet-tongu'd 198:4
make the a. weep 200:19

[Milton] wrote of A. and God 39:16
on the side of the a. 76:8
Praise Him, A. 122:24
Sons of men and a. say 241:7
that neither..a. 35:10
tongues of men and of a. 35:20
walk the a. 139:12
where a. fear to tread 164:13
women are a. 52:5
Anger: more in sorrow than in a. 185:18
wishes, fears, a. 119:1
Anglais: Les a. s'amusent tristement selon l'usage de leur pays 222:11
Angles: they were called A. 98:14
Angli vocarentur 98:14
Angling or float fishing 116:12
Anglo-Saxon: an A. Messenger 58:8
Angry: Be a., and dispatch 183:4
Be ye a., and sin not 36:12
Speak no a. word 2:9
Such a. passions rise 239:7
when thou art a. 170:18
with a. prayers 105:13
Anguis: Latet a. in herba 236:24
Anguish: When pain and a. 180:13
With a. moist 120:11
Angulus: mihi praeter omnis A. ridet 109:12
Animal: Man is..a political a. 10:15
poor, bare, forked a. 195:12
tool-using a. 55:20
Animal: cet a. est très méchant 9:3
Animalculous: beings a. 93:19
Animals: All a. are equal 159:15
a. went in one by one 7:13
live with a. 242:14
paragon of a.! 187:4
Wild a. never kill 88:10
Animated bust 97:13
Animula vagula blandula 99:3
Anna: Here thou, great A.! 165:3
Annabel Lee: I and my A. 163:14
Annals: a. of the poor 97:12
War's a. will cloud 100:4
whose a. are blank 55:10
writ your a. true 184:19
Anne: as Saint A., the mother of Mary 161:9
Tell 'em Queen A.'s dead 67:18
Anne, ma soeur Anne, ne vois-tu rien venir? 162:8
Anni: Labuntur a. 109:14
Annie Laurie: And for bonny A. 77:25
Annihilating all that's made 140:7
Annihilation: in A.'s Waste 85:9
Annoy: and sewers a. 146:22
does it to a. 56:19
Annoyance: To his extreme a. 21:19
Annual income twenty pounds 74:1
Anoint: with oil a. 181:8
Anointed: a. king 206:12
a. my head 169:2
Anointing: a. Spirit 172:11
Another: absent one from a. 23:31
a. to hear 233:8
as true as a. 49:12
But for a. gives its ease 39:5
Can I see a.'s grief 39:14
Can I see a.'s woe 39:14
in a.'s trouble 96:6
members one of a. 36:11
one from a. 23:31
when comes such a.? 194:14
Answer: A. a fool 26:26
a. came there none 58:1, 180:1
a. made it none 185:17
a. to 'Hi' 56:2
dusty a. 142:7
give a.! 125:4
give me your a., do! 72:1

Answer (cont.)
  never offer to a. this — 220:14
  soft a. turneth away wrath — 26:16
  Thurlow's a. — 217:19
  would not stay for an a. — 15:5
Answered: a. never a word — 134:13
  hath Caesar a. it — 194:3
  no one a. — 73:5
  They only a. — 21:9
Ant: Go to the a. — 26:8
Antelope: deer and the a. play — 105:5
Anthem: plaintive a. fades — 121:7
Anthems: and a. clear — 144:9
Anthropophagi: of the Cannibals..
  the A. — 204:22
Antic: a. disposition — 186:17
  dance an a. hay — 138:9
Anti-Christ: looks't like A. — 117:9
Antick: Old father a. — 190:7
  there the a. sits — 206:15
Antidote: oblivious a. — 200:1
Antique: a. pageantry — 144:19
  a. pillars — 144:9
  from an a. land — 214:5
  nude and a. — 224:3
  ye a. towers — 98:5
Antiquity: write for A.! — 129:14
Antony: A. shall be brought
  drunken forth — 182:24
  A., who lost the world — 79:27
Anvil: What the a.? — 39:2
Anxiety: taboo'd by a. — 91:23
Anxious: a. for to shine — 92:20
Anybody: is there a. there? — 73:4
  Then no one's a. — 91:14
Anything: And what I do in a. — 103:21
  A., to me is sweeter — 106:5
  hardly mind a. else — 114:20
  Wot's the good of A.? — 62:3
Anywhere: Go a. in England — 212:15
Apace: Work a. — 72:18
Ape: like an angry a. — 200:19
  man an a. or an angel? — 76:8
  sedulous a. — 220:22
Apella the Jew — 110:12
Apes: a. and peacocks — 25:9, 140:20
  for dogs and a.! — 43:17
  that a. humility — 218:17
Apes: vos non vobis mellificatis a. — 237:10
Apollo: after the songs of A. — 197:1
  A.'s first — 54:20
  A.'s laurel bough — 139:2
  as is A.'s lute — 144:2
  in fealty to A. hold — 121:9
Apollyon: his name is A. — 46:8
Apologize: I never a. — 212:6
Apology: a favourite a. — 73:24
Apostle in the high aesthetic band — 92:22
Apostolick: Catholick and A.
  Church — 167:19
Apothecary: good a. — 195:21
Apparel: a. oft proclaims the man — 185:21
  My gay a. — 206:16
  neatness of a. — 241:19
Apparelled in celestial light — 246:7
Apparition: lovely a. — 248:4
Appeal: I a. unto Caesar — 34:48
Appear: A. like mice — 195:19
  bright original a. — 89:24
  everything would a. — 39:21
  what I may a. to the world — 153:17
  which indeed a. beautiful — 32:9
Appearances: Keep up a. — 62:10
Appears: when a woman a. — 89:18
Appelles: regular habit of A. — 163:12
Appétit: L'a. vient en mangeant — 174:4
Appetite: a. grows by eating — 174:4
  a. may sicken — 209:2
  increase of a. — 185:11

  wait on a. — 199:9
Appetites: And not their a. — 205:7
  cloy The a. they feed — 182:16
Applaud: Till thou a. the deed — 199:6
Applause! delight! — 118:4
Apple: An' there vor me the a.
  tree — 18:10
  a. of an eye — 168:28
  like an a.-tree — 177:8
  My a. trees will never get across — 88:9
  shade of the old a. tree — 244:8
  when you've got an a. — 234:19
Apple-pie: A was an a. — 155:2
  to make an a. — 86:19
Apples: a., cherries, hops, and
  women — 75:16
  comfort me with a. — 27:15
  eggs, a., and cheese — 124:15
  golden a. of the sun — 250:10
  Ripe a. drop — 140:6
  silver a. of the moon — 250:10
  stolen, be your a. — 112:5
Apple-tart: To eat with a. — 221:13
Apprehend: would but a. some joy — 203:19
Apprehension: a. of the good — 206:5
  in a. how like a god! — 187:4
  is most in a. — 200:21
Appris: rien a. ni rien oublié — 225:2
  rien oublié et..rien a. — 80:11
Approach: Beats my a. — 123:11
Approbation..is praise indeed — 150:15
Appropriate: to be the a. title — 112:12
Approve: a. better things — 160:7
  a. By his lov'd mansionry — 198:2
Après nous le déluge — 163:19
April: A., A., Laugh thy girlish
  laughter — 239:5
  A. is the cruellest month — 81:23
  A., June, and September — 96:8
  A., June, and November — 158:7
  A.'s in the west wind — 141:6
  March winds and A. showers — 6:5
  Men are A. when they woo — 184:11
  Now that A.'s there — 44:1
  of an A. day — 210:1
  Sweet A. showers — 234:14
  Three A. perfumes — 211:13
  to A.'s breeze — 82:14
  Whanne that A. with his shoures — 60:8
Aprons: made themselves a. — 23:15
Arabia: perfumes of A. — 199:30
Arabs: like the A. — 133:15
Araby: sing these songs of A. — 244:10
Arbitrator: common a., Time — 209:1
Arcadia: et in A. ego — 10:1
Arch: broken a. of London Bridge — 136:21
  experience is an a. — 230:13
Arch Fear in a visible form — 45:3
Archangel a little damaged — 129:12
Arched: that a. the flood — 82:14
Archer: busy a. — 216:30
Arches: a. of the years — 232:7
Architecture: A. in general — 179:10
  A. of the world — 139:10
Arcs: On the earth the broken a. — 43:6
Arden: now am I in A. — 183:10
Ardent: most a. of my desires — 142:15
Ardeur: une a. dans mes veines
  cachée — 174:10
Arduous: No height is too a. — 108:15
Are: Here we a.! — 128:28
  tell you who you a. — 61:5
Area: at a. gates — 81:20
Arethusa: In wanton A. — 138:13
Argentines sleep firmly — 69:8
Argifying: good of a.? — 128:18
Argo: loftier A. cleaves the main — 213:12
Argue: A. as you please — 154:11
  he could a. still — 95:8

Arguing: I am not a. with you — 242:1
  In a. too — 95:8
Argument: any other kind of a. — 220:14
  heard great a. — 85:7
  highth of this great a. — 145:11
  knockdown a. — 58:5, 79:14
  without great a. — 189:7
Aright: how to live a. — 108:13
A-ripening: His greatness is a. — 192:14
Arise: and a., a. — 77:8
  A., shine — 29:1
  I will a. — 33:22, 250:9
  Let God a. — 170:6
  thoughts that a. in me — 225:14
Arising from sullen earth — 210:13
Aristocrat who banks with Coutts — 91:9
Arithmetic: branches of A. — 57:5
Ark: straight out of the A. — 217:15
Arly: agèd Uncle A.! — 131:3
Arm: A! A! it is..the cannon's opening roar! — 51:2
  gather the lambs with his a. — 28:14
  I bit my a. — 65:14
  long a. of coincidence — 59:17
  on his mother's a. — 246:9
  strength with his a. — 32:38
  Sufficient is Thine A. alone — 239:14
Arma: a. virumque cano — 236:3
  cedant a. togae — 63:14
  nunc a...hic paries habebit — 110:2
Armadas: till the great A. come — 153:5
Armchair: for loving that old a.? — 68:23
Armed: A. neutrality — 244:12
  a. with more than complete steel — 139:15
  strong man a. — 33:10
  Thrice is he a. — 192:7, 213:4
Armies: ignorant a. clash — 11:9
Arming: a. me from fear — 41:13
  kings are a. — 180:15
Armour: a. is his honest thought — 249:10
  a. of light — 35:14, 166:23
  his a. wherein he trusted — 33:11
  my a. and the lute — 110:2
  no a. against fate — 216:24
  put your a. on — 241:13
  whole a. of God — 36:13, 14
Armourers: thrive the a. — 191:5
Arms: A. I sing — 236:3
  A., take your last embrace! — 208:5
  azured a. — 138:13
  Come to my a. — 57:14
  corners of the world in a. — 193:8
  defy th' Omnipotent to a. — 145:12
  entrusted with a. — 244:16
  everlasting a. — 24:25
  every man in a. — 246:2
  hug it in mine a. — 200:22
  if my love were in my a. — 8:10
  in the nurse's a. — 183:20
  muscles of his brawny a. — 134:10
  So he laid down his a.! — 106:22
  take a. against a sea of troubles — 187:13
  to my a. restore — 68:14
  To war and a. I fly — 134:20
  vigour from our a. — 47:7
  what can ail thee, Knight at a. — 120:10
Army: a. marches on its stomach — 9:1
  a. of unalterable law — 142:1
  a. would be a base rabble — 47:3
  noble a. of martyrs — 166:12
  terrible as an a. — 27:19
Aroint thee, witch! — 197:5
Aromatic pain — 164:15, 244:15
Arose: a. as one man — 24:34
  A. from out the azure main — 232:13
Arques: we fought at A. — 103:1
Array: to summon his a. — 136:8
Arrayed: not a. like one of these — 30:28
Arrest: strict in his a. — 189:28

Arrive: than to a. — 221:6
Arrived: day of glory has a. — 177:17
Arrow: a. that flieth — 170:19
  I shot an a. — 133:12
  With my bow and a. — 159:4
Arrows: a. in the hand of the giant — 171:23
  his sharp a. tries? — 216:30
  my a. of desire! — 38:16
  slings and a. — 187:13
Arsenal of democracy — 176:16
Arsenic and Old Lace — 123:4
Art: anything but his a. — 212:20
  a. constantly aspires — 161:10
  A. for a.'s sake — 69:6
  A. is a jealous mistress — 82:16
  A. is too precise — 104:11
  a. To find the mind's construction — 197:13
  but is it A.? — 125:1
  Desiring this man's a. — 210:13
  next to Nature, A. — 129:20
  thou a. with me — 181:8
  unpremeditated a. — 215:3
  use no a. — 186:23
  What a. can wash her guilt — 95:21
  what a., Could twist — 39:2
  with less a. — 186:22
Art: L'a. pour l'a. — 69:6
Artful Dodger, — 75:8
Arthur: slowly answer'd A. from the barge — 227:1
Article: be snuff'd out by an a. — 51:25
Articles: A. of the Christian Faith — 167:32
Articulate monotony — 220:7
Artificer: great a. — 221:19
Artist: more of an a. — 122:11
  portrait of the a. — 118:17
  true a. will let his wife starve — 212:20
  What an a. dies — 153:3
Artistic: to give a. verisimilitude — 92:13
Arts: a., the academes — 196:16
  as One of the Fine A. — 73:14
  France, mother of a. — 20:14
  No a.; no letters — 105:9
  these thine a. — 236:18
Ascend: a. to heaven — 84:12
  that would a. the brightest heaven — 191:2
Ash: Oh! the oak, and the a. — 6:15
  Than Oak, and A. — 127:24
Ashamed: a. with the noble shame — 124:4
  shall not be a. — 171:23
  to beg I am a. — 33:25
Ashbuds: More black than a. — 226:13
Ashes: A. and sparks — 214:4
  a. of his fathers — 136:9
  a. to a. — 168:20
  cinders, a., dust — 120:15
  handful of grey a. — 69:4
  in a. ending! — 59:5
  into a. all my lust — 140:12
Asia: pampered Jades of A. — 139:13
Aside: often turn a. — 125:5
Ask: all I a. is a tall ship — 141:2
  all we ought to a. — 122:14
  A. a p'liceman! — 176:3
  A., and it shall be given you — 30:33
  Belike you a. of me — 59:2
  do not a. to see — 153:15
  dost a. me blessing — 196:6
  exerted herself to a. — 13:21
  only a. for information — 74:11
  Pray, a. not — 109:2
  We a. and a. — 11:20
Asked: King a. — 143:13
  Nobody a. you — 159:3
  You a. for it — 148:18
Askelon: in the streets of A. — 24:47
Asking: a. too much — 54:12

Asking (cont.)
first time of a. 168:5
think not of a. 109:1
Asleep: and he lies fast a. 85:1
Half a. as they stalk 100:4
houses seem a. 249:4
on a half-reap'd furrow sound a. 119:18
such a tide as moving seems a. 226:6
sucks the nurse a.? 183:4
When men were all a. 41:7
Aspect: distraction in 's a. 187:11
sweet a. of princes 192:14
terrible a. 191:8
Aspen: quivering a. 180:13
Right as an a. leaf 60:27
Aspersion upon my'parts of speech! 216:10
Asphodel: amaracus, and a. 229:4
Aspires: a. towards the condition of music 161:10
Aspiring: to have a. minds 139:10
Ass: call great Caesar a. 183:4
for your dull a. 189:19
law is an a. 75:10
nor his a. 167:17
white curd of a.'s milk? 165:7
Wild A. 85:1
Assail: scholar's life a. 117:2
Assassination: absolutism moderated by a. 4:7
if the a...trammel up the consequence 198:3
Assassins: que MM. les a. commencent 119:14
Assembled: Once again a. here 45:20
Assert: a. eternal Providence 145:11
a. my firm belief 176:13
Assist: I want you to a. me 117:4
Assuaged: half a. for Itylus 223:28
Assurance: make a. double sure 199:21
Assured: of what he's most a. 200:19
Astolat: lily maid of A. 226:21
Astonished: always a. and delighted 161:3
a. at my own moderation! 64:2
Astonishment: Your a.'s odd 4:1
Astray: like sheep have gone a. 28:21
Asunder: let no man put a. 168:15
let not man put a. 31:41
when afar and a. 40:15
At: wonder what you're a. 56:24
Atahualpa: who strangled A. 136:20
Ate: He a. and drank 105:15
With A. by his side 193:21
Athæneum, that was the name! 221:10
Atheist: a. half believes a God 250:18
village a. 62:2
Athens: as refin'd as ever A. heard 11:3
gods of A. 163:7
Ye men of A. 34:42
Athirst: him that is a. 37:27
Atkins: Thank you Mister A. 127:20
Atlanta: from A. to the sea 249:8
Atlantic: 'twas in the broad A. 6:17
Atlantic Ocean: pushing away the A. 218:4
Atomic globule 91:28
Atoms: concurrence of a. 160:16
Attachment: a. à la Plato 92:22
Attack: dared a. my Chesterton 21:20
I shall a. 86:14
to lead such dire a. 136:13
Attacked: when..a. it defends itself 9:3
Attained: The heights..Were not a. 133:22
Attempt: Never literary a. 111:22
Attempted: Something a. 134:11
Attend, all ye 136:5
Attendance: To dance a. 193:2
Attended: on his way a. 246:11
Attention: listened to with such a. 176:7
to draw my a.? 78:11
with diligence and a. 14:25

Attic: mellow glory of the A. stage 11:14
O A. shape! 120:22
Atticum: Sal A. 163:11
Attire: wild in their a. 197:8
Attitude: Fair a.! 120:22
Attorney: rich a.'s Elderly ugly daughter 93:33
to an A.'s firm 93:10
you find your a. 91:25
Attractive: metal more a. 188:12
Attribute: a. to awe 202:5
a. to God himself 202:5
Auburn: Sweet A.! 95:3
Audace: De l'a., et encore de l'a. 72:8
Aude: sapere a. 108:7
Audentis Fortuna iuvat 236:22
Audi partem alteram 13:8
Audience: fit a. find 146:20
Aught remains to do 176:5
Augury: we defy a. 189:26
Augustus was a chubby lad 105:15
Aunt: an a. in Yucatan 21:23
Aunt Jane observed, the second time 96:11
Auntie, did you feel no pain 96:9
Aunts: cousins and his a.! 93:9
for me and my a. 210:5
Auream quisquis mediocritatem 109:13
Austerlitz: Voilà le soleil d'A. 152:3
Austria: Don John of A. 61:19
Austrian army, awfully arrayed 3:10
Author: a. and finisher 36:35
a. and giver 167:2
a. of peace 166:14
expected to see an a. 161:3
prefer being the a. 245:8
Authority: every shadow of a. 47:7
little brief a. 200:19
man under a. 31:5
Authors: much exposed to a. 240:18
We a., Ma'am 76:13
Automatic: with a. hand 82:2
Autumn: breath of A.'s being 214:1
to yellow a. turn'd 211:13
Autumnal: deep, a. tone 214:4
Thick as a. leaves 146:4
Autumn-fields: happy A. 229:13
Auxilio: non tali a..Tempus eget 236:12
Availeth: struggle naught a. 64:10
Avails: what a. the sceptred race! 129:19
Avalanche: Beware the awful a.! 133:19
Avarice: dreams of a. 115:24, 149:11
Avaunt: and bid them a. 109:16
Ave Caesar 9:16
Ave Mari: With an A. 217:7
Avenge: A., O Lord 147:16
will a. me of this..clerk! 103:13
Avenger: enemy, and the a. 168:22
Avenues: lawns and a. 125:8
Avernus: descent to A.! 236:15
Avert this omen 63:20
Aves: Sic vos non vobis nidificatis a. 237:10
Avilion: island-valley of A. 227:3
Avoid: pray you, a. it 188:1
Avon: Sweet Swan of A.! 118:9
Awaits alike th' inevitable hour 97:12
Awake: A.! for Morning 84:15
A. my soul 123:1
Christians a. 50:14
do not lie a. 242:14
keep her still a. 208:7
Smiles a. you 73:1
stab my spirit broad a. 221:24
to a. out of sleep 35:14
you're lying a. 91:23
Awaked: so the Lord a. 170:12
Aware: I am a. 81:20
whom England bore, shaped, made a. 42:11
Away: are a'wede a. 82:12

A., I'm bound to go 6:14
A. went Gilpin 69:27
come a. 27:16
let us a. 11:10
stretch far a. 214:7
Sweet, when they've cleared a. 53:9
was put a. 162:16
went a. with a flea in 's ear 19:16
wish he'd stay a. 141:17
yesterday . . that she went a.? 11:12
Awe: attribute to a. 202:5
have not Thee in a. 127:6
keep even kings in a. 72:10
Nature in a. to him 145:7
wonder and a. 119:10
Aweary: I am a. 228:18
Awful: an a. warmth 122:9
keeps 'is side-arms a. 125:3
Awkward: with an a. shame 165:13
Awkward squad fire over me 49:6
Awoke: a. one morning and found
myself famous 52:18
A. one night from a deep dream 112:2
I a., and behold it was a dream 46:14
I a., it rained 66:1
Awry: currents turn a. 187:13
strike not a. 150:5
Axe: also the a. is laid 30:6
a.'s edge did try 140:8
let the great a. fall 189:17
Axis: soft under-belly of the A. 63:4
Aye: for a. to dwell 229:5
Ayes: of A. and Noes 85:11
Aylmer: Rose A., all were thine 129:19
Azores: At Flores in the A. 230:2
Azure: Day's a. eyes 213:17
in its a. hue 54:3
Thine a. sister 214:1
with a. moss 214:2

B

B bit it 155:2
Baa, baa, black sheep 155:4
Babbled: a' b. of green fields 191:6
Babe: acts like a b. 128:8
b. leaps up 246:9
birth-strangled b. 199:16
naked new-born b. 198:4
Babes: b. and sucklings 168:22
Old men, and b. 66:6
Bab-lock-hithe: Thames at B. 11:24
Baby: Bye, b. bunting 155:6
Cry, b., cry 155:10
Down comes the b. 38:9
my b. at my breast 183:4
When B.'s cries grew hard to
bear 96:14
When the first b. laughed 18:19
Where a Mother laid her B. 2:10
Where did you come from, b.
dear? 137:9
Baby Doll: You called me B. 100:17
Babylon: B. is fallen 37:21
B., the great 37:22
How many miles to B.? 155:19
I was a King in B. 102:15
waters of B. 171:24
Bacchus and his revellers 146:20
'Baccy for the Clerk 127:10
Bachelor: who will live a b. 204:7
Back: at my b. I always hear 140:12
B. and side go bare 221:25
b. in the Closet lays 85:10
b. o'beyont 180:14
borne me on his b. 189:20
Come you b. 126:11
hair that lay along her b. 126:11
I will b. the masses 94:5

never come b. to me 225:15
never turned his b. 45:10
no come b. again? 151:11
On the bat's b. 208:20
sent'st it b. to me 117:19
Shall lure it b. 85:12
slid from his b. 127:1
soon find a way b. 108:8
that rubs its b. 81:16
those before cried 'B.!' 136:13
wallet at his b. 208:27
Will you no come b. again? 106:8
with harness on our b. 200:7
with his b. to the East 65:3
yet my soul drew b. 104:1
Back rooms: boys in the b. 19:28
Backs: beast with two b. 204:17
With our b. to the wall 99:4
Backward: In the dark b. 208:8
look b. to their ancestors 47:13
Backwards and forwards 105:18
Bacoun was nat fet for hem 60:20
Bad: b. die late 72:16
b. masters 132:1
b., then, to be misunderstood? 82:21
believe a thing to be b. 143:19
For being a little b. 201:5
How sad and b. 43:15
Mad, b., and dangerous 129:4
nothing either good or b. 187:2
Of this b. world 21:16
or a b. peace 88:3
She was not really b. at heart 21:11
so many shocking b. hats 240:16
so much b. in the best of us 105:12
To that b. eminence 146:10
when she was b. 134:14
Bade me fight 250:7
Badge: b. of all our tribe 201:18
Red B. of Courage 70:24
Badly written 243:19
Bag and baggage 94:3, 184:5
Bags: Three b. full 155:4
Bah to you 93:2
Bahram: And B., that great Hunter 85:1
Baiae: in B.'s bay 214:2
Bait in the fishes' mouth 8:15
Baiting-place of wit 217:1
Baits: good news b. 147:8
Baked: funeral b. meats 185:13
You have b. me too brown 57:10
Baker: Pat-a-cake b.'s man 157:9
Baker Street irregulars 78:19
Balance: b. of power 238:12
in nice b. 164:1
Balanced: I b. all 250:7
Balances: art weighed in the b. 29:18
Bald: fierce and b. 179:4
otherwise b. and unconvincing
narrative 92:13
Ball: After the b. is over 100:15
B. no question makes 85:11
I am the bowler and the b. 130:2
sceptre and the b. 191:15
Urge the flying b. 98:6
Ballad: met with a b. 53:6
with a woful b. 183:20
Ballads: Of b., songs and snatches 91:27
to make all the b. 86:12
Ballot is stronger 132:6
Balls: And elliptical billiard b. 92:9
Match'd our rackets to these b. 191:4
Balm: b. in Gilead? 29:5
B. of hurt minds 198:13
b. of woe 217:1
calm is in that b. 154:13
'Tis not the b. 191:15
wash the b. 206:12
Balmy sleep! 250:15

Banbury: To B. came I   41:3
Banbury Cross: Ride a cock-horse
  to B.   157:17
Band: b. of brothers   153:2, 192:4
  b. of glorious Angels   152:8
  Cassock, b., and hymn-book too   243:2
  happy b. of pilgrims   152:16
  high aesthetic b.   92:22
  humbler b.   70:20
  lordly b.   70:20
  when the b. begins to play   127:20
Bandersnatch: frumious B.!'   57:14
Bands: from servile b.   249:11
  loose the b. of Orion?   25:43
  pursue Culture in b.   241:22
  strong as iron b.   134:10
  With b. of rosy hue   112:8
Bandusiae: O fons B.   109:24
Bandy civilities   114:23
Bane: Deserve the precious b.   146:8
Bang: b. these dogs of Seville   230:4
  b.—went saxpence!   173:10
  Not with a b.   81:13
  Who shout and b.   21:21
Bangs: And b. me most severely   55:3
Banish: B. not him   190:15
  should b. all sin   94:10
  With night we b. sorrow   105:2
Bank: As I sat on a sunny b.   3:14
  b. and shoal of time   198:3
  from the B. to Mandalay   126:13
  goes to sleep at a b.   113:7
  I know a b.   203:9
  man who broke the B.   90:17
  pregnant b.   77:6
  upon a b. of violets   209:2
Banker: he thought he saw a B.'s
  Clerk   56:9
Banks: b. and braes   49:4
  on the b. of the Nile   216:12
  upon the b. of Thames   118:9
  who b. with Coutts   91:9
Banner: b. over me was love   27:14
  b. with the strange device   133:17
  royal b.   205:10
  star-spangled b.   123:7
  thy b., torn, but flying   51:4
Banners: an army with b.   27:19
  Confusion on thy b. wait   97:4
  Hang out our b.   200:2
  royal b. forward go   87:7
Baptism: Ministration of B.   167:31
Bar: gold b. of Heaven   177:15
  I have crost the b.   226:6
  moaning of the b.   226:6
  When I went to the B.   91:20
Barabbas: B. was a publisher   54:9
  B. was a robber   34:24
Barbarians: his young b. all at
  play   51:5
Bard: blame not the b.   149:16
  by the lover and the b.   43:7
  Hear the voice of the B.!   38:18
Bardolph: banish B.   190:15
Bards: b. sublime   133:14
  last of all the B.   180:4
  Which b. in fealty   121:9
Bare: Back and side go b.   221:25
  B. ruin'd choirs   211:8
  boundless and b.   214:7
  child she b.?   70:4
  cupboard was b.   157:3
  one b. hour to live   138:14
  silent, b.   249:4
  when the heavens are b.   246:8
Barefoot: children go b.   212:20
  while the b. friars   90:12
Bare-legg'd beggarly son of a gun   53:7
Bareness: old December's b.   211:12

Bares: foeman b. his steel   93:20
  Sea that b. her bosom   249:5
Bargain: dateless b.   208:5
  never was a better b. driv'n   216:29
Barge: answer'd Arthur from the b.   227:1
  b. she sat in   182:15
Bark: delight to b. and bite   239:6
  dogs did b.   69:28
  every wandering b.   211:16
  his b. cannot be lost   197:6
  let no dog b.!   201:8
  tall anchoring b.   195:19
  they b. at me   195:15
  watch-dogs b.   208:9
  watch-dog's honest b.   51:13
Barkis is willin'   74:6
Barks: Nicean b. of yore   163:16
Barley: fields of b.   227:23
  Sitting on a heap of B.   131:3
Barlow: O my Hornby and my B.   232:11
Barn: sit in a b.   157:1
Baron: 'Good!' said the B.   124:19
Barred: On a spot that's always b.   92:9
Barren: A b. superfluity of words   89:4
  among these b. crags   230:12
  I am but a b. stock   82:5
  leave this b. spot   53:13
  to a b. strand   117:3
Barricade: some disputed b.   181:11
Barricks: single men in b.   127:23
Bars: beside the glowing b.   250:11
  Between their silver b.   86:10
  iron b. a cage   134:11
  look out through the same b.   130:3
Basan: bulls of B.   168:34
Base: Ere the b. laws   79:19
  Majors at the B.   179:4
Baser: I give to b. life   183:3
  of the b. sort   34:40
Bashful: a b. young potato   92:22
  maiden of b. fifteen   216:19
Basia: Da mi b. mille   59:1
Basingstoke: with hidden meaning—
  like B.   93:28
Basking: lie a-b. in the sun   93:23
Bassoon: heard the loud b.   65:7
Bat: black b., night   228:20
  I am the batsman and the b.   130:2
  On the b.'s back   208:20
  Twinkle, twinkle, little b.!   56:24
  where the weak-ey'd b.   67:12
  Wool of b.   199:14
Bataillons: Dieu..pour les gros b.   237:18
Bath: sore labour's b.   198:13
Bathe in fiery floods   200:23
Bathing: caught the Whigs b.   76:7
Bathing machine: a large b.   91:24
Baths of all the western stars   230:15
Bâton: le b. de maréchal   151:16
Bats: b. in the belfry   162:16
  Do cats eat b.?   56:11
Batsman: And a ghostly b.   232:11
  I am the b. and the bat   130:2
  if the b. thinks he's bowled   130:2
Battalions: But in b.   189:11
  God is..for the big b.   237:18
Batter my heart   77:12
Battle: Agreed to have a b.   57:18
  b. done   165:21
  Ben B. was a soldier   106:22
  braved..the b.   54:6
  delight of b.   230:13
  field of b.   221:5
  foremost in b.   16:9
  he smelleth the b.   25:44
  in the midst of the b.!   25:1
  lit the b.'s wreck   102:7
  noise of b. roll'd   226:25
  nor the b. to the strong   27:3

old Sarah B. 129:6
See the front o' b. lour! 48:30
to b. for freedom 112:14
When the b.'s lost 197:2
While the b. rages 54:6
who is in b. slain 95:2
Battle-line: far-flung b. 127:3
Battlements: Towers, and b. 144:14
  Under my b. 197:15
Battles: And b. long ago 248:9
  fought my b. 110:2
  God of b.! 192:1
  high-engender'd b. 195:5
Bauble: prettiest b. you ever saw 238:5
Baubles: Take away these b. 71:10
Bawdy: when he was talking b. 129:9
Bawl: and roar and b. 21:21
  As loud as he could b. 69:28
Bay: and b. the moon 194:17
  bet on de b. 87:8
  in Baiae's b. 214:2
Bayed: that b. the whisp'ring wind 95:5
Bayonets: Chains are worse than b. 113:12
  with our b. turning 245:4
Bays: oak, or b. 140:4
Bay-tree: like a green b. 169:14
Be: Continues to b. 129:2
  ever this should b.! 65:14
  From all I may b. 51:7
  it might b. 57:19
  must ever b. 246:13
  that he seem'd to b. 79:8
  To b., or not to b. 187:13
  where they would b. 171:9
Beach: not the only pebble on the b. 41:1
  walk upon the b. 195:19
Beaches: fight on the b. 62:21
Beachy Head: by way of B. 61:22
Beaded: With b. bubbles 121:3
Bead-rolls: Set in our b. 217:7
Beads: for a set of b. 206:16
  take in his b. 142:14
Beak: b. from out my heart 163:17
Beaker full of the warm South 121:3
Beale: Miss Buss and Miss B. 6:6
Be-all: Might be the b. 198:3
Beam: b. that is in thine own eye? 30:31
  full midday b. 148:10
Beaming in one eye 74:20
Beamish: my b. boy! 57:14
Beams: from happy human eyes 221:24
  b. of lightsome day 180:5
  chaste b. 203:7
  Some b. of wit 79:24
  throws his b.! 202:14
  tricks his b. 145:4
  white moon b. 123:12
Bean: a not too French French b.! 92:22
  home of the b. and the cod 40:11
Bean-rows: Nine b. will I have 250:9
Beans: Full o' b. 222:18
Bear: B. his mild yoke 147:17
  B. of Very Little Brain 143:17
  b. the whips and scorns 187:13
  b. thee in their hands 170:20
  b. with a sore head 139:18
  conceive, and b. a son 27:30
  could I b. that too 205:13
  flood may b. me far 226:6
  How a b. likes honey? 143:16
  no man alive could b. it 212:19
  pain to the b. 137:1
  pursued by a b. 210:4
  rather b. those ills 187:13
  so b. ourselves 62:22
  still less the b.! 88:8
  suppos'd a b.! 203:19

To love, and b. 215:1
Who would fardels b. 187:13
Bear-baiting: Puritan hated b. 137:1
Beard: b. of formal cut 183:20
  long grey b. 65:4
  Old Man with a b. 130:15
  singeing of the King of Spain's B. 78:26
Bearded like the pard 183:20
Beareth all things 35:21
Bear-like: But b. I must fight 200:8
Bears: B. all its sons away 239:14
  b. his blushing honours 192:14
  But b. it out 211:16
  dancing dogs and b. 105:13
  Let b. and lions growl 239:6
Beast: A b., but a just b. 3:5
  b., that wants discourse 185:11
  b. with two backs 204:17
  Blonde b. 154:7
  drinks like a b. 128:8
  good for man nor b. 8:15
  man and bird and b. 66:7
  name of the b. 37:20
  questing b. 137:20
  When people call this b. to mind 20:17
  you hugly b.! 222:15
Beastie, Wee, sleekit, cow'rin, tim'rous b. 48:25
Beastly: Don't let's be b. 69:13
Beasts: b. did leap 18:12
  b. that perish 169:24
  both small and great b. 171:4
Beat: b. high for praise 149:13
  b. him when he sneezes 56:19
  b. on the rocky shore 130:20
  b. the drums! 150:10
  b. the earth with free step 109:8
  b. the ground 144:1
  b. upon my whorlèd ear 107:13
  B. wild 154:13
  heart would hear her and b. 228:20
  May b. in Belgrave Square 91:19
  They shall b. their swords 27:22
  Tom was b. 158:13
  water which they b. 182:15
  We must b. the iron 80:2
  when thy heart began to b. 39:2
Beaten: a b. path 83:4
Beating: almost hear the b. of his wings 41:10
  glory of b. the French 245:8
  mend his pace with b. 189:19
Beatitude: ninth b. 165:16
Beats: B. my approach 123:11
  b. upon a throne 226:15
Beatus..qui procul negotiis 108:14
Beaumont: bid B. lie 118:4
Beauteous: b. eye of heaven 193:6
  Commands the b. files 235:7
  I love all b. things 41:6
  It is a b. evening 246:15
  promise such a b. day 211:3
Beauties: meaner b. of the night 249:13
Beautified with our feathers 98:13
Beautiful: appear b. outward 32:9
  Are b. and fair 246:8
  as thou art b. 226:20
  b. and free 215:1
  b. and ineffectual angel 12:5
  b. and swift 213:7
  B. Dreamer 87:16
  b. Soup! 57:11
  How b. they stand! 102:11
  How b. Thy mercy-seat 83:14
  How b. upon the mountains 28:18
  meet on that b. shore 22:6
  My b., my b.! 154:12
  name of which was B. 46:6

Beautiful (cont.)
of a b. countenance 24:43
Oh, how b.! 125:9
yet so b. 86:9
Beautifully: and b. less 172:19
Beauty: all that b. 97:12
b. and length of days 224:2
b. draws us 165:2
B. in the eye of the beholder 111:23, 238:2
B. is truth 120:23
b. of a thousand stars 138:13
b. of the morning 249:4
b. of the world! 187:4
b. shall no more be found 140:12
b. that hath not some strangeness 14:8
B. that must die 120:24
B. unadorn'd 20:12
b. 's charming 180:15
B.'s ensign 208:4
b.'s summer dead 211:13
Coming in solemn b. 140:19
England, home and b. 40:18
extent of its b. and power 137:3
For b. lives with kindness 210:2
for b.'s heightening 12:1
grew in b., side by side 102:9
her b. and her chivalry 50:23
seizes as b. 122:7
Shall within one B. meet 140:3
She dwells with B. 120:24
She walks in b. 52:12
some b. lies 144:14
Spring, nor Summer b. 77:4
Such seems your b. still 211:13
that life was B. 107:6
thing of b. 120:1
to b. grew 82:15
What is b. 139:11
whose b. is past change 107:15
winds of March with b. 210:8
With the moon's b. 247:18
yet doth b., like a dial-hand 211:13
Becks: gold and silver b. me 193:4
Nods, and b. 144:12
Become: to b. what we now see him will that it should b. 114:17
119:11
Becomes: hardly b. any of us 105:12
It b. a pleasure 243:13
Becoming: sweet thing and b. 109:18
Bed: A B., a b., 16:4
and so to b. 162:4
as little as my b. 123:2
as upon a b. 140:9
at the foot of the b. 143:15
B. be blest that I lie on 1:17
B. in the bush 221:15
called me from my b. 97:2
Come, let's to b. 155:8
dark wintry b. 214:1
die—in b. 179:5
Each within our narrow b. 58:21
Four angels to my b. 1:17
go to b. making a calculation 74:7
go to b. with the lamb 41:4
heaped for the beloved's b. 215:10
Holy angels guard thy b.! 239:11
I in my b. again! 8:10
in a manger for His b. 2:10
in an earthy b. 228:20
in the ocean b. 145:4
kick his wife out of b. 222:14
laid in b. majestical 191:15
light you to b. 157:8
made his pendent b. 198:2
my Lord Tomnoddy went home to b.! 17:10
my second best b. 212:6
nicer to lie in b. 130:10
not a b. of roses 221:5

on the foot of the b. 74:13
pillow on a b. 77:6
put them to b. 158:6
rouse them from their lowly b. 97:11
so he on his b. 239:12
take up thy b. 34:3
weans in their b. 143:4
Welcome to your gory b. 48:30
Bedeck: We shift and b. 224:3
Bedecked: so b., ornate 147:5
Bedfellows: Poverty has strange b. 136:3
with strange b. 208:14
Bedford and Exeter 192:4
Bedonebyasyoudid: Mrs. B. is coming 124:5
Bedrape: bedeck and b. us 224:3
Beds: borders, b. and shrubberies 125:8
when I came unto my b. 209:20
Bedside: very good b. manner! 173:16
Bedürfnissen: jedem nach seinen B. 140:15
Bee: I am the b. 84:14
little busy b. 239:9
Where the b. sucks 208:20
Beechen: plot of b. green 121:2
Beef: first with b. 231:19
pig had roast b. 158:9
roast b. of England 84:6
stole a piece of b. 158:3
Your b., pork, and mutton 124:15
Beefy face 126:14
Bee-keeping: How to Make B. Pay 96:15
Bee-loud: in the b. glade 250:9
Bee-mouth: while the b. sips 120:24
Been: and those who would have b. 41:16
b. and gone and done? 90:20
It might have b. 101:2, 242:17
thing that hath b. 26:35
where have you b.? 157:14
Which having b. 246:13
Beer: b. and skittles 53:8, 141:15
chronicle small b. 204:27
only a b. teetotaller 212:11
talk o' gin an' b. 125:11
Beer-sheba: even to B. 24:33
Bees: A swarm of b. in May 3:15
b. makes your honey 237:10
innumerable b. 229:19
stung to death by savage b. 96:15
Yellow b. 214:9
Beetle: And the poor b. 200:21
b. wheels 97:8
where the b. winds 67:12
Beetles: B. black 203:11
gross as b. 195:19
Befell: What foolish Harriet b. 106:1
Before: all b. them 146:25
all b. us lie 140:12
as it was b. 209:2
B. the rising sun 239:14
Come ye b. Him 123:5
Going on b. 18:7
I see b. me 198:9
if they knew it b. 108:1
is preferred b. me 33:47
look b. and after 215:5
or have been b. 51:7
or what went b. 20:2
sinned..b. thee 33:22
those b. cried 'Back!' 136:13
Beg: b. cold comfort 193:7
b. the core 234:19
to b. I am ashamed 33:25
Began: when my life b. 247:10
Begat: fathers that b. us 29:37
Beget a temperance 188:7
Beggar: absent-minded b. 124:10
Beggared all description 182:15
Beggarly son of a gun 53:7
Beggar-maid: lov'd the b. 207:19

Beggars: pays us, poor b.   128:6
When b. die   193:14
Begging: nor. . b. their bread   169:13
Begin: b. as heresies   112:11
B. at the beginning   57:13
Beginning: Begin at the b.   57:13
b. and the ending   37:13
b. of the end   225:4
b. of wisdom   171:11
Before the b. of years   224:1
end of the b.   63:2
In the b.   23:4
quiet homes and first b.   21:12
true b. of our end   203:20
Beginnings: start again at your b.   125:15
Begone, dull care!   3:16
Begot: How b.   202:11
Begotten: b. by despair   140:2
flowers b.   223:29
only b. Son   34:1
Beguile the time   198:1
Begun: b., continued, and ended   167:29
He who has b. his task   108:7
not yet b. to fight   117:7
Behave: b. mannerly at table   221:11
Doth not b. itself unseemly   35:21
How well did I b.   110:18
Behaviour: check to loose b.   220:5
Beheld your devotions   34:42
Behemoth: Behold now b.   26:1
Behest: falls at Thy b.   82:11
Behind: can Spring be far b.?   214:4
close b. him tread   66:5
Get thee b. me   31:34
in what remains b.   246:13
led his regiment from b.   91:5
that comes b.   223:26
they look b.   98:7
those b. cried 'Forward!'   136:13
we leave b.   64:11
Behold: b., and see   29:8
B. her, single in the field   248:7
B. the man   34:25
B. thy mother!   34:27
b. thy son!   34:27
mayest in me b.   211:8
when I b.   247:10
Beholder: eye of the b.   111:23, 238:2
Beholdest: Why b. thou the mote   30:31
Beholds: he b. the light   246:11
Being: and have our b.   34:43
Belfry: bats in the b.   162:16
clock in the b. strikes one   249:9
in the b. sits   230:9
Belgium: And B.'s capital   50:23
Belgrade: battery besieged B.   3:10
Belgrave Square: May beat in B.   91:19
Belial: sons of B.   79:9, 146:5
Belican: hold more than his b.   142:14
Belief: assert my firm b.   176:13
Beliefs and forsaken b.   12:3
two contradictory b.   159:17
Believe: b. also in me   34:16
B. it or not   175:12
B. me   149:12
B. the man with experience   236:23
Do you b. in fairies?   18:22
Firmly I b.   153:13
I b. verily   169:7
If you b. that   240:23
little ones which b. in me   31:38
Lord, I b.   32:33
must b. it, not I   110:12
That I b.   82:4
ye b. in God   34:16
you will b. anything   240:23
Believed: against hope b. in hope   35:2
nearer than when we b.   35:14
Believes: half b. a God   250:18

Believeth: whosoever b. in him   34:1
Bell: B., book, and candle   193:4
crier rung the b.   20:1
for whom the b. tolls   77:23
sexton toll'd the b.   106:23
Silence that dreadful b.!   204:31
sound as a b.   204:11
surly sullen b.   211:7
to toll the b.   100:9
Twilight and evening b.   226:6
unto the B. at Edmonton   69:22
word is like a b.   121:7
Belle Dame sans Merci   120:14
Bells: b. I hear   242:10
b. of St. Clement's   157:6
b. of Shandon   173:1
b. on her toes   157:17
b. they sound on Bredon   111:1
b. they sound so clear   110:19
b. were ringing   94:10
evening b.   226:11
ring O b.!   242:11
Ring out, wild b.   227:18
ring the b. of Heaven   105:13
sweet b. jangled   188:6
They now ring the b.   238:9
where b. have knoll'd   183:19
With silver b.   156:16
Bellum: praeparet b.   235:12
Belly: But b. . . send thee good ale   221:25
does not mind his b.   114:20
fair round b.   183:20
Jonah was in the b. of the fish   29:26
Whose God is their b.   36:17
Belong: To b. to other nations   93:14
Beloved: Ah, my B.   85:3
B. from pole to pole   65:23
Dearly b. brethren   166:7
Escape me? never B.   44:8
for the b.'s bed   215:10
I would go, O my b.   94:16
lovely that are not b.   161:14
My b. is mine   27:18
my b. Son   30:7
shall prove B. over all   127:18
Below: all creatures here b.   123:3
Man wants but little drink b.   106:12
Belted you an' flayed you   125:12
Bend: b. to the oar   39:23
I b. and I break not   86:16
Bending: Angels b. near the earth   181:10
b. down beside the glowing bars   250:11
head is b. low   87:12
Within his b. sickle   211:16
Bends: b. the gallant mast   71:16
b. with the remover   211:16
each to his great Father b.   66:6
Though she b. him   134:7
When the bough b.   38:9
Beneath: B. the shadow of Thy throne   239:14
b. the trees   247:3
round b. it   235:11
Benefit o' the Clergy   68:7
Benefits: As b. forgot   184:2
Benevolence: beans and b.!   222:18
Benison: b. of hot water   41:18
For a b. to fall   104:16
Bent: Are idly b.   207:3
b. with thickset fruit   177:8
more b. to serve   147:17
to the top of my b.   188:19
Bereaved: as if b. of light   39:10
Bermudas: remote B. ride   139:25
Berries: b. moulded on one stem   203:15
pluck your b. harsh   144:20
Berry: God could have made a better b.   50:11
O sweeter than the b.   89:8
Berth: happened in his b.   106:23

Bertie: I'm Burlington B. 100:13
Beside: B. me singing 84:18
  B. the lake 247:3
  B. the Seaside 94:8
  shall fall b. thee 170:19
Bespangling: dew b. herb 104:9
Best: All is for the b. 237:11
  any other person's b. 101:9
  at the very b. 8:15
  B. and brightest 213:14
  b. and happiest moments 215:17
  b. is like the worst 126:15
  b. is the enemy of the good 237:14
  b. is yet to be 45:4
  b. men are moulded 201:5
  b. on these occasions 75:18
  b. portion of a good man's life 248:18
  b. to be done for the country 240:21
  Brightest and b. 101:14
  did his very b. 57:20
  doing his b. 243:14
  he is at b. 218:8
  He prayeth b. 66:7
  how much the b.! 87:17
  is always the b. 86:18
  loveliest and b. 21:16, 85:4
  Not to be born is b. 218:10
  one another's b. 77:6
  One should never put on one's b.
    trousers 112:14
  our b. men are dead! 173:20
  Send forth the b. 128:5
  so much bad in the b. of us 105:12
  Stolen sweets are b. 63:9
  That action is b. 112:10
  'tis b., to use myself 77:15
  who loved him the b. 124:2
  who loveth b. 66:7
Bestial: what remains is b. 204:33
Bestow: I b. all my goods 35:21
  is powerless to b. 83:1
Bestowed: well b. 187:9
Best-regulated families 74:12
Bestride the narrow world 193:11
Bet: I b. my money 87:8
  once a pound 73:8
  Somebody b. on de bay 87:8
Beteem the winds 185:11
Bethlehem: B. thou dost all excel 58:22
  come ye to B. 9:14, 159:6
  thou B. 29:28
Betray: All things b. thee 232:8
  that men b. 95:21
Betrayed: We are b. 142:4
Betrayest: who is. Me 232:8
Better: appear the b. reason 146:11
  baffled to fight b. 45:10
  become much more the b. 201:5
  B. by far 177:11
  b. man than I am 125:12
  b. men than we 125:9
  b. only guessing 64:4
  b. than a play 60:2
  b. than a thousand 170:15
  b. than all 67:4
  b. than light 101:5
  b. that ten guilty persons 38:8
  b. to be left 68:16
  b. to wear out 71:15
  far, far b. thing 75:34
  for b. for worse 168:12
  getting b. and b. 69:5
  give place to b. men 71:11
  God hath no b. praise 41:6
  He builded b. 82:15
  He is no b. 13:22
  it is b. to marry 35:16
  it were b. for him 31:38, 33:30
  make a b. mousetrap 83:4

man hath no b. thing 26:43
much b. done in Shakespeare 80:4
nae b. than he should be 48:14
no b. than you should be 19:10
not for the b. 8:6
preach a b. sermon 83:4
something b. than his dog 228:6
worst is b. 101:9
write a b. book 83:4
Beware: all should cry, B.! 66:15
  B. of desp'rate steps 70:1
  B. of false prophets 31:3
  B. of the dog 162:12
  B. the pine-tree 133:19
  bid you b. 127:2
  may b. of thee 185:21
Beweep my outcast state 210:13
Bewitch: Do more b. me 104:11
Beyond: back o' B. 180:14
  die b. my means 244:2
  is there anything b.? 41:19
Bezonian: Under which king, B.? 190:34
Bibendum: nunc est b. 109:8
Bible: English B...would alone
  suffice 137:3
  for the B. tells me so 239:1
Bicker down a valley 225:17
Bicycle made for two 72:1
Bid: And do as you're b. 80:21
  I b. you beware 127:2
Bidding: at his b. speed 147:17
Bide the pelting 195:8
Bier: his watery b. 144:20
Big: are b. with mercy 70:6
  four times as b. 130:16
  too b. for his station 225:1
Bigger: great deal b. than I am 55:21
  no b. than his head 195:19
  no b. than the moon 65:12
Big-Sea-Water: shining B. 134:4
Bill: b. will hold more than his beli-
  can 142:14
  defects of the B. 178:11
  Who's 'im B.? 173:6
Billabong: camped by a b. 161:12
Billee: youngest he was little B. 231:19
Billet: Every bullet has its b. 244:6
Billiard: And elliptical b. balls 92:9
  The b. sharp 92:9
Billiards: to play b. well 219:5
Billingsgate: Alias, B. 250:3
Billowing: sail in amply b. gown 21:21
Billows: b. smooth and bright 57:20
Billy: B., in one of his nice new
  sashes 96:13
  to poke poor B. 96:13
  waited till his b. boiled 161:12
Bin of wine 221:22
Bind: bids me b. my hair 112:8
  b. their kings in chains 172:7
  b. your sons to exile 128:5
  to b. another to its delight 39:6
  to b. up the brokenhearted 29:2
Binds so dear a head 213:6
Biography: art of B. 22:9
  B. is about chaps 22:9
  b. of great men 55:13
  only b. 82:18
Bird: b. in a gilded cage 129:3
  B. is on the Wing 84:19
  b. made his pendent bed 198:2
  b. my lady loved 58:25
  b. of dawning 185:4
  B. of Time 84:17
  B. thou never wert 215:3
  half angel and half b. 45:6
  immortal B. 121:6
  in the sight of any b. 26:5
  like a fluttered b. 230:2

man and b. and beast 66:7
perceive a young b. in this
  bush 130:16
rare b. on the earth 119:4
regretted that he was not a b. 175:14
Shall I call thee b. 245:15
she, poor b., as all forlorn 18:12
Sweet b., that shunn'st the
  noise 144:6
sweet b.'s throat 183:13
widow b. sate mourning 213:11
wise old b. 173:13
wonderful b. is the pelican 142:14
Birdie: B. rest a little longer 230:7
What does little b. say 230:6
Birds: b. began to sing 158:1
b. did sing 18:12
B. in their little nests 239:8
b. of the air fell a-sighing 159:4
b. of the air have nests 31:7
b. sit brooding 196:20
feathers that make fine b. 1:20
full of b.' cries 141:6
like b. i' the cage 196:6
melodious b. sing madrigals 139:7
nest of singing b. 113:15
no b. sing 120:10
one of the early b. 68:20
pretty b. do sing 152:6
singing of b. is come 27:16
song of the b. 99:2
sweet b. O how they sing 210:5
sweet b. sang 211:8
when b. do sing 184:12
ye little b. 49:4
you b. make nests 237:10
Bird-song at morning 221:17
Birmingham: we went to B. 61:22
Birnam Wood do come 200:5
Birth: b. as rare 140:2
b. will be a. .mouse 107:21
Border, nor Breed, nor B. 124:13
coming to b. 159:19
famous by their b. 206:7
give b. to verses 118:19
Land of our b. 124:17
new b. of freedom 132:8
Our b. is but a sleep 246:11
quicken a new b. 214:4
Repeats the story of her b. 1:12
sunshine is a glorious b. 246:8
virtue, and not b. that makes us
  noble 19:21
wherein our Saviour's b. 185:4
Birthright: selleth his b. for a mess
  of pottage 4:6
Shall we sell our b. for a mess of
  potash? 238:17
sold his b. unto Jacob 23:27
Birth-strangled babe 199:16
Bis dat qui cito dat 224:12
Biscuits: captain's b. 231:19
Bit: B b. it 155:2
every poet. .b. by him 223:26
have a little b. 158:4
I b. my arm 65:14
little b. off the top 151:5
though he had b. me 195:23
Went mad and b. the man 95:14
Bitch-goddess SUCCESS 113:1
Bite: b. some other of my generals 90:6
b. the hand that fed them 47:14
dost not b. so nigh 184:2
jaws that b. 57:14
man recover'd of the b. 95:16
nor slow worm b. thee 104:13
smaller fleas to b. 'em 223:26
To b. so good a man 95:15
Bites: wind b. shrewdly 186:2

Biting: good b. falchion 196:10
Bits: shatter it to b. 86:1
Bitter: B. constraint 144:20
b. tears to shed 69:2
brought me b. news 69:2
love grows b. 224:10
make misfortunes more b. 14:20
mirth that has no b. springs 124:18
shed a b. tear 57:21
thou b. sky 184:2
with a b. look 243:5
Bitterly thought of the morrow 245:6
Bitterness: b. of death 24:42
b. of life 56:7
no hatred or b. 59:4
tears no b. 135:17
Black: as b. as they might be 16:17
big b. block 92:5
b., and midnight hags 199:18
b. as a tar-barrel 57:18
B. as the Pit 102:13
Devil damn thee b. 199:31
Hump that is b. and blue 126:3
I am b. 27:12, 39:10
in b. and white 117:15
like a b. swan 119:4
More b. than ashbuds 226:13
not so b. as they are painted 133:10
Two lovely b. eyes 64:15
Yellow, and b., and pale 214:1
Blackbird: came a little b. 158:1
Blackbirds: Four and twenty b. 158:1
Black-ey'd: When b. Susan came
  aboard 89:30
Blackguards: we aren't no b. too 127:23
Bladders: that swim on b. 192:14
Blade: b. struck the water 64:17
bloody blameful b. 204:1
Blades: two b. of grass 223:2
Blade-straight: Steel-blue and b. 221:19
Blame: Alike reserved to b. 165:6
b. not the bard 149:16
Dispraise or b. 147:10
full of b. 212:1
Blameless: of a b. life 226:15
Blaming it on you 125:14
Blanch: Tray, B., and Sweet-heart 195:15
Blank: A b., my Lord 209:10
whose annals are b. 55:10
Blanket of the dark 197:41
Blankets: rough male kiss of b. 41:17
Blaspheming: brooding and b. 62:2
Blast: b. of war 191:8
First B. of the Trumpet 129:1
from the stormy b. 239:14
striding the b. 198:4
wings on the b. 52:10
Blasted: B. with ecstasy 188:6
b. with excess of light 98:11
Blaze: b. forth the death of princes 193:14
b. of noon 147:3
into sudden b. 145:1
rash fierce b. 206:6
Bleaching: white sheet b. 210:5
Bleak: In the b. mid-winter 177:9
Bleats articulate monotony 220:7
Bled: where some buried Caesar b. 85:2
wi' Wallace b. 48:30
Bleed: do we not b.? 201:27
I b.! 214:3
Bleeding piece of earth 193:20
Blemish: and without b. 9:4
Blenheim: I dine at B. once a week 6:10
Bless: and b. us 170:4
B. relaxes 39:20
B. the squire 74:2
guard and b. our fatherland 111:13
how to load and b. 119:17
Lord b. thee 24:13

Bless (cont.)
Thee at hand to b. 135:17
to b. the turf 67:15
Blessed: all generations shall call
me b. 32:37
always to be b. 164:14
B. are the poor in spirit 30:11
B. are the pure 122:19
b. art thou among women 32:36
b. be the name of the Lord 25:26
B. is the man 165:16
B. Trinity 102:1
call her b. 26:33
it is twice b. 202:5
more b. to give 34:46
nor b. abode 141:5
Blessedness: in single b. 203:1
Blesseth him that gives 202:5
Blessing: as a boon and a b. to
men 8:5
behold us with Thy b. 45:20
dismiss us with Thy b. 45:21
dost ask me b. 196:6
give us his b. 170:5
health is the second b. 238:15
most need of b. 198:12
my b. season 185:21
truly it's a b. 64:4
Blessings: all the b. of this life 166:31
B. in disguise 104:17
b. on the falling out 229:7
break in b. 70:6
from whom all b. flow 123:3
Heavenly b. 239:11
Blest: be for ever b. 111:12
B. be the man 212:5
b. him in their pain 230:3
milk and honey b. 152:14
Blew: all the winds that b. 229:1
b. his silly brains out 232:4
he b. Soul-animating strains 248:2
slug-horn to my lips and b. 43:14
Blind: b. as they that won't see 223:17
B. guides 32:8
b. leaders of the b. 31:30
b. life within the brain 227:2
De b. hoss 87:9
halt, and the b. 33:17
In his heart is a b. desire 224:2
love is b. 201:23
Mad, b...king 215:8
right to be b. sometimes 152:19
Blindly: never loved so b. 48:5
Blindness: 'eathen in 'is b. 125:3
heathen in his b. 101:16
To help him of his b. 210:2
Blinds let through the day 111:10
Blind-worms: Newts and b. 203:10
Blink: stars began to b. 247:16
Blinking: of a b. idiot 201:25
Bliss: b. in proof 212:2
b. of solitude 247:5
B. was it in that dawn 246:1
everlasting b. 138:11
excels all other b. 80:17
perfect b. 139:10
soul in b. 196:1
sum of earthly b. 146:21
Where ignorance is b. 98:10
Blisses: finds he mortal b. 214:9
Blithe: be you b. and bonny 204:9
b., and debonair 144:11
Hail to thee b. Spirit 215:3
How b. the throstle sings 248:14
No lark more b. than he 37:29
O b. new-comer 245:15
Block: a big black b. 92:5
chip of the old 'b.' 47:19
Blockhead ever wrote 115:8

Blocks: you b., you stones 193:9
Blonde beast 154:7
Blonde Bestie 154:7
Blondes: Gentlemen Prefer B. 134:15
Blood: against flesh and b. 36:14
B. and iron 38:4
b. be the price 127:12
b. is nipp'd 196:20
b. is strong 181:7
B. is thick, but water's thin 91:26
b. more stirs 190:8
b. of Christians is seed 231:10
B. of Jesus 37:33
b., toil, tears and sweat 62:20
b. was frozen slowly 228:1
b. will have b. 199:11
blush'd with b. 120:4
Christ's b. streams 138:14
Felt in the b. 248:17
flesh and b. so cheap 107:4
freeze thy young b. 186:7
from kindred b. 47:6
glories of our b. 216:24
I am in b. 199:12
I smell the b. 195:14
in my youth's hot b. 109:25
It will have b. 199:11
make thick my b. 197:15
Norman b. 227:22
of his country's b. 95:15
purged away but with b. 42:14
red b. reigns 210:5
sheds his b. with me 192:4
sucked the b. 65:14
summon up the b. 191:8
to have had so much b. in him 199:28
to stir men's b. 194:12
wash this b. 198:15
We be of one b. 128:10
when the moon was b. 61:16
who sheddeth man's b. 23:22
with the b. of patriots 113:3
with the b. of the saints 37:22
Young b. must have its course 123:18
Bloodless lay the untrodden snow 53:15
Bloody: and the b. sweats 243:6
Be b., bold, and resolute 199:20
b. and invisible hand 199:6
b., full of blame 212:1
My head is b. 102:13
sang within the b. wood 81:22
Bloom: b. is gone 12:2
b. on a woman 18:24
flowers that b. in the spring 92:14
here tulips b. 42:5
How can ye b. 49:4
is hung with b. 110:15
saw the water-lily b. 227:25
to look at things in b. 110:15
Where fairer Tempes b. 213:12
where the lemon-trees b.? 94:16
Blooming: Left b. alone 149:18
Blooms each thing 152:6
Blossom: b. as the rose 28:9
B. by b. the spring begins 223:29
b. in purple and red 228:20
b. in their dust 216:25
Under the b. 208:20
Blossoms: b. of my sin 186:12
It b. through the year! 216:8
to-morrow b. 192:14
Blot: blackens every b. 226:15
Blotted: never b. out a line 117:12
Would he had b. a thousand 117:12
Blow: Angel trumpets b. 147:14
another deadly b.! 247:11
B., b. thou winter wind 184:1
B., bugle, b. 229:10
B. him again to me 229:9

b. his wreathed horn   249:5
B. me about in winds!   205:18
B. out, you bugles   41:16
B. soft o'er Ceylon's isle   101:16
b. up your horn   156:10
B., wind! come, wrack!   200:7
B., winds   195:4
b. your own trumpet   93:24
b. your trumpets, Angels   77:8
breathe and b.   229:9
gets his b. in fust   213:4
Liberty's in every b.!   49:1
north wind doth b.   157:1
return the b.   54:14
shall b. her clarion   214:1
stormy winds do b.   54:6
Sweet air b. soft   105:2
this b. might be the be-all   198:3
wind doth b.   196:20
word and a b.   79:14, 207:29
Bloweth: wind b. where it
  listeth   33:50
Blown: B. about   116:7
b. with restless violence   200:23
figure of b. youth   188:6
Flower that once hath b.   85:6
rooks are b.   227:8
Song on your bugles b.   102:17
Blows: b. his nail   196:20
by the Water b.   84:16
meanest flower that b.   246:14
never b. so red   85:2
Unkempt about those hedges b.   42:5
When the wind b.   38:9
wild thyme b.   203:9
wind b. it back   38:17
wind that b.   73:18
yon far country b.   111:5
Blowy: Snowy, Flowy, B.   88:16
Blücher: Napoleon forgot B.   62:15
Bludgeonings of chance   102:13
Blue: b. days at sea   221:17
b. remembered hills   111:5
b. ribbon of the turf   76:18
b. sky   248:19
breeches were b.   66:10, 218:16
clear b. sky   101:11
dark b. Ocean   51:8
hands are b.   131:4
hump that is black and b.!   126:3
in the central b.   228:9
lace my bodice b.   112:8
Little boy b.   156:10
little tent of b.   243:4
Presbyterian true b.   49:18
violets b.   196:19
Blues: Twentieth-Century B.   69:11
Blunder: At so grotesque a b.   22:13
it is a b.   40:12
It wad frae mony a b. free us   48:23
Blundered: Some one had b.   226:1
Blund'ring kind of melody   79:10
Blunt: plain b. man   194:11
Blush: B.'d with blood   120:4
b. to find it fame   165:13
born to b. unseen   97:15
it bring a b.   75:11
Blushful Hippocrene   121:3
Blushing: b. flow'rs shall rise   165:1
his b. honours   192:14
Blut und Eisen   38:4
Blynken: Wynken, B., and Nod   84:3
Board: above the b.   99:7
all came on b.   91:25
forcing her on b.   117:4
I struck the b.   103:19
Boarded: Youth are b., clothed   74:25
Boards: all the b. did shrink   65:14
Boast: B. not .. of tomorrow   26:28

b. of heraldry   97:12
b. thee, death   183:5
For frantic b. and foolish word   127:7
Boastings: Such b. as the Gentiles
  use   127:6
Boat: b. he can sail   233:5
pea-green b.   131:6
took a b. and went to sea   231:19
Boatman, do not tarry!   53:17
Boats: b. began to near the win-
  ning-post   64:17
messing about in b.   96:16
Bob-tail: on de b. nag   87:8
Bode: Doth that b. weeping   205:14
Bodice: b., aptly lac'd   172:19
lace my b. blue   112:8
Bodies: b. of those that made such
  a noise   81:6
b. of unburied men   240:11
our dead b. must tell the tale   179:19
Bodkin: with a bare b.?   187:13
Body: Absent in b.   35:15
age and b. of the time   188:10
b. did contain a spirit   190:23
b. of a weak and feeble woman   82:9
b. of England's   42:11
commit his b. to the deep   172:10
commit his b. to the ground   168:20
companion of the b.   99:3
exercise is to the b.   220:6
fretted the pigmy b.   79:5
gave his b.   207:2
Gin a b.   48:11
give my b. to be burned   35:21
having seen his b.   232:4
in his whole b.   223:15
in mind, b., or estate   166:29
its b. brevity   66:12
John Brown's b.   99:6
my poor father's b.   185:11
no b. to be kicked?   233:15
nor a b. to kick   217:19
resurrection of the b.   172:10
sound mind in a sound b.   119:9
their distempered b.   119:6
wished to see my dead b.   100:9
with a b. fill'd   191:15
with my b. I thee worship   168:14
Boil: We b. at different degrees   83:3
Boiled: b. leg of mutton   75:30
passion b. and bubbled   232:4
waited till his billy b.   161:12
Boilers: parcel of b.   115:24
Boiling: sea is b. hot   57:22
with b. oil   92:12
Bois: je b. dans mon verre   151:7
nous n'irons plus aux b.   17:7
Bois-Bou-long: As I walk along
  the B.   90:17
Bold: a b. peasantry   95:4
bloody, b., and resolute   199:20
b. as a lion   26:29
b. spirit in a loyal breast   206:2
speak out loud and b.   121:9
Boldly: spurr'd b. on   79:10
Boldness, and again B.   72:8
Bole: round the elm-tree b.   44:1
Bombast: serious swelling into b.   80:3
Bond: I will have my b.   202:3
look to his b.   201:26
take a b. of fate   199:21
that great b.   199:6
'tis not in the b.   202:7
Bondage: spirit of b.   35:7
Bonds: My b. in thee   211:9
Bone: B. of my b.   23:13
bright hair about the b.   77:14
get her poor dog a b.   157:3
To a rag and a b.   128:1

Bones: b. lie scattered 147:16
can these b. live? 29:15
fever in my b. 126:14
for his honour'd b. 147:12
full of dead men's b. 32:9
lay my b. amongst you 245:10
Of his b. are coral made 208:11
Rattle his b. 154:8
that moves my b. 212:5
town of monks and b. 66:9
valley which was full of b. 29:14
where my b. shall be thrown 209:9
Bonfire: to the everlasting b. 198:17
Bong-tree: land where the B.
  grows 131:7
Bonhomie: Overcame his natural b. 22:11
Bonnet: In her latest new b. 76:24
Bonnets: room for the b. of Bonny
  Dundee 179:20
Bonnie wee thing 48:10
Bonny: be you blithe and b. 204:9
Bonny Dundee: bonnets of B. 179:20
Bono: cui b. 63:22
Bononcini: Signor B. 50:12
Booh to you 93:2
Boojum: If your Snark be a B.! 56:4
  Snark was a B. 56:6
Book: Bell, b. and candle 193:4
  B. of Life begins 243:26
  B. of Verse—and Thou 84:18
  B. of Verses underneath the
    Bough 84:19
  b. where men may read strange
    matters 198:1
  bred in a b. 196:14
  damned, thick, square b. 94:7
  drown'd my b. 208:19
  Go, litel b. 61:1
  Go, little b., and wish to all 221:22
  good b. 148:8
  Great b., great evil 53:5
  Hers of the B. 174:3
  hotch-potch of my b. 119:14
  In thy b. record 147:16
  kill a good b. 148:7
  knows this out of the b. 75:2
  longest chapter in the b. 244:3
  melancholy b. 70:21
  Nature's mystic b. 140:13
  never read a b. before reviewing it 218:1
  Not on his picture, but his b. 118:3
  Or frowst with a b. 126:4
  printed in a b.! 25:34
  publishing a b., next May 96:15
  substance of the b. 128:29
  take down this b. 250:11
  that mine adversary had written
    a b. 25:38
  There is a b. who runs may read 122:18
  We present you with this B. 69:1
  What is the use of a b.? 56:10
  while thy b. doth live 118:4
  write a better b. 83:4
  write In a b. 39:8
Books: B., and my food 221:24
  B. are well written 243:19
  b. in the running brooks 183:9
  b., the arts, the academes 196:16
  b. to be read but not curiously 14:25
  b...to be read only in parts 14:25
  borrowers of b. 129:7
  but his b. were read 21:15
  fate of b. 141:16
  lenders' b. 195:11
  Of making many b. 27:9
  old b., old wines 95:24
  read of in b. 17:11
  some b. are to be tasted 14:25
  spectacles of b. 80:3

to Cambridge b. he sent 43:3
toil o'er b. 89:27
true University..a collection of
  b. 55:14
Boon: sordid b.! 249:5
  They came as a b. and a blessing 8:5
Boot: B., saddle, to horse 43:13
  hey for b. and horse 123:18
Bootless: with my b. cries 210:13
Boots: at the heels of their b. 86:19
  B.—b.—b.—b. 124:16
  Great Big Waterproof B. 143:8
  lick the blooming b. 125:11
  what b. it to repeat 85:8
  what b. it with uncessant care 145:1
  who cleans the b. 91:9
Bo-peep: Little B. 156:9
Borden: Lizzie B. took an axe 6:3
Border: all the wide B. 180:8
  B. chivalry 180:4
  B., nor breed, nor birth 124:13
  thin, flowery b. 129:11
Borders: invade the b. of my realm 82:9
  Of b., beds and shrubberies 125:8
Bore: dust whom England b. 42:11
  Hills of the Chankly B. 130:20
  My mother b. me 39:10
  they b. her up 189:18
  way to be a b. 237:19
  who b., 'mid snow and ice 133:17
Bores through his castle wall 206:15
Born: as of one b. out of due time 35:24
  as well as b. 118:8
  before the god of love was b. 77:13
  being b., to die? 15:15
  blackest Midnight born 144:10
  B. 1820, still going strong 3:18
  B. and educated in this country 90:7
  b. for the Universe 95:17
  b. into the world alive 91:21
  b. of the exclusive worship 113:1
  B. of the sun 219:7
  B. on a Monday 158:2
  b. to blush unseen 97:15
  b. when I was consul! 63:24
  Bred and b. in a brier-patch! 100:20
  children b. of thee 226:18
  darling of the Gods was b. 140:10
  Else, wherefore b.? 226:17
  Ere you were b. 211:13
  Every moment one is b. 231:2
  Godolphin Horne was nobly b. 21:2
  he that is b. King of the Jews? 30:1
  house where I was b. 107:1
  I was b. sneering 91:28
  Is not b., and does not die 217:16
  Man is b. free 177:18
  Man that is b. of woman 25:31
  Never was b. 222:3
  none of woman b. 199:20
  Not to be b. is best 218:10
  not to be b., or being b. 15:15
  powerless to be b. 11:15
  Saviour of the World was b. 50:14
  some men are b. great 209:12
  sucker b. every minute 18:14
  that ever I was b. 186:16
  Then surely I was b. 61:16
  they are b. so 74:22
  time to be b. 26:38
  to the manner b. 186:3
  under that was I b. 204:8
  unto us a child is b. 27:32
  wast not b. for death 121:14
  We were not b. to sue 206:13
  Where were you b.? 222:3
  whereof it is b. 201:6
  who are b. of thee? 22:7
  You took the trouble to be b. 19:8

Borne: B. before her on a shutter 232:4
b. his faculties 198:4
b. it in my youth's hot blood 109:25
b. me on his back 189:20
b. with philosophy 74:12
he hath b. our griefs 28:20
It is b. in upon me 100:12
Borogroves: mimsy were the b. 57:14
Boroughs: bright b. 107:16
Borrioboola-Gha: natives of B. 73:23
Borrow: must b. its mirth 243:3
Borrower: Neither a b., nor a
lender be 185:21
Borrowers of books 129:7
Borrowing: b. dulls the edge 185:21
goeth a b. 234:9
Bosom: carry them in his b. 28:14
Cleanse the stuff'd b. 200:1
From thy full b. 172:19
heart out of the b. 110:17
in Arthur's b. 191:6
into Abraham's b. 33:28
into the b. of the lake 229:17
Leaning across the b. of the
urgent west 41:8
Let me to Thy B. fly 241:8
ocean's b. 139:25
on the b. of the earth 206:14
Sea that bares her b. 249:5
slip into my b. 229:17
thorns that in her b. lodge 186:13
wear thee in my b. 48:10
wife of thy b. 24:19
wring his b. 95:21
Bosomed high in tufted trees 144:14
Bosom-friend: Close b. 119:17
Bosoms: and brush their b.? 45:12
Boston: And this is good old B. 40:11
Bo'sun: and a b. tight 91:3
Boswell is a very clubable man 116:4
Botanize: went down to b. 62:2
Both: accepting b. of them 159:17
Bother: B. Mrs. Harris! 74:24
B. the flowers that bloom 92:15
long words B. me 143:17
Bottle: b. of salvation 174:13
leave the b. 74:21
nor a b. to give him 74:15
pass the b. round 242:20
Bottles: new wine into old b. 31:11
Bottom: at the b. of our garden 88:12
bless thee, B.! 203:13
b. of good sense 115:25
b. of the deep 190:9
can't touch de b. 87:9
Which will reach the b. first? 96:10
Bottomless: key of the b. pit 37:23
To b. perdition 145:12
Bottoms of my trousers 81:19
Bough: along the b. 110:15
beneath the b. 84:18
hangs on the b. 208:20
on the orchard b. 44:1
touch not a single b.! 150:12
underneath the B. 84:19
Upon a wintry b. 213:11
When the b. bends 38:9
Boughs: And oft between the b. is
seen 42:6
on the pendent b. 189:18
That the lowest b. 44:1
Upon those b. 211:8
whose b. are bent 177:8
Bought it at any price 63:26
Boulogne: old man of B. 8:3
Bound: And b. on that journey 91:25
as a man is b. to do 230:5
B. each to each 247:10
b. in To saucy doubts 199:8

b. Upon a wheel of fire 196:1
earth. .b. by gold chains 227:2
Is b. in shallows 194:19
Slumber's chain has b. me 150:1
to them that are b. 29:2
was too small a b. 190:23
With a leap and a b. 67:2
Boundary of the march of a nation 161:1
Bounded in a nut-shell 187:3
Boundless: amid the b. main 41:14
b. and bare 214:7
Bounds: do their b. divide 79:6
thy b. be set 22:7
very b. of Britain 224:14
Bountiful: My Lady B. 83:18
Bourgeoisie: British B. 217:6
Bourn: from whose b. 187:13
our b. of Time and Place 226:6
Bout: many a winding b. 144:19
Bovril prevents that sinking feeling 3:19
Bow: as unto the b. 134:7
B., b., ye lower middle classes 91:16
b. myself in the house of
Rimmon 25:18
B. themselves when he did sing 192:13
breaketh the b. 169:21
Bring me my b. 38:16
drew a b. at a venture 25:17
Eigg on the starboard b. 221:21
every knee should b. 36:15
not b. down to them 167:7
set my b. in the cloud 23:23
What of the b.? 78:1
With my b. and arrow 159:4
Bowed his comely head 140:9
Bowels: in the b. of Christ 71:6
Bower: keep a b. quiet for us 120:1
smooth-swarded b. 229:4
to the b. they came 229:4
Bowery: And b. hollows 227:3
Showery, Flowery, B. 88:16
Bowl: B. of Night 84:15
called for his b. 157:2
Come, landlord, fill the flowing b. 3:21
crabs hiss in the b. 196:20
golden b. be broken 27:8
In a b. to sea 162:2
that inverted B. 85:13
trowl the brown b. 180:19
Went to sea in a b. 158:11
with my friendly b. 165:10
Bowler: I am the b. and the ball 130:2
wild b. thinks he bowls 130:2
Bowling: b. of a ghost 232:11
lies poor Tom B. 73:19
Bows: B. down to wood 101:16
in his blindness b. down 125:3
Bow-windows to the house 74:7
Bow-wow: Big B. strain 181:5
b., the watch-dogs bark 208:9
Bow-wows: to the demnition b. 75:6
Box: b. where sweets compacted
lie 104:7
Worth a guinea a b. 8:17
Boy: beamish b.! 57:14
b. fell dead 44:7
b. playing on the sea-shore 153:17
b. stood on the burning deck 102:7
b.'s will 133:24
b. that looks after the sheep? 156:10
carried by an orphan b. 108:4
Chatterton, the marvellous b. 247:19
hearty, healthy b. 105:15
horrid wicked b. 105:16
I saw a little vulgar B. 18:1
Let the b. win his spurs 81:3
Little b. blue 156:10
Little B. kneels 143:15
little tiny b. 209:20

Boy (cont.)
Love is a b. 49:26
modest, good-humoured b. 20:8
one for the little b. 155:4
That every b. and every gal 91:21
to your little b. 56:19
Upon the growing b. 246:11
what a good b. am I 156:11
where is my wandering b.
    tonight? 6:18
your Idiot B. 246:4
Boyaux: les b. du dernier prêtre 142:15
Boyhood: I were as in my b. 214:3
Boys: B. and girls come out to play 155:5
b...Are level now with men 182:21
b. in the back rooms 19:28
b. of the Old Brigade 240:1
chant to maidens and to b. 109:16
Cheer! B., cheer! 137:10
flies to wanton b. 195:18
liquor the growing b. 115:20
little wanton b. 192:14
men that were b. 22:1
pretty-dimpled b. 182:15
till the b. come home 87:4
trust in God, my b. 38:5
What are little b. made of? 158:14
when the b. came out to play 155:15
Brace ourselves to our duty 62:22
Bracelet of bright hair 77:14
Braces: Damn b. 39:20
Bradford: there goes John B. 40:17
Bradshaw: vocabulary of 'B.' 78:17
Brae: waly, waly, doun the b. 17:2
Braes: Ye banks and b. 49:4
Brag: left this vault to b. of 198:19
Nor shall death b. 210:12
Braid those flaxen locks 108:18
Braids: twisted b. of lilies 144:3
Brain: blind life within the b. 227:2
b. of heaven 142:1
glean'd my teeming b. 122:3
heat-oppressèd b.? 198:9
In what furnace was thy b.? 39:2
might injure the b. 56:16
of Very Little B. 143:17
o'ercomes the feeble b. 244:15
schoolmasters puzzle their b. 95:20
That thy b. must know 215:6
written troubles of the b. 200:1
Brains: blew his silly b. out 232:4
b. they punched in 240:3
Cudgel thy b. 189:19
Brake: nymphs in the b. 224:9
Bramble-dew: eyes of gold and b. 221:19
Branch: B. shall grow 28:1
Cut is the b. 139:2
withered b. 133:19
Branches ne'er remember 122:6
Branchy between towers 107:11
Brandished: with his b. steel 197:4
Brandy: B. for the Parson 127:10
must drink b. 115:20
Brass: All that was ever writ in b. 118:3
as sounding b. 35:20
As well in b. 118:3
Were b. impregnable 206:15
Brattle: Wi' bickering b.! 48:25
Brave: ally to the b. 236:22
b. man with a sword! 243:5
b. Music of a *distant* Drum 84:20
Fortune aids the b. 231:7
home of the b. 123:7, 212:7
How sleep the b. 67:14
None but the b. 79:11
not too late tomorrow to be b. 11:4
passing b. 139:9
That b. vibration 104:15
Toll for the b. 70:9, 10

What's b. 182:22
When I was clean and b. 110:18
Braved: Whose flag has b. 54:6
Bravery: all her b. on 147:5
Bravest: boy who was b. of all 6:18
Braw, bricht, moonlicht nicht 130:8
Brawl: I'll rail and b. 208:7
Bray: I will be the Vicar of B., Sir! 5:9
Brazil, where the nuts come from 232:6
Breach: honour'd in the b. 186:3
Once more unto the b. 191:8
Bread: ate his b. in sorrow 55:23
begging their b. 169:13
b., and the games of the circus 119:8
b. eaten in secret 26:11
B. I dip in the river 221:15
b. of adversity 28:8
b. of affliction 25:16
broth without any b. 158:6
Cast thy b. upon the waters 27:5
cramm'd with distressful b. 191:15
cutting b. and butter 232:12
eat b. to the full 24:6
Eating b. and honey 158:1
fetch you your b. 124:15
half-penny-worth of b. 190:16
He took the B. 82:4
Here with a Loaf of B. 84:18
if his son ask b. 30:34
Loaf of B.—and Thou 84:19
looked to government for b. 47:17
not live by b. alone 24:17, 30:8
our daily b. 30:32
quarrel with my b. and butter 223:11
Royal slice of b.? 143:13
Some gave them white b. 156:8
that b. should be so dear 107:4
thou shalt eat b. 23:16
White b. and butter 156:13
Breadth: length without b. 83:10
Break: and shall b. In blessings 70:6
B., b., b. 225:14
B. forth into joy 28:19
b. of day 97:2, 201:3, 210:13
bruised reed shall he not b. 28:16
even if my heart b. 102:3
I bend and I b. not 86:16
Never doubted clouds would b. 45:10
Take and b. us 102:17
thieves b. through 30:23
to b. known rules 71:12
took the Bread and b. it 82:4
Until the day b. 27:18
which condition if he b. 71:17
Breakers: angry b. roar 130:20
Breaketh the bow 169:21
Breakfast: B., supper, dinner 44:22
Where shall we our b. take? 16:17
Breakfasts: Where the M.F.H.
    sleeps he b. 222:16
Breaking: B. the silence 248:8
cheerfulness was always b. in 81:7
grey dawn b. 141:2
grey dawn is b. 71:3
vainly b. 64:10
Breaks: nearly b. my heart 113:8
Breast: beat his b. 65:7
boiling, bloody b. 204:1
from out thy b. 51:20
in a loyal b. 206:2
in the b. of every man 191:5
in the human b. 164:14
Lean'd her b. up-till a thorn 18:12
marched b. forward 45:10
my baby at my b. 183:4
Of thy chaste b. 134:20
Or knock the b. 147:10
sooth a savage b. 68:3
soul wears out the b. 52:14

that with dauntless b. 97:15
upon this b.! 133:18
With sweetness fills the b. 58:23
Breastie: panic's in thy b. 48:25
Breastplate: What stronger b. 192:7
Breasts: B. more soft than a
dove's 224:9
b. of the nymphs 224:9
Come to my woman's b. 197:15
her b. are dun 212:3
They bore within their b. 14:1
Warring within our b. 139:10
Breath: Allowing him a b. 206:15
borne away with every b. 52:8
b. can make them 95:4
b. of Autumn's being 214:1
b. of the night-wind 11:8
call the fleeting b. ? 97:13
down and out of b. 190:26
draw thy b. in pain 190:3
endures for a b. 224:1
every thing that hath b. 172:8
heaven's b. smells wooingly 198:2
mouth-honour, b. 199:32
my quiet b. 121:6
of Cytherea's b. 210:8
short of b. 179:4
thou no b. at all ? 196:11
thy b. be rude 184:1
to the latest b. 164:22
Weary of b. 106:20
with tenderer b. 224:9
Breathe: b. among the pleasant
villages 146:22
b. and blow 229:9
b. his native air 165:14
knock, b., shine 77:12
like the air we b. 222:13
long as men can b. 210:12
must pause to b. 52:14
never b. a word 125:15
thereon didst only b. 117:19
to b. were life 230:19
Yet did I never b. 121:9
Breathed o'er Eden 122:20
Breathes: B. there the man 180:6
b. upon a bank of violets 209:2
Enjoys the air it b. 248:12
Breathing: and quiet b. 120:1
b. English air 42:11
b. of the common wind 248:20
B. out threatenings 34:34
in fast thick pants were b. 66:14
In the sound his b. kept 214:9
Breathless: b. on thy fate! 133:13
B., we flung us 42:4
B. with adoration 246:15
Bred: B. en bawn in a brier-patch! 100:20
b. in a book 196:14
b. to the sea 139:21
I am American b. 143:2
where is fancy b. 202:1
without father b. 144:4
Bredon: summertime on B. 110:19
Breeches: his b. were blue 66:10, 218:6
made themselves b. 23:15
what leg you shall put into your
b. 114:16
Breed: Border, nor B., nor Birth 124:13
endless war still b. 148:4
Fear'd by their b. 206:7
happy b. of men 206:7
little neglect may b. mischief 88:5
most b. and haunt 198:2
Send forth the best ye b. 128:5
Breeding: oxen of his own b. 108:14
true b. of a gentleman 51:16
Breeds: Or lesser b. 127:6
Breeze: braved..the b. 54:6

dancing in the b. 247:3
the tossing b. 12:2
to April's b. 82:14
Breezes: b. and the sunshine 53:12
through the spicy b. 101:16
Breezy: b. call 97:11
B., Sneezy, Freezy 88:16
Breitmann: Hans B. gife a barty 131:19
Brent: bonny brow was b. 48:20
Brer Fox, he lay low 100:19
Brethren: Dearly beloved b. 166:7
least of these my b. 32:17
Brevity: body b. 66:12
B. is the soul of wit 186:21
Brewery: O take me to a b. 5:5
Brewing: trouble b. 128:28
Brick: 'Eave 'arf a b. at 'im 173:6
found it b. 52:21
Bridal: b. of the earth 104:6
dance at our b. 180:11
Bride: encounter darkness as a b. 200:22
happy b. 225:16
prepared as a b. 37:25
unravish'd b. 120:18
Bridegroom out of his chamber 168:30
Bridesmaid: happy b. 225:16
Bridge: And keep the b. with me 136:11
By the b. 82:14
Horatius kept the b. 136:16
Women, and Champagne, and B. 21:18
Brief life is here our portion 152:10
Brier: thorough b. 203:6
Brier-patch: Bred en bawn in a b.! 100:20
Brig: mate of the Nancy b. 91:3
Brigade: boys of the Old B. 240:1
Bright: All b. and glittering 249:4
Among the heather b. 58:12
as b. as day 155:5
as it was b. 235:11
Behold the b. original 89:24
billows smooth and b. 57:20
bracelet of b. hair 77:14
B. and fierce and fickle 229:14
b. boroughs 107:16
B., b. as day 250:12
b. day is done 182:23
b. dew is shaking 71:2
B. is the ring of words 221:18
b. particular star 182:7
b. reversion in the sky 164:5
B. star, would I were steadfast 121:8
B. the vision 138:6
b. with sinuous rills 66:14
but a b. lily grow 118:11
excellently b. 117:11
he shone b. 65:6
her eye was b. 65:2
land is b. 64:10
light of the b. world dies 40:13
memory is fair and b. 235:9
moon be still as b. 52:13
O the moon shines b. 82:1
one b. star 65:16
outshine Myriads though b. 145:14
so calm, so b. 104:6
spirit still, and b. 248:5
Thy majesty how b. 83:14
Tiger, tiger, burning b. 39:1, 4
Where the b. Seraphim 147:14
young lady named B. 45:24
Brighter: look b. when we come 51:13
Brightest: ascend the b. heaven 191:2
Best and b., come away! 213:14
B. and best of the sons 101:14
B. in dungeons 51:9
Brightly: log was burning b. 94:10
Brightness: B. falls from the air 152:5
Clothed with transcendent b. 145:14
Brilliancy: Send thy light and b. 130:5

Brillig: 'Twas b. 57:14
Brim: by the river's b. 274:14
  Filled to the b. 92:2
  winking at the b. 121:3
Bring: b. again Zion 28:19
  b. all heaven 144:9
  b. back the hour 246:13
  b. forth her increase 170:5
  b. his sheaves 171:21
  B. hither the fatted calf 33:23
  b. me forth 169:2
  B. me my bow 38:16
  b. the philosophic mind 246:13
  b. with thee jest 144:12
  from above did b. 145:6
  I b. you good tidings 32:42
  in my hand I b. 234:1
  what a day may b. forth 26:28
Bringeth: b. them unto the haven 171:9
  that b. good tidings 28:18
Brink of danger 173:26
Brinkmanship: boasting of his b. 220:19
Brioche: qu'ils mangent de la b. 138:8
Briskly: in driving b. 115:12
Bristol: three sailors from B. city 231:19
Britain: ambassador from B.'s crown 78:23
  B. a fit country for heroes 90:3
  B. would fight on alone 63:1
  I've lost B. 127:8
  very bounds of B. 224:14
  When B. first..Arose 232:13
  Yet B. set the world ablaze 91:22
Britannia: B. needs no bulwarks 54:7
  B., rule the waves 232:13
  B. rules the waves 54:2
  B., the pride of the ocean 212:7
British: blood of a B. man 195:14
  B. Bourgeoisie 217:6
  B. public 136:23
  B. soldier can stand up 212:12
  B. soldier fights 151:14
  Come you back, you B. soldier 126:11
  Dirty B. coaster 140:21
  except the B. War Office 212:12
  maxim of the B. people 62:19
  Our ships were B. oak 12:12
  twice tricked by the B. 19:29
British Commonwealth: B. . . . lasts
    for a thousand years 62:22
British Empire: liquidation of the B. 63:3
British Nation: greatness of the B. 1:10
Briton: I glory in the name of B. 90:7
Britons never will be slaves 232:13
Broach'd: bravely b. 204:1
Broad: and b. is the way 31:1
  B. and deep continueth 127:15
  fair these b. meads 181:7
  She's the B. 219:19
Broke: all hell b. loose? 146:18
  b. no promise 164:25
  b. under me 192:14
  man who b. the Bank 90:17
Broken: b. and contrite heart 169:28
  Laws were made to be b. 154:10
  London Bridge is b. down 156:14
  On the earth the b. arcs 43:6
  pitcher be b. at the fountain 27:8
  Promises and pie-crust..b. 223:8
  When the lute is b. 213:16
Broken-hearted: half b. 52:16
  ne'er been b. 48:5
  to bind up the b. 29:2
Bronze: lungs of b. 21:21
Brooches: make you b. 221:17
Brood of Folly 144:4
Brooding: birds sit b. 196:20
  b. and blaspheming 62:2
  love b. there 244:11
Brook: aslant a b. 189:18

Fell in the weeping b. 189:18
  hidden b. 66:3
  Where the b. and river meet 133:23
Brooks: books in the running b. 183:9
  Shallow b. 144:14
  that strow the b. 146:4
Broom: sent with b. before 204:4
Broth without any bread 158:6
Brothel: scene..laid in a B. 129:9
Brothels: Keep thy foot out of b. 195:11
Brother: Big b. is watching you 159:16
  B. clasps the hand of b. 18:9
  B., I am too old 60:4
  b. whom someone should save 235:1
  b.'s tears 59:3
  called him B. 247:18
  closer than a b. 26:21
  dawn is my b. 21:13
  hateth his b. 37:12
  I am distressed for thee, my b. 25:1
  mote that is in thy b.'s eye 30:31
  My b., good morning 21:13
  my b.'s keeper? 23:18
  My father's b. 185:11
  Shall be my b. 192:4
  stick more close than a b. 127:19
Brotherhood: Love the b. 37:4
Brother Jonathan 239:3
Brothers: all the b. too 209:11
  B. and Sisters 127:2
  B. we find our fellow-men 179:11
  b. who strove to leave Pelion 109:20
  Romans were like b. 136:12
  So the two b. 120:8
  Such a band of b. 153:2
  we band of b. 192:4
Brought: B. death into the world 145:9
  b. her warrior 229:15
  b. me to my last dregs 79:21
  never b. to mind 48:6
  we b. nothing into this world 36:29
Brow: bonny b. was brent 48:20
  in a b. of Egypt 203:19
  lily on thy b. 120:11
  on the rocky b. 51:19
  rugged mountain's b. 96:10
  Shine upon my b. 175:6
  upon the b. of labor 45:15
  wring the b. 180:13
Brown: all the trees are b. 123:18
  falling on the city b. 41:7
  From those b. hills 41:15
  John B.'s body 99:6
  long, and lank, and b. 65:18
  with the light b. hair 87:15
  Ye myrtles b. 144:20
Browne: to Sir Thomas B. 220:22
Browning: Carlyle, Tennyson, B. 173:20
Browning: entsichere ich meinen B. 117:5
Bruce: wham B. has aften led 48:30
Bruised: he was b. for our iniquities 28:21
Brunck: most learn'd professor, B. 165:18
Brunswick: Hamelin Town 's in B. 44:18
Brush: hang and b. their bosoms? 45:12
Brushwood sheaf 44:1
Brutal and insolent soldiery 83:7
Brute: Chuck him out, the b.! 127:21
  Feed the b.! 173:19
Brute: Et tu, B.? 53:1, 193:17
Brutes without you 159:22
Brutish: poor, nasty, b. 105:9
Brutus: Caesar had his B. 103:9
  he had praised B. 224:17
  noble B. 194:3
  were I B. 194:13
Bubble: and cauldron b. 199:13
  b. on the fountain 180:3
  mostly froth and b. 96:6
  Seeking the b. reputation 183:20

Bubbled: passion boiled and b. 232:4
Bubbles: With beaded b. 121:3
Buckets: silly b. on the deck 66:1
Buckingham: so much for B. 63:6
Buckingham Palace: changing
  guard at B. 143:7
Buckler: thy shield and b. 170:19
Bud: nip him in the b. 175:15
  worm i' the b. 209:10
Buds: darling b. of May 210:12
  Driving sweet b. 214:1
Buffalo: where the b. roam 105:5
Buffer: say a poor b. lies low 243:1
Buffet: to b. me 36:4
Buffeted: much b. he 236:3
Buffoon: fiddler, statesman, and b. 79:8
Buffs: Steady the B. 128:22
Bug: flap this b. 165:8
Bugle: Blow, b., blow 229:10
  Bring the good old b. 249:7
Bugle-horn: upon the b. 228:4
Bugles: Blow out, you b. 41:16
  Song on your b. blown 102:17
Build: And a small cabin b. 250:9
  b. his house in the woods 83:4
  b. the lofty rhyme 144:20
  Except the Lord b. 171:22
  I will b. my church 31:33
  I would b. that dome 66:15
  That they may b. from age to age 124:17
Builded: He b. better than he knew 82:15
  was Jerusalem B. here? 38:16
Builders: which the b. refused 171:15
Builds: and b. a Heaven 39:5
Built: are b. with air 117:13
  b. An absolute trust 197:13
  b. their nests in my beard! 130:15
  I b. my soul 229:5
  Till we have b. Jerusalem 38:16
Bull: Cock and a B. 220:18
Bull and Bush: Down at the old B. 233:18
Bullet: Every b. has its billet 244:8
  stronger than the b. 132:6
  with a b. through his heart 231:17
Bullets: b. made of platinum 20:18
Bulls of Basan 168:34
Bully boy 180:19
Bulwarks: Britannia needs no b. 54:7
Bumbast: to b. out a blank verse 98:13
Bunches of knot-grass 120:4
Bundle: b. of contradictions 68:2
  b. of prejudices 129:5
Bunk: History is b. 87:2
Buoy: her cock a b. 195:19
Burbled as it came! 57:14
Burden: borne the b. and heat 32:4
  b. bear 208:9
  heavy b. of responsibility 81:5
  my b. is light 31:21
  White Man's b. 128:5
Burg: Ein feste B. ist unser Gott 135:12
Burglar: enterprising b. 93:22
Burial-ground God's-Acre! 133:21
Buried: And b. once 206:16
  b. him darkly 245:4
  b. in the king's highway 206:16
  B. on Sunday 158:2
  Lie a-b. in one grave 7:20
  may be so b. 167:30
  not b. in consecrated ground 100:9
  outworn b. age 211:6
  some b. Caesar 85:2
  To b. merit 117:2
  when they b. him 226:10
Buries: universal darkness b. all 164:3
Burlington: I'm B. Bertie 100:13
Burma girl a-settin' 126:11
Burn: better to marry than to b. 35:16
  b. out themselves 206:6

candles b. their sockets 111:10
I rage, I melt, I b. 89:7
shall not b. thee 171:17
Shall yet terrific b. 54:8
To b. always 161:11
torches to b. bright 207:17
we b. daylight 207:15
Burned: b. is Apollo's laurel bough 139:2
  B. on the water 182:15
  bush b. with fire 23:38
  give my body to be b. 35:21
Burneth the chariots 169:21
Burning: boy stood on the b. deck 102:7
  in b. row 147:14
  In depths of the b. light! 83:14
  Keep the home fires b. 87:4, 154:15
  log was b. brightly 94:10
  of b. gold! 38:16
  plucked out of the b. 29:24
  speech is a b. fire 224:2
  Tiger! Tiger! b. bright 39:1, 4
Burnished: changes on the b. dove 228:5
  like a b. throne 182:15
  of the b. sun 201:19
Burns: B., Shelley, were with us 44:11
  candle b. at both ends 143:1
Burnt: b. the topless towers 138:12
  Night's candles are b. out 208:2
Burnt-offerings: delightest not in b. 169:28
Burr: kind of b. 201:4
Burrow: so near his b. 142:17
Burst: b. out singing 179:6
  came a b. of thunder 102:8
  first that ever b. 65:11
  see the mast b. open 86:9
  think to b. out 145:1
Bursts come crowding through the
  leaves 11:18
Burthen: And this the b. of his
  song 37:30
  Ever to b. thine 215:11
  weep their b. 230:10
Bury: B. the Great Duke 228:24
  come to b. Caesar 194:3
  dead b. their dead 31:8
Bus: Descending from the b. 56:9
  not even a b. I'm a tram 100:12
  She tumbled off a b. 96:11
Buses: ain' no 'b. runnin' 126:13
Bush: Bed in the b. 221:15
  b. burned with fire 23:38
  b. suppos'd a bear 203:19
  every common b. afire 43:4
  four times as big as the b.! 130:16
  good wine needs no b. 184:16
  perceive a young bird in this b.! 130:16
  sits in the b. 180:18
  thorough b. 20:63
Business: All the b. of war 240:15
  B. as usual 62:19
  B. first 231:15
  b. in great waters 171:7
  b. of America 68:25
  b. of everybody 136:18
  b. of life 240:15
  by particular b. 216:17
  damned serious b. 240:14
  end of this day's b. 194:22
  engaged in big b. 177:4
  everybody's b. is nobody's b. 238:14
  far from schemes of b. 108:14
  minded their own b. 56:18
  settled Hoti's b. 43:19
  This b. will never hold water 63:10
Buss: Miss B. and Miss Beale 6:6
Bust: or animated b. 97:13
  raise the tardy b. 117:2
Busy: b. haunts of men 102:12
  b. hum of men 144:18

Busy (cont.)
B. old fool   77:18
b. world is hushed   153:12
how b. I must be this day   12:17
I would be b. too   239:10
little b. bee   239:9
No-wher so b. a man   60:15
Butcher'd to make a Roman holiday   51:5
Butchers: meek and gentle with
  these b.   193:20
Butler: Groom, the B., and the
  Cook   91:9
Butt: here is my b.   205:17
with the b. end of it   96:3
Butter: B. and eggs   53:6
b. in a lordly dish   24:29
b. no parsnips   180:20
b. will only make us fat   94:12
Could we have some b.?   143:13
cutting bread and b.   232:4
do like a little bit of b.   143:14
it was the best b.   56:23
ladling b.   176:4
quarrel with my bread and b.   223:11
your bread and your b.   124:15
Buttercup: I'm called Little B.   93:5
Buttercups and daisies   111:17
Buttered: dig for b. rolls   58:13
on the b. side   161:16
Butterflies: gilded b.   196:6
Butterfly: breaks a b.   165:7
b. upon the road   126:20
Butting through the Channel   140:21
Button: little round b. at top   86:19
undo this b.   196:11
Buttons: taken of 'is b. off   125:2
Buttress: jutty, frieze, b.   198:2
Buxom, blithe   144:11
Buy: as thy purse can b.   185:21
come and b.   104:8
I will b. with you   201:13
no man might b. or sell   37:20
that money cannot b.   238:15
what the Vintners b.   85:16
what would you b.?   20:1
Buyer: if a b. can be found   179:1
Buying: For b. or selling   234:10
By and by: in the coming b.   93:1
sweet b.   22:6
Bye, baby bunting   155:6
Byng: Kentish Sir B.   43:12
Byway: and the b. nigh me   221:15
Byword: a b. among the people   25:7
Byzantium: Soldan of B.   61:18

C
C cut it   155:2
Ça ira   9:2
Caballero: El C. de la Triste Figura 59:8
Cabbage-leaf: to cut a c.   86:19
Cabbages: of c.—and kings   57:22
Cabin: And a small c. build   250:9
Make me a willow c.   209:4
Cabin'd: But now I am c.   199:8
Cabots talk only to God   40:11
Cacoethes: scribendi c.   119:6
Cadiz Bay: reeking into C.   44:2
Caelum non animum mutant   108:9
Caesar: appeal unto C.   34:48
C. had his Brutus   103:9
C.'s spirit   193:21
call great C. ass   183:4
come to bury C.   194:3
every wound of C.   194:13
Imperious C.   189:21
loved C. less   194:1
O mighty C.!   193:18

Regions C. never knew   69:20
Render therefore unto C.   32:7
some buried C.   85:2
unto C. shalt thou go   34:49
word of C.   194:6
Café: in every street c.   99:10
Cage: bird in a gilded c.   129:3
birds i' the c.   196:6
nor iron bars a c.   134:19
Robin Redbreast in a C.   38:11
Cain: and the first city C.   69:18
drunk and raising C.   124·12
Cake: Bake me a c.   157:9
Let them eat c.   138:8
Some gave them plum c.   156:8
Cakes: no more c. and ale   209:6
Calais: 'C.' lying in my heart   140:18
to show light at C.   114:18
Calamity: makes c. of so long life 187:13
more than a public c.   219:2
Calculation: c. shining   74:20
making a c.   74:7
Calculus: integral and differential c. 93:19
Calender: my good friend, the c.   69:23
Calf: c. and the young lion   28:2
fatted c.   33:23
when he killed a c.   12:18
Call: breezy c.   97:11
c. back yesterday   206:13
c. her blessed   26:33
C. him on the deep sea   153:5
c. me not fool   183:16
c. of the running tide   141:3
C. of the Wild   133:11
c. the cattle home   124:1
c. the fleeting breath?   97:13
c. up your men   179:20
c. ye upon him while he is near   28:24
c. your neighbours in   155:9
Dunno what to c. him   220:3
help Thy children when they c.   124:17
let me always c. you   83:20
one clear c. for me   226:6
please God to c. me   168:1
Shall I c. thee bird   245:15
to c. thee mine   137:15, 235:4
To honour we c. you   88:18
wake and c. me early   228:21
was good enough to c. it   96:7
wild c. and a clear c.   141:3
Called: c. her his lady fair   128:1
C. him soft names   121:6
c. me from my bed   97:2
c. the Holy Roman Empire   237:16
c. unto thee   171:25
Come when you're c.   80:21
many are c.   32:6
never c. me mother   245:12
they c. him Sunny Jim   99:12
to be c. thy son   33:22
Calling: dignity of this high c.   47:5
heard one c. 'Child'   103:20
temple-bells are c.   126:15
their mercenary c.   111:11
Callooh,! Callay!   57:14
Calls: hour c. not   236:12
If anybody c.   22:12
Calm: a c. so deep   249:4
all our c.   154:13
c. and free   246:15
c., as it was bright   235:11
c. of mind   147:11
season of c. weather   246:12
so cool, so c.   104:6
Calmness: smallest space of c.   20:2
Calumny: Envy and c.   213:8
shalt not escape c.   188:5
Calypso: Ulysses leaves once more
  C.   213:12

Cam: my C. and Isis   164:2
Cambridge: for C. people rarely
  ʝ⸱ smile   42:8
  more attractive than C.   15:16
  To C. books   43:3, 234:3
Cambridgeshire: and C., of all Eng-
  land   42:7
Came: answer c. there none   180:1
  c. out by the same door   85:7
  c. unto him delicately   24:42
  He c. unto his own   33:45
  I c., I saw, I conquered   53:2
  Tell them I c.   73:5
  they all c. on board   91:25
Cameelious Hump   126:3
Camel: and swallow a c.   32:8
  C.'s hump is an ugly lump   126:2
  easier for a c.   32:1
  in shape of a c.?   188:18
Camelot: look'd down to C.   227:25
Campaigns: whose c. are over   110:2
Campaspe: Cupid and my C.   135:14
Campbells are comin'   7:14
Can: fill up my c.   179:20
  He who c.   212:24
  therefore I c.   119:12
  What we c. we will be   123:15
  While we c.   118:12
Canakin: Let me the c. clink   204:29
Canary: mine host's C. wine   120:17
Cancel: C. and tear to pieces   199:6
  to c. half a line   85:12
Candid: from the c. friend   54:14
Candle: Bell, book, and c.   193:4
  burning a farthing c.   114:18
  c. burns at both ends   143:1
  c. of understanding   29:30
  c. to light you to bed   157:8
  c...which shall not be put out   29:30
  fit to hold a c.   50:12
  half a c.   130:19
  hold their farthing c.   250:14
  light a c. to the sun   216:28
  light such a c.   130:6
  little c. throws its beams!   202:14
  out, brief c.   200:4
  we did not see the c.   202:14
Candle-ends: his intimate friends
  called him 'C.'   56:3
Candle-light: Can I get there by c.?   155:19
  sit in the c.   176:11
Candles: c. burn their sockets   111:10
  Night's c.   208:2
  Their c. are all out   198:8
Candour: to justify mine own c.   117:12
Cannibals that each other eat   204:22
Cannon: C. to right of them   226:3
  even in the c.'s mouth   183:20
  the c.'s opening roar   51:2
Cannon-ball took off his legs   106:22
Cannot: He who c.   212:24
Canoe: paddle his own c.   139:20
Canon 'gainst self-slaughter   185:11
Canons of Christ-Church   115:6
Canopy: most excellent c.   187:4
Canossa: Nach C. gehen wir nicht   38:3
Canst: Give all thou c.   247:6
Can't! Don't! Sha'n't! Won't!   127:1
Cant: Clear your mind of c.   116:3
Cantering: Steadily c. through   128:3
Canyon: in a c.   149:7
Cap: my considering c.   19:17
  stuck a feather in his c.   17:6
Capable of nothing   188:7
Capacity: c. of the reader   141:6
  transcendent c.   55:9
Capax: omnium consensu c. imperii   225:1
Cape: round the C.   44:16
Cape St. Vincent.. Nobly, nobly C.   44:2

Cape Turk: doubled C.   142:9
Capital mistake   78:4
Capitol: musing amidst the ruins of
  the C.   90:12
Capon: with good c. lined   183:20
Capreis: epistula venit a C.   119:7
Caps: red roses crest the c. I know   232:11
  threw their c.   184:17
Captain: and a c. bold   91:3
  And a right good c. too!   93:6
  C., art tha sleepin' there below?   153:5
  c. of my soul   102:14
  C. of the Gate   136:9
  C. of the Pinafore   93:6
  C.'s hand on his shoulder   153:6
  crew of the c.'s gig   91:3
  Foremost c. of his time   228:25
  my C. lies   242:11
  O C.! my C.!   242:10
  plain russet-coated c.   71:5
  train-band c.   69:21
Captains: C. and the Kings depart   127:4
  C. couragious   16:9
  C. of industry   55:19
  thunder of the c.   25:44
Captive: foes they c. make   59:18
  led us away c.   171:28
Captives: liberty to the c.   29:2
  serve your c.' need   128:5
Captivity: led c. captive   170:7
  Turn our c.   171:21
Car: or the c. rattling   51:1
Caravan: and the C. starts   85:9
  Put up your c.   105:14
  Where my c. has rested   231:12
Caravanserai: this batter'd C.   84:22
Carcass: hew him as a c.   193:13
  Wheresoever the c. is   32:13
Card: cut it on his c.   127:17
Cards: play'd at c. for kisses   135:14
Care: Age is full of c.   210:10
  be this thy c.   236:18
  Begone, dull c.   3:16
  Black C.   109:17
  c.'ll kill a cat   117:14
  c. o' th' main chance   49:28
  full of c.   72:13
  hath any c.   39:5
  he need not c.   86:12
  I c. for nobody   37:30
  I c. not two-pence   19:11
  Lift her with c.   106:20
  Nor c. beyond today   98:8
  ravell'd sleave of c.   198:13
  short-lived c.   152:10
  sought it with c.   56:5
  Take c. of the sense   57:4
  uncessant c.   145:1
  weary fu' o' c.   49:4
  What c. I   244:18
  whose wish and c.   165:14
  woman who did not c.   128:1
  woman's tender c.   70:4
  wrinkled C.   144:13
Cared: Gallio c. for none of these
  things   34:44
Career open to talents   55:6, 151:18
Careful: so c. of the type   227:12
  wery c. o' vidders   75:21
Careless: c. shoe-string   104:11
  sitting c.   119:18
Carelessness: looks like c.   243:10
Cares: against eating c.   144:19
  c. that infest the day   133:15
  If no one c. for me   37:30
  is deprest with c.   89:18
  Whose constant c.   106:14
Careth for the strangers   172:5
Cargo of ivory   140:20

Caricature: With a c. of a face   92:15
Carlisle: roused the burghers of C.   136:6
Carlyle, Tennyson, Browning   173:20
Carnage: where his c...cease   50:18
Carol: Heard a c.   228:1
Carpenter: Walrus and the C.   57:21
Carpet: on c. consideration   209:18
Carriage: I can't afford a c.   72:1
  very small second class c.   91:24
Carried: and c. our sorrows   28:20
  c. about with every wind   36:10
  c. by an orphan boy   180:4
  c. by the angels   33:28
Carrière: La c. ouverte aux talents
                                   55:6, 151:18
Carries: He c. weight   69:28
Carrow: late slain at C.   217:7
Carry: all Earth's volumes c.   59:20
  c. nothing out   36:29
  c. the wealth of the Indies   115:18
  could c. all he knew   95:8
  lancers shall c. me   243:1
  must c. knowledge   115:18
  To c. off the latter   162:1
Carthage: C. must be destroyed   58:24
  To come again to C.   202:10
Carthaginian faith   179:2
Cartridge-boxes: holsters and c.   212:8
Cartridge-pouch: carries in his c.   151:16
Carve: c. heads upon cherry-stones   116:5
  c. him as a dish   193:13
  c. it on his tombstone   127:17
  c. on every tree   184:3
Carved: c. out his passage   197:4
  We c. not a line   245:7
Carven: garlanded with c. imag'ries   120:4
Casca: envious C.   194:8
Case: C. is concluded   13:11
  Having nothing to do with the c.   92:14
  in c. anything turned up   74:7
  lady in the c.   51:23, 91:4
  when a lady's in the c.   89:29
Cased: Take your hare when it is c.   94:6
Casement high   120:4
Casements: Charm'd magic c.   121:6
Cash: Ah, take the C.   84:20, 21
  and the c. that goes therewith   61:13
  when c. payment   55:8
Cashmere: tales of wild C.   244:10
Casques that did affright the air   191:3
Cassius the last of the Romans   224:17
Cassock, band, and hymn-book   243:2
Cassowary: If I were a c.   243:2
Cast: C. away the works of darkness   166:33
  c. into my teeth   194:18
  c. into the..fiery furnace   29:17
  c. it from thee   31:39
  c. me in the teeth   169:17
  c. off the works of darkness   35:14
  c. one's eyes so low   195:19
  c. out into outer darkness   31:6
  c. out my shoe   170:2
  c. out of the world   174:16
  C. thy bread upon the waters   27:5
  c. ye your pearls   30:32
  die is c.   53:3
  first c. a stone   34:6
  he c. into the sea   33:30
  His noses c. is of the roman   86:11
  I will in no wise c. out   34:5
  let us c. lots   29:25
  Our loving lot was c.   106:19
  pale c. of thought   187:13
  when I c. mine eyes   104:15
Casting down their golden crowns   102:1
Castitatem: Da mihi c.   13:3
Castle: Bores through his c. wall   206:15
  c., called Doubting-Castle   46:11
  c. hath a pleasant seat   198:2

hung in the c. hall   19:4
man's house is his c.   65:1
our c.'s strength   200:2
splendour falls on c. walls   229:10
Castlereagh: mask like C.   213:18
Castles: all the c. I have, are built
  with air   117:13
  make c. than in Spayne   60:23
Cat: care'll kill a c.   117:14
  c. and the fiddle   155:17
  C. He walked by himself   128:16
  c. may look at a king   57:2
  c. would watch a mouse   223:18
  crooked c.   158:5
  Hanging of his c.   41:3
  harmless necessary c.   202:4
  he was a fine c.   116:2
  how the c. jumps   181:6
  I shall bell the c.   3:4
  It was the c.!   93:12
  like the poor c.   198:6
  made a c. laugh   163:6
  pavilion c.   130:2
  Runcible C. with crimson whiskers   131:12
  to swing a c.   74:13
  to tear a c. in   203:3
  ways of killing a c.   124:7
  What c.'s averse to fish?   98:2
  worried the c.   158:5
Cataract: wild c. leaps   229:10
Cataracts and hurricanoes   195:4
Catch: c. as c. can   86:19
  c. him once upon the hip   201:15
  c. the conscience of the king   187:12
  c. the nearest way   197:14
  c. With his surcease success   198:3
  claws that c.!   57:14
  First c. your hare   94:6
Catch'd: ere th'are c.   50:1
Catching: Somebody's c. it now   127:1
Catechism: scarce had said his C.   232:3
Categorical: one c. imperative   119:11
Cathay: cycle of C.   228:15
Catholick and Apostolick Church   167:19
Catiline: abuse our patience, C.?   63:16
Cats: do c. eat bats?   56:11
  every sack had seven c.   155:3
  rain c. and dogs   223:16
Cattle: a lowly c. shed   2:10
  c. are grazing   247:9
  go and call the c. home   124:1
Caudle: Mrs. C.'s Curtain Lectures   113:10
Caught: And c. our youth   42:10
  c. an everlasting cold   240:13
  c. my foot in the mat   98:18
  c. the Sultan's Turret   84:15
  how I c. it   201:6
  I c. this morning   107:17
Cauldron bubble   199:13
Cause: c. of dullness in others   87:1
  devotion to that c.   132:8
  for the C.   136:7
  in the justice of our c.   99:4
  it is the c.   205:15
  know c. or just impediment   168:5
  Report me and my c. aright   190:1
  try the whole c.   56:14
  what high c.   140:10
  whose c. this evil is upon us   29:25
Causes: c. of things   237:7
  home of lost c.   12:3
Cautiously: do c.   10:5
Cavaliero: perfect c.   50:16
Cave: Idols of the C.   15:11
  misty eastern c.   213:20
  Stygian c. forlorn   144:10
Cave canem   162:12
Cavern: In a c.   149:7
  or mossy c.   120:17

Caverns measureless to man   66:14, 15
Caves: From the fountain and the c.   66:15
  unfathom'd c.   97:15
  with c. of ice!   66:15
Caviare to the general   187:7
Cawdor: and C.   197:14
  C. shall sleep no more   198:14
Cease: and c. to be   227:5
  c. upon the midnight   121:6
  I may c. to be   122:3
  I will not c.   38:16
  maketh wars to c.   169:21
  tender care c.   70:4
  that love may never c.   104:2
  That time may c.   138:14
  they shall c. [tongues]   35:21
Ceased: When Lucy c. to be   248:3
Cedamus: nos c. Amori   237:3
Cedarn: a c. cover   66:14
Cedarwood: Sandalwood, c.   140:20
Cela est bien qui   237:13
Celebrated: c., cultivated, under-
  rated   91:6
  c. wish   129:6
Celestial: from thy c. seat   130:5
  in c. light   246:7
  with c. fire   172:11
Celia: Come, my C.   118:12
Celibacy has no pleasures   116:24
Cell: Each in his narrow c.   97:10
  in a dungeon c.   92:9
Cells: contented with their c.   247:12
Censorious: Crabbed old c. men   58:26
Censure: take each man's c.   185:21
Centipede was happy   71:1
Centre: c. of the household   212:15
  fire's c.   219:6
Centre: mon c. cède   86:14
Centuries: All c. but this   92:1
  forty c. look down   152:1
  great march of the c.   237:1
  through what wild c.   73:2
Century: c. of the common man   238:1
  c. on which we are entering   238:1
  fierce intellectual life of our c. 12:3
  lain for a c.   228:20
Cerberus: give that C. a sop   68:5
  Of C. and blackest Midnight born 144:10
Ceremony: but for c.   191:15
  thrice-gorgeous c.   191:15
Certain: c. of nothing   122:7
  It is c.   231:11
  little and c. compass   40:4
  One thing is c.   85:6
  said to be c.   88:4
Certainties: hot for c.   142:7
Certifieth: one night c. another   168:29
Certum est quia impossibile est   231:11
Cervicem: unam c.   53:4
Cesspool: London, that great c.   78:20
Cetera quis nescit?   160:2
Ceylon: soft o'er C.'s isle   101:16
Chadband: it is, says C.   73:26
Chafes: surge that on the..pebbles c. 195:19
Chaffinch: While the c. sings   44:1
Chain: has a watch and c.   176:3
  Slumber's c.   150:1
  what the c.?   39:2
Chainless: of the c. mind   51:9
Chains: bind their kings in c.   172:7
  bound by gold c.   227:2
  C. and slaverie!   48:30
  C. are worse than bayonets   113:12
  he is in c.   177:18
  in adamantine c.   145:12
  lose but their c.   140:14
Chair: flood of tears and a sedan c. 75:29
  has one vacant c.!   134:1
  jumping from the c.   112:4

mouse under the c.   157:14
  seated in thy silver c.   117:11
  tilts up his c.   105:18
Chairman: My God, Mr. C.   64:2
Chairs: Two old c.   130:19
Chaise: all in a c. and pair   69:22
Cham: great C. of literature   218:5
Chamber: bridegroom out of his c.   168:30
  get you to my lady's c.   189:20
  in my lady's c.   155:16
  To thy c. window   213:13
Champagne: not a c. teetotaller   212:11
  Women, and C., and Bridge   21:18
Chance: bludgeonings of c.   102:13
  By c., or nature   210:12
  care o' th' main c.   49:28
  if she c. to nod   208:7
  to prove our c.   78:28
  you haven't a c.   93:24
Chancellor: A rather susceptible C. 91:18
Chances of this mortal life   167:27
Chandelle: au soir, à la c.   176:11
Change: C. and decay   135:16
  c. and loss in the heavens   110:6
  C. but the name   110:8
  c. for the worse   8:6
  C. in a trice   224:4
  Ethiopian c. his skin   29:6
  grooves of c.   228:14
  is past c.   107:15
  many c. and pass   213:10
  more things c.   119:13
  necessary not to c.   83:16
  Neither to c.   215:1
  not necessary to c.   83:16
  They c. their sky   108:9
  Times c.   10:7
  we c. with them   160:10
  With rapid c.   166:5
  would not c. for thine   117:19
Changé: nous avons c. tout cela   148:19
Change: plus ça c.   119:13
Changed: c. all that   148:19
  how c. from him   145:14
  living things are c.   135:9
  we shall all be c.   35:29
Changeful is woman always!   236:14
Changes: c. and chances   167:27
  One, who never c.   235:8
  plot hath many c.   173:27
Changest: O Thou, who c. not   135:16
Changeth: old order c.   227:1
Changing: c. scenes of life   225:7
  in a c. age   78:12
  of your c. face   250:11
  They're c. guard   143:7
Chankly Bore: Hills of the C.   130:20
Channel: Butting through the C.   140:21
  drum them up the C.   153:4
  you are crossing the C.   91:24
Chant: How can ye c.   49:4
  now c. to maidens   109:16
Chanted: C. loudly   228:1
  c. snatches of old tunes   189:18
Chanticleer: strain of strutting C. 208:9
Chaos: C. is come again   205:3
  dread empire, C.!   164:3
  reign of C.   146:6
Chapels: are nice in c.   112:5
  c. had been churches   201:9
Chap-fallen: quite c.?   189:20
Chapman: heard C. speak   121:9
Chapter: c. of accidents   61:11, 244:3
  repeat a complete c.   115:17
Character: leave my c. behind me   216:17
  lofty c. of Wife   74:12
  look thou c.   185:21
  reap a c.   175:4
Characters of hell to trace   97:5

Charge: c. over thee | 170:20
Take thou in c. this day | 136:14
upon this c. | 191:9
wild c. they made | 226:5
Charged: c. with the grandeur of God | 107:12
How c. with punishments | 102:14
Charing Cross: betwixt Heaven and C. | 232:10
tide of human existence is at C. | 115:2
went out to C. | 162:5
Chariot: beneath thy c. wheel | 107:10
Bring me my c. | 38:16
Swing low, sweet c. | 7:10
Time's winged c. | 140:12
Chariotest to their dark wintry bed | 214:1
Chariots: burneth the c. | 169:21
His c. of wrath | 96:19
put their trust in c. | 168:32
Charity: and have not c. | 35:20
C. begins at home | 42:20
C...is kind | 35:21
C. shall cover the multitude of sins | 37:6
C. suffereth long | 35:21
faith, hope, c. | 35:22
greatest of these is c. | 35:22
in all things, c. | 19:2
in love and c. | 167:22
living need c. more than the dead | 11:6
with c. for all | 132:9
Charles: C. the First, his Cromwell | 103:9
C. the First walked and talked | 6:1
For C. King of England | 136:7
In good King C.'s golden days | 5:9
navy of C. the Second | 137:2
out of King C.'s head | 74:10
Charlie: C. came to our town | 106:7
C. he's my darling | 106:7
C. is my darling | 151:12
live or die wi' C. | 106:6
o'er the water to C. | 106:6
Charlotte: had a love for C. | 232:4
Charm: c. from the sky | 161:17
c. thee to a tear | 244:10
power to c. | 185:4
What c. can soothe | 95:21
Charmed: bear a c. life | 200:10
c. it with smiles | 56:5
C. magic casements | 121:6
Charmer: voice of the c. | 169:29
were t'other dear c. away | 89:21
Charming: beauty's c. | 180:15
c. is divine philosophy | 144:2
O most c. pug | 86:11
Charmingly: so c. curled | 123:17
Charms: endearing young c. | 149:12
Music has c. | 68:9
Charter: c. of thy worth | 211:9
this was the c. | 232:13
Charybdis: Scylla and C. | 215:16
Chase: c. e'en now the fliers | 64:10
heated in the c. | 225:6
new mistress now I c. | 134:20
To c. the glowing Hours | 51:1
unhurrying c. | 232:8
Chasm: romantic c. | 66:14
Chassis: world in a state of c. | 159:7
Chaste: as c. as ice | 188:5
c. and fair | 117:11
c. beams of the wat'ry moon | 203:7
fair, the c. | 184:3
Of thy c. breast | 134:20
you c. stars | 205:15
Chasten: To c. and subdue | 248:19
Chasteneth: Whom the lord loveth he c. | 36:36
Chastised: been a little c. | 29:33
c. you with whips | 25:10

Chastisement of our peace | 28:21
Chastity: Give me c. | 13:3
Chatham: Great C. with his sabre drawn | 4:14
Chatter: only idle c. | 92:21
Chatterings: In multitudinous c. | 142:6
Chatterton, the marvellous boy | 247:19
Chaucer: C., who had geneyus | 238:19
lodge thee by C., or Spenser | 118:4
Chavender: fine stuffed c. | 178:13
Cheap: c. and chippy chopper | 92:5
hold their manhoods c. | 192:4
how potent c. music is | 69:15
Cheat: c. thee of a sigh | 244:10
fancy cannot c. so well | 121:7
lucrative to c. | 64:8
may c. at cards genteelly | 115:3
Cheated: of being c., as to cheat | 49:29
Check: c. to loose behaviour | 220:5
rod to c. | 245:19
Cheek: Feed on her damask c. | 209:10
into the c. of the young person | 75:11
leans her c. upon her hand | 207:21
might touch that c. | 207:21
on thy c. | 120:11
pale grew thy c. | 52:16
smite thee on thy right c. | 30:18
upon the c. of night | 207:18
wither'd c. | 180:4
Cheeks: c. were so red | 123:17
crack your c.! | 195:4
Fat ruddy c. | 105:15
glow the delicate c. | 182:15
in thy c. | 208:14
make pale my c. | 244:18
rosy lips and c. | 211:16
Cheer: be of good c. | 34:22
C.! Boys, c.! | 137:10
c. but not inebriate | 70:18
C. for a halt | 127:1
c. up, my lads | 88:18
C. up, the worst is yet to come | 113:13
greet the unseen with a c. | 45:9
make good c. | 234:7
piped with merry c. | 39:8
scarce forbear to c. | 136:15
songs of happy c. | 39:8
Cheerful: c. countenance | 26:17, 171:2
c. hearts now broken | 150:1
c., merry Dr. Brighton | 231:13
God loveth a c. giver | 36:2
looking as c. as any man | 162:5
with c. voice | 123:5
Cheerfulness was always breaking in | 81:7
Cheering: nor c. crowds | 250:7
Cheers: give three c. | 93:7
Cheese: and a pound of c. | 53:6
dreamed of c. | 221:4
smells of c. | 222:19
Cheeses: eggs, apples, and c. | 124:15
Chelsea: outer C. to the Strand | 126:14
Chemist: was c., fiddler | 79:8
Chequer-board: all a c. of Nights and Days | 85:10
Chequered: in the c. shade | 144:16
Cherchez la femme | 80:9
Cherchons la femme | 80:9
Cherish: Love, c., and to obey | 168:13
to love and to c. | 168:12
Cheroot: whackin' white c. | 126:12
Cherries: c., hops, and women | 75:16
there c. grow | 54:11
Cherry: 'C. ripe' themselves do cry | 54:11
C. ripe, ripe, ripe, I cry | 104:8
like to a double c. | 203:15
Loveliest of trees, the c. | 110:15
ruddier than the c. | 89:8
To see the c. hung with snow | 110:15
Cherry-stones: carve heads upon c. | 116:5

Cherub: Fall'n c. 146:1
Cherubins: young-eyed c. 202:11
Chest: on the dead man's c. 220:23
ten-times-barr'd-up c. 206:2
Chesterton: dared attack my C. 21:20
Chestnut: spreading c. tree 134:10
Chestnuts: had c. in her lap 197:5
pull their c. out of the fire 19:29
Chevalier: young C. 106:7
Chevalier sans peur et sans reproche 9:4
Chewing little bits of string 21:3
Chicken: c. in his pot 102:18
neck wrung like a c. 63:1
she's no c. 223:12
Some c.! 63:1
Chickens: count their c. 50:1
curses are like young c. 218:15
Don't count your c. 1:21
pretty c. and their dam 199:27
Chid: And you'll never be c. 80:21
Chide: c., and fight 239:8
dare to c. me 68:23
lest He returning c. 147:17
trumpets 'gan to c. 120:3
Chief: brilliant c. 136:1
c. end of man? 216:26
Chieftain to the Highlands 53:17
Child: any c. of man 172:4
any christom c. 191:6
as an angel is the English c. 39:10
As yet a c. 165:4
C. is father of the Man 247:10
c. of dirt 165:8
c. of God 167:32
c. of hell 191:15
c. she bare? 70:4
c. should always say what's
true 221:11
c. that's born on the Sabbath
day 156:17
c.'s amang you 48:29
Defend. .this thy c. 168:4
Elephant's C. 128:13
Every c. may joy to hear 39:8
Fancy's c. 144:19
Get with c. a mandrake root 77:16
Heav'n born c. 145:7
Here a little c. I stand 104:16
I heard one calling, 'C.' 103:20
I understood as a c. 35:22
I was a c. 163:14
knows his own c. 201:21
little c. shall lead them 28:2
Look upon a little c. 241:12
mid-May's eldest c. 121:5
Monday's c. 156:17
nicest c. I ever knew 21:1
old Adam in this c. 167:30
on a cloud I saw a c. 39:8
painted c. 165:8
She was an aggravating c. 21:11
spoil the c. 49:26
spoils the c. 107:2
thankless c. 195:3
To be my c. 196:3
Train up a c. 26:22
unto us a c. is born 27:32
When I was a c. 35:22
Where is my c.? 50:19
would not coddle the c. 114:26
Childhood: In my days of c. 129:16
Womanhood and c. fleet 133:23
Childish: c. toy 139:4
put away c. things 35:22
Childishly: suck'd on country
pleasures, I 77:7
Childishness: is second c. 183:20
Children: become as little c. 31:37
called the c. of God 30:11

call'd you c. 195:5
c. all gone 156:7
C. begin by loving their parents 243:27
c. born of thee 226:18
c. cried in the streets 150:17
c. go barefoot 212:20
c. like the olive branches 171:24
c. of one family 239:8
c. of our country 177:17
c. of the kingdom 31:6
C. of the Lord 2:9
c. scream'd 69:28
c. stood watching 124:2
c. sweeten labours 14:20
c.'s teeth are set on edge 29:12
Come, dear c., let us away 11:10
devour. .each one of her c. 235:13
eager c. cry 99:5
even so are the young c. 171:23
Frail c. of dust 96:20
Friend for little c. 142:20
had so many c. 158:6
her c. rise up 26:33
holdeth c. from play 217:2
Listen, my c. 133:25
mother for her c. 38:1
never knows the c. 139:19
Oh, help Thy c. 124:17
old men and c. 172:6
on behalf. .of their c. 178:18
procreation of c. 168:6
see the c. sport 246:12
suffer the little c. 32:34
To whom the lips of c. 152:7
upon the c. 167:7
We are but little c. weak 2:11
When the voices of c. 39:11
Child Roland to the dark tower
came 195:14
Child-wife: only my c. 74:14
Chill: bitter c. it was! 120:2
Chilly: I feel c. 45:12
now, although the room grows c. 96:13
Chimborazo, Cotopaxi 234:6
Chime: evening c. 150:2
Chimes at midnight 190:31
Chimney: and smoked like a c. 17:16
from the c. corner 217:2
Chimney-piece: bottle on the c. 74:21
Chimney-sweepers: As c. 184:22
China: from C. to Peru 117:1
outer C. 'crost the Bay 126:11
Chinee: heathen C. is peculiar 101:3
Chinese wouldn't dare to 69:8
Chippy: cheap and c. chopper 92:5
Chit-chat: divine c. of Cowper 129:8
Chivalry: age of c. is gone 47:14
age of c. is past 124:8
and true c. 206:7
beauty and her c. 50:23
Border c. 180:4
Choice: Each to his c. 127:18
in my c. 146:3
more difficult the c. 2:15
takes your c. 173:4
Choicer than the Mermaid Tavern? 120:17
Choir: full-voiced c. 144:9
Sweet singing in the c. 7:17
Choirs: Bare ruin'd c. 211:8
Choking her with cream 124:7
Choose: c. their place of rest 146:25
I c. it to mean 58:5
Let's c. executors 206:14
to c. or reject 80:5
To c. The Jews 83:13
use any language you c. 91:23
will c. her dwelling 79:23
Chopper: cheap and chippy c. 92:5
c. to cut off your head 157:8

Chops and Tomata sauce 75:24
Chord: one c. of music 172:23
Chortled: He c. in his joy 57:14
Chorus: sang the c. 249:8
Chorus-ending from Euripides 43:9
Chosen: but few are c. 32:6
thy c. music 248:13
Choughs: crows and c. 195:19
Christ (see also Jesus): C. being
raised from the dead 35:4
C. is the path 149:1
C. is thy strength 149:1
C., the Lord is risen 241:7
C. walking on the water 232:10
C.'s blood streams 138:14
in the bowels of C. 71:6
member of C. 167:32
Ring in the C. 227:20
through C. which strengtheneth
me 36:21
unto his captain C. 207:2
whole state of C.'s Church 167:20
Christ-Church: dine with the
Canons of C. 115:6
Christendom: wisest fool in C. 103:3
Christened on Tuesday 158:2
Christian: Articles of the C. Faith 167:32
as little as a C. can 78:24
C., doth thou see them? 152:10
C. hearts 122:18
C. men, rejoice 152:12
Fled with a C.! 201:24
for C. service 206:7
hadn't got a C. 173:12
hate him for he is a C. 201:14
lawful for C. men 172:15
naturally C. 231:9
of all C. kings 191:5
Onward, C. soldiers 18:7
persuadest me to be a C. 34:51
souls of C. people 61:13
to form C. men 12:13
wastin' C. kisses 126:12
you were a C. slave 102:15
Christianity: begins by loving C. 67:4
faults of the age come from C. 16:1
his C. was muscular 76:16
Christians: blood of C. is seed 231:10
call themselves C. 166:28
C., awake 50:14
Onward, C. 242:5
Christmas: At C. play 234:7
C. comes but once a year 234:7
C. Day in the workhouse 217:5
C. is coming 3:20
C. should fall out in the Middle of
Winter 1:9
eating a C. pie 156:11
On C. Day in the morning 3:14
Christopher Robin: C. is saying his
prayers 143:15
C. went down with Alice 143:7
Chronicle small beer 204:27
Chronicles: abstracts and brief c. 187:9
Chub: chavender, or c. 178:13
Chubby: Augustus was a c. lad 105:15
Chuck: C. him out 127:21
C. it, Smith 61:13
dearest c. 199:6
Chunking: 'ear their paddles c. 126:11
Church: At Trinity C. 90:16
bells have knoll'd to c. 183:19
Catholick and Apostolick C. 167:19
c. with psalms must shout 103:18
C.'s one foundation 222:1
Come all to c. 111:1
figure in a country c.? 223:4
loving his own sect or c. 67:4
no salvation exists outside the c. 13:7

not been in the inside of a c. 114:12
stands the C. clock 42:9
whole state of Christ's C. 167:20
will I build my c. 31:33
Church-door: Housbondes at c.,
she hadde fyve 60:16
Churches: chapels had been c. 201:9
Churchyard: lie in Mellstock c. 100:3
Churlish: reply c. 184:14
Cigar: good c. is a Smoke 124:14
Cinara: when poor C. was queen 110:4
Cinders: c., ashes, dust 120:15
sat among the c. 156:12
Circle: weave a c. round him 66:15
wheel is come full c. 196:8
Circle-citadels there 107:16
Circled: in her c. orb 207:24
Circulating library in a town 216:8
Circumcised dog 205:20
Circumlocution Office 74:18
Circumspice: si monumentum re-
quiris, c. 250:1
Circumstance: fell clutch of c. 102:13
pomp, and c. 205:10
slave of c. 52:8
such perilous c. 186:1
Circumstances: concatenation of c. 240:5
creature of c. 100:11
Circumstantial: C. evidence 233:9
lie c. 184:14
Circus: bread, and the games of the
c. 119:8
Cistern: wheel be broken at the c. 27:8
Citadel: with peaceful c. 120:21
Cite: devil can c. Scripture 201:16
Cities: c. of men 230:13
flower of c. all 80:14
He saw the c. of many men 106:17
Seven c. warr'd for Homer 105:1
Towered c. 144:18
Citizen: c. of no mean city 34:47
first requisite of a good c. 177:1
Roman c. 63:18
Citizens: heat of fellow c. 109:19
City: C. now doth..wear 249:4
C. of Dreadful Night 233:3
c. of our God 154:2
c. that is set on a hill 30:13
corrupting the youth of the c. 163:7
decline and fall of the c. 90:12
depart out of that..c 31:12
except the Lord keep the c. 26:4, 171:22
falling on the c. brown 41:7
first c. Cain 69:18
hope of the C. of God 141:5
I John saw the holy c. 37:25
long in c. pent 122:2
long in populous c. pent 146:22
many a noble c. 58:22
of no mean c. 34:47
on the field and c. 231:17
rose-red c. 46:26
so improved the c. 52:21
that great c. 37:21
that sweet C. 12:1
through the c. 170:1
Towery c. 107:11
upper ten thousand of the c. 244:9
venal c. 179:1
very famous c. 67:19
City Road: Up and down the C. 138:2
Civet: ounce of c. 195:21
Civil: assent with c. leer 165:6
c. to folk he ne'er saw 10:8
Too c. by half 216:13
What dire effects from c. discord
flow 1:16
Civilities: bandy c. with my Sovereign 114:23

Civility: I see a wild c. 104:11
Civilization: great elements of modern c. 55:5
Civilized by man 142:12
Civis Romanus sum 63:18
Clad: c. in the beauty 138:13
naked every day he c. 95:12
Claim: last territorial c. 105:8
Claims: thousand c. to reverence 230:1
Clair: ce qui n'est pas c. 175:13
Clamour: And with the c. 208:7
public will always c. for 107:5
Clamouring for what is wrong 109:19
Clamours: dread c. counterfeit 205:10
Clap on Dutch bottoms 54:12
Clapper: tongue is the c. 204:11
Clapper-clawing: and one another c. 49:27
Clara threw the twins 96:10
Clarence is come 207:8
Claret is the liquor for boys 115:20
Clarion: cock's shrill c. 97:11
shall blow her c. 214:1
Sound, sound the c. 150:3
Clasp: deadly terrors c. 39:2
Clasps: gross c. 204:18
He c. the crag 226:9
Classes: masses against the c. 94:5
ye lower middle c.! 91:16
Clause: servant with this c. 103:22
Claw: in tooth and c. 227:13
Claws: c. that catch 57:14
pair of ragged c. 81:18
Clay: Hark you, John C. 118:10
house of c. 83:12
of c. and wattles made 250:9
potter and c. endure 45:5
tenement of c. 79:5
that wraps their c. 67:15
turn'd to c. 189:21
Clean: c. hearth 129:6
c., verb active 75:2
did not love c. linen 114:10
hands ne'er be c.? 199:29
I shall be c. 169:26
licked the platter c. 156:5
Make me a c. heart 169:27
small and white and c. 150:14
Then I was c. and brave 110:18
took them c. away 157:15
wash this blood c. 198:15
Cleaned: I c. the windows 93:10
Cleanliness is..next to godliness' 241:19
Cleans: who c. the boots 91:9
Cleanse the stuff'd bosom 200:1
Cleansed: If the doors of perception were c. 39:21
Clear: as c. as a whistle 50:13
bells they sound so c. 110:19
came upon the midnight c. 181:10
c. as the sun 27:19
c. blue sky 101:11
c. call 141:3, 226:6
c. fire 129:6
hath been so c. 198:4
how thin and c. 229:11
in honour c. 164:25
is as c. as the day 172:1
one c. call for me! 226:6
One truth is c. 164:17
sad thoughts doth c. 235:9
stain'd the water c. 39:8
they could get it c. 57:21
very loud and c. 58:6
What is not c. 175:13
Cleared: were only c. away 57:21
Clearing-house of the world 59:13
Clears: c. us of this deed 198:16
fill the Cup that c. 85:3

Cleave: c. to the roof of my mouth 171:28
c. unto his wife 23:14
Cleaves: Argo c. the main 213:12
Cleft: c. for me 233:23
who c. the Devil's foot 77:16
Clementine: and his daughter C. 149:7
Clenches: degenerating into c. 80:3
Cleopatra: some squeaking C. 182:23
Cléopâtre: nez de C...plus court 161:4
Clergy: without the benefit o' the C. 68:7
Clergymen: men, women, and c. 217:17
to have with c. to do 78:24
Clerical: on lissom, c., printless toe 42:6
Clerk: 'Baccy for the C. 127:10
C. ther was of Oxenford 60:13
saw a Banker's c. 56:9
this one upstart c. 103:13
Clever: all the good people were c. 245:13
c. men at Oxford 96:17
c. so rude to the good 245:13
who can be c. 123:14
Client: here..is our c. 78:13
Cliff: from c. and scar 229:11
Cliffs: solitary c. wheeled by me 246:6
Climate: is much more common where the c.'s sultry 51:11
Climates: And manners, c. 230:11
Climax of vice 119:2
Climb: c. not at all 82:17, 174:14
Fain would I c. 174:14
whose last steps I c. 213:15
Climbing after knowledge 139:10
Climbs: slow moon c. 230:15
Climb'st: thou c. the skies! 216:30
Clime: happy fire-side c. 48:9
that sweet golden c. 39:7
Climes: cloudless c. 52:12
Cling: I'll c. to you 143:5
to thy Cross I c. 234:1
Clinging heaven 232:10
Clings to many 119:6
Clink: Let me the canakin c. 204:29
Clip an angel's wings 120:16
Clive: what I like about C. 22:10
Cloak: knyf under the c. 60:17
with his martial c. 245:5
without my c. 211:3
Clock: by Shrewsbury c. 190:26
c. in the belfry 249:9
c. struck one 155:18
c. will strike 138:14
forgot to wind up the c.? 220:13
mouse ran up the c. 155:18
Stands the Church c. 42:9
Clod: become a kneaded c. 200:23
Clods: man harrowing c. 100:4
Cloistered: fugitive and c. virtue 148:9
Close: C. beside a leafy thicket 131:3
c. me in 168:34
c. the shutters fast 70:18
c. the wall up 191:8
c. upon the growing boy 246:11
c. your eyes 66:15
draw the curtain c. 192:8
hush in the c. tonight 153:6
porpoise c. behind us 57:7
Stick c. to your desks 93:11
stick more c. 127:19
Swift to its c. 135:16
walking c. at hand 57:21
Closed his eyes in endless night 98:11
Closer: friend that sticketh c. 26:21
Closet: in the C. lays 85:10
Closing: Before my c. eyes 135:17
diapason c. full 79:16
Cloth: coarse c. she saw 70:22
On a c. untrue 92:9
Clothed C., and in his right mind 32:30
C. in white samite 226:16

Clothed (*cont.*)
is c. with derision 224:2
Naked, and ye c. me 32:16
Clothes: Hanging out the c. 158:1
Her c. spread wide 189:18
Kindles in c. a wantonness 104:11
liquefaction of her c. 104:15
Nothing to wear but c. 123:10
She wears her c. 223:13
spoiling her nice new c. 156:12
walked away with their c. 76:7
When he put on his c. 95:12
Clothing: c. is of wrought gold 169:19
in sheep's c. 31:3
Cloth-of-gold of tissue 182:15
Cloud: c. . . like a man's hand 25:12
c. of witnesses 36:35
Do you see yonder c. 188:18
lift me as . . a c.! 214:3
lonely as a c. 247:3
On a c. I saw a child 39:8
one silvery c. 229:4
set my bow in the c. 23:23
swift c. to fly 214:3
through the dark c. 87:4
When the c. is scattered 213:16
will c. into night 100:4
Clouded: c. with a doubt 227:3
through his c. heaven 247:18
upon our c. hills? 38:16
Clouding: sea rising, nor sky c. 41:8
Cloudless: Of c. climes 52:12
Clouds: c. ye so much dread 70:6
deep thunder c. form 96:19
Never doubted c. would break 45:10
O c., unfold! 38:16
Pack, c., away 105:2
Sees God in c. 164:14
trailing c. of glory 246:11
tumult in the c. 250:7
White c. on the wing 2:18
with c. descending 241:16
Cloud-topped: Behind the c. hill 164:14
Cloudy: And the skies are not c. 105:5
be among her c. trophies 120:24
Huge c. symbols 122:4
Clover: knee deep in c. 129:13
Clown: by emperor and c. 121:6
Cloy: other women c. 182:16
Club: best c. in London 75:12
Clubable: very c. man 116:4
Clusters of the vine 140:6
Clutch: fell c. of circumstance 102:13
let me c. thee 198:9
we c. thee! 232:9
Coach: Come, my c.! 189:10
drive a c. and six 175:11
indifference and a c. and six! 67:16
Coaches: and four-horse c. 108:9
Coach-house: with a double c. 218:17
Coal: cargo of Tyne c. 140:21
England's own c. 124:15
Coals: Heap c. of fire 26:24
Coarse cloth she saw 70:22
Coast: near the shadowy c. 232:11
On the c. of Coromandel 130:19
Coaster: Dirty British c. 140:21
Coat: c. is so warm 156:3
c. of many colours 23:32
His c. was red 218:16
riband to stick in his c. 44:9
sake of a ribboned c. 153:6
with his c. so gray? 97:2
Coats: a hole in a' your c. 48:29
Cobbler should not judge 163:13
Cobham: brave C.! 164:22
Cock: before the c. crow 32:19
C. and a Bull 220:18
c. that crowed in the morn 158:8

c.'s shrill clarion 97:11
Crito, we owe a c. 218:7
crowing of the c. 185:4
Diminish'd to her c. 195:19
head-waiter at the C. 231:4
Cock-a-diddle-dow 208:9
Cock a doodle doo! 155:7
Cock-horse: Ride a c. 157:17
Cockle shells: silver bells, and c. 156:16
Cockles and mussels! 5:8
Cockney: much of C. impudence 178:8
Cockpit: this c. hold the vasty fields 191:3
Cock) Robin: Who killed C.? 159:4
Cocks: drown'd the c.! 195:4
Cocksure of anything 141:18
Cod: home of the bean and the c. 40:11
Coddle: would not c. the child 114:26
Coeli: et ruant c. 239:4
Coelitus: emitte c. lucis tuæ radium 130:5
Cœur: Le c. a ses raisons 161:7
Coffee: with c. spoons 81:17
Coffin: On my black c. 209:9
Cogimur: omnes eodem c. 109:11
Cogito, ergo sum 73:15
Cohort of the damned 125:6
Cohorts: his c. were gleaming 52:9
Coign of vantage 198:2
Coil: Lulled by the c. 214:2
off this mortal c. 187:13
Coin: pays him in his own c. 223:19
Coincidence: long arm of c. 59:17
Cold: Alpine mountains c. 147:16
beg c. comfort 193:7
caught an everlasting c. 240:13
c. and heavy mist 106:21
c. as paddocks 104:16
c. doth not sting 152:6
c. in the earth 41:15
c. untroubled heart 54:4
cup of c. water 31:17
Fallen c. and dead 242:11
foot and hand go c. 221:24
heart grown c. 213:8
in his c. grave 60:18
It is c. winter's night 16:18
it is very c. 186:2
lie c. and low 214:1
lie in c. obstruction 200:23
never let his soup get c. 105:15
one c. winter's day 105:15
(penny ice and c. meat) 91:25
shake against the c. 211:8
shelter me from the c. 22:1
Three winters c. 211:13
'tis bitter c. 185:2
was a-c. 120:2
wind was c. 180:4
Colder: C. thy kiss 52:16
pleasanter the c. 50:4
Coldly she turns 149:17
Cole: Old King C. 157:2
Coleridge said 129:9
Coliseum: While stands the C. 51:6
Collateral: puff c. 216:1
Collections: mutilators of c. 129:7
College: I am Master of this c. 20:5
Collusive: puff c. 216:1
Cologne: wash your city of C. 66:9
Colonel: C. of the Knuts 244:14
C.'s Lady 126:8
Colonies: My hold of the c. 47:6
Colonnade: of the cool c. 70:7
Colonus: Singer of sweet C. 11:14
Colossal: decay of that c. wreck 214:7
Colossus: cut a C. from a rock 116:5
Like a C. 193:11
Colour: an effect of c. 107:18
c. she abhors 209:14
giveth his c. in the cup 26:23

her c. is natural 216:16
horse of that c. 209:8
Colours: coat of many c. 23:32
in gay, fine c. 103:4
Under whose c. 207:2
Column: a steamy c. 70:18
fifth c. 148:13
men of the c. 123:13
Comb: With a c. and a glass in her hand 6:20
Combattu: nous avons c. à Arques 103:1
Combined: knotted and c. locks 186:7
Combines the manners of a Marquis 93:25
Combustion: and c. down 145:12
Come: c. again with joy 171:21
C. all to church 111:1
C., all ye faithful 159:6
c. and buy 104:8
C., and he cometh 31:5
C., and trip it 144:13
c. away 27:16
C. back! c. back! 54:1
C., fill the cup 84:17
C. hither 14:4
C. Hup! 222:15
C. on and hear 22:17
c. out of Nazareth? 33:48
C. over into Macedonia 34:39
C. unto me 31:20
C. up and see me 241:21
C. when you're called 80:21
C. with old Khayyám 85:6
c. ye in peace 180:11
c. ye in war 180:11
compel them to c. in 33:18
Curates, long dust, will c. and go 42:6
death will c. when it will c. 193:14
dreaming on things to c. 211:14
from the wrath to c.? 30:5
I knew he'd c. 106:4
I will c. 111:1
in a life to c. 164:14
is to c. 37:16
King of glory shall c. in 169:4
let 'em all c.! 128:28
look brighter when we c. 51:13
love is c. to me 177:8
mine hour is not yet c. 33:49
nor things to c. 35:10
O c., O c., Emmanuel 152:15
oxen are c. about me 168:34
seen it c. and go 216:16
Shape of Things to C. 241:4
she'll c. to you 19:26
Softly c. 159:14
Suffer me to c. to thee 241:12
therefore I cannot c. 33:16
Thy kingdom c. 30:22
till the boys c. home 87:4
time has c. 57:22
'tis not to c. 189:26
to this favour she must c. 189:20
What's to c. is still unsure 209:5
whistle, and I'll c. to you 49:3
will they c. 190:17
Will you no c. back 106:8
worst is yet to c. 113:13
Comedy: world is a c. 238:7
Comely: black, but c. 27:12
bowed his c. head 140:9
how c. it is 147:6
Comes: C. at the last 206:15
C. the blind Fury 145:1
Lo! he c. with clouds descending 241:16
rainbow c. and goes 246:8
w'en de great day c. 101:1
Comest: Rarely, rarely, c. thou 215:7
when thou c. into thy kingdom 33:40

Cometh: c. unto you 217:2
Him that c. to me 34:5
night c. 34:11
no man c. unto the Father 34:19
tell whence it c. 33:50
whence c. my help 171:16
Comets: there are no c. seen 193:14
Comfort: another c. like to this 204:28
beg cold c. 193:7
c. me with apples 271:5
c. ye my people 28:11
naught for your c. 61:14
of c. and despair 212:4
Of c. no man speak 206:14
rod and staff me c. still 181:8
rod and thy staff c. me 169:2
that c. cruel men 61:20
tidings of c. and joy 4:12
to c., and command 248:5
waters of c. 169:2
Comfortable: c. estate of widowhood 89:12
Comfortably: liv'd c. so long together 89:9
Speak ye c. 28:11
Comforted: hath c. his people 28:19
they shall be c. 30:11
Comforters: miserable c. 25:32
Comforts: and c. flee 135:16
Comic wit degenerating 80:3
Comical: I often think it's c. 91:21
Coming: and thy c. in 171:18
c. of the Lord 111:15
c. to the sacrifice? 120:21
do you see anything c.? 162:8
eye will mark our c. 51:13
Hold the fort, for I am c. 39:22
I'm c., I'm c. 87:12
my c. down 150:4
she-bear, c. up the street 86:19
She is c. 228:20
true love's c. 209:5
who c. after me 33:47
Command: And, wide as his c. 79:3
at heaven's c. 232:13
but to c. 206:3
more invitation than c. 220:5
not in mortals to c. success 1:4
That shall c. my heart 70:27
to comfort, and c. 248:5
Commandest: Give what thou c. 13:5
Commandment of the Magistrate 172:15
Commandments: holy will and c. 167:32
keep his c. 27:10
Where there aren't no Ten C. 126:11
Commands the beauteous files 235:7
Commencement de la fin 225:4
Commend: all our swains c. her? 210:2
I c. my spirit 33:42
to blame, or to c. 165:6
to c. their friend 117:12
Comment is free 179:17
Commentators each dark passage shun 250:14
Commerce: In matters of c. 54:12
wealth and c. 138:4
whole of that c. 46:28
Commit: his body to the deep 172:10
that themselves c. 201:23
we c. thee 168:16
Commodities: levied upon c. 116:14
Common: breathing of the c. wind 248:20
c. task 122:14
every c. sight 246:7
happiness of the c. man 23:3
Is much more c. 51:11
light of c. day 246:11
nor lose the c. touch 125:16
not already c. 133:6
nothing c. did 140:8
Commonplace, said Holmes 78:21

Commons faithful to their system 137:12
Common-sense: Rich in saving c. 228:25
Commonwealth: C. last for a thou-
  sand years 62:22
  C. of Nations 177:5
Communication: Let your c. be 30:17
Communications: Evil c. 35:27
Communities: hated all nations..
  and c. 223:6
Compact: imagination all c. 203:19
Compacted: sweets c. lie 104:7
Companion of the body 99:3
Companions: her lovely c. 149:18
  I have had c. 129:16
  old c. in adversity 45:16
Company: commonly better c. 114:6
  c. of the heavenly host 38:13
  conversation in a mixed c. 61:12
  crowd is not c. 14:14
  Crowds without c. 90:11
  except the present c. 159:11
  In sooth a goodly c. 17:11
  in that man's c. 192:4
  justice from a c. 217:19
  out of the ladies' c. 182:6
  Take the tone of the c. 61:6
  three is c. and two none 243:8
  To bear him c. 134:12
  Vandyke is of the c. 88:13
  With a goodly c. 66:6
  with-outen any c. 60:18
Compare: can c. unto thee! 212:7
  c. thee to a summer's day? 210:12
  no place can c. 244:11
  there's none that can c. 7:7
Comparisons: c. are odious 77:3
  c. are odorous 204:13
Compass: all the c. of the notes 79:16
  bending sickle's c. 211:16
  c. of the world 169:3
  little and certain c. 40:4
  to the top of my c. 188:17
Compassed: we also are c. about 36:35
Compel: and c. them to come in 33:18
Competition: all forms of c. 64:9
Complain: by the tide of Humber
  would c. 140:11
  heard him c. 239:12
  to the moon c. 97:9
Complaining: soft c. flute 79:17
Complete: c. freedom of movement 174:2
  c. in itself 10:16
  more than c. steel 139:15
Completer: Stolen kisses much c. 112:5
Complexion: for my c. 201:19
  his gold c. dimm'd 210:12
  That schoolgirl c. 7:11
Complicated state of mind 92:21
Complies: He that c. against his will 50:3
Composition: Mad c.! 193:3
Compositions: Read over your c. 115:1
Compound for sins 49:19
Comprehend: faculties can c. 139:10
Comprehended: darkness c. it not 33:44
Comprehends some bringer 203:19
Comprehensive: most c. soul 80:3
Comprendre: tout c. 219:22
Comrade: c. of thy wanderings 214:3
  new-hatch'd, unfledg'd c. 185:21
Comrades chase e'en now the fliers 64:10
Concatenation: Fearful c. 240:5
Concave: tore hell's c. 146:6
Conceal: cannot all c. 51:7
Concealed: in yon smoke c. 64:10
Concealment, like a worm 209:10
Conceit: and vain c. 206:15
  forms to his c.? 187:11
  to his own c. 187:11
Conceive: c. a melancholy book 70:21

I c. you may use 91:23
  tongue to c. 203:18
  virgin shall c. 27:30
Conceived: hath my mother c. me 169:25
  invented what I c. 112:12
Conceives delight 146:22
Concentrated all in self 180:6
Concentrates: it c. his mind 115:13
Concern: and its largest c. 12:9
  matter they had no c. in 223:22
Concert: Saints on earth in c. sing 241:17
Concluded: case is c. 13:11
Conclusion: a foregone c. 205:11
Conclusive: verdict of the world is c. 13:6
Concord: c. of sweet sounds 202:13
  lover of c. 166:14
Concordia discors 108:10
Concurrence of atoms 160:16
Condemn: c. you to death 56:14
  neither do I c. thee 34:7
  nor the years c. 38:2
Condemned: C. alike to groan 98:9
  you yourself are much c. 194:15
Condemns neatness of apparel 241:19
Condition: as any man..in that c. 162:5
  shall gentle his c. 192:4
  whine about their c. 242:14
Conditions: sorts and c. of men 166:27
Conduct: c. is three-fourths of our
  life 12:9
  c. to the prejudice of good order 3:23
  sometimes our c. 127:23
  under Teucer's c. 108:19
Cones: And eat the c. 88:9
  with c. upon them 134:4
Confederate: in games C. 246:5
Conference a ready man 14:26
Confessed: before the world c. 111:12
  ev'rywhere c. 116:27
Confidence: expected with c. 74:12
  fight with growing c. 62:21
Confident: glad c. morning 44:12
Confined: c. from home 164:14
  cribb'd, c. 199:8
Confinement: keep her in c.! 119:5
Confines: Shall in these c. 193:21
Confirmations strong 205:8
Conflict: field of human c. 62:23
Confound their politics 55:1
Confounded: confusion worse c. 146:13
Confused: unformed and c. 160:5
Confusedly: Ribbands to flow c. 104:11
Confusion: C. on thy banners wait 97:4
  C. worse confounded 146:13
Confute: how to c. him 181:13
Congrès: Le c. ne marche pas 132:5
Conjecture: are not beyond all c. 43:1
Conned: learn'd and c. by rote 194:18
Conquer: cannot c. America 162:19
  fight and we'll c. 88:13
  shalt thou c. 68:22
  She stoops to c. 95:23
  we will c. 20:3
  wont to c. others 206:9
Conquered: c. at last 163:15
  I came, I saw, I c. 53:2
  perpetually to be c. 46:29
  Thou hast c. 118:18, 224:10
  to have c...half the world 181:12
Conquering hero comes! 150:10
Conqueror: proud foot of a c. 193:8
Conquest: C.'s crimson wing 97:4
  shameful c. of itself 206:9
Conquests: Are all thy c...shrunk 193:18
  carnage and c. cease! 50:18
Conscience: C. avaunt 63:7
  c. doth make cowards 187:13
  c. of the king 187:12
  corporation to have a c. 233:15

next to a good c. 238:15
Nonconformist c. 20:9, 243:17
some c. of what they did 71:5
Whose c. with injustice 192:7
Conscious stone to beauty grew 82:15
Consecrate: cannot c...this ground 132:8
Consecrated: not buried in c. ground 100:9
Consecration, and the poet's dream 247:13
Consent: all with one c. 208:28
I will ne'er c. 51:12
Consequence: servitude is at once the c. 71:17
trammel up the c. 198:3
Consequences: c. will be..what they will be 49:15
damn the c. 143:19
Conservative: Or else a little C.! 91:21
Consider it not so deeply 198:11
Considerably agitated 75:29
Consideration: on carpet c. 209:18
Considered: ne'er c. it, as loth 49:20
Considering: C. how to run my c. cap 71:1; 19:17
Consolation: c. in a distressed one 13:17
peace and c. 147:11
Conspire: with Fate c. 86:1
Conspiring with him how to load 119:17
Constabulary: When c. duty's to be done 93:21
Constant: c. as the northern star 193:16
One here will c. be 46:20
To one thing c. never 204:9
Whose c. cares 106:14
Constitution: does not agree with my c. 233:6
Every country has its own c. 4:7
principle of the English c. 38:7
venerable parts of our c. 47:7
Constraint: Bitter c. 144:20
by c. of Heaven 236:3
Constructing tribal lays 125:13
Construction: To find the mind's c. 197:13
Consule: natam me c. 63:24
Consult Brother Jonathan 239:3
Consumed the midnight oil? 89:27
Consummation: 'tis a c. 187:13
Consummatum est 34:28
Contagion: c. of the world's slow stain 213:8
foul c. spread 145:3
Contain: c., and nourish all the world 196:16
I c. multitudes 242:15
Contemned: Utterly be c. 27:20
Contemplates: thing it c. 215:1
Contemplation: Beneath thy c. 152:14
For c. he and valour 146:16
Contempt: no c. 147:10
pour c. on all my pride 239:16
Content: C. to breathe his native air 165:14
Farewell c! 205:10
he's c. with a vegetable love 92:22
My soul hath her c. 204:28
Oh sweet c.! 72:18
to c. you 203:20
travellers must be c. 183:10
with equal advantage c. 54:12
Contented: c. least 210:13
c. with their cells 247:12
king shall be c. 206:16
then ye c. your souls 126:1
Contentment: Preaches c. 126:20
Continency: gift of c. 168:8
Give me..c. 13:3
Thou imposest c. 13:5
Continent: brought forth upon this c. 132:8
C. will not suffer 76:6
overspread the c. 159:20

Continents: three separate c. 78:15
Continue thine for ever 168:4
Continued: begun, c., and ended 167:29
Continueth: their work c. 127:15
Continuous as the stars 247:4
Contradict: Do I c. myself? 242:15
Contradictions: bundle of c. 68:2
Contrapshun what he call a Tar-Baby 100:18
'Contrariwise' continued Tweedledee 57:19
Contrary: goes c. with me 74:5
runneth not to the c. 132:14
trial is by what is c. 148:9
Contrite: broken and c. heart 169:28
humble and a c. heart 127:4
Contrive: Nature always does c. 91:21
Contrived by man 115:7
Control: lease of my true love c. 211:14
Contumely: proud man's c. 187:13
Convent: at their c.'s narrow room 247:12
Conversation: c. in a mixed company 61:12
in c. with Her Majesty 76:13
John Wesley's c. is good 115:15
Conversations: without pictures or c.? 56:10
Conversion: Till the c. of the Jews 140:11
Convert: shall c. my life 169:2
Converted: Except ye be c. 31:37
Convincing: And thought of c. 95:18
Convoy: crowns for c. 192:4
Coodle: Lord C. would go out 73:27
Cook: c. was a good c. 178:15
Duke's son—c.'s son 124:11
Groom, the Butler and the C. 91:9
I am a c. 91:3
Cool: cheeks which they did c. 182:15
c. kindliness of sheets 41:17
c. of the day 23:15
c. repentance came 181:1
of the c. colonnade 70:7
so c., so calm 104:6
Cooled: c. a long age 121:3
warmed and c. 201:27
Coolibah: shade of a c. tree 161:12
Coop't: Whereunder crawling c. 85:13
Coot: haunts of c. and hern 225:17
Copernicus: and C. [was misunder-stood] 82:21
Cophetua: When King C. 207:19
Copper: C. for the craftsman 124:19
hot and c. sky 65:12
Cor: ulterius c. lacerare nequit 223:27
Coral: C. is far more red 212:3
India's c. strand 101:15
of his bones are c. made 208:11
Corbies: I heard twa c. 16:19
Cord: Or ever the silver c. 27:8
Cordelia: my child C. 196:3
Core: beg the c. 234:19
In my heart's c. 188:11
Corinth: that can get to C. 108:11
Corioli: Volscians in C. 184:19
Cormorant devouring Time 196:13
Corn: amid the alien c. 121:6
better stop raising c. 131:16
c. was orient 234:2
cow's in the c. 156:10
fields of c. where Troy 160:4
like ripe c. 177:16
make two ears of c. 223:2
so thick with c. 170:3
sowing his c. 158:8
there was c. in Egypt 23:34
treadeth out the c. 24:20
Corner: c. in the thing I love 205:7
c. of heaven 244:11
from the chimney c. 217:2
head-stone in the c. 171:15

Corner (cont.)
sat in the c.   156:11
Sits the wind in that c.?   204:10
there's some c. of a foreign field   42:11
world in ev'ry c. sing   103:18
Corners: all the c. of the earth   170:22
imagined c.   77:8
three c. of the world   193:8
Cornet: sound of the c.   29:16
Cornfield: o'er the green c.   184:12
Cornish: twenty thousand C. men   101:6
Coromandel: On the coast of C.   130:19
Coronet: her c. weeds   189:18
Coronets: more than c.   227:22
crowns and c.   191:5
Corporal sufferance   200:21
Corporation: expect a c. to have a
conscience   233:15
Corps: ce c. qui s'appelait..le saint
empire romain   237:16
Corpse: frozen c. was he   134:13
like a c.   214:1
lovely c.   74:23
Corpulent man of fifty   112:7
Correct: All present and c.   3:8
Correggios: Raphaels, C., and stuff   95:19
Corridors: Through the c. of Time   133:14
Corrival: wear without c.   190:9
Corroborative: Merely c. detail   92:13
Corrupt: c. good manners   35:27
c. the minds   162:18
Power tends to c.   1:1
progeny yet more c.   109:23
should c. the world   227:1
Corrupted: with injustice is c.   192:7
Corruptible must put on incorrup-
tion   35:30
Corruption: turned into c.   172:10
Corse: As his c. to the rampart   245:3
My poor c.   209:9
Cortez: like stout C.   121:9
Cossack commanders cannonading
come   3:10
Cost: rich-proud c.   211:6
whatever the c. may be   62:21
Coster: When the c.'s finished   93:23
Costly thy habit   185:21
Cottage: before his c. door   218:12
c. of gentility!   218:17
He passed a c.   218:17
Love and a C.   67:16
there's a c. small   160:21
Cottages: poor men's c.   201:9
Cotton is King   62:6
Cotton-tail, and Peter   165:22
Couch: on my c. I lie   247:5
There I c.   208:20
Couch grass: From the heaps of c.   100:4
Coughing drowns the parson's saw   196:20
Councils: climates, c., governments   230:13
wisdom from our c.   47:7
Counsel: darkeneth c. by words   25:39
sometimes c. take   165:3
spirit of c.   28:1
Counsellor: shall be called..C.   27:32
Counsellors: In the multitude of c.   26:12
Counsels: all good c.   166:18
By his c. guide   175:2
Mix with your sage c.   110:7
Count: all men c. with you   125:16
I c. but loss   239:16
I c. myself   206:10
Counted: c. them at break of day   51:19
we c. our spoons   82:17
Countenance: cheerful c.   26:17, 171:2
c. more in sorrow   185:18
did the C. Divine   38:16
disinheriting c.   216:20
fiery sighs, and sorrowful c.   49:10

grim grew his c.   16:5
Knight of the Sorrowful C.   59:8
lift up his c.   24:13
light of his c.   170:4
of a beautiful c.   24:43
Counter: All things c.   107:15
Countercheck quarrelsome   184:14
Counterfeit: c. a gloom   144:7
dread clamours c.   205:10
Counterpane: pleasant land of c.   221:10
Countest: Who c. the steps of the
sun   39:7
Counties: And see the coloured c.   110:19
Forget six c.   150:14
Counting out his money   158:1
Counting-house: King was in his c.   158:1
Countries: preferreth all c. before
his own   160:1
Country: after the fashion of their
c.   222:11
Anybody can be good in the c.   243:22
Born and educated in this c.   90:7
By all their c.'s wishes   67:14
children of our c.   177:17
c. green   121:3
c. he has turned into a desert   47:11
c. in town   139:24
c. lane   160:21
c. messes   144:15
died to save their c.   21:14
do our c. loss   192:3
every c. but his own   54:13, 92:1
Every c. has the government it
deserves   139:17
figure in a c. church?   223:4
fit c. for heroes   90:3
for his c.'s good   89:25
friend of every c.   54:13
from a far c.   26:25
go down into the c.   243:9
God made the c.   70:14
God's own c.   4:13
good of his c.   249:14
how I love my c.   163:2
I loath the c.   68:18
I love thee still—My C.!   70:15
I vow to thee, my c.   219:18
My c.! oh, my c.!   163:4
My c., 'tis of thee   217:14
My soul, there is a c.   235:7
of his c.'s blood   97:15
on behalf of their c.   178:18
Our c., right or wrong   72:14
pleasant c.'s earth   207:2
pretty c. folks   184:12
pride that pulls the c. down   204:30
save in his own c.   31:29
Saviour of 'is c.   127:21
she is my c. still   62:7
spare your c.'s flag   242:16
stake in the c.   244:16
suck'd on c. pleasures   77:7
their c.'s pride   95:4
to all the c. dear   95:6
to say to his c.   161:1
treason to his c.   116:18
undiscover'd c.   187:13
We left our c. for our c.'s good   18:26
yon far c. blows   111:5
Countrymen: Friends, Romans, c.   194:3
many of your c.   114:7
Courage: All goes if c. goes   18:18
As to moral c.   151:17
C. in your own   96:6
C. is the thing   18:18
c. never to submit   145:15
c. to be wise   108:7
endurance, and c.   179:19
fresh c. take   70:6

my c. and skill | 46:22
my c. prove | 183:3
of a good c. | 24:26
Red Badge of C. | 70:24
screw your c. | 198:7
three-o'clock in the morning c. | 233:7
unprepared c. | 151:17
with a good c. | 169:11
With c., love and joy | 89:17
Courage: c. de l'improviste | 151:17
c.,..le diable est mort! | 175:3
Couragious: captains c. | 16:9
Couriers: sightless c. of the air | 198:14
Course: c. of one revolving moon | 79:8
earth's diurnal c. | 254:14
finished my c. | 36:33
must stand the c. | 195:16
nature's changing c. | 210:12
nature's second c. | 198:13
steer a middle c. | 141:9
to run his c. | 168:30
took the regular c. | 57:5
what c. others may take | 103:10
Young blood must have its c. | 123:18
Courses: planets in their radiant c. | 166:5
stars in their c. | 24:28
Court: before the C. | 73:21
Her c. was pure | 230:1
Keeps Death his c. | 206:15
she will c. you | 117:18
So c. a mistress | 117:18
Talk of c. news | 196:6
Courted by all the winds | 147:5
Courteous: retort c. | 184:14
Courtesy: mirror of all c. | 192:12
very pink of c. | 207:27
Courtier's, soldier's, scholar's, eye | 188:6
Courtly foreign grace | 230:5
Courts: in the c. of the sun | 61:18
into the c. of the Lord | 170:13
keep the C. | 85:1
one day in thy c. | 170:15
Cousins: and his c. and his aunts! | 93:9
Coutts: who banks with C. | 91:9
Covenanted: And they c. with him | 32:18
Cover: cedarn c.! | 66:14
C. her face | 240:8
C. my defenceless head | 241:10
darkness shall c. me | 172:1
green underwood and c. | 223:29
Covered it all over | 174:16
Covers: that c. me | 102:13
Covet: Thou shalt not c. | 64:9, 167:17
Cow: c. is kept for every three acres | 152:24
c. jumped over the moon | 155:17
c. with the crumpled horn | 158:8
friendly c. | 221:13
I never saw a Purple C. | 46:24
Three acres and a c. | 67:9
till the c. comes home | 19:23
Coward: c. does it with a kiss | 243:5
No c. soul is mine | 41:13
Cowards: C. die many times | 193:14
make c. of us all | 187:13
Nonconformist Conscience makes c. | 20:9
Cowper: divine chit-chat of C. | 129:8
Cows in the corn | 156:10
Cowslip: In a c.'s bell | 208:20
Coxcomb: to hear a c. | 178:8
Coy: c., and hard to please | 180:13
Lord, make me c. | 104:5
Coyness: This c., Lady | 140:11
Cozenage: greatest c. | 71:12
Crabbed: C. age and youth | 210:10
c. old censorious men | 58:26

harsh, and c. | 144:2
Crabs: roasted c. hiss | 196:20
set limed twigs for c. | 58:13
Crack: C. nature's moulds | 195:4
to the c. of doom? | 199:23
Cracked: It c. and growled | 65:8
mirror. | 227:25
Crackling of thorns | 26:39
Cracks a noble heart | 190:5
Cradle: Between the c. and the grave | 80:18
c. of the fairy queen? | 203:12
c. will fall | 38:9
c. will rock | 38:9
from the c. to the grave | 70:21
hand that rocks the c. | 238:3
in the c. of the deep | 244:4
In the c. where it lies | 202:1
Out of the c. | 242:12
procreant c. | 198:2
traveller from the c. | 214:10
Craft so long to learn | 105:6
Crag: clasps the c. | 226:9
Crags: among these barren c. | 230:12
At the foot of thy c. | 225:15
Cram Within this wooden O | 191:3
Crammed: just as they..were c. | 247:15
Cramped by narrow means | 119:3
Cranks: Quips and c. | 144:12
Crannied: Flower in the c. wall | 226:12
Crannies: pluck you out of the c. | 226:12
Crave: forbids to c. | 80:17
Craven: Thro' c. fears | 226:14
Crawling: Whereunder c. coop't | 85:13
Crazy: I'm half c. | 72:1
Cream: choking her with c. | 124:7
Do c. and mantle | 201:7
gives me c. | 221:11
Sugar and c. | 155:11
Cream-faced loon! | 199:31
Create: c. he can | 214:9
I c. new heavens | 29:3
must himself c. the taste | 249:6
Created: C. half to rise | 164:19
God c. the heaven | 23:4
Nothing can be c. | 135:8
Thou hast c. us for thyself | 13:2
Creates: hope till Hope c. | 215:1
Creation: false c. | 198:9
from that equal c. | 113:2
Our c., preservation | 166:31
She is His new c. | 222:1
since the c. of the world | 220:13
up and down de whole c. | 87:11
Creator: Remember now thy C. | 27:7
Creators of odd volumes | 129:7
Creature: c. of circumstances | 100:11
Drink, pretty c. | 247:16
excellent c. | 76:15
heaven-eyed c. | 246:3
I am a lone lorn c. | 74:5
kill the poor c. | 89:5
kills a reasonable c. | 148:7
nor any other c. | 35:10
Creatures: All c. great and small | 2:7
death of his fellow-c. | 88:10
delicate c. | 205:7
man is distinguished from all other c. | 1:15
Praise Him, all c. | 123:3
Credat Iudaeus Apella, Non ego | 110:12
Credit: c. for the rest | 62:10
greatly to his c. | 93:13
Have done my c...wrong | 85:15
let the C. go | 84:21
Of c. and renown | 69:21
Credite posteri | 109:15
Creed: His c. no parson ever knew | 78:24
in a c. outworn | 249:5

Creeds: dust of c. outworn   214:8
  in half the c.   227:16
  in our casual c.   11:25
  Vain are the thousand c.   41:14
Creeks: back through c.   64:10
Creep: c. home   123:18
  C. in our ears   202:1
  to make your flesh c.   75:17
  Wit that can c.   165:9
Creeping: c. like snail   183:20
  things c.   171:4
Creeps: C. in this petty pace   200:4
  time c. along   112:17
Creetur: lone lorn c.   74:5
Crept: c. silently to Rest   85:4
  music c. by me   208:10
Cressid: Where C. lay that night   202:9
Crew: c. of the captain's gig   91:3
  darling of our c.   73:19
  ghastly c.   66:2
Cribbed, confin'd   199:8
Cricket: c. on the hearth   144:7
  On his nose there was a C.   131:3
Cried: c. in the streets   150:17
  ev'ry soul c. out   69:28
  nor c. aloud   102:13
  one c. unto another   27:27
  voice of him that c.   27:27
  When Agamemnon c. aloud   81:22
Crier rung the bell   20:1
Cries: full of birds' c.   141:6
  man who turnips c.   116:9
  red rose c.   228:20
  with my bootless c.   210:13
Crieth: the voice of him that c.   28:12
Crillon: Hang yourself, brave C.   103:1
Crime: consequence of his c.   71:17
  c. of being a young man   162:17
  c. to love too well?   164:4
  let the punishment fit the c.   92:8
  Napoleon of c.   78:8
  This coyness were no c.   140:11
  treason was no c.   79:9
  worse than a c.   40:12
Crime: pire qu'un c...une faute   40:12
Crimes: and the worst of c.   212:16
  c. of this guilty land   42:14
  of the c., follies   90:14
  Successful c.   79:26
Crimes: que de c...en ton nom   176:8
Criminal: British c. law   78:7
Crimson: Conquest's c. wing   97:4
  Enthrals the c. stomacher   104:11
  Is c. in thy lips   208:4
Crispian: feast of C.   192:4
Critic, you have frowned   248:1
Critical: nothing if not c.   204:26
Criticism: every wind of c.   116:7
  father of English c.   116:21
Critics: will true c. please   241:20
Critique: kill'd off by one c.   51:25
Crito, we owe a cock   218:7
Croaks the fatal entrance   197:15
Crocodile: c.'s tears   49:10
  How doth the little c.   56:13
Crocodiles: wisdom of the c.   15:6
Crocus brake like fire   229:4
Cromek: O! Mr. C.—, how do ye do?   38:14
Cromwell: Charles the First, his C.   103:9
  C. guiltless of his country's blood   97:15
  that C. knocked about   133:3
Crooked: c. shall be made straight   28:12
  There was a c. man   158:5
Crop: kingly c.   72:12
Crop-headed Parliament swing   43:12
Croppy: Hoppy, c.   88:16
Cross: At the c. her station keeping   233:21
  c. shines forth   87:7
  c. when he comes home   173:19

Hold Thou Thy C.   135:17
  no c. deserves no crown   174:1
  No C., No Crown   162:3
  survey the wondrous C.   239:16
  to thy C. I cling   234:1
  upon a c. of gold   45:15
Cross-bow: With my c.   65:10
Crossed: may be c. in love   216:5
Crosses: E'en c. from his sov'reign
  hand   104:17
Cross-gartered: to see thee ever c.   209:13
Crossing: while c. the river   132:11
  you are c. the Channel   91:24
Cross-patch, Draw the latch   155:9
Crost: I have c. the bar   226:6
Crow: a monstrous c.   57:18
  an upstart c.   98:13
  and the c. makes wing   199:6
Crowd: amid a c. of stars   250:11
  c. into a shade   165:1
  c. is not company   14:14
  Far from the madding c.   98:1
  I saw a c.   247:3
  pass in a c.?   223:4
  uninitiate c.   109:16
Crowded: busy scenes of c. life   117:1
  One c. hour   150:3
Crowding: thy white sails c.   41:8
Crowds: C. without company   90:11
  nor cheering c.   250:7
  talk with c.   125:16
Crowed: that c. in the morn   158:8
Crow-flowers   189:18
Crowing: on the c. of the cock   185:4
Crown: Ambassador from Britain's c.   78:23
  better than his c.   202:5
  broke his c.   156:4
  c. imperial   191:15, 210:8
  c. o' the earth   182:21
  fighting for the c.   156:8
  from the c. to the toe   197:15
  fruition of an earthly c.   139:10
  give thee a c. of life   37:14
  hairy gold c.   128:6
  head that wears a c.   190:30
  holly bears the c.   7:17
  influence of the C. has increased   12:15
  Life's fresh c.   20:1
  no cross deserves no c.   174:1
  No Cross, No C.   162:3
  power of the C. has increased   12:15
  Sceptre and c.   216:24
  sorrow's c. of sorrow   228:7
  strike his father's c.   191:4
  That c. the wat'ry glade   98:5
  this c. of thorns   45:15
  Thy joy and c.   149:1
  tripled C.?   174:3
  within the hollow c.   206:15
Crowned: c. with summer sea   227:3
  Peace is c. with smiles   235:7
  was c. with thorns   122:21
Crowning mercy   71:7
Crowns: c. and coronets   191:5
  c. for convoy   192:4
  c. imperial   191:5
  c. resign   137:15
  end c. all   209:1
  Give c. and pounds   110:16
  I'd c. resign   235:4
  last act c. the play   173:27
  their golden c.   102:1
Crows and choughs   195:19
Crowsfeet: Til c. be growe   60:24
Crucem: iuxta c. lacrimosa   233:21
Crucible: God's C.   251:3
Crucify: thou shalt not c. mankind   45:15
Crucis: fulget c. mysterium   87:7
Crude: harsh and c.   144:20

Cruel: comfort c. men | 61:20
c. men of Rome | 193:9
c., not to trust | 212:1
c., only to be kind | 189:4
Here is c. Frederick | 105:16
Let me be c. | 188:21
Cruellest: April is the c. month | 81:23
Cruelly: I am c. used | 13:20
Cruelty: Of direst c. | 197:15
pride, c., and ambition | 174:16
Crumbs which fell from the ...
table | 31:31, 33:27
Crunch: so..c. on | 44:22
Crush: do c. their wine | 140:6
Crust: upper c. | 93:15
with water and a c. | 120:15
Cry: all should c., Beware | 66:15
any loud c. | 56:2
but that we still should c. | 15:15
But (when..thou canst not sadder)
c. | 232:10
C., baby, c. | 155:10
c. goes up, 'How long?' | 222:2
C., 'Havoc!' | 193:21
c. of his hounds | 97:2
c. unto the Lord | 171:8
cuckoo's parting c. | 12:2
do not c. | 73:1
harlot's c. | 38:12
I heard a voice c. | 198:13
in glorious c. | 84:11
made them c. | 155:15
makes me c. to tell | 106:1
Need a body c.? | 48:11
no language but a c. | 227:11
ripe, ripe, I c. | 104:8
sickening c. | 61:16
stones would..c. out | 33:35
sudden c. of pain! | 220:9
swoon'd, nor utter'd c. | 229:15
War is still the c. | 50:20
we c., Abba, Father | 35:7
What shall I c.? | 28:13
when owls do c. | 208:20
when we c. to Thee | 242:9
Crying: c. at the lock | 143:4
c. with all her might | 143:11
heavenly host c. | 38:13
infant c. in the night | 227:11
no more..c. | 37:26
voice of one c. | 30:4
Crystal: river of c. light | 84:3
Cuckoo: C., jug-jug | 152:6
c. then, on every tree | 196:19
c.'s parting cry | 12:2
In spring-time from the c.-bird | 248:8
O C.! Shall I call Thee bird | 245:15
weather the c. likes | 100:5
Cuckoo-buds of yellow hue | 196:19
Cudgel thy brains | 189:19
Cue: With a twisted c. | 92:9
Cuff neglectful | 104:11
Cui bono | 63:22
Culpa: O felix c. | 148:12
Cultivate our garden | 237:13
Cultivated: celebrated, C., Under-
rated | 91:6
c. entirely by the spade | 142:24
Culture: man of c. rare | 92:20
pursue C. in bands | 241:22
Whenever I hear the word c. | 117:5
Cumbered about much serving | 33:9
Cunctando: Unus homo..c. | 83:5
Cunning: c. at his trade | 124:19
forget her c. | 171:28
is as c. as you | 119:5
Cup: Ah, fill the C. | 85:8
colour in the c. | 26:23
Come, fill the C. | 84:17

Come fill up my c. | 179:20
c. of cold water | 31:17
c. shall be full | 169:2
Fill high the c. | 51:21
fill the C. that clears | 85:3
Have drunk their C. | 85:4
in a Shallow C. | 85:15
kiss but in the c. | 117:19
let this c. pass from me | 32:20
my c. overflows | 181:8
Take a c. | 155:9
Cupboard: Went to the c. | 157:3
Cupid: C. and my Campaspe | 135:14
C.'s darts do not feel | 6:6
C.'s fiery shaft | 203:7
Young Adam C. | 207:19
Cupids: all ye Loves and C. | 58:25
like smiling C. | 182:15
Cups: c., that cheer | 70:18
in their flowing c. | 192:4
Cur: ears of the old c. | 49:23
Cura: atra C. | 109:17
Curate: pale young c. | 93:30
Curates: by wild c. | 217:20
C., long dust, will come | 42:6
Curb your magnanimity | 122:11
Curd: white c. of ass's milk? | 165:7
Cure: c. for this ill | 126:4
c. the disease | 14:15
thy life, thy c. | 235:8
Curfew: C. must not ring | 233:10
c. tolls the knell | 97:8
Curiosity: satiable c. | 128:13
Curiouser and curiouser! | 56:12
Curl: make your hair c. | 93:26
Who had a little c. | 134:14
Curled: and c. up on the floor | 101:4
charmingly c. | 123:17
Curly locks | 155:11
Current: take the c. when it serves | 194:19
Currents: c. turn awry | 187:13
Curs of low degree | 95:13
Curse: An orphan's c. | 65:21
and c. my fate | 210:13
C. God, and die | 25:27
c. in a dead man's eye | 65:21
c. is come upon me, | 227:25
c. of marriage! | 205:7
c. to party strife | 245:20
Never was heard such a terrible c.! | 17:13
that c. our race | 91:4
Cursed me with his eye | 65:17
Curses: C. are like young chickens | 218:15
C., not loud | 199:32
Curst: C. be he that moves my
bones | 212:5
C. himself | 218:21
c. the hand | 16:7
Curtain: draw the c. close | 192:8
iron c. | 63:5, 94:11, 234:5
lets the c. fall | 164:3
Ring down the c. | 174:6
Curtains: c. of Solomon | 27:12
Let fall the c. | 70:18
through c. call on us? | 77:18
Curtsey while you're thinking | 57:15
Curtsied when you have | 208:9
Curzon: My name is George
Nathaniel C. | 6:9
Cushion: sit on a c. | 155:11
Custom: Against good c. | 181:20
c. more honour'd in the breach | 186:3
C., that unwritten law | 72:10
nor c. stale | 182:16
one good c. | 227:1
receipt of c. | 31:9
Customers: people of c. | 217:12
Cut: beard of formal c. | 183:20
C c. it | 155:2

Cut (cont.)
   c. and came again   70:22
   c. him out in little stars   208:1
   C. is the branch   139:2
   c. it on his card   127:17
   C. off even in the blossoms of
     my sin   186:12
   c. off out of the land of the living 28:22
   it is c. down   170:17
   laurels all are c.   111:8
   most unkindest c. of all   194:9
   or c. a throat   51:16
   throat they c. from ear to ear   240:3
   to c. a cabbage-leaf   86:19
   to c. any one   58:16
   Your servant's c. in half   96:12
Cyclads: sleep young C.   213:12
Cycle of Cathay   228:15
Cycno: nigro.. simillima c.   119:4
Cymbal: or a tinkling c.   35:20
   talk but a tinkling c.   14:14
Cymbals: upon the loud c.   172:8
   well-tuned c.   172:8
Cynara: faithful to thee, C.   77:26
Cynic: What is a c.?   243:18
Cynosure of neighbouring eyes   144:14
Cypress: In sad c.   209:9
   Nor waves the c.   229:16
   shady c. tree   177:12
Cyprian: forsake her C. groves   79:23
Cytherea: Or C.'s breath   210:8

D

D.: I never use a big, big D.   93:8
Da quod iubes   13:5
Dacian: There was their D. mother   51:5
Daddy's gone a-hunting   155:6
Dads: get leave of your d.   3:22
Daffodils: D. that come before   210:8
   dances with the d.   247:5
   Fair d., we weep to see   104:10
   host of golden d.   247:3
   in the west wind, and d.   141:6
   When d. begin to peer   210:5
Daffy-down-dilly   155:12
Dagger: D. of the mind   198:9
   Is this a d.?   198:9
Daggers: been at d.-drawing   49:27
   d. in men's smiles   198:20
   speak d.   188:21
Daily: D. devours apace   145:3
   d. farther from the east   246:11
   d., nearer God   122:14
   d. rations   74:2
   our d. bread   30:22
   we d. see   101:2
Dainties: not fed of the d.   196:14
Dairy: nightly rob the d.   118:2
Dairymaid: Queen asked the d.   143:13
Daisies: Buttercups and d.   111:17
   d., and long purples   189:18
   d. smell-less   19:24
   lie upon the d.   92:21
   When d. pied   196:19
   with d. pied   144:14
Daisy: D., D., give me your answer
   do   72:1
   There's a d.   189:15
Dale: doxy, over the d.   210:5
   over hill, over d.   203:6
   through wood and d.   66:15
Dalhousie wrote   173:8
Dalliance: primrose path of d.   185:20
   silken d. in the wardrobe   191:5
Dam: pretty chickens and their d.   199:27
Damaged: Archangel, a little d.   129:12
Damask: Feed on her d. cheek   209:10

Dame: d. has lost her shoe   155:7
   one for the d.   155:4
Dame Partington was seen   218:4
Damn: D. braces   39:20
   d. thee black   199:31
   once was a man who said, 'D.'   100:12
Damna tamen.. reparant caelestia
   lunae   110:6
Damnable: by all that's d.!   216:21
Damnation: deep d.   198:4
Damned: be d. perpetually   138:14
   cohort of the d.   125:6
   d. be him   200:12
   D. disinheriting countenance   216:20
   D. from here to Eternity   125:7
   d. nice thing   240:14
   no soul to be d.   233:15
   Publish and be d.   241:2
   silent and all d.!   247:15
   those d. dots   62:17
Damning: by d. those they have
   no mind to   49:19
Damnosa hereditas   88:14
Damozel: blessed d.   177:15
Damp: d. fell round the path of
   Milton   248:2
   d. souls of housemaids   81:20
Damsel with a dulcimer   66:15
Dan: from D. even to Beer-sheba   24:33
Danaos: timeo D.   236:9
Dance: come and join the d.   57:9
   D. and Provençal song   121:3
   d. at our bridal   180:17
   D. little lady   69:10
   d. ne moe atte hallie daie   60:7
   each d. the others   73:8
   on with the d.   51:1
   To d. attendance   193:2
   will you join the d.?   57:8
   with their goat feet d.   138:9
Danced: d. by the light of the moon   131:9
   d. till doomsday   68:6
   star d.   204:8
   ye have not d.   31:19
Dances: but it d.   132:5
   d. with the daffodils   247:5
   with d. and delights   203:9
Dancing: d. in the breeze   247:3
   D. in the chequered shade   144:16
   d., to put they pale, lost lilies   77:27
   manners of a d. master   114:2
   'mid these d. rocks   66:15
   past our d. days   207:16
Dane: Roman than a D.   190:2
   Saxon, and Norman and D.   231:3
Danger: above noise and d.   235:7
   bright eyes of d.   221:14
   brink of d.   173:26
   d. of violent death   105:9
   d.'s troubled night   54:8
   five-and-twenty per cent. of its
     d.   222:13
   Oft in d.   242:5
   out of this nettle, d.   190:12
   run into any kind of d.   166:15
Dangerous: a d. thing   164:9
   d. to know   129:4
   d. to meet it alone   241:22
   Many a d. temptation   103:4
Dangers: all perils and d.   166:20
   d. of the seas   160:19
   with d. compass'd round   146:20
Daniel come to judgment!   202:6
Dank: wind was wild and d.   124:1
Danket: nun d. alle Gott   71:14
Danny Deever: hangin' D.   125:2
Danube: his rude hut by the D.   51:5
Dapple-dawn-drawn Falcon   107:17
Dappled: for d. things   107:14

Dare: D. frame thy fearful
  symmetry?   39:4
  D. its deadly terrors   39:2
  fain deny, and d. not   199:32
  'I d. not' wait upon 'I would' 198:6
  who shall d. to chide me   68:23
  You who d.   142:8
Dared: Determined, d., and done 217:9
  none hath d.   174:16
Dares: Whisper who d.!   143:15
Darien: on a peak in D.   121:9
Daring: that d. young man   132:4
Dark: across the d. wave   235:1
  after that the d.   226:6
  Among these d. satanic mills?   38:16
  at one stride comes the d.   65:15
  blanket of the d.   197:15
  d. amid the blaze of noon   147:3
  d. and silent grave   174:15
  d. and true   229:14
  d. as Erebus   202:13
  d. as winter   53:15
  d. is his path   96:19
  d., the serpent-haunted sea   86:5
  d. world and wide   147:17
  each d. passage shun   250:14
  fear to go in the d.   14:12
  Hellish d.   222:19
  in the d. backward   208:8
  Irrecoverably d.   147:3
  leap in the d.   105:10
  leap into the d.   212:15
  lie awake in the d.   242:14
  night is d.   153:15
  this d. world of sin?   37:33
  through the d. cloud   87:4
  Trotting through the d.   127:10
  ways that are d.   101:3
  we are for the d.   182:23
  What d. days seen   211:12
  What in me is d.   145:11
Darkened: eyes were d. wholly   228:1
Darkening: and d. the sky   175:15
Darkens: night d. the streets   146:5
Darker: d. than death or night   215:1
  sky grows d. yet   61:14
Darkling I listen   121:6
Darkly: buried him d.   245:4
  see through a glass d.   35:22
Darkness: awful d. and silence   130:20
  Cast away the works of d.   166:33
  cast off the works of d.   35:14
  d. and light   172:1
  d. at noon-day   70:8
  D. came down on the field   231:17
  d. comprehended it not   33:44
  d. deepens   135:16
  d. falls   82:11
  d. is no d.   172:1
  d. of this world   36:14
  d. shall cover me   172:1
  d. visible   145:13
  d. which may be felt   24:4
Dawn on our d.   101:14
  encounter d. as a bride   200:22
  in d., and with dangers   146:20
  in d. pin'd   181:9
  into outer d.   31:6
  leaves the world to d.   97:8
  light shineth in d.   33:44
  lighten our d.   166:20
  out into the d.   101:5
  people that walked in d.   27:31
  Prince of d.   195:13, 222:7
  that walketh in d.   170:19
  them that sit in d.   32:39
  universal d. buries all   164:3
  voice in the d.   134:9
Darksome: spent the d. hours   55:23

Darling: Charlie, he's my d.   106:7
  Charlie is my d.   151:12
  D., I am growing old   175:6
  d. of my heart   55:2
  d. of our crew   73:19
  d. of the Gods   140:10
  d. of the Spring   245:16
  my d. from the power of the dog 169:1
  Oh, my d. Clementine!   149:7
Dart: D., with heedful mind   20:4
  Time shall throw a d.   43:2
Dash: to d. through thick and thin 69:25
Dastard in war   180:10
Dastards: fools and d.   103:13
Data: before one has d.   78:4
Date: all too short a d.   210:12
Dateless bargain   208:5
Daub: and d. his Visage   85:14
Daughter: D. am I   126:19
  d. of Elysium   179:11
  d. of the gods   226:8
  D. of the Moon   134:4
  Don't put your d. on the stage 69:9
  farmer's d.   53:6
  had taken his little d.   134:12
  harping on my d.   186:24
  King of Spain's d.   156:2
  King's d. is all glorious   169:19
  King's d. o' Noroway   16:13
  Lord Ullin's d.   53:18
  My d.! O my ducats!   201:24
  my Soul, my d.   232:10
  O fairer d.   109:4
  on her d.   82:1
  One fair d.   187:6
  rich attorney's elderly ugly d. 93:33
  Sea-King's d.   231:3
  so is her d.   29:11
  Stern d.   245:19
  washed the colonel's d.   8:7
  whipped her little d.   156:12
Daughters: d. of my father's house 209:11
  fairest of her d.   146:17
  sons and your d. shall prophesy 29:22
  two pernicious d.   195:5
  ye of Jerusalem   27:12
  your d. do not like them   157:4
Dauntless: d. in war   180:9
  d. the slug-horn   43:14
  that with d. breast   97:15
Dauphin: daylight's d.   107:17
David: D. [slain] ..his ten thousands 24:45
  D.'s word   59:5
  Once in royal D.'s city   2:10
Dawn: before d. of day   82:12
  Bliss was it that d.   246:1
  d. comes up like thunder   126:11
  d. is my brother   21:13
  D. on our darkness   101:14
  d. on the other   21:13
  day may d.   236:5
  for the D. of Nothing   85:9
  from d. to gloom   214:9
  grey d. breaking   141:2
  grey d. is breaking   71:2
  next day after d.   191:15
Dawning: bird of d.   185:4
Daws: for d. to peck at   204:16
Day: all d. long   123:14
  all on a summer d.   57:12
  All on a summer's d.   157:15
  alternate Night and D.   84:22
  as bright as d.   155:5
  as on a summer's d.   120:7
  As some d. it may happen   91:30
  as the night the d.   185:21
  at peep of d.   230:6
  at the break of d.?   97:2
  at the opening d.   239:14

Day (cont.)
before dawn of d.   82:12
beware of the d.   56:4
blinds let through the d.   111:10
break of d., lights   201:3
Bright, bright as d.   250:12
bright d. is done   182:23
burden and heat of the d.   32:4
but a penny a d.   157:18
By night or d.   246:7
clear as the d.   172:1
close of d.   53:9
cold winter's d.   105:15
Come again another d.   157:16
compare thee to a summer's d.   210:12
cool of the d.   23:15
counted them at break of d.   51:19
current literature of the d.   50:6
darkest d.   70:1
d. after   51:15
d. brought back my night   148:2
d. but one   40:13
d. he overcame the Nervii   194:7
d. in toil   173:24
d. is at hand   35:14
d. is called the feast of Crispian 192:4
d. is past and gone   16:18
d. may dawn   236:5
d. of glory   177:17
d. of temptation   170:25
D. of wrath   59:5, 180:7
d. returns too soon   52:15
d. that is dead   225:15
d. Thou gavest   82:11
d. too much   62:4
d. when heaven was falling   111:11
d. without a line   163:12
d.'s at the morn   44:24
D.'s azure eyes   213:17
death of each d.'s life   198:13
dreams happy as her d.   42:11
each d. that Fortune gives you   109:1
end of a perfect d.   40:6
end of this d.'s business   194:22
Ere I had ever seen that d.   185:13
every d. in every way   69:5
every d. of my life   220:23
every d. speaks a new scene   173:27
every d. to be lost   116:8
every dog has its d.   40:9
every dog his d.   123:18
eye of pitiful d.   199:6
fairer than the d.   244:18
feats he did that d.   192:4
fight another d.   95:2
fills my thoughts by d.   222:14
first, last, everlasting d.   77:1
for a year and a d.   131:7
foul and fair a d.   197:7
frabjous d.   57:14
from d. to d.   200:4
from this d. forward   168:12
from this d. to the ending   192:4
gather honey all the d.   239:9
Give us this d.   30:22
goes all the d.   210:7
good d. to you   93:2
Good things of d.   199:6
Gwine to run all d.!   87:8
he fell . . a summer's d.   146:9
He sailed on a d.   221:20
He that outlives this d.   192:4
He that shall live this d.   192:4
I have lost a d.   233:20
I have seen the d.   196:10
if she be a d.   223:12
in a summer's d.   203:5
in the evil d.   36:14
Infinite d. excludes the night   239:15

intenser d.   214:2
is this d. leichter   82:5
jocund d.   208:2
Just for one d.   105:14
keeps their fallen d.   161:9
knell of parting d.   97:8
known a better d.   180:4
labour night and d.   46:20
lark at break of d.   210:13
life's little d.   135:16
light of common d.   246:11
listen all d.   56:17
long d. wanes   230:15
long love's d.   140:11
love is sweet for a d.   224:10
maddest merriest d.   228:21
make perpetual d.   138:14
murmur of a summer's d.   11:23
named a trysting d.   136:8
natural d.   138:14
neither night not d.   197:6
night be turned to d.   172:1
not cloudy all d.   105:5
now's the d.   48:30
Now the d. is over   18:6
of an April d.   210:1
of an empty d.   150:13
of lightsome d.   180:5
of this immortal d.   214:10
on a stormy d.   131:5
one d. at the organ   172:22
One d. end it   209:1
one d. in thy courts   170:15
One d. telleth another   168:29
our short d.   58:26
please you every d.   209:20
prevail upon the d.   79:24
promise such a beauteous d.   211:3
raineth every d.   209:20
rest for one d.   68:5
rest not d. and night   37:16
rested the seventh d.   167:11
rise for me . . night and d.   227:2
shall this d. light such a candle 130:6
She set out one d.   45:24
Shillin' a d.   127:9
since my d. began   231:1
Sister, the whole d. long   55:27
sufficeth that the d. will end   194:22
Sufficient unto the d.   30:29
sunbeam in a winter's d.   80:18
support us all the d. long   153:12
Sweet d., so cool   104:6
take the whole long d.?   177:13
Take thou in charge this d.!   136:14
that dreadful d.   180:7
that flieth by d.   170:19
There's night and d.   40:8
third d. comes a frost   192:14
this and every d.   122:15
this d. we must part   71:2
this fair d.   213:14
through the roughest d.   197:12
till the d. when I'll be going   123:12
until the d. break   27:18
until the hasting d.   104:10
welcome d.   105:2
what a d. may bring forth   26:28
when this d. is nam'd   192:4
Will the d.'s journey   177:13
without all hope of d.   147:3
Day-labour: Doth God exact d.?   147:17
Daylight: and the d.'s past   150:2
  Kingdom of d.'s dauphin   107:17
  long and lone d.   213:20
  we burn d.   207:15
  When d. comes   64:10
Days: after many d.   27:5
  all our d. are gone   170:18

all the d. of my life   167:32, 169:2
all the d. that's in the week   55:4
Ancient of d.   29:19, 96:18
as thy d.   24:24
blue d. at sea   221:17
brave d. of old   136:12
Chequer-board of Nights and D.   85:10
D. and moments   58:21
d. of man   171:1
d. of our age   170:18
d. of our youth   52:7
d. that are gone   219:1
d. that are no more   229:13
d. when I was fair   176:11
d., which are at best but dull   235:10
down the d.   232:7
evil d. come not   27:7
fall'n on evil d.   146:20
Forty d. and forty nights   218:6
full of d., riches, and honour   25:23
full of sweet d.   104:7
green d. in forests   221:17
halcyon d.   192:5
half my d.   147:17
heard in ancient d.   121:6
In good King George's glorious d.   91:22
in the d. of thy youth   27:7
in those d.   23:21
is of a few d.   25:31
Length of d.   26:6, 224:2
light of other d.   150:1
live laborious d.   145:1
look'd on better d.   183:19
mad March d.   140:21
man in his hasty d.   41:6
married within these three d.   79:25
My salad d.   182:13
past our dancing d.   207:16
pride of former d.   149:13
seemed unto him but a few d.   23:30
seen better d.   208:24
Sev'n whole d.   104:3
Six d. shalt thou labour   167:9
story of our d.   174:15
strength which in old d.   230:15
that thy d. may be long   167:12
Thirty d. hath September   158:7
Three whole d. together   222:8
Time in hours, d.   235:11
trample on my d.   235:10
What dark d. seen!   211:12
which shall for a few d.   137:5
winding up d. with toil   191:15
wish my d. to be   247:10
wrought in ancient d.   136:5
Day-star: sinks the d.   145:4
Dazzle: mine eyes d.   240:8
De: the enclitic *D.*   43:19
Dea: vera incessu patuit d.   236:6
Dead: are over and d.   224:7
are their rivals d.   161:13
at d. of night   245:4
beauty's summer d.   211:13
been d. many times   161:9
being raised from the d.   35:4
best men are d.   173:20
boy fell d.   44:7
curse in a d. man's eye   65:21
d. and gone   120:17, 189:9
D.! and .. never called me
  mother   245:12
d. and turn'd to clay   189:21
d. bury their d.   31:8
d. ere his prime   144:20
D., for a ducat   188:24
d. from the waist down   43:19
d. man out of mind   169:10
d. man win a fight   16:3
d. men rise up never   224:6

d. men's fingers call them   189:18
d. shall live   79:18
D. Sir John Vanburgh   83:12
d. YESTERDAY   85:8
dear, d. women   45:12
Down among the d. men   80:19
Drive my d. thoughts   214:4
earth, which bears thee d.   190:23
England mourns for her d.   38:1
faith without works is d.   36:39
Fallen cold and d.   242:11
finished and d.   143:2
for a century d.   228:20
For y'er a lang time d.   3:17
from these honoured d.   132:8
full of d. men's bones   32:9
gathered flowers are d.   86:7
he is d.   213:6
Homer, being d.   105:1
I am d. and opened   140:18
I would that I were d.   228:18
If I were a d. leaf   214:3
In the d. vast   185:16
in the dust lies d.   213:16
is a d. Indian   215:20
leaves d. are driven   214:1
little fairy falls down d.   18:20
live a life half d.   147:4
living need charity more than
  the d.   11:6
living with the d.   58:21
Lycidas is d.   144:20
mie love ys d.   60:7
mourn for me when I am d.   211:7
nobody is wished to see my d. body   100:9
not d.—but gone before   176:6
o'er the d.   102:7
of a day that is d.   225:15
Of their d. selves   227:6
on the face that was d.   245:6
one d. lamb is there!   134:1
our d. bodies   179:19
our Spartan d.!   51:20
out of the d. land   81:23
over the rich d.   41:16
patient, being d.   161:15
Queen Anne's d.   67:18
queen..is d.   200:4
renown and grace is d.   198:19
sea gave up the d.   37:24
sea give up her d.   172:10
sheeted d.   185:3
their sorrow is not d.   145:4
There are no d.   137:16
this my son was d.   33:24
to be said for being d.   22:10
to my d. heart   221:24
told me you were d.   69:2
took their wages and are d.   111:11
When I am d.   21:15, 140:18, 177:12
when the rose is d.   215:10
Where the d. leaf fell   120:7
with our English d.!   191:8
with soul so d.   180:6
would waken the d.   97:2
youth stone d.   179:5
Dead-born: it fell d. from the press   111:22
Deadlock: Holy D.   103:17
Deadly: another d. blow!   247:11
are its d. terrors   39:2
more d. than the male   125:5
Dead March: hear the D. play   125:2
Deaf: And trouble d. heaven   210:13
as a d. adder   169:29
turn the d. ear   223:22
Deal: d. of sack   190:16
don't d. in lies   125:14
new d. for the American people   176:12
square d.   177:4

Dealer in magic and spells 93:31
Dealings: All his d. are square 99:7
Dean: D. of Christ Church 219:19
  I am the D. 219:20
  sly shade of a Rural D. 42:6
Deans: dowagers for d. 229:6
Dear: bread should be so d. 107:4
  in grief for one so d.? 109:7
  terrible and d. 213:20
  thou art too d. 211:9
  to all the country d. 95:6
Dearer than his horse 228:6
Dearest: met my d. foe 185:13
Death: after my d. 122:10
  after your d. 187:9
  Angel of D. 41:10, 52:10
  any man's d. diminishes me 77:23
  Be thou faithful unto d. 37:14
  bitterness of d. 24:42
  blaze forth the d. of princes 193:14
  boast thee, d. 183:5
  brought d. into the world 145:9
  come away, d. 209:9
  condemn you to d. 56:14
  danger of violent d. 105:9
  darker than d. 215:1
  d., a necessary end 193:14
  d. after life 219:10
  d. be not proud 77:9
  D. closes all 230:15
  D. cometh soon or late 136:9
  d. could not daunt 16:9
  D. 'ere thou hast slain another 43:2
  d. hath no more dominion 35:4
  d. hath ten thousand doors 240:7
  d. in my University 153:11
  D. is a fearful thing 200:23
  D. is d. 102:17
  D. joins us to the great majority 251:1
  D. lays his icy hand 216:24
  d. of each day's life 198:13
  d. of Nelson 219:2
  d. of poor Cock Robin 159:4
  d. shall be no more 77:10
  d. so noble 147:10
  d. the journey's end 79:28
  d., thou shalt die 77:10
  d. us do part 168:12
  d.'s dark vale 181:8
  d.'s pale flag 208:4
  defend to the d. 237:20
  die many times before their d. 193:14
  die not, poor d. 77:9
  dull cold ear of d. 97:13
  enemy that shall be destroyed is d. 35:25
  faith that looks through d. 246:13
  fear d.? to feel the fog in my
    throat 45:2
  fed on the fullness of d. 224:10
  fell sergeant, d. 189:28
  For d. and life 154:13
  foreknowledge of d. 224:2
  Gone to her d.! 106:20
  hard at d.'s door 171:6
  His d., which happen'd in his
    berth 106:23
  importune d. awhile 182:19
  In life, in d. 135:17
  in that sleep of d. 187:13
  in the ranks of d. 149:15
  in the shadow of d. 32:39
  in their d. they were not divided 24:48
  Into the valley of D. 226:2
  jaws of d. 226:4
  joy before d. 224:9
  just and mighty D. 174:16
  Keeps D. his court 206:15
  land of the shadow of d. 27:31
  Life, the shadow of d. 224:1

living d. 147:4
love with easeful d. 121:6
make d. proud to take us 182:22
Men fear d. 14:12
much possessed by d. 82:3
My part of d. 209:9
name that sat on him was D. 37:17
never taste of d. but once 193:14
Nor shall d. brag 210:12
nothing..certain except d. and
  taxes 88:4
O d. where is thy sting? 35:31
O D. where is thy sting-a-ling-a-
  ling? 6:12
of the d. of kings 206:15
opportune moment of his d. 224:16
or give me d.! 103:10
Pale D. 108:16
preached to d. 217:20
rendezvous with D. 181:11
report of my d. 234:21
sense of d. 200:21
so make Life, and D. 123:14
some one's d. 43:9
something after d. 187:13
stroke of d. 116:22
strong in d. 164:22
studied in his d. 197:13
sweats to d. 190:11
thank you 'most to d. 234:19
that neither d., nor life 35:10
there shall be no more d. 37:26
Think thee Milton, D. 251:2
this life, this d. 250:7
To what we fear of d. 201:1
torture and d. of his fellow creatures 88:10
up the line to d. 179:4
valley of the shadow of d. 169:2
wages of sin is d. 35:5
was not born for d. 121:6
Was stung to d. 96:15
way to dusty d. 200:4
we are in d. 168:19
we owe God a d. 190:32
Where is d.'s sting? 135:17
which is d. to hide 147:17
Deathbed: gon to hys d. 60:7
Death penalty: abolish the d. 119:14
Deaths: by feigned d. 77:15
  more d. than one 243:6
Debate: Rupert of D. 136:1
Debauch his friend's wife 115:3
Debauched with ease 79:4
Debonair: blithe and d. 144:11
Deboshed fish 208:15
Debt: more than millions of d. 47:7
Debtors: we forgive our d. 30:22
Debts: forgive us our d. 30:22
  pays all d. 208:17
  to Pay Old D. 141:10
Decay: and men d. 95:4
  change and d. 135:16
  muddy vesture of d. 202:11
  our love hath no d. 77:1
  pigmy body to d. 79:5
  Round the d. 214:7
  woods d. 230:10
Decays: glimmering and d. 235:10
Deceased: 'e is frequent d. 128:8
  He first d. 249:12
Deceitful: heart is d. 29:7
Deceits of the world 166:23
Deceive: O Sleep, again d. me 68:14
  practise to d. 180:12
  we d. ourselves 37:8
Deceived: be not d. 36:8
  mine eye may be d. 211:13
  we desire to be d.? 49:15

Deceiver: gay d.   67:21
Deceivers: Men were d.   204:9
Deceiving elf   121:7
December: D. when they wed   184:11
  drear-nighted D.   122:6
  old D.'s bareness   211:12
Decembers: and fifteen wild D.   41:15
Decent: in the d. obscurity   90:13
Decently and in order   35:23
Decide: comes the moment to d.   135:3
  d. accordingly   138:5
Decision: in the valley of d.   29:23
Deck: and the whole d.   86:9
  boy stood on the burning d.   102:7
  silly buckets on the d.   66:1
  Walk the d.   242:11
Decks: d. the rural pavender   178:13
  he fell upon their d.   230:5
  rose upon their d.   230:5
Declaration that nothing was now left   74:7
Declare: hear the girls d.   90:17
  him d. I unto you   34:42
  I heard him d.   57:10
  nothing to d.   244:1
  then, I d.   105:18
  ye are to d. it   168:5
Declared: eye sublime d.   146:16
Decline: writing the d. and fall   90:12
Declined into the vale of years   205:6
Declines: from fair sometime d.   210:12
Decree: stately pleasure-dome d.   66:14
Dedicate: d. a portion of that field 132:8
  d. this nation   176:14
  we cannot d.   132:8
Dedicated to the proposition   132:8
Dedications: refusing d.   240:18
Deduced: principles d. from it
  [history]   102:2
Dee: Across the sands of D.   124:1
  lived on the river D.   37:29
Deed: blow the horrid d.   198:4
  by a nobler d.   59:18
  clears us of this d.   198:16
  d. is everything   94:14
  d. of dreadful note   199:5
  d. of shame   136:10
  d. without a name   199:19
  good d. in a naughty world   202:14
  matchless d.'s achieved   217:9
  Till thou applaud the d.   199:6
  To do the right d.   81:21
  unlucky d. relate   205:20
  will for the d.   223:14
Deeds: D., not words shall speak me   19:14
  d. of derring do   93:27
  d. of mercy   202:5
  good d. past   208:27
  Renowned for their d.   206:7
  Such evil d.   135:7
  thrice famous d.   136:5
  your better d.   19:20
Deep: bottom of the d.   190:9
  Broad and d. continueth   127:15
  By the d. sea   51:7
  calm so d.!   249:4
  D. and crisp   152:13
  d. and dark blue ocean   51:8
  d. damnation   198:4
  d. moans round   230:15
  drank d.   85:1
  from the vasty d.   190:17
  her home is on the d.   54:7
  his body to the d.   172:10
  in terms too d. for me   92:21
  in the cradle of the d.   244:4
  natural philosophy, [makes men] d. 14:27
  not loud but d.   199:32
  of their shadows d.   250:11
  on a sunnier d.   213:12

One d. calleth another   169:16
one is of the d.   220:7
Out of the d.   171:25
out the boundless d.   226:6
rolling d.   179:3
singularly d. young man   92:21
some precept d.   166:5
sweep through the d.   54:6
'tis buried d.   121:7
to such a d. delight   66:15
too d. for his hearers   95:18
too d. for tears   246:14
very d. did rot   65:14
wonder in the d.   171:7
Deep-brow'd Homer   121:9
Deep-delved earth   121:3
Deepens: darkness d.   135:16
Deeper: D. than did ever plummet
  sound   208:19
  d. than the depth of waters   177:15
  much d. waters   78:9
Deeply: Consider it not so d.   198:11
  more d. interfused   248:19
Deep-meadowed: lies d.   227:3
Deep-mouth'd welcome   51:13
Deer: a-chasing the d.   48:27
  I was a stricken d.   70:17
  running of the d.   7:17
  Where the d. and the antelope
    play   105:5
Defaced: by Time's fell hand d.   211:6
Defeat: possibilities of d.   235:17
Defect: the chief d. of Henry King   21:3
Defects: among the d. of the Bill   178:11
Defence: Lord is thy d.   171:17
  our d. is sure   239:14
Defenceless: Cover my d. head   241:10
Defend: D., O Lord, this thy child   168:4
  d. thee under his wings   170:19
  d. to the death   237:20
  d. us from all perils   166:20
  shall d. our island   62:21
Defended: howsoe'er d.   134:1
  What God abandoned, these d.   111:11
Defender: Faith's d.   50:15
Defenders: nor such d.   236:12
Defendeth the fatherless   172:5
Defends itself   9:3
Defensive: as a moat d.   206:7
Defer: let me not d. or neglect it   98:15
Defiled: He that toucheth pitch shall
  be d.   29:35
Definitions: homely d.   67:8
Defoe: to D., to Hawthorne   220:22
Defy: d. the foul fiend   195:11
  d. th' Omnipotent   145:12
  To d. Power   215:1
Degrading: so d. a profession   178:1
Degree: curs of low d.   95:13
  exalted them of low d.   32:38
Degrees: boil at different d.   83:3
  Fine by d.   172:19
  I may by d.   68:18
Deified: are we d.   247:19
Deject: of ladies most d.   188:6
Dejected Mariana   201:2
Delay: In d. there lies no plenty   209:5
  law's d.   187:13
Delayed till I am indifferent   113:22
Delaying: by d. saved the state   83:5
Delectable: came to the D. Moun-
  tains   46:12
Delenda est Carthago   58:24
Delia: While D. is away   112:17
Deliberate speed   232:8
Delicacy: lives only in the d.   161:9
Delicate: air is d.   198:2
  call these d. creatures   205:7
  What d. stripling   108:18

L

Delicately: came unto him d.   24:42
Delicta maiorum immeritus lues   109:22
Delight: All for your d.   203:20
    Applause,! d.!   118:4
    dogs d. to bark   239:6
    doth with d.   246:8
    drunk d. of battle   230:13
    each thing met conceives d.   146:22
    Energy is Eternal D.   39:15
    impulse of d.   250:7
    labour we d. in   198:18
    land of pure d.   239:15
    lookers-on feel most d.   49:29
    Moon of my D.   86:2
    Mother of the Fair D.   177:14
    our sole d.   146:1
    paint the meadows with d.   196:19
    phantom of d.   248:4
    space for d.   224:2
    Spirit of D.   215:7
    Teach us d. in simple things   124:18
    temple of d.   120:24
    that give d.   208:18
    'tis my d.   6:16
    to its d.   39:6
    to such a deep d.   66:15
    toys for your d.   221:17
    which men miscall d.   213:8
    with dances and d.   203:9
Delighted: you have d. us long
    enough   13:19
Delightest not in burnt-offerings   169:28
Delights: man d. not me   187:4
    To scorn d.   145:1
Deliver: d. thee from the snare   170:19
    d. us from evil   30:22
Deliverance: after d.   173:26
Deliverer: hands of their d.   147:6
Delivereth: he d. them   171:8
Delivers the Goods   141:7
Delos: where D. rose   51:17
Deluding: vain d. joys   144:4
Déluge: Aprés nous le d.   163:19
Delusion: a d., a mockery   73:11
Demands my soul   239:17
Dementat prius   80:15
Demented: not one is d.   242:14
Demesne: ruled as his d.   121:9
Demi-paradise   206:7
Democracy: A d...government of
    all the people   160:22
    arsenal of d.   176:16
    D. resumed her reign   21:18
    safe for d.   244:13
Democritus: rideret D.   108:12
Demolished: is d. but by himself   22:14
Demoniac frenzy   146:24
Demon-lover: wailing for her d.   66:14
Demonstrandum: quod erat d.   83:9
Denied: hast not d. him   168:33
    is d. to me   181:5
    may not be d.   141:2
Denies: nature d. the power   118:19
    she d. you   117:18
Denmark: in the state of D.   186:6
    may be so in D.   186:14
Deny: thou shalt d. me thrice   32:19
    to palliate or d.   162:17
    will this health d.   80:19
    would fain d.   199:32
Denying: I'm not d.   81:8
Deoch-an-doris: wee d.   130:8
Depart: ere you d.   185:12
    he will not d. from it   26:22
    Let him d.   192:4
    ready to d.   129:20
    ye d. out of that house   31:12
Departed: D. never to return   49:5
    glory is d.   24:39

Departing: and, d., leave behind us   133:27
    at my d.   4:10
Depend upon it, Sir   115:13
Deposed: by the ghosts they have
    d.   206:15
    must he be d.?   206:16
    some have been d.   206:15
Depress'd: by poverty d.   116:27
Deprest with cares   89:18
Deprived of everlasting bliss!   138:11
Depth: far beyond my d.   192:14
    in the d. be praise   153:14
    in the d. of the sea   31:38
    nor height nor d.   35:10
Depths of burning light   83:14
Deputy: books to be read by d.   14:25
Derangement of epitaphs!   216:11
Derides: wrinkled Care d.   144:13
Derision: clothed with d.   224:2
    Uglification, and D.   57:5
Derive: This doctrine I d.   196:16
Derring: deeds of d. do: 93:27
Descend: into the Dust d.   85:5
Descended: D. of so many royal
    kings   183:6
    when we have d.   110:6
Descends from on high   237:1
Descent to Avernus!   236:15
Descried: when 'tis d.   79:26
Description: answered the d.   83:19
    beggar'd all d.   182:15
    from the truth of the d.   181:5
Desdemona: O D.! D.! dead   205:18
Desert: and the d. shall rejoice   28:9
    country he has turned into a d.   47:11
    d. of wire, concrete roads   151:10
    every man after his d.   187:10
    Fret not to roam the d.   154:12
    Life is the d.   251:1
    make straight in the d.   28:12
    on the d. air   97:15
    Stand in the d.   214:5
Deserts: D. of vast eternity   140:12
    his d. are small   149:6
Deserve: best d. the precious bane   146:8
Deserves: d. no crown   174:1
    d. the fair   79:11
    government it d.   137:19
Desiderio: quis d..tam cari capitis? 109:7
Design: My d. is to make what
    haste   71:13
Designated: ever after d.   180:16
Designing: I am d. St. Paul's   22:12
Desipere in loco   110:7
Desire: arrows of d.   38:16
    d. more love   183:8
    d. of the moth   215:13
    given him his heart's d.   168:33
    In his heart is a blind d.   224:2
    mixing memory and d.   81:23
    nearer to the Heart's D.   86:1
    not to get your heart's d.   212:22
    nought for your d.   61:14
    soul hath a d.   170:13
    we d. to be deceived?   49:15
    wonder and a wild d.   45:6
    yearning in d.   230:14
Desires: all d. known   167:4
    all holy d.   166:18
    him who d. peace   235:12
    most ardent of my d.   142:15
Desirest: d. no sacrifice   169:28
    d. the water-brooks   169:15
Desiring this man's art   210:13
Desirous: else on earth d.?   89:17
Desks: Stick close to your d.   93:11
Desolated: province they have d.   94:3
Desolation: abomination of d.   32:12
Despair: begotten by d.   140:2

Do not d. 173:2
endure my own d. 238:13
hurried question of D. 50:19
in Hell's d. 39:5
in his d. 218:21
Look upon my works..and d. 214:6
Of comfort and d. 212:4
Rash-embrac'd d. 202:2
some divine d. 229:13
wasting in d. 244:18
Desperate: Beware of d. steps 70:1
D. deeds 93:27
D. diseases require d. remedies 84:1
No lot is d. 108:19
tempt not a d. man 208:3
Despise: can gold d.? 98:2
Money, I d. it 92:24
shalt thou not d. 169:28
whom I can d. so entirely 212:14
Despised: cast out..and d. 174:16
d. and dying king 215:8
d. old man 195:5
He is d. and rejected 28:20
Despising: myself almost d. 210:13
Despite: come but in d. 203:20
D. those titles 180:6
Despond: slough was D. 46:4
Despondency and madness 247:19
Despondently: Sprouting d. 81:20
Despotism: of anarchy and d. 215:16
Destined: Abode his d. Hour 84:23
His fall was d. 117:3
Destiny: and d. obscure 97:12
Our manifest d. 159:20
reap a d. 175:4
Where D. with Men 85:10
Destroy: come to d. the law 30:15
our sense d. 179:11
Whom God would d. 80:15
Destroyed: Carthage must be d. 58:24
last enemy that shall be d. 35:25
When once d. 95:4
Destroyer and preserver 214:1
Destroyeth: sickness that d. 170:19
Destruction: dealing d.'s devasta-
ting doom 3:10
pride goeth before d. 26:20
that leadeth to d. 31:1
to their d. draw 77:1
Destructive: war is d. of his material
body 113:12
Detail: Merely corroborative d. 92:13
Deteriora sequor 160:7
Determinate: are all d. 211:9
Determined, dared, and done 217:9
Detest: hate and d...man 223:6
Detests: fashion she d. 209:14
Detract: to add or d. 132:8
Detrimenti: ne quid res publica d.
caperet 63:23
Deum: Te D. laudamus 10:6
Deus disponit 122:22
Deutschland über alles 83:17
Development: this work of d. 19:28
Deviates into sense 79:23
Device: banner with the strange
d. 133:17
nor d...in the grave 27:2
of rare d. 66:15
panes of quaint d. 120:4
Devil: children of the d. 230:4
cleft the D.'s foot 77:16
d. and all his works 167:32
d. can cite Scripture 201:16
d. damn thee black 199:31
D. having nothing else to do 21:19
D. howling 'Ho'! 219:21
d. understands Welsh 190:19
d. was sick 151:2

D. whispered behind the leaves 125:1
d. will come 138:14
D.'s walking parody 61:16
Drink and the d. 221:1
first Whig was the D. 115:19
if the d. dress her not 183:1
of the D.'s party 39:16
shame the d. 118:10, 190:18
wedlock's the d. 52:5
What the d. 148:17
world, the flesh, and the d. 166:23
your adversary the d. 37:7
Devils: D. are not so black 133:10
d. incarnate 191:7
One sees more d. 203:19
wrote..of D. and Hell 39:16
Devon: If the Dons sight D. 153:4
started that morning from D. 91:25
Dévorât: la Révolution..d...tous ses
enfants 235:13
Devotees: no genuine d. 112:16
Devotion: d. to something afar 215:13
Farwel my book and my d. 60:21
is the heart's d. 215:11
last full measure of d. 132:8
object of universal d. 112:16
sailor's d. 212:7
we take increased d. 132:8
Devotions: and beheld your d. 34:42
next to her d. 129:6
Devour: might d. in turn 235:13
shed tears when they would d. 15:6
whom he may d. 37:7
Devoured: which are d. as fast 208:27
Devourer of all things 160:8
Devouring: d. Time 196:13
Time's d. hand? 41:2
Devours: Daily d. apace 145:3
Devoutly to be wish'd 187:13
Dew: bright d. is shaking 71:2
d. on the mountain 180:3
d. shall weep 104:6
d. was falling fast 247:16
d. will rust them 204:19
fever d. 120:11
rained a ghastly d. 228:9
resolve itself into a d. 185:11
sea of d. 84:3
see the d. bespangling herb 104:9
that they were filled with d. 66:1
Walks o'er the d. 185:5
Dewdrops: showers and d. 177:12
Dew-pearled: hill-side's d. 44:24
Dewy: full of d. wine 121:5
Di: quem d. diligunt 163:8
Diabolical: tree of d. knowledge 216:8
Dial: drew a d. from his poke 183:16
Dial-hand: beauty, like a d. 211:13
Diamond: like a d. in the sky 225:10
more of rough than polished d. 61:9
Diamonded with panes 120:4
Diana: D.'s foresters 190:6
Great is D. 34:45
Diapason closing full 79:16
Dicere: nec possum d. quare 139:22
Dick, the shepherd 196:20
Dickens: what the d. his name is 202:19
Dicky-bird why do you sit? 92:16
Dictatorship of the proletariat 140:17
Dictionaries: to make d. 116:13
Dictionary: a walking d. 59:20
Did: Alone I d. it 184:19
And d. it very well 91:22
never forget what they d. 132:8
Dido with a willow 202:10
Die: Beauty that must d. 120:24
before that spirit d. 221:24
being born, to d. 15:15
but we shall d. 102:17

Die (cont.)
by feigned deaths to d.   77:15
coop't we live and d.   85:13
Cowards d. many times   193:14
Curse God and d.   25:27
Dar'st thou d.?   200:21
death, thou shalt d.   77:10
determine to d. here   20:3
D. because a woman's fair   244:18
d. before they sing   66:13
d. beyond my means   244:2
d. by inches   103:6
d. here in a rage   223:5
d.—in bed   179:5
d. in the last ditch   47:20, 244:5
d. in their glory   111:2
d. is cast   53:3
D. my dear Doctor   160:17
d. not, poor death   77:9
D. of a rose   164:15
d. on mine own sword?   200:9
d. with harness on our back   200:7
do and d.   226:2
do we not d.?   201:27
does not d.   217:6
either do or d.   19:13
Ere their story d.   100:4
For thou must d.   104:6
for tomorrow we d.   35:26
for tomorrow we shall d.   28:6
gladly d.   221:23
good d. early   72:16
Guards d.   53:10
harken ere I d.   229:4
how can man d. better   136:9
how to d.   165:20
I must d.   77:15, 152:5
I will d. in peace   245:9
If I must d.   200:22
If I should d. before I wake   6:11
If I should d., think only this   42:11
If it were now to d.   204:28
if thou d. a martir   60:29
If we are mark'd to d.   192:3
Is not to d.   53:14
is to d.   95:21
John Barleycorn should d.   48:22
laws and learning d.   138:4
lay me doun and d.   77:25
let me d.   247:10
let us d. to make men free   111:16
Let us do or d.   49:1
living d.   79:18
man can d. but once   190:32
may sicken, and so d.   209:2
More deaths than one must d.   243:6
must be free or d.   247:1
not made to d.   227:4
not to live, but to d. in   42:21
or bravely d.?   164:5
or I d.   234:1
perceives it d. away   246:11
quiet d.   180:15
Ride on to d.   143:6
sail..until I d.   230:15
seems it rich to d.   121:6
shall Trelawny d.?   101:6
sing before they d.   66:13
speak or d.   190:34
suffer and d.   236:1
sure to d.   149:19
taught us how to d.   233:17
that d. unmarried,   210:8
that one man should d.   34:14
they d. in yon rich sky   229:12
They that d. by famine   103:6
those about to d.   222:10
those who are about to d.   9:16
thou shalt surely d.   23:10

time to d.   26:38
to d., and go we know not where   200:23
To d. for fatherland   109:18
To d.: to sleep   187:13
To d. will be an awfully big
   adventure   18:21
to d. with us   192:4
to fight is but to d.   230:4
to live and to d.!   44:10
We shall d. alone   161:6
We would not d.   192:4
weep or she will d.   229:15
When beggars d.   193:14
when good Americans d.   10:9, 243:23
when he shall d.   208:1
when soft voices d.   215:10
Who saw him d.?   159:5
who would wish to d.?   40:8
wish to d.   90:17
yet I love her till I d.   7:22
Died: d. as one   197:13
d. in a good old age   25:23
D. on Saturday   158:2
d. to make men holy   111:16
dog it was that d.   95:16
fell upon their decks and .. d.   230:5
I had d. for thee   25:4
lik'd it not, and d.   249:12
not have d. in vain   132:8
our fathers d.   124:18
Prince of glory d.   239:16
she d. young   240:8
should have d. hereafter   200:4
so groan'd and d.   89:28
They d. to save their country   21:14
When he d. the little children
   cried   150:17
when my father d.   189:15
where my fathers d.   217:14
who d. before the god of love   77:13
Diem perdidi   233:20
Dies: artist d. with me   153:3
As when a giant d.   200:21
Call no man happy till he d.   18:8
d. ere he knows it   43:18
d. the swan   230:10
d. young   163:8
Every moment d. a man   231:2
for ever d.   85:6
Function never d.   245:17
Grows, lives and d.   203:1
he that d. pays all debts   208:17
king never d.   38:6
light of a whole life d.   40:13
light of the bright world d.   40:13
loves, and weeps, and d.   213:12
tumult and the shouting d.   127:4
when his father d.   116:9
worm that never d.   42:3
Dies: irae, d. illa   59:5
nulla d. sine linea   163:12
Diet: d. unparalleled   74:25
immortal d.   174:13
Dieth: being raised from the dead
   d. no more   35:4
Dieu: D. me pardonnera   102:6
D...pour les gros bataillons   237:18
si D. n'existait pas   237:15
Difference to me!   248:3
Different: boil at d. degrees   83:3
How d., how very d.   5:4
other naturs thinks d.   74:22
so d. from her picture   103:14
something d. from either   81:24
would have been d.   161:4
Differential calculus   93:19
Difficult: D. indeed is it   119:3
first step that is d.   72:15
Difficulty: my only d.   80:5

Diffugere nives, redeunt iam gramina
   campis   110:5
Dig: d. for buttered rolls   58:13
   D. the grave   221:3
   d. till you gently perspire   126:4
   forbear to d. the dust   212:5
   I cannot d.   33:25
   Many a d. in the ribs   222:14
   to d. him up   212:14
Digest: inwardly d. them   166:34
Digestion: good d. wait on appetite   199:9
Diggeth: He that d. a pit   27:4
Dight: richly d.   144:9
Dignities: all her d.   190:9
Dignity: d. of this high calling   47:5
   with silent d.   98:18
Diligence: with d. and attention   14:25
Diligently: as d. as I have served
   the king   245:11
Dim: adazzle, d.   107:15
   greater glory d. the less   202:14
   into the forest d.   121:3
   lights are d.   159:14
   Through the d. night   214:10
   Vext the d. sea   230:13
Dim-discovered spires   67:13
Dimensions of this mercy   71:7
Dimidium facti qui coepit habet   108:7
Diminished to her cock   195:19
Diminishes: increases rather than d.   80:5
Dimmed: now d. and gone   150:1
Dinah: Vilikins and his D.   7:20
Dine: D. with Jack Wilkes   115:10
   go to inns to d.   61:25
   going to d. with some men   22:12
   I d. at Blenheim once a week   6:10
   If this should stay to d.   56:9
   should d. at Edmonton   69:30
   sooner d. with Jack Ketch   115:10
   to d. with the Canons   115:6
   when he sat down to d.   61:28
Dined: I have d. to-day   217:18
   They d. on mince   131:9
Dines: where the MFH d. he sleeps   222:16
Ding: Always d., dinging   150:16
   D. dong bell   155:13, 202:1, 208:12
   hey d. a d. d.   184:12
Dinge: Zwei D. erfüllen das Gemüth   119:10
Dingo: Yellow-Dog D. behind   126:5
Dining: while they thought of d.   95:18
Dinna ye hear it?   242:18
Dinner: better is a d. of herbs   26:18
   breakfast, d., supper   44:22
   rice pudding for d.   143:12
   then have d.   58:2
   three hours' march to d.   101:11
   What gat ye to your d.?   16:8
   won't eat her d.   143:11
Dinner-bell: tocsin of the soul—the d.   51:24
Dinner-knives: broken d.   125:9
Dint of pity   194:10
Diogenes: I would be D.   2:6
Diplomacy: Dollar d.   4:2
Dipt: I d. into the future   228:8
Dirck: I galloped, D. galloped   44:5
Direct: lie d.   184:14
   puff d.   216:1
Directions: find d. out   186:20
   off in all d.   130:12
Directly: Go d.—see   173:11
Direful spring   106:15
Dirge: their d. is sung   67:15
Dirt: instead of d. and poison   223:1
   painted child of d.   165:8
   poverty, hunger, and d.   107:3
Dirty British coaster   140:21
Dis aliter visum   236:11
Disappointed: d. by that stroke of
   death   116:22

never be d.   165:16
   pangs of d. love   178:4
   unhousel'd, d.   186:12
Disapprove: I d. of what you say   237:20
Disaster: meet with Triumph and
   D.   125:14
Disasters: to see d.   47:14
Disbelief: willing suspension of d.   67:5
Disc: a round d. of fire   38:13
Discerning: Gives genius a better d.   95:20
   very well d.   234:3
Discharge: no d. in that war   26:42, 124:16
   to d. my duties   81:5
Disciple: d. whom Jesus loved   34:30
   in the name of a d.   31:17
Discipline: good order and military
   d.   3:23
Discontent: divine d.   124:4
   winter of our d.   207:4
Discontented with the divine dis-
   content   124:4
Discord: Harmony in d.   108:10
Discouragement: there's no d.   46:20
Discouraging word   105:5
Discourse: and d. in novel phrases   92:21
   beast, that wants d.   185:11
Discourst in Three Questions   182:2
Discretion: better part of valour is
   d.   190:9
   d. be your tutor   188:8
   years of d.   168:3
Discussing their duty   242:14
Disdain: For thee to d. it   215:12
Disdained: too falsely d.   215:12
Disdainful smile   97:12
Disdaining fortune   197:4
Disdains all things   160:1
Disease: cure the d.   14:15
   life is an incurable d.   69:19
   long d., my life   165:5
   Meet the d.   162:9
   remedy is worse than the d.   14:23
   shapes of foul d.   227:20
   strange d. of modern life   11:26
Diseases: Desperate d.   84:1
   Subject to the same d.   201:27
Disgrace: When in d.   210:13
Disgruntled: if not actually d.   245:1
Disguise: Blessings in d.   104:17
   D. fair nature   191:8
Dish: a lordly d.   24:29
   dainty d.?   158:1
   d. fit for the gods   193:13
   d. ran away   155:17
   for a d. of wood   206:15
   is a d. for a king   210:5
   woman is a d. for the gods   183:1
Dished: we have d. the Whigs   220:1
Dishes: not wash d.   155:11
Dishonourable graves   193:11
Disinheriting countenance   216:20
Disinterested: seldom so d.   1:2
Dislike the matter   182:14
Disliked: who d. gravy   217:16
Dislikings: likings and d.   129:5
Dismal: with a d. headache   91:23
Dismay: Let nothing you d.   4:11
Dismayed: be thou d.   24:26
   Was there a man d.?   225:21
Dismembered: in his d. state   110:11
Dismiss: Lord, d. us   45:21
Dismissed: d. with hard words   161:15
   rudely be d.   67:3
   With peace and consolation hath
   d.   147:11
Disobedience: Man's first d.   145:9
Disobeyed: seventh time d.   161:15
Disorder: spring . . of all d.   47:7
   sweet d. in the dress   104:11

Dispatch: be angry and d. 183:4
Dispelled: mist is d. 89:18
Displeasing: not d. to us 175:16
Disposed: when I am so d. 74:21
Disposes: God d. 122:22
Disposition: antic d. 186:17
  so heavily with my d. 187:4
Dispraise or blame 147:10
Dispraised: Of whom to be d. 147:1
Disprized: pangs of d. love 187:13
Dispute: none to d. 70:19
  such high d. 50:12
Disputed: some d. barricade 181:11
Dissatisfied: Not one is d. 242:14
Dissipation without pleasure 90:11
Dissolve: d. me into ecstasies 144:9
  Fade far away, d. 121:4
Dissolving dream 213:12
Dissonance: barb'rous d. 146:20
Distance: d. is nothing 72:15
  d. lends enchantment 54:3
  sixty second's worth of d. run 125:16
Distance: La d. n'y fait rien 72:15
Distant: d. drum 84:20, 21
  far d., storm-beaten ships 137:18
  Ye d. spires 98:5
Distempered: their d. body 119:6
Distilled: is the rose d. 203:1
Distinction: no d. among the upper
  ten thousand 244:9
Distracted: lay d. in the ditch 71:1
Distraction: Ambition, D. 57:5
  d. in 's aspect 187:11
  into a fine d. 104:11
Distress: All pray in their d. 39:12
  incapable of her own d. 189:18
  out of their d. 171:8
Distressed: consolation in a d. one 13:17
  d., in mind, body, or estate 166:29
  I am d. for thee 25:1
  sore d.? 152:9
District: and of that d. I prefer 42:7
Disturb: d. this hallow'd house 204:4
  d. your season due 144:20
Disturbs: presence that d. me 248:19
Ditch: both shall fall into the d. 31:30
  die in the last d. 47:20, 244:5
  dull as d. water 75:14
  lay distracted in the d. 71:1
Ditch-delivered by a drab 199:16
Ditties: Pipe to the spirit d. 120:19
  Sing no more d. 204:9
Ditty: sung a dolefull'st d. 18:12
Diurnal: earth's d. course 245.14
Diver in deep seas 161:9
Divers: in d. tones 227:6
Divers-colour'd fans 182:15
Diversion: country d. 68:18
Divide: do their bounds d. 79:6
  mountains d. us 181:7
Divided: d. against itself 132:7
  in death they were not d. 24:48
  thy kingdom is d. 29:18
Dividing: by d. we fall 76:1
Divine: ask a drink d. 117:19
  did the Countenance D. 38:16
  d. his real thought 51:16
  good d. that follows his own in-
    structions 201:10
  Hand that made us is D. 1:14
  human form d. 39:13
  Love..so D. 239:17
  Makes drudgery d. 103:22
  she song the service d. 60:12
  some d. despair 229:13
  tale of Troy d. 144:8
  to forgive, d. 164:12
  what power d. 66:9
  what the form d. 129:19

Divinest: two d. things 112:9
Divinities: introducing new d. 163:7
Divinity: d. that shapes our ends 189:24
  piece of d. in us 42:20
  such d. doth hedge a king 189:13
Division: D. is as bad 6:8
  Woe weeps out her d. 117:10
Dizzy: How fearful and d. 195:19
Djinn: On the resident D. 93:32
Do: but I d. it! 92:29
  but to d. and die 226:2
  can d. no other 135:10
  didn't want to d. it 137:6
  D. as you would be done by 61:7
  d. as you're bid 80:21
  d. nothing upon my self 77:21
  d. this, and he doeth it 31:5
  D. what thou wilt 174:5
  either d., or die 19:13
  first thing we d. 192:9
  Go and d. thou likewise 33:8
  how d. ye d.? 38:14
  how not to d. it 74:18
  I'll d., I'll d. 197:5
  know not what they d. 33:39
  seemly so to d. 123:6
  that d. thereafter 171:11
  This will never d. 113:5
  To d. it as for Thee 103:21
  what have I to d. with thee? 33:49
  what I d. in any thing 103:21
  What is there I would not d.? 102:16
  which I would not, that I d. 35:6
Doasyouwouldbedoneby: her name
  is Mrs. D. 124:6
Doctor: D. and Saint 85:7
  merry D. Brighton 231:13
  What sort of a D. is he? 173:16
Doctrine: d. of the enclitic De 43:19
  every wind of d. 36:10
  this d. I derive 196:16
Doeg, brought without knowing 79:10
Does: I wonder why he d.? 143:16
Dog: better than his d. 228:6
  Beware of the d. 162:12
  circumcised d. 205:20
  d. at Kew 164:7
  d. in a manger 234:12
  d. it was that died 95:16
  d. returneth to his vomit 26:27
  d. to gain some private ends 95:14
  d. was found 95:13
  d.'s walking on his hinder legs 114:19
  every d. has its day 40:9
  every d. his day 123:18
  get her poor d. a bone 157:3
  grin like a d. 170:1
  If you call a d. Hervey 113:16
  incident of the d. 78:11
  Is thy servant a d.? 25:19
  lean d., a keen d. 137:13
  little d. laughed 155:17
  living d. is better 27:1
  Mine enemy's d. 195:23
  power of the d. 169:1
  rather be a d. 194:17
  to a d. to tear 127:2
  tongue of d. 199:14
  tossed the d. 158:8
  When a d. bites a man 72:2
  when a man bites a d. 72:2
  whose d. are you? 164:7
  Why should a d...have life 196:11
  wild d., and alone 137:13
Dogged as does it 234:4
Doggedly: set himself d. 113:17
Dogs: As many d. there be 95:13
  better I like d. 176:9
  dancing d. 195:13

d. did bark | 69:28
d. delight to bark | 239:6
d. eat of the crumbs | 31:31
d. in the town | 158:4
d. of war | 193:21
Lame d. over stiles | 123:15
leave Now for d. | 43:17
little d. and all | 195:15
Mad d. and Englishmen | 69:8
rain cats and d. | 223:16
these d. of Seville | 230:4
throw physic to the d. | 200:1
Uncover, d., and lap | 208:23
Doing: Be not weary in well d. | 36:25
D. or suffering | 146:1
In d. of either | 234:10
see what she's d. | 173:11
up and d. | 133:28
Doing-good: As for D. | 233:6
Doings: in all our d. | 167:28
Doit: Give no d. | 58:26
Dole: I mete and d. | 230:12
Doleful: one in d. dumps | 213:5
Dolendum est primum ipsi tibi | 107:20
Doll: prettiest d. in the world | 123:17
sweet little d. | 123:17
Dollar: almighty d. | 7:12, 112:16
D. Diplomacy | 4:2
Dolores: splendid and sterile D. | 224:5
Dolorous midland sea | 224:11
Dome: build that d. | 66:15
d. of many-coloured glass | 213:10
d. of pleasure | 66:15
that rounded Peter's d. | 82:15
that sunny d. | 66:15
Domes: Ships, towers, d. | 249:4
Domestic: Malice d. | 199:4
Dominations: Thrones, D., Prince-
doms | 146:19
Domine, defende nos | 94:9
Dominion: dark d. | 142:1
death hath no more d. | 35:4
d. of the world | 137:18
d. over the nations | 236:18
we hold d. over palm and pine | 127:3
Dominions: His Majesty's D. | 154:9
sun does not set in my d. | 179:12
Dominus: d. illuminatio mea | 26:3
nisi d. frustra | 26:4
Domus sua cuique est.. refugium | 65:1
Don: remote and ineffectual D. | 21:20
turn my back upon D. or devil | 230:4
Done: anything remained to be
d. | 135:6
be d. decently | 35:23
been and gone and d. | 90:20
bright day is d. | 182:23
but thine be d. [will] | 33:37
cried out—Well d.! | 69:28
Determined, dared, and d. | 217:9
d. all I could | 113:20
d. like lightning | 117:16
enemy hath d. this | 31:26
forgot as soon as d. | 208:27
Great things are d. | 38:15
had d. for the rest | 221:1
has half d. it | 108:7
Have d. my credit | 85:15
having d. all | 36:14
I don't think it would have d. | 240:14
I have only d. my duty | 230:5
if it is not d. | 212:18
If it were d. | 198:3
It is well d. | 183:6
Let justice be d. | 239:4
long day's task is d. | 182:18
may fairly be d. | 153:9
may yet be d. | 230:15
might have d. with us | 64:4

much better d. in Shakespeare | 80:4
not d. well | 114:19
Old Kaspar's work was d. | 218:12
our fearful trip is d. | 242:10
required to be d. | 74:18
seen to be d. | 104:19
So little d. | 175:9, 227:14
something attempted, something
d. | 134:11
surprised to find it d. | 114:19
than I have ever d. | 75:34
that our duty has been d.! | 91:11
that which shall be d. | 26:35
Think nothing d. | 176:5
thou hast d. | 174:16
Thy will be d. | 30:22
traveller's journey is d. | 39:7
Were it not better d. | 145:1
What have I d. for you | 102:16
what shall be d. in the dry? | 33:38
what was to be d.? | 17:10
what's d. is d. | 199:3
when love is d. | 40:13
which we ought to have d. | 166:9
ye have d. it unto me | 32:17
Dong with the Luminous Nose! | 131:1
Donkey wot wouldn't go | 23:2
Donne: Dr. D.'s verses are like the
peace of God | 112:18
John D., Anne D., Un-done | 77:24
with D., whose muse | 66:11
Dons: If the D. sight Devon | 153:4
these regal D.! | 21:21
Don't: Can't! D.! | 127:1
Doodah!, doodah! | 87:8
Doodle: Sir Thomas D. wouldn't
come in | 73:27
Doom: d. impending | 59:5
His d.'s extremely hard | 92:9
I met my d. | 90:16
regardless of their d. | 98:8
to the crack of d. | 199:23
to the edge of d. | 211:16
Doomsday: danced till d. | 68:6
Dooney: play on my fiddle in D. | 250:8
Door: As the d. on its hinges | 239:12
at my wee, small d. | 73:10
beaten path to his d. | 83:4
before his cottage d. | 218:12
by the same D. | 85:7
d. flew open | 106:3
d. stood open | 65:3
dust behind the d. | 204:4
form from off my d.! | 163:17
get up and bar the d. | 16:6
hard at death's d. | 171:6
I stand at the d. | 37:15
Knock at the d. | 157:5
knocking on the moonlit d. | 73:4
living river by the d. | 221:22
No d. can keep them out | 103:18
of the big front d. | 93:10
outside the fast-closed d. | 111:14
posts of the d. moved | 27:27
Shut the d. after you | 80:21
that grows beside thy d. | 107:10
two-handed engine at the d. | 145:3
Door-keeper in the house of my
God | 170:15
Doors: death hath ten thousand d. | 240:7
d. of perception | 39:21
thousand d. to let out life | 141:12
ye everlasting d. | 169:4
Doorways are alternate Night and
Day | 84:22
Dots: those damned d. | 62:17
Double: D., d. toil and trouble | 199:13
D. think | 159:17
Doubled Cape Turk | 142:9

Doubt: begin to d.   200:5
  clouded with a d.   227:3
  defence of philosophic d.   15:23
  in honest d.   227:16
  no manner of d.   91:7
  no possible d. whatever   91:7
  One may not d. that   41:20
  through the night of d.   18:8
  when all men d. you   125:14
  When in d. win the trick   111:19
Doubted: never d. clouds would
    break   45:10
Doubtful: in d. things, liberty   19:2
Doubting-Castle   46:11
Doubts: To saucy d.   199:8
Dove: all the d.   70:26
  Beside the springs of D.   248:3
  burnished d.   228:5
  more soft than a d.'s   224:9
  She is coming, my d.   228:20
Dove-cot: eagle in a d.   184:19
Dover: chalk cliffs of D.   15:22
Doves: as harmless as d.   31:13
  moan of d.   229:19
Dowagers for deans   229:6
Dower: faith's transcendent d.   245:18
Down: as the sun went d.   124:2
  don't go d. with me   143:10
  d. and away below   11:10
  d. to the sea in ships   171:7
  d. to the seas again   141:2
  He that is d.   46:17
  lay me d. and dee   77:25
  level d. as far as themselves   114:15
  never go d. to the end   143:10
  pack-horse on the d.   150:14
  Piping d. the valleys   39:8
  put d. the mighty   32:37
  sit thee d. and write   39:8
  soon came d. again   69:26
  toss'd you d. into the field   85:11
  turneth it upside d.   172:5
  Up and d. the City Road   138:2
  When Kempenfelt went d.   70:11
  when they were d.   7:21
  who pulls me d.   138:14
Downhearted: Are we d.?   3:13, 128:28
  We are not d.   59:14
Downs: in the D. the fleet was
    moored   89:30
Downstairs: kick you d.   56:17
  Upstairs and d.   143:4, 155:16
Doxy: d., over the dale   210:4
  Orthodoxy is my d.   238:16
Drab: Ditch-deliver'd by a d.   199:16
Drag: would d. to hell   65:21
Dragon-green, the luminous   86:5
Drags its slow length along   164:11
Drain: by the town d.   219:17
Drained: irresistibly d.   78:20
Drake, he's in his hammock   153:5
Drama's laws   116:28
Drank: and d. deep   85:1
  He ate and d.   105:15
Draught of vintage!   121:3
Draw: d. but twenty miles   139:13
  gentleman to haul and d.   78:27
  rank mist they d.   145:3
  to d. my attention?   78:11
  to d. tears from me   107:20
  to their destruction d.   77:1
Drawers: and flannel d.   89:5
  d. of water   24:27
Drawn: but have d. his wit   118:3
  hast d. together   174:16
  is d. to them   119:10
  long d. out   144:19
  wine of life is d.   198:19
Draws: Though she d. him   134:7

Dread: d. and fear of kings   202:5
  d. of something after death   187:13
  for mighty d.   225:9
  so much d.   70:6
  that I may d.   123:2
  walk in fear and d.   66:5
  what d. grasp   39:2
  what d. hand?   39:2
  with holy d.   66:15
Dreadful: called thee mighty and d.   77:9
  deed of d. note   199:5
  d. state   73:27
  Matilda told such D. Lies   21:8
  that d. day   180:7
Dreadfully: He is d. married   238:20
Dream: as a d. dies   239:14
  as a d. doth flatter   211:10
  behind, a dream   212:2
  dissolving d.   213:12
  d. of joye   60:23
  d. of London   150:14
  d. of peace   112:2
  d. of the soft look   250:11
  d. you are crossing   91:24
  each age is a d.   159:19
  freshness of a d.   246:7
  glory and the d.   246:10
  I d. of Jeanie   87:15
  I have had a d.   203:17
  If you can d.   125:14
  in a d. of passion   187:11
  it was a d.   46:14
  Life is but an empty d.   133:26
  love's young d.   149:14
  not d. them, all day long   123:14
  or a waking d.?   121:7
  perchance to d.   187:13
  poet's d.   247:13
  shall d. dreams   29:22
  sight to d. of   66:8
  sweet d.   141:4
  they d. of home   87:4
  what my d. was   203:18
Dreamed: I slept, and d.   107:6
  never d...wrong would triumph   45:10
Dreamer: Beautiful D.   87:16
  d. of dreams   24:18
  this d. cometh   23:33
Dreaming: D. like a love-adept   214:9
  d. on both   200:20
  d. on things to come   211:14
  o'er the d. earth   214:1
Dreams: beyond the d. of avarice
                                 115:24, 149:11
  dreamer of d.   24:18
  dreamers of d.   159:18
  d. happy as her day   42:11
  d. of joy   213:20
  d. to sell   20:1
  dreamt of in d.   17:11
  I have bad d.   187:3
  I have spread my d.   250:6
  in d. behold the Hebrides   181:7
  into the land of my d.   123:12
  Is it some d.?   238:18
  my d. all come true   123:12
  not make d. your master   125:14
  rise from d. of thee   213:13
  sleep full of sweet d.   120:1
  Than this world d. of   227:2
  tread on my d.   250:6
  waken from his summer d.   214:2
  what d. may come   187:13
  wovest d. of joy   213:20
Dreamt: d. of in your philosophy   186:16
  I d. I dwelt   46:2
Dreamy lullaby   91:27
Drear: epitaph d.   126:17
Drear-nighted December   122:6

Dreary: My life is d.   228:18
Dregs: to my last d.   79:21
Drenched our steeples   195:4
Dress: come to thee for d.   234:1
  d. of thought   241:20
  if the devil d. her not   183:1
  modest d.   241:20
  Peace, the human d.   39:13
  sweet disorder in the d.   104:11
  that ever went with evening d.!   127:11
Dressed: All d. up   49:7, 242:6
  nature to advantage d.   160:10
  with garlands d.?   120:21
Dresses: neat-handed Phyllis d.   144:15
Dressing eels   166:5
Drest in a little brief authority   200:19
Drew: d. a dial from his poke   183:16
  d. from out the boundless deep   226:6
  D. nearer to me   104:1
  I d. my snickersnee   92:10
  yet my soul d. back   104:1
Dried up and withered   170:17
Drifts: thro' scudding d.   230:13
Drink: ask a d. divine   117:19
  Aunt Jobiska made him d.   131:11
  Come and have a d. with me   233:18
  D. and the devil   221:1
  D. deep   164:9, 185:12
  d. it up   155:9
  D. no longer water   36:28
  d. oblivion   142:3
  d. of Adam's ale   172:21
  D., pretty creature, d.!   247:16
  d., puppy, d.   242:20
  D. to me only   117:19
  D. to the lass   216:19
  glass I d. from   151:7
  hero must d. brandy   115:20
  I will d. life   230:13
  let a soldier d.   204:29
  Let us eat and d.   28:6, 35:26
  Man wants but little d.   106:12
  Nor any drop to d.   65:14
  not. .d. with you   201:13
  Now we must d.   109:8
  shall give to d.   31:17
  sit and d. with me   22:1
  That I might d.   121:3
  There are five reasons we should
    d.   2:5
  tippled d. more fine   120:17
  to eat and to d.   26:43
Drinking: D. is the soldier's pleasure   79:512
  d. up ta water   14:3
  knave in d.   180:19
Drinks: d. like a beast   128:8
  it's a long time between d.   5:13
Drive: But d. far off   146:20
  D. my dead thoughts   214:4
  d. nature out   108:8
  nor d. her away   156:3
  That I was used to d.   111:3
Driven: all are d. one road   109:11
  better bargain d.   216:29
  D. by the spheres   235:11
  d. into a desperate strait   141:9
  leaves dead are d.   214:1
  white as d. snow   210:9
Drives away his fear   154:1
Driving: d. of Jehu   25:20
  in d. briskly   115:12
Drizzle: blasted English d.   126:14
Dromedary trots   66:11
Droning: his d. flight   97:8
Droop: begin to d.   199:6
  honest folk d.   43:12
Drooping head   145:4
Droops: D. on the little hands   143:15
  Now d. the milk-white peacock   229:16
Drop: d. about my head   140:6
  D. thy pipe   39:8
  heard a pin d.   176:7
  His eyes d. out   133:9
  Nor any d. to drink   65:14
  one d. would save my soul   138:14
  Droppeth as the gentle rain   202:5
Droppy: Croppy, D.   88:16
Drops: little d. of water   55:26
  little water d.   139:1
  these are gracious d.   194:10
Dropt: D. from the zenith   146:9
  D. in her lap   85:2
Dross: all is d.   138:12
Drought of Marche   60:8
Drown: can the floods d. it   27:20
  I'll d. my book   208:19
  That tears shall d. the wind   198:4
Drowned: chance of being d.   114:6
  d. the cocks   195:4
  have d. my Glory   85:15
  pluck up d. honour   190:9
  were d. in the depth of the sea   31:38
Drowns the parson's saw   196:20
Drowse: begin to droop and d.   199:6
Drows'd with the fume of poppies   119:18
Drowsy: And d. tinklings   97:1
  d. numbness   121:8
  d. syrups   205:9
  of a d. man   193:5
Drudge: harmless d.   114:4
  his mother d.   212:20
Drudgery: Makes d. divine   103:22
Drum: d. them up the Channel   153:4
  like a soft d.   123:11
  listenin' for the d.   153:5
  Music of a distant d.   84:20
  Not a d. was heard   245:3
  rumble of a distant d.   84:21
  spirit-stirring d.   205:10
  Take my d. to England   153:4
Drums: bangin' er de d.?   101:1
  beat the d.   150:10
  when the d. begin to roll   127:22
Drunk: d. and raising Cain   124:12
  d. delight of battle   230:13
  d. the milk of Paradise   66:15
  d. with sight of power   127:6
  eaten and d. enough   108:13
  got d.   165:18
  hath not d. ink   196:14
  Have d. their Cup   85:4
Drunkard: rolling English d.   61:21
Drunken: brought d. forth   182:23
  d. of things Lethean   224:10
  d. sailor   8:12
  got more d.   165:18
  stagger like a d. man   171:8
  still had d. heads   209:20
Dry: But oh, I am so d.!   5:5
  keep your powder d.   38:5
  what shall be done in the d.?   33:38
Dryad: light-winged D.   121:2
Dubious: and a d. hand   117:3
Dublin: In D.'s fair city   5:8
Ducat: Dead, for a d.   188:24
Ducats: O my d.! O my daughter!   201:24
Duchess: that's my last D.   44:14
  The D.! The D.!   56:15
Duchess of Malfi: I am D. still   240:6
Duck: As the D. and the Kan-
    garoo   131:2
Ducks: Four d. on a pond   2:18
Duke: Bury the Great D.   228:24
  D. of Plaza Toro   91:6
  D.'s son—cook's son   124:11
  Earl, the Marquis, and the D.   91:9
  everybody praised the D.   218:14
Dukes were three a penny   91:13

Dulce: D. et decorum est pro patria
   mori   109:18
  D. *ridentem Lalagen amabo*   109:6
Dulcimer: damsel with a d.   66:15
  sound of the. . d.   29:16
Dull: as d. as ditch water   75:14
  but d. and hoary   235:10
  do not d. thy palm   185:21
  d. as night   202:13
  d. it is to pause   230:13
  D. would he be   249:4
  is d. work   116:13
  not only d. in himself   87:1
  Sherry [Thomas Sheridan] is d.   114:17
  so d. and heavy   204:9
  splendidly d.   228:19
  stirring d. roots   81:23
  Though it's d.   123:15
  Vexing the d. ear   193:5
Duller: And d. shouldst thou be   186:9
Dullness: cause of d. in others   87:1
Dulls the edge   185:21
Dumb: Oh, noisy bells, be d.   111:1
  sheep. . is d.   28:21
Dumb-shows: inexplicable d.   188:7
Dummheit: mit der D. kämpfen Götter   179:13
Dumps: As one in doleful d.   213:5
  of d. so dull   204:9
Dun: her breasts are d.   212:3
Duncan: D. hath borne his faculties   198:4
  D. is in his grave   199:4
  fatal entrance of D.   197:14
Dunfermline: King sits in D. town   16:12
Dungeon: in a d. cell   92:9
  vapour of a d.   205:7
Dungeons: brightest in d.   51:9
Dunmow: in Essex at D.   60:20
Dunsinane: do come to D.   200:5
  to high D. hill   199:22
Duodecimos: band of d.   70:20
Dupe: played with a d.   71:4
Dupes: hopes were d.   64:10
Dupree: Weatherby George D.   143:9
Durst not have used that word   82:10
Dusk: in the d. with a light behind
  her   93:34
Dusky: d. night   84:11
  Trusty, d., vivid   221:19
Dust: All valiant d.   127:7
  blossom in their d.   216:25
  but some d. and a shadow   110:6
  cinders, ashes, d.   120:15
· come to d.   184:22
  curates, long d., will come   42:6
  D. hath closed Helen's eye   152:5
  D. into D.   85:5
  d. of creeds outworn   214:8
  d. return to the earth   27:8
  D. thou art   23:17, 133:26
  d. to d.   168:20
  d. whom England bore   42:11
  d. would hear her   228:20
  forbear to dig the d.   212:5
  Frail children of d.   96:20
  grave and d.   174:15
  Guilty of d. and sin   104:1
  in a handful of d.   81:24
  in the d. be equal   216:24
  into the D. descend   85:5
  Less than the d.   107:10
  lick the d.   170:9
  licks the d.   165:9
  light in the d.   213:16
  Make d. our paper   206:14
  not without d. and heat   148:9
  provoke the silent d.   97:13
  quintessence of d.   187:4
  richer d. concealed   42:11
  shake off the d. of your feet   31:12

sun which makes a d.   162:8
sweep the d.   204:4
To the vile d.   180:6
turn to d.   140:12
with age and d.   174:15
writes in the d.   15:14
Dusty: d. answer   142:7
  way to d. death   200:4
Dutch: fault of the D.   54:12
  my dear old D.   62:4
Duties: brace ourselves to our d.   62:22
  If I had no d.   115:12
  Property has its d.   79:1
  teach new d.   135:4
  to discharge my d.   81:5
Dutiful: hang your husband and be
  d.   89:13
Duty: constabulary d.   93:21
  daily stage of d.   123:1
  D. of an Opposition   62:16, 219:23
  d. to have done the highest   226:19
  d. to try to prevent it   143:19
  d. towards God   167:33
  d. towards my Neighbour   167:33
  Every subject's d.   191:13
  I have done my d.   152:22, 230:5
  Love is then our d.   89:19
  more than a moral d.   243:13
  my d. to warn you   78:7
  no d. . . was so trying   113:4
  Nor law, nor d.   250:7
  O D.!   245:19
  our bounden d.   167:24
  path of d.   229:2
  that life was D.   107:6
  that our d. has been done   91:11
  their d. to God   242:14
  this is a d., not a sin   241:19
  to do my d.   168:1
  when love and d. clash   229:8
  whole d. of man   27:10
  will do his d.   152:20
Dwarfish whole   66:12
Dwell: alone d. for ever   11:13
  d. in the house of the Lord   169:2
  d. in the tents   170:15
  d. in thy tabernacle   168:27
  enter in and d. there   31:24
  for aye to d.   229:5
  He's made to d.   92:9
  Here will I d.   138:12
  on earth do d.   123:5
  that d. in the land   27:31
  they that d. therein   169:3
  to d. a weeping hermit   67:15
  to d. in adamantine chains   145:12
  to d. together   171:26
  with vilest worms to d.   211:7
Dwelling: come nigh thy d.   170:20
  d. is the light   248:19
  Upon the dull earth d.   210:2
  will choose her d.   79:23
Dwellings: amiable are thy d.   170:13
Dwells: She d. with Beauty   120:24
Dwelt: and d. among us   33:46
  d. in the land of Nod   23:19
  have d. secure   239:14
  I dreamt I d.   46:2
  She d. among the untrodden
    ways   248:3
Dwindle, peak, and pine   197:6
Dyes: splendid d.   120:4
Dying: as a d. man to d. men   19:1
  but, d., has made us rarer gifts   41:16
  despised and d. king   215:8
  doubly d.   180:6
  dream that is d.   159:19
  echoes d., d., d.   229:10
  I am d., Egypt   182:19

it had a d. fall 209:2
like a d. lady 215:13
Tomorrow will be d. 104:14
Truth sits on the lips of d. men 11:21
unconscionable time d. 60:5
unmoved see thee d. 75:19
with the d. sun 40:13
Dyke: Feb. fill the d. 234:13
Dynastic: a simple d. arrangement 98:20
Dynasties: Though D. pass 100:4

E

Each: Bound e. to e. 247:10
e. according to his abilities 140:15
e. without the other! 134:7
To e. his suff'rings 98:9
Eager: nipping and an e. air 186:2
Eagerly: did e. frequent 85:7
Eagle: By all the e. 70:26
e. in a dove-cot 184:19
e. mewing her mighty youth 148:10
In and out the E. 138:2
way of an e. 26:31
when with e. eyes 121:9
Eagles: e. be gathered together 32:13
swifter than e. 24:48
Where his e. never flew 69:20
with wings as e. 28:15
Ear: beat upon my whorlèd e. 107:13
came o'er my e. 209:2
dull cold e. of death? 97:13
e. of man hath not seen 203:18
flea in his e. 11:2
flea in 's e. 19:16
from e. to e. 240:3
Give e. unto my song 95:10
Give every man thine e. 185:21
In a believer's e. 154:1
in an Ethiop's e. 207:17
lies in the e. 196:18
Oon e. it herde 60:28
sensual e. 120:19
shouted in his e. 58:6
Stop thine e. 180:15
through mine e. 144:9
to soothe thine e. 67:11
turn the deaf e. 223:22
Unpleasing to a married e.! 196:19
Vexing the dull e. 193:5
Earl: The E., the Marquis, and the
  Dook 91:9
Early: call me e. 228:21
e. generations of mankind 108:14
E. in the morning 102:1
E. one morning 4:4
good die e. 72:16
had it been e. 113:22
one of the e. birds 68:21
Right e. in the year 106:7
Walking so e. 180:18
Early-rising: As yet the e. sun 104:10
Earnest: I am in e. 89:3
Life is e.! 133:26
Earnestly: truly and e. repent 167:22
Ear-piercing fife 205:10
Ears: blow in our e. 191:8
Creep in our e. 202:11
e., and hear not 171:13
e. like errant wings 61:16
Enemy e. are listening 9:9
He that hath e. to hear 32:28
hedges e. 223:25
I have e. in vain 121:6
lend me your e. 194:3
make two e. of corn 223:2
pluck'd the ripen'd e. 229:7
shout about my e. 61:17

split the e. 188:7
that stoppeth her e. 169:29
Earsight: eyes deceive me e.? 238:18
Earth: abominations of the e. 37:25
above heaven and e. 172:6
air, e., and skies 248:20
all e. to love 127:18
all E.'s volumes 59:20
Angels bending near the e. 181:10
anywhere else on e. 99:2
arising from sullen e. 210:13
as they on e. were cramm'd 247:15
At the round e.'s imagined corners 77:8
aught else on e. 89:17
bleeding piece of e. 193:20
bridal of the e. 104:6
Cold in the e. 41:15
corners of the e. 170:22
Could frame in e. 219:12
crown o' the e. 182:21
deep-delved e. 121:3
dust return to the e. 27:8
e., and every common sight 246:7
e. bring forth 170:5
e. doth like a snake renew 213:12
E. has many a noble city 58:22
E. has not anything 249:4
e. his sober inn 54:10
e. in an earthy bed 228:20
e. in fast thick pants 66:14
e. is not too low 103:18
e. is the Lord's 35:19, 169:3
e. is the sepulchre 233:12
e. of majesty 206:7
e. received her frame 239:14
E.! render back 51:20
e. reply 241:7
e. . . rolled with visible motion 246:6
e. shall be fill'd with the glory of
  God 2:3
e. shall be full of the knowledge 28:3
e. shall pass away 180:7
E. stood hard as iron 177:9
e., that bears thee dead 190:23
e. to e. 168:20
e. was nigher heaven 44:25
E. will slumber o'er us 10:2
E.'s crammed with heaven 43:4
e.'s diurnal course 245:14
e.'s foundations stay 111:11
E.'s joys grow dim 135:16
E.'s shadows fly 213:10
E.'s vain shadows flee 135:17
English e. and sky 102:17
every man upon this e. 136:9
first e. were passed away 37:25
flowers appear on the e. 27:16
for e. too dear 207:17
foundations of the e. 25:41
from which e. 174:15
fruits of the e. 166:25
giants in the e. 23:21
girdle round about the e. 203:8
glance from heaven to e. 203:19
glory from the e. 246:8
God created the heaven and the e. 23:4
goodly frame, the e. 187:4
Heaven and e.! 185:11
Heaven and e. in ashes 59:5
heaven on e. 146:15
heroic for e. too hard 43:7
I create . . a new e. 29:3
I will move the e. 10:13
If he were on e. 108:12
In that rich e. 42:11
in the e. beneath 167:7
inhabitants o' the e. 197:8
is of the e. 35:28
It fell to e. 133:12

Earth (cont.)
it would be hell on e. 212:19
known upon e. 170:4
lards the lean e. 190:11
Lay her i' the e. 189:22
Let saints on e. 241:17
Lie heavy on him, E.! 83:12
life of men on e. 20:2
made heaven and e. 167:11
mighty of the e. 147:6
militant here in e. 167:20
more things in heaven and e. 186:16
Moved e. and heaven 230:15
new heaven and a new e. 37:22
nook of e.'s surface 109:12
not on things on the e. 36:22
now beat the e. 109:8
o'er the dreaming e. 214:1
on e. do dwell 123:5
on e. peace 32:43
on the bosom of the e. 206:14
On the e. the broken arcs 43:6
over the whole e. 242:14
Peace on e. 241:15
Peace on the e. 181:10
rare bird on the e. 119:4
replenish the e. 23:9
round e.'s human shores 121:8
sad old e. 243:3
salt of the e. 30:12
shall not perish from the e. 132:8
sleeps in e. 246:3
stand at the latter day upon the
e. 25:35
Standing on e. 146:20
That e. affords 80:17
they shall inherit the e. 30:11
This e., this realm, this England 206:7
though the e. be moved 169:20
though they come from the ends
of the e.! 124:13
Till E. and Sky stand 124:13
to and fro in the e. 25:24
to that pleasant country's e. 207:2
treasures upon e. 30:23
two paces of the vilest e. 190:23
unawakened e. 214:4
Upon the dull e. dwelling 210:2
water under the e. 167:7
when e.'s foundations fled 111:11
whole e. is full of his glory 27:27
whole round e. 227:2
will be done in e. 30:22
work i' the e. so fast? 186:15
wrong left unredressed on e. 124:8
Ye know on e. 120:23
Yours is the E. 125:16
Earthly: all e. things above 219:18
e. power 202:5
fruition of an e. crown 139:10
sum of e. bliss 146:21
touch of e. years 245:14
Earthquake: Lord was not in the e. 25:14
Earthy: in an e. bed 228:20
is of the earth, e. 35:28
Ease: another's loss of e. 39:6
at e. for aye to dwell 229:5
debauched with e. 79:4
E. after war 219:10
full-throated e. 121:2
gives its e. 39:5
greatest of e. 132:4
ill at e. 172:22
in our hours of e. 180:13
infinite heart's e. 191:14
live at home at e. 160:19
rots itself in e. 186:9
take mine e. 190:21
Thy fortress, and thy e. 235:8

Easeful: in love with e. Death 121:6
Easier for a camel 32:1
Easily: is not e. provoked 35:21
East: 'eard the E. a-callin' 126:13
e. of Suez 126:15
from the e. must travel 246:11
from the e., nor from the west 170:10
goes out to the E. 128:8
gorgeous E. 249:1
Hunter of the E. 84:15
It is the e. 207:20
man with his back to the E. 65:3
morn purples the e. 146:20
Oh, E. is E. 124:13
seen his star in the e. 30:1
three kings into the e. 48:22
When the wind is in the e. 8:15
who tried to hustle the E. 126:17
wise men from the e. 30:1
Eastern: misty e. cave 213:20
not by e. windows only 64:1
Eastertide: white for E. 110:15
Easy: E. live 180:15
From all the e. speeches 61:20
If to do were as e. 201:9
my yoke is e. 31:21
not e. to tell what it is 115:9
not so. e. as you seem to think 96:4
take love e. 250:5
Eat: dogs e. of the crumbs 31:31
e. a missionary 243:2
e. bread to the full 24:6
e. it in haste 24:5
e. my supper there 249:3
e. the cones 88:9
e. the fat of the land 23:36
e. to live 148:14
hath not e. paper 196:14
I see what I e. 56:22
Let them e. cake 138:8
Let us e. and drink 28:6, 35:36
Nothing to e. but food 123:10
pig was e. 158:13
shalt thou e. bread 23:16
that each other e. 204:22
thou shalt not e. of it 23:10
to e., and to drink 26:43
To e. with apple-tart 221:13
we must e. we 232:1
will not e. with you 201:13
won't e. her dinner 143:11
Eaten: bread e. in secret 26:11
e. every one 58:1
e. me out of house 190:29
e. thee for a word 196:17
hath even e. me 170:8
have e. and drunk enough 108:13
often e. oysters 90:19
that the locust hath e. 29:21
Eater: out of the e. 24:31
Eateth: Why e. your master 31:10
Eating: against e. cares 144:19
appetite grows by e. 174:4
e. pâtés de foie gras 218:2
e. too much lettuce 166:2
Eats: seeking the food he e. 183:15
Ebb and flow by the moon 196:6
Ecce homo 34:25
Echo: e. answers 'Where?' 50:19
E. beyond 140:1
e. is not faint at last 129:22
Echoes: e. roll from soul to soul 229:12
set the wild e. flying 229:10
stage but e. back 116:28
Echoing: My e. song 140:12
or the e. horn 97:11
Eclipse: E. first 159:12
in the moon's e. 199:15
total e. 147:3

Economists: That of sophisters, e. 47:14
Écrasez l'infâme 237:17
Ecstasies: Dissolve me into e. 144:9
Ecstasy: Blasted with e. 188:6
  In such an e.! 121:6
  maintain this e. 161:11
  Or wak'd to e. 97:14
Eden: This other E. 206:7
  Through E. took their solitary
    way 146:25
  voice that breathed o'er E. 122:20
  With loss of E. 145:9
Edge: axe's e. did try 140:8
  plugging tooth on e. 210:5
  to the e. of doom 211:16
Editis annalibus laudatoque M.
  Bruto C. Cassium Romanorum
  ultimum dixisset 224:17
Edmonton: should dine at E. 69:30
  Unto the Bell at E. 69:22
Edom: over E. will I cast out my
  shoe 170:2
Educated: Born and e. in this
  country 90:7
  treason of the e. classes 22:4
Education: liberal e. 103:7, 220:5
  travel..is a part of e. 15:4
Edward: proud E.'s power 48:30
  winding-sheet of E.'s race 97:5
Edwin: let me always call you E. 83:20
Eels: dressing e. 166:5
Effect: between the e. and it! 197:15
  what e. these men will have 240:22
Efficacious: more e. 116:25
Effort: But if that e. be too great 6:7
  e. very nearly killed her 21:8
  mighty e. of will 22:11
  written without e. 116:10
Eftsoons his hand dropt he 65:5
Egestas: duris urgens in rebus e. 237:5
Egg: as an e. is full of meat 207:28
  e. boiled very soft 13:12
  got a bad e. 173:21
Eggs: as a weasel sucks e. 183:14
  boil e. in your shoes 131:15
  Butter and e. 53:6
  e., apples, and cheese 124:15
Eglantine: and with e. 203:9
Egypt: I am dying, E. 182:19
  in a brow of E. 203:19
  there was corn in E. 23:34
Eheu fugaces 17:9, 109:14
Eigg on the starboard bow 221:21
Eight: Pieces of e.! 221:3
Einstein: Let E. be! 219:21
Either: How happy could I be with
  e. 89:21
Elaine the fair 226:21
Elbow: My right e. 92:11
Elected silence 107:13
Elects: told us of his e. 150:9
Elegant: You e. fowl! 131:7
Elegantiae arbiter 224:18
Elementary, said he 78:6
Elemented: which e. it 77:20
Elements: e. so mix'd in him 194:24
  fram'd us of four e. 139:10
  I tax not you, you e. 195:5
  that was before the e. 42:22
Elephant: at the E. 209:15
  E.'s Child 128:13
  thought he saw an E. 56:7
Elephants never forget an injury 178:16
Elevated: joy of e. thoughts 248:19
Eleven: tells you he's only e. 91:25
Elf: deceiving e. 121:7
Elfland: horns of E. 229:11
Elgin: He stands in E.'s place 78:23
Eli, Eli, lama sabachthani? 32:25

Eliminated the impossible 78:16
Eliot: George E.! 173:20
Eliza: That so did take E. 118:9
Elizabeth: no scandal about Queen
  E.? 216:2
  Servant to Queen E. 98:16
Ellen: wed the fair E. 180:10
Elliptical billiard balls 92:9
Elms: immemorial e. 229:19
Elm-tree: Round the e. bole 44:1
Eloquent, just, and mighty Death! 174:16
Elsewhere: Hath had e. its setting 246:11
  ne'er met with e. 161:17
Elves: And the e. also 104:13
Elysium: Sleeps in E. 191:15
  What E. have ye known 120:17
Elysium: Tochter aus E. 179:11
Embalmed and treasured 148:8
Embark: When I e. 226:6
Embarras: L'e. des richesses 2:15
Embarrassing: e. young 89:6
Embattled: Here once the e.
  farmers 82:14
Embers: glowing e. 144:7
Emblazonings: dim e. 120:4
Emblem: e. of my own perpetual
  residence 153:11
Embodied paradox 68:2
Embodiment: is the true e. 91:17
Embody the Law 91:17
Embrace: none..do there e. 140:12
  right hand doth e. me 27:15
  stronger faith e. 134:20
  take your last e.! 208:5
  to e. me she inclined 148:2
Emerald: men of the E. Isle 78:30
Emergunt: Haud facile e. 119:3
Eminence: To that bad e. 146:10
Emmanuel: O come, O come, E. 152:15
Emotion: morality touched by e. 12:8
Emotions: purgation of such e. 10:16
Emperor: by e. and clown 121:6
  had he never been e. 225:1
Empire: Another mighty E. 247:11
  course of e. 22:16
  E. is a Commonwealth of Nations 177:5
  great e. and little minds 47:4
  Joy, E. and Victory 215:1
  loungers of the E. 78:20
  metropolis of the e. 64:14
  nor Roman, nor an e. 237:14
  rod of e. 97:14
  savage wilderness into a glorious
  e. 47:5
  thy dread e. 164:3
  To found a great e. 217:12
  With an e.'s lamentation 228:24
Empire: ni romain, ni e. 237:16
Empires: faiths and e. gleam 213:12
  Vaster than e. 140:11
Employ: should life e. 89:17
Emptorem: si e. invenerit 179:1
Empty: e., swept, and garnished 31:23
  of an e. day 150:13
  sent e. away 32:38
  turn down an e. Glass! 86:3
Emulation: Shouting their e. 184:17
Enamelled: her e. skin 203:9
  set in e. meadows 238:5
Enamour: which most e. us 50:17
Enamoured on peace 63:26
Enchanted: as holy and e. 66:14
  e. woods 142:8
Enchanter: from an e. 214:1
Enchantment: distance lends e. 54:3
Enclitic: the e. De 43:19
Encounter darkness as a bride 200:22
Encourager: pour e. les autres 237:11
Encumbers him with help? 113:22

End: at the e. of a perfect day   40:6
  at their wit's e.   171:8
  beginning of the e.   225:4
  bring our years to an e.   170:18
  comes in the e. despondency   247:19
  death the journey's e.   79:28
  e. crowns all   209:1
  e. of it again   168:30
  e. of Solomon Grundy   158:2
  e. of the beginning   63:2
  e. of this day's business   194:22
  fight on to the e.   99:4
  God be at my e.   4:10
  hasten to their e.   211:5
  look to the e.   10:5
  made a good e.   189:16
  making many books there is no e.   27:9
  my journey's e.   205:17
  My patience is now at an e.   105:7
  sans E.!   85:5
  served no private e.   164:25
  something ere the e.   230:15
  then the e. is known   194:22
  there's an e. on't   114:24
  This is not the e.   63:2
  Though the e. in sight   45:8
  till you come to the e.   57:13
  to e. as superstitions   112:11
  to make an e.   230:13
  to the e. of the road   130:9
  to the e. of the town   143:10
  true beginning of our e.   203:20
End-all: be-all and the e.   198:3
Endearing young charms   149:12
Endears: all the more e.   229:7
Ended: begun, continued, and e.   167:29
Ending: in ashes e.!   59:5
  the beginning and the e.   37:13
Endless: Closed his eyes in e. night 98:11
  one e. night   58:26
  pure and e. light   235:11
  sold for e. rue   110:17
  To e. years the same   239:14
Endlessly rocking   242:12
Endow: I thee e.   168:14
Ends: at both e.   143:1
  come from the e. of the earth!   124:13
  divinity that shapes our e.   189:24
  e. with Revelations   243:26
  that e. the night   239:14
  to make both e. meet   88:11
  undiscovered e.   21:12
Endurance, and courage   179:19
Endure: can long e.   132:8
  e. for a night   169:8
  e. the toothache   204:15
  government cannot e. permanently   132:7
  Men must e.   196:5
  potter and clay e.   45:5
  will not e.   209:5
Endured: much is to be e.   116:23
Endures for a breath   224:1
Endureth: e. all things   35:21
  mercy e. for ever   171:27
  praise of it e. for ever   171:11
Enemies: because of thine e.   168:22
  e. shall lick the dust   170:9
  e. that trouble me   169:17
  let his e. be scattered   170:6
  make thine e. thy footstool   171:10
  naked to mine e.   193:1
  smote his e.   170:12
  speak with their e.   171:23
Enemy: effect these men will have
    on the e.   240:22
  e. faints not   64:10
  e. hath done this   31:26
  e. of the good   237:14
  How goes the e.?   175:7

I impeach the common e.   47:11
  last e.   35:25
  Mine e.'s dog   195:23
  near'st and dearest e.   190:20
  Our friends, the e.   22:15
  see no e.   183:13
  spoils of the e.   138:7
  still the e.   168:22
Energy is Eternal Delight   39:15
Enfants: e. de la patrie   177:17
  Les e. terribles   89:6
Enforcement: gentleness my strong
    e.   183:19
Engaged: All that men are e. in   119:1
Engendered in the eyes   202:1
Engine: An e. that moves   100:12
  two-handed e. at the door   145:3
Engineer hoist with his own petar   189:5
Engines: you mortal e.   205:10
England: all the youth of E.   191:5
  always be an E.   160:21
  Be E. what she will   62:7
  bow was made in E.   78:1
  defence of E.   15:22
  did E. help me   44:3
  dust whom E. bore   42:11
  E. and Saint George!   191:9
  E., bound in   206:8
  E.! did I know till then   247:2
  E. expects that every man   152:20
  E. forget her precedence   148:11
  E. has been in a dreadful state   73:27
  E. has saved herself   162:22
  E. hath need of thee   247:7
  E., home and beauty   40:18
  E. is a garden   125:8
  E. is a nation of shopkeepers   151:15
  E. is a paradise for women   49:11
  E. is the mother of Parliaments   41:12
  E. is the paradise of women   86:13
  E. mourns for her dead   38:1
  E., my E.?   102:16
  E., that was wont to conquer   206:9
  E. to be the workshop   76:6
  E., with all thy faults   70:15
  E.'s green and pleasant Land   38:16
  E.'s pleasant pastures   38:16
  further off from E.   57:9
  gentlemen in E.   192:4
  gentlemen of E.   160:19
  get me to E.   42:7
  Go anywhere in E.   212:15
  high road that leads him to E.!   114:13
  how can I help E.?   44:3
  If E. to itself   193:8
  in E...only one sauce   54:19
  in E...sixty different religions   54:19
  meteor flag of E.   54:8
  of a king of E. too   82:9
  of those men in E.   192:2
  Oh, to be in E.   44:1
  Old E. to adorn   127:24
  old E.'s winding sheet   38:12
  our noble E.'s praise   136:5
  poorest he that is in E.   174:12
  stately homes of E.   102:11
  Take my drum to E.   153:4
  That is for ever E.   42:11
  this E.   206:7
  This E. never did.   193:8
  Wake up, E.   90:9
  we are the people of E.   61:24
  what should they know of E.   125:4
  where E. is finished   143:2
  whoever wakes in E.   44:1
  With E.'s own coal   124:15
  Ye Mariners of E.   54:6
English: among the E. Poets   122:10
  as an angel is the E. child   39:10

Between E. earth and sky 102:17
blasted E. drizzle 126:14
E...are..foul-mouthed 101:12
E. Bible..alone suffice 137:3
E. unofficial rose 42:5
made our E. tongue 219:15
really nice E. people 212:15
rolling E. drunkard 61:21
under an E. heaven 42:11
when you can't think of the E. 57:16
with our E. dead! 191:8
Englishman: and not one E. 238:11
cleave to the heart of a true
E. 1:10
E., and Friend! 247:18
E. thinks he is moral 212:21
He is an E.! 93:13
heart of every E. 179:19
one E. could beat three French-
men 1:10
Englishmen: E. detest a siesta 69:8
Honest E. 123:15
Mad dogs and E. 69:8
We be all good E. 230:4
Engrossing death 208:5
Enhances: while it e. 74:12
Enjoy: cannot e. it 113:22
e. him for ever 216:26
go out and e. it 217:13
he can thoroughly e. 56:20
that private men e.! 191:14
we may e. them 166:25
what I most e. 210:13
Enjoyed: I have e. greatly 230:13
I once e.! 70:2
little to be e. 116:23
Enjoys: e. his own again 160:20
E. the air it breathes 248:12
Enkindles: it e. the great 49:14
Ennemi: l'e. du bien 237:14
Ennemis: nos amis, les e. 22:15
Enormous through the Sacred
Town 21:21
Enough: never had e. 90:19
that is e. 56:17
Enriches: that which not e. him 205:4
Ensign: Beauty's e. 208:4
Ensue: seek peace, and e. it 169:12
Enter: e. on far-reaching hopes 108:17
littlest fish may e. in 42:2
shall not e. into the kingdom 31:37
they e. in and dwell there 31:24
ye who e. here 72:5
Entering: century on which we are
e. 238:1
Enterprises: e. of great pith 187:13
impediments to great e. 14:17
Enterprising burglar 93:22
Enters: him that e. next 207:3
Entertain: to e. divine Zenocrate 139:12
Entertained angels 36:37
Entertainment: dull thy palm with
e. 185:21
Enthrals the crimson stomacher 104:11
Enthusiastic: with e. tone 92:1
Entire: E. and whole 219:18
e. of it self 77:22
Scheme of Things e. 86:1
Entrance: e. to a quarrel 185:21
fatal e. 197:15
From my first e. 104:1
Entrances: and their e. 183:20
Entrate: voi ch'e. 72:5
Entrusted with arms 244:16
Entuned in hir nose ful semely 60:12
Envieth: charity e. not 35:21
Envy: attracts the e. of the world 46:28
E. and calumny 213:8
E., hatred, and malice 166:22

e. of less happier lands 206:7
e. of thy happy lot 121:2
Toil, e., want 117:2
Ephesians: Diana of the E. 34:45
Epicure would say 217:18
Epigram: What is an E.? 66:12
Epilogue: good play needs no e. 184:16
Epistle: wordy and lengthy e. 119:7
Epitaph: And the e. drear 126:17
better have a bad e. 187:9
Epitaphs: derangement of e. 216:11
of worms, and e. 206:14
Epitome: all mankind's e. 79:8
Epochs: In e. when cash payment 55:8
Equal: All animals are e. 159:15
all men are created e. 8:9, 113:2, 132:8
All shall e. be 91:9
And faith shines equal 41:13
compel us to be e. 18:15
in the dust be e. made 216:24
more e. than others 159:15
Equality: e. in the servants' hall 18:15
Liberty! E.! Fraternity! 9:7
We wish, in a word, e. 15:21
Equator: as far as the E. 231:19
Equi: lente currite noctis e. 138:14
Equitem: post e...Cura 109:17
Equivalent: without an e. 116:18
Equivocate: I will not e. 89:3
Equivocation of the fiend 200:5
Erebus: dark as E. 202:13
Erect: above himself he can e. him-
self 72:3
Eremite: sleepless E. 121:8
Eric: and call me E. 83:20
Eros: Unarm, E. 182:18
Err: To e. is human 164:12
Errand: in thy joyous E. 86:3
Errands: run on little e. 91:10
Errant: ears like as wings 61:16
Erred: We have e. 166:8
Erring: check the e. 245:19
e. lace 104:11
Error: a stalking-horse to e. 40:5
All men are liable to e. 133:8
but e. is immense 40:4
If this be e. 211:16
in endless e. 164:19
that he is in an e. 133:7
Esau: E...is a hairy man 23:28
E. selleth his birthright 4:6
Escape: E. me? Never 44:8
shalt not e. calumny 188:5
ten guilty persons e. 38:8
who should e. whipping? 187:10
Escaped with the skin of my teeth 25:33
Eschew evil 169:12
Espagnol: je parle e. à Dieu 60:6
Espouse the everlasting Sea 249:2
Esprit: L'e. de l'escalier 76:2
Espy: And then the heaven e. 103:21
Essence: glassy e. 200:19
Essex: in E. at Dunmowe 60:20
Estate: came to man's e. 209:20
e. o' the world 200:6
fourth e. of the realm 136:19
holy e. of Matrimony? 168:10
low e. of his handmaiden 32:37
mind, body or e. 166:29
Not born in any high e. 2:11
order'd their e. 2:8
Estates: Three E. in Parliament 55:15
Esteemed: we e. him not 28:20
Estimate: know'st thy e. 211:9
Estranged: your e. faces 232:10
Et tu, Brute? 53:1, 193:17
Étais: tu n'y é. pas 103:1
État: L'E. c'est moi 134:17
Eternal: assert e. Providence 145:11

Eternal (*cont.*)
 Energy is E. Delight 39:15
 e. joys of heaven 138:11
 e. lids apart 121:8
 E. Passion! E. Pain! 11:18
 e. silence 161:5, 230:13
 E. spirit of the chainless mind! 51:9
 E. summer 51:17, 210:12
 e. triangle 7:15
 Hope springs e. 164:14
 is e. vigilance 71:17
 lay hold on e. life 36:31
 lose not the things e. 166:36
 our e. home 239:14
 our e. life 166:14
 pulse in the e. mind 42:11
 Resurrection to E. life 168:20
 swear an e. friendship 54:16
 swear e. friendship 217:16
 When in e. lines 210:12
Eternally: we wake e. 77:10
Eternity: ages of e. 55:26
 and E. in an hour 38:10
 Deserts of vast e. 140:12
 E. is in love with the productions of time 39:18
 from here to E. 125:7
 I saw E. 235:11
 Rise to all e. 241:11
 white radiance of E. 213:10
Ethereal: from th' e. sky 145:12
Etherized: Like a patient e. 81:14
Ethiop: in an E.'s ear 207:17
Ethiopian: Can the E. change his skin 29:6
Etiquette: It isn't e. 58:16
Eton: playing fields of E. 240:17
Étranglé: le dernier des rois..é. 142:15
Etrurian: where th' E. shades 146:4
Eugene Aram: And E. walked between 106:21
Eugenia: Listen, E. 11:18
Eureka! 10:12
Euripides: chorus-ending from E. 43:9
Europe: all over E. 98:17
 fifty years of E. 228:15
 glory of E. is extinguished 47:14
 iron curtain across E. 234:5
 last territorial claim.. in E. 105:8
 save E. by her example 162:22
 slain this year in E. 238:11
 Thames was the noblest river in E. 1:10
Eve: and E. span 8:13, 99:11
 fallen sons of E. 61:26
 noon to dewy E. 146:9
 O pensive E. 67:11
 thro' the land at e. 229:7
 when the e. is cool? 42:18
Even: At e. ere the sun was set 234:22
 keep your mind e. 109:10
 stilled at e. 177:15
Evening: at e. spinning by the fire 176:11
 beauteous e. 246:15
 e. bells 226:11
 e. chime 150:2
 e. comes 153:12
 e. of my age 178:3
 fairer than the e. air 138:13
 in preparation for the e. meal 245:2
 in the e. it is cut down 170:17
 like an e. gone 239:14
 Never morning wore to e. 227:7
 Shadows of the e. 18:6
 Soon as the e. shades prevail 1:12
 Soup of the e. 57:11
 summer's e. 194:7, 218:12
 Sunset and e. star 226:6
 that ever went with e. dress! 127:11

 turns as I, this e. 44:3
 Twilight and e. bell 226:6
 until the e. 171:3
 welcome peaceful e. in 70:18
 When the e. is spread out 81:14
 your shadow at e. 81:24
Even-song: But to the e. 104:10
Event: e. has happened 47:10
 from this great e. 147:11
 greatest e. 87:17
Eventide: fast falls the e. 135:16
Events: coming e. 53:16
Eventum: ad e. festinat 108:1
Ever: enjoy him for e. 216:26
 e. and for e. when I move 230:13
 e. this should be! 65:14
 For e., and for e., farewell 194:21
 For e. wilt thou love 120:20
 gone, and for e.! 180:3
 grow for e. and e. 229:12
 Hardly e.! 93:7
 I go on for e. 225:18
 is a joy for e. 120:1
 Jesus Christ the same..for e. 36:38
 may be for e. 71:2
 possession for e. 233:11
 talked on for e. 101:10
 There's the life for e. 221:15
 world spin for e. 228:14
 would you live for e.? 88:7
Everlasting: caught an e. cold 240:13
 espouse the e. Sea 249:2
 e. arms 24:25
 e. bliss! 138:11
 e. Father 27:32
 E. had not fix'd 185:11
 first, last, e. day 77:1
 From e. Thou art God 239:14
 from e. to e. 234:2
 should..have e. life 34:1
 thy e. kingdom 168:4
 to the e. bonfire 198:17
 ye e. doors 169:4
Evermore: but e. came out 85:7
 this time forth for e. 171:18
 waters rolling e. 246:12
Ever-rolling stream 239:14
Everybody: business of e. 136:18
 e.'s business 238:14
Every day, in e. way 69:5
Everyone: E. likes flattery 76:15
 e. will say 92:21, 22
Everything: Earth and e. that's in it 125:16
 E. passes 9:10
 e. that hath breath 172:8
 e. would appear..as it is 39:21
 good in e. 183:9
 is to say e. 237:19
 laugh at e. 19:7
 Of e. that's excellent 91:17
 place for e. 217:11
 price of e. 243:18
 Rum Go e. is 241:3
 sans e. 183:20
 Was e. by starts 79:8
Everywhere: out of the e. 137:9
Evidence: circumstantial e. 233:99
 it's not e. 75:26
Evil: all e. shed 42:11
 Be not overcome of e. 35:12
 deliver us from e. 30:22
 do e., that good may come 35:1
 Eschew e. 169:12
 E. be thou my Good 146:14
 E. communications 35:27
 e. days come not 27:7
 e. news rides post 147:8
 e. that men do 194:3

e. tongues 146:20
e. which I would not 35:6
fall'n on e. days 146:20
fear no e. 169:2
for the good or e. side 135:3
free of e. done 124:18
Great book, great e. 53:5
in the e. day 36:14
is the e. thereof 30:29
knowledge of good and e. 23:10
necessary e. 160:13
no e. happen unto thee 170:20
Of moral e. 248:15
overcome e. with good 35:12
Resist not e. 30:18
root of all e. 36:30
Such e. deeds 135:7
sun to rise on the e. 30:19
that call e. good 27:26
thinketh no e. 35:21
vice itself lost half its e. 47:15
whose cause this e. is upon us 29:25
Evils: greatest of e. 212:16
necessary e. 110:26
Evil-speaking: my tongue from e. 167:34
Evolution: Some call it e. 58:17
Ewe: at the e. milking 82:12
Exact: very rigid and e. 123:13
Exactitude: L'e. est la politesse des rois 134:18
Exaggeration: report of my death.. an e. 234:21
Exalted: Every valley shall be e. 28:12
e. them of low degree 32:38
Satan e. sat 146:10
shall be e. 33:15
Exalteth: whosoever e. himself 33:15
Example: E. is always more effica- cious 116:25
profit by their e. 103:9
Exceed: reach should e. his grasp 43:8
Excel: different men e. 62:9
dost all e. 58:22
Excellent: an e. creature 76:15
everything that's e. 91:17
'E!' I cried 78:6
e. to have a giant's strength 200:18
Name only is e. 172:6
Parts of it are e.! 173:21
situation e. 86:14
Excelling: all isles e. 79:23
Excels: it e. all other bliss 80:17
She e. each mortal thing 210:2
Excelsior! 133:17
Excess: Give me e. of it 209:2
light's e. 179:11
Nothing in e. 9:11
wasteful and ridiculous e. 193:6
Exchange one for the other 216:29
Excise. A hateful tax 116:14
Exciseman: De'il's Awa' Wi' the E. 48:15
Excite your languid spleen 92:22
Excited: When he's e. 93:26
Exciting: found it less e. 91:5
Excludes: day e. the night 239:15
Excuse: e. for the glass 216:19
hoped that they would e. it 60:5
I will not e. 89:3
Excuses no man 181:13
Execution: smok'd with bloody e. 197:4
Executioner: mine own E. 77:21
Executors: Let's choose e. 206:14
Exempt from public haunt 183:9
Exercise: what e. is to the body 220:6
Exertions: by her e. 162:22
Exeter: Bedford and E. 192:4
Exhausted: range of e. volcanoes 76:9
Exile: bind your sons to e. 128:5

Exiles: e. from our fathers' land 181:7
which none save e. feel 14:1
Exist: if God did not e. 237:15
Existait: Si Dieu n'e. pas 237:15
Existed: greatest geniuses that ever e. 238:6
whether it e. before 122:7
Existence: full tide of human e. 115:2
woman's whole e. 51:14
Exit pursued by a bear 210:4
Exits: For men to take their e. 240:7
They have their e. 183:20
Expanse: one wide e. 121:9
Expectancy and rose of the fair state 188:6
Expectation: sits E. in the air 191:5
Expected with confidence 74:12
Expects: England e. that every man 152:20
Expedient: It is e. for us 34:14
things are not e. 35:18
Expendable: They Were E. 242:7
Expenditure: annual e. 74:8
Expense: at the e. of two? 64:5
calculation of the e. 74:7
e. of spirit 212:1
Experience: acquist of true e. 147:11
Believe the man with e. 236:23
e. is an arch 230:13
hope over e. 114:27
Some by e. 68:13
travel.. is a part of e. 15:4
What e. and history teach 102:2
Experto credite 236:23
Expires: the wretched child e. 21:4
Expiring: E. frog! 75:19
thus e. do foretell 206:6
Explain: I would rise to e. 101:3
Expose thyself to feel 195:9
Exposed: much e. to authors 240:18
Express: how e. and admirable! 187:4
of shape e. 172:19
what I can ne'er e. 51:7
Expressed: n'er so well e. 164:10
Expresses: young man e. himself 92:21
Expression: an indolent e. 21:22
geographical e. 142:16
his favourite e. 74:7
Extensive: e. and peculiar observation with e. view 75:20, 117:1
Extenuate: nothing e. 205:20
Extinguishes: it e. the small 49:14
Extol: How shall we e. thee 22:7
Extravagant: flaunting, e. quean 216:19
plays e. matches 92:9
Extreme: Perplex'd in the e. 205:20
Savage, e., rude 212:1
Exuberance of his own verbosity 76:11
Exult O shores 242:11
Exultations: Thy friends are e., agonies 248:20
Exulting: people all e. 242:10
Eye: apple of an e. 168:28
as it were in the e. 148:7
beaming in one e. 74:20
beauteous e. of heaven 193:6
crowes feet be growe under your e. 60:24
curse in a dead man's e. 65:21
cursed me with his e. 65:17
dark and fiery e.! 154:12
e. for e. 24:7
e. of a needle 32:1
e. of heaven shines 210:12
e. of man hath not heard 203:18
E. of newt 199:14
e. of the beholder 111:23, 238:2
e. sublime 146:16
e. will mark our coming 51:13
Fair nature's e. 138:14
far as human e. could see 228:8

Eye (cont.)
finger in your e. 155:10
first your e. I ey'd 211:13
from every e. 95:21
glittering e. 65:4
Half hidden from the e.! 248:3
heart and hand, and e. 180:15
her e. was bright 65:2
horrid deed in every e. 198:4
I have only one e. 152:19
If thine e. offend thee 31:39
immortal hand or e. 39:1, 4
In my mind's e. 185:14
in the e. of Phoebus 191:15
in thy brother's e. 30:31
lack-lustre e. 183:16
lend the e. 191:8
mine e. may be deceiv'd 211:13
more than meets the e. 125:8
neither e. to see 131:20
On it may stay his e. 103:21
poet's e. 203:19
reverent e. must see 41:20
Scarf up the tender e. 199:6
scholar's e. 188:16
see e. to e. 28:19
soft black e. 149:19
such a wistful e. 243:4
Task-Master's e. 147:15
twinkling of an e. 35:29, 169:8
upon that inward e. 247:5
welcome in your e. 198:1
wink the other e. 90:17
with his keener e. 140:8
with my little e. 159:5
with open e. 60:9
with sovereign e. 211:2
with unshut e. 11:11
worm's e. point of view 173:23
Eyebrow: Made to his mistress' e. 183:20
Eyeless: E. in Gaza 147:2
vast and e. 236:13
Eyelids: from your e. wip'd a tear 183:19
tinged the e. 161:9
tir'd e. 228:17
With e. heavy and red 107:3
Eyes: as long as her e. could see 110:14
before mine e. 144:9
before my closing e. 135:17
before my very e. 75:23
bright e. of danger 221:16
cast one's e. so low! 195:19
Close up his e. 192:8
Day's azure e. 213:17
doth to her e. repair 210:2
engender'd in the e. 202:1
e. deceive me earsight? 238:18
e. have they, and see not 171:13
E., look your last! 208:5
e. of men...idly bent 207:3
e. so shiny blue 220:3
e. that shone 150:1
e., the break of day 201:3
e. were darken'd 228:1
For whose e. 108:18
fortune and men's e. 210:13
frightened look in its e. 217:6
From women's e. 196:16
full of e. within 37:16
gather to the e. 229:13
Get thee glass e. 195:22
God be in my e. 4:10
good for sore e. 223:9
haddocks' e. 58:12
happy human e. 221:24
Hath not a Jew e.? 201:27
Her e. the glow-worm lend thee 104:13
Her e. were deeper 177:15
her undazzled e. 148:10

His e. drop out! 133:9
His flashing e. 66:15
I have a pair of e. 75:27
In his e. foreknowledge 224:2
in Huncamunca's e. 84:10
lids of Juno's e. 210:8
lift up mine e. 171:16
Lift up thine e. 149:1
look your e. had once 250:11
look'd from thoughtful e. 161:15
lost to your e. 20:2
make e. at me 233:19
Make thy two e...start 186:7
mind has a thousand e. 40:13
mine e. dazzle 240:8
Mine e. have seen the glory 111:15
My mistress' e. 212:3
night has a thousand e. 40:13
Night hath a thousand e. 135:15
of neighbouring e. 144:14
one whose subdu'd e. 205:20
ope their golden e. 184:20
or e. can see 210:12
pearls that were his e. 208:11
Pure e. 122:18
Sans e. 183:20
satisfy our e. 249:13
shut her wild, wild e. 120:13
Soft e. look'd love 50:23
Stretch one's E. 21:8
Take a pair of sparkling e. 91:12
tears are in my e. 141:6
tears from their e. 37:18, 26
Tears in his e. 187:11
tempts your wand'ring e. 98:4
tir'd e. 228:17
to tear each other's e. 239:7
to turn thine e. 117:2
turn'st mine e. into my very soul 189:1
Two lovely black e. 64:15
West in her e. 65:3
what my e. are to rest upon 220:23
when I cast my e. 104:15
when with eagle e. 121:9
where you turn your e. 165:1
whites of their e. 173:22
Whose little e. glow 104:13
with e. of flame 57:14
With e. of gold 221:19
With e. severe 183:20
with judicious e. 234:3
With magic in my e. 100:17
with rainy e. 206:14
with thine e. 117:19
wonder in your e. 176:11
Eyesight and speech 224:2

F

Fables: old wives' f. 36:27
Fabula: mutato nomine de te f.
narratur 110:8
Face: as he has hit his f. 118:3
bears a lovely f. 72:18
Beefy f. 126:14
caricature of a f. 92:15
classic f. 163:16
Cover her f. 240:8
damned Tyburn-f. 68:7
Each turned his f. 65:17
f. of heaven 122:2, 138:10
f. that launch'd a thousand ships 138:12
fair of f. 156:17
find one f. there 123:18
garden in her f. 54:11
hid his f. 250:11
His f. when he repeats his verses 129:12
how wan a f.! 216:30

in the public's f. 178:8
kissing with golden f. 211:2
Lord make his f. shine 24:13
loved its silly f. 174:19
lying on his f. 231:17
make the f. of heaven so fine 208:1
mind's construction in the f. 197:13
mist in my f. 45:2
never see my f. again 227:2
night's starr'd f. 122:4
no glorious morning f. 221:24
of a foolish f. 179:8
of your changing f. 250:11
on the f. that was dead 245:6
on the sea's f. 141:2
one Autumnal f. 77:4
Pity a human f. 39:13
rogue's f. 68:7
see my Pilot f. to f. 226:6
seek His F. 149:1
She has a lovely f. 228:2
she painted her f. 25:21
shining morning f. 183:20
silent f. 247:17
Since I noo mwore do zee your f. 18:11
stand f. to f. 124:13
sweat of thy f. 23:16
then f. to f. 35:22
Was never f. so pleased my
    mind 7:22
who saw the f. of God 138:11
with twain he covered his f. 27:27
Your f...is as a book 198:1
Faces: by their f. see 247:15
    f. are but a gallery of pictures 14:14
    foreign f. 223:28
    grind the f. of the poor 27:23
    hid as it were our f. 28:20
    In nice clean f. 17:12
    old familiar f. 129:16
    your estranged f. 232:10
Facilis descensus Averni 236:15
Facing fearful odds 136:9
Faction: name of a f. 116:19
Facts: f. are sacred 179:17
    to his imagination for his f. 216:23
Faculties: borne his f. 198:4
    from each according to his f. 15:21
    whose f. can comprehend 139:10
Faculty: infinite in f. 187:4
Fade: eternal summer shall not f. 210:12
    f. away suddenly 170:17
    F. far away, dissolve 121:4
    f. into the light of common day 246:11
    flourish, or may f. 95:4
    Nothing of him that doth f. 208:11
    When can their glory f.? 226:5
    with thee f. away 121:3
Faded and gone 149:18
Fades: Now f. the glimmering land-
    scape 97:8
Fadeth: flower f. 28:13
Fading: f. rose 120:11
    Fast f. violets 121:5
    Life is f. 175:6
Faery: in f. lands forlorn 121:6
Fähigkeiten: jeder nach seinen F. 140:15
Fail: And we'll not f. 198:7
    flag or f. 62:21
    If we should f. 198:7
    soul does not f. you 108:9
    they shall f. [prophecies] 35:21
Failed: Light that F. 128:19
Faileth: Charity never f. 35:21
Fain would I climb 82:7, 174:14
Faint: Damn with f. praise 165:6
    F. heart never won fair lady 91:26
    F., yet pursuing 24:30
    not f. at last 129:22

shall walk, and not f. 28:15
They f. on hill 229:12
We f. beneath 244:15
Fainted: utterly have f. 169:7
Faintly: f. as tolls 150:2
    f., gentle springs 117:10
Faints: enemy f. not 64:10
    sense f. picturing them 214:2
Fair: All this f. 140:3
    beautiful and f. 246:8
    called her his lady f. 128:1
    chaste and f. 117:11
    days when I was f. 176:11
    deserves the f. 79:11
    died young and f. 152:5
    every f. from f. 210:12
    F. and learned 43:2
    f. and unpolluted flesh 189:22
    f. as a star 248:3
    f. as is the rose in May 60:22
    f. as the moon 27:19
    F., fat, and forty 181:3
    F. is foul, and foul is f. 197:2
    F. nature's eye 138:14
    F. quiet 140:5
    F. stood the wind for France 78:28
    f., the chaste 184:3
    F. the fall of songs 221:18
    f. to outward view 65:2
    Fat, f. and forty 159:10
    foul and f. a day 197:7
    ful f. and fetisly 60:12
    Full and f. ones 104:8
    Going to the f. 157:19
    Holy, f., and wise 210:2
    how f. she be? 244:18
    How sweet and f. 238:4
    in a f. ground 127:18
    just as pure and f. 91:19
    kind as she is f. 210:2
    magnificent f. play 78:7
    man right f. 212:4
    most divinely f. 226:8
    my f. one 27:16
    never won f. lady 91:26
    of that f. thou ow'st 210:12
    Sabrina f. 144:3
    sae fresh and f. 49:4
    she be f. 120:20
    She f., divinely f. 146:23
    to show more f. 249:4
    trees that grow so f. 127:24
    very memory is f. 235:9
    well and f. 147:10
    Whither away f. rover 41:8
    Woman true and f. 71:17
    Young, and so f. 106:20
Fairer: f. far than this fair day 213:14
    f. than the day 244:18
    f. than the evening air 138:13
    O f. daughter 109:4
Fairest: f. isle 79:23
    f. of her daughters 146:17
Fairies: beginning of f. 18:19
    do you believe in f.? 18:22
    f. at the bottom of our garden 88:12
    I don't believe in f. 18:20
    rewards and f. 68:27
Fairly: tried it f. 233:6
Fairy: by f. hands 67:15
    like a f. 149:8
    loveliest f. in the world 124:6
    Mr. W. Liiley believes it was a F. 12:20
    no f. takes 185:4
    to wrap a f. in 203:9
Fairy-tale of olden times 102:4
Faith: Articles of the Christian F. 167:32
    author and finisher of our f. 36:35

Faith (cont.)
Carthaginian f. 179:2
Ever the f. endures 102:17
f. and morals hold 247:1
f. as a grain of mustard seed 31:36
f. shines equal 41:13
f. that looks through death 246:13
f. unfaithful 226:22
F. without works 36:39
F.'s Defender 50:15
f.'s transcendent dower 245:18
fight of f. 36:31
fruit of the spirit is..f. 36:7
I have kept the f. 36:33
just shall live by f. 34:52
more f. in honest doubt 227:16
my f. that every flower 248:12
now abideth f. 35:22
our f. our pride 124:18
poetic f. 67:5
Sea of F. 11:8
simple f. than Norman blood 227:22
staff of f. 174:13
stronger f. embrace 134:20
though I have all f. 35:21
Who thee by f. 111:12
Faithful: Be thou f. unto death 37:14
come all ye f. 9:14, 159:6
f. and just to me 194:5
f. in love 180:9
f. to their system 137:12
good and f. servant 32:14
I have been f. 77:26
in action f. 164:25
these words are true and f. 37:26
Faithfulness and truth 170:19
Faithless: but f. was she 11:13
f. and stubborn 170:11
Faiths and empires gleam 213:12
Falchion: good biting f. 196:10
Falcon: dapple-dawn-drawn F. 107:17
f., towering in her pride of place 199:1
Fall: another thing to f. 200:15
before a f. 26:20
by dividing we f. 76:1
cradle will f. 38:9
Fair the f. of songs 221:18
f. o' the snow 118:11
F. out, and chide 239:8
fear I to f. 82:7, 174:14
fear to f. 249:11
fears no f. 46:17
For a benison to f. 104:16
had a great f. 156:1
half to f. 164:19
His f. was destined 117:3
it had a dying f. 209:2
Let it the curtains f. 70:18
lets the curtain f. 164:3
on other souls may f. 79:23
on the F. of the Rupee 243:12
shall f. into it 27:4
shall f. into the ditch 31:30
some by virtue f. 200:16
then let f. your..pleasure 195:5
thousand shall f. 170:19
we f. to rise 45:10
weep thy f. tonight 104:6
what a f. was there 194:10
which f. from their masters' table 31:31
worship and f. down 170:23
writing the decline and f. 90:12
Fallen: Babylon is f. 37:21
f. at length 229:1
F. cold and dead 242:11
f. on evil days 146:20
how are the mighty f. 24:47, 25:1
How art thou f. from heaven 28:4
O how f.! 145:14

soldier's pole is f. 182:21
Ye are f. from grace 36:6
Falleth: flower thereof f. away 37:3
where it f. 27:6
Falling: catch a f. star 77:16
dew was f. fast 247:16
F. from that willow-tree 96:9
Gently f. on thy head 239:11
if my leaves are f. 214:4
large white flakes f. 41:7
like a f. star 146:9
Falls: darkness f. 82:11
f. by its own weight 109:21
f. like Lucifer 192:14
f. on the other 198:4
fast f. the eventide 135:16
like a thunderbolt he f. 226:9
then he f. 192:14
False: all was f. and hollow 146:11
be f. to any man 185:21
Beware of f. prophets 31:3
f. Sextus 136:10
love f. or true 250:11
men would be f. 135:13
not bear f. witness 167:16
Ring out the f. 227:19
what is f. within 142:4
Falsehood: strife of Truth with F. 135:3
Falsely: too f. disdained 215:12
Falseness: produce in us a f. 178:9
Falstaff: F. sweats to death 190:11
sweet Jack F. 190:15
Falter: nor f., nor repent 215:1
Faltered: I have f. 221:24
Fame: blush to find it f. 165:13
f. can never heal 14:1
F. is the spur 145:1
f. soon spread around 69:28
fool to f. 165:4
heir of f. 147:12
hope of a season's f. 153:6
Man dreams of f. 226:24
Till love and f. 122:5
Fam'd: as she is f. to do 121:7
Familiar: Be thou f. 185:21
f. in his mouth 192:4
old f. faces 129:16
Families: best-regulated f. 74:12
happy f. resemble each other 233:22
two f. in the world 59:11
Family: children of one f. 239:8
my f. pride 91:28
Famine: They that die by f. 103:6
Famous: f. by their birth 206:7
found myself f. 52:18
now praise f. men 29:37, 127:15
was a f. victory 218:14
Fan: her f. spread 68:17
shall f. the glades 165:1
Fancies flee away 46:20
Fancy: all your f. paints 127:23
Ever let the f. roam 120:6
f. cannot cheat so well 121:7
f. dies 202:1
f. from a flower-bell 43:9
f. I am sick 221:8
f. outwork nature 182:15
F.'s child 144:19
I f. 92:12
little of what you f. 133:2
not expressed in f. 185:21
of most excellent f. 189:20
where is f. bred? 202:1
young man's f. 228:5
Fancy-free 203:7
Fanged: pavements f. 66:9
Fanny: pretty F.'s way 161:2
Fans: divers-colour'd f. 182:15
Fantastic: light f. round 144:1

light f. toe | 144:13
such f. tricks | 200:19
with f. garlands | 189:18
Far: F. and few | 131:4
f. and wide | 102:9
f. as human eye could see | 228:8
F., f. ahead | 64:12
f., f. away | 97:2, 250:12
f. from the land | 149:17
F. from us | 160:3
f. to go | 156:17
I am f. from home | 153:15
lads are f. away | 87:4
old Kentucky home f. away | 87:10
Over the hills and f. away | 89:15, 158:12
Peace to him that is f. off | 28:26
so near and yet so f. | 227:17
thus f. shalt thou go | 161:1
Farce is over | 174:6
Fardels: Who would f. bear | 187:13
Fare thee well | 8:1
Fares: Ill f. the land | 95:4
Farewell: bade the world f. | 54:5
But f. it | 186:23
F.! a long f. | 192:14
f. hope | 146:14
f. king | 206:15
F. Leicester Square | 244:7
F. my book | 60:21
F. rewards | 68:27
F. the tranquil mind | 205:10
F., thou art too dear | 211:9
f. to the shade | 70:7
hail and f. | 59:3
sadness of f. | 226:6
Far-flung battle-line | 127:3
Farie: Mr. W. Lilley believes it was
a F. | 12:20
Farmer: f. sowing his corn | 158:8
ran after the f.'s wife | 158:10
Farmers: once the embattled f. | 82:14
Three jolly f. | 73:8
Farms: pleasant villages and f. | 146:22
what f. are those? | 111:5
Far-off: unhappy, f. things | 248:9
Farrago: nostri f. libelli | 119:1
Far-reaching: enter on f. hopes | 108:17
Far-stretched greatness | 174:16
Farthest: Among the f. Hebrides | 248:8
F. Thule | 237:4
Farthing: burning a f. candle | 114:18
hold their f. candle to the sun | 250:14
never pay a f. for it | 71:9
paid the uttermost f. | 30:16
Farthings: sold for two f. | 33:13
Fascinates: it f. me | 113:8
Fascination: f. few can resist | 92:11
Fashion: after the f. of their
country | 222:11
f. she detests | 209:14
glass of f. | 188:6
high Roman f. | 182:22
in my f. | 77:26
marriage ever out of f. | 50:2
of a vegetable f. | 92:22
Fashion'd so slenderly | 106:20
Fast: as f. as they are made | 208:27
close the shutters f. | 70:18
crowding in so f. upon me | 80:5
dew was falling f. | 247:16
drop tears as f. | 205:20
f. as you can | 157:9
F. fading violets | 121:5
grew f. and furious | 49:2
hold f. that which is good | 36:24
stream runs f. | 150:2
than a hermit's f. | 120:15
twice as f. as that | 57:17
were falling f. | 133:17

wind that follows f. | 71:16
work i' the earth so f. | 186:15
Fast-closed: outside the f. door | 111:14
Fastened on her prey | 174:10
Faster: can't work any f. | 157:18
f. we counted our spoons | 82:17
good deal f. | 56:18
to follow f. | 182:15
Will you walk a little f. | 57:7
Fastest: travels the f. | 128:7
Fasting: f. in the wild | 218:6
thank heaven, f. | 184:6
Fat: butter will only make us f. | 94:12
eat no f. | 156:5
Fair, f. and forty | 181:3
F., fair and forty | 159:10
f. of the land | 23:36
F. ruddy cheeks | 105:15
f. white woman | 68:28
I will feed f. | 201:15
Jeshurun waxed f. | 24:23
than the f. weed | 186:9
Who's your f. friend? | 45:14
Fatal vision | 198:9
Fate: breathless on thy f. | 133:13
by time and f. | 230:15
curse my f. | 210:13
F. cannot harm me | 217:18
f. of the great wen | 64:14
fears his f. too much | 149:6
heart for any f. | 133:28
in unknown f. | 204:28
It is the customary f. | 112:11
master of my f. | 102:14
my life, my f. | 228:20
no armour against f. | 216:24
take a bond of f. | 199:21
That Time and F. | 85:4
untoward f. | 51:25
with F. conspire | 86:1
Fate-exiled, to Italy | 236:3
Fates: masters of their f. | 193:11
Father: Cry not when his f. dies | 116:9
daughters of my f.'s house | 209:11
everlasting F. | 27:32
F., dear f., come home | 249:9
F., forgive them | 33:39
F., I cannot tell a lie | 239:2
F., I have sinned | 33:22
F. in Heaven | 124:17
F., into thy hands | 33:42
F. is rather vulgar | 74:19
f. of it | 34:10
f. of the Man | 247:10
f...to that thought | 190:33
f.'s sword | 149:15
go to my f. | 33:22
Honour thy f. | 167:12
In my F.'s house | 34:17
It is a wise f. | 201:21
Lead us, Heavenly F. | 81:2
leave his f. and his mother | 23:14
My f. feeds his flocks | 106:14
my f.'s brother | 185:11
my poor f.'s body | 185:11
no man cometh unto the F. | 34:19
Our F., which art in heaven | 30:22
Praise him, Son and Holy Ghost | 123:3
rather have a turnip than his f. | 116:9
strike his f.'s crown | 191:4
tho' f. and mither | 49:3
thy f. lies | 208:11
to his great F. bends | 66:6
we cry, Abba, F. | 35:7
when my f. died | 189:15
without f. bred | 144:4
Fatherland: guard and bless our f. | 111:13
To die for f. | 109:18
Fatherless and widow | 172:5

Fathers: ashes of his f.   136:9
   exiles from our f.s' land   181:7
   f. have eaten sour grapes   29:12
   f. that begat us   29:37
   God of our f.   127:3
   our f. died   124:18
   our f. worshipped   147:16
   sins of the f.   167:7
   slept with his f.   25:11
   When your f. tempted me   170:26
   where my f. died   217:14
Fathers-forth: He f.   107:15
Fathom: Full f. five   208:11
Fathom-line could never touch   190:9
Fatling: young lion and the f.   28:2
Fatted calf   33:23
Fatter: valley sheep are f.   162:1
Fault: a grievous f.   194:3
   f., dear Brutus   193:11
   has no kind of f. or flaw   91:17
   Just hint a f.   165:6
   O happy f.   148:12
Faulted: by wherein he most f.   117:12
Faultily faultless   228:19
Faults: All his f. observ'd   194:18
   moulded out of f.   201:5
   With all her f.   62:7
   with all thy f.   70:15
Faustus: That F. may repent   138:14
Favour: To have found f.   108:11
   to this f. she must come   189:20
   whom the gods f.   163:8
Favoured: hail thou that art highly
   f.   32:36
Favourite: a f. apology   73:24
   f. has no friend   98:3
   his f. expression   74:7
   his f. sin   218:17
Favours: hangs on princes' f.   192:15
   middle of her f.   187:1
   that f. fools   117:8
Fawning publican   201:13
Fay ce que vouldras   174:5
Fealty: Which bards in f.   121:9
Fear: again to f.   35:7
   arming me from f.   41:13
   continual f. and danger   105:9
   dread and f. of kings   202:5
   dreams of joy and f.   213:20
   drives away his f.   154:1
   F. God   25:25, 27:10, 37:4
   f. in children is increased with tales   14:12
   'F. not', said he   225:9
   f. not what men say   46:20
   f. of having to weep   19:7
   f. of the Lord   28:1, 171:10
   f. thy nature   197:14
   f. I to fall   82:7, 174:14
   f. to fall   249:11
   For f. of which   211:13
   freedom from f.   176:17
   Have nothing else to f.   225:8
   He is F.   127:13
   Him serve with f.   123:5
   hope and f. set free   224:6
   I f. the Danaans   236:9
   I f. thee, ancient Mariner   65:18
   I f. thy kisses   215:11
   I will f. no evil   169:2
   I will show you f.   81:24
   imagining some f.   203:19
   incidents arousing pity and f.   10:16
   Knight without f.   9:4
   men as had the f. of God   71:5
   men f. death   14:12
   needst not f. mine   215:11
   no f. in love   37:11
   only thing we have to f.   176:13
   O word of f.   196:19

perfect love casteth out f.   37:11
   possess them not with f.   192:1
   shuddering f.   202:2
   so long as they f.   63:19
   strange that men should f.   193:14
   to f. that the Revolution   235:13
   To what we f. of death   201:1
   walk in f.   66:5
   What need we f. who knows it   199:28
   will be not f.   169:20
   will I f. none ill   181:8
   with f. and trembling   36:16
Feared: As if they f. the light   222:6
   be f., and kill with looks   206:15
   I f. it might injure the brain   56:16
   just as I f.   130:15
Fearest: that f. nor sea rising   41:8
Fearful: Death is a f. thing   200:23
   facing f. odds   136:9
   f. and hideous   236:13
   F. concatenation   240:5
   How f. and dizzy   195:19
   our f. trip is done   242:10
   snatch a f. joy   98:7
   thy f. symmetry   39:1, 4
   Ye f. saints   70:5
Fearfully and wonderfully made   172:2
Fearless: Stepping f. through the
   night   18:9
Fears: f. do make us traitors   199:25
   f. his fate too much   149:6
   f. may be liars   64:10
   for fifty hopes and f.   43:9
   Humanity with all its f.   133:13
   I had no human f.   245:14
   its joys and f.   246:14
   More pangs and f. than wars   192:15
   Not mine own f.   211:14
   past Regrets and Future F.   85:3
   Present f.   197:11
   saucy doubts and f.   199:8
   serves and f.   141:13
   sympathy with hopes and f.   215:4
   That f. his fellowship   192:4
   Thro' craven f.   226:14
   When I have f.   122:3
   wishes, f., anger   119:1
Feast: at any good man's f.   183:19
   door stood open at our f.   65:3
   f. his neighbours   192:4
   great f. of languages   196:17
   nourisher in life's f.   198:13
   pomp and f.   144:19
Feasts: moveable f.   166:6
Feat: an empty f.   64:8
Feather: stuck a f. in his cap   17:6
Feathered: f. race   88:8
   from the f. grass   120:7
Feathers: beautified with our f.   98:13
   f. that make fine birds   1:20
   for all his f., was a-cold   120:2
   safe under his f.   170:19
Featly: Foot it f.   208:9
Feats: f. he did that day   192:4
   'twas one of my f.   52:6
Feb, fill the dyke   234:13
February: Excepting F. alone   158:7
   F. hath twenty-eight alone   96:8
Fecisti nos ad te   13:2
Fed: and are not f.   145:3
   bite the hand that f. them   47:17
   f. and watered   53:12
   f. on the fullness of death   224:10
   grown by what it f. on   185:11
   Had f. the feeling   139:11
   not f. of the dainties   196:14
   on honey-dew hath f.   66:15
   with gazing f.   202:1
Federation of the world   228:10

Fee: hold the gorgeous east in f. 249:1
Feeble: And f. as frail 96:20
f. God 89:7
weak and f. woman 82:9
Feebleness: all else is f. 236:1
Feed: appetites they f. 182:16
f. me in a green pasture 169:2
F. on her damask cheek 209:10
F. the brute 173:19
f. the swine 155:11
guide us, keep us, f. us 81:2
He shall f. his flock 28:14
He that doth me f. 104:4
I will f. fat 201:15
to f. in air 214:1
to f. the poor 35:21
Feedeth: he f. among the lilies 27:18
Feeding: forty f. like one 247:9
Feeds: father f. his flocks 106:14
f. on the aërial kisses 214:9
meat it f. on 205:5
Feel: thing that could not f. 245:14
to f. what wretches f. 195:8
tragedy to those that f. 238:7
We uncomfortable f. 93:20
Feeling: as old as he's f. 67:10
f. of inward tranquillity 83:1
f. of their masters' thoughts 139:11
greater f. to the worse 206:5
One f. too falsely disdained 215:12
sensible to f. 198:9
With the gratifying f. 91:11
Feelings: violent f. 178:9
Feels: young man f. his pockets 111:10
Feet: beautiful..are the f. 28:18
did those f. in ancient time 38:16
dreams under your f. 250:6
f. beneath her petticoat 222:6
Keep Thou my f. 153:15
little snow-white f. 250:5
More instant than the F. 232:8
palms before my f. 61:17
pansy at my f. 246:10
shake the dust off your f. 31:12
shall with their goat f. 138:9
shoes from off thy f. 24:1
shoes on your f. 24:5
spirit in my f. 213:13
tempt with wand'ring f. 146:12
They wash their f. 82:1
to guide our f. 32:27
tremble under her f. 228:20
turf beneath my f. 101:11
underneath our F. 85:8
what dread f.? 39:2
where subjects' f. 206:16
Whose f. they hurt 171:5
with flying f. 51:1
with lifted f. 20:4
with reluctant f. 133:23
with twain he covered his f. 27:27
Feigned necessities 71:12
Feigning: most friendship is f. 184:1
Felicity: from f. awhile 190:3
green f. 122:6
sole f. 139:10
Felix..opportunitate mortis 224:16
F. qui potuit..cognoscere causas 237:7
Fell: all of us f. down 194:10
f. among thieves 33:6
F. in the fire 96:13
f. sergeant, death 189:28
f. upon the sanded floor 161:16
foremost fighting, f. 51:3
From morn to noon he f. 146:9
I do not love you, Dr. F. 42:16
It f. to earth 133:12
my f. purpose 197:15
one f. swoop 199:27

seeds f. by the wayside 31:25
they all f. to playing 86:19
We f. out 229:7
where the dead leaf f. 120:7
with flowers that f. 224:1
Fella: on the unjust f. 40:14
Felled: poplars are f. 70:7
Feller: Sweetest li'l f. 220:3
Fellow: Hail, f., well met 223:23
He's a Good F. 85:14
no f. in the firmament 193:16
of his f. creatures 88:10
periwig-pated f. 188:7
Poor f.? 51:25
Fellow-feeling makes one wondrous kind 89:2
Fellow-men: find our f. 179:11
that loves his f. 112:3
Fellow-rover: laughing f. 141:4
Fellows: Certain lewd f. 34:40
mighty fine f. 221:7
Fellowship: fears his f. 192:4
half-fac'd f. 190:9
right hands of f. 36:5
Felt: darkness which may be f. 24:4
f. a calm so deep 249:4
F. in the blood 248:17
heart has f. the tender passion 89:23
I have f. a presence 248:19
never f. a wound 207:20
What freezings have I f. 211:12
Female: F. of sex 147:5
f. of the species 125:5
polished f. friend 242:19
What f. heart 98:2
Femina: varium et mutabile semper f. 236:14
Femme: en un mot, elle est f. 174:9
Fen of stagnant waters 247:7
Fences: Good f. make good neighbours 88:9
Ferments and frets 50:4
Fern: sparkle out among the f. 235:17
Ferry: row us o'er the f. 53:17
Fertile: miles of f. ground 66:14
Fester: Lilies that f. 211:12
Festina lente 222:9
Fetch: f. the age of gold 145:8
f. you your bread 124:15
Fetters: reason Milton wrote in f. 39:16
Feu: ce qu'est au f. le vent 49:14
Feud: Fhairshon swore a f. 14:2
Fever: and f. dew 120:11
f. call'd 'Living' 163:15
f. in my bones 126:14
f. of life is over 153:12
life's fitful f. 199:4
weariness, the f. and the fret 121:4
Fever-trees: set about with f. 128:14
Février: Generals Janvier and F. 154:4
Few: alas! too f. 248:2
but f. are chosen 32:6
Far and f. 131:4
F. and short were the prayers 245:6
f. could know 248:3
gain of a f. 223:21
so f. who can grow old 220:4
so much owed..to so f. 62:23
they are f. 213:19
to so f. 62:23
very f. to love 248:3
we happy f. 192:4
Fhairshon swore a feud 14:2
Fiat justitia et ruant coeli 239:4
F. lux 23:5
Fickle: f. is the South 229:14
f. thing..is woman 236:14
Whatever is f. 107:15
Fiction: in a f. 187:11
stranger than f. 52:3

Fiddle: cat and the f. 155:17
  I the second f. 219:20
  played on an old f. 50:9
  play on my f. in Dooney 250:8
Fiddle de-dee: He replied fish f. 131:10
Fiddler: And the f.'s standing by 3:22
  Was chemist, f., statesman 79:8
Fiddlers: called for his f. 157:2
Fiddling-stick: lost his f. 155:7
Fidgety Phil 105:18
Fidus quae tela gerebat Achates 236:4
Fie: F., foh, and fum 195:14
  F. on't! 185:11
Field: as a flower of the f. 171:1
  as the flower of the f. 28:13
  Beside a f. of grain 160:21
  corner of a foreign f. 42:11
  dedicate a portion of that f. 132:8
  f. is full of shades 232:11
  f. of battle 221:5
  f. of human conflict 62:23
  f. of world policy 176:14
  first foe in the f. 134:20
  Happy f. 120:17
  he rushed into the f. 51:3
  hill or f. or river 229:12
  his presence on the f. 240:20
  lilies of the f. 30:28
  on flood and f. 236:3
  possess the f. 64:10
  single f. 246:10
  single in the f. 248:7
  that lay f. to f. 27:25
  though the f. be lost 145:15
  till the f. ring again 40:16
  tills the f. 230:10
  toss'd you down into the f. 85:11
Fields: babbled of green f. 191:6
  f. of corn where Troy 160:4
  fight in the f. 62:21
  grass comes again in the f. 110:5
  hills and f. 139:6
  in Flanders f. 137:8
  little tyrant of his f. 97:15
  no f. of amaranth 129:22
  open unto the f. 249:4
  playing f. of Eton 240:17
  vasty f. of France 191:3
  walk through the f. 68:28
Fiend: defy the foul f. 195:11
  equivocation of the f. 200:5
  foul F. coming over the field 46:8
  frightful f. 66:5
  swung the f. 142:1
Fiends: from the f. that plague thee 65:10
Fierce: bright and f. and fickle 229:14
  If I were f. 179:4
  look not so f. 139:1
  one f. hour 61:17
Fiery: bathe in f. floods 200:23
  Cupid's f. shaft 203:7
  f. sighs 49:10
  f. soul 79:5
  that very f. particle 51:25
Fife: ear-piercing f. 205:10
  fill the f. 150:3
  Thane of F. 199:29
  that practised on a f. 56:7
Fifteen: and f. wild Decembers 41:15
  bashful f. 216:19
Fifth column 148:13
Fifth of November: Please to re-
  member the F. 7:3, 157:12
Fifty: corpulent man of f. 112:7
Fifty-score strong 43:12
Fig: sewed f. leaves together 23:15
Fig tree: under his f. 29:27
Fight: bade me f. 250:7
  baffled to f. better 45:10

bear-like I must f. 200:8
Britain would f. on alone 63:1
cannot f. against the future 94:2
chide, and f. 239:8
dead man win a f. 16:3
f. on the seas 62:21
F. the good f. 36:31, 149:1
fought a good f. 36:33
from Mental F. 38:16
gone to f. the French 118:15
growl and f. 239:6
Let's f. till six 58:2
must f. on to the end 99:4
never rise and f. again 95:2
no stomach to this f. 192:4
not yet begun to f. 117:7
Shall we f. 230:4
Strength without hands to f. 224:1
to f. is but to die 230:4
Ulster will f. 62:12
We don't want to f. 8:8, 112:1
we shall f. on the beaches 62:21
We'll f. and we'll conquer 88:18
Who this great f. did win 218:14
Fighter: Am I no a bonny f.? 220:21
Fighteth: none other that f. 166:13
Fighting: and foremost f., fell 51:3
  f. for the crown 156:8
  I was f. as low as ever 79:21
Fights: British soldier f. 151:14
  he that f. and runs away 5:1
  he who f. and runs away 95:2
  knows what he f. for 71:5
Figs grew upon thorn 61:16
Figure: foolish f. 186:23
  f. in a country church 223:4
  f. of blown youth 188:6
  f. that thou here seest 118:3
  make me the fixed f. 205:13
  Steal from his f. 211:13
  strangest f. 44:21
Figures: prove anything by f. 55:7
Filches from me my good name 205:4
Files: Commands the beauteous f. 235:7
  f. of time 228:13
Filia: matre pulchra f. pulchrior 109:4
Filigree: with f. hedges 238:5
Fill: Come f. up my cup 179:20
  f. it in a silver tassie 48:18
  f. the Cup 84:17, 85:8
  world can never f. 70:2
Filled: F. to the brim 92:2
  f. with dew 66:1
  he hath f. the hungry 32:38
  they shall be f. 30:11
Fills: with pleasure f. 247:5
Filthy: f. air 197:2
  greedy of f. lucre 36:26
Fin: and under that Almighty F. 42:2
  winks the gold f. 229:16
Finally he paid 83:15
Find: by searching f. out God 25:30
  f. one face there 123:18
  f. out his uncouth way 146:12
  F. out, if you can 223:23
  f. out what you don't know 240:15
  o'erjoy'd was he to f. 69:24
  rather f. strength 246:13
  seek, and ye shall f. 30:33
  seeking shall f. Him 43:18
  seeks abroad may f. 119:18
  sin will f. you out 24:16
  therein I f. 80:17
  thou shalt f. it 27:5
  to f. an author 161:3
  to f., and not to yield 230:15
  we f. at the end 40:6
  when we hope to f. 145:1

Who can f. a virtuous woman? 26:32
you f. your attorney 91:25
Findeth: He that f. his life 31:16
  thy hand f. to do 27:2
Finds: Nor seeks nor f. 214:9
Fine: as one of the F. Arts 73:14
  exquisitely f. 164:16
  face of heaven so f. 208:1
  f. and private place 140:12
  F. by degrees 172:19
  in gay, f. colours 103:4
  London is a f. town 67:19
  Makes that and th' action f. 103:22
  mine has been a f. one 40:9
  too f. a point upon it 73:24
Finest: This was their f. hour 62:22
Finger: f. in your eye 155:10
  F. of birth-strangled babe 199:16
  goodness in her little f. 223:15
  keep thy f. 180:15
  Moving F. writes 85:12
  slow and moving f. 205:13
Fingers: dead men's f. 189:18
  f. held the pen 70:11
  forc'd f. rude 144:20
  in the cool stream thy . wet 11:24
  my f. wandered 172:22
  Rings on her f. 157:17
  With f. weary 107:3
Finger-stalls: In fitless f. 92:9
Finish, good lady 182:23
Finished: heroically hath f. 147:9
  I have f. my course 36:33
  It is f. 34:28
Finisher: author and f. 36:35
Fire: Against my f. 195:23
  are sword and f. 226:18
  as it is with f. 132:1
  at their hearts the f.'s centre 219:6
  before the f. of life 129:20
  bush burned with f. 23:38
  celestial f. 172:11
  chariot of f. 38:16
  clear f., a clean hearth 129:6
  coals of f. 26:24
  crocus brake like f. 229:4
  don't let the awkward squad f. 49:6
  Don't one of you f. 173:22
  every time she shouted 'F.!' 21:9
  Fell in the f. 96:13
  F. burn 199:13
  F. first! 101:7
  f. is dying 142:2
  F. of Spring 84:17
  f. which in the heart resides 11:17
  fretted with golden f. 187:4
  frighted with false f. 188:15
  frowst with a book by the f. 126:4
  gulfs of liquid f. 205:18
  house is on f. 156:7
  I am f. and air 183:3
  I sit beside my lonely f. 2:1
  Lord was not in the f. 25:14
  Muse of f. 191:2
  nodding by the f. 250:11
  penal f. 145:12
  pull their chestnuts out of the f. 19:29
  right Promethean f. 196:16
  round disc of f. 38:13
  Sit by the f. 155:9
  speech is a burning f. 224:2
  spinning by the f. 176:11
  stir the f. 70:18
  thorough f. 203:6
  two irons in the f. 19:12
  what wind is to f. 49:14
  wheel of f. 196:1
  when his pistol misses f. 96:3
  wi' the f. of old Rome 83:6

youth of England are on f. 191:5
Firebrand plucked out of the burn-
  ing 29:24
Fired: And f. the shot 82:14
Fire-fly wakens 229:16
Fire-folk: O look at all the f. 107:16
Fires: and f. us with courage 89:17
  His violent f. 206:6
  Keep the home f. burning 87:4, 154:15
  thought-executing f. 195:4
Fireside: no f. howso'er defended 134:1
Firewood, iron-ware 140:21
Firmament: F. sheweth his handy-
  work 168:29
  no fellow in the f. 193:16
  o'erhanging f. 187:4
  spacious f. on high 1:11
  streams in the f. 138:14
Firmly I believe 153:13
Firmness in the right 132:9
Firs with cones upon them 134:4
First: as at f. 173:19
  F. come I 20:5
  f. shall be last 32:3
  f. step that is difficult 72:15
  f. that ever burst 65:11
  f. to do so in France 40:2
  for which the f. was made 45:4
  from f. beginning 21:12
  Glorious F. of June 64, 13, 151:3
  If at f. 105:4
  leave off f. 29:36
  night that f. we met 19:5
  She is the f. 219:20
  truly keeps his f. 77:1
  worse than the f. 31:24
Fish: f. out of the water 182:6
  f. say, they have their stream 41:19
  He has gone to f. 131:12
  in the belly of the f. 29:26
  littlest f. may enter in 42:2
  there shall be no more land, say f. 42:3
  Thou deboshed f. 208:15
  What cat's averse to f.? 98:2
Fished: Who f. the murex up? 44:26
Fisher: skilful f. goes not forth 8:15
Fishermen that walk upon the
  beach 195:19
Fishers: f. of men 30:10
  Three f. went sailing 124:2
Fishes: bait in the f.' mouth 8:15
  f. of the sea 168:24
  talk like little f. 96:4
  when f. flew 61:16
Fishified: flesh how art thou f.! 207:26
Fishing: angling or float f. 116:12
  f. up the moon 162:2
Fish-like: ancient and f. smell 208:13
Fishy form and mind 42:2
Fit: f. form to serve 128:8
  Is f. for treasons 202:13
  it is not f. 71:11
  Let the punishment f. the crime 92:8
Fitful: life's f. fever 199:4
Fitless finger-stalls 92:9
Fits: periodical f. of morality 136:23
Fittest: Survival of the F. 219:3
Fitting for a princess 183:6
Five: f. in f. score 165:17
  f. sparrows 33:11
  Full fathom f. 208:11
Five-pound note: Wrapped up in
  a f. 131:6
Fixed: Everlasting had not f. 185:11
  great gulf f. 33:29
  have they f. the where and
  when? 101:6
  make me the f. figure 205:13
Flabbiness: moral f. 113:1

Flag: death's pale f.   208:4
  f. that makes you free   249:8
  meteor f. of England   54:8
  old f. flyin'   153:5
  shall not f.   62:21
  spare your country's f.   242:16
  Their f. to April's breeze   82:1
  whose f. has braved   54:6
Flag-flapper: Jelly-bellied F.   127:16
Flagons: stay me with f.   27:15
Flakes: in large white f. falling   41:7
Flame: adding fuel to the f.   147:7
  f. that lit the battle's wreck   102:7
  hard, gemlike f.   161:11
  so full of subtil f.   19:9
  thin smoke without f.   100:4
  with eyes of f.   57:14
Flamens: Here lies two F.   54:20
Flames in the forehead   145:4
Flaming from th' ethereal sky   145:12
Flanders: F. mare   103:14
  grow in F. fields   137:8
Flanks: all her silken f.   120:21
Flannel: Get her a f. waistcoat   89:5
Flannelled: With the f. fools   126:1
Flap: let me f. this bug   165:8
Flap-dragon: easier swallowed than
  a f.   196:17
Flash: f. upon that inward eye   247:5
  passed almost in a f.   20:2
Flashes: by f. of lightning   67:7
  f. of merriment   189:20
Flashing: his f. eyes   66:15
Flashy: lean and f. songs   145:3
Flask of Wine   84:18
Flat: f. and unprofitable   185:11
  he is many times f.   80:3
  very f., Norfolk   69:16
Flats: fifty different sharps and f.   44:19
Flatter: as a dream doth f.   211:10
  F. the mountain-tops   211:2
  not f. me at all   71:9
Flattered: world hath f.   174:16
Flattering: that f. unction   189:3
  with a f. word   243:5
Flattery: everyone likes f.   76:15
  Or f. soothe the dull cold ear   97:13
  paid with f.   116:18
Flaunting, extravagant quean   216:19
Flavour: gives it all its f.   70:16
Flaw: no kind of fault or f.   91:17
Flax: smoking f.   28:16
Flaxen: those f. locks   108:18
Flayed: belted you and f. you   125:12
Flea: between a louse and a f.   116:1
  f. hath smaller fleas   223:26
  f. in his ear   11:2
  f. in 's ear   19:16
Fleas: f. that tease   22:3
  Great f. have little f.   150:11
Flectere si nequeo superos   236:20
Fled: all but he had f.   102:7
  earth's foundations f.   111:11
  F. with a Christian   201:24
  how Love f.   250:11
  I f. Him   232:7
  I waked, she f.   148:2
  snows have scattered and f.   110:5
  that I am f.   211:7
  Whither is f. the visionary gleam?   246:10
Flee: and comforts f.   135:16
  f. before him   170:6
  shadows f. away   27:18
  They f. from me   250:2
  warned you to f.   30:5
Fleece was white as snow   99:5
Fleeces: you sheep bear f.   237:10
Fleet: in the Downs the f. was moor'd   89:30
  so long as we took care of our f.   1:10

Fleeting: call the f. breath   97:13
  f. years   109:14
  pleasure of the f. year   211:12
Fleets: ten thousand f.   51:8
Flere: si vis me f.   107:20
Flesh: All f. is as grass   28:13, 37:3
  all f. shall see it   28:12
  As if this f.   206:15
  closed up the f.   23:12
  fair and unpolluted f.   189:22
  f. and blood so cheap   107:4
  f., f., how art thou fishified!   207:26
  f. is weak   32:21
  f. of my f.   23:13
  heart and my f. rejoice   170:13
  lusts of the f.   167:32
  make your f. creep   75:17
  sat by the f. pots   24:6
  shocks that f. is heir to   187:13
  that ever took f.   82:21
  they shall be one f.   23:14
  thorn in the f.   36:4
  too solid f.   185:11
  upon all f.   29:22
  way of all f.   68:15, 182:4, 240:9
  weariness of the f.   27:9
  Word was made f.   33:46
  world, the f., and the devil   166:23
  wrestle not against f.   36:14
Fleshly School of Poetry   45:17
Flew: Out f. the web   227:25
  Up f. the windows   69:28
  where his eagles never f.   69:20
Flicker: run-stealers f.   232:11
Fliers: e'en now the f.   64:10
Flies: As f. to wanton boys   195:18
  he f. through the air   132:4
  immortal f.   42:3
  it still f. you   117:18
  Life f.   85:6
  murmurous haunt of f.   121:5
  see, where it f.!   138:12
  Then she f. away   230:7
Flieth: arrow that f.   170:19
Flight: by sudden f.   133:22
  confused alarms of struggle and f.   11:9
  his droning f.   97:8
  His f. was madness   199:25
  puts the Stars to F.   84:15
  short day takes f.   58:26
  Swift be thy f.   213:20
  Thy soul's f.   199:2
Flights upon the banks of Thames   118:9
Flinders: Little Polly F.   156:12
Fling: Garden of Repentance f.   84:17
  I'll have a f.   19:22
Flits by on leathern wing   67:12
Float upon his watery bier   144:20
Floated midway on the waves   66:15
Floating: his f. hair   66:15
Floats: that f. on high   247:3
Flock: feed his f.   28:14
  silent was the f.   120:2
  There is no f.   134:1
Flocks: feeds his f.   106:14
  like f. to feed   214:1
  While shepherds watched their f.   225:9
Flood: and nearly spoiled ta F.   14:3
  f. may bear me far   226:6
  home in a f. of tears   75:20
  on f. and field   236:3
  taken at the f.   194:19
  ten years before the F.   140:11
  that arched the f.   82:14
  Thorough f.   203:6
  with a f. of tears   74:7
Flooding: silent, f. in, the main   64:10
Floods: bathe in fiery f.   200:23
  can the f. drown it   27:20

Floor: and I swept the f. 93:10
  beneath the watery f. 145:4
  curled up on the f. 101:4
  fell upon the sanded f. 161:16
  f. of heaven 202:11
  on a granary f. 119:18
Floors: Scuttling across the f. 81:18
Flopsy, Mopsy, Cotton-tail 165:22
Flora: Tasting of F. 121:3
Florence: Rode past fair F. 120:8
Flores: At F. in the Azores 230:2
Flotilla: Where the old F. lay 126:11
Flourish: all things f. 165:1
  Princes and Lords may f. 95:4
  they f. at home 6:15
Flourished: bloody treason f. 194:10
Flourisheth as a flower 171:1
Flourishing like a green bay-tree 169:14
Flout 'em and scout 'em 208:16
Flow: ebb and f. by the moon 196:6
  f. of soul 165:10
  from whom all blessings f. 123:3
  plaintive numbers f. 248:9
  pleasant fruits do f. 54:11
Flower: as the f. of the field 28:13
  ev'ry f. is united 89:14
  flourisheth as a f. 171:1
  f. enjoys the air 248:12
  f. is born to blush unseen 97:15
  f. of cities all 80:14
  f. of the grass 37:3
  f. of their age 24:36
  F. that once hath blown 85:6
  f. thereof falleth away 37:3
  from every opening f. 239:9
  glory in the f. 246:13
  grows the f. of Peace 235:8
  Heaven in a Wild F. 38:10
  I sipt each f. 89:14
  leaves and f. 240:11
  lightly like a f. 227:21
  like the innocent f. 198:1
  Little f. 226:12
  little western f. 203:7
  meanest f. that blows 246:14
  No f. upon the ground 213:11
  not a f. sweet 209:9
  pluck this f., safety 190:12
  this same f. that smiles today 104:14
  white f. of a blameless life 226:15
Flower-bell: a fancy from a f. 43:9
Flower-de-luce being one 210:8
Flower-pots: your damned f. 45:7
Flowers: all its twined f. 119:18
  azure moss and f. 214:2
  blushing f. 165:1
  bringeth vo'th May f. 6:5
  chalic'd f. that lies 184:20
  Do spring May f. 234:14
  f. appear on the earth 27:16
  f. begotten 223:29
  F. I leave you 231:12
  F. in the garden 221:22
  f. of the forest 64:16, 82:12
  f. that bloom in the spring 92:14
  gathered f. are dead 86:7
  Insnared with f. 140:6
  like sleeping f. 249:5
  lull'd in these f. 203:9
  no f. be planted on my grave 100:9
  No f., by request 2:2
  of fruits, and f. 120:4
  Oh, the pretty f. 111:17
  play with f. 191:6
  with f. that fell 224:1
Flowery: As you walk your f. way 92:22
  Showery, F. 88:16
Flowing: f. sea 71:16
  seiz'd fast the f. mane 69:26

Flown: night has f. 228:20
Flows: and whence it f. 246:11
  how sweetly f. 104:15
Flowy: Snowy, F. 88:16
Fluently: she spak ful faire and f. 60:12
Flung: f. himself upon his horse 130:12
  f. roses 77:27
  f. the stone 84:15
  we f. us on the windy hill 42:4
Flute: soft complaining f. 79:17
  sound of the..f. 29:16
Flutes: sound of lyres and f. 161:9
  tune of f. 182:15
Fluttered: like a f. bird 230:2
Fluttering and dancing 247:3
Flux: All is f. 103:15
Fly: F. away, breath 209:9
  F., envious Time 148:6
  f. to others 187:13
  His praise may thither f. 103:18
  I cannot f. 200:8
  I do f. 208:20
  'I,' said the F. 159:5
  is not worth a f. 3:15
  Let me to Thy Bosom f. 241:8
  little way to f. 84:17
  or shall we f.? 230:4
  said a spider to a f. 111:18
  Seem to f. 117:18
  swift cloud to f. 214:3
  They f. forgotten 239:14
  Up above the world you f. 56:24
  with twain he did f. 27:27
Fly fishing may be a very pleasant
    amusement 116:12
Flying: banner torn but f. 51:4
  f. from far away 230:2
  quickly f. 58:21
  set the wild echoes f. 229:10
  snow came f. 41:7
  Time is f. 237:8
  Urge the f. ball 98:6
Flying-fishes: Where the f. play 126:11
Foam: dank with f. 124:1
  f. on the river 180:3
  opening on the f. 121:6
  ships on the f. 128:6
  Too full for sound and f. 226:6
Foe: but half his f. 146:7
  erect and manly f. 54:14
  first f. in the field 134:20
  His f. was folly 107:8
  I fear no f. 135:17
  manxome f. 57:14
  met my dearest f. 185:13
  sail to meet the f. 153:5
  to match another f. 54:6
Foeman: beneath the f.'s frown 78:23
  When the f. bares his steel 93:20
Foes: From the f. they captive
    make 59:18
  in presence of my f. 181:8
  neither f. nor loving friends 125:16
  Oh, my f. 143:1
Fog: a f., Miss 73:22
  hover through the f. 197:2
  to feel the f. in my throat 45:2
  yellow f. 81:16
Fogs: his rising f. 79:24
Fold: f. their tents 133:15
  in their ancient f. 147:16
  in woolly f. 120:2
  like a wolf on the f. 52:9
  loves to f. his legs 115:15
  securely f. you 175:2
  So f. thyself 229:17
Folded: and f. it right 110:14
Folding of the hands to sleep 26:9
Folds: f. shall be full of sheep 170:3

Folds (*cont.*)
lull the distant f. 97:8
now f. the lily 229:17
Foliage: In the dark f. 94:16
Folios: mighty f. first 70:20
Folk: emptied of this f. 120:21
fluttered f. and wild 128:5
F. dance like a wave 250:8
matches of the Southron f. 232:11
Than longen f. to goon 60:9
'Tis ever thus with simple f. 93:36
Folks: F. of a surly Tapster 85:14
O yonge fresshe f. 61:2
pretty country f. 184:12
Some f. rail against other f. 84:8
where de old f. stay 87:11
You ain't heard nothin' yet, F. 117:6
Follies: and f. of the age 59:7
f., and misfortunes 90:14
pretty f. 201:23
Follow: Albatross did f. 65:9
And it must f. 185:21
F. a shadow 117:18
F. your spirit 191:9
shall f. me 169:2
Followed: loved him so, f. him 44:10
With which she f. 185:11
Following: F. his plough 247:19
from f. after thee 24:35
Follows: of what f. 20:2
yet she f. 134:7
Follow up! 40:16
Folly: according to his f. 26:26
brood of F. 144:4
F.'s at full length 61:4
His foe was f. 107:8
most loving mere f. 184:1
noise of f. 144:6
persist in his f. 39:19
returneth to his f. 26:27
some brief f. 110:7
stoops to f. 82:2, 95:21
'Tis f. to be wise 98:10
uses his f. 184:14
Fond: men would be f. 135:14
not so f. of me 173:19
so f. of handling the leaves 216:8
some are f. of French 141:1
Fonder: Absence makes the heart
grow f. 3:6, 19:3
Fondly: gaze on so f. today 149:12
If with me you f. stray 89:15
Fons: O f. Bandusiae 109:24
Font: in the porphyry f. 229:16
Food: better f. 114:6
Books, and my f. 221:24
fed with the same f. 201:27
F. enough for a week 142:14
f. of love 209:2
for f. or play 65:9
Nothing to eat but f. 123:10
Seeking the f. he eats 183:15
Fool: answer a f. 26:26
become a f. and jester! 191:1
Busy old f. 77:18
Call me not f. 183:16
f. all the people 132:10
f. at forty 250:13
f. at the other 116:12
f. hath said 168:26
f. returneth to his folly 26:27
f. sees not the same tree 39:17
f. there was 128:1
f. to fame 165:4
I am Fortune's f. 207:31
I have played the f. 24:46
if the f. would persist 39:19
is a f. indeed 250:13
laughter of a f. 26:39

life time's f. 190:22
more f. I. 183:10
not Time's f. 211:16
play the Roman f. 200:9
poor f. is hang'd 196:11
poor venemous f. 183:4
Remains a f. 135:11
They f. me 188:19
to live a f. 19:9
Wisest f. in Christendom 103:3
worthy f. 183:18
Foolish: being young and f. 250:5
f., fond old man 196:2
f. thing was but a toy 209:20
Leave then thy f. ranges 235:8
never said a f. thing 176:2
women are f. 81:8
Fools: as dull f. suppose 144:2
by f. like me 123:9
flannelled f. 126:1
f. rush in 164:13
f. who came to scoff 95:7
have lighted f. 200:4
how f. are vexed 72:18
I am two f. 77:19
mostly f. 55:16
shoal of f. 68:17
Silence is the virtue of f. 14:7
suffer f. gladly 36:3
that favours f. 117:8
To suckle f. 204:27
What a parcel of f. 103:13
what f. these mortals be 203:14
world is full of f. 9:6
world is made up...of f. 45:18
Foot: at the f. of the bed 143:15
Both f. and hand go cold 221:25
caught my f. in the mat 98:18
cleft the Devil's f. 77:16
F. it featly 208:9
heard his f. 73:6
hurt not thy f. 170:20
on the f. of the bed 74:13
One f. in sea 204:9
proud f. of a conqueror 193:8
right-hand f. 58:14
sleep thegither at the f. 48:21
thy f. out of brothels 195:11
We're f.-slog..sloggin' 124:16
with impartial f. 108:16
With leaden f. 112:17
with shining F. 86:3
words a f. and a half long 107:19
Footed: fiery-f. steeds 207:32
Foot-in-the-grave young man 93:4
Foot-path: jog-on the f. way 210:7
Footprints on the sands of time 133:27
Footsteps: distant f. echo 133:14
f. he hath turned 180:6
plants his f. 70:5
Footstool: enemies thy f. 171:10
Foppery of the world 195:2
Forbid: and f. them not 32:34
Life's short span f. us 108:17
live a man f. 197:6
that I am f. 186:7
Forbidden: fruit of that f. tree 145:9
Forbids to crave 80:17
Force: Ev'ry member of the f. 176:3
f. of temporal power 202:5
F. without mind falls 109:21
no argument but f. 43:3
no f. 245:14
overcomes by f. 146:7
spent its novel f. 228:6
use of f. alone 46:29
Forced: momently was f. 66:14
Forcing her on board 117:4
Forefathers: rude f. of the hamlet 97:10

Foregone conclusion 205:11
Forehand and vantage of a king 191:15
Forehead: Flames in the f. 145:4
  in the middle of her f. 134:14
  of the godlike f. 246:3
Foreheads: free f. 230:15
Foreign: and the f. faces 223:28
  corner of a f. field 42:11
  f. levy 199:4
  on a f. strand 180:6
Foreknowledge of death 224:2
Foremost: none who would be f. 136:13
Forest: even as the f. is 214:4
  flowers of the f. 64:16, 82:12
  f. primeval 133:16
  into the f. dim 121:3
  lost to the f. 180:2
  rose the f. 134:4
  upon the f. bare 213:11
Foresters: Diana's f. 190:6
Forests: and f. walked 61:16
  f. ancient as the hills 66:14
  from the f. shook three summers 211:13
  green days in f. 221:17
  in the f. of the night 39:14
Foretell: do f. of him 206:6
  Who can f. 140:10
Forever: man has f. 43:17
Forfeit: our deadly f. 145:6
  shall f. fair renown 180:6
Forget: courage to f. 2:1
  dissolve, and quite f. 121:4
  do not quite f. 61:24
  f. and forgive 196:4
  f. and smile 177:11
  F. not 147:16
  if I f. thee 12:17, 171:28
  If thou wilt f. 177:12
  Lest we f. 127:3
  never f. an injury 178:16
  Old men f. 192:4
  That will f. thee 248:20
  we f. because we must 11:7
Forgetful: Be not f. to entertain
  strangers 36:37
  yet she may f. be 70:4
Forgetfulness: Not in entire f. 246:11
Forgetting: sleep and a f. 246:11
Forgive: do they f. them 243:27
  Father, f. them 33:39
  forget and f. 196:4
  f. us our debts 30:22
  f. us our trespasses 166:11
  God may f. you 82:6
  I could f. a man 129:8
  Love, f. us 120:15
  much to f. 143:2
  one woman can f. another 89:11
  to f., divine 164:12
  To f. wrongs 215:1
  will f. me 122:11
  You will f. this..fraud 89:23
Forgiveness: ask of thee f. 196:6
  f. free of evil 124:18
Forgot: accents are soon f. 213:16
  all shall be f. 192:4
  As benefits f. 184:2
  by the world f. 164:6
  f. as soon as done 208:27
  f. my Clementine 149:9
  I have f. much 77:27
  Should ever be f. 157:12
Forgotten: f. pastime 180:17
  grief f. 223:29
  hast thou f. 71:2
  have f. nothing 80:11
  I am clean f. 169:10
  not..f. before God? 33:13
  Our God's f. 173:26

Forked animal 195:12
Forks: pursued it with f. 56:5
Forlorn: as all f. 18:12
  faery lands f. 121:6
  F.! the very word 121:7
  make me less f. 249:5
Form: f. and pressure 188:10
  f. from off my door 163:17
  f. of things unknown 203:19
  F. remains 245:17
  Human f. divine 39:13
  I like definite f. 220:23
  in a visible f. 45:3
  in f., in moving 187:4
  mould of f. 188:6
  no time to lick it into t. 49:8
  of fishy f. and mind 42:2
  pretty f. to the lips 74:19
  unmatch'd f. 188:6
  what the f. divine 129:19
Forming in the air 175:15
Forms: by f. unseen 67:15
  f. more real 214:9
  f. to his conceit? 187:11
Fors: quem F. dierum cumque dabit 109:1
Forsake her Cyprian groves 79:23
Forsaken: never the righteous f. 169:13
  why hast thou f. me? 32:25
Forsaking all other 168:11
Forsworn: so sweetly were f. 201:3
Fort: Hold the f. 39:22
Forth: bring me f. 169:2
Forties: Hungry F. 235:2
Fortis fortuna adiuvat 231:7
Fortitude of mind 113:14
Fortnight: to be hanged in a f. 115:13
Fortress: A petty f. 117:3
  f. built by nature 206:7
  Thy f. and thy ease 235:8
Fortuitous: Accidental and f. 160:16
Fortunate: at best but f. 218:8
  on the f. hit 105:11
Fortune: disdaining f. 197:4
  Each day that F. gives you 109:1
  F. aids the brave 231:7
  F. favoured him 224:16
  F. is ally to the brave 236:22
  F. that favours fools 117:8
  given hostages to f. 14:17
  heaven hath sent me f. 183:16
  I am F.'s fool 207:31
  in adverse f. 40:1
  in disgrace with f. 210:13
  in possession of a good f. 13:18
  leads on to f. 194:19
  my face is my f. 159:2
  of outrageous f. 187:13
Forty: Every man over f. 213:2
  Fair, fat, and f. 181:3
  Fat, fair and f. 159:10
  fool at f. 250:13
  for f. years 62:4
  F. days and f. nights 218:6
  f. feeding like one 247:9
  F. years on 40:15
  with f. pounds a year 95:6
Forty-three: very well pass for f. 93:34
Forward: f. let us range 228:14
  marched breast f. 45:10
  royal banners f. go 87:7
  this day f. 168:12
  those behind cried 'F.!' 136:13
Forwards: backwards and f. 105:18
Foster-child of silence 120:18
Fou: I wasna f. 48:13
Fought: f. a good fight 36:33
  f. for life 219:6
  f. upon his stumps 213:5
  he had f. so long 207:2

Fought (cont.)
I have f. for Queen and Faith 230:5
stars in their courses f. 24:28
That f. with us 192:4
we f. at Arques 103:1
what they f. each other for 218:13
Foul: f. and fair a day 197:7
f. and pestilent congregation 187:4
f. contagion spread 145:3
F., I to the fountain 234:1
f. is fair 197:2
f., strange and unnatural 186:8
many a f. and midnight murther 97:7
Murder most f. 186:8
shapes of f. disease 227:20
some f. play 185:19
think f. scorn 82:9
ways be f. 196:20
Foul-mouthed nation 101:12
Found: dog was f. 95:13
f. in thy heart to sing 224:7
f. it less exciting 91:5
f. out by accident 129:15
f. them worthy 29:33
he still has f. 215:18
I have f.! 10:12
if a buyer can be f. 179:1
in the snow was f. 133:20
lost, and is f. 33:24
ne'er be f. 139:1
no more be f. 140:12
To f. a great empire 217:12
when f., make a note of 74:15
where I've f. it 126:7
while he may be f. 28:24
Foundation: Church's one f. 222:1
f. of morals and legislation 22:8
Foundations: when earth's f. fled 111:11
when I laid the f. of the earth 25:41
Fount: level with their f. 149:5
Slow, slow, fresh f. 117:10
Fountain: bubble on the f. 180:3
f. of honour 15:7
From the f. and the caves 66:15
mighty f. 66:14
of the f. of the water 37:27
perpetual f. of good sense 80:7
pitcher be broken at the f. 27:8
rise like a f. for me 227:2
summer-dried f. 180:2
Thou of Life the F. art 241:11
to the f. fly 234:1
Fountains: Afric's sunny f. 101:15
rolls his f. 213:12
Founts: white f. falling 61:16
Four-footed: of all f. things 61:16
Four-horse coaches 108:9
Fourscore: f. and upward 196:2
F. years 170:18
Four-square: stood f. 229:1
Fourth estate 55:15, 136:19
Fous: le monde est plein de f. 9:6
Fowl: You elegant f. 131:7
Fowles: smale f. maken melodye 60:9
Fowls of the air 168:24
Fox: I loves the f. less 222:17
Or a f. from his lair 97:2
Foxes: f. have holes 31:7
little f. 27:17
take us the f. 27:17
Frabjous: O f. day! 57:14
Frail children of dust 96:20
Frailty: F., thy name is woman 185:11
noblest f. 182:5
Frame: Are all the human f. requires 21:4
Could f. in earth 219:12
Could f. thy fearful symmetry? 39:1
earth received her f. 239:14

this goodly f. 187:4
universal f. began 79:16
Framed: Nature that f. us 139:10
France: better in F. 220:11
Fair stood the wind for F. 78:28
first to do so in F. 40:12
F., mother of arts 20:14
in F. of the best rank 185:21
King of F. went up the hill 156:6
lived a singer in F. 224:11
marshal of F. 151:16
nearer is to F. 57:9
vasty fields of F. 191:3
We shall fight in F. 62:21
France, mère des arts 20:14
Francesca di Rimini 93:3
Frankfort: I went to F. 165:18
Frankie and Johnny were lovers 4:8
Frankincense: gold, and f., and myrrh 30:2
Frappé: darling's now completely f.! 96:14
Fraternity: Liberty! Equality! F.! 9:7
Fratresque tendentes 109:20
Fraud: f. of men 204:9
this just, this pious f. 89:23
Frauds: Well stored with pious f. 47:12
Fraught: With some pain is f. 215:5
F. with a later prize 213:12
Freckled: Whatever is fickle, f. 107:15
Fred: Here lies F., who was alive and is dead 4:17
Frederick: Here is cruel F. 105:16
Free: beautiful and f. 215:1
calm and f. 246:15
Comment is f. 179:17
die to make men f. 111:16
each way f. 104:15
flag that makes you f. 249:8
half slave and half f. 132:7
himself from God he could not f. 82:15
home of the brave and the f. 212:7
hope and fear set f. 224:6
I am as f. as nature 79:19
in my soul am f. 134:19
less f. than thou 214:3
must be f. or die 247:1
Man is born f. 177:18
O'er the land of the f. 123:7
or wholly f. 79:22
our will is f. 114:24
that Greece might still be f. 51:18
thou art f. 11:20
Thought is f. 208:16
truth shall make you f. 34:8
valiant man and f. 227:20
We that have f. souls 188:14
who are so f. 88:18
Who will f. me 103:12
Freed: f. from servile bands 249:11
From the thousands He hath f. 59:18
Freedom: battle for f. and truth 112:14
complete f. of movement 174:2
f. in my love 134:19
f. of speech 176:17
F. shall awhile repair 67:15
F. shrieked 54:5
idea of f. 160:22
is perfect f. 166:14
Let f. ring 217:14
new birth of f. 132:8
with F.'s lion-banner 54:2
Yet F.! yet thy banner 51:4
Freedoms: four essential f. 176:17
Freely: far too f. moved to tears 21:5
F. let me take of Thee 241:11
of the water of life f. 37:27
Freeman butters Stubbs 176:4
Freeze: F., f., thou bitter sky 184:2

f. thy young blood 186:7
mountain-tops that f. 192:13
Freezing stream below 213:11
Freezings: What f. have I felt 211:12
French: For F. of Paris 60:12
F., or Turk 93:14
F. she spak ful faire 60:12
Gentlemen of the F. Guard 101:7
glory of beating the F. 245:8
gone to fight the F. 118:15
is not F. 175:13
not too F. F. bean 92:22
some are fond of F. 141:1
speak in F. 57:16
taken from the F. 215:21
to men [I speak] F. 60:6
we F. stormed Ratisbon 44:6
Frenchmen: Fifty million F. 99:1
one Englishman could beat three
F. 1:10
Frenzy: demoniac f. 146:24
fine f. rolling 203:19
Frequent: did eagerly f. 85:7
Frequented: more f. rows 70:20
Fresh: f. as is the month of May 60:11
f. as paint 217:10
O yonge f. folkes 61:2
sae f. and fair? 49:4
Since first I saw you f. 211:13
to f. woods 145:5
Freshness of a dream 246:7
Fret: fever and the f. 121:4
F. not to roam the desert 154:12
Nuns f. not 247:12
Why f. about them 85:8
Frets: Ferments and f. 50:4
struts and f. his hour 200:4
Fretted: f. the pigmy body 79:5
f. with golden fire 187:4
Freude, schöner Götterfunken 179:11
Friar: F. Bacon and F. Bungay 98:12
many a f. 17:11
Friars: while the barefoot f. 90:12
Friday: F.'s child 156:17
takes my man F. with me 72:17
Worse on F. 158:2
Friend: As f. remember'd not 184:2
Believe me, my young f. 96:16
candid f. 54:14
Englishman and F. 247:18
fav'rite has no f.! 98:3
F. for little children 142:20
F., go up higher 33:14
f. that sticketh closer 26:21
F. to Sir Philip Sidney 98:16
f. to truth 164:25
Good f., for Jesu's sake 212:5
guide, philosopher, and f. 164:21
He was my f. 194:5
I finds a f. 73:17
loses both itself and f. 185:21
loss of a dear f. 219:2
lost no f. 164:25
may debauch his f.'s wife 115:3
my f. here didn't see 96:9
my good f. the calender 69:23
not a f. greet 209:9
polished female f. 242:19
soul of a f. 40:6
that love my f. 194:11
those who call them f. 227:2
to commend their f. 117:12
To me, fair f. 211:13
want a f. in need 74:15
Who's your fat f.? 45:14
wise f. of mine 238:14
would not call that man my f. 129:8
Friendless: f. bodies of unburied men 240:11
no man so f. 136:4

Friendly: f. cow, all red and white 221:13
nor yet is it f. 106:10
Friends: all their f. could say 131:5
best of f. must part 8:1
F. and loves 141:5
F., Romans, Countrymen 194:3
f. thou hast 185:21
f. were poor but honest 182:8
good thoughts his only f. 54:10
How to win F. 55:25
laughter, learnt of f. 42:11
lay down his life for his f. 34:20
love of f. 21:12
loving f. and youths 66:6
loving f. can hurt you 125:16
make..f. of the mammon 33:26
misfortunes of our best f. 175:16
Oh, my f. 143:1
old f., old times 95:24
Our f., the enemy 22:15
our f. the murderers 119:14
party of f. and relations 91:25
remembering my good f. 206:10
Thy f. are exultations 248:20
'Tis hard to part when f. are dear 17:8
troops of f. 199:32
with f. possess'd 210:12
Friendship: eternal f. 54:16, 217:16
keep his f. in constant repair 114:5
most f. is feigning 184:1
Frieze: no jutty, f., buttress 198:2
Frighted: F. the reign of Chaos 146:6
f. with false fire? 188:15
Frighten her into marriage 117:4
Frightened: f. both the heroes so 57:18
f. look in its eyes 217:6
Frightful fiend 66:5
Frights: it f. the isle 204:30
Frigidaire: popped him in the F. 96:14
Frisk: I'll have a f. with you 113:19
Fritter-my-wig! 56:2
Fro: reel to and f. 171:8
Frog: and toe of f. 199:14
expiring f. 75:19
f. he would a-wooing go 155:14
Frogs and snails 158:14
Frolic: ever with a f. welcome 230:15
f. and the gentle 246:3
Front: fair large f. 146:16
iron curtain drawn down upon
their f. 63:5
Frost: killing f. 192:14
Thaw not the f. 213:6
third day comes a f. 192:14
Frosts are slain 223:29
Frosty wind made moan 177:9
Froth: mostly f. and bubble 96:6
or idlest f. 41:14
Frown: beneath the foeman's f. 78:23
Frowned: Critic, you have f. 248:1
Frowst with a book 126:4
Frozen: blood was f. slowly 228:1
comes f. home 196:20
f. corpse was he 134:13
f. wind crept 213:11
is f. music 179:10
that he'd be f. stiff 96:14
through the f. grass 120:2
Frugal: f. swain 106:14
She had a f. mind 69:24
Fruit: bless with f. 119:17
f. of that forbidden tree 145:9
f. of the Spirit 36:7
reach the ripest f. 139:10
thickset f. 177:8
will long for the f. 216:8
Fruitful: as the f. vine 171:24
Be f. and multiply 23:8
in a very f. hill 27:24

Fruitfulness: mellow f.   119:17
Fruition: sweet f.   139:10
Fruits: all pleasant f.   54:11
  By their f.   31:4
  imag'ries of f.   120:4
  kindly f. of the earth   166:25
Fruit-tree: all these f. tops   207:24
Frumious Bandersnatch   57:14
Frustrate: F. their knavish tricks   55:1
  to each f. ghost   45:8
Fry me!   56:2
Fuel: adding f. to the flame?   147:7
Fugaces: Eheu f. Anni labuntur   17:9
  Eheu f., Postume, Postume   109:14
Fugit interea, f. inreparabile tempus   237:8
Fugitive and cloistered virtue   148:9
Fulfil: not to destroy but to f.   30:15
Fulfils: God f. himself   227:1
Full: cup shall be f.   169:2
  diapason closing f.   79:16
  F. and fair ones   104:8
  f. of eyes within   37:16
  f. of good works   34:37
  F. of the true   121:3
  Serenely f.   217:18
  so f. within   221:25
  Too f. for sound   226:6
Fullness: fed on the f. of death   224:10
  and the f. thereof   35:19
Full-throated ease   121:2
Full-voiced quire   144:9
Fumble with the sheets   191:6
Fume of poppies   119:18
Fun: mirth and f. grew fast   49:2
  taken my f. where I've found it   126:7
  till the Toad in f.   71:1
  What Jolly F.   174:19
Function: F. never dies   245:17
  whole f. suiting   187:11
Fundamentally: was f. sensible   115:25
Funeral: costlier f.   226:10
  f. bak'd meats   185:13
  not a f. note   245:3
Funny: F. peculiar or f. ha-ha   101:8
  Isn't it f.   143:16
Fur: make the f. fly   49:23
  my f. and whiskers   56:15
Furca: Naturam expellas f.   108:8
Furious: fast and f.   49:2
  queen was in a f. passion   57:1
Furiously: he driveth f.   25:20
Furnace: burning fiery f.   29:17
  in what f. was thy brain   39:2
  sighing like f.   183:20
Furnish: coldly f. forth   185:13
  f. all we ought to ask   122:14
Furnished: My table thou hast f.   181:8
Furnishing: advantage of f. very few materials   90:14
Furniture: with the f.   212:6
Furrow: half-reaped f.   119:18
  plough my f. alone   177:6
Furrows: sounding f.   230:15
Further: f. off from England   57:9
  nothing can touch him f.   199:4
  Trip no f.   209:5
Fury: Allaying both their f.   208:10
  Comes the blind F.   145:1
  full of sound and f.   200:4
  f. of the many-headed monster   141:13
  nor Hell a f.   68:10
Fust: gets his blow in f.   213:4
Future: And time f.   81:10
  cannot fight against the f.   94:2
  dipt into the f.   228:8
  hopes of f. years   133:13
  past Regrets and F. Fears   85:3
  present, past, and f.   38:18

Futurity: no reference to f.   115:12
Futurum: quid sit f. cras   109:1

G

Gab: gift of the g.   139:21
Gad! she'd better!   55:24
Gadier: isles of Javan or G.   147:5
Gaels: great G. of Ireland   61:15
Gage: hope's true g.   174:13
Gai: toujours g., archy   139:16
Gaiety of nations   116:22
Gaily the Troubadour   19:6
Gain: g. of a few   223:21
  he shall g. the whole world   31:35, 32:32
  My richest g.   239:16
  painful inch to g.   64:10
  set down for g.   109:1
  To g. the timely inn   199:7
  world to g.   140:14
Gaiters: gas and g.   75:5
Galère: dans cette g.   148:17
Gales: cool g. shall fan   165:1
  'mid the equinoctial g.   6:17
Galilean: conquered, O G.   118:18
  O pale G.   224:10
  Pilot of the G. lake   145:2
  Wilt thou yet take all, G.?   224:9
Galilee: nightly on deep G.   52:9
Galileo: and G. [was misunderstood]   82:21
Gall: milk for g.   197:15
  wormwood and the g.   29:9
Gallant: A very g. gentleman   12:18
  bends the g. mast   71:16
  nation of g. men   47:14
Gallantry: men call g.   51:11
Galled: Let the g. jade wince   188:14
Galleon: a ghostly g.   155:1
Gallery: faces are but a g. of pictures   14:14
  g. in which the reporters sit   136:19
Gallia .. in partes tres   52:23
Gallimaufry .. of all other speeches   219:15
Gallio cared for none of those things   34:44
Gallop apace   207:32
Galloped: l g., Dirck g.   44:5
Galumphing: went g. back   57:14
Gambols: your g.? your songs?   189:20
Game: g.'s afoot   191:9
  g. which a sharper once played   71:4
  how you played the g.   175:10
  more than a g.   111:21
  play the g.!   153:6
  rigour of the g.   129:6
  start some g.   101:11
  time to win this g.   78:25
Games: in g. Confederate   246:5
Gamesmanship   166:3
Gamesters: see more than g.   14:13
Gang: old g.   62:13
Ganges: by the Indian G.' side   140:11
Garb: In the g. of old Gaul   83:6
Garde: la G. meurt   53:10
Garden: Come into the g., Maud   228:20
  cultivate our g.   237:13
  England is a g.   125:8
  fairies at the bottom of our g.   88:12
  first g. made   69:18
  Flowers in the g.   221:22
  G. by the Water blows   84:16
  g. in her face   54:11
  g. is a lovesome thing   42:17
  Glory of the G.   125:8
  God Almighty first planted a g.   14:16
  How does your g. grow?   156:16
  Hyacinth the G. wears   85:2
  in a g. grew   215:2
  maid was in the g.   158:1
  man and a woman in a g.   243:26

Nearer God's Heart in a g.   99:2
she went into the g.   86:19
Through this same G.   86:2
unweeded g.   185:11
walked over yon g. green   16:4
walking in the g.   23:15
Gardener: Adam was a g.   125:10, 192:10
half a proper g.'s work   125:10
will come the G.   86:7
Gardens: bordered by its g.   150:14
by the salley g.   250:5
g. are not made by singing   125:9
g. bright   66:14
walks through parks and g.   67:22
Garish: to the g. sun   208:1
Garland: immortal g.   148:9
wither'd is the g. of the war   182:21
Garlanded: All g.   120:4
Garlands: let us g. bring   210:2
with fantastic g.   189:18
with g. drest?   120:21
Garment: like a g.   249:4
Winter G. of Repentance   84:17
Garnished: Empty, swept, and g.   31:23
Garter: I like the G.   141:19
Garvalies: and the G.   86:19
Gas: All is g. and gaiters   75:5
Gasp: at the last g.   29:39
It made one G.   21:8
Gate: A-sitting on a g.   58:11
at the g. of the year   101:5
Captain of the G.   136:9
enemies in the g.   171:23
here at the g. alone   228:20
how strait the g.   102:14
lark at heaven's g. sings   184:20
no latch ter de golden g.?   101:1
passion-flower at the g.   228:20
Sings hymns at heaven's g.   210:13
Strait is the g.   31:2
Wide is the g.   31:1
willow cabin at your g.   209:4
Gates: at area g.   81:20
g. of hell   31:33
men shut their g.   209:20
O ye g.   169:4
twelve g. were twelve pearls   37:28
within thy g.   167:10
Gath: Tell it not in G.   24:47
Gather: g. honey all the day   239:9
G. ye rosebuds   104:14
shall g. the lambs   28:14
we'll g. and go   106:6
Gathered: eagles be g. together   32:13
g. flowers are dead   86:7
two or three are g. together   31:40, 166:17
Gathering: saw the swallows g.   142:45
Gathers round him   176:6
Gaudeamus igitur   10:2
Gaudy: neat but not g.   241:20
Neat, not g.   129:11
one other g. night   182:17
rich, not g.   185:21
Gaul and I've lost G.   127:8
G...is divided into three parts   52:23
In the garb of old G.   83:6
Gaunt: Old John of G.   206:1
siege of the city of G.   16:9
Gauzy: wrapped in a g. veil   215:14
Gave: g. up the years to be   41:16
he g. his only begotten Son   34:1
never g. you kingdom   195:5
sea g. up the dead   37:24
The Lord g.   25:26
They g. it me   58:4
Gavest: The day Thou g.   82:11
Gawds: praise new-born g.   208:28
Gawdy: her g. trim   145:7

Gay: a g. deceiver   67:21
good and g.   156:17
her heart was warm and g.   99:10
in g., fine colours   103:4
My g. apparel   206:16
ornate, and g.   147:5
Gaza: Eyeless in G.   147:2
Gaze: g. on so fondly   149:12
turns from their g.   149:17
Gazed: steadfastly g.   245:6
still they g.   95:8
Gazelle: nurs'd a dear g.   149:19
Gazing: With g. fed   202:1
Geese: all his own g. are swans   238:8
g. are getting fat   3:20
swans of others are g.   238:8
Gehenna: Down to G.   128:7
Gem: G. of all joy   80:14
g. of purest ray serene   97:15
Gemlike: hard, g. flame   161:11
General: caviare to the g.   187:7
Generals: bite some other of my g.   90:6
Russia has two g.   154:4
Generation: O g. of vipers   30:5
One g. passeth away   26:34
one g. to another   170:16
stubborn g.   170:11
third and fourth g.   167:7
Generations: all g. shall call me blessed   32:37
early g. of mankind   108:14
No hungry g.   121:6
Generous: like g. wine   50:4
most select and g.   185:21
Génie: le g...aptitude à la patience   45:23
Geniumque loci...precatur   236:19
Genius: Chaucer, who had g.   238:19
except my g.   244:1
G. does what it must   142:13
G...first of all   55:9
G. is..great aptitude for patience   45:23
G. is one per cent. inspiration   81:1
g. of the Constitution!   162:20
G. of the place   236:19
g...supreme capacity   50:5
Gives g. a better discerning   95:20
Milton...was a g.   116:5
Ramp up my g.   118:1
recognizes g.   78:18
you believe yourself to be a great g.!   19:8
Geniuses: One of the greatest g.   238:6
Gennesareth: Not of G., but Thames!   232:10
Genteelly: committed very g.   115:3
Gentile: might of the G.   52:11
Gentiles: Such boastings as the G. use   127:6
Gentility: cottage of g.!   218:21
Gentle: faintly, g. springs   117:10
frolic and the g.   246:3
G. and low   196:9
g. voices calling   87:12
His life was g.   194:24
shall g. his condition   192:4
Sleep! it is a g. thing   65:23
That I am meek and g   193:20
verray parfit g. knight   60:10
Gentleman: Be a little g.   105:17
breeding of a g.   51:16
cannot make a g.   47:12
fine old English g.   6:8
finish'd g.   52:1
g. to haul and draw   78:27
Prince of Darkness is a g.   195:13, 222:7
talking about being a g.   222:18
very gallant g.   12:12
Who was then a g.?   8:13, 99:11

Gentlemen: g. and there were seamen 137:2
g. of England 160:19
G. of the French Guard 101:7
G. Prefer Blondes 134:15
G.-rankers 125:7
Great-hearted g. 43:12
seamen were not g. 137:2
while the G. go by! 127:10
You g.'s g. 216:9
Gentleness: fruit of the spirit is..g. 36:7
g. my strong enforcement 183:19
Gently: g. lead 28:14
roar you as g. 203:4
use all g. 188:7
Genuine night 79:24
Genus: g. immortale manet 237:9
hoc g. omne 110:9
Geographical expression 142:16
Geography: different from G. 22:9
G. is about maps 22:9
George: Amelia was praying for G. 231:17
England and Saint G.! 191:9
for King G. upon the throne 118:15
G. goes to sleep at a bank 113:7
in good King G.'s glorious days 91:22
George the Third: and G. 103:9
G. Ought never to have occurred 22:13
Georgie Porgie 155:15
Germ..of all virtue 124:4
German: a G. who smoked like a
chimney 17:15
and to my horse-G. 60:6
Herman's a G. 165:17
Germans: beastly to the G. 69:13
G. in Greek 165:17
Germany, G. over all 83:17
Germens: all g. spill at once 195:4
Gesang: Wein, Weib und G. 135:11
Gesanges: auf Flügeln des G. 102:5
Gesetz: das moralische G. in mir 119:10
Get: And g. me to England 42:7
G. thee behind me 31:34
other is to g. it 212:22
plenty to g. 75:26
We will g. everything out of her 90:2
Gets: pleased with what he g. 183:15
Getting and spending 249:5
Get-up, sweet Slug-a-bed 104:9
Ghastly: rain'd a g. dew 228:9
We were a g. crew 56:2
with a g. pang 65:17
Ghost: I'll make a g. of him 186:5
milk-white peacock like a g. 229:16
Since g. there's none to affright
thee 104:13
some old lover's g. 77:13
to each frustrate g. 45:8
Vex not his g. 196:12
Ghosties: From ghoulies and g. 4:9
Ghostly: And a g. batsman 232:11
moon was a g. galleon 155:1
Ghosts: haunted by the g. 206:15
like g. from an enchanter 214:1
Ghoulies: From g. and ghosties 4:9
Giant: and like a g. refreshed 170:12
as a g. 168:30
as when a g. dies 200:21
Giant Despair 46:11
in the hand of the g. 171:23
To have a g.'s strength 200:18
To use it like a g. 200:18
Giants: there were g. in the earth 23:21
Gibber: squeak and g. 185:3
Gibbon: and G.'s elegant [style] 67:22
Eh! Mr. G.? 94:7
Gibes: Where be your g. now? 189:20
Giddy multitude 141:13
Gift: g. of the gab 139:21
Time with a g. of tears 224:1

Gift-horse: look a g. in the mouth 49:20
Gifts: All good g. around us 53:12
But, dying, has made us rarer g. 41:16
g. for men 170:7
g. of God are strown 101:16
hands proffer g. 236:9
or his own g. 147:17
presented unto him g. 30:2
seven-fold g. 172:11
Gig: crew of the captain's g. 91:3
Gigadibs the literary man 43:10
Giggles: wriggles and g. 105:18
Gilbert, the Filbert 244:14
Gild: G.,,.the ruins 180:5
To g. refined gold 193:6
Gilded: bird in a g. cage 129:3
but g. loam 206:2
g. butterflies 196:6
g. monuments 211:4
Gilding pale streams 211:2
Gilds: eternal summer g. them 51:17
Gilead: balm in G.? 29:5
Gilpin: G. long live he 69:31
John G. 69:21
Gimble: gyre and g. 57:14
Gin: talk o' g. an' beer 125:11
Ginger shall be hot 209:7
Gipfeln: über allen G. ist Ruh' 94:15
Gipsy: Time, you old g. man 105:14
vagrant g. life 141:4
Gird up now thy loins 25:40
Girded: g. with praise 96:18
he has g. on 149:15
Girdle: folds of a bright g. 11:8
g. round the earth 203:8
Girdled round 66:14
Girl: Burma g. a-settin' 126:11
fair little g. 110:14
g. I left behind me 7:16
Home is the g.'s prison 213:1
like a green g. 186:1
Poor Little Rich G. 69:12
That every boy and every g. 91:21
There was a little g. 134:14
to the sweetest g. 244:7
We all love a pretty g. 37:31
Girl-graduates: sweet g. 229:6
Girlish: Laugh thy g. laughter 239:5
Weep thy g. tears! 239:5
with g. glee 92:2
Girls: At g. who wear glasses 160:18
Boys and g. come out 155:5
g. are level now with men 182:21
g. that are so smart 55:2
Golden lads and g. 184:22
hear the g. declare 90:17
Kissed the g. 155:15
What are little g. made of? 158:14
where g. are so pretty 5:8
with the g. be handy 17:5
Gitche Gumee: shores of G. 134:4
Give: all other things g. place 89:29
bottle to g. him! 74:15
do not g. it yet 13:3
don't g. way to hating 125:14
G. all thou canst 247:6
g. him a stone? 30:34
g. me indifference 67:16
g. me liberty 103:10
g. me my soul again 138:12
g. my love good-morrow! 105:2
G. thanks unto him 169:8
g. thee a crown of life 37:14
g. them the other harmony 80:5
g. to drink 31:17
g. unto this last 32:5
G. us this day 30:22
I g. my body to be burned 35:21
I will g. you rest 31:20

more blessed to g. 34:46
My sword, I g. to him 46:22
praise to g. 118:4
such as I have g. I thee 34:32
What shall we g. him? 156:13
What will ye give me 32:18
which the world cannot g. 166:19
Given: g. him a name 36:15
g. him his heart's desire 168:33
g. our hearts away 249:5
it shall be g. you 30:33
never g. in vain 110:17
not have g. me over 245:11
son is g. 27:32
Unto every one that hath shall
be g. 32:15
Giver: author and g. 167:2
God loveth a cheerful g. 36:2
Givers: when g. prove unkind 188:2
Gives: g. twice who gives soon 224:11
this g. life to thee 210:12
Giveth! shepherd g. his life 34:12
Giving: And you're g. a treat 91:25
g. your heart 127:2
loving and g. 156:17
Glad: g. confident morning 44:12
G. did I live 221:23
g. me with its soft black eye 149:19
I was g. 171:19
Let us live then and be g. 10:2
maketh g. the heart of man 17:12
moments of g. grace 250:11
shall be g. for them 28:9
shew ourselves g. 170:21
Then are they g. 171:9
Gladder: heart is g. 177:8
Glade: in the bee-loud g. 250:9
That crown the wat'ry g. 98:5
Glades: shall fan the g. 165:1
Gladly: and g. die 221:23
g. wolde he lerne 60:14
suffer fools g. 36:3
Gladness: begin in g. 247:19
Teach me half the g. 215:6
Gladstone: What's the matter with
G.? 98:19
Glamis: G. hath murder'd sleep 198:14
G. thou art 197:14
Glance: g. from heaven to earth 203:19
in the g. of the Lord! 52:11
Glass: dome of many-coloured g. 213:10
excuse for the g. 216:19
Fill ev'ry g. 89:17
Get thee g. eyes 195:22
g. I drink from 151:7
g. of fashion 188:6
Grief with a g. that ran 224:1
Man that looks on g. 103:21
more brilliant than g. 109:24
see through a g. darkly 35:22
turn down an empty G.! 86:3
With a comb and a g. in her
hand 6:20
Glasses: girls who wear g. 160:18
Wiv a ladder and some g. 18:27
Glassy: around the g. sea 102:1
His g. essence 200:19
Gleam: visionary g.? 246:10
Gleamed upon my sight 248:4
Gleaming: cohorts were g. 52:9
Gleams that untravell'd world 230:13
Glee: fill'd one home with g. 102:9
songs of pleasant g. 39:8
with girlish g. 92:2
Glen: Down the rushy g. 2:17
sides of this long g. 229:4
Glide: shall for ever g. 245:17
Glides: Still g. the Stream 245:17
Glideth: river g. 249:4

Glimmering: g. landscape 97:8
Mere g. 235:10
Glimmers on to me 229:16
Glimpses that would make me less
forlorn 249:5
Glistens: when the wine-cup g. 180:15
Glittering: All bright and g. 249:4
g. eye 65:4
g. like the morning star 47:14
how that g. taketh me! 104:15
Gloaming: In the g., O, my darling 159:14
Roamin' in the G. 130:11
Gloat: Hear me g.! 128:23
Globes: use of the g. 74:25
Globule: primordial, atomic g. 91:28
Gloom: amid the encircling g. 153:15
counterfeit a g. 144:7
from dawn to g. 214:9
Inspissated g. 114:25
Shine through the g. 135:17
through hours of g. 11:17
Gloria: Sic transit g. mundi 122:23
Gloriam: Ad majorem Dei g. 9:15
Gloried: where Jamshyd g. 85:1
Glories: g. of our blood 216:24
g. pass away 135:16
g...shrunk 193:18
I see Heaven's g. shine 41:13
not the meanest of g. 108:11
Glorify: To g. God 216:26
Glorious: G. First of June 64:13, 151:3
g. morning face 221:24
g. thing, I ween 91:8
G. things of thee are spoken 154:2
had a g. time 79:9
in g. cry 84:11
In good King George's g. days! 91:22
is a g. birth 246:8
is all g. within 169:19
it is a g. thing 93:16
Made g. summer 207:4
seen a g. light 181:9
That g. song of old 181:10
Glory: All g., laud, and honour 152:7
alone with his g. 245:7
cataract leaps in g. 229:10
crowned with g. now 122:21
day of g. has arrived 177:17
days of our g. 52:7
die in their g. 111:2
don't know what you mean by 'g.' 58:5
G. and loveliness 122:1
g. and the dream? 246:10
g. and the freshness 246:7
g. be to God for dappled things 107:14
g. from the earth 246:8
g. in the flower 246:13
g. in the name of Briton 90:7
g. is departed 24:39
g., jest, and riddle 164:19
g. of beating the French 245:8
g. of Europe 47:14
g. of God 9:15, 168:29
g. of man 37:3
g. of rulers 23:3
g. of the coming of the Lord 111:15
G. of the Garden 125:8
g. of the Lord 28:12, 29:1, 32:41
g. of the world 122:23
G. of youth 221:21
g. shone around 225:9
G. to God in the highest 32:43
G. to Man 224:8
G. to the new-born King 241:15
g.'s thrill is o'er 149:13
gown of g. 174:13
greater g. dim the less 202:14
hath its ancient g. 129:12
Have drown'd my G. 85:15

Glory (*cont.*)

hope of g.	166:32
in a sea of g.	192:14
in an air of g.	235:10
King of G.	104:2, 169:4, 169:5
Land of Hope and G.	22:7
like thy g., Titan	215:1
mellow g. of the Attic stage	11:14
not without g.	110:2
paths of g.	97:12
power, and the g.	30:22
Prince of g. died	239:16
rainbow's g.	213:16
return the g. of your prime?	213:15
Saints in g. stand	250:12
Solomon in all his g.	30:28
There's g. for you!	58:5
to g. we steer	88:18
trailing clouds of g.	246:11
uncertain g.	210:1
Vain pomp and g.	192:14
walked in g.	247:19
way to g.	229:2
What Price G.	3:2
When can their g. fade?	226:5
Where is that g. now?	221:21
who to your g. came	11:1
whole earth is full of his g.	27:27
whose g. is in their shame	36:17

Gloucester: Salisbury and G. 192:4
Glove: g. upon that hand 207:21
  hand and g. 70:12
Gloves: through the fields in g. 68:28
Glow: g. the delicate cheeks 182:15
  gold oranges g. 94:16
  shines forth in mystic g. 87:7
  Whose little eyes g. 104:13
Glowed in his soul 221:21
Glowing: beside the g. bars 250:11
  g. embers 144:7
  To chase the g. Hours 51:1
Glows the lily 86:6
Glow-worm: Her eyes the g. lend thee 104:13
Gnashing: weeping and g. of teeth 31:6
Gnat: strain at a g. 32:8
Go: About the woodlands I will g. 110:15
  all have to g. through it 113:6
  as cooks g. 178:15
  donkey wot wouldn't g. 23:2
  far to g. 156:17
  g., and sin no more 34:7
  g. at once 199:10
  G. directly 173:11
  g. into the house 171:19
  G., litel book 61:1
  G. out into the darkness 101:5
  G. out into the highways 33:18
  I do not g. 77:15
  I would g., O my beloved 94:16
  in the way he should g. 26:22
  let them g. 204:9
  no place to g. 49:7
  nowhere to g. 242:6
  see ere thou g. 234:15
  seen it come and g. 216:16
  softly g. 159:14
  sup before we g. 155:8
  thus far shalt thou g. 161:1
  to g. again to my travels 60:4
  to g. at a certain hour 115:15
  to g. away at any rate 6:7
  unto Caesar shalt thou g. 34:49
  wherever I g. 48:27
  who will g. for us? 27:28
  Will g. with you along 104:10
Goal: final g. of ill 227:10
  g. stands up 111:4
  grave is not its g. 133:26
Goals: muddied oafs at the g. 126:1

Goat: fleecy hairy g. 21:22
  with their g. feet 138:9
Goats: better than sheep or g. 227:2
Goblets: My figur'd g. 206:16
Goblins: of sprites and g. 210:3
God: abusing of G.'s patience 202:15
  according to G.'s holy ordinance 168:12
  afire with G. 43:4
  after G.'s ordinance 168:10
  America is G.'s crucible 251:3
  angels of G. ascending 23:29
  Around the throne of G. 152:8
  as had the fear of G. 71:5
  attribute to G. 202:5
  before the g. of love 77:13
  But for the grace of G. 40:17
  Cabots talk only to G. 40:11
  called the children of G. 30:11
  called . . The mighty G. 27:32
  canst thou . . find out G. ? 25:30
  child of G. 167:32
  city of our G. 154:2
  coming down from G. 37:25
  Cry G. for Harry! 191:9
  Curse G., and die 25:27
  daily, nearer G. 122:14
  doubtless G. never did 50:11
  enter into the kingdom of G. 32:1
  eternal G. is thy refuge 24:25
  Fear G. 37:4
  feeble G. 89:7
  For G. hath made them so 239:6
  for G. is love 37:9
  For they shall see our G. 122:19
  freedom . . to worship G. 176:11
  From everlasting Thou art G. 239:14
  from G. he could not free 82:15
  gifts of G. 101:1
  Glory be to G. 107:14
  glory of G. 168:29
  Glory to G. in the highest 32:43
  G. Almighty first planted a garden 14:16
  G. Almighty made 'em 81:8
  G. and sinners reconciled 241:15
  G. be in my head 4:10
  G. be merciful to me 33:34
  G. be merciful unto us 170:4
  G. be with you 175:2
  G. bless the King 50:15
  G. bless us every one! 74:3
  G. bless you! 3:20
  G. cannot change the past 1:22
  G. caused a deep sleep 23:12
  G. created the heaven 23:4
  G. disposes 122:22
  G. doth not need 147:17
  G. fulfils himself 227:1
  G. gives all men 127:18
  G. gives us to see the right 132:9
  G. has not said a word! 45:1
  G. hath joined together 31:41, 168:15
  G. hath made man upright 26:41
  G. hath no better praise 41:6
  G., I thank thee 33:33
  G. in his mercy 228:2
  G. in Three Persons 102:1
  G. into the hands 147:6
  G. is a Spirit 34:2
  G. is always for the big battalions 237:18
  G. is gone up 169:22
  G. is making the American 251:3
  G. is no respecter of persons 34:38
  G. is not mocked 36:8
  G. is One 153:13
  G. is our hope 169:20
  G. is Three 153:13
  G. is working His purpose out 2:3
  G. knows 128:26
  G. loveth a cheerful giver 36:2

G. made him   201:12
G. made the country   70:14
G. made the wicked Grocer   61:25
G. made them, high or lowly   2:8
G. make thee good   226:20
G. may forgive you   82:6
G. moves in a mysterious way   70:5
G. must think it exceedingly odd   129:2
G. my Saviour   32:37
G. of battles!   192:1
G. of love   104:4
G. of our fathers   127:3
G...order'd their estate   2:8
G. proved them   29:33
G. rest you merry   4:11
G. said 'Let there be light'   23:5
G. save our gracious King!   54:22
G. save the king   24:40, 54:22
G. save the Queen   124:9
G. save thee   65:10
G. saw that it was good   23:7
G. shall give us his blessing   170:5
G. shall wipe away all tears   37:18, 26
G. so loved the world   34:1
G. tempers the wind   220:12
G. the first garden made   69:18
G. threw him from..heaven   138:10
G. to be his guide   46:17
G. who loveth us   66:7
G. who made him   125:10
G. who made thee mighty   22:7
G. will pardon me   102:6
G.'s great Judgment Seat   124:13
G.'s own country   4:13
G.'s pampered people   79:4
greater glory of G.   9:15
Had I but served G.   245:11
Had I but serv'd my G.   193:1
half believes a G.   250:18
He for G. only   146:16
He is the Lord our G.   170:24
here is G.'s plenty   80:6
highway for our G.   28:12
holy Lamb of G.   38:16
honest G.   50:7
hope of the City of G.   141:5
how like a g.!   187:4
How odd of G.   83:13
If a man say, I love G.   37:12
If G. be for us   35:9
if g. be pleased   81:4
If G. did not exist   237:15
if there be a G.   6:13
in G.'s sight   177:14
in the hand of G.   29:32
in the house of my G.   170:15
in the living G.   170:13
into the hand of G.   101:5
is G. indeed   123:5
jealous G.   167:7
justify G.'s ways to man   111:7
justify the ways of G. to Men   145:11
keep G.'s holy will   167:32
kills the image of G.   148:7
kingdom of G.   31:1, 34; 33:31
know that I am G.   169:21
know what G. and man is   226:12
leap up to my G.   138:14
Let G. arise   170:6
lively Oracles of G.   69:1
Lord G. Almighty!   37:16, 38:13, 102:1
Lord G. made them all   2:7
Lord G. of Hosts   127:3
Lord thy G. is with thee   24:26
love G. whom he hath not seen?   37:12
men that G. made mad   61:15
mills of G.   134:2
music sent up to G.   43:7
My duty towards G.   167:33

My G. and King   103:18
My G., how wonderful   83:14
my King and my G.   170:13
Name of the Lord thy G.   167:8
nearer G.'s Heart   99:2
no G. could please   79:4
No man hath seen G.   37:10
noblest work of G.   164:20
not..forgotten before G.?   33:13
not tempt the Lord thy G.   30:9
Now G. be praised   245:9
Now, G. be thanked   42:10
Now thank we all our G.   71:14, 244:17
O G.! Oh Montreal!   50:10
of such is the kingdom of G.   32:34
one G. only   64:5
only G. can make a tree   123:9
only thou, O G.   166:13
others call it G.   58:17
ought to obey G.   34:33
Our G. and soldiers   173:26
Our G., our help   239:14
Our G.'s forgotten   173:26
out of the mouth of G.   30:8
owe G. a death   190:32
peace of G.   36:19, 112:18, 167:25
please G. to call me   168:1
Praise G. from whom all blessings
    flow   123:3
presume not G. to scan   164:18
put upon the Providence of G.   71:12
Put your trust in G.   38:5
sacrifice of G.   169:28
safe stronghold our G. is still   135:12
saw the face of G.   138:11
Scourge of G.   139:14
Sees G. in clouds   164:14
separate us from the love of G.   35:10
Serve G. and mammon   30:27
serve G. and the King   153:7
she for G. in him   146:16
spirit shall return unto G.   27:8
Teach me, my G. and King   103:21
their duty to G.   242:14
them that love G.   35:8
There is no G.   64:4, 168:26
they shall see G.   30:11
three person'd G.   77:12
throws himself on G.   43:18
thy G. my G.   24:35
Thy G. reigneth!   28:18
Thy G., thy life   235:8
To glorify G.   216:26
to G. to praise and pray   44:3
to the unknown G.   34:42
to walk humbly with thy G.?   29:29
true G.'s priest   54:20
trust G.   45:4
'Twas G. the word that spake it   82:4
unchanging law of G.   160:22
under the Providence of G.   60:1
very sure G. walks in mine   42:18
voice of G.!   2:4, 175:8, 245:19
voice of the Lord G.   23:15
we come from G.   246:11
We praise thee, O G.   10:6
we were G.'s spies   196:6
What G. abandoned   111:11
whole armour of G.   36:13, 14
whom G. would destroy   80:15
whose G. is their belly   36:17
will of G. prevail   12:6
with G. all things are possible   32:2
with the grandeur of G.   107:12
Word was with G.   33:43
wrote of Angels and G.   39:16
ye believe in G.   34:16
Goddess: G., excellently bright   117:11
    G. indubitable   236:6

Godfathers and Godmothers 167:32
God-intoxicated man 154:14
Godlike: of the g. forehead 246:3
Godliness: Cleanliness is, indeed,
   next to g. 241:19
Godly: g., righteous, and sober life 166:10
   Still a g. race he ran 95:11
Godmothers: Godfathers and G. 167:32
Gods: are we to the g. 195:18
   By the nine g. he swore 136:8
   darling of the G. was born? 140:10
   daughter of the g. 226:8
   dish fit for the g. 193:13
   dish for the g. 183:1
   fit love for G. 146:23
   g. are just 196:7
   g. help them that help themselves 1:19
   I thank whatever g. 102:13
   May the g. avert this omen 63:20
   nights and suppers of g.! 110:13
   none other g. 167:5
   temples of his G.? 136:9
   that strove with g. 230:15
   to talk about the G. of late 51:25
   Whatever g. may be 102:13, 224:6
   whom the g. favour 163:8
God's-Acre! 133:21
Goes: comes and g. 246:8
   g. contrairy with me 74:5
   How g. the enemy? 175:7
   ship that g. 73:18
Goest: whither thou g. 24:35, 27:2
Goeth: Go, and he g. 31:5
   g. on his way 171:21
   whither it g. 33:50
   Who g. a borrowing 234:9
   wind g. over it 171:1
Going: all g. to heaven 88:13
   At the g. down of the sun 38:2
   g. to St. Ives 155:3
   g. up the stair 141:17
   not worth g. to see 115:21
   order of your g. 199:10
   thy g. out 171:18
   Where are you g. to 124:15, 159:1
    175:6
Gold: among the g. 227:2
   Bound by g. chains 98:2
   can g. despise? 145:8
   fetch the age of g. 180:15
   From the red g. 52:9
   gleaming in purple and g. 193:4
   g. and silver becks me 124:19
   G. is for the mistress 94:16
   g. oranges glow 21:21
   hearts of g. 169:19
   her clothing is of wrought g. 210:12
   his g. complexion dimm'd 143:15
   little g. head 227:20
   lust of g. 38:16
   of burning g.! 191:15
   of g. and pearl 44:16
   path of g. 202:11
   patines of bright g. 182:15
   poop was beaten g. 30:2
   presented unto him. .g. 41:16
   rarer gifts than g. 121:9
   realms of g. 224:11
   ruin and g. 34:32
   Silver and g. have I none 67:19
   streets are paved with g. 193:6
   To gild refined g. 181:10
   touch their harps of g. 164:1
   truth with g. she weighs 45:15
   upon a cross of g. 45:12
   what's become of all the g. 221:19
   With eyes of g. 101:15
Golden: down their g. sand 250:10
   g. apples of the sun 27:8
   g. bowl be broken

g. daffodils 247:3
G. opinions 198:5
G. slumbers kiss your eyes 73:1
g. years return 213:12
hast thou g. slumbers? 72:18
Jerusalem the g. 152:14
Kissing with g. face 211:2
loves well the g. mean 109:13
no latch ter de g. gate? 101:1
on every g. scale! 56:13
that sweet g. clime 39:7
their g. crowns 102:1
To add to g. numbers 72:18
We take the G. Road 86:8
Goldsmith: Here lies Nolly G. 89:1
   Olivarii G., Poetae 115:11
Gone: All, all are g. 129:16
   all our days are g. 170:18
   been and g. and done? 90:20
   but g. before 154:13, 176:6
   dead and g. 120:17
   faded and g. 149:18
   God is g. up 169:22
   g., and for ever! 180:3
   G. to her death! 106:20
   g. up on high 170:7
   g. with the wind 77:27
   He's g. 147:7
   I have g. here and there 211:15
   it is g. 171:1
   Iram indeed is g. 84:16
   lad that is g. 221:20
   like an evening g. 239:14
   lost and g. for ever 149:7
   My peace is g. 94:13
   Now dimm'd and g. 150:1
   odds is g. 182:21
   something that is g. 246:10
   they are g. 120:5
   to be g. 71:13
   we are g. 170:18
   when thou art g. 215:10
Gongs: struck regularly, like g. 69:17
Good: all g. to me is lost 146:14
   any g. thing therefore that I can
    do 98:15
   apprehension of the g. 206:5
   Be g., sweet maid 123:14
   be of g. cheer 34:22
   bringeth g. tidings 28:18
   can be g. in the country 243:22
   cannot be g. 197:10
   corrupt g. manners 35:27
   do evil, that g. may come 35:1
   Do g. by stealth 165:13
   does you g. 133:2
   don't look too g. 125:14
   doubt that, somehow, g. shall
    come 41:20
   enemy of the g. 237:14
   Eschew evil, and do g. 169:12
   evil and of g. 248:15
   Evil be thou my G. 146:14
   for his country's g. 89:25
   for the g. of his country 249:14
   for the g. or evil side 135:3
   fought a g. fight 36:33
   fountain of g. sense 80:7
   Full of g. works 34:37
   general g. 46:27
   go about doing g. 71:3
   God make thee g. 226:20
   God saw that it was g. 23:7
   g. and gay 156:17
   g. and joyful a thing 171:26
   g. are so harsh 245:13
   g. as she 43:2
   g. die early 72:14
   G. fences make g. neighbours 88:9

g. for sore eyes 223:9
G., great and joyous 215:1
g. in everything 183:9
g. is oft interred 194:3
g. men and true? 204:12
g. new baits 147:8
g. news from a far country 26:25
g. of argifying? 128:18
g. of the people 63:11
G. people all 95:10
'G.!' said the Baron 124:19
g. servants 132:1
g. shepherd giveth his life 34:12
g. that I would I do not 35:6
g. will to man 181:10
g. will toward men 32:43
Hanging is too g. for him 46:10
He's a G. Fellow 85:14
highest g. 63:13
how g. is it! 26:19
I will be g. 235:15
If all the g. people were clever 245:13
It is always g. 19:12
know what were g. to do 201:9
Life is g. 102:17
many a g. tune 50:9
may see your g. works 30:14
neither g. for man nor beast 8:15
never was a g. war 88:3
not g. that the man should be alone 23:11
nothing either g. or bad 187:2
nothing so g. 131:11
of a g. man's life 248:18
of all g. things 167:2
of g. report 36:20
only g. thing left to me 151:8
overcome evil with g. 35:12
Rich in g. works 36:32
so much g. in the worst 105:12
Such g. things 167:1
sun to rise..on the g. 30:19
that call evil g. 27:26
that which is g. 36:24
thou g. and faithful servant 32:14
To bite so g. a man 95:15
To do aught g. 146:1
too g. to be lost 129:18
tree of the knowledge of g. 23:10
turns none to g. 234:8
very, very g. 134:14
what g. came of it 218:14
what is g. for them 71:8
When she was g. 134:14
where de g. niggers go 87:14
will do him little g. 114:14
with g. things 32:38
won my right g.-will 137:15, 235:4
work together for g. 35:8
wos wery g. to me 73:25
Good-bye: G. Piccadilly 244:7
G. to all that 97:3
Goodliness: All the g. thereof 28:12
Goodly: and g. to look at 24:43
With a g. company 66:6
Good-morning: Bid me 'G.' 17:8
Good-morrow: give my Love g.! 105:2
Goodness: And g. only knowses 61:27
fruit of the spirit is..g. 36:7
g. faileth never 15:20
g. in her little finger 223:15
g. of the Lord 169:7
of great g. 172:3
Good-night: Dear work! G.! G.! 110:14
G., sweet prince 190:5
say g. till it be morrow 207:25
Goods: all his worldly g. 130:19
bestow all my g. 35:21
his g. are in peace 33:10

Man Who Delivers the G. 141:7
precious as the G. they sell 85:16
Goose: every g. a swan 123:18
that g. look? 199:31
Goosey goosey gander 155:16
Gorge: my g. rises 189:20
Gorgeous: let g. Tragedy 144:8
My g. palace 206:16
Gorging Jack 231:19
Gorm: When Mrs. G. (Aunt Eloise) 96:15
Gory: Welcome to your g. bed 48:30
Goschen: I forgot G. 62:15
Got: I've g. a little list 91:30
Gotham: Three wise men of G. 158:11
Gott-betrunkener Mensch 154:14
Götter: Mit der Dummheit kämpfen G. 179:13
Gouvernement: le g. qu'elle mérite 137:19
Govern: g. thou my song 146:20
He that would g. others 141:8
No king could g. 79:4
such should g. 19:21
Government: attachment to their g. 47:3
G.,..a necessary evil 160:13
g. it deserves 137:19
g. of the people 132:8
g. shall be upon his shoulder 27:32
How can the G. be carried on? 240:21
increase of his g. 27:32
looked to g. for bread 47:17
object of g. in peace 23:3
there has been no G. 73:27
Governments: councils, g. 230:13
G. never have learned 102:2
Gown: and a green g. 155:12
for an almsman's g. 206:16
g. of glory 174:13
sail in amply billowing g. 21:21
Grace: but for the g. of God 40:17
courtly foreign g. 230:5
every g.! 129:19
fallen from g. 36:6
for love of g. 189:3
full of g. 156:17
God's good g. 149:1
G. me no g. 206:11
grow old with a good g. 220:4
hath such g. 77:4
have g. to use it 147:15
heart of g. 93:17
inward and spiritual g. 168:2
lend her g. 228:2
look to thee for g. 234:1
means of g. 166:32
ministers of g. 186:4
moments of glad g. 250:11
petitionary g. 225:19
renown and g. is dead 198:19
such g. did lend her 210:2
sweet attractive g. 146:16
tender g. of a day 225:15
that g. may abound? 35:3
Thy G. may give 124:17
with thy heavenly g. 168:4
with what g. 86:6
Graceful: Thy g. air 86:11
Graces do not seem to be natives 61:9
Gracious: be g. unto thee 24:13
hallow'd and so g. 185:4
Heaven's all g. King 181:10
Lord is g. 172:3
Gradualness: inevitability of g. 240:2
Graecas: Ad G. Kalendas 52:12
Grain: Beside a field of g. 160:21
g...generally given to horses 116:16
g. of mustard seed 31:27, 36
in a G. of Sand 38:10
to swell the g. 53:12

Grammar: Heedless of g. 17:14
With g., and nonsense 95:20
Gramophone: puts a record on the g. 82:2
Grampian: on the G. hills 106:14
Granary: on a g. floor 119:18
Grand: hoary woods are g. 181:7
it would be g.! 57:21
sound so g. 173:1
that g. old man 154:11
Grandchild: His little g. 218:12
Grandeur: Nor g. hear 97:12
with the g. of God 107:12
Grandmother: as my g. used to say 59:11
may not marry his G. 172:17
Grandsire's grandsire 237:9
Grandsires: was worse than our g. 109:23
Grandstand: rushed past the g. 76:23
Grange: at the moated g. 201:2
Grant their requests 166:17
Grantchester: The lovely hamlet G. 42:7
Grape: Joy's g. 120:24
Grapes: fathers have eaten sour g. 29:12
where the g. of wrath 111:15
Grapeshot: whiff of g. 55:11
Grapple them to thy soul 185:21
Grappling in the central blue 228:9
Grasp: should exceed his g. 43:8
To g. this sorry Scheme 86:1
what dread g. 39:2
Grass: All flesh is as g. 37:3
All flesh is g. 28:13
are but as g. 171:1
eateth g. as an ox 26:1
flower of g. 37:3
from the feather'd g. 120:7
g. comes again in the fields 110:5
g. looking green 162:8
g. withereth 28:13, 37:3
green g. above me 177:12
I fall on g. 140:6
I leave you on the g. 231:12
kissed the lovely g. 42:4
like the g. 170:17
lurks in the g.! 236:24
or two blades of g. 223:2
people is g. 28:13
splendour in the g. 246:13
Star-scattered on the G. 86:3
through the frozen g. 120:2
Grassy: search the g. knolls 58:13
Grate: dying in the g. 142:2
G. on their scrannel pipes 145:3
Gratifying: With the g. feeling 91:11
Grating: Nor harsh nor g. 248:19
Gratitude: shall our g. sleep? 54:17
Grave: Between the cradle and the g. 80:18
dark and silent g. 174:15
Dig the g. 221:23
dread The g. as little 123:2
Duncan is in his g. 199:4
earth, and g., and dust 174:15
from the cradle to the g. 70:21, 214:10
g. is not its goal 133:26
g.'s a fine and private place 140:12
her heart in his g. 149:17
In cold g. she was lain 17:1
labour to his g. 191:15
lead but to the g. 97:12
lie a-buried in one g. 7:20
lies a mould'ring in the g. 99:6
like Alcestis from the g. 148:1
little light g., an obscure g. 206:16
never find my g. 209:9
no flowers be planted on my g. 100:9
no work..in the g. 27:2
now in his cold g. 60:18

O g., where is thy victory? 35:31
on this side of the g. 129:22
secrets of the g. 161:9
she is in her g. 248:3
thought shall be my g. 208:22
untimely g. 54:21
verse you g. for me 221:23
Where, g., thy victory? 135:17
with sorrow to the g. 23:35
With the old world to the g. 102:15
within its g. 214:1
work of g. purpose 107:18
Gravel paths: weeds from g. 125:9
Gravelled for lack of matter 184:9
Graven: any g. image 167:7
Gravender: eat my g. 178:13
Graver: wherein the g. had a strife 118:3
Graves: among the g. 81:6
dishonourable g. 193:11
g. are sever'd 102:9
g. stood tenantless 185:3
Let's talk of g. 206:14
watch from their g.! 44:11
Gravy: who disliked g. 217:16
Gray: see Grey
Graymalkin: I come, G.! 197:2
Grazing: cattle are g. 247:9
satyrs g. on the lawns 138:9
Great: All g. men make mistakes 62:15
all things both g. and small 66:7
enkindles the g. 49:14
Good, g. and joyous 215:1
g. and original writer 249:6
g. and wide sea 171:4
G. book g. evil 53:5
g. gulf fixed 33:29
G. is Diana 34:45
g. is truth 29:31, 42:12
G. things are done 38:15
G. wits are sure to madness 79:6
he is always g. 80:3
his weaknesses are g. 124:10
irregularly g. 136:1
name in story 52:7
No g. man lives in vain 55:13
pearl of g. price 31:28
promised something g. 51:25
Rightly to be g. 189:7
rudely g. 164:18
Silence alone is g. 236:1
some men are born g. 209:12
that g. city 37:21
that g. Hunter 85:1
those who were truly g. 219:6
thou wouldst be g. 197:14
tidings of g. joy 32:42, 225:9
To be g. 82:21
Great Birnam wood 199:22
Great Britain: G. is going to make war 23:1
natives of G. 61:9
nobody in G. 73:27
Greater: G. are none 127:24
g. feeling to the worse 206:5
G. love hath no man 34:20
G. than their knowing! 127:15
g. than we know 245:18
half is g. than the whole 104:18
Thy necessity is yet g. than mine 217:3
Greatest: as the g. he 174:12
g. event 87:17
g. of these is charity 35:22
g. pleasure I know 129:15
is the g. treason 81:21
procures the g. happiness 112:10
Great-Heart 46:16
Great-hearted gentlemen 43:12
Great Illusion 3:3
Greatness: be not afraid of g. 209:12
far-stretched g. 174:16

g. is a-ripening | 192:14
g. thrust upon them | 209:12
our g. may not fail | 226:14
some achieve g. | 209:12
squeaking Cleopatra boy my g. | 182:24
to all my g.! | 192:14
Grecian: Of all the G. woes | 106:15
towards the G. tents | 202:9
Greece: glory that was G. | 163:16
isles of G.! | 51:17
that G. might still be free | 51:18
Greedy of filthy lucre | 36:26
Greek: and less G. | 118:6
Germans in G. | 165:17
it was G. to me | 193:12
questioned him in G. | 56:8
without G. Contrived to talk | 51:25
Greek Kalends: pay at the G. | 52:22
Greeks: came first, the G. or the Romans | 76:15
When G. joined G. | 131:18
Green: all the trees are g. | 123:18
Flora country g. | 121:3
grass looking g. | 162:8
g. and yellow melancholy | 209:10
g. days in forests | 221:17
g. for a season | 224:10
G. grow the rashes O | 48:19
g. in judgment | 182:13
heads are g. | 131:4
heard on the g. | 39:11
In England's g. and pleasant | 38:16
In pastures g. | 181:8
In the morning it is g. | 170:17
like a g. girl | 186:1
Little Johnny G. | 155:13
memory be g. | 185:6
on ilka g. loaning | 82:12
Plot of beechen g. | 121:2
sported on the g. | 218:12
Their g. felicity | 122:6
things in a g. tree | 33:38
To what g. altar | 120:21
wearin' o' the G. | 7:2
which yet are g. | 211:13
Greenery: spots of g. | 66:14
Greenery-yallery Grosvenor Gallery | 93:4
Green-ey'd monster | 205:5
Greenland: From G.'s icy mountains | 101:15
Greenly: done but g. | 189:12
Greensleeves was all my joy | 4:15
Greenwood: Under the g. tree | 183:13
Greet: G. the unseen | 45:9
how should I g. thee? | 52:17
Grenadier: British G. | 7:7
Greville: Fulke G., Servant to Queen Elizabeth | 98:16
Grew: g. in beauty | 102:9
only one g. before | 223:2
still the wonder g. | 95:8
to beauty g. | 82:15
we g. together | 203:15
Grey: few locks..are g. | 218:22
good g. head | 228:25
grown g. from Thy breath | 224:10
head grown g. in vain | 213:8
little g. home | 244:11
my g. hairs with sorrow | 23:35
old and g. | 250:11
pilgrim g. | 67:15
This g. spirit | 230:14
tresses g. | 180:4
when the morn is g. | 53:9
with his coat so g.? | 97:2
Grey-green: great g., greasy Limpopo | 128:14
Greyhounds: like g. in the slips | 191:9
Grief: acquainted with g. | 28:20

bore within their breasts the g. | 14:1
Can I see another's g. | 39:14
g. forgotten | 223:29
G. with a glass that ran | 224:1
he cried in g. | 54:1
in g. for one so dear? | 109:7
Smiling at g. | 209:10
Thus g. still treads | 68:13
Griefs: he hath borne our g. | 28:20
Grieve: Do not let this parting g. thee | 8:1
made to g. on account of me | 100:9
We will g. not | 246:13
Grieved: And much it g. my heart | 248:11
Grievous: More g. torment | 120:15
Grievously hath Caesar answer'd it | 194:3
Grim grew his countenance | 16:5
Grin: ending with the g. | 56:21
g. like a dog | 170:1
owned with a g. | 218:17
Grind: g. exceeding small | 134:2
G. the faces of the poor | 27:23
Grinds: with exactness g. | 134:2
Grinning: g. at his pomp | 206:15
mock your own g.? | 189:20
Groan: Condemn'd alike to g. | 98:9
hear each other g. | 121:4
Groaned: so g. and died | 89:28
Groans: record their g. | 147:16
Grocer: God made the wicked G. | 61:25
Groined: And g. the aisles | 82:15
Grolle: ich g. nicht | 102:3
Gromboolian: Over the great G. plain | 130:20
Groom, the Butler, and the Cook | 91:9
Grooves: g. of change | 228:14
In predestinate g. | 100:12
Gross: g. as beetles | 195:19
g. clasps | 204:18
rank and g. | 185:11
Grossness: by losing all its g. | 47:15
Grosvenor Gallery: greenery-yallery G. | 93:4
Grot: in some pleasant g.? | 108:18
Grotesque: from the g. to the horrible | 78:14
so g. a blunder | 22:13
Ground: and beat the g. | 144:1
Betwixt the stirrup and the g. | 53:11
cannot hallow this g. | 132:8
commit his body to the g. | 168:20
grow upon a spot of g. | 223:2
haunted, holy g. | 50:22
in a fair g. | 127:18
is holy g. | 24:1
miles of fertile g. | 66:14
native air in his own g. | 165:14
never touch the g. | 190:9
No flower upon the g. | 213:11
Off the g. | 73:8
On the holy g. | 152:11
passion that left the g. | 43:7
seated on the g. | 225:9
sit upon the g. | 206:15
when he has reached g. | 113:22
Groundlings: ears of the g. | 188:7
Grove: meadow, g., and stream | 246:7
Groves: forsake her Cyprian g. | 79:23
o'er shady g. they hover | 240:11
valleys, g., hills | 139:6
Grow: a Branch shall g. | 28:1
g. for ever and for ever | 229:12
g. into a hound | 242:20
heads do g. beneath their shoulders | 204:22
His praises there may g. | 103:18
How does your garden g.? | 156:16
how they g. | 30:28
I g. old | 81:19

Grow (cont.)
I shall g. old 247:10
more we g. 231:10
not the wiser g. 163:18
observing me g. slack 104:1
They shall not g. old 38:2
to g. upon a spot 223:2
trees that g. so fair 127:24
vegetable love should g. 140:11
where de wool ought to g. 87:13
where they do g. 104:8
Growed: I 'spect I g. 222:4
Growest: to time thou g. 210:12
Groweth: green, and g. up 170:17
Growing: Darling, I am g. old 175:6
Say I'm g. old 112:4
Upon the g. boy 246:11
Growl: bears and lions g. 239:6
Growled: It cracked and g. 65:8
Grown: and g. old 45:12
g. but what it fed on 185:11
g. full straight 139:2
When we are g. 124:17
Grown-up: spoke in quiet g. wise 161:15
Grows: G., lives, and dies 203:1
or g. by kind 80:17
that g. beside thy door 107:10
when it g. and smells 117:19
willow g. aslant 189:18
Gr-r-r- there go 45:7
Grub: gravender, or g. 178:13
old ones, g. 212:8
Grubbing weeds 125:9
Grubby hand 126:14
Grudge: ancient g. I bear him 201:15
Gruel: Make the g. thick 199:16
nice smooth g. 13:14
Grumble: we g. a little 96:1
Grundy: Solomon G. 158:2
What will Mrs. G. think? 150:16
Grunt: To g. and sweat 187:13
Gruntled: far from being g. 245:1
Gruvvelling: hankering and g. 234:19
Guard: Be on your g.! 9:9
calls not Thee to g. 127:7
changing g. 143:7
Gentlemen of the French G. 101:7
g. and bless our fatherland 111:13
G. us, guide us 81:2
Holy angels thy bed! 239:11
That g. our native seas 54:6
who is to g. the guards 119:5
Guarding: And, g., calls not Thee 127:7
Guards: G. die 53:10
Up G. 241:1
who is to guard the g. 119:5
Gudgeons: To swallow g. 50:1
Guerdon: fair g. 145:1
Guessing: better only g. 64:4
g. what was at the other side 240:15
Guest: g. of summer 198:2
nigh-related g. 67:3
speed the going g. 165:11
Guests: pass among the G. 86:3
Unbidden g. 192:6
Guide: By His counsels g. 175:2
God to be his g. 46:17
Guard us, g. us 81:2
g. our feet 32:39
g., philosopher, and friend 164:21
into the haven g. 241:8
light to g. 245:19
Providence their g. 146:25
Thou wert my g. 164:21
Guides: Blind G. 32:8
Guiding-star of a whole brave nation 150:17
Guile: packed with g. 42:8
Guilt: dwell on g. and misery 13:15

only art her g. to cover 95:21
punishment of his g. 71:17
pure from g. 109:5
war without its g. 222:13
wash her g. away? 95:21
Guiltless of his country's blood 97:15
Guilty: crimes of this g. land 42:14
G. of dust and sin 104:1
ten g. persons 38:8
Guinea: somewhat like a g.? 38:13
Worth a g. a box 8:17
Guinea-pig: lift a g. 133:9
Guineas: pounds and g. 110:16
Guitar: sang to a small g. 131:6
Touch'd his g. 19:6
Gulf: great g. fixed 33:29
Gulfs will wash us down 230:15
Gull's way 141:4
Gum: Drop..med'cinable g. 205:20
Gun: son of a g. 53:7
Gunga Din 125:12
Gunpowder: G., Printing, and the Protestant Religion 55:5
G. Treason and Plot 7:3, 157:12
till the g. ran out at the heels 86:19
Guns will make us powerful 94:12
Gusty: among the g. trees 155:1
Guts of the last priest 142:15
Gutter: Homesickness for the g. 13:1
We are all in the g. 243:16
Guzzling Jimmy 231:19
Gwine to run all night! 87:8
Gyre: Did g. 57:14
Gyves: With g. upon his wrist 106:21

H

Habit: Costly thy h. 185:21
reap a h. 175:4
regular h. of Appelles 163:19
Habitation: local h. 203:19
Habits: O what h. 63:17
Hackney Marshes: you could see to H. 18:27
Haddocks: hunt for h.' eyes 58:12
Haggards ride no more 220:8
Hags: black and midnight h. 199:18
rags, and h. 66:9
Ha-ha: funny h. 101:8
Ha-ha-ha, you and me 4:16
Hail: falls not h. 227:3
h. and farewell 59:3
H., master 32:22
H. to thee, blithe Spirit 215:3
Hair: amber-dropping h. 144:3
bids me bind my h. 112:8
bracelet of bright h. 77:14
h. has become very white 56:16
h. soft-lifted 119:18
h. that lay along her back 177:16
h. to stand on end 186:7
hank of h. 128:1
her h. in one long yellow string 44:27
his floating h. 66:15
hyacinth h. 163:16
in their golden h. 229:6
make your h. curl 93:26
She smooths her h. 82:2
soft brown h. 53:6
stars in her h. were seven 177:15
sugar my h. 57:10
tangles of Neæra's h. 145:1
tore his h. 218:21
vine-leaves in his h. 112:15
with a single h. 165:2
with the light brown h. 87:15
Hairs: h. of your head 31:14
How ill white h. become a fool 191:1
If h. be wires 212:3

in my gray h.   245:11
my gray h. with sorrow   23:35
Hairy: is a h. man   23:28
Halcyon: h. days   192:5
in a h. sea   177:8
Hale: You are h.   218:22
Half: h. as worth doing   96:16
H. asleep as they stalk   100:4
H. hidden from the eye   248:3
h. is greater than the whole   104:18
h. my days   147:17
h. seas over   223:10
h. was not told me   25:8
know one h. as much   96:17
Teach me h. the gladness   215:6
Too civil by h.   216:13
your servant's cut in h.   96:12
youth shows but h.   45:4
Half-believers in our casual creeds   11:25
Half-devil and half-child   128:5
Half-dozen of the other   139:19
Halfpenny will do   3:20
Half-reaped: on a h. furrow   119:18
Hall: Absolute across the h.   21:21
bears logs into the h.   196:20
hung in the castle h.   19:4
meat in the h.   221:22
sitting in his h.   124:19
Hallow: seems to h. us there   161:17
Hallowed: h. and so gracious   185:4
H. be thy name   30:22
his h. relics   147:12
Halls: Amphitrite's destined h.   213:17
dwelt in marble h.   46:2
through Tara's h.   149:13
Halt: Cheer for a h.   127:1
h. and the blind   33:17
Ham: Noah begat Shem, H.   23:20
Hambre: La mejor salsa..el h.   59:9
Hamelin Town's in Brunswick   44:18
Hamlet: lovely h. Grantchester   42:7
rude forefathers of the h.   97:10
tragedy of H.   181:4
Hamlets brown   67:13
Hammer: h., h., h.   173:9
What the h.   39:2
Hammock: Drake, he's in his h.   153:5
Hand: admire his sleight of h.   49:29
at thy right h.   170:19
Beneath whose awful H.   127:3
bite the h. that fed them   47:17
bloody and invisible h.   199:6
Both foot and h. go cold   221:25
Brother clasps the h. of brother   18:9
by the h. of the Lord   24:6
cheek upon her h.   207:21
clean from my h.   198:15
crosses from his sov'reign h.   104:17
curst be the h.   16:7
day is at h.   35:14
Death lays his icy h.   216:24
dubious h.   117:3
every man's h. against him   23:25
fear thy skinny h.   65:18
glove upon that h.   207:21
go into his h. and pierce it   25:22
God's Almighty h.   53:12
grubby h.   126:14
had no h. in them   109:22
h. and glove   70:12
h. for h.   24:7
h. in h.   48:21, 131:9, 146:25, 154:16
h. of war   206:7
h. out of plackets   195:11
H. that made us is divine   1:14
h. that rocks the cradle   238:3
h. that rounded Peter's dome   82:15
h. that rules the world   238:3
Head, heart, and h.   124:18

Heaving up my either h.   104:16
His h. will be against every
    man   23:25
his hat in his h.   116:11
His sickle in his h.   134:3
holds him with his skinny h.   65:5
If you want to win her h.   41:1
immortal h.   39:1, 4
in her left h. riches   26:6
in her right h.   26:6
In his h.   170:22
in the h. of God   29:32
in the h. of the giant   171:23
in the palm of your h.   38:10
in your medieval h.   92:22
Joy, whose h.   120:24
kindlier h.   227:20
Kingdom of Heaven is at h.   30:3
left h. is under my head   27:15
length of days is in her right h.   26:6
let not thy left h.   30:20
like a man's h.   25:12
lilies in her h.   177:15
man have the upper h.   168:25
man's h. is not able to taste   203:18
moon on the one h.   21:13
Nothing in my h. I bring   234:1
our times are in His h.   45:4
put your h. into the h. of God   101:5
right h. doth embrace me   27:15
right h. forget her cunning   171:28
right h. shall hold me   172:1
saw the air..with your h.   188:7
shall thy h. lead me   172:1
sheep of his h.   170:24
Sit thou on my right h.   171:9
skinny hand   65:5, 18
stretch forth thy mighty h.   111:13
sweeten this little h.   199:30
Sword sleep in my h.   38:16
take the Cash in h.   84:20
then join in h.   76:1
there's a h.   48:8
this h. hath offended   70:25
Thy h. great Anarch!   164:3
time's devouring h.   41:2
Time's fell h. defac'd   211:6
touch of a vanish'd h.   225:15
toward my h.?   198:9
upon thy right h.   171:17
Vacant heart and h.   180:15
wander h. in h.   154:16
what dread h.   39:2
Whatsoever thy h. findeth   27:2
who will stand on either h.   136:11
with automatic h.   82:2
with a muckrake in his h.   46:15
with a willow in her h.   202:10
Your h., your tongue   198:1
your staff in your h.   24:45
Handel: compar'd to H.   50:12
Handful: for a h. of silver   44:9
h. of grey ashes   69:4
in a h. of dust   81:24
Handkerchief: he had no little h.   18:2
Handle: h. toward my hand   198:9
hands, and h. not   171:13
I polished up that h.   93:10
old jug without a h.   130:19
tools to him that can h. them   55:6
Handling: fond of h. the leaves 216:8
Handmaid perfect   177:14
Handmaiden: low estate of his h.   32:37
Hands: bear thee in their h.   170:20
before rude h. have touch'd it   118:11
by fairy h.   67:15
Come, knit h.   144:1
Droops on the little h.   143:15
for idle h. to do   239:10

Hands (cont.)

h., and handle not 171:13
h. are blue 131:4
h. from picking 167:34
h. of their deliverer 147:6
h. prepared the dry land 170:22
h. proffer gifts 236:9
h. still 20:4
H., that the rod of empire 97:14
Hath not a Jew h. 201:27
Into my h. 140:6
into thy h. 33:42, 169:9
laid violent h. 168:18
large and sinewy h. 134:10
lift not h. of prayer 227:2
Lift not thy h. 85:13
little h. were made to take 20:16
little h. were never made 239:7
Pale h. I loved 107:9
right h. of fellowship 36:5
soon wring their h. 238:9
Their h. outstretched 236:17
then take h. 208:9
these h. ne'er be clean? 199:29
tinged the eyelids and the h. 161:9
warmed both h. 129:20
with crooked h. 226:9
With heart and h. 244:17
With my own fair h. 223:3
without h. to fight 224:1
Handsaw: know a hawk from a h. 187:5
Handsome man 67:21
Handywork: sheweth his h. 168:29
Hang: all h. separately 88:6
all h. together 88:6
clambering to h. 189:18
h. a man first 148:20
h. here on yonder wall 110:2
H. out our banners 200:2
h. them on the horns o' the moon 184:17
H. upon his pent-house 197:6
H. your husband 89:13
H. yourself, brave Crillon 103:1
none, or few, do h. 211:8
she would h. on him 185:11
used to h. and brush 45:12
Hanged: If I were h. 126:16
knows he is to be h. 115:13
millstone were h. about his neck 31:38, 33:30
to see Major-general Harrison h. 162:5
we h. them up 171:28
Hanging: h. Danny Deever 125:2
h. is too good for him 46:10
h. of his cat 41:3
Hanging-look to me 68:7
Hangman: louse for the h. 117:14
Hangs: H. my helpless soul 241:9
h. upon the cheek of night 207:18
that h. on the bough 208:20
Thereby h. a tail 205:1
thereby h. a tale 183:17, 208:6
Hank of hair 128:1
Hankering and gruvvelling 234:19
Hanover: by famous H. city 44:18
Hansom-cabs: wheels of h. 58:13
Hanyfink: Wot's the good of H. 62:3
Happen: no evil h. unto thee 170:20
some day it may h. 91:30
Happened: ever h. in the world 87:17
Happier: less h. lands 206:7
remembering h. things 228:7
Happiest: best and h. moments 215:17
h. nations 81:9
h. time of..the..new year 228:21
h. women 81:9
Happily: thousand hearts beat h. 50:23
Happiness: by which so much h. is produced 115:7

greatest h. for the greatest numbers 112:10
greatest h. of the greatest number 22:8
h. of the common man 23:3
lifetime of h. 212:19
promoting the..h. of the human race 47:5
pursuit of h. 8:9, 113:2
recall a time of h. 72:7
result h. 74:8
seek h. in yachts 108:9
task of h. 221:24
too happy in thine h. 121:2
Happy: as h. prologues 197:9
be h. while y'er leevin 3:17
being too h. 121:2
Call no man h. 218:8
Centipede was h. 71:1
dreams h. as her day 42:11
earthlier h. 203:1
envy of thy h. lot 121:2
h. as kings 221:14
h. band of pilgrims 152:16
h. bells 227:19
h. breed of men 206:7
h., fair with orchard lawns 227:3
h. families resemble each other 233:22
H. field 120:17
H., h. tree 122:6
H. he, who has availed 237:7
h. is the blameless vestal 164:6
H. is the man 171:23
h. issue 166:30
h. low, lie down! 190:30
h. noise to hear 110:19
H. the man 108:14, 165:14
H. the people 55:10
h. the wanderer 20:15
he won't be h. till he gets it 5:2
How h. could I be with either 89:21
How h. is he born 249:10
How to be H. though Married 100:2
is to have been h. 40:1
lot is not a h. one 93:21
many a h. accident 142:18
nothing else so h. 206:10
now to be most h. 204:28
salute the h. morn 50:14
so long as you're h.? 141:15
songs of h. cheer 39:8
There is a h. land 250:12
this the h. morn 145:6
thrice h. he 140:13
thy h. pipe 39:8
we h. few 192:4
Who is the h. Warrior? 246:2
who so h. 131:2
wrote my h. songs 39:8
Happy Isles: touch the H. 230:15
Harbinger: perfume her h. 147:5
Hard: Baby's cries grew h. to bear 96:14
Dere's no more h. work 87:14
H...as nails 75:9
h. at death's door 171:6
h. be the task 58:18
h. pounding this 240:19
h. to please 180:13
heroic for earth too h. 43:7
His doom's extremely h. 92:9
It is h. for thee 34:36
It is h. if I cannot start 101:11
way of the transgressors is h. 26:14
work h. at doing nothing 108:9
Harden not your hearts 170:25
Hardihood, endurance, and courage 179:19
Hardly becomes any of us 105:12
Hardy: H. went down 62:2
Kiss me, H. 153:1
Hare: First catch your h. 94:6

h. limp'd trembling 120:2
Take your h. 94:6
to start a h. 190:8
Hares: little hunted h. 105:13
Hark: But h. 123:11
H., H.! Bow, wow 208:9
H.! h.! the lark 184:20
H., my soul! 70:3
H.! the herald-angels sing 241:15
O h., O hear! 229:11
Harken ere I die 229:3
Harlot's cry 38:12
Harlots: mother of h. 37:22
Harm: do me no h. 156:3
do so much h. 71:3
h. may come to the state 63:23
no h. in looking 222:20
shall h. Macbeth 199:20
Harmless: as h. as doves 31:13
h. necessary cat 202:4
Harmonies: tumult of thy mighty h. 214:4
Harmonious: h. sisters 147:13
Such h. madness 215:6
Harmony: From h., from heavenly h. 79:16
From h. to h. 79:16
H. in discord 108:10
h. is in immortal souls 202:11
h. of prose 80:5
That air and h. 172:19
touches of sweet h. 202:11
Harness: between the joints of the h. 25:17
wait in heavy h. 128:5
with h. on our back 200:7
Harp: h., his sole remaining joy 180:4
H. not on that string 207:10
h. that once 149:13
I'll hang my h. 8:1
sound of . . the h. 29:16
To one clear h. 227:6
wild h. slung behind him 149:15
Harping on my daughter 186:24
Harps: As for our h. 171:28
touch their h. of gold 181:10
Harriet: What foolish H. befell 106:1
Harrow: h. up thy soul 186:7
toad beneath the h. 126:20
Harrowing: man h. clods 100:4
Harry: God for H.! 191:9
little touch of H. 191:11
Harsh: good are so h. 245:13
h. and crabbed 144:2
h. world-use 179:11
in this h. world 190:3
Not h. nor grating 248:19
out of tune and h. 188:6
your berries h. 144:20
Hart: Like as the h. 169:15
Harvest: Raise the song of H.-home 2:13
Harwich: in a steamer from H. 91:24
Has beens: one of the h. 106:18
Haste: eat it in h. 24:5
H. thee Nymph 144:12
I said in my h. 171:14
in h. to ride 69:26
make what h. I can 71:13
marry'd in h. 68:13
Oh, make h.! 85:9
repent in h. 68:13
why such h.? 89:28
You h. away so soon 104:10
Hasten: H. slowly 222:9
h. to their end 211:5
Hastens: He ever h. to the issue 108:1
Hasting: Until the h. day 104:10

Hasty: are so h. 216:9
man in his h. days 41:6
na start awa sae h. 48:25
Hat: away went h. 69:27
By his cockle h. 189:8
great big waterproof h. 143:8
in a shocking bad h. 222:21
In his h. a Railway-Ticket 131:3
in that lewd h.! 117:9
my h. and wig 69:29
my h. upon my head 116:11
never passes a church without pulling off his h. 114:12
runcible h. 130:18
Where did you get that hat? 176:10
wid my h. caved in 87:8
With his h. in his hand 116:11
Hatched: chickens before they are h. 1:21
ere th'are h. 50:1
Hatchet: with my little h. 239:2
Hate: from my only h. 207:18
h. and detest . . man 223:6
h. and pain 213:8
h. anyone that we know 101:13
h. him for he is a Christian 201:14
h. so long as they fear 63:19
I h. all Boets and Bainters 90:4
I h., I love 59:2
I h. ye 192:14
immortal h. 145:15
much to h. here 143:2
nought did I in h. 205:19
Persian luxury . . I h. 109:9
that h. him flee 170:6
Hated: ever h. all nations 223:6
Or being h. 125:14
Hateth: and h. his brother 37:12
spareth the rod h. his son 26:15
Hath: every one that h. 32:15
Hating: give way to h. 125:14
Hatred: and h. therewith 26:18
Envy, h., and malice 166:22
I must have no h. 59:4
love to h. turn'd 68:10
Hats: so many shocking bad h. 240:16
Haughty spirit before a fall 26:20
Haul: gentleman to h. and draw 78:27
Haunt: exempt from public h. 183:9
most breed and h. 198:2
murmurous h. 121:5
shapes that h. 214:9
Haunted: beneath a waning moon was h. 66:14
by h. stream 144:19
h., holy ground 50:22
Some h. by the ghosts 206:15
Haunts: busy h. of men 102:12
h. of coot and hern 225:17
Have: if you h. it [charm] 18:24
other folks h. 84:8
such as I h. 34:32
To h. and to hold 168:12
Have-his-carcase 75:32
Havelock: pipes o' H. sound 242:18
Haven: h. under the hill 225:15
rowing home to h. 140:20
Safe into the h. guide 241:8
unto the h. 171:9
Have-nots: Haves and the H. 59:11
Havoc: 'Cry, H.!' 193:21
Hawk: know a h. from a handsaw 187:5
Hawked at and kill'd 199:1
Hawthorne 220:22
Hay: dance an antic h. 138:9
is worth a load of h. 3:15
tumbling in the h. 210:5
Haycock: under the h. fast asleep 156:10
Hazard: into the h. 191:4

Hazlitt: cannot write like H. 221:7
  played the sedulous ape to H. 220:22
He: because h. was h. 149:2
  h. and they together 105:13
  where was h. 102:8
Head: all my imperfections on my
  h. 186:12
  anointed my h. 169:2
  At his h. a grass-green turf 189:9
  away with his h. 67:23
  bear with a sore h. 139:18
  binds so dear a h. 213:6
  black wires grow on her h. 212:3
  blessings on your h. 70:6
  bowed his comely h. 140:9
  cannot get out of my h. 102:4
  coals of fire upon his h. 26:24
  Cover my defenceless h. 241:10
  crown on her h. 128:6
  cut off your h. 157:8
  drop about my h. 140:6
  gently falling on thy h. 239:11
  God be in my h. 4:10
  good grey h. 228:25
  had no wool on de top of his h. 87:13
  hairs of your h. 31:14
  h. as old and white as this 195:5
  h. grown grey 213:8
  H., heart, and hand 124:18
  h. is as full of quarrels 207:28
  h. is bending low 87:12
  H. that once was crowned 122:21
  h. under his wing 157:1
  h...with oil anoint 181:8
  his heavy h. 239:12
  his poor little h. 92:17
  If you can keep your h. 125:14
  into my h. 74:10
  left hand is under my h. 27:15
  little gold h. 143:15
  my hat upon my h. 116:11
  My h. is bloody 102:13
  no bigger than his h. 195:19
  no roof to shroud his h. 105:1
  not so long by the h. 196:17
  Off with his h.! 57:1, 63:6
  once lovely h. 85:2
  or in the h. 202:1
  pops its h. into the shop 86:19
  precious jewel in his h. 183:9
  repairs his drooping h. 145:4
  rest thy weary h. 133:18
  Singe my white h. 195:4
  sky over my h. 101:11
  Stamps o'er his H. 85:1
  stand on your h. 56:16
  That one small h. 95:8
  this old gray h. 242:16
  tired her h. 25:21
  to lay his h. 31:7
  trample on their sovereign's h. 206:16
  turns no more his h. 66:5
  Uneasy lies the h. 190:30
  Violet's reclining h. 77:6
  which way the h. lies 174:18
  why not upon my h.? 206:16
  with monstrous h. 61:16
Headache: with a dismal h. 91:23
Head-In-Air: Little Johnny H. 106:2
Heads: carve h. upon cherry-stones 116:5
  h. are green 131:4
  h. do grow beneath their
    shoulders 204:22
  H. I win 71:4
  h. never raising 247:9
  Lift up your h. 169:4
  shall your houseless h. 195:7
  still had drunken h. 209:20
Head-stone: is become the h. 171:15

Headstrong: h. as an allegory 216:12
  h., moody, murmuring race 79:4
Head-waiter: O plump h. 231:4
Heal: h. me of my grievous wound 227:3
  Physician, h. thyself 33:2
  that fame can never h. 14:1
Healed: h. by the same means 201:27
  with his stripes we are h. 28:12
Healing spells 179:11
Heals his wounds 154:1
Health: he that will this h. deny 80:19
  h. and quiet breathing 120:1
  h. is the second blessing 238:15
  h. on both 199:9
  in sickness and in h. 168:12
  Look to your h. 238:15
  no h. in us 166:9
  Say that h. and wealth 112:4
  thy saving h. 170:4
Healthy: hearty, h. boy 105:15
Heap: on a h. of barley 131:3
  one h. of all your winnings 125:15
  struck all of a h. 216:7
Heaped: on the h. rose-leaves 108:18
Hear: almost h. the beating of his
  wings 41:10
  another to h. 233:8
  Come on and h. 22:17
  did ye not h. it? 51:1
  Dinna ye h. it 242:18
  ears, and h. not 171:13
  every child may joy to h. 39:8
  good news yet to h. 61:23
  Hark I h. them 208:12
  He that hath ears to h. 32:28
  he wept to h. 39:8
  h. each other groan 121:4
  h. his word 70:3
  h., oh, h. 214:1
  h. the larks so high 110:19
  H. the other side 13:8
  H. the voice of the Bard 38:18
  h. thee and rejoice 245:15
  H. them, read, mark, learn 166:34
  h. us when we cry to Thee 242:9
  I always h. 140:12
  I h. but their low lone song? 55:27
  I h. you 111:1
  Lord, h. my voice 171:25
  love to h. the story 143:3
  music that I care to h. 107:13
  My heart would h. her 228:20
  never h. the west wind 141:6
  news to h. 69:2
  Nor grandeur h. 97:12
  O hark, O h.! 229:11
  O stay and h. 209:5
  shall h. it by and by 43:7
  They never would h. 223:22
  To h. the angels sing 181:10
  voice I h. 121:6
  we cannot h. it 202:11
  when you will h. me 76:5
  will h. his voice 170:25
  you shall h. 133:25
Heard: ain't h. nothin' 117:6
  cannot be h. so high 195:19
  children are h. on the green 39:11
  enough that he h. it once 43:7
  eye of man hath not h. 203:18
  h. a pin drop 176:7
  h. great argument 85:7
  h. him say again 110:17
  h. his foot 73:6
  H. melodies are sweet 120:19
  h. on the hill 39:11, 71:2
  h. round the world 82:14
  h. the mingled measure 66:15
  I have h., I hear thee 245:15

I have h. with admiring submission 83:1
I h. a voice 247:16
I will be h. 89:3
if they had h. of the loss 219:2
is h. in our land 27:16
Isn't generally h. 93:29
I've heard them lilting 82:12
more he h. 173:13
never was h. 248:8
Not a drum was h. 245:3
shall be h. for their much speaking 30:21
then is h. no more 200:4
thou hast h. me also 169:1
trumpet shall be h. 79:18
was h. in ancient days 121:6
Where seldom is h. 105:5
Hearers: edification of the h. 47:12
hurries his h. 108:1
too deep for his h. 95:18
Hearest: thou h. the sound thereof 33:50
Hearing often-times 248:19
Hears: h. him in the wind 164:14
neither h., nor sees 245:14
Hearse: Underneath this sable h. 43:2
Heart: Absence makes the h. grow
fonder 3:6, 19:3
all that mighty h. 249:3
awful warmth about my h. 122:9
Batter my h. 77:12
beak from out my h. 163:17
Because h. is pure 230:8
But not your h. away 110:16
but some h. did break 227:7
Calais lying in my h. 140:18
cracks a noble h. 190:5
darling of my h. 55:2
even if my h. break 102:3
Faint h. never won 91:26
Fare thee well, great h. 190:23
felt along the h. 248:17
fire which in the h. resides 11:17
For heathen h. 127:7
found in thy h. to sing? 224:7
given his h.'s desire 168:33
God be in my h. 4:10
grieved my h. to think 248:11
Head, h., and hand 124:18
h. and my flesh 170:13
h. and stomach of a king 82:9
h. as sound as a bell 204:11
h. be full of the spring 224:7
h. be still as loving 52:13
h. but one 40:13
h. for any fate 133:28
h. grown cold 213:8
h. has its reasons 161:7
H. 'How goes it?' 21:17
h. is deceitful 29:7
h. is gladder 177:8
h. is Highland 181:7
h. is like a rainbow shell 177:8
h. is like a singing bird 177:8
h. is like an apple-tree 177:8
h. leaps up 247:10
H. must bear the longest part 103:18
h. must pause to breathe 52:14
h. of grace 93:17
h. of my mystery 188:17
H. of oak 88:18
h. out of the bosom 110:17
h. runs away 67:23
h. to report 203:18
h. upon my sleeve 204:16
h. with pleasure fills 247:5
h. would fain deny 199:32
her h. in his grave 149:17

her h. was warm and gay 99:10
his h. was one of those 50:17
hold me in thy h. 190:3
humble and a contrite h. 127:4
I am sick at h. 185:2
I haven't the h. 96:13
If the h. be right 174:18
if the h. of a man is deprest 89:18
If thy h. fails thee 82:7, 174:14
in his h. is a blind desire 224:2
In my h. 104:3, 118:15
in the h. 202:1
in the triumph of his h. 1:10
infinite h.'s ease 191:14
into my h. and air that kills 111:5
is the h.'s devotion 215:11
joy to his mighty h. 125:1
larger h. 227:20
laughter of her h. 99:10
Let not your h. be troubled 34:16
Lift up your h. 241:14
lock'd my h. in a case o' gowd 17:3
love with all my h. 221:13
Make me a clean h. 169:27
makes my h. go pit-a-pat 44:20
maketh glad the h. of man 171:2
maketh the h. sick 26:13
man after his own h. 24:41
man's h. is small 127:18
meditation of my h. 168:31
Mercy has a human h. 39:13
merry h. 26:17, 210:7
My h. aches 121:1
My h. is heavy 94:13
My h. is inditing 169:18
my h. new open'd 192:14
my h. of h. 188:11
My h. would hear her 228:20
my h.'s abhorrence 45:7
My h.'s in the Highlands 48:27
my h.'s right there 244:7
my sullen h. 221:24
nearer to the H.'s Desire 86:1
nearly breaks my h. 113:8
no longer tear his h. 223:27
not to get your h.'s desire 212:22
of giving your h. 127:2
of the h.'s affections 122:7
on my h. they tread 206:16
One is nearer God's H. 99:2
our h. cannot be quieted 13:2
perform with all your h. 236:1
pourest thy full h. 215:3
pure in h. 30:11, 122:19
Rise in the h. 229:13
said in his h. 168:26
Shakespeare unlocked his
h. 44:4, 248:1
shall command my h. 70:27
She was not really bad at h. 21:11
sink h. and voice 152:14
Spring Thou up within my h. 241:11
stabb'd me to the h. 89:7
stirred the h. 179:19
tears out the h. of it 128:29
than a h. untainted 192:7
thanks to the human h. 246:14
there will your h. be 30:25
this h. all evil shed 42:11
thou voice of my h. 71:2
through the sad h. 121:6
Thy h. must teach alone 99:9
tiger's h. 98:13, 192, 11
to my dead h. 221:24
touch the h. of man! 236:7
true love hath my h. 216:29
truth from his h. 168:27
twist the sinews of thy h. 39:2
understanding in thine h. 29:30

Heart (cont.)
untroubled h. of stone 54:4
Vacant h. and hand 180:15
wear him in my h.'s core 188:11
weighs upon the h. 200:1
What female h. 98:2
what his h. thinks 204:11
when thy h. began to beat 39:2
where my h. is turning ebber 87:11
With a bullet through his h. 231:17
with a hungry h. 230:13
With h. and hands 244:17
With h. and soul 152:11
your h. has felt the tender
  passion 89:23
Heart-ache: end the h. 187:13
Hearth: by this still h. 230:12
clean h. 129:6
cricket on the h. 144:7
from his lonely h. 246:3
unextinguished h. 214:4
Hearths: behalf..of their h. 178:18
Hearts: all h. be open 167:4
cheerful h. now broken 150:1
Christian h. 122:18
creeds that move men's h. 41:14
given our h. away 249:5
harden not your h. 170:24
h. just as pure and fair 91:19
h. of gold 21:21
h. of oak 12:12
h., that once beat high 149:13
heedless h. 98:4
imagination of their h. 32:38
in h. at peace 42:11
in the h. of his fellow-citizens 131:17
in the h. of kings 202:5
Incline our h. 167:6
Kind h. are more than coronets 227:22
Knave of H. 57:12, 157:15
men with splendid h. 42:7
O valiant h. 11:9
opposed free h. 230:15
Queen of H. 57:12, 157:15
steal away your h. 194:11
temper of heroic h. 230:14
that inspir'd their h. 139:11
their h. were set 162:2
thousand h. beat happily 50:23
to live in h. 53:14
Two h. that beat as one 99:9
while your h. are yearning 87:4
wore at their h. 219:6
you hard h. 193:9
Hearty: h. old man 218:22
plump and h. 105:15
Heat: burden and h. 32:4
h. o' the sun 184:22
hid from the h. 168:30
not the h. of fellow citizens 109:19
not without dust and h. 148:9
Heated in the chase 225:6
Heath: likewise a wind on the h. 40:8
Upon the h. 197:2
Heathen: as the h. do 30:21
For h. heart 127:7
h. Chinee is peculiar 101:3
h. in his blindness 101:16, 125:3
h. so furiously rage 168:21
pokes the h. out 125:3
Heather: among the h. bright 58:12
Heaths: on these lone h. 101:11
Heat-oppressèd brain 198:9
Heaven: above h. and earth 172:6
All this and h. too 103:8
ascend the brightest h. 191:2
Ascend to H. 84:12
as it is in h. 30:22
as near to h. by sea 90:18

at H.'s command 232:13
at h.'s gate 184:20, 210:13
beauteous eye of h. 193:6
betwixt h. and Charing Cross 232:10
brain of h. 142:1
bring all h. before mine eyes 144:9
builds a h. 39:5
by constraint of h. 236:3
clinging h. 232:10
co-heirs of the angels in h. 98:14
comrade of thy wanderings over h. 214:3
corner of h. 244:11
dearest foe in h. 185:13
Earth's crammed with h. 43:4
earth was nigher h. 44:25
enter into the kingdom of h. 31:37
eternal joys of h. 138:11
ever-moving spheres of h. 138:14
eye of h. shines 210:12
face of h. 122:2, 138:10, 208:1
Father in H. 124:17
first h...passed away 37:25
floor of h. 202:11
from God out of h. 37:25
gentle rain from h. 202:5
glance from h. to earth 203:19
go to h. 60:29
God created the h. 23:4
God's in his h. 44:24
gold bar of H. 177:15
H. and earth in ashes 59:5
H. and earth! Must I remember! 185:11
H. and earth shall pass away 180:7
h. be in these lips 138:12
h. has no rage 68:10
h. hath sent me fortune 183:16
h. in a Wild Flower 38:10
H. is comin' clost ter you 220:3
H. lies about us 246:11
h. on earth 146:15
h. peep through 197:14
H. rejects the lore 247:6
H. smiles 213:12
h. such grace did lend her 210:2
H. will help you 86:15
H.'s all gracious King 181:10
h.'s breath 198:2
h.'s cherubim 198:4
H.'s light for ever shines 213:10
H.'s morning breaks 135:17
H.'s thought was otherwise 236:11
High H. rejects 247:6
his clouded h. 247:18
how art thou fallen from h. 28:4
humbler h. 164:14
husbandry in h. 198:8
I have sinned against h. 33:22
I saw a new h. 37:25
I see H.'s glories shine 41:13
idea of h. is 218:2
if H. be inflexible 236:20
if it find h. 199:2
in h.'s despite 39:6
in the h. a perfect round 43:6
in the h. above 167:7
inheritor of the kingdom of h. 167:32
Is he in h.? 159:13
Is it, in h. 164:4
jolly h. above 221:15
joy shall be in h. 33:20
kindred points of h. 248:6
kingdom of h. 30:3, 31:27, 167:32
Leave her to h. 186:13
Lord made h. 167:11
make a H. of Hell 146:2
make the face of h. so fine 208:1
Moon of H. 86:2
more things in h. and earth 186:16
moved earth and h. 230:15

on the walls of h. 139:12
open face of h. 122:2
or what's a h. for? 43:8
pledges of H.'s joy 147:13
purpose under the h. 26:38
Puts all h. in a rage 38:11
quit the port o' H. 153:4
Remembrance fallen from h. 224:1
ring the bells of H. 105:13
sent from H. above 53:12
sent the gentle sleep from H. 65:23
serve in h. 146:3
smells to h. 188:22
Son of H.'s eternal King 145:6
spark from H. 11:25
steep and thorny way to h. 185:20
thank h., fasting 184:6
That from H., or near it 215:3
that h. of all their wish 42:3
theirs is the kingdom of h. 30:11
then the h. espy 103:21
though not in h. 104:3
Threw him from the face of h. 138:10
to h. or to hell 198:10
to shun the h. 212:2
top of it reached to h. 23:29
treasures in h. 30:24
tricks before high h. 200:19
trouble deaf h. 210:13
under an English h. 42:11
uttermost part of the h. 168:30
was very h. 246:1
We are all going to h. 88:13
when h. was falling 111:11
which art in h. 30:22
winds of h. 185:11
Heaven-born child 145:7
Heaven-eyed creature 246:3
Heavenly: company of the h.
host 38:13
even in h. place 216:30
from h. harmony 79:16
H. blessings without number 239:11
h. mug 86:11
h. paradise 54:11
Lead us, H. Father 81:2
Which h. truth imparts 122:18
with h. alchymy 211:2
ye h. host 123:3
Heavens: change and loss in the h. 110:6
h. are not too high 103:18
H. declare the glory of God 168:29
h. fill with shouting 228:9
h. themselves blaze forth 193:14
I create new h. 29:3
Sing, ye h. 241:7
starry h. above me 119:10
starry h. above that plain 233:4
though the h. fall 239:4
when the h. are bare 246:8
ye h. adore Him 122:24
Heavily: so h. with my disposition 187:4
Heaviness: h. may endure for a night 169:8
in our h. 171:28
Heaving up my either hand 104:16
Heavy: and are h. laden 31:20
cold and h. mist 106:21
eyelids h. and red 107:3
Lie h. on him 83:12
list to the h. part 117:10
long and h. task 236:1
My heart is h. 94:13
so dull and h. 204:9
wait in h. harness 128:5
He-bear in his pride 125:5
Hebrides: Among the farthest H. 248:8
behold the h. 181:7
Hectic red 214:1
Hector: of H. and Lysander 7:7

Hecuba: What's H. to him 187:11
Hedge: doth h. a king 189:13
sheet bleaching on the h. 210:5
Hedge-hogs: Thorny h. 203:10
Hedges: and h. ears 223:25
Go out into the..hedges 33:18
unkempt about those h. blows 42:5
with filigree h. 238:5
Heed: H. not the rolling waves 39:23
lesson you should h. 105:4
never h. naught else 126:13
Nor h., nor see 214:9
Nor h. the rumble 84:21
Heeded: it h. not 215:4
Heedless: and h. hearts 98:4
H. of grammar 17:14
Heels: At his h. a stone 189:9
fair pair of h. 190:13
gunpowder ran out at the h. 86:19
h. are nimble 155:19
h. of pleasure 68:13
with winged h. 191:5
Heifer: lead'st thou that h. 120:21
Heigh-ho! sing h.! 184:1
Height: although his h. be taken 211:16
h. of this great argument 145:11
No h. is too arduous 108:15
nor h., nor depth 35:10
reached a middle h. 142:1
What pleasure lives in h.? 229:18
Heights: h. by great men reached 133:22
on the towering h. 130:20
Heir: h. of all the ages 228:13
h. of fame 147:12
that flesh is h. to 187:13
Held: h. to the last man 99:4
H. we fall to rise 45:10
Helen: hath closed H.'s eye 152:5
H., thy beauty 163:16
I wish I were where H. lies 16:7
Sees H.'s beauty 203:19
Sweet H. 138:12
Helen of Troy: mother of H. 161:9
Helena: that is not H. 138:12
Helican: how the h. 142:14
Hell: all h. broke loose 146:18
begin raising h. 131:16
bells of H. 6:12
better to reign in h. 146:3
builds a h. 39:6
characters of h. 97:5
child of h. 191:15
come hot from h. 193:21
dunnest smoke of h. 197:14
gates of h. 31:33
h. for horses 49:11
H. is murky 199:28
h. of horses 86:13
h. on earth 212:19
H. shall be unleashed 236:20
in H.'s despair 39:5
Is he in h.? 159:13
leads men to this h. 212:2
Madness risen from h. 224:1
make a Heav'n of H. 146:2
mouth of h. 226:4
nor H. a fury 68:10
riches grow in h. 146:8
this is h. 138:11
to heaven or to h. 198:10
tore h.'s concave 146:6
vast h. can hold 203:19
with the Smoke of H. 85:14
would drag to h. 65:21
wrote..of devils and h. 39:16
Hellas: brighter H. 213:12
Hell-fires: dreamin' h. to see 126:7
Hellish dark 222:19
Hell-kite: O h.! 199:27

Hells: with ten thousand h.   138:11
Helm: Pleasure at the h.   97:6
Helmet: saw the h. and the plume   227:25
Help: cannot h. it   114:7
  Come over into Macedonia, and
    h. us   34:39
  did England h. me   44:3
  encumbers him with h.   113:22
  from whence cometh my h.   171:16
  gods h. them   1:19
  H. of the helpless   135:16
  h. thou my unbelief   32:33
  H. yourself   86:15
  how can I h. England?   44:3
  I can't h. it   91:28, 151:9, 243:15
  Lord h. you!   67:18
  no h. in them   172:4
  O h. Thy children   124:17
  our h. in ages past   239:14
  since there's no h.   78:29
  to It for h.   85:13
  very present h.   3:9, 169:20
  we have no h. but Thee   81:2
  without the h. and support   81:5
Helped: great man h. the poor   136:12
Helpers: other h. fail   135:16
Helping, when we meet them   123:15
Helpless: Hangs my h. soul   241:9
  Help of the h.   135:16
  H., look to thee   234:1
Help meet: will make him an h.   23:11
Helter skelter, hang sorrow   117:14
Hempen: What h. homespuns   203:12
Hems: clinging Heaven by the h.   232:10
Hen: big fat h.   157:5
  Two Owls and a H.   130:15
Hence: endure their going h.   196:5
  H., O h.   236:16
  hundred years h.   75:3
Henchard: Michael H.'s Will   100:9
Hent: merrily h. the stile-a   210:7
Heraclitus: they told me, H.   69:2
Herald-angels sing   241:15
Heraldries: 'mong thousand h.   120:4
Heraldry: of h.   97:12
Herb: dew bespangling h.   104:9
Herbs: dinner of h.   26:18
  h. and other country messes   144:15
Hercules: Some talk..of H.   7:7
  Than I to H.   185:11
Herd: lowing h.   97:8
  numerous was the h.   79:7
  that left the h.   70:17
Here: But H. or There   85:11
  featly h. and there   208:9
  H. today and gone tomorrow   20:11
  H. we are!   128:28
  I have gone h. and there   211:15
  neither h. nor there   205:14
  Nothing is h. for tears   147:10
  Out of the everywhere into h.   137:9
  We are not h.   203:20
  We seek him h.   159:13
  ye who enter h.   72:5
Hereafter: h. for ever hold his peace   168:9
  'tis not h.   209:5
Heresies: begin as h.   112:11
Heritage: undefiled h.   124:17
Herman's a German   165:17
Hermit: a weeping h.   67:15
  than a h.'s fast   120:15
Hermitage: for a h.   134:19, 206:16
Hermits are contented   247:12
Hern: haunts of coot and h.   225:17
Hero: conquering h. comes   150:10
  he who aspires to be a h.   115:20
  h. to his valet   68:29
  seemed a h.   50:16
  where her young h. sleeps   149:17

Herod: out-herods H.   188:7
Heroes: for h. to live in   90:3
  frightened both the h.   57:18
  of all the world's brave h.   7:7
  speed glum h.   7:7
  thin red line of h.   179:4
Heroic: h. for earth too hard   43:7
  temper of h. hearts   230:15
Heroine: when a h. goes mad   216:4
Héros: point de h. pour son valet   68:29
Herren-Moral und Sklaven-Moral   154:5
Herring: H. boxes without topses   149:8
  Neighbours o'er the H. Pond   80:16
Herrings: red h. grow in the wood   156:15
Hervey: If you call a dog H.   113:16
Herz: Mein H. ich will dich fragen   99:9
Hesitate: and h. dislike   165:6
Hesitation: wavering and h.   174:6
Hesperus: H. entreats thy light   117:11
  It was the schooner H.   134:12
Heterodoxy is another man's doxy   238:16
Hew: Not h. him as a carcass   193:13
Hewers of wood   24:27
Hey: Sing H. to you   93:2
  then h. nonny, nonny   72:18, 204:9
  With a h.   184:12
Hey diddle diddle   155:17
Hic jacet   174:16
Hickory, Dickory, Dock   155:18
Hid: cannot be h.   30:13
  he h. himself among women   43:1
  h. as it were our faces   28:20
  h. his face   250:11
  I h. from Him   232:6
  lay h. in night   164:8
  no secrets are h.   167:4
  relics should be h.   147:12
  there is nothing h.   168:30
Hidden: half h. from the eye   248:3
  h. in my veins   174:10
  h. in the light of thought   215:4
  teems with h. meaning   93:28
Hide: death to h.   147:17
  H. me, O my Saviour   241:8
  his h. is sure to flatten 'em   20:18
  in a player's h.   98:13
  in a woman's h.   192:11
  Let me h. myself   233:23
  that must for ever h. me   192:14
  To h. her shame   95:21
Hideous: and h. wenches   66:9
  fearful and h.   236:13
  With h. ruin   145:12
Hides a sword   191:5
Hierophant: Muses' h.   109:16
High: between the h. and low   217:1
  cannot be heard so h.   195:19
  casement is   120:4
  descends from on h.   237:1
  floats on h.   247:3
  gone up on h.   170:7
  hear the larks so h.   110:19
  heav'ns are not too h.   103:18
  h. and lifted up   27:27
  H. and palmy state   185:3
  h. man, with a great thing to pur-
    sue   43:18
  h. promises   107:18
  h. that proved too h.   43:7
  h. thinking   247:8
  H. though his titles   180:6
  h. time to awake out of sleep   35:14
  I'm the H.   219:19
  in service h.   144:9
  joy runs h.   102:17
  on the h. horse   42:13
  sing both h. and low   209:5
  spirit from on h.   65:21

strange and h.   140:2
sunk low but mounted h.   145:4
Tempest still is h.   241:8
that's as h.   49:17
wickedness in h. places   36:14
High-Churchman: furious H. was I   5:9
High-engender'd battles   195:5
Higher: Friend, go up h.   33:14
knows nothing h.   78:18
sea rises h.   61:14
Highest: Glory to God in the h.   32:43
h. good   63:13
to have loved the h.   226:19
Highland: heart is H.   181:7
solitary H. lass   248:7
where is your H. laddie gone?   118:15
Highlands: chieftain to the H.   53:17
my heart's in the H.   48:27
Highly: thou that art h. favoured   32:36
Highway: buried in the king's h.   206:16
h. for our God   28:12
Highwayman came riding   155:1
Highways: Go out into the h.   33:18
Hill: Behind the cloud-topped h.   164:14
city that is set on a h.   30:13
down the green h.   66:14
every..h. shall be made low   28:12
flung us on the windy h.   42:4
from the h.   11:22
hanged on the highest h.   126:16
haven under the h.   225:15
heard on the h.   39:11, 71:2
high eastern h.   185:5
h. will not come to Mahomet   14:9
home from the h.   221:23
in a very fruitful h.   27:24
other side of the h.   240:15
Over h., over dale   203:6
rest upon thy holy h.   168:27
upon a little h.   120:9
valley, rock, or h.   249:14
went up the h.   156:6
Hills: ancient as the h.   66:14
Before the h. in order stood   239:14
blue remembered h.   111:5
fight in the h.   62:21
from those brown h.   41:15
great h. of the South Country   21:24
h. like young sheep   171:12
H. of the Chankly Bore   130:20
o'er vales and h.   247:3
old brown h.   141:6
Over the h. and far away   89:15, 158:12
strength of the h.   170:22
though the h. be carried   169:20
unto the h.   171:16
upon our clouded h.   38:16
valleys, groves, h.   139:6
Hill-side: h.'s dew-pearled   44:24
up the h.   121:7
Him: God made h.   201:12
H. that walked the waves   145:4
mindful of h.   168:23
Himalayan peasant   125:5
Himmel: der bestirnte H. über
mir   119:10
Himself: demolished but by h.   22:14
does not know h.   86:17
for h. alone   216:6
he h. has said it   93:13
he h. said it   63:12
Lord of h.   249:11
loving h.   67:4
master of h.   141:8
never to h.   180:6
seed of ruin in h.   11:16
Hinder: in the h. parts   170:12
Hinds: soil'd by rude h.   70:22
Hindu: we'll send the mild H.   8:8

Hindus and Argentines   69:8
Hinges: door on its h.   239:12
Hinky, dinky, parley-voo   178:6
Hint: Just h. a fault   165:6
my h. to speak   204:22
Hip: have thee on the h.   202:8
once upon the h.   201:15
smote them h. and thigh   24:32
Hippocrene: blushful H.   121:3
Hippopotamus: it was a H.   56:9
shoot the H.   20:18
Hire: labourer is worthy of his h.   33:5
Hired: as one of thy h. servants   33:22
Hireling: state h.   116:19
His: and I am H.   104:4
Hiss: roasted crabs h.   196:20
Hissed along the polished ice   246:5
Histories make men wise   14:27
History: by tale or h.   203:2
experience and h. teach   102:2
few materials for h.   90:14
have no h.   81:9
H. came to a full-stop   181:19
H. is bunk   87:2
h. of the world   55:13, 161:4
liquid h.   48:2
never learned anything from h.   102:2
properly no h.   82:18
strange eventful h.   183:20
what's her h.?   209:10
world's h.   179:14
Hit: h., a very palpable h.   189:27
h. it off as they should   245:13
on the fortunate h.   105:11
Hitch your wagon to a star   83:2
Hither: Come h.   183:13
H. and thither moves   85:10
their coming h.   196:5
Which brought us h.   246:12
Hive for the honey bee   250:9
Hives: chosen to fill our h.   223:1
Hoar: show his h. leaves   189:18
Hoarse: h. or mute   146:20
raven himself is h.   197:14
Hoary: dull and h.   235:10
h. woods are grand   181:7
Hodgepodge of all other speeches   219:15
Hoe: long row to h.   135:1
take a large h.   126:4
Hoist with his own petar   189:5
Hold: He will h. thee   228:6
h. fast that which is good   36:24
h. his peace   168:9
h. Infinity   38:10
h. me in thy heart   190:3
h. more than his belican   142:14
H. off! unhand me!   65:5
H. the fort   39:22
h. the gorgeous East in fee   249:1
I h. his dear   216:29
I h. you here   226:12
if these should h. their peace   33:35
It cannot h. you long   95:10
right hand shall h. me   172:1
To cry H., h.!   197:14
To have and to h.   168:12
Holdeth: children from play   217:2
Hole: better 'ole   15:19
h. in a' your coats   48:29
h. where his tail came   218:16
h. where the tail came   66:10
poisoned rat in a h.   223:5
stick'n in a big mud h.   87:9
stop a h.   189:21
Holes: foxes have h.   31:7
Holiday: butcher'd to make a
Roman h.   51:5
in a h. humour   184:8
sunshine h.   144:16

Holiest: Praise to the H.   153:14
Holiness: h. of the heart's affections   122:7
remembrance of his h.   169:8
Hollo: mariner's h.   65:9
Holloa: and we'll h.   242:20
Hollow: all was false and h.   146:11
plucked a h. reed   39:8
We are the h. men   81:12
within the h. crown   206:15
Hollows: And bowery h.   227:3
Holly: h. and the ivy   7:17
h. branch shone   19:4
unto the green h.   184:1
Holsters: by the inside of his h.   212:8
Holy: all h. desires   166:18
as h. and enchanted   66:14
carol, mournful, h.   228:1
close your eyes with h. dread   66:15
died to make men h.   111:16
haunted, h. ground   50:22
H. angels guard thy bed   239:11
H. Deadlock   103:17
H., fair, and wise   210:2
H., H., H., is the Lord of hosts   27:27
H., H., H.! Lord God Almighty!
   37:16, 38:13, 102:1
h. Lamb of God   38:16
h. rest   153:12
h. sages once did sing   145:6
h. time is quiet   246:15
h. will and commandments   167:32
I John saw the h. city   37:25
is h. ground   24:1
keep h. the Sabbath-day   167:9
neither h., nor Roman   237:16
O h. simplicity   112:9
On the h. ground   152:11
proofs of h. writ   205:8
Holy day: Our triumphant h.   5:17
Holy Ghost: Come H.   172:11
Father, Son, and H.   123:3
Holy Roman Empire: calls itself
the H.   237:16
Homage: owes no h. unto the sun   42:20
Home: any more at h. like you?   99:8
as we draw near h.   51:13
blest by suns of h.   42:11
bring h. knowledge   115:18
bring h. the wealth   115:18
call the cattle h.   124:1
can't find my way h.   158:9
Charity begins at h.   42:20
come happily h. at last   20:15
come h. to roost   218:15
come h. to supper   74:7
come h. with me now   249:9
comes frozen h. in pail   196:20
comes marching h. again   8:14
comes safe h.   192:4
Comin' for to carry me h.   7:10
confined from h.   164:14
cramped by narrow means at h.   119:3
Creep h.   123:18
cross when he comes h.   173:19
England, h. and beauty   40:18
far from h.   153:15, 206:7
for the old Kentucky h.   87:10
God, who is our h.   246:11
have brought me h.   163:16
her h. is on the deep   54:7
h. art gone   184:22
h. from sea   221:23
h. from the hill   221:23
H. is h.   63:27
H. is the girl's prison   213:1
H. is the sailor   221:23
h. of the brave   123:7, 212:7
h. on the rolling deep   179:3

H. sweet h.   161:17
H. they brought her warrior   229:15
h. where the buffalo roam   105:5
I go back h.   87:8
Keep the h. fires burning   87:4, 154:15
little grey h. in the west   244:11
live at h. at ease   160:19
millions at h.   128:6
no place like h.   161:17
of heaven and h.   248:6
old folks at h.   87:11
our eternal h.   239:14
out of house and h.   109:29
pig stayed at h.   158:9
Pleasure never is at h.   120:6
princes are come h. again   193:8
Rowing h. to haven   140:20
they dream of h.   87:4
They fill'd one h.   102:9
till the boys come h.   87:4
till the cow comes h.   19:23
toddle safely h.   179:5
Turns again h.   226:6
went straight h.   75:29
When I was at h.   183:10
when sick for h.   121:6
wish him safe at h.   118:15
Homely: it be never so h.   63:27
my h. definitions   67:8
tend the h.   145:1
Their h. joys   97:12
Homer: deep-brow'd H.   121:9
sage H.'s rule   165:11
Seven cities warr'd for H.   105:1
single exception of H.   212:14
When H. smote 'is bloomin' lyre   128:4
Homerus: bonus dormitat H.   108:3
Homes: from quiet h.   21:12
stately h. of England   102:11
Homesickness for the gutter   13:1
Homespuns: What hempen h.   203:12
Homeward: ploughman h. plods   97:8
Homines: quot h. tot sententiae   231:8
Homme: L'h. est né libre   177:18
L'h. n'est qu'un roseau   161:8
Homo: h. proponit   122:22
h. sum   231:6
Honest: h. and true   5:14, 141:14
H. Englishmen   123:15
h. folk droop   43:12
h. God   50:7
h. labour   72:18
h. man sent to lie abroad   249:14
h. man's the noblest work   164:20
I'm h.   142:19
indifferent h.   188:4
is his h. thought   249:10
poor but h.   182:8
She was poor but she was h.   7:5
watchdog's h. bark   51:13
whatsoever things are h.   36:20
Honesty: saving of thine h.   150:5
Thy h. and love   204:31
Honey: bees make your h.   237:10
Eating bread and h.   158:1
fill our homes with h.   223:1
flowing with milk and h.   24:2
gather h. all the day   239:9
How a bear likes h.   143:16
is there h.   42:9
milk and h. blest   152:14
sucked the h.   188:6
took some h.   131:6
You are my h.   84:14
Honey-bee: hive for the h.   250:9
Honey-dew: He on h. hath fed   66:15
Honey-suckle: You are my h.   84:14
Honneur: Tout est perdu fors l'h.   87:18
Honorificabilitudinitatibus   196:17

Honour: All is lost save h. 87:18
As h., love 199:32
but all in h. 205:19
Can h.'s voice 97:13
died..full..of h. 25:23
do h. his memory 117:12
drowned h. 190:9
fountain of h. 15:7
giving h. unto the wife 37:5
glory, laud, and h. 152:7
greater share of h. 192:3
H. all men 37:4
h. rooted in dishonour 226:22
h. the king 37:4
h. thereof 81:4
H. thy father 167:12
h.'s at the stake 189:7
h.'s thought 191:5
I h. him 194:2
in her left hand riches and h. 26:6
in h. clear 164:25
jealous in h. 183:20
louder he talked of his h. 82:17
Lov'd I not h. more 134:20
Man being in h. 169:24
mine h. is my life 206:2
my Robe of H. 85:16
Old age hath yet his h. 230:15
peace I hope with h. 76:10
peace with h. 59:16
post of h. 1:5
prophet is not without h. 31:29
quaint h. 140:12
roll of h. 64:1
safety, h...of the realm 60:1
signed with their h. 219:7
There H. comes 67:15
To h. we call you 88:18
To pluck bright h. 190:9
while the h. thou hast got 49:25
Honourable: all h. men 194:4
h. murderer 205:19
h. retreat 184:5
Honoured: but h. of them all 230:13
followed him, h. him 44:10
for his h. bones 147:12
h. me of late 198:5
is h. for them 41:6
Honouring: not so much h. thee 117:19
Honours: blushing h. 192:14
of its just h. 248:1
Hoofs: when the plunging h. 73:6
Hook: draw out leviathan with an
while thy h. spares 26:2
Hoops of steel 119:18
Hoo-ray and up she rises 185:21
Hope: against h. believed in h. 8:12
All h. abandon 35:1
As giving it a h. 72:5
farewell h. 117:19
for the h. of glory 146:14
h. and fear set free 166:32
H. deferred 224:6
H., for a season 26:13
h. I don't intrude? 54:5
h. of day 163:20
h. of posterity 147:3
h. of the City of God 166:4
H. springs eternal 141:5
h. that keeps up a wife's spirits 164:14
h.'s true gage 89:12
Land of H. and Glory 174:13
Never to h. again 22:7
no very lively h. of success 192:15
Nor in h. the world can show 218:3
not another's h. 77:15
now abideth faith, h. 238:13
nursing the unconquerable h. 35:22
11:27

Of h. to rise 249:11
one more rich in h. 210:13
our h. and strength 169:20
Our h. for years to come 239:14
pursued it with..hope 56:5
sure and certain h. 168:20
tender leaves of h. 192:14
their h. full of immortality 29:33
through h. 245:18
to his h. has giv'n 164:14
to h. till H. creates 215:1
triumph of h. 114:27
when we h. to find 145:1
Where there is life, there's h. 89:28
which H. thinks infinite 215:1
Hopeful: Hey, but I'm h. 92:24
Hopefully: To, travel h. 221:4
Hopeless: perennially h. 73:21
Hopes: enough for fifty h. and fears 43:9
far-reaching h. 108:17
h. of future years 133:13
h. of man 116:22
h. were dupes 64:10
sympathy with h. 215:4
Hopeth all things 35:21
Hoppy, Croppy 88:16
Hops: cherries, h., and women 75:16
Horace: what H. says is 17:9
Horatius: out spake brave H. 136:9
Horde: ravenous h. 91:25
Horizon: saw her just above the h. 47:14
Horn: blow up your h. 156:10
crumpled h. 158:8
echoing h. 97:11
his wreathed h. 219:8, 249:5
h. of the hunter 71:2
huntsman winds his h. 84:11
small but sullen h. 67:12
sound of his h. 97:2
With his hounds and his h. 97:2
Hornby: O my H. and my Barlow 232:11
Horned Moon 65:16
Horner: Little Jack H. 156:11
Horns: from the h. of the unicorns 169:1
h. of Elfland 229:11
h. of the moon 184:17
Horny-handed sons of toil 119:16
Horresco referens 236:10
Horrible: from the grotesque to the h. 78:14
less than h. imaginings 197:11
more h. than that 65:21
O. h.! most h.! 186:12
your h. pleasure 195:5
Horrid: blow the h. deed 198:4
h. shapes 144:10
h. wicked boy 105:16
never sees h. night 191:15
she was h. 134:14
Horrors: supp'd full with h. 200:3
Horse: at his h.'s side 69:26
behold a pale h. 37:17
boot and h. 123:18
Boot, saddle, to h. 43:13
dark h. 76:23
De blind h. 87:9
dog, a h., a rat have life 196:11
Fifty thousand h. and foot 124:11
flung himself upon his h. 130:12
for want of a h. 88:5
Give a man a h. 233:5
help Hyperion to his h. 191:15
h. of that colour 209:8
h. was lost 48:5
I knew two things about the h. 5:7
king to Oxford sent a troop of h. 43:3, 234:3
lady upon a white h. 157:17
little dearer than his h. 228:6

Horse (cont.)
my kingdom for a h.!   207:12
nothing but talk of his h.   201:11
sword, a h., a shield   134:20
to buy the h.   191:5
to my h. [I speak] German   60:6
upon the high h.   42:13
will lend his h. to go   69:23
With an old h. that stumbles   ·   100:4
Horsed upon the sightless couriers   198:4
Horseman: mounts on the h.'s
  pillion   109:17
Horses: All the king's h.   156:1
generally given to h.   116:17
hell for h.   49:11
hell of h.   86:13
no h. are kept   142:24
or shoeing h.   166:5
saddle your h.   179:20
some [put their trust] in h.   168:32
to swap h.   132:11
Hosannas: sweet H. ring   152:7
Hose: His youthful h.   183:20
Hospes comesque corporis   99:3
Host: h. of golden daffodils   247:3
soundless-clapping h.   232:11
ye heavenly h.   123:3
Hostages: given h. to fortune   14:17
Hostile: Universe is not h.   106:10
Hosts: Lord God of H.   127:3
  Lord of H.   27:27, 169:5, 170:13
Hot: benison of h. water   41:18
come h. from hell   193:21
h. and copper sky   65:12
h. for certainties   142:7
h. i' the mouth   209:7
iron while it is h.   80:2
piping h.   49:25
sea is boiling h.   57:22
three h. Junes   211:13
too h. the eye of heaven   210:12
Hot cross buns: two a penny h.   157:4
Hotch-potch: form the h. of my book   119:1
Hoti: settled H.'s business   43:19
Hound: by the faithful h.   133:20
grow into a h.   242:20
loves the h. more   222:17
nought good a sleping h. to wake   60:26
whelp and h.   95:13
Hounds: carcass fit for h.   193:13
cry of his h.   97:2
h. all join   84:11
h. of spring   223:28
With his h. and his horn   97:2
Hour: Abode his H. or two   84:22
come most carefully upon your h.   185:1
eternity in an h.   38:10
every h. is saved   230:13
fought a long h.   190:26
from h. to h.   183:17
his destin'd H.   84:23
h. calls not   236:12
h. of thoughtless youth   248:19
h. to play   153:6
h. when earth's foundations fled   111:11
I also had my h.   61:17
I chang'd ev'ry h.   89:14
Improve each shining h.   239:9
inevitable h.   97:12
let this hour be but a year   138:14
living at this h.   247:7
mine h. is not yet come   33:49
musing there an h. alone   51:18
not an h. more or less   196:2
nothing can bring back the h.   246:13
now's the h.   48:30
occupation for an idle h.   13:17
one bare h. to live   138:14
One crowded h.   150:3

One far fierce h.   61:17
struts and frets his h.   200:4
This was their finest h.   62:22
Time and the h.   197:12
to go at a certain h.   115:15
who has matched us with His h.   42:10
wonder of an h.   50:21
Hourly: May h. trample   206:16
Hours: about the space of two h.   34:45
brief h. and weeks   211:16
h. of gloom fulfilled   11:17
h. of insight   11:17
h. will take care of themselves   61:8
howling at all h.   249:5
in our h. of ease   180:13
leaden-stepping h.   148:6
silent h. of night   131:3
spent the darksome h.   55:23
sweetest h. that e'er I spend   48:19
Time in h.   235:11
to chase the glowing H.   51:1
what peaceful h.   70:2
House: bow-windows to the h.   74:7
build his h. in the woods   83:4
daughters of my father's h.   209:11
depart out of that h.   31:12
disturb this hallow'd h.   204:4
dwell in the h. of the Lord   169:2
Except the Lord build the h.   172:22
h. are many mansions   34:17
h. divided against itself   32:27, 132:7
h. in the high wood   22:1
h. is on fire   156:7
H. is pleased to direct me   131:20
h. of clay   83:12
h. of my God   170:15
h. that Jack built   158:8
h. was filled with smoke   27:27
h. where I was born   107:1
h. with deep thatch   22:1
h. with lawns   221:22
I would say to the H.   62:20
in my mother's h.   126:19
into the h. of the Lord   171:19
join h. to h.   27:25
lodger in my own h.   95:22
man's h. is his castle   65:1
moat defensive to a h.   206:7
nourished in my h.   103:13
out of h. and home   190:29
Peace be to this h.   33:4
save..in his own h.   31:29
Set thine h. in order   28:10
sparrow hath found her an h.   170:13
star of their h.   237:9
substance of his h. for love   27:20
Taffy came to my h.   158:3
that h. cannot stand   32:27
There's nae luck about the h.   8:2
walls of thine h.   171:24
within the h.   209:4
zeal of thine h.   170:8
Household: centre of the h.   212:15
Houseless heads   195:7
Housemaids: damp souls of h.   81:20
walks with fifty h.   126:14
House of Peers throughout the war   91:22
Houses: for the h. in between   18:22
h. go wheeling back   233:4
h. thick   146:22
plague o' both your h.   207:30
very h. seem asleep   249:4
Housewife that's thrifty   216:19
Hovels: of poor men's h.   108:16
Hover: over shady groves they h.   240:11
Hovers: soft wind h.   94:16
How-de-doo: Here's a h.   92:7
Howe, and the Glorious First of
  June!   151:3

Howled: roared and h. 65:8
Howling: When thou liest h. 189:22
winds that will be h. 249:5
Hubbard: Old Mother H. 157:3
Hudibras: Quoth H., I smell a rat 49:21
Hue: add another h. unto the
rainbow 193:6
bands of rosy h. 112:8
in its azure h. 54:3
native h. of resolution 187:13
your sweet h. 211:13
Hues: With living h. 214:1
Hug it in mine arms 200:22
Hugger-mugger to inter him 189:12
Hulk: Here a sheer h. 73:19
Hum: busy h. of men 144:18
smell and hideous h. 94:9
still the steeples h. 111:1
Human: are all the h. frame requires 21:4
full tide of h. existence 115:2
happy h. eyes 221:24
He held the h. race in scorn 21:2
H. life is everywhere 116:23
h. race, to which..my readers
belong 62:1
I had no h. fears 245:14
love the h. form divine 39:13
Mercy has a h. heart 39:13
milk of h. kindness 197:14
nothing h. alien from me 231:6
Peace the h. dress 39:13
Pity a h. face 39:13
purest of h. pleasures 14:16
spring out of h. suffering 246:13
thanks to the h. heart 246:14
thorough knowledge of h. nature 13:16
To err is h. 164:12
Treatise of H. Nature 111:22
utmost bound of h. thought 230:14
wish I loved the H. Race 174:19
Humani nil a me alienum puto 231:6
Humanity: h. with all its fears 133:13
music of h. 248:19
religion of h. 160:14
Humber: by the tide of H. 140:11
Humble: Be it ever so h. 161:17
He that is h. 46:17
h. Allen 165:13
h. and a contrite heart 127:4
h. though they be 55:26
Humbled: spare the h. 236:18
Humblest: I am the 'umblest per-
son 74:9
Humbleth: he that h. himself 33:15
Humbly: to walk h. 29:29
Humbug: considered him a h. 75:15
Humiliation: valley of H. 46:7
Humility: modest stillness and h. 191:8
pride that apes h. 218:17
Humour: in a holiday h. 184:8
in this h. woo'd..won? 207:7
liveliest effusions..of h. 13:16
there's the h. of it 202:16
unconscious h. 50:6
Humoured: and h. thus 206:15
Hump: Camel's h. is an ugly lump 126:2
We get the h. 126:3
Humph yourself! 128:12
Humpty Dumpty 156:1
Hunacamunca: in H.'s eyes 84:10
Hung: h. aloft the night 121:8
h. loose upon society 113:18
h. those lips 189:20
Hunger: In poverty, h. 107:3
sauce in the world is h. 59:9
which do h. 30:11
Hungry: he hath filled the h. 32:38
h. as a hunter 129:10

H. Forties 235:2
h. sheep look up 145:3
no h. generations 121:6
she makes h. 182:16
with a h. heart 230:13
Hunt for haddocks' eyes 58:12
Hunted: little h. hares 105:13
Hunter: Bahram, that great H. 85:1
horn of the h. 71:2
hungry as a h. 129:10
h. home from the hill 221:23
H. of the East 84:15
Nimrod the mighty H. 23:24
O Little H. 127:13
snare of the h. 170:19
Hunting: a-h. we will go 84:11
ain't the h. 173:9
Daddy's gone a-h. 155:6
Good h. 128:9
H. fills my thoughts 222:14
H. is all that's worth living for 222:13
I'm weary wi' h. 16:8
we daren't go a-h. 2:17
Huntress: Queen and h. 117:11
Huntsman winds his horn 84:11
Hurled: H. headlong 145:12
in endless error h. 164:19
world and all her train were h. 235:11
Hurly-burly: when the h.'s done 197:2
Hurrah! hurrah! we bring the
Jubilee! 249:8
Hurricanoes: cataracts and h. 195:4
Hurries his hearers 108:1
Hurry: old man in a h. 62:14
Hurrying near 140:12
Hurt: Balm of h. minds 198:13
give delight and h. not 208:18
h. not thy foot 170:20
h. with the same weapons 201:27
if I don't h. her 156:3
loving friends can h. you 125:16
nothing to h. her 232:4
whose feet they h. 171:5
Hurting: You are h. be! 128:15
Hurts: ain't the 'unting as h. 173:9
Husband: bride adorned for her h. 37:25
Hang your h. 89:13
H., I come 183:3
H.'s to Aleppo gone 197:5
Husbandry: dulls the edge of h. 185:21
h. in heaven 198:8
Husbands at chirche-dore she hadde
fyve 60:16
Hush: an old man who said 'H.!' 130:16
breathless h. in the Close 153:6
Hushed: air is h. 67:12
busy world is h. 153:12
Hussy: Away h. 89:13
Hustle: tried to h. the East 126:17
Hut: leave my little wooden h. 141:21
Love in a h. 120:15
where his rude h. 51:5
Hyacinth: That every H. 85:2
Thy h. hair 163:16
Hyades: the rainy H. 230:13
Hymn: our parting h. 150:2
Hymn-book: Cassock, band, and h. 243:2
Hymns: Singing h. unbidden 215:4
sings h. at heaven's gate 210:13
Hyperion: help H. to his horse 191:15
H. to a satyr 185:11
Hypocrite in his pleasures 116:6
Hyssop: purge me with h. 169:26

I

I: as well as I 243:6
Even less am I 107:10
Here am I 27:28

I (cont.)
I am a man 247:10
I am that I am 24:3
I am the State 134:17
I ought, therefore I can 119:12
I was I 149:2
I will arise 250:9
Than I to Hercules 185:11
what am I? 227:11
Iacta alea est 53:3
Iambics march from short 67:2
Ice: along the polished i. 246:5
caves of i. 66:15
chaste as i. 188:5
i. was here 65:8
it is good to break the i. 14:11
'mid snow and i. 133:17
over thin i. 82:20
penny i. and cold meat 91:25
thick-ribbèd i. 200:23
to smooth the i. 193:6
Iceland: Natural History of I. 115:17
I-chabod 24:39
Icicles hang by the wall 196:20
Icily regular 228:19
Icy: Greenland's i. mountains 101:15
i. hand 216:24
Ida: O mother I. 229:3
Idea: i. of freedom 160:22
i. of heaven 218:2
kind of i. 55:6
Ides of March 193:10, 193:15, 194:16
Idiot: i. who praises 92:1
of a blinking i. 201:25
over the village i. 62:2
tale told by an i. 200:4
your I. Boy 246:4
Idle: be not i. 49:13, 115:22
for i. hands to do 239:10
I too, my lord, have not been i. 5:12
I. singer 150:13
If you are i. 115:22
Most 'scruciating i. 128:11
my words are i. 240:10
Never less i. 63:15
only i. chatter 92:21
Idleness is only the refuge 61:10
Idlest froth amid the boundless
main 41:14
Idly: wandered i. 172:22
Idol: 'eathen i.'s foot 126:12
Idolatry: this side i. 117:12
Idols: four classes of I. 15:11
the I. I have loved 85:15
Ignoble: crowd's i. strife 98:1
Ignorance: but for their i. 117:12
I. madam, pure i. 114:3
I. of the law 181:13
no sin but i. 139:4
Where i. is bliss 98:10
Ignorant of what he's most assur'd 200:19
Ignorantly: ye i. worship 34:42
Ignotum pro magnifico est 224:14
Ilium: topless towers of I. 138:12
Ill: Cannot be i. 197:10
cure for this i. 126:4
ever to do i. 146:1
final goal of i. 227:10
if it is i. 217:6
i. at ease 172:22
in his actions be so i.! 141:11
It is an i. wind 234:8
Looking i. 222:5
Nought shall go i. 203:16
Took i. on Thursday 158:2
will I fear none i. 181:8
woman colour'd i. 212:4
Ill-clad, ill-nourished 176:15
Ill-favoured thing 184:13

Ill-housed: one-third of a nation i. 176:15
Ill-nourished: ill-clad, i. 176:15
Ills: bear those i. 187:13
hast'ning i. a prey 95:4
I. have no weight 135:17
of i. to come 98:8
sure one for all i. 174:17
what i. the scholar's life 117:2
Ill-spent: mark of an i. youth 219:5
Ill-tempered: Some think him i. 130:17
Illume: lake-reflected sun i. 214:9
Illumine: What in me is dark i. 145:11
Illusion: Great I. 3:3
Illustrious: my i. predecessors 84:4
Ill-weav'd ambition 190:23
Image: any graven i. 167:7
i. of war 222:13
kills the i. of God 148:7
scatter'd his Maker's i. 79:3
Imageries: garlanded with carven i. 120:4
Imaginary necessities 71:12
Imagination: abhorred in my i. 189:20
as i. bodies forth 203:19
if i. amend them 204:2
i. all compact 203:19
in the i. of their hearts 32:38
strong i. 203:19
to his i. for his facts 216:23
to sweeten my i. 195:21
truth of i. 122:7
Imagine a vain thing? 168:21
Imagined corners 77:8
Imaginings: less than horrible i. 197:11
Imbower: High over-arch'd i. 146:4
Immanuel: shall call his name I. 27:30
Immense: but error is i. 40:4
i., of fishy form 42:2
Immoral: moral or i. book 243:19
Immorality: of vice and i. 84:7
Immortal: i. Bird 121:6
i. diet 174:13
i. flies 42:3
i. garland 148:9
i. hate 145:15
i. Jove 205:10
i. lodgings 183:2
i. with a kiss 138:12
is in i. souls 202:11
lost the i. part of myself 204:33
of that i. sea 246:12
orient and i. wheat 234:2
race abides i. 237:9
this i. day 214:10
to i. verse 144:19
warn the i. souls 139:12
What i. hand 39:1, 4
Where saints i. reign 239:15
Immortality: load of i. 122:9
must put on i. 35:30
Nurslings of i. 214:9
their hope full of i. 29:33
they gave, their i. 41:16
Immortals: President of the I. 100:10
Impart: cannot i. it 113:22
seven-fold gifts i. 172:11
Impartial: with i. foot 108:16
Impeachment: I own the soft i. 216:14
Impediment: cause or just i. 168:5
Impediments: admit i. 211:16
i. to great enterprises 14:17
Imperative: categorical i. 119:11
Imperfections: all my i. on my
head 186:12
Imperial: crown i. 191:15
i. votaress 203:7
Of the i. theme 197:9
Imperious mother of sweet loves 110:4
Impetuous: Be thou me, i. one! 214:4
Impious men bear sway 1:5

Implication: puff by i. 216:1
Importunate: rashly i. 106:20
Impose the law of peace 236:18
Impossibility: upon i. 140:2
Impossible: because it is i. 231:11
eliminated the i. 78:16
i. to be silent 47:10
I. to carry the heavy burden 81:5
In two words: i. 96:5
That not i. she 70:27
with men this is i. 32:2
Impostors: treat those two i. 125:14
Impotently: rolls i. on 85:13
Impregnable: Were brass i. 206:15
Imprisoned: i. in the viewless
winds 200:23
who i. Montezuma 136:20
Imprisonment: penury, and i. 201:1
Improbable: however i. 78:16
Impropriety: to indulge in without
i. 91:23
Improve: I. each shining hour 239:9
I. his shining tail 56:13
Improved: so i. the city 52:21
Imprudently married the barber 86:19
Impudence: much of Cockney i. 178:8
Impulse: i. from a vernal wood 248:15
lonely i. of delight 250:7
share the i. of thy strength 214:3
very slave..of i. 52:8
Impunity: No one provokes me
with i. 10:3
Impurer: from th' i. matter 50:4
Impurity: we bring i. 148:9
Impute: the sin I i. 45:8
In: I. and out the Eagle 138:2
never out nor i. 79:10
Who's i. 196:6
Inactivity: masterly i. 137:12
Inalienable: rights inherent and i. 113:2
Inapprehensible, we clutch thee! 232:9
Incantation of this verse 214:4
Incapable of her own distress 189:18
Incarnadine: multitudinous seas i. 198:15
Incarnate: devils i. 191:7
Incense-bearing tree 66:14
Incense-breathing Morn 97:11
Inceptis gravibus plerumque et
magna professis 107:18
Inch: every i. a king 195:20
painful i. to gain 64:10
retreat a single i. 89:3
Inchcape Rock 218:20
Inches: die by i. 103:6
Incident: curious i. of the dog 78:11
Inclination: as i. leads him 114:14
Incline our hearts 167:6
Income: annual i. twenty pounds 74:8
moderate i. 129:18
Inconceivable: is something i. 91:28
Inconstancy: this i. is such 134:20
Inconstant moon 207:24
Incorruptible: seagreen I. 55:12
Incorruption: must put on i. 35:30
Increase: bring forth her i. 170:5
daily i. in thy holy Spirit 168:4
i. of appetite 185:11
may his tribe i.! 112:2
were to i. his store 106:14
Increases: as their wealth i. 139:5
i. rather than diminishes 80:5
its loveliness i. 120:1
Population..i. 138:1
Increaseth: knowledge i. sorrow 26:37
Increasing: one i. purpose runs 228:11
Increment: Unearned i. 142:21
Incurable: i. disease 69:19
now i. 119:6
Indebted to his memory 216:23

Independent: created equal and i. 113:2
With an i. air 90:17
Index: marble i. 247:17
India: in the name of the people of I. 47:11
I.'s coral strand 101:15
Indian: by the i. Ganges' side 140:11
like the base I. 205:20
Lo, the poor I. 164:14
only good I. 215:20
Indictment: drawing up an i. 47:2
Indies: wealth of I. 115:18, 232:4
Indifference: give me i. 67:16
with affected i. 13:16
Indifferent: delayed till I am i. 113:22
I am myself i. honest 188:4
it is simply i. 106:10
Indignatio: facit i. versum 118:19
saeva i...cor lacerare 223:27
Indignation: I. would give birth 118:19
Where fierce i. 223:27
Indignor quandoque bonus dormitat
Homerus 108:3
Indirections: By i. 186:20
Inditing of a good matter 169:18
Individual: liberty of the i. 142:22
Individualism: system of rugged i. 107:7
Individuals: love is towards the i. 223:6
worth of the i. 142:23
Indolent expression 21:22
Indubitable: Goddess i. 236:6
Indulge: choose to i. in 91:23
Indulgent: tout comprendre rend
très i. 219:22
Industry: Captains of i. 55:19
Inebriate: cheer but not i. 70:18
Ineffectual: Remote and i. Don 21:20
Inevitability of gradualness 240:2
Inexactitude: terminological i. 62:18
Infallible: none of us i. 232:12
only i. rule 222:12
Infâme: quoi que vous fassiez,
écrasez l'i. 237:17
Infancy: in our i. 246:11
Infant: describe the i. phenomenon 75:4
i. crying in the night 227:11
i., mewling and puking 183:20
Like i. slumbers 122:17
mother with i. 147:16
Infection: against i. 206:7
Infest: cares that i. the day 133:15
Infidel: has played the I. 85:16
Infini: l'i. me tourmente 151:9
Infinite: appear as it is, i. 39:21
fellow of i. jest 189:20
Her i. variety 182:16
idea of the i. 151:9
i. in faculty 187:4
king of i. space 187:3
knowledge i. 139:10
of these i. spaces 161:5
which Hope thinks i. 215:1
Infinity: hold i. 38:10
Infirm: i. and old 180:4
poor, i., weak 195:5
Infirmities: thine often i. 36:28
Infirmity: last i. of noble mind 145:1
Inflexible: if Heaven be i. 236:20
Influence: and i. People 55:25
corrupt i. 47:7
i. of the Crown 12:15
Spheres of i. 7:8
that pervading i. 74:12
Influences: sweet i. of Pleiades 25:43
Inform: do i. against me 189:6
Information: only ask for i. 74:11
Informed the tenement of clay 79:5
Infusing him with self 206:15
Inglorious: mute i. Milton 97:15
Ingrateful man! 195:4

Ingratitude: as man's i. 184:1
Ingratitudes: monster of i. 208:27
Inhabitants: not like th' i. o' the earth 197:8
Inhabits: being help'd, i. there 210:2
Inherent: rights i. and inalienable 113:2
Inherit: they shall i. the earth 30:11
Inheritance: Ruinous i. 88:14
Inhumanity: Man's i. to man 48:24
Iniquities: bruised for our i. 28:21
Iniquity: i. of us all 28:21
　rejoiceth not in i. 35:21
Injure: might i. the brain 56:16
Injuries: adding insult to i. 149:10
Injury: never forget an i. 178:16
Injustice: with i. is corrupted 192:7
Ink: hath not drunk i. 196:14
　i. were temper'd 196:15
Inland far we be 246:12
Inlets: creeks and i. making 64:10
Inn: as a good tavern or i. 115:7
　do you remember an i.? 22:2
　his sober i. 54:10
　I count it not an i. 42:20
　in mine i. 190:21
　no room for them in the i. 32:40
　To gain the timely i. 199:7
　welcome at an i. 215:18
　world's an i. 79:28
Inn-door: up to the old i. 155:1
Innisfree: go to I. 250:9
Innocence: bring not i. into the world 148:9
　I. thy Sister 140:5
Innocent: I. is the heart's devotion 215:11
　i. of the knowledge 199:5
　i. sleep 198:13
　look like the i. flower 198:1
　Minds i. and quiet 134:19
　than one i. suffer 38:8
Inns: and go to i. to dine 61:25
Innumerable: i...bees 229:19
　i. company of the heavenly host 38:13
Inops: Magnas inter opes i. 110:1
Inscriptions: in lapidary i. 115:5
Insensibility: stark i. 113:14
Inside: Turn the dark cloud i. out 87:4
Insight: tasks in hours of i. 11:17
Insipid: many times flat, i. 80:3
Insnare: imperial race i. 165:2
Insnared with flow'rs 140:6
Insolence: i. of office 187:13
　pride and i. 138:10
　supports with i. 116:18
　with i. and wine 146:5
Insolent: brutal and i. soldiery 83:7
Inspiration: Genius is one per cent. i. 81:1
Inspire: our souls i. 172:11
Inspired: prophet new i. 206:6
　that i. their hearts 139:11
Inspires: wine i. us 89:17
Inspissated gloom 114:25
Instances: and modern i. 183:20
Instancy: majestic i. 232:8
Instant: rose both at an i. 190:26
Institution: in such a glorious i. 47:3
　it's an i. [cricket] 111:21
Instructions: follows his own i. 201:10
Instruments: make i. to plague us 196:7
Insufferable: Oxford that has made me i. 20:8
Insult: adding i. to injuries 149:10
　threatened her with i. 47:14
Intangible: O world i. 232:9
Integer vitae scelerisque purus 109:5
Integral: good at i. and differential calculus 93:19
Intellect: Is it weakness of i.? 92:17
Intelligence: started at the i. 219:2

Intelligible: if not i., without Greek. 51:25
Intended: We had i. you to be 21:7
Intent: first avow'd i. 46:20
　sides of my i. 198:4
Inter: hugger-mugger to i. him 189:12
Interest: I du in i. 135:2
　lend fresh i. 52:4
Interested him no more 101:4
Interesting: renders ordinary.. things i. 181:5
　statements was i. 234:18
Interference: No i. 174:2
Interfused: more deeply i. 248:19
Intermission of pain 181:15
Interred with their bones 194:3
Interrupt a man with such a silly question? 220:13
Intersections: between the i. 116:15
Interstices between the intersections 116:15
Interval: make a lucid i. 79:24
Intervals: lucid i. and happy pauses 15:8
　lucid i. of life 245:20
Interviews: from these our i. 51:7
Intolerable: i. one 160:13
　possession of it is i. 235:6
Intreat me not 24:35
Intrinsicate: this knot i. 183:4
Introduced: when I'm i. to one 174:19
Intrude: I hope I don't i. 163:20
Intrudes: society, where none i. 51:7
Invade: dare to i. the borders 82:9
　i. the sphere of private life 141:20
Invalid: invaluable permanent i. 243:9
Invectives: with sharp i. 250:3
Invent: necessary to i. him 237:15
Invented: i. an invaluable permanent invalid 243:9
　i. what I conceived 112:12
　When I i. the phrase 105:11
Inventer: il faudrait l'i. 237:15
Invention: brightest heaven of i. 191:2
　it is a happy i. 9:13
　my own i. 58:10
Inventions: sought out many i. 26:41
Inverted: that i. Bowl 85:13
Invincible: none i. as they 69:20
　Puts i. might 147:6
　shaking her i. locks 148:10
Inviolable shade 11:27
Invisible: bloody and i. hand 199:6
　O world i. 232:9
　visible and i. 167:18
Invitation: more i. than command 220:5
Invoke the genius of the Constitution 162:20
Involved: I am i. in Mankind 77:23
Inward: of i. tranquillity 83:1
　upon that i. eye 247:5
Inwardly they are ravening wolves 31:3
Inwards: he looked i. 80:3
Iohannes fac totum 98:13
'Ipse dixit.' 'Ipse' autem erat Pythagoras 63:12
Iram indeed is gone 84:16
Ire: Juno's unslumbering i. 236:3
Ireland: great Gaels of I. 61:15
Iris: livelier i. 228:5
Iron: as strong as links of i. 47:6
　Blood and i. 38:4
　Cold I. 124:19
　hard as i. 177:9
　i. bars a cage 134:19
　i. curtain 63:5, 94:11, 234:5
　i. entered into his soul 171:5
　i. shuts amain 145:2
　reeking tube and i. shard 127:7

sound of i. on stone   73:6
strong as i. bands   134:10
We must beat the i.   80:2
with links of i.   172:7
wreathe i. pokers   66:11
Ironies: Life's Little I.   100:8
Irons: two i. in the fire   19:12
Iron-ware and cheap tin trays   140:21
Irrecoverably: lost my voice most i.   240:13
Irregularly great   136:1
Irregulars: Baker Street i.   78:19
Irresistibly drained   78:20
Irreverent to my tutor   113:14
Iser: flow of I.   53:15
Isis: my Cam and I.   164:2
Island: defend our i.   62:21
  no man is an i.   77:22
  shieling of the misty i.   181:7
  snug little I.   73:20
  throughout the whole i.   115:17
  tight little I.!   73:20
Islands: Round many western i.   121:9
Island-story: rough i.   229:2
Isle: A ship, an i.   86:10
  Beside a pumice i.   214:2
  Fairest I.   79:23
  i. is full of noises   208:18
  I. of Beauty   19:3
  it frights the i.   204:30
  men of the Emerald I.   78:30
  o'er Ceylon's i.   101:16
  scepter'd i.   206:7
Isle of Man: Kelly from the I.   151:4
Isles: all i. excelling   79:23
  bound for the i.   147:5
  i. of Greece   51:17
Isolation: in that which is called i.   96:7
  our splendid i.   96:7
Israel: beauty of I.   24:47
  Now I. loved Joseph   23:32
  ransom captive I.   152:15
  sweet psalmist of I.   25:5
  to be ruler in I.   29:28
Issue: happy i.   166:30
  hastens to the i.   108:1
Issues: to fine i.   200:13
Issuing on a summer's morn   146:22
Isthmus of a middle state   164:18
Italian: Or perhaps I.   93:14
  to women [I speak] I.   60:6
Italien aux femmes   60:6
Italien ist ein geographischer
  Begriff   142:16
Italy: Fate-exiled, to I.   236:3
  I. a paradise for horses   49:11
  I. is a geographical expression   142:16
Itch: inveterate i. of writing   119:6
  Mine eyes do i.   205:14
Itching palm   194:15
Itself: divided against i.   32:27
  Not of i., but thee   117:19
Itur: sic i. ad astra   236:21
Itylus: half assuaged for I.   223:28
Iudicium: per legale i. parium
  suorum   137:17
Iuppiter pluvius   233:16
Iustum et tenacem propositi   109:19
Iuvabit: Forsan et haec olim memi-
  nisse i.   236:5
Iuventa: Non ego hoc ferrem calidus i. 109:25
Ivory: cargo of i. and apes and pea-
  cocks   25:9, 140:20
Ivy: i. never sere   144:20
  Just like the i.   143:5
  myrtle and i.   52:7
Ivy-bloom: bees in the i.   214:9
Ivy-mantled: yonder i. tow'r   97:9
Ivy-tree: the oak, and the ash, and
  the bonny i.   6:15

J

Jabberwock: beware the J.   57:14
  J. with eyes of flame   57:14
Jack: gorging J.   231:19
  J. and Jill   156:4
  J. and Joe   128:28
  J. shall have Jill   203:16
Jackdaw sat on the Cardinal's chair!   17:11
Jacket: his j. was red   66:10
  my tarpaulin j.   243:1
Jacky shall have a new master   157:18
Jacob: J. served seven years   23:30
  sold his birthright unto J.   23:27
  traffic of J.'s ladder   232:10
Jade: let the galled j. wince   188:14
Jades: pampered J. of Asia   139:13
Jail: being in a ship is being in a j. 114:6
  but a j.   74:7
  patron and the j.   117:2
  to get himself into j.   114:6
Jam to-morrow   58:3
James: and our J.   118:9
  J. J. Morrison Morrison   143:9
  work of Henry J.   98:20
Jamshyd: J.'s Sev'n-ring'd cup   84:16
  where J. gloried   85:1
Jane: Willie shall dance with J.   3:22
Jangled: sweet bells j.   188:6
Janvier: General J.   154:4
Japanese don't care to   69:8
Japheth: Noah begat Shem, Ham
  and J.   23:20
Jargon of the schools   172:18
Jarndyce and Jarndyce   73:21
Jasper of jocunditie   80:14
Javan: isles of J.   147:5
Jaws: j. of Death   226:4
  j. that bite   57:14
Jay: thrush and the j.   210:5
Jealous: am a j. God   167:7
  j. in honour   183:20
  j. mistress   82:16
  one not easily j.   205:20
  to the j. confirmations   205:8
Jealousy: beware..of j.   205:5
  green-ey'd j.   202:2
Jeanie with the light brown hair   87:15
Jehu: driving of J.   25:20
Jelly: Out, vile j.   195:17
Jelly-bellied Flag-flapper   127:16
Je-ne-sais-quoi young man   93:3
Jenkin: jolly J.   180:19
Jenny kissed me   112:4
Jeopardy of their lives   25:6
Jerusalem: hath redeemed J.   28:19
  If I forget thee O J.   171:28
  J. my happy home   5:3
  J. the golden   152:14
  new J.   37:25
  peace of J.   171:20
  prefer not J.   171:28
  There's J.   232:3
  Till we have built J.   38:16
  was J. builded here?   38:16
  waste places of J.   28:19
  ye daughters of J.   27:12
Jeshurun waxed fat   24:23
Jesse: stem of J.   28:1
Jest: bring with thee j.   144:12
  fellow of infinite j.   189:20
  glory, j., and riddle   164:19
  j.'s prosperity   197:18
  Life is a j.   89:26
  tells the j.   67:3
  to put his whole wit in a j.   19:9
  to use myself in j.   77:15
Jested: He j., quaff'd, and swore   78:22
Jester: become a fool and j.   191:1

Jests: He j. at scars 207:20
to his memory for his j. 216:23
Jesu: for J.' sake 212:5
J., by a nobler deed 59:18
J., lover of my soul 241:8
J., Mary and Joseph they bare 5:10
J., the very thought 58:23
O J., thou art standing 111:14
Jesus (see also Christ): Blood of J. 37:33
Gentle J. 241:12
J. Christ her little child 2:10
J. Christ her Lord 222:1
J. Christ is risen to-day 5:17
J. Christ, the same 36:38
J. loves me 239:1
J. shall reign 239:13
J. speaks 70:3
J. [was misunderstood] 82:21
looking unto J. 36:35
name of J. 36:15
Stand up for J. 80:8
sweet reasonableness of J. 12:11
sweet the name of J. sounds 154:1
which is in Christ J. 35:10
whom J. loved 34:30
With the Cross of J. 18:7
ye belong to J. 2:9
Jeunesse: si j. savoit 83:8
Jew: Hath not a J. eyes? 201:27
This is the J. 165:15
Jewel: immediate j. of their souls 205:4
j. in a..chest 206:2
my j. it should tine 48:10
rich j. 207:18
wears yet a precious j. 183:9
Jewels: give my j. for a set of beads 206:16
Jewry: in stubborn J. 206:7
Jews: J., a headstrong, moody, murmuring race 79:4
that is born King of the J. 30:1
Till the conversion of the J. 140:11
To choose The J. 83:13
Jigging veins 139:8
Jimmy: guzzling J. 231:19
Jingo: but, by J. 8:8, 112:1
By the living J. 96:2
Jinks: pastime of high j. 180:17
Joan: greasy J. 196:20
Johnny has got his J. 3:22
Job: as poor as J. 190:28
patience of J. 37:1
we will finish the j. 62:23
Jobiska: Aunt J. made him drink 131:11
Joblillies: and the J. 86:19
Jocund: and J. day 208:2
Jocunditie: jasper of j. 80:14
Joe: Jack and J. 128:28
Poor old J. 87:12
Jog: J. on, j. on 210:7
might j. on with 129:18
John: and I J. saw the holy city 37:25
Don J. of Austria 61:19
J. had Great Big Waterproof Boots on 143:8
O No J.! 7:1
Matthew, Mark, Luke, and J. 1:17
There St. J. mingles 165:10
John Anderson my jo 48:20
John Barleycorn 48:22
John Gilpin was a citizen 69:21
Johnny: Frankie and J. were lovers 4:8
J. has got his Joan 3:22
When J. Comes Marching Home 8:14
Johnny-head-in-air 106:2, 173:2
Johnny underground 173:2
Johnson: Cham of Literature, Samuel J. 218:5
J.'s style was grand 67:22
no arguing with J. 96:3

Join: Come and j. the dance 57:9
hounds all j. 84:11
that j. house to house 27:25
then j. in hand 76:1
will you j. the dance? 57:8
Joined: j. the great majority 162:13
j. together in holy Matrimony 168:5
What therefore God hath j. 31:41
whom God hath j. together 168:15
Joint: remove the j. 58:16
time is out of j. 186:19
Jollity: youthful j. 144:12
Jolly: j. Jenkin 180:19
life is most j. 184:1
there was a j. miller 37:29
three j. Farmers 73:8
Jonah: lot fell upon J. 29:25
Jonathan: Saul and J. 24:48
Jones: John J. may be described 106:18
Jonquille o'ercomes the feeble brain 244:15
Jonson: J.'s learnèd sock 144:19
O rare Ben J. 118:14
Jordan: I looked over J. 7:10
Joris: and J., and he 44:5
Joseph: Israel loved J. 23:32
Jesu, Mary and J. they bare 5:10
Joshua the son of Nun 24:9
Jostle: Philistines may j. 92:22
Jostling: by j. in the street 38:15
Journalism: but why j.? 16:1
Journalists say a thing..isn't true 22:5
Journey: And bound on that j. 91:25
death the j.'s end 79:28
I woll this j. be his 81:4
my j.'s end 205:17
traveller's j. is done 39:7
Will the day's j. 177:13
Journeys: his successive j. run 239:13
J. end in lovers meeting 209:5
Jove: Immortal J. 205:10
might I of J.'s nectar 117:19
when J.'s planet rises 44:3
Jowett: my name is J. 20:5
Joy: apprehend some j. 203:19
Break forth into j. 28:19
but j. cometh 169:8
can burst J.'s grape 120:24
chortled in his j. 57:14
come again with j. 171:21
courage, love and j. 89:17
dreams of j. and fear 213:20
dreme of j. 60:23
every child may j. to hear 39:8
everybody saw with j. 105:15
fruit of the spirit is..j. 36:7
Gemme of all j. 80:14
Glad tidings of great j. 225:9
good tidings of great j. 32:42
is a j. for ever 120:1
j. before death 224:9
j. of elevated thoughts 248:19
j. propos'd 212:2
j. runs high 102:17
J. shall be in heaven 33:20
J. thy shrine we tread 179:11
J. whose hand is ever at his lips 120:24
let j. be unconfined 51:1
Life, J., Empire 215:1
of work and j. 41:16
pledges of Heaven's j. 147:13
scrip of j. 174:13
sees it in his j. 246:11
shall reap in j. 171:21
snatch a fearful j. 98:7
sole remaining j. 180:4
sons of God shouted for j. 25:42
Thy j. and crown 149:1
tidings of comfort and j. 4:11
tidings of great j. 32:42, 225:9

walked in glory and in j.   247:19
was j. to his mighty heart   125:1
wept with j.   39:8
Joyful: and j. rise   123:1
  good and j. a thing   171:26
  J. and triumphant   9:14, 159:6
  j. school-days   129:16
  With a j. spirit   230:5
Joyous: Good, great and j.   215:1
  in thy j. errand   86:3
Joys: eternal j. of heaven   138:11
  its j., and fears   246:14
  j. and varied pursuits   119:1
  j. in another's loss of ease   39:6
  made for j.   89:19
  minds me o' departed j.   49:5
  our j., and all we have   174:15
  raise your j.   241:7
  Such present j.   80:17
  Their homely j.   97:12
  Thy j. when shall I see?   5:3
  vain deluding j.   144:4
  visionary j.   68:14
  What lasting j.   242:19
Jubilee: we bring the J.   249:8
Jubjub: beware the J. bird   57:14
Judah: sight of J.'s seer   138:6
Judge: after a time they j. them   243:27
  as sober as a J.   84:5
  cobbler should not j.   163:13
  Forbear to j.   192:8
  I am a J.   93:35
  I'll be j.   56:14
  indifferent j.   217:1
  J. And a good j. too   93:35
  j. not   30:30, 33:3
  j. not me   53:11
  J. not the play   173:27
  J. of taste   224:18
  Sole j. of truth   164:19
  wise young j.   202:6
Judged: shall not be j.   33:3
  that ye be not j.   30:30
Judgement: Daniel come to J.   202:6
  God's great J. Seat   124:13
  green in j.   182:13
  legal j. of his peers   137:17
  reserve thy j.   185:21
  what j. I had   80:5
  world's j.   179:14
Judges: I will vanquish..my J.   153:10
Judy O'Grady: 126:8
Jug: J. of Wine   84:19
  old j. without a handle   130:19
Juggler's sleight   49:29
Julia: When as in silks my J.
    goes   104:15
  Where my J.'s lips do smile   104:8
Juliet is the sun   207:20
Julius: mightiest J. fell   185:3
  towers of J.   97:7
July: swarm of bees in J.   3:15
  'twas in Margate last J.   18:1
Jumblies: Lands where the J. live   131:4
Jump the life to come   198:3
Jumping on his mother   93:23
Jumps: how the cat j.   181:6
June: April, J., and November   158:7
  April, J., and September   96:8
  brilliant night in J.   162:2
  Glorious First of J.   64:13, 151:3
  lately sprung in J.   48:28
  leafy month of J.   66:3
  she needs not J.   12:1
  swarm of bees in J.   3:15
Junes: three hot J.   211:13
Jungle: Law of the J.   126:9
  Through the J.   127:13
Juniper: under a j. tree   25:13

Juno: fell J.   236:3
  lids of J.'s eyes   210:8
Jupiter: in the Temple of J.   90:12
  J. the rain-bringer   233:16
  than flaming J.   138:13
Jury: I'll be j.   56:14
  Trial by j.   73:11
Just: actions of the j.   216:25
  and meanly j.   117:2
  beast, but a j. beast   3:5
  chiefly on the j.   40:14
  faithful and j. to me   194:5
  gods are j.   196:7
  hath his quarrel j.   192:7, 213:4
  He's j.—nae better   48:14
  j., and mighty Death!   174:16
  j. man and firm of purpose   109:19
  j. shall live by faith   34:52
  ninety and nine j. persons   33:20
  of its j. honours   248:1
  raineth on the j.   40:14
  sendeth rain on the j.   30:19
  this j., this pious fraud   89:23
  Thou art j.   227:4
  whatsoever things are j.   36:20
Justice: expected j. from a company? 217:19
  J., in fair round belly   183:20
  j. of my quarrel   139:15
  j. of our cause   99:4
  J. should not only be done   104:19
  kind of wild j.   14:21
  Let j. be done   239:4
  mercy seasons j.   202:5
  of eternal j.   160:22
  plucks j. by the nose   200:14
  Poetic j.   164:1
  Though j. be thy plea   202:5
  what j. requires   138:5
Justified: alone are j.   79:26
  To j. God's ways   145:11
Justify: J. the ways of G.   145:11
  To j. God's ways   111:7
Justly: to do j.   29:29
Jutty: no j., frieze   198:2
J'y suis, j'y reste   137:14

                    K

Kalends: pay at the Greek K.   52:22
Kangaroo: Duck and the K.   131:2
  Old Man K.   126:5
Kansas had better stop   131:16
Kaspar: Old K.'s work was done   218:12
Kathleen Mavourneen!   71:2
Keats: John K., who was kill'd off   51:25
  porridge had John K.?   44:26
  Who killed John K.?   52:6
Kedar: tents of K.   27:12
Keel: doth k. the pot   196:20
Keen: k. dog   137:13
  tooth is not so k.   184:1
Keener: with his k. eye   140:8
Keep: Guard us, guide us, k. us   81:2
  If you can k. your head   125:14
  K. me as the apple of an eye   168:28
  k. one from going nude   123:10
  K. the home fires burning   87:4, 154:15
  k. thee in all thy ways   170:20
  k. thee only unto her   168:11
  k. up appearances   62:10
  k. your powder dry   38:5
  K. yourself to yourself   75:22
  Lord k. the city   171:22
  love to k. it by me   113:8
  subtle ways I k.   82:13
  they should k. who can   247:20
  to k. her alive   89:5
  to k. in the same place   57:17
  to k. this law   167:6

Keeper: k. stands up 111:4
　Lord himself is thy k. 171:17
　my brother's k. 23:18
Keeping: by k. men off 89:10
　Saints their watch are k. 222:2
Kelly: anybody here seen K.? 151:4
Kempenfeit: brave K. 70:10
Ken: swims into his k. 121:9
Kennst du das Land 94:16
Kensal Green: by way of K. 61:23
Kent: everybody knows K. 75:16
Kentucky: for the old K. home 87:10
Kept: I have k. the faith 36:33
　k. thy truth 147:16
　reached and k. 133:22
　that I k. my word 73:5
Ketch: as soon dine with Jack K. 115:10
Kettle: put the k. on 157:13
Kew: dog at K. 164:7
　K. in lilac-time 154:16
Key: k. of the bottomless pit 37:23
　taken away the k. of knowledge 33:12
　with this k. 248:1
　with this same k. 44:4
Keys: half that's got my k. 96:12
　Over the noisy k. 172:22
　Two massy k. 145:2
Khayyám: come with old K. 85:6
Kick: k. his wife out of bed 222:14
　k. you downstairs 56:17
　nor a body to k. 217:19
　to k. against the pricks 34:36
Kicked: Jeshurun..k. 24:23
　k. down stairs 48:1
　no body to be k. 233:15
Kid: leopard shall lie down with the k. 28:2
Kidney: man of my k. 202:21
Kill: care'll k. a cat 117:14
　fatted calf, and k. it 33:23
　I'll k. you if you quote it 46:25
　k. a man as k. a good book 148:7
　k. a wife with kindness 208:7
　k. all the lawyers 192:9
　k. an admiral 237:11
　k. the poor creature at once 89:5
　k. us for their sport 195:18
　k. with looks 206:15
　never k. for sport 88:10
　prepared to k. one another 212:18
　Thou shalt not k. 64:6
Killed: hawk'd at and k. 199:1
　I'm k., Sire! 44:7
　not k. it 199:3
　some sleeping k. 206:15
　Who k. Cock Robin? 159:4
　Who k. John Keats? 52:6
　Woman K. with Kindness 105:3
Killeth: letter k. 36:1
Killing: For k. of a mouse on
　　Sunday 41:3
　k. Kruger with your mouth 124:9
　K. no Murder 182:2
　k. sin 221:24
　More ways of k. a cat 124:7
Kills: and air that k. 111:5
　k. the thing he loves 243:5
Kin: All their kith and k. 110:9
　little less than k. 18:5
　little more than k. 185:7
　makes the whole world k. 208:28
Kind: best in this k. 204:2
　cruel, only to be k. 189:4
　every poet in his k. 223:26
　had been k. 113:22
　Is she k. as she is fair? 210:2
　K.. cheerful, merry 231:13
　less than k. 185:7
　makes one wond'rous k. 89:2
　nor to his k. 242:14

occasion of this k. 243:13
　of a transcendental k. 92:21
　or grows by k. 80:17
　rather more than k. 18:5
　seek for k. relief 39:14
　squamous, omnipotent, and k. 42:2
　There is a lady sweet and k. 7:22
Kindle: cannot k. when we will 11:17
Kindles in clothes a wantonness 104:11
Kindliness: cool k. of sheets 41:17
Kindly: never lov'd sae k. 48:5
Kindness: acts of k. and of love 248:18
　any k. that I can show 98:15
　beauty lives with k. 210:2
　kill a wife with k. 208:7
　K. in another's trouble 96:6
　milk of human k. 197:14
　tak a cup o' k. yet 48:7
　with lavish k. 101:16
　Woman Killed with K. 105:3
Kindred: k. points of heaven 248:6
　Table of K. 172:16
King: All the k.'s horses 156:1
　anointed k. 206:12
　as I have served the K. 245:11
　cat may look at a k. 57:2
　conscience of the k. 187:12
　Cotton is K. 62:6
　despised and dying k. 215:8
　doth hedge a k. 189:13
　every inch a k. 195:20
　farewell k. 206:15
　follow the K. 226:17
　Glory to the new-born K. 241:15
　God bless the K. 50:15
　God save our gracious k. 54:22
　God save the k. 24:40, 54:22
　great and mighty k. 176:2
　heart and stomach of a k. 82:9
　Heaven's all-gracious K. 181:10
　Heaven's eternal K. 145:6
　Honour the K. 37:4
　I serv'd my k. 193:1
　I was a K. in Babylon 102:15
　In sleep a k. 211:10
　in the k.'s highway 206:16
　is a dish for a k. 210:5
　Is't not the k.? 195:20
　K. asked 143:13
　k. can do no wrong 38:7
　k. enjoys his own 160:20
　K. found her so different 103:14
　k. is but a man 191:12
　k. may make a nobleman 47:18
　k. never dies 38:6
　K., observing with judicious eyes 234:3
　K. of all kings 5:11
　K. of France went up the hill 156:6
　K. of Glory 104:2, 169:4, 169:5
　K. of infinite space 187:3
　K. of peace 104:2
　K. of shreds and patches 189:2
　k. over the Water 7:18
　k. sate on the rocky brow 51:19
　k. shall be contented 206:16
　k. shall do it 206:16
　k. should have bought it 63:26
　K. sits in Dunfermline 16:12
　K. that ruled 54:20
　K. to Oxford sent 43:3, 234:3
　K. was in his counting-house 158:1
　K.'s daughter 16:13, 169:19
　k.'s name is a tower of strength 207:11
　Long live the k. 69:31
　lose the name of k. 206:16
　more royalist than the k. 9:5
　mortal temples of a k. 206:15
　my duties as K. 81:5
　My God and K. 103:18

my K. and my God 170:13
no k. could govern 79:4
not offended by a k. 150:6
passing brave to be a k. 139:9
patriot k. 40:3
Ruin seize thee, ruthless K. 97:4
running 'fore the k. 191:15
see the last k: 142:15
serve God and the K. 153:7
set before the K. 158:1
So excellent a k. 185:11
stood for his K. 43:12
Teach me, my God and K. 103:21
that an idle k. 230:12
To be a Pirate K. 93:16
Under which K. 190:34
vantage of a k. 191:15
What must the k. do now? 206:16
Who is the K. of glory? 169:5
year's pleasant k. 152:6
Kingdom: best walls of this k. 69:7
children of the k. 31:6
enter into the k. of heaven 31:37
God hath numbered thy k. 29:18
His k. stretch 239:13
k. against k. 32:11
k. for it was too small 190:23
k. of daylight 107:17
K. of God is within you 33:31
k. of heaven 30:3, 31:27, 167:32
my k. for a horse! 207:12
My large k. for a little grave 206:16
My mind to me a k. is 80:17
never gave you k. 195:5
no peasant in my k. 102:18
of such is the k. of God 32:34
rich man to enter into the k. 32:1
theirs is the k. of heaven 30:11
thine everlasting k. 168:4
thine is the k. 30:22
Thy k. come 30:22
thy k. is divided 29:18
when thou comest into thy K. 33:40
Kingdoms: good states and k. 121:9
Kingly: k. crop 72:12
State is K. 147:17
Kings: as happy as k. 221:14
bind their k. 172:7
blood of queens and k. 120:4
Captains and the K. depart 127:4
change my state with k. 210:13
Conquering k. their titles take 59:18
descended of so many royal k. 183:6
Divine Right of K. 164:2
dread and fear of k. 202:5
in the hearts of k. 202:5
keep even k. in awe 72:10
K. are by God appointed 5:9
k. of the sea 11:13
lays his icy hand on k. 216:24
Mad k.! 193:3
mirror of all Christian k. 191:5
must k. neglect 191:14
Of cabbages—and k. 57:22
of K.' palaces 108:16
of the death of k. 206:15
politeness of k. 134:18
royal throne of k., 206:7
son of a hundred K. 124:11
sport of k. 222:13
There were three k. 48:22
walk with K. 125:16
when k. are arming 180:15
womb of royal k. 206:7
Kinquering Congs 219:16
Kinship with the stars 142:2
Kipling: Rudyards cease from k. 220:8
Kirk: walk together to the k. 66:6
Kirkconnell: On fair K. lea! 16:7

Kiss: Ae fond k. 48:3
colder thy k. 52:16
does it with a k. 243:5
Gin a body k. a body 48:11
immortal with a k.! 138:12
k. and part 78:29
k. and tell 68:8
K. me, Hardy 153:1
K. me times a thousand 59:1
k. of the sun 99:2
K. till the cow comes home 19:23
Or leave a k. 117:19
rough male k. of blankets 41:17
seal with a righteous k. 208:5
Then come k. me 209:5
Kissed: Curtsied when you have,
and k. 208:9
had I wist, before I k. 17:3
k. again with tears 229:7
k. for forty years 178:6
k. her little sister 149:9
k. him 32:22
K. the girls 155:15
k. the lovely grass 42:4
k. the maiden 158:8
lips that I have k. 189:20
toyed and k. 89:10
Kisses: fear thy k. 215:11
feeds on the aërial k. 214:9
my k. bring again 201:3
of many thousand k. 182:19
play'd at cards for k. 135:14
Stolen k. 112:5
wastin' Christian k. 126:12
With k. four 120:13
Kissing: K. with golden face 211:2
when the k. had to stop 45:11
Kitbag: Pack up your troubles in
your old k. 12:14
Kith: All their k. and kin 110:9
Kits: every cat had seven k. 155:3
Knappeth the spear 169:21
Knave: K. of Hearts 57:12, 157:15
petty sneaking k. 38:14
spy a k. in drinking 180:19
Knaves: 'Gainst k. and thieves 209:20
of fools and k. 45:18
Knee: every k. should bow 36:15
k. deep in clover 129:13
Kneel: I'll k. down 196:6
k. before the Lord 170:23
Kneels: Not one k. to another 242:14
is done upon his k. 184:6
Knees: Down on your k. 125:10
k. that summons me 208:12
like a rising k. 198:10
overpowering k. 50:23
ring fancy's k. 51:24
their k. is rung 202:1
toll the k. of parting day 67:15
Knelt down with angry prayers 97:8
Knew: and k. their mind 105:13
better than he k. 106:17
could carry all he k. 82:15
if they k. it before 95:8
they perfectly k. 108:1
which all men k. 128:3
Knife: keen k. see not the wound 228:25
like a whetted k. 197:14
smyler with the k. 141:4
war even to the k. 60:17
with a carving k. 50:20
Knight: gentle k. 158:10
k. dubbed with unhatched rapier 219:9
K. of the Sorrowful Countenance 209:18
K. without fear 59:8
many a k. 9:4
17:11

Knight (cont.)
  never was k.   180:9
  varray parfit gentil k.   60:10
  what can ail thee, K. at arms?   120:10
  White K. said   58:10
Knightly: ever the k. years were
  gone   102:15
Knit: Come, k. hands   144:1
Knits up the ravell'd sleave   198:13
Knitting: twisted braids of lilies k.   144:3
Knock: k. and it shall be opened   30:33
  k., breathe, shine, and seek   77:12
  k. the breast   147:10
  stand at the door, and k.   37:15
Knock-down argument   58:5, 79:14
Knocked: k. about a bit   133:3
  k. 'em in the Old Kent Road   62:5
  K. on my sullen heart   221:24
Knocking: k. on the moonlit door   73:4
  Some one came k.   73:10
Knocks: he k. you down   96:3
  k. at the doors   108:16
  Whoever k.   199:17
Knolled: bells have k. to church   183:19
Knolls: search the grassy k.   58:13
Knot: certain k. of peace   217:1
  this k. intrinsicate   183:4
Knot-grass: bunches of k.   120:4
Knots: true-love k.   66:11
Knotted and combined locks   186:7
Know: all the world doth k.   69:23
  all ye need to k.   120:23
  dangerous to k.   129:4
  did I k. till then   247:2
  does not k. himself   86:17
  few could k.   248:3
  greater than we k.   245:18
  hate anyone that we k.   101:13
  I do not k.   59:2
  I k. not why   229:7
  I k. thee not   191:1
  K. all there is to be knowed   96:17
  k. not why I am sad   102:4
  k. one half as much   96:17
  k. that I am God   169:21
  K. then thyself   164:17
  k. thyself   9:12
  K. you the land   94:16
  now I k. in part   35:22
  now I k. it   89:26
  one land I k.   42:7
  rest who does not k.?   160:2
  shall k. it no more   171:1
  that a man might k.   194:22
  That thy brain must k.   215:6
  that we k. not of   187:13
  then shall I k.   35:22
  this I k.   239:1
  To k. all   219:22
  to k. for whom the bell tolls   77:23
  we k. in part   35:21
  We k. our will is free   114:24
  we k. thee   232:9
  What do I k.?   149:4
  What should they k. of England   125:4
  what you don't k.   240:15
  ye shall k. them   31:4
  yet I k.   246:8
  you yourselves do k.   194:12
Knoweth: he that loveth not k. not   37:9
Knowing: For lust of k.   86:8
  Greater than their k.   127:15
  though without k.   79:10
Knowledge: all k. to be my province   15:9
  by words without k.   25:39
  climbing after k.   139:10
  diabolical k.   216:8
  full of the k. of the Lord   28:3
  he that increaseth k.   26:37

  in k. of whom   166:14
  innocent of the k.   199:5
  Is k. that I, too, have wept   151:8
  K. comes   228:12
  K. itself is power   15:12
  k. of a lifetime   242:3
  k. of nothing   74:1
  love and k. of you   183:8
  Mr. Weller's k. of London   75:20
  must carry k. with him   115:18
  nor k...in the grave   27:2
  out-topping k.   11:20
  price for k.   233:17
  spirit of..k.   28:1
  such k. is not for us   109:2
  taken away the key of k.   33:12
  to follow k.   230:14
  too much k.   164:18
  tree of k.   23:10
  what I don't know isn't k.   20:5
  where k. fails   224:14
  whether there be k.   35:21
Known: all desires k.   167:4
  even as also I am k.   35:22
  hast never k.   121:4
  k. a better day   180:4
  k. by the sobriquet   75:8
  k. of old   127:3
  k. upon earth   170:4
  safer than a k. way   101:5
  seen and k.   230:13
  than have ever k.   75:34
  till I am k.   113:22
  what Elysium have ye k.   120:17
  what should not be k.   86:8
Knows: everybody k.   220:3
  He k. the world   86:17
  k. not what to do   155:7
  k. nothing higher   78:18
  k. this out of the book   75:2
  k. what he fights for   71:5
  k. wot's wot   75:31
  k. ye not   55:23
  no man k.   73:2
  That now she k.   238:4
  where no one k.   84:16
  who k. how he may report   147:7
  who k., who k.?   86:9
Knuts: Colonel of the K.   244:14
Köhln, a town of monks   66:9
Kosciusko: as K. fell   54:5
Kosmos: untented K.   221:16
Kotched: will be k. out late   101:1
Kruger: killing K. with your mouth   124:9
Kubla Khan: did K.   66:14
Kultur: Wenn ich Kultur höre   117:5

                      L

Labor omnia vicit   237:5
Laborare: orare est l.   10:4
Laborious: live l. days   145:1
Labour: all ye that l.   31:20
  brow of l.   45:15
  for two days' l.   242:3
  Honest l.   72:18
  I'll l. night and day   46:20
  In works of l.   239:10
  l. and sorrow   170:18
  l. and the wounds   64:10
  l. is but lost   171:22
  l. of an age   147:12
  L. of love   36:23
  l. we delight in   198:18
  learn and l. truly   168:1
  Learn to l.   133:28
  Mountains will be in L   107:21
  Never-flinching l.   237:5
  of all his l.   26:34

Six days shalt thou l. 167:9
sore l.'s bath 198:13
time for l. 224:2
true success is to l. 221:6
With profitable l. 191:15
work, and to his l. 171:3
Labourer: l. is worthy of his hire 33:5
Labouring: sweet to the l. man 46:13
Labours: Children sweeten l. 14:20
take of my l. 113:22
who from their l. rest 111:12
Labyrinth: peopled l. of walls 213:17
Labyrinthine: down the l. ways 232:7
Lace: Arsenic and Old L. 123:4
erring l. 104:11
l. my bodice blue 112:8
Laced: aptly l. 172:19
Laces for a lady 127:10
Lack: can I l. nothing 169:2
l. of many a thing 211:1
Lacked: if he l. anything 76:4
If I l. any thing 104:1
Lackey: like a l. 191:15
Lack-lustre: with l. eye 183:16
Lacks: If anyone anything l. 93:32
Lad: Augustus was a chubby l. 105:15
could that l. be I? 221:20
l. that is gone 221:20
many a lightfoot l. 111:6
When I was a l. 93:10
Ladder: l. set up on earth 23:29
traffic of Jacob's l. 232:10
wiv a l. and some glasses 18:27
Laddie: Highland l. gone 118:15
Laden: and are heavy l. 31:20
too deeply l. 215:11
Ladies: come from a l.' seminary 92:3
Good-night l. 189:10
meet for l.' love 110:2
of l. most deject 188:6
on the tables of young l. 137:5
out of the l.' company 182:6
Ladling: While l. butter 176:4
Lads: cheer up, my l.! 88:18
Come lasses and l. 3:22
Golden l. and girls 184:22
l. that will die in their glory 111:2
Though your l. are far away 87:4
Lady: ain't a l. livin' 62:4
called her his l. fair 128:1
Charlotte was a married l. 232:4
Colonel's L. 126:8
Dance, Little L. 69:10
experience of the l. 83:1
Finish, good l. 182:23
I do not [know the l.] 129:17
I think this l. to be my child 196:3
Laces for a l. 127:10
l. doth protest too much 188:13
l. in the case 51:23, 89, 29, 91:4
L. of Shalott 227:25
l. that's known as Lou 182:1
like a dying l. 215:14
My fair l. 156:14
My L. Bountiful 83:18
My l. sweet 184:20
never won fair l.! 91:26
Our L. of Pain 224:5
see a fine l. 157:17
There is a l. sweet and kind 7:22
Weep no more, my l. 87:10
young l. named Bright 45:24
Ladybird, ladybird, fly away
home 156:7
Lady-smocks all silver-white 196:19
Laid: for ever l. 97:10
he l. many heavy loads 83:12
l. me down with a will 221:23
let me be l. 209:9

Lord hath l. on him 28:21
So he l. down his arms! 106:22
sun is l. to sleep 117:11
These l. the world away 41:16
Lain for a century 228:20
Lair: fox from his l. 97:2
Laissez faire, laissez passer 174:2
Lake: Beside the l. 247:3
bosom of the l. 229:17
Galilean l. 145:2
wither'd from the l. 120:10
Lake-reflected sun 214:9
Lakes: shakes across the l. 229:10
Lalage: I've lost L.! 127:8
Lalagen: dulce ridentem L. amabo 109:6
Lalun is a member of the most
ancient profession 128:21
Lamb: as a l. to the slaughter 28:21
go to bed with the l. 41:4
he who made the L. 39:3
holy L. of God 38:16
L., the frolic 246:3
l. was sure to go 99:5
Little L., who made thee? 39:9
Mary had a little l. 99:5
one dead l. is there! 134:1
save one little ewe l. 25:3
song about a l. 39:8
to the shorn l. 220:12
wolf also shall dwell with the l. 28:2
Lambs: gather the l. 28:14
Lame dogs over stiles 123:15
Lament: l. not the days 219:1
universal Nature did l. 144:21
Lamentation: With an empire's l. 228:24
Lamented: ye have not l. 31:19
Lamp: Slaves of the L. 11:5
smell too strong of the l. 220:15
unlit l. 45:8
When the l. is shattered 213:16
Lamps: change old l. for new ones? 10:10
l. are going out 98:17
l. shone o'er fair women 50:23
Lancaster: time-honour'd L. 206:11
Lancelot: Not L., nor another 226:19
Sang Sir L. 227:24
Lancers: six stalwart l. 243:1
Land: abroad throughout the l. 41:10
ancestral l. 108:14
by l. an' sea 128:4
by sea as by l.! 90:18
charter of the l. 232:13
cleaner, greener l. 126:14
crimes of this guilty l. 42:14
England's green & pleasant L. 38:16
England's the one l. 42:7
every three acres of l. 142:24
exiles from our fathers' l. 181:7
far from the l. 149:17
fat of the l. 23:36
her l. reposed 230:1
Ill fares the l. 95:4
in a strange l.? 171:28
in the l. of Nod 23:19
in the l. of the living 169:7
Into the l. of my dreams 123:12
is heard in our l. 27:16
Know you the l. 94:16
l. flowing with milk 24:2
l. in which it seemed 228:16
l. is bright 64:10
l. is cultivated 142:24
L. of Hope and Glory 22:7
L. of our birth 124:17
l. of pure delight 239:15
l. of sand and ruin 224:11
l. of such dear souls 206:7
L. of the pilgrims' pride 217:14
L. where my fathers died 217:14

Land (cont.)
l. where the Bong-tree grows   131:7
l. which the Lord thy God giveth
   thee   167:12
law of the l.   137:17
livin' in the l.   62:4
make .. the pleasant l.   55:26
Marching to the Promised L.   18:8
my native l.!   180:6
No l. can compare unto thee!   212:7
O'er all the pleasant l.   102:11
o'er L. and Ocean   147:17
O'er the l. of the free   123:7
on sea or l.   247:13
out of the dead l.   81:23
out of the l. of the living   28:22
pleasant l. of counterpane   221:12
prepared the dry l.   170:22
stranger in a strange l.   23:37
Sweet l. of liberty   217:14
that dwell in the l.   27:31
There is a happy l.   250:12
There shall be no more l.   42:3
There's l. I see!   232:3
There's the l., or cherry-isle   104:8
thing of sea or l.?   147:5
this dear, dear l.   206:7
thro' the l. at eve   229:7
through the l.   79:3
to spy out the l.   24:14
traveller from an antique l.   214:5
Where lies the l.   64:12
where the l.   64:12
Landing grounds: fight on the l.   62:21
Landlady: l. can be reduced   130:14
Landlord: Come, l., fill the flowing
   bowl   3:21
Land-lubbers lying down below   6:20
Landmark: he that removeth his
   neighbour's l.   24:21
Lands: comes from the west l.   141:6
in faery l. forlorn   121:6
in lonely l.   226:9
l. beyond the sea   247:2
l. were fairly portioned   136:12
l. where the Jumblies live   131:4
less happier l.   206:7
though not of l.   249:11
tilled his l.   248:10
Landscape: glimmering l.   97:8
Landscapes: if l. were sold   220:23
one of those marine l.   76:9
Lane: lives down the l.   155:4
While there's a country l.   160:21
Language: best chosen l.   13:16
in our l. should perish   137:3
l. that would make your hair curl   93:26
l. was not powerful enough   75:4
Learned his great l.   44:10
My l. fails!   21:7
my l. is plain   101:3
no l. but a cry   227:11
obscurity of a learned l.   90:13
some entrance into the l.   15:4
use any l. you choose   91:23
Languages: great feast of l.   196:17
instructed in all the l.   74:25
l. living and dead   74:25
Languid: art thou l.   152:9
excite your l. spleen   92:22
Languors of virtue   224:4
Lank: long, and l.   65:18
Lap: chestnuts in her l.   197:5
Dropt in her L.   85:2
old enough to l.   242:20
Uncover, dogs, and l.   208:23
Lapidary inscriptions   115:5
Lapland is remarkable   114:13
Lards the lean earth   190:11

Large: as l. as life   58:9
I am l.   242:15
is not l.   151:7
Largest: Shout with the l.   75:18
Lark: Hark! hark! the l.   184:20
l. from her light wing   71:2
l., that tirra-lirra chants   210:5
l.'s on the wing   44:24
Like to the l.   210:13
no l. more blithe   37:29
We rise with the l.   41:4
Larks: and hear the l. so high   110:19
Four L. and a Wren   130:15
mount l. aloft   105:2
Larkspur listens   228:20
Lars Porsena of Clusium   136:8
Lasciate ogni speranza   72:5
Lascivious Moor   204:18
Lash: and l. the vice   59:7
Lass: Drink to the l.   216:19
every l. a queen   123:18
Highland l.!   248:7
l. so neat   137:15, 235:4
l. that loves a sailor!   73:18
l. unparallel'd   183:5
lover and his l.   184:12
Sweet l. of Richmond
   Hill   137:15, 235:4
Lasses: are spent among the l.   48:19
Come l. and lads   3:22
L. a'lilting   82:12
Lassie: but a l. yet   106:9
I love a l.   130:7
Last: Comes at the l.   206:15
conquered at l.   163:15
first shall be l.   32:3
give unto this l.   32:5
It did not l.   219:21
judge above his l.   163:13
L. came, and l. did go   145:2
l. man in   153:6
l., not least   193:19
l. of all   74:3
l. of life   45:4
l...of my desires   142:15
L. of the Mohicans   68:26
l. out a night in Russia   200:17
l. thing I shall do!   160:17
look thy l. on all things   73:3
noblest offspring is the l.   22:16
peace at the l.   153:12
poor l. I lay   182:19
to my l. dregs   79:21
will not l. the night   143:1
Lasting: What l. joys   242:19
Latch: Draw the l.   155:9
no l. ter de golden gate?   101:1
Latchet: whose shoe's l.   33:47
Late: and the bad die l.   72:16
comes l. in life   113:11
honour'd me of l.   198:5
l. and soon   249:5
not too l. to-morrow   11:4
sinners'll be kotched out l.   101:1
So l. into the night   52:13
too l. to seek a newer world   230:15
Latericiam: quam l. accepisset   52:21
Latin: small L.   118:6
Latter: carry off the l.   162:1
Laud: Glory, l., and honour   152:7
Laudamus: Te Deum l.   10:6
Laudant illa sed ista legunt   139:23
Laudator temporis acti   108:2
Laugh: do we not l.?   201:27
l. a siege to scorn   200:2
L. and the world laughs   243:3
l. at any mortal thing   51:22
l. at gilded butterflies   196:6
l. at the sight   108:12

l. broke into a thousand pieces 18:19
L. thy girlish laughter 239:5
l. to scorn 199:20
l. to see how fools are vexed 72:18
loud l. 95:5
made a cat l. 163:6
make myself l. at everything 19:7
shall l. and sing 170:3
Laughable: single l. little mouse 107:21
Laughed: L. in the sun 42:4
little dog l. 155:17
When the first baby l. 18:19
Laughing: and he l. said to me 39:8
And l. is heard 39:11
l. fellow-rover 141:4
Laughter: her sweet l. 109:6
l. and the love of friends 21:12
L. holding both his sides 144:13
l., learnt of friends 42:11
l. of a fool 26:39
l. of her heart 99:10
Laugh thy girlish l. 239:5
man is distinguished..by..l. 1:15
'mid l. free 8:1
mirth and l. 51:15
Our sincerest l. 215:5
present l. 209:5
under running l. 232:7
weeping and with l. 136:16
Launch'd a thousand ships 138:12
Laurel: and the l. stands tall 94:16
Apollo's l. bough 139:2
L. is green for a season 224:10
l., the palms and the paean 224:9
Laurels: l. all are cut 17:1, 111:8
l. to paeans 63:14
O ye l. 144:20
worth all your l. 52:7
Laus: non ultima l. est 108:11
Lave: Let the l. go by me 221:15
Lavender water tinged with
pink 131:1
Lavinia: She is L. 208:25
Lavinian: and her L. strand 236:3
Lavish: with l. kindness 101:16
Law: all men know the l. 181:13
become a universal l. 119:11
British criminal l. 78:7
come to destroy the l. 30:15
Dusty purlieus of the l. 227:15
his own a l. to each 231:8
I, my Lords, embody the L. 91:17
If the l. supposes that 75:10
Ignorance of the l. 181:13
impose the l. of peace 236:18
is the chief l. 63:11
l. is an ass 75:10
L. is the true embodiment 91:17
L. of the Jungle 126:9
l. of the land 137:17
l.'s delay 187:13
moral l. within me 119:10
more ought l. to weed it out 14:21
my l. the seventh time 161:15
Necessity hath no l. 71:12, 224:13
Nor l., nor duty 250:7
Old father antick, the l. 190:7
this is l., I will maintain 5:9
this is the royal L. 69:1
to keep this l. 167:6
unalterable l. 142:1
unchanging l. of God 160:22
unwritten l. 72:10
windward of the l. 62:8
windy side of the l. 209:17
without the L. 127:6
Lawful: all things are l. 35:18
is it not l. 32:5
is l. prize 98:4

on their l. occasions 172:9
that which is l. 29:13
Lawn: hurrying thro' the l. 229:19
l. about the shoulders 104:11
L. as white 210:9
Lawns: fair with orchard l. 227:3
grazing on the l. 138:9
house with l. 221:22
l. and avenues 125:8
Laws: as for Thy l. 103:22
base l. of servitude 79:19
breaking up of l. 226:18
drama's l. 116:28
France, mother..of l. 20:14
here obedient to their l. 217:4
l. and learning die 138:4
L. are inoperative 63:21
L. were made to be broken 154:10
l. which keep the planets 166:5
Unequal l. 230:12
war has its l. 153:9
who should make the l. 86:12
Lawyers: kill all the l. 192:9
Woe unto you, l.! 33:12
Lay: he l. low 100:19
l. distracted in the ditch 71:1
l. field to field 27:25
L. her i' the earth 189:22
l. it on with a trowel 76:15
l. like a warrior 245:5
l. my bones amongst you 245:10
L. not up for yourselves 30:23
L. up for yourselves 30:24
let us l. aside every weight 36:35
may l. her young 170:13
not where to l. his head 31:7
where he l. 214:2
Lays: constructing tribal l. 125:13
She l. it on 68:3
Lazy: l. leaden-stepping hours 148:6
looking l. at the sea 126:15
Lea: standing on this pleasant l. 249:5
wind slowly o'er the l. 97:8
Lead: are lapp'd in l. 18:13
gently l. those 28:14
l. but to the grave 97:12
L., kindly Light 153:15
l. me forth 169:2
l. such dire attack 136:13
L. us, Heavenly Father 81:2
l. us not into temptation 30:12
life is this I l.! 140:6
little child shall l. them 28:2
scald like molten l. 196:1
thy hand l. me 172:1
to l. a new life 167:22
Leaden: l.-stepping hours 148:6
With l. foot 112:17
Leaders: blind l. of the blind 31:30
with l. of mankind 108:11
Leadest thou that heifer 120:21
Leadeth: he l. me 181:8
that l. to destruction 31:1
Leads men to this hell 212:2
Leaf: are in tiny l. 44:1
If I were a dead l. 214:3
last red l. 227:8
lift me as..a l. 214:3
no l. upon the forest bare 213:11
Right as an aspes l. 60:27
where the dead l. fell 120:7
yellow l. 199:32
Leafy: a l. thicket 131:3
in the l. month 66:3
top of l. Olympus 109:20
League: Half a l. 225:20
she hadna sail'd a l. 16:5
Lean: lards the l. earth 190:11
l. and flashy songs 145:3

Lean (cont.)
l. and pale 215:14
l. dog 137:13
Leaning: L. across the bosom of the urgent West 41:8
L. together 81:12
Leans her cheek 207:21
Leap: an easy l. 190:9
great l. in the dark 105:10
l. into the dark 42:15
l. up to my God 138:14
look before you ere you l. 49:28
Look ere thou l. 234:15
with a l. and a bound 67:2
Leaps: cataract l. in glory 229:10
heart l. up 247:10
Lear: How pleasant to know Mr. L. 130:17
Learn: craft so long to l. 105:6
gladly wolde he l. 60:14
I am to l. 201:6
l. about women 126:7
l. and labour truly 168:1
L. to labour 133:28
to l. their letters 215:19
We live and l. 163:18
Learned: naturally l. 80:3
fair and l. 43:2
Jonson's l. sock 144:19
l. and conn'd by rote 194:18
l. body wanted loyalty 234:3
l. his great language 44:10
l. the secrets of the grave 161:9
l. to look on nature 248:19
never l. anything from history 102:2
never l. to stray 98:1
of a l. language 90:13
this l. man 139:2
Learning: enough of l. to misquote 52:4
laws and l. 138:4
l. here in London 126:13
little l. 164:9
loyal body wanted l. 234:3
Men of polite l. 103:7
much l. doth make thee mad 34:50
nonsense and l. 95:20
weight of l. 227:21
Whence is thy l. 89:27
Learnt: and l. nothing 80:11
laughter, l. of friends 42:11
They have l. nothing 225:2
Lease: and summer's l. 210:12
l. of my true love 211:14
Least: last, not l. 193:19
Myself not l. 230:13
one of the l. of these my brethren 32:17
Leather: sick o' wastin' l. 126:14
Leathern: flits by on l. wing 67:12
Leave: how I l. my country! 163:3
I l. my work 55:3
Intreat me not to l. thee 24:35
L. her to heaven 186:13
l. me here a little 228:4
l. my character behind 216:17
l. my little wooden hut 141:21
l. the bottle 74:21
l. the Wise 85:6
L. then thy foolish ranges 235:8
Or l. a kiss 117:19
to l. the scene 108:13
why dost thou l. me? 68:14
Leaven: Pleasure with pain for l. 224:1
Leaves: among the l. 121:4
as the l. grow on the tree 250:5
bursts come crowding through the l.! 11:18
cover'd up in l. 121:5
fond of handling the l. 216:8
How green are thy l.! 179:16
if my l. are falling 214:4

l. and flowers do cover 240:11
l. dead are driven 214:1
l. on the trees 110:5
l. them all about 125:3
l. they are so green 16:18
Like withered l. 214:4
only l. me fifty more 110:15
put on its l. again 86:9
Shatter your l. 144:20
shows his hoar l. 189:18
tender l. of hope 192:14
Thick as autumnal l. 146:4
Ulysses l. once more 213:12
When yellow l. 211:8
With lisp of l. 223:28
Leaving: like the l. it 197:13
Leavy: summer first was l. 204:9
Lectures: Mrs. Caudle's Curtain L. 113:10
Led: hath l. me 213:13
He l. his regiment from behind 91:5
L. go! 128:15
l. us away captive 171:28
Leda: and, as L. 161:9
Lee: Of the River L. 173:1
settled on the l. 50:4
Leer: assent with civil l. 165:6
Lees: and the mere l. 198:19
drink life to the l. 230:13
Left: as we that are l. 38:2
better to be l. 68:16
for a handful of silver he l. 44:9
I have a l. shoulder-blade 92:11
l. him alone with his glory 245:7
l. me naked 193:1
let not thy l. hand 30:20
locks which are l. you 218:22
Thou hast l. behind 248:20
We are l...alone 247:11
What of soul was l. 45:11
Left-hand: Into a l. shoe 58:14
Leg: he has a l. 142:10
nursing his l. 74:13
took him by the left l. 155:16
what l. you shall put into your breeches 114:16
which l. goes after which? 71:1
You make a l. 207:1
Legem: iudicium parium..vel per l. terrae 137:17
Leges: Silent enim l. inter arma 63:21
Legion: L. of the lost ones 125:6
my name is L. 32:29
Legiones: Vare, l. redde 52:20
Legions: give me back my l. 52:20
Legislation: foundation of morals and l. 22:8
Legislators of the world 215:15
Legs: never have stood upon his l. 74:4
slimy things did crawl with l. 65:14
took off his l. 106:22
Walk under his huge l. 193:11
when his l. were smitten off 213:5
who loves to fold his l. 115:15
Leicester Square: Farewell L. 244:7
Leichter: queen of Scots is this day l. 82:5
Leisure: at l. marry'd 68:13
is never at l. 115:15
polish it at l. 80:2
repent at l. 68:13
Lemon: squeeze out of a l. 90:2
Lemons: Oranges and l. 157:6
Lemon-trees: where the l. bloom? 94:16
Lend: Few l. 234:9
Her eyes the glow-worm l. thee 104:13
l. me your ears 194:3
l. the eye 191:9
l. us Thine aid! 101:14

such grace did l. her 210:2
Will l. his horse to go 69:23
Lender: nor a l. be 185:21
Lenders: pen from l.' books 195:11
Length: A line is l. 83:10
drags its slow l. 164:11
dreary l. 73:21
fall'n at l. 229:1
go the l. of twopence 220:23
l. of days 224:2
Lengthen: till the shades l. 153:12
Lengthy: wordy and l. epistle 119:7
Lente: l., l., currite noctis equi 138:14
Leopard: l. [change] his spots 29:6
l. shall lie down with the kid 28:2
Lesbia mine, let's live 58:26
Less: And the little l. 43:11
beautifully l. 172:19
l. he spoke 173:13
L. than the dust 107:10
l. will you settle to one 126:7
neither more nor l. 58:5
nicely-calculated l. 247:6
Lessen from day to day 57:6
Lesson: l. you should heed 105:4
still harder l.! 165:20
Lessons: reason they're called l. 57:6
Let: will not l. my play run 73:13
Lethe: on L. wharf 186:9
Lethean: drunken of things L. 224:10
Letter: l. killeth 56:7
l. killeth 36:1
not of the l. 36:1
To change the name, and not the
l. 8:6
Letters: l. for a spy 127:10
No arts; no l. 105:9
pause awhile from l. 117:2
to learn their l. 215:19
Lettuce: eating too much l. 166:2
Level: lone and l. sands 214:7
Levellers wish to level down 114:15
Leviathan: draw out l. 26:2
there is that L. 171:4
Levity: little judicious l. 221:9
Levy: foreign l. 199:4
Lewd: Certain l. fellows 34:40
Lex: Salus populi suprema est l. 63:11
Lexicographer: a writer of dic-
tionaries 114:4
Liable: are l. to error 133:8
Liar: and a fluent l. 126:21
He is a l. 34:12, 37:12
Pagett, M.P., was a l. 126:21
they only answered 'Little l.!' 21:9
Liars: All men are l. 171:14
fears may be l. 64:10
L. ought to have good memories 216:27
Libelli: pro captu lectoris. . fata
l. 141:16
Liberal: a l. education 103:7, 220:5
Is either a little L. 91:21
Liberal Party: watchword of the
great L. 41:11
Liberté! Égalité! Fraternité! 9:7
l.! que de crimes. . en ton nom! 176:8
Libertine: puff'd and reckless l. 185:20
Liberty: as primordial condition
of L. 15:21
conceived in l. 132:8
Enjoy such l. 134:19
give me l. 103:10
given l. to man 71:17
in doubtful things, l. 19:2
L.! Equality! Fraternity! 9:7
l. of the individual 142:22
l. plucks justice 200:14
L.! thou art 51:9
L.'s in every blow 49:1

life and l., and the pursuit of
happiness 113:2
life, l. and the pursuit of happiness 8:9
Sweet land of l. 217:14
thy chosen music, L.! 248:13
to proclaim l. 29:2
tree of l. 113:3
wrote at l. 39:16
Liberty-Hall: This is L. 95:26
Library: circulating l. in a town 216:8
Libre: né l., et partout il est dans les
fers 177:18
Licentious: all l. passages 90:13
rapacious and l. soldiery 47:9
Licentiousness: uncontrouled l. 83:7
Licht: Mehr L.! 95:1
Lick: l. the bloomin' boots 125:11
l. the dust 170:9
no time to l. it into form 49:8
Licks: pride that l. the dust 165:9
Liddell: this is Mrs. L. 219:20
Lids: eternal l. apart 121:8
sweeter than the l. of Juno's eyes 210:8
Lie: all before us l. 140:12
Beaumont l. a little further 118:4
country folks would l. 184:12
do not l. awake 242:14
dost thou l. so low? 193:18
fain wald l. down 16:8
here let her l.! 79:20
I cannot tell a l. 239:2
In a cowslip's bell I l. 208:20
is a true l. 118:16
isn't told a l. 127:10
let him l. 80:19
let me l. 221:23
l. as quietly among the graves 81:6
L. at the proud foot 193:8
l. circumstantial 184:14
l. direct 184:14
L. heavy on him 83:12
l. in her pavilion 182:15
l. in the Soul 118:16
l. open unto the fields 249:4
l. too deep for tears 246:14
l. upon the daisies 92:21
loves to l. with me 183:13
makes me down to l. 181:8
nicer to l. in bed 130:10
obedient to their laws we l. 217:4
on my couch I l. 247:5
sweets compacted l. 104:7
they l. cold and low 214:1
to l. abroad 249:14
under Dust to l. 85:5
Lied: but it l. 21:17
Or being l. about 125:14
Lies: before us l. 149:1
don't deal in l. 125:14
father of l. 34:10
he l. fast asleep 85:1
Heaven l. about us 246:11
here l. my wife 79:20
In the cradle where it l. 202:1
in thy possession l. 183:5
l. beneath your spell? 107:9
l. deep-meadowed 227:3
l. where he longed to be 221:23
Matilda told such Dreadful L. 21:8
now l. he there 194:6
poor buffer l. low 243:1
Rest is L. 85:6
that way madness l. 195:7
thy father l. 208:11
tills the field and l. beneath 230:10
Life: all that l. can afford 115:14
all the days of my l. 167:32
all your l. 75:21
Anythin' for a quiet l. 75:33

Life (cont.)

balance with this l.   250:7
bear a charmed l.   200:10
before the fire of l.   129:20
bitterness of l.   56:7
blessings of this l.   166:31
Brief l.   152:10
business of l.   240:15
busy scenes of crowded l.   117:1
careless of the single l.   227:12
chances of this mortal l.   167:27
changing scenes of l.   225:7
comes late in l.   113:11
conduct is three-fourths of our l.   12:9
cool sequester'd vale of l.   98:1
days of my l.   169:2
death after l.   219:10
death of each day's l.   198:13
Demands..my l.   239:17
ever saw in my l.   238:20
ever saw in your l.   240:14
every day of my l.   220:23
fever of l. is over   153:12
For death and l.   154:13
fought for l.   219:6
full of l., and splendour   47:14
give to baser l.   183:3
Give to me the l. I love   221:15
giveth his l.   34:12
he is tired of l.   115:14
he that findeth his l.   31:16
her l. serene   230:1
her lonely l.   162:6
His l. was gentle   194:24
I am..the l.   34:19
I will drink l.   230:13
I will give thee a crown of l.   37:14
I would spend my l.   115:12
in a l. to come   164:14
in his pleasure is l.   169:8
In l., in death   135:17
in l.'s feast   198:13
in poetry, no less than in l.   12:5
in that state of l.   168:1
In the midst of l.   168:19
in this transitory l.   167:21
In tragic l.   142:4
intend to lead a new l.   167:22
jump the l. to come   198:3
knot intrinsicate of l.   183:4
large as l.   58:9
last of l.   45:4
lay hold on eternal l.   36:31
Lay hold on l.   149:1
leadeth unto l.   31:2
l. and liberty   113:2
L. flies   85:6
l. for a man like me   221:15
L. for l.   24:7
l. heroic   147:9
L. is a jest   89:26
l. is a watch   224:2
l. is an incurable disease   69:19
L. is as tedious   193:5
l. is everywhere a state   116:23
L. is fading   175:6
L. is good   102:17
L. is just one damned thing   111:20
l. is most jolly   184:1
L. is mostly froth and bubble   96:6
L. is real!   133:26
L. is the desert   251:1
l. is very sweet   40:8
L. is with such all beer and skittles   53:8
l., liberty, and the pursuit of
     happiness   8:9
L., like a dome   213:10
l. of man   105:9
l. of men on earth   20:2

l. of sensations   122:8
l. of struggles   237:5
l. on the ocean wave   179:3
l. piled on l.   230:13
l. so short   105:6
L., the shadow of death   224:1
l. the solitude   251:1
l. time's fool   190:22
l. was duty   107:6
L.! we've been long together   17:8
L. with its way   149:1
L. worth living?   173:15
L.'s but a span   204:29
L.'s but a walking shadow   200:4
l.'s dull round   215:18
l.'s first native source   219:14
L.'s fitful fever   199:4
l.'s little day   135:16
L.'s Little Ironies   100:8
L.'s short span   108:17
light of a whole l. dies   40:13
live a l. half dead   147:4
long disease, my l.   165:5
love is of a man's l.   51:14
lucid intervals of l.   245:20
luxuries of l.   151:1
makes calamity of so long l.   187:13
man lay down his l.   34:20
Marriage is like l.   221:5
mine honour is my l.   201:1
most loathèd worldly l.   201:1
my l. is done   206:2
My l. is dreary   228:18
my l., my fate   228:20
my way of l.   199:32
need thou hast in l. of me   107:10
Not so much l.   120:7
Nothing in his l.   197:13
O world! O l.!   213:15
of a blameless l.   226:15
of a good man's l.   248:18
of glorious l.   150:3
of the Well of L.   85:9
our eternal l.   166:14
Our l.'s star   246:11
poorest he..hath a l. to live   174:12
preservation of l.   113:2
rat, have l.   196:11
reck'd not of the l. he lost   51:5
rest of his dull l.   19:9
resurrection and the l.   34:13
road of our l.   72:4
shamed l.   200:23
should have everlasting l.   34:1
should l. employ   89:17
slits the thin-spun l.   145:1
so make L., and Death   123:14
so sweet in l.   149:14
sober l.   166:10
sought the simple l.   70:23
sphere of private l.   141:20
spirit giveth l.   36:1
storm of l.   241:8
strange disease of modern l.   11:26
sublime of human l.   48:9
success in l.   161:11
such is L.   74:16
sunset of l.   53:16
that l. was Beauty   107:6
that neither..l.   35:10
There's the l. for ever   221:15
this gives l. to thee   210:12
This is alone L.   215:1
this our l.   142:7, 183:9
thorns of l.!   214:3
those who live call L.   215:9
Thou of l.   241:11
Though that l. is past   110:2
thought's the slave of l.   190:22

threatened its l. 56:5
Thy God, thy l. 235:8
time of this mortal l. 166:33
to a l. beyond l. 148:8
to breathe were l. 230:13
to let out l. 141:12
two tragedies in l. 212:22
torch of l. 135:9
uncorrupt l. 168:27
under a weary l. 187:13
vagrant gypsy l. 141:4
very spice of l. 70:16
voyages of their l. 194:19
walls about our l. 206:15
water of l. 37:27
what is this l. 72:13
when l.'s path is steep 109:10
when my l. began 247:10
Where there is l. 89:28
who saw l. steadily 11:14
whole l. long 135:11
wine of l. is drawn 198:19
wond'rous l. 140:6
worthy womman al hir l. 60:16
Life-blood of a master spirit 148:8
Lifeless ocean 66:15
Life-line: Throw out the l. 235:1
Lifetime: knowledge of a l. 242:3
l. of happiness 212:19
lit again in our l. 98:17
Lift: Here I l. them up to Thee 104:16
L. her with care 106:20
l. not hands of prayer 227:2
L. not the painted veil 215:9
L. not thy hands 85:13
l. up mine eyes 171:16
L. up thine eyes 149:1
L. up your heads 169:4
L. up your heart 241:14
L. up your voice 241:14
Light: all was l. 164:8
all ye stars and l. 122:24
are the l. of the world 30:13
armour of l. 35:14, 166:33
a-roving By the l. of the
  moon 52:15
as if bereav'd of l. 39:10
As if they fear'd the l. 222:6
as l. as air 47:6
better than l. 101:5
blinding l. 153:6
brings the l. 150:1
comes in the l. 64:10
danced by the l. of the moon 131:9
darkness and l. 172:1
dim religious l. 144:9
far faster than l. 45:24
from her l. wing 71:2
gave him l. 224:2
Give me a l. 101:5
gives a lovely l. 143:1
happy realms of l. 145:14
he beholds the l. 246:11
Heaven's l. for ever shines 213:10
Hesperus entreats thy l. 117:11
how my l. is spent 147:17
in celestial l. 246:7
In depths of burning l.! 83:14
In the dusk with the l. behind
  her! 93:34
in the l. of thought 215:4
infant crying for the l. 227:11
into the l. of things 248:14
into the world of l. 235:9
know what l. is 115:9
Lead, kindly L. 153:15
Let there be l. 23:5, 6
Let your l. so shine 30:14
l. a candle of understanding 29:30

l. a candle to the sun 216:28
l. deny'd? 147:17
l. dies 164:43
l. fantastic toe 144:13
l. in the dust 213:16
L. is the descent 236:15
l. of a whole life dies 40:13
l. of common day 246:11
l. of his countenance 170:4
l. of setting suns 248:19
l. of Terewth 73:26
l. of the bright world dies 40:13
l. quivering aspen 180:13
L. she was 149:8
l. shineth in darkness 33:44
l. such a candle 130:6
L. that Failed 128:19
l. that never was 247:13
L. thickens 199:6
l. to counterfeit 144:7
l. to guide 245:19
l.'s excess 179:11
long l. shakes 229:10
Lord is my l. 26:3
More l.! 95:1
my burden is l. 31:21
Night, the shadow of l. 224:1
No l. 145:13
Noose of L. 84:15
of crystal l. 84:3
or with taper l. 193:6
progeny of l. 146:19
pure and endless l. 235:11
pure and l. 122:17
pursuit of sweetness and l. 12:6
Put out the l. 205:16
seen a glorious l. 181:9
seen a great l. 27:31
Send thy l. and brilliancy 130:5
Servants of L. 11:5
something of angelic l. 248:5
spring of l. 65:2
such a l. affliction 152:16
sweetness and l. 12:6, 223:1
than your l. 249:13
that fierce l. 226:15
thy l. is come 29:1
to give l. 32:39
Trifles l. as air 205:8
Truth will come to l. 201:22
upon them hath the l. shined 27:31
we lose this l. 118:13
what l. through yonder window
  breaks? 207:20
Whose l. doth trample 235:10
with excess of l. 98:11
with the l. brown hair 87:15
Light Brigade: Forward the L.! 225:21
Lighten: L. our darkness 166:20
l. with celestial fire 172:11
Lighter: is l. than vanity 46:9
Lightfoot: many a l. lad 111:6
Lighthouse: took the sitivation at
  the l. 75:33
Lightning: by flashes of l. 67:7
done like l. 117:16
in thunder, l. 197:2
Lights: l. are dim and low 159:14
l. begin to twinkle 230:15
L. that do mislead the morn 201:3
They are but broken l. 227:5
Lightsome: of l. day 180:5
Light-winged Dryad 121:2
Like: and when l. her 86:4
I know what I l. 20:10
l. this sort of thing 132:12
look upon his l. again 185:15
with what thou dost l. 234:13
Liked it not and di'd 249:12

Likeness of anything 167:7
Likewise: Go, and do thou l. 33:8
Likings: made up of l. 129:5
Lilacs: breeding l. out of the dead land 81:23
Lilac-time: Kew in l. 154:16
Lilies: he feedeth among the l. 27:18
  l. in her hand 177:15
  l. of all kinds 210:8
  l. of the field 30:28
  l...of virtue 224:4
  L. that fester 211:11
  Lotos and l. 229:4
  pale lost l. 77:27
  twisted braids of l. 144:3
  white l. grow 54:11
Lillabullero 220:14
Lilting: I've heard them l. 82:12
Lily: but a bright l. grow 118:11
  glows the l. 86:6
  I see a l. 120:11
  l. of the valleys 27:13
  l. whispers 228:20
  Now folds the l. 229:17
  to paint the l. 193:6
  with a poppy or a l. 92:22
Limb: of wind and l. 49:22
Limbs of a poet 110:11
Limed: set l. twigs 38:13
Limelight: not sit in the l. 19:28
Limit: quiet l. of the world 230:11
Limited: must be thus far l. 142:22
  my wision's l. 75:27
  terse but l. 78:17
Limped: hare l. trembling 120:2
Limpopo: greasy L. River 128:14
Linages: Dos l. sólos..el tenir y el no tenir 59:11
Linden: On L., when the sun was low 53:15
Linden Lea: low in L. 18:10
Line: day without a l. 163:12
  in the high aesthetic l. 92:20
  l. is length 83:10
  l. upon l. 28:7
  lives along the l. 164:16
  Marlowe's mighty l. 118:5
  never blotted out a l. 117:12
  Pass it along the l.! 127:1
  thin red l. 178:12
  Thin red l. of 'eroes 127:22
  to cancel half a L. 85:12
  up the l. to death 179:4
  We carved not a l. 245:7
  will the l. stretch out 199:23
Linea: Nulla dies sine l. 163:12
Lineaments: moulded the changing l. 161:9
Linen: did not love clean l. 114:10
Linen-draper: I am a l. bold 69:23
Lines: of l. like these 53:6
  town-crier spoke my l. 188:7
  When in eternal l. 210:12
Linger longer Lucy 98:21
Lingering: sit l. here 235:9
  Something l. 92:12
Lingers: wisdom l. 228:12
Lining: There's a silver l. 87:4
Links: as strong as l. of iron 47:6
  with l. of iron 172:7
Lin-lan-lone of evening bells 226:11
Lion: as a roaring l. 37:7
  as bold as a l. 26:29
  better than a dead l. 27:1
  calf and the young l. 28:2
  hungry l. roars 204:3
  L. and the Lizard 85:1
  L. and the unicorn 156:8
  Save me from the l.'s mouth 169:1
  to rouse a l. 190:8

Lion-banner: with Freedom's l. 54:2
Lions: bears and l. growl 239:6
  stronger than l. 24:48
Lip: stiff upper l. 58:18
Lips: Be through my l. 214:4
  From my l. would flow 215:6
  hand is ever at his l. 120:24
  heaven be in these l. 138:12
  If you your l. would keep from slips 5:6
  Is crimson in thy l. 208:4
  Julia's l. do smile 104:8
  last I lay upon thy l. 182:19
  let me put my l. to it 74:21
  l...seal with a righteous kiss 208:5
  l. suck forth my soul 138:12
  moulded by the l. of man 231:1
  of unclean l. 27:27
  On a poet's l. 214:9
  pretty form to the l. 74:19
  request of his l. 168:33
  rosy l. and cheeks 211:16
  slug-horn to my l. 43:14
  take those l. away 201:3
  than her l.'s red 212:3
  those l. that I have kissed 189:20
  Truth from his l. 95:7
  truth sits upon the lips 11:21
  very good words for the l. 74:19
  when I ope my l. 201:8
  When the l. have spoken 213:16
  whom the l. of children 152:7
  With his l. he travaileth 224:2
Liquefaction: That l. of her clothes 104:15
Liquidity: a purpose in l. 41:20
Liquor: good l., I stoutly maintain 95:20
  l. for boys 115:20
Lisp: With l. of leaves 223:28
Lisped in numbers 165:4
Lissom: on l., clerical, printless toe 42:6
List: get sweets into your l. 112:4
  I've got a little l. 91:30
  never even observed in the l. 76:23
Listen: Darkling I l. 121:6
  I can l. all day 56:17
  L. all in silence 109:16
  L., my children 133:25
  L. to my tale of woe 84:2
  L. where thou art sitting 144:3
  Stop; look; l. 235:3
  world should l. 215:6
Listened: Sheridan was l. to 176:7
Listening: as I am l. now 215:6
  Enemy ears are l. 9:9
Listens: larkspur l. 228:20
  When the people l. 180:15
Listeth: bloweth where it l. 33:50
Lit: we shall not see them l. again 98:17
Literary: Gigadibs the l. man 43:10
  unsuccessful l. man 21:22
Literature: current l. of the day 50:6
  every other branch of classical l. 74:25
  great Cham of l. 218:5
  in the locks of l. 231:5
Littérature: tout le reste est l. 235:14
Little: be it ever so l. 113:20
  for having too l. to do 126:2
  here a l. 28:7
  it was a very l. one 139:12
  lies within a l. 40:4
  l. of us left 230:4
  l. of what you fancy 133:2
  L. One! 220:10
  l. things affect l. minds 76:20
  l. to do 75:26
  l. to relate 58:11
  l. we see in Nature 249:5
  Man wants but l. 95:9, 250:17
  nor that l., long 250:17

Nor wants that l. long | 95:9
offering too l. | 54:12
think too l. | 79:7
though thou be l. | 29:28
Were all too l. | 230:13
Littlenesses: thousand peering l. | 226:15
Littlest fish may enter in | 42:2
Live: as ye both shall l. | 168:11
by which we l. | 246:14
can these bones l. | 29:15
cannot l. together | 210:10
coop't we l. and die | 85:13
dead shall l. | 79:18
Easy l. | 180:15
eat to l. | 148:14
for heroes to l. in | 90:3
for in him we l. | 34:43
Glad did I l. | 221:23
He that shall l. this day | 192:4
How to l. well | 231:18
I do not wish to l. | 143:2
I l. alone | 250:9
I must l. | 10:14, 178:1
if to l. | 192:3
ill report while you l. | 187:9
in the midst of whom they l. | 40:7
just shall l. by faith | 34:52
know how to l. aright | 108:13
Lesbia mine, let's l. | 58:26
l. a man forbid | 197:6
l. about her waist | 187:1
l. as they l. elsewhere | 3:1
l. at home at ease | 160:19
l. in the best of..worlds | 52:19
l. laborious days | 145:1
l. more nearly as we pray | 122:15
L. pure | 226:17
l. till to-morrow | 70:1
l. upon our daily rations | 74:2
l. with animals | 242:14
l. with me | 139:6
L. within the sense | 215:10
May l. to fight | 95:2
merrily shall I l. now | 208:20
not l. by bread alone | 24:17, 30:8
not to l., but to die in | 42:20
one bare hour to l. | 138:14
poor Will must l. | 172:21
see me, and l. | 24:10
shall l. behind me | 190:3
Should L. alone | 9:6
taught us how to l. | 233:17
Teach him how to l. | 165:20
Teach me to l. | 123:2
teaching nations how to l. | 148:11
tell me whom you l. with | 61:5
that l. to please | 116:28
that nation might l. | 132:8
those who l. call Life | 215:9
to l. a fool | 19:9
to l. and to die | 44:10
to l. in hearts | 53:14
to l. i' the sun | 183:15
to l. together | 168:10
To l. without him | 249:12
We l. and learn | 163:18
we'll l., and pray | 196:6
while thy book doth l. | 118:4
while you l. | 90:18
would you l. for ever? | 88:7
wouldn't l. under Niagara | 55:22
Lived: all l. together | 158:5
As long as he l. | 150:17
Had we l. | 179:19
I have l. long enough | 199:32
l. in the tide of times | 193:20
l. thousands of years ago | 242:14
She l. unknown | 248:3
should have l. comfortably | 89:9

who has never lov'd, has never l. | 89:22
Wot l. in Lyon's Inn | 240:3
Lively Oracles of God | 69:1
Liver: notorious evil l. | 167:3
question of the L. | 173:15
Livery: shadow'd l. | 201:19
Lives: gave their l. | 132:8
Grows, l., and dies | 203:1
in jeopardy of their l. | 25:6
in their l. fought for life | 219:6
l. after them | 194:3
l. along the line | 164:16
l. by selling something | 220:20
l. down the lane | 155:4
l. more l. than one | 243:6
L. of great men | 133:27
l. only in the delicacy | 161:9
make our l. sublime | 133:27
no man l. forever | 224:6
she l. in our alley | 55:2
So long l. this | 210:12
start their working l. | 125:9
Living: be happy while y'er l. | 3:17
Blend the l. | 58:21
By the l. jingo | 96:2
drudge for his l. | 212:20
earned a precarious l. | 4:5
fever called 'L.' | 163:15
get mine own l. | 168:1
in the land of the l. | 169:7
life worth l. | 173:15
l. air | 248:19
l. at this hour | 247:7
l. die | 79:18
l. need charity more than the dead | 11:6
l. to be dedicated | 132:8
more real than l. man | 214:9
out of the land of the l. | 28:22
Plain l. | 247:8
snake is l. yet | 21:23
that's worth l. for | 222:13
too much love of l. | 224:6
tribes of l. things | 135:9
When I am l. in the Midlands | 21:24
with riotous l. | 33:21
works hard for its l. | 156:17
Livingstone: Dr. L., I presume? | 220:2
Lizard: Lion and the L. | 85:1
Llama is a woolly sort of..goat | 21:22
Load: how to l. and bless | 119:17
l. every rift | 122:11
l. of immortality | 122:9
somebody's l. has tipped | 127:1
Loads: laid many heavy l. on thee | 83:12
Loaf: a L. of Bread | 84:18, 19
Loam: men are but gilded l. | 206:2
Loan oft loses both itself | 185:21
Loaning: on ilka green l. | 82:12
Loathed: Hence, l. Melancholy | 144:10
most l. worldly life | 201:1
Lobster: voice of the l. | 57:10
Local: l. habitation | 203:19
not l. prejudices | 46:27
Loch Lomond: On the bonnie, bonnie banks o' L. | 7:4
Lochinvar: O, young L. | 180:8
Lock: crying at the l. | 143:4
put on a l.! | 119:5
Locked up in steel | 192:7
Locks: braid those flaxen l. | 108:18
by the l. | 190:9
Curly l. | 155:11
few l. which are left you | 218:22
her invincible l. | 148:10
in the l. of literature | 231:5
l. to part | 186:7
l. were like the raven | 48:20
Open l. | 199:17

Locust: that the l. hath eaten 29:21
Lodge: in her bosom l. 186:13
  will not l. thee by Chaucer 118:4
Lodged with me useless 147:17
Lodger: L.'s such a nice young
  man 151:6
  mere l. in my own house 95:22
Lodgers: full of l. at present 75:13
Lodgest: where thou l. 24:35
Lodging: give us a safe l. 153:12
  Towards Phoebus' l. 207:32
Lofty character of Wife 74:12
Log: l. was burning brightly 94:10
  on a l. 75:19
Log-Cabin to White House 232:5
Logic: That's l. 57:19
Logicians: If we may believe our l. 1:15
Logs: bears l. into the hall 196:20
Loin: ungirt l. 45:8
Loins: Gird up now thy l. 25:40
  With your l. girded 24:5
Loitering: Alone and palely l. 120:10
London: as L. is to Paddington 54:15
  been up to L. 157:14
  best club in L. 75:12
  chief advantage of L. 142:17
  City of L. remains . . . the clear-
    ing-house 59:13
  dream of L. 150:14
  lived in L. 113:18
  L. is a fine town 67:19
  L. particular 73:22
  L., that great cesspool 78:20
  L., thou art of townes 80:13
  L., thou art the flower 80:14
  L.'s lasting shame 97:7
  lungs of L. 162:20
  man is tired of L. 115:14
  Mr. Weller's knowledge of L. 75:20
  Of famous L. town 69:21
  to merry L. came 219:14
London Bridge: broken arch of L. 136:21
  L. . . greater . . than any of the
    Seven Wonders 1:10
  L. is broken down 156:14
Lone: l. and level sands 214:7
  walking by his wild l. 128:17
Lonely: l. as a cloud 247:3
  none of these so l. 41:16
  rapture on the l. shore 51:7
Lonesome: on a l. road 66:5
Long: ages l. ago 120:5
  battles l. ago 248:9
  craft so l. to learn 105:6
  from l. to short 67:1
  from short to l. 67:2
  I have loved so l. 85:15
  I l. to talk 77:13
  It cannot hold you l. 95:10
  it shan't be l. 61:3
  l. and heavy task 236:1
  l. and wide 161:16
  l., l. trail 123:12
  l. shot 78:10
  look at them l. and l. 242:14
  Lord, how l. ? 27:29
  music loud and l. 66:15
  nor that little l. 250:17
  Nor wants that little l. 95:9
  nothing l. 79:8
  short and the l. of it 202:18
  So l. lives this 210:12
  that thy days may be l. 167:12
  thou art l. 65:18
  'Tis three feet l. 248:16
  to last l. 152:21
  to study a l. silence 240:12
  way was l. 180:4
Longer: endure you a little l. 68:18

l. will tarry 78:28
  sit here any l. 71:11
Longeth: so l. my soul 169:15
Longing: desire and longing 170:13
  l. for de old plantation 87:11
Longings: Immortal l. 183:2
  l. to two things 119:8
Longsuffering: fruit of the spirit is
  . .l. 36:7
  l. and of great goodness 172:3
Look: cat may l. at a king 57:2
  cradle to the grave I l. 70:21
  Don't l. at me 173:18
  don't l. too good 125:14
  dream of the soft l. 250:11
  frightened l. in its eyes 217:6
  goodly to l. at 24:43
  how ungentlemanly he can l. 222:21
  I stand and l. at them 242:14
  if he'll only l. in 93:32
  let us l. for the woman 80:9
  l. a gift-horse in the mouth 49:20
  l. and a voice 134:9
  l. around 250:1
  L. at the stars! 107:16
  l. before you ere you leap 49:28
  L. ere thou leap 234:15
  l. not thou upon the wine 26:23
  l. out through the same bars 130:3
  l. through my tears 232:11
  l. to his bond 201:26
  L. up at the skies 107:16
  l. upon his like again 185:15
  L. upon my works 214:6
  l. upon myself 210:13
  L. upward to the skies 152:16
  l. well at her 219:19
  must not l. to have 199:32
  shall she l. 86:2
  Stop; l. ; listen 235:3
  that goose l. ? 199:31
  they l. behind 98:7
  to l. at things in bloom 110:15
  To l. on nature 248:19
  Twelve-pound l. 18:23
  We l. before and after 215:5
  with a bitter l. 243:5
Looked: he l. again 56:9
  I have l. upon 246:10
  l., and sank 142:1
  She l. at me 120:12
  upon which the Grand Army
    never l. 137:18
  who l. with such a wistful eye 243:4
Looker-on: patient l. 173:27
Lookers-on: l. feel most delight 49:29
  l. many times see more 14:13
Looketh forth as the morning 27:19
Looking: in my l. 4:10
  l. at the stars 243:16
  l. on it 183:16
  l. unto Jesus 36:35
  no harm in l. 222:20
Looks: as she l. 67:10
  kill with l. 206:15
  man that l. on glass 103:21
  stolen l. 112:5
  that l. through death 246:13
Loom: she left the l. 227:25
Loon: cream-faced l.! 199:31
  grey beard l.! 65:5
Looped and window'd raggedness 195:8
Loose: all hell broke l. 146:18
  we l. wild tongues 127:6
Loosed: silver cord be l. 27:8
Loosely: and l. lying 41:7
Loquimur: Dum l., fugerit . . Aetas 109:3
Lord: abomination unto the L. 3:9
  Angel of the L. 32:41, 225:10

Avenge, O L. 147:16
because you are a great L. 19:8
before the L. 23:24
blessed be the name of the L. 25:26
children of the L. 2:9
Christ Jesus our L. 35:10
coming of the L. 111:15
courts of the L. 170:13
died by the hand of the L. 24:6
earth is the L.'s 35:19, 169:3
even the L. of hosts 169:5
Except the L. build 171:22
except the L. keep the city 26:4, 171:22
fear of the L. 28:1, 171:10
glory of the L. 28:12, 29:1,
32:41, 230:3
goodness of the L. 169:7
Great l. of all things 164:19
He is the L. 170:24
house of the L. 169:2, 170:15, 171:19
I pray the L. my soul to keep 6:11
I pray the L. my soul to take 6:11
I replied 'My L.' 103:20
in the glance of the L. 52:11
it is the L. 70:3
it is the L.'s passover 24:5
kneel before the L. 170:23
knowledge of the L. 28:3
labour proved l. of all 237:5
L. among wits 114:1
L. be with thee 24:44
L. behold us 45:20
L. bless thee 24:13
L., dismiss us 45:21
L. God Almighty 37:16, 38:13, 102:1
L. God of Hosts 127:3
L. hath laid on him 28:21
L. have mercy 152:5
L. hear my voice 171:25
L. help you 67:18
L. how long 27:29
L. is my light 26:3
L. is my shepherd 169:2
L. is thy defence 171:17
L. is with thee 32:36
L., now lettest thou thy servant 33:1
L. of himself 249:11
L. of Hosts 27:27, 169:5, 170:13
L. of our far-flung battle-line 127:3
L. remember me 33:40
L. said unto my L. 171:9
L. shall raise me up 174:15
L. sitting upon a throne 27:27
L., thou hast been our refuge 170:16
L. watch between me and thee 23:31
L., with me abide 135:16, 17
L. ye know 123:5
L.'s my shepherd 181:8
Love is l. of all 237:3
mouth of the L. 28:12
my soul doth magnify the L. 32:37
Name of the L. thy God 167:8
not tempt the L. 30:9
Praise the L. 87:5, 122:24, 172:8
Praise the name of the L. 172:6
Rejoice in the L. always 36:18
remember the name of the L. 168:32
saith the L. 35:11
Seek ye the L. 28:24
Sing to the L. 123:5
Sing unto the L. 169:11
speak, L.; for thy servant heareth 24:37
spirit of the L. 28:1, 13
thank the L. 53:12
that sought the L. aright 48:12
that wait upon the L. 28:15
voice of the L. God 28:15
way of the L. 28:12, 30:4
what does the L. require 29:29

whom the L. loveth 36:36
Lordly: l. band 70:20
butter in a l. dish 24:29
Lords may flourish 95:4
Lordships: on their l.'s pleasures 193:2
Lore: All the l. its scholars need 122:18
Heaven rejects the l. 247:6
mystical l. 53:16
Lorn: lone l. creetur 74:5
Lose: l. and start again 125:15
l. his own soul? 31:35, 32:32
l. the name of action 187:13
l. this light 118:13
must he l. the name of king? 206:16
neither a soul to l. 217:19
no wise l. his reward 31:17
nothing to l. 140:14
shall l. it 31:16
some day you will l. them all 131:10
tails you l. 71:4
to l. itself in the sky 43:7
to l. myself in a mystery 42:19
To l. one parent 243:10
To win or l. it all 149:6
Losers: all are l. 59:15
Loses: l. both itself 185:21
Who l. and who wins 196:6
Losing: Are l. theirs 125:14
Loss: another's l. of ease 39:6
breathe a word about your l. 125:15
change and l. in the heavens 110:6
Gain I count but l. 239:16
l. of a dear friend 219:2
to do our country l. 192:3
upon thy so sore l. 232:10
With l. of Eden 145:9
Lost: all good to me is l. 146:14
All is l. save honour 87:18
All is not l. 145:15
all time is l. 222:13
battle's l. and won 197:2
be l. in me 229:17
cannot be l. 197:6
every day to be l. 116:8
had l. his wits 95:15
has l. her shoe 155:7
he was l., and is found 33:24
I have l. a day 233:20
I have l. my voice 240:13
I've l. Britain 127:8
labour is but l. 171:22
like l. sheep 166:8
l. and gone for ever 149:7
l. awhile 153:16
l. to the forest 180:2
never to see it l. 47:20
no love l. 117:17
Not l. but gone before 103:11, 154:13
pale, l. lilies 77:27
rider was l. 88:5
sheep which was l. 33:19
shoe was l. 88:5
that you won or l. 175:10
though the field be l. 145:15
to have loved and l. 227:9
too good to be l. 129:18
what's l. upon the roundabouts 59:12
who l. no friend 164:25
world well l. 79:13
Lot: envy of thy happy l. 121:2
l. has fallen to me 127:18
No l. is desperate 108:19
our loving l. was cast 106:19
Policeman's l. 93:21
remember L.'s wife 33:32
Sack the l.! 84:13
Loth: ne'er considered it as l. 49:20
Lothario: gallant, gay L. 178:5
Lotos and lilies 229:6

Lots: let us cast l. 29:25
Lou: Linger longer L. 98:21
  that's known as L. 182:1
Loud: as l. as he could bawl 69:28
  l. uplifted 147:14
  music l. and long 66:15
  needn't shout so l. 58:6
  not l. but deep 199:32
  speak out l. 121:9
  Triton blowing l. 219:8
  upon the l. cymbals 172:8
  very l. and clear 58:6
  waxed very l. 142:6
Louder he talked of his honour 82:17
Loud-hissing: bubbling and l. urn 70:18
Loudly: Chanted l. 228:1
Louis: Son of Saint L. 84:12
Loungers of the Empire 78:20
Louse: a l. for the hangman 117:14
  between a l. and a flea 116:1
  l. in the locks of literature 231:5
Love: absence is to l. 49:14
  acquainted with l. 113:21
  acts of kindness and of l. 248:18
  Ah L.! 86:1
  all earth to l. 127:18
  All for L. 79:13, 219:11
  all for the l. of you 72:11
  all l. at first 50:4
  As honour, l. 199:32
  as she did l. 120:12
  banner over me was l. 27:14
  be in l. with night 208:1
  be my l. 139:6
  before the god of l. 77:13
  But I do l. thee 205:3
  but not for l. 184:10
  corner in the thing I l. 205:7
  courage, l. and joy 89:17
  course of true l. 203:2
  deep and heavy was the l. 16:4
  desire more l. 183:8
  did not l. clean linen 114:9
  disappointed l. 178:4
  dull sublunary lovers' l. 77:20
  faithful in l. 180:9
  fit l. for Gods 146:23
  fitter l. for me 77:15
  food of l. 209:2
  for a good man's l. 184:6
  for all his l. 53:12
  For ever wilt thou l. 120:20
  for God is l. 37:9
  for l. of grace 189:3
  For thy sweet l. 210:13
  freedom in my l. 134:19
  fruit of the Spirit is l. 36:7
  God of l. 104:4
  greater l. hath no man 34:20
  heartily l. John, Peter 223:6
  Him whom you l. 246:4
  how L. fled 250:11
  I am sick of l. 27:15
  I could not l. thee 134:20
  I do not l. thee 42:16, 139:22
  I hate, I l. 59:2
  I l. a lassie 130:7
  I l. all beauteous things 41:6
  I l. everything that's old 95:24
  I l. it 68:23
  I l. not man the less 51:7
  I l. thee still 70:15
  I never had but one true l. 17:1
  I will l. Thee 104:2
  I would l. you 140:11
  if a man say, I l. God 37:12
  if my l. were in my arms 8:10
  if that name thou l. 245:19
  in l. and charity 167:22
  in l. with easeful death 121:6
  in l. with the productions of time 39:18
  it's l. that makes the world go round 5:15, 57:3, 91:26
  King of L. 15:20
  know me well, and l. me 149:19
  labour of l. 36:23
  laggard in l. 180:10
  lease of my true l. 211:14
  let me l. 77:2
  life I l. 221:15
  like to l. three more 222:8
  long l.'s day 140:11
  lost the world for l. 79:27
  l. a lover 82:19
  L. alters not 211:16
  l. and a cottage 67:16
  l., and a space for delight 224:2
  l. and do what you will 13:9
  l., and man's unconquerable mind 248:20
  l. and murder will out 68:4
  L. bade me welcome 104:1
  l. but one day 55:4
  l., cherish, and to obey 168:13
  L. doth her eyes repair 210:2
  L., forgive us! 120:15
  l. grows bitter 224:10
  l. he had for her 23:30
  l. her so sincerely 55:3
  L. in a hut 120:15
  L. in a palace 120:15
  l. is a boy 49:26
  l. is blind 201:23
  L. is like the measles 113:6
  L. is Lord of all 237:3
  L. is not l. 211:16
  l. is sweet for a day 224:10
  l. is then our duty 89:19
  l. is towards individuals 223:6
  l. itself have rest 52:14
  L. itself shall slumber 215:10
  l. me little, l. me long 6:4
  l. of friends 21:12
  l. of money 36:30
  l. our occupations 74:2
  l. seeketh not itself 39:5
  l. seeketh only Self 39:6
  L. so amazing 239:17
  L. that endures for a breath 224:1
  l. that makes the world go round 57:3, 91:26
  l. the brotherhood 37:4
  l., the human form divine 39:13
  l. those who l. you 237:17
  l. thy neighbour 24:12, 31:42
  l. to all men 124:18
  l. to hatred turned 68:10
  l. to hear the story 143:3
  l. to keep it by me 113:8
  l. to me was wonderful 25:1
  l. with all my heart 221:13
  L.'s like the measles 113:11
  L.'s not Time's fool 211:16
  L.'s young dream 149:14
  loved with a l. 163:14
  made me l. you 137:6
  man's l. is of a man's life 51:14
  many waters cannot quench l. 27:20
  may be crossed in l. 216:5
  me and my true l. 7:4
  meet for ladies' l. 110:2
  most power to hurt us that we l. 19:19
  my dear l. sits him down 8:1
  my l. and I did meet 250:5
  My l. and I would lie 110:19
  my l. is come to me 177:8
  my L.'s like a red red rose 48:28
  My l. is of a birth as rare 140:2

My l. she's but a lassie 106:9
My only l. 207:18
My true l. hath my heart 216:29
my wand'ring l. 68:14
New every morning is the l. 122:13
no fear in l. 37:11
no l. lost 96:1, 117:17
Now with his l. 60:18
O lyric l. 45:6
of the woman I l. 81:5
off with the old l. 5:14, 141:14
our l. and toil 124:17
our l. hath no decay 77:1
pangs of dispriz'd l. 187:13
passing the l. of women 25:1
passionate l. repeated 129:22
perfect l. casteth out fear 37:11
prosper that l. thee 171:20
quick-ey'd l. 104:1
rise up, my l. 27:16
sate mourning for her l. 213:11
Seals of l. 201:3
separate us from the l. of God 35:10
service of my l. 219:18
shackles of an old l. 226:22
She never told her l. 209:10
should I your true l. know 189:8
So I fell in l. 93:33
so you l. me long 104:12
Soft eyes look'd l. 50:23
sports of l. 118:12
spring of l. 210:1
substance of his house for l. 27:20
Sweet lovers l. the spring 184:12
sweetest l., I do not go 77:15
take l. easy 250:5
temper'd with L.'s sighs 196:15
that l. had been sae ill to win 17:3
that l. may never cease 104:2
That l. my friend 194:11
them that l. God 35:8
thoughts of l. 228:5
Through l. 245:18
Thy honesty and l. 204:31
thy l. prove likewise variable 207:24
To give my L. good-morrow 105:2
To l. and bear 215:1
To l. and fame 122:5
to l. and to cherish 168:12
to l. her 220:5
to l. mercy 29:29
To l. the lovely 161:14
to l. too well 164:4
To Mercy, Pity, Peace, and L. 39:12
to see her was to l. her 48:4
too much l. of living 224:6
true l.'s coming 209:5
vegetable l. 92:22, 140:11
very few to l. 248:3
waft her l. 202:10
we all l. a pretty girl 37:31
We l. the precepts 106:11
well of l. 65:2
What is l.? 209:5
What l. I bore to thee 247:2
What l. is 99:9
What makes the lamb l. Mary so? 99:5
when I l. thee not 205:3
when I was in l. with you 110:18
when l. and duty clash 229:8
when l. is done 40:13
where I and my L. wont to gae 17:2
where l. is 26:18
where there is no l. 14:14
whose l. would follow me 126:16
with l. brooding there 244:11
with l. false or true 250:11
with l.'s wound 203:7

Woman wakes to l. 226:24
words of l. 150:1
yet I I l. her till I die 7:22
yield we, too, to l.! 237:3
Love-adept: Dreaming like a l. 214:9
Loved: better l. ye canna be 151:11
better l. you'll never be 106:8
bird my lady l. 58:25
burning Sappho l. 51:17
did till we l. 77:7
disciple whom Jesus l. 34:30
for I I l. the man 117:12
God so l. the world 34:1
he l. so long 176:6
I have l. long since 153:16
I have l. so long 85:15
L. accents 213:16
l. Caesar less 194:1
l. I not honour more 134:20
l. not at first sight 139:3, 184:7
l. not wisely 205:20
l. one all together 44:15
l. passing well 187:6
l. the beggar-maid 207:19
l. thee since my day began 231:1
l. the Human Race 174:19
l. the pilgrim soul in you 250:11
l. when all was young 123:18
l. with a love 163:14
l. your beauty 250:11
l. your moments of glad grace 250:11
must be l. 208:25
never l. so kindly 48:5
never to have been l. 68:16
never to have l. 227:9
nor no man ever l. 211:16
Out upon it, I have l. 222:8
Pale hands I l. 107:9
poor man l. the great 136:12
some we l. 85:4
to have l. and lost 227:9
to have l. the highest 229:19
we that had l. him so 44:10
Who ever l. 139:3, 184:7
who has never l., has never lived 89:22
who l. him best 124:2
why I l. him 149:2
with those that l. me 230:13
Love-in-idleness 203:7
Loveliest: l. and best 85:4
l. and the best 21:16
Loveliness: a miracle of l. 92:11
Glory and l. 122:1
her l. I never knew 65:2
l. increases 120:1
portion of the l. 213:9
This Adonis l. 112:7
Lovely: all things l. 73:3
art more l. 210:12
bears a l. face 72:18
Do l. things 123:14
extremely l. thing 91:2
gives a l. light 143:1
he made more l. 213:9
kissed the l. grass 42:4
l. and pleasant 24:48
l. apparition 284:4
l. hamlet Grantchester 42:7
l. is the rose 246:8
L. wee thing 48:10
l. woman in a rural spot 112:6
more l. than the monarch of the sky 138:13
O l. O most charming pug 86:11
once l. head 85:2
she has a l. face 228:2
To love the l. 161:14
whatsoever things are l. 36:20
When l. woman stoops 82:2, 95:21

Lover: as true a l.   183:11
  by the l. and the bard   43:7
  cannot prove a l.   207:6
  give repentance to her l.   95:21
  I sighed as a l.   90:10
  I've got one l.   141:21
  love a l.   82:19
  l., all as frantic   203:19
  l. and his lass   184:12
  l. of concord   166:14
  L. of my soul   241:8
  l., Sighing like furnace   183:20
  Lunatic, the l.   203:19
  pale and wan, fond l.   222:5
  sad true l.   209:9
  some old l.'s ghost   77:13
  such a constant l.   222:8
Lovers: dull sublunary l.   77:20
  in l meeting   209:5
  l. are round her   149:17
  l. cannot see   201:23
  l. fled away   120:5
  l.' seasons run   77:18
  pair of star-crossed l.   207:13
  Sweet l. love the spring   184:12
Loves: a-waiting for their ain dear
  l.!   16:15
  Come, all ye L.   58:25
  Friends and l. we have none   141:5
  I l. the fox less   222:17
  I l. the 'ound more   222:17
  Jesus l. me   239:1
  kills the thing he l.   243:5
  lass that l. a sailor   73:18
  l., and weeps, and dies   213:12
  l. not woman, wine and song   135:11
  l. to lie with me   183:13
  l. to live i' the sun   183:15
  l. well the golden mean   109:13
  l. what he knows   71:5
  mother of sweet l.   110:4
  seat..of l.   79:23
  that l. his fellow-men   112:3
  Two l. have I   212:4
  who l. to fold his legs   115:15
  wings of the L.   224:9
Love-sick: L. all against our will   92:18
  Twenty l. maidens   92:18
  winds were l.   182:15
Lovesome thing   42:17
Lovest: l. thou me   70:3
  who l. all   124:17
Loveth: God l. a cheerful giver   36:2
  he that l. not   37:9
  l. not his brother   37:12
  who l. well   66:7
  whom the Lord l.   36:36
Loving: by l. their parents   243:27
  for l., and for saying so   77:19
  heart be still as l.   52:13
  l. and giving   156:17
  l. friends   66:6
  most l. mere folly   184:1
  night was made for l.   52:15
  nor l. friends can hurt you   125:16
  Our l. lot was cast   106:19
  so l. to my mother   185:11
  talks a lot of l.   126:14
Loving-kindness and mercy   169:2
Low: between the high and L.   217:1
  cast one's eyes so l.   195:19
  dim and l.   159:14
  earth is not too l.   103:18
  exalted them of l. degree   32:38
  fighting as l. as ever   79:21
  gentle and l.   196:9
  he that is l.   46:17
  head is bending l.   87:12
  lie cold and l.   214:1

L., l., breathe and blow   229:9
l. man seeks a little thing   43:18
mountain and hill shall be made l.   28:12
poor buffer lies l.   243:1
sing both high and l.   209:5
Sweet and l.   229:9
what is l. raise   145:11
Lowells: where the L. talk to the
  Cabots   40:11
Lower: ye l. middle classes   91:16
Lowest: reduced to her l. terms   130:14
Lowing: l. at the skies   120:21
  l. herd   97:8
Lowly: as in the l. air of Seven Dials   91:19
  Chanted l.   228:1
  from their l. bed   97:11
  In l. pomp   143:6
Loyal: in a l. breast   206:2
  L. Achates   236:4
  l. body wanted learning   234:3
Loyalties: impossible l.   12:3
Loyalty: learned body wanted l.   234:3
  when l. no harm meant   5:9
Lucid: L. intervals and happy
  pauses   15:8
  l. intervals of life   245:20
  make a l. interval   79:24
Lucifer: falls like L.   192:15
  O L., son of the morning   28:4
Luck: As good l. would have it   202:20
  there's nae l. about the house   8:2
Lucky to touch it   127:9
Lucrative: so l. to cheat   64:8
Lucy: Linger longer L.   98:21
  When L. ceased to be   248:3
Lugete, O Veneres Cupidinesque   58:25
Lugger: on board the l.   117:4
Lui: Parce que c'était l.   149:2
Luke: Matthew, Mark, L., and John   1:1
Lull the distant folds   97:8
Lullaby: And dreamy l.   91:27
  will sing a l.   73:1
Lulled: l. by the coil   214:2
  L. in these flowers   203:9
Lumber of the schools   223:24
Lumen: cui l. ademptum   236:13
Luminous, the dark   86:5
Lump: Camel's hump is an ugly l.   126:2
Lunatic, the lover, and the poet   203:19
Lunch and at close of day   53:9
Luncheon: supper, dinner, l.   44:22
Lungs: l. of London   162:20
  with l. of bronze   21:21
Lure: Shall l. it back   85:12
Lurks in the grass   236:24
Luscious clusters   140:6
Lust: for l. of knowing   86:8
  into ashes all my l.   140:12
  Is l. in action   212:1
  l. is perjur'd   212:1
  l. of gold   227:20
Lusts: sinful l. of the flesh   167:32
Lute: as is Apollo's l.   144:2
  my armour and the l.   110:2
  Orpheus and his l.   192:13
  rift within the l.   226:23
  When the l. is broken   213:16
Luther: and L. [was misunderstood]   82:21
Luxuries of life   151:1
Luxury: Persian l.   109:9
Lycidas is dead   144:20
Lydian: soft L. airs   144:19
Lying: and loosely l.   41:7
  in his grave is l.   149:17
  is given to l.   190:26
  l. and slandering   167:34
  when you're l. awake   91:23
  who was l. on his face   231:17
  you and I be l.   58:21

Lynn: set out from L. 106:21
Lyonnesse: set out for L. 100:6
Lyon's Inn: Wot lived in L. 240:3
Lyre: living l. 97:14
  Make me thy l. 214:4
  'Omer smote 'is bloomin' l. 128:4
Lyres: as the sound of l. 161:9
Lysander: of Hector and L. 7:7

M

Mab, the Mistress-Fairy 118:2
Mac: Pat and M. and Tommy 128:28
Macaroni: called it M. 17:6
Macaulay: as Tom M. is of every-
  thing 141:18
  M. is well for a while 55:22
Macbeth: M. does murder sleep 198:13
  shall harm M. 199:20
  to meet with M. 197:2
Macduff: M. was from his mother's
  womb 200:11
Mace: the m., the crown imperial 191:15
Macedonia: come over into M. 34:39
Machine: you're a m. 212:10
Mackerel: Not so the m. 88:8
Macte nova virtute, puer 236:21
Mad: but m. north-north-west 187:5
  He first sends m. 80:15
  M., bad, and dangerous 129:4
  m., blind. .king 215:8
  m. dogs and Englishmen 69:8
  M. in pursuit 212:2
  m. it was 43:15
  M. World! Mad Kings! 193:3
  M. World, My Masters 41:5, 225:12
  men that God made m. 61:15
  much learning doth make thee
  m. 34:50
  Oh! he is m., is he? 90:6
  pleasure sure, In being m. 80:1
  That he is m. 186:23
  Went m. and bit the man 95:14
  when a heroine goes m. 216:4
Madagascar: Jerusalem and M. 232:3
Madam: Thank you, m. 137:4
Maddest merriest day 228:21
Madding: far from the m. crowd's 98:1
Made: all that's m. 140:7
  as fast as they are m. 208:27
  as wos ever m. 75:32
  he m. and loveth all 66:7
  he m. it 170:22
  he who m. the lamb 39:3
  I am m. all things 35:17
  m. known 169:18
  of a friend we've m. 40:6
  who m. thee? 39:9
  who m. you? 222:4
  whom thou hast m. 171:4
Mademoiselle from Armenteers 178:6
Madly: rode m. off 130:12
Madman: That is the m. 203:19
Madmen: which none but m. know 80:1
Madness: despondency and m. 247:19
  harmonious m. 215:6
  His flight was m. 199:25
  m. of many 223:21
  M. risen from hell 224:1
  moon-struck m. 146:24
  sure to m. 79:6
  that way m. lies 195:7
  this be m., yet there is method 186:26
  very midsummer m. 209:16
Madrigals: melodious birds sing m. 139:7
Magic: charmed m. casements 121:6
  dealer in m. 93:31
  With m. in my eyes 100:7

Magistrate: commandment of the
  M. 172:15
Magna est veritas 29:31, 42:12
Magnanimity: curb your m. 122:11
  m. in politics 47:4
Magnas inter opes inops 110:1
Magnificent: it is m. 40:10
  mild and m. eye 44:10
Magnifique: C'est m.,. .pas la guerre 40:10
Magnitude: having m., complete in
  itself 10:16
Magnus ab integro saeclorum 237:1
Mahomet: from M. to Moses 166:5
  M. will go to the hill 14:9
Maid: Abyssinian m. 66:15
  Be good, sweet m. 123:14
  Come down, O m. 229:18
  fair cruel m. 209:9
  I heard a m. sing 4:4
  m. and her wight 100:4
  m. is mine 117:4
  m. was in the garden 158:1
  m. whom there were none to
  praise 248:3
  many a m. 144:16
  my pretty m. 159:1
  nor his m. 167:17
  of wedded m. 145:6
  silver for the m. 124:19
  there was a fair m. dwellin' 16:2
  Thou M. Divine 179:11
  way of a man with a m. 26:31
  we there did espy a fair pretty m. 6:20
  wink for every pretty m. 222:20
Maiden: how could you use a poor
  m. so? 4:4
  I sing of a m. 5:11
  in m. meditation 203:7
  let the m. understand 41:1
  m. all forlorn 158:8
  m. of bashful fifteen 216:19
  Many a rose-lipt m. 111:6
  neater, sweeter m. 126:14
  'O stay', the m. said] 133:18
  Prithee, pretty m. 92:24
  Tell me, pretty m. 99:8
Maidens: All her m. watching 229:15
  all the m. pretty 67:19
  as many m. be 65:2
  For dear to m. 161:13
  long may the m. sit 16:15
  now chant to m. 109:16
  Twenty love-sick m. 92:18
  Young men and m. 172:6
  youths and m. gay 66:6
Maids: m. are May 184:11
  m. dance in a ring 152:6
  most incident to m. 210:8
  our cold m. 189:18
  pretty m. all in a row 156:16
  three little m. from school 92:2
  three little m. who, all unwary 92:3
Maimed: poor and the m. 33:17
  spent and m. 123:18
Main: all her might and m. 143:11
  amid the boundless m. 41:14
  Argo cleaves the m. 213:12
  arose from out the azure m. 232:13
  care o' th' m. chance 49:28
Maintain: I stoutly m. 95:20
Maisie: Proud M. 180:18
Maîtresses: j'aurai des m. 90:5
Majestic instancy 232:8
Majestical: in bed m. 191:15
  this m. roof 187:4
Majesty: earth of m. 206:7
  His M.'s dominions 154:8
  in conversation with Her M. 76:13
  please your M. 57:13

Majesty (cont.)
ride on in m. 143:6
Thy m. how bright 83:14
to awe and m. 202:5
touching in its m. 249:4
what a strength and m. 151:14
Major-General: modern M. 93:18
Majority: joined the great m. 162:13
to the great m. 251:1
Majors: live with scarlet M. 179:4
Make: could not well m. out 218:13
He did us m. 123:5
I m. all things new 37:26
m. himself a nuisance 142:22
m. me as one of thy hired servants 33:22
m. the most of what we get 85:5
m. what haste I can 71:13
Scotsman on the m. 18:25
territorial claim which I have to m. 105:8
what the word did m. it 82:4
Maker: scatter'd his M.'s image 79:3
serve therewith my M. 147:17
the Lord our M. 170:23
Makes: man who m. no mistakes 162:14
Malade: un homme gravement m. 154:3
Malady: m. most incident to maids 210:8
medicine worse than the m. 19:15
Male: more deadly than the m. 125:5
rough m. kiss of blankets 41:17
Malherbe: Enfin M. vint 40:2
Malice: Envy, hatred, and m. 166:22
M. domestic 199:4
m. toward none 132:9
set down aught in m. 205:20
Malignant and turban'd Turk 205:20
Malmsey and Malvoisie 20:13
Malt: ate the m. 158:8
M. does more than Milton can 111:7
Malvoisie: of Malmsey and M. 20:13
Mammon: of the m. of unrighteousness 33:26
serve God and m. 30:27
Mammy: Looking at his m. 220:3
Man: aged, aged m. 58:11
ambition of m. 174:16
any child of m. 172:4
arose as one m. 24:34
as a young m. 118:17
as I am a m. 196:3
be false to any m. 185:21
Blessed is the m. 165:16
Blest be the m. 212:5
blood of a British m. 195:14
both m. and bird 66:7
Breathes there a m. 180:6
But m., proud m. 200:19
came to the making of m. 224:1
century of the common m. 238:1
chief end of m. 216:26
closing full in M. 79:16
contrived by m. 115:7
crooked m. 158:5
daring young man. 132:4
days of m. 171:1
despis'd old m. 195:5
each m. kills the thing he loves 243:5
England expects that every m. 152:20
every m. in arms 246:2
Every m. meets his Waterloo 162:15
Every m. over forty 213:2
Every m. thinks meanly of himself 115:16
every m. upon this earth 136:9
Every moment dies a m. 231:2
excuses no m. 181:13
father to the M. 247:10
find a m. 161:3
foolish, fond old m. 196:2
~~Foot-in-the-grave~~ young m. 93:4

for I loved the m. 117:12
Gird up now thy loins like a m. 25:40
given liberty to m. 71:17
glory of m. 37:3
Glory to M. 224:8
Go west young m. 218:11
God hath made m. upright 26:41
goodliest m. of men 146:17
good will to m. 181:10
great m. helped the poor 136:12
Greater love hath no m. 34:20
grew within this learned m. 139:2
hang a m. first 148:20
happiness of the common m. 23:3
Happy is the m. 171:23
Happy the m. 165:14
He was a m. 185:15
heart of m. 171:2
hearty old m. 218:22
held to the last m. 99:4
honest m. 164:20
hopes of m. 116:22
how can m. die better 136:9
how poor a thing is m. 72:3
I am a m. 231:6
I am a smooth m. 23:28
I heard a wise m. say 110:16
I love not m. the less 51:7
if the heart of a m. 89:18
in that m.'s company 192:4
in the breast of every m. 191:5
in the mind of m. 248:19
ingrateful m.! 195:4
inner m. 36:9, 168:17
interrupt a m. 220:13
is m. an ape 76:8
It prejudices a m. 218:1
It's that m. again 119:15
just m. and firm of purpose 109:19
justify God's ways to m. 111:7
king is but a m. 191:12
know what God and m. is 226:12
Let no such m. be trusted 202:13
let not m. put asunder 31:41
life for a m. like me 221:15
life of m. 105:9
little m., little m.! 82:10
low m. seeks a little thing 43:18
m. after his own heart 24:41
m. all tattered and torn 158:8
m. and a woman in a garden 243:26
m. and his wife 128:25
M. being in honour 169:24
m. can die but once 190:32
M. comes and tills 230:10
m. delights not me 187:4
m. doth not live by bread 24:17
M. dreams of fame 226:24
m. forbid 197:6
M. goeth forth 171:3
m. has forever 43:17
M. has his will 106:13
m. have the upper hand 168:25
m. he was to all the country dear 95:6
m. in his hasty days 41:6
m. in the wilderness 156:15
m. is a tool-using animal 55:20
m. is always so near his burrow 142:17
m. is an embodied paradox 68:2
m. is as old 67:10
M. is born free 177:18
M. is born unto trouble 25:29
M. is by nature a political animal 10:15
M. is distinguished from all other creatures 1:15
m. is of the earth 35:28
M. is only a reed 161:8
M. is the master of things 224:8
m. lay down his life 34:20

m. leave his father 23:14
m. may not marry 172:17
m. more sinned against 195:6
M. never is. . blessed 164:14
m. of culture rare 92:20
m. of my kidney 202:21
m. of propertee 92:24
m. of sorrows 28:20
m. of unclean lips 27:27
m. perceives it die away 246:11
M. proposes 122:22
m. right fair 212:4
M. shall not live by bread 30:8
m. should be alone 23:11
m. so various 79:8
m. that hath no music 202:13
m. that's marred 182:10
m. under authority 31:5
M. wants but little 95:9, 250:17
M. who delivers the goods 141:7
m., who first from the shores of
   Troy 236:3
m. who is always talking 222:12
m. who is not passion's slave 188:11
m. who makes no mistakes 162:14
m. who said 'Damn' 100:12
m. who stood at the gate 101:5
m. who turnips cries 116:9
m. who wasn't there 141:17
m. with his back to the East 65:3
m. with seven wives 155:3
M. without religion 100:11
m. would give all his substance 27:20
m.'s a m. for a' that 48:17
M.'s imperial race insnare 165:2
M.'s inhumanity to m. 48:24
m.'s the gowd for a' that 48:16
m.'s unconquerable mind 248:20
marry—and no m. 76:19
measureless to m. 66:14, 15
met an old m. 155:16
mighty m. is he 134:10
mildest manner'd m. 51:16
Misery acquaints a m. 208:14
more real than living m. 214:9
more wonderful than m. 218:9
most married m. 238:20
nature first made m. 79:19
no m. can serve two masters 30:26
No m. does 243:11
No m. has a right 161:1
no m. is a hero 68:29
no m. is an island 77:22
no m. lives forever 224:6
no m. remember me 100:9
no m. so friendless 136:4
noblest work of m. 50:7
noselessness of m. 61:27
now I am a m. 247:10
of a good m.'s life 248:18
Of M.'s first disobedience 145:9
of the m. of many wiles 106:16
oft proclaims the m. 185:21
old m. in a hurry 62:14
old m. to have had so much
   blood 199:28
old m. with a beard 130:15
on our hands a sick m. 154:3
Once to every m. 135:3
One m. by delaying 83:5
One m. in a thousand 127:19
one m. in his time 183:20
one m. loved 250:11
one thing to show a m. 133:7
only m. is vile 101:16
Parliament of m. 228:10
particularly pure young m. 92:22
pass for a m. 201:12
past the wit of m. 203:17

piece of work is a m.! 187:4
plain, blunt m. 194:11
play the m. 130:6
poor m. loved the great 136:12
power of m. 199:20
proper m. 203:5
rich m. to enter into 32:1
right m. in the right place 113:4
ruins of the noblest m. 193:20
running a m. down 223:7
sabbath was made for m. 32:26
saw a m. who looked 243:4
so becomes a m. 191:8
Son of m. 31:7, 168:23
spar'd a better m. 190:24
strong m. after sleep 148:10
strong m. armed 33:10
study of mankind is m. 164:18
such a nice young m. 151:6
teach you more of m. 248:15
that a m. might know 194:22
that one m. should die 34:14
that the new m. 167:30
their murder'd m. 120:8
There was once a m. who said 129:2
This is the state of m. 192:14
This was a m.! 194:24
Thou madest m. 227:94
Time, you old gipsy m. 105:14
to temper m. 159:22
touch the heart of m. 236:7
unaccommodated m. 195:12
unclubable m. 114:22
unsuccessful literary m. 21:22
unto the m. is woman 134:7
valiant m. and free 227:20
way of a m. 26:31
What bloody m. is that? 197:3
What is a m. profited 31:35
What is m. 168:23
What m. has made of m. 248:11
what profit hath a m. 26:34
when a dog bites a m. 72:2
when a m. bites a dog 72:2
when no m. can work 34:11
when no m. pursueth 26:29
When the right m. rings them 221:18
Where was then the pride of m. 99:11
who sheddeth m.'s blood 23:22
who's m. 223:23
whole duty of m. 27:10
woes of m. 236:7
you'll be a M. 125:16
young m. married 127:17, 182:10
young m.'s fancy 228:5
You're not a m. 212:10
Mandalay: come you back to M.! 126:11
Mandragora: Not poppy, nor m. 205:9
Mandrake: get with child a m. root 77:16
Mane: seiz'd fast the flowing m. 69:26
Manger: dog in the m. 234:12
   in a m. for His bed 2:10
   in the rude m. lies 145:7
   One born in a m. 235:7
Manger pour vivre 148:14
Manhood taken by the Son 153:13
Manhoods: hold their m. cheap 192:4
Mania of owning things 242:14
Manifestly. . be seen to be done 104:19
Mankind: All m. love a lover 82:19
   all m.'s epitome 79:8
   better service of m. 223:2
   early generations of m. 108:14
   I am involved in M. 77:23
   misfortunes of m. 90:14
   proper study of m. 164:18
   spectator of m. 1:7
   survey m. 117:1
   thus furnishing m. 223:1

Mankind (cont.)
what was meant for m. 95:17
with the leaders of m. 108:11
words among m. 214:4
you and all m. 225:9
you shall not crucify m. 45:15
Manna: tongue dropt m. 146:11
Manner: after this m. 30:22
m. of his speech 182:14
mildest m.'d man 51:16
no m. of doubt 91:7
State in wonted m. keep 117:11
very good bedside m. 173:17
Mannerly: behave m. 221:9
Manners: And m., climates 230:13
corrupt good m. 35:27
for m.' sake 29:36
M. are not so polite 126:18
m. of a dancing master 114:2
m. of a Marquis 93:25
old m., old books 95:24
Manor: sold a goodly m. 182:11
Mansion: Back to its m. call 97:13
Mansionry: his lov'd m. 198:2
Mansions: there are many m. 34:17
Mantle: cast his m. upon him 25:15
do cream and m. 201:7
russet m. clad 185:5
twitch'd his m. blue 145:5
You all do know this m. 194:7
Mantovano: I salute thee, M. 231:1
Manure: its natural m. 113:3
Manus: tendebantque m. ripae
ulterioris 236:17
Manxome foe 57:14
Many: for m. are called 32:6
for we are m. 32:29
madness of m. 223:21
owed by so m. 62:23
they among so m. 34:4
Ye are m. 213:19
Many-coloured: dome of m. glass 213:10
Many-fountain'd Ida 229:3
Many-headed monster 141:13, 165:12
Many-splendoured thing 232:10
Map: roll up that m. 163:1
Marathon: mountains look on M. 51:18
Marble: and m. to retain 50:17
in m. halls 46:2
in thy m. vault 140:12
left it m. 52:21
m. index of a mind 247:17
Not m. 211:4
this in m. 19:20
March: front of M. 226:13
ides of M. 193:10, 193:15, 194:16
mad M. days 140:21
m. is o'er the mountain waves 54:7
m. of the centuries 237:1
M. winds and April showers 6:5
Remember M. 194:16
take the winds of M. 210:8
three hours' m. to dinner 101:11
Marched: but m. breast forward 45:10
he m. them up to the top 7:21
m. on their stomachs 181:18
m. rank on rank 142:1
m. them along 43:12
Märchen: ein M. aus alten Zeiten 102:4
Marches: howe'er my m. be 123:11
Marching: His soul is m. on 99:6
m. as to war 18:7
m. through Georgia 249:7
M. to the Promised Land 18:8
Mare: a Flander's m. 103:14
have his m. again 203:16
Margate: 'twas in M. last July 18:1
Margin: meadow of m. 216:15
whose m. fades 230:13

Mariana: dejected M. 201:2
Maries: Queen had four M. 16:10
Marine: one of those m. landscapes 76:9
Mariner: an ancient m. 65:4
haul and draw with the m. 78:27
m. hath his will 65:5
Mariners: My m. 230:15
ye m. of England 54:6
Marion's nose 196:20
Mark: it is an ever-fixed m. 211:1
m. him well 180:6
m. it with B 157:9
Matthew, M., Luke, and John 1:17
read, m. 166:34
save he that had the m. 37:20
Marked: Have you m.'d 118:11
m. to die 192:3
Market: pig went to m. 158:9
Market-place: Idols of the m. 15:11
Marks: nobody m. you 204:6
Marksmen: you are all m. 173:21
Marlowe's mighty line 118:5
Marmoream..relinquere 52:21
Marquis: Earl, the M., and the
Dook 91:9
manners of a M. 93:25
Marred: man that's m. 182:10
young man m. 127:17
Marriage: curse of m.! 205:7
frighten her into m. 117:4
m. has many pains 116:24
M. is like life 221:5
M. is popular 212:25
m. of true minds 211:16
merry as a m. bell 50:23
stylish m. 72:1
was m. ever out of fashion? 50:2
Marriage-feast: sweeter than the m. 66:6
Married: Charlotte was a m. lady 232:4
he is dreadfully m. 238:20
How To Be Happy Though M. 100:2
I have m. a wife 33:16
if we had ever been m. 89:9
I'm to be m. today 91:15
imprudently m. the barber 86:19
In m. life three is company 243:8
let us be m. 131:7
M. on Wednesday 158:2
m. past redemption 79:25
m. the man 158:8
M. to immortal verse 144:19
m. with mine uncle 185:11
mocks m. men 196:19
most m. man 238:20
till anes we m. be 16:4
to be m. within these three days 79:25
unpleasing to a m. ear 196:19
young man m. 127:17, 182:10
Marrow-bone: stole a m. 158:3
Marry: At leisure m.'d 68:13
better to m. than to burn 35:16
every woman should m. 76:19
going to m. Yum-Yum 92:6
m.'d in haste 68:13
m. for munny 228:23
may not m. his grandmother 172:17
persons about to m. 173:3
when a man should m. 14:19
will you m. me? 92:24
Mars: seat of M. 206:7
Marshal of France 151:16
Martha was cumbered about much
serving 33:9
Martial: with his m. cloak 245:5
Martin: Saint M.'s summer 192:5
Martlet: temple-haunting m. 198:2
Martyr: if thou dये a m. 60:29
Martyrs: noble army of m. 166:12
Marvel more and more 20:17

Mary: Blessed M.'s son 206:7
Jesu, M. and Joseph they bare 5:10
M. had a little lamb 99:5
M., M., quite contrary 156:16
M. was that Mother mild 2:10
mother of M. 161:9
to M. Queen the praise 65:23
Mary-buds: winking M. 184:20
Mary Jane: *What* is the matter
  with M.? 143:11
Mask: He had a m. 213:18
  m., and antique pageantry 144:19
Mass: confused m. 160:5
Masses: bow ye m. 96:16
  m. against the classes 94:5
Mast: above the m. did stand 65:12
  bends the gallant m. 71:16
  to see the m. burst open 86:9
Master: Man is the m. of things 224:8
  m. of himself 141:8
  m. of my fate 102:14
  m. o' the Tiger 197:5
  m. of them all 124:19
  my m. comes like any Turk 55:3
  not make dreams your m. 125:14
  of a m. spirit 148:8
  one for the m. 155:4
  Who's m. 223:23
  Why eateth your m. with publicans 31:10
  With her great M. 145:7
Masters: bad m. 132:1
  from their m.' table 31:31
  Mad World, My M. 41:5, 225:12
  m. of their fates 193:11
  morality of m. 154:5
  no man can serve two m. 30:26
  of their m.' thoughts 139:11
  people are the m. 47:8
  prevail on our future m. 215:19
Mat: caught my foot in the m. 98:18
Match: and a m. to win 153:6
  m. another foe! 54:6
Matched: m. our rackets 191:4
  M. with an aged wife 230:12
  who has m. us with His hour 42:10
Matches: m. of the Southron folk 232:11
  plays extravagant m. 92:9
Mate: and the m. of the *Nancy* brig 91:3
  Made my m. 221:19
  took unto herself a M. 249:2
Mater: stabat m. dolorosa 233:21
Materials: very few m. for history 90:14
Mates: and m. and slays 85:10
Mathematics [make men], subtile 14:27
Matilda: come a-waltzing M. 161:12
Matre pulchra filia pulchrior 109:4
Matrimony: holy estate of M. 168:10
  in holy M. 168:5
Matter: doth mince this m. 204:32
  for lack of m. 184:9
  from th' impurer m. 50:4
  in waking, no such m. 211:10
  More m. with less art 186:22
  No m. 173:7
  not much dislike the m. 182:14
  of a good m. 169:18
  root of the m. 25:36
  What is M.? 173:7
  What is the m. 143:11
Matters: It m. not how strait the
  gate 102:14
  may read strange m. 198:1
Matthew, Mark, Luke, and John 1:17
Maturing: of the m. sun 119:17
Maud: Come into the garden, M. 228:20
Mavourneen: Kathleen M. 71:2
Maxim of the British people 62:19
Maximum of temptation 212:25
May: be it what it m. 109:1

Bringeth vo'th M. flowers 6:5
Come what come m. 197:12
darling buds of M. 210:12
Do spring M. flowers 234:14
fair as is the rose in M. 60:22
fresh as is the month of M. 60:11
gathering nuts in M. 4:19
Maids are M. 184:11
meads in M. 244:18
merry month of M. 16:11, 18:12
mid-M.'s eldest child 121:5
outlives not M. 224:10
Queen o' the M. 228:21
swarm of bees in M. 3:15
while ye m. 104:14
Maypole: away to the M. hie 3:22
  m. in the Strand 41:2
Mazy: with a m. motion 66:15
Me: think only this of m. 42:11
  to come unto m. 32:34
  To m. did seem 246:7
  too much of m. 93:1
Meadow: in m. or plain 223:28
  sheep's in the m. 156:10
  through a m. of margin 216:15
  when m., grove, and stream 246:7
Meadows: Do paint the m. 196:19
  m. green 211:2
  M. trim 144:14
  past the near m. 121:7
  set in enamelled m. 238:5
Meads: fair these broad m. 181:7
  m. in May 244:18
Meal: for the evening m. 245:2
Mean: And that's what I m. 92:15
  choose it to m. 58:5
  know not what they m. 229:13
  loves well the golden m. 109:13
  say what you m. 56:22
Meander: As streams m. 149:5
  m. through a meadow of margin 216:15
Meanest: m. flower that blows 246:14
  not the m. of glories 108:11
Meaning: faint m. make pretence 79:24
  m. doesn't matter 92:21
  teems with hidden m. 93:28
Meanings packed up into one word 58:7
Meanly: All m. wrapt 145:7
  thinks m. of himself 115:16
Means: by right m. if you can 108:6
  cramped by narrow m. 119:3
  die beyond my m. 244:2
  For the m. of grace 166:32
  I don't know what it m. 91:1
Measles: Love is like the m. 113:6
Measure: heard the mingled m. 66:15
  m. every wand'ring planet 139:10
  m. my mind against his 212:14
  shrunk to this little m. 193:18
  stateliest m. 231:1
  treasure beyond m. 91:10
  What shame or m. 109:7
Measured: I have m. out my life 81:17
  I've m. it 248:16
Measureless to man 66:14, 15
Meat: all manner of m. 171:6
  came forth m. 24:31
  egg is full of m. 207:28
  give them m. 171:4
  penny ice and cold m. 91:25
  m. in the hall 221:22
  mock the m. it feeds on 205:5
  On our m., and on us all 104:16
Meats: funeral bak'd m. 185:13
Medes: given to the M. and Persians 29:18
Medias: in m. res 108:1
Mediator: Our M. and Advocate 166:26
Medicine: m. worse than the malady 19:15
  Shall ever m. thee 205:9

Medieval: in your m. hand   92:22
Medio tutissimus ibis   160:6
Mediocrity knows nothing higher   78:18
Meditate: strictly m.   145:1
Meditation: in maiden m.   203:7
let us all to m.   192:8
m. of my heart   168:31
Mediterranean: blue M.   214:2
Meed of some melodious tear   144:20
Meek: blessed are the m.   30:11
faculties so m.   198:4
m. and mild   241:12
That I am m. and gentle   193:20
Meekness: fruit of the spirit is . .m. 36:7
Meet: if I should m. thee   52:17
If we do m. again   194:21
m. and right   167:23
my love and I did m.   250:5
never the twain shall m.   124:13
still m. for ladies' love   110:2
till we m. again   175:2
we three m. again   197:2
when men and mountains m.   38:15
when we m. them   123:15
Meeter: deemed it m.   161:1
Meeting: as if I was a public m.   235:18
end in lovers m.   209:5
Meets: m. his Waterloo   162:15
more than m. the eye   125:8
Meilleur: le m. des mondes possibles 237:12
Melancholy: can soothe her m.   95:21
divinest M.   144:5
green and yellow m.   209:10
Hence, loathed M.   144:10
m. book   70:21
moping m.   146:24
most m.   144:6
suck m. out of a song   183:14
trick of m.   182:11
Veil'd M.   120:24
Mellow fruitfulness   119:17
Mellowing year   144:20
Mellstock: lie in M. churchyard   100:3
Melodies: Heard m. are sweet   120:19
Melodious: in some m. plot   121:2
m. birds   139:7
some m. tear   144:20
Melody: blund'ring kind of m.   79:10
Luve's like the m.   48:28
smale fowles maken m.   60:9
song and a m.   171:28
Melons: stumbling on m.   140:6
Melrose: view fair M.   180:5
Melt: crown of the earth doth m.   182:21
I rage, I m.   89:7
too solid flesh would m.   185:11
Melted: have m. into spring   41:15
Melting: are m. and reforming   251:3
Member: m. of Christ   167:32
m. of the force   176:3
Members one of another   36:11
Membra: etiam disiecti m. poetae   110:11
Même: plus c'est la m. chose   119:13
Memorable: that m. scene   140:8
Memorial: that have no m.   29:37
Memories: Liars ought to have
  good m.   216:27
Memory: do honour his m.   117:12
few precepts in thy m.   185:21
Fond M.   150:1
how sweet their m.   70:2
indebted to his m.   216:23
m. be green   185:6
m. of man runneth not   132:14
mixing m. and desire   81:23
Pluck from the m.   200:1
son of m.   147:12
very m. is fair   235:9
Vibrates in the m.   215:10

Men: all good English m.   230:4
all honourable m.   194:4
all m. are created equal   132:8
All m. are liars   171:14
all m. count with you   125:16
all the king's m.   156:1
all things to all m.   35:17
All those m. have their price   238:10
among unknown m.   247:2
arduous for mortal m.   108:15
are the best m.   191:10
Beneath the rule of m.   136:2
best m. are dead   173:20
better m. than we go out   125:9
biography of great m.   55:13
bodies of unburied m.   240:11
brave m.   50:23
busy haunts of m.   102:12
busy hum of m.   144:18
By keeping m. off   89:10
call up your m.   179:20
cities of m.   230:13
creeds that move m.'s hearts   41:14
cruel m. of Rome   193:9
dead m. rise up never   224:6
die to make m. free   111:16
died to make m. holy   111:16
Down among the dead m.   80:19
eyes of m.   207:3
fishers of m.   30:10
For m. may come   225:18
For m. must work   124:3
fraud of m.   204:9
give place to better m.   71:11
going to dine with some m.   22:12
good m. and true   204:12
good will toward m.   32:43
goodliest man of m.   146:17
happy breed of m.   206:7
Heart of oak are our m.   88:18
his m. Look'd at each other   121:9
honour all m.   37:4
I see m. as trees   32:31
in the sight of m.   29:33
just m. long opprest   147:6
Let us now praise famous m.
                         29:37, 127:15
life of m. on earth   20:2
light shine before m.   30:14
love to all m.   124:18
many m., many women   114:8
m. and women merely players   183:20
M. are April   184:11
m. be so strong   170:18
m. better than sheep or goats   227:2
m. decay   95:4
M. have died   184:10
m. in nations   51:19
m., like satyrs   138:9
M. may have rounded   142:9
m. might shun the awful shop   61:25
M. must endure   196:5
M. of few words   191:10
M. of little showing   127:15
m. of the Emerald Isle   78:30
M. seldom make passes   160:18
m. that strove with gods   230:14
m. that were boys   22:1
m. the more vicious grow   160:10
m. to take their exits   240:7
M. were deceivers   204:9
m. whose heads do grow   204:22
m., women, and clergymen   217:17
m. would be false   135:13
more I see of m.   176:9
nation of gallant m.   47:14
Nor public m.   250:7
not as other m. are   33:33
Not unbecoming m. that strove   230:15

obey God rather than m.   34:33
of sinful m.   166:35
of those m. in England   192:2
old m. and children   172:6
Old m. forget   192:4
old m. from the chimney corner   217:2
purgatory of m.   86:13
quit you like m.   35:32
Quit yourselves like m.   24:38
schemes o' mice and m.   48:26
sepulchre of famous m.   233:12
shadows of us m.?   117:18
So long as m. can breathe   210:12
So many m.   231:8
some m. are born great   209:12
Sons of m. and angels   241:7
sort of m. whose visages   201:7
sorts and conditions of m.   166:27
stories of savage m.   46:28
that m. betray   95:21
That m. call age   41:16
that private m. enjoy!   191:14
thoughts of m.   228:11
Three wise m. of Gotham   158:11
to match the m.   81:8
Two stern-faced m.   106:22
vainly m. themselves amaze   140:4
War Between M. and Women   233:13
ways of God to M.   145:11
we are the hollow m.   81:12
we petty m.   193:11
we've got the m.   112:1
what effect these m. will have   240:22
when m. and mountains meet   38:15
When m. were all asleep   41:7
When two strong m.   124:13
where Destiny with M.   85:10
Where m. with splendid hearts   42:7
which all m. knew!   228:25
wise m. three   162:2
with the tongues of m.   35:20
world of m.   44:16
Ye m. of Athens   34:42
Young m. and maidens   172:6
Mend: not m. his pace   189:19
  seek to m.   77:12
  times will not m.   160:20
Mene, mene, tekel, upharsin   29:18
Mens: m. sana in corpore sano   119:9
  m. sibi conscia recti   236:8
Mental: cease from M. Fight   38:16
Mentioned: players have often m.
  it   117:12
Mercenary: Followed their m. call-
  ing   111:11
Merchants: with Eastern m.   161:9
Mercies: thanks for m. past receive   45:21
Merciful: blessed are the m.   30:11
  God be m. to me   33:34
  God be m. unto us   170:4
  gracious, and m.   172:3
  M. and Mighty!   102:1
Mercuries: English M.   191:5
Mercury: words of M.   197:1
Mercy: big with m.   70:6
  crowning m.   71:7
  dimensions of this m.   71:7
  for M. has a human heart   39:13
  God in his m.   228:2
  God's gracious m.   168:16
  Have m. on thy people   127:7
  Have m. on us   166:21
  Lord have m.   152:5
  loving-kindness and m.   169:2
  m. endureth for ever   171:27
  M. I asked   53:11
  m. is above this sceptred sway   202:5
  m. mild   241:15
  quality of m.   202:5

render the deeds of m.   202:5
they shall obtain m.   30:11
to love m.   29:29
to M., Pity, Peace, and Love   39:12
to the m. of a rude stream   192:14
  when m. seasons justice   202:5
Mercy-seat: how beautiful Thy m.   83:14
Meredith climbed towards the sun   62:2
Merit: by m. raised   146:10
  no damned m. in it   141:19
  patient m.   187:13
  To buried m.   117:2
Merits: Let him who m.   152:17
Mermaid: done at the M.   19:9
  married to a m.   6:17
Mermaid-like   189:18
Mermaid Tavern: Choicer than the
  M.   120:17
Merriest: maddest, m. day   228:21
Merrily: After summer m.   208:20
  m. we'll whoop   242:20
Merriment: flashes of m.   189:20
  This m. of parsons   115:23
Merry: all their wars are m.   61:15
  as m. as a marriage bell   50:23
  eat..drink..to be merry   26:43
  for to-night we'll m. be   3:21
  God rest you m.   4:11
  it is good to be m. and wise   5:14
  m. and sad to tell   20:1
  m. and wise   5:14, 141:14
  m. Dr. Brighton   231:13
  m. heart   26:17
  m. monarch   176:1
  m. month of May   16:11, 18:12
  M. of soul   221:20
  m. yarn   141:4
  never m. when I hear sweet music   202:12
  piped with m. cheer   39:8
  turn his m. note   183:13
  we were m.   65:3
  with a m. noise   169:22
Mess: In every m.   73:17
  m. of potash   238:17
Messe: Paris vaut bien une m.   103:2
Messenger: an Anglo-Saxon M.   58:8
  m. of Satan   36:4
Messengers: bade his m. ride forth   136:8
Messes: other country m.   144:15
Messieurs les gardes françaises   101:7
Messing about in boats   96:16
Met: Hail fellow, well m.   223:23
  how first he m. her   232:4
  Jenny kissed me when we m.   112:4
  never m.   48:5
  night that first we m.   19:5
Metal more attractive   188:12
Metals: of m. twain   145:2
Metaphysic: high as m. wit   49:17
Mete: I m. and dole   230:12
Meteor flag   54:8
Method: no objection to this m.   220:15
  there is m. in it   186:26
Methodist: morals of a M.   93:25
Methods: by different m.   62:9
  you know my m.   78:5
Metropolis: m. of the empire   64:14
  m. of the north   226:7
Mewing her mighty youth   148:10
Mewling and puking   183:20
Mexique: beyond the M. bay   140:1
Mezzo: nel m. del cammin   72:4
Mice: appear like m.   195:19
  best laid schemes o' m.   48:26
  like little m.   222:6
  Three blind m.   158:10
Michelangelo: Talking of M.   81:15
Mickle: makes a m.   59:10
Microcosm of a public school   76:22

Microscopes of hextra power   75:27
Midday: full m. beam   148:10
  our m. sweat   173:23
  out in the m. sun   69:8
Middle: m. of her favours   187:1
  m. of the night   57:20, 185:16
  safely in the m.   160:6
  steer a m. course   141:9
Middle age: wives..companions for
  m.   14:18
Middle Class was quite prepared   21:7
Middle classes: ye lower m.   91:16
Midian: troops of M.   152:11
Midlands: when I am living in the M. 21:24
Midnight: black and m. hags   199:18
  blackest M. born   144:10
  came upon the m. clear   181:10
  cease upon the m.   121:6
  chimes at m.   190:31
  consumed the m. oil   89:27
  foul and m. murther   97:7
  m. never come   138:14
  our m. oil   173:24
  sighed upon a m. pillow   183:11
Midnoon: It was the deep m.   229:4
Midshipmite: and a m.   91:3
Midst: I in the m. of them   31:40
  in the m. of life   168:19
  in the m. of the sea   169:20
  in the m. of whom they live   40:7
  into the m. of the story   108:1
Midsummer madness   209:16
Midway: floated m. on the waves   66:15
  wing the m. air   195:19
Mid-winter: in the bleak m.   177:9
Mien: her m. carries much more
  invitation   220:5
  I fear thy m.   215:11
Mieux: je vais de m. en m.   69:5
  Le m. est l'ennemi du bien   237:14
  Tout est pour le m.   237:12
Might: all her m. and main   143:11
  do it with thy m.   27:2
  m. of the Gentile   52:11
  Puts invincible m.   147:6
  sadness of her m.   120:24
  shining with all his m.   57:20
  spirit of..m.   28:1
  thy saw of m.   184:7
  to be strengthened with m.   36:9
  with all thy m.   149:1
Might-have-been: I don't want to
  be a m.!   18:16
Mightier: make thee m. yet   22:7
Mightiest: m. in the m.   202:5
Mighty: all that m. heart   249:4
  all the proud and m.   80:18
  called..The M. God   27:32
  each a m. Voice   248:13
  God who made thee m.   22:7
  hear the m. waters   246:12
  how are the m. fallen   24:47, 25:1
  is m. offensive   115:23
  joy to his m. heart   125:1
  Look on my works ye M.   214:6
  m. above all things   29:31
  m. of the earth   147:6
  Merciful and M.!   102:1
  Nimrod the m. hunter   23:24
  put down the m.   32:38
  rushing m. wind   34:31
  some have called thee m.   77:9
  stretch forth thy m. hand   111:13
Milan: Retire me to my M.   208:22
Mild: his m. and magnificent eye   44:10
  meek and m.   241:12
Mildest: m. manner'd man   51:16
Mile: tires in a m.-a   210:7
  walked a crooked m.   158:5

Miles: draw but twenty m. a day?   139:13
  five m. meandering   66:15
  How many m. to Babylon?   155:19
  hundred m. away   100:6
  m. around the wonder grew   110:18
  People come m. to see it   92:11
Militant here in earth   167:20
Military: good order and m. discipline   3:23
  to be left to m. men   225:5
Milk: drunk the m. of Paradise   66:15
  flowing with m.   24:2
  m. and honey blest   152:14
  m. comes frozen home   196:20
  m. of human kindness   197:14
  take my m. for gall   197:14
  trout in the m.   233:9
  white curd of ass's m.   165:7
Milked the cow   158:8
Milk-white peacock   229:16
Milky Way: or m.   164:14
  twinkle on the m.   247:4
Mill: at the m. with slaves   147:2
Mill, John Stuart: By a mighty
  effort of will   22:11
Miller: there was a jolly m.   37:29
Million: aiming at a m.   43:18
  pleased not the m.   187:7
Millionaire: he must be a m.   90:17
Millions: m. at 'ome   128:6
  multiplying m.   159:20
Mills: dark Satanic m.   38:16
  m. of God   134:2
Millstone: m. were hanged about
  his neck   31:38, 33:30
Mill-wheel: except the m.'s sound 213:11
Milton: for not enjoying M.   129:8
  Malt does more than M. can   111:7
  M.! thou shouldst be living   247:7
  M...was a genius   116:5
  M. was for us   44:11
  mute inglorious M.   97:15
  reason M. wrote in fetters   39:16
  round the path of M.   248:2
  Think thee M.   251:2
  which M. held   247:1
Miminy piminy   93:3
Mimsy: all m.   57:14
Mince: doth m. this matter   204:31
  They dined on m.   131:9
Mind: bring the philosophic m.   246:13
  brought all to m.   250:7
  But to my m.   186:3
  calm of m.   147:11
  cannot m. my wheel   129:21
  Clear your m. of cant   116:3
  Come back into my m.   21:24
  complicated state of m.   92:21
  concentrates his m.   115:13
  dagger of the m.   198:9
  dead man out of m.   169:10
  distressed in m.   166:29
  Farewell the tranquil m.   205:10
  first started to my m.   90:12
  Force without m.   109:21
  fortitude of the m.   113:14
  frailty of the m.   182:5
  he that does not m. his belly   114:20
  in his right m.   32:30
  In my m.'s eye   185:14
  in the m. of man   248:19
  index of a m.   247:17
  is thy m. perplexed?   72:18
  keep your m. even   109:10
  knew their m.   106:17
  last infirmity of noble m.   145:1
  let the world m. him   43:18
  man's unconquerable m.   248:20
  measure my m. against his   212:14

m. conscious of the right 236:8
m. has a thousand eyes 40:13
m. is clouded with a doubt 227:3
m. is its own place 146:2
m.'s construction 197:13
my m. forbids to crave 80:17
My m. to me a kingdom is 80:17
narrowed his m. 95:17
never brought to m.? 48:6
Never m. 173:7
noble m. is here o'erthrown 188:6
nobler in the m. 187:13
not in my perfect m. 196:2
of fishy form and m. 42:2
of the chainless m.! 51:9
out of m. 64:11, 77:27
pulse in the eternal m. 42:11
quiet m. 134:20
seized their troubled m. 225:9
she had a frugal m. 69:24
so pleased my m. 7:22
sound m. 119:9
that spoke the vacant m. 95:5
they have no m. to 49:19
'Tis strange the m. 51:25
to a m. diseas'd 200:1
to speak one's m. 243:13
to the noble m. 188:2
Two things fill the m. 119:10
untutored m. 164:14
vacant m. 191:15
ways of my own m. 232:6
what he is pleased to call his m. 22:19
What is m. 173:7
worked her m. to such a pitch 71:1
Mindless of its just honours 248:1
Minds: Balm of hurt m. 198:13
corrupt the m. 162:18
great actions speak great m. 19:21
great empire and little m. 47:4
happiest and best m. 215:17
idols which beset men's m. 15:11
inspir'd their hearts, Their m. 139:11
little things affect little m. 76:20
marriage of true m. 211:16
M. innocent and quiet 134:19
refuge of weak m. 61:10
religion of feeble m. 47:16
to have aspiring m. 139:10
Mine: and the maid is m. 117:4
Excavating for a m. 149:7
He is m. 104:4
I will pledge with m. 117:19
m. has been a fine one 40:9
m. he cannot miss 216:29
My beloved is m. 27:18
necessity is yet greater than m. 217:3
needst not fear m. 215:11
O mistress m.! 209:5
to call thee m. 137:15, 235:4
vengeance is m. 35:11
Wilt thou be m.? 155:11
wish it were only m.! 127:1
Miner: Dwelt a m. 149:7
Mingle: to m. with the Universe 51:7
Mingled: heard the m. measure 66:15
Minion: Like valour's m. 197:4
Morning's m. 107:17
Minions of the moon 190:6
Minister: m. to a mind diseas'd 200:1
must m. to himself 200:1
stickit m. 180:16
Ministering angel 180:13
Ministers: errands for the M. of
State 91:10
m. of grace 186:4
m. reminded me 76:9
murdering m. 197:14
servile m. 195:5

Ministries: Times has made many m. 15:18
Ministry of all the talents 7:19
Minnehaha, Laughing Water 134:6
Minnows: Triton of the m. 184:18
Minority is always right 112:12
Minstrel: M. was infirm 180:4
wandering M. I 91:27
Minstrel Boy: M. to the war 149:15
Minute: about once in a m. 57:1
fill the unforgiving m. 125:16
in a m. 74:4
sucker born every m. 18:14
Minutes: m. hasten to their end 211:5
so the little m. 55:26
take care of the m. 61:8
Miracle: a m. of loveliness 92:11
a m. of rare device 66:15
Miracles: m. are past 182:9
m. do not happen 12:7
Miranda: remember an Inn, M.? 22:2
Mirror: and smash his m. 9:6
m. cracked 227:25
m. of all Christian kings 191:5
m. of all courtesy 192:12
m. up to nature 188:9
Mirrors of the sea 86:10
Mirth: in my m. 171:28
m. and fun grew fast 49:2
m. and laughter 51:15
m. that has no bitter springs 124:18
must borrow its m. 243:3
present m. 209:5
song of the birds for m. 99:2
sunburnt m. 121:3
Mischief: either of virtue or m. 14:17
may breed m. 88:5
Satan finds some m. 239:10
wait on nature's m. 197:14
Mischievous: this animal is very m. 9:3
Miserable: m. comforters 25:32
m. sinners 166:21
to be weak is m. 146:1
Miseries: Is bound in..m. 194:19
Misery: dwell on guilt and m. 13:15
happiness in m. 72:7
M. acquaints a man 208:14
result m. 74:8
vale of m. 170:14
worst sting of m. 40:1
Misfortune: M. of our best friends 175:16
regarded as a m. 243:10
Misfortunes: make m. more bitter 14:20
m. of mankind 90:14
Mislead the morn 201:3
Mislight: No will-o'-th'-wisp m.
thee 104:13
Mislike me not 201:19
Misplaced: find those words m. 68:13
Misquote: enough of learning to m. 52:4
Miss: mine he cannot m. 216:29
whatever M. T. eats 73:7
Missed: health and wealth have m.
me 112:4
who never would be m. 91:30
Misses a unit 43:18
Missing so much 68:28
Missionary: I would eat a m. 243:2
Missouri: cross the wide M. 6:14
Mist: grey m. 141:2
in the m. of tears 232:6
m. in my face 45:2
m. is dispell'd 89:18
rank m. they draw 145:3
Through the cold and heavy m. 106:21
Mistake: a capital m. 78:4
made any such m. 75:3
m. was made 74:10
Mistaken: possible you may be m. 71:6
unless I am m. 78:13

Mistakes: All great men make m. 62:15
  man who makes no m. 162:14
Mistletoe hung in the castle hall 19:4
Mistook: he who, not m. 140:13
Mistress: But m. in my own 126:19
  Gold is for the m. 124:19
  in ev'ry port a m. find 90:1
  jealous m. 82:16
  made to his m.' eyebrow 183:20
  m. still the open road 221:16
  My m.' eyes 212:3
  new m. now I chase 134:20
  O m. mine 209:5
  So court a m. 117:18
Mistresses: I shall have m. 90:5
  wives are young men's m. 14:18
Mists: Season of m. 119:17
Misty: m. mountain tops 208:2
  m. solitudes 128:3
Misunderstood: To be great is to be m. 82:21
Mites: threw in two m. 32:35
Mithras, God of the Morning 127:14
Mixed: conversation in a m. company 61:12
  elements so m. in him 194:24
Mizpah 23:31
Moab is my wash-pot 170:2
Moan: And made sweet m. 120:12
  everything did banish m. 18:12
  m. of doves 229:19
Moaning: m. of the bar 226:6
  now they are m. 82:12
Moans: deep m. round 230:15
Moat: as a m. defensive 206:7
Moated: at the m. grange 201:2
Mob: to do what the m. do 75:18
Mobled queen 187:8
Mock: doth m. the meat it feeds on 205:5
  M. on 38:17
  m. their useful toil 97:12
  m. your own grinning 189:20
  They m. the air 97:4
Mocked: God is not m. 36:8
Mockery: delusion, a m. 73:11
Mocking-bird: Out of the m.'s throat 242:12
Model: very m. of a modern Major-General 93:18
Moderate: taking care to m. his voice 220:13
Moderation: astonished at my own m.! 64:2
  easier than perfect m. 13:10
Modest: m. dress 241:20
  m. stillness 191:8
  quip m. 184:14
Modester: people ought to be m. 55:21
Modesty of nature 188:8
Modified rapture 92:4
Mohicans: Last of the M. 68:26
Moi: Parce que c'était m. 149:2
Moist: with anguish m. 120:11
Mole: Well said, old m.! 186:15
Moles: Rudis indigestaque m. 160:5
Molly Malone: sweet M. 51:8
Molten: like m. lead 196:1
Mome: and the m. raths 57:14
Moment: every m. dies a man 231:2
  Every m. one is born 231:2
  great pith and m. 187:13
  in a m., in the twinkling 35:29
  in a m. travel thither 246:12
  m. to decide 135:3
  one M. in Annihilation's Waste 85:9
  To be a m.'s ornament 248:4
Moments: best and happiest m. 215:17
  days and m. 58:21
  m. of glad grace 250:11
  m. which he calls his own 176:6

Monarch: merry m. 176:1
  m. of all I survey 70:19
  m. of the sky 138:13
  throned m. 202:5
  with a m.'s voice 193:21
Monarchize: to m. 206:15
Monarchy of wit 54:20
Monday: betwixt a Saturday and M. 55:4
  Born on a M. 158:2
  hanging of his cat on M. 41:3
  M.'s child 156:17
  on a M. morning 106:7
Mondes: le meilleur des m. possibles 237:12
Money: blessing that m. cannot buy 238:15
  Counting out his m. 158:1
  ever wrote, except for m. 115:8
  go where m. is 228:23
  I bet my m. 87:8
  love of m. 36:30
  marry for m. 228:23
  M. by right means 108:6
  M., I despise it 92:24
  m. is like muck 14:22
  m. the sinews of war 15:2
  No m. 174:11
  pays your m. 173:4
  pleasant to have m. 64:3
  plenty of m. 131:6
  Put m. in thy purse 204:25
  time is m. 88:1
  way the m. goes 138:2
  we've got the m. too 112:1
Mongrel: Both m., puppy, whelp 95:13
Monk: devil a m. wou'd be 151:2
  many a m. 17:11
Monkey: for a m. 201:28
Monkeys: wilderness of m. 201:28
Monks: town of m. 66:9
Monotony: articulate m. 220:7
Monster: green-ey'd m. 205:5
  many-headed m. 141:13, 165:12
  m. fearful and hideous 236:13
  m. of ingratitudes 208:27
  to scare the m. 125:5
Monstrous: a m. crow 57:18
  Is it not m. 187:11
  M. Regiment of Women 129:1
  O m.! 190:16
  with m. head 61:11
Monstrum horrendum, informe, ingens 236:13
Montaigne 220:22
Monte Carlo: who broke the bank at M. 90:17
Montezuma: who imprisoned M. 136:20
Month: a year, a m., a week 138:14
  fresh as is the m. of May 60:11
  is the cruellest m. 81:23
  leafy m. of June 66:3
  little m. 185:11
  This is the m. 145:6
  yet within a m. 185:11
Months: mother of m. 223:28
  twelve m. in all the year 16:11
Montreal: Oh M.! 50:10
Monument: his m. look around 250:1
  patience on a m. 209:10
  thou art a m. 118:4
Monuments: gilded m. 211:4
  oases of preserved m. 151:10
Monumentum: Si m. requiris 250:1
Mood: melting m. 205:20
  vacant or in pensive m. 247:5
Moody: headstrong, m., murmuring race 79:4
Moon: a-roving by the light of the m. 52:15
  bares her bosom to the m. 249:5
  bay the m. 194:7
  beneath a waning m. 66:14

beneath the visiting m. — 182:21
by the light of the m. — 131:9
by yonder blessed m. — 207:24
Come from the dying m. — 229:9
Daughter of the M. — 134:4
ebb and flow by the m. — 196:6
fair as the m. — 27:19
fishing up the m. — 162:2
from the pale-fac'd m. — 190:9
hang them on the horns o' the m. — 184:17
hornèd m. — 65:16
how sad steps, O M. — 216:30
I saw the new m. — 16:41
in the m.'s eclipse — 199:15
inconstant m. — 207:24
jumped over the m. — 155:17
minions of the m. — 190:6
m. be still as bright — 52:13
m. doth shine — 155:5
m. doth with delight — 246:8
m. is my sister — 21:13
M. of Heaven — 86:2
m. of moons — 73:26
M. of my Delight — 86:2
m. on the one hand — 21:13
m. shines bright — 82:1
m. takes up the wondrous tale — 1:12
m. was a ghostly galleon — 155:1
m.'s soft pace — 247:18
moving M. — 65:22
neither the m. by night — 171:17
no bigger than the M. — 65:12
old m. in her arms — 16:14
one revolving m. — 79:8
sickle m. — 86:10
silver apples of the m. — 250:10
slow m. climbs — 230:14
Sun and m. rejoice — 122:24
sun, m., and stars — 40:8
swear not by the m. — 207:24
to the m. complain — 97:9
wat'ry m. — 203:7
when the m. shall rise — 249:13
When the m. shone — 202:14
when the m. was blood — 61:16
white m. beams — 123:12
With the m.'s beauty — 247:18
Moonlight: braw, bricht, m. nicht — 130:8
how sweet the m. — 202:11
pale m. — 180:5
ribbon of m. — 155:1
Moonlit: knocking on the m. door — 73:4
Moons: swift m. make up again — 110:6
Till m. shall wax — 239:13
Moonshine: transcendental m. — 55:18
Moon-struck madness — 146:24
Moor: lascivious M. — 204:18
over the purple m. — 155:1
Mop: with m. and pattens — 218:4
Moping owl — 97:9
Mopsy: Flopsy, M., Cotton-tail — 165:22
Moral: Englishman thinks he is m. — 212:21
m. law within me — 119:10
m. man was Werther — 232:4
m. of that is — 57:3
m. or an immoral book — 243:19
more than a m. duty — 243:13
Of m. evil — 248:15
symptom of the m. flabbiness — 113:1
To point a m. — 117:3
Moral philosophy is but an hand-
    maid to religion — 14:5
Morality: m. of masters — 154:5
m. of slaves — 154:5
m. touched by emotion — 12:8
not simple m. — 12:8
periodical fits of m. — 136:23
talk of m. — 80:28
Morals: faith and m. hold — 247:1

foundation of m. — 22:8
m. of a whore — 114:2
with the m. of a Methodist — 93:25
Morbo: Venienti occurrite m. — 162:9
More: are m. than they — 227:5
brave, that are no m. — 70:9
cried 'No m.' — 103:19
death shall be no m. — 77:10
has asked for m. — 75:7
interested him no m. — 101:4
m. he heard — 173:13
m. they are the same — 119:13
neither m. nor less — 58:5
nicely-calculated less or m. — 247:6
No m. of that — 205:20
Oh, never m. — 213:15
Oh, the little m. — 43:11
sees no m. — 176:6
Morem: Contra bonum m. — 181:20
Mores: O tempora, O m. ! — 63:17
Mori: pro patria m. — 109:18
Moriar: Non omnis m. — 110:3
Morituri te salutant — 9:16, 222:10
Morn: crowed in the m. — 158:8
day's at the m. — 44:24
From m. to night — 177:13
From m. to noon he fell — 146:9
incense-breathing M. — 97:11
issuing on a summer's m. — 146:22
look, the m. — 185:5
mislead the m. — 201:3
m. of song — 222:2
no sleep till m. — 51:1
On a winter's m. — 131:5
peeping in at m. — 107:1
salute the happy m. — 50:14
sang from m. till night — 37:29
this pious m. — 120:21
this the happy m. — 145:6
ushers in the m. — 84:11
when m. purples the east — 146:20
when the m. is grey — 53:9
with the m. — 153:16
yet 'tis early m. — 228:4
Morning: Against the m. star — 213:12
beauty of the m. — 249:4
birdsong at m. — 221:17
but with the m. — 181:1
come again in the m. — 216:16
early in the m. — 8:12, 102:1
early one m. — 4:4
forehead of the m. sky — 145:4
from his lair in the m. — 97:2
glad confident m. — 44:12
glorious m. face — 221:24
glorious m. have I seen — 211:2
God of the M. — 127:14
Heaven's m. breaks — 135:17
How splendid in the M. — 86:6
I caught this m. m.'s minion — 107:17
if m. skies — 221:24
in the m. it is green — 170:17
in the m. of the world — 44:25
in the m. we will remember — 38:2
joy cometh in the m. — 169:8
like the m. star — 47:14
looketh forth as the m. — 27:19
m. cometh — 28:5
M. in the Bowl of Night — 84:15
m.'s at seven — 44:24
Never m. wore to evening — 227:7
New every m. — 122:13
nice to get up in the m. — 130:10
on a cold and frosty m. — 4:19
on a Monday m. — 106:7
pay thy m. sacrifice — 123:1
scent the m. air — 186:11
sees some m., unaware — 44:1
shining m. face — 183:20

Morning (cont.)
son of the m.! | 28:4
sons of the m.! | 101:14
three-o'-clock in the m. courage | 233:7
two o'clock in the m. courage | 151:17
when the m. stars sang | 25:42
who started that m. | 91:25
wings of the m. | 172:1
your shadow at m. | 81:24
Morrison Weatherby | 143:9
Morrow: Of the night for the m. | 215:13
thought of the M. | 245:6
till it be m. | 207:25
watching for the m. | 55:23
Mors: Pallida M. aequo..pede | 108:16
Mortal: arduous for m. men | 108:15
chances of this m. life | 167:27
Come, thou m. wretch | 183:4
finds he m. blisses | 214:9
here came a m. | 11:13
laugh at any m. thing | 51:22
m. must put on immortality | 35:30
m. temples of a king | 206:15
sing with m. voice | 146:20
tend on m. thoughts | 197:15
this m. coil | 187:13
whose m. taste | 145:9
you m. engines | 205:10
Mortalibus: Nil m. ardui est | 108:15
Mortality: m. her tears | 236:7
to frail m. shall trust | 15:14
Mortals: fools these m. be | 203:14
'tis not in m. to command
success | 1:4
we m. are capable of | 238:15
Mortify a wit | 165:12
Morts: Il n'y a pas de m. | 137:16
Mos: suo' quoique m | 231:8
Moses: from Mahomet to M. | 166:5
Moss: gather no m. | 234:16
overgrown with azure m. | 214:2
Mossy: by a m. stone | 248:3
or m. cavern | 120:17
Most: make the m. of it | 103:9
m. of what we yet may spend | 85:5
pleased the m. | 73:18
Mote that is in thy brother's eye | 30:31
Moth: desire of the m. | 215:13
where m. and rust doth corrupt | 30:23
Mother: as is the m. | 29:11
behold thy m. | 34:27
by her m. wit | 219:12
call me early, m. dear | 228:21
does your m. know that you are
out? | 18:4
England is the m. of Parliaments | 41:12
from his m.'s womb | 200:11
his m. drudge | 212:20
Honour thy father and thy m. | 167:12
in my m.'s house | 126:19
jumping on his m. | 93:23
man leave . . his m. | 23:14
m. bids me bind my hair | 112:8
m. for her children | 38:1
M., for the love of grace | 189:3
M., I cannot mind my wheel | 129:21
m. of harlots | 37:22
M. o' mine | 126:16
m. of months | 223:28
M. of the Fair Delight | 177:14
M., Wife, and Queen | 230:1
my m. bore me | 39:10
never called me m. | 245:12
O m. Ida | 229:3
of a fair m. | 109:4
on his m.'s arm | 246:9
Pembroke's m. | 43:2
rhyming m. wits | 139:8
rolled m. with infant | 147:16

so loving to my m. | 185:11
Stood the mournful m. | 233:21
tell your m. it wasn't I | 155:10
there was their Dacian m. | 51:5
tho' father and m. | 49:3
Took great care of his M. | 143:9
virgin m. born | 145:6
where a M. laid her baby | 2:10
Who was your m.? | 222:3
your m. and I should have liv'd | 89:9
Motherland, we pledge to thee | 124:18
Mothers: become like their m. | 243:11
Moths: unfading m. | 42:3
Motion: Hath m. | 211:13
I fear..thy m. | 215:11
in his m. like an angel | 202:11
little m. in the air | 213:11
next to the perpetual m. | 75:32
no m. has she now | 245:14
sensible warm m. | 200:23
with a mazy m. | 66:15
Motions: m. of his spirit | 202:13
to thy m. lovers' seasons run? | 77:18
Motives meaner than your own | 181:17
Motley: made myself a m. | 211:15
m.'s the only wear | 183:18
Motor Bus: Can it be a M.? | 94:9
Mould: m. of form | 188:16
scratched with a stick in the m. | 125:1
Moulded: m. by the lips of man | 231:1
m. out of faults | 201:5
m. the changing lineaments | 161:9
Mouldering: lies a-m. in the grave | 99:6
Moulds: crack nature's m. | 195:4
Moulmein: old M. Pagoda | 126:11
Moult away his wings | 222:8
Mount: By m. and stream | 102:9
may not m. on thee again | 154:12
m. larks aloft | 105:2
m. up with wings | 28:15
pants its source to m. | 149:5
Mount Abora: singing of M. | 66:15
Mountain: along the m. side | 247:19
dew on the m. | 180:3
every m...shall be made low | 28:12
from yonder m. height | 229:18
gone on the m. | 180:2
m. sheep are sweeter | 162:1
o'er the rugged m.'s brow | 96:10
on the misty m. tops | 208:2
Over all the m. tops | 94:15
robes the m. | 54:3
say unto this m. | 31:36
sun looked over the m.'s rim | 44:16
up the airy m. | 2:17
watches from his m. walls | 226:9
Woods or steepy m. | 139:6
Mountain-built with peaceful cita-
del | 120:21
Mountains: Alpine m. cold | 147:16
Among our ancient m. | 132:13
Among the m. | 226:25
Delectable M. | 46:12
Greenland's icy m. | 101:15
Hellas rears its m. | 213:12
how beautiful upon the m. | 28:18
m. divide us | 181:7
m. look on Marathon | 51:18
m. skipped | 171:12
M. will be in labour | 107:21
one of the m. | 248:13
paced upon the m. | 250:11
that I could remove m. | 35:21
walk upon England's m. | 38:16
when men and m. meet | 38:15
Mountain-side: From every m. | 217:14
Mountain-tops: Flatter the m. | 211:2
M. that freeze | 192:13
Mounted: but m. high | 145:4

Mourn: haste to m. 58:25
makes countless thousands m. 48:24
No longer m. for me 211:7
now can never m. 213:8
they that m. 30:11
Mourned: we have m. unto you 31:19
would have m. longer 185:11
Mourners: no m. walk behind me 100:9
Mournful: in m. numbers 133:26
m. and slow 243:1
m., holy 228:1
m. truth 116:27
Stood the m. mother 233:21
with m. tread 242:11
Mourning: m. of a mighty nation 228:24
widow bird sate m. 213:11
Mourns: England m. for her dead 38:1
Mourra: On m. seul 161:6
Mouse: birth will be a..m. 107:21
cat would watch a m. 223:18
caught a crooked m. 158:5
for killing of a m. 41:3
little m. under the chair 157:14
m. ran up the clock 155:18
Not a m. 204:4
Mouse-trap: make a better m. 83:4
Mouth: down in the m. 68:11
Familiar in his m. 192:4
from the lion's m. 169:1
God be in my m. 4:10
he opened not his m. 28:21
hot i' the m. 209:7
if you m. it 188:7
in the cannon's m. 183:20
killing Kruger with your m. 124:9
look a gift horse in the m. 49:20
make a m. at you 234:19
make his m. to water 49:24
m. of Hell 226:4
m. of the Lord 28:12
m. of very babes 168:22
out of the m. of God 30:8
purple-stained m. 121:3
roof of my m. 171:28
upon my m. 140:6
words of my m. 168:31
Mouth-honour, breath 199:32
Mouths and speak not 171:13
Moutons: Retournons à nos m. 9:8
Move: But it does m. 88:15
creeds that m. men's hearts 41:14
ever when I m. 230:13
I will m. Thee 104:2
looking well can't m. her 222:5
prayers would m. me 193:16
to m. immediately upon your works 97:1
we live and m. 34:43
Moveable Feasts 166:6
Moved: have m. me not 221:24
I, singularly m. 161:14
like a cast shadow m. 235:11
m. among my race 221:24
m. and spoke 161:15
though the earth be m. 169:20
Movement: freedom of m. 174:2
Moves: an engine that m. 100:12
having writ m. on 85:12
Hither and thither m. 85:10
It m. us not 249:5
Moving: always m. 139:10
art m. everywhere 214:1
in form, in m. 187:4
M. Finger writes 85:12
slow and m. finger 205:13
Mow: more ye m. us down 231:10
Mr. Dick justly observed to me 74:13
Mrs. Crupp had indignantly assured him 74:13

Mrs. Gummidge's words 74:5
Mrs. Worthington: on the stage M. 69:9
Much: how m. it is 43:11
is too m. for us 249:5
m. learning doth make thee mad 34:50
M. of a muchness 235:5
none too m. 125:16
so m. and so m. 68:28
so m. owed 62:23
so m. to do 175:9, 227:14
talk too m. 79:7
Tho' m. is taken 230:15
though m. I want 80:17
too m. of me 93:1
won't be m. for us 56:9
Mucho: Muchos pocos hacen un m. 59:10
Muck: money is like m. 14:22
m. of sweat 96:2
Muckrake in his hand 46:15
Muck-rakes: men with the m. 177:2
Mud: me name is M. 73:12
one sees the m. 130:3
shall come of water and of m. 41:20
stick'n in a big m. hole 87:9
Muddied oafs 126:1
Muddle through 41:9
Muddy vesture of decay 202:11
Mug: and heavenly m. 86:11
Mules of politics 166:4
Mull was a-stern 221:21
Multiplication is vexation 6:8
Multiply: be fruitful, and m. 23:8
Multitude: giddy m. 141:13
in the m. of counsellors 26:12
m. is always in the wrong 76:3
Multitudes: I contain m. 242:15
m. in the valley of decision 29:23
pestilence-stricken m. 214:1
Multitudinous: M. chatterings 142:6
M. seas 198:15
Mum's the word 67:17
Munch on 44:22
Munched: and m., and m. 197:5
Muove: E pur si m. 88:15
Murder: does m. sleep 198:13
foul and midnight m. fed 97:7
Killing no M. 182:2
met M. in the way 213:18
M...as One of the Fine Arts 73:14
m. cannot be hid long 201:22
m. most foul 186:8
m. will out 68:4
shalt do no m. 167:13
to m. and to rafish 14:2
Murdered: All m. 206:15
and their m. man 120:8
hath m. sleep 198:14
Murderer: honourable m. 205:19
Murderers: our friends the m. 119:14
Murdering ministers 197:14
Murderous, bloody, full of blame 212:1
Murex: who fished the m. up? 44:26
Murky: Hell is m. 199:28
Murmur: I do not m. 102:3
M. a little sadly 250:11
m. of a summer's day 11:23
to prevent that m. 147:17
Murmuring: headstrong, moody, m. race 79:4
m. of innumerable bees 229:19
m. surge 195:19
Murmurous haunt of flies 121:5
Murmurs: As for m., mother 96:1
Mus: nascetur ridiculus m. 107:21
Muscles of his brawny arms 134:1
Muscular: his Christianity was m. 76:16
Muse: M. of fire 191:2
Rise, honest M.! 164:24
Tell me M. 106:16

Muse (*cont.*)
thankless M. 145:1
whose m. on dromedary trots 66:11
Mused: many a m. rhyme 121:6
m. a little space 228:2
never m. on sorrow 54:4
Muses: M.' hierophant 109:16
M. on admired themes 139:11
Music: all kinds of m. 29:16
condition of m. 161:10
don't know anything about m. 20:10
fled is that m. 121:7
frozen m. 179:10
hear sweet m. 202:12
heavy part the m. bears 117:10
how potent cheap m. is 69:15
let the sounds of m. 202:11
man that hath no m. in himself 202:13
mind the m. and the step 17:5
m. arose with its voluptuous swell 50:23
m. be the food of love 209:2
m. crept by me 208:10
m. hath charms 68:9
m. in its roar 51:7
m. sent up to God 43:7
M. shall untune the sky 79:18
M. that gentlier 228:17
m. that I care to hear 107:13
M. when soft voices die 215:10
of his m. vows 188:6
Oh, the brave M. 84:20
one chord of m. 172:23
She shall have m. 157:17
soul of m. shed 149:13
still, sad m. 248:19
They were thy chosen m. 248:13
We are the m. makers 159:18
will make the m. mute 226:23
with m. loud and long 66:15
your voice is m. 20:10
Musical: most m. 144:6
m. as Apollo's lute 144:2
Musing there an hour 51:18
Musk of the rose 228:20
Musk-rose: coming m. 121:5
Musk-roses: sweet m. 203:9
Must: Is m. a word to be addressed
to princes? 82:10
Mustard: grain of m. seed 31:27, 36
Pass the m. 93:36
Mustn't; tell her she m. 173:11
Mutamur: *nos et m. in illis* 160:10
nos m. in illis 10:7
Mutantur: *Tempora m.* 10:7, 160:10
Mute: are not soon m. 129:22
hangs as m. 149:13
hoarse or m. 146:20
m. inglorious Milton 97:15
will make the music m. 226:23
Mutilators of collections 129:7
Mutiny: to rise and m. 194:13
Mutton: beef, pork, and m. 124:15
boiled leg of m. 75:20
Muzzle: thou shalt not m. the ox 24:20
Myriads: M. of rivulets 229:19
outshine m. though bright 145:14
Myrrh: presented unto him..m. 30:2
Myrtle: m. and ivy 52:7
m. is still 94:16
Myrtles: which a grove of m. made 18:12
ye m. brown 144:20
Myself: Do I contradict m. 242:15
M. not least 230:13
M. when young 85:7
Said I to m. 91:20
to keep m. from being afraid 79:15
Mysterious: God moves in a m. way 70:5
m. priest 120:21
Mystery: for a m. and a sign 61:25

heart of my m. 188:17
I shew you a m. 35:29
in m. our soul abides 11:17
m. of things 196:6
to lose myself in a m. 42:19
Mystic: As you walk your m. way 92:21
m., wonderful 226:16
shines forth in m. glow 87:7

N

N or M. 167:32
Nag: de bob-tail n. 87:8
Nail: blows his n. 196:20
for want of a n. 88:5
tooth and n. 125:5
Nails: Hard..As n. 75:9
Naked: And he but n. 192:7
like a n. new-born babe 198:4
n. and ye clothed me 32:16
N., come to thee 234:1
n. every day he clad 95:12
N. they came 229:4
n. to mine enemies 193:1
pale, stiff, n. 99:3
poor n. wretches 195:8
Nakedness: in utter n. 246:11
Name: above every n. 36:15
age without a n. 150:3
at the n. of Crispian 192:4
Change but the n. 110:8
change the n. 8:6
confess'd thy name 111:12
crimes committed in thy n. 176:8
deed without a n. 199:19
filches from me my good n. 205:4
for his own n.'s sake 181:8
gathered together in my n. 31:40
give a grosser n. 189:18
given him a n. 36:15
glory in the n. of Briton 90:7
Good n. in man and woman 205:4
habitation and a n. 203:19
hallowed be thy n. 30:22
He left the n. 117:3
his N. only is excellent 172:6
his n. shall be called 27:32
his n. that sat on him was Death 37:17
his N.'s sake 169:2
I am become a n. 230:13
if that name thou love 245:19
King's n. is a tower of strength 207:11
lose the n. of action 187:13
lose the n. of king 206:16
Me n. is Mud 73:12
My n. is Norval 106:14
My n. is Ozymandias 214:6
n. great in story 52:7
n. of Jesus 36:15
not n. it to you 205:15
or the number of his n. 37:20
praise the N. of the Lord 172:6
proud his n. 180:6
remember the N. of the Lord 168:32
rose by any other n. 207:23
shadow of a glorious n. 135:5
she lost her honest n. 7:5
take the N. of the Lord 167:8
there is no n. 129:22
thy n. is woman 185:11
three things in my n. 167:32
to that n. 183:3
To this I put my n. 100:9
together in thy N. 166:17
weak witness of thy n. 147:12
what a wounded n. 190:3
What is your n.? 167:32
What's in a n.? 207:23
what n. Achilles assumed 43:1

what the dickens his n. is 202:19
Who gave you this n.? 167:32
whose n. was writ in water 122:11
write against your n. 175:10
Nameless: n., unremembered acts 248:18
Namely novelty 107:5
Names: and such great n. as these 7:7
Call'd him soft n. 121:6
Then shall our n. 192:4
unpopular n. 12:3
Nancy: mate of the N. brig 91:3
Napier: Admiral N., K.C.B. 232:3
Napoleon: N.'s armies 181:18
N. forgot Blücher 62:15
N. of crime 78:8
Narrative: bald and unconvincing n. 92:13
Narrow: convent's n. room 247:12
Each in his n. cell 97:10
each within our n. bed 58:21
n. is the way 31:2
two n. words 174:16
Narrow'd his mind 95:17
Nasty: solitary, poor, n. 105:9
something n. in the woodshed 90:15
take the n. soup away 105:15
Nation: assembly of one n. 46:27
brought forth..a new n. 132:8
clearly top n. 181:19
dedicate this n. 176:14
for n. shall rise against n. 32:11
foul-mouthed n. 101:12
lift up sword against n. 27:22
make the laws of a n. 86:12
march of a n. 161:1
mourning of a mighty n. 228:24
n. not governed 46:29
n. of gallant men 47:14
n. of shop-keepers 1:2, 151:15, 217:12
N. spoke to a N. 126:19
no n. was ever ruined by trade 88:2
noble and puissant n. 148:10
that the n. might live 132:8
to every man and n. 135:3
whole brave n. 150:17
Nation: une n. de boutiquiers 151:15
Nations: among all n. 170:4
Commonwealth of N. 177:5
extends over many n. 78:15
formed two n. 76:21
gaiety of n. 116:22
happiest in n. 81:9
hated all n. 223:6
intercourse with foreign n. 72:14
let fierce contending n. know 1:6
men in n. 51:19
n.' airy navies 228:9
over the n. 236:18
Rome is above the N. 127:14
See n. slowly wise 117:2
teaching n. how to live 148:11
To belong to other n. 93:14
truth whereby the n. live 124:17
Native: breathe his n. air 165:14
fast by their n. shore 70:9
first n. source 219:14
for his n. shore 213:12
I am n. here 186:3
my n. land 180:6
n. of the rocks 113:21
n. wood-notes 144:19
thus the n. hue 187:13
Natives of Great Britain 61:9
Natura: Si n. negat 118:19
Natural: by n. piety 247:10
her colour is n. 216:16
twice as n. 58:9
Natural philosophy [makes men]
    deep 14:27

Natural Selection 72:9
Naturalists: So, n. observe 223:26
Nature: as free as n. 79:19
books to read N. 80:3
can lay on n. 201:1
Crack n.'s moulds 195:4
Disguise fair n. 191:8
drive n. out 108:8
Fair n.'s eye 138:14
fancy outwork n. 182:15
fear thy n. 197:14
For all that n. 219:12
fortress built by N. 206:7
great n.'s second course 198:13
had a strife with N. 118:3
If n. denies the power 118:19
if thou hast n. in thee 186:12
is not in N. 114:17
Little we see in N. 249:5
Love not man the less, but N.
    more 51:7
mirror up to n. 188:9
modesty of n. 188:8
N. always does contrive 92:21
N. and N.'s laws 164:8
N. be your teacher 248:14
N. I loved 129:20
N. in awe to him 145:7
N. made thee 159:22
N., red in tooth 227:13
N. that fram'd us 139:10
n. to advantage dressed 164:10
n.'s changing course 210:12
N.'s priest 246:11
One touch of n. 208:28
paid the debt of n. 83:15
part of n. 219:4
rank and gross in n. 185:11
read in N.'s mystic book 140:13
so priketh hem n. 60:9
that N. might stand up 194:24
that N. yields 70:23
thorough knowledge of human n. 13:16
Tir'd N.'s sweet restorer 250:15
'tis their n. too 239:6
to look on n. 248:19
Treatise on Human N. 111:22
universal N. did lament 144:21
visitings of n. 197:15
wait on n.'s mischief! 197:14
weakest thing in n. 161:8
Yet simple n. 164:14
Naught (see also Nought): Doth
    Job fear God for n.? 25:25
n. for your comfort 61:14
n. for your desire 61:14
N. venture, n. have 234:11
say n. 236:1
Navies: nations' airy n. 228:9
Navy: in the n. of Charles 137:2
n. nothing but rotten timber 47:3
n. under the providence of God 60:1
Ruler of the Queen's N. 93:10
Nay: and your n., n. 37:2
your communication be..n. 30:17
Nazareth: any good thing come out
    of N.? 33:48
Neæra: tangles of N.'s hair 145:1
Near: as n. to heaven 90:18
hurrying n. 140:12
peace..to him that is n. 28:26
port is n. 242:10
She is n. 228:20
so n. and yet so far 227:17
while he is n. 28:24
Nearer: n. is to France 57:9
n. to the Heart's Desire! 86:1
now is our salvation n. 35:14
Nearest: Do the work that's n. 123:15

Neat: lass so n.   137:15, 235:4
N., but not gaudy   241:20
n., not gaudy   129:11
Neat-handed Phyllis   144:15
Neatness of apparel   241:19
Necessaries: provided with all n.   74:25
Necessary: n. and fundamental principle   38:7
  n. not to change   83:16
  n. to invent him   237:15
  n. to salvation   172:12
  not n. to change   83:16
  notes are often n.   116:26
Necessitas non habet legem   224:13
Necessities: dipense with its n.   151:1
Necessity: I do not see the n.   10:14
  n. has no law   224:13
  n. hath no law   71:12
  no virtue like n.   206:4
  not an accident but a n.   219:4
  teach thy n. to reason   206:4
  Thy n. is yet greater than mine   217:3
Neck: a millstone were hanged
  about his n.   33:30
  glossy n.   154:12
  had but one n.   53:4
  her n. wrung like a chicken   63:1
  n. is very short   150:5
  n. or nought   69:27
  some n.!   63:1
  yoke of usury upon his n.   108:14
Nectar: Jove's n. sup   117:19
Nectared: of n. sweets   144:2
Nectarine and curious peach   140:6
Need: all ye n. to know   120:23
  England hath n. of thee   247:7
  God doth not n.   147:17
  in my sore n.   214:3
  Less than the n.   107:10
  n. of a world   44:16
  n. was the sorest   180:2
  never want a friend in n.   74:15
  sorrow, n., sickness   167:21
  stress of n.   237:5
  want or n.?   104:4
Needest: What n. thou   147:12
Needle: eye of a n.   32:1
  Plying her n.   107:3
Needs: according to his n.   15:21, 140:15
  What n. my Shakespeare   147:12
Neglect: do not n. it   218:7
  let me not defer or n. it   98:15
  little n. may breed mischief   88:5
  must kings n.   191:14
Neglected: pleased to have his all
  n.   113:20
Neglectful: cuff n.   104:11
Neglects me dreadfully   173:19
Neiges: les n. d'antan   236:2
Neighbour: duty towards my N.   167:33
  false witness against thy n.   167:16
  feast his n.   192:4
  love thy n.   24:12, 31:42
  policy of the good n.   176:14
Neighbours: among the graves of
  their n.   81:5
  call your n. in   155:9
  charity with your n.   167:22
  good fences make good n.   88:9
  N. o'er the Herring Pond   80:16
  what is happening to our n.   59:14
Neighing: Farewell the n. steed   205:10
Nell: Pretty witty N.   162:7
Nelson: death of N.   219:2
  N. touch   152:17, 153:7
Nemo: N. me impune lacessit   10:3
  N. repente fuit turpissimus   119:2
Nephew: beamish n.   56:4
Neptune: great N.'s ocean   198:15

Nerves: feels for my poor n.   13:20
Nervii: overcame the N.   194:7
Nervous: vocabulary..is n. and
  terse   78:17
Nest: and the swallow a n.   170:13
  in her n. at peep of day   230:6
  n. is in a watered shoot   177:8
  n. of singing birds   113:15
  tumble-down n.   244:11
Nests: built their n. in my beard   130:15
  in their little n.   239:8
  you birds make n.   237:10
Net: carried a n.   162:2
  in vain the n. is spread   26:5
  N. Anything reticulated   116:15
Nettle: out of this n.   190:12
Nettles: n., daisies, and long purples 189:18
Neutrality: Armed n.   244:12
  just for a word—'n.'   23:1
Never: N. do to-day   173:5
  N., n., n.   196:11
  n. the twain shall meet   124:13
  n. to himself   180:6
  n. to return   237:8
  seldom or n.   245:13
  What, n.?   93:7
Never-flinching labour   237:5
Nevermore: Quoth the Raven, 'N.'   163:17
New: bringer of n. things   230:13
  I make all things n.   37:26
  N. every morning   122:13
  no n. thing   26:35
  on with the n.   5:14, 141:14
  ring in the n.   227:19
  something n. from Africa   163:9
  Whether it be n. or old   221:25
New-born: Glory to the n. King   241:15
  like a naked n. babe   198:4
  praise n. gawds   208:28
New-comer: O blithe n.   245:15
New deal   176:12
New-found-land   77:5
New-hatched, unfledg'd comrade   185:21
News: brought me bitter n.   69:2
  evil n. rides post   147:8
  good n. baits   147:8
  good n. from a far country   26:25
  good n. yet to hear   61:23
  n. that's fit to print   159:8
  N. value   175:1
  talk of court n.   196:6
  that is not n.   72:2
New South Wales: go out and
  govern N.   21:7
Newt: Eye of n.   199:14
Newton: and N. [was misunder-
  stood]   82:21
  Let N. be!   164:8
  N., with his prism   247:17
Newts, and blind-worms   203:10
New World: I called the N.   53:18
New Year: and the N. in   94:10
  happiest time..N.   228:21
New Zealand: some traveller from
  N.   136:21
Nexus: sole n. of man   55:8
Nez: Le n. de Cléopâtre   161:4
Niagara: wouldn't *live* under N.   55:22
Nice: all that's n.   158:14
  n. to get up in the morning   130:10
Nicean barks of yore   163:16
Nicely-calculated less or more   247:6
Nicer: world would be n.   245:13
Nicest child I ever knew   21:1
Nicole, bring my slippers   148:15
Niger: left bank of the N.   73:22
Niggers: whar de good n. go   87:14
Nigh: shall not come n. thee   170:19
Nigh-related: poor n. guest   67:3

Night: all n. long we have not stirred 45:1
all n. sleeps 191:15
alternate N. and Day 84:22
any terror by n. 170:19
armies clash by n. 11:9
at dead of n. 245:4
awoke one n. 112:2
be in love with n. 208:1
black bat, n. 228:20
Bowl of N. 84:15
braw, bricht, moonlicht n. 130:8
brilliant n. in June 162:2
By n. an atheist 250:18
By n. or day 246:7
City of Dreadful N. 233:3
cold winter's n. 16:18
come, seeling n. 199:6
Come, thick n. 197:14
dangers of this n. 166:20
danger's troubled n. 54:8
darker than death or n. 215:1
day brought back my n. 148:2
day excludes the n. 239:15
dull as n. 202:13
dusky n. 84:11
earned a n.'s repose 134:11
endless n. 58:26, 98:11
first sweet sleep of n. 213:13
follow as the n. the day 185:21
For one n. 86:7
from morn till n. 37:29
from morn to n. 177:13
genuine n. 79:24
goes off at n. 216:16
gwine to run all n.! 87:8
hung aloft the n. 121:8
in beauty like the n. 52:12
In such a n. 202:9
in the forests of the n. 39:1, 4
in the n., my soul 232:10
In the silent n. 58:12
infant crying in the n. 227:11
It is not n. 122:16
labour n. and day 46:20
last n., among his fellow roughs 78:22
last out a n. 200:17
lay hid in n. 164:8
long n. of waiting 123:12
may endure for a n. 169:8
meaner beauties of the n. 249:13
middle of the n. 57:20, 185:16
neither n. nor day 197:6
neither the moon by n. 171:17
Never sees horrid n. 191:15
n. be turned to day 172:1
n. certifieth another 168:29
n. cometh 34:11
n. has a thousand eyes 40:13
N. hath a thousand eyes 135:15
n. is as clear as the day 172:1
n. is dark 153:15
n. is drawing nigh 18:6
n. is far spent 35:14
n. of weeping 222:2
n. that first we met 19:5
n. that should banish all sin 94:10
N., the shadow of light 224:1
n. to do with sleep? 143:20
n. was made for loving 52:15
N.'s candles are burnt out 208:2
n.'s starr'd face 122:4
of Chaos and old N. 146:6
Of the n. for the morrow 215:13
Oft in the stilly n. 150:1
on a shining n. 6:16
On a starred n. 142:1
on a starry n. 246:8
one other gaudy n. 182:17
Or in the n. 203:19

Out of the n. 102:13
passing n. 121:6
perpetual n. 118:13
rest not day and n. 37:16
returned home the previous n. 45:24
rise for me..n. and day 227:2
saw Eternity the other n. 235:11
shades of n. 133:17
shadow of our n. 213:8
she shall watch all n. 208:7
should have stood that n. 195:23
silent hours of n. 131:3
singeth all n. 185:4
sleep in the n. 224:2
slepen al the n. 60:9
so late into the n. 52:13
soft stillness and the n. 202:11
sound of revelry by n. 50:23
Spirit of N. 213:20
star-shine at n. 221:17
stepping fearless through the n. 18:9
that ends the n. 239:14
that n. we went to Birmingham 61:22
that pass in the n. 134:9
there's n. and day 40:8
things that go bump in the n. 4:9
Through the dim n. 214:10
Through the n. of doubt 18:8
tire the n. in thought 173:24
touch of Harry in the n. 191:11
upon the cheek of n. 207:17
upward in the n. 133:22
walks the n. 73:9
watch in the n. 170:17
watched their flocks by n. 225:9
Watchman, what of the n.? 28:5
when n. darkens the streets 146:5
While n.'s black agent 199:6
will cloud into n. 100:4
will not last the n. 143:1
witching time of n. 188:20
With n. we banish sorrow 105:2
Nightcap: bring his n. with him 222:16
give me my n. 148:15
Night-gown: in his n. 143:4
Nightingale: as 'twere any n. 203:4
bright n. amorous 223:28
n. in the sycamore 221:22
save the n. alone 18:12
Nightingales are singing 81:22, 123:12
Nightly: n. rob the dairy 118:2
n. sings the staring owl 196:20
n. to the listening Earth 1:12
visit'st my slumbers n. 146:20
Nights: Chequer-board of N. 85:10
down the n. 232:6
Forty days and forty n. 218:7
long wintry n. 130:20
n. and suppers of gods! 110:13
n. are longest there 200:17
n. are wholesome 185:4
n. with sleep 191:15
Night-time: of the dog in the n. 78:11
Nihilo: de n. nihilum 162:10
Nil: n. desperandum Teucro 108:19
n. posse creari De nilo 135:8
Nile: on the banks of the N. 216:12
serpent of old N. 182:12
waters of the N. 56:13
Nimble and light 155:19
Nimbly and sweetly 198:2
Nimrod the mighty hunter 23:24
Nine: N. bean-rows 250:9
n. times n. 197:6
ninety and n. 33:20
Nine-fifteen: Romance brought up the n. 126:6
Nine-tenths: reach of the n. 40:7
Ninety and nine 33:20

Nineveh: Is one with N.   127:5
Quinquireme of N.   140:20
Ninny: a mere n.   50:12
Niobe: Like N., all tears   185:11
Nip him in the bud   175:15
Nipped: blood is n.   196:20
Nipping and an eager air   186:2
Nips his root   192:14
No: the people cried 'O n.!'   18:3
Noah: N. begat Shem   23:20
N. he often builds to his wife   61:28
who married N.'s daughter   14:3
Nobility: N. carries its obligations   132:3
our old n.   138:4
Noble: cracks a n. heart   190:5
death so n.   147:10
Earth has many a n. city   58:22
How n. in reason!   187:4
n. and most sovereign reason   188:6
n. and puissant nation   148:10
n. mind is here o'erthrown   188:6
n. savage ran   79:19
Thou are n. and nude   224:3
to the n. mind   188:2
virtue not birth that makes us n.   19:21
what's n.   182:22
whose n. qualities   119:3
work of n. note   230:15
Nobleman: king may make a n.   47:18
underrated n.   91:6
Nobler: Jesu, by a n. deed   59:18
n. in the mind   187:13
Nobles with links of iron   172:7
Noblesse oblige   132:3
Noblest: n. Roman of them all   194:23
n. work of man   50:7
time's n. offspring   22:16
Nobly: Godolphin Horne was n. born   21:2
N., n. Cape St. Vincent   44:2
n. planned   248:5
Nobody: business of n.   136:18
I care for n.   37:30
n. is on my side   13:20
n.'s business   238:14
Noctes cenaeque deum!   110:13
Nod: if she chance to n.   208:7
in the land of N.   23:19
n. or a wink   222:20
Wynken, Blynken, and N.   84:3
Nodding by the fire   250:11
Nods, and becks   144:12
Noes: of Ayes and N.   85:11
Noise: above n. and danger   235:7
dumb-shows and n.   188:7
happy n. to hear   110:19
n. like of a hidden brook   66:3
n. of battle roll'd   226:25
n. of folly   144:6
n. of the water-pipes   169:16
pleasant n.   66:3
that made such a n.   81:6
with a merry n.   169:22
Noiseless: kept the n. tenor   98:1
Noises: isle is full of n.   208:18
like n. in a swound   65:8
Noisome: from the n. pestilence   170:19
Noisy: n. bells, be dumb   111:1
over the n. keys   172:22
Nokomis: wigwam of N.   134:4
Noll: for shortness call'd N.   89:1
Nominate: boldly n.   118:1
Nonconformist conscience   20:9, 243:17
None: answer came there n.   58:1
answer made it n.   185:17
don't ask me to take n.   74:21
I strove with n.   129:20
I'll n. of it   200:1
Let n. admire   146:8
loves we have n.   141:5

malice toward n.   132:9
Never had n.!   222:3
n. can thee secure   235:8
n. of us infallible   232:12
n. too much   125:16
n. was for a party   136:12
n. who would be foremost   136:13
pig had n.   158:9
poor dog had n.   157:3
seen of n.   120:24
sure I have n.   56:16
There's n. of these so lonely   41:16
there were n. to praise   248:3
turns n. to good   234:8
yet n. knows well   212:2
Nonny: hey n., n.   72:18, 204:10
Nonsense: grammar, and n.   95:20
n. of the old women   220:17
through sense and n.   79:10
Nonumque prematur in annum   108:5
Nook of earth's surface   109:12
Noon: blaze of n.   147:3
bloody Sun at n.   65:12
From morn to n. he fell   146:9
from n. to dewy eve   146:9
Has not attain'd his n.   104:10
pleasant noise till n.   66:3
returned ere n.   178:14
Noon-day: darkness at n.   70:8
destroyeth in the n.   170:19
Noose: in a N. of Light   84:15
Norfolk: very flat, N.   69:16
Norman: N. blood   227:22
Saxon and N. and Dane   231:3
Normans: not like us N.   126:18
Noroway: the king's daughter of
N.   16:13
North: gray metropolis of the N.   226:7
n. wind doth blow   157:1
North-easter: Welcome wild N.   123:16
Northern: that the N. States will..
muddle through   41:9
North-north-west: but mad n.   187:5
Norval: My name is N.   106:14
Norway has noble wild prospects   114:13
Nose: by the n.   200:14
Cleopatra's n.   161:4
entuned in hir n. ful semely   60:12
his n. cast is of the roman   86:11
Marion's n.   196:20
n. was as sharp as a pen   191:6
on his n. there was a Cricket   131:3
ring at the end of his n.   131:7
snapped off her n.   158:1
spectacles on n.   183:20
to wipe his little n.   18:2
Noselessness of Man   61:27
Noses: got no n.   61:26
n. have they and smell not   171:13
Nostalgie de la boue   13:1
Not: easier to say what it is n.   115:9
N. bloody likely   213:3
Note: deed of dreadful n.   199:5
from my lowest n.   188:17
make a n. of   74:15
merry n.   196:20
not a funeral n.   245:3
turn his merry n.   183:19
work of noble n.   230:15
world will little n.   132:18
Note-book: Set in a n.   194:18
Notes: all the compass of the n.   79:16
N. are often necessary   116:26
pierce in n.   144:19
These rough n.   179:19
Nothing: ain't heard n. yet   117:6
all for n.   187:11
can I lack n.   169:2
carry n. out   36:29

Did n. in particular 91:22
for saying n. 201:8
for the Dawn of N. 85:9
forgotten n. 80:11, 225:2
hard at doing n. 108:9
having n. 249:11
I am n. 35:21
I have n. to declare 244:1
I have n. to offer 62:20
it profiteth me n. 35:21
it was n. more 247:14
knowledge of n. 74:1
knows n. higher 78:18
learnt n. 80:11
n. a year 222:22, 231:18
N. beside remains 214:7
n. but talk of his horse 201:11
N. can be created 135:8
n. can bring back the hour 246:13
N. can come out of n. 162:10
n. common did 140:8
n. either good or bad 187:2
n. else to do 21:19
n. if not critical 204:26
N. in his life 197:13
N. in my hand I bring 234:1
N. is ever done 212:18
n. left remarkable 182:21
n. long 79:8
n. to do with the case 92:14
N. venture 91:26
n. was now left 74:7
n. which has yet been contrived 115:7
N. win 91:26
reason knows n. of 161:7
signifying n. 200:4
value of n. 243:18
we brought n. into this world 36:29
when you have n. to say 68:1
who expects n. 165:16
Nothingness: pass into n. 120:1
to n. do sink 122:5
Notice you have been pleased to take 113:22
Notion: and foolish n. 48:23
Notorious evil liver 167:3
Nought (see also Naught): neck or n. 69:27
N. could be done 17:10
n. shall make us rue 193:8
Nourish all the world 196:16
Nourished: how n. 202:1
n. in my house 103:13
Novel: discourse in n. phrases 92:21
it is only a n. 13:16
last fashionable n. 137:5
spent its n. force 228:6
Novelty: namely n., n., n. 107:5
November: April, June, and N. 158:7
Fifth of N. 7:3, 157:12
thirty days hath N. 96:8
Now: If it be n. 189:26
let me do it n. 98:15
somebody's catching it n.! 127:1
tell us n. 230:4
Where are you n.? 107:9
Nowhere: rest n. 159:12
Swear n. 77:17
with n. to go 242:6
Nox est perpetua una dormienda 58:26
Nuclear: edge of the n. abyss 220:19
Nude: keep one from going n. 123:10
noble and n. 224:3
Nuffink: Why—N.! 62:3
Nuisance: make himself a n. 142:22
Number: full of a n. of things 221:14
More by your n. 249:13
or the n. of his name 37:20
promoting the..number..of the human race 47:5

Numbered: hairs..are all n. 31:14
hath n. thy kingdom 29:18
he was n. with the transgressors 28:23
n. in the roll 237:9
Numberless: shadows n. 121:2
Numbers: for the greatest n. 112:10
for the n. came 165:4
in mournful n. 133:26
lisped in n. 165:4
plaintive n. flow 248:9
to add to golden n. 72:18
Numbness: drowsy n. 121:1
Numerous: but far more n. 79:7
Nun: quiet as a n. 246:15
the son of N. 24:9
Nuncheon: take your n. 44:22
Nunnery: from the n. 134:20
Get thee to a n. 188:3
Nunnes: Among the N. Black 217:7
Nuns fret not 247:12
Nurse: in the n.'s arms 183:20
most kindly n. 219:14
sucks the n. asleep 183:4
This n. 206:7
Nursed: n. a dear gazelle 149:19
threw the twins she'd n. 96:10
Nurseries: Public schools are the n. 84:7
Nurses: old men's n. 14:18
Nursing his leg 74:13
Nurslings of immortality 214:9
Nut: I had a little n. tree 156:2
Nut-brown ale 144:17
Nutmeg: silver n. 156:2
Nuts: where the n. come from 232:6
Nut-shell: bounded in a n. 187:3
Nymph: Haste thee N. 144:12
N., in thy orisons 188:1
Nymphs: breasts of the n. 224:9
tell me, N. 66:9
Ye N. that reign 66:9

O

Oafs: muddied o. at the goals 126:1
Oak: Heart of o. 88:18
hearts of o. 12:12
liv'd in an o. 173:13
o., and the ash 6:15
o., or bays 140:4
our ships were British o. 12:12
Than O., and Ash 127:24
Oak-cleaving thunderbolts 195:4
Oar: bend to the o. 39:23
Oars: o. keep time 150:2
o. were silver 182:15
Oases: isolated o. 151:10
Oaten: aught of o. stop 67:11
Oath: man is not up on o. 115:5
sworn a solemn o. 48:22
Oaths: full of strange o. 183:20
Oats..given to horses 116:16
Obdurate: if too o. 221:24
Obedience: troops of friends 199:32
Obedient to their laws 217:4
Obermann 220:22
Obey: don't o. no orders 125:3
Love, cherish, and to o. 168:13
ought to o. God 34:33
whom three realms o. 165:3
Obeyed as a son 90:10
Obeys: she o. him 134:7
Object: My o. all sublime 92:8
o. strange and high 140:2
o. to an aged parent 74:17
Objection: no o. to this method 220:15
Obligations: Nobility carries its o. 132:3
Obliged: always o. to go 115:15
Oblique: puff o. 216:1

O

Oblivion: alms for o.   208:27
  drink o.   142:3
  mere o.   183:20
Oblivious: sweet o. antidote   200:1
Obscure: and destiny o.   97:12
Obscurity: emerge from o.   119:3
  in the decent o.   90:13
Observance: than the o.   186:3
Observation with extensive view   117:1
Observed: all his faults o.   194:18
  justly o. to me   74:13
Observers: observed of all o.   188:6
Obstruction: lie in cold o.   200:23
Occasion: o. of this kind   243:13
  sad o. dear   144:20
  when some o. is presented to him   80:3
Occasions: all o. do inform against
  me   189:6
  best on these o.   75:18
  New o.   135:4
  upon their lawful o.   172:9
Occupation: o. for an idle hour   13:17
  Othello's o.'s gone   205:10
  pleasant o.   91:18
Occupations: love our o.   74:2
Occur: accidents will o.   74:12
Ocean: deep and dark blue O.   51:8
  fall into the o.   139:1
  great Neptune's o.   198:15
  great o. of truth   153:17
  in the o. bed   145:4
  life on the o. wave   179:3
  lifeless o.   66:15
  make the mighty o.   55:26
  o. of life   134:9
  o.'s bosom   139:25
  O.'s nursling   213:17
  o'er land and o.   147:17
  painted o.   65:13
  pride of the o.   212:7
  round o.   248:19
  unfathom'd caves of o.   97:15
Octavios: light o.   70:20
Odd: and this was o.   57:20
  as o. as can be   73:7
  How o. of God   83:13
  scarcely o.   58:1
  think it exceedingly o.   129:2
Odds: facing fearful o.   136:9
  o. is gone   182:21
  what's the o.   141:15
Ode: I intended an O.   76:24
Oderint, dum metuant   63:19
Odes to every zephyr   123:16
Odi et amo   59:2
Odious: comparisons are o.   77:3
Odorous: comparisons are o.   204:13
  o. perfume   147:5
Odour: stealing and giving o.   209:2
Odours: hues and o. plain   214:1
  O., when sweet violets sicken   215:10
Odyssey: surge and thunder of the
  O.   130:1
O'erjoy'd was he to find   69:24
O'er-picturing that Venus   182:15
Off with the old love   5:14, 141:14
Offence: O. is rank   188:22
  where the o. is   189:17
Offences: sins and o.   169:6
Offend: coy and tender to o.   104:5
  if thine eye o. thee   31:39
  shall o. one of these little ones   31:38
Offended: not o. the king   150:6
  this hand hath o.   70:25
  who should be o.   129:8
Offenders: society o.   91:30
Offends me to the soul   188:7
Offensive: is mighty o.   115:23
Offer: never o. to answer this   220:14

Offering too little   54:12
Office: clear in his great o.   198:4
  during his o.   79:9
  insolence of o.   187:13
  o. of a wall   206:7
  to do thine o.   150:5
Office boy to an attorney's firm   93:10
Office boys: By o. for o.   178:17
Offspring: time's noblest o. is the last 22:16
Oft: How o. hereafter   86:2
  O. in danger, o. in woe   242:5
  seen thee o.   119:18
  What o. was thought   164:10
Often: how o. have I said to you   78:16
  how o. you and I   69:3
Often-times: hearing o.   248: 9
Oft-times: same that o. hath
  Charm'd   121:6
Ogled: sighed and pined and o.   232:4
Oil: anointed my head with o.   169:2
  midnight oil   89:27, 173:24
  o. to make him   171:2
  with boiling o.   92:12
  with o. anoint   181:8
Old: as o. as he's feeling   67:10
  glorious song of o.   181:10
  grow o. along with me   45:4
  grow to be o.   22:1
  grown o.   45:12
  I am growing o.   112:4, 175:6
  I grow o.   81:19
  I love everything that's o.   95:24
  I shall grow o.   247:10
  In the brave days of o.   136:12
  infirm and o.   180:4
  known of o.   127:3
  lonely and poor of o.   41:16
  never be o.   111:2
  nine days o.   157:10
  now am o.   169:13
  o. and as true   126:9
  o. come forth to play   144:16
  o. enough to lap   242:20
  o. men shall dream dreams   29:22
  O. men's nurses   14:18
  o. with service   192:14
  redress the balance of the O.   54:18
  Ring out the o.   227:19
  sad, O. earth   243:3
  so o. a ship   86:9
  they shall grow not o.   38:2
  those shoes were o.   185:11
  We're o. and tough   232:2
  When all the world is o.   123:18
  when he is o.   26:22
  When you are o. and gray   250:11
  whether it be new or o.   221:25
  Woman as o. as she looks   67:10
  you and I are o.   230:15
  You are o., Father William
                         56:16, 218:22, 219:1
  you are very o.   176:11
  you never can be o.   211:13
Old Bailey: bells of O.   157:7
Older than the rocks   161:9
Old Kent Road: knocked 'em in the O. 62:5
Olive-branches: like the o.   171:24
Oliver Twist has asked for more!   75:7
Olympum: Ossae .. involvere O.   237:6
Olympus: top of leafy O.   109:20
Omega: I am Alpha and O.   37:13
Omen: avert this o.   63:20
Omen: Procul o. abesto !   160:3
  Quod di o. avertant   63:20
Omit: you may o.   243:12
Omnes eodem cogimur   109:11
Omnia: Non o. possumus omnes   237:2
  O. vincit Amor: et nos cedamus
    Amori   237:3

Omnipotent: defy th' O. 145:12
  Power, which seems o. 215:1
  squamous, o., and kind 42:2
Omnis: Non o. moriar 110:3
On: you keep them o. 89:10
Onaway! Awake 134:8
Once: can die but o. 190:32
  go at o. 199:10
  I thought so o. 89:26
  Not o. or twice 229:2
  that o. hath blown 85:6
  Yet o. more 144:20
  Your eyes had o. 250:11
One: All for o. 80:10
  Animals went in o. by o. 7:13
  bless us every o.! 74:3
  But that's all o. 209:20
  from twelve to o. 69:8
  nobby o. 176:10
  not o., but all mankind's epitome 79:8
  O. and all 94:3
  O. born in a manger 235:7
  o. by o. back 85:10
  o. by o. crept 85:4
  o. for the master 155:4
  O. remains 213:10
  o. to speak 233:8
  O., two, buckle my shoe 157:5
  O. who never changes 235:8
  rather see than be o.! 46:24
  very little o. 139:17
  when only o. is shining 248:3
  Where I made o. 86:3
One-and-twenty: When I was o. 110:16
One-horse town 234:20
Ones: sets of great o. 196:6
Onward: go o. the same 100:4
  O., Christian soldiers 18:7
  O., Christians, o. go 242:5
  upward still, and o. 135:4
Ope: to o. their golden eyes 184:20
  when I o. my lips 201:8
Open: all hearts be o. 167:4
  door flew o. 106:3
  door stood o. 65:3
  o. and notorious 167:3
  O., locks 199:17
  O. Sesame! 10:10
  o. unto the fields 249:4
  to see the mast burst o. 86:9
Opened: dead and o. 140:18
  he o. not his mouth 28:21
  it shall be o. 30:33
  When the pie was o. 158:1
Openeth: he o. not his mouth 28:21
Opening: and the o. of the prison 29:2
  at the o. day 239:14
  every o. flower 239:9
Opes: golden o. 145:2
Ophir: from distant O. 140:20
Opinion: gave it for his o. 223:2
  Is of his own o. still 50:3
  My o. is 41:9
  o. of His Majesty's Government 62:18
Opinions: golden o. 198:5
  New o. are always suspected 133:6
  so many o. 231:8
  stiff in o. 79:8
Opium of the people 140:16
Opponent: to an o. motives meaner 18:17
Opportunities: wise man will make
    more o. 14:10
Opportunity: maximum of o. 212:25
  o. makes a thief 15:10
Oppose: was to o. everything 219:23
Opposed: and o. free hearts 230:15
  suspected and usually o. 133:6
Opposing: by o. end them 187:13
Opposition: duty of an O. 62:16, 219:23

Her Majesty's O. 15:17
'His Majesty's O.' 105:11
Oppressed: he was o. 28:21
  just men long o. 147:6
Oppressor: o. of all 47:11
  o.'s wrong 187:13
Optimist proclaims that we live 52:19
Oracle: I am Sir O. 201:8
Oracles: lively O. of God 69:1
Oracular: use of my o. tongue 216:11
Oranges: gold o. glow 94:16
  O. and lemons 157:6
Orare est laborare 10:4
Orator: I am no o. 194:11
Orb: in her circled o. 207:24
  lighted on this o. 47:14
  not the smallest o. 202:11
Orbis: Securus iudicat o. terrarum 13:6
Orchard: fair with o. lawns 227:3
  on the o. bough 44:1
Ordained: are o. of God 35:13
  hast thou o. strength 168:22
Ordains for each one 127:18
Order: decently, and in o. 35:23
  hills in o. stood 239:14
  old o. changeth 227:1
  o. of your going 199:10
  o...this matter better 220:11
  set thine house in o. 28:10
  words in the best o. 67:8
Orders: don't obey no o. 125:3
Ordinance: God's holy o. 168:12
Ordinary: renders o. 181:5
Ordo: saeclorum nascitur o. 237:1
Ore: new spangled o. 145:4
  of your subject with o. 122:11
Organ: let the pealing o. blow 144:9
  one day at the o. 172:22
  playing of the merry o. 7:17
Orient: corn was o. 234:2
Original: All things counter, o. 107:15
  behold the bright o. 89:24
  great and o. writer 249:6
Orion: loose the bands of O. 25:43
Orisons: Nymph, in thy o. 188:1
Orlando: Run, run, O. 184:3
Ornament: O. to her profession 46:18
  serve..for o. 14:24
  To be a moment's o. 248:4
Ornate and gay 147:5
Orphan: an o.'s curse 65:21
  carried by an o. boy 180:4
Orpheus: another O. 213:12
  O. with his lute 192:13
Orthodoxy is my doxy 238:16
Oscar: You will, O., you will 242:4
Ossa: to pile O. on Pelion 237:6
Other: each without the o.! 134:7
  forsaking all o. 168:11
  I am o. than I was 110:4
  not as o. men are 33:33
  turn to him the o. [cheek] 30:18
  used no o. 173:17
Others: cause of dullness in o. 87:1
  more you 'ave known o' the o. 126:7
  to encourage the o. 237:11
  what course o. may take 103:10
Otherwise: Heaven's thought was
    o. 236:11
Otiosum: Numquam se minus o. esse 63:15
Oublié: rien appris, ni rien o. 225:2
  rien o. et..rien appris 80:11
Oude: I've O. 173:8
Ought: hadn't o. to be 101:2
  I o. 119:12
Oun: properly based O. 43:19
Ounce of civet 195:21
Ours: that is o. 249:5
Ourselves: But in o. 193:11

Ourselves (*cont.*)
in o. that we are thus   204:24
to see o.   48:23
Out: get o. and enjoy it   217:13
In and o. the Eagle   138:2
never o. nor in   79:10
No door can keep them o.   103:18
O., damned spot!   199:28
o. of sight   64:11
O. of the deep   171:25
O., o., brief candle!   200:4
pluck it o.   31:39
shall not be put o.   29:30
who's o.   196:6
Outcast: my o. state   210:13
Outer: into o. darkness   31:6
Outgrabe: mome raths o.   57:14
Outlive this powerful rhyme   211:4
Outlives: he that o. this day   192:4
o. not May   224:10
Outrageous fortune   187:13
Outshine: didst o.   145:14
Outside: put him o.   113:7
Out-soared the shadow   213:8
Outstayed his welcome   67:3
Outstretched: Their hands o.   236:17
Outstrip thy skiey speed   214:3
Outward: appear beautiful o.   32:9
o. and visible sign   168:2
Outwork: fancy o. nature   182:15
Outworn: dust of creeds o.   214:8
in a creed o.   249:5
o. buried age   211:6
Oven: put it in the o.   157:9
Over: after the ball is o.   100:15
are gone o. me   169:16
farce is o.   174:6
not have given me o.   245:11
thousand summers are o.   224:7
Over-arch'd: High o. imbower   146:4
Overcame: o. his natural bon-
homie   22:11
o. the Nervii   194:7
Over-canopied   203:9
Overcome: be not o. of evil   35:12
I have o. the world   34:22
not to be o.   145:15
Overcomes: Who o. by force   146:7
Over-driven: only o.   221:8
Overflows: and my cup o.   181:8
Overhung with smoke   150:14
Overpowering knell   51:24
Overthrow: thou dost o.   77:9
Overthrown: Empire o.   247:11
Oves: non vobis vellera fertis o.   237:10
Owe: o. me no subscription   195:5
we o. a cock   218:7
Owed: dearest thing he o.   197:13
Owl: moping o.   97:9
mousing o.   199:1
O. and the Pussy-cat   131:6
o., for all his feathers   120:2
o. liv'd in an oak   173:13
sings the staring o.   196:20
white o. in the belfry   230:9
Owlet: my little o.!   134:5
Owls: Two O. and a Hen   130:15
when o. do cry   208:20
Own: before his o.   160:1
but at least it is my o.   151:7
but mine o.   184:13
came unto his o.   33:45
every country but his o.   92:1
falling like its o.?   214:4
I o. the soft impeachment   216:14
mistress in my o.   126:19
my o., my native land!   180:6
to do what I will with mine o.   32:5
unfeeling for his o.   98:9

unless they is 'ls o.   125:3
which he calls his o.   176:6
Owned: it must be o.   61:9
o. with a grin   218:17
treason is not o.   79:26
Owning: mania of o. things   242:14
Owns: whom nobody o.   154:8
Ox: as an o. goeth to the slaughter   26:10
eateth grass as an o.   26:1
nor his o.   167:17
stalled o.   26:18
thou shalt not muzzle the o.   24:20
Oxen: many o. are come about
me   168:34
with o. of his own breeding   108:14
Oxenford: Clerk ther was of O.   60:13
Oxford: clever men at O.   96:17
leave O. by the town drain   219:17
never seen O. since   153:11
O...more attractive than Cam-
bridge   15:16
O. that has made me insufferable   20:8
To O. sent a troop of horse   43:3, 234:3
Oxlips: bold o.   210:8
here o. and the nodding violet   203:9
Oyster: o. may be crossed in love   216:5
world's mine o.   202:17
Oysters: often eaten o.   90:19
Ozymandias: My name is O.   214:6

P

Pace: Creeps in this petty p.   200:4
moon's soft p.   247:18
no p. perceiv'd   211:13
not mend his p. with beating   189:19
unperturbèd p.   232:8
Paced upon the mountains   250:11
*Pacem: Qui desiderat p., praeparet
bellum*   235:12
solitudinem..p. appellant   224:15
Paces: P. about her room   82:2
two p. of the vilest earth   190:23
Pacific: star'd at the P.   121:9
Pacisque imponere morem   236:18
Pack: I will p., and take a train   42:7
P., clouds, away   105:2
Somebody's p. has slid   127:1
Pack-horse on the down   150:14
Packs and sets   196:6
Paddington: as London is to P.   54:15
Paddle his own canoe   139:20
Paddles: 'ear their p. chunkin'   126:11
p. in a halcyon sea   177:8
Paddock calls   197:2
Paddocks: Cold as p.   104:16
Paddy: O P. dear, an' did ye hear   7:2
Paean: palms and the p.   224:9
Paeans: laurels to p.   63:14
Pagan: I'd rather be a P.   249:5
Page: beautiful quarto p.   216:15
Pageantry: antique p.   144:19
Pagett, M.P., was a liar   126:21
Paid: not p. to think   126:10
p. the debt of nature   83:15
p. with flattery   116:17
p. with sighs a plenty   110:17
we ha' p. in full!   127:12
Pail: fetch a p. of water   156:4
frozen home in p.   196:20
Pain: and all the p.   223:28
aromatic p.   164:15, 244:15
blest him in their p.   230:3
did you feel no p.   96:9
draw thy breath in p.   190:3
Eternal P.   11:18
first feel p. yourself   107:20
hasn't a p.   143:12

hate and p. 213:8
I feel no p. dear mother now 5:5
intermission of p. 181:15
neither shall there be any more
  p. 37:26
No p. felt she 44:27
Our Lady of P. 224:5
p. and anguish 180:13
p. to the bear 137:1
physics p. 198:18
piercing p. 221:24
pleasures banish p. 239:15
sudden cry of p. 220:9
tender for another's p. 98:9
what p. it is to part! 89:16
with no p. 121:6
with p. for leaven 224:1
With some p. is fraught 215:5
Pains: for my p. 204:23
His present and your p. 191:4
marriage has many p. 116:24
must have taken him a great deal
  of. p. 114:17
p. my sense 121:1
Paint: flinging a pot of p. 178:8
fresh as p. 217:10
let her p. an inch thick 189:20
p. the meadows 196:19
to p. my picture truly 71:9
to p. the lily 193:6
Painted: black as they are p. 133:10
idle as a p. ship 65:13
Lift not the p. veil 215:9
not so young as they are p. 20:6
p. on the wall 44:14
Painter: As with the p.'s work 108:4
Painters: I hate all Boets and
  Bainters 90:4
two p. in the world 242:2
Paint-pots: Throws aside his p. 107:19
Paints: all your fancy p. 127:23
Pair: Blest p. of Sirens 147:13
chaise and p. 69:22
fair p. of heels 190:13
p. o' patent double million..of
  hextra power 75:27
p. of ragged claws 81:18
Pal: split on a p. 128:26
Palace: cypress in the p. walk 229:16
keepeth his p. 33:10
Love in a p. 120:15
My gorgeous p. 206:16
p. fit for you and me 221:17
very stately p. 46:6
Palaces: and of kings' p. 108:16
Mid pleasures and p. 161:17
princes' p. 201:9
saw in sleep old p. 214:2
within thy p. 171:20
Palate: against his p. fine 120:24
Pale: at which the world grew p. 117:3
behold a p. horse 37:17
by the p. moonlight 180:5
in the winter's p. 210:5
lean and p. 215:14
Or make p. my cheeks 244:18
over p. 203:6
p., and hectic red 214:1
p. and wan, fond lover? 222:5
P. Death 108:16
P. grew thy cheek 52:16
P. hands I loved 107:9
p., lost lilies out of mind 77:27
p., stiff, naked 99:3
p. young curate 93:30
Prithee, why so p.? 222:5
turn not p. 57:9
turned p. 219:2
Which keeps me p.! 199:6

Pale-fac'd: from the p. moon 190:9
Palely: Alone and p. loitering 120:10
Palestine: in sunny P. 140:20
Pall: In sceptred p. 144:8
  p. thee in the dunnest smoke 197:15
Palliate: to p. or deny 162:17
Palls: everything p. 9:10
Palm: an itching p. 194:15
bear the p. 152:17
Dominion over p. and pine 127:3
dull thy p. 185:21
in the p. of your hand 38:10
To win the p. 140:4
Palmam qui meruit, ferat 152:17
Palmer: for a p.'s walking staff 206:16
Palms: other p. are won 246:14
p. and the paean 224:9
p. before my feet 61:17
Palm-trees: wind is in the p. 126:11
Palmy: high and p. state 185:3
Palpable: very p. hit 189:27
Pampered: God's p. people 79:4
p. Jades of Asia 139:13
Pan: the great god P. 43:5
Panem et circenses 119:8
Panes of quaint device 120:4
Pang: finds a p. as great 200:21
with a ghastly p. 65:17
Pangs: More p. and fears than
  wars 192:14
p. of disappointed love 178:4
p. of dispriz'd love 187:13
Panjandrum: and the grand P. 86:19
Pansies, that's for thoughts 189:14
Pansy at my feet 246:10
Pantaloon: lean and slipper'd p. 183:20
Pants: As p. the hart 225:6
fast thick p. 66:14
p. its source to mount 149:5
Papa: The word P. 74:17
Paper: any news in the p. 13:21
Golly, what a p.! 221:10
hath not eat p. 196:11
Make dust our p. 206:14
scrap of p. 23:4
Paraclete: Come, thou holy P. 130:5
Paradise: Before we go to P. 61:23
drunk the milk of P. 66:15
England is a p. for women 49:11
England is the p. of women 86:13
heav'nly p. 54:11
is a p. 201:1
shalt thou be with me in P. 33:41
Wilderness is P. 84:18
Paradox: an embodied p. 68:2
Paragon of animals! 187:4
Paramour: shalt be my p. 138:13
Parcel: p. of boilers 115:24
What a p. of fools 103:13
Parcere subiectis 236:18
Parching: to the p. wind 144:20
Pard: bearded like the p. 183:20
Pard-like Spirit 213:7
Pardon: God might p. her 82:6
God will p. me 102:6
kiss of the sun for p. 99:2
O! p. me 193:20
Parent: an aged p. 74:17
To lose one p. 243:10
Parents: by loving their p. 243:27
Paris: Good Americans..go to P.
  10:9, 243:23
last time I saw P. 99:10
P. is well worth a mass 103:2
Paris vaut bien une messe 103:2
Parish: all the world as my p. 241:18
Park: over p. 203:6
Parks: levelled walks through p. 67:22
p. were the lungs of London 162:21

Parliament: crop-headed P. 43:12
  In the P. of man 228:10
  p. is a deliberative assembly 46:27
  P. is not a congress 46:27
  P. speaking through reporters 55:16
  Three Estates in P. 55:15
  When I first came into P. 219:23
Parliaments: the mother of P. 41:12
Parlour: party in a p.? 247:15
  queen was in the p. 158:1
  Will you walk into my p.? 111:18
Parlous state 184:4
Parma: foul scorn that P. 82:9
Parody: devil's walking p. 61:16
Parsnips: butter no p. 180:20
Parson: Brandy for the P. 127:10
  drowns the p.'s saw 196:20
  His creed no p. ever knew 78:24
  If P. lost his senses 105:13
  p. own'd his skill 95:8
Parsons: merriment of p. 115:23
Part: day we must p.? 71:2
  death us do p. 168:12
  For mine own p. 193:12
  immortal p. of myself 204:33
  kiss and p. 78:29
  List to the heavy p. 117:10
  Must bear the longest p. 103:18
  now I know in p. 35:22
  p. of all that I have met 230:13
  p. of nature 219:4
  p. to tear a cat in 203:3
  so he plays his p. 183:20
  too precise in every p. 104:11
  uttermost p. of the heaven 168:30
  we know in p. 35:21
  we prophesy in p. 35:21
  what pain it is to p.! 89:16
Parted: never p. 48:5
  p. are those 40:15
  seeming p. 203:15
  When we two p. 52:16
Particle: that very fiery p. 51:25
Particular: a London p. 73:22
  called away by p. business 216:17
  Did nothing in p. 91:22
Parting: Do not let this p. grieve
    thee 8:1
  p. is such sweet sorrow 207:25
  p. was well made 194:21
Partition: union in p. 203:15
Partitions: thin p. do their bounds
    divide 79:6
Parts: in the hinder p. 170:12
  my p. of speech! 216:10
  P. of it are excellent! 173:21
  plays many p. 183:20
Parturient montes 107:21
Party: none was for a p. 136:12
  of the Devil's party 39:16
  p. in a parlour? 247:15
  P. is the madness of many 223:21
  p. of friends and relations 91:15
  Stick to your p. 76:12
  to p. gave up 95:17
  to p. strife 245:20
Pass: all ye that p. by? 29:8
  as p. on the seas 172:9
  come to a pretty p. 141:20
  glories p. away 135:16
  glory of the world p. away! 122:23
  I keep, and p. 82:13
  let this cup p. from me 32:20
  many change and p. 213:10
  may not p. away! 125:10
  never P. into nothingness 120:1
  O! let him p. 196:12
  o'er the green cornfield did p. 184:12
  p. for a man 201:12

P. it along the line! 127:1
p. man's understanding 167:1
p. the ammunition 87:5
p. the bottle round 242:20
p. through things temporal 166:36
pay us, p. us 61:24
shall p. away 180:7
ships that p. in the night 134:9
They shall not p. 162:11
Though Dynasties p. 100:4
through it p. 103:21
to p. through this world but once 98:1
who could p. by 249:4
Will she p. in a crowd? 233:4
with shining Foot shall p. 86:3
you shall p. 86:4
Passage: a p. which you think is
    particularly fine 115:1
  carv'd out his p. 197:4
  each dark p. shun 250:14
  p. to remorse 197:15
Passages: and licentious p. 90:13
Passe: Tout p., tout casse, tout lasse 9:10
Passed: For as I p. by 34:42
  former things are p. away 37:26
  glory and loveliness have p. away 122:1
  p. away a glory 246:8
  p. by on the other side 33:7
  plucked them as we p.! 106:19
  So he p. over 46:23
  will have p. away 70:1
Passeront: Ils ne p. pas 162:11
Passes: never p. a church 114:12
  seldom make p. 160:18
Passeth: One generation p. away 26:34
  p. all understanding 36:19, 167:25
  soon p. it away 170:18
Passing-bell: some cost a p. 20:1
Passing of the Third Floor Back 113:9
Passion: all p. spent 92:22
  Eternal P.! 11:18
  felt the tender p. 89:23
  have no p. for it 114:10
  in a dream of p. 187:11
  p. boiled and bubbled 232:4
  p. hidden in my veins 174:10
  p. shall have spent 228:6
  p. that left the ground 43:7
  Queen was in a furious p. 57:1
  sentimental p. 147:11
  tear a p. to tatters 188:7
  That is not p.'s slave 188:11
  their fury, and my p. 208:10
  whirlwind of p. 188:7
  your ruling p. 164:22
Passion-flower at the gate 228:20
Passions: never let such angry p.
    rise 239:7
  P. spin the plot 142:4
  with our p. as it is with fire 132:1
Passport: his p. shall be made 192:4
Past: Even God cannot change the
    p. 1:22
  in ages p. 239:14
  of things p. 211:1
  One short sleep p. 77:10
  p. as a watch 170:17
  p. our dancing days 207:16
  Though that life is p. 110:2
  where all p. years are 77:16
  Who present, p. 38:18
  winter is p. 27:16
Pastime: After youthful p. had 10:2
  to take his p. 171:4
Pastoral song 67:11
Pastors: some ungracious p. 185:20
Pasture: feed me in a green p. 169:2
  people of his p. 170:24
  sell the p. 191:5

Pastures: and p. new   145:5
  England's pleasant p.   38:16
  lie in p. green   181:8
  p. still   107:13
Pat: Now might I do it p.   188:23
  P. and Mac and Tommy   128:28
Pat-a-cake, baker's man   157:9
Patch: purple p. or two   107:18
Patches: of shreds and p.   91:27, 189:2
Pater noster qui   217:7
Paternal: few p. acres   165:14
Pâtés de fois gras to..trumpets   218:2
Path: beaten p.   83:4
  Christ is the p.   149:1
  dark is his p. .   96:19
  p. of duty   229:2
  p. of gold   44:16
  primrose p. of dalliance   185:20
  round the p. of Milton   248:2
  that found a p.   121:6
  when life's p. is steep   109:10
'Pathetic Fallacy'   178:9
Pathless: pleasure in the p. woods   51:7
Pathos: true p.   48:9
Paths: all her p. are peace   26:7
  make his p. straight   30:4
  p. of glory   97:12
  p. of righteousness   169:2, 181:8
Patience: abuse our p.   63:16
  abusing of God's p.   202:15
  great aptitude for p.   45:23
  In your p. possess ye   33:36
  like p. on a monument   209:10
  My p. is now at an end   105:7
  p. of Job   37:1
  run with p.   36:35
  Talk him out of p.   205:2
  with p. he stands   134:2
  your gracious p.   204:21
Patient: kill the p.   14:15
  Like a p. etherized   81:14
  like nature's p.   121:8
  not so p.   190:28
  p. looker-on   173:27
  p. must minister   200:1
  who was p., being dead   161:15
Patines of bright gold   202:11
Patria: Pro p., pro liberis   178:18
Patrician: regular p.   93:15
Patrick: No more St. P.'s Day   7:2
Patriot: P. king   40:3
  p. of the world alone   54:13
Patriotism: p. is not enough   59:4
  P. is the last refuge   115:4
Patriots: blood of p.   113:3
  True p. we   18:26
Patron: Is not a P., my Lord   113:22
  p., and the jail   117:2
  P. commonly a wretch..   116:17
Patrons: drama's p.   116:28
Pattens: with mop and p.   218:4
Patter: unintelligible p.   93:29
Pattern: made him our p.   44:10
Pattle: Wi' murd'ring p.   48:25
Paul, thou art beside thyself   34:50
Pauper: only a p.   154:8
  p. in the midst of wealth   110:1
Pauperum tabernas Regumque turris   108:16
Pause: And p. awhile from letters   117:2
  dull it is to p.   230:13
  Must give us p.   187:13
Pauses: happy p.   15:8
Paved with gold   67:19
Pavements: And p. fang'd   66:9
Pavender: decks the rural p.   178:13
  p., or pub   178:13
Pavilion: lie in her p.   182:15
Pavilioned in splendour   96:18
Paving-stones: on these gritty p.   126:14

Paw: with privy p.   145:3
Paws: massive p. of elder persons   20:16
  my dear p.!   56:15
Pay: Bloomin' good p.   127:9
  never p. a farthing for it   71:9
  now I must p. for my fun   126:7
  p. at the Greek Kalends   52:22
  p. given to a state hireling   116:18
  p. it, therefore   218:7
  p. the piper   68:6
  p. thy morning sacrifice   123:1
  p. us, pass us   61:24
  saved the sum of things for p.   111:11
  to P. Old Debts   141:10
  When will you p. me?   157:7
  wonders what's to p.   111:10
Payment: cash p.   55:8
Pays: He that dies p. all debts   208:17
  p. him in his own coin   223:19
  p. us but with age   174:15
  p. your money   173:4
Pea: nothing left but one split p.   231:19
Peace: all her paths are p.   26:7
  arts of war and p.   51:17
  author of p.   166:14
  brought you back p.   76:10
  calls it—p.!   50:18, 224:15
  certain knot of p.   217:1
  chastisement of our p.   28:21
  come ye in p.   180:11
  deep dream of p.   112:2
  depart in p.   33:1
  enamoured on p.   63:26
  first in p.   131:17
  flower of P.   235:8
  fruit of the Spirit is..p.   36:7
  give thee p.   24:13
  God gave her p.   230:1
  him who desires p.   235:12
  his goods are in p.   33:10
  hold his p.   168:9
  I am for P.   41:11
  I will die in p.   245:9
  If these should hold their p.   33:35
  impose the law of p.   236:18
  In hearts at p.   42:11
  In p. there's nothing   191:8
  increase of his..p.   27:32
  into the way of p.   32:39
  keep p. between   197:15
  King of p.   104:2
  Let wars yield to p.   63:14
  My p. is gone   94:13
  not to send p., but a sword   31:15
  object of government in p.   23:3
  on earth p.   32:43
  or a bad p.   88:3
  Over all the mountain tops is p. 94:15
  p. and consolation   147:11
  p. at the last   153:12
  P. be to this house   33:4
  P. be within thy walls   171:20
  p. for our time   59:16
  P. hath her victories   148:5
  p. I hope with honour   76:10
  p. in our time   166:13
  P. its ten thousands   165:19
  P. more destructive of the man-
    hood   113:12
  p. of God   36:19, 167:25
  p. of Jerusalem   171:20
  P. on earth   241:15
  P. on the earth   181:10
  P.! p.!   29:4, 183:4
  P., perfect p.   37:33
  P., the human dress   39:13
  P. to him that is far off   28:26
  p. which the world cannot give   166:19
  p. with honour   59:16

Peace (cont.)
Prince of P. 27:32
saying, P., p. 29:4
seek p. 169:12
soft phrase of p. 204:20
star of p. return 54:8
Sweet P. is crown'd 235:7
that publisheth p. 28:18
There is no p. 28:17, 29:4
thousand years of p. 227:20
to Mercy, Pity, P., and Love 39:12
until I come in p. 25:16
We love p. 113:12
weak piping time of p. 207:5
whispers P. within 37:33
work us a perpetual p. 145:6
Peaceful: welcome p. ev'ning in 70:18
what p. hours 70:2
with p. citadel 120:21
Peacemakers: blessed are the p. 30:11
Peach: curious p. 140:6
Peacock: milk-white p. 229:16
Peacocks: Ivory, and apes and p. 25:9, 140:20
p. strutting by 125:8
Proud as p. 182:3
Pea-green boat 131:6
Peak: p., and pine 197:6
Silent upon a p. 121:9
Peal: wildest p. for years 105:13
Pealing: let the p. organ blow 144:9
Pear: and a golden p. 156:2
Pearl: One p. of great price 31:28
robe of gold and p. 191:15
threw a p. away 205:20
Pearls: cast ye your p. 30:32
p. that were his eyes 208:11
twelve gates were twelve p. 37:28
Peasant: Himalayan p. 125:5
no p. in my kingdom 102:18
p. slave am I 187:11
rends the p. 125:5
Peasantry: bold p. 95:4
Pease-porridge hot 157:10
Pebble: finding a smoother p. 153:17
not the only p. on the beach 41:1
Pebbled: towards the p. shore 211:5
Pebbles: idle p. 195:19
Peccavi—I've Scinde 173:8
Peck: For daws to p. at 204:16
Peculiar: extensive and p. 75:20
Funny p. 101:8
heathen Chinee is p. 101:3
Pede: p. libero Pulsanda tellus 109:8
Peel: D'ye ken John P. 97:2
Peep: and p. about 193:11
at p. of day? 230:6
p. through the blanket 197:15
treason can but p. 189:13
Peeping: Came p. in at morn 107:1
Peer: hath not left his p. 144:20
When daffodils begin to p. 210:5
Peerage: gained a p. 152:18
Peers: battle with my p. 230:13
legal judgement of his p. 137:17
Pejor: fit semper tempore p. homo 160:10
Peleus: wrath of P.' son 106:15
Pelf: power, and p. 180:6
Pelican: wonderful bird is the p. 142:14
Pelio: Imponere P. Ossam 237:6
Pelion: imposuisse Olympo 109:20
Pelops: Thebes, or P.' line 144:8
Pelting of this pitiless storm 195:8
Pembroke: P.'s mother 43:2
Pen: as sharp as a p. 191:6
Before my p. has glean'd 122:3
far less brilliant p. 20:7
fingers held the p. 70:11
made a rural p. 39:8

p. from lenders' books 195:11
p. is mightier 136:2
p. of a ready writer 169:18
poet's p. 203:19
sad words of tongue or p. 242:17
touch a p. to write 196:15
words of tongue and p. 101:2
Penal fire 145:12
Penance: and p. more will do 66:4
hath p. done 66:4
Pendant: about the p. world! 200:23
Pendent: made his p. bed 198:2
Pendre: Ils commencent ici par faire p. 148:20
Pends-toi, brave Crillon 103:1
Peneus: new P. rolls his fountains 213:12
Penny: but a p. a day 157:18
Dukes were three a p. 91:13
In for a p. 91:26
One a p. 157:4
p. ice and cold meat 91:25
p. plain 220:23
Please to put a p. in the old man's hat 3:20
Penny-fights: sent to p. 125:11
Pens: all the p. 139:11
Let other p. 13:15
Pension: P. an allowance 116:18
p. list of the republic 64:1
Pensive: O p. Eve 67:11
vacant or in p. mood 247:5
Pent: long in city p. 122:2
populous city p. 146:22
Pent-house: Hang upon his p. 197:6
Penury and imprisonment 201:1
People: All p. that on earth 123:5
all sorts of p. 198:5
all the good p. were clever 245:13
are the p. of England 61:24
byword among the p. 25:7
comfort ye my p. 28:11
common p. of the skies 249:13
fool all the p. 132:10
For Cambridge p. rarely smile 42:8
give the p. a square deal 177:4
God's pampered p. 79:4
good of the p. 63:11
Good p. all 95:10
government of the p. 132:8
Happy are the p. 55:10
has such p. in 't 208:21
hath comforted his p. 28:19
indictment against an whole p. 47:2
influence P. 55:25
look after our p. 179:18
love of the p. 47:3
Many p. prize it 92:24
No p. do so much harm 71:3
nuisance to other p. 142:22
of all the p. 160:22
opium of the p. 140:16
p. all exulting 242:10
p. and governments never have learned 102:2
p. are the masters 47:8
p. arose as one man 24:34
p. came to theirs 105:13
P. come miles to see it 92:11
p. imagine a vain thing? 168:21
p. keep even kings in awe 72:10
p. of customers 217:12
p. of his pasture 170:24
p. of unclean lips 27:27
P. ought to be modester 55:21
p. perish 26:30
p. that walked in darkness 27:31
P. will not look forward 47:13
Privileged and the P. 76:21
really nice English p. 212:15

should die for the p. 34:14
some of the p. all the time 132:10
some p...may be Rooshans 74:22
some p. talk of morality 80:20
stiffnecked p. 24:8
supports the p. 116:16
surely the p. is grass 28:13
Thy mercy on Thy P. 127:7
thy p. shall be my p. 24:35
Understanded of the p. 172:14
voice of the p. 2:4, 175:8
What kind of p. 62:25
when the p. listens 180:15
Peopled half the world 181:12
Peoples: souls of Christian p. 61:13
sullen p. 128:5
Pepper: p. when he pleases! 56:20
pickled p. 157:11
Perceive: I p. that in all things 34:42
Perceived: no pace p. 211:13
Perceives it die away 246:11
Perceiving: art of p. 74:18
Perception: doors of p. 39:21
Perdere: Quem Juppiter vult p. 80:15
Perdition: P. catch my soul 205:3
To bottomless p. 145:12
Perdu: Tout est p. fors l'honneur 87:18
Perennially hopeless 73:21
Peres; Thy Kingdom is divided 29:18
Perfect: end of a p. day 40:6
Entire and whole and p. 219:18
not in my p. mind 196:2
Peace, p. peace 37:33
p. bliss 139:10
p. cavaliero 50:16
p. woman 248:5
verray p. gentil knight 60:10
Perfection: The pursuit of p. 12:6
very pink of p. 95:25
Perform: His wonders to p. 70:5
P. with all your heart 236:1
Perfume: curious P. 12:20
odorous p. 147:5
throw a p. on the violet 193:6
Perfumed: and so p. 182:15
o'er a p. sea 163:16
Perfumes: All the p. of Arabia 199:30
steeped in liquid p. 108:18
Perhaps: great p. 174:7
the grand P. 43:9
Peril: For those in p. 242:9
Perilous: knew the p. rock 218:19
Of p. seas 121:6
such p. circumstance 186:1
that p. stuff 200:1
Perils: from all p. and dangers 166:20
Through p. both of wind and limb 49:22
When our p. are past 54:17
Periodical fits of morality 136:23
Perish: beasts that p. 169:24
city soon to p. 179:1
in our language should p. 137:3
people p. 26:30
P. the thought! 63:8
shall not p. from the earth 132:13
shall p. unconsoled 130:2
shall p. with the sword 32:23
should not p. 34:1
Perished in his pride 247:19
Perishes: everything p. 9:10
Periwig-pated fellow 188:7
Permitted: were p. to make all the ballads 86:12
Pernicious: most p. woman! 186:14
two p. daughters 195:5
Perpetual: make P. day 138:14
my own p. residence 153:11
next to the p. motion 75:32

p. fountain of good sense 80:7
p. shame 170:12
work us a p. peace 145:6
Perpetually: Stealthily and p. 41:7
Perplexed: is thy mind p.? 72:18
p. in the extreme 205:20
Perplexing: is p. enough 235:6
Persecutest: why p. thou me? 34:35
Persepolis: ride in triumph through P.? 139:9
Persian luxury 109:9
Persians: given to the Medes and P. 29:18
Persicos odi, puer, apparatus 109:9
Persist: fool would p. in his folly 39:19
Person: any other p.'s best 101:9
cheek of the young p.? 75:11
her own p. 182:15
I am the 'umblest p. 74:9
Like a well-conducted p. 232:4
looking for a p. 217:16
there's no sich a p. 74:24
Persons: God in Three P. 102:1
massive paws of elder p. 20:16
ninety and nine just p. 33:20
no respect..of p. 209:6
no respecter of p. 34:38
p. about to marry 173:3
p. of some substance 244:16
p. who are accused 73:11
resentment towards p. 153:8
ten guilty p. 38:8
why these two p. 168:5
Perspiration: and ninety-nine per cent. p. 81:1
Perspire: till you gently p. 126:4
Persuaded: For I am p. 35:10
thou hast p. 174:16
Persuadest: thou p. me to be a Christian 34:51
Pert as a schoolgirl 92:2
Pervading: that p. influence 74:12
Peru: from China to P. 117:1
Pessimist fears this is true 52:19
Pestilence: noisome p. 170:19
p. that walketh 170:19
Pestilence-stricken multitudes 214:1
Pestilent: foul and p. congregation 187:4
Pet: kept it for a p. 21:23
Petal: Now sleeps the crimson p. 229:16
Petar: hoist with his own p. 189:5
Peter: Cotton-tail, and P. 165:22
Shock-headed P. 106:5
that rounded P.'s dome 82:15
Thou art P. 31:33
Peterkin: Quoth little P. 218:14
Peter Piper picked a peck 157:11
Peto: Banish P. 190:15
Petticoat: feet beneath her p. 222:6
tempestuous p. 104:11
With a yellow p. 155:12
Petty: Creeps in this p. pace 200:4
p. fortress 117:3
p. sneaking knave 38:14
Peut-être: un grand p. 174:7
Pews: Talk about the p. 61:13
Phagocytes: Stimulate the p. 212:13
Phantom: She was a p. of delight 248:4
Phenomenon: infant p. 75:4
Phil: But fidgety P. 105:18
Philip: appeal from P. drunk to P. sober 3:11
see if P. can 105:17
Philippi: Ay, at P. 194:20
Philistines may jostle 92:22
Philistinism! 12:4
Philosopher: guide, p., and friend 164:21
never yet p. 204:15
to be a p. 81:7

Philosophic: bring the p. mind   246:13
Philosophy: borne with p.   74:12
  charming is divine p.!   144:2
  in your p.   186:16
  moral p. is but an handmaid to
    religion   14:5
  P., the lumber of the schools   223:24
  P. will clip an Angel's wings   120:16
Phoebus: and P. sprung!   51:17
  behold Bright P.   210:8
  in the eye of P.   191:15
  P. 'gins arise   184:20
  Towards P.' lodging   207:32
Phrase: ancient Saxon p.   133:21
  England invented the p.   15:17
  soft p. of peace   204:20
  When I invented the p.   105:11
Phrases: discourse in novel p.   92:21
Phyllis: neat-handed P.   144:15
Physic: p. to the dogs   200:1
  Take p., pomp   195:9
Physician: P., heal thyself   33:2
  Time is the great p.   76:17
Physics pain   198:18
Pianist: do not shoot the p.   243:14
Piccadilly: Good-bye P.   244:7
  If you walk down P.   92:22
Picking: from p. and stealing   167:34
Pickle: many a p.   59:10
Pickle herring: plague o' these p.!   209:3
Pickwick, the Owl, and the Waverley
    pen   8:5
Pickwickian: in its P. sense..   75:15
Picninnies: there were present the
    P.   86:19
Pictura: Ut p. poesis   108:4
Picture: different from her p.   103:14
  Look here, upon this p.   188:25
  Not on his p.   118:3
  paint my p. truly   71:9
Pictures: without p.   56:10
Picturing: sense faints p. them   214:2
Pie: Baked in a p.   158:1
  Eating a Christmas p.   156:11
  p. may be produced   130:13
  pudding and p.   155:15
  to make an apple-p.   86:19
Pieces: Cancel and tear to p.   199:6
  Men!for P. plays   85:10
  P. of eight!   221:3
  thirty p. of silver   32:18
Pie-crust: Promises and p.   223:8
Pied: daisies p.   144:14, 196:19
Piedmontese: by the bloody P.   147:16
Pieman: met a p.   157:19
Pier: I walk'd upon the p.   18:1
Pierce: meeting soul may p.   144:19
Pierced: hath p. to the rote   60:8
Pierian: taste not the P. spring   164:9
Pies: one of Bellamy's veal p.   163:5
Piety: all thy P. nor Wit   85:12
  by natural p.   247:10
  to p. more prone   2:12
Pig: little p. went to market   158:9
  p. in a poke   234:10
  Stole a p.   158:13
Piggy-wig stood   131:7
Pig-lead: Road-rail, p.   140:21
Pigmy: fretted the p. body   79:5
Pigs: As p. do in a poke   150:8
  whether p. have wings   57:22
Pilate: Jesting P.   15:5
  P. saith unto him   34:23
Piled: in p. stones   147:12
Pilgrim: loved the p. soul   250:11
  Onward goes the p. band   18:8
  p. grey   67:15
  To be a p.   46:20
Pilgrimage: quiet p.   54:10

succeed me in my p.   46:22
  thus I'll take my p.   174:13
Pilgrimages: to goon on p.   60:9
Pilgrims: happy band of p.   152:16
  p. of the year   142:6
  p.' pride   217:14
  p. to th' appointed place   79:28
Pillar of salt   23:26
Pillars: antique p.   144:9
Pillion: mounts on the horseman's
    p.   109:17
Pillow: sigh'd upon a midnight p.   183:11
  where, like a p.   77:6
Pilot: P. of the Galilean lake   145:2
  p. that weathered the storm   54:17
  see my P. face to face   226:6
Piminy: miminy, p.   93:3
Pimpernel: demmed, elusive P.   159:13
Pimples: these roughnesses, p.,
    warts   71:9
Pin: heard a p. drop   176:7
  pinn'd it wi' a siller p.   17:3
  with a little p.   206:15
Pinafore: Captain of the P.   93:6
Pine: Dominion over palm and p.   127:3
  peak, and p.   197:6
  We p. for what is not   215:5
Pined: he sighed and p.   232:4
  long in darkness p.   181:9
Pines: cones under his p.   88:9
Pine-tree: O p.   179:16
Pine-trees: black and gloomy p.   134:4
Piney: between the p. sides   229:4
Pinions: with p. skim the air   88:8
Pink: My face is p.   6:10
  P. pills for pale people   4:3
  very p. of courtesy   207:27
  very p. of perfection   92:25
  Pinnace, like a fluttered bird   230:2
Pioneers: P.! O P.   242:13
Pious: In p. times   79:2
  this just, this p. fraud   89:23
  this p. morn?   120:21
  with p. frauds   47:12
Pipe: called for his p.   157:2
  P. a song   39:8
  P. me to pastures still   107:13
  p. that song again   39:8
  P. to the spirit ditties   120:19
  put that in your p.   17:16
Piped: I p. with merry cheer   39:8
  We have p. unto you   31:19
Piper: pay the p.   68:6
  P. pipe that song again   39:8
  p.'s son   158:12
Pipers: especially p.!   44:23
  hundred p.   151:13
Pipes: on their scrannel p.   145:3
  p. and whistles in his sound   183:20
  p. o' Havelock sound!   242:18
  ye soft p.   120:19
Piping: P. down the valleys wild   39:8
  p. songs   39:8
  p. time of peace   207:5
Pips: until you can hear the p.
    squeak   90:2
Pirate: To be a P. King   93:16
Pistol: when his p. misses fire   96:3
Pistols: young ones carry p.   212:8
Piston: and p. stroke   150:14
Pit: bottomless p.   37:23
  He that diggeth a p.   27:4
  monster of the p.   165:12
  wretched, blind, p. ponies   105:13
Pit-a-pat: makes my heart go p.!   44:20
Pitch: bumping p.   153:6
  He that toucheth p.   29:35
  roller, p., and stumps   130:2
  worked her mind to such a p.   71:1

Pitch-and-toss: one turn of p.   125:15
Pitcher be broken at the fountain   27:8
Pitchfork: out with a p.   108:8
   thrown on her with a p.   223:13
Pith: great p. and moment   187:13
Pitied: pity, and be p.   183:19
Pitiful: of p. day   199:6
   'Twas p.   204:23
Pitiless: this p. storm   195:8
Pitt is to Addington   54:15
Pity: dint of p.   194:10
   incidents arousing p.   10:16
   it was great p.   18:12
   know what 'tis to p.   183:19
   more's the p.   141:15
   never a saint took p.   65:19
   P. a human face   39:13
   p., like a naked new-born babe   198:4
   P. my simplicity   241:12
   'Tis P. She's a Whore   87:3
   'tis true 'tis p.   186:23
   To Mercy, P., Peace, and Love   39:12
   yet the p. of it   205:12
Place: all other things give p.   89:29
   bourne of Time and P.   226:6
   even in heavenly p.   216:30
   everything in its p.   217:11
   fine and private p.   140:12
   Genius of the p.   236:19
   in a better p.   183:10
   mind is its own p.   146:2
   Never the time and the p.   44:15
   no p. can compare   244:11
   no p. to go   49:7
   p. for everything   217:11
   p. of rest   146:25
   p. thereof shall know it   171:1
   p. where the tree falleth   27:6
   p. within the meaning of the Act   3:11
   Remove hence to yonder p.   31:36
   respect of p.   209:6
   right man in the right p.   113:4
   savage p.!   66:14
   shall now give p.   71:11
   solitary p.   28:9
   stands in Elgin's p.   78:23
   take our p.   124:17
   take your p. there   123:18
   till there be no p.   27:25
   to keep in the same p.   57:17
   to prepare a p. for you   34:18
   to th' appointed p.   79:28
   Upon the p. beneath   202:5
   what a p. to plunder!   39:24
   Where the p.?   197:2
   yielding to p. new   227:1
Places: all p. were alike to him   128:16
   before all other p.   109:12
   Fills the shadows and windy p.   223:28
   in sundry p.   166:7
   in the right p.   50:8
   into what p. wilt thou now go   99:3
   keep their ancient p.   232:10
   P. where they sing   166:16
   rough p. plain   28:12
   slain in thine high p.   25:1
   two p. at once   175:14
   upon thy high p.   24:47
   wickedness in high p.   36:14
Placid: so p. and self-contain'd   242:14
Plackets: thy hand out of p.   195:11
Plague: any p. come nigh   170:20
   instruments to p. us   196:7
   p. o' both your houses!   207:30
   p. of his sentiments!   216:18
   p. o' these pickle herring!   209:3
   that p. thee   65:10
Plagues: of all the p.   54:14
Plain: above that p.   233:4

as on a darkling p.   11:9
fill a spacious p.   70:20
Gromboolian p.   130:20
in meadow or p.   223:28
my language is p.   101:3
p., blunt man   194:11
P. living   247:8
pricking on the p.   219:9
rough places p.   28:12
Plainer: in p. words   129:5
Plainly: And, to deal p.   196:2
Plains: On the p. of Timbuctoo   243:2
Plain-speaking: apology for p.   73:24
Plaintive: p. anthem fades   121:7
   p. numbers flow   248:9
Plan: simple p.   247:20
   still his 'simple p.'   78:24
Planco: Consule P.   109:25
Planet: every wand'ring p.   139:10
   When a new p. swims   121:9
Planets: And all the p., in their turn   1:13
   keep the p.   166:5
   no p. strike   185:4
Planned: A whole I p.   45:4
   nobly p.   248:5
Plant: P. thou no roses   177:12
   Sensitive P.   215:2
Plantation: longing for de old p.   87:11
Planted: flours be p. on my grave   100:9
Plants: p. did spring   18:12
   p. his footsteps   70:5
Plaster: grow into p. saints   127:23
Platinum: bullets made of p.   20:18
Plato: attachment à la P.   92:22
   P. is dear to me   10:17
Platter: licked the p. clean   156:5
Play: At Christmas p.   234:7
   before the p. is done   173:27
   Better than a p.   60:2
   came out to p.   155:15
   come out to p.   155:5
   come forth to p.   144:16
   for food or p.   65:9
   gently will p.   156:3
   good p. needs no epilogue   184:16
   hear the Dead March p.   125:2
   holdeth children from p.   217:2
   hour to p.   153:6
   I doubt some foul p.   185:19
   Judge not the p.   173:27
   last act crowns the p.   173:27
   learned to p.   158:12
   little victims p.!   98:8
   magnificent fair p.   78:7
   nor wilt thou p.   99:3
   our p. is done   209:20
   p. a set   191:4
   p. on; give me excess of it   209:2
   p. on my fiddle   250:8
   p...pleased not the million   187:7
   p. the man   130:6
   P. up! and p. the game!   153:6
   p. with flowers   191:6
   p.'s the thing   187:12
   that he could p.   158:12
   to p. billiards well   219:5
   To see that Interesting P.   21:10
   when the band begins to p.   127:20
   will not let my p. run   73:13
   winds that hold them p.   147:5
   ye soft pipes, p. on   120:19
   You would p. upon me   188:17
   young barbarians all at p.   51:5
Played: how you p. the game   175:10
   I have p. the fool   24:46
   p. on an old fiddle   50:9
   p. the Infidel   85:16
   p. the sedulous ape   220:22
   You have p. enough   108:13

Player: a poor p.   200:4
  as strikes the P. goes   85:11
  in a p.'s hide   98:13
Players: as many of your p. do   188:7
  men and women merely p.   183:20
  p. have often mentioned it   117:12
  see the p. well bestowed?   187:9
Playing: and they all fell to p.   86:19
  p. fields of Eton   240:17
  p. on the sea-shore   153:17
  purpose of p.   188:9
Playmates: I have had p.   129:16
Plays: Men for Pieces p.   85:10
  p. extravagant matches   92:9
  p. many parts   183:20
  P. such fantastic tricks   200:19
Plaything-house that I got   238:5
Plaza Toro: Duke of P.!   91:6
Plea: justice be thy p.   202:5
Plead: every man will p.   181:13
  Will p. like angels   198:4
Pleasance: Youth is full of p.   210:10
Pleasant: all the p. land   102:11
  bread eaten in secret is p.   26:11
  England's p. pastures   38:16
  green and p. Land   38:16
  hath a p. seat   198:2
  How p. to know Mr. Lear!   130:17
  in some p. grot?   108:18
  make...the p. land   55:26
  of our p. vices   196:7
  on this p. lea   249:5
  p. it is to have money   64:3
  p. noise   66:3
  p. occupation   91:18
  p. waters   173:1
  songs of p. glee   39:8
  think him p. enough   130:17
Pleasanter: proves the p. the colder   50:4
Pleasantness: ways of p.   26:7
Please: does greatly p.   219:10
  hard to p.   180:13
  live to p.   116:28
  no God could p.   79:4
  not difficult to p.   53:8
  only Self to p.   39:6
  seeketh not itself to p.   39:5
  strive to p. you   209:20
  will p. themselves   74:22
  will true critics p.   241:20
Pleased: face so p. my mind   7:22
  in whom I am well p.   30:7
  p. to have his all neglected   113:20
  p. with what he gets   183:15
  toast that p. the most   73:18
Pleases: every prospect p.   101:16
Pleaseth: Or if he p.   103:21
Pleasing: surest method..of p.   61:7
Pleasure: aching P.   120:24
  But the privilege and p.   91:10
  dissipation without p.   90:11
  dome of p.   66:15
  Doubtless the p. is as great   49:29
  greatest p. I know   129:15
  heart with p. fills   247:5
  heels of p.   68:13
  I have no p. in them   27:7
  in his p. is life   169:8
  It becomes a p.   243:13
  it gave p.   137:1
  Its the rich wot gets the p.   7:6
  on p. she was bent   69:24
  p. afterwards   231:15
  P. at the helm   97:6
  p. in the pathless woods   51:7
  P. never is at home   120:6
  p. of the fleeting year!   211:12
  P...the intermission of pain   181:15
  P. with pain for leaven   224:1

read without p.   116:10
  soldier's p.   79:12
  stock of harmless p.   116:22
  There is a p. sure   80:1
  thy most pointed p.   221:24
  What p. lives in height?   229:18
  when Youth and P. meet   51:1
  would have been my p.   226:19
  Your horrible p.   195:5
Pleasure-dome: stately p.   66:14
  sunny p.   66:15
Pleasure-house: lordly p.   229:5
Pleasures: all the p. prove   139:6
  cannot understand the p.   13:13
  celibacy has no p.   116:24
  hypocrite in his p.   116:6
  Mid p. and palaces   161:17
  on their lordships' p.   193:2
  p. banish pain   239:15
  p., joys, and varied pursuits   119:1
  p. with youth pass away   219:1
  purest of human p.   14:16
  Seat of p.   79:23
  suck'd on country p.   77:7
  Take their p. sadly   222:11
Pledge: I p. you   176:12
  I will p. with mine   117:19
  to p. my toast   172:20
  we p. to thee   124:17
Pledges of Heaven's joy   147:13
Pleiades: sweet influences of P.   25:43
Plenteousness within thy palaces   171:20
Plenty: but just had p.   48:13
  here is God's p.   80:6
  paid with sighs a p.   110:17
  p. to get   75:26
  there lies no p.   209:5
  though ever so p.   52:7
Pleuré: d'avoir quelquefois p.   151:8
Plie: Je p. et ne romps pas   86:16
Plight: p. thee my troth   168:12
  when this p.   236:5
Plods: ploughman homeward p.   97:8
Plot: now the p. thickens   45:19
  Passions spin the p.   142:4
  p. hath many changes   173:27
  some melodious p.   121:2
  This blessed p.   206:7
Plough: Following his p.   247:19
  late at p.   100:3
  p. my furrow alone   177:6
  Speed his p.   59:19
  We p. the fields   53:12
Ploughing: Is my team p.   111:3
Ploughman: heavy p. snores   204:3
  p. homeward plods   97:8
Ploughs and p. again   108:14
Plowshares: swords into p.   27:22
Pluck: P. from the memory   200:1
  p. it out   31:39
  p. one thorn   108:13
  p. out the heart   188:17
  p. this flower, safety   190:12
  p. till time and times   250:10
  p. up drowned honour   190:9
  P. up thy spirits   150:5
  p. you out of the crannies   226:12
  p. your berries   144:20
  To p. bright honour   190:9
Plucked: firebrand p. out of the
    burning   29:24
  I p. a hollow reed   39:8
  We p. them as we passed!   106:19
Plum: pulled out a p.   156:11
Plume: helmet and the p.   227:25
Plumed: Farewell the p. troop   205:10
Plummet: did ever p. sound   208:19
Plump and hearty   105:15
Plunder: What a place to p.!   39:24

Plündern: Was für p.!   39:24
Plunging: When the p. hoofs   73:6
Plying her needle   107:3
Plymouth Hoe: dreamin' arl the
    time o' P.   153:5
Pobble who has no toes   131:10
Pobbles are happier   131:13
Pocket: wid a p. full of tin   87:8
Pocket-money: furnished with p.   74:25
Pockets: young man feels his p.   111:10
Poem lovely as a tree   123:8
Poems are made by fools   123:9
Poesis: Ut pictura p.   108:4
Poet: any p. ever writ   80:4
    durst p. touch a pen   196:15
    every p., in his kind   223:26
    good p.'s made   118:8
    he was a true P.   39:16
    Like a P. hidden   215:4
    limbs of a p.   110:11
    lunatic, the lover, and the p.   203:19
    On a p.'s lips   214:9
    p.'s dream   247:13
    so with the p.'s [work]   108:4
    truth the p. sings   288:7
Poetic: constitutes p. faith   67:5
    P. Justice   164:1
Poetry: Fleshly School of P.   45:17
    in p., no less than in life   12:5
    In whining P.   77:19
    P. is the record   215:17
    p.=the best words   67:8
    what is p.?   115:9
Poets: among the English P.   122:10
    by p. styl'd   49:26
    clever young p.   67:8
    I hate all Boets and Bainters   90:4
    of all modern, and perhaps ancient
    p.   80:3
    P. are the unacknowledged legis-
    lators   215:15
    p. in our youth   247:19
    p. [make men] witty   14:27
    that ever p. held   139:11
    youthful p. dream   144:19
Poins: banish P.   190:15
Point: any p. to which   78:11
    one fixed p.   78:12
    p. me to the skies   135:17
    p. of view   173:23
    To point a moral   117:3
    too fine a p. upon it   73:24
Point d'argent, point de Suisse   174:11
Points of heaven   248:6
Poised: I am p.   20:4
Poison: if you p. us   201:27
    Instead of dirt and p.   223:1
    nor steel, nor p.   199:4
    to p. the wells   153:9
    Turning to P.   120:24
Poisoned: Some p. by their wives   206:15
Poke: As pigges do in a p.   150:8
    drew a dial from his p.   183:16
    pig in a p.   234:10
Pokers: wreathe iron p.   66:11
Pole: Beloved from p. to p.   65:23
    Black..from p. to p.   102:13
    rapt above the P.   146:20
    soldier's p. is fall'n   182:21
    spread the truth from p. to p.   1:13
    wid a ten-foot p.   87:9
Policeman: Ask a p.!   176:3
    p.'s lot   93:21
Policy: field of world p.   176:14
Polish it at leisure   80:2
Polished: along the p. ice   246:5
    I p. up the handle   93:10
    p. female friend   242:19
    rough than p.   61:9

Polite: Men of p. learning   103:7
    not so p.   126:18
Political: man is..a p. animal   10:15
    P. Ravishment   94:1
Politician: scurvy p.   195:22
Politicians: whole race of p.   223:2
Politics: Confound their p.   55:1
    Magnanimity in p.   47:4
    mules of p.   166:4
    p. to puns   166:5
    range of practical p.   94:4
    They shoved him into p.   21:6
Poll: talk'd like poor P.   89:1
Polly: O P., you might have toy'd   89:10
    P. put the kettle on   157:13
Poltagrue: tempt my Lady P.   21:19
Polygamy: Before p. was made a sin   79:2
Pomp: all our p. of yesterday   127:5
    grinning at his p.   206:15
    In lowly p.   143:6
    p., and circumstance   205:10
    p., and feast   144:19
    p. of pow'r   97:12
    Sultan with his P.   84:22
    Take physic, p.   195:9
    tide of p.   191:15
    Vain p. and glory   192:14
Pompey: Knew you not P.?   193:9
Pomps and vanity   167:32
Pond: have their stream and p.   41:19
    like a standing p.   201:7
    o'er the Herring P.   80:16
Ponies: Five and twenty p   127:10
    wretched, blind, pit p.   105:13
Pools are filled with water   170:14
Poop was beaten gold   182:15
Poor: annals of the p.   97:12
    Art thou p.   72:18
    certain p. widow   32:35
    faces of the p.   27:23
    great man helped the p.   136:12
    how p. a thing is man!   72:3
    its the p. wot gets the blame   7:6
    lonely and p. of old   41:16
    makes me p. indeed   205:4
    none so p.   194:6
    of p. men's hovels   108:16
    p. always ye have with you   34:15
    p., and the maimed   33:17
    p. bare, forked animal   195:12
    p. but honest   182:8
    p. have become poorer   215:16
    p. in spirit   30:11
    p., infirm, weak   195:5
    P. Little Rich Girl   69:12
    P. man at his gate   2:8
    p. man had nothing   25:3
    p. man loved the great   136:12
    P. old Joe   87:12
    Rich gifts wax p.   188:2
    scandalous and p.   176:1
    She was p. but she was honest   7:5
    solitary, p., nasty   105:9
    Though I be p.   142:19
    to feed the p.   35:21
Poorer: for richer for p.   168:12
    poor have become p.   215:16
Poorest he that is in England   174:12
Pop goes the weasel!   138:2
Popery: never be in danger of p.   1:10
Poplars are fell'd   70:7
Popped: I p. him in the Frigidaire   96:14
Poppies: fume of p.   119:18
    though p. grow   137:8
Poppy: Not p., nor mandragora   205:9
    with a p. or a lily   92:22
Popular: Marriage is p.   212:25
Population when unchecked   138:1
Populos: regere imperio p., Romane   236:18

Populous city   146:22
Porcelain: rogue in p.   142:11
Pork: And pickled p. they loaded   231:19
  Your beef, p., and mutton   124:15
Porpentine: fretful p.   186:7
Porphyry: in the p. font   229:16
Porpoise close behind us   57:7
Porridge: What p. had John Keats?   44:26
Porringer: take my little p.   249:3
Port: In every p. a wife   73:17
  In every p. he finds a wife   37:32
  in ev'ry p. a mistress find   90:1
  p. after stormy seas   219:10
  p. for men   115:20
  p. is near   242:10
  Rum on the p.   221:21
Portals: whose P. are alternate
    Night and Day   84:23
Porter: moon shines bright on Mrs. P. 82:1
  Oh, mister p.   133:4
Portion: best p. of a good man's life 248:18
  Brief life is here our p.   152:10
  p. of the loveliness   213:9
Portioned: lands were fairly p.   136:12
Portmanteau: like a p.   58:7
Portrait of a blinking idiot   201:25
Position: Every p. must be held   99:4
Possess: P. it merely   185:11
  p. the field   64:10
  P. them not with fear   192:1
  p. ye your souls   33:36
Possessed: much p. by death   82:3
  with friends p.   210:13
Possessing: too dear for my p.   211:9
Possession: and in p. so   212:2
  in thy p. lies   183:5
  Nor lose p.   210:12
  p. for ever   233:11
  put him in p. of truth   133:7
Possibilities: in the p. of defeat   235:17
Possible: best of all p. worlds 52:19, 237:12
  with God all things are p.   32:2
Post: evil news rides p.   147:8
  speed and p. o'er Land   147:17
Post-chaise: driving briskly in a p.   115:12
Posterity: hope of p.   166:4
  I had not told p. this   117:12
  look forward to p.   47:13
  Thy p. shall sway   69:20
  We are always doing..something
    for P.   1:16
Posts of the door moved   27:27
Postumus, the fleeting years   109:14
Posture of a whore   182:24
Pot: chicken in his p. every Sunday   102:18
  doth keel the p.   196:20
  flinging a p. of paint   178:8
  Put on the p.   155:8
  thorns under a p.   26:39
Potage: selleth his birthright for a
    mess of p.   4:6
Potash: for a mess of p.?   238:17
Potato: a bashful young p.   92:22
Potatoes, poultry, prunes   74:19
Potent: how p. cheap music is   69:15
Potomac: All quiet along the P.   137:7
Potter and clay endure   45:5
Pouch on side   183:20
Poule: tous les dimanches sa p.   102:18
Poultry, prunes and prism   74:19
Pound: give thee a silver p.   53:17
  in for a p.   91:26
  once bet a p.   73:8
  'Tis for a thousand p.!   69:28
Pounding: Hard p. this   240:19
Pounds: crowns and p.   110:16
  with forty p. a year   95:6
Poured out the red   41:16
Pourest thy full heart   215:3

Pouring forth thy soul   121:6
Poverty: by p. depress'd   116:27
  In p., hunger   107:3
  P. has strange bedfellows   136:3
  worst of crimes is p.   212:16
Powder: keep your p. dry   38:5
  when your p. 's runnin' low   153:4
Power: accursed p.   21:18
  All p. is not to all   237:2
  Almighty P.   145:12
  balance of p.   238:12
  call our p. to account?   199:28
  consecrated it far above our p.   132:8
  drunk with sight of p.   127:6
  earthly p.   202:5
  enduring p.   12:10
  extent of its beauty and p.   137:3
  force of temporal p.   202:5
  Knowledge itself is p.   15:12
  most p. to hurt us   19:19
  nature denies the p.   118:19
  nor p. of speech   194:12
  nor witch hath p.   185:4
  of ample p.   248:19
  pomp of p.   97:12
  p., and pelf   180:6
  p., and the glory   30:22
  p. of man   199:20
  p. of the Crown   12:15
  p. of the dog   169:1
  P. tends to corrupt   1:1
  To defy P.   215:1
  to pant beneath thy p.   214:3
  ungodly in great p.   169:14
  Unlimited p.   162:18
  wad some P. the giftie gie us   48:23
  who have the p.   247:20
Powerful: Guns will make us p.   94:12
  not p. enough   75:4
  outlive this p. rhyme   211:4
Powerless: is p. to bestow   83:1
  p. to be born   11:15
Powers: lay waste our p.   249:5
  nor p.   35:10
  p. that be ordained   35:13
  P. that will work   248:20
  Virtues, P.   146:19
  wrestle..against p.   36:14
  ye heavenly P.   55:23
Power-State: conception of the P.   225:13
Practice: P. drives me mad   6:8
  very good p.   178:2
Practise to deceive!   180:12
Praemia: sua p. laudi   236:7
Praemissi: not amissi, but p.   103:11
Praise: against empty p.   164:1
  beat high for p.   149:13
  Damn with faint p.   165:6
  girded with p.   96:18
  God hath no better p.   41:6
  His p. may thither fly   103:18
  I will p. Thee   104:3
  if there be any p.   36:20
  is p. indeed   150:15
  Let us now p. famous men 29:37, 127:15
  none to p.   248:3
  not to p. him   194:3
  our noble England's p.   136:5
  p. a fugitive and cloistered virtue 148:9
  p. above heaven   172:6
  p. be given!   65:23
  P. God, from whom   123:3
  P. him   107:15, 172:8
  p. new-born gawds   208:28
  p. of it endureth   171:11
  P. the Lord   87:5, 122:24, 172:8
  p. the Name of the Lord   172:6
  p. to give   118:4
  P. to the Holiest   153:14

song of p. be sung   165:21
Those they p.   139:23
turn to God to p.   44:3
We p. thee, O God   10:6
were no small p.   147:1
Praised: everybody p. the Duke   218:14
  p. him to his face   230:5
Praises: His p. there may grow   103:18
  sing p.   169:11
  who p., with enthusiastic tone   92:1
Praising: doing one's p.   50:8
Prattle: and her sweet p.   109:6
  his p. to be tedious   207:3
Pray: After this manner therefore p. 30:22
  All p. in their distress   39:12
  all together p.   66:6
  If I could p. to move   193:16
  live, and p., and sing   196:6
  live more nearly as we p.   122:15
  nor p. with you   201:13
  One to watch, and one to p.   1:17
  P., ask not   109:2
  P. for my soul   227:2
  p. for the peace   171:20
  P. love me little   104:12
  remain'd to p.   95:7
  to p. for you at St. Paul's   218:3
  To p. is to work   10:4
  To whom the Romans p.   136:14
  turn to God to praise and p.   44:3
  wash your hands and p.   125:10
  we do p. for mercy   202:5
  Whene'er he went to p.   95:11
Prayed: Having p. together   104:10
  who often. . have p.   62:11
Prayer: he made his p.   128:1
  in p. in my sore need   214:3
  let the P. re-echo   132:13
  More things are wrought by p.   227:2
  Your p. must be   119:9
Prayers: Christopher Robin is say-
    ing his p.   143:15
  fall to thy p.   191:1
  short were the p.   245:6
  with angry p.   105:13
  would not say his p.   155:16
Prayeth: He p. well   66:7
Praying: Amelia was p.   231:17
  insisted on people p. with him   114:9
  now he is p.   188:23
  past p. for   190:14
Preach: as never sure to p. again   19:1
  P. a better sermon   83:4
  p. it long!   164:2
Preached: he practis'd what he p.   11:3
  I p. as never sure   19:1
  p. to death   217:20
Preacher: advantage of the p.   47:12
  no mean p.   248:14
  saith the P.   26:34
Preaches contentment   126:20
Preaching: woman's p.   114:19
Precedency: point of p.   116:1
Precept: for p. must be upon p.   28:7
  more efficacious than p.   116:25
  some p. deep   166:5
Precepts: few p. in thy memory   185:21
  We love the p.   106:11
Precious: One half so p.   85:16
  This p. stone   206:7
Precise: Is too p. in every part   104:11
Predecessors: my illustrious p.   84:4
Predestinate: In p. grooves   100:12
Prefer: And of that district I p.   42:7
Preferred: is p. before me   33:47
Pregnant bank   77:6
Prejudices: bundle of p.   129:5
  it p. a man so   218:1
Preliminary: puff p.   216:1

Prepare: go to p. a place   34:18
  O! p. it   209:9
  p. a table   169:2
  p. for war   235:12
  P. ye the way of the Lord   28:12, 30:4
Prepared: p. as a bride   37:25
  The Middle Class was quite p.   21:7
Presbyter: New P.   148:3
Presbyterian true blue   49:18
Presence: conspicuous by its p.   178:11
  his p. on the field   240:20
  I have felt a p.   248:19
  whose unseen p.   214:1
Present: but p. in spirit   35:15
  His p. and your pains   191:4
  if this p. were the world's last
    night?   77:11
  No time like the p.   138:3
  p. far too small   239:17
  P. mirth hath p. laughter   209:5
  p. my true account   147:17
  Such p. joys   80:17
  there were p. the Picninnies   86:19
  things p.   35:10
  un-birthday p.   58:4
  Who p., past   38:18
Presentation: under the p. of that 184:15
Presented: p. unto him gifts   30:2
  when some occasion is p.   80:3
Presenting Thebes   144:8
Preservation: our creation, p.   166:31
  p. of life   113:2
Preserve thy going out   171:18
Preserved: each slight variation..is p. 72:9
President of the Immortals   100:10
Press: dead-born from the p.   111:22
  If you p. me to say   149:12
  not p. you like slaves   88:18
  the P. was squared   21:7
  You shall not p. down upon the
    brow of labor   45:15
Press-men: so we be named P.   11:5
Pressure: form and p.   188:10
Prest: all their Vintage p.   85:4
Presume: Dr. Livingstone, I p.?   220:2
Pretence: faint meaning make p.   79:24
Pretences: make p.   71:12
Pretender: God bless..the P.   50:15
Pretty: All my p. ones?   199:27
  all the maidens p.   67:19
  everything that p. is   184:20
  It's p., but is it Art?   125:1
  Oh, the p. flowers   111:17
  p. ring time   184:12
  p. sweeting   209:5
  Tell me, p. maiden   99:8
  very p. weoman   86:11
  We all love a p. girl   37:31
  Which is p.   91:1
  with a p. woman   115:12
Pretty-dimpled boys   182:15
Prevail: and shall p. [truth]   42:12
  p. on our future masters   215:19
  p. upon the day   79:24
  shall not p.   31:33
Prevail'd with double sway   95:7
Prevaricate: thou dost p.   49:21
Prevent: P. us, O Lord   167:28
  right to p. it   143:19
Prey: fastened on her p.   174:10
  p. to all   164:19
  to hast'ning ills a p.   95:4
Preys: to their p. do rouse   199:6
Price: men have their p.   238:10
  pearl of great p.   31:28
  p. for knowledge   233:17
  p. is far above rubies   26:32
  p. of admiralty   127:18
  p. of everything   243:12

Prick: If you p. us 201:27
    Pat it and p. it 157:9
    p. and sting her 186:13
    To p. the sides 198:4
Pricking: By the p. of my thumbs 199:17
    p. on the plain 219:9
Pricks: hard for thee to kick against
    the p. 34:36
Pride: all the p., cruelty 174:16
    aspiring p. 138:10
    he-bear in his p. 125:5
    He that is low no p. 46:17
    high-blown p. 192:14
    my family p. 91:28
    our faith, our p. 124:18
    perished in his p. 247:19
    pilgrims' p. 217:14
    pour contempt on all my p. 239:16
    P. goeth before destruction 26:20
    p. of ancestry 166:4
    p. of former days 149:13
    p. of place 199:1
    p. of the ocean 212:7
    P., pomp, and circumstance 205:10
    p. that apes humility 218:17
    p. that licks the dust 165:9
    p. that pulls the country down 204:30
    soldier's p. 44:7
    spite of p. 164:17
    their country's p. 95:4
    three summers' p. 211:13
    Whare was than the p. of man 99:11
Priest: ghastly p. doth reign 136:17
    guts of the last p. 142:15
    I tell thee, churlish p. 189:22
    mysterious p. 120:21
    Nature's p. 246:11
    old P. writ large 148:3
    p. who slew the slayer 136:17
    this turbulent p.? 103:12
    true God's p. 54:20
    waked the p. 158:8
Priestcraft: ere p. did begin 79:2
Priestlike: at their p. task 121:8
Priketh: So p. hem nature 60:9
Primal: In the p. sympathy 246:13
Prime: dead ere his p. 144:20
    glory of your p.? 213:15
Prime Minister: The next P. but
    three 21:7
Prime-roses: pale p. 210:8
Primeval: forest p. 133:16
Primordial atomic globule 91:28
Primrose: p. by a river's brim 247:14
    p. path of dalliance 185:20
    p. way 198:17
Prince: 'God bless the P. of Wales!' 132:13
    Good-night, sweet p. 190:5
    p. of darkness 195:13, 222:7
    P. of Denmark being left out 181:4
    P. of glory died 239:16
    P. of Peace 27:32
    p.'s palaces 201:9
Princedoms: Dominations, P., Vir-
    tues 146:19
Princes: a word to be addressed to
    p.? 82:10
    blaze forth the death of p. 193:14
    hangs on p.' favours! 192:14
    her p. are come home 193:8
    monuments of p. 211:4
    P. and lords may flourish 95:4
    Put not your trust in p. 172:4
    sweet aspect of p. 192:14
Princess: fitting for a p. 183:6
Principalities: against p. 36:14
    nor p. 35:10
Principibus placuisse viris 108:11
Principle: don't believe in p. 135:2

fundamental p. 38:7
I have called this p. 72:9
Principles: Damn your p.! 76:12
    he has good p. 114:12
    p. deduced from it 102:2
    p. of eternal justice 160:22
Print: faith, he'll p. it 48:29
    p. would then surpass 118:3
    that's fit to p. 159:8
Printed in a book! 25:34
Printing and the Protestant Re-
    ligion 55:5
Printless: On lissom, clerical, p. toe 42:6
Prism: Newton, with his p. 247:17
    prunes and p. 74:12
Prison: do not a p. make 134:19
    Home is the girl's p. 213:1
    in a wall'd p. 196:6
    in p., and ye came unto me 32:16
    let's away to p. 196:6
    opening of the p. 29:2
    What is a ship but a p.? 49:9
Prisoners: which p. call the sky 243:14
Prison-house: secrets of my p. 186:7
    Shades of the p. 246:11
Prithee pretty maiden 92:24
Private: fine and p. place 140:12
    p. advantage of the preacher 47:12
    sphere of p. life 141:20
    tempted by a p. whim 21:19
    to gain some p. ends 95:14
Privates: her p. we 187:1
Privato: Maior p. visus 225:1
Privilege: accursed power which
    stands on P. 21:18
    But the p. and the pleasure 91:10
Privileged and the People 76:21
Privy: with p. paw 145:3
Prize: Christ the p. 149:1
    Fraught with a later p. 213:12
    is lawful p. 98:4
    Many people p. it 92:24
    p. the thing ungain'd 208:26
    p. we sought 242:10
    win you such a p.! 152:16
Problem: a three-pipe p. 78:2
Proceed: all just works do p. 166:18
Proceedeth: that p. out of the
    mouth of God 30:8
Proceedings: And the subsequent p. 101:4
Procés: puis ils lui font son p. 148:20
Process: In p. of the seasons 211:13
    p. of the suns 228:11
    such was the p. 204:22
Proclaim: sensual world p. 150:3
    to p. liberty 29:2
Proclaims: apparel oft p. the man 185:21
Proconsul: great P. 136:22
Procrastination is the thief of time 250:16
Procreant cradle 198:2
Procreation: for the p. of children 168:6
Proctors: prudes for p. 229:6
Procul, o procul este, profani 236:16
Procures the greatest happiness 112:10
Prodigality: perennial spring of all p. 47:7
Produce: unless I p. something 137:5
Produced: may be p. any number
    of times 130:13
    so much happiness is p. 115:7
Productions of time 39:18
Profane: For me to p. it 215:12
    O p. one! 41:3
Profaned: they have desolated and
    p. 94:3
    too often p. 215:12
Profess and call themselves 166:28
Profession: an ornament to her p. 46:18
    most ancient p. 128:21
    so degrading a p. 178:1

Professions: hated..all p. 223:6
p. which are full 233:6
Professor: that most learn'd p. 165:18
Proffer: hands p. gifts 236:9
Profit: It surely was my p. 226:19
p. by their example 103:9
To whose p. 63:21
What p. hath a man 26:34
Profitable: With p. labour 191:15
Profited: What is a man p. 31:35
Profiteth: it p. me nothing 35:21
Profits: little p. that an idle king 230:12
Profligate and thin 251:2
Progeny: p. of light 146:19
p. yet more corrupt 109:23
Progress: makes no p. 132:5
Proletarier: Die P. haben nichts..als
    ihre Ketten...P., vereinigt euch! 140:14
Prologues: As happy p. 197:9
Promethean: right P. fire 196:16
Promise: broke no p. 164:25
p. and vow 167:32
p. such a beauteous day 211:3
Whose p. none relies on 176:2
Promised: What thou art p. 197:14
Promises: and high p. 107:18
P. and pie-crust 223:8
Promontory: sterile p. 187:4
Promotion cometh neither from the
    east 170:10
Pronounced: as I p. it to you 188:7
Proof: antique pillars massy p. 144:9
bliss in p. 212:2
Proofs: As p. of holy writ 205:8
Prop: my very p. 201:20
Proper: our p. stations 74:2
p. man 203:5
Properly: never did anything p. 131:15
There is p. no history 82:18
Property: give me a little snug p. 80:20
man of p. 92:24
P. has its duties 79:1
P. is theft 172:25
Prophecies: there be p. 35:21
Prophecy: trumpet of a p.! 214:4
Prophesy: sons and your daughters
    shall p. 29:22
we p. in part 35:21
Prophesying war! 66:15
Prophet: p. is not without honour 31:29
p. new inspir'd 206:6
Prophetic: nor the p. soul 211:14
Prophets: Beware of false p. 31:3
to destroy..the p. 30:15
Propinquity does it 238:22
Proportion: some strangeness in the
    p. 14:8
Propose: and p. nothing 219:23
Proposes: Man p. 122:22
Propositions: by a series of p. 130:14
Propriété: La p. c'est le vol 172:25
Propriety: From her p. 204:31
Prose: harmony of p. 80:5
in p. or rhyme 145:10
not p. is verse 148:16
p. = words in their best order 67:8
speaking p. 148:15
Prose: Tout ce qui n'est point p. est vers 148:16
Prospect: every p. pleases 101:16
Prospects: noble wild p. 114:13
Prosper: For if it p. 100:14
shall p. that love thee 171:20
Treason doth never p. 100:14
Prosperity: jest's p. 196:18
Protect: I'll p. it now 150:12
Protection: mercy and p. 168:16
Protest: lady doth p. too much 188:13
Protestant: Printing, and the P.
    Religion 55:5

Protestantism: All p. is a sort of
    dissent 47:1
p. of the Protestant religion 47:1
Proteus: Have sight of P. 249:5
Protoplasmal: to a p. primordial 91:28
Proud: all the p. and mighty 80:18
Death be not p. 77:9
make death p. 182:22
man, p. man 200:19
P. as peacocks 182:3
p. foot of a conqueror 193:8
p. his name 180:6
P. Maisie 180:18
p. man's contumely 187:13
p.,..untroubled heart 54:4
scattered the p. 32:38
very stiff and p. 58:6
war down the p.! 236:18
With p. thanksgiving 38:1
Proudly-arched and glossy neck 154:12
Prove: all the pleasures p. 139:6
cannot p. a lover 207:6
I shall p. it 50:13
let us p. 118:12
now to p. our chance 78:28
P. all things 36:24
shall p. Beloved 127:18
to p. a villain 207:6
Proved: and upon me p. 211:16
God proved them 29:33
p. me, and saw my works 170:26
Which was to be p. 83:9
Provençal: Dance, and P. song 121:3
Proverb: according to the p. 80:6
p. and a byword 25:7
Southern p. 180:20
There is a Spanish p. 61:5
Proverbs: in the P. of Solomon 74:15
Providence: assert eternal P. 145:11
P. their guide 146:25
put upon the P. of God 71:12
There's a special p. 189:26
under the P. of God 60:1
Province: all knowledge to be my
    p. 15:9
Provisos: O horrid p.! 68:20
Provocation: as in the p. 170:25
Provoke the silent dust 97:13
Provoked: is not easily p. 35:21
Provokes: No one p. me with im-
    punity 10:3
Prow: Youth on the p. 97:6
Prowl and p. around? 152:11
Prudes for proctors 229:6
Prunes and prism 74:19
Pruninghooks: spears into p. 27:22
Prussian: French, or Turk or P. 93:14
Prussians: others may be P. 74:22
Psalmist: sweet p. of Israel 25:5
Psalms: Church with p. must shout 103:18
glad in him with p. 170:21
Psaltery: sound of the..p. 29:16
Pub: pavender, or p. 178:13
Public: as if I was a p. meeting 235:18
British p. 136:23
exempt from p. haunt 183:9
microcosm of a p. school 76:22
Nor p. men 250:19
P. schools are the nurseries 84:7
than a p. calamity 219:2
which the p. will always clamour 107:5
Publican: fawning p. 201:14
Publicans: with p. and sinners? 31:10
Publish: P. and be damned 241:2
p. it not in the streets 24:47
Publisher: Barabbas was a p. 54:9
Pudding: p. and pie 155:15
solid p. 164:1
Puellis Vixi p. nuper idoneus 110:2

Puer: Quis. .p. in rosa Perfusus   108:18
Puffed: is not p. up   35:21
   p. and reckless libertine   185:20
Puffing is of various sorts   216:1
Pug: O most charming p.   86:11
Pugging: set my p. tooth on edge   210:5
Puissant: noble and p. nation   148:10
Puking: mewling and p.   183:20
Pull for the shore   39:23
Pulls: who p. me down?   138:14
Pulsanda: pede libero P. tellus   109:8
Pulse: feel that p. no more   149:13
   My p. like a soft drum   123:11
   p. in the eternal mind   42:11
Pumice: Beside a p. isle   214:2
Pumpkins: Where the early p. blow   130:19
Punch: Some sipping p.   247:15
Punched: brains they p. in   240:3
Punctuality is the politeness of
   kings   134:18
Punica fide   179:2
Punished: be p. in the sight of men   29:33
Punishment: Let the p. fit the crime   92:8
   Oh, p.!   72:18
   p. of his guilt   71:17
Punishments: How charged with p.   102:14
Puns: politics to p.   166:5
Punt: slow p. swings around   11:24
Puppy: Both mongrel, p., whelp   95:13
   drink, p., drink   242:20
Puppy-dogs' tails   158:14
Pure: as p. as snow   188:5
   Because my heart is p.   230:8
   blessed are the p.   30:11
   every p. and wise spirit   82:21
   Her court was p.   230:1
   his p. soul   207:2
   just as p. and fair   91:19
   land of p. delight   239:15
   Live p., speak true   226:17
   most particularly p. young man   92:22
   p. and endless light   235:11
   p. and light   122:17
   p. from guilt   109:5
   p. in heart   122:19
   so p. of old   147:16
   to the p. all things are p.   129:9
   Truth is rarely p.   243:7
   Unto the p. all things are p.   36:34
   Whatsoever things are p.   36:20
Purgation of such emotions   10:16
Purgatory of men   86:13
Purge me with hyssop   169:26
Purged: will never be p. away   42:14
Puritan hated bear-baiting   137:1
Puritane-one: I saw a P.   41:3
Purlieus: Dusty p. of the law   227:15
Purple: gleaming in p. and gold   52:9
   I never saw a p. cow   46:24
   in p. and red   228:20
   p. patch or two   107:18
   P. the sails   182:15
   p. with love's wound   203:7
Purples: daisies, and long p.   189:18
   P. the east   146:20
Purple-stained mouth   121:3
Purpose: My p. is   209:8
   one increasing p. runs   228:11
   p. in liquidity   41:20
   Shake my fell p.   197:15
   time to every p.   26:38
Purpureus. .pannus   107:18
Purse: as thy p. can buy   185:21
   put into his p.   192:4
   Put money in thy p.   204:25
   Who steals my p.   205:4
Pursue: it will p.   117:18
   to p. my reason   42:19
   who p. Culture   241:22

Pursued: p. by a bear   210:4
   p. it with forks   56:5
Pursueth: when no man p.   26:29
Pursuing: Faint yet p.   24:30
   still p.   133:28
Pursuit: and the p. of happiness   8:9, 113:2
   Mad in p.   212:2
   unspeakable in full p.   243:24
Pursuits: varied p.   119:1
Pusillanimity: as we abhor p.   113:12
Pussy: beautiful p. you are   131:6
   I like little p.   156:3
   Owl and the P.-cat   131:6
   P. cat, p. cat   157:14
   P.'s in the well   155:13
Put: hath p. down the mighty   32:37
   P. it down a we   75:25
   p. off till to-morrow   173:5
   p. on the armour of light   35:14, 166:23
   shall never be p. out   130:6
   When he p. on his clothes   95:12
Puzzle: schoolmasters p. their brain   95:20
Pyramid: star-y-pointing p.?   147:12
Pyramides: du haut de ces p.   152:1
Pyrenees: high P.   22:3
Pyrénées: Il n'y a plus de P.   134:16
Pyrrha: P...is wooing thee   108:18
Pythagoras: 'Ipse' autem erat P.   63:12
   P. was misunderstood   82:21
Python: Who bought a P.   21:23

Q

Quad: about in the Q.   4:1, 129:2
Quaesieris: Tu ne q., scire nefas   109:2
Quaff'd: jested, q., and swore   78:22
Quaint: panes of q. device   120:4
   yet most q.   19:24
Quake: she gan to q.   60:27
Quaker: knaw'd a Q. feller   228:23
Qualis: Non sum q. eram   110:4
   Q. artifex pereo!   153:3
Quality: and all q.   205:10
   q. of mercy   202:5
   resting q.   193:16
Quarrel: entrance to a q.   185:21
   forgot their q.   57:18
   hath his q. just   192:7, 213:4
   justice of my q.   139:15
   q. with my bread and butter   223:11
   sudden and quick in q.   183:20
   to find q. in a straw   189:7
Quarrels: full of q.   207:28
Quarrelsome: countercheck q.   184:14
Quart: For a q. of ale   210:5
Quartered safe out 'ere   125:11
Quarterly: 'I,' says the Q.   52:6
   nothing a-year paid q.   222:22
Quarto: beautiful q. page   216:15
Quartos, their well-order'd ranks   70:20
Quean: flaunting, extravagant q.   216:19
Queen: Come not near our fairy q.   203:10
   cradle of the fairy q.?   203:12
   every lass a q.   123:18
   home life of our own dear Q.!   5:4
   look at the q.   157:14
   mobled q.   187:8
   Most Gracious Q.   6:7
   Mother, Wife and Q.   230:1
   Q. and huntress   117:11
   Q. asked   143:13
   q...is dead   200:4
   Q. of Hearts   57:12, 157:15
   Q. of Scots is this day leichter   82:5
   Q. o' the May   228:21
   Q. was in a furious passion   57:1
   q. was in the parlour   158:1
   regular Royal Q.!   91:8

Queens: blood of q. 120:4
Q. have died young 152:5
Queer: ill-tempered and q. 130:17
Queer Street is full of lodgers 75:13
Quell the mighty 147:6
Quench: Many waters cannot q. love 27:20
shall he not q. 28:16
Quest: and what thy q.? 41:8
Questing beast 137:20
Question: hurried q. of Despair 50:19
no q. makes 85:11
Others abide our q. 11:20
q...about everything was 75:11
struck out of the q. 55:17
such a silly q.? 220:13
that is the q. 187:13
Questioning: sweetly q. 104:1
Questions: answered three q. 56:17
Discourst in Three Q. 182:2
Them that asks no q. 127:10
though puzzling q. 43:1
Quick: q. in quarrel 183:20
Touched to the q. 44:7
Quicken: q. a new birth! 214:4
within the sense they q. 215:10
Quick-eyed: but q. love 104:1
Quickly: q. flying 58:21
were done q. 198:3
Quiet: All q. along the Potomac 137:7
All Q. on the Western Front 175:5
Anythin' for a q. life 75:33
Be q.! 9:9
Fair q. 140:5
From q. homes 21:12
In q. she reposes 11:19
innocent and q. 134:19
keep a bower q. 120:1
Let it be kept q. 108:5
q. as a nun 246:15
q. die 180:15
q. shadows falling 159:14
q. sleep 141:4
q. waters 181:8
scallop-shell of q. 174:13
what may q. us 147:10
Quietly: as q. among the graves 81:6
Quietness: bride of q. 120:18
Quietus: might his q. make 187:13
Quills: upon the fretful porpentine 186:7
Quince: slices of q. 131:9
Quinquireme of Nineveh 140:20
Quinta: La q. columna 148:13
Quintessence of dust 187:4
Quip modest 184:14
Quips and cranks 144:12
Quire: full-voiced q. 144:9
Quires: In Q. and Places 166:16
Quit: q. you like men 35:32
q. yourselves like men 24:38
Quiver full of them 171:23
Quivering aspen 180:13
Quote: I'll kill you if you q. it! 46:25
Quo vadis? 34:21
Quousque tandem abutere, Catilina,
patientia nostra? 63:16

R

Rabbit: Gone to get a r. skin 155:6
r. in a snare 220:9
Rabbits: four little R. 165:22
Rabble: army would be a base r. 47:3
Race: Another r. hath been 246:14
feather'd r. 88:8
He held the human r. in scorn 21:2
headstrong, moody, murmuring r. 79:4
human r. 62:1
man's imperial r. 165:2
men and women with our r. 124:17

moved among my r. 221:24
new and better r. 237:1
he rides a r.! 69:28
r. abides immortal 237:9
r. is not to the swift 27:3
r. that is set before us 36:35
r. that long in darkness pin'd 181:9
run out thy r. 148:6
Run the straight r. 149:1
sceptred r.! 129:19
slinks out of the r. 148:9
still a godly r. he ran 95:11
that curse our r. 91:4
type of all her r. 78:33
unto a savage r. 230:12
whole r. of politicians 223:2
winding-sheet of Edward's r. 97:5
wins the r. 133:5
Races: all the r. of Europe 251:3
glory..of r. 23:3
Rachel: seven years for R. 23:30
Rack: upon the r. of this tough
world 196:12
weather'd every r. 242:10
Racker: Ihr R., wollt ihr ewig leben? 88:7
Rackets: match'd our r. 191:4
Radiance: r. sprung from God 179:11
white r. of Eternity 213:10
Radiant: in their r. courses 166:5
Rag: To a r. and a bone 128:1
Rage: die here in a r. 223:5
furiously r. together 168:21
hard-favour'd r. 191:8
Heav'n has no r. 68:10
I r., I melt 89:7
Puts all Heaven in a R. 38:11
r.! blow! 195:4
Rages: While the battle r. 54:6
Ragged: pair of r. claws 81:18
Raggedness: looped and window'd
r. 195:8
Rags: And r., and hags 66:9
to very r. 188:7
unwomanly r. 107:3
Rail: I'll r. and brawl 208:7
r. against other folks 84:8
Railway: with a r.-share 56:5
Railway-Ticket: In his hat a R. 131:3
Raiment: in sparkling r. bright 2:14
Rain: as the gentle r. 202:5
falls not hail, or r. 227:3
few small drops of r. 17:1
or in r.? 197:2
r. is over and gone 27:16
r. it raineth every day 209:20
r. it raineth on the just 40:14
R., r., go away 157:16
ripple of r. 223:28
sendeth r. on the just 30:19
small r. down can r. 8:10
soft refreshing r. 53:12
summer r. 221:24
vollying r. 12:2
wind and the r. 209:20
with spring r. 82:13
would r. cats and dogs 223:16
Rainbow: add another hue unto
the r. 193:6
like a r. shell 177:8
r. comes and goes 246:8
r. in the sky 247:10
r.'s glory is shed 213:16
Rain-bringer: Jupiter, the r. 233:16
Rained: r. a ghastly dew 228:9
when I awoke, it r. 66:1
Raineth: rain it r. every day 209:20
rain it r. on the just 40:14
Rainy: r. Hyades 230:13
with r. eyes 296:14

Raise: can r. a thirst | 126:15
I can r. Thee | 104:3
Lord shall r. me up | 174:15
R. your joys | 241:7
what is low r. | 145:11
Raised: by merit r. | 146:10
Christ being r. | 35:4
r. not a stone | 245:7
r. up in him | 167:30
Raising: heads never r. | 247:9
r. up a people of customers | 217:12
Raison: La r. du plus fort | 86:18
Rake: a r. among scholars | 136:24
R.'s progress | 231:14
Raking: stop r. the muck | 177:2
Rally behind the Virginians | 20:3
Ramp up my genius | 118:1
Rampage: on the R. | 74:16
Ramparts: to the r. we hurried | 245:3
Rams: skipped like r. | 171:12
Ran: Grief with a glass that r. | 224:1
in he r. | 106:3
noble savage r. | 79:19
Sunset r. | 44:2
Range: forward let us r. | 228:14
r. of practical politics | 94:4
Ranges: thy foolish r. | 235:8
Rangoon: from R. to Mandalay? | 126:11
Rank: best r. and station | 185:21
in the name of every r. | 47:11
marched, r. on r. | 142:1
my offence is r. | 188:22
r. and gross | 185:11
r. is but the guinea's stamp | 48:16
r. mist they draw | 145:3
you will r. as an apostle | 92:22
Ranks: even the r. of Tuscany | 136:15
r. of death | 149:15
well-order'd r. | 70:20
Ransom: Of the world's r. | 206:7
r. captive Israel | 152:15
Rapacious and licentious soldiery | 47:9
Raphaels: talk'd of their R. | 95:19
Rapid: With r. change | 166:5
Rapids are near | 150:2
Rapier: unhatched r. | 209:18
Rapt: r. above the Pole | 146:30
r. one | 246:3
Rapture: Modified r.! | 92:4
r. on the lonely shore | 51:7
Raptures: no Minstrel r. swell | 180:6
r. and roses of vice | 224:4
Rara avis | 119:4
Rare: birth as r. | 140:2
by the r. advantage | 90:14
man of culture r. | 92:20
miracle of r. device | 66:15
O r. Ben Jonson | 118:14
r. bird on the earth | 119:4
Rarely: and r. simple | 243:7
R., r., comest thou | 215:7
Singing so r. | 180:18
Rarer: But, dying, has made us r.
gifts | 41:16
Rarest: thought was the r. | 233:7
Rascals, would you live for ever? | 88:7
Rashes: green grow the r. O | 48:19
Rashly importunate | 106:20
Rat: horse, a r. have life | 196:11
How now a r. | 188:24
I smell a r. | 49:21, 175:15
killed the r. | 158:8
like the sound of a r. | 44:20
poisoned r. in a hole | 223:5
r. without a tail | 197:5
Ratcliffe Road: Rolling down the R. | 124:12
Rated: in the Rialto you have r. me | 201:17
Rather: proof that he had r. | 116:9
Raths: and the mome r. | 57:14

Rations: live upon our daily r. | 74:2
Ratisbon: we French stormed R. | 44:6
Rattle: R. his bones | 154:8
spoiled his nice new r. | 57:18
Rattlesnake: he saw a r. | 56:8
Ravell'd sleave of care | 198:13
Raven: locks were like the r. | 48:20
r. himself is hoarse | 197:14
Ravening: they are r. wolves | 31:3
Ravenous horde | 91:24
Ravens: three r. sat on a tree | 16:17
Ravishment: Political r. | 94:1
Raw: looks red and r. | 196:20
Ray: admits no r. | 79:24
of purest r. serene | 97:15
r. of rays | 73:26
Raze out the written troubles | 200:1
Reach: above his r. | 160:1
is it, then, beyond the r. | 40:7
man's r. | 43:8
themselves do r. | 140:6
Until we r. | 139:10
Which will r. the bottom first? | 96:10
Reached: r. a middle height | 142:1
r. and kept | 133:22
Read: but they r. the others | 139:23
ever I could r. | 203:2
his books were r. | 21:15
May r. strange matters | 198:1
never r. a book before reviewing
it | 218:1
ought to r. just as inclination | 114:14
R., mark, learn, and inwardly
digest | 166:34
R. over your compositions | 115:1
r. the causes of things | 237:7
r. without pleasure | 116:10
slowly r. | 250:11
Take up and r. | 13:4
that all may r. | 39:8
What do you r.? | 186:25
who runs may r. | 122:18
wits to r. | 118:4
Reader: capacity of the r. | 141:16
Readers: many of my r. belong | 62:1
Readiness is all | 189:26
Reading: like r. Shakespeare | 67:7
R. is to the mind | 220:6
R. maketh a full man | 14:26
Reads: what he r. as a task | 114:14
Ready: We always are r. | 88:18
Real: Forms more r. | 214:9
Life is r.! | 133:26
Realm: borders of my r. | 82:9
fourth estate of the r. | 136:19
safety,. . of this r. | 60:1
this r., this England | 206:7
whole r. of nature | 239:17
Realms: happy r. of light | 145:14
in the r. of gold | 121:9
whom three r. obey | 165:3
Reap: as you sow, you are like to r. | 49:28
r. a habit | 175:4
r. in joy | 171:21
shall r. the whirlwind | 29:20
Sows, and he shall not r. | 224:2
that shall he also r. | 36:8
Reaped: never should be r. | 234:2
Rear: to r. the tender thought | 232:14
Rears: Hellas r. its mountains | 213:12
Reason: appear the better r. | 146:11
conquers r. still | 164:23
discourse of r. | 185:11
erring r.'s spite | 164:17
feast of r. | 165:10
general r. of the whole | 46:27
How noble in r.! | 187:4
In R.'s ear they all rejoice | 1:14
kills r. itself | 148:7

most sovereign r.   188:6
neither rhyme nor r.   150:7
not to r. why   226:2
r. of the strongest   86:18
r. of this thusness?   238:21
right deed for the wrong r.   81:21
tell me the r.   218:22, 219:1
to pursue my r.   42:19
to r. thus   206:4
We know no r.   157:12
What's the r.?   100:14
Will know the r. why?   101:6
without any other r.   133:6
works to make r.   12:6
Reasonableness: sweet r. of Jesus   12:11
Reasons: heart has its r.   161:7
    never give your r.   138:5
    r. will certainly be wrong   138:5
Recall: I shudder to r. it   236:10
    R. a time of happiness   72:7
Receipt of custom   31:9
Receive: r. my soul at last   241:8
    to give than to r.   34:46
    Wax to r.   50:17
Received: have r. the Spirit   35:7
    his own r. him not   33:45
    not r. the spirit of bondage   35:7
Rechabite poor Will must live   172:21
Reckless: puff'd and r. libertine   185:20
Reckoning: No r. made   186:12
Recks not his own rede   185:20
Reclining: violet's r. head   77:6
Recognizes: talent instantly r.
    genius   78:18
Reconciled: God and sinners r.   241:15
Record: In thy book r.   147:16
    puts a r. on the gramophone   82:2
    r. of the best   215:17
Recovered: man r. of the bite   95:16
    may not r. be   60:30
    we have never r.   81:11
Recruity: 'arf-made r.   128:8
Recte: Si possis r.   108:6
Red: Coral is far more r.   212:3
    eyelids heavy and r.   107:3
    His coat was r.   218:16
    His jacket was r.   66:10
    If the r. slayer think he slays   82:13
    in purple and r.   228:20
    looks r. and raw   196:20
    Luve's like a r. r. rose   48:28
    Making the green one r.   198:15
    never blows so r.   85:2
    pays us poor beggars in r.   128:6
    poured out the r.   41:16
    R. Badge of Courage   70:24
    r. blood reigns   210:5
    r. in tooth and claw   227:13
    so red and so white   123:17
    thin r. line   178:12
    wine when it is r.   26:23
Redbreast: Call for the robin r.   240:11
    Robin R. in a Cage   38:11
Rede: recks not his own r.   185:20
Redeem: he that doth r. her thence   190:9
Redeemed: hath r. Jerusalem   28:19
Redeemer: I know that my r.
    liveth   25:35
    mighty a R.   148:12
    my strength, and my r.   168:31
    To Thee, R.   152:7
Redemption: married past r.   79:25
    Our great r.   145:6
Redemptorem: tantum meruit habere
    R.   148:12
Red-legged scissor-man   106:3
Reduced: landlady can be r.   130:14
Reed: bruised r.   25:22, 28:16
    Man is only a r.   161:8

pluck'd a hollow r.   39:8
    r. shaken with the wind?   31:18
    thinking r.   161:8
Reeds: Down in the r. by the river?   43:5
Reeking: In r. tube   127:7
    one glorious blood-red, r.   44:2
Reel: They r. to and fro   171:8
Reference: no r. to futurity   115:12
References: always to verify your r.   178:2
Refining: still went on r.   95:18
Reform: Peace, retrenchment and r.   41:11
Reforming: melting and r.!   251:3
Refreshed: r. with wine   170:12
    tree of liberty must be r.   113:3
Refuge: God is thy r.   24:25
    last r. of a scoundrel   115:4
    Other r. have I none   241:9
    r. of weak minds   61:10
    thou hast been our r.   170:16
Refusal: great r.   72:6
Refuse: if you please r.   140:11
    r. to set his hand to a rope   78:27
Refute: can r. a sneer?   160:15
    I r. it   114:21
Regard: should be without r.   199:3
    Strict R. for Truth   21:8
Regarded: he hath r. the low estate   32:37
Regardless of their doom   98:8
Regiment: comes up the R.   125:3
    led his r. from behind   91:5
    Monstrous R. of Women   129:1
    R.'s in 'ollow square   125:2
    within our breasts for r.   139:10
Region of thick-ribbèd ice   200:23
Regions Caesar never knew   69:20
Register of the crimes   90:14
Regret: one thing I r.   56:8
Regrets: And the wild r.   243:6
    past R. and Future Fears   85:3
Regretted that he was not a bird   175:14
Regular: icily r.   228:19
    took the r. course   57:5
Regularly: struck r., like gongs   69:17
Reign: Democracy resumed her r.   21:18
    doubted his ability to r.   225:1
    Frighted the r. of Chaos   146:6
    ghastly priest doth r.   136:17
    His r. is marked   90:14
    Jesus shall r.   239:13
    may r. secure   146:3
    to r. in hell   146:3
    To r. is worth ambition   146:3
    Where saints immortal r.   239:15
Reigns: no crude surfeit r.   144:2
    R. solely in the breast   191:5
Reject: choose or r.   80:5
Rejected: despised and r. of men   28:20
    When my sonnet was r.   129:14
Rejects: high Heaven r.   247:6
Rejoice: again I say, R.   36:18, 241:14
    before Him, and r.   123:5
    Christian men, r.   152:12
    desert shall r.   28:9
    hear thee and r.   245:15
    heart and my flesh r.   170:13
    I r. The lot has fallen   127:18
    r. before Him   122:24
    R. in the Lord alway   36:18
    R. with me   33:19
Rejoiced: my spirit hath r.   32:37
Rejoices: His world r.   244:17
Rejoiceth: r. as a giant   168:30
    r. in the truth   35:21
    R. not in iniquity   35:21
Relate: little to r.   58:11
    unlucky deeds r.   205:20
Related: so nearly r.   160:11
Relations: party of friends and r.   91:25
    squire and his r.   74:2

Relaxes: Bless r.   39:20
Release: deadly forfeit should r.   145:6
  prisoner's r.   217:1
Releasing: gives thee r.   211:9
Relent: make him once r.   46:20
Relics: that his hallow'd r.   147:12
Relief: And not seek for kind r.?   39:14
  be a r. to me   212:14
  For this r.   185:2
Relies: none r. on   176:2
Relieve: How does it r. you   108:13
Religio: Tantum r. potuit suadere
  malorum   135:7
Religion: could r. prompt   135:7
  handmaid to r.   14:5
  Man without r.   100:11
  One r. is as true   49:12
  Printing, and the Protestant R.   55:5
  r. but a childish toy   139:4
  r. is allowed to invade   141:20
  R. is by no means a proper sub-
    ject   61:12
  r. is powerless to bestow   83:1
  R...is the opium   140:16
  r. most prevalent   47:1
  r. of feeble minds   47:16
  r. of humanity   160:14
  slovenliness is no part of r.   241:19
  some [talk] of r.   80:20
  true meaning of r.   12:8
Religion: Die R...das Opium   140:16
Religions: sixty different r.   54:19
Religious: dim r. light   144:9
Relished: by which he is to be r.   249:6
Rem: quocumque modo r.   108:6
Remain: and r. with you   167:26
  r. in the uttermost parts   172:1
Remained: anything r. to be done   135:6
  had so long r.   66:1
  r. some time   56:21
  r. to pray   95:7
Remains: aught r. to do   176:5
  Form r.   245:17
  in what r. behind   246:13
  Little r.   230:13
  Nothing besides r.   214:7
  what r. is bestial   204:33
  whatever r.   78:16
Remark: r. all these roughnesses   71:9
  Which I wish to r.   101:3
Remarkable: nothing left r.   182:21
Remedies: desperate r.   84:1
Remedy: r. against sin   168:7
  r. is worse than the disease   14:23
  sharp r.   174:17
  with all r.   199:3
Remember: branches ne'er r.   122:6
  calmness to r.   2:1
  I r., I r.   107:1
  If I do not r. thee   171:28
  Lord, r. me   33:40
  Must I r.?   185:11
  never can r.   76:14
  no man r. me   100:9
  nor long r.   132:8
  Please to r.   7:3, 157:12
  r. and be sad   177:11
  R. Lot's wife   33:32
  r. not the sins   169:6
  r. the name of the Lord   168:32
  r. with advantages   192:4
  shall be sweet to r.   236:5
  We will r. them   38:2
  Yet will I r. thee   70:4
Remembered: are r. not   213:16
  As friend r. not   184:2
  Be all my sins r.   188:1
  blue r. hills   111:5
  freshly r.   192:4

shall be r.   192:4
  time r.   223:29
  we r. thee, O Sion   171:28
Remembering: r. happier things   228:7
  r. my goods friends   206:10
Remembrance: for a r. of his holi-
  ness   169:8
  R. fallen from heaven   224:1
  that's for r.   189:14
Remind: lives of great men all r. us   133:27
Reminding: always r. us   238:22
Reminiscence sing   242:12
Remorse: Farewell r.   146:14
  passage to r.   197:15
Remote and ineffectual Don   21:20
Re-mould it nearer   86:1
Remove: it doth r. those things   77:20
  R. hence to yonder place   31:36
  so that I could r. mountains   35:21
  visionary joys r.?   68:14
Remover: bends with the r.   211:16
  with the r. to remove   211:16
Render therefore unto Caesar   32:7
Rendezvous with Death   181:11
Renew: r. a right spirit   169:27
  shall r. their strength   28:15
Renounce the devil   167:32
Renown: forfeit fair r.   180:6
  Of credit and r.   69:21
  r. and grace is dead   198:19
Renowned for their deeds   206:7
Rent: what a r.   194:8
Repair: in constant r.   114:5
  Love doth to her eyes r.   210:2
  shall awhile r.   67:15
  we will then r.   69:22
Repairs his drooping head   145:4
Repay: I will r.   35:11
Repeat: same tale r.   246:10
  what boots it to r.   85:8
Repeats: he r. his verses   129:12
Repent: earnestly r.   167:22
  nor falter, nor r.   215:1
  r. at leisure   68:13
  r. in haste   68:13
  R. ye   30:3
Repentance: cool r. came   181:1
  To give r.   95:21
  which need no r.   33:20
  Winter Garment of R.   84:17
Repented: and much r.   51:12
Repenteth: one sinner that r.   33:20
Repetitions: Use not vain r.   30:21
Replenish the earth   23:9
Reply: r. churlish   184:14
  R., r.   202:1
  Their's not to make r.   226:2
Report: how he may r.   147:7
  ill r. while you live   187:9
  of good report   36:20
  R. me and my cause aright   190:1
  r. of my death   234:21
Reporters: in which the r. sit   136:19
  speaking through r.   55:16
Repose: and r. is taboo'd   91:23
  earned a night's r.   134:11
  it may find r. in thee   13:2
Reposed: her land r.   230:1
Reposes: In quiet she r.   11:19
Reprehend: If I r. any thing   216:11
Representation: Taxation without
  r.   159:4
Reproof valiant   184:14
Reprove: check the erring and r.   245:19
Republic: pension list of the r.   64:1
Reputation: I have lost my r.   204:33
  Is spotless r.   206:2
  Seeking the bubble r.   183:20
  sold my R.   85:15

Repute: its r. nothing 94:14
Request of his lips 168:33
Requests: grant their r. 166:17
Requiem: To thy high r. 121:6
Require: thought 'e might r. 128:4
Required to be done 74:18
Requited: both alike r. 173:26
Resemble: I r. her to thee 238:4
Resentment: to get up r. 153:8
Reserve thy judgement 185:21
Reserved: Alike r. to blame 165:6
Reside in thrilling region 200:23
Residence: my own perpetual r. 153:11
Resign: I'd crowns r. 137:15, 235:4
Resist: few can r. 92:11
  I can r. everything 243:15
  R. not evil 30:18
Resistance: principle of r. 47:1
Resolute: bloody, bold, and r. 199:20
Resolution: native hue of r. 187:13
  pull in r. 200:5
Resolve: we here highly r. 132:8
Resort: r. of mirth 144:7
  To which I most r. 231:4
Respect: no r. of place 209:6
  There's the r. 187:13
Respectable: Not one is r. 242:14
Respecter: no r. of persons 34:38
Responsibility: heavy burden of r. 81:5
Rest: after the r. of it had gone 56:21
  All the r. have thirty-one 96:8
  be at r. for one day 68:5
  because they are at r. 171:9
  crept silently to R. 85:4
  do r. but true 193:8
  done for the r. 221:1
  far, far better r. 75:34
  gentle wings may r. 179:11
  Gets him to r. 191:15
  give thee credit for the r. 62:10
  holy r. 153:12
  I will give you r. 31:20
  long ago at r. 69:4
  love itself have r. 52:14
  never r. 139:10
  Now she's at r. 79:20
  R. is Lies 85:6
  r. is mere fine writing 235:14
  r. is silence 190:4
  r. nowhere 159:12
  R., r., perturbed spirit! 186:18
  r. to some faint meaning 79:24
  r. upon thy holy hill? 168:27
  r. who does not know? 160:2
  Said 'Good Night', and gone to
    r. 21:16
  sing thee to thy r.! 190:5
  taking his r. 245:5
  Their place of r. 146:25
  there did it r. 120:7
  they r. not day and night 37:16
  To talk about the r. 105:12
  waive the R. 84:20
  weary be at r. 25:28
  who from their labours r. 111:12
  who sink to r. 67:14
  without r. 147:17
Rested: my caravan has r. 231:12
  r. the seventh day 167:11
Restless: as the r. Spheres 139:10
Restore: healing spells r. 179:11
  r. my wand'ring love 68:14
  soul he doth r. again 181:8
Restorer: sweet r. 250:15
Rests: r. a little longer 230:7
  R. and expatiates 164:14
Result: r. happiness 74:8
  r. misery 74:8
Resurrection: I am the r. 34:13

r. of the body 172:10
  R. to Eternal Life 168:20
Retain: marble to r. 50:17
Reticulated: Anything r. 116:15
Retirement: there must be no r. 99:4
Retort courteous 184:14
Retournons à nos moutons 9:8
Retrace: Thy steps r. 93:17
Retreat: honourable r. 184:5
  I will not r. 89:3
  my right is in r. 86:14
Retrenchment: I am for Peace, r. 41:11
Retrograde: be not r. 118:1
Return: bid time r. 206:13
  never to r. 49:5, 237:8
  r. the blow 54:14
  r. the glory 213:15
  spirit shall r. unto God 27:8
  unto dust shalt thou r. 23:17
Returned: R. ere noon 178:14
  Then ye r. to your trinkets 126:1
Returneth: dog r. his vomit 26:27
Returning were as tedious 199:12
Returns: No traveller r. 187:13
Revealed: r. in her step 236:6
  shall be r. 28:12
Revelations: ends with R. 243:26
Revelry: feast, and r. 144:19
  sound of r. by night 50:23
Revenge: R. is a kind of wild justice 14:21
  shall we not r.? 201:27
  spur my dull r.! 189:6
  study of r. 145:15
Revenges: brings in his r. 209:19
Revere: ride of Paul R. 133:25
Reverence: claims to r. 230:1
  to do him r. 194:6
Reverent eye 41:20
Reversion: bright r. in the sky 164:5
Reviewing: before r. it 218:1
Revive: Could I r. within me 66:15
Reviving: how r. 147:6
Révolte: C'est une r.? 175:17
Revolts: it r. me 91:29
Revolution: that the R., like
    Saturn 235:13
Révolution: Non, Sire, c'est une r. 175:17
Revolver: reach for my r. 117:5
  safety catch of my r. 117:5
Revolving: one r. moon 79:8
Reward: in no wise lose his r. 31:17
  nothing for r. 219:11
Rewarded: shall be greatly r. 29:33
Rewards: Farewell r. 68:27
  virtue hath her r. 236:7
Rhetorician: sophistical r. 76:11
Rhine: river R., it is well known 66:9
  Rupert of the R.! 136:7
  shall wash the river R.? 66:9
  think of the R. 15:22
  watch on the R. 179:15
Rhodopè: no voices, O R.! 129:22
Rhyme: build the lofty r. 144:20
  could not get a r. for roman 86:11
  in prose or r. 145:10
  many a mused r. 121:6
  neither r. nor reason 150:7
  outlive this powerful r. 211:4
Rialto: What news on the R.? 201:13
Rib: Smote him under the fifth r. 25:2
  Riband to stick in his coat 44:9
Ribbands to flow confusedly 104:11
Ribbon: blue r. of the turf 76:18
  r. of moonlight 155:1
Ribbons: with r. rare 112:8
Ribs: dig in the r. 222:14
  they roar their r. out! 93:36
  took one of his r. 23:12
Ribstone Pippin: Right as a R.! 21:17

Rice: Beside the ungather'd r. 134:3
r. pudding again 143:11
Rich: Art thou r. 72:18
crumbs..from the r. man's table 33:27
If I ever become a r. man 22:1
into something r. 208:12
It's the rich wot gets the pleasure 7:6
one more r. in hope 210:13
over the r. Dead 41:16
passing r. 95:6
Poor Little R. Girl 69:12
potentiality of growing r. 115:24
r. beyond the dreams of avarice
115, 24, 149:11
R. gifts wax poor 188:2
r. have become richer 215:16
r. he hath sent empty away 32:38
R. in good works 36:32
R. in saving common-sense 228:25
R. man in his castle 2:8
r. man to enter into 32:1
r., not gaudy 185:21
R.-proud cost 211:6
seems it r. to die 121:6
too r. for use 207:17
When I grow r. 157:7
yon r. sky 229:12
Richard's himself again 63:7
Richer: for r. for poorer 168:12
rich have become r. 215:16
R. than all his tribe 205:20
Riches: full.. of r. 25:23
in her left hand r. 26:6
Infinite r. 139:5
r. grow in hell 146:7
Richesses: L'embarras des r. 2:15
Richest: My r. gain 239:16
Richmond Hill: Sweet lass of R.
137:15, 235:4
Richness: Here's r.! 75:1
Ricordarsi: Che r. del tempo felice 72:7
Rid: to get r. of a temptation 243:21
Ride: about the woodland r. 110:15
bade his messengers r. forth 136:8
doth r. abroad 69:31
Haggards r. no more 220:8
horse he can r. 233:5
in haste to r. 69:26
remote Bermudas r. 139:25
R. a cock-horse 157:17
r. in triumph 139:9
r. of Paul Revere 133:25
R. on! R. on 143:6
Rider was lost 88:5
Rides: evil news r. post 147:8
he r. a race! 69:28
r. down the sky 84:11
R. in the whirl-wind 1:3
r. upon the storm 70:5
Ridiculous: no spectacle so r. 136:23
sublime and the r. 160:11
sublime to the r. 96:11, 152:2
Riding: highwayman came r. 155:1
Ridley: Be of good comfort Master
R. 130:6
Rifiuto: Il gran r. 72:6
Rift: r. of your subject 122:11
r. within the lute 226:23
Riga: young lady of R. 8:4
Right: by r. means if you can 108:6
conscious of the r. 236:8
defend to the death your r. 237:20
doeth the thing which is r. 168:27
endeavours to do r. 177:4
every-single-one-of-them-is-r. 125:13
firmness in the r. 132:9
folded it r. 110:14
He's all r. 98:19
in his r. mind 32:30

in the r. places 50:8
it is r.? 56:16
judgement will probably be r. 138:5
lawful and r. 29:13
may she always be in the r. 72:14
meet and r. 167:23
minority is always r. 112:13
My r. elbow 92:11
my r. is in retreat 86:14
my r. there is none 70:19
of r. and wrong he taught 11:3
our country r. or wrong 72:14
r. hands of fellowship 36:5
r. man in the r. place 113:4
r. to prevent it 143:19
r. wrong 226:17
smite thee on thy r. cheek 30:18
So the heart be r. 56:16
though r. were worsted 45:10
To do the r. deed 81:21
to see the r. 132:9
to set it r. 186:19
Ulster will be r. 62:12
what thy r. hand doeth 30:20
Whatever is, is r. 164:17
when the r. man 221:18
Righteous: Be not r. over much 26:40
r., and sober life 166:10
r. are bold as a lion 26:29
saw I the r. forsaken 169:13
seal with a r. kiss 208:5
Righteousness: paths of r. 169:2, 181:8
thirst after r. 30:11
what r. really is 12:11
which makes for r. 12:10
Right-hand foot 58:14
Rights: as well as its r. 79:1
certain unalienable r. 8:9
r. he has trodden under foot 47:11
r. inherent and inalienable 113:2
Rigid: very r. and exact 123:13
Rigour of the game 129:6
Rills: with sinuous r. 66:14
Rimmon: bow myself in the house
of R 25:18
Ring: Bright is the r. of words 221:18
Curfew must not r. 233:10
dance in a r. 152:6
Let freedom r. 217:14
Let us all r. fancy's knell 202:1
r. at the end of his nose 131:7
R. down the curtain 174:6
r. in the new 227:19
r. O bells 242:11
r. of pure and endless light 235:11
R. out, wild bells 227:18
Round both the shires they r. 110:19
showed me a r. 201:28
They now r. the bells 238:9
Till the field r. again 40:16
'Twould r. the bells of Heaven 105:13
what shall we do for a r.? 131:7
With this R. I thee wed 168:14
Ringed with the azure world 226:9
Ringing: r. plains 230:13
r. the Old Year out 94:10
Rings on her fingers 157:17
Riot: blaze of r. 206:6
Riotous: with r. living 33:21
Riotously with the throng 77:27
Rip: Let her r.! 174:8
Ripe: Cherry r. 54:11, 104:8
R. apples drop 140:6
we r. and r. 183:17
yellow like r. corn 177:16
Ripened: pluck'd the r. corn 229:7
Ripeness is all 196:5
Riper: of R. Years 167:31
Ripest: reach the r. fruit 139:10

Ripped: untimely r.   200:11
Ripple of rain   223:28
Rire: Je me presse de r.   19:7
Rise: blushing flow'rs shall r.   165:1
  Can never r. and fight   95:2
  dead men r. up never   224:6
  from the r. to set   191:15
  half to r.   164:19
  I r. at ten-thirty   100:13
  I would r. to explain   101:3
  joyful r.   123:1
  maketh his son to r.   30:19
  may r. again   118:13
  nation shall r. against nation   32:11
  Of hope to r.   249:11
  R. in the heart   229:13
  r., r. again   138:14
  R., take up thy bed   34:3
  R. to all eternity   241:11
  R. up, my love   27:16
  set and r. again   58:26
  shall r. to Thee   102:1
  Some r. by sin   200:16
  we fall to r.   45:10
  We r. with the lark   41:4
  when the moon shall r.?   249:13
  when you r.   73:1
Risen: Christ, the Lord is r. today 241:7
  is r. upon thee   29:1
  Madness r. from hell   224:1
Rises: Soul that r. with us   246:11
  when the sun r.   38:13
  while Jove's planet r.   44:3
Rising: Before the r. sun   239:14
  His r. fogs   79:24
  is r. once again   86:2
  Proteus r. from the sea   249:5
  r. to meet you   81:24
  That fearest nor sea r.   41:8
Risk it on one turn   125:15
Rivals: are their r. dead   161:13
River: Away, you rolling r.   6:14
  Bread I dip in the r.   221:15
  by the r.'s brim   247:14
  Down in the reeds by the r.?   43:5
  either side the r. lie   227:23
  foam on the r.   180:3
  hill or field or r.   229:12
  living r. by the door   221:22
  On a tree by a r.   92:16
  r. glideth   249:4
  r. of crystal light   84:3
  sacred r.   66:14, 66:15
  There's one more r. to cross   7:13
  town by r. or sea shore   120:21
  weariest r.   224:6
  Where the brook and r. meet   133:23
  while crossing the r.   132:11
Rivers: and r. wide   144:14
  as the r. in the south   171:21
  shallow r.   139:7
  Washed by the r.   42:11
Rivulet: neat r. of text   216:15
Rivulets: Myriads of r.   229:19
Road: all are driven one r.   109:11
  'ard 'igh r.   173:9
  at the other end of the r.   141:5
  butterfly upon the r.   126:20
  high r. that leads him   114:13
  middle of the r.   72:4
  O ye'll tak' the high r.   7:4
  old lost r.   128:3
  on a lonesome r.   66:5
  r. to bring us   122:14
  r. was a ribbon   155:1
  r. wind up-hill   177:13
  rolling English road   61:21
  Rose crossed the r.   76:24
  still the open r.   221:16

They are upon the r.   69:29
They shut the r. through the
  woods   128:2
  tipped off in the r.   127:1
  to the end of the r.   130:9
  We take the Golden R.   86:8
  winding r. before me   101:11
Road-rail pig-lead   140:21
Roam: but never r.   248:6
  Ever let the fancy r.   120:6
  Fret not to r. the desert   154:12
  her ways to r.   42:11
  long wont to r.   163:16
  Sadly I r.   87:11
  though we may r.   161:17
  where the buffalo r.   105:5
Roaming: R. in the Gloamin'   130:11
  r. with a hungry heart   230:13
  where are you r.?   209:5
Roar: and music in its r.   51:7
  cannon's opening r.   51:2
  r. their ribs out!   93:36
  r. you as gently   203:4
  set the table on a r.?   189:20
  who shout and bang and r.   21:21
Roared: r. and howled   65:8
  Well r., Lion   204:3
Roareth: What is this that r. thus? 94:9
Roaring: as a r. lion   37:7
Roars: hungry lion r.   204:3
Roast: pig had r. beef   158:9
  r. beef of England   84:6
  r. me in sulphur!   205:18
  to rule the r.   172:20
Rob: nightly r. the dairy   118:2
Robbed: and r. me of my Robe of
  Honour   85:16
Robber: Barabbas was a r.   34:24
Robe: my R. of Honour   85:16
  r. of gold and pearl   191:15
Robes the mountain   54:3
Robin: Call for the r. redbreast   240:11
  Christopher R. went down   143:7
  R. Redbreast in a cage   38:11
  Sweet R. sits in the bush   180:18
  what will poor r. do then?   157:1
Robs: R. me of that   205:4
  R. not one light seed   120:7
Rock: cradle will r.   38:9
  R. of ages   233:23
  R. them, r. them   73:1
  serpent upon a r.   26:31
  they knew the perilous r.   218:19
  upon this r.   31:33
  valley, r., or hill   249:4
Rock-a-bye-baby on the tree top   38:9
Rocked in the cradle of the deep   244:4
Rocking: endlessly r.   242:12
Rocklike: shake in his r. soul   109:19
Rocks: down the r.   147:16
  from r. to roses   166:5
  hand that r. the cradle   238:3
  native of the r.   113:21
  r. among which she sits   161:9
  these dancing r.   66:15
  twinkle from the r.   230:15
  With r. and stones   245:14
Rod: He that spareth his r.   26:15
  r. and staff me comfort still   181:8
  r. and thy staff comfort me   169:2
  r. of empire   97:14
  r. out of the stem of Jesse   28:1
  r. to check   245:19
  spare the r.   49:26
  spares the r.   107:2
  spoils the rod   107:2
Rode: r. madly off   130:12
  R. past fair Florence   120:2
  R. the six hundred   226:8

Roe: following the r. 48:27
Rogue: dainty r. 142:11
r.'s face? 68:7
what a r. 187:11
Rogues: and hear poor r. 196:6
And see the r. flourish 43:12
Roll: nearer waters r. 241:8
numbered in the r. 237:9
r. and rumble 150:8
R. down their golden sand 101:15
r. from soul to soul 229:12
r. leaf-crowned Olympus 237:6
r. of honour 64:1
R. on, thou deep 51:8
R. up that map 163:1
when the drums begin to r. 127:22
Rolled: bottoms of my trousers r. 81:19
r. mother with infant 147:16
R. round in earth's diurnal course 245:14
Roller, pitch, and stumps 130:2
Rolling: heed not the r. waves 39:23
Over the r. waters 229:9
R. down the Ratcliffe Road 124:12
r. English drunkard 61:21
r. rapidly 53:15
stone that is r. 234:16
waters r. evermore 246:12
Rolls: dig for buttered r. 58:13
Peneus r. his fountains 213:12
R. impotently on 85:13
Roma locuta est 13:11
Romae: Si fueris R. 3:1
Roman: antique R. 190:2
Before the R. came 61:21
Butcher'd to make a R. holiday 51:5
could not get a rhyme for r. 86:11
high R. fashion 182:22
I am a R. citizen 63:18
live in the R. style 3:1
noblest R. of them all 194:23
nor R., nor an empire 237:16
noses cast is of the r. 86:11
play the R. fool 200:9
R., be this thy care 236:18
R. by a R. 182:20
than such a R. 194:17
Roman Conquest was..a good thing 181:17
Romance: Confound R.! 126:6
of a high r. 122:4
spirit of r. is dead 124:8
Romanorum ultimum 224:17
Romans: first, the Greeks or the R. 76:14
Friends, R. 194:3
last of the R. 224:17
R. were like brothers 136:12
To whom the R. pray 136:14
Romantic chasm 66:14
Romanus: Civis R. sum 63:18
populus R. unam cervicem 53:4
Rome: cruel men of R. 193:9
grandeur that was R. 163:16
It was at R. 90:12
I've lost R. 127:8
loved R. more 194:1
move the stones of R. 194:13
O happy R. 63:24
of Christian R. 82:15
palmy state of R. 185:3
R. has spoken 13:11
R. is above the Nations 127:14
R. shall stand 51:6
when R. falls 51:6
wi' the fire of old R. 83:6
Romeo: Give me my R. 208:1
wherefore art thou R.? 207:22
Ronsard sang of me 176:11
Ronyon: rump-fed r. 197:5
Roof: had no roof to shroud his head 105:1

r. of my mouth 171:28
this majestical r. 187:4
Rooks are blown 227:8
Rooky: to the r. wood 199:9
Room: always r. at the top 240:4
convent's narrow r. 247:12
Fifty springs are little r. 110:15
Give ample r. 97:5
glowing embers through the r. 144:7
I left the r. with silent dignity 98:18
in a little r. 139:5
In the r. the women come and go 81:15
Is r. enough 190:23
jail has more r. 114:6
no r. for them in the inn 32:40
Paces about her r. 82:2
r. for the bonnets 179:20
r. grows chilly 96:13
R. to deny ourselves 122:14
three paces thro' the r. 227:25
to make thee a r. 118:4
Who sweeps a r. 103:22
Roost: come home to r. 218:15
Root: hath perced to the r. 60:8
laid unto the r. of the trees 30:6
mandrake r. 77:16
nips his r. 192:14
r. and all 226:12
r. of all evil 36:30
r. of the matter 25:36
Rooted sorrow 200:1
Roots: branch shall grow out of his r. 28:1
Rope: to set his hand to a r. 78:27
Rose: At last he r. 145:5
blossom as the r. 28:9
burst open with a r. 86:9
But R. crossed the road 76:24
Die of a r. 164:15
English unofficial r. 42:5
fading r. 120:11
fair as is the r. in May 60:22
Go, lovely R.! 238:4
is the r. distill'd 203:1
last r. of summer 149:18
lovely is the r. 246:8
Luve's like a red red r. 48:28
mighty lak' a r. 220:3
musk of the r. 228:20
red r. cries 228:20
r. by any other name 207:23
R. leaves, when the r. is dead 215:10
r. of Sharon 27:13
r. of the fair state 188:6
R. that cannot wither 235:8
R. the black and gloomy pine-trees 134:4
r. upon their decks 230:5
Roves back the r. 73:2
so red the R. 85:2
supplication to the r. 86:6
under the r. 37:31
when the r. is dead 215:10
white r. weeps 228:20
with all its R. 84:16
Rosebuds: Gather ye r. 104:14
Roseleaf: Only a r. down 20:1
Rose-leaves: on the heaped r. 108:18
Rose-lipt: Many a r. maiden 111:6
Rosemary: that's for remembrance 189:14
Rose-red city 46:26
Roses: Flung r. 77:27
from rocks to r. 166:5
It was the time of r. 106:19
my own red r. 232:11
not a bed of r. 221:5
Plant thou no r. 177:12
r. of vice 224:4
r., r., all the way 44:17

She wore a wreath of r. 19:5
Strew on her r. 11:19
sweet days and r. 104:7
Where r...grow 54:11
Rosy: bands of r. hue 112:8
'Cause another's r. are? 244:18
r. lips and cheeks 211:16
r. wreath 117:19
Ross: sing the Man of R.! 164:24
Rot: and to r. 200:23
R. inwardly 145:3
very deep did r. 65:14
we r. and r. 183:17
Rote: learn'd, and conn'd by r. 194:18
Rots itself in ease 186:9
Rotten in the state 186:6
Rotundity: thick r. o' the world 195:4
Rough: more of r. 61:9
our r. island-story 229:2
r. male kiss of blankets 41:17
r. places plain 28:12
winter and r. weather 183:13
Rough-hew them 189:24
Roughly: Speak r. 56:19
Visit her face too r. 185:11
Roughnesses: remark all these r. 71:9
Roughs: Last night, among his
  fellow r. 78:22
Round: dangers compass'd r. 146:20
girdled r. 66:14
go r. a good deal faster 56:18
having once turned r. 66:5
heard r. the world 82:14
in the heaven, a perfect r. 43:6
life's dull r. 215:18
light fantastic r. 144:1
pass the bottle r. 242:20
r. about thy table 171:24
r. beneath it 235:11
r. ocean 248:19
R. or two before 85:4
r. the Cape 44:16
that makes the world go r.!
                  5:15, 57:3, 91:26
trivial r. 122:14
Roundabouts: lost upon the r. 59:12
Rounded: hand that r. Peter's
  dome 82:15
r. Seraglio Point 142:9
Roundelay: synge untoe mie r. 60:7
Rounds the mortal temples 206:15
Rouse: r. him at the name 192:4
shall r. them from their lowly
  bed 97:11
to r. a lion 190:8
to their preys do r. 199:6
Rousing herself 148:10
Rousseau: Mock on..R. 38:17
Rout: on r. 146:13
Rover: Sir Ralph the R. 218:21
Whither away, fair r. 41:8
Roves back the rose 73:2
Roving: go no more a r. 52:13
Row: darned long r. 135:1
halt and a r. 127:1
in burning r. 147:14
R., brothers, r. 150:2
r. us o'er the ferry 53:17
Rowing home to haven 140:20
Rows: more frequented r. 70:20
Royal: regular R. Queen! 91:8
r. banner 205:10
r. banners forward go 87:7
r. throne of kings 206:7
this is the r. Law 69:1
womb of r. kings 206:7
Royaliste: plus r. que le roi 9:5
Royalty: when you come to R. 76:15
Rub: there's the r. 187:13

Rubies: price is far above r. 26:32
price of wisdom is above r. 25:37
Shouldst r. find 140:11
Rubs: that r. its back 81:16
Ruby: ancient R. 84:16
Ruddier: O r. than the cherry 89:8
Ruddy: Fat r. cheeks 105:15
he was r. 24:43
Rude: Before r. hands 118:11
But only rather r. and wild 21:11
By the r. bridge 82:14
R. am I in my speech 204:20
r. forefathers of the hamlet 97:10
Savage, extreme, r. 212:1
so r. to the good! 245:13
thy breath be r. 184:1
where his r. hut 51:5
whose r. throats 205:10
Rudely: not r. be dismist 67:3
Rudyards cease from kipling 220:8
Rue: nought shall make us r. 193:8
sold for endless r. 110:17
wear your r. with a difference 189:15
Ruffle up your spirits 194:13
Rugged: r. mountain's brow 96:10
system of r. individualism 107:7
Ruh': Meine R.' ist hin 94:13
Über allen Gipfeln Ist R.' 94:15
Ruhnken: learn'd professor, R. 165:18
Ruin: bears the seed of r. 11:16
he that tastes woman, r. meets 89:20
hideous r. 145:12
land of sand and r. 224:11
Red r. 226:18
R. seize thee 97:4
r. upon r. 146:13
Ruined: Bare r. choirs 211:8
r. by trade 88:2
Ruinous inheritance 88:14
Ruins: Gild..the r. 180:5
one of the r. 133:3
r. of St. Paul's 136:21
r. of the Capitol 90:12
r. of the noblest man 193:20
Rule: Beneath the r. of men 136:2
declared absolute r. 146:16
golden r. 212:23
good old r. 247:20
little r. 80:18
only infallible r. 222:21
R. of three doth puzzle me 6:8
sage Homer's r. 165:11
to r. the roast 172:20
Rule, Britannia   6:17, 232:13
When you've shouted R. 124:9
Ruled as his demesne 121:9
Ruler of the Queen's Navee 93:10
Rulers of the darkness of this world 36:14
Rules: hand that r. the world 238:3
no golden r. 212:23
simple little r. and few 21:23
to break known r. 71:12
Ruling: your r. passion 164:22
Rum: and a bottle of r. 221:1
R. on the port 221:21
what a R. Go 241:3
Rumble: roll and r. 150:8
r. of a distant Drum 84:21
Rumming: Tunning of Elynour R. 217:8
Rumours: Wars and r. of wars 32:10
Rump-fed ronyon 197:5
Run: Considering how to r. 71:1
good r. I have 222:14
Gwine to r. all night! 87:8
hasting day has r. 104:10
his successive journeys r. 239:13
in the long r. 142:23
is smiling as they r. 61:18
is to be r. for 148:9

Run (cont.)
  let us r. with patience   36:35
  nearest r. thing   240:14
  r. about through the city   170:1
  r. into any kind of danger   166:15
  R., Orlando   184:3
  r. out thy race   148:6
  see how they r.!   158:10
  shall r. to and fro   29:34
  Still as they r.   98:7
  Sweet Thames, r. softly   219:13
  they shall r.   28:15
  Time will r. back   145:8
  to r. his course   168:30
  to r. them into verse   80:5
  who r. across the sea   108:9
Runcible: ate with a r. spoon   131:9
  r. cat   131:12
  weareth a r. hat   130:18
Rung: their knell is r.   67:15
Runnable stag   72:12
Runneth: memory of man r. not   132:14
Running: ain' no 'buses r.   126:13
  books in the r. brooks   183:9
  call of the r. tide   141:3
  r. a man down   223:7
  r. into the warmint   242:14
  R. it never runs from us   77:1
  r. of the deer   7:17
  takes all the r.   57:17
  Time..will have been r.   109:3
  under r. laughter   232:7
Runs: fights and r. away   5:1, 95:2
  Running it never r. from us   77:1
  r. the world away   188:16
  stream r. fast   150:2
  time r.   138:14
  Time's wheel r. back   45:5
  which r. with rapid change   166:5
  who r. may read   122:18
Run-stealers: as the r. flicker   232:11
Rupee: Fall of the R.   243:12
Rupert: R. of Debate   136:1
  R. of the Rhine   136:7
Rural: in a r. spot!   112:6
  made a r. pen   39:8
  sly shade of a R. Dean   42:6
Rus in urbe   139:24
Rush: as we r. in the train   233:4
  fools r. in   164:13
  stars r. out   65:15
Rushing mighty wind   34:31
Russell, let me always call you
    Edwin   83:20
Russet: in r. mantle clad   185:5
Russet-coated: plain r. captain   71:5
Russia: last out a night in R.   200:17
  R. has two generals   154:4
Russian: he might have been a R.   93:14
Russians: some people may be R.   74:22
Rust: dew will r. them   204:19
  Less than the r.   107:10
  moth and r. doth corrupt   30:23
  To r. unburnished   230:13
  wear out than r. out   71:15, 242:8
Rustling: white and r. sail   71:16
Ruth: sad heart of R.   121:6
Rye: acres of the r.   184:12
  Before the Roman came to R.   61:21
  Coming through the r.   48:11
  fields of barley and of r.   227:23
  pocket full of r.   158:1

                    S

Sabbath: born on the S. day   156:17
  keep holy the S.-day   167:9
  S. of the Lord thy God   167:9
  s. was made for man   32:26

Sabidius: do not love you S.   139:22
Sabrina fair   144:3
Sacerdos: Musarum s.   109:16
Sack: intolerable deal of s.   190:16
  S. the lot!   84:13
Sackbut: sound of the..s.   29:16
Sacks: each wife had seven s.   155:3
Sacred: facts are s.   179:17
  s. river   66:14, 15
  truths to be s. and undeniable   113:2
Sacred Heart: near the Convent of
    the S.   81:22
Sacred Town: enormous through
    the S.   21:21
Sacrifice: coming to the s.   120:21
  desireth no s.   169:28
  pay thy morning s.   123:1
  s. of God   169:28
  Thine ancient s.   127:4
Sad: all their songs are s.   61:15
  how s. and bad   43:15
  is there not s. stuff?   90:8
  know not why I am s.   102:4
  Merry and s. to tell   20:1
  More s. are these   101:2
  remember and be s.   177:11
  s. heart of Ruth   121:6
  s. music of humanity   248:19
  s. occasion   144:20
  s. old earth   243:3
  s. thoughts doth clear   235:9
  s. words of tongue   242:17
  Say I'm s.   112:4
  Sing no s. songs   177:12
  tell s. stories   206:15
  why I am so s.   201:6
  wrought in a s. sincerity   82:15
  Your s. tires   210:7
Sadder: canst not s. cry   232:10
Saddest: s. are [words]   101:2
  tell of s. thought   215:5
Saddle: Boot, s., to horse   43:13
  s. your horses   179:20
Sadly: Murmur, a little s.   250:11
  S. I roam   87:11
  take their pleasures s.   222:11
Sadness: s. of farewell   226:6
  s. of her might   120:24
  sweet though in s.   214:4
Saecla: mutantur s. animantum   135:9
Saeva: Ubi s. indignatio..lacerare
    nequit   223:27
Safe: comes s. home   192:4
  More s. I sing   146:20
  quartered s. out 'ere   125:11
  s. for democracy   244:13
  S. into the haven guide   241:8
  s. under his feathers   170:19
  see me s. up   150:4
  Winds somewhere s. to sea   224:6
  wish him s. at home!   118:15
Safeguard of the West   249:1
Safely: s. in the middle   160:6
  that I may tread s.   101:5
Safer: and s. than a known way   101:5
Safest: when we're s.   43:9
Safety: multitude of counsellors..
    s.   26:12
  pluck this flower, s.   190:12
  release the s. catch   117:5
  s. is in our speed   82:20
  s.,..of the realm   60:1
Sage: Mix with your s. counsels   110:7
Sages: all the s. can   248:15
  holy s. once did sing   145:6
Said: fool hath s.   168:26
  he himself has s. it   93:13
  He himself s. it   63:12
  How often have I s. to you   78:16

never s. a foolish thing 176:2
S. I to myself 91:20
That is well s. 237:13
there's no more to be s. 4:16
Well s. 186:15
when they s. unto me 171:19
Sail: boat he can s. 233:5
comes i' faith full s. 68:17
cried, A s.! 65:14
I'll thither s. 197:5
of my utmost s. 205:17
s. and s. 11:11
s. on, O Ship of State! 133:13
s. to meet the foe 153:5
To s. beyond the sunset 230:15
when we set s. 6:20
white and rustling s. 71:16
white s.'s shaking 141:2
Sailed: he s. on a day 221:20
s. away for a year and a day 131:7
s. off in a wooden shoe 84:3
Sailing: Comes this way s. 147:5
Three fishers went s. 124:2
Sailor: drunken s. 8:12
Home is the s. 221:23
lass that loves a s.! 73:18
No man will be a s. 114:6
of the s.'s devotion 212:7
Pull for the shore s. 39:23
s.'s wife 197:5
Sailor-boys: and we jolly s. 6:20
Sailors: s. from Bristol 231:19
s. when away 90:1
Sails: Purple the s. 182:15
S. fill'd 147:5
s. made on 66:3
thy white s. crowding 41:8
we our s. advance 78:28
Saint: Doctor and S. 85:7
late espoused s. 148:1
never a s. took pity 65:19
St. Agnes' Eve 120:2
St. Ann's: sing at S. 150:2
St. Clement's: bells of S. 157:6
St. Ives: As I was going to S. 155:3
St. John: There S. mingles 165:10
Saint Martin's summer 192:5
St. Patrick's Day: no more S. we'll keep 7:2
St. Paul's: I am designing S. 22:12
pray for you at S. 218:3
ruins of S. 136:21
Saints: all the S. adore Thee 102:1
blood of the s. 37:22
Fear Him, ye s. 225:8
For all the s. 111:12
grow into plaster s. 127:23
Let s. on earth 241:17
pair of carved s. 206:16
s. have dwelt secure 239:14
S. in glory stand 250:12
S. their watch are keeping 222:2
slaughtered s. 147:16
twilight s. 120:4
Where s. immortal reign 239:15
Ye fearful s. 70:6
Sais: Que s.-je? 149:4
Sake: for his Name's s. 169:2
for the teacher's s. 106:11
For whose dear s. 124:18
loseth his life for my s. 31:16
own name's s. 181:1
s. of a ribboned coat 153:6
s. of my little nut tree 156:2
Saki: O S. you shall pass 86:4
Sal Atticum 163:11
Salad: My s. days 182:13
Salamis: sea-born S. 51:19
Salisbury and Gloucester 192:4

Sallies: never s. out 148:9
Salley: Down by the s. gardens 250:5
Sally: make a sudden s. 225:17
none like pretty S. 55:2
Salsa: La mejor s...hambre 59:9
Salt: became a pillar of s. 23:26
if the s. have lost his savour 30:12
s. of the earth 30:12
time with my s. tears 117:10
up and down the s. seas? 124:15
Salt-caked smoke stack 140:21
Salted: wherewith shall it be s.? 30:12
Salus: S. extra ecclesiam non est 13:7
S. populi suprema est lex 63:11
Salute: I s. thee, Mantovano 231:1
s. the happy morn 50:14
those about to die s. thee 222:10
those who are about to die s. you 9:16
Salvation: bottle of s. 174:13
necessary to s. 172:12
No s. exists outside the church 13:7
none of us should see s. 202:5
now is our s. nearer 35:14
that publisheth s. 28:18
Work out your own s. 36:16
Samarkand: Golden Road to S. 86:8
Same: he is much the s. 13:22
it would be all the s. 75:3
Jesus Christ the s. 36:38
just the s. as that! 176:10
more they are the s. 119:13
Not the s. thing 56:22
s. as me! 128:4
Samian: with S. wine! 51:21
Samite: Clothed in white s. 226:16
Samphire: that gathers s. 195:19
Samson hath quit himself 147:9
Sanctifies: influence which s. 74:12
Sand: down their golden s. 101:15
in a Grain of S. 38:10
land of s. 224:11
little grains of s. 55:26
on the edge of the s. 131:9
quantities of s. 57:21
s. against the wind 38:17
Sandal: And his s. shoon 189:8
Sandals were for Clementine 149:8
Sandalwood, cedarwood 140:20
Sands: Across the s. of Dee 124:1
Come unto these yellow s. 208:9
lone and level s. 214:7
on the s. of time 133:27
Sang: Ful wel she s. 60:12
I s. the same again 39:8
morning stars s. together 23:42
Ronsard s. of me 176:11
s. as he sat 161:12
S. Sir Lancelot 227:24
s. to a small guitar 131:6
s. within the bloody wood 81:22
sweet birds s. 211:8
worked and s. 37:29
Sank: And s. in tumult 66:15
looked and s. 142:1
Sans: S. teeth, s. eyes 183:20
S. Wine, S. Song 85:5
Sapientia: De S. Veterum 15:13
Sappho: burning S. 51:17
Sashes: in one of his nice new s. 96:13
Sat: chair she s. in 112:4
he that s. upon the throne 37:26
sang as he s. 161:12
s. at any good man's feast 183:19
s. by the flesh pots 24:6
s. down and wept 171:28
s. down under a juniper tree 25:13
s. under a tree 110:14
Satan: Get thee behind me, S. 31:34

Satan (cont.)
  messenger of S.   36:4
  S. exalted sat   146:10
  S. finds some mischief   239:10
Satanic: dark S. mills?   38:16
Satchel: schoolboy, with his s.   183:20
Satin: always goes into white s.   216:4
Satire: author of s.   178:1
  S. or sense   165:7
Satisfied: am s.   233:6
  I shall not be s.   137:5
Satisfies: where most she s.   182:16
Satisfy: poorly s. our eyes   249:13
Saturday: betwixt a S. and Monday   55:4
  Died on S.   158:2
  S.'s child   156:17
Saturn: that the Revolution, like S.   235:13
Saturnia: redeunt S. regna   237:1
Satyr: Hyperion to a s.   185:11
Satyrs: men, like s.   138:9
Sauce: best s. in the world   59:9
  Chops and Tomata s.   75:24
  only one s.   54:19
Saucy: To s. doubts   199:8
Saul: S. and Jonathan   24:48
  S. hath slain his thousands   24:45
  S., S., why persecutest thou me?   34:35
Savage: noble s. ran   79:19
  S., extreme, rude   212:1
  s. in his blindness   101:16
  s. place!   66:14
  sooth a s. breast   68:9
  So s. and Tartarly   52:6
  unto a s. race   230:12
Save: died to s. their country   21:14
  himself he cannot s.   32:24
  One drop would s. my soul   138:14
  s. his soul   29:13, 138:14
  S. me from the lion's mouth   169:1
  s. me, oh, s. me   54:14
  someone should s.   235:1
Saved: And s. the sum of things   111:11
  by delaying s. the state   83:45
  has s. herself   162:22
  He s. others   32:24
  only s. the world   21:14
  s. from that eternal silence   230:13
Saviour: God my S.   32:37
  Hide me, O my S.   241:8
  S. of 'is country   127:21
  S. of the world was born   50:14
  'tis thy S.   70:3
  Wash me, S.   234:1
  Wherein our S.'s birth   185:4
Savoir être à soi   149:3
Savour: lost his s.   30:12
Saw: drowns the parson's s.   196:20
  ever s. in my life   238:20
  ever s. in your life   240:14
  everybody s. with joy   105:15
  God s. that it was good   23:7
  He s.; but blasted   98:11
  I find thy s. of might   184:7
  I s. a child   39:8
  I s., I conquered   53:2
  Ne'er s. I   249:4
  s. my works   170:26
  s. the swallows gathering   142:5
  vision once I s.   66:15
Saws: Full of wise s.   183:20
Saxon: ancient S. phrase   133:21
  S. and Norman   231:3
  S. is not like us Normans   126:18
Say: all their friends could s.   131:5
  always s. what's true   221:9
  disapprove of what you s.   237:20
  everyone will s.   92:21, 22
  I s. to this man, Go   31:5
  If we s. that we have no sin   37:8

  is all that they can s.   64:12
  press me to s.   149:2
  s. to all the world   194:24
  s. what you mean   56:22
  s. what you will   68:16
  Though I s. it   19:25
  When you have nothing to s.   68:1
  will s. unto him   33:22
  yet I s. unto you   30:28
  your right to s. it   237:20
Saying: For loving, and for s. so   77:19
  keep on s. it long enough   22:5
  wild waves s.   55:27
Scabbard: threw away the s.   63:25
Scabbards: leaped from their s.   47:14
Scald: mine own tears do s.   196:1
Scale: On every golden s.!   56:13
  s. the stars!   236:21
  with her lifted s.   164:1
Scallop-shell of quiet   174:13
Scan: presume not God to s.   164:18
Scandal: No s. about Queen Elizabeth   216:2
Scandalous and poor   176:1
Scapegoat: a s. into the wilderness   24:11
Scar: from cliff and s.   229:11
Scarce: S. seemed a vision   214:3
  Show s. so gross   195:19
Scarcity: on the very first s.   47:17
Scare: to s. the monster   125:5
Scarf up the tender eye   199:6
Scarlet: His sins were s.   21:15
  In S. town   16:2
  sins be as s.   27:21
  though the s. line was slender   123:13
Scars: He jests at s.   207:20
  show his s.   192:4
Scatter: S., as from an unextinguished hearth   214:4
  s. the good seed   53:12
Scattered: bones lie s.   147:16
  enemies are s.   170:6
  hath s. the proud   32:38
  s. his Maker's image   79:3
  snows have s. and fled   110:5
  When the cloud is s.   213:16
Scatterest: as thou s. them   170:17
Scene: Last s. of all   183:20
  little s.   206:15
  see the distant s.   153:15
  Speaks a new s.   173:27
  that memorable s.   140:8
  to leave the s.   108:13
Scenes: changing s. of life   225:7
  watch the busy s.   117:1
Scent: amber s.   147:5
  s. the morning air   186:11
Sceptic: for the s. side   164:18
  What ever s. could inquire for   49:16
Sceptre: My s. for a palmer's walking staff   206:16
  S. and crown   216:24
  s. and the ball   191:15
  s. shows the force   202:5
Sceptred: In s. pall   144:8
  s. race!   129:19
  this s. isle   206:7
Scheme: this sorry S. of Things   86:1
Schemes: far from s. of business   108:14
Scherzando! ma non troppo   91:2
Scholar: a s. among rakes   136:24
  let a s. all Earth's volumes   59:20
  s.'s eye   188:6
  s.'s life assail   117:2
Scholars: all the lore its s. need   122:18
School: After the s. of Stratford atte Bowe   60:12
  microcosm of a public s.   76:22
  special reason for hating s.   20:8

Three little maids from s.   92:2
Unwillingly to s.   183:20
Schoolboy: Every s. knows   136:20, 225:11
s.'s tale   50:21
whining s.   183:20
School-days: my joyful s.   129:16
Schoolgirl: Pert as a s.   92:2
That s. complexion   7:11
Schoolmasters: Let s. puzzle their
brain   95:20
Schools: jargon of the s.   172:18
lumber of the s.   223:24
Public s. are the nurseries   84:7
Schooner Hesperus   134:12
Science: proud s.   164:14
Scientia potestas est   15:12
Scinde: I've S.   173:8
Scire nefas   109:2
Scissor-man: red-legged s.   106:3
Scoff: fools, who came to s.   95:7
Scoffing his state   206:15
Scold: You may s. a carpenter   114:11
Scope: that man's s.   210:13
Scorer: One Great S.   175:10
Scores: wipers of s. out   44:23
Scorn: and think foul s.   82:9
for the time of s.   205:13
He held the human race in s.   21:2
I s. to change my state   210:13
laugh a siege to s.   200:2
laugh to s.   199:20
S. not the Sonnet   248:1
To s. delights   145:1
Scorned: a woman s.   68:10
Scornful: rather s. tone   58:5
Scorns: whips and s. of time   187:13
Scorpions: chastise you with s.   25:10
Scotched: We have s. the snake   199:3
Scotchman: noblest prospect which
a S. ever sees   114:13
Scotland: And I'll be in S. afore
ye   7:4
in S. supports the people   116:16
Stands S. where it did ?   199:26
Scots, wha hae wi' Wallace bled   48:30
Scotsman: a s. on the make   18:25
Scott: not even Sir Walter S.   212:14
Scoundrel: is a s.   213:2
last refuge of a s.   115:4
Scourge of God   139:14
Scout: Flout 'em, and s. 'em   208:16
Scrannel: on their s. pipes   145:3
Scrap of paper   23:1
Scraps: s. are good deeds   208:27
stolen the s.   196:17
Scratched with a stick   125:1
Screamed: children s.   69:28
Screw your courage   198:7
Scribble: Always s., s., s.!   94:7
Scribendi cacoethes   119:6
Scrip: s. of joy   174:13
with s. and scrippage   184:5
Scrippage: with scrip and s.   184:5
Scripture: any text of S.   241:19
devil can cite S.   201:16
S. moveth us   166:7
Scroll: charged with punishments
the s.   102:14
Scudding: Thro' s. drifts   230:13
Scurvy politician   195:22
Scutcheon: shielded s.   120:4
Scuttled: ever s. ship   51:16
Scuttling across the floors   81:18
Scylla and Charybdis   215:16
Scythe: poor crooked s.   216:24
Sea: around the glassy s.   102:1
as the waters cover the s.   2:3, 28:3
At the bottom of the deep blue s.   6:17
blue days at s.   221:17

bred to the s.   139:21
by land an' s.   128:4
By the deep s.   51:7
by the winter s.   226:25
Call him on the deep s.   153:5
cold gray stones, O s.!   225:14
crown'd with summer s.   227:3
dead across the s.   38:1
dolorous midland s.   224:11
Down to a sunless s.   66:14
drowned in the depth of the s.   31:38
eastward to the s.   126:11
espouse the everlasting S.   249:2
fishes of the s.   168:24
flowing s.   71:16
from over the s.   231:3
go down to the s.   171:7
great and wide s.   171:4
gurly grew the s.   16:5
he cast into the s.   33:30
he that commands the s.   15:3
home from s.   221:23
if we gang to s.   16:14
In a bowl s.   162:2
in a halcyon s.   177:8
in a s. of glory   192:14
In a Sieve they went to s.!   131:5
in peril on the s.   242:9
in the rough rude s   206:12
Into that silent s.   65:11
kingdom by the s.   163:14
kings of the s.   11:13
lands beyond the s.   247:2
like a wave of the s.   250:3
like stars on the s.   52:9
lonely s. and the sky   141:2
midst of the s.   169:20
mirrors of the s.   86:10
mount, and stream, and s.   102:9
near to heaven by s.   90:18
never go to s.   93:11
never, never sick at s.!   93:7
no more s.   37:25
no stir in the s.   218:18
o'er a perfumed s.   163:16
of a sudden came the s.   44:16
of that immortal s.   246:12
One foot in s.   204:9
one is of the s.   248:13
on s. or land   247:13
On such a full s.   194:19
on the s.'s face   141:2
or not having been at s.   115:16
Out of the s. came he!   65:6
Over the s. to Skye   221:20
Owl and the Pussy-cat went to
s.   131:6
plants his footsteps in the s.   70:5
rising from the s.   249:5
run across the s.   108:9
safe to s.   224:6
sailed the wintry s.   134:12
s., and all that in them is   167:11
s. gave up the dead   37:24
s. is boiling hot   57:22
s. is his   170:22
s. of dew   84:3
S. of Faith   11:8
s. of troubles   187:13
s. rises higher   61:14
S. shall give up her dead ?   172:10
S. that bares her bosom   249:5
S.! the s.!   250:4
serpent-haunted s.   86:5
set in the silver s.   206:7
ship in the midst of the s.   26:31
strawberries grow in the s. ?   156:15
sun was shining on the s.   57:20
Sussex by the s.!   127:18

Sea (cont.)
That fearest nor s. rising | 41:8
thing of s. or land ? | 147:5
took a boat and went to s. | 231:19
Upon the slimy s. | 65:14
uttermost parts of the s. | 172:1
Vext the dim s. | 230:13
We'll o'er the s. | 106:6
Went down into the s. | 65:6
Went to s. in a bowl | 158:11
went to s. in a Sieve | 131:4
When I put out to s. | 226:6
whisper, o'er the s. | 65:15
wide wide s.! | 65:19
Wind of the western s. | 229:9
with the triumphant s. | 206:8
Within a walk of the s. | 22:1
world's tempestuous s. | 81:2
wrinkled s. beneath him | 226:9
yonder is the s. | 43:20
Sea-banks: Upon the wild s. | 202:10
Sea-change: suffer a s. | 208:12
Seagreen Incorruptible | 55:12
Sea-King's daughter | 231:3
Seal: did my spirit s. | 245:14
Sealed in vain | 201:3
Sealing-wax: like sticks of s. | 74:4
ships and s. | 57:22
Seals of love | 201:3
Seam: sew a fine s. | 155:11
Sea-mark of my utmost sail | 205:17
Seamen: gentlemen were not s. | 137:2
is all her s. know | 64:12
s. in the navy | 137:2
Sea-nymphs hourly ring his knell | 208:12
Sear: into the s. | 199:32
Search the grassy knolls | 58:13
Searching: Canst thou by s. find out
God ? | 25:30
I am s. everywhere! | 220:10
Seas: across the floors of silent s. | 81:18
dangers of the s. | 160:19
desperate s. | 163:16
down to the s. again | 141:2
half s. over | 223:10
multitudinous s. | 198:15
Of perilous s. | 121:6
pass on the s. | 172:9
port after stormy s. | 219:10
silence of the s. | 248:8
That guard our native s. | 54:6
through strange s. | 247:17
up and down the salt s. ? | 124:15
waste of s. | 181:7
While the raging s. did roar | 6:20
Sea-sand: ribbed s. | 65:18
Sea-shore: playing on the s. | 153:17
town by river or s. | 120:21
Seaside: I Do Like To Be Beside the
S. | 94:8
Season: ever 'gainst that s. | 185:4
Hope, for a s. | 54:5
In a summer s. | 130:4
is green for a s. | 224:10
meat in due s. | 171:4
my blessing s. | 185:21
of a s.'s fame | 153:6
s. made for joys | 89:19
s. of calm weather | 246:12
S. of mists | 119:17
there is a s. | 26:38
word spoken in due s. | 26:19
your s. due | 144:20
Seasons: all the S. | 161:14
From s. such as these ? | 195:8
In process of the s. | 211:13
lovers' s. run ? | 77:18
Seat: from thy celestial s. | 130:5
God's great Judgment S. | 124:13

hath a pleasant s. | 198:2
s. of Mars | 206:7
s. of pleasures | 79:23
upon the s. | 72:1
Seated: S. in thy silver chair | 117:11
s. on the ground | 225:9
S. one day at the organ | 172:22
Seats: mighty from their s. | 32:38
Second: To their own s. and sober
thoughts | 103:5
Second class: very small s. carriage | 91:24
Secret: bread eaten in s. | 26:11
her s. none can utter ? | 174:3
Secret: Le s. d'ennuyer est..de tout
dire | 237:19
Secrets: forbid to tell the s. | 186:7
no s. are hid | 167:4
Sect: loving his own s. | 67:4
Sectes: soixante s. religieuses | 54:19
Secure: He is s. | 213:8
may reign s. | 146:3
none can thee s. | 235:8
saints have dwelt s. | 239:14
seek to make s. | 176:17
Security to persons | 73:11
Securus iudicat orbis terrarum | 13:6
Sedan: flood of tears and a S. chair | 75:29
Sedge is wither'd | 120:10
See: all flesh shall s. it | 28:12
as others s. us! | 48:23
behold, and s. | 29:8
by their faces s. | 247:15
can s. no more | 246:7
do not s. the signal! | 152:20
eat what I s.! | 56:22
eyes have they, and s. not | 171:13
far as human eye could s. | 228:8
Here shall he s. | 183:13
I never hope to s. one | 46:24
I s. how the helican | 142:14
I should like to s. | 142:15
into the wilderness to s. ? | 31:18
lovers cannot s. | 201:23
May I be there to s.! | 69:31
may s. your good works | 30:14
neither eye to s. | 131:20
no man s. me | 24:10
Nor heed, nor s. | 214:9
not worth going to s. | 115:21
or eyes can s. | 210:12
People come miles to s. it | 92:11
reverent eye must s. | 41:20
s. all, nor be afraid! | 45:4
S. and approve | 160:7
s. thee still | 198:9
s. the works of the Lord | 171:7
that I shall never s. | 123:8
Then I shall s. thee again? | 194:20
they shall s. our God | 122:19
they that won't s. | 223:17
Thus may we s. | 183:16
To s. such sport | 155:17
Wait and s. | 12:16
we s. through a glass | 35:22
Seed: a grain of mustard s. | 31:27, 36
beareth forth good s. | 171:21
blood of Christians is s. | 231:10
garden that grows to s. | 185:11
nor his s. begging | 169:13
Robs not one light s. | 120:7
scatter the good s. | 53:12
Seeds: Some s. fell by the wayside | 31:25
winged s. | 214:1
Seeing: Worth s. ? | 115:21
Seek: I s. and adore them | 41:6
sadly to s. | 165:17
s. a great perhaps | 174:7
s., and ye shall find | 30:33
s. for kind relief ? | 39:14

s. the beauteous eye of heaven   193:6
s. through the world   161:17
s. to make secure   176:17
s. to mend   77:12
S. ye the Lord   28:24
sometime did me s.   250:2
to s. a newer world   230:15
To strive, to s.   230:15
We s. him here   159:13
What you s. is here   108:9
Seeketh not her own   35:21
Seeking: S. after that sweet   39:7
s. the bubble reputation   183:20
S. the food he eats   183:15
s. whom he may devour   37:7
unperplext S. shall find   43:18
Seeks: Nor s. nor finds   214:9
s. abroad may find   119:18
Seeling: Come, s. night   199:6
Seem: things not what they s.   133:26
To me did s.   246:7
Seemly: it is s. so to do   123:6
Seems: I know not 's.'   185:9
Seen: As I have s.   77:4
Because thou art not s.   184:1
England's pleasant pastures s.?   38:16
Ere I had ever s. that day   185:13
fine things to be s.   61:23
God whom he hath not s.?   37:12
have s. a great light   27:31
he was s. of me also   35:24
I have s. the day   196:10
Much have I s.   230:13
No man hath s. God   37:10
s. of none   120:24
s. thee oft   119:18
things which I have s.   246:7
To have s. what I have s.   188:6
what dark days s.!   211:12
When I have s.   211:6
whom one has never s.   153:8
Seer: Judah's s.   138:6
Sees: A fool s. not the same tree   39:17
He s. it in his joy   246:11
neither hears nor s.   245:14
s. it and does it   43:18
s. no more   176:6
See-saw Margery Daw   157:18
Seething: ceaseless turmoil s.   66:14
Seigneur: Parce que vous êtes un
    grand s.   19:8
Seize: Ruin s. thee   97:4
Seldom: 'tis s. or never   245:13
Where s. is heard   105:5
Select: most s. and generous   185:21
Selection: term of Natural S.   72:9
Self: all in s.   180:6
entire of it s.   77:22
I do nothing upon my s.   77:21
Infusing him with s.   206:15
only S. to please   39:6
to my sole s.!   121:7
To sun my s.   84:10
to thine own s. be true   185:21
Self-contained: placid and s.   242:14
Self-slaughter: canon 'gainst s.!   185:11
Sell: as the Goods they s.   85:16
dreams to s.   20:1
no man might buy or s.   37:20
s. with you   201:13
to s. for one shilling   131:8
Selling: For buying or s.   234:10
lives by s. something   220:20
Selves: stepping-stones of their dead
    s.   227:6
Semele: hapless S.   138:13
Semen est sanguis Christianorum   231:10
Seminary: Come from a ladies' s.   92:3
Semper eadem   82:8

Sempronius: we'll do more, S.   1:4
Send: Here am I; s. me   27:28
never s. to know for whom the
    bell tolls   77:23
not to s. peace   31:15
Whom shall I s.   27:28
Sends: He first s. mad   80:15
Sensational: It is somewhat too s.   243:12
Sensations: life of s.   122:8
S. sweet   248:17
Sense: bottom of good s.   115:25
deviates into s.   79:24
fountain of good s.   80:7
Live within the s.   215:10
our s. destroy   179:11
pains my s.   121:1
Satire or s.   165:7
s. faints picturing them   214:2
s. of being well-dressed   83:1
s. of death   200:21
s...of ills to come   98:8
s. sublime   248:19
Take care of the s.   57:4
Through s. and nonsense   79:10
(Whose soul is s.)   77:20
Senseless: worse than s. things!   193:9
Senses: If Parson lost his s.   105:13
our gentle s.   198:2
Sensibility: a dissociation of s.   81:11
Sensible: s. to feeling   198:9
s. warm motion   200:23
was fundamentally s.   115:25
Sensitive Plant in a garden grew   215:2
throughout the s. world   150:3
Sensual: Not to the s. ear   120:19
s. from Heaven above   53:12
Sent: music s. up to God   43:7
s. from Heaven above   53:12
s. him down the sky   69:3
s.'st it back to me   117:19
s. thee late   117:19
Sentimental passion   92:22
Sentiments: plague of his s.!   216:18
Them's my s.!   231:16
Sentinels: to warn s.   139:12
Sentry: Where stands a winged
    s.   235:7
Separate: shall be able to s. us   35:10
Separately: to class them s.   160:11
September: April, June and S.   96:8
Thirty days hath S.   158:7
Sepulcre: s. in stubborn Jewry   206:7
s. of famous men   233:12
Whited s.   32:9
Sequestered: cool s. vale of life   98:1
Seraglio Point: rounded S.   142:9
Seram: Pone s., prohibe   119:5
Seraphim: Where the bright S.   147:14
Seraphims: Above it stood the s.   27:27
Sere: ivy never s.   144:20
Serene: and that unhoped s.   41:16
her life s.   230:1
its pure s.   121:9
of purest ray s.   97:15
Serenely full   217:18
Serener: From waves s. far   213:12
Serfs: With vassals and s.   46:2
Sergeant: This fell s.   189:28
This is the s.   197:3
Serious: damned s. business   240:14
s. swelling into bombast   80:3
too s...to be left   225:5
Sermon: preach a better s.   83:4
Sermons: s. and soda-water   51:15
S. in stones   183:9
Serpent: be the s. under't   198:1
s. of old Nile?   182:12
s. upon a rock   26:31
sharper than a s.'s tooth   75:14, 195:3
Serpent-haunted sea   86:5

P

Serpents: wise as s. 31:13
Servant: good and faithful s. 32:14
Is thy s. a dog 25:19
nor his s. 167:17
say..to my s. 31:5
s. with this clause 103:22
thy s. depart in peace 33:1
Your s.'s cut in half 96:12
Servants: as one of thy hired s. 33:22
equality in the s.' hall 18:15
good s. 132:1
s. he with new acquist 147:11
Serve: can s. two masters 30:27
cannot s. God and mammon 30:26
fit to s. as a soldier 128:8
Him s. with fear 123:5
In Which We S. 69:14
S. God and the King 153:7
s. in Heav'n 146:3
s. in the wars 172:15
They also s. 147:17
they s. him best 147:17
time to s. and to sin 224:2
To s. your captives' need 128:5
Served: Had I but s. God 245:11
Had I but s. my God 193:1
I s. a term 93:10
Youth will be s. 40:9
Serves: S. and fears 141:13
s. it in the office of a wall 206:7
take the current when it s. 194:19
Serveth not another's will 249:10
Service: did me yeoman's s. 189:25
done the state some s. 205:20
duty and s. 167:24
For Christian s. 206:7
s. of my love 219:18
s. to his country 223:2
song the s. divyne 60:12
Weary and old with s. 192:14
whose s. is perfect freedom 166:14
Servile ministers 195:5
Serving: cumbered about with much s. 33:9
Servitude: base laws of s. 79:19
s. is at once the consequence 71:17
Sesquipedalia verba 107:19
Sessions: to the s. of sweet silent thought 211:1
Set: ere the s. of sun 197:2
from the rise to s. 191:15
hearts were s. 162:2
it is I s. it down 186:14
play a s. 191:4
s. himself doggedly to it 113:17
sun does not s. 179:12
Sets: packs and s. 196:6
sun never s. 154:9
Setting: Hath had elsewhere its s. 246:11
light of s. suns 248:19
Stars are s. 85:9
with the s. sun 146:9
Settle: less will you s. to one 126:7
Settlement: Act of S. 175:11
Settling: Stealthily and perpetually s. 41:7
Seven: not one in s. 104:3
S. cities warr'd for Homer 105:1
s. maids with s. mops 57:21
S. whole days 104:3
taketh..s. other spirits 31:24
Seven Dials: lowly air of S. 91:19
Seven-fold gifts 172:11
Seven-ringed: Jamshyd's S. Cup 84:16
Seventeen: Sweet S. 225:19
Seven Wonders of the World: London Bridge..greater piece of work than any of the S. 1:10
Sever: how soon we must s.? 71:2

then we s. 48:3
To s. for years 52:16
Severed: graves are s. 102:9
Severely: bangs me most s. 55:3
Severity: with its usual s. 67:6
Severn: out to S. strode 61:21
Seville: these dogs of S. 230:4
Sewers: and s. annoy 146:22
reign o'er s. 66:9
Sewing as long as her eyes could see 110:14
Sex: Female of s. 147:5
Is S. Necessary? 233:14
weaker s. 2:12
Sexes: in the name of both s. 47:11
old women (of both s.) 220:17
there are three s. 217:17
Sexton: no s. be asked to toll the bell 100:9
went and told the s. 106:23
Sextus: false S. 136:10
Shabby: for tamed and s. tigers 105:13
Shackles of an old love 226:22
Shade: chequered s. 144:16
crowd into a s. 165:1
farewell to the s. 70:7
gentlemen of the s. 190:6
in a green s. 140:7
inviolable s. 11:27
s. of a coolibah tree 161:12
s. of the old apple tree 244:8
Sitting in a pleasant s. 18:12
sitting in the s. 125:9
sly s. of a Rural Dean 42:6
variable as the s. 180:13
wander'st in his s. 210:12
with Amaryllis in the s. 145:1
Shades: field is full of s. 232:11
s. of night 133:17
S. of the prison-house 246:11
till the s. lengthen 153:12
where th' Etrurian s. 146:4
Shadow: but a walking s. 200:4
dust and a s. 110:6
every s. of authority 47:7
flits a s. 127:13
Follow a s. 117:18
in the land of the s. of death 27:31
in the s. of death 32:39
in whose dim s. 136:17
like a vast s. 235:11
lose the substance by grasping at the s. 1:18
No probable, possible s. of doubt 91:7
out-soared the s. 213:8
s. of a glorious name 135:5
s. of the dome of pleasure 66:15
s. of Thy Throne 239:14
under the s. of thy wings 168:28
valley of the s. of death 169:2
With the s. of Thy wing 241:10
Your s. at morning 81:24
Shadowed livery 201:19
Shadows: are but s. 204:2
Are s., not substantial 216:24
but the s. of us men? 117:18
cast their s. before 53:16
Earth's s. fly 213:10
Earth's vain s. flee 135:17
Fills the s. 223:28
of their s. deep 250:11
quiet s. falling 159:14
s. flee away 27:18
s. numberless 121:2
S. of the evening 18:6
Shadowy: near the s. coast 232:11
Shadwell: But S. never deviates 79:24
Shady: o'er s. groves 240:11
Shaft: Cupid's fiery s. 203:7

Shake: may be used to s. 20:16
s. against the cold 211:8
s. in his rocklike soul 109:19
S. my fell purpose 197:15
S. off dull sloth 123:1
s. off the dust of your feet 31:12
With a s. of his poor little head 92:17
Shaken: and is never s. 211:16
reed s. with the wind? 31:18
To be well s. 67:24
Shake-scene: only S. in a country 98:13
Shakespeare: as an honour to S. 117:12
as great part of S.? 90:8
as I despise S. 212:14
for gentle S. cut 118:3
like reading S. 67:7
much better done in S. 80:4
My S., rise 118:4
S., undoubtedly wanted taste 238:6
S. unlocked his heart 44:4, 248:1
S. was of us 44:11
sweetest S. 144:19
That S. drew 165:15
tongue that S. spake 247:1
What needs my S. 147:12
Shaking: bright dew is s. 71:2
s. her invincible locks 148:10
white sail's s. 141:2
Shalimar: beside the S. 107:9
Shall: His absolute 's.'? 184:18
Shallow: By s. rivers 139:7
in a S. Cup 85:15
S. brooks 144:14
Shallows: Is bound in s. 194:19
Shalott: Lady of S. 227:25
Shame: Ain't it all a blooming s. 7:6
ashamed with the noble s. 124:4
glory is in their s. 36:17
I think it s. 108:3
London's lasting s. 97:7
or momentary s. 13:16
perpetual s. 170:12
S. it is to see 123:16
s. the devil 118:10, 190:18
To hide her s. 95:21
waste of s. 212:1
What s. or measure 109:7
with an awkward s. 165:13
wrought the deed of s. 136:10
Shamed: And s. life a hateful 200:23
Shameful: s. conquest of itself 206:9
'tis a s. sight 239:8
Shandon: bells of S. 173:1
Shank: his shrunk s. 183:20
Shape: in s. of a camel? 188:18
O Attic shape! 120:22
of s. express 172:19
S. of Things to Come 241:4
Shaped: whom England bore, s. 42:11
Shapen in wickedness 169:25
Shapes: 'Mongst horrid s. 144:10
Of s. that haunt 214:9
s. of foul disease 227:20
Turns them to s. 203:19
Shard: reeking tube and iron s. 127:7
Share: Did s. it 209:9
greater s. of honour 192:3
s. the impulse of thy strength 214:3
with a railway-s. 56:5
Sharks: Among the s. and whales 6:17
Sharon: rose of S. 27:13
Sharp: billiard s. 92:9
s. as a pen 191:6
s. remedy 174:17
short, s. shock 92:5
sting is not so s. 184:2
With s. invectives 250:3
Sharper: a s. once played 71:4
s. than a serpent's tooth 75:14, 195:3

Sharps: fifty different s. and flats 44:19
Shatter: s. it to bits 86:1
S. your leaves 144:20
Shattered: When the lamp is s. 213:16
Shaven: all s. and shorn 158:8
She: none but s. 224:11
S., and comparisons are odious 77:3
unexpressive s. 184:3
Sheaf: and the brushwood s. 44:1
Shearers: sheep before her s. 28:21
Shears: with th' abhorred s. 145:1
Sheath: sword outwears its s. 52:14
sword was in the s. 70:11
Sheaves: bring his s. 171:21
She-bear: a great s. 86:19
s. thus accosted 125:5
Shed: a lowly cattle s. 2:10
all evil s. 42:11
bitter tears to s. 69:2
from the straw-built s. 97:11
prepare to s. them 194:7
soul of music s. 149:13
Sheds: he to-day that s. his blood 192:4
Sheen of their spears 52:9
Sheep: All we like s. 28:21
as a s. before her shearers 28:21
Baa, baa, black s. 155:4
better than s. or goats 227:2
full of s. 170:3
half-witted s. 220:7
hungry s. look up 145:3
I have found my s. 33:19
in s.'s clothing 31:3
like lost s. 166:8
like young s. 171:12
lost her s. 156:9
mountain s. are sweeter 162:1
return to our s. 9:8
s. of his hand 170:24
s.'s in the meadow 156:10
valley s. are fatter 162:1
Who were thy s. 147:16
With His s. 175:2
you s. bear fleeces 237:10
Sheer: Here, a s. hulk 73:19
Sheet: weave old England's wind- ing s. 38:12
wet s. and a flowing sea 71:16
white s. bleaching 210:5
Sheeted: and the s. dead 185:3
Sheets: cool kindliness of s. 41:17
fumble with the s. 191:6
Shell: like a rainbow s. 177:8
prettier s. than ordinary 153:17
Shelley: Burns, S., were with us 44:11
did you once see S. 44:13
Shells: and cockle s. 156:16
Shelter: s. from the stormy blast 239:14
s. me from the cold 22:1
Sheltered: In youth it s. me 150:12
Shelves: symmetry of s. 129:7
Shem: Noah begat S. 23:20
Shenandoah: Oh S., I long to hear you 6:14
Shepherd: Dead s. 184:7
Dick, the s. 196:20
God of love my S. is 104:4
good s. giveth his life 34:12
his flock like a s. 28:14
King of Love my S. is 15:20
Lord is my s. 169:2
Lord's my s. 181:8
s. in Virgil 113:21
slighted, s.'s trade 145:1
they call you, S. 11:22
Shepherds: liberal s. 189:18
While s. watch'd 225:9
Sheridan was listened to 176:7
Shew: I s. you a mystery 35:29
S. ourselves glad 170:21

Shield: be thy s. and buckler 170:19
sword, a horse, a s. 134:20
trusty s. 135:12
Shielded scutcheon 120:4
Shieling: lone s. of the misty island 181:7
Shift: let me s. for myself 150:4
We s. and bedeck 224:3
Shifted: He s. his trumpet 95:19
Shilling: S. a day 127:9
to sell for one s. 131:8
Shine: anxious for to s. 92:20
Arise, s. 29:1
as the stars that s. 247:4
face to s. upon thee 24:13
I see Heaven's glories s. 41:13
knock, breathe, s. 77:12
Let your light so s. 30:14
moon doth s. 155:5
scatteringly doth s. 140:3
S. forth upon our clouded hills? 38:16
s. in use! 230:13
s. the traffic 232:10
S. through the gloom 135:17
S. upon my brow 175:6
they shall s. 29:34
Shined: hath the light s. 27:31
Shines: And faith s. equal 41:13
cross s. forth 87:7
forever s. 213:10
O the moon s. bright 82:1
Shineth: light s. in darkness 33:44
Shingles: naked s. of the world 11:8
Shining: Improve each s. hour 239:9
s. in the sky 248:3
s. morning face 183:20
s. on the sea 57:20
s. out of the other 74:20
Somewhere the sun is s. 100:16
stars are s. bright 213:13
through the dark cloud s. 87:4
with s. Foot 86:3
Ship: in a s. is being in a jail 114:6
painted s. 65:13
s., an isle 86:10
s. has weather'd every rack 242:10
s. in the midst of the sea 26:31
s. that goes 73:18
s. was still 218:18
so old a s. 86:9
stately s. of Tarsus 147:5
tall s. 141:2
That ever scuttled s. 51:16
There was a s. 65:5
to which the ship would go! 64:12
What is a s. but a prison? 49:9
Whither, O splendid s. 41:8
Ships: down to the sea in s. 171:7
For the Thracian s. 223:28
Heart of oak are our s. 88:18
I saw three s. 5:10
I spied three s. come sailing by 3:14
launched a thousand s. 138:12
Of shoes—and s. 57:22
Our s. were British oak 12:12
s., by thousands 51:19
s. on the foam 128:6
S. that pass in the night 134:9
S., towers, domes 249:4
stately s. go on 255:15
storm-beaten s. 137:18
There go the s. 171:4
We've got the s. 112:1
Shire for men who understand 42:7
Shires: Round both the s. 110:19
Shoal: bank and s. of time 198:0
s. of fools 68:17
Shock: sensation of a short, sharp s. 92:5
we shall s. them 193:8
Shock-headed Peter 106:5

Shocks: thousand natural s. 187:13
Shod: All s. with steel 246:5
Shoe: Buckle my s. 157:5
cast out my s. 170:2
for want of a s. 88:5
has lost her s. 155:7
Into a left-hand s. 58:14
Sailed off in a wooden s. 84:3
s. was lost 88:6
whose s.'s latchet 33:47
woman who lived in a s. 158:6
Shoeing: or s. horses 166:5
Shoes: boil eggs in your s. 131:15
Of s.—and ships 57:22
put off thy s. 24:1
s. on your feet 24:5
s. were far too tight 131:3
s. were number nine 149:8
those s. were old 185:11
Shoe-string: careless s. 104:11
Shone: And he s. bright 65:6
eyes that s. 150:1
glory s. around 225:9
s. one woman 224:11
S. round him 102:7
When the moon s. 202:14
Shoon: And his sandal s. 189:8
in her silver s. 73:9
Shoot: do not s. the pianist 243:14
S., if you must 242:16
teach..how to s. 232:14
Shooting-stars attend thee 104:13
Shoots: he s. his wit 184:15
Shop: pops its head into the s. 86:19
shun the awful s. 61:25
Shopkeepers: governed by s. 217:12
nation of s. 1:2, 151:15, 217:12
Shore: beat on the rocky s. 130:20
Fast by their native s. 70:2
for his native s. 213:12
hang it by the s. 153:9
high s. of this world 191:15
meet on that beautiful s. 22:6
on s. 230:13
on the s. of the wide world 122:5
on this world's s. 154:13
one on s. 204:9
pull for the s. 39:23
rapture on the lonely s. 51:7
sport upon the s. 246:12
stretch from s. to s. 239:13
To his own native s. 163:16
towards the pebbled s. 211:5
woods on s. look dim 150:2
yearning for the farther s. 236:17
Shoreditch: bells of S. 157:7
Shores: earth's human s. 121:8
Exult O s. 242:11
from the s. of Troy 236:3
s. of Gitche Gumee 134:4
Shorn: all shaven and s. 158:8
tempers the wind..to the s. lamb 220:12
Short: brutish, and s. 105:9
find it wond'rous s. 95:10
from long to s. 67:1
from s. to long 67:2
life so s. 105:6
my neck is very s. 150:5
One s. sleep past 77:10
s. and the long of it 202:18
S. as the watch 239:14
s., sharp shock 92:5
Shorten I the stature 142:3
Shot: a very long s.! 78:10
fired the s. 82:14
he that s. so trim 207:19
I s. an arrow 133:12
I s. the Albatross 65:10
Off s. the spectre-bark 65:15

Shoulder: Captain's hand on his s.   153:6
    government shall be upon his s.   27:32
    what s., and what art   39:2
Shoulder-blade: I have a left s.   92:11
Shoulders: Do grow beneath their s.   204:22
    lawn about the s.   104:11
    Their s. held the sky   111:11
    Turns his sides and his s.   239:12
Shout: Church with psalms must s.   103:18
    needn't s. so loud!   58:6
    s. about my ears   61:17
    s. that tore hell's concave   146:6
    S. with the largest   75:18
    Who s. and bang   21:21
Shouted in his ear   58:6
Shouting: heavens fill with s.   228:9
    S. their emulation   184:17
    thunder of the captains, and the
        s.   25:44
    tumult and the s. dies   127:4
Shouts to scare the monster   125:5
Shovel: take a large hoe and a s.   126:4
Show: all things s. it   89:26
    I will s. you fear   81:24
    s. his scars   192:4
    to s. more fair   249:4
    which passeth s.   185:10
    world can s.   77:15
Showed: he that s. strength   32:37
Showers: Aprille with his s. sote   60:8
    March winds and April s.   6:5
    s. and dewdrops   177:12
    Small s. last long   206:6
    Sweet April s.   234:14
Showery: Blowy, S.   88:16
Showing: Men of little s.   127:15
Shreds and patches   91:27, 189:2
Shrewdly: air bites s.   186:2
Shriek: short shrill s.   67:12
Shrieked: And Freedom s.   54:5
Shrieking and squeaking   44:19
Shrieks and sights unholy   144:10
Shrill: and the s. trump   205:10
    short s. shriek   67:12
Shrine: s. of the sailor's devotion   212:7
    sovran s.   120:24
    Thy s. we tread   179:11
Shrink: all the boards did s.   65:14
Shroud: My s. of white   209:9
    no roof to s. his head   105:1
Shrubberies: borders, beds and s.   125:8
Shrunk: how much art thou s.!   190:23
    S. to this little measure?   193:18
Shudder: I s. to recall it   236:10
Shuddering fear   202:2
Shuffled off this mortal coil   187:13
Shun: each dark passage s.   250:14
    let me s. that   195:7
    s. the awful shop   61:25
    To s. the heaven   212:2
    Who doth ambition s.   183:15
Shut: men s. their gates   209:20
    s. her wild, wild eyes   120:13
    S. the door after you   80:21
Shuts: iron s. amain   145:2
    S. up the story   174:15
Shutter: Borne before her on a s.   232:4
Shutters: close the s. fast   70:18
Shuttle: musical s.   242:12
Sibyl: with S.'s blending   59:5
Sick: devil was s.   151:2
    do not make me s.   242:14
    I am s. at heart   185:2
    I am s., I must die   152:5
    I am s. of love   27:15
    never, never s. at sea!   93:7
    not fancy I am s.   221:8
    on our hands a s. man   154:3
    s., and ye visited me   32:16

    s., O Lord, around thee   234:22
    when s. for home   121:6
Sicken: may s., and so die   209:2
    when sweet violets s.   215:10
Sickening cry   61:16
Sickle: His s. in his hand   134:3
    s. moon   86:10
    Within his bending s.'s compass   211:16
Sicklied o'er   187:13
Sickly: kind of s. smile   101:4
Sickness: in s. and in health   168:12
    s. that destroyeth   170:19
    sorrow, need, s.   167:21
Side: along the mountain s.   247:19
    Back and s. go bare   221:25
    for the sceptic s.   164:18
    Hear the other s.   13:8
    measured it from s. to s.   248:16
    on every s.   168:34
    on the buttered s.   161:16
    on the side of the angels   76:8
    other side of the hill   240:15
    passed by on the other s.   33:7
    pouch on s.   183:20
    serfs at my s.   46:2
    s. by s.   102:9
    sounded..on the other s.   46:23
    Time is on our s.   94:2
    wrong side of thirty   223:12
Side-arms: keeps 'is s. awful   125:3
Sides: between the piney s.   229:4
    holding both his s.   144:13
    s. of my intent   198:4
    turns his s.   239:12
Sidney: Friend to Sir Philip S.   195:8
    S.'s sister   98:16
Siècles: du haut de ces pyramides
    quarante s.   43:2
Siege: laugh a s. to scorn   152:1
Siesta: Englishmen detest a s.   200:2
Sieve: in a S. I'll..sail   69:8
    went to sea in a S.   197:5
Sigh: cheat thee of a s.   131:4
    hear them s.   244:10
    I s. the lack   90:17
    May s. to think   211:1
    Perhaps 'twill cost a s.   215:18
    shadow and a s.   17:8
    S. no more   127:13
    s. not so   204:9
    Some a light s.   204:9
Sighed: he s. and pined   20:1
    I s. as a lover   232:4
    s. and looked unutterable things   90:10
    s. his soul   233:1
    s. upon a midnight pillow   202:9
Sighing: fell a-s.   183:11
    round her, s.   159:4
Sighs: fiery s.   149:17
    paid with s. a plenty   49:10
    temper'd with Love's s.   110:17
    thousand thousand s.   196:15
    world of s.   209:9
Sight: acceptable in thy s.   204:23
    every common s.   66:8
    feeling as to s.!   246:7
    gleamed upon my s.   198:9
    glimmering landscape on the s.   248:4
    in God's s.   97:8
    in the s. of any bird   177:14
    laugh at the s.   26:5
    loved not at first s. ?   108:12
    out of s.   139:3, 184:7
    punished in the s. of men   64:11
    s. of Proteus   29:33
    s. of that immortal sea   249:5
    s. of you is good   246:12
    s. so touching   223:9
                                        249:4

Sight (cont.)
  s. to dream of   168:31
  thousand ages in Thy s.   239:14
  thousand years in thy s.   170:17
  'tis a shameful s.   239:8
  too small for s.   195:19
  vanish'd from my s.   39:8
  what a s. it were   118:9
Sighted: we have s. fifty-three! 230:2
Sightless: s. couriers   198:4
  your s. substances   197:15
Sights: and s. unholy   144:10
  few more impressive s.   18:25
  Her s. and sounds   42:11
  s. as youthful poets dream 144:19
Sign: I have a s.   42:18
  In this s.   68:22
  mystery and a s.   61:25
  outward and visible s.   168:2
Signal: do not see the s.!   152:19
  Only a s. shown   134:9
Signify: what does that s.   74:13
Signifying nothing   200:4
Signs of the times   31:32
Silence: awful darkness and s. reign 130:20
  darkness again and a s.   134:9
  Elected S.   107:13
  eternal s.   161:5, 230:13
  Foster-child of s.   120:18
  Listen all in s.!   109:16
  rest is s.   190:4
  S. alone is great   236:1
  s. and tears   52:16,17
  S. is the virtue of fools   14:7
  s. of the seas   248:8
  s. surged softly backward 73:6
  S. that dreadful bell   204:31
  slowly s. all   226:23
  to study a long s.   240:12
Silence: Le s. éternel de ces espaces 161:5
  seul le s. est grand   236:1
Silent: Comes s., flooding in 64:10
  floors of s. seas   81:18
  impossible to be s.   47:10
  In the s. night   58:12
  Into that s. sea   65:11
  provoke the s. dust   97:13
  s. and all damned!   247:15
  s., bare   249:4
  s. face   247:17
  s. hours of night   131:3
  s. over Africa   44:3
  S., upon a peak   121:9
  s. was the flock   120:2
  slow s. walk   100:4
  sweet s. thought   211:1
  toward the s. tomb   245:18
  why art thou s.   71:2
Silently: crept s. to Rest   85:4
  How s.   216:30
  Slowly, s., now the moon 73:9
Silk: thing of s.   165:7
Silken: all her s. flanks   120:21
  s. dalliance   191:5
Silks: Whenas in s.   104:15
Silly: s. buckets on the deck 66:1
  such a s. question?   220:13
Silver: Between their s. bars 86:10
  fill it in a s. tassie   48:18
  for a handful of s.   44:9
  gold and s. becks me   193:4
  in her s. shoon   73:9
  in the s. sea   206:7
  oars were s.   182:15
  Or ever the s. cord   27:8
  Seated in thy s. chair 117:11
  S. and gold have I none 34:32
  s. apples of the moon   250:10
  s. for the maid   124:19

  s. threads   175:8
  That tips with s.   207:29
  There's a s. lining   87:4
  thirty pieces of s.   32:14
  With s. bells   156:16
Silvery cloud   229:4
Simmery Axe: Number seventy, S.! 93:32
Simon: real S. Pure   59:6
Simon the Cellarer   20:13
Simple: and never s.   243:7
  in s. things   124:18
  s. plan   78:24, 247:20
  so trim, so s.?   108:18
  sought the s. life   70:23
Simple Simon   157:19
Simplex munditiis   108:18
Simplicitas: O sancta s.!   112:9
Simplicity: In his s. sublime 228:25
  Pity my s.   241:12
Sin: Be ye angry, and s. not 36:12
  blossoms of my s.   186:12
  dark world of s.?   37:33
  go, and s. no more   34:7
  go away and s. no more   6:7
  Guilty of dust and s.   104:1
  He that is without s.   34:6
  his favourite s.   218:17
  If we say that we have no s. 37:8
  in s. hath my mother conceived me 169:25
  killing s.   221:24
  Milton, Death, and S.   251:2
  no s. but ignorance   139:4
  polygamy was made a s. 79:2
  remedy against s.   168:7
  Shall we continue in s.   35:3
  should banish all s.   94:10
  s. I impute   45:8
  s. which doth so easily beset us 36:35
  s. will find you out   24:16
  Some rise by s.   200:16
  this is a duty not a s.   241:19
  time to serve and to s. 224:2
  wages of s.   35:5
Since: But s. that I   77:15
Sincere: of soul s.   164:25
Sincerely: love her so s.   55:3
Sincerest: Our s. laughter 215:5
Sincerity: Wrought in a sad s. 82:15
Sinews: Stiffen the s.   191:8
Sinful: Do no s. action   2:9
  of s. men   166:35
Sing: birds began to s.   158:1
  Bow themselves when he did s. 192:13
  die before they s.   66:13
  'eard men s.   128:4
  found in thy heart to s.? 224:7
  hear the angels s.   181:10
  holy sages once did s.   145:6
  How charmingly sweet you s.! 131:7
  How shall we s.   171:28
  in concert s.   241:17
  I s. the Sofa   70:13
  Lhude s. cuccu!   7:9
  live, and pray, and s.   196:6
  More safe I s.   146:20
  no birds s.   120:10
  Now let us s.   69:31
  O Goddess, s.!   106:15
  O, how they s.!   210:5
  O s. unto my roundelay 60:7
  Of thee I s.   217:14
  pretty birds do s.   152:6
  reminiscence s.   242:12
  shall laugh and s.   170:3
  s. a lullaby   73:1
  S. a song of sixpence   158:1
  s. another song   249:7
  s. before they die   66:13
  s. both high and low   209:5

S. 'Hey to you' 93:2
S. it as we used to s. it 249:7
S. me a song of a lad 221:20
s. My God and King 103:18
s. the Man of Ross! 164:24
s. thee to thy rest! 190:5
s. to me 107:13
S. to the Lord 123:5
s. together 28:19
S. unto the Lord 169:11
S. us one of the songs 171:28
Still wouldst thou s. 121:6
Then to Silvia let us s. 210:2
they began to s. 91:2
We'll s. at St. Ann's 150:2
We will s. one song 87:10
When birds do s. 184:12
where they s. 166:16
Who would not s. 144:20
Singe my white head! 195:4
Singeing of the King of Spain's
    Beard 78:26
Singer: against the s. 180:15
idle s. 150:13
lived a s. in France 224:11
sans S. 85:5
S. of sweet Colonus 11:14
When the s. sings them 221:18
Singest of summer 121:2
Singeth: S. a quiet tune 66:3
s. all night 185:4
Singing: Beside me s. 84:18
For ever s. as they shine 1:14
like a s. bird 177:8
made by s. 125:9
nest of s. birds 113:15
nightingales are s. 81:22, 123:12
S. hymns unbidden 215:4
S. of Mount Abora 66:15
S. so rarely 180:18
s. will never be done 179:7
suddenly burst out s. 179:6
Sweet s. in the choir 7:17
time of the s. of birds 27:16
were s. vespers 90:12
who are s. today 40:15
Singing-boys: six little S. 17:12
Single: careless of the s. life 227:12
come not s. spies 189:11
I wish I were s. again 5:16
s. in the field 248:7
s. men in barricks 127:23
Sings: Another Orpheus s. 213:12
at heaven's gate s. 184:20
blithe the throstle s.! 248:14
like an angel s. 202:11
s. hymns at heaven's gate 210:13
tell me what she s.? 248:9
truth the poet s. 228:7
when she s. 117:10
When the singer s. them 221:18
While the chaffinch s. 44:1
with him who s. 227:6
Singularly deep young man 92:21
Sink: to nothingness do s. 122:5
who s. to rest 67:14
Sinking: like a s. star 230:14
Someone is s. today 235:1
Sinking feeling: Bovril prevents
    that s. 3:19
Sinks: It s...ready to depart 129:20
o'er sewers and s. 66:9
s. the day-star 145:4
Sinn: kommt mir nicht aus dem S. 102:4
Sinned: I have s. against heaven 33:22
More s. against 195:6
Sinner: be merciful to me a s. 33:34
one s. that repenteth 33:20
Say, poor s. 70:3

Sinners: God and s. reconciled 241:15
miserable s. 166:21
we are s. all 192:8
with publicans and s.? 31:10
Sinning: sinned against than s. 195:6
Sins: and weep for their s. 242:14
Be all my s. remember'd 188:1
Compound for s. 49:19
cover the multitude of s. 37:6
His s. were scarlet 21:15
manifold s. 166:7
repent you of your s. 167:22
s. and offences 169:6
s. be as scarlet 27:21
s. of the fathers 167:7
s. of your sires 109:22
Sinuous: with s. rills 66:14
Sion: bring against S. 28:19
remembered thee, O S. 171:28
saith unto S. 28:18
S. city of our God 154:2
songs of S. 171:28
Walk about S. 169:23
Sipping: Some s. punch 247:15
Sips: while the bee-mouth s. 120:24
Sipt: I s. each flower 89:14
Sire: I'm killed, S.! 44:7
Sirens: Blest pair of S. 147:13
What song the S. sang 43:1
Sires: Our s.' age was worse 109:23
sins of your s. 109:22
Sisera: fought against S. 24:28
Sister: Innocence thy S. 140:5
kissed her little s. 149:9
moon is my s. 21:13
my s., good night 21:13
O s. swallow 224:7
shall my s. be 189:22
Sidney's s. 43:2
Thine azure s. 214:1
Sisters: And so do his s. 93:9
Are s. under their skins! 126:8
Brothers and S. 127:2
harmonious s. 147:13
weird s. 199:24
Sit: birds s. brooding 196:20
He won't s. still 105:18
Here will we s. 202:11
I shall at last s. down 123:11
is not to s. still 126:4
Piper, s. thee down 39:8
s. and drink with me 22:1
s. and look at it 113:8
s. in the candle-light 176:11
s. on a cushion 155:11
s. thou a patient looker-on 173:27
S. thou on my right hand 171:10
S. thou still 180:15
s. upon the ground 206:15
that s. in darkness 32:39
that you should s. here 71:11
Though I s. down now 76:5
To s. still for once 105:17
Trees, where you s. 165:1
We would s. down 140:11
where men s. 121:4
Sits: Expectation in the air 191:5
s. in the bush 180:18
there the antick s. 206:15
Sitting: A-s. on a gate 58:11
end of it's s. 126:7
S. at the receipt of custom 31:9
s. careless 119:18
s. in the air! 107:16
s. in the shade 125:9
Was s. in the sun 218:12
where thou art s. 144:3
Situation: s. excellent 86:14
took the s. at the lighthouse 75:33

Six: a coach and s.! 67:16
  fight till s. 58:2
  s. of one 139:19
Sixpence: *bang* went s.! 173:10
  found a crooked s. 158:5
  song of s. 158:1
Sixty seconds' worth of distance run 125:16
Skating over thin ice 82:20
Skelter: Helter s. 117:14
Sketch: first rude s. 125:1
  s. the ruins of St. Paul's 136:21
Skiddaw: red glare on S. 136:6
Skies: air, earth, and s. 248:20
  blown about the s. 227:8
  if morning s. 221:24
  Look up at the s.! 107:16
  Look upward to the s. 152:16
  lowing at the s. 120:21
  people of the s. 249:13
  point me to the s. 135:17
  s. are not cloudy 105:5
  starry s. 52:12
  thou climb'st the s.! 216:30
  watcher of the s. 121:9
Skiey: outstrip thy s. speed 214:3
Skilful in the wars 235:7
Skill: his utmost s.! 249:10
  my courage and s. 46:22
  or of s. 239:10
  parson own'd his s. 95:8
  use all your s. 71:9
Skim: with pinions s. the air 88:8
Skin: Can the Ethiopian change his
    s. 29:6
  enamell'd s. 203:9
  Gone to get a rabbit s. 155:6
  s. of my teeth 25:33
  stuff my s. 221:25
Skin-deep: that are but s. 103:4
Skinny: holds him with his s. hand 65:5
  I fear thy s. hand! 65:18
Skins: Are sisters under their s.! 126:8
Skip: would have made them s. 196:10
Skipped: mountains s. 171:12
Skittles: all beer and s. 53:8, 141:15
Sky: About us in the s. 110:19
  Above the bright blue s. 142:20
  blue s. of spring 2:18
  bridal of the earth and s. 104:6
  charm from the s. 161:17
  clear blue s. 101:11
  darkening the s. 175:15
  diamond in the s.! 225:10
  English earth and s. 102:17
  forehead of the morning s. 145:4
  from th' ethereal s. 145:12
  gathering in the s. 142:5
  held the s. suspended 111:11
  hot and copper s. 65:12
  hovers from the s. 94:16
  inverted Bowl we call The S. 85:13
  Is shining in the s. 248:3
  Like a teatray in the s. 56:24
  Living air and the blue s. 248:19
  lonely sea and the s. 141:2
  monarch of the s. 138:13
  Music shall untune the s. 79:18
  old and as true as the s. 126:9
  prisoners call the s. 243:4
  rainbow in the s. 247:10
  reversion in the s. 164:5
  rides down the s. 84:11
  sea rising, nor s. clouding 41:8
  sent him down the s. 69:3
  s. changes when they are wives 184:11
  s. grows darker yet 61:14
  spread out against the s. 81:14
  Steal across the s. 18:6
  They change their s. 108:9

thou bitter s. 184:2
Till Earth and S. 124:13
to lose itself in the s. 43:7
to the s. 249:4
went up the s. 65:22
wide and starry s. 221:23
With all the blue ethereal s. 1:11
Skye: Beyond the Isle of S. 16:3
  Over the sea to S. 221:20
Slab: thick and s. 199:16
Slack: observing me grow s. 104:1
Slain: Death, ere thou hast s.
    another 43:2
  frosts are s. 223:29
  late s. at Carrow 217:7
  Or if the s. think he is s. 82:13
  shall himself be s. 136:17
  s. by a fair cruel maid 209:9
  S. by the bloody Piedmontese 147:16
  s. his thousands 24:45
  s. in thine high places 25:1
  s. this year in Europe 238:11
  s. upon thy high places 24:47
  some s. in war 206:15
  thou s. the Jabberwock? 57:14
  who is in battle s. 95:2
Slandering: lying, and s. 167:34
Slanted: romantic chasm which s. 66:14
Slap-dash: I s. down in the mouth 68:11
Slaughter: as a lamb to the s. 28:21
  goeth to the s. 26:10
  threatenings and s. 34:34
  when it comes to s. 125:11
Slaughtered saints 147:16
Slave: as the wretched s. 191:15
  been s. to thousands 205:4
  half s. and half free 132:7
  here I stand, your s. 195:5
  peasant s. am I 187:11
  That is not passion's s. 188:11
  thought's the s. of life 190:22
  very s. of circumstance 52:8
  you were a Christian S. 102:15
Slavery: Chains and s.! 48:30
Slaves: at the mill with s. 147:2
  either to be wholly s. 79:22
  morality of s. 154:5
  never will be s. 232:13
  not press you like s. 88:18
Slayer: If the red s. think he slays 82:13
  priest who slew the s. 136:17
Slays: and mates, and s. 85:10
  If the red slayer think he s. 82:13
  War its thousands s. 165:19
Sleave: ravell'd s. of care 198:13
Sleep: after-dinner's s. 200:20
  awaked as one out of s. 170:12
  balmy s.! 250:15
  Between a s. and a s. 224:2
  birth is but a s. 246:11
  by a s. to say we end 187:13
  Can s. so soundly 191:15
  Cawdor shall s. no more 198:14
  deep s. to fall upon Adam 23:12
  Do I wake or s.? 121:7
  even as a s. 170:17
  first sweet s. of night 213:13
  folding of the hands to s. 26:9
  full of s. 250:11
  Glamis hath murder'd s. 198:14
  goes to s. at a bank 113:7
  good run I have in my s. 222:14
  How s. the brave 67:14
  In s. a king 211:10
  in that s. of death 187:13
  innocent s. 198:13
  little s. 26:9
  Macbeth does murder s. 198:13
  night to do with s.? 143:20

nights with s. 191:15
No s. till morn 51:1
Now I lay me down to s. 6:11
O S, again deceive me 68:14
O S., why dost thou leave me? 68:14
Oh S.! it is a gentle thing 65:23
One short s. past 77:10
quiet s. 141:4
saw in s. 214:2
shall our gratitude s.? 54:17
S. after toil 219:10
s. firmly 69:8
s. full of sweet dreams 120:1
s. in the night 224:2
S. is sweet 46:13
s. like a top 72:11
S. no more! 198:13
S., pretty wantons 73:1
S. shall neither night nor day 197:6
S. that knits 198:13
S., the certain knot of peace 217:1
s. thegither at the foot 48:21
S. to wake 45:10
S. we must one endless night 58:26
strong man after s. 148:10
sun is laid to s. 117:11
Sword s. in my hand 38:16
That s. all the night 60:9
there s. Young Cyclads 213:12
to awake out of s. 35:14
To die: to s. 187:13
To s.: perchance to dream 187:13
to that sweet s. 205:9
we must s. 182:18
We shall not all s. 35:29
We shall not s. 137:8
Sleeping: and wakened us from s. 42:10
like s. flowers 249:5
s. hound to wake 60:26
s. woods 66:3
some s. kill'd 206:15
Sleepless: s. Eremite 121:8
s. soul 247:19
Sleeps: he s. well 199:4
Now s. the crimson petal 229:16
s. as sound 173:2
s. in earth 246:3
s. in Elysium 191:15
s. the pride 149:13
s. upon this bank! 202:11
where the M.F.H. dines he s. 222:16
where the M.F.H. s. he break-
    fasts 222:16
while my pretty one, s. 229:9
young hero s. 149:17
Sleepy-head 155:8
Sleeve: heart upon my s. 204:16
Snatch the s. of to-day 109:3
strip his s. 192:4
Sleeves: Tie up my s. 112:8
Sleight: a juggler's s. 49:29
Slender: scarlet line was s. 123:13
Slenderly: Fashion'd so s. 106:20
Slept: I s., and dreamed 107:6
not s. one wink 184:21
On a poet's lips I s. 214:9
s. with his fathers 25:11
while their companions s. 133:22
Slew: I s. him 194:2
Slices of quince 131:9
Slid: s. from his back 127:1
That s. into my soul 65:23
Slide: Let the world s. 19:27
Slighted: our soldiers s. 173:26
s., shepherd's trade 145:1
Slime: slimier s. 42:1
Slimy things 65:14, 20
Slings and arrows 187:13
Slinks out of the race 148:9

Slip: Since he gave us all the s.? 45:13
Slippered: lean and s. pantaloon 183:20
Slippers: bring me my s. 148:15
Slipping: are s. by 109:14
    s. underneath our Feet 85:8
Slips: like greyhounds in the s. 191:9
    S. of yew 199:15
Slithy: and the s. toves 57:14
Slits the thin-spun life 145:1
Sliver: envious s. 189:18
Slivered in the moon's eclipse 199:15
Sloane Square: came on board at S. 91:25
Slog: We're foot-s.-s.-s.-sloggin' 124:16
Sloth: Shake off dull s. 123:1
Slough: name of the s. 46:4
Slovenliness is no part of religion 241:19
Slow: and more s. 140:11
    mournful, and s. 243:1
    S. and steady 133:5
    s. howe'er my marches be 123:11
    S., s., fresh fount 117:10
    wandering steps and s. 146:25
    With swift, s. 107:15
Slower: Yet, s., yet 117:10
Slowly: And s. read 250:11
    blood was frozen s. 228:1
    hasten s. 222:9
    See nations s. wise 117:2
    s., silently, now the moon 73:9
Slow-worm: or s. bite thee 104:13
Slug-a-bed: Get-up, sweet S. 104:9
Sluggard: Go to the ant, thou s. 26:8
    voice of the s. 239:12
Slug-horn: Dauntless the s. 43:14
Slumber: I must s. again 239:12
    lie still and s. 239:11
    little s. 26:9
    shall s. on 215:10
    s. did my spirit seal 245:14
    S.'s chain 150:1
Slumbering: what, s. still? 71:2
Slumbers: Golden s. kiss your eyes 73:1
    hast thou golden s.? 72:18
    Like infant s. 122:17
    soul is dead that s. 133:26
    Visit'st my s. 146:20
Slung atween the round shot 153:5
Sly shade of a Rural Dean 42:6
Small: All things both great and s. 66:7
    extinguishes the s. 49:14
    his deserts are s. 149:6
    Is it s.? 130:16
    still s. voice 25:14
    too s. for sight 195:19
    was too s. a bound 190:23
    wee, s. door 73:10
Smart: girls that are so s. 55:2
    lief pray with Kit S. 114:9
Smattering of everything 74:1
Smell: actions of the just s. sweet 216:25
    daisies s.-less 19:24
    fish-like s. 208:13
    I s. a rat 49:21, 175:15
    I s. the blood 195:14
    noses have they, and s. not 171:13
    s. and hideous hum 94:9
    s. far worse that weeds 211:11
    s. too strong of the lamp 220:15
    would s. as sweet 207:23
Smelleth: he s. the battle 25:44
Smells: s. of cheese! 222:19
    s. to heaven 188:22
    s. wooingly here 198:2
    violet s. to him 191:12
    when it grows and s. 117:19
Smile: Cambridge people rarely s. 42:8
    disdainful s. 97:12
    forget and s. 177:11
    Julia's lips do s. 104:8

Smile (cont.)
  kind of sickly s.   101:4
  one may s., and s.   186:14
  S. at us   61:24
  s., s., s.   12:14
  s. we would aspire to
    those Angel faces s.   192:14
                                      153:16
  we shall s.!   194:21
  With s. so sweet   235:4
  without the s.   67:3
Smiled: Has s. and said 'Good
  Night'   21:16
  Never S. Again!   102:10
  s. a kind of sickly smile   101:4
  Until she s. on me   65:2
Smiles: charmed it with s.   56:5
  daggers in men's s.   198:20
  Heaven s.   213:12
  Peace is crown'd with s.   235:7
  s. so sweet   137:15
  s., the tears   150:1
  that s. to-day   104:14
  wreathed s.   144:12
Smiling: by your s., you seem to say
  so   187:4
  is s. as they run   61:18
  S. at grief   209:10
  s., damned villain!   186:14
Smite: ready to s. once   145:3
  s. the sounding furrows   230:15
  whosoever shall s. thee   30:18
Smith: Chuck it, S.!   61:13
Smithy: village s. stands   134:10
Smitten: legs were s. off   213:5
Smoke: and s. it!   17:16
  dunnest s. of hell   197:15
  good cigar is a S.   124:14
  house was filled with s.   27:27
  in yon s. concealed   64:10
  overhung with s.   150:14
  salt-caked s. stack   140:21
  thin s. without flame   100:4
  with the S. of Hell   85:14
Smoked: s. with bloody execution   197:4
  Who s. like a chimney   17:15
Smokeless: in the s. air   249:4
Smoking: seed her first a-s.   126:12
  s. flax   28:16
Smooth: billows s. and bright   57:20
  that soon s. away trouble   41:17
  never did run s.   203:2
  To s. the ice   193:6
Smoothed: Then s. her work   110:14
Smoother: finding a s. pebble   153:17
Smoothes: She s. her hair   82:2
Smoothly: makes verse run s.   40:2
Smoothness: may give it s.   188:7
Smote: And s. him thus   205:20
  He s. his enemies   170:12
  S. him under the fifth rib   25:2
  S. him with the edge of the sword   24:15
  s. them hip and thigh   24:31
Smutch'd: Before the soil hath s. it ?   118:11
Snail: beloved s.   57:9
  creeping like s.   183:20
  s.'s on the thorn   44:24
  whiting to a s.   57:7
  Worm nor s.   203:11
Snails: Frogs and s.   158:14
Snake: like a s. renew   213:12
  like a wounded s.   164:11
  s. lurks in the grass!   236:24
  Nor s., or slow-worm   104:13
  S. is living yet   21:23
  s. throws her enamell'd skin   203:9
  We have scotch'd the s.   199:3
Snakes: Concerning s.   115:17
  spotted s.   203:10
Snap-dragon growing on the walls   153:11

Snapped: s. 'em off   74:4
  s. off her nose   158:1
Snapper-up of unconsidered trifles   210:6
Snare: delusion, a mockery, and a s.   73:11
  rabbit in a s.   220:9
  s. of the hunter   170:19
Snark: S. be a Boojum!   56:4
  S. was a Boojum   56:6
Snarling: silver, s. trumpets   120:3
Snatch: And s. a fearful joy   98:7
  S. the sleeve of to-day   109:3
Snatches: Of ballads, songs and s.   91:27
  s. of old tunes   189:18
Sneaking: petty s. knave   38:14
Sneer: refute a s. ?   160:15
  teach the rest to s.   165:6
Sneering: I was born s.   91:28
  without s.   165:6
Sneezed: Not to be s. at   67:20
Sneezes: beat him when he s.   56:19
Sneezy, Freezy   88:16
Snicker-snack: blade went s.!   57:14
Snickersnee: I drew my s.!   92:10
Snores: heavy ploughman s.   204:3
Snorting steam   150:14
Snow: across the s.   227:19
  as pure as s.   188:5
  fall o' the s.   118:11
  Half-buried in the s.   133:20
  If s. be white   212:3
  Its fleece was white as s.   99:5
  lay the untrodden s.   53:15
  melted like s.   52:11
  'mid s. and ice   133:17
  sends the s. in winter   53:12
  s. came flying   41:7
  S. had fallen   177:9
  s. lay round about   152:13
  s. on s.   177:9
  To see the cherry hung with s.   110:15
  we shall have s.   157:1
  white as driven s.   210:9
  white as s.   27:21
  whiter than s.   169:26
Snows: s. have scattered   110:5
  s. of yesteryear?   236:2
Snow-white: little s. feet   250:5
Snowy, Flowy   88:16
Snuff: only took s.   95:19
Snuffed: be s. out by an article   51:25
Snug: little s. property   80:20
  s. little Island   73:12
So: but feel 'tis s.   59:2
  if it was s.   57:19
  used to be s.   148:19
Soap: charmed it with..s.   56:5
  used your s.   173:17
  What! no s.?   86:19
Soar: that s. above   134:19
  Type of the wise who s.   248:6
Sobbing: and a-s.   159:4
Sober: as s. as a Judge   84:5
  Be s., be vigilant   37:7
  righteous and s. life   166:10
  Their s. wishes   98:1
  To their own second and s.
    thoughts   103:5
  To-morrow we'll be s.   3:21
Socialists: We are all S.   100:1
Society: hung loose upon s.   113:18
  list of s. offenders   91:30
  no s.; and which is worst of all   105:9
  s., where none intrudes   51:7
  well-being of s.   177:2
Sock: Jonson's learnèd s.   144:19
Sockets: candles burn their s.   111:10
Socrates: and S. [was misunder-
  stood]   82:21
  S. is charged   163:7

Sod: become a s. 121:6
Soda-water: Sermons and s. 51:15
  wash their feet in s. 82:1
Sodden and unkind 21:24
Sods with our bayonets turning 245:4
Sofa: I sing the S. 70:13
  wheel the s. round 70:18
Soft: But, s., what light 207:20
  dream of the s. look 250:11
  moon's s. pace 247:18
  more s. than a dove's 224:9
  O so s. 118:11
  own the s. impeachment 216:14
  s., and sweet 140:3
  s. answer 26:16
  s. complaining flute 79:17
  s. was the sun 130:4
  Sweet air blow s. 105:2
  voice was ever s. 196:9
  when s. voices die 215:10
Soft-lifted: Thy hair s. 119:18
Softly: silence surged s. 73:6
  s. and suddenly vanish 56:4
  S. come 159:14
  S. she was going up 65:22
  Speak s. 176:18
  Thames, run s. 219:13
Softness: For s. she and sweet
  attractive grace 146:16
Soi: savoir être à s. 149:3
Soil: Before the s. hath smutch'd it? 118:11
  s. may best deserve 146:8
Soil'd by rude hinds 70:22
Solar walk 164:14
Sold: if landscapes were s. 220:23
  s. a goodly manor 182:11
  s. for endless rue 110:17
  s. for two farthings 33:13
  s. his birthright 23:27
  s. my Reputation 85:15
  spoils were fairly s. 136:12
  thou'rt s. 154:12
Soldan of Byzantium 61:18
Soldier: always tell an old s. 212:8
  as the s. said 75:26
  Ben Battle was a s. bold 106:22
  British s. can stand up 212:12
  British s. fights 151:14
  come you back, you British s. 126:11
  Drinking is the s.'s pleasure 79:12
  fit to serve as a s. 128:8
  for not having been a s. 115:16
  in the vaunting style of a s. 78:26
  let a s. drink 204:29
  s., and afeard? 199:28
  s. carries in his cartridge-pouch 151:16
  S. full of strange oaths 183:20
  s.'s a man 204:29
  s.'s pole is fall'n 182:21
  s.'s pride 44:7
  s.'s, scholar's, eye 188:6
  wot the ten-year s. tells 126:13
Soldiers: having s. under me 31:5
  Old s. never die 6:19
  Onward, Christian s. 18:7
  Our God and s. 173:26
  our s. slighted 173:26
  S. of Christ 241:13
  They mustered their s. 16:9
Soldiery: brutal and insolent s. 83:7
  rapacious and licentious s. 47:9
Soleil: le s. d'Austerlitz 152:3
Solemn: in s. stillness lay 181:10
  s., mournful, and slow 243:1
  s. stillness holds 97:8
Soliciting: supernatural s. 197:10
Solitary: Be not s. 49:13, 115:22
  if you are s. 115:22
  s. Highland lass! 248:7

s. place 28:9
s., poor, nasty 105:9
till I am s. 113:22
Solitude: And s.; yet not alone 146:20
  bliss of s. 247:5
  in the midst of a vast s. 136:21
  life the s. 251:1
  makes a s. 50:18
Solitudes: misty s. 128:3
Solitudinem: Ubi s. faciunt 224:15
Solomon: curtains of S. 27:12
  even S. in all his glory 30:28
  Proverbs of S. 74:15
  S. says 127:19
  which is S.'s 27:11
Solum: nec minus s. quam cum solus 63:15
Some: Lo! s. we loved 85:4
Somebody: every one is s. 91:14
  Let's stop s. 103:16
Somehow: doubt that, s., good 41:20
Some one came knocking 73:10
Something: from doing s.! 103:16
  s. ere the end 230:15
  S. lingering 92:12
  Time for a little s. 143:18
  To add s. more 88:18
  unless I produce s. 137:5
  Which is s. between 91:24
Somewhat: More than s. 178:7
Somewhere: But s., beyond space 42:1
  S. the sun is shining 100:16
Son: behold thy s.! 34:27
  blessed Mary's S. 206:7
  conceive, and bear a s. 27:30
  Duke's s.—cook's s. 124:11
  Every wise man's s. 209:5
  gave his only begotten S. 34:1
  good man teach his s. 192:4
  hateth his s. 26:15
  if his s. ask bread 30:34
  leichter of a fair s. 82:5
  Manhood taken by the S. 153:13
  my beloved S. 30:7
  My little S. 161:15
  obeyed as a s. 90:10
  Praise Father, S., and Holy Ghost 123:3
  s. is given 27:32
  s. of a gun 53:7
  s. of a hundred Kings 124:11
  S. of Heaven 145:6
  s. of his old age 23:32
  S. of man 31:7, 168:23
  s. of memory 147:12
  S. of Saint Louis 84:12
  s. of the morning! 28:4
  This my s. was dead 33:24
  worthy to be called thy s. 33:22
  wrath of Peleus' s. 106:15
Song: burden of my s. 6:4
  burthen of his s. 37:30
  ends the s. 164:11
  for a s. 182:11
  Give ear unto my s. 95:10
  glorious s. of old 181:10
  govern thou my s. 146:20
  Her symphony and s. 66:15
  low lone s.? 55:27
  morn of s. 222:2
  My echoing s. 140:12
  new s. 169:11
  On the wings of s. 102:5
  One grand sweet s. 123:14
  our s. shall rise 102:1
  pastoral s. 67:11
  pipe that s. again 39:8
  Provençal s. 121:3
  required of us then a s. 171:22
  sang a most topical s. 8:3
  sans S. 85:5

Song (cont.)
self-same s.   121:6
Sing a s. of sixpence   158:1
sing another s.   249:7
Sing the Lord's s.   171:28
sold my Reputation for a S.   85:15
s. of a lad   221:20
s. of praise be sung   165:21
s. of songs   27:11
s. of the birds   99:2
s. was wordless   179:7
suck melancholy out of a s.   183:14
till I end my S.   219:13
To the S. on your bugles   102:17
We will sing one s.   87:10
What s. the Syrens sang   43:1
will I frame my s.   61:3
wind's s.   141:2
woman, wine and s.   135:11
Songs: all their s. are sad   61:15
Are summer s.   210:5
Fair the fall of s.   221:18
lean and flashy s.   145:3
of ballads, s. and snatches   91:27
Our sweetest s.   215:5
piping s.   39:8
Sing no sad s.   177:12
s. of Apollo   197:1
s. of Araby   244:10
s. of Sion   171:28
there shall the Sussex s. be sung   22:1
thy s. of happy cheer   39:8
wrote my happy s.   39:8
your gambols? your s. ?   189:20
Sonne: Die S. geht. . nicht unter   179:12
Sonnet: Scorn not the S.   24:1
turned to a S.   76:24
When my s. was rejected   129:14
Sons: all the s. of God shouted   25:42
as the s. of the waves?   88:18
Bears all its s. away   239:14
bind your s. to exile   128:5
fallen s. of Eve   61:26
give them to your s.   157:4
Horny-handed s. of toil   119:16
s. and your daughters shall pro-
  phesy   29:22
s. of Belial   79:9, 146:5
S. of men and angels   241:7
s. of the morning!   101:14
Their s., they gave   41:16
We their s. are more worthless   109:23
Soon: day returns too s.   52:15
forgot as s. as done   208:27
how s. we must sever ?   71:2
late and s.   249:5
wak'd me too s.   239:12
You haste away so s.   104:10
Soothe can s. her melancholy   95:21
s. a savage breast   68:9
to s. thine ear   67:11
Soothes his sorrows   154:1
Soothing: In the s. thoughts   246:13
Sop: give that Cerberus a s.   68:5
Sophisters: that of s.   47:14
Sophistical rhetorician   76:11
Sophonisba! Oh!   233:2
Soporific: is 's.'   166:2
Sordid boon!   249:5
Sore: bear with a s. head   139:18
good for s. eyes   223:9
s. labour's bath   198:13
thy so s. loss   232:10
Sorest: need was the s.   180:2
Sorrow: any s. like unto my s.   29:8
ate his bread in s.   55:23
Brief s.   152:10
hang s.   117:14
increaseth knowledge increaseth s.   26:37

labour and s.   170:18
more in s.   185:18
never mused on s.   54:4
no more. . s.   37:26
not a word of s.   245:6
not be in s.   39:14
parting is such sweet s.   207:25
rooted s.   200:1
s., need, sickness   167:21
s.'s crown of s.   228:7
sphere of our s.   215:13
There is no greater s.   72:7
Through the night of doubt and s.   18:8
With night we banish s.   105:2
with s. to the grave   23:35
Write s.   206:14
your s. is not dead   145:4
Sorrowful: and s. countenance   49:10
Knight of the S. Countenance   59:8
Sorrowing: Goeth a s.   234:9
Sorrows: carried our s.   28:20
man of s.   28:20
soothes his s.   154:1
s. of your changing face   250:11
When shall my s. have an end   5:3
When s. come   189:11
Sorry: dreadful s.   149:7
this s. Scheme of Things   86:1
Sort: like this s. of thing   132:12
of every s.   95:10
of the baser s.   34:40
Sorts: all s. and conditions of men   166:27
all s. of people   198:5
of various s.   216:1
Sought: never s. in vain   48:12
prize we s.   242:10
s. it with thimbles   56:5
s. out many inventions   26:41
s. the simple life   70:23
Soul: Awake my s.   123:1
call upon my s. within the house   209:4
captain of my s.   102:14
change their sky, not their s.   108:9
cold waters to a thirsty s.   26:25
convert my s.   169:2
Could force his s.   187:11
Deliver my s.   169:1
Dull would he be of s.   249:4
echoes roll from s. to s.   229:12
every subject's s.   191:13
ev'ry s. cried out   69:28
fiery s.   79:5
flattering unction to your s.   189:3
flow of s.   165:10
For that sweet s.'s sake   217:7
gets the s.   142:7
give me my s. again   138:12
glowed in his s.   221:21
Grapple them to thy s.   185:21
Hangs my helpless s.   241:9
Hark, my s.!   70:3
heart, and s., and voice   152:12
his pure s.   207:2
His s. is marching on!   99:6
His s. shall taste   120:24
I built my s.   229:5
I pray the Lord my s. to take   6:11
if an even s.   108:9
if I have a s.!   6:13
if that s. were fled   149:13
in my s. am free   134:19
In mystery our s. abides   11:17
in the night, my S.   232:10
into my very s.   189:1
iron entered into his s.   171:5
largest and most comprehensive s.   80:3
lie in the S.   118:16
Little s., wandering   99:3
lose his own s. ?   31:35, 32:32

loved the pilgrim s. 250:11
Lover of my s. 241:8
meeting s. may pierce 144:19
Merry of s. 221:20
merry old s. 157:2
my prophetic s.! 186:10
My s. doth magnify the Lord 32:37
My s. hath her content 204:28
my s. is white 39:10
My s., there is a country 235:7
my unconquerable s. 102:13
neither a s. to lose 217:19
No coward s. is mine 41:13
no s. to be damned 233:15
nor the prophetic s. 211:14
of s. sincere 164:25
offends me to the s. 188:7
One drop would save my s. 138:14
Perdition catch my s. 205:3
pouring forth thy s. 121:6
Pray for my s. 227:2
receive my s. 241:8
repent and save his s. 138:14
save his s. alive 29:13
shake in his rocklike s. 109:19
sigh'd his s. 202:9
sleepless s. 247:19
slid into my s. 65:23
so longeth my s. 169:15
s. abhorred 171:6
s. aspiring 149:5
s. hath a desire 170:13
s. he doth restore again 181:8
s. in agony 65:19
s. in bliss 196:1
s. is dead that slumbers 133:26
S. more bent to serve 147:17
s. of a friend 40:6
s. of music 149:13
s. of Philip Sparrow 217:7
S. of the Age! 118:4
s. of wit 186:21
s. proud science never taught 164:14
s. remembering my good friends 206:10
s., sit thou 173:27
S. that rises with us 246:11
s., uneasy 164:14
s. wears out the breast 52:14
stature of my s. 142:3
stolen my s. away! 234:6
suck forth my s. 138:12
Sun of my s.! 122:16
thirst that from the s. 117:19
Thy s.'s flight 199:2
to bear my s. away 1:17
tocsin of the s. 51:24
'twas not my s. that swore 83:11
veil of the s. 224:2
Was not spoken of the s. 133:26
What of s. was left 45:11
(Whose s. is sense) 77:20
wit its s. 66:12
with s. so dead 180:6
witness of the s. 231:9
Would harrow up thy s. 186:7
Yet my s. drew back 104:1
Soul-animating strains 248:2
Souls: But the s. of Christian peoples 61:13
damp s. of housemaids 81:20
for all sparrows' s. 217:7
immediate jewel of their s. 205:4
is in immortal s. 202:11
land of such dear s. 206:7
on other s. may fall 79:24
Our s. have sight 246:12
our s. inspire 172:11
Our s., whose faculties 139:10
poor misguided s. 130:2

possess ye your s. 33:39
S. of poets dead and gone 120:17
s. of the righteous 29:32
S. that have toil'd 230:15
then ye contented your s. 126:1
try men's s. 160:12
Two s. with but a single thought 99:9
warn th' immortal s. 139:12
We that have free s. 188:14
Sound: as the s. of lyres 161:9
bells they s. so clear 110:19
call him up the S. 153:5
deep s. strikes 50:23
Except the mill-wheel's s. 213:11
full of s. and fury 200:4
In the s. his breathing kept 214:9
like the s. of a rat 44:20
like the sweet s. 209:2
pipes and whistles in his s. 183:20
pipes o' Havelock s.! 242:18
sleeps as s. 173:2
s. as a bell 204:11
s. me from my lowest note 188:17
s. mind in a s. body 119:9
s. my echoing song 140:12
s. of a great Amen 172:23
s. of a voice 225:15
s. of his horn 97:2
s. of iron on stone 73:6
s. of revelry 50:23
s. of the cornet 29:16
s. so grand on 173:1
S., s. the clarion 150:3
S. the trumpets 150:10
s. upon the bugle-horn 228:4
Sweet is every s. 229:19
thou hearest the s. thereof 33:50
to the s. of trumpets 218:2
Too full for s. and foam 226:6
whispering s. 70:7
with the s. of the trump 169:22
Sounding: as s. brass 35:20
Soundless-clapping host 232:11
Soundly: Can sleep so s. 191:15
Sounds: concord of sweet s. 202:13
Her sights and s. 42:11
let the s. of music 202:11
S. and sweet airs 208:18
s. of woe 204:9
s. will take care 57:4
Soup: beautiful s.! 57:11
I won't have any s. to-day 105:15
never let his s. get cold 105:15
S. of the evening 57:11
Take the s. away! 105:15
Soup-and-fish: Donning the s. 245:2
Sour: fathers have eaten s. grapes 29:12
sweet, s. 107:15
Source: life's first native s. 219:14
South: fickle is the S. 229:14
full of the warm S. 121:3
good s. wind 65:9
In the s. suburbs 209:15
nor yet from the s. 170:10
rivers in the s. 171:21
South Country: hills of the S. 21:24
Southern: in the s. wild 39:10
South Kensington: Sloane Square and S. Stations 91:25
Southron: of the S. folk 232:11
Sovereign: civilities with my S. 114:23
most s. reason 188:6
trample on their s.'s head 206:16
with s. eye 211:2
Sovran shrine 120:24
Sow: For, as you s. 49:28
S. an act 175:4
s. in tears 171:21

Soweth: whatsoever a man s.   36:8
Sown: have s. the wind   29:20
  nor was ever s.   234:2
Sows, and he shall not reap   224:2
Space: about the s. of two hours   34:45
  beyond s. and time   42:1
  king of infinite s.   187:3
  mused a little s.   228:2
  s. for delight   224:2
Spaces: infinite s.   161:5
Spacious: fill a s. plain   70:20
Spade: crooked scythe and s.   216:24
  entirely by the s.   142:24
  nominate a s. a s.   118:1
  S.! with which Wilkinson   248:10
Spain: king of S.'s daughter   156:2
  make castels than in S.   60:23
  old tunes of S.   140:19
  Singeing the King of S.'s beard   78:26
  S...should dare to invade   82:9
  they were not left to S.   230:3
Spake: I s. as a child   35:22
  out s. brave Horatius   136:9
  that s. it   82:4
  tongue that Shakespeare s.   247:1
Span: life's but a s.   204:29
  Life's short s.   108:17
  spick and s.-new   49:25
Spangled: new s. ore   145:4
Spaniards: thrash the S. too   78:25
Spanish: fond of S. wine   141:1
  S. ships of war   230:2
  To God I speak S.   60:6
Spare: original, s., strange   107:15
  s. that tree!   150:12
  s. the rod   49:26
  to s. the humbled   236:18
Spared a better man   190:24
Spares: and s. the rod   107:2
  s. the child   107:2
  that s. these stones   212:5
Spareth: he that s. his rod   26:15
Spark from heaven!   11:25
Sparkle: s. out among the fern   225:17
  They s. still   196:16
Sparkling: Take a pair of s. eyes   91:12
Sparks: Ashes and s.   214:4
  like s. among the stubble   29:34
  s. fly upward   25:29
Sparrow: fall of a s.   189:26
  'I,' said the S.   159:4
  My lady's s.   58:25
  soul of Philip S.   217:7
  s. hath found her an house   170:13
Sparrows: five s.   33:13
Spartan: remnant of our S. dead!   51:20
Spartans: Go, tell the S.   217:4
Speak: did he stop and s.?   44:13
  Even while we s.   109:3
  I s. of the things   169:18
  it cannot s.!   56:8
  Let him now s.   168:9
  might have been supposed to s.   51:25
  mouths, and s. not   171:13
  my hint to s.   204:22
  neither s. they   171:13
  nor tongue to s.   131:20
  O! couldst thou s.   183:4
  Of comfort no man s.   206:14
  one to s.   233:8
  only s. right on   194:12
  s. daggers   188:21
  s. each other in passing   134:9
  S. in French   57:16
  S., Lord   24:37
  S. no more   189:1
  S. not when the people   180:15
  S. of me as I am   205:20
  s. of something   246:10

s., or die!   190:34
S. softly   176:18
S. the speech   188:7
s. the tongue   247:1
s. true   226:17
s. when he is spoken to   221:11
S. when you're spoken to!   58:15
s. with their enemies   171:23
S. ye comfortably   28:11
  that can s. so well   141:11
  to s. one's mind   243:13
  To whom you s., of whom you s.   5:6
  two to s. the truth   233:8
  upon which it is difficult to s.   47:10
Speakest: Thou s. wiser   183:12
Speaketh the truth   168:27
Speaking: for their much s.   30:21
  in my s.   4:10
  s. prose   148:15
Speaks: S. a new scene   173:27
  s. to thee   70:3
Spear: Bring me my s.!   38:16
  knappeth the s.   169:21
Spears: sheen of their s.   52:9
  s. into pruninghooks   27:22
Species: female of the s.   125:5
Spectacle: no s. so ridiculous   136:23
Spectacles: s. of books   80:3
  With s. on nose   183:20
Spectator of mankind   1:7
Spectators: pleasure to the s.   137:1
Spectre-bark: Off shot the s.   65:15
Sped: O, he's s.   58:25
Speech: aspersion upon my parts of
    s.!   216:10
  Eyesight and s.   224:2
  freedom of s.   176:17
  make a s.   12:19
  malevolent s.   117:12
  manner of his s.   182:14
  nor power of s.   194:12
  Rude am I in my s.   204:20
  s. is a burning fire   224:2
  Speak the s.   188:7
Speeches: From all the easy s.   61:20
  Hodgepodge of all other s.   219:15
Speed: all thy winged s.   154:12
  at his bidding s.   147:17
  Be wise with s.   250:13
  Deliberate s.   232:8
  Good s. to thy youthful valour   236:21
  outstrip thy skiey speed   214:3
  safety is in our s.   82:20
  s. glum heroes   179:4
  S. his plough   59:19
  s. the going guest   165:11
  Whose s. was far faster   45:24
Spell: Who lies beneath your s.?   107:9
Speller: wuss s. I know of   238:19
Spells: dealer in magic and s.   93:31
  healing s.   179:11
Spem nos vetat incohare longam   108:17
Spend: hours that e'er I s.   48:19
  I would s. my life   115:12
  of what we yet may s.   85:5
  s. our midday sweat   173:24
Spending: Getting and s.   249:5
Spenser: by Chaucer, or S.   118:4
  sweet S.   247:18
Spent: all passion s.   147:11
  how my light is s.   147:17
  night is far s.   35:14
  s. and maimed   123:18
  s. its novel force   228:6
Sphere: cheering the elevated s.   47:14
  in the world's storm-troubled s.   41:13
  s. of our sorrow   215:13
  s. of private life   141:20
Sphere-born harmonious sisters   147:13

Spheres: as the restless S.   139:10
Driv'n by the s.   235:11
ever-moving s.   138:14
S. of action   132:2
S. of influence   7:8
start from their s.   186:7
Spherical: body is perfectly s.   130:18
Spice: s. of wit   221:22
Sugar and s.   158:14
very s. of life   70:16
Spices: woodbine s.   228:20
Spick and span-new   49:25
Spicy: s. nut-brown ale   144:17
though the s. breezes   101:16
Spider: said a s. to a fly   111:18
s.'s touch   164:16
Spiders: Weaving s.   203:11
Spies: come not single s.   189:11
we were God's s.   196:6
Spill: all germens s.   195:4
Spin: great world s. for ever   228:14
neither do they s.   30:28
Passions s. the plot   142:4
Sit by the fire and s.   155:9
Spinis de pluribus una   108:13
Spinners: long-legg'd s.   203:11
Spinning by the fire   176:11
Spires: dim-discover'd s.   67:13
excepting its s.   153:11
her dreaming s.   12:1
What s., what farms   111:5
Ye distant s.   98:5
Spirit: anointing S.   172:11
Be thou, S. fierce   214:4
before that s. die   221:24
Blessed be the poor in s.   30:11
body did contain a s.   190:23
Caesar's s.   193:21
clear s. doth raise   145:1
delighted s.   200:23
Eternal s. of the chainless mind!   51:9
every pure and wise s.   82:21
expense of s.   212:1
Follow your s.   191:9
fruit of the S.   36:7
gentlier on the s. lies   228:17
God is a S.   34:2
Hail to thee, blithe S.!   215:3
haughty s. before a fall   26:20
I commend my s.   33:42, 169:9
I will pour out my s.   29:22
in thy holy S.   168:4
Is a bold s.   206:2
is a troubled s.   169:28
motions of his s.   202:13
my s. hath rejoiced   32:37
no s. can walk   185:4
Not of the letter, but of the s.   36:1
of a master s.   148:8
pard-like S.   213:7
perturbed s.!   186:18
Pipe to the s. ditties   120:19
present in s.   35:15
received the S. of bondage   35:7
renew a right s.   169:27
Sing it with a s.   249:7
slumber did my s. seal   245:14
s. bloweth and is still   11:17
s. from on high   65:21
s. giveth life   36:1
s. in my feet   213:13
S. in the inner man   36:9
s. indeed is willing   32:21
s. is too deeply laden   215:11
S. of adoption   35:7
S. of Delight!   215:7
S. of Night!   213:20
s. of the Lord bloweth   28:13
s. of the Lord shall rest   28:1

s. shall return   27:8
stab my s.   221:24
This gay s.   230:14
To be strengthened..by his S.   36:9
vexation of s.   26:36
whether a good s. or a bad?   12:20
With a joyful s.   230:5
worship him in s.   34:2
worser s.   212:4
yet a s. still   248:5
Spirits: By our own s.   247:19
Come, you s.   197:15
Pluck up thy s.   150:5
S. are not finely touch'd   200:13
s. from the vasty deep   190:17
s. of just men   147:6
taketh..seven other s.   31:24
that keeps up a wife's s.   89:12
Which like two s.   212:4
Would ruffle up your s.   194:13
Spirit-stirring drum   205:10
Spiritual: against s. wickedness   36:14
inward and s. grace   168:2
Spiritus: Veni, Sancte S.   130:5
Spite: And, s. of pride   164:17
cursed s.   186:19
S. of cormorant   196:13
Spleen: excite your languid s.   92:22
Splendid: fallen a s. tear   228:20
How s. in the morning   86:6
men with s. hearts   42:7
s. and sterile Dolores   224:5
Whither, O s. ship   41:8
with how s. stars   86:10
Splendour: full of life, and s.   47:14
lone s.   121:8
Pavilioned in s.   96:18
s. falls on castle walls   229:10
s. in the grass   246:13
s. of a sudden thought   43:16
steep in his first s.   249:4
Split: s. on a pal   128:26
s. the ears of the groundlings   188:7
to make all s.   203:3
tongue shall be s.   158:4
Spoil: s. the child   49:26
that s. the vines   27:17
Spoiling her nice new clothes   156:12
Spoils: He never s. the child   107:2
s. of the enemy   138:7
s. shrunk to this   193:18
s. were fairly sold   136:12
stratagems, and s.   202:13
Spoke: a s. among your wheels   19:18
less he s.   173:13
moved and s.   161:15
s. not a word of sorrow   245:6
s. with a certain what-is-it   245:1
that s. the vacant mind   95:5
Spoken: mouth of the Lord hath s. it   28:12
never have s. yet   61:24
of thee are s.   154:2
speak when he is s. to   221:11
Speak when you're s. to!   58:15
When the lips have s.   213:16
word s. in due season   26:19
words of love then s.   150:1
Spoon: a runcible s.   131:9
Is worth a silver s.   3:15
ran away with the spoon   155:17
Spoons: we counted our s.   82:17
with coffee s.   81:17
Sport: all the s. is stale   123:18
For 'tis the s.   189:5
kill us for their s.   195:18
never kill for s.   88:10
see the children s.   246:12
s. of kings   222:13
S. that wrinkled Care derides   144:13

Sport (cont.)
To see such s. 155:17
To s. with Amaryllis 145:1
Sported on the green 218:12
Sports of love 118:12
Sportsman: fit to be called a s. 222:14
Sporus: Let S. tremble 165:7
Spot: barren s. 53:13
for each one s. 127:18
in a rural s.! 112:6
On a s. that's always barred 92:9
Out, damned s.! 199:28
reach the S. 86:3
Tip me the black s. 221:2
Spotless: Is s. reputation 206:2
Spots: leopard [change] his s.? 29:6
sunny s. of greenery 66:14
Spout till you have drench'd 195:4
Sprat: Jack S. could eat no fat 156:5
Spread: fame soon s. around 69:28
Her clothes s. wide 189:18
her fan s. 68:17
not good except it be s. 14:22
When the evening is s. out 81:14
Spreading of the hideous town 150:14
Spree: out on the s. 125:7
Spring: can S. be far behind? 214:4
darling of the S.! 245:16
direful s. 106:15
flowers that bloom in the s. 92:14
found in the s. to follow? 224:7
full of the s.? 224:7
have melted into s. 41:15
hounds of s. 223:28
in the Fire of S. 84:17
In the S. a livelier iris 228:5
In the S. a young man's fancy 228:5
In the s. time 184:12
No S., nor Summer beauty 77:4
O s. of Bandusia 109:24
perennial s. of all prodigality 47:7
Pierian s. 164:9
plants did s. 18:12
sister of the s. shall blow 214:1
s. begins 223:29
s. of light 65:2
s. of love 210:1
s. out of human suffering 246:13
S. Thou up within my heart 241:11
Sweet lovers love the s. 184:12
Sweet: 104:7, 152:6
with s. rain 81:23
year's at the s. 44:24
Springs: Beside the s. of Dove 248:3
no bitter s. 124:18
O faintly, gentle s. 117:10
take from seventy s. 110:15
Three beauteous s. 211:13
water at those s. 184:20
Spring-time: In s. from the Cuckoo-
bird 248:8
Sprites: And, sweet s. 208:9
I have one of s. 210:3
Sprouting despondently 81:20
Sprung: and Phoebus s.! 51:17
s. from my only hate! 207:18
whence he s. 180:6
Spur: Fame is the s. 145:1
I have no s. 198:4
s. my dull revenge! 189:6
Spurns that patient merit 187:13
Spurr'd boldly on 79:10
Spurs: Let the boy win his s. 81:3
Now s. the lated traveller 199:7
that s. too fast 206:6
Spy: letters for a s. 127:10
S. a knave in drinking 180:19
that ever you did s. 111:18
to s. out the land 24:14

Squamous, omnipotent, and kind 42:2
Square: All his dealings are s. 99:7
in 'ollow s. 125:2
Squat: Being urban, s. 42:8
Squeak and gibber 185:3
Squeaking: Shrieking and s. 44:19
Squeeze: s. a right-hand foot 58:14
s. out of a lemon 90:2
Squire: And the S., and Lady Susan 100:3
Bless the s. 74:2
many a s. 17:11
Squire Widdrington: as ever was S. 79:21
Stab my spirit 221:24
Stabb'd me to the heart 89:7
Stable-place sufficed 177:10
Stables are the real centre 212:15
Stacks: all ready in s. 93:32
Staff: By his cockle hat and s. 189:8
rod and s. me comfort still 181:8
rod and thy s. comfort me 169:2
s. of faith 174:13
s. of my age 201:20
s. of this bruised reed 25:22
your s. in your hand 24:5
Stag: A runnable s. 72:12
Stage: actor leaves the s. 207:3
agree on the s. 216:3
All the world's a s. 183:20
at its first s. 162:9
daily s. of duty 123:1
daughter on the s. 69:9
his hour upon the s. 200:4
mellow glory of the Attic s. 11:14
s. but echoes back 116:28
traffic of our s. 207:14
well-trod s. 144:19
wonder of our s.! 118:4
Stages: his s. may have been 215:18
Stagger like a drunken man 171:8
Stagnant: fen of s. waters 247:7
Stain: many a s. 70:22
of the world's slow s. 213:8
Stain'd: I s. the water clear 39:8
Stains: Innumerable of s. 120:4
S. the white radiance 213:10
Stair: As I was going up the s. 141:17
Staircase wit 76:2
Stairs: kicked down s. 48:1
threw him down the s. 155:16
Stake: honour's at the s. 189:7
s...in such a glorious institution 47:3
s. in the country 244:16
tied me to a s. 200:8
tied to the s. 195:16
To the thumbscrew and the s. 230:3
Stale: all the sport is s. 123:18
nor custom s. 182:16
s., flat, and unprofitable 185:11
Stalk: Half asleep as they s. 100:4
Stalking-horse: folly like a s. 184:15
s. to error 40:5
Stalky: Uncle S. 128:24
Stalled ox 26:18
Stalwart: six s. lancers 243:1
Stamp: but the guinea's s. 48:16
Stamping: went s. about 57:1
Stamps o'er his Head 85:1
Stand: above the mast did s. 65:12
By uniting we s. 76:1
Come, s. beside my knee 14:4
done all, to s. 36:14
glorious Angels always s. 152:8
Here a little child I s. 104:16
here I s. 195:5
How beautiful they s.' 102:11
I s. and look at them 242:14
I s. at the door 37:15
must s. the course 195:16
only s. and wait 147:17

s. a tip-toe   192:4
s. alone, and think   122:5
s. face to face   124:13
S. in the desert   214:5
s. like greyhounds   191:9
S. not upon the order of your
    going   199:10
s. on your head   56:16
s. out of my sun   76:4
S. up!—s. up for Jesus!   80:8
still doth s.   211:13
to s. and stare?   72:13
Standard: glorious s. launch   54:6
Standest: s. meekly by   154:12
    whereon thou s. is holy   24:1
Standfast: Mr. S.   46:21
Standing: S. on earth   146:20
    s. on this pleasant lea   249:5
    S., with reluctant feet   133:23
    thou art s.   111:14
Stands: And s. about the woodland
    ride   110:15
    goal s. up   111:4
    s. in Elgin's place   78:23
    s. the Church clock   42:9
    Where he s.   45:3
    with patience he s.   134:2
Stanley: Here S. meets   136:1
Stans pede in uno   110:10
Star: Against the morning s.   213:12
    bright particular s.   182:7
    Bright s.   65:16, 121:8
    catch a falling s.   77:16
    constant as the northern s.   193:16
    desire of the moth for the s. 215:13
    Fair as a s.   248:3
    glittering like the morning s. 47:14
    Hitch your wagon to a s.   83:2
    like a falling s.   146:9
    like a sinking s.   230:14
    O eastern s.!   183:4
    our life's S.   246:11
    seen his s. in the east   30:1
    s. of peace return   54:8
    s. of stars   73:26
    s. of their house   237:9
    s. or two beside   65:22
    s. to every wandering bark   211:16
    s. to steer her by   141:2
    Sunset and evening s.   226:6
    Teucer's s.   108:19
    There was a s. danced   204:8
Starboard: Eigg on the s. bow   221:21
Star-cross'd lovers   207:13
Stare: all the world would s.   69:30
    to stand and s.?   72:13
Staring: sings the s. owl   196:20
Starred: night's s. face   122:4
    On a s. night   142:1
Starry: and s. skies   52:12
    on a s. night   246:8
    s. heavens above me   119:10
    s. heavens above that plain   233:4
    wide and s. sky   221:23
Stars: amid a crowd of s.   250:11
    at the s...he looked   142:1
    continuous as the s.   247:4
    cut him out in little s.   208:1
    Far beyond the s.   235:7
    how splendid s.   86:10
    in the beauty of a thousand s. 138:13
    is not in our s.   193:11
    kinship with the s.   142:2
    like s. on the sea   52:9
    Look at the s.!   107:16
    looking at the s.   243:16
    one [sees] the s.   130:3
    Owl looked up to the S.   131:6
    Praise Him, all ye s.   122:24

puts the S. to Flight   84:15
scale the s.!   236:21
S. are setting   85:9
s. are shining bright   213:13
s. began to blink   247:16
s. in her hair   177:15
s. in their courses   24:28
s. move still   138:14
s. rush out   65:15
sun, moon, and s.   40:8
true as the s. above   4:8
western s.   230:15
When the morning s. sang   25:42
Whilst all the s. that round her   1:13
    burn
    with s. to see   221:15
    you chaste s.!   205:15
Star-scattered on the Grass   86:3
Star-shine at night   221:17
Star-spangled banner   123:7
Start: and s. a wing!   232:10
    lose, and s. again   125:15
    s. some game   101:11
    s. the world along   249:7
    Straining upon the s.   191:9
    than to s. a hare   190:8
    Would s. and tremble   228:20
Started: first s. to my mind   90:12
    s. at the intelligence   219:2
    who s. that morning   91:25
Starts: and the Caravan s.   85:9
    Was everything by s.   79:8
Starve: let his wife s.   212:20
Star-y-pointing pyramid?   147:12
State: all were for the s.   136:12
    change my s. with kings   210:13
    complicated s. of mind   92:21
    done the s. some service   205:20
    dreadful s.   73:27
    errands for the Ministers of S. 91:10
    harm come to the s.   63:23
    his S. is Kingly   147:17
    I am the S.   134:17
    in his dismembered s.   110:11
    in its worst s.   160:13
    in that s. of life   168:1
    last s. of that man   31:24
    my outcast s.   210:13
    my s...sings hymns   210:13
    O Ship of S.!   133:13
    of a middle s.   164:18
    of our blood and s.   216:24
    of the fair s.   188:6
    parlous s.   184:4
    saved the s.   83:5
    Scoffing his s.   206:15
    S. in wonted manner keep   117:11
    s. of both his universities   234:3
    This is the s. of man   192:14
    traduc'd the s.   205:20
    vessel of the s.   215:16
    with idle s.   97:4
    worth of a S.   142:23
Stately: A s. pleasure-dome   66:14
    full of s. views   125:8
    s. homes of England   102:11
Statements was interesting   234:18
States: many goodly s.   121:9
Statesman: chemist, fiddler, s.   79:8
    S., yet friend to truth!   164:25
    witty s.   55:7
Station: At the cross her s.   233:21
    best rank and s.   185:21
    post of honour is a private s.   1:5
    too big for his s.   225:1
Stationary: nothing is s.   103:15
Stations: our proper s.   74:2
    Sloane Square and South Ken-
        sington S.   91:25

Statue: Where the s. stood 247:17
Statues: s. on the terraces 125:8
Stature: Her s. tall 51:10
s. of my soul 142:3
Status quo: restored the s. 219:21
Stay: here I s. 137:14
Not making a s. 104:13
O! s. and hear 209:5
'O s.', the maiden said 133:18
On it may s. his eye 103:21
S. me with flagons 27:15
S., s., until the hasting day 104:10
where de old folks s. 87:11
Will you not s. 105:14
Steadfast: I were s. as thou art 121:8
Steadfastness: With s. and careful
truth 124:17
Steady: Slow and s. 133:5
S., boys, s. 88:18
S. the Buffs 128:22
Steal: break through and s. 30:23
in which I s. 51:7
silently s. away 133:15
s. away your hearts 194:11
S. from his figure 211:13
s. my thunder! 73:13
Thou shalt not s. 64:8, 167:15
Stealing: from picking and s. 167:34
S. and giving odour! 209:2
Steals: Who s. my purse 205:4
Stealth: Do good by s. 165:13
good action by s. 129:15
Stealthily and perpetually 41:7
Steam: snorting s. 150:14
Steamer: in a s. from Harwich 91:24
Steamers: where are you going to,
all you Big S. 124:15
Steamy column 70:18
Steed: Farewell the neighing s. 205:10
his s. was the best 180:8
Steeds: fiery-footed s. 207:32
His s. to water 184:20
Steel: All shod with s. 246:5
bares his s. 93:20
lock'd up in s. 192:7
more than complete s. 139:15
nor s., nor poison 199:4
tipped with s. 178:12
with his brandish'd s. 197:4
with hoops of s. 185:21
Steel-true and blade-straight 221:19
Steep: more beautifully s. 249:4
No towers along the s. 54:7
s. and thorny way 185:20
when life's path is s. 109:10
Steep-down gulfs of liquid fire! 205:18
Steeped in liquid perfumes 108:18
Steeples: And still the s. hum 111:1
drench'd our s. 195:4
In s. far and near 110:19
pews and s. 61:13
Steer: cannot s. a middle course 141:9
star to s. her by 141:2
to glory we s. 88:18
Stem: moulded on one s. 203:15
out of the s. of Jesse 28:1
Stenches: two and seventy s. 66:9
Step: at one s. 119:2
first s. that is difficult 72:15
one s. enough 153:15
only one s. from the sublime 152:2
revealed in her s. 236:6
s. is short 96:11
There is but one s. 78:14
with free s. 109:8
Stephen: On the Feast of S. 152:13
Stepped in so far 199:12
Stepping-stones: rise on s. 227:16
Steps: beware of desp'rate s. 70:1

how sad s. 216:30
s. of the Sun 39:7
Thy s. retrace 93:17
wandering s. and slow 146:25
whose last s. 213:15
With s. solemn 243:1
Sterile: splendid and s. Dolores 224:5
s. promontory 187:4
Stern: Mull was a-s. 221:21
S. daughter 245:19
Stern-faced: Two s. men 106:21
Stick: carry a big s. 176:18
I shall s. 201:4
scratched with a s. 125:1
s. and a string 116:12
S. close to your desks 93:11
S. to your party 76:12
to s. in his coat 44:9
Sticking in a big mud hole 87:9
Sticking place: to the s. 198:7
Stickit minister 180:16
Sticks: like s. of sealing-wax 74:4
Pick up s. 157:5
Stiff: pale, s., naked 99:3
S. in opinions 79:8
s. upper lip 58:18
that he'd be frozen s. 96:14
very s. and proud 58:6
Stiffen the sinews 191:8
Stiffnecked people 24:8
Stile: against a crooked s. 158:5
merrily hent the s.-a 210:7
Stiles: Lame dogs over s. 123:15
Still: Be s. then 169:21
He won't sit s. 105:18
I love thee s. 70:15
is lying s.! 249:4
is not to sit s. 126:4
lie s. and slumber 239:11
over the s. stream 121:7
see thee s. 198:9
she is my country s. 62:7
ship was s. 218:18
sit s. for once 105:17
Sit thou s. 180:15
s., sad music 248:19
s. small voice 25:14
voice that is s.! 225:15
Stilled at even 177:15
Stillness: a solemn s. holds 97:8
in solemn s. lay 181:10
modest s. 191:8
soft s. and the night 202:11
Stilly: in the s. night 150:1
Stimulate the phagocytes 212:13
Sting: Cold doth not s. 152:6
O death, where is thy s.? 35:31
prick and s. her 186:13
s. is not so sharp 184:2
Where is death's s.? 135:17
worst s. of misery 40:1
Stings: stinks and s. 165:8
there were s. in their tails 37:19
Stinks: several s.! 66:9
s. and stings 165:8
Stir: Is not to s. 189:7
No s. in the air 218:18
No s. of air 120:7
Now s. the fire 70:18
s. it and stump it 93:24
To s. men's blood 194:12
Stirred: we have not s. 45:1
Stirring dull roots 81:23
Stirrup: Betwixt the s. and the ground 53:11
I sprang to the s. 44:5
Stirs: blood more s. 190:8
Stitch: S.! s.! s.! 107:3
Stock: I am but a barren s. 82:5
public s. of harmless pleasure 116:22

Stockings: who commended thy
  yellow s. 209:13
Stocks: hurt in the s. 171:5
  worshipped s. and stones 147:16
Stole: He s. the tarts 57:12, 157:15
  s. in and out 222:6
Stolen: s. be your apples 112:5
  s. my soul away! 234:6
  s. sweets 63:9, 112:5
  s. the scraps 196:17
  S. waters are sweet 26:11
Stoles: nice white s. 17:12
Stomach: army marches on its s. 9:1
  hath no s. 192:4
  heart and s. of a king 82:9
  wine for thy s.'s sake 36:28
Stomacher: Enthrals the crimson s. 104:11
Stomachs: march on their s. 181:18
Stone: against a s. 170:20
  At his heels a s. 189:9
  Bows down to wood an' s. 101:16, 125:3
  by a mossy s. 248:3
  conscious s. 82:15
  first cast a s. at her 34:6
  flung the S. 84:15
  give him a s.? 30:34
  legs of s. 214:5
  raised not a s. 245:7
  sound of iron on s. 73:6
  s. that is rolling 234:16
  S. walls do not a prison 134:19
  s. which the builders refused 171:15
  This precious s. 206:7
  Turn but a s. 232:10
  Two things stand like s. 96:6
  Under this s. 83:12
  untroubled heart of s. 54:4
  Water like a s. 177:9
Stones: cold gray s. 225:14
  in piled s. 147:12
  move the s. of Rome 194:13
  over the s. 154:8
  Sermons in s. 183:9
  s. would immediately cry out 33:35
  that spares these s. 212:5
  throw s. at him 212:14
  with murderous s. 66:9
  With rocks, and s. 245:14
  worshipped stocks and s. 147:16
  You blocks, you s. 193:9
Stony: o'er the s. street 51:1
Stood: I s. tip-toe 120:9
  never have s. upon his legs 74:4
  s. against the world 194:6
  s. awhile in thought 57:14
  s. from everlasting 234:2
  They s. 111:11
  We have s. alone 96:7
  where I had s. before 213:15
  Where the Statue s. 247:17
Stoop: unable to s. 43:12
Stoops: She s. to conquer 95:23
  s. to folly 95:21
Stop: did he s. and speak 44:13
  Let's s. somebody 103:16
  Must have a s. 190:22
  s. a hole 189:21
  S.; look; listen 235:3
  S. thine ear 180:15
  S. up the access. . to remorse 197:15
  then s. 57:13
  when the kissing had to s.? 45:11
Stoppeth one of three 65:4
Stops: runs back or s. 45:5
  seem to know my s. 188:17
Store: amid thy s.? 119:18
  were to increase his s. 106:14
Storied: Can s. urn 97:13
  s. windows 144:9

Stories: s. of savage men 46:28
  tell sad s. 206:15
Storm: directs the s. 1:3
  fled away into the s. 120:5
  On the wings of the s. 96:19
  pilot that weathered the s. 54:17
  pitiless s. 195:8
  rides upon the s. 70:5
  S. and stress 128:27
  S. in a Teacup 22:18
  s. of life 241:8
Storm-beaten: far distant, s. ships 137:18
Storm-clouds brood 130:20
Stormed: we French s. Ratisbon 44:6
Storms: all thy waves and s. 169:16
  Ere the winter s. begin 2:13
  sudden s. are short 206:6
Storm-troubled: world's s. sphere 41:13
Stormy: Across the s. water 54:1
  from the s. blast 239:14
  on a s. day 131:5
  port after s. seas 219:10
  While the s. winds 54:6
Story: Ere their s. die 100:4
  love to hear the s. 143:3
  midst of the s. 108:1
  My s. being done 204:23
  name great in s. 52:7
  no reason to doubt the s. 76:13
  old in s. 229:10
  Still is the s. 136:16
  s. of our days 174:15
  s. shall the good man teach 192:4
  Tell me the old, old s. 99:13
  that is another s. 128:20, 220:16
  To tell my s. 190:3
  what is all this s. about? 220:18
Stout: so s. a gentleman 190:23
Stoutly: I s. maintain 95:20
Strachan: Stood waiting for Sir
  Richard S. 4:14
Straight: And s. was a path of gold 44:16
  crooked shall be made s. 28:12
  grown full s. 139:2
  Lay them s. 157:5
  make his paths s. 30:4
  make s. in the desert 28:12
  s. out of the Ark 217:15
Strain: angels sung this s. 232:13
  Big Bow-Wow s. 181:5
  That s. again! 209:2
  which s. at a gnat 32:8
Strained: is not s. 202:5
Straining upon the start 191:9
Strains: Soul-animating s. 248:2
  s. of unpremeditated art 215:3
  S. unheard 109:16
Strait: how s. the gate 102:14
  Into a desperate s. 141:9
  S. is the gate 31:2
Strand: I walk'd along the S. 116:11
  India's coral s. 101:15
  Let's all go down the S. 58:20
  Maypole in the S. 41:2
  on a foreign s.! 180:6
  outer Chelsea to the S. 126:14
  to a barren s. 117:3
Strange: How s. it seems 44:13
  original, spare, s. 107:15
  read s. matters 198:1
  Sing. .in a s. land? 171:28
  something rich and s. 208:12
  s. and high 140:2
  s., and unnatural 186:8
  s. as it may seem 233:6
  s. that men should fear 193:14
  stranger in a s. land 23:37
  through s. seas 247:17
  truth is always s. 52:2

Strange (cont.)
'twas s. 204:23
with s. bedfellows 208:14
Strangeness: some s. in the propor-
tion 14:8
Stranger: a s., and ye took me in 32:16
I, a s. and afraid 111:9
S. than fiction 52:3
s. that is within thy gates 167:10
wilful s. 221:16
Strangers: careth for the s. 172:5
to entertain s. 36:37
Strangled: And s. her 44:27
last king s. 142:15
who s. Atahualpa 136:20
Stratagems, and spoils 202:13
Stratford atte Bowe: schole of S. 60:12
Straw: of wretched s. 145:3
Take a s. 181:14
to find quarrel in a s. 189:7
Strawberries: feed upon s. 155:11
s. grow in the sea? 156:15
Straw-built: from the s. shed 97:11
Stray: never learn'd to s. 98:1
never taught to s. 164:14
you'd fondly s. 89:15
Strayed: erred, and s. 166:8
thou hast surely s. 93:17
Stream: by haunted s. 144:19
By mount, and s. 102:9
ever-rolling s. 239:14
freezing s. below 213:11
have their s. and pond 41:19
in the glassy s. 189:18
meadow, grove, and s. 246:7
Of a rude s. 192:14
over the still s. 121:7
Still glides the S. 245:17
s. runs fast 150:2
talk was like a s. 166:5
Trailing in the cool s. 11:24
Streamers: fan spread and s. out 68:17
s. waving 89:30, 147:5
Streams: As s. meander 149:5
crystalline s. 214:2
for cooling s. 225:6
Gilding pale s. 211:2
s. in the firmament 138:14
S. like the thunder-storm 51:4
Street: by jostling in the s. 38:15
from s. to s. 38:12
howling down the s. 158:13
o'er the stony s. 51:1
she-bear coming up the s. 86:19
Streets: cried in the s. 150:17
Darkens the s. 146:5
fight. . in the s. 62:21
publish it not in the s. 24:47
s. are paved with gold 67:19
Strength: Christ is thy s. 149:1
from s. to s. 170:14
hath shewed s. 32:38
impulse of thy s. 214:3
my s., and my redeemer 168:31
our castle's s. 200:2
our hope and s. 169:20
Phoebus in his s. 210:8
rather find s. 246:13
shall renew their s. 28:15
so shall thy s. be 24:24
s. is as the s. of ten 230:8
s. of the hills 170:22
s. then but labour 170:18
s. which in old days 230:15
S. without hands to smite 224:1
thou ordained s. 168:22
To have a giant's s. 200:18
tower of s. 207:11, 229:1
what a s. and majesty 151:14

Strengthened: To be s. with might 36:9
Strengtheneth: which s. me 36:24
Strenuous: whose s. tongue 120:21
Stress: and the s. of need 237:5
Storm and s. 128:27
Stretch: His kingdom s. 239:13
sands s. far away 214:7
s. forth thy mighty hand 111:13
S. him out longer 196:12
Stretched: things which he s. 234:17
Strewn: mirrors of the sea are s. 86:10
Stricken: I was a s. deer 70:17
Strict in his arrest 189:28
Stride: at one s. comes the dark 65:15
Striding: s. behind you 81:24
S. the blast 198:4
Strife: each eager s. 117:1
ignoble s. 98:1
in ceaseless s. 154:13
none was worth my s. 129:20
s. is o'er 165:21
s. of truth with falsehood 135:3
to party s. 245:20
Wherein the graver had a s. 118:3
Strike: afraid to s. 165:6
clock will s. 138:14
S. flat 195:4
S. it when your powder's running
low 153:4
s. not awry 150:5
S. through 79:24
Strikes: as s. the Player 85:11
deep sound s. 50:23
String: a stick and a s. 116:12
Harp not on that s. 207:10
long yellow s. 44:27
was chewing little bits of s. 21:3
Strip his sleeve 192:4
Stripe for stripe 24:7
Stripes: cut 'is s. away 125:2
with his s. we are healed 28:21
Stripling: What delicate s. 108:18
Strive: need'st not s. 64:6
To s., to seek 230:15
Striven: ne'er have s. 214:3
Stroke: piston s. 150:14
s. of death 116:22
to the tune of flutes kept s. 182:15
wit bear a s. 234:10
Strokes: amorous of their s. 182:15
Strong: as s. as links of iron 47:6
battle to the s. 27:3
Be s. and of a good courage 24:26
blood is s. 181:7
but s. in will 230:15
evidence is very s. 233:9
fifty thousand s. 249:7
men be so s. 170:18
out of the s. 24:31
Quit you like men, be s. 35:32
smell too s. of the lamp 220:15
still going s. 3:18
s. man after sleep 148:10
s. man armed 33:10
wants that little s. 106:12
Stronger: little wings are s. 230:7
s. than lions 24:48
Strongest: reason of the s. 86:18
Stronghold: safe s. our God is still 135:12
Strove: A little still she s. 51:12
I s. with none 129:20
s. to rule the roast 172:20
that s. with gods 230:15
Strow: that s. the brooks 146:4
Strown: gifts of God are s. 101:16
let there be s. 209:9
Struck: I s. him 161:15
I s. the board 103:19
s. all of a-heap 216:7

s. one chord   172:23
    women should be s.   69:17
Struggle: confused alarms of s.   11:9
    Gods..s. in vain   179:13
    s. naught availeth   64:10
Struggles: life of s.   237:5
Struggling for life   113:22
Struts and frets his hour   200:4
Strutting: peacocks s. by   125:8
    strain of s. Chanticleer   208:9
Stubble: like sparks among the s.   29:34
Stubborn generation   170:11
Stubbs butters Freeman   176:4
Stuck: s. all with yew   209:9
    S. in my throat   198:12
Studied in his death   197:13
Studies serve for delight   14:24
Study: much s. is a weariness   27:9
    to s. a long silence   240:12
Stuff: I s. my skin   221:25
    Is there not sad s.?   90:8
    listen..to such s.?   56:17
    such volumes of s.!   130:17
    that perilous s.   200:1
    What s. 'tis made of   201:6
Stuffed: Cleanse the s. bosom   200:1
Stultitiam: Misce s. consiliis   110:7
Stumbles: old horse that s.   100:4
Stumbling on melons   140:6
Stump: stir it and s. it   93:24
Stumps: fought upon his s.   213:5
    roller, pitch, and s.   130:2
Stung: s. by the splendour   43:16
    Was s. to death   96:15
Stupidity: an excess of s.   114:17
    With s. the gods..struggle   179:13
Sturm und Drang   128:27
Stygian: In S. cave forlorn   144:10
Style: any s. of writing untouched   115:11
    in a high s.   12:19
    just the proper s.!   176:10
    S. is the dress of thought   241 20
    s. is the man himself   45:22
    s. was grand   67:22
    vaunting s. of a soldier   78:26
Style: Le s. est l'homme même   45:22
    le s. naturel   161:3
Stylish marriage   72:1
Subdue: it [force] may s.   46:29
    to chasten and s.   248:19
Subject: a proper s. [religion]   61:12
    Every s.'s duty   191:13
    every s.'s soul   191:13
    get back to the s.   9:8
    no s. of which any poet ever
        writ   80:4
    rift of your s.   122:11
    s. to the same diseases   201:27
    Unlike my s.   61:3
Subjects: My s. for a pair of carved
        saints   206:16
    where s.' feet   206:16
Sublime: and eye s.   146:16
    bards s.   133:14
    In his simplicity s.   228:25
    make our lives s.   133:27
    My object all s.   92:8
    One step above the s.   160:11
    sense s.   248:19
    s. and the ridiculous   160:11
    s. to the ridiculous   96:11, 152:2
Sublime: Du s. au ridicule   152:2
Sublimities: one of his s.   129:18
Sublunary: Dull s. lovers' love   77:20
Submerged Tenth   40:7
Submission: with admiring s.   83:1
Submit: Must he s.?   206:16
    never to s.   145:15
Subscrib'd: These articles s.   68:19

Subscription: owe me no s.   195:5
Subsequent: And the s. proceedings   101:4
Subsistence only increases   138:1
Substance: lose the s. by grasping at
        the shadow   1:18
    persons of some s.   244:16
    s. of a book   128:29
    Wasted his s.   33:21
    would give all his s.   27:20
Substances: sightless s.   197:15
Substantial: not s. things   216:24
Subtile: mathematics [make men] s.   14:27
Subtle ways   82:13
Subtopia   151:10
Suburbs: In the south s.   209:15
Succeed: you don't s.   105:4
Success: his surcease s.   198:3
    is s. in life   161:11
    no very lively hope of s.   218:3
    of the bitch-goddess S.   113:1
    'Tis not in mortals to command s.   1:4
    true. is to labour   221:6
Successful crimes   79:26
Successive: his s. journeys run   239:13
Succour: calls not for such s.   236:12
    died to s. me!   16:7
Such: not any s. here   78:27
Suck: s. forth my soul   138:12
    s. melancholy out of a song   183:14
Suck-a-Thumb: naughty little S.   106:4
Sucked: But s. on country pleasures   77:7
    I s. the blood   65:14
Sucker born every minute   18:14
Sucking dove: as any s.   203:4
Suckle fools   204:27
Suckled in a creed outworn   249:5
Sucklings: babes and s.   168:22
Sucks: as a weasel s. eggs   183:14
    s. the nurse asleep?   183:4
    Where the bee s.   208:20
Sudden: of a s. came the sea   44:16
    s. and quick in quarrel   183:20
Suddenly: fade away s.   170:17
Sue: not born to s.   206:3
Suez: somewheres east of S.   126:15
Suffer: s. and die   236:1
    S. me to come to thee   241:12
    s. the slings and arrows   187:13
    S. to redeem our loss   5:17
    than one innocent s.   38:8
    To s. woes   215:1
    ye s. fools gladly   36:3
    you must s.   109:22
Sufferance: In corporal s.   200:21
    s. is the badge   201:18
Suffered: I have..s. greatly   230:13
Suffering: Doing or s.   146:1
    Out of human s.   246:13
Sufferings: saith my s.   139:11
    To each his s.   98:9
Suffice: would alone s.   137:3
Sufficeth: old rule s. them   247:20
Sufficient: S. is Thine Arm alone   239:14
    s. unto oneself   149:3
    S. unto the day   30:29
    'Tis s. to say   80:6
Sugar: I must s. my hair   57:10
    S. and cream   155:11
    S. and spice   158:14
Suggest: do s. me still   212:4
Suit: certainly not s. me   92:22
Suiting: whole function s.   187:11
Suits: trappings and the s. of woe   185:10
Sullen: Knocked on my s. heart   221:24
    small but s. horn   67:12
    surly s. bell   211:7
Sulphur: roast me in s.!   205:18
Sulphurous and thought-executing
    fires   195:4

Sultan: caught the S.'s Turret   84:15
   How S. after S.   84:22
Sultry: where the climate's s.   51:11
Sum: saved the s. of things   111:11
   s. of earthly bliss   146:21
Summer: after many a s.   230:10
   After s. merrily   208:20
   all on a s. day   57:12
   All on a s.'s day   157:15
   Are s. songs   210:5
   as on a s.'s day   120:7
   beauty's s. dead   211:13
   compare thee to a s.'s day?   210:12
   crown'd with s. sea   227:3
   Eternal s. gilds them   51:17
   eternal s. shall not fade   210:12
   from his s. dreams   214:2
   guest of s.   198:2
   In a s. season   130:1
   in a s.'s day   203:5
   issuing on a s.'s morn   146:22
   It was a s. evening   218:12
   last rose of s.   149:18
   Made glorious s.   207:4
   murmur of a s.'s day   11:23
   Noon to dewy eve, A s.'s day   146:9
   nor S. beauty   77:4
   Saint Martin's s.   192:5
   Since s. first was leavy   204:9
   Singest of s.   121:2
   s. eves   144:19
   S. has set in   67:6
   S. is icumen in   7:9
   s. rain   221:24
   S. with flowers that fell   224:1
   s.'s lease   210:12
   s.'s wonderland   154:16
   'Twas on a s.'s evening   194:7
   when the s. is shed?   224:7
Summer-dried fountain   180:2
Summers: many s. in a sea of glory   192:14
   thousand s. are over   224:7
   three s.' pride   211:13
Summertime on Bredon   110:19
Summit: from the s. of these pyramids   152:1
Summits: snowy s. old in story   229:10
Summon: I s. up remembrance   [211:1
   s. up the blood   191:8
   To s. his array   136:8
Summons: s. thee to heaven or to hell   198:10
Summum bonum   63:13
Sun: all men 'neath the s.!   124:18
   as the s. went down   124:2
   At the going down of the s.   38:2
   aweary of the s.   200:6
   Before the rising s.   239:14
   beneath the S.   127:24
   better thing under the s.   26:43
   bloody S. at noon   65:12
   Born of the s.   219:7
   by the time this s. be set   230:4
   by this s. of York   207:4
   candle to the s.   216:28, 250:14
   clear as the s.   27:19
   Close to the s.   226:9
   courts of the s.   61:18
   early-rising s.   104:10
   ere the set of s.   197:2
   ere the s. was set   234:22
   except their s., is set   51:17
   go out in the mid-day s.   69:8
   golden apples of the s.   250:10
   heat o' the s.   184:22
   Juliet is the s.   207:20
   just as the s. was rising   4:4
   kiss of the s. for pardon   99:2
   labour..under the s.?   26:34

lake-reflected s.   214:9
Laughed in the s.   42:4
lie a-basking in the s.   93:23
maketh his s. to rise   30:19
nothing like the s.   212:3
Now the s. is laid to sleep   117:11
of the burnished s.   201:19
of the maturing s.   119:17
owes no homage unto the s.   42:22
rising of the s.   7:17
sitting in the s.   218:12
So that the s. shall not burn thee   171:17
soft was the s.   130:4
Somewhere the s. is shining   100:16
stand out of my s. a little   76:4
steps of the s.   39:7
S. and moon, rejoice   122:24
S. came up   65:6
s. climbs slow   64:10
s. does not set   179:12
s. go down upon your wrath   36:12
s. has gone in   217:13
s. looked over the mountain's rim   44:16
s., moon, and stars   40:8
s. more beautifully steep   249:4
s. never sets   154:9
s. of Austerlitz   152:3
S. of my soul!   122:16
s. of suns   73:26
s. which makes a dust   162:8
S.'s rim dips   65:15
tabernacle for the s.   168:30
tired the s.   69:3
to live i' the s.   183:15
to s. myself   84:10
to the garish s.   208:1
too much i' the s.   185:8
travelled a short while towards the s.   219:7
under the s.   26:35
unruly S.   77:18
when the s. rises   38:13
when the s. set   51:19
when the s. was low   53:15
where e'er the s.   239:13
where the s. came peeping   107:1
With the dying s.   40:13
with the setting s.   146:9
with the s.   123:1
Sunbeam in a winter's day   80:18
Sunburnt mirth!   121:3
Sunday: Buried on S.   158:2
   chicken in his pot every S.   102:18
   Here of a S. morning   110:19
   killing of a mouse on S.   41:3
Sunder: knappeth the spear in s.   169:21
Sunflower! weary of time   39:7
Sung: angels s. this strain   232:13
   Sappho loved and s.   51:17
   song of praise be s.   165:21
   s. of Border chivalry   180:4
   their dirge is s.   67:15
Sunk: s. beneath the wave   70:9
   s. low, but mounted high   145:4
   S. though he be   145:4
Sunless: Down to a s. sea   66:14
Sunnier: on a s. deep   213:12
Sunny: Afric's s. fountains   101:15
   s. pleasure-dome   66:15
   s. spots of greenery   66:14
Sunny Jim: called him S.   99:12
Suns: blest by s. of home   42:11
   light of setting s.   248:19
   process of the s.   228:11
   S. may set   58:26
   S., that set   118:13
Sunset: sail beyond the s.   230:15
   S. and evening star   226:6

s. of life 53:16
s. ran 44:2
there's a s.-touch 43:9
Sunshine: breezes and the s. 53:12
s. holiday 144:16
S. is a glorious birth 246:8
thunder and the s. 230:15
Sup: Jove's nectar s. 117:19
s. before we go 155:8
Superbos: debellare s. 236:18
Supererogation: Works of S. 172:13
Superfluity: barren s. of words 89:4
Superior: I am a most s. person 6:9
Superman: teach you the s. 154:6
Supernatural soliciting 197:10
Supersede the last fashionable novel 137:5
Superstition: s. in avoiding s. 15:1
s. is the religion 47:16
Superstitions: to end as s. 112:11
Superstitious: ye are too s. 34:42
Supped full with horrors 200:3
Supper: breakfast, s., dinner 44:22
come home to s. 74:7
eat my s. there 249:3
Sings for his s. 156:13
Suppers: nights and s. of gods! 110:13
Supplication: throws his s. to the
  rose 86:6
Supplied: can never be s. 95:4
Support: help and s. 81:5
raise and s. 145:11
s. us all the day long 153:12
Supports the people 116:16
Surcease: his s. success 198:3
Sure: but of this be s. 146:1
I'm perfectly s. 56:16
I'm s.—s.—s. 73:10
make assurance double s. 199:21
s. in all His ways 153:14
Surfeit: no crude s. 144:2
Surfeiting: that, s., the appetite 209:2
Surge: murmuring s. 195:19
s. and thunder 130:1
Surged: how the silence s. 73:6
Surly: hear the s. sullen bell 211:7
of a s. Tapster 85:14
Surmise: with a wild s. 121:9
Surpassed: something to be s. 154:6
Surprise: gave rise to no little s. 17:13
Oh! what a s.! 64:15
Surprised: s. to find it done 114:19
you don't feel s. 91:25
Surrender: do not s. 53:10
No terms except unconditional s. 97:1
we shall never s. 62:21
Survey: I s. the wondrous Cross 239:16
monarch of all I s. 70:19
s. of all the world 190:22
Under this stone, Reader, s. 83:12
Survival of the fittest 219:3
Susan: black-ey'd 89:30
Susceptible: A rather s. Chancellor! 91:18
Suspected: are always s. 133:6
Suspended: held the sky s. 111:11
Suspension: willing s. of disbelief 67:5
Sussex: shall the S. songs be sung 22:1
S. by the sea! 127:18
Sutor: Ne supra crepidam s. *iudicaret* 163:13
Swaggering could I never thrive 209:20
Swagman: Once a jolly s. 161:12
Swain: frugal s. 106:14
Swains: all our s. commend her? 210:2
Swallow: and s. a camel 32:8
and the s. a nest 170:13
come before the s. 210:8
O tell her, S. 229:14
S., my sister 224:7
s. twitt'ring 97:11
to lap and to s. 242:20

Swallowed: easier s. than a flap-
  dragon 196:17
Swallows: saw the s. 142:5
Swamp: to botanize in the s. 62:2
Swan: dies the s. 230:10
every goose a s. 123:18
like a black s. 119:4
Sweet S. of Avon! 118:9
Swanee Ribber: Way down upon de
  S. 87:11
Swans: All his own geese are s. 238:8
s. of others are geese 238:8
S. sing before they die 66:13
Swap horses 132:11
Swarm: took the s. 96:15
Swarry: a friendly s. 75:30
Swat: Akond of S.? 131:14
Swath: Spares the next s. 119:18
Sway: a little s. 80:18
prevail'd with double s. 95:7
this sceptred s. 202:5
Thy posterity shall s. 69:20
Swayed: rod of empire might have s. 97:14
Swear: And s. no where 77:17
by yonder blessed moon I s. 207:24
I dare s. you have 216:16
s. an eternal friendship 54:16
s. eternal friendship 217:16
s. not by the moon 207:24
Sweat: Agony and bloody s. 166:24
blood, toil, tears and s. 62:20
muck of s. 96:2
our midday s. 173:24
s. of thy face 23:16
They do not s. 242:14
To grunt and s. 187:13
Sweats: and the bloody s. 243:6
S. in the eye of Phoebus 191:15
s. to death 190:11
Sweeping: come s. by 144:8
in s. triumph 76:23
Sweeps: Who s. a room 103:22
Sweet: actions of the just smell s. 216:25
at his own s. will 249:4
both s. things 40:8
flowers so s. 214:2
Heard melodies are s. 120:19
How charmingly s. 131:7
how it was s.! 43:15
How s. and fair 238:4
How s. the moonlight 202:11
How s. the name of Jesus 154:1
how s. their mem'ry 70:2
if Today be s.! 85:8
is a s. thing and becoming 109:18
life is very s., brother 40:8
look s. upon the seat 72:1
love is s. for a day 224:10
Nature's s. restorer 250:15
nothing half so s. 149:14
O so s. 118:11
Oh s. content! 72:18
red s. wine of youth 41:16
Sensations s. 248:17
Sleep is s. 46:13
soft, and s. 140:3
Stolen waters are s. 26:11
S. air blow soft 105:2
S. and low 229:9
s. and twenty 209:5
s. are the uses of adversity 183:9
S. Auburn! 95:3
S. day, so cool 104:6
s. disorder in the dress 104:11
s. influences of Pleiades 25:43
S. is every sound 229:19
s. little doll 123:17
s. o' the year 210:5
S. seventeen 225:19

Sweet (cont.)

S., sour	107:15
S. spring	104:7
s. though in sadness	214:4
s. to hear the watchdog's honest bark	51:13
s. to remember	236:5
that s. golden clime	39:7
There is a lady s. and kind	7:22
'Tis not so s.	209:2
to forget one's wisdom is s.	110:7
with smile so s.	235:4
with smiles so s.	137:15
would smell as s.	207:23
Sweeten: to s. my imagination	195:21
Sweeter: Anything to me is s.	106:5
mountain sheep are s.	162:1
O s. than the berry	89:8
s. far to me	66:6
s. than the marriage-feast	66:6
S. thy voice	229:19
Sweetest: Our s. songs	215:5
Possibly s.	53:9
s. hours that e're I spend	48:19
to the s. girl	244:7
Sweetheart: Tray, Blanch and S.	195:15
Sweeting: pretty s.	209:5
Sweetly: how s. flows	104:15
Nimbly and s.	198:2
so s. were forsworn	201:3
s. questioning	104:1
Sweetness: came forth s.	24:31
every s.	139:11
folds the lily all her s.	229:17
linked s.	144:19
may, with s.	144:9
s. and light	12:6, 223:1
waste its s.	97:15
With s. fills the breast	58:23
Sweets: get s. into your list	112:4
nectared s.	144:2
Stolen s.	63:9, 112:5
S. to the sweet	189:23
where s. compacted lie	104:7
Swell: its voluptuous s.	50:23
Swelled up, to rest	77:6
Swelling: a s. wisibly	75:23
serious s. into bombast	80:3
to the s. act	197:9
Swept: and I s. the floor	93:10
Empty, s. and garnished	31:23
S. it for half a year	57:21
Swift: beautiful and s.	213:7
race is not to the s.	27:3
S. be thy flight!	213:20
S. to its close	135:16
With s., slow	107:15
Swifter than eagles	24:48
Swim: that s. on bladders	192:14
Swims into his ken	121:9
Swine: feed the s.	155:11
pearls before s.	30:32
Swing: to s. a cat	74:13
Swings: pulls up on the s.!	59:12
S. backwards and forwards	105:18
Swiss: No S.	174:11
Swoln with wind	145:3
Swooned: She nor s.	229:15
Swoop: At one fell s.?	199:27
Sword: are s. and fire	226:18
brave man with a s.!	243:5
die on mine own s.?	200:9
embrace a s.	134:20
eye, tongue, s.	188:6
father's s.	149:15
first drew the s.	63:25
hides a s.	191:5
His s. was in the sheath	70:11
lift up s. against nation	27:22

mightier than the s.	136:2
my soul from the s.	169:1
My s., I give to him	46:22
my S. sleep in my hand	38:16
never stained thy s.	107:10
peace, but a s.	31:15
shall perish with the s.	32:23
Smote him with the edge of the s.	24:15
s. outwears its sheath	52:14
s., the mace	191:15
they that take the s.	32:23
took his vorpal s.	57:14
unsmote by the s.	52:11
with s. will open	202:17
Swords: beat their s. into plowshares	27:22
Keep up your bright s.	204:19
s. must have leaped	47:14
Swore: And s. the dog had lost his wits	95:15
jested, quaff'd, and s.	78:22
'twas not my soul that s.	83:11
Sworn a solemn oath	48:22
Swound: like noises in a s.!	65:8
Sycamore: nightingale in the s.!	221:22
Syllable: last s. of recorded time	200:4
Sylvia: Who is S.?	210:2
Symbols: Huge cloudy s.	122:4
Symmetry: s. of shelves	129:7
thy fearful s.?	39:1, 4
Sympathize: so to s.	145:7
Sympathy: In the primal s.	246:13
s. with hopes and fears	215:4
Symphony: Her s. and song	66:15
Syrups: drowsy s. of the world	205:9
System: faithful to their s.	137:12
Systems: Our little s. have their day	227:5

T

T: to a T	83:19
Tabernacle: shall dwell in thy t.	168:27
t. for the sun	68:30
Table: behave mannerly at t.	221:11
from their masters' t.	31:31
My t. thou hast furnished	181:8
prepare a t. before me	169:2
rich man's t.	33:27
round about thy t.	171:24
set the t. on a roar?	189:20
sit still..at the t.	105:17
t. of green fields	191:16
T. of Kindred	172:16
who has made you a bad t.	114:11
Table Bay: going to T.!	124:11
Tables: marriage t.	185:13
on the t. of young ladies	137:5
Taboo'd: repose is t.	91:23
Tackle: and t. trim	147:5
Taffy was a Welshman	158:3
Tail: At such a little t. behind	20:17
beginning with the end of the t.	56:21
Improve his shining t.	56:13
not pull her t.	156:3
rat without a t.	197:5
thereby hangs a t.	205:1
treading on my t.	57:7
up by the t.	133:9
waving his wild t.	128:17
where his t. came through	218:16
where the t. came through	66:10
Tails: bring their t. behind them	156:9
cut off their t.	158:10
stings in their t.	37:19
t. you lose	71:4
Taisez-vous!	9:9

Take: Ah, t. the Cash   84:20, 84:21
  believe, and t. it   82:4
  don't ask me to t. none   74:21
  Freely let me t. of Thee   241:11
  Rise, t. up thy bed   34:3
  T. and break us   102:17
  T. away these baubles   71:10
  T. her up tenderly   106:21
  t. into the air   121:6
  t. my pilgrimage   174:13
  t. those lips away   201:3
  T. up and read   13:4
  That they should t.   247:20
  to t. my last voyage   105:10
  to t. under my wing   92:15
  We t. the Golden Road   86:8
  Wilt thou yet t. all   224:9
Taken: Lord hath t. away   25:26
  shall be t. away   32:15
  t. at the flood   194:19
  t. away the key   33:12
  t. from the French   215:21
  t. my fun   126:7
  when t.   67:24
Takes: and him that t.   202:5
  No fairy t.   185:4
  t. my man Friday with me   72:17
  t. your choice   173:4
Taking his rest   245:5
Taking-off: damnation of his t.   198:4
Talbot: Warwick and T.   192:4
Tale: by t. or history   203:2
  I could a t. unfold   186:7
  must tell the t.   179:19
  my t. of woe   84:2
  of yourself that t. is told   110:8
  or adorn a t.   117:3
  round unvarnish'd t.   204:21
  sad t.'s best for winter   210:3
  same t. repeat   246:10
  schoolboy's t.   50:21
  t. of a tub   150:9, 240:10
  t. that is told   170:18
  t. to tell of the hardihood   179:19
  t. told by an idiot   200:4
  Tell t., tit!   158:4
  thereby hangs a t.   183:17, 208:6
  twice-told t.   52:4, 193:5
  With a t. forsooth   217:2
Talent: T. does what it can   142:13
  t. instantly recognizes genius   78:18
  that one T.   147:17
Talents: career open to t.   151:18
  ministry of all the t.   7:19
Tales: t. of wild Cashmere   244:10
  tell old t.   196:6
Talk: have out his t.   115:15
  I long to t.   77:13
  In after-dinner t.   228:22
  leave the Wise to t.   85:6
  should t. like little fishes   96:4
  t. but a tinkling cymbal   14:14
  T. him out of patience   205:2
  t. of culture   117:5
  t. o' gin an' beer   125:11
  t. of his horse   201:11
  t. of many things   57:22
  t. of morality   80:20
  t. of some strict Testing   85:14
  t. of wills   206:14
  t. too much   79:7
  t. too wise   125:14
  t. was like a stream   166:5
  t. with crowds   125:16
  t. with them too   196:6
  t. with you   201:13
  To t. about the rest   105:12
  to t. on for ever   101:10
Talked: but t. like poor Poll   89:1

He [Coleridge] t. on for ever   101:10
  louder he t. of his honour   82:17
  t. of their Raphaels   95:19
  worse than being t. about   243:20
Talking: he will be t.   204:14
  man who is always t.   222:12
  T. of Michelangelo   81:15
  tired the sun with t.   69:3
  will still be t.   204:6
Talks: way it t.   174:19
Tall: divinely t.   226:8
  Her stature t.   51:10
Tamburlaine, the Scourge of
  God   139:14
Tame: Be not too t. neither   188:8
Tamed: For t. and shabby tigers   105:13
Tangere: Noli me t.   34:29
Tangled web we weave   180:12
Tangles of Neæra's hair   145:1
Tannenbaum: O T., O T.   179:16
Taper: or with t. light   193:6
Tapster: of a surly T.   85:14
Tara: through T.'s halls   149:13
Tarantara   93:20
Ta-ra-ra-boom-de-ay   179:9
Tarbaby: what he call a T.   100:18
Tar-barrel: black as a t.   57:18
Tardy: raise the t. bust   117:2
Tarpaulin: Wrap me up in my t.
  jacket   243:1
Tarquin: great house of T.   136:8
Tarried: too long we have t.   131:7
Tarry: do not t.!   53:17
  T. a while   155:8
Tarsus: ship of T.   147:5
Tartarly: So savage and T.   52:6
Tarts: made some t.   57:12, 157:15
  stole the t.   57:12, 157:15
Task: at their priestlike t.   121:8
  common t.   122:14
  dedicated to the great t.   132:8
  delightful t.   232:14
  hard be the t.   58:18
  He who has begun his t.   108:7
  long and heavy t.   236:1
  long day's t.   182:18
  never will be our t.   146:1
  t. of happiness   221:24
  thy worldly t.   184:22
  weary t. fordone   204:3
  what he reads as a t.   114:14
  What is our t.?   90:3
Task-Master: my great T.'s eye   147:15
Tasks in hours of insight   11:17
Tassie: fill it in a silver t.   48:18
Taste: hand is not able to t.   203:18
  His soul shall t.   120:24
  Judge of t.   224:18
  Let me t. your ware   157:19
  must create the t.   249:6
  sans t.   183:20
  T. not   164:9, 180:15
  undoubtedly wanted t.   238:6
  Well of Life to t.   85:9
  whose mortal t.   145:9
Tasted: deliberately t. two worms   219:17
  Some books are to be t.   14:25
Tastes: he that t. woman   89:20
Tasting of Flora   121:3
Tat: Die T. ist alles   94:14
Tattered and torn   158:8
Tatters: tear a passion to t.   188:7
Tattle: give no doit for t.   58:26
Taught: if thou wouldst be t.   99:6
  is he born and t.   249:10
  t. us how to die   233:17
  t. us how to live   233:17
Tavern: as a good t.   115:7
  There is a t. in the town   8:1

Tax: hateful t. 116:14
  I t. not you 195:5
Taxation without representation 159:21
Taxes: nothing..certain, except..t. 88:4
Te Deum laudamus 10:6
Tea: all have t. 157:13
  and sometimes t. 165:3
  is there honey still for t.? 42:9
  some sipping t. 247:15
  some'll swallow t. 141:1
Teach: Doth t. us all 139:10, 202:5
  gladly t. 60:14
  T. him how to live 165:20
  t. his son 192:4
  T. me half the gladness 215:6
  T. me, my God 103:21
  T. me to live 123:2
  t. the morals of a whore 114:2
  t. the rest to sneer 165:6
  t. the torches to burn 207:17
  t. the young idea 232:14
  T. us delight 124:18
  T. us to bear the yoke 124:17
  t. you more of man 248:15
  t. you the superman 154:6
  t. you to drink 185:12
  Thy heart must t. alone 99:9
  what you t. them first 114:16
Teacher: for the t.'s sake 106:11
  Nature be your t. 248:14
  t. did reply 99:5
Teaches: he who cannot, t. 212:24
Teaching: follow mine own t. 210:10
  precedence of t. 148:11
Teacup: Storm in a T. 22:18
Team: Is my t. ploughing 111:3
Tear: Cancel and t. to pieces 199:6
  charm thee to a t. 244:10
  droppe the brynie t. 60:7
  from your eyelids wip'd a t. 183:19
  no longer t. his heart 223:27
  Perhaps 'twill cost a sigh, a t. 17:8
  shed a bitter t. 57:21
  some melodious t. 144:20
  splendid t. 228:20
  to a dog to t. 127:2
  to t. a cat in 203:3
  To t. each other's eyes 239:7
Tears: all thy Tears wash out a
    Word 85:12
  bitter t. to shed 69:2
  blood, toil, t. and sweat 62:20
  brother's t. 59:3
  crocodile's t. 49:10
  home, in a flood of t. 75:29
  if you have t. 194:7
  in the mist of t. 232:7
  kiss'd again with t. 229:7
  Like Niobe, all t. 185:11
  look through my t. 232:11
  mine own t. 196:1
  mortality her t. 236:7
  Nothing is here for t. 147:10
  shall wipe away all t. 37:18, 26
  silence and t. 52:16, 17
  smiles, the t. 150:1
  sow in t. 171:21
  stood in t. 121:6
  t. are in my eyes 141:6
  T., idle t. 229:13
  T. in his eyes 187:11
  t. no bitterness 135:17
  t. shall drown the wind 198:4
  that shed t. when they would
    devour 15:6
  though our t. 213:6
  Time with a gift of t. 224:1
  time with my salt t. 117:10
  to draw t. from me 107:20

To remember with t.! 2:18
  too deep for t. 246:14
  Was far too freely moved to t. 21:5
  Weep thy girlish t.! 239:5
  with a flood of t. 74:7
Tease: fleas that t. 22:3
  thus t. me together 89:21
Teases: Because he knows it t. 56:19
Teatray: Like a t. in the sky 56:24
Tedious: as t. as a twice-told tale 193:5
  prattle to be t. 207:3
  Returning were as t. 199:12
Teeming: glean'd my t. brain 122:3
Teems: that t. with hidden mean-
    ing 93:28
Teeth: cast into my t. 194:18
  cast me in the t. 169:17
  children's t. are set on edge 29:12
  Sans t. 183:20
  skin of my t. 25:33
  weeping and gnashing of t. 31:6
  With thy sharp t. 183:4
Teetotaller: only a beer t. 212:11
Tekel: Mene, Mene, T., Upharsin 29:18
Tell: cannot t. a lie 239:2
  canst not t. whence it cometh 33:50
  His praise forth t. 123:5
  kiss and t. 68:8
  makes me cry to t. 106:1
  never t. why 93:5
  not easy to t. 115:9
  not to t.! 66:8
  T. it not in Gath 24:47
  T. me, pretty maiden 99:8
  t. of saddest thought 215:5
  t. sad stories 206:15
  t. the towers therof 169:23
  t. thee everything 58:11
  t. you three times 56:1
  that I cannot t. 218:14
  Which angel voices t. 143:3
  why I cannot t. 42:16
  Will no one t. me 248:9
  would t. one anything 243:25
  you must not t. us 75:26
Telleth: one day t. another 168:29
Telling: I am t. you 242:1
  t. a man he was wrong 64:15
Tells: t. the jest 123:11
  t. thee I come 67:3
Temper: t. of heroic hearts 230:15
  To t. man 159:22
Temperance: beget a t. 188:7
  fruit of the spirit is..t. 36:7
Temperate: and more t. 210:12
Tempers: God t. the wind 220:12
Tempes: Where fairer T. bloom 213:12
Tempest: t...whirlwind of passion 188:7
  While the t. still is high 241:8
Tempests: looks on t. 211:16
Tempest-tost: shall be t. 197:6
Tempestuous: In the t. petticoat 104:11
  world's t. sea 81:2
Temple: his train filled the t. 27:27
  in the T. of Jupiter 90:12
  t. of delight 120:24
Temple-bells: an' the t. they say 126:11
  t. are callin' 126:15
Temple-haunting martlet 198:2
Temples: t. of his Gods? 136:9
  theatres, and t. 249:4
Tempora mutantur 10:7, 160:10
Temporal: force of t. power 202:5
  things t. 166:36
Tempt: not t. the Lord 30:9
  T. not a desperate man 208:3
  t. with wand'ring feet 146:12
  to t. my Lady Poltague 21:19
Temptation: day of t. 170:25

except t. 243:15
last T. 81:21
lead us not into t. 30:22
Many a dangerous t. 103:4
maximum of t. 212:25
to get rid of a t. 243:21
under t. to it 133:8
Temptations: in spite of all t. 93:14
Tempted: one thing to be t. 200:15
  T., and yet undefiled 218:6
  t. by a private whim 21:19
  When your fathers t. me 170:26
Tempts: Not all that t. 98:4
Tempus: fugit inreparabile t. 237:8
  nec defensoribus istis T. eget 236:12
  T. abire tibi est 108:13
  T. edax rerum 160:8
Ten: for t. guilty persons 38:8
  from t. to four 113:7
  it's now t. o'clock? 143:4
  T. to make 153:6
Tenantless: graves stood t. 185:3
Tend: t. the homely 145:1
  to th' appointed place we t. 79:28
Tended: however watched and t. 134:1
Tender: and t. to offend 104:5
  felt the t. passion 89:23
  Scarf up the t. eye 199:6
  t. for another's pain 98:9
  t. is the North 229:14
Tenderly: Take her up t. 106:20
Tenderness: Thanks to its t. 246:14
Tenders: shoal of fools for t. 68:17
Tenement of clay 79:5
Ten-foot: wid a t. pole 87:9
Tennyson: Carlyle, T., Browning 173:20
Tenor: noiseless t. of their way 98:1
1066, And All That 181:16
Tent: I rede you t. it 48:29
  little t. of blue 243:4
  summer's evening in his t. 194:7
Tenth: Submerged T. 40:7
Ten-thirty: I rise at t. 100:13
Ten thousand times ten thousand 2:14
Ten-times-barr'd-up chest 206:2
Tents: fold their t. 133:15
  t. of Kedar 27:12
  t. of ungodliness 170:15
  towards the Grecian t. 202:9
Tereu, Tereu 18:12
Terewth: light of T. 73:26
Term: I served a t. 93:10
Termagant: o'erdoing T. 188:7
Terminological inexactitude 62:18
Terms: in t. too deep for me 92:21
  reduced to her lowest t. 130:14
Terraces: statues on the t. 125:8
Terrible: t. and dear 213:20
  t. as an army 27:19
  t. aspect 191:8
Terrifies: eternal silence..t. me 161:5
Terrify: they t. me 240:21
Territorial: last t. claim 105:8
Terror: any t. by night 170:19
Terse: nervous and t. 78:17
Tertium Quid: and a T. 128:25
Tess: ended his sport with T. 100:10
Test: there lies the t. 62:10
Testimonium animae naturaliter
  Christianae 231:9
Testing: strict T. of us 85:14
Tête d'Armée 152:4
Teucro: Nil desperandum T. duce 108:19
Text: any t. of Scripture 241:19
  My English t. is chaste 90:13
  neat rivulet of t. 216:15
Thames: clear T. 150:14
  every drop of the T. 48:2
  not of Gennesareth, but T.! 232:10

stripling T. 11:24
Sweet T. 219:13
T. was the noblest river in Europe 1:10
upon the banks of T. 118:9
Thane of Fife 199:29
Thank: God, I t. thee 33:33
  I t. whatever Gods 102:13
  Now t. we all our G. 71:14, 244:17
  t. the Lord 53:12
  t. with brief thanksgiving 224:6
  T. you, madam 137:4
  t. you 'most to death 234:19
Thanked: Now, God be t. 42:10
Thankless child! 195:4
Thanks: For this relief much t. 185:2
  Give t. unto him 169:8
  give t. unto thee 172:2
  T. to its tenderness 246:14
Thanksgiving: thank with brief t. 224:6
  With proud t. 38:1
That: And t...Is T. 143:8
Thatch: house with deep t. 22:1
Thatch-eaves: round the t. run 119:17
Thaw: T., and resolve 185:11
  T. not the frost 213:6
Theatre: As in a t. 207:3
  Her Aunt was off to the t. 21:10
  Idols of the T. 15:11
Theatres, and temples 249:4
Thebes: Presenting T. 144:8
Thee: for weariness of t. 77:15
  it tolls for t. 77:23
Theft: Property is t. 172:25
Theirs: And people came to t. 105:13
Them: begins with t. 119:5
  Is honoured for t. 41:6
  when you do call for t.? 190:17
Theme: imperial t. 197:9
Themes: on admired t. 139:11
Theorize before one has data 78:4
There: But Here or T. 85:11
  featly here and t. 208:9
  gone here and t. 211:15
  had I not been t. 240:14
  I would like to be t. 181:6
  Is there anybody t.? 73:4
  we seek him t. 159:13
  when she got t. 157:3
  you were not t. 103:1
Thereby: t. hangs a tail 205:1
  t. hangs a tale 183:17, 208:6
Therein: all that t. is 169:3
Thereon: But thou t. 117:19
Thermopylae: old man of T. 131:15
  to make a new T.! 51:20
Thick: Blood is t. 91:26
  dash through t. and thin! 69:25
  dash'd through t. and thin 79:10
  lay it on so t. 50:8
  Make the gruel t. 199:16
  make t. my blood 197:15
  Through t. and thin she follow'd 49:22
Thickens: Light t. 199:6
Thicket: leafy t. 131:3
Thick-ribbèd ice 200:23
Thickset: with t. fruit 177:8
Thief: Opportunity makes a t. 15:10
  Taffy was a t. 158:3
  t. of time 250:16
Time, you t. 112:4
Thieves: Fell among t. 33:6
  'Gainst knaves and t. 209:20
  where t. break through 30:23
Thigh: smote them hip and t. 24:31
Thimbles: sought it with t. 56:5
Thin: but water's t. 91:26
  dash through thick and t.! 69:25
  dash'd through thick and t. 79:10
  how t. and clear 229:11

Thin (cont.)
  over t. ice 82:20
  profligate, and t. 251:2
  t., but not too t. 13:14
  t. partitions 79:6
  t. red line 178:12
  Through thick and t. she follow'd 49:22
Thine: not my will, but t. 33:37
  She be only t. 140:3
  would not change for t. 117:19
Thing: any good t. come out of Nazareth? 33:48
  any good t. therefore that I can do 98:15
  any t. that is his 167:17
  Bad T. 181:19
  damned nice t. 240:14
  dearest t. he owed 197:13
  each t. met conceives delight 146:22
  English for a t. 57:16
  excels each mortal t. 210:2
  far, far better t. 75:34
  first t. we do 192:9
  good and joyful a t. 171:26
  greatest t. in the world 149:3
  how poor a t. is man! 72:3
  If I lack'd any t. 104:1
  ill-favoured t. 184:13
  is a dang'rous t. 164:9
  it is a gentle t. 65:23
  it is a glorious t. 93:16
  kills the t. he loves 243:5
  last t. civilized 142:12
  last t. I shall do! 160:17
  laugh at any mortal t. 51:22
  lovesome t. 42:17
  man hath no better t. 26:43
  many-splendoured t. 232:10
  most valuable t. 69:1
  never said a foolish t. 176:2
  no new t. under the sun 26:35
  one damned t. after another 111:20
  one t. is certain 85:6
  only good t. left to me 151:8
  only t. we have to fear 176:13
  play's the t. 187:12
  that extremely lovely t. 91:2
  T. became a trumpet 248:2
  t. it contemplates 215:1
  t. of beauty 120:1
  t. that hath been 26:35
  t. which is right 168:27
  this sort of t. 132:12
  Thou art the t. itself 195:12
  to every t. there is a season 26:38
  'twere no bad t. 66:13
  unattractive old t. 92:15
  very odd t. 73:7
  want of a t. 235:6
  was, however a Good T. 181:17
  What a little t. to remember 2:18
Things: affection on t. above 36:22
  all four-footed t. 61:16
  all other t. give place 89:29
  All t. are lawful 35:18
  all t. are not expedient 35:18
  All t. bright and beautiful 2:7
  all t. lovely 73:3
  all t. necessary 172:12
  all t. to all men 35:17
  All t. wise and wonderful 2:7
  approve better t. 160:7
  believeth all t. 35:21
  better t. and leave the worse 20:16
  bringer of new t. 230:13
  cared for none of these t. 34:44
  devourer of all t. 160:8
  do these t. in a green tree 33:38
  dreaming on t. to come 211:14

filled the hungry with good t. 32:38
  fine t. to be seen 61:23
  for dappled t. 107:14
  for the t. of itself 30:29
  former t. are passed away 37:26
  Glorious t. of thee 154:2
  Good t. of day 199:6
  Great t. are done 38:15
  I can do all t. 36:21
  I make all t. new 37:26
  I speak of the t. 169:18
  In all T. thee to see 103:21
  in all t. ye are too superstitious 34:42
  in simple t. 124:18
  insists on the other t. 154:11
  light of t. 248:14
  looked unutterable t. 233:1
  lord of all t. 164:19
  lose not the t. eternal 166:36
  love all beauteous t. 41:6
  mania of owning t. 242:14
  more t. change 119:13
  mystery of t. 196:6
  nor t. present 35:10
  not substantial t. 216:24
  Of unseen t. above 99:13
  one of the blessedest t. 75:32
  Prove all t. 36:24
  put away childish t. 35:22
  read the causes of t. 237:7
  remembrance of t. past 211:1
  remove those t. 77:20
  Shape of T. to Come 241:4
  slimy t. 65:14, 20
  Such good t. 167:1
  T...are what they are 49:15
  t. be done decently 35:23
  t. creeping 171:4
  t. remain 64:10
  t. that are Caesar's 32:7
  t. that are tender and unpleasing 14:11
  t. that go bump in the night 4:9
  T. unattempted 145:10
  t. which he stretched 234:17
  think on these t. 36:20
  this sorry Scheme of T. 86:1
  thousand, thousand slimy t. 65:20
  three t. which the public 107:5
  to higher t. 227:6
  to look at t. in bloom 110:15
  To see the t. thou dost not 195:22
  To talk of many t. 57:22
  two noblest of t. 223:1
  unhappy, far-off t. 248:9
  what t. they be 214:9
  What t. we have seen 19:9
  Who wondrous t. hath done 244:17
  with God all t. are possible 32:2
Think: comedy to those that t. 238:7
  do they t. we are? 62:25
  Double t. 159:17
  grieved my heart to t. 248:11
  Haply I t. on thee 210:13
  I sometimes t. 85:2
  I t. that I shall never see 123:8
  I t., therefore I am 73:15
  If you can t. 125:14
  little do you t. 160:19
  May sigh to t. 215:18
  not paid to t. 126:10
  often t. it's comical 91:21
  stand alone and t. 122:5
  t. foul scorn 82:9
  T., in this batter'd Caravanserai 84:22
  t. not well of me 244:18
  t. on these things 36:20
  t. thee Milton 251:2
  t., this heart 42:11
  t. to burst out 145:1

t. to wed it   182:7
t. which way   140:11
who greatly t.   164:5
Who t. too little   79:7
Thinkest: whom thou t.   77:9
Thinketh no evil   35:21
Thinking: ain't t. about it   234:4
high t.   247:8
in my t.   4:10
sittin' and t.   126:7
then to t.!   101:11
t. makes it so   187:2
T. nothing done   135:6
t. of the days that are no more   229:13
t. reed   161:8
t. what to say   57:15
Thinks: she t. o' me   126:11
when he t...full surely   192:14
Thin-spun: slits the t. life   145:1
Third Floor: Passing of the T.
   Back   113:9
Thirst: can raise a t.   126:15
t. that from the soul   117:19
which do hunger and t.   30:11
Thirsty: waters to a t. soul   26:25
Thirty: T. pieces of silver   32:18
wrong side of t.   223:12
This: All t. and heaven too   103:8
But who is t.   147:5
should come to t!   185:11
Thither: canst get but t.   235:8
Hither and t. moves   85:10
Thorn: figs grew upon t.   61:16
Oak, and Ash, and T.   127:24
on the virgin t.   203:1
one t. out of many?   108:13
snail's on the t.   44:24
t. in the flesh   36:4
Thorns: And to those t.   186:13
crackling of t.   26:39
crowned with t.   122:21
this crown of t.   45:15
t. of life   214:3
Thorny: steep and t. way   185:20
Thou: and T.   84:18
T. also   160:9
Thought: Adds to the t.   61:4
any unproportion'd t.   185:21
divine his real t.   51:16
dress of t.   241:20
Each t. on the woman   124:2
Every third t.   208:22
Heaven's t. was otherwise   236:11
honour's t.   191:5
I t. as a child   35:22
I t. of Chatterton   247:19
I t. so once   80:26
I took t.   112:12
In the light of t.   215:4
is his honest t.   249:10
long, long t.   133:24
mind of t.   119:10
never been t. of   76:23
no t. for the morrow   30:29
pale cast of t.   187:13
Perish the t.!   63:8
rear the tender t.   232:14
seas of t.   247:17
splendour of a sudden t.   43:16
stood awhile in t.   57:14
sweet silent t.   211:1
tell of saddest t.   215:5
than I had t.   78:9
they t. of dining   95:18
T. is free   208:16
t. of convincing   95:18
t. of the morrow   245:6
t.'s wildernesses   214:9
time for labour and t.   224:2

tire the night in t.   173:24
To a green t.   140:7
Two souls with but a single t.   99:9
uffish t.   57:14
utmost bound of human t.   230:14
very t. of Thee   58:23
We t. that it possibly could   245:13
wrought, and t. with me   230:15
Thought-executing fires   195:4
Thoughtless: hour of t. youth   248:19
Thoughts: are above my t.   71:7
Drive my dead t.   214:4
Give thy t. no tongue   185:21
gives..back the t.   42:11
Good t. his only friends   54:10
In the soothing t.   246:13
joy of elevated t.   248:19
make t. your aim   125:14
My t. are not your t.   28:25
of their masters' t.   139:11
rather than of t.!   122:8
sad t. doth clear   235:9
second and sober t.   103:5
so thy t., when thou art
   gone   215:10
that's for t.   189:14
t...come crowding in   80:5
t. of love   228:5
t. of men   228:11
t. that arise in me   225:14
T. that do often lie   246:14
'Unting fills my t.   222:14
Yet in these t.   210:13
Thousand: better than a t.   170:15
kiss me a t. times   59:1
One man in a t.   127:19
ten t. at thy right hand   170:19
t. doors   141:12
t. shall fall   170:19
Thousands: slain his t.   24:45
Thracian: For the T. ships   223:28
Thrall: Hath thee in t.!   120:14
Thrash: to t. the Spaniards too   78:25
Thread: Feels at each t.   164:16
Plying her needle and t.   107:3
Threadneedle Street: The Old
   Lady of T. in Danger   94:1
Threatening: presence of t. tyrant 109:19
Threatenings: breathing out t.   34:34
Three: at ten to t.?   42:9
Dukes were t. a penny   91:13
Though he was only t.   143:9
two or t. are gathered   166:17
Three-pipe problem   78:2
Threescore years and ten   110:15, 170:18
Threw: God t. him   138:10
They t. their caps   184:17
t. a pearl away   205:20
T. him down the stairs   155:16
Thrice: thou shalt deny me t.   32:19
T. is he armed   192:7, 213:4
T. welcome   245:16
Thrice-gorgeous ceremony   191:15
Thrift: T., t., Horatio!   185:13
Thrifty: housewife that's t.   216:19
Thrill: Glory's t. is o'er   149:13
Thrilling: voice so t.   248:8
Thrive: could I never t.   209:20
Now t. the armourers   191:5
Throat: mocking-bird's t.   242:12
or cut a t.   51:16
Stuck in my t.   198:12
Three times her little t. around   44:27
t. they cut   240:3
through their t.   171:13
to feel the fog in my t.   45:2
took him by the t.   205:20
undulating t.   21:22
Unto the sweet bird's t.   183:13

Throats: whose rude t.   205:10
Throne: Around the t. of God   152:8
  beats upon a t.   226:15
  he that sat upon the t.   37:26
  like a burnish'd t.   182:15
  Lord sitting upon a t.   27:27
  royal t. of kings   206:7
  shadow of Thy T.   239:14
  t. he sits on   191:15
  T. sent word to a T.   126:19
  up to the T.   128:7
Thrones, Dominations   146:19
Throng: swift Anapaests t.   67:2
  with the t.   77:27
Throstle: How blithe the t. sings!   248:14
Through and through   57:14
Throw: t. away the dearest thing   197:13
  t. it up into the air   181:14
  T. out the life-line   235:1
  T. physic to the dogs   200:1
  t. sand against the wind   38:17
  t. stones at him   212:14
Thrown: about the shoulders t.   104:11
  t. on her with a pitchfork   223:13
Throws: he t. his supplication   86:6
  T. aside his paint-pots   107:19
  t. himself on God   43:18
Thrush: t. and the jay   210:5
Thule: Ultima T.   237:4
Thumb: put in his t.   156:11
Thumbs: pricking of my t.   199:17
Thumbscrew: To the t. and the
    stake   230:3
Thunder: all-shaking t.   195:4
  burst of t. sound   102:8
  dawn comes up like t.   126:11
  deep t. clouds form   96:19
  In t., lightning   197:2
  steal my t.!   73:13
  surge and t.   130:1
  t. of the captains   25:44
  took the t.   230:15
Thunderbolt: like a t. he falls   226:9
Thunderbolts: oak-cleaving t.   195:4
Thunder-storm: Streams like the t.   51:4
Thurlow's answer   217:19
Thursday: T.'s child   156:17
  Took ill on T.   158:2
Thus: Why is this t.?   238:21
Thusness: reason of this t.   238:21
Thyme: wild t. blows   203:9
Thyself: love thy neighbour as t.
                                 24:12, 31:42
Tiber: father T.   136:14
Tickle: if you t. us   201:27
Tide: by the t. of Humber   140:11
  call of the running t.   141:3
  full t. of human existence   115:2
  such a t. as moving seems asleep   226:6
  t. in the affairs of men   194:19
  t. of pomp   191:15
  t. of times   193:20
  turning o' the t.   191:6
Tidings: Glad t. of great joy   225:9
  good t. of great joy   32:42
  that bringeth good t.   28:18
  t. of comfort and joy   4:11
Tie: in whose t.   104:11
  T. up my sleeves   112:8
Tied: t. me to a stake   200:8
  t. to the stake   195:16
Tierney: Mr. T., a great Whig
    authority   219:23
Ties which, though light as air   47:6
Tiger: action of the t.   191:8
  his t.'s heart   98:13
  master o' the T.   197:5
  one poor t.   173:12
  rode with a smile on a t.   8:4

smile on the face of the t.   8:4
  t.'s heart   192:11
Tiger-moth's deep damask'd wings   120:4
Tigers: tamed and shabby t.   105:13
Tight: and a bo'sun t.   91:3
  shoes were far too t.   131:3
  t. little Island!   73:20
Tile: Where did you get that t.   176:10
Tilled: hath t. his lands   248:10
Tills: Man comes and t.   230:10
Tilts up his chair   105:18
Timber: navy nothing but rotten
    t.   47:3
Timbuctoo: On the plains of T.   243:2
Time: abysm of t.   208:8
  age and body of the t.   188:10
  all of the olden t.   6:2
  all of the t.   132:10
  at the same t.   86:19
  Aunt Jane observed, the second
    t.   96:11
  bank and shoal of t.   198:3
  Before this t. to-morrow   152:18
  beguile the t.   198:1
  beyond space and t.   42:1
  bid t. return   206:13
  Bird of T.   84:17
  born out of due t.   35:24
  brief chronicles of the t.   187:9
  but for all t.!   118:7
  by T.'s fell hand   211:6
  common arbitrator, T.   209:1
  corridors of T.   133:14
  dear t.'s waste   211:1
  destroyed by T.'s devouring
    hand?   41:2
  devouring t.   196:13
  died from t. to t.   184:10
  envious T.   148:6
  Even such is t.   175:14
  files of t.   228:13
  first t. ever Caesar put it on   194:7
  for the t. of scorn   205:13
  good t. coming   137:11
  gracious is the t.   185:4
  gude t. coming   181:2
  had a glorious t.   79:9
  half as old as t.!   46:26
  hath seen God at any t.   37:10
  he said 'What's t.?'   43:17
  holy t. is quiet   246:15
  I shall achieve in t.   92:8
  in ancient t.   38:16
  in due t.   166:25
  in my t. to be a philosopher   81:7
  In the spring t.   184:12
  in the t. of their visitation   29:34
  it is high t.   35:14
  keep t. with my salt tears   117:10
  kill an admiral from t. to t.   237:11
  last syllable of recorded t.   200:4
  Love's not T.'s fool   211:16
  Made weak by t.   230:15
  many a t.   121:6
  may write at any t.   113:17
  never the t. and the place   44:15
  No t. like the present   138:3
  O Life! O t.!   213:15
  oars keep t.   150:2
  Old T. is still a-flying   104:14
  on the sands of t.   133:27
  Once upon a t.   128:25, 165:21
  one man in his t.   183:20
  peace for our t.   59:16
  piping t. of peace   207:5
  plenty of t. to win   78:25
  pretty ring t.   184:12
  productions of t.   39:18
  respect..of t.   209:6

seventh t. disobey'd | 161:15
slow t. | 120:18
some of the t. | 132:10
That, in our t. | 124:17
That T. and Fate | 85:4
that t. is money | 88:1
That t. may cease | 138:14
that wastes her t. | 238:4
thief of t. | 250:16
this t. forth | 171:18
till t. and times are done | 250:10
T. and the hour | 197:12
t. creeps along | 112:17
T. for a little something | 143:18
t. for labour | 224:2
t. for such a word | 200:4
t. for you to leave | 108:13
t. future | 81:10
t. has come | 57:22
T. hath..a wallet | 208:27
T. in hours | 235:11
t. is drawing near | 2:3
T. is flying | 237:8
T. is on our side | 94:2
t. is out of joint | 186:19
T. is slipping | 85:8
T. is the great physician | 76:17
T., like an ever-rolling stream | 239:14
T. makes ancient good | 135:4
t. of the singing of birds | 27:16
t. of this mortal life | 166:33
t. past | 81:10
T. present | 81:10
t. remembered | 223:29
t. runs | 138:14
T. shall moult away his wings | 222:8
t. shall throw a dart | 43:2
T., the churl | 109:3
T. the devourer | 160:8
t. to be born | 26:38
t. to die | 26:38
t. to every purpose | 26:38
t. when meadow | 246:7
t. which to us is uncertain | 20:2
t. will come | 76:5
T. will run back | 145:8
T. with a gift of tears | 224:1
T. y-lost | 60:30
T., you old gypsy man | 105:14
T., you thief | 112:4
t.'s fool | 190:22
T.'s noblest offspring | 22:16
T.'s wheel runs back | 45:5
T.'s winged chariot | 140:12
to t. thou grow'st | 210:12
unconscionable t. | 60:5
want to know the t. | 176:3
was the t. of roses | 106:19
We have no t. | 72:13
weary of t. | 39:7
whips and scorns of t. | 187:13
whirligig of t. | 209:19
witching t. | 188:20
world enough and t. | 140:11
Time-Machine | 241:5
Timeo Danaos et dona ferentis | 236:9
Times: ever lived in the tide of t. | 193:20
    fairy-tale of olden t. | 102:4
    In pious t. | 79:2
    mortal t. afford | 206:2
    old t., old manners | 95:24
    our t. are in His hand | 45:4
    O what t. | 63:17
    signs of the t. | 31:32
    tell you three t. | 56:1
    time and t. are done | 250:10
    T. change | 10:7, 160:10
    t. that try men's souls | 160:12
    t. will not mend | 160:20

Times: The T. has made many
    ministries | 15:18
Timor mortis conturbat me | 80:12
Tin: cheap t. trays | 140:21
    wid a pocket full of t. | 87:8
Tinged the eyelids | 161:9
Tinkling: a t. cymbal | 14:14, 35:20
Tinklings: And drowsy t. | 97:8
Tiny Tim, the last of all | 74:3
Tip: T. me the black spot] | 221:2
    Within the nether t. | 65:16
Tipped: load has t. | 127:1
Tipperary: long way to T. | 244:7
Tippled drink more fine | 120:17
Tips with silver | 207:24
Tiptoe: days stands t. | 208:2
    I stood t. | 120:9
    stand a t. | 192:4
Tire the night in thought | 173:24
Tired: not be t. by waiting | 125:14
    now the t. waves | 64:10
    T. of his dark dominion | 142:1
    t. of life | 115:14
    t. the sun with talking | 69:3
    when a man is t. of London | 115:14
Tires: He t. betimes | 206:6
Tirez: Messieurs..t. | 101:7
    T. le rideau, la farce est jouée | 174:6
Tirling at the window | 143:4
Tirra lirra: lark that t. chants | 210:5
    T., by the river | 227:24
Tissue: cloth-of-gold of t. | 182:15
Titan: like thy glory, T. | 215:1
Titania: There sleeps T. | 203:9
Title: farced t. | 191:15
    gained no t. | 164:25
    my courage prove my t.] | 183:3
    t. of 'agnostic' | 112:12
Titles: Despite these t. | 180:6
    High through his t. | 180:6
    kings their t. take | 59:18
Titwillow: Sang Willow, t. | 92:16
Toad: As intelligent Mr. T. | 96:17
    rather be a t. | 205:7
    t. beneath the harrow | 126:20
    t., ugly and venomous | 183:9
    Until the T. in fun | 71:1
Toast: Let the t. pass | 216:19
    never had a piece of t. | 161:16
    pledge my t. | 172:20
    standing t. | 73:18
    t. before each martial tune | 151:3
Toasted-cheese | 56:3, 221:4
Toasts of the young men | 159:10
Toby: My uncle T. | 220:14
Tocsin of the soul | 51:24
To-day: clears T. of past Regrets | 85:3
    do no work t. | 192:2
    gaze on so fondly t. | 149:12
    I have dined t. | 217:18
    if T. be sweet! | 85:8
    I'm to be married t. | 91:15
    in the giving vein t. | 207:9
    Jesus Christ the same..t. | 36:38
    Never do t. | 173:5
    never jam t. | 58:3
    Nor care beyond t. | 98:8
    Snatch the sleeve of t. | 109:3
    T., beneath the foeman's frown | 78:23
    t. he puts forth | 192:14
    T. if ye will hear | 170:25
    T. shalt thou be with me | 33:21
    wasn't there again t. | 141:17
    who are singing t. | 40:15
Toddle: I'd t. safely home | 179:5
Toe: and t. of frog | 199:14
    from the crown to the t. | 197:15
    from top to t. | 52:2
    light fantastic t. | 144:13

Toes: bells on her t. 157:17
Pobble who has no t. 131:10
pretty little t. 156:12
without their t. 131:13
Together: all hang t. 88:6
All things work t. 35:8
loved one all t. 44:15
We've been t. 62:4
What God hath joined t. 31:41
Toil: day in t. 173:24
Hath thy t. o'er books 89:27
honour and its t. 230:15
Horny-handed sons of t. 119:16
mock their useful t. 97:12
Our love and t. 124:17
Remark each anxious t. 117:1
Sleep after t. 219:10
they t. not 30:28
t. and trouble 199:13
T., envy, want 117:2
Winding up days with t. 191:15
Toiled: Souls that have t. 230:15
Toiling upward in the night 133:22
Told: as he was t. 105:15
as they are t. 42:5
had I been t. 121:9
never t. anybody 128:17
Still is the story t. 136:16
tale that is t. 170:18
Two truths are t. 197:9
Went and t. the sexton 106:24
Tolerant: makes one t. 219:22
Toll: to t. me back 121:7
to t. the bell 100:9
T. for the brave 70:9, 10
Tolle lege 13:4
Tolls: for whom the bell t. 77:23
Tom: T. bears logs 196:20
T. he was a piper's son 158:12
T.'s a-cold 195:10
Tomata sauce: chops and t. 75:24
Tomb: monument, without a t. 118:4
toward the silent t. 245:18
Tombstone: carve it on his t. 127:17
Tommy: it's T. this an' T. that 127:20
Pat and Mac and T. 128:28
To-morrow: Before this time t. 152:18
Boast not..of t. 26:28
for t. we die 35:26
for t. we shall die 28:6
here to-day, and gone t. 20:11
jam t. 58:3
(Live till t.) 70:1
put off till t. 173:5
Take therefore no thought for t. 30:29
This, no t. hath 77:1
T., and t., and t. 200:4
t. blossoms 192:14
T. to fresh woods 145:5
T. will be dying 104:14
trust as little as you may to t. 109:3
Unborn T. 85:8
What shall be t. 109:1
Why, T. I may be 85:3
Tom-tit: little t. 92:16
Tone: deep, autumnal t. 214:4
rather scornful t. 58:5
take the t. of the company 61:6
that t. of voice 173:18
with enthusiastic t. 92:1
Tones: I fear..thy t. 215:11
in divers t. 227:6
Sweet t. 213:16
Tongue: eye, t., sword 188:6
Give thy thoughts no t. 185:21
his t. speaks 204:11
hold your t., and let me love 77:2
let my t. cleave 171:28
made our English t. 219:15

My t. is the pen 169:18
never in the t. 196:18
not t. to speak 131:20
that my t. could utter 225:14
t. dropt manna 146:11
t. from evil-speaking 167:34
t. in every wound 194:13
t. is the clapper 204:11
t. of dog 199:14
t. shall be split 158:4
t. that Shakespeare spake 247:1
t. to conceive 203:18
trippingly on the t. 188:7
'Twas but my t. 83:11
use of my oracular t. 216:11
whose strenuous t. 120:24
with double t. 203:10
words of t. and pen 101:2, 242:17
Your hand, your t. 198:1
Tongueless vigil 223:28
Tongues: evil t. 146:20
Finds t. in trees 183:9
loose wild t. 127:6
Though I speak with the t. 35:20
whether there be t. 35:21
To-night: Curfew must not ring t. 233:10
find it out t. 199:2
For t. we'll merry be 3:21
weep thy fall t. 104:6
Took: spirit that ever t. flesh 82:21
t. them quite away! 57:12
t. unto herself a Mate 249:2
ye t. me in 32:16
Tool-using animal 55:20
Tools: Give us the t. 62:23
Their working t. 234:4
t. to him 55:6
Without t. he is nothing 55:20
Tooth: in t. and claw 227:13
pugging t. on edge 210:5
sharper than a serpent's t. 75:14, 195:3
t. and nail 125:5
t. for t. 24:7
t. is not so keen 184:1
Toothache: endure the t. patiently 204:15
Tooth-point: where each t. goes 126:20
Top: always room at the t. 240:4
from t. to toe 52:2
little bit off the t. 151:5
sleep like a t. 72:11
wool on de t. of his head 87:13
Topless towers of Ilium? 138:12
Topses: Herring boxes without t. 149:8
Torch: hand on the t. of life 135:9
Torches: teach the t. to burn 207:17
Tore his hair 218:21
Tories own no argument but force 43:3
Torment: is a t. to me 151:9
More grievous t. 120:15
shall no t. touch them 29:32
Tormented with ten thousand hells 138:11
Torn: tattered and t. 158:8
Torrent: for in the very t. 188:7
t. of darkness 155:1
Torture: and t. not again 213:8
t. and death of his fellow creatures 88:10
Toss'd: and He that t. 85:11
Tossing about 91:24
Toss-pots still had drunken heads 209:20
Totter: Now we maun t. down 48:21
Totters: Who t. forth 215:14
Touch: Can t. him not 213:8
exquisite t. 181:5
lose the common t. 125:16
Lucky to t. it 127:9
might t. that cheek 207:21
One t. of nature 208:28
spider's t. 164:16

T. me not 34:29
T. not a single bough! 150:12
t. of a vanish'd hand 225:15
t. of earthly years 245:14
t. the Happy Isles 230:14
t. the heart of man! 236:7
t. their harps of gold 181:10
we t. thee 232:9
Touched: Before rude hands have t.
  it? 118:11
not finely t. 200:13
t. none that he did not adorn 115:11
Touches of sweet harmony 202:11
Touching: sight so t. 249:4
Tough: interesting, but t. 234:18
old and t. 232:2
rather t. worm 92:17
Toujours gai, archy 139:16
Tous pour un 80:10
Tout passe, t. casse, t. lasse 9:10
Toves: slithy t. 57:14
Tower: ivory t. 178:14
to the dark t. came 195:14
t. of strength 207:11, 229:1
yonder ivy-mantled t. 97:9
Towered cities 144:18
Towering in her pride of place 199:1
Towers: branchy between t. 107:11
No t. along the steep 54:7
saw in sleep old palaces and t. 214:2
ships, t., domes 249:4
tell the t. thereof 169:23
topless t. of Ilium? 138:12
T., and battlements 144:14
walls and t. 66:14
whispering from her t. 12:3
ye antique t. 98:5
Towery city 107:11
Town: all around the t. 156:8
Charlie came to our t. 106:7
circulating library in a t. 216:8
country in t. 139:24
dogs in the t. 158:4
in that t. a dog was found 95:13
leave Oxford by the t. drain 219:17
London is a fine t. 67:19
man made the t. 70:14
new come to t. 155:12
of the hideous t. 150:14
one-horse t. 234:20
out of the t. 124:2
Rins through the t. 143:4
to the end of the t. 143:10
What little t. 120:21
Town-crier: lief the t. spoke my
  lines 188:7
Towns: London, thou art of t. 80:13
Toy: childish t. 139:4
foolish thing was but a t. 209:20
Toyed: you might have t. 89:10
Toys: All is but t. 198:19
t. for your delight 221:17
Trace: characters of hell to t. 97:5
I can t. my ancestry 91:28
Traces: on winter's t. 223:28
Track: Around the ancient t. 142:1
Come flying on our t. 233:4
Trade: cunning at his t. 124:19
dreadful t.! 195:19
It is His t. 102:6
It is not your t. 114:11
old t.'s plyin' 153:5
ruined by t. 88:2
slighted, shepherd's t. 145:1
Some way of common t. 206:16
Tradesmen: ye t., bow, ye masses 91:16
Tradition approves all forms of
  competition 64:9
Traduced the state 205:20

Traffic: t. of Jacob's ladder 232:10
t. of our stage 207:14
Trafficked for strange webs 161:9
Tragedies: two t. in life 212:22
Tragedy: go litel myn t. 61:1
let gorgeous T. 144:8
That is their t. 243:11
t. is the imitation of an action.. 10:16
t. to those that feel 238:7
Tragic: in t. life 142:4
Trahison des clercs 22:4
Trail: long, long t. 123:12
Trailing: But t. clouds of glory 246:11
Train: as we rush in the t. 233:4
his t. filled the temple 27:27
loose t. 144:3
pack, and take a t. 42:7
T. up a child 26:22
world and all her t. 235:11
Train-band captain 69:21
Traitors: fears do make us t. 199:25
Tram: I'm a t. 100:12
Trammel up the consequence 198:3
Tramp of the twenty-two men 40:16
Trample: May hourly t. 206:16
t. down abuses 237:17
Whose light doth t. 235:10
Trampling out the vintage 111:15
Tranquil: Farewell the t. mind 205:10
Tranquillity: inward t. 83:1
Transcendent: Clothed with t.
  brightness 145:14
faith's t. dower 245:18
Transcendental: of a t. kind 92:21
t. moonshine 55:18
Transgressions: wounded for our t. 28:21
Transgressors: numbered with the
  t. 28:23
way of the t. is hard 26:14
Transitory life 167:21
Translated: thou art t. 203:13
Translation: Not a t. 215:21
Transmitter of a foolish face 179:8
Trapeze: on the flying t. 132:4
Trappings and suits of woe 185:10
Trash: steals t. 205:4
Travaileth: With his lips he t. 224:2
Travel: from the east must t. 246:11
in a moment t. thither 246:12
Make me t. forth 211:3
To t. hopefully 221:6
t...is a part of education 15:4
Travelled: Much have I t. 121:9
t. a short while 219:7
Traveller: anybody there, said the
  t. 73:4
no t. returns 187:13
Now spurs the lated t. 199:7
some t. from New Zealand 136:21
t., by the faithful hound 133:20
t. from an antique land 214:5
t. from the cradle 214:10
where the t.'s journey 39:7
Travellers must be content 183:10
Travelling: So it is in t. 115:18
Travels: land she t. from 64:12
to go again on my t. 60:4
t. the fastest 128:7
Tray, Blanch, and Sweet-heart 195:15
Trays: cheap tin t. 140:21
Tread: beetle that we t. upon 200:21
close behind him t. 66:5
I with mournful t. 242:11
on my heart they t. 206:16
so airy a t. 228:20
that I may t. safely 101:5
Thy shrine we t. 179:11
t. on my dreams 250:6
T. softly 250:6

Tread (cont.)
  t. thee down — 121:6
  where angels fear to t. — 164:13
  where'er we t. — 50:22
  Where'er you t. — 165:1
Treading on my tail — 57:7
Treason: bloody t. — 194:10
  for t. to his country — 116:18
  Gunpowder T. and Plot — 7:3, 157:12
  If this be t. — 103:9
  is the greatest t. — 81:21
  love grows bitter with t. — 224:10
  none dare call it t. — 100:14
  t. can but peep — 189:13
  'T.' cried the Speaker — 103:9
  T. doth never prosper — 100:14
  T. has done his worst — 199:4
  t. is not own'd — 79:26
  t. of the educated classes — 22:4
  t. was no crime — 79:9
Treasons: fit for t. — 202:13
Treasure: purest t. — 206:2
  That we t. beyond measure — 91:10
  Where your t. is — 30:25
Treasured: embalmed and t. — 148:8
Treasures: Lay not up..t. upon
  earth — 30:23
  Lay up..t. in heaven — 30:24
Treat: And you're giving a t. — 91:25
Treble: towards childish t. — 183:20
Tree: as the leaves grow on the t. — 250:5
  But there's a t. — 246:10
  carve on every t. — 184:3
  dew bespangling herb and t. — 104:9
  evergreen t. of diabolical know-
    ledge! — 216:8
  finds that this t. — 129:2
  happy, happy t. — 122:6
  heart is like an apple-t. — 177:8
  I had a little nut t. — 156:2
  incense-bearing t. — 66:14
  Of that forbidden t. — 145:9
  On a t. by a river — 92:16
  on every t. — 196:19
  only God can make a t. — 123:9
  poem lovely as a t. — 123:8
  Rock-a-bye-baby on the t. top — 38:9
  sat under a t. — 110:14
  sat under the T. — 125:1
  sees not the same t. — 39:17
  shade of a coolibah t. — 161:12
  shade of the old apple t. — 244:8
  shady cypress t. — 177:12
  spare that t. — 150:12
  spare the beechen t. — 53:13
  spreading chestnut t. — 134:10
  that's why the t. — 4:1
  there vor me the apple t. — 18:10
  things in a green t. — 33:38
  three ravens sat on a t. — 16:17
  t. of liberty — 113:3
  t. of the knowledge — 23:10
Tumtum t. — 57:14
  under a juniper t. — 25:13
  under his fig t. — 29:27
  Under the greenwood t. — 183:13
  where the t. falleth — 27:6
Trees: all the t. are brown — 123:18
  all the t. are green — 123:18
  All the t. they are so high — 16:18
  among the gusty t. — 155:1
  as the Arabian t. — 205:20
  beneath the t. — 247:3
  Dryad of the t. — 121:2
  Finds tongues in t. — 183:9
  I see men as t. — 32:31
  in tufted t. — 144:14
  laid unto the root of the t. — 30:6
  laurel-t. are cut — 17:7

leaves on the t. — 110:5
Loveliest of t. — 110:15
My apple t. — 88:9
Of all the t. — 7:17
  stones, and t. — 254:14
  tall ancestral t. — 102:11
  t. and the houses go wheeling — 233:4
  T. did grow — 18:12
  t. in whose dim shadow — 136:17
  t. that are therein — 171:28
  t. that grow so fair — 127:24
  T., where you sit — 165:1
  vext garden-t. — 12:2
  with his lute made t. — 192:13
Trelawny: And shall T. die? — 101:6
Tremble: Let Sporus t. — 165:7
  t. with tenderer breath — 224:9
  Would start and t. — 228:20
Trembler: no t. in the world — 41:13
Trembling: hare limp'd t. — 120:2
  T. at that — 213:15
  with fear and t. — 36:16
Trencher-man: valiant t. — 204:5
Trespasses: forgive us our t. — 166:11
Tresses: and t. grey — 180:4
  Fair t. — 165:2
Trial: purifies us is t. — 148:9
  T. by jury itself — 73:17
Triangle: eternal t. — 7:15
Tribal: constructing t. lays — 125:13
Tribe: badge of all our t. — 201:18
  Idols of the t. — 15:11
  may his t. increase! — 112:2
  Richer than all his t. — 205:20
Tribes of living things — 135:9
Tribulation: In the world ye shall
  have t. — 34:22
Trice: Change in a t. — 224:4
Trick: t. of melancholy — 182:11
  t. worth two of that — 190:10
  when the long t.'s over — 141:4
  win the t. — 111:19
Tricks: for t. that are vain — 101:3
  Frustrate their knavish t. — 55:1
  such fantastic t. — 200:19
  t. hath strong imagination — 203:19
  t. his beams — 145:4
Tried: I have t. too in my time — 81:7
  she for a little t. — 249:12
Trifle: careless t. — 197:13
Trifles: T. light as air — 205:8
  unconsidered t. — 210:6
Trim: and tackle t. — 147:5
  he that shot so t. — 207:19
  her gawdy t. — 145:7
  Meadows t. — 144:14
  so t., so simple? — 108:18
Trimmings: with the usual t. — 75:30
Trinity: At T. Church I met my
  doom — 90:16
  Blessed T.! — 102:1
  T. had never been unkind to me — 153:11
Trinkets: ye returned to your t. — 126:1
Trip: Come, and t. it — 144:13
  our fearful t. is done — 242:10
  T. no further — 209:5
Triple-arched: high and t. — 120:4
Trippingly on the tongue — 188:7
Triton: hear old T. blow his
  wreathed horn — 249:5
  T. blowing loud — 219:8
  T. of the minnows? — 184:18
Triumph: I t. still — 135:17
  In sweeping t. — 76:23
  meet with T. — 125:14
  ride in t. — 139:9
  Victor's t. won — 165:21
  wrong would t. — 45:10
Triumphant: Joyful and t. — 9:14, 159:6

Triumphs: joys and t.   241:7
  t...shrunk   193:18
Trochee trips   67:1
Troia: Iam seges est ubi T. fuit   160:4
Troilus methinks mounted the
  Troyan walls   202:9
Troop: And, pressing a t.   43:12
  plumed t.   205:10
  sent a t. of horse   43:3, 234:3
Troops: t. of friends   199:32
  t. of Midian   152:11
Trophies: her cloudy t.   120:24
  her weedy t. and herself   189:18
Troth: I wonder by my t.   77:7
  plight thee my t.   168:12
  tell t. and shame the devil   118:10
Trots: dromedary t.   66:11
Trotting through the dark   127:10
Trotwood: You know, T.   74:13
Troubadour: Gaily the T.   19:6
Trouble: capacity for taking t.   50:5, 55:9
  enemies that t. me   169:17
  getting its possessors into t.   50:5
  in their t.   171:8
  Kindness in another's t.   96:6
  Man is born unto t.   25:29
  Man..is full of t.   25:31
  only t. is   59:14
  putting some of the t.   74:10
  soon smooth away t.   41:17
  them that t. me   169:2
  there's t. brewing   128:28
  toil and t.   199:13
  t. deaf heaven   210:13
  t. enough of its own   243:3
  t., sorrow, need, sickness   167:21
  very present help in time of t.
                                           3:9, 169:20
  You took the t. to be born   19:8
Troubled: is a t. spirit   169:28
  Let not your heart be t.   34:16
  no more was by it t.   232:4
  t. with her lonely life   162:6
Troubles: pack up your t.   12:14
  sea of t.   187:13
  written t. of the brain   200:1
Troubling: wicked cease from t.   25:28
Trousers: bottoms of my t. rolled   81:19
  put on one's best t.   112:14
Trout: find a t. in the milk   233:9
Trowel: laid on with a t.   183:7
  lay it on with a t.   76:14
  lays it on with a t.   68:3
Trowl the brown bowl   180:19
Troy: from the shores of T.   236:3
  tale of T. divine   144:8
  where T. once was   160:4
  Where's T.?   41:2
  windy T.   230:13
Troyan: mounted the T. walls   202:9
True: always say what's t.   221:11
  course of t. love   203:2
  dark and t.   229:14
  do rest but t.   193:8
  dreams all come t.   123:12
  Full of the t.   121:3
  good men and t.   204:12
  he was a t. Poet   39:16
  honest and t.   5:14, 141:14
  If it is not t.   9:13
  Is t. of most   64:11
  kept truth falsely t.   226:22
  Law is the t. embodiment   91:17
  love false or t.   250:11
  no one so t.   209:9
  old and as t.   126:9
  One religion is as t. as another   49:12
  Presbyterian t. blue   49:18
  ring in the t.   227:19
so young..and t.   195:1
tell me t.   92:23
these words are t.   37:26
they know isn't t.   22:5
three times is t.   56:1
'tis t. 'tis pity   186:23
'tis t., 'tis t.   110:17
to thine own self be t.   185:21
t. as the stars above   4:8
T. to the kindred points   248:6
vivid, t.   221:19
Whatsoever things are t.   36:20
woman t. and fair   77:17
True-love: into t. knots   66:11
Truly: Firmly I believe and t.   153:13
  learn and labour t.   168:1
  t. and earnestly repent   167:22
Trump: at the last t.   35:29
  shrill t.   205:10
  sound of the t.   169:22
Trumpet: blow your own t.   93:24
  First Blast of the T.   129:1
  shifted his t.   95:19
  Thing became a t.   248:2
  t. of a prophecy!   214:4
  t. shall be heard   79:18
Trumpets: all the t. sounded   46:23
  blow your t., Angels   77:8
  blowin' er de t.   101:1
  He saith among the t.   25:44
  silver snarling t.   120:3
  Sound the t.   150:10
  to the sound of t.   218:2
  t. waken the Wall   127:14
Trumpet-tongu'd: angels t.   198:4
Trunk: So large a t. before   20:17
Trunkless legs of stone   214:5
Trust: absolute t.   197:13
  never t. a woman   243:25
  not to t.   212:1
  Or t. me   93:24
  put not your t. in princes   172:4
  Put your t. in God   38:5
  takes it in t.   174:15
  that puts her t.   127:7
  to frail mortality shall t.   15:14
  t. as little as you may   109:3
  t. God   45:4
  t. in chariots   168:32
  t. that somehow good   227:10
  you can t. yourself   125:14
Trusted: his armour wherein he t.   33:11
  Let no such man be t.   202:13
Trusty, dusky, vivid   221:19
Truth: battle for freedom and t.   112:14
  Beauty is t.   120:23
  better than T.   67:4
  careful t.   124:17
  dearer still is t.   10:17
  faithfulness and t.   170:19
  friend to t.   164:25
  great is T.   29:31, 42:12
  great ocean of t.   153:17
  heavenly t. imparts   122:18
  I am..the t.   34:19
  I held it t.   227:6
  in possession of t.   133:7
  keep abreast of T.   135:4
  kept thy t.   147:16
  mainly he told the t.   234:17
  make t. serve as a stalking-horse   40:5
  mournful t.   116:27
  must be the t.?   78:16
  must be t.   122:7
  no t. in him   34:9
  One t. is clear   164:17
  rejoiceth in the t.   35:21
  simple t. his utmost skill   249:10
  Sole judge of t.   164:19

Truth (cont.)
spread the t. from pole to pole   1:13
Strict Regard for T.   21:8
strife of T. with Falsehood   135:3
tell t., and shame the devil   118:10, 190:18
That lies like t.   200:5
T. comes out in wine   163:10
t. from his heart   168:27
T. from his lips   95:7
t. is always strange   52:2
t. is not in us   37:8
T. is rarely pure   243:7
t. lies within a little   40:4
t. of imagination   122:7
t. of the description   181:5
t. shall make you free   34:8
t. sits upon the lips of dying men   11:21
t. the poet sings   228:7
t. universally acknowledged   13:18
t. whereby the nations live   124:17
T. will come to light   201:22
t. with gold she weighs   164:1
two to speak the t.   233:8
What is t.?   15:5, 34:23
worship him...in t.   34:2
Truths: fate of new t.   112:11
hold these t. to be sacred   113:2
tell him disagreeable t.   136:4
T. as refined as ever Athens heard   11:3
t. to be self-evident   8:9
Two t. are told   197:9
Try: axe's edge did t.   140:8
t. him afterwards   148:20
t. the whole cause   56:14
T., t. again   105:4
Tu: Et t., Brute?   53:1, 193:17
T. quoque   160:9
Tub: tale of a t.   150:9, 240:10
Tube: In reeking t.   127:7
Tubs: from alternate t.   176:4
Tucker: Little Tommy T.   156:13
Tuesday: Christened on T.   158:2
T.'s child   156:17
Tulgey: through the t. wood   57:14
Tulips: Here t. bloom   42:5
Tullus: rich old T.   110:6
Tumble: Must t. down   216:24
turn and t.   150:8
Tumble-down nest   244:11
Tumbled off a bus   96:11
Tumbling: came t. after   156:4
lie t. in the hay   210:5
Tumtum: rested he by the T. tree   57:14
Tumult: made such a noise and t.   81:6
sank in t.   66:15
t. and the shouting dies   127:4
t. in the clouds   250:7
t. of thy mighty harmonies   214:4
Tune: all the t. that he could play   158:12
before each martial t.   151:3
many a good t.   50:9
out of t. and harsh   188:6
Singeth a quiet t.   66:3
sweetly play'd in t.   48:28
t. of flutes   182:15
voices keep t.   150:2
we are out of t.   249:5
Tuneful: soon mute, however t.   129:22
Tunes: slow old t.   140:19
snatches of old t.   189:18
Tunning of Elynour Rumming   217:8
Turban'd: malignant and a t. Turk   205:20
Turbulent: this t. priest   103:12
Turf: blue ribbon of the t.   76:18
grass-green t.   189:9
green t. beneath my feet   101:11
To bless the t.   67:15
Turk: A French, or T., or Proosian   93:14

comes like any T.   55:3
malignant and a turban'd t.   205:20
unspeakable T.   55:17
Turkey: It was a t.!   74:4
Turmoil: ceaseless t. seething   66:14
Turn: he will t. it over   22:19
pass, and t. again   82:13
t. and live with animals   242:14
t. and tumble   150:8
T. but a stone   232:10
t. down an empty Glass   86:3
t. his merry note   183:13
t. to dust   140:12
where you t. your eyes   165:1
Turned: Each t. his face   65:17
footsteps he hath t.   180:6
having once t. round   66:5
in case anything t. up   74:7
One who never t. his back   45:10
t. into corruption   172:10
we have t. every one   28:21
Turneth it upside down   172:5
Turning: t. o' the tide   191:6
where my heart is t. ebber   87:11
Turnips: man who t. cries   116:9
Turns: t. as I, this evening   44:3
t. into Miss T.   73:7
t. no more his head   66:5
Turtle: voice of the t. is heard   27:16
Tuscany: even the ranks of T.   136:15
Tutor: discretion be your t.   188:8
irreverent to my t.   113:14
Tu-whit   196:20
Twain: never the t. shall meet   124:13
of metals t.   145:2
with t. he covered his face   27:27
Twang: a most melodious t.   12:19
Tweedledum and Tweedledee   50:12, 57:18
Twelve: sleep firmly from t. to one   69:8
t. gates were t. pearls   37:28
T.-pound Look   18:23
Twentieth-Century Blues   69:11
Twenty: sweet and t.   209:5
T. love-sick maidens   92:18
T. will not come again   110:15
Twenty-two: tramp of the t. men   40:16
Twice: it is t. bless'd   202:5
Not once or t.   229:2
t. as fast   57:17
t. as natural   58:9
Twice-told tale   52:4, 193:5
Twigs: set limed t.   58:13
Twilight: T. and evening bell   226:6
t. saints   120:4
Twined: all its t. flowers   119:18
Twinkle: lights begin to t.   230:15
t. on the milky way   247:4
Twinkle, twinkle little bat   56:24
Twinkle, twinkle, little star   225:11
Twinkling of an eye   35:29, 169:8
Twins: Clara threw the t.   96:10
Twist: could t. the sinews   39:2
No more t.!   166:1
Twisted: With a t. cue   92:9
Twittering: swallow t.   97:11
Two: about the space of t. hours   34:45
at the expense of t.   64:5
bicycle made for t.   72:1
don't want t.   141:21
in t. words: im-possible   96:5
sold for t. farthings   33:13
takes t. to speak the truth   233:8
trick worth t.   190:10
t. hit it off   245:13
t. o'clock in the morning courage   151:17
T. things fill the mind   119:10
Where t. or three are gathered together   166:17
Two-handed engine   145:3

Two-pence: I care not t. 19:11
  t. coloured 220:23
Tyburn-face: damn'd T. 68:7
Tyger: t. burning bright 39:1, 4
Tyne: cargo of T. coal 140:21
Type: so careful of the t. 227:12
  t. of all her race 78:23
  T. of the wise 248:6
Tyrannous to use it like a giant 200:18
Tyranny: Taxation .. is t. 159:20
Tyrant: little t. of his fields 97:15
  threatening t. 109:19
Tyrants: blood of patriots and t. 113:3
Tyre: Is one with Nineveh and T. 127:5

U

U and non-U 177:7
Übermenschen: Ich lehre euch den Ü. 154:6
Uffish thought 57:14
Uglier yet is the Hump we get 126:2
Uglification: Distraction, U. 57:5
Ugly and venomous 183:9
Ullin: Lord U.'s daughter 53:18
Ulster will fight 62:12
Ultima Thule 237:4
Ulubrae: is at U. 108:9
Ulva: chief of Ulva's isle 53:18
Ulysse: Heureux qui comme U. 20:15
Ulysses: new U. leaves 213:12
Umbra: magni nominis u. 135:5
Umbrella: steals the just's u. 40:14
Umpire the pavilion cat 130:2
Un: Tous pour u. 80:10
Unaccommodated man 195:12
Unacknowledged legislators 215:15
Unadorned: beauty u. 20:12
Unanel'd: unhousel'd, disap-
  pointed, u. 186:12
Unanimity: their u. is wonderful! 216:3
Unarm, Eros 182:18
Unattempted: Things u. 145:10
Unattractive: most u. old thing 92:15
Unawakened earth 214:4
Unaware: sees, some morning, u. 44:1
Unbecoming: so u. to a woman 243:17
Unbelief: help thou mine u. 32:33
Unbidden: Singing hymns u. 215:4
  u. guests 192:6
Un-birthday present 58:4
Unborn To-morrow 85:8
Unbottom'd: dark u. infinite abyss 146:12
Unbowed: bloody, but u. 102:13
Unbred: thou age u. 211:13
Unburied: bodies of u. men 240:11
Unburnished: To rust u. 230:13
Uncertain: time which to us is u. 20:2
  U., coy 180:13
Unchang'd to hoarse or mute 146:20
Uncharitableness: all u. 166:22
Uncle: married with mine u. 185:11
  u. me no u. 206:11
Uncle Tom Cobbleigh and all 17:4
Unclean: man of u. lips 27:27
Unclubable man 114:22
Uncomfortable: he is only u. 212:21
  We u. feel 93:20
Unconcern: looks with u. 113:22
Unconditional . . surrender 97:1
Unconfined: let joy be u. 51:1
Unconquerable: man's u. mind 248:20
  my u. soul 102:13
  nursing the u. hope 11:27
Unconscious humour 50:6
Unconsidered trifles 210:6
Unconsoled: shall perish u. 130:2
Uncontrollable: less free than thou,
  O u.! 214:3
Uncontrouled licentiousness 83:7

Unconvincing: bald and u. narrative 92:13
Uncorrupt life 168:27
Uncouth: His u. way 146:12
  makes ancient good u. 135:4
Uncreating word 164:3
Unction: that flattering u. 189:3
Undazzled: her u. eyes 148:10
Undefiled: Tempted, and yet u. 218:6
  u. heritage 124:17
Undeniable: truths to be sacred and
  u. 113:2
Under: to take u. my wing 92:15
Under-belly: soft u. of the Axis 63:4
Underground: who might well be u. 91:30
Underlings: that we are u. 193:11
Underneath are the everlasting
  arms 24:25
Underrated: celebrated, cultivated,
  u. 91:6
Undersized: a bit u. 91:25
Understand: cannot u. what is
  happening 59:14
  if I could u. 226:12
  let the maiden u. 41:1
  shire for men who u. 42:7
  wot do they u. 126:14
Understanded of the people 172:14
Understanding: a candle of u. 29:30
  good u. 171:11
  hath no u. 169:24
  in my u. 4:10
  pass all u. 112:18
  pass man's u. 167:1
  passeth all u. 36:19, 167:25
  spirit of . . u. 28:1
Understood: I u. as a child 35:22
Undertones of War 39:25
Underwood: green u. and cover 223:29
Undid: And what they u. did 182:15
Undiscovered: lay all u. before me 153:17
  to the u. ends 21:12
  u. country 187:13
Undone: another victory, we are u. 14:6
  I am u. 27:27
  left u. 166:9
  were now u. 200:6
Undoubtedly be seen to be done 104:19
Undulating throat 21:22
Unearned increment 142:21
Uneasy lies the head 190:30
Uneatable: pursuit of the u. 243:24
Unedicated: so u. 238:19
Unequal laws 230:12
Unespied: ocean's bosom u. 139:25
Unexercised and unbreathed 148:9
Unexpressive she 184:3
Unextinguished hearth 214:4
Unfading moths 42:3
Unfaithful: And faith u. 226:22
Unfathomed caves of ocean 97:15
Unfed sides 195:8
Unfledged comrade 185:21
Unfold: could a tale u. 186:7
  O clouds, u.! 38:16
Unforgiving: fill the u. minute 125:16
Unformed and confused mass 160:5
Unfortunate: One more u. 106:20
Unfurled: to April's breeze u. 82:14
Ungained: prize the thing u. 208:26
Ungathered: Beside the u. rice 134:3
Ungentlemanly he can look 222:21
Ungirt loin 45:8
Ungodly: u. in great power 169:14
  way of the u. 172:5
Ungracious pastors 185:20
Unhand: Hold off! u. me 65:5
  U. me, gentlemen 186:5
Unhappy: I'm so u. 96:14
  respectable or u. 242:14

Unhappy (cont.)
u., far-off things 248:9
u. in its own way 233:22
Unhatched: with u. rapier 209:18
Unheard: Strains u. 109:16
those u. are sweeter 120:19
Unholy: sights u. 144:10
Unhonour'd: Unwept, u. 180:6
Unhoped: and that u. serene 41:16
Unhousel'd, disappointed 186:12
Unhurrying: with u. chase 232:8
Unicorn: lion and the u. 156:8
Unicorns: horns of the u. 169:1
Uniform: When I first put this u. on 92:19
Uninitiate crowd 109:16
Uninitiated: ye that are u. 236:16
Unintelligible patter 93:29
Union: O U. strong and great 133:13
u. in partition 203:15
Unit: Misses a u. 43:18
Unite: Workers of the world, U. 8:16, 140:14
United: ev'ry flower is u. 89:14
Uniting: By u. we stand 76:1
Unity: dwell together in u. 171:26
In necessary things, u. 19:2
Univers: Il connaît l'u. 86:17
Universal: a u. law 119:11
object of u. devotion 112:16
u. frame began 79:16
Universe: born for the U. 95:17
I accept the u. 55:24
over the u. 214:4
To mingle with the U. 51:7
to understand the U. 55:21
U. is not hostile 106:10
Universities: state of both his u. 234:3
University: true U. 55:14
unto death in my U. 153:11
We are the U. 219:19
Unjust: on the u. fella 40:14
sendeth rain on the..u. 30:19
Unkempt about those hedges blows 42:5
Unkind: art not so u. 184:1
I am u. 134:20
sodden and u. 21:24
when givers prove u. 188:2
Unkindness: I tax not you..with u. 195:5
Unknowable: O world u. 232:9
Unknown: among u. men 247:2
She lived u. 248:3
Things standing thus u. 190:3
to the u. God 34:42
tread safely into the u. 101:5
Whose worth's u. 211:16
Unleashed: Hell shall be u.! 236:20
Unlit lamp 45:8
Unlocked: Shakespeare u. his heart 44:4, 248:1
Unloose: I am not worthy to u. 33:47
Unmarried: That die u. 210:8
Unmoved: Can I u. 75:19
Unnatural: cruel, not u. 188:21
strange, and u. 186:8
Unnumber'd idle pebbles 195:19
Unofficial: English u. rose 42:5
Unparalleled: diet u. 74:25
lass u. 183:5
Unperplext seeking 43:18
Unperturbèd pace 232:8
Unpolluted: fair and u. flesh 189:22
Unpopular: I was not u. there 20:8
Unpremeditated art 215:3
Unprofitable: flat, and u. 185:11
Unproportion'd thought 185:21
Unrest which men miscall delight 213:8
Unrighteousness: of the mammon of u. 33:26
tents of u. 170:15

Unruly: u. Sun 77:18
u. wills 166:35
Unseemly: behave itself u. 35:12
Unseen: born to blush u. 97:15
By forms u. 67:15
Greet the u. 45:9
leave the world u. 121:3
Of u. things above 99:13
Unsex me here 197:15
Unsifted in such perilous circumstance 186:1
Unslumbering: Juno's u. ire 236:3
Unsmote by the sword 52:11
Unspeakable: u. in full pursuit 243:24
u. Turk 55:17
Unstained in life 109:5
Unsuccessful literary man 21:22
Unsung: unhonour'd, and u. 180:6
Unsure: is still u. 209:5
Untainted: than a heart u. 192:7
Untender: so young, and so u.? 195:1
Untie: knot of life at once u. 183:4
Untouched: any style of writing u. 115:11
Untravell'd world 230:13
Untrimmed: changing course u. 210:12
Untrodden: beside the u. ways 248:3
Untrue: On a cloth u. 92:9
Untune the sky 79:18
Unutterable: deep, u. woe 14:1
looked u. things 233:1
Unutterably vain 41:14
Unvarnished: round u. tale 204:21
Unwary: who all u. 92:3
Unweeded garden 185:11
Unwept: U., unhonour'd 180:6
watery bier u. 144:20
Unwillingly to school 183:20
Unwomanly rags 107:3
Unworthy: merit of the u. 187:13
Unwritten law 72:10
Unwrung: withers are u. 188:14
Up: And when they were u. 7:21
u. and doing 133:28
U. and down the City Road 138:2
u. Guards and at them 241:1
u. she rises 8:12
Up-gathered now like sleeping flowers 249:5
Upgrowth: germ and first u. 124:4
Upharsin: Mene, Mene, Tekel, U. 29:18
Up-hill: road wind u. 177:13
Uphold you 175:2
Up-lifted Angel trumpets 147:14
Upper: stiff u. lip 58:18
u. ten thousand 244:9
Upright: God hath made man u. 26:41
Uprising: wakening and u. prove 122:13
Upside down: turned the world u. 34:41
turneth it u. 172:5
Upstairs: U. and downstairs 143:4, 155:16
Upstart: of this one u. clerk! 103:13
u. crow 98:13
Up-tails all 117:14
Upward: They must u. still 135:4
Urania: govern thou my song U. 146:20
Urban: being u., squat 42:8
Urbem: U...excoluit adeo 52:21
U. *venalem..perituram* 179:1
Urgent: bosom of the u. West 41:8
Urn: bubbling and loud-hissing u. 70:18
Can storied u. 97:13
Us: Between u. and you 33:29
won't be much for u. 56:9
Use: as others u. 145:1
grace to u. it 147:15
I conceive you may u. 91:23
too rich for u. 207:17
U. every man after his desert 187:10
what's the u. of Hanyfink? 62:3

Used: be well u.   187:9
  it u. to be so   148:19
  u. no other   173:17
  will be u. against you   78:7
Useful: mock their u. toil   97:12
Useless: Lodg'd with me u.   147:17
Uses: For other's u.   205:7
  u. of adversity   183:9
Ushers in the morn   84:11
Using more than once   76:13
Usual: Business as u.   62:19
Usury: no yoke of u.   108:14
Utter: as words could never u.   232:4
  her secret none can u. ?   174:3
  in u. nakedness   246:11
Utterance: Action, nor u.   194:12
Uttermost: paid the u. farthing   30:16
  u. part of the heaven   168:30
  u. parts of the sea   172:1
Uzziah: In the year that king U.
  died   27:27

                V

Vacant: and v. mind   191:15
  has one v. chair!   134:1
  V. heart and hand   180:15
  v. or in pensive mood   247:5
Vadis: Quo v.?   34:21
Vae victis   133:1
Vagrant gypsy life   141:4
Vain: after me—in v.!   86:2
  all but in v.   60:23
  grown grey in v.   213:8
  I have ears in v.   121:6
  I watched in v.   86:9
  In v. with lavish kindness   101:16
  Name of the Lord thy God in v.   167:8
  never given in v.   110:17
  never sought in v.   48:12
  No great man lives in v.   55:13
  not have died in v.   132:8
  seal'd in v.   201:3
  struggle in v.   179:13
  Surely in v. the net is spread   26:5
  sweep over thee in v.   51:8
  'tis all in v.!   38:17
  tricks that are v.   101:3
  unutterably v.   41:14
  Use not v. repetitions   30:21
  V. are the thousand creeds   41:14
  v. conceit   206:15
  v. deluding joys   144:4
  V. pomp and glory   192:14
  watchman waketh but in v.
                        26:4, 171:22
Vale: cool sequester'd v. of life   98:1
  death's dark v.   181:8
  v. of misery   170:14
  v. of years   205:6
Vales: from our lovely v.   132:13
  o'er v. and hills   247:3
Valet: hero to his v.   68:29
  to his very v. seem'd a hero   50:16
Valiant: All v. dust   127:7
  As he was v.   194:2
  O v. hearts   11:1
  reproof v.   184:14
  v. man and true   230:5
  v. never taste of death   193:14
  v. trencher-man   204:5
Valiant-for-Truth   46:19
Valley: bicker down a v.   225:17
  Every v. shall be exalted   28:12
  in the v. of decision   29:23
  Piping down the v. wild   39:8
  v. of Humiliation   46:7
  v. of the shadow   169:2
  v., rock, or hill   249:4

v. sheep are fatter   162:1
v. which was full of bones   29:14
Valley-glades: in the next v.   121:7
Valleys: lily of the v.   27:13
  v. also shall stand   170:3
  v., groves, hills   139:6
Vallombrosa: brooks in V.   146:4
Valour: better part of v.   190:25
  Like v.'s minion   197:4
  who would true v. see   46:20
  youthful v.   236:21
  he and v. formed   146:16
Valuable: most v. thing   69:1
Value: and the v. of nothing   243:18
  News v.   175:1
  v. it next to a good conscience 238:15
Vampire: like the v.   161:9
Vanbrugh: Dead Sir John V.   83:12
Vandyke is of the company   88:13
Vanish: it shall v. away   35:21
  softly and suddenly v.   56:4
Vanished: it v. quite slowly   56:21
  touch of a v. hand   225:15
  v. from his lonely hearth   246:3
Vanity: All is v.   26:36
  is lighter than v.   46:9
  pomps and v.   167:32
  V. of vanities   26:34
Vanity-Fair: beareth the name of V. 46:9
Vanquish: I will v.   153:10
Vanquished: shall never v. be   199:22
  though v., he could argue still   95:8
  Valiantly v.   182:20
  Woe to the v.   133:1
Vantage: coign of v.   198:2
  v. of a king   191:15
Vapour of a dungeon   205:7
Vapours: congregation of v.   187:4
  v. weep their burthen   230:10
Variable: prove likewise v.   207:24
  v. as the shade   180:13
Variation: which each slight v.   72:9
Variety: her infinite v.   182:16
  V.'s the very spice of life   70:16
Vassals: With v. and serfs   46:2
Vast: In the dead v. and middle of
  the night   185:16
  Two v. and trunkless legs   214:5
  v. and eyeless   236:13
  v. solitude   136:21
Vaster: V. than empires   140:11
Vasty: from the v. deep   190:17
  v. fields of France ?   191:3
Vats: parcel of boilers and v.   115:24
Vault: in thy marble v.   140:12
  left this v. to brag of   198:19
Vaunt-couriers   to   oak-cleaving
  thunderbolts   195:4
Vaunteth: charity v. not itself   35:21
Vaunting ambition   198:4
Veal: one of Bellamy's v. pies   163:5
Vegetable: of a v. fashion   92:22
  v. love   92:22, 140:11
Veil: for the v. of the soul   224:2
  in a gauzy v.   215:14
  Lift not the painted v.   215:9
  Put on his v. and took the swarm 96:15
Veil'd Melancholy   120:24
Vein: in the giving v.   207:9
Veins: hidden in my v.   174:10
  Jigging v.   139:8
Velasquez: Why drag in V. ?   242:2
Venerable parts of our constitution 47:7
Veneres Cupidinesque   58:25
Venetian: Beat a V.   205:20
Vengeance is mine   35:11
Veni, vidi, vici   53:2
Venice: there at V. gave   207:2
  V. lies   213:17

Venomous: poor v. fool 183:4
ugly and v. 183:9
Venture: bow at a v. 25:17
damn her at a v. 129:17
Naught v. 234:11
Nothing V. 91:26
Ventured: I have v. 192:14
Ventures: Or lose our v. 194:19
Venus: Goddess V. 174:10
O'er-picturing that V. 182:15
V. here will choose her dwelling 79:23
Verbosa et grandis epistula 119:7
Verbosity: exuberance of his own v. 76:11
Verdict of the world 13:6
Verge enough 97:5
Verify: always to v. your references 178:2
Verisimilitude: artistic v. 92:13
Veritas: In vino v. 163:10
Vernal: from a v. wood 248:15
Vero: Se non è v. 9:13
Verre: je bois dans mon v. 151:7
Vers: Tout ce qui n'est point prose est
v. 148:16
Verse: a Book of V. 84:18
bumbast out a blank v. 98:13
immortal v. 144:19
incantation of this v. 214:4
Lies the subject of all v. 43:2
makes v. run smoothly 40:2
Ne'er a v. to thee 123:16
not prose is v. 148:16
to run them into v. 80:5
v. you grave for me 221:23
Voice and V. 147:13
Verses: A Book of V. 84:19
give birth to v. 118:19
murmur my v. 176:11
v. are like the peace of God 112:18
when he repeats his v. 129:12
Vespers: singing v. 90:12
Vessel: v. of the state 215:16
weaker v. 37:5
Vestal: blameless v.'s lot! 164:6
Vesture: muddy v. of decay 202:11
Veterum: De Sapientia V. 15:13
Vex not his ghost 196:12
Vexation: Multiplication is v. 6:8
vanity and v. of spirit 26:36
Vexed: how fools are v. 72:18
Vexilla regis prodeunt 87:7
Vexing the dull ear 193:5
Vibrates in the memory 215:10
Vibration: That brave v. 104:15
Vice: And lash the v. 59:7
climax of v. 119:2
end in sight was a v. 45:8
nurseries of all v. 84:7
roses of v. 224:4
V. itself lost half its evil 47:15
When v. prevails 1:5
Vices: Most v. may be committed
very genteelly 115:3
of our pleasant v. 196:7
Vicious: more v. grow 160:10
Vicisti, Galilæe 118:18
Victim must be found 91:30
Victims: little v. play! 98:8
Victis: Vae v. 133:1
Victor: To the v. belong 138:7
V.'s triumph won 165:21
whichever side may call itself the v. 59:15
Victories: Peace hath her v. 148:5
Victory: another v., we are undone 14:6
Empire and V. 215:1
O grave, where is thy v.? 35:31
Or to v. 48:30
'twas a famous v. 218:14
Where, grave, thy v.? 135:17
Victuals: about their v. 53:8

Video meliora, proboque 160:7
Vieille: Quand vous serez bien v. 176:11
Vieillesse: si v. pouvoit 83:8
View: lends enchantment to the v. 54:3
made myself a motley to the v. 211:15
point of v. 173:23
v. fair Melrose 180:5
we v. thee 232:9
with extensive v. 117:1
View-hollo: Peel's v. 97:2
Viewless: in the v. winds 200:23
Views: full of stately v. 125:8
Vigil: tongueless v. 223:28
yearly on the v. 192:4
Vigilance: is eternal v. 71:17
Vigilant: Be sober, be v. 37:7
Vigny plus secret 178:14
Vile: be he n'er so v. 192:4
From this v. world 211:7
only man is v. 101:16
Out, v. jelly! 195:17
To the v. dust 180:6
v. Whig 114:28
Vilikins and his Dinah 7:20
Village: through an Alpine v. 133:17
v. smithy stands 134:10
Village-Hampden: Some v. 97:15
Villages: in these peculiar v. 112:16
pleasant v. and farms 146:22
Villain: No v. need be! 142:4
prove a v. 207:6
smile, and be a v. 186:14
smiling, damned v.! 186:14
Vinces: In hoc signo v. 68:22
Vine: as the fruitful v. 171:24
clusters of the v. 140:6
every man under his v. 29:27
V. her ancient Ruby yields 84:16
Vine-leaves in his hair 112:15
Vines: that spoil the v. 27:17
v. that round the thatch-eaves
run 119:17
Vineyard: My wellbeloved hath a v. 27:24
Vino: In v. veritas 163:10
Vintage: all their V. prest 85:4
draught of v.! 121:3
Vintners: what the V. buy 85:16
Violence: with restless v. 200:23
Violent: All v. feelings 178:9
danger of v. death 105:9
Laid v. hands 168:18
Violet: nodding v. 203:9
throw a perfume on the v. 193:6
V., amaracus, and asphodel 229:4
v. by a mossy stone 248:3
v. smells to him 191:12
v.'s reclining head 77:6
Violets: Fast fading v. 121:5
I would give you some v. 189:15
May v. spring! 189:22
upon a bank of v. 209:2
v. blue 196:19
v. dim 210:8
when sweet v. sicken 215:10
Vipers: generation of v. 30:5
to extirpate the v. 14:2
Virgil: shepherd in V. 113:21
Virgin: and v. mother born 145:6
Now the V. returns 237:1
on the v. thorn 203:1
v. shall conceive 27:30
Virginians: Rally behind the V. 20:3
Virginity: long preserved v. 140:12
Virtue: either of v. or mischief 14:17
fugitive and cloistered v. 148:9
if there be any v. 36:20
keep your v. 125:16
languors of v. 224:4
make ambition v.! 205:10

no v. like necessity   206:4
Silence is the v. of fools   14:7
some by v. fall   200:16
upgrowth of all v.   124:4
V.! a fig!   204:24
v., and not birth that makes us
  noble   19:21
v. hath her rewards   236:7
What every v.   129:19
Virtues: Princedoms, v., Powers   146:19
  that his v.   198:4
Virtuous: because thou art v.   209:7
  find a v. woman?   26:32
Vis consili expers   109:21
Visage: all his v. wann'd   187:11
  daub his V.   85:14
Visages: whose v. do cream   201:7
Visible: darkness v.   145:13
  outward and v. sign   168:2
  v. and invisible   167:18
Vision: Bright the v.   138:6
  fatal v.   198:9
  In a v. once I saw   66:15
  life is a watch or a v.   224:2
  more delightful v.   47:14
  my v.'s limited   75:27
  Scarce seemed a v.   214:3
  V. of the world   228:8
  Was it a v.?   121:7
  Where there is no v.   26:30
Visionary: fled the v. gleam?   246:10
  v. joys   68:14
Visions: shall see v.   29:22
Visit her face   185:11
Visitation: in the time of their v. 29:34
Visited: sick and ye v. me   32:16
Visitest: that thou v. him   168:23
Visiting: Beneath the v. moon   182:21
Visitings: compunctious v.   197:15
Vitae summa brevis   108:17
Vitro: splendidior v.   109:24
Vivamus, mea Lesbia, atque
  amemus   58:26
Vive: Il faut que je v.   10:14, 178:1
  V. l'Intérieur!   181:18
Vivid: left the v. air   219:7
  Trusty, dusky, v.   221:19
Vivre: manger pour v.   148:14
Vogue la galère!   174:8
Voice: aggravate my v.   203:4
  All with one v.   34:45
  big manly v.   183:20
  broken v.   187:11
  but a wandering v.   245:15
  but few thy v.   185:21
  Can honour's v.   97:13
  certain what-is-it in his v.   245:1
  cheerful v.   123:5
  daughter of the v. of God   245:19
  distant v.   134:9
  each a mighty V.   248:13
  Hear the v. of the Bard!   38:18
  heard the v. of the Lord   23:15
  Heart, and soul, and v.   152:12
  heart and v.   152:14
  I heard a v. cry   198:13
  I heard a v.; it said   247:16
  it is the v. of the world   42:20
  let thy v. rise   227:2
  Lift up your v.   241:14
  look and a v.   134:9
  Lord hear my v.   171:25
  lost my v. most irrecoverably   240:13
  more weighty v.   14:11
  public v.   116:28
  sing with mortal v.   146:20
  sound of a v. that is still   225:15
  still small v.   25:14
  Sweeter thy v.   229:19

that tone of v.   173:18
thou v. of my heart?   71:2
to moderate his v.   220:13
utter forth a glorious v.   1:14
V. and Verse   147:13
V. beat   232:8
v. I hear   121:6
v. in every wind   98:7
V. of God   2:4, 175:8
v. of him that cried   27:27
v. of him that crieth   28:12
v. of one crying   30:4
v. of the charmer   169:29
v. of the lobster   57:10
V. of the people   2:4, 175:8
v. of the sluggard   239:12
v. of the turtle   27:16
v. said, Cry   28:13
v. so thrilling   248:8
v. that breathed o'er Eden   122:20
v. was ever soft   196:9
watchdog's v.   95:5
will hear his v.   170:25
with a monarch's v.   193:21
your v. is music   20:10
Voices: Ancestral v.   66:15
  angel v.   143:3
  gentle v. calling   87:12
  hands and v.   244:17
  there are no v.   129:22
  Two v. are there   220:7, 248:13
  v. keep tune   150:2
  when soft v. die   215:10
  When the v. of children   39:11
  with many v.   230:15
Void: left an aching v.   70:2
Volcanoes: range of exhausted v.   76:9
Volley'd and thunder'd   226:3
Volscians: flutter'd your V.   184:19
Voltaire: Mock on, V.   38:17
Volumes: creators of odd v.   129:7
  written such v.   130:17
Voluptuous: with its v. swell   50:23
Vomit: dog returneth to his v.   26:27
Vorhang: ein eiserner V. herunter-
  senken   94:11
Vorpal: took his v. sword   57:14
Votaress: imperial v.   203:7
Voulu: Vous l'avez v.   148:18
Vovi—I've Oude   173:8
Vow: I v. to thee, my country   219:18
  promise and v.   167:32
Vows: of his music v.   188:6
Vox populi, vox dei   2:4, 175:8
Voyage: my last v.   105:10
  v. of their life   194:19
Voyage: fait un beau v.   20:15
Voyaging through strange seas   247:17
Vulgar: but by no means v.   185:21
  Father is rather v.   74:17
  it's v.   173:14
  little v. Boy   18:1
Vulgus: Odi profanum v.   109:16

W

Wabe: in the w.   57:14
Wacht: Die W. am Rhein   179:15
Wade: should I w. no more   199:12
Waft her love   202:10
Wafted abroad   228:20
Wages: ta'en thy w.   184:22
  took their w. and are dead   111:11
  w. of sin is death   35:5
Wagon: Hitch your w. to a star   83:2
Wags: how the world w.   183:16
Wail: needs must I w.   213:5
  new w. my dear times' waste   211:1
  nothing to w.   147:10

Wailing: By woman w. 66:14
Waist: Dead from the w. down 43:19
live about her w. 187:1
to thy slender w. 172:19
Waistcoat: Get her a flannel w. 89:5
Waistcoat-buttons: work them into
w. 58:12
Wait: good digestion w. 199:9
If you can w. 125:14
lily whispers, 'I w.' 228:20
only stand and w. 147:17
These w. all upon thee 171:4
they that w. upon the Lord 28:15
to labour and to w. 133:28
W. and see 12:16
Waiting: long night of w. 123:12
tired by w. 125:14
Waive the Rest 84:20
Wake: a sleping hound to w. 60:26
Do I w. or sleep? 121:7
go and w. them 58:6
Sleep to w. 45:10
w. and call me early 228:21
W. up, America 88:17
W. up, England 90:9
we w. eternally 77:10
when they w. him up 113:7
Waked: I w., she fled 148:2
Or w. to ecstasy 97:14
w. me too soon 239:12
Waken: trumpets w. the Wall! 127:14
w. from his summer dreams 214:2
w. thou with me 229:16
would w. the dead 97:2
Wakened us from sleeping 42:10
Wakening: Our w. and uprising
prove 122:13
Wakens: fire-fly w. 229:16
Wakes: whoever w. in England 44:1
woman w. to love 226:24
Waketh: watchman w. but in vain
26:4, 171:22
Waking: find him ware an' w. 153:5
in..w., no such matter 211:10
or a w. dream? 121:7
Wales: God bless the Prince of W.! 132:13
Walk: as I w. along the Bois Bou-
long 90:17
As you w. your flowery way 92:22
As you w. your mystic way 92:21
Doth w. in fear 66:5
If you w. down Piccadilly 92:22
in the palace w. 229:16
me to w. doth make 181:8
no murners w. behind me 100:9
no spirit can w. 185:4
Now w. the angels 139:12
shall w., and not faint 28:15
slow silent w. 100:4
solar w. 164:14
staff of faith to w. upon 174:13
think which way to w. 140:11
to w. humbly with thy God? 29:29
W. about Sion 169:23
w. in the same 167:32
w. into my parlour? 111:18
W. the deck my Captain lies 242:11
w. through the fields 68:28
w. through the valley 169:2
w. together to the kirk 66:6
W. under his huge legs 193:11
W. upon England's mountains 38:16
w. with Kings 125:16
w. with you 201:13
w. ye in it 28:9
Where'er you w. 165:1
Will you w. a little faster? 57:7
Within a w. of the sea 22:1
Walked: Eugene Aram w. between 106:21

forests w. 61:16
Him that w. the waves 145:4
I w. along the Strand 116:11
people that w. in darkness 27:31
w. away with their clothes 76:7
w. by himself 128:16
w. in glory 247:19
w. straight out of the Ark 217:15
w. through the wilderness 46:3
Walketh: pestilence that w. 170:19
w. about 37:7
Walking: As I was w. all alane 16:19
but a w. shadow 200:4
I nauseate w. 68:18
men as trees, w. 32:31
w. close at hand 57:21
w. dictionary 59:20
w. in an air of glory 235:10
w. in the garden 23:15
W. so early 180:18
w. up and down in it 25:24
Walking staff: for a palmer's w. 206:16
Walks: liked the way it w. 174:19
very sure God w. in mine 42:18
W. o'er the dew 185:5
W. the night 73:9
Wall: close the w. up 191:8
Flower in the crannied w. 226:12
hang here on yonder w. 110:2
icicles hang by the w. 196:20
in the office of a w. 206:7
old oak w. 19:4
painted on the w. 44:14
standing like a stone w. 20:3
through his castle w. 206:15
trumpets waken the W.! 127:14
Watch the w., my darling 127:10
whitewash on the w. 8:7
With our backs to the w. 99:4
Wallace: wi' W. bled 48:30
Wallet at his back 208:27
Walls: be within thy w. 171:20
labyrinth of w. 213:17
on the outward w. 200:2
on the w. of heaven 139:12
snap-dragon growing on the w. 153:11
Stone w. do not a prison 134:19
upon the w. of thine house 171:24
w. about our life 206:15
W. have tongues 223:25
Washes its w. 44:18
watches from his mountain w. 226:9
With w. and towers 66:14
wooden w. 69:7
Walnuts: Across the w. and the
wine 228:22
Walrus and the Carpenter 57:21
Waltzing Matilda 161:12
Waly, waly, up the bank 17:2
Wan: how w. a face! 216:30
pale and w., fond lover? 222:5
Wander: w. forth the sons of Belial 146:5
w. hand in hand 154:16
Whither shall I w.? 155:16
Wandered: fingers w. idly 172:22
w. all our ways 174:15
Wanderer: Happy the w. 20:15
weary, wayworn w. 163:16
Wandering: but a w. voice? 245:15
Poor w. one! 93:17
tempt with w. feet 146:12
tempts your w. eyes 98:4
W. between two worlds 11:15
w. minstrel I 91:27
w. on a foreign strand! 180:6
where is my w. boy to-night? 6:18
Wanderings: comrade of thy w. 214:3
Wane: wax and w. no more 239:13
who know'st no w. 86:2

Wanes: long day w.   230:15
Waning: beneath a w. moon   66:14
Wann'd: all his visage w.   187:11
Want: and do not w. it   113:22
    freedom from w.   176:17
    I'll not w.   181:8
    though much I w.   80:17
    Toil, envy, we.   117:2
    w. of a thing   235:6
    We don't w. to fight   112:1
    What can I w.?   104:4
    what they w.   71:8
Wanted: not be w. these ten years   163:1
Wanting: art found w.   29:18
Wanton: As flies to w. boys   195:18
    w. wiles   144:12
Wantonness: in clothes a w.   104:11
Wantons: Sleep, pretty w.   73:1
Wants: Man w. but little   95:9, 250:17
    w. that little strong   106:12
War: All the business of w.   240:15
    arts of w. and peace   51:17
    blast of w.   191:8
    come out of this w.   238:1
    come ye in w.   180:11
    dastard in w.   180:10
    dauntless in w.   180:9
    dogs of w.   193:21
    Ease after w.   219:10
    engaged in a great civil w.   132:8
    First in w.   131:17
    garland of the w.   182:21
    going to the w.   61:19
    Great Britain is going to make w.   23:1
    image of w.   222:13
    In w...there are no winners   59:15
    infection and the hand of w.   206:7
    inoperative in w.   63:21
    it is not w.   40:10
    learn w. any more   27:22
    Marching as to w.   18:7
    Minstrel Boy to the w.   149:15
    money the sinews of w.   15:2
    never was a good w.   88:3
    no discharge in that w.   26:42
    no discharge in the w.!   124:16
    No less renowned than w.   148:5
    object of government in..w.   23:3
    of glorious w.!   205:10
    prepare for w.   235:12
    prophesying w.!   66:15
    some slain in w.   206:15
    take as much and as little of the w.   15:3
    then was the tug of w.!   131:18
    throughout the w.   91:22
    To w. and arms I fly   134:20
    Undertones of W.   39:25
    used to w.'s alarms   106:22
    W. between Men and Women   233:13
    w. but endless w. still breed?   148:4
    w. has its laws   153:9
    w. is destructive   113:12
    W. is much too serious   225:5
    W. its thousands slays   165:19
    W. that will end W.   241:6
    W., w. is still the cry   50:20
    W.'s annals   100:4
    weapons of w. perished!   25:1
    What did you do in the Great W.?   8:11
    when the w. is done   179:5
Warble his native wood-notes   144:19
Wardrobe: in the w. lies   191:5
Ware: Let me taste your w.   157:19
    should dine at W.   69:30
Warfare: her w. is accomplished   28:11
    legitimate w.   153:9
Waring: What's become of W.   45:13
Warm: a w. wind   141:6
    coat is so w.   156:3
    her heart was w.   99:10
    keep himself w.   157:1
    sensible w. motion   200:23
Warmed: I w. both hands   129:20
    w. and cooled   201:27
Warmest welcome   215:18
Warming his five wits   230:9
Warmint: running into the w.   222:14
Warmth: an awful w.   122:9
    w. to swell the grain   53:12
Warn: duty to w. you   78:7
    To w., to comfort   248:5
    w. th' immortal souls   139:12
Warned: be w. by my lot   126:7
    Oh, my friends, be w. by me   21:4
    who hath w. you to flee   30:5
Warning: Give w. to the world   211:7
    steal away, give little w.   17:8
War Office: except the British W.   212:12
Warp: Though thou the waters w.   184:2
    Weave the w.   97:5
Warr'd: Seven cities w. for Homer   105:1
Warring within our breasts   139:10
Warrior: lay like a w.   245:5
    they brought her w. dead   229:15
    Who is the happy W.?   246:2
Warriors: France, mother..of w.   20:14
Wars: and the big w.   205:10
    For all their w. are merry   61:15
    Let w. yield to peace   63:14
    maketh w. to cease   169:21
    serve in the w.   172:15
    skilful in the w.   235:7
    thousand w. of old   227:20
    W. and rumours of w.   32:10
Warts: roughnesses, pimples, w.   71:9
Warwick and Talbot   192:4
Was: which w., and is   37:16
Wash: not w. dishes   155:11
    Shall henceforth w. the river
        Rhine?   66:9
    They w. their feet   82:1
    thou shalt w. me   169:26
    w. her guilt away?   95:21
    W. me in the water   8:7
    W. me, Saviour   234:1
    w. out a Word   85:12
    w. the balm   206:12
    w. this blood   198:15
    w. your hands and pray   125:10
Washed by the rivers   42:11
Washing: by taking in one another's
        w.   4:5
Wash-pot: Moab is my w.   170:2
Wassailing: Here we come a-w.   4:18
Waste: dear times' w.   211:1
    in Annihilation's W.   85:9
    lay w. our powers   249:5
    seemed w. of breath   250:7
    w. howling wilderness   24:22
    w. its sweetness   97:15
    w. of seas   181:7
    w. of shame   212:1
    ye w. places of Jerusalem   28:19
Wasted his substance   33:21
Wastes: that w. her time   238:4
Wasting: sick o' w. leather   126:14
    w. in despair   244:18
Watch: as a w. in the night   170:17
    Has a w. and chain   176:3
    One to w., and one to pray   1:17
    Saints their w. are keeping   222:2
    She shall w. all night   208:7
    they w. from their graves!   44:11
    w. between me and thee   23:31
    w. on the Rhine   179:15
    w. that ends the night   239:14
    W. the wall, my darling   127:10
    will w. from dawn to gloom   214:9

Watchdog: w.'s honest bark 51:13
w.'s voice 95:5
Watch-dogs bark 208:9
Watched: however w. and tended 134:1
I w. in vain 86:9
w. their flocks by night 225:9
Watcher of the skies 121:9
Watches: She w. him 223:18
Watching: And w., with eternal lids 121:8
Big brother is w. you 159:16
children stood w. 124:2
w. for the morrow 55:23
Watchman: w. waketh but in vain 26:4, 171:22
W. what of the night? 28:5
Watchword of the great Liberal party 41:11
Water: Across the stormy w. 54:1
be changed into little w. drops 139:1
before it beat the w. 134:4
benison of hot w. 41:18
blade struck the w. 64:17
burn'd on the w. 182:15
But limns the w. 15:14
but w.'s thin 91:26
by the W. blows 84:16
By w. and the Word 222:1
Christ walking on the w. 232:10
cup of cold w. 31:17
dipping into the w. 64:17
do your work on w. 125:11
don't care where the w. goes 61:28
drawers of w. 24:27
Drink no longer w. 36:28
dull as ditch w. 75:14
fish out of the w. 182:6
fountain of the w. 37:27
His steeds to w. 184:20
Is wetter w. 42:1
King over the W. 7:18
Lavender w. tinged with pink 131:11
Little drops of w. 55:26
little w. clears us 198:16
made his mouth to w. 49:24
never hold w. 63:10
pools are filled with w. 170:14
Shall be in w. writ 19:20
Shall come of w. and of mud 41:20
stain'd the w. clear 39:8
struggling for life in the w. 113:22
was writ in w. 122:12
w. in the rough rude sea 206:12
W. like a stone 177:9
w. of affliction 25:16
w. under the earth 167:7
W., w., every where 65:14
w. which they beat 182:15
W. your damned flower-pots 45:7
We'll o'er the w. 106:6
with w. and a crust 120:15
Water-brooks: desireth the w. 169:15
Watered: fed and w. 53:12
Waterfall: From the w. 134:6
Water-lily: saw the w. bloom 227:25
Waterloo: meets his W. at last 162:15
W. was won 240:17
Water-pipes: noise of the w. 169:16
Waterproof: Great Big W. Boots 143:8
Waters: as the w. cover the sea 2:3, 28:3
Cast thy bread upon the w. 27:5
cold w. to a thirsty soul 26:25
depth of w. 177:15
fen of stagnant w. 247:7
hear the mighty w. 246:12
in great w. 171:7
Many w. cannot quench love 27:20
moving w. 121:8
much deeper w. 78:9
Over the rolling w. 229:9

pleasant w. 173:1
pour the w. of the Nile 56:13
quiet w. by 181:8
Stolen w. are sweet 26:11
thou the w. warp 184:2
To see thee in our w. 118:9
upon the w. 208:10
w. of comfort 169:2
W. on a starry night 246:8
While the nearer w. roll 241:8
Watery: beneath the w. floor 145:4
crown the w. glade 98:5
his w. bier 144:20
Watson: Good old W.! 78:12
You know my methods, W. 78:5
Wattles: of clay and w. made 250:9
Wave: across the dark w. 235:1
All sunk beneath the w. 70:9
blue w. rolls 52:9
cool, translucent w. 144:3
life on the ocean w. 179:3
lift me as a w. 214:3
like a w. of the sea 250:8
long may it w. 123:7
over the western w. 213:20
w. to pant 214:3
w.'s intenser day 214:2
winning w. 104:11
Wavering: all w. and hesitation 174:9
Waves: all thy w. 169:16
as the sons of the w.? 88:18
Britannia rules the w. 54:2
Floated midway on the w. 66:15
Heed not the rolling w. 39:23
Him that walked the w. 145:4
Like as the w. 211:5
march is o'er the mountain w. 54:7
w. serener far 213:12
What are the wild w. saying 55:27
while the tired w. 64:10
wild w. whist 208:9
Wax: w. and wane no more 239:13
W. to receive 50:17
with honey and w. 223:1
Waxed very loud 142:6
Way: broad is the w. 31:1
catch the nearest w. 197:14
gull's w. 141:4
has but a little w. 84:17
His uncouth w. 146:12
I am going a long w. 227:3
I am the w. 34:19
into the w. of peace 32:39
Life with its w. 149:1
make w. for those who do 108:13
moves in a mysterious w. 70:5
My centre is giving w. 86:14
narrow is the w. 31:2
New W. to Pay Old Debts 141:10
noiseless tenor of their w. 98:1
on his w. attended 246:11
on thy w. 104:13
or milky w. 164:14
plods his weary w. 97:8
Prepare ye the w. of the Lord 28:12, 30:4
pretty Fanny's w. 161:2
roses, roses, all the w. 44:17
safer than a known w. 101:5
shall not pass this w. again 98:15
Some w. of common trade 206:16
soon find a w. back 108:8
there was but one w. 191:6
think which w. to walk 140:11
This is the w. the world ends 81:13
This is the w., walk ye in it 28:9
took their solitary w. 146:25
turned..to his own w. 28:21
up-hill all the w.? 177:13

walk your flowery w.   92:22
walk your mystic w.   92:21
was the w. to glory   229:2
W. down upon de Swanee Ribber   87:11
w. may be known   170:4
w. of a man   26:31
w. of all flesh   68:15, 182:4, 240:9
w. of an eagle   26:31
w. of the ungodly   172:5
w. of transgressors   26:14
w. to be a bore   237:19
w. was long   180:4
went his w.   84:22
winning w.   68:12
woman has her w.   106:13
working out its w.   79:5
Ways: among the untrodden w.   248:3
consider her w.   26:8
down the labyrinthine w.   232:7
justify God's w. to man   111:7
keep thee in all thy w.   170:20
light in his w.   224:2
strayed from thy w.   166:8
subtle w.   82:13
sure in all His w.   153:14
wandered all our w.   174:15
w. be foul   196:20
w. of pleasantness   26:7
w. that are dark   101:3
your w. my w.   28:25
Wayside: fell by the w.   31:25
Wayworn: weary, w. wanderer   163:16
Weak: body of a w. and feeble
    woman   82:9
but the flesh is w.   32:21
Made w. by time   230:15
poor, infirm, w.   195:5
to be w. is miserable   146:1
We are but little children w.   2:11
Weaker: W. sex   2:12
w. vessel   37:5
Weakest thing in nature   161:8
Weak-ey'd: where the w. bat   67:12
Weakness: amiable w.   84:9, 216:22
Is it w. of intellect ?   92:17
no w., no contempt   147:10
Weaknesses: his w. are great   124:10
Wealth: all that w. e'er gave   97:12
as their w. increases   139:5
health and w. have missed me   112:4
nor w. nor blessed abode   141:5
pauper in the midst of w.   110:1
poor man's w.   217:1
promoting the w...of the human
    race   47:5
such w. brings   210:13
w. a well-spent age   54:10
w. and commerce   138:4
w. of the Indies   115:18, 232:4
Where w. accumulates   95:4
Worldly w. he cared not for   88:11
Wean'd: were we not w. till then?   77:7
Weans: Are the w. in their bed   143:4
Weapon: and his w. wit   107:8
trusty shield and w.   135:12
Weapons: hurt with the same w.   201:27
to wear w.   172:15
w... Achates bore   236:4
w. of war perished!   25:1
Wear: I will w. him   188:11
might w...all her dignities   190:9
Motley's the only w.   183:18
Nothing to w. but clothes   123:10
to w. ourselves   139:10
to w. weapons   172:15
w. my heart upon my sleeve   204:16
w. of winning   21:12
w. out than rust out   71:15, 242:8
w. the beauty of the morning   249:4

w. the bottoms of my trousers   81:19
w. your rue   189:15
we'll w. out   196:6
Weare: name was Mr. William W.   240:3
Wearies: It w. me   201:6
Weariest: w. and most loathèd   201:1
w. river   224:6
Weariness: For w. of thee   77:15
study is a w.   27:9
w. of the flesh   27:9
w., the fever, and the fret   121:4
Wears: She w. her clothes   223:13
That every Hyacinth the Garden w.   85:2
w. yet a precious jewel   183:9
Weary: Age shall not w. them   38:2
Art thou w.   152:9
Be not w. in well doing   36:25
How w., stale   185:11
I sae w.   49:4
plods his w. way   97:8
run, and not be w.   28:15
Say I'm w.   112:4
Sun-flower! w. of time   39:7
w. and ill at ease   172:22
W. and old with service   192:14
w. be at rest   25:28
W. of breath   106:20
W. se'nnights   197:6
With fingers w.   107:3
Weasel: as a w. sucks eggs   183:14
it is like a w.   188:18
Pop goes the w.!   138:2
Weather: come wind, come w.   46:20
different kinds of good w.   178:10
first talk is of the w.   116:20
If it prove fair w.   222:8
no such thing as bad w.   178:10
season of calm w.   246:12
Through pleasant and through
    cloudy w.   17:8
under the w.   221:8
w. the cuckoo likes   100:5
winter and rough w.   183:13
Weathered every rack   242:10
Weave: Shall w. old England's   38:12
tangled web we w.   180:12
W. a circle round him   66:15
W. the warp   97:5
Weaves: He w., and is clothed   224:2
Web: Out flew the w.   227:25
She left the w.   227:25
tangled w. we weave   180:12
Webs: trafficked for strange w.   161:9
Webster was much possessed by
    death   82:3
Wed: And think to w. it   182:7
I thee w.   168:14
December when they w.   184:11
Wedded: to thy w. wife   168:10
w. maid   145:6
Wedding-day: It is my w.   69:30
To-morrow is our w.   69:22
Wedding-Guest stood still   65:5
Wedlock's the devil   52:5
Wednesday: Married on W   158:2
W.'s child   156:17
Wee: At my w., small door   73:10
pig cried, W., w., w.!   158:9
Weed: Less than the w.   107:10
than the fat w.   186:9
Weeds: grubbing w.   125:9
her coronet w.   189:18
smell far worse than w.   211:11
winter w. outworn   213:12
Worthless as withered w.   41:14
Week: a w., a natural day   138:14
days that's in the w.   55:4
Food enough for a w.   142:14
Middle of Next W.   56:8

Weeks: brief hours and w. 211:16
 once in three w.! 222:14
Weel: Come w., come wo 106:6
Ween: a glorious thing, I w. 91:8
Weep: dew shall w. 104:6
 Fair daffodils, we w. to see 104:10
 for fear of having to w. 19:7
 I w. for Adonais 213:6
 make the angels w. 200:19
 now you w. 194:10
 She must w. 229:15
 That he should w. for her? 187:11
 that I may not w. 51:22
 To w. there 209:9
 vapours w. their burthen 230:10
 W., and you w. alone 243:3
 w. for their sins 242:14
 W. no more, my lady 87:10
 W. thy girlish tears! 239:5
 women must w. 124:3
Weeping: Doth that bode w.? 205:14
 dwell a w. hermit 67:15
 goeth on his way w. 171:21
 mournful mother w. 223:21
 night of w. 222:2
 there shall be w. 31:6
 W...for the morrow 55:23
 With w. and with laughter 136:16
Weeps: loves, and w., and dies 213:12
 turns from their gaze, and w. 149:17
 white rose w. 228:20
 Woe w. out her division 117:10
Wee Willie Winkie 143:4
Weib: Wein, W. und Gesang 135:11
Weighed: art w. in the balances 29:18
Weighs upon the heart? 200:1
Weight: falls by its own w. 109:21
 He carries w.! 69:28
 Ills have no w. 135:17
 lay aside every w. 36:35
 Wearing all that w. 227:21
 willing to pull his w. 177:1
Wein, Weib und Gesang 135:12
Weird sisters 199:24
Welcome: Bay deep-mouth'd w. 51:13
 Love bade me w. 104:1
 outstay'd his w. 67:3
 Thrice w. 245:16
 warmest w. 215:18
 w. day 105:2
 w. in your eye 198:1
 W. the coming [guest] 165:11
 W., wild North-easter! 123:16
 with a frolic w. 230:15
Welcomes at once all the world 10:8
Welcomest: often w. when they are
 gone 192:6
Welfare: safety, honour, and w. of
 this realm 60:1
Welfare-State 225:13
Well: All is not w. 185:19
 all shall be w. 203:16
 Be not weary in w. doing 36:25
 came to know me w. 149:19
 can do all things w.? 62:9
 cried out—W. done! 69:28
 did it very w. 91:22
 loved passing w. 187:6
 mark him w. 180:6
 not done w. 114:19
 not feeling very w. 173:20
 not wisely but too w. 205:20
 nothing but w. 147:10
 of the W. of Life 85:9
 perfectly w. 143:12
 prayeth w. 66:7
 Pussy's in the w. 155:13
 so w. as I 243:6
 that can speak so w. 141:11

That is w. said 237:13
They know not w. 82:13
think not w. of me 244:18
to love too w.? 164:4
to play billiards w. 219:5
'twill all be w. 85:14
use it for a w. 170:14
W. done, thou good and faithful 32:14
 w. of love 65:2
 yet none knows w. 212:2
Well-being of society 177:2
Wellbeloved: My w. hath a vine-
 yard 27:24
Well-conducted: Like a w. person 232:4
Well-dressed: sense of being w. 83:1
Well-order'd ranks 70:20
Wells: My name is John Welling-
 ton W. 93:31
 to poison the w. 153:9
Well-trod stage 144:19
Well-tuned cymbals 172:8
Welsh: devil understands w. 190:19
Welter to the parching wind 144:20
Weltgeschichte: Die W. ist das Welt-
 gericht 179:14
Wen: fate of the great w. 64:14
Wenceslas: Good King W. 152:13
Wench: fit only for a w. 141:1
Wenches: hideous w. 66:9
Went: as cooks go she w. 178:15
 as in I w. 85:7
 at the other out it w. 60:28
 When I w. to the Bar 91:20
Weoman: very pretty w. 86:11
Wept: he w. to hear 39:8
 I, too, have w. 151:8
 sat down and w. 171:28
 They w. like anything 57:21
 w. with joy 39:8
Werther had a love for Charlotte 232:4
Weser: river W. 44:18
Wesley: John W.'s conversation 115:15
West: bosom of the urgent w. 41:8
 come out of the w. 180:8
 Go w., young man 218:11
 home in the w. 244:11
 nor from the w. 170:10
 O wild W. Wind 214:1
 safeguard of the W. 249:1
 sailing away to the w. 124:2
 W. is W. 124:13
 wind is in the w. 8:15
 with the W. in her eyes 65:3
West Port: open the W. 179:20
Westen: Im W. nichts Neues 175:5
Western: all the w. stars 230:15
 over the w. wave 213:20
 Wind of the w. sea 229:9
Western Front: All Quiet on the
 W. 175:5
Westminster Abbey: gained a peer-
 age, or W. 152:13
 I very often walk by myself in W. 1:8
Westward: But w., look 64:10
 W. the course of empire 22:16
Wet: dirty and w. 223:23
 have w. them o'er 59:3
 hir joly whistle wel y-w. 60:19
 w. sheet and a flowing sea 71:16
Wetter water 42:1
Whale: and the w.'s way 141:4
 Very like a w. 188:18
Whales: Among the sharks and w. 6:17
 they would talk like w. 96:4
 Where great w. come sailing 11:11
What: He knew w.'s w. 49:17
 She knows w.'s w. 75:31
What-Ho! She bumps! 58:19
What: is-it-certain w. 245:1

Wheat: orient and immortal w.   234:2
Wheel: beneath thy chariot w.   107:10
  breaks a butterfly upon a w.?   165:7
  cannot mind my w.   129:21
  Time's w. runs back   45:5
  w. broken at the cistern   27:8
  w. is come full circle   196:8
  w. of fire   196:1
  w. the sofa round   70:18
  w.'s kick   141:2
Wheeling: houses go w. back   233:4
Wheels: a spoke among your w.   19:18
  all the w. run down   123:18
  For w. of hansom-cabs   58:13
Whelp: Both mongrel, puppy, w.   95:13
When: the where and w.?   101:6
Whenas in silks   104:15
Whence: and w. it flows   246:11
  from w. he sprung   180:6
Where: an echo answers—'W.?'   50:19
  But w. is he   62:9
  If so be, you ask me w.   104:8
  knew not w.   133:12
  w. and when?   101:6
Wherefore: he had a w.   49:16
Whetted: like a w. knife   141:4
Whiff of grapeshot   55:11
Whiffling: Came w.   57:14
Whig: a vile W.   114:28
  first W. was the Devil   115:19
  W. The name of a faction   116:19
Whigs: caught the W. bathing   76:7
  For W. admit no force   43:3
  We have dished the W.?   220:1
Whim: tempted by a private w.   21:19
Whimper: but a w.   81:13
Whimpering to and fro   125:4
Whine: do not sweat and w.   242:14
Whining: In w. Poetry   77:19
  w. schoolboy   183:20
Whipped: have such a fellow w.   188:7
  w. her little daughter   156:12
  w. them all soundly   158:6
Whipping: who should 'scape w.?   187:10
  who would bear the w.   187:13
Whips: chastised you with w.   25:10
Whirled: leaf is w. away   227:8
Whirligig of time   209:19
Whirlwind: shall reap the w.   29:20
  w. of passion   188:7
Whiskers: Cat with crimson w.!   131:12
  my fur and w.!   56:15
Whisper: far-heard w.   65:15
  W. who dares!   143:15
Whispered behind the leaves   125:1
Whispering: And the w. sound   70:7
  bay'd the w. wind   95:5
  Come w. by   100:4
  w. from her towers   12:3
Whispers: lily w.   228:20
  w. peace within   37:33
Whist: good game at w.   129:6
  wild waves w.   208:9
Whistle: as clear as a w.   50:13
  hir joly w. wel y-wet   60:19
  w., and I'll come to you   49:3
  W. and she'll come to you   19:26
Whistles in his sound   183:20
Whistling: w. half a dozen bars   220:14
  W. to keep myself from being
    afraid   79:15
Whit: Not a w.   189:26
White: crimson petal, now the w.   229:16
  fat w. woman   68:28
  Gardener in w.   86:7
  hair has become very w.   56:16
  in black and w.   117:15
  In large w. flakes falling   41:7
  Its fleece was w. as snow   99:5

my soul is w.   39:10
O so w.!   118:11
so red and so w.   123:17
Take up the W. Man's burden   128:5
thy w. sails crowding   41:8
Wearing w. for Eastertide   110:15
w. and rustling sail   71:16
W. as an angel   39:10
W. founts falling   61:18
w. rose weeps   228:20
your sins..as w. as snow   27:21
Whited sepulchres   32:9
White House: Log-cabin to W.   232:5
Whiter: I shall be w.   8:7
Whites of their eyes   173:22
Whitewash on the wall   8:7
Whither: and w. it goeth   33:50
  W. away, fair rover   41:8
  W., O splendid ship   41:8
  W. goest thou?   34:21
  w. thou goest   24:35
Whithersoever thou goest   24:26
Whiting: said a w. to a snail   57:7
Whitman: daintily dressed Walt W.   62:2
Whole: a dwarfish w.   66:12
  A w. I planned   45:4
  Entire and w.   219:18
  half is greater than the w.   104:18
  saw it w.   11:14
Wholesome: nights are w.   185:4
Wholly: Either to be w. slaves   79:22
Whoop: merrily we'll w.   242:20
Whore: morals of a w.   114:2
  posture of a w.   182:24
  'Tis Pity She's a W.   87:3
Whorled: beat upon my w. ear   107:13
Why: fail to see w.   178:1
  For every w.   49:16
  he knows not w.   227:4
  Though I could never tell w.   93:5
Wicked: God made the w. Grocer   61:25
  heart is..desperately w.   29:7
  horrid w. boy   105:16
  more w. than himself   31:24
  no peace..unto the w.   28:17
  Something w. this way comes   199:17
  this w. world   167:32
  When the w. man turneth away   29:13
  w. cease from troubling   25:28
  w. flee   26:29
  w. saith   64:4
  worse than w.   173:14
Wickedness: shapen in w.   169:25
  sins and w.   166:7
  spiritual w. in high places   36:14
Wicket: flannelled fools at the w.   126:1
Widdicombe Fair: I want for to go
    to W.   17:4
Widdrington: as ever was Squire
    W.   79:21
Wide: dark world and w.   147:17
  far and w.   102:9
  great and w. sea   171:4
  long and w.   161:16
  rivers w.   144:14
  shore of the w. world   122:5
  two feet w.   248:16
  Under the w. and starry sky   221:23
  w. as his command   79:3
  W. is the gate   31:1
  world too w.   183:20
Wider: w. still and w.   22:7
Widow: a certain poor w.   32:35
  fatherless and w.   172:5
  W. at Windsor   128:6
  w. bird sate mourning   213:11
  w. of fifty   216:19
Widowhood: comfortable estate of
  w.   89:12

Widows: careful o' w. 75:21
Wielder of the stateliest measure 231:1
Wife: All the world and his w. 10:8, 223:20
  cleave unto his w. 23:14
  covet thy neighbour's w. 167:17
  dwindle into a w. 68:19
  give unto my w. 212:6
  He that hath w. and children 14:17
  Here lies my w. 79:20
  his w. looked back 23:26
  honour unto the w. 37:5
  hope that keeps up a w.'s spirits 89:12
  I have married a w. 33:16
  In every port a w. 73:17
  In every port he finds a w. 37:32
  in want of a w. 13:18
  kick his w. out of bed 222:14
  kill a w. with kindness 208:7
  let his w. starve 212:20
  letter from his w. 56:7
  lofty character of W. 74:12
  Man and his W. 128:25
  Match'd with an aged w. 230:12
  may debauch his friend's w. 115:3
  Mother, W., and Queen 230:1
  My w., who, poor wretch 162:6
  ran after the farmer's w. 158:10
  Remember Lot's w. 33:32
  sailor's w. 197:5
  Thane of Fife had a w. 199:29
  There's my w. 219:19
  to thy wedded w. 168:10
  w...as the fruitful vine 171:24
  w. could eat no lean 156:5
  w. of thy bosom 24:19
Wig: Away went hat and w.! 69:27
  My hat and w. 69:29
Wight: a maid and her w. 100:4
Wigwam: that lights the w.? 134:5
  w. of Nokomis 134:4
Wild: But only rather rude and w. 21:11
  Call of the W. 133:11
  down the valleys w. 39:8
  fasting in the w. 218:6
  fifteen w. Decembers 41:15
  fluttered folk and w. 128:5
  Heaven in a W. Flower 38:10
  her w., w. eyes 120:13
  in the southern w. 39:10
  It was the winter w. 145:7
  Ring out, w. bells 227:18
  tales of w. Cashmere 244:10
  walking by his w. lone 128:17
  western wind was w. 124:1
  what w. centuries 73:2
  When w. in woods 79:19
  W. animals never kill 88:10
  W. Ass 85:1
  w. call 141:3
  w. desire 45:6
  w. dog 137:13
  w. regrets 243:6
  W. Spirit 214:1
  with a w. surmise 121:9
  withered, and so w. 197:8
Wilderness: crying in the w. 30:4
  into the w. to see? 31:18
  man in the w. 156:15
  savage w. into a glorious empire 47:5
  scapegoat into the W. 24:11
  singing in the W. 84:18
  temptation in the w. 170:25
  that crieth in the w. 28:12
  waste howling w. 24:22
  When they make a w. 224:15
  w. and the solitary place 28:9
  W. is Paradise 84:18
  w. of monkeys 201:28
  w. of this world 46:3

Wildernesses: thought's w. 214:9
Wiles: man of many w. 106:16
  wanton w. 144:12
Wilhelmine: His little grandchild W. 218:12
Wilkes: Dine with Jack W. 115:10
Wilkinson hath tilled 248:10
Will: at his own sweet w. 249:4
  be it what it w. 164:23
  boy's w. 133:24
  complies against his w. 50:3
  God's holy w. 167:32
  good w. to man 181:10
  good w. toward men 32:43
  laid me down with a w. 221:23
  Man has his w. 106:13
  Mariner hath his w. 65:5
  Michael Henchard's W. 100:9
  mighty effort of w. 22:11
  not another's w. 249:10
  not my w., but thine 33:37
  our w. is free 114:24
  poor W. must live 172:21
  Say what you w. 68:16
  strong in w. 230:15
  take the w. for the deed 223:14
  Thy w. be done 30:22
  unconquerable w. 145:15
  w. that it should become 119:11
  W. you, won't you 57:8
  won my right good w. 137:15, 235:4
William: W. Dewy, Tranter Reuben 100:3
  You are old, Father W. 56:16, 218:22, 219:1
Williams: Dr. W.'s pink pills for pale people 4:3
Willie shall dance with Jane 3:22
Willing: Barkis is w. 74:6
  spirit indeed is w. 32:21
  W. to wound 165:6
Will-o'-th'-Wisp: No W. mislight thee 104:13
Willow: Hey w. waly O! 92:24
  Make me a w. cabin 209:4
  Sang W., titwillow 92:16
  w. grows aslant a brook 189:18
  with a w. in her hand 202:10
Willow-tree: a weeping w. 8:1
  al under the w. 60:7
  Falling from that w. 96:9
Wills: and talk of w. 206:14
  unruly w. 166:35
Willy: So W., let me and you be wipers 44:23
Win: Heads I w. 71:4
  How to w. Friends 55:25
  If you want to w. her hand 41:1
  match to w. 153:6
  nothing w. 91:26
  this great fight did w. 218:14
  time to w. this game 78:25
  To w. or lose it all 149:6
  To w. the palm 140:4
  w. his spurs 81:3
  w. the trick 111:19
  would w. me 66:15
Winced: I have not w. 102:13
Wind: against the w. 51:4
  air goes by in a w. 20:4
  bay'd the whisp'ring w. 95:5
  Blow, blow, thou winter w. 184:1
  Blow, w.! 200:7
  breath of the night w. 11:8
  breathing of the common w. 248:20
  by the winnowing w. 119:18
  Come w., come weather 46:20
  every w. of doctrine 36:10
  Fair stood the w. for France 78:28
  forgot to w. up the clock? 220:13

Frosty w. 177:9
frozen w. 213:11
gone with the w. 77:27
good south w. 65:9
hear a voice in every w. 98:7
hears him in the w. 164:14
is the w.'s will 133:24
It is an ill w. 234:8
likewise a w. on the heath 40:8
Lord was not in the w. 25:14
Nor ever w. blows loudly 227:3
north w. doth blow 157:1
O wild West W. 214:1
O, W. 214:4
of w. and limb 49:22
parching w. 144:20
reed shaken with the w.? 31:18
rushing, mighty w. 34:31
sand against the w. 38:17
shall drown the w. 198:4
soft w. hovers 94:16
streamers waving in the w. 89:30
swoln with w. 145:3
they have sown the w. 29:20
to keep the w. away 189:21
'twas but the w. 51:1
warm w. 141:6
west w. 141:6
western w. was wild 124:1
Western w., when wilt thou
  blow 8:10
what w. is to fire 49:14
When the w. blows 38:9
which way the w. is 181:14
whose w. did seem to glow 182:15
w. and the rain 209:20
w. bloweth where it listeth 33:50
w. blows it back 38:17
w. doth blow 17:1, 196:20
w. goeth over it 171:1
w. in that corner? 204:10
w. is in the east 8:15
w. is in the north 8:15
w. is in the palm-trees 126:11
w. is in the south 8:15
w. is in the west 8:15
w. of criticism 116:7
W. of the western sea 229:9
w. slowly o'er the lea 97:8
w. that blows 73:18
w. that follows fast 71:16
w. was a torrent of darkness 155:1
w. was cold 180:4
w.'s like a whetted knife 141:4
w.'s song 141:2
Winder, a casement 75:2
Winding: a w. road before me 101:11
many a w. bout 144:19
weave old England's w. sheet 38:12
W.-sheet of Edward's race 97:5
W. up days with toil 191:15
Window: and looked out at a w. 25:21
little w. where the sun 107:1
through yonder w. breaks? 207:20
Tirling at the w. 143:4
To thy chamber w. 213:13
Window'd raggedness 195:8
Window-panes: upon the w. 81:16
Windows: eastern w. only 64:10
I cleaned the w. 93:10
maid that showed at the w. 222:20
storied w. 144:9
through w.,..call on us? 77:18
up flew the w. all 69:28
Winds: all the w. that blew! 229:1
Blow me about in w.! 205:18
Blow, w. 195:4
in the viewless w. 200:23
March w. and April showers 6:5

Rough w. do shake 210:12
take the w. of March 210:8
where the beetle w. 67:12
While the stormy w. 54:6
w. his horn 84:11
w. of heaven 185:11
W. of the World 125:4
W. somewhere safe to sea 224:6
w. that hold them play 147:5
w. that will be howling 249:5
w. were love-sick 182:15
Windsor: Widow at W. 128:6
Windward of the law 62:8
Windy: and w. places 223:28
flung us on the w. hill 42:4
plains of w. Troy 230:13
w. side of the law 209:17
Wine: Across the walnuts and the
  w. 228:22
bin of w. 221:22
do crush their w. 140:6
Drinking the blude-red w. 16:12
fetch to me a pint o' w. 48:18
Flask of W. 84:18
fond of Spanish w. 141:1
full of dewy w. 121:5
Good w.—a friend 2:5
good w. needs no bush 184:16
I'll not look for w. 117:19
it doesn't get into the w. 61:28
Jug of W. 84:19
like generous w. 50:4
little w. for thy stomach's sake 36:28
mine host's Canary w.? 120:17
new w. into old bottles 31:11
red Sweet w. of youth 41:16
refreshed with w. 170:12
Sans W. 85:5
sweet white w. 140:20
Truth comes out in w. 163:10
when the w. is in, the wit is out 19:30
w. and women 51:15
W. has play'd the Infidel 85:16
w. inspires us 89:17
w. of life is drawn 198:19
W. that maketh glad 171:2
w. when it is red 26:23
with insolence and w. 146:5
with Samian w.! 51:21
woman, w., and song 135:11
Women and w. 89:17
Wine-cup: when the w. glistens 180:15
Wines: old w. 95:24
Wing: Bird is on the W. 84:17
Conquest's crimson w. 97:4
crow makes w. 199:6
flits by on leathern w. 67:12
from her light w. 71:2
head under his w. 157:1
lark's on the w. 44:24
shadow of Thy w. 241:10
start a w.! 232:10
to take under my w. 92:15
w. the midway air 195:19
Winged: Where stands a w. sentry 235:7
w. seeds 214:1
With w. heels 191:5
Wings: almost hear the beating of
  his w. 41:10
beating..luminous w. 12:5
bug with gilded w. 165:8
clip an Angel's w. 120:16
deep-damask'd w. 120:4
defend thee under his w. 170:19
each one had six w. 27:27
errant w. 61:16
gentle w. may rest 179:11
moult away his w. 222:8
On the w. of song 102:5

Wings (*cont.*)
On the w. of the storm   96:19
pigs have w.   57:22
shadow of thy w.   168:28
spread his w. on the blast   52:10
Till the little w. are stronger   230:7
w. of the Loves   224:9
w. of the morning   172:1
with w. as eagles   28:15
Wink: not slept one w.   184:21
see them w. the other eye   90:17
w. for every pretty maid   222:20
Winking: w. at the brim   121:3
w. Mary-buds   184:20
Winks: Nor w. the gold fin   229:16
Winning: a w. way   68:12
the wear of w.   21:12
w. wave   104:11
Winning-post: as the boats began to near the w.   64:17
Winnings: make one heap of all your w.   125:15
Winnowing wind   119:18
Wins: Who loses, and who w.   196:6
Winter: As dark as w.   53:15
blow, thou w. wind   184:1
But w. and rough weather   183:13
by the w. sea   226:25
Christmas should fall out in the Middle of W.   1:9
cold w.'s day   105:15
cold w.'s night   16:18
Ere the w. storms begin   2:13
furious w.'s rages   184:22
fury of the w.   20:2
How like a w.   211:12
If W. comes   214:4
in the w.'s pale   210:5
It was not in the w.   106:19
It was the w. wild   145:7
most love W.   161:14
On a w.'s morn   131:5
on w.'s traces   223:28
sad tale's best for w.   210:3
sends the snow in w.   53:12
sunbeam in a w.'s day   80:18
W. Garment of Repentance   84:17
w. is past   27:16
w. of our discontent   207:4
w. weeds outworn   213:12
Winters: Three w. cold   211:13
Wintry: dark w. bed   214:1
sailed the w. sea   134:12
Upon a w. bough   213:11
Wipe: shall w. away all tears   37:18, 26
Wipers: be w. of scores   44:23
Wire: desert of w.   151:10
Wires: Across the w. the electric message came   13:22
If hairs be w.   212:3
Wisdom: beginning of w.   171:11
Here is w.   69:1
nor w., in the grave   27:2
pray for w. yet   2:1
price of w.   25:37
seldom the truest w.   47:4
spirit of w.   28:1
to forget one's w. is sweet   110:7
W. and Wit are little seen   61:4
w. from our councils   47:7
w. lingers   228:12
w. of the ancients   15:13
Wise: are reputed w.   201:8
Be w. with speed   250:13
being darkly w.   164:18
consider her ways and be w.   26:8
every pure and w. spirit   82:21
Every w. man's son   209:5
from letters to be w.   117:2

Full of w. saws   183:20
Have the courage to be w.   108:7
he would become w.   39:19
Histories make men w.   14:27
Holy, fair, and w.   210:2
I heard a w. man say   110:16
I knew a very w. man   86:12
in no w. lose his reward   31:17
leave the W.   85:6
merry and w.   5:14, 141:14
Nor ever did a w. one   176:2
not worldly w.   173:25
See nations slowly w.   117:2
talk too w.   125:14
that a w. man sees   39:17
that w. bird   173:13
There came w. men   30:1
Three w. men of Gotham   158:11
'Tis folly to be w.   98:10
Type of the w.   248:6
we were very, very w.   65:3
w. and masterly inactivity   137:12
w. as serpents   31:13
w. father that knows his own child   201:21
w. friend of mine   238:14
w. man will make more opportunities   14:10
w. men three   162:2
ye yourselves are w.   36:3
Wisely: Be w. worldly   173:25
never so w.   169:29
Wiser: not the w. grow   163:18
Thou speakest w.   183:12
Wisest fool in Christendom   103:3
Wish: as I would w. to do   81:5
celebrated w.   129:6
should w. to be   246:2
that heaven of all their w.   42:3
who would w. to die?   40:8
whose w. and care   165:14
w. he'd stay away   141:17
w. my days to be   247:10
w. to all   221:22
w. to die   90:17
w. to draw my attention?   78:11
w. was father..to that thought   190:33
Wished: Devoutly to be w.   187:13
you w. him to talk   101:10
Wishes: country's w. blest!   67:14
Their sober w.   98:1
w., fears, anger   119:1
Wistful: such a w. eye   243:4
Wit: all thy Piety nor W.   85:12
As metaphysic w. can fly   49:17
at their w.'s end   171:8
Attic w.   163:11
baiting-place of w.   217:1
but have drawn his w.   118:3
by her mother w.   219:12
comic w. degenerating   80:3
his weapon w.   107:8
I have neither w.   194:12
let w. bear a stroke   234:10
liveliest effusions of w.   13:16
monarchy of w.   54:20
mortify a w.   165:12
past the w. of man   203:17
shoots his w.   184:15
Some beams of w.   79:24
soul of w.   186:21
spice of w.   221:22
Staircase w.   76:2
that w. is in other men   190:27
to put his whole w. in a jest   19:9
True w.   164:10
when the wine is in, the w. it out   19:30
Wisdom and W. are little seen   61:4
w. among Lords   114:1

w. is out 19:30, 204:14
w. its soul 66:12
W. that can creep 165:9
w.'s the noblest frailty 182:5
Witch: nor w. hath power 185:4
Witching time of night 188:20
Wither: Age cannot w. her 182:16
  Rose that cannot w. 235:8
Withered: are w. away 64:16
  dried up, and w. 170:17
  His w. cheek 180:4
  It could not w. be 117:19
  Like w. leaves 214:4
  So w., and so wild 197:8
  they w. all 189:15
  w. is the garland of the war 182:21
  Worthless as w. weeds 41:14
Withereth: Fast w. too 120:11
  grass w. 28:13, 37:3
Witherington needs must I wail 213:5
Withers are unwrung 188:14
Within: be w. thy walls 171:20
  kingdom of God is w. you 33:31
  what is false w. 142:4
Withstand: to w. in the evil day 36:14
Withstood: tyrant of his fields w. 97:15
Witness: bear false w. 167:16
  weak w. of thy name? 147:12
  w. of the soul 231:9
Witnesses: cloud of w. 36:35
Wits: dog had lost his w. 95:15
  rhyming mother w. 139:8
  warming his five w. 230:9
  we have w. to read 118:4
  w. are sure to madness..alli'd 79:6
Wittles: We have no w. 232:1
Witty: It shall be w. 61:3
  poets [make men] w. 14:27
  w. in myself 190:27
  w., profligate 251:2
Wive: came..to w. 209:20
Wives: changes when they are w. 184:11
  man with seven w. 155:3
  Old w.' fables 36:27
  poison'd by their w. 206:15
  W. are young men's mistresses 14:18
Wo: Come weel, come w. 106:6
Woe: all our w. 145:9
  balm of w. 217:1
  can I see another's w. 39:14
  deep unutterable w. 14:1
  full of w. 156:17
  Listen to my tale of w. 84:2
  oft in w. 242:5
  prov'd, a very w. 212:2
  sounds of w. 204:9
  trappings and the suits of w. 185:10
  W. is me! for I am undone 27:27
  w. is me, to have seen 188:6
  W. to the vanquished 133:1
  W. unto them 27:25
  W. unto you 33:12
  W. weeps out her division 117:10
Woeful: with a w. ballad 183:20
Woes: Of all the Grecian w. 106:15
  To suffer w. 215:1
  with old w. 211:1
  w. of man 236:7
  w. that curse our race 91:4
Woke: I w., and found 107:6
Wolf: grim w. with privy paw 145:3
  w. behowls the moon 204:3
  w. on the fold 52:9
  w. shall dwell with the lamb 28:2
Wollop: D'ye think I'd w. him 23:2
Wolves: they are ravening w. 31:3
Woman: always the w. 78:3
  as far as one w. can forgive 89:11
  bloom on a w. 18:24

By w. wailing 66:14
Can a w.'s tender care 70:4
Did ever w...interrupt a man 220:13
Die because a w.'s fair 244:18
dumpy w. 51:10
Each thought on the w. 124:2
Every w. should marry 76:19
excellent thing in w. 196:9
fat white w. 68:28
fickle thing..is w. 236:14
find a virtuous w. 26:32
God..made he a w. 23:12
he that tastes w. 89:20
in a w.'s hide 192:11
influence of W. 74:12
Let us look for the w. 80:9
man and a w. in a garden 243:26
most pernicious w.! 186:14
my w.'s breasts 197:15
none of the w. born 199:20
nor w. neither 187:4
O w.! lovely w.! 159:22
of the w. I love 81:5
perfect w. 248:5
saw the w. drunken with the blood 37:22
she is a w. 174:9, 208:25
She was a worthy w. 60:16
shone one w. 224:11
so unbecoming to a w. 243:17
thy name is w.! 185:11
'Tis w.'s whole existence 51:14
unto the man is w. 134:7
weak and feeble w. 82:9
when a w. appears 89:18
When lovely w. stoops to
  folly 82:2, 95:21
Wilt thou have this w. 168:10
with a pretty w. 115:12
w. as old as she looks 67:10
W., behold thy son! 34:27
w. colour'd ill 212:4
W. has her way 106:13
W. in our hours of ease 180:13
w. in this humour woo'd 207:7
w. is a dish for the gods 183:1
w. is only a w. 124:14
W. Killed with Kindness 105:3
w. sat, in unwomanly rags 107:3
w. scorn'd 68:10
w. true and fair 77:17
w. wakes to love 226:24
W., what have I to do with thee? 33:49
W. who Did 2:16
w. who did not care 128:1
w. who lived in a shoe 158:6
w. who tells one her real age 243:25
W. will be the last thing 142:12
w., wine and song 135:11
w. with the West in her eyes 65:3
w.'s preaching 114:19
w.'s workhouse 213:1
Womanhood and childhood fleet! 133:23
Womb: from his mother's w. 200:11
  w. of royal kings 206:7
Women: are not w. truly 117:18
  As men and w. 124:17
  blessed art thou among w. 32:36
  cherries, hops, and w. 75:16
  Dear dead w. 45:12
  England is a paradise for w. 49:11
  England is the paradise of w. 86:13
  experience of w. 78:15
  From w.'s eyes 196:16
  happiest w. 81:9
  he hid himself among w. 43:1
  learn about w. 126:7
  many men, many w. 114:8
  men and w. merely players 183:20
  men, w., and clergymen 217:17

Women (cont.)
Monstrous Regiment of W.   129:1
nonsense of the old w.   220:17
O! see my w.   182:21
old w. (of both sexes)   220:17
other w. cloy   182:16
passing the love of w.   25:1
shone o'er fair w.   50:23
than war or w. have   192:14
War Between Men and W.   233:13
were w. never so fair   135:13
where the w. come and go   81:15
wine and w.   51:15
W., and Champagne, and Bridge 21:18
W. and elephants   178:16
W. and wine   89:17
w. are angels   52:5
w. are foolish   81:8
w. are not so young as they are
  painted   20:6
w. become like their mothers 243:11
w. must weep   124:3
w. should be struck   69:17
Won: battle's lost and w. 197:2
not that you w.   175:10
other palms are w.   246:14
therefore may be w.   208:25
woman in this humour w.?   207:7
w. in the playing fields of Eton 240:17
w. my right good-will   137:15, 235:4
Wonder: all a w.   45:6
around the w. grew   110:18
ever-increasing w.   119:10
I w. by my troth   77:7
I w. now   96:10
One can only w.   22:13
still the w. grew   95:8
w. grows   224:14
w. in your eyes   176:11
w. of an hour!   50:21
w. of our stage!   118:4
w. that would be   228:8
w. what you are!   225:10
Wonderful: all his words most w. 153:14
by all that's w.!   216:21
how w. Thou art!   83:14
is more w. than man   218:9
mystic, w.   226:16
shall be called W.   27:32
their unanimity is w.   216:3
to this w. year   88:18
'W.!' I ejaculated   78:21
Wonderfully: concentrates his mind
  w.   115:13
fearfully and w. made   172:2
Wonderland: summer's w.   154:16
Wonders: his w. in the deep 171:7
Of all the w.   193:14
W. are many   218:9
w. to perform   70:5
Wont: any longer as thou art w. 99:3
Wonted: State in w. manner 117:11
Woo: Men are April when they w. 184:11
Wood: Bows down to w. and
  stone   101:16, 125:3
for a dish of w.   206:16
from a vernal w.   248:15
Hewers of w.   24:27
house in the high w.   22:1
in a w. a Piggy-wig stood   131:7
is in the w.   180:18
Of true w.   78:1
red herrings grow in the w.   156:15
sang within the bloody w.   81:22
Through w. and dale   66:15
to the rocky w.   199:6
tulgey w.   57:14
w. of English bows   78:1
Woodbine: with luscious w. 203:9

Wooden: cram within this w. O 191:3
Sailed off in a w. shoe   84:3
w. walls   69:7
Woodland: stands about the w. ride 110:15
w. spices   228:20
Woodlands: About the w. I will go 110:15
Woodman, spare that tree! 150:12
Wood-notes: native w.   144:19
Woodshed: in the w.   90:15
Woods: build his house in the w. 83:4
enchanted w.   142:8
hoary w. are grand   181:7
in the middle of the w.   130:19
pleasure in the pathless w.   51:7
road through the w.   128:2, 3
sleeping w.   66:3
to fresh w.   145:5
we will go no more to the w.   17:7
We'll to the w. no more   111:8
Wet Wild W.   128:17
wild in w.   79:19
w. decay   230:10
w. on shore   150:2
W. or steepy mountain   139:6
Wooed: therefore may be w. 208:25
woman in this humour w.   207:7
Woof: Weave the w.   97:5
Wooing: is w. thee   108:18
would a-w. go   155:14
Wool: had no w. on de top of his
  head   87:13
Have you any w.?   155:4
W. of bat   199:14
Woolly fold   120:2
Word: according to thy w.   33:1
answered never a w.   134:13
by every w.   30:8
By water and the W.   222:1
discouraging w.   105:5
durst not have used that w.   82:10
eaten thee for a w.   196:17
foolish w.   127:7
God has not said a w.!   45:1
hear his w.   70:3
hear the w. culture   117:5
His w. was still, Fie   195:14
In the beginning was the W.   33:43
meanings packed up into one w. 58:7
Mum's the w.   67:17
never breath a w.   125:15
not a w. of sorrow   245:6
O w. of fear   196:19
One w. is too often profaned 215:12
perhaps we have not the w.   12:4
some with a flattering w.   243:5
speak no angry w.   2:9
suit the action to the w.   188:8
That I kept my w.   73:5
thy uncreating w.   164:3
time for such a w.   200:4
To neither a w. will I say   89:21
'Twas God the w.   82:4
used the w. in its Pickwickian
  sense   75:15
wash out a W.   85:12
what the w. did make it   82:4
When I use a w.   58:5
whose lightest w.   186:7
w. and a blow   79:14, 207:17
w. is like a bell   121:7
w. of Caesar   194:6
w. spoken in due season   26:19
w. that teems with hidden meaning   93:28
W. was made flesh   33:46
you've spoken the foremost w. 16:6
Wordless: song was w.   179:7
Words: all his w. most wonderful 153:14
alms-basket of w.   196:17

barren superfluity of w. 89:4
Bright is the ring of w. 221:18
deeds, not w. shall speak me 19:14
find those w. mis-plac'd 68:13
fine w. butter no parsnips 180:20
For all sad w. 242:17
his w. a foot and a half long 107:19
in plainer w. 129:5
In two w: im-possible 96:5
long w. bother me 143:17
Men of few w. 191:10
my w. among mankind 214:4
my w. are idle 240:10
neither wit, nor w. 194:12
report thy w. 147:7
these w. are true 37:26
two narrow w. 174:16
whose w. are of less weight 14:11
With hard w. 161:15
w. could never utter 232:4
w. of love 150:1
w. of Mercury 197:1
w. of my mouth 168:31
w. of tongue and pen 101:2, 242:17
w. that have been so nimble 19:9
w. were now written 25:34
w., w., w. 186:25
you will find the following w. 74:15
Wordsworth: to W. 220:22
W., both are thine 220:7
Wordy and lengthy epistle 119:7
Work: all things w. together 35:8
can't w. any faster 157:18
Dere's no more hard w. 87:14
Do the w. that's nearest 123:15
do your w. on water 125:11
Either man's w. 147:17
For men must w. 124:3
goeth forth to his w. 171:3
I leave my w. 55:3
I like w. 113:8
men who do the w. 19:28
noblest w. of God 164:20
noblest w. of man 50:7
Nothing to do but w. 123:10
Old Kaspar's w. was done 218:12
our w. is done! 153:12
Powers that will w. 248:20
said 'Dear w.!' 110:14
smoothed her w. 110:14
Some w. of noble note 230:15
sooner than w. at anything 212:20
That do no w. today 192:2
their w. continueth 127:15
there is no w...in the grave 27:2
this w. of development 19:28
To make dictionaries is dull w. 116:13
to pray is to w. 10:4
warm w., Hardy 152:21
We w. hard at doing nothing 108:9
What a piece of w. is a man! 187:4
when no man can w. 34:11
when your w. is finished 125:10
w. apace 72:18
w. i' the earth so fast 186:15
w. of grave purpose 107:18
W. out your own salvation 36:16
years to be of w. 41:16
Worked: He w. and sang 37:29
Workers: w. have nothing to
    lose 140:14
W. of the world, unite 8:16, 140:14
Workhouse: Christmas Day in the
    w. 217:5
woman's w. 213:1
Working: from her w. 187:11
Their w. tools 234:9
w. out its way 79:5
Works: all just w. 166:18

All our w. 167:29
devil and all his w. 167:32
Faith without w. 36:39
Full of good w. 34:37
In w. of labour 239:10
Look on my w. 214:6
move immediately upon your w. 97:1
Rich in good w. 36:32
saw my w. 170:26
see the w. of the Lord 171:7
see your good w. 30:14
w. hard for its living 156:17
w. of darkness 35:14, 166:33
W. of Supererogation 172:13
Workshop of the world 76:6
World: All's right with the w. 44:24
all the w. as my parish 241:18
all the w. doth know 69:23
All the w. over 94:5
all the w. should stare 69:30
all the w. will be in love 208:1
All the w. wonder'd 226:5
All the w.'s a stage 183:20
All this the w. well knows 212:2
Architecture of the w. 139:10
are conveyed to the w. 13:16
attracts the envy of the w. 46:28
at which the w. grew pale 117:3
bade the w. farewell 54:5
banish all the w. 190:15
beauty of the w. 187:4
before the w. confess'd 111:12
best sauce in the w. 59:9
bestride the narrow w. 193:11
born into the w. alive 91:21
bring not innocence into the w. 148:9
Britain set the w. ablaze 91:22
Brought death into the w. 145:9
brought nothing into this w. 36:29
busy w. is hushed 153:12
cast out of the w. 174:16
cease in all the w. 169:21
clearing-house of the w. 59:13
compass of the w. 169:3
conquered..half the w. 181:12
dark w. of sin 37:33
darkness of this w. 36:14
Deceits of the w. 166:23
Deign on the passing w. 117:2
dominion of the w. 137:18
drowsy syrups of the w. 205:9
estate o' the w. 200:6
ever happened in the w.! 87:17
fact the whole w. knows 131:13
Federation of the w. 228:10
fled from this vile w. 211:7
foppery of the w. 195:2
for the w., I count it not an inn 42:21
gain the whole w. 31:35, 32:32
give the w. a progeny 109:23
Give warning to the w. 211:7
glory of the w. 122:23
God so loved the w. 34:1
great while ago the w. began 209:20
greatest thing in the w. 149:3
Had we but w. enough 140:11
hand that rules the w. 238:3
He knows the w. 86:17
heard round the w. 82:14
high shore of this w. 191:15
His w. rejoices 244:17
history of the w. 55:13, 161:4
how the w. wags 183:16
I called the New W. 54:18
I have overcome the w. 34:22
impressive sights in the w. 18:25
in a better w. 183:8
in a naughty w. 202:14
In a w. I never made 111:9

World (*cont.*)

in hope the w. can show 77:15
In the morning of the w. 44:25
In the whole wide w. 222:8
in the w.'s storm-troubled sphere 41:13
In the w. ye shall have tribulation 34:22
in this dark w. 147:17
in this harsh w. 190:3
in this W. much wrong 85:15
in this w. nothing can be said 88:4
into the w. of light 235:9
leave the w. unseen 121:3
leaves the w. to darkness 97:8
Let all the w. 103:18
Let the great w. spin 228:14
Let the w. mind him! 43:18
Let the w. slide 19:27
light of the bright w. dies 40:13
light of the w. 30:13
lost the w. for love 79:27
love that makes the w. go round! 57:3
loveliest fairy in the w. 124:6
Mad w.! Mad kings! 193:3
mad W., My Masters 41:5, 225:12
makes the whole w. kin 208:28
makes the w. go round 5:15, 57:3, 91:26
most ancient profession in the w. 128:21
naked shingles of the w. 11:8
need of a w. of men 44:16
nothing in the whole w. 243:17
Nothing is ever done in this w. 212:18
nourish all the w. 196:16
O brave new w. 208:21
O W. intangible 232:9
O w. invisible 232:9
O w.! O life! 213:15
O'er the w.'s tempestuous sea 81:2
Of the w.'s ransom 206:7
of the w.'s slow stain 213:8
Of this bad w. 21:16
on this w.'s shore 154:13
One half of the w. 13:13
only one thing in the w. 243:20
or the W. Well Lost 79:13
patriot of the w. 54:13
peopled half the w. 181:12
pomp and glory of this w. 192:14
prettiest doll in the w. 123:17
quiet limit of the w. 230:11
rack of this tough w. 196:12
reprehend any thing in this w. 216:11
riddle of the w.! 164:19
Ring'd with the azure w. 226:9
round about the pendent w.! 200:23
round the w. away 123:18
round the w. for ever 11:11
runs the w. away 188:16
Saviour of the W. 50:14
say to all the w. 194:24
seek a newer w. 230:15
seek through the w. 161:17
set the w. on sixe and sevene 60:29
shore of the wide w. 122:5
should corrupt the w. 227:1
since the creation of the w. 220:13
soul of the wide w. 211:14
start the w. along 249:7
stood against the w. 194:6
survey of all the w. 190:22
that, has the w. here 43:18
that the w. has seen 125:1
These laid the w. away 41:16
they only saved the w. 21:14
thick rotundity o' the w. 195:4
this little w. 206:7
this wicked w. 167:32
this w. has got 112:6
three corners of the w. 193:8
through the sensual w. 150:3

Till the w. is wrought 215:4
to pass through this w. but once 98:15
To see the W. 38:10
to the ending of the w. 192:4
turned the w. upside down 34:41
two families in the w. 59:11
two painters in the w. 242:2
unacknowledged legislators of the w. 215:15
untravell'd w. 230:13
Up above the w. 56:24, 225:10
uses of the w. 185:11
verdict of the w. 13:6
Vision of the w. 228:8
voice of the w. 42:20
way the w. ends 81:13
What I may appear to the w. 153:17
What is this w.? 60:18
When all the w. is young 123:18
when Rome falls—the W. 51:6
which the w. cannot give 166:19
whole w. is in a state of chassis 159:7
whom the w. hath flattered 174:16
wilderness of this w. 46:3
Winds of the W. 125:4
With the old w. to the grave 102:15
Workers of the w. 8:16, 140:14
workshop of the w. 76:6
W. and all her train 235:11
w. and his wife 10:8, 223:20
w. and they 70:12
w. can never fill 70:2
w. forgetting 164:6
w. founded on four essential freedoms 176:17
w. has grown grey 224:10
w. in general knows 131:11
w. in solemn stillness 181:10
w. is a comedy 238:7
w. is charged 107:12
w. is full of fools 9:6
w. is given to lying! 190:26
w. is made up..of fools 45:18
w. is so full of a number of things 221:14
w. is too much with us 249:5
w. laughs with you 243:3
w. must be made safe 244:13
w. of sighs 204:23
w. should listen 215:6
w. to gain 140:14
w. too wide 183:20
w. was all before them 146:25
w. where England is finished 143:2
w. will give thee credit 62:10
w. will make a beaten path 83:4
w. would be nicer 245:13
w. would go round 56:18
w.'s an inn 79:28
w.'s great age 213:12
w.'s history 179:14
w.'s judgement 179:14
w.'s last night? 77:11
w.'s my oyster 202:17
Worldly: all my w. goods 168:14
Be wisely w. 173:25
loathèd w. life 201:1
not w. wise 173:25
thy w. task 184:22
W. wealth he cared not for 88:11
Worldly-Wise-Man: name was Mr. W. 46:5
Worlds: and what w. away! 43:11
best of all possible w. 52:19, 237:12
So many w. 227:14
wandering between two w. 11:15
World-use: harsh w. 179:11
Worm: And the w. that never dies 42:3
rather tough w. 92:17
w. at one end 116:12

w. i' the bud 209:10
w. nor snail 203:11
w.'s eye point of view 173:23
Worms: I was one of the w. 68:20
of w. and epitaphs 206:14
tasted two w. 219:17
with vilest w. to dwell 211:7
w. have eaten them 184:10
w. shall try 140:12
Wormwood and the gall 29:9
Worn: With fingers weary and w. 107:3
Worrying: what's the use of w.? 12:14
Worse: but follow w. 160:7
for better for w. 168:12
greater feeling to the w. 206:5
is w. than the first 31:24
it is w. than a crime 40:12
nobody seemed one penny the w. 17:13
W. on Friday 158:2
w. than being talked about 243:20
w. than our grandsires 109:23
w. than senseless things! 193:9
w. than wicked 173:14
w. when it comes late 113:11
Worship: come let us w. 170:23
come to w. him 30:1
freedom..to w. God 176:17
I thee w. 168:14
nor w. them 167:7
only object of w. 7:12
pay no w. to the garish sun 208:1
they that w. him 34:2
whom therefore ye ignorantly w. 34:42
With which I w. thine 215:11
w. him is spirit 34:2
Worshipped stocks and stones 147:16
Worst: best is like the w. 126:15
His w. is better 101:9
leave the w. ones 20:16
make the w. appear the better reason 146:11
so much good in the w. 105:12
Treason has done his w. 199:4
which is w. of all 105:9
w. are no worse 204:2
w. is yet to come 113:13
w. sting of misery 40:1
Worth: charter of thy w. 211:9
half so much w. doing 96:16
none was w. my strife 129:20
nor words, nor w. 194:12
Slow rises w. by poverty depress'd 116:27
Whose w.'s unknown 211:16
w. a guinea a box 8:17
w. of a State 142:23
w. of the individuals 142:23
Worthless: are more w. than they 109:23
W. as withered weeds 41:14
Worthy: am no more w. 33:22
found them w. 29:33
I am not w. to unloose 33:47
labourer is w. of his hire 33:5
She was a w. woman 60:16
Worts: went to W. 165:18
Wot prawce Selvytion nah? 212:17
Would: wait upon 'I w.' 198:6
Wound: heal me of my grievous w. 227:3
help to w. itself 193:8
see not the w. it makes 197:15
that never felt a w. 207:20
tongue in every w. 194:13
Willing to w. 165:6
with love's w. 203:7
w. for w. 24:7
Wounded: he was w. 28:21
what a w. name 190:3
You're w. 44:7

Wounds: heals his w. 154:1
labour and the w. 64:10
these w. had I 192:4
Wrack: come, w.! 200:7
Wrap: w. a fairy in 203:9
W. me up in my tarpaulin jacket 243:1
w. the baby bunting in 155:6
Wrapped: All meanly w. 145:7
w. in a gauzy veil 215:14
W. up in a five-pound note 131:6
Wraps: that w. their clay 67:15
Wrath: chariots of w. 96:19
day of w. 59:5, 180:7
from the w. to come? 30:5
his w. endureth 169:8
sun go down upon your w. 36:12
thy w. can send 54:14
turneth away w. 26:16
where the grapes of w. are stored 111:15
w. of Peleus' son 106:15
Wreath: a rosy w. 117:19
she wore a w. of roses 19:5
Wreathe iron pokers 66:11
Wreathed: and w. smiles 144:12
his w. horn 219:8, 249:5
Wreck: creates from its own w. 215:1
decay of that colossal w. 214:7
lit the battle's w. 102:7
Wrecks of a dissolving dream 213:12
Wren: Four Larks and a W. 130:15
robin redbreast and the w. 240:11
Sir Christopher W. said 22:12
Wrestle: For we w. not against flesh 36:14
Wretch: Come, thou mortal w. 183:4
Excellent w.! 205:3
such a w. 191:15
who, poor w. 162:6
w., concentred all in self 180:6
w. who supports with insolence 116:18
Wretched: most deject and w. 188:6
w. is that poor man 192:14
Wretches: How shall w. live like us 94:9
Poor naked w. 195:8
what w. feel 195:9
Wriggles: He w. 105:18
Wring: And w. his bosom 95:21
soon w. their hands 238:9
w. the brow 180:13
Wrist: With gyves upon his w. 106:21
Writ: All that was ever w. in brass 118:3
and, having w. 85:12
any poet ever w. 80:4
I never w. 211:16
proofs of holy w. 205:8
shall be in water w. 19:20
was w. in water 122:12
w. your annals true 184:19
Write: cannot w. like Hazlitt 221:7
he said unto me, W. 37:26
I will w. for Antiquity! 129:14
may w. at any time 113:17
sit thee down and w. 39:8
touch a pen to w. 196:15
w. a better book 83:4
w. against your name 175:10
W. me as one that loves 112:3
W. sorrow 206:14
Writer: Every great and original w. 249:6
no eminent w. 212:14
of a ready w. 169:18
Writes: The Moving Finger w. 85:12
w. in the dust 15:14
Writing: any style of w. untouched 115:11
idea of w. 90:12
itch of writing 119:6
mere fine w. 235:14
that in his w. 117:12
w. maketh..an exact man 14:26

Written: Books are well w., or badly
  w.   243:19
  that mine adversary had w. a
    book   25:38
  that my words were now w.   25:34
  What I have w.   34:26
  w. troubles of the brain   200:1
  w. without effort   116:10
Wrong: always in the w.   73:16, 78:8
  clamouring for what is w.   109:19
  do no w.   203:10
  Fifty million Frenchmen can't be
    w.   99:1
  he done her w.   4:8
  if you w. us   201:27
  in this World much w.   85:15
  king can do no w.   38:7
  multitude is always in the w.   76:3
  of right and w. he taught   11:3
  oppressor's w.   187:13
  our country, right or w.   72:14
  right deed for the w. reason   81:21
  Should suffer w. no more   136:8
  telling a man he was w.   64:15
  to govern w.   164:1
  w. left unredressed   124:8
  w. or irreverent   113:14
Wrongs darker than death   215:1
Wrote: ever w., except for money   115:8
  I w. my happy songs   39:8
  I'm sorry, now, I w. it   46:25
  Who w. like an angel   89:1
Wrought: Eyesight and speech they
  w.   224:2
  Till the world is w.   215:4
  w., and thought with me   230:15
  W. in a sad sincerity   82:15
Wynken, Blynken, and Nod   84:3

                    X

Xanadu: In X.   66:14

                    Y

Yachts: seek happiness in y.   108:9
Yankee Doodle, keep it up   17:5
Yarn: a merry y.   141:4
Yea: Let your y. be y.   37:2
  Your communication be y., y.   30:17
Year: Another y.   247:11
  as y. succeeds to y.   2:3
  at the gate of the y.   101:5
  blossoms through the y.   216:8
  called me Baby Doll a y. ago   100:17
  comes but once a y.   234:7
  ever-running y.   191:15
  for half a y.   57:21
  forty pounds a y.   95:6
  in each leap y.   158:7
  In the y. that king Uzziah died   27:27
  mellowing y.   144:20
  on nothing a y.   231:18
  pilgrims of the y.   142:6
  pleasure of the fleeting y.   211:12
  Right early in the y.   106:7
  season of the y.   6:16
  sweet o' the y.   210:5
  That time of y.   211:8
  till the ninth y.   108:5
  to this wonderful y.   88:18
  twelve months in all the y.   16:11
  y., a month, a week   138:14
  y. and a day   131:7
  y. is going   227:19
  y.'s at the spring   44:24
  y.'s pleasant king   152:6
Yearly on the vigil   192:4

Yearning: while your hearts are y.   87:4
  y. for the farther shore   236:17
Years: after long y.   52:17
  arches of the y.   232:7
  beginning of y.   224:1
  braved a thousand y.   54:6
  bring our y. to an end   170:18
  ever the Knightly y.   102:15
  fifty y. of Europe   228:15
  fleeting y.   109:14
  for forty y.   62:4
  for y. to come   239:14
  forty y. on   40:15
  from his earliest y.   21:5
  gave up the y. to be   41:16
  golden y. return   213:12
  Hasn't been kissed in forty y.   178:6
  in hours, days, y.   235:11
  in the y. to be   124:17
  Into the vale of y.   205:6
  lived thousands of y. ago   242:14
  may be for y.   71:2
  nor the y. condemn   38:2
  Of boyhood's y.   150:1
  of earthly y.   245:14
  of my three score y.   110:15
  of Riper Y.   167:31
  restore to you the y.   29:21
  Sev'n thousand Y.   85:3
  seven y. were gane and past   16:16
  ten y. before the Flood   140:11
  thousand y. in thy sight   170:17
  through many y.   237:9
  through the y. to be.!   124:18
  To endless y. the same   239:14
  to remember for y.   2:18
  To sever for y.   52:16
  where all past y. are   77:16
  wildest peal for y.   105:13
  y. draw nigh   27:7
  Y. glide away   17:9
  y. of discretion   168:3
  y. that bring the philosophic
    mind   246:13
  y. to come   250:7
Yellow: Come unto these y. sands   208:9
  green and y. melancholy   209:10
  thy y. stockings   209:13
  to y. autumn turn'd   211:13
  When y. leaves   211:8
  Y., and black   214:1
  y. fog   81:16
  y. like ripe corn   177:16
  y. primrose was to him   247:14
Yellow-Dog Dingo behind   126:5
Yeoman: did me y.'s service   189:25
Yesterday: all our pomp of y.   127:5
  but as y.   170:17
  call back y.   206:13
  dead Y.   85:8
  jam y.   58:3
  Jesus Christ the same y.   36:38
  nor y.   77:1
  Which thou ow'dst y.   205:9
  with Y.'s Sev'n thousand Years   85:3
Yesterdays: our y. have lighted
    fools   200:4
Yesteryear: snows of y.   236:2
Yet: be with us y.   127:3
Yew: never a spray of y.   11:19
  of true wood, of y.-wood   78:1
  Slips of y.   199:15
  stuck all with y.   209:9
Yield: find, and not to y.   230:15
  is to y. to it   243:21
  never to submit or y.   145:15
Yields: ancient Ruby y.   84:16
Yo-ho-ho   221:1
Yoke: bear his mild y.   147:17

bear the y. in his youth 29:10
my y. is easy 31:21
no y. of usury 108:14
Teach us to bear the y. 124:17
Yonghy-Bonghy-Bò 130:19
Yore: as it hath been of y. 246:6
Yorick: Alas! poor Y. 189:20
York: by this sun of Y. 207:4
noble Duke of Y. 7:21
You and I are old 230:15
Young: all the world is y. 123:18
as a y. man 118:17
as she doth her y. ones 49:8
being y. and foolish 250:5
crime of being a y. man 162:17
dies y. 163:8
embarrassing y. 89:6
I have been y. 169:13
lay her y. 170:13
Myself when y. 85:7
O y. fresshe folkes 61:2
Queens have died y. and fair 152:5
she died y. 240:8
so y., and so untender? 195:1
that are with y. 28:14
to be y. was very heaven! 246:1
We were y. 65:3
went to the Bar as a very y. man 91:20
when he was y. 158:12
you loved when all was y. 123:18
y. and old 144:16
Y., and so fair 106:20
y. and tender 232:2
y. man feels his pockets 111:10
y. man married 127:17
y. man said 56:16
your y. men shall see visions 29:22
Youngest: not even the y. of us 232:12
Yours: We are y. 102:17
Yourself: Help y. 86:15
keep y. to y. 75:22
Yourselves: not for y. 237:10
Youth: all the y. of England 191:5
bear the yoke in his y. 29:10
bear the yoke in y. 124:17
caught our y. 42:10
corrupting the y. 163:7
Crabbed age and y. 210:10

days of our y. 52:7
figure of blown y. 188:6
from her earliest y. 21:8
Glory of y. 221:21
If y. knew 83:8
ill-spent y. 219:5
in my y. 56:16
in my y.'s hot blood 109:25
in the days of thy y. 27:7
in y. it sheltered me 150:12
made every y. cry well-a-way 16:2
mewing her mighty y. 148:10
neither y. nor age 200:20
Of thoughtless y. 248:19
pleasures with y. 219:1
poets in our y. 247:19
Sweet wine of y. 41:16
takes in trust our y. 174:15
thoughts of y. 133:24
To many a y. 144:16
when Y. and Pleasure meet 51:1
y. are boarded, clothed 74:25
y., I do adore thee 210:11
Y. is full of pleasance 210:10
Y. on the prow 97:6
Y. shows but half 45:4
y. stone dead 179:5
y., who daily farther from the east 246:11
Y. will be served 40:9
Y.'s a stuff 209:5
Y.'s the season 89:19
Youthful: y. poets dream 144:19
y. valour 236:21
Youths and maidens gay! 66:6
Yucatan: I had an aunt in Y. 21:23
Yum-Yum: going to marry Y. 92:6

Z

Zeal: with half the z. 193:1
z. of thine house 170:8
Zealous: always z. for his country's good 89:25
Zèle: N'ayez pas de z. 225:3
Zenith: Dropt from the z. 146:9
Zenocrate: entertain divine Z. 139:12
Zephyr: Odes to every z. 123:16
Zoo: may see at the z. 126:2

GREEK INDEX

A

Ἄγαν : μηδὲν ἄ. 9 : 11
Ἄειδε : μῆνιν ἄ., θεά, Πηληϊάδεω Ἀχιλῆος 106 : 15
Ἀλεκτρυόνα : τῷ Ἀσκληπιῷ ὀφείλομεν ἀ. 218 : 7
Ἀλέξανδρος : εἰ μὴ Ἀ. ἤμην 2 : 6
Ἀμελήσητε : ἀλλὰ ἀπόδοτε καὶ μὴ ἀ. 218 : 7
Ἄνθρωπον : πάντων χρημάτων ἄ. μέτρον εἶναι 172 : 24
Ἀνθρώπου : πολλὰ τὰ δεινὰ κοὐδὲν ἀ. δεινότερον
    πέλει 218 : 9
Ἀπόδοτε : ἀλλὰ ἀ. καὶ μὴ ἀμελήσητε 218 : 7
Ἀσκληπιῷ : τῷ Ἀ. ὀφείλομεν ἀλεκτρυόνα 218 : 7
Ἄστεα : πολλῶν δ' ἀνθρώπων ἴδεν ἀ. 106 : 17
Ἀχαιοῖς : ἣ μυρί' Ἀ. ἄλγε' ἔθηκε 106 : 15
Ἀχιλῆος : μῆνιν ἄειδε, θεά, Πηληϊάδεω Ἀ. 106 : 15

B

Βιβλίον : μέγα β. μέγα κακόν 53 : 5
Βίος : ὁ β. βραχύς, ἡ δὲ τέχνη μακρή 105 : 6
Βραδέως : σπεῦδε β. 222 : 9
Βραχύς : ὁ βίος β., ἡ δὲ τέχνη μακρή 105 : 6

Γ

Γῆ : ἀνδρῶν γὰρ ἐπιφανῶν πᾶσα γ. τάφος 233 : 12
Γῆν : δός μοι ποῦ στῶ καὶ κινῶ τὴν γ. 10 : 13

Δ

Δαιμόνια : ἕτερα δὲ δ. καινά 163 : 7
Δεινὰ : πολλὰ τὰ δ. κοὐδὲν ἀνθρώπου δεινότερον
    πέλει 218 : 9

E

Ἐπιφανῶν : ἀνδρῶν γὰρ ἐ. πᾶσα γῆ τάφος 233 : 12
Εὕρηκα 10 : 12
Εὐτυχέα : ἐπισχεῖν μηδὲ καλέειν κω ὄλβιον, ἀλλ'
    εὖ. 218 : 8

H

Ἥμισυ : πλέον ἥ. παντός 104 : 18

Θ

Θάλαττα θάλαττα 250 : 4
Θεοὺς οὓς ἡ πόλις νομίζει οὐ νομίζοντα 163 : 7

K

Κείμεθα : ἄγγειλον Λακεδαιμονίοις ὅτι τῇδε κ. 217 : 4
Κτῆμα ἐς ἀεί 233 : 11

Λ

Λακεδαιμονίοις : ἄγγειλον Λ. ὅτι τῇδε κείμεθα 217 : 4
Λόγον : μὴ φῦναι τὸν ἅπαντα νικᾷ λ. 218 : 10

M

Μακρή : ὁ βίος βραχύς, ἡ δὲ τέχνη μ. 105 : 6
Μένει : πάντα ῥεῖ, οὐδὲν μ. 103 : 15
Μέτρον : πάντων χρημάτων ἄνθρωπον μ. εἶναι 172 : 24
Μῆνιν ἄειδε, θεά, Πηληϊάδεω Ἀχιλῆος 106 : 15

N

Νομίζοντα : θεοὺς οὓς ἡ πόλις νομίζει οὐ ν. 163 : 7
Νόον : πολλῶν δ' ἀνθρώπων . . . ν. ἔγνω 106 : 17

O

Ὄλβιον : ἐπισχεῖν μηδὲ καλέειν κω ὄ. 218 : 8
Ὀμώμοχ' : ἡ γλῶσσ' ὄ. 83 : 11
Ὀφείλομεν : τῷ Ἀσκληπιῷ ὀ. ἀλεκτρυόνα 218 : 7

Π

Παντός : πλέον ἥμισυ π. 104 : 18
Πειθόμενοι : τοῖς κείνων ῥήμασι π. 217 : 4
Πολιτικόν : ἄνθρωπος φύσει π. ζῷον 10 : 15
Πολύτροπον : ἄνδρα μοι ἔννεπε, Μοῦσα, π. 106 : 16

P

Ῥεῖ : πάντα ῥ., οὐδὲν μενει 103 : 15
Ῥήμασι : τοῖς κείνων ῥ. πειθόμενοι 217 : 4

Σ

Σεαυτόν : γνῶθι σ. 9 : 12
Σπεῦδε βραδέως 222 : 9
Στῶ : δός μοι ποῦ σ. 10 : 13
Σωκράτη φησὶν ἀδικεῖν . . . 163 : 7

T

Τάφος : ἀνδρῶν γὰρ ἐπιφανῶν πᾶσα γῆ τ. 233 : 12
Τελευτήσῃ : πρὶν δ' ἂν τ., ἐπισχεῖν μηδὲ καλέειν
    κω ὄλβιον 218 : 8
Τέχνη : ὁ βίος βραχύς, ἡ δὲ τ. μακρή 105 : 6
Τραγῳδία : ἐστιν οὖν τ. .. 10 : 16

Φ

Φῦναι : μὴ φ. τὸν ἅπαντα νικᾷ λόγον 218 : 10